Reader's Digest

FIX-IT-YOURSELF MANUAL

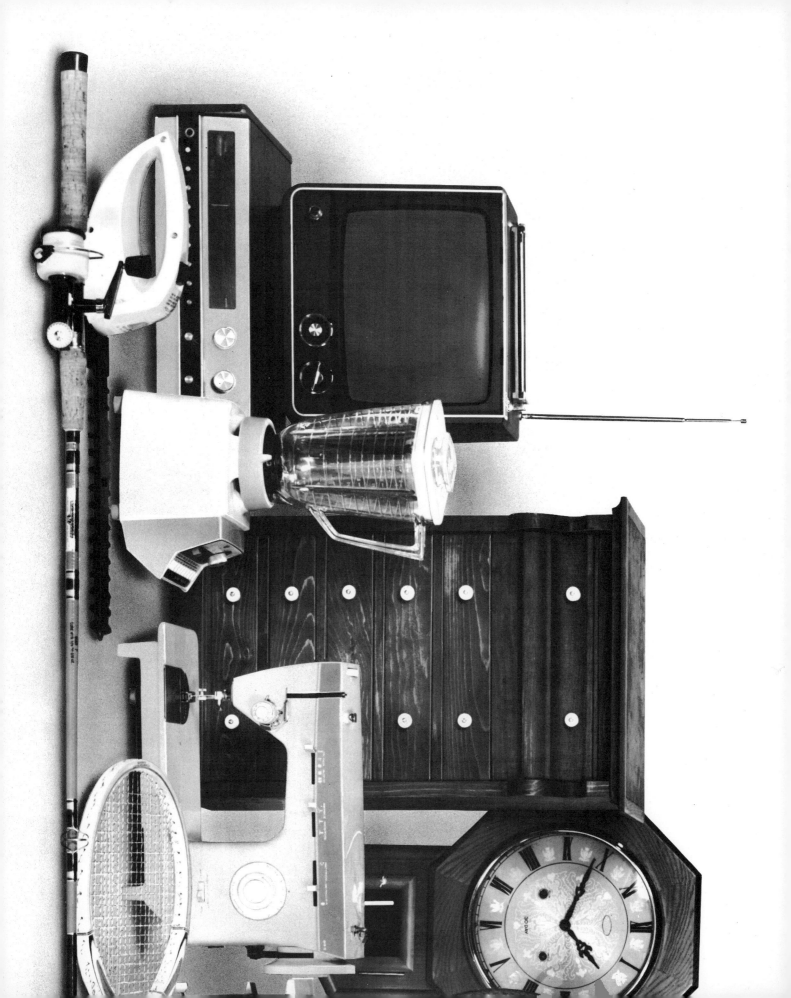

Reader's Digest

FIX-IT-YOURSELF MANUAL

The Reader's Digest Association, Inc.
Pleasantville, New York/Montreal

Fix-it-yourself Manual

The credits and acknowledgments that appear on the facing page are hereby made a part of this copyright page.

Copyright © 1977 The Reader's Digest Association, Inc.
Copyright © 1977 The Reader's Digest Association (Canada) Ltd.
Copyright © 1977 Reader's Digest Association Far East Ltd.
Philippine Copyright 1977 Reader's Digest Association Far East Ltd.

Library of Congress Catalog Card Number 77-73634
ISBN 0-89577-040-7
Printed in the United States of America
Ninth Printing, March 1982

Staff

Project Director John Speicher
Section Editors Paul Ahrens
Wade Hoyt
Norman Mack

Associate Editors Laura Dearborn
Florence Hamsher
Richard Compton
William Dasheff
James L. Forsht
Sarah W. French

Copy Editor Robert V. Huber
Editorial Assistant Marguerite Anderson

Group Art Director David Trooper
Associate Art Director Albert D. Burger
Art Associates Morris Karol
David Lindroth
Joel Musler
Judy Skorpil

Art Assistant Lisa Grant

Contributors

Contributing Writers
John S. Bowman
Peter Chaitin
Tony Chiu
Sydney Wolfe Cohen
Richard Compton
William Dasheff
James L. Forsht
Sarah W. French
Donna Harris
Edmund H. Harvey
Frank B. Latham
John Maury Warde

Contributing Artists
Dominic Colacchio
Don Coles
Ron Bertuzzi
Thomas Erik Fornander
Marilyn Grastorf
Henry Grindall
Arthur D. Gustafson
Rudie Hampel
Edward P. Hauser
George Kelvin
Earl L. Kvam
John A. Lind Corp.
Max Menikoff
Hisanori Morimoto
Bohdan Osyczka
Ken Rice
Bill Rudrow/Nancy Mazza
Jim Silks/Randall Lieu
Ray Skibinski
Lou Sklarsky
Dan Todd
Michael Vivo
Whitman Studio, Inc.

Contributing Photographers
Joseph Barnell
Ernest Coppolino
W. A. Sonntag

Technical Consultants
George Daniels, Chief Consultant
Tim Snider, General Consultant
Gordon Alexander
Walter Andrews
Robert H. Baker
Frank Bandera
Joe Bates
Steve Bottino
Archie P. Brill
N. R. Cooper
George Daniti
Nicholas De Palma
Reginald De Palma
James DiMeglio
Martin J. Donahue
Fentress Dorn
Thomas Elliot
Samuel A. Ernst
Donald Fausel
David Fiedler
Martin Forscher
Bill Geraghty
Fred Gildea
Peter Gillotti
Martens E. Goos
Leon Grabowski
Frank Granelli
Russ Haiskey
Leon R. Greenman
H. J. Hennigan
Walter L. Jacob
Donald W. Jagger
Joseph J. Knolczynski
R. J. Kronschnabel
Floyd J. Leach
J. J. McWilliams
Frank Monsky
Dough Nash
Charles F. Ne-Jame
J. D. Norton
Bob Paris
Harold Paris
James G. Patton
Tom Philb n
Emile Piasecki
Don Prieto
Ken Reisinger
Bill Ridgway
C. A. Ritchie
Norris Rosenbaum
Nancy Russell
Tom W. Stever
Donald P. Stone
Joseph Tripodi
Sol Weinstein
Paul Weissler
Richard C. Wolff
Gary Young

The editors are grateful for the assistance provided by the following manufacturers and organizations:

Albert Constantine & Son, Inc.
Allcraft Tool & Supply Company, Inc.
Amana Refrigeration, Inc.
Amerace Corporation
American Grease Stick Co.
American Motors Corp.
American Society for Testing & Materials
AMF Inc., Lawn & Garden Div.
Anchor Post Products, Inc.
The Anderson Company
Anglo-American Distribution, Ltd.
Arno Adhesive Tapes, Inc.
Association of Home Appliance Manufacturers
Automotive Information Council
Automotive Parts & Accessories Association
L. L. Bean, Inc.
Berkley & Co.
Bernzomatic Corporation
Bio-Lab Inc.
The Black & Decker Mfg. Co.
Briggs & Stratton Corp.
Brookstone Company
Brother International Corp.
Brown & Sharpe Mfg. Co.
Bruner Corporation
The Brunswick Corporation
Calgon Corp.
Caloric Corporation
Castrol (U.S.A.)
Champion Parts Rebuilders, Inc.
Champion Spark Plug Company
Chevron Chemical Co.
Chrysler Corporation
The Coleman Company, Inc.
Colt Industries Inc., Fairbanks Morse Pump Division
The Columbia Mfg. Co., Inc.
Conrad's Bicycle Shop
The Cooper Group
Culligan U.S.A.
Decorator's Emporium Div. of Goos Lumber Co.
Deere & Company
Dennco (Metro Bicycles)

De Palma Bros.
Dixson, Inc.
Duo-Fast Corporation
Dupli-Color Products
Dur-A-Flex, Inc.
Eastern Mountain Sports, Inc.
Eaton Corporation
Echlin Manufacturing Co.
Eico Electronic Instrument Co., Inc.
Emerson Electric Co.
Evinrude Motors Div. of Outboard Marine Corp.
Federal Chemical Co. Inc.
Fibre Glass—Evercoat Co. Inc.
The Firestone Tire & Rubber Company, Inc.
Fisher Corporation
Ford Motor Company
Frederick—Willys Co., Inc.
Frigidaire Div. of General Motors
The Garcia Corporation
General Battery Corp.
General Electric Co.
Goulds Pumps, Inc.
Gravely Div. of Clark—Gravely Corp.
Grumman Boats Div. of Grumman Allied Industries, Inc.
Harley—Davidson Motor Co., Inc.
Harvey Hubbell, Inc.
Harvey—Westbury Corporation
Havahart Traps
Hayward Manufacturing Co., Inc.
Heli—Coil Products
Hoffco, Inc., Comet Industries
Holsclaw Brothers, Inc.
Homlite Div. of Textron Inc.
Honeywell
The Hoover Company
Hopco Products
E. F. Houghton & Co.
Industrial Fasteners Institute
Institute of Electrical & Electronics Engineers

International Harvester Company
Jaw Manufacturing Company
Jayward Manufacturing Company, Inc.
Johnson Outboards Div. of Outboard Marine Corp.
Kastar, Inc.
K. D. Manufacturing Co.
Ken's Hardware
Kensington/Koni Shock Absorbers
Kester Solder Company
KitchenAid Division, Hobart Corporation
Kohler Co.
Life Industries Corporation
Loctite Corporation
Luger Industries, Inc.
McCulloch Corporation
McQuay—Norris Manufacturing Company
Mansfield Sanitary, Inc.
Melnor Industries
Minwax
Molded Fiber Glass Boat Co.
Moor & Mountain Equipment
Muskin Corp.
National Pest Control Association
National Swimming Pool Institute
Ne—Jame Company, Inc.
L. R. Nelson Corporation
Norelco Div. North American Phillips Corp.
Northern Instruments, Inc.
Norton Company
Oatey Company
Old Town Canoe Company
OMC—Lincoln
Owens—Corning Fiberglas Corp.
Peerless Enterprises, Inc.
J. C. Penney Company
Penreco
Petroleum Chemicals Company
Pirelli Tire Corporation
Polaroid Corp.
Power Tools Inc.
The Prestolite Co. an Eltra Co.
Pylon Manufacturing Corporation
Rain Jet Corporation

Recreational Equipment, Inc. Co-Op
The Ridge Tool Company
Rockwell International
ROKA International Corporation
Russell, Burdsall & Ward, Inc.
Schwinn Bicycle Company
O. M. Scott & Sons Co.
Sears, Roebuck and Co.
Seymour Smith & Son, Inc.
Simplicity Manufacturing Co., Inc.
Simpson Electric Company
The Singer Company
Skil Corporation
Society of Automotive Engineers
Sparkomatic Corporation
Sperex Corporation
Standard Motor Products, Inc.
Standard—Thomson Corp.
The Stanley Works
State Industries, Inc.
State Stove and Manufacturing Co., Inc.
Summit Grinding & Machine Company
The Tappan Co.
3-M Company
The Toro Company
Trico Products Corp.
True Temper Corporation
Union Carbide Corporation
U.S. Department of Agriculture
U.S. Office of Consumer Affairs
U.S. Suzuki Motor Corp.
U.S. Trademark Association
Very Important Products, Inc.
Volkswagen of America, Inc.
Wagner Electric Corporation
Wall—Lenk Mfg. Co.
Water Systems
Wen Products, Inc.
R. D. Werner Co., Inc.
Whirlpool Corporation

Table of Contents

About this book. Modern technology has enriched our lives with a variety of machines and appliances that work for us, transport us, and amuse us. When one of them breaks, however, we are often left groping for answers. How much will the repair cost? How long will it take? Can we be sure that the job will be done correctly? Usually there are two ways to solve the problem—either pay out large sums of money to a shop, or try to remedy things ourselves.

This book shows you how to follow the second, more economical path. Be sure to consult the charts that accompany the text in the various sections. The charts are there to help you find a defect quickly and take the right repair action. In some places you will see cross references to related pages and sections. This arrangement permits the grouping of basic information that would otherwise have to be repeated in too many scattered places. If you have a question about a technical term or a repair step, and no page reference

appears next to it, look it up in the index at the end of this volume.

Anyone can use this book, whether he or she be an old hand or just a beginner at repair work. After experiencing the satisfaction of finding and replacing a defective $2 part that would otherwise cost $20 or $30 to have a professional repairman replace, you will quickly appreciate how much you can save by referring to a book as useful, detailed, and complete as this one. Even if you have no intention of making your own repairs, you will value this volume as a money-saving ready reference in dealing with today's highly expensive professional repairmen.

Around the Home

Such common household articles as lamps, doorbells, and window shades occasionally break or require adjustment. This section tells how to repair such items. It also covers the basics of plumbing and includes a comprehensive, up-to-date chart on the properties and uses of the many modern adhesives available for work inside and outside the home.

contents

Adhesives

Properties and uses

A large and growing number of adhesives is available on the market today. Some are specialized. For example, Resorcinol, because of its strong water resistance, is excellent for repairing boats and outdoor furniture. Others, such as the PVA adhesives—commonly called white glues—are fine for general household use. The chart that begins below and continues on the two following pages is designed to help you determine the most appropriate adhesive for a specific job.

Setting and curing time. Setting time is the interval before the glue hardens. Curing time is the period it takes the bond to reach maximum strength. An object should not be used until the adhesive has cured. Fast-setting and instantaneous adhesives are ideal for bonding objects that are difficult or impossible to clamp. If you will need time to make minor adjustments before the glue sets, use fast-setting but not instantaneous glues, which set almost immediately or in seconds.

Water resistance. Remember that PVA adhesives and water-based adhesives, including casein and hide glues, are water soluble. They should not be used on objects that will be exposed to dampness or weather.

Preparation of surfaces. Clean surfaces thoroughly. Wood should always be stripped or sanded free of wax, paint, and varnish. Read labels carefully for instruction in safety and application. If a drop of glue etches the surface of a plastic, it will probably bond that material.

Adhesive	Sample brand names	Typical uses	Components	Application	Setting and curing time	Strength	Flexibility	Water resistance	Solvent
Acrylic	3 Ton Adhesive	For fast, extra-strong bonding of wood, metal, glass, outdoor furniture; used in boat building	Two parts, liquid and powder; mix amount needed just before use	Apply with brush, putty knife, or strip of wood, depending on job	Sets in as little as 5 min; cures overnight	6,000 pounds per square inch (psi)	Rigid	Waterproof	Acetone (nail polish remover)
Acrylonitrile	Pliobond	For metal, glass, fabrics, carpets and tents, boat sails; not recommended for furniture joints	One part, liquid; ready to use	Apply adhesive to both surfaces; use a brush for large jobs; for small jobs, apply from tube	Sets almost immediately; cures in 24–48 hr, depending on type and method of application	2,000–3,000 psi	Highly flexible	Waterproof	Acetone (nail polish remover)
Aliphatic	Titebond, Se-Cur-It Resin	General purpose adhesive for furniture building and repair, cabinet work	One part, liquid; ready to use (generally in squeeze bottle)	Apply from squeeze bottle	Clamp for at least 45 min, while it sets; cures overnight	2,000–3,500 psi	Rigid	Water soluble; do not use on outdoor furniture	Warm water
Bolt-locking compound (anaerobic resins)	Locktite Lock N' Seal (temporary bond), Locktite Stud N' Bearing Mount (permanent bond), Permatex Locknut	For locking threads of bolts and screws; will harden in absence of air between closely fitted metal parts	One part, liquid; ready to use	Squeeze from tube or bottle	Sets in about 15 min; cures overnight for most bonds, in 24 hr for steel to steel bonds	Red, maximum strength; blue, medium strength; purple, low strength	Rigid	Waterproof and resistant to gasoline, oil, and other solvents	Soap and water before hardening
Casein glues	National Casein Co. No. 30	Traditional furniture glue; good for such oily woods as teak and lemon; good gap filler; will leave stain marks on redwood, other softwoods	One part, powder; mix with water	Apply with brush, roller, or strip of wood, depending on the job	Clamp for 5–6 hr while glue sets; cures overnight	3,200 psi	Rigid	Moderate; not waterproof	Warm water
Cellulose	Duco Cement (clear) Ambroid (amber)	For wood, mold work, china, glass, most fabrics. Check for usability on plastics by testing on small area (see text, above)	One part, liquid; ready to use	Apply directly from tube. Use strip of wood to apply from can. Strength is increased by applying two coats to both surfaces, letting first coat set until gummy before applying second coat	Sets to 60% of strength in 2 hr; cures to 90% in 2 days	3,500 psi	Moderately flexible	Waterproof	Acetone (nail polish remover)
Contact cement	Weldwood Contact Cement, Goodyear Contact Cement	For bonding laminated plastic to countertops	One part, liquid; ready to use	Apply with brush or roller to both surfaces	Allow cement to stand about 15 min before joining surfaces. Sets almost immediately			High	Acetone (nail polish remover)

Adhesive	Sample brand names	Typical uses	Components	Application	Setting and curing time	Strength	Flexibility	Water resistance	Solvent
Epoxy	Fiberglass Evercoat Epoxy, Weldwood Epoxy, Devcon Clear Epoxy, Devcon UW, Miracle Fast-Set Epoxy (5 min)	For wood, metal, china, glass, most other materials. Especially good for bonding two dissimilar materials, such as metal to glass	Two parts, both syrupy liquids; mix equal amounts just before using (see text, p.13)	Apply with strip of wood, putty knife, brush, or matchstick	Sets at room temperature in 5 min to overnight, depending on type; cures in 3 hr to several days (Devcon UW will cure at 0°F in 2–3 weeks)	3,400 psi	Rigid to semirigid	Waterproof	Acetone (nail polish remover). Not easily removed; use expendable brushes
Hide glue, flake (flakes can be stored dry for long periods)	Usually carries retailer's name	For construction and repair of wood furniture	One part, flakes; soak until smooth and brushable in water heated to 130°F	Apply with brush; work fast—glue stiffens as it cools. Cannot be applied cold	Sets and cures in about 8 hr at 70°F	3,200 psi	Rigid	Water soluble; do not use on outdoor furniture	Warm water
Hide glue, liquid	Franklin Liquid Hide Glue	For construction and repair of wood furniture	One part, liquid; ready to use	Apply with brush, roller, or strip of wood, depending on job	Sets and cures in about 8 hr at 70°F	3,200 psi	Rigid	Water soluble; do not use on outdoor furniture	Warm water
Hot-melt	Thermgrip Hot Melt, Swingline Hot Melt	For everything but a few plastics. Good for quick repairs on leather and fabrics; good gap filler for loose furniture joints	One part, cartridges in stick form; place into chamber of an electrically heated gun	Apply with electric glue gun	Sets and cures in 1 to 2 min	250 psi or more	Moderately flexible	Waterproof	Acetone (nail polish remover)
Latex-base adhesive	Devcon Patch, Sears Stitchless Mender, Duralite Formula 55, Franklin Indoor/Outdoor Carpet Adhesive	Fabrics, carpet, paper, cardboard	One part, liquid; ready to use	Apply directly from tube; use brush or strip of wood to apply from can	Sets almost immediately; cures in about 1 hr	250 psi or more	Flexible	Water resistant	Lighter fluid
Liquid solder (household cement with metallic particles for coloring effect)	Ross Liquid Solder, Liquid Steel	Bonds aluminum, tin, other metals and materials, but do not use to solder electrical connections	One part, liquid; ready to use	Squeeze from tube; apply to both surfaces and press together at once	Sets in 8 hr; cures overnight	Up to 3,500 psi	Moderately flexible	Water resistant	Acetone (nail polish remover)
Mastic	Ruscoe Pan-L Bond, Franklin Construction Adhesive, Webtex 200 Acoustical Adhesive	For ceiling, wall, and floor tiles, plywood panels, concrete, asphalt, leather, textiles	One part, either a water-base synthetic latex or a rubber resin; both are ready to use	If in a can, use stick or notched trowel; if in a tube, fit tube into a caulking gun	Sets in few seconds up to 1 hr; cures in 24 hr	250 psi or more	Flexible or rigid, depending on type	Water resistant	Usually mineral spirits. Follow the instructions for type being used
Polyester	Fiberglass-Evercoat Polyester, Pettit Polyester Resin	Used on fiberglass boats; bonds fiberglass to wooden hulls	Two parts, resin and activator; mix just before using	Add activator and brush on	Usually sets in less than an hour. Cures over a longer period. See instructions for type being used		Rigid	Waterproof	Acetone (nail polish remover). Not easily removed; use expendable brushes

Adhesives

Properties and uses (continued)

Adhesive	Sample brand names	Typical uses	Components	Application	Setting and curing time	Strength	Flexibility	Water resistance	Solvent
Polyvinyl acetate (PVA, or white glue)	Elmer's Glue-All, DuPont White Glue, Sears White Glue	For general household repairs, furniture, interior woodwork, paper, ceramics	One part, liquid; ready to use	For small jobs use applicator on bottle; for large jobs, use a brush	Sets in about 8 hr at 70°F; cures in 24 hr	3,200 psi (tensile strength is good, but will creep under steady stress)	Rigid	Soluble; do not use on materials to be exposed to water	Soap, warm water
Polyvinyl chloride (PVC)	Sheer Magic	For quick repairs and craft work; china, marble, glass, wood, porcelain, metal	One part, liquid; ready to use	Apply directly from tube or use a wood paddle	Sets in minutes. Cures over a longer period. See brand specifications	Depends on material being bonded	Semirigid	Water resistant	Acetone (nail polish remover)
Resorcinol	Elmer's Waterproof Glue, Sears Waterproof Resorcinol Glue, U.S. Plywood Waterproof Resorcinol Glue	For extra strong wood repairs; outdoor furniture, boat building	Two parts, liquid and powder; mix only amount needed depending on the job and area	Apply with brush, roller, or strip of wood, depending on the job	Sets and cures in 10 hr at 70°F, in 6 hr at 80°F, in 3½ hr at 90°F	3,400 psi	Rigid	Waterproof	Cool water before hardening; can not be removed after hardening
Silicone sealant	Dow Silicone Adhesive, General Electric Silicone Seal, Sears Silicone Adhesive Sealant	For caulking sinks, bathtubs, windows, doors. Also bonds tiles, glass, metal, porcelain, wood. May contain toxic ingredients; do not use in dishwashers or aquariums	One part, liquid; ready to use	Apply directly from tube, or from can, using spatula	Sets in 1 hr; cures in about 24 hr		Flexible	Waterproof	Excess can be peeled or scraped from some materials
Styrene butadiene (rubber base cement)	Black Magic (black), Brite Magic (white)	Versatile adhesive for use on metal, glass, many plastics; replacement of loose tiles, bricks; reattachment of wall fixtures to tile or metal walls	One part, thick paste; ready to use	Use spatula, putty knife, or trowel on large jobs; apply directly from tube on small jobs	Sets and cures in about 48 hr	Depends on material being bonded	Rigid	Waterproof	Mineral spirits, such as turpentine
"Super" glue, or instant glue (cyanoacrylate)	Krazy Glue, Duro Super Glue-3, Sears Super Glue #3	Bonds most plastics, metals, vinyl, rubber, ceramics, but not paper, cardboard, fabrics, and wood; do not to use on polyethelene or teflon	One part, liquid; ready to use	Cautiously apply one or several drops directly from tube; do not get any on your skin	Sets in seconds; cures in ½ hr to 12 hr	Up to 5,000 psi	Rigid to semirigid	Highly water resistant	Acetone (nail polish remover)
Urea formaldehyde	Weldwood Plastic Resin Glue, Elmer's Plastic Resin Glue, Craftsman Plastic Resin Glue	For extra strong furniture and cabinet repairs	One part, powder; mix with water as per instructions just before using	Apply with brush, roller, or spatula, depending on the job	Sets in 9-13 hr at 70°F; cures in 24 hr	3,000 psi	Rigid	Highly water resistant after curing time	Soap, warm water before hardening
Water-phase epoxy	Dur-A-Poxy	Can be used as waterproof coating over masonry, as protection for pointing in chimneys; also can be mixed into cement	Two parts, both liquid; mix equal amounts just before using	Apply with brush or roller when used as waterproof coating; with trowel or putty knife when mixed with cement	Varies; see the instructions for type used; sets and cures faster when mixed with cement		Moderately flexible	Waterproof after hardening	Soap and water before hardening

Epoxy compound

In the past decade, epoxy compound has become one of the most popular all-purpose adhesives. It is exceptionally strong, and will bond just about any material except rubber and certain plastics. It also has good gap-filling and caulking properties, and because it is waterproof it can be used to repair leaking water pipes.

Epoxy comes in two tubes, one containing a resin and the other a hardener. The two substances are mixed together in equal amounts just before the adhesive is applied. With most brands a moderate mixing error will not significantly affect bonding strength. Epoxy does not harden by evaporation but by a chemical process known as polymerization. The molecules of the resin and those of the hardener bond to form new and larger molecules.

Some epoxy adhesives set in a matter of minutes but complete the chemical curing process only after several days. Others set in several hours and take a day or longer to reach maximum strength. Objects mended with epoxy will often seem ready to use after the glue has set, for the joint will look and feel deceptively hard. But the polymerization process is not complete until the adhesive has fully cured, and objects should not be used until this occurs.

Not all epoxy label instructions are clear with respect to setting and curing times at different temperatures. As a rule, therefore, it is wise to allow for a longer curing time for epoxy than that given on the label.

While most epoxy adhesives recommend that repair work be done at room temperature, some brands will cure at temperatures below 40°F, and are convenient for outdoor repair work in cold weather. However, the curing time at such temperatures may be several times longer than the curing time at room temperature.

Use the type of epoxy that suits the job to be done: fast-setting for small jobs, slow-setting for large ones, such as repairing fiberglass boat hulls. Although epoxy is expensive, its strength, flexibility, and ability to bond most materials make it a good buy.

Instant glues

The new, so-called "super" glues require the application of only a drop or two to make an instantaneous bond of exceptionally high strength. They are not strictly speaking contact cements, which are applied to both surfaces and permitted to become tacky before the surfaces are joined. But as with contact cements, surfaces joined by instant glues bind immediately on contact.

Instant glues are most effective with nonporous materials: glass, metal, porcelain, and most plastics. They are not recommended for use on paper or wood. Because of their setting speed, these glues are ideal for mending small objects, such as eyeglass frames, that can be held in the hand rather than clamped. Instant glues are not suited to long glue lines or to large repair jobs.

Instant glues must always be used cautiously, as they bond skin. Squeeze the tube gently and carefully to avoid squirting, and point the tube away from your face and eyes. Always keep instant glues out of the reach of young children.

Tapes

Tapes may not provide the lasting bond that is attainable with glue; nonetheless, they are convenient for patching fabrics and some harder materials.

Carpet tape: This double-faced adhesive tape is used to anchor rugs and carpets. The tape is first applied to the floor; the paper coating on top is then peeled away uncovering a second adhesive surface to which the carpet is anchored.

Tent tape: This heavy-duty, waterproof, all-purpose cloth tape is good for repairing tents, carpeting, and leaking hoses.

Aluminum tape: This waterproof tape is made of aluminum foil. It does not tarnish or rust, and can be used to repair leaking rainspouts and as a seal for metal surfaces.

Clear tapes: Clear vinyl waterproof tapes can be used where transparency is desirable, as in the patching of ripped plastic rainwear.

Masking tape: This heavy paper tape is intended primarily for use as a guide in painting straight lines. However, it has many possible uses, including clamping glued surfaces.

Hot-melt glue

Hot-melt glue has only recently become available as a household adhesive. It is extensively used in industry because it sets quickly and is easy to apply. The adhesive cartridge, or glue stick, is inserted into the electrically heated chamber of a glue gun. There are two types of glue guns. In one type the cartridge is fed automatically by means of a trigger. In the other, the glue sticks are pushed through the melting chamber by the thumb. Both release a stream of hot, melted glue, which sets by cooling in a minute or less.

Hot-melt glue can be used on a variety of materials including metal and glass. For the best bond, heat both gluing surfaces to about 150°F before the glue is applied. Although not as strong as epoxy compound or instant glues, hot-melt glue is convenient and effective for gluing joints that cannot easily be clamped. Because it is flexible, hot-melt glue is excellent for repairing leather, canvas, and other fabrics, and can in some cases be used as a substitute for sewing, as in fastening a zipper to a fabric. It is also handy in model making. Smooth surfaces should be roughened with fine sandpaper before gluing.

Hot-melt glue can also be used for caulking, and special caulking cartridges are available. Glue guns should be used carefully. Not only is the glue hot, but the nozzle and forward part of the melting chamber reach a temperature of about 400°F, and remain hot enough to burn for several minutes after the gun is turned off.

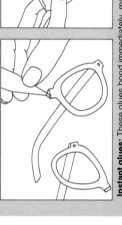

Mixing epoxy: To assure proper mixture of resin and hardener, squeeze out equal amounts side by side on a piece of glass or foil. Mix the two together.

Instant glues: These glues bond immediately, making them ideal for repairs where clamping is difficult or impossible. Here, broken eyeglasses are mended.

Bookbinding

Tools and materials

Repairing a book is largely a matter of cutting, pasting, and measuring accurately. In most cases, you can do this at home, but a valuable book should be taken to a professional book-binder.

The most essential tools are a bone folder—a special tool made of bone for creasing, folding, or smoothing—and a mat knife, scalpel, or sharp utility knife. Other basic tools include a square or a straightedge and a triangle, scissors, and brushes. Materials you will need include adhesives, cheesecloth, scrap paper for a gluing surface, and wax paper. Tools and materials are listed for each job.

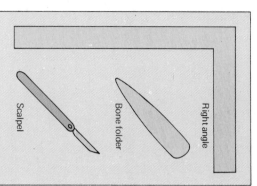

Right angle

Bone folder

Scalpel

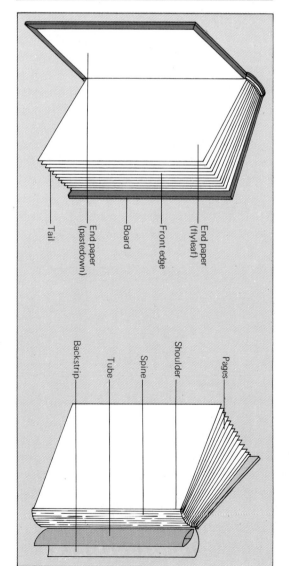

End paper (flyleaf)

Front edge

Board

End paper (pastedown)

Tail

Pages

Shoulder

Spine

Tube

Backstrip

Gluing

Two types of adhesives are used for book repair, quick-drying white (polyvinyl acetate) glue and slower drying flour paste.

White glue is used where permanent flexibility is desired. Before using, thin with water until glue dripped from a brush back into container blends into the surface smoothly.

Flour paste is used where flexibility is not required. To make it, add ¼ teaspoon flour to 1½ teaspoons water, stir until smooth, then cook to consistency of thin cream sauce. Use unenriched wheat flour of fine pastry grade. Commercial wall-paper paste may be substituted.

Glue quickly, using largest practical brush. Hold piece to be glued on scrap paper and brush glue from center outwards. Discard scrap paper to avoid putting clean work on it.

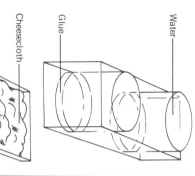

Water

Glue

Cheesecloth

Brush

Place glue and water containers in a third container to avoid spillage by tipping. When working with brushes, be careful not to drip glue. Brushes should be in glue, in water, or thoroughly cleaned with water and stored, bristles up, in jar.

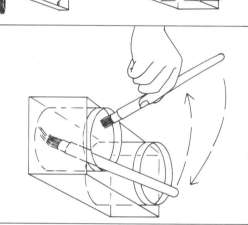

To avoid spreading glue all over brush handle and rim of glue container, always wipe off excess glue on rim nearest you. In returning brush to glue, place handle against far, clean edge of rim. Brushes should be in glue, in water, or thoroughly cleaned with water and stored, bristles up, in jar. Use damp cheesecloth to wipe up excess glue.

Caring for books

Before opening any book that is dusty, hold it tightly shut and clean it with a silicone-treated cloth, usually available at five-and-ten and houseware stores. Always brush from the spine to the front edge.

If the pages are soiled, some surface dirt can be removed with a soft, clean pencil eraser. Use a soft brush to whisk away the eraser dust.

Mold and leather

Mold may be hidden from view but it can be detected by its distinctive musty odor. It can cause damage and spread to other books. Do not try to remove mold yourself, since this requires the employment of chemicals. Take the book to a professional bookbinder.

Leather-bound books should be oiled every five years to pro-tect the leather against drying out and to restore color and sur-face sheen. Use neatsfoot oil or a special mixture of neatsfoot oil and lanolin, available at book-binding supply stores. Place the book on a piece of scrap paper and rub the oil well into the cover, applying it with your fingers or a soft cloth. Be careful not to get oil onto the pages or any parts of the binding that are not made of leather. Let stand overnight. Next day, wipe off any excess oil and gently polish the leather with a soft cloth.

Opening a new book incor-rectly can break its spine. Do not snap it open; instead, set the book down on its spine, hold onto the pages and let the covers drop. Then gently fold down a few pages at a time, starting at each cover and working alter-nately toward the middle.

Repairing a torn or cut page

Paper is made of matted and glued fibers; when the paper is torn those fibers are wrenched apart. Repair a tear by brushing a line of glue along one of the torn edges and rejoining the edges (see right).

When paper is cut, there are no wrenched-apart fibers. Repair with a gummed, transparent tape. Do not use shiny cellophane tape, as it becomes brittle with age, and its glue will stain the page. Snip off a length of tape slightly longer than the cut. Line up edges of cut and position tape so that one end extends over edge of page. Smooth tape down; trim the long end with a pair of scissors.

Fibers in torn edge as seen under magnification

1. Place wax paper under torn page. Lift torn edge carefully and brush thin line of white glue along one edge only.

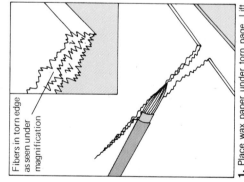

2. Line up edges of tear so print matches. Press with dry cheesecloth. Move wax paper so page does not stick; press again.

Tipping in a loose page

Each book page is half a folded sheet. The fold is the axis the page turns on. When a page tears loose along the fold, replace the fold with a new hinge.

Tools
Straightedge, knife, brush, bone folder

Materials
Onion skin bond, wax paper, white glue, scrap paper

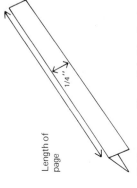

Length of page

Making a new hinge: Cut strip of onion skin bond ½ in. wide and to exact length of page. Fold in half lengthwise.

Repairing a frayed corner

One of the first signs of wear in a book generally occurs at the corners. First, the corner becomes bent with use; then, the cloth begins to work loose or is torn from the boards, and the boards split. If left unrepaired, the corners will eventually break off, no longer protecting the book pages. When this happens, the whole cover must be replaced.

Repairing a corner is simple. Inspect your books. If any have worn corners, follow the instructions at right.

Tools
Bone folder, ⅜- to ½-inch brush

Materials
Thin flour paste

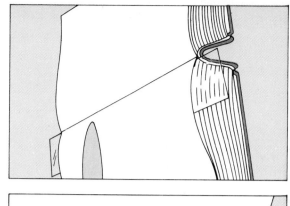

1. Using a narrow brush, work thin solution of flour paste between loose layers of board and book cloth at the corner.

2. Press together firmly with fingers to mold corner into shape. Smooth cloth with bone folder if necessary. Let dry.

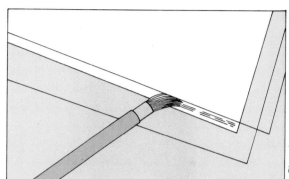

1. On page following loose page, line up straight edge of a strip of wax paper ¼ in. from spine to act as gluing guide. Apply glue sparingly to ¼-in. band along spine.

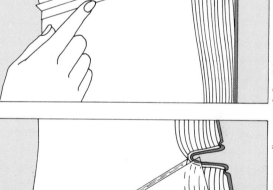

2. Carefully position one side of hinge along ¼-in. band of glue. Tuck hinge fold well back into spine of book. Press into place with fingers or bone folder.

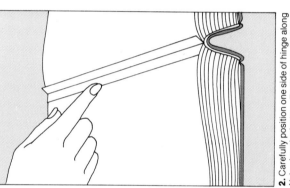

3. Place loose page, even-numbered side up, on scrap paper. Use strip of wax paper as gluing guide; lightly brush ¼-in. band of glue along edge of page.

4. Align page at head, tail, and front edge. Hold in position while smoothing page onto hinge with bone folder. Hinge and page should come together automatically.

Bookbinding

Making a tube

A tube is used when re-covering a book or replacing the cover's sections are shaped to provide spine to strengthen the book. To make a tube, first cut a piece of brown paper slightly longer than the spine of the book and a little over twice its width. Center the paper on the spine; measure and mark it with pencil to the exact width of spine.

Fold the paper lengthwise at each mark, forming a tube with the edges overlapping. Mark the length of the spine on the tube and cut it to size. Apply a thin line of white glue to the inside of the overlapping edge; rub down to seal the tube, which will be glued to both the backstrip and spine of book.

Tools
Scissors, pencil, brush
Materials
Brown paper, white glue, scrap paper

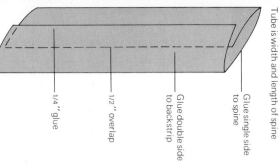

Tube is width and length of spine

Glue single side
to spine

Glue double side
to backstrip

1/2" overlap

1/4" glue

Replacing a spine

Books are sewn in sections; the sections are shaped to provide a curve at the back, and a shoulder along the spine against which the boards rest flat. The cloth hinges between boards and spine often break, and the cover comes apart from the book. If the boards are in good condition, repair by simply attaching a new spine.

Book cloth for the spine is available from bookbinding supply stores. Use a light cardstock for the backstrip.

Clean the old boards by trimming ragged edges of the end papers and cutting away a narrow strip of book cloth along the spine, exposing bare board to which the new spine cloth will be glued. Clean book spine by first picking off old, dry material with a knife. Soften remaining material with white glue thinned to consistency of skim milk; scrape book clean. Reshape book by tapping head on a flat surface; push any loose sections back into place.

Always test-fit cover before gluing it to book. Position book on right-hand board so that board extends evenly beyond pages at head, tail, and front edge. Bring cover around and close it on book. Crease hinges with bone folder. Finally, glue a connecting strip along the spine inside each cover to replace the broken hinges of the end papers.

Tools
Straightedge, utility or mat knife, bone folder
Materials
Book cloth, light cardstock, new tube, white glue, scrap paper

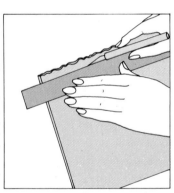

1. Cut away ¼-in. strip of cloth along spine edge of the book's old boards. Trim end papers even with boards.

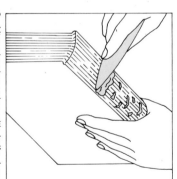

2. After cleaning spine with knife, brush thinned glue onto spine to soften remaining material; clean off with bone folder.

New tube

3. Apply unthinned white glue along spine, let dry. Make tube. Glue its single side to spine, using white glue. Smooth down.

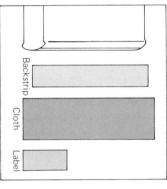

Backstrip

Cloth

Label

4. Cut backstrip to board's length, spine's width; cut cloth ½ in. longer than boards, 2 in. wider than spine. Trim label.

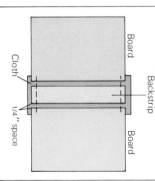

Cloth

Backstrip

Board

Board

1/4" space

5. Center backstrip on glued cloth; place boards ¼ in. away on each side. Fold over cloth ends and rub them down.

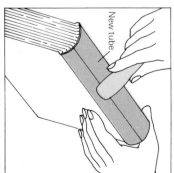

6. Place book on right-hand board. Bring cover around and close it on book. Test fit before gluing tube to backstrip.

7. Apply glue. Refit book into cover. Crease hinge on back and front cover with blunt end of bone folder. Let dry.

8. Cut two connecting strips for hinges (p.15). Glue each, tucking fold into spine. Smooth edges down on board and flyleaf.

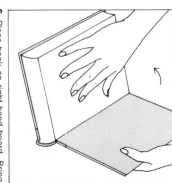

9. Glue back of trimmed label; position correctly on spine. Cover with wax paper and rub smooth with bone folder.

Making new end papers

An end paper is a sheet of paper folded in half, cut to fit the book pages, and tipped in along the spine. Half is glued over inside of the cover, the rest is left as the flyleaf.

Books are not always perfectly rectangular. Measure length of end papers at both front and back of book, width at both top and bottom. The end papers must be cut so that the grain runs parallel to the spine; otherwise, the boards will warp when the paper is glued down. To determine grain, cut small strip of paper and dampen it. It will curl along grain.

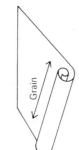

Tools
Bone folder, brush, straightedge, mat knife, pencil, brush
Materials
Bond paper, white glue

1. Lay folded paper under first book page, fold along spine. Mark to length of page and trim with knife and straight edge.

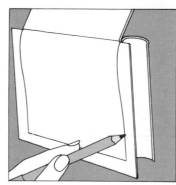

2. Make slight bend along fold, as wide as depth of shoulder curve, so that end paper will fit snugly against spine.

3. With bend against shoulder, mark width of end paper even with front edge of book. Cut to size, using straight edge and knife.

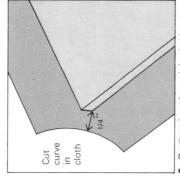

4. Brush narrow line of glue along bend. Align end paper and fit bend into shoulder curve. Smooth down. Tip in other paper.

Fitting a new cover

A new cover is made with two boards, a backstrip, a tube, and the book cloth—available from bookbinding supply stores. Cut the boards from heavy cardboard using old boards for size.

Cut the cloth large enough to cover the book, and overlap it ⅝ inch all around. On the wrong side, center the backstrip and space the boards ¼ inch away on either side. Be sure that the boards are squared on the cloth. Mark their exact position, using a pencil and a square.

Glue boards and backstrip in place, using a mixture of half white glue and half flour paste. The dampness of the glue will warp the boards slightly. Once the end papers are glued down, the boards will warp back in the opposite direction to lie flat.

Tools
A 2-inch brush, bone folder, scissors, weight, square
Materials
Book cloth, glue/paste mixture, cardboard, a light cardstock, brown paper, scrap paper

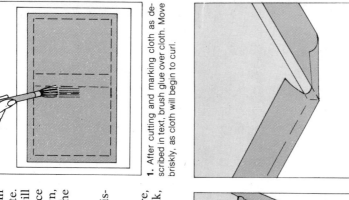

1. After cutting and marking cloth as described in text, brush glue over cloth. Move briskly, as cloth will begin to curl.

Cut curve in cloth   ¼″

2. Position boards and backstrip along marked lines. Curve corners of cloth, leaving ¼ in. extending beyond boards.

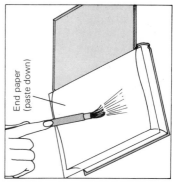

3. Fold cloth over tightly at top and bottom of boards. Rub with folder, pressing cloth down between boards and backstrip.

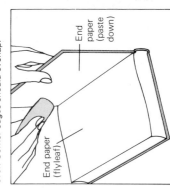

4. Pinch and tuck in overhang at top and bottom corners. Fold cloth at sides tightly over. Corner edges should overlap.

End paper (flyleaf)

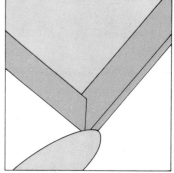

End paper (paste down)

5. After laying clean paper over right side of cover and rubbing smooth, round corners by gently tapping with folder.

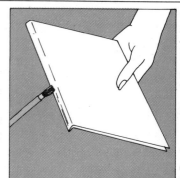

End paper (paste down)

6. Glue cover on book (p.16). Open front cover; glue end paper; close cover. Repeat on back. Weight down two minutes.

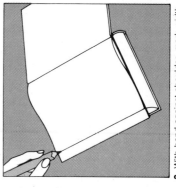

End paper (paste down)

7. Open cover *only* 90°. Smooth down end paper with folder. Wipe off excess glue. Repeat on back. Weight down overnight.

China, porcelain, and glass

Mending techniques

Because an exact fit is essential in mending glass, porcelain, and china, you need time to adjust the pieces precisely before the glue sets. Instantaneous adhesives are therefore not recommended—they set too quickly. A clear epoxy is generally effective (see *Adhesives*, pp.10-13). It is waterproof, provides a strong bond, and has good gap-filling properties.

Before gluing, thoroughly clean and dry the broken surfaces. Assemble the pieces dry and note how they fit. Then, apply a light coat of glue along

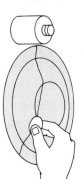
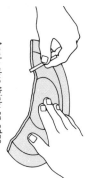

one edge of the break with a matchstick or small spatula. Join the pieces. Wipe off the

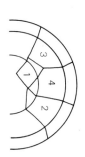

Apply glue thinly on edge.

Remove excess glue with solvent.

excess glue with a cotton swab dipped in the appropriate solvent (see *Adhesives*). The less glue used the better; a thin film will usually do. Remember that glue itself takes up space. If you mend an item shattered into many pieces, thick glue joints will deform the restored piece.

Next, clamp and support the glued piece either by using one of the methods shown at right,

or one of your own invention. As you put clamping pressure on the piece and adjust its alignment, you may force more glue out of joints. Again, wipe away any excess, using a solvent.

It is probable that more glue will ooze from cracks as the pieces sets. All glues pass through a stage where they are strong enough to hold the piece together, though not completely hardened. This stage will vary depending on the setting and curing time of the glue you use. During this stage the glue is still soft enough to be removed with a solvent, and you should make a final removal of excess glue before it completely cures.

When mending objects with many breaks, glue the pieces one or two at a time. Study the pieces and put them together dry to determine the most sensi-

ble order of assembly, then glue them in this order.

Devising supports often requires ingenuity. Plasticine is helpful; a malleable, plastic substance, it holds any shape you give it. Molds and masking tape are also useful.

You can easily fashion a homemade mold, using either wax or plaster (see illustrations at right). Molds are helpful in reassembling many small pieces; they hold them in place while the glue dries.

Determine order of gluing.

Plate supports

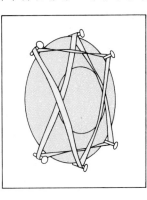

Drive nails in a circle slightly larger than radius of plate. Stretch rubber bands over plate to create clamping pressure.

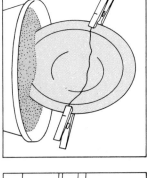

Anchor the larger piece of the plate in a basin filled with dirt or sand. Use clothes pins to clamp the pieces.

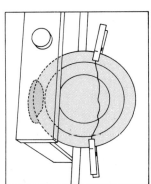

You can use a drawer to hold the plate immobile if you buffer the points of contact with lumps of Plasticine.

Improvised supports

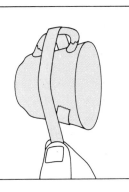

A glued cup handle can be held firmly in position by vertical and horizontal strips of masking tape encircling the cup.

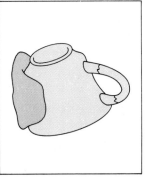

A cup can be supported by lumps of Plasticine, with the force of gravity supplying the clamping pressure.

Ingenuity at work: Three sand-filled cans anchor sticks; Plasticine on ends of sticks support a glass with a broken stem.

Wax mold

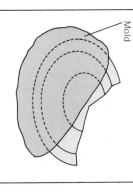

1. Molds are ideal for plates. Heat paraffin until it softens, then pack it around bottom on unbroken side of plate.

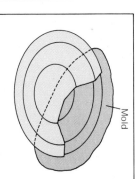

2. Let the mold set, then shift it around to the broken side; slip it carefully under the plate, and align it.

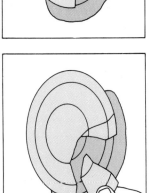

3. Fit the broken pieces into the mold. If there are many, first glue only a few. Let them set, then glue the additional pieces.

Doorbells, buzzers, and chimes

Troubleshooting signaling systems

Signaling systems such as doorbells, buzzers, and chimes consist of a pushbutton, a signaling unit, and a transformer. A typical home circuit is shown here in cross section.

It is normally safe to work on faulty signaling systems without shutting off the main power. However, the transformer may be defective, either relaying no current or failing to reduce it. Therefore, first check the transformer with a volt-ohm meter, as illustrated at the right side of this page. If the transformer is producing too much power or no power at all, it should be replaced. If it is working properly, you may check out the system without turning off the main power.

Next, check the whole system for breaks in the wiring; splice any you find. If the transformer is working properly and all wiring is intact, dismantle the pushbutton and test it by shorting it with a screwdriver, as shown in the center illustration at the bottom of this page. The button's contact points may have been corroded by exposure to weather, and need cleaning. Repeated use can weaken the button's internal spring mechanism. If this seems to be the case, replace the button.

If the button is working properly, check wiring connections inside the signaling unit—the chimes or bell. Poorly connected wiring at either the transformer or signaling unit can cause a system to ring continuously or not at all. If all tests lead you to conclude that the signaling unit itself is faulty, replace it.

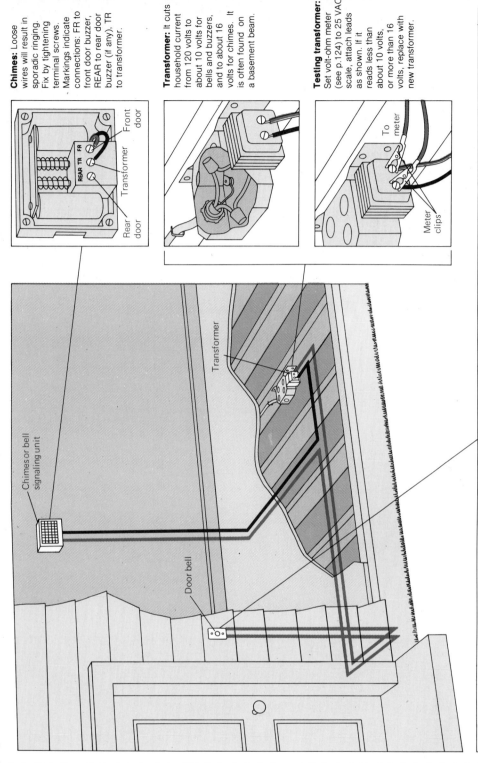

Chimes or bell signaling unit

Transformer

Door bell

Chimes: Loose wires will result in sporadic ringing. Fix by tightening terminal screws. Markings indicate connections: FR to front door buzzer, REAR to rear door buzzer (if any), TR to transformer.

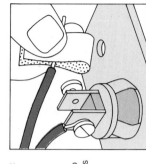

Front door

Transformer

Rear door

Transformer: It cuts household current from 120 volts to about 10 volts for bells and buzzers, and to about 16 volts for chimes. It is often found on a basement beam.

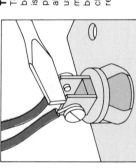

Testing transformer: Set volt-ohm meter (see p.124) to 25 VAC scale, attach leads as shown. If it reads less than about 10 volts, or more than 16 volts, replace with new transformer.

To meter

Meter clips

Cleaning corroded terminals: Either spray them with an electrical contact cleaner (p.123) or remove wires and sand all corrosion from wires and screws with fine sandpaper, as shown. Wires will spark if they touch.

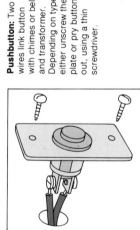

Testing the button: To avoid a shock, be sure transformer is functioning properly (see test, above right). Then, use a screwdriver to make contact across both terminals. If chimes sound, replace the button.

Pushbutton: Two wires link button with chimes or bell and transformer. Depending on type, either unscrew the plate or pry button out, using a thin screwdriver.

Doorknobs, locks, and hinges

Typical locks

Many lock problems can be solved by a simple repair or adjustment. Even when more complicated work is necessary, your ability to disassemble the lock and take the right part to the locksmith will save you the expense of a house call. Several common types of door locks and lock mechanisms are illustrated on this page; specific problems and repairs are discussed and illustrated on the two following pages. Many of these repairs entail a delicate process of trial and error.

Rim lock: The cylinder extends through the entire thickness of the door. The lock is held in place by screws mounted from the inside, often accessible only after removing the lock case. A loose fitting ring on the front of the cylinder prevents tampering from the outside.

Mortise lock: This lock is installed in a recess cut in the edge of the door. A threaded lock cylinder is screwed into the unit and secured by setscrews, which engage a slot in the side of the cylinder. Note: The setscrews are often concealed by a false plate that covers the lock face.

Locksets: These locks have doorknobs at both ends. Exterior models have a lock cylinder in the outside knob, which is accessible only by removing the unit from the inside. Depressing a spring catch removes the knob and rose, exposing the mounting plate. Interior types, or privacy locks, may be opened from the outside by turning the slotted spindle—accessible through a hole in the knob. Screws in the rose fasten the whole unit.

Rim lock

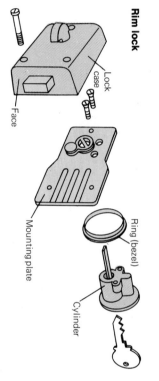

Cylinder
Lock case
Face
Setscrew
Mounting plate
Ring (bezel)
Cylinder

Mortise lock

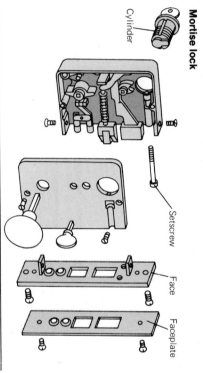

Face
Faceplate

Lockset/exterior type

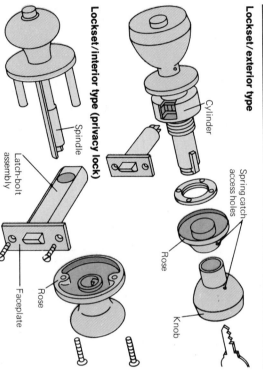

Cylinder
Spring catch access holes
Rose
Knob

Lockset/interior type (privacy lock)

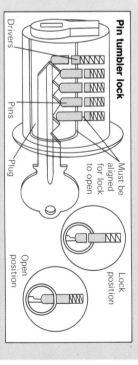

Spindle
Latch-bolt assembly
Rose
Faceplate

How common lock mechanisms work

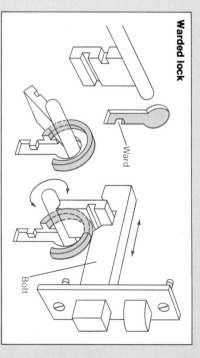

Warded lock

The key is cut to avoid the obstacles, called wards, that block the keyway and the path of rotation. As the key is turned, its top engages the notch in the bolt and moves it forward or backward.

Ward
Bolt

Disc tumbler lock

Disc tumblers extend into the shell when locked, preventing the plug from turning. The correct key repositions them within the diameter of the plug, allowing it to turn. A fixed cam, or tail, at the end of the plug acts as the bolt.

Disc tumblers
Bolt
Plug

Pin tumbler lock

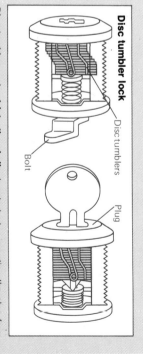

Drivers protruding into tumbler shafts prevent the plug from turning. The correct key, notched to raise pin segments flush with the plug surface, forces drivers above the shear line and enables the plug to turn, opening the lock.

Drivers
Pins
Plug
Must be aligned for lock to open
Lock position
Open position

Troubleshooting lock problems

Problem	Probable Cause	Repair
Proper key hard to insert or remove; plug sticks before turning	Key is worn; rough spots on key	Have a new key made by a locksmith to replace a worn key. If the key is a new, but poorly cut duplicate, you can try filing away rough spots yourself. Black the key in a candle flame; insert it into the lock, and turn it slightly. Remove the key and file down shiny spots. Repeat this procedure until the key works properly
Proper key does not always work	Loose plug	Remove cylinder and tighten cam screws. If play persists, remove cam and carefully file down the plug shoulder so that the cam can be screwed more closely against the cylinder
Entire cylinder turns when key is turned	Loose or broken cylinder setscrews	On a rim lock, check and tighten screws holding cylinder. On a mortise lock, check and tighten setscrews in lock face, in edge of door (see illustrations at right)
Proper key is difficult to turn	Lock and latch parts need cleaning; broken cylinder components	Remove the lock and latch parts from the door and soak them in cleaning solvent; scrub surfaces with a toothbrush. Lubricate sparingly with powdered graphite. Spray some graphite into cylinder. Broken components require locksmith
Proper key cannot be fully inserted, or becomes wedged in keyway	Obstruction in keyway; damaged keyway; usually indicates that lock has been tampered with	Carefully remove wedged key with pliers. Remove broken key or metal fragments with broken-key extractor (see illustrations, p.22). Replace lock
Plug turns but dead bolt does not	Cam or tang is disengaged from bolt mechanism	Check rim lock for loose cylinder screws (see illustrations, this page). On rim and mortise locks, check cam or tang, and bolt mechanism. Some parts may be loose, broken, or out of position
Key is difficult to turn when door is closed; easy when door is open	Dead bolt rubs against strike plate in door frame	Bolt and strike plate must be realigned. Strike plate opening may be filed larger; door hinges or frame may require alterations (see illustrations, p.22)
Lock frozen; key will not penetrate	Moisture in lock expands when frozen, binding cylinder components	Gradually insert warmed key in cylinder. Remove key and reheat as necessary. Wear gloves. Alcohol or de-icing spray may help. Turn key carefully to avoid tumbler damage

Spindle adjustment

Problems with latches can often be corrected by realigning the spindle (which may consist of two components). Remove the spindle for inspection by detaching the doorknobs. Check the spindle and setscrews for stripped threads and replace any stripped elements with new parts. Center the spindle in the shaft and reposition the knobs so that they fit snugly against the escutcheons but do not bind.

Misaligned spindle

Properly aligned spindle

Cylinder adjustment and removal

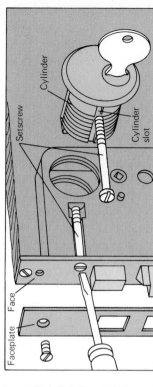

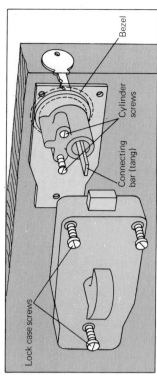

To tighten loose cylinder in a mortise lock, tighten the setscrew or screws on the face in the edge of the door. Sometimes they are concealed beneath a false plate. Be sure the screws seat in the cylinder slot. Loosening the setscrews permits the cylinder to be unscrewed for removal. Turn it out with key, as shown above at right, or use a wrench.

To remove a rim lock, first unscrew the case (left), then unfasten the screws holding the cylinder (right). If cylinder does not seat flush, a large washer, called a bezel, may be placed around it on the exterior of the door. The connecting bar, or tang, can be filed down to the proper size if it is too long.

Three common spindles

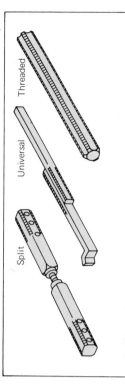

Split type: Remains fixed on one doorknob; adjust by realigning threaded parts.
Universal type: Both portions must seat in shaft; adjust before attaching knobs.
Threaded type: Tighten knobs against escutcheon, back off quarter turn.

Doorknobs, locks, and hinges

Problem hinges

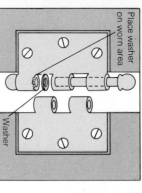

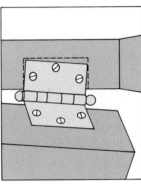

Restore worn metal in old hinges by placing metal washers between the lower hinge where shown.

For proper latch and strike plate alignment, hinge pins must be plumb, top and bottom. This hinge is out of alignment.

Broken key removal

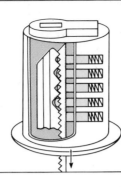

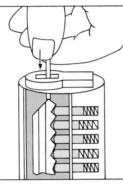

An extractor made from a coping saw blade can be inserted through the keyhole to pull out a broken key shank.

With the cylinder removed, a stiff wire can be inserted through slot in cam to push broken key out from the rear.

Lost keys: emergency entry

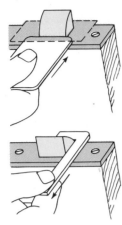

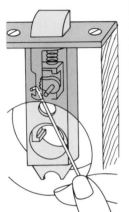

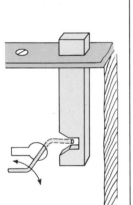

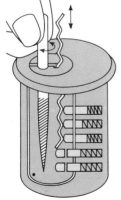

Prying back the latch: Press latch into door, left, with credit card or plastic. If bevel faces other way, cut card to L-shape, insert, and pull back.

Privacy lock: Remove doorknobs. Retract broken latch by inserting hooked paper clip through mounting screw hole into latch section.

Warded lock: Thin wire bent at right angles bypasses lock wards, engages notch in bolt. Turn pick with one hand, steady it in keyway with other.

Pin or disc tumbler: Apply rotational pressure with a small nail file while sawing back and forth with irregular wire pick to hit tumbler combination.

Door and door frame alignment

Problems with the door latch often result from misaligned hardware or warped woodwork. For a door to swing well, an exactly vertical pivot point must be achieved by careful alignment of the hinge pins. The strike plate and doorstop must be positioned so that the latch makes proper contact with the

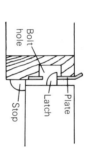

Latch, strike plate, doorstop alignment.

strike plate and the door is flush with the doorstop. If the door will not latch, the plate may have to be reset. Where misalignment is slight, file the edges of the plate to restore clearance. If the door rattles, relocate the stop nearer the bolt hole.

Shimming, chiseling, and planing. In an old house, a door latch may no longer make contact with the strike plate. Move the door closer to the latch jamb

strike plate and the door by shimming. Make the shim by using the plate as a pattern; be sure to cut the bolt hole accurately.

If the latch side of the door rubs or sticks against the jamb, chisel the hinge mortises deeper. If the problem is caused by built-up paint on the jamb and the edge of the door, remove the buildup with paint remover, a scraper, and sandpaper. Doors that bind only in one corner may be corrected by shimming the hinge diagonally opposite the bind, provided this will bring the hinge pins plumb. Carefully planing down the door's high spots may prove to be the only workable solution.

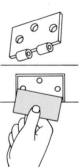

Restore worn metal by shimming with a washer placed between the hinges and the bottom knob of the hinge pin, as illustrated at left. Tighten loose screws or replace them with longer ones. Restore old screw holes with glue-coated wood plugs; drill new pilot holes.

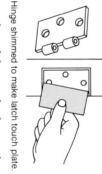

Doors that resist turning all the way on their hinges probably have excess paint on the hinge jamb. Remove the build-up or shim the hinges to adjust the door's position.

Lost keys. A locksmith can make a new key for any lock. But it pays to keep a record of the numbers on your keys, including your auto ignition keys, since locksmiths can make duplicates of any key simply on the basis of its code.

Fabrics, leather, and zippers

Gluing fabrics and leather

It is often more appropriate to mend leather, rubber, and certain heavy fabrics, such as vinyl and canvas, with glue and patches than to attempt to repair them by sewing. Luggage, shoes, bags, and vinyl and leather upholstery frequently suffer rips or slashes that can be repaired by gluing a patch under the tear. A slash in a leather jacket can similarly be mended by undoing the lining and gluing a patch on the inside of the jacket behind the tear. When leather stitching loosens or breaks, seams can frequently be rejoined with an appropriate adhesive. Larger holes in leather can be neatly mended with two patches, as illustrated below.

Heavy rubber cements and contact cements are preferred for most fabric, rubber, and leather repair work. Among these, clear silicone adhesives are unaffected by laundering and drycleaning. For a full description of the properties of modern glues, including those suitable for leather and fabric repair, see *Adhesives*, pp.10–13.

Patches should match torn materials in texture, color, and flexibility. Repair kits, containing patches, are available at hardware stores and notions counters. Often patches for fabric can be identically matched by cutting them from an inside or underpart of the garment or upholstery.

To make a neat, flush patch on vinyl or leather: 1. Use a razor blade to cut out a circle or square around the hole. This need not match the material. **3.** Trace the hole on paper and cut a patch to this pattern. **2.** Glue backing behind the hole. Glue patch in place on the backing.

Repairing zippers

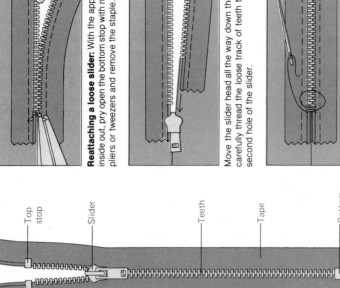

Top stop · Slider · Teeth · Tape · Bottom stop

One of the most common problems with zippers is that the slider head comes off of one or both tracks of teeth. At the lower end of the zipper you will see a metal staple, or stop, which binds the two tracks together. This staple prevents the slider from coming off at the bottom. If the staple is defective or missing, you can make a stop to replace it by sewing the tapes together just over the bottom teeth. The stitching should hold the teeth tightly together and should have enough loops to make the stop firm. There are also stops at the top of each track to prevent the slider from pulling off at either side. These can be restored in the same way as the bottom stop.

If the cause of the problem is a bent slider, bent or missing teeth, or a separation of one of the tracks from the material of the tape, it is better to sew in a whole new zipper. However, you can temporarily retrack any slider as illustrated at right. (For plastic zippers, see p.467.)

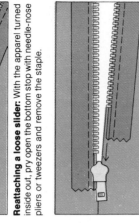

Reattaching a loose slider: With the apparel turned inside out, pry open the bottom stop with needle-nose pliers or tweezers and remove the staple.

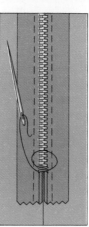

Move the slider head all the way down the teeth and carefully thread the loose track of teeth through the second hole of the slider.

Work the slider head up both tracks and then crimp the staple back into place with pliers or make a new stop with stitching, as shown.

Cleaning carpets

Carpeting should be regularly cleaned for more than appearance's sake. While daily or weekly vacuuming is sufficient for superficial cleaning, with time and wear dirt becomes deeply embedded in the fibers and can ruin the carpet.

Two commercial home shampooing methods are commonly available for removing deeply ingrained dirt. In one, entailing the use of a spray can, the shampoo is sprayed onto the carpet in sections and worked in with a damp sponge. After it has dried, it is vacuumed away.

Another method calls for the use of a shampooing machine. Machines are available for rental in many areas. They clean by means of rotating brushes, which scrub a liquid shampoo into the carpet. This method is generally more effective than the spray can, though the drying time is longer—up to six hours. (See also *Stain removal*, p.47.)

You may prefer to buy or rent a shampooing machine to shampoo your carpet. Instructions come with the machines.

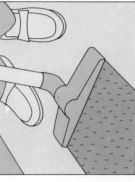

Allow about an hour for the foam to dry. When the carpet is dry, thoroughly vacuum the entire carpet free of residue.

Spray foam over a section of the carpet, then work the foam into the fibers with a sponge. Do the whole carpet by sections.

Jewelry

Jewelry tools

Because of the delicacy of the work, jewelry repair requires special tools. You may need three sets of smooth-jawed, 4½-inch pliers—chain-nose for small, hard-to-reach places, round-nose for rounded surfaces, and flat-nose for larger areas. Ordinary household pliers have ribbed jaws, which will leave scratches on jewelry.

Other useful tools are wire clippers, a jeweler's saw frame with very thin blades (graded in size from 2/0 for very fine work to 1 or 2 for general), beeswax to make cutting easier, needle files sized especially for jewelry, and a jeweler's ring mandrel for reshaping rings. Instant glue or epoxy compound will refix a stone. A jeweler's magnifier with an adjustable stand can be helpful. Its lens turns to any angle and the stand leaves both hands free to work.

All the necessary tools and materials are available from a jeweler's supply house or craft shop. Often you can substitute a household item for a jeweler's tool. Any smooth metal surface can replace the steel block used to repair bent metal. The wooden hammer from your child's toy workbench can be your mallet for pounding out dents.

As you become more proficient, you will probably do more complicated repairs that require soldering. For this you will need easy (silver) solder, flux, a gas-air torch with lighter, an asbestos block or coil wire, a pair of copper tongs, and pickling solution. Instructions and illustrations for soldering your jewelry appear on page 31.

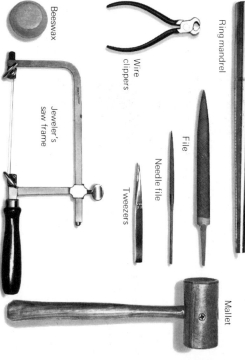

Round-nose

Chain-nose

Flat-nose

Propane (gas-air) torch

Asbestos coil

Beeswax

Epoxy Adhesive

Epoxy Hardener

Jeweler's saw frame

Wire clippers

Ring mandrel

File

Needle file

Tweezers

Mallet

Flint striker

Solder

FLUX

Binding wire

Copper tongs

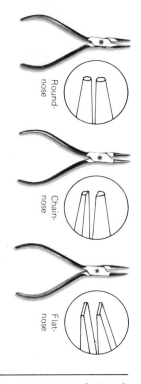

Emery sticks

Jewelers use an emery stick to smooth surfaces roughened by filing. You can make one with emery paper. Do same with polishing paper for shining.

Materials
Emery paper; stick, rubber bands

Tool
Nail or other pointed tool

Place a sheet of emery paper wrong side up on a board or other cutting surface. Lay the stick along the width of the paper. Score paper with a nail or other pointed tool. Turn the stick and score paper again.

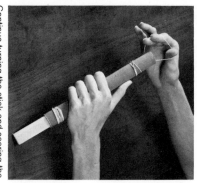

Continue turning the stick and scoring the paper until the entire sheet is wrapped very snugly around the stick. Trim off any excess paper. Fasten the paper with rubber bands or thumb tacks.

Cleaning jewelry

Jewelry should be cleaned often to keep it bright. Put a tablespoonful of detergent into a pint of hot water. Mix in a few drops of ammonia. (Do *not* use ammonia for pearls, amber, or other porous jewels.) Clean article with soft brush. Rinse in hot water; dry. Polish with chamois cloth. If piece has stones, pour all water through strainer to catch any stones that may have fallen free.

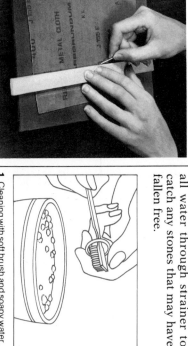

1. Cleaning with soft brush and soapy water.

2. Rinsing in clear hot water.

3. Polishing with chamois cloth.

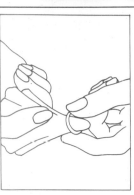

Restringing a necklace

Any string of beads or pearls should be checked for weak spots from time to time. If you find one weak spot, there are probably others, and the entire necklace should be restrung. A broken string of beads should also be entirely restrung on a new cord. It is always wiser to restring on new cord than to try to repair the old cord with knots and splices.

Craft shops carry beading cord in varying thicknesses with a beading needle attached. You can also buy packets of individual beading needles (fine steel wire with an eye). If the smallest bead will accommodate it, a darning needle and nylon thread can be used.

Material
Beading cord or nylon thread
Tools
Beading needle and darning needle or two darning needles, round-nose pliers, chain-nose pliers

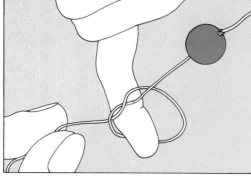
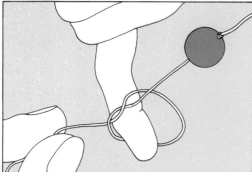

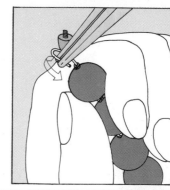

Attaching a clasp

Be sure that your old clasp is in good working order before reattaching it.
Materials
Epoxy cement, water-base glue
Tools
Wire clippers or scissors, darning needle, chain-nose pliers

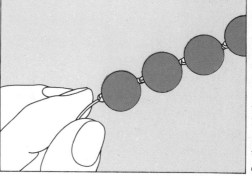

1. Slip the end of the cord through the link on the clasp. Knot link tightly against the last knot in the string. Clip off excess cord, leaving length equal to the last bead plus the two knots.

2. Stiffen end of cord by applying a water-base glue. When dry, grasp cord end in pliers and push it into the hole in the last bead until only the knot shows. Secure knot with epoxy compound.

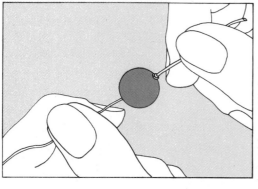
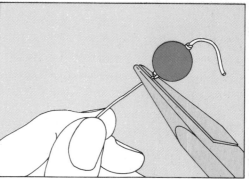

1. Thread the needle. If a beading needle is used and its eye is too small for the cord to pass through, force one jaw of round-nose pliers through the eye until it is large enough to take the cord.

2. After threading needle, make a knot in the cord, leaving at least 1½ in. at the end. Thread the first bead and slide it along the cord to the knot. The bead should lie tightly against the knot.

3. Make a loose loop in the cord. Insert your little finger through the loop and guide it down the cord toward bead. Be careful not to let the loop tighten into a knot before it reaches the bead.

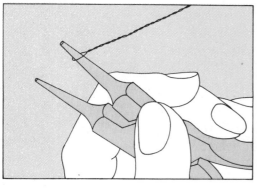
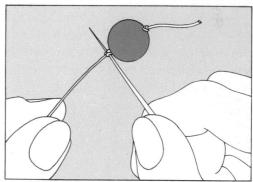

4. When the loop is almost to the bead, slip your little finger out of the loop and insert the darning needle. Pull cord tight, pushing knot firmly against the bead. Remove the needle.

5. Hold the cord in your fingers. Grasp it close to the knot with chain-nose pliers and push knot gently but firmly against the bead to tighten securely. Thread the next bead and repeat the procedure.

Continue stringing one bead at a time, knotting between beads. Make sure each knot is tight against the adjacent bead before threading the next bead. When restringing is complete, attach the clasp.

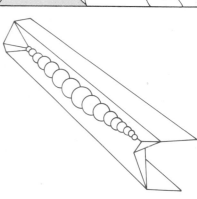

Make a trough for beads by folding a sheet of bond paper into an M shape. Fold each end, as shown above, to prevent beads from falling out. Place beads in trough in the same order as on old cord.

Fold-over clasp

Tightening a fold-over clasp on a bracelet requires only a pair of pliers.

Tool
Chain-nose pliers

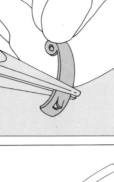

Misshapen

Repaired

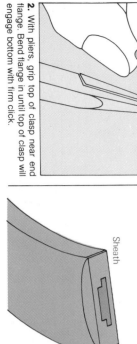

1. Open the clasp. With clasp held firmly in your fingers, grip top with pliers. Gently bend length of arm back into a curve.

2. With pliers, grip top of clasp near end flange. Bend flange in until top of clasp will engage bottom with firm click.

V-spring clasps

Clasps on some bracelets and necklaces have a V-spring that slides into a sheath. The spring is more likely to need repair, but the sheath may require work.

Tools
Small knife, tape, flat-nose pliers, steel block, emery stick

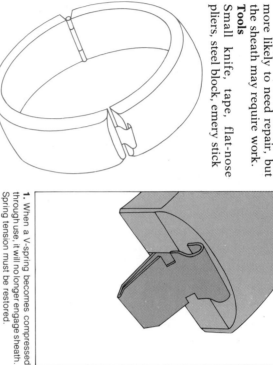

Sheath

V-spring

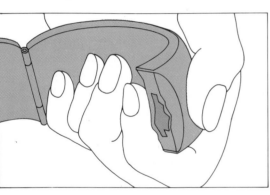

1. When a V-spring becomes compressed through use, it will no longer engage sheath. Spring tension must be restored.

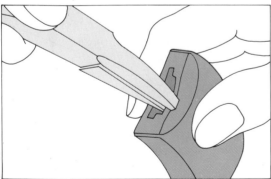

2. Brace spring against forefinger. Insert knife blade wrapped with tape between leaves of spring; twist to open slightly.

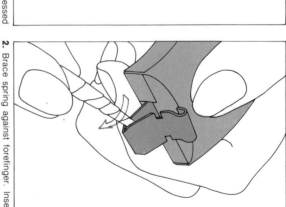

3. Spring should then engage with a firm click. If it does not, widen opening by prying leaves further apart.

1. If the sheath is bent out of shape, it will not hold the spring. You can repair sheath with pliers and a steel block.

2. Grasp top of sheath with pliers and bend it back into its original shape. Reshape bottom of the sheath in the same way.

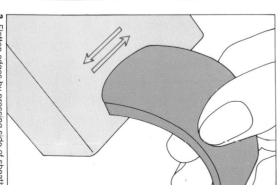

3. Flatten edges by pressing side of sheath against steel block and rubbing back and forth. Smooth with emery stick.

Straightening a bent pin

A bent pin stem can tear a fine fabric. If not repaired, it may slip from its catch, causing a brooch to fall off. In time, the back of the pin stem will work loose from ball joint.

Tools
Flat-nose pliers, emery stick, needle file

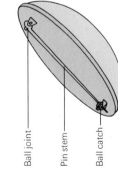

Ball joint — Pin stem — Ball catch

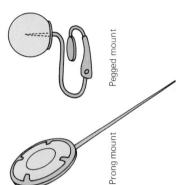

1. To straighten bent pin stem, hold brooch firmly in hand, grasp pin stem with pliers near ball joint and bend back into shape.

2. To straighten bent pin point, grasp it with pliers and bend flat. File point to attain taper, and smooth with emery stick.

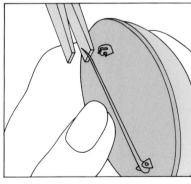

3. To adjust pin stem tension, grasp the pin stem close to the joint and bend it to bring point well behind catch.

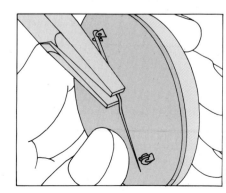

4. Pin stem will then have maximum tension, allowing it to snap securely into catch. Smooth any roughness with emery stick.

Riveting a pin

When a pin has fallen out of its socket, it must be riveted back into place. If old rivet, or wire, is missing, buy new wire in matching color from craft shop or jeweler's supply house. Be sure it is of a diameter that fits snugly into socket holes.

Material
Matching wire
Tool
Flat-nose pliers

Set pin stem into socket, making sure all holes are aligned. With pliers, hold old rivet or piece of new wire (cut slightly longer than width of socket). Carefully thread wire through all of the holes (left). Fix rivet firmly in place by squeezing with the pliers both ends of the wire that protrude from the socket holes (right).

Tightening a ball catch

If the latch on the ball catch is loose, pin stem may slip from catch. This is an easy repair.

Tool
Flat-nose pliers

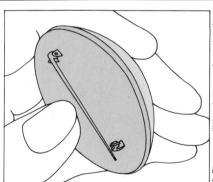

To tighten a loose ball catch, position the latch so that its nubs are straight up. Grasp catch in jaws of pliers and squeeze firmly. Move latch to a closed position. It should be tight enough to remain closed until it is moved manually.

Resetting a loose stone

Almost any loose stone can be reset right at your kitchen table. For a prong mount, you will need chain-nose pliers; for a pegged mount, epoxy compound. The compound must be handled with care. Read all instructions on package, paying particular attention to warnings.

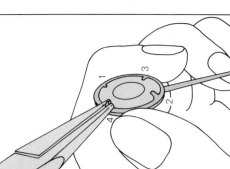

Pegged mount

Prong mount

To refasten stone to pegged mount, first squeeze a little epoxy compound or contact cement onto a strip of cardboard. Apply it with a needle to both the peg and the hole in the stone. Press peg and stone together. Let dry 20 minutes.

1. To replace stone in prong mount, slide stone into mount. Grasp first prong with pliers and bend into position. Do the same with the prong directly opposite. This will hold stone in place.

2. Bend the third and fourth prongs into position. Be sure stone is firmly in place. If any prongs are worn or missing, secure stone with cement after roughening base of mount with emery paper.

27

Jewelry

Making new links

New links for mending a broken chain or reattaching an eardrop can be made at home. Obtain matching wire and a metal rod in the size and shape of links to be matched—square, rectangular, or round. A round drill bit will form oval as well as round links.

Materials
Round soft wire, beeswax

Tools
Drill bit or metal rod, flat-nose pliers, chain-nose pliers, jeweler's saw

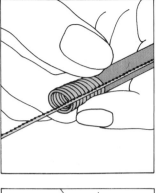

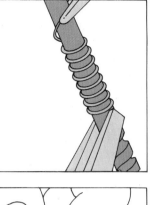

1. Make a hook in one end of a length of wire. Insert hook in last twist of groove in drill bit. Grasp bit with flat-nose pliers and wind wire tightly around shank of bit.

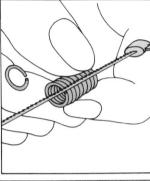

2. Close the last loop by squeezing end of wire firmly against the shank with chain-nose pliers. To shape wire for making oval links, wind it around bit at 45° angle.

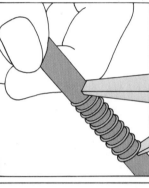

3. Squeeze all of the loops together with chain-nose pliers to form a coil that are exactly uniform—both in their size and in their shape.

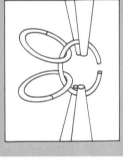

4. Rub beeswax on saw blade to facilitate cutting. Slide coil to end of drill bit. Angle saw slightly and saw along spine of coil until first links fall free.

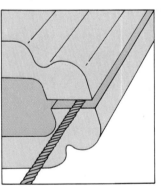

5. Remove coil from the drill bit shank and continue sawing one link at a time to avoid cutting fingers. Links will be easier to work with if left open until used.

Twisting wire

Besides providing new links for a twisted wire chain in need of repair, twisted wire can turn an unattractive piece of jewelry into an unusual and interesting accessory. Bond it to the rim of pin with epoxy compound, shape it into a loop for a handsome eardrop, or fashion a new companion piece for an old favorite.

Materials
Matching soft round wire, epoxy compound or instant glue

Tools
Flat-nose pliers, clamp-on vise

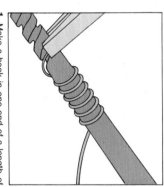

1. After bending a length of wire in half and squeezing folded end tightly with pliers, turn the wire around and twist the loose ends together as shown above.

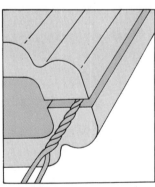

2. Secure folded end of wire in vise, grip opposite end with pliers, and begin turning to right. Continue turning until twist is evenly distributed along length of wire.

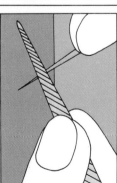

3. Reverse the position of wire in vise. Begin turning wire to right again, continuing until the second twist is uniform. The twisted wire is now ready for use.

Closing links

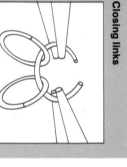

To attach a new link or reattach an opened link, begin by widening the opening. Grip each side with round-nose pliers and twist until link slips easily through adjacent link.

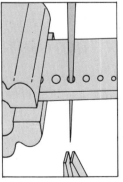

Bend sides of link into alignment. Tighten by pressing ends of link together until solidly joined. A drop of instant glue or cold solder will assure a strong bond.

Drawing wire

Knowing how to draw wire can be useful in jewelry repair. A draw plate is a flat piece of metal with a series of graduated holes numbered on the plate's face. The wire becomes thinner as it is passed front to back through a succession of ever smaller holes. To keep wire from becoming brittle, heat over gas flame to soften; wash in warm, soapy water; resume drawing.

Material
Soft round wire

Tools
Household pliers, coarse file, large and small draw plates, clamp-on vise

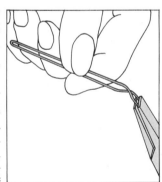

Brace the wire in a notch in the edge of an old table or workbench. File a point on the wire, turning wire as you file. Make a round, tapered point long enough to pass through draw plate and provide a secure grip for the pliers from the other side.

Clamp draw plate into vise. Find the hole that accommodates thickness of wire. Grip wire with pliers and pull through. Continue pulling wire through progressively smaller holes until thin enough for use. Do not skip holes or wire will break.

Repairing rings

Two of the most common ring repairs can be done at home with considerable savings. Both are uncomplicated and not at all difficult for the nonprofessional to master.

The first of these repairs is restoring a bent shank to its original shape. A plain band can often be straightened just by pushing it firmly down over a jeweler's mandrel or a tapered smooth steel bar. If the ring has a deep-set prong mounting, however, a special grooved mandrel will be required to prevent any damage to the stone. A badly bent shank may also require pounding with a wooden mallet.

A twisted box, or mount, can also be turned back into position. If the box consists of a stone setting and the prongs have loosened, you may have to reset the stone (p.27) after making the repair.

A few Do's and Don'ts when repairing rings: Do *not* try to repair a band inlaid with precious or semiprecious stones. Their settings are usually delicate and easily damaged. Take valuable rings, and even expensive costume pieces, to a professional jeweler. *Never* use a metal hammer when your pounding surface is also metal. Always use wood to metal or metal to wood. A wooden mallet should do the trick; if it does not, the damage is evidently extensive enough to require the expert touch of a professional jeweler.

Tools
Round-nose pliers, ring mandrel, wooden mallet, steel block, emery stick, polishing paper

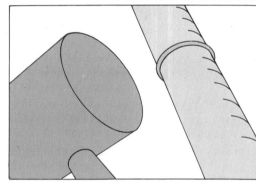

1. If the mount is twisted, it must be straightened before the shank is repaired. Hold the shank firmly in one hand. Grasp the mount at its base with the pliers and gently bend it back to align with shank.

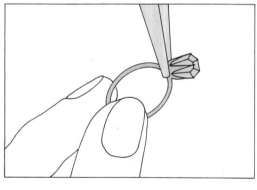

2. To correct a bent shank, slide the ring onto mandrel. Push ring down so that it is held firmly on the mandrel. Pound shank with mallet, turning mandrel as you do. Work shank until it is round again.

3. If shank needs leveling, grip ring tightly by the mount and hold against steel block. Pound shank with mallet until it is completely straight. Slide ring back on mandrel; pound out any remaining dents.

Attaching a ring guard

When a ring is slightly large for the finger, it is much less expensive to buy a card of ring guards in assorted sizes and attach one yourself than to have it put on by a jeweler.

Tool
Chain-nose pliers

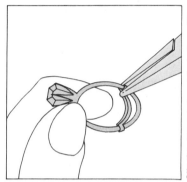

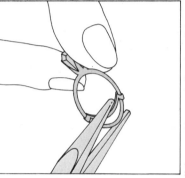

Slip the ring guard over the bottom of the shank and center it. Squeeze the flanges together at each end with pliers.

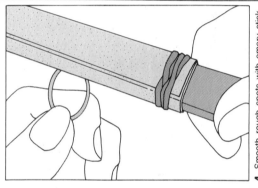

4. Smooth rough spots with emery stick. Restore shine by buffing with polishing paper. If outside of band is etched or otherwise decorated, use a very light touch both in smoothing and polishing.

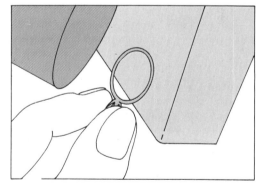

If the guard has made the ring a little too tight, grip the center of guard and shank with pliers and squeeze slightly.

Making a ring polisher

You can make a ring polisher using the following materials and tools: polishing paper, a nail, a vise, a jeweler's saw frame with a fine blade, a variable speed electric drill, and pliers whose jaws are covered with masking tape.

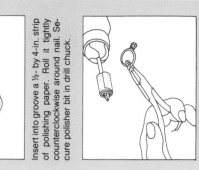

Grip the nail, point up, in the vise. Fasten a thin blade into the jeweler's saw frame and cut a groove into center of nail point.

Insert into groove a ½- by 4-in. strip of polishing paper. Roll it tightly counterclockwise around nail. Secure polisher bit in drill chuck.

Hold ring by mount, or hold band in taped jaws of pliers. Run the drill at slow speed around the inside and outside of the shank.

Clip-back earrings

The repair most often needed on a clip-back earring is adjustment of the tension in the clip. Tension is applied through a spring that is either a part of the back or set inside a sheath that is part of the back. Before working with the spring, try bending the neck. This is often all that need be done to adjust tension.

Tool
Chain-nose pliers

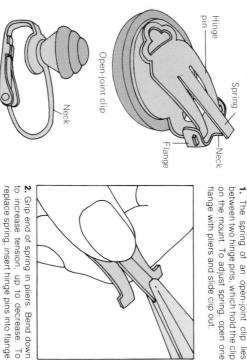

Hinge pin · Spring · Open-joint clip · Neck · Flange · Sheathed clip · Neck

1. The spring of an open-joint clip lies between two hinge pins, which hold the clip on the mount. To adjust spring, open one flange with pliers and slide clip out.

2. Grip end of spring in pliers. Bend down to increase tension, up to decrease. To replace spring, insert hinge pins into flange holes and squeeze flanges together.

Post earrings

When a post breaks, buy a new one for a few cents from a craft shop. Clip off the remnants of the old post and file the contact point smooth. Set new post into position to determine exact bonding point. Incorrect positioning will cause earring to hang off center. Apply epoxy compound to mount and to base of screw wire. Hold firmly together for a few minutes. Put the earring aside and let it dry for 20 minutes.

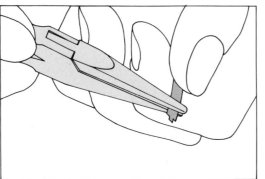

Grip neck of open-joint clip (left) with pliers. To relax tension, bend back from mount; to tighten, bend forward. Bend neck of sheathed clip (right) away from mount to loosen, towards it to tighten.

Adjusting spring tension in a pair of cuff links

When the spring in a rocker arm or swivel bar cuff link loses its tension, the cuff link will no longer stay in place. Pliers and a penknife can be used to put the cuff link quickly back into good working order.

Tools
Small knife, darning needle, chain-nose pliers

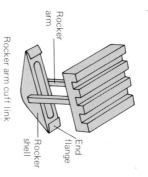

Rocker arm · Rocker arm cuff link · End flange · Rocker shell · Cover · Spring · Shell · Rocker arm

1. Hold rocker arm firmly in your fingers with cover of shell facing up. Pry open one end flange with the point of the knife. This will release the cover.

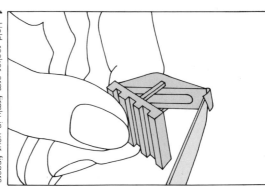

2. The thin strip of steel now exposed is the spring of the rocker arm. Lift up the end of the spring with the needle and shake spring onto working surface.

3. Bend each end of the spring downward until the length of the spring forms an even curve. With ends still pointing down, drop the spring back into the shell.

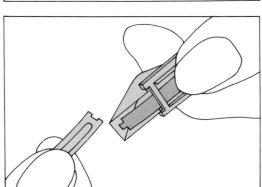

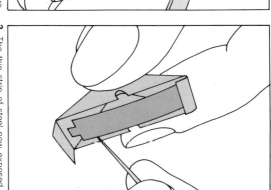

4. Place the rocker arm over spring. Slide cover under closed flange; press firmly into place. Close open flange with pliers. Rocker arm should click when moved.

Soldering silver

A new back can be bonded to a solid silver mount with easy (silver) solder. Soldering is not recommended for gold plate or other alloys commonly used in costume jewelry, as the pickling solution will remove the plating as well as the discoloration left by soldering.

The best heating tool to use is a gas-air torch. The correct flame will quickly heat the piece just enough to cause the solder to flow.

Materials
Flux, easy solder, wire

Tools
Small brush, gas-air torch, file, asbestos block or coil, tweezers

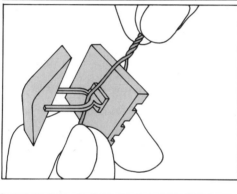

1. File any old solder off back of mount. Wipe away all filings. The metal must be clean and smooth in order for the joint to bond securely. With a small brush, apply a little flux to the entire mount and to the base of the rocker arm.

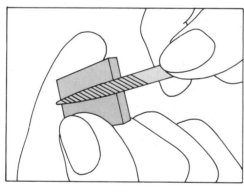

2. Position the arm on the mount and wire the two pieces together. Place cuff link on an asbestos block or coil. If you use a coil, pins can be inserted around cuff link to hold it steady during soldering. Apply flux again around the base of the arm.

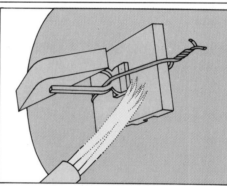

3. Cut a 1/16-in. piece of solder. Grip in pliers and dip into flux. Place solder next to base of arm. Heat flux slowly with torch to dry it out. Flux may bubble; a white crust will form. Heat should not be enough to melt solder at this point.

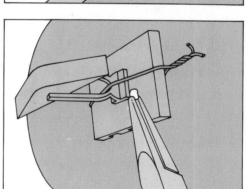

4. Check to see that solder is still in place. Direct flame tip to heat mount around base of arm; solder will begin to flow under base. Remove torch as soon as solder melts. Allow cuff link to cool slightly; snip off wire; pickle cuff link.

Correct flame in gas-air torch is a 5-in. blue flame with soft, slightly yellow tip. Too yellow a flame does not give enough heat; too much blue creates oxide deposits.

Too much gas

Too much air

Correct mixture of gas and air

Light blue
Darker blue
Trace of yellow

Pickling

After soldering, remove flux by dipping joint into pickling solution. A commercial pickling powder added to water—1 tablespoon powder to 1 pint water—is much safer to use than the old mixture of 1 part sulfuric acid to 16 parts water. Always handle pickling solution with care. After use, store in a covered Pyrex jar.

Use a copper or Pyrex saucepan as a container for the solution and a pair of copper tongs or loop of copper wire to hold the piece during pickling.

Since the spring in the rocker arm is steel, it must be kept out of the pickling solution. If it is not, the entire cuff link will discolor and the solution be made unusable by chemical reaction.

After the cuff link has been washed and dried, smooth with emery stick, and polish.

Tools
Saucepan, tongs

1 pint water

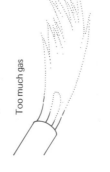

1 level tbsp. pickling powder

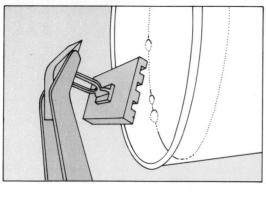

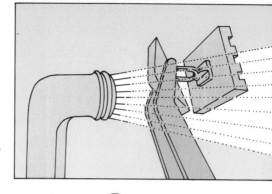

1. Heat pickling solution on stove until it begins simmering. *Do not boil.* Grasp cuff link in tongs just below rocker back. Lower carefully into solution.

2. When flux disappears from soldered area, remove cuff link from solution and rinse with warm water. Clean with soap and water. Dry with a soft cloth.

Lamps, outlets, and switches

Troubleshooting a broken lamp

If a lamp flickers, first be sure that the problem is not simply a loose or damaged harp. If the loose or damaged bulb. If the lamp will not light, check for a loose or burned-out bulb or a blown fuse or tripped circuit breaker (see *Electricity in the home*, pp.126-127). If the problem is not in the bulb, fuse, or the circuit, it may be either in

the switch or the lamp's wiring.

Unplug the lamp and examine the cord for fraying, cracks, bare wires, or loose connections at metal tube through which the cord passes from the base to the switch. You need not always re-right, the switch is probably broken. To replace the switch, follow Steps 1 through 5 of the illustrated instructions below. To replace the cord, follow all of

the steps in the drawings below. Note: In the exploded view at right the lamp has an internal metal tube through which the cord passes from the base to the switch. You need not always re-move this tube when rewiring a lamp. After you have pried off the felt base cover, disconnected the cord leads from the switch,

and then pulled the cord out of the lamp from the bottom, you may be able to simply feed a new cord back up through the tube. But, depending on the na-ture of your lamp, you may find it more convenient to remove the tube altogether before rewiring it, a procedure that is shown in the illustrations below.

Rewiring a lamp and replacing its switch

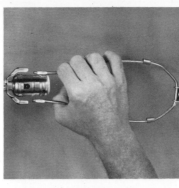

1. Unplug lamp. Slide sleeves up arms of harp to expose the clips. Unclip the harp by pressing the arms together.

2. Depress outer shell of socket at area marked *Press*. Pull off shell with its en-closed insulating sleeve intact.

3. Unscrew wires from their terminals and remove the old switch. You will then be ready to install the new switch.

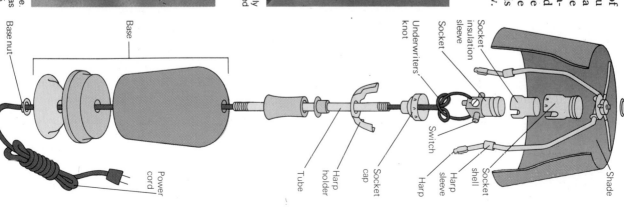

4. The new switch shown here is partly disassembled. In practice, there is no need to remove insulating sleeve from shell.

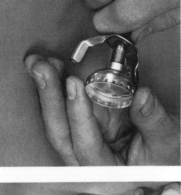

5. Before connecting switch, tie an Un-derwriters' knot (if not already present) to prevent wires from pulling off terminals.

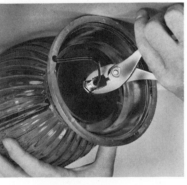

6. To remove cord for rewiring untie Un-derwriters' knot and unscrew socket cap. Slide off harp holder and any fixtures.

7. Turn the lamp over and use a wrench or a pair of pliers to unscrew the nut that se-cures the tube to the base.

8. Pull old wire from tube, feed in new wire. Reassemble lamp in same order it was taken apart. Knot top of wire as in Step 5.

Base nut

Base

Power cord

Socket insulation sleeve

Socket

Underwriters' knot

Tube

Harp holder

Socket cap

Switch

Harp

Harp sleeve

Socket shell

Shade

Replacing a switch

If a light fixture fails to work when its wall switch is turned on, the switch may be defective. Before testing the switch, unscrew the fuse or trip the circuit breaker to shut off its power. (see *Electricity in the home*, pp.126–127). Remove the switch plate (referring to the illustration below), pull out the switch, and unscrew the wires.

There are two ways to test a switch. You may disconnect at least one of its wires and test it with a volt-ohm meter (see p.124) or you may hook up a new switch to see if it will solve the problem. To test with a new switch, attach its wires in the same positions you found the wires on the old switch. Restore circuit power and turn the switch on. (Note: You need not completely install the new switch to make the test if you wear insulating gloves and avoid touching the terminals.) If the light works, install the new switch. If it does not, have an electrician check the wiring.

Replacing an outlet

If a lamp or an appliance does not work when plugged into an electrical outlet, and the problem does not lie with a fuse or circuit breaker, the outlet may be defective. To check it, plug in a lamp you know is working. If the lamp does not go on, the outlet is probably the cause.

When replacing an outlet, refer to the illustration below. Turn off the power to the outlet by unscrewing a fuse or tripping a breaker before proceeding.

Many new outlets are made with an additional terminal for grounding; it connects to the third prong on three-wire plugs when they are inserted into the outlet. Older house wiring systems, however, do not have a grounding wire inside the outlet box to which this terminal may be attached. If you are replacing an old outlet with this newer type, connect the ground terminal with a short piece of wire to any screw inside the box. But to be sure the box itself is properly grounded, call an electrician.

Fluorescent lamps

If a fluorescent lamp flickers or will not light, unplug it or shut off power to it at the fuse box. Remove the tube and then use long-nose pliers to carefully straighten any bent pins on the tube or socket contacts in the fixture. Spray the pins and socket contacts with electrical contact cleaner (p.123) or clean them with sandpaper. Remove any socket residue with a toothbrush. Reinstall the tube and restore power to the lamp.

If the problem persists, replace the tube. If the new tube does not light, replace the starter (see illustrations at right and below); if the lamp still does not come on, replace the ballast. Note: Not all fluorescent lamps have starters.

New tubes often shimmer the first 100 hours of use. If the fixture hums while in operation, tighten any loose ballast connections. If the noise continues, replace the ballast with a special low-noise unit.

Wear gloves to replace tubes. They are fragile and may explode if dropped or jarred. Tubes will last much longer if allowed to burn without frequent interruption than if repeatedly turned on and off. Manufacturers rate tube life by the number of such starts.

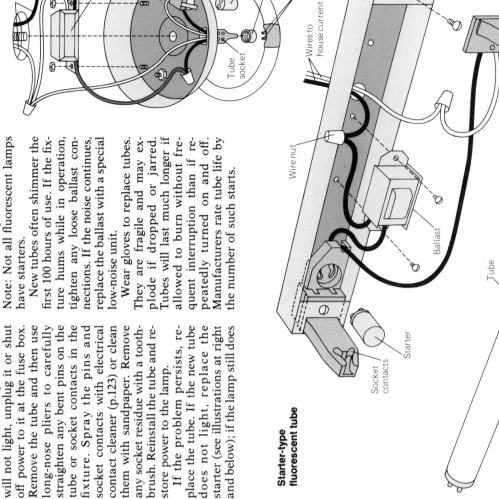

Circular tube fixture with starter

Wires to house current · Wire nut · Ballast · Tube · Starter · Cap nut · Tube pins · Tube socket · Starter

Starter-type fluorescent tube

Wires to house current · Wire nut · Ballast · Socket contacts · Starter · Tube · Tube pins

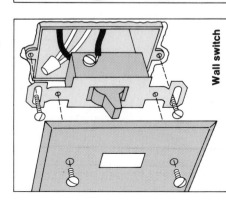

Wall outlet

Ground wires · Green · Silver

Wall switch

Plumbing

Tools and materials

By purchasing a few basic tools and materials and keeping them on hand, you can be prepared to meet most plumbing emergencies quickly and efficiently. When a particular repair calls for a special tool, you can buy it at the time the job comes up. There are certain tools—such as a power auger for clearing main drain lines—that you may prefer to rent.

Be sure you have an adjustable wrench; one of these is as good as a complete set of open-end wrenches for working with nuts and fittings of varying sizes. A pair of pipe wrenches will let you tackle most household drains, traps, and pipe fittings. Plastic pipe requires the use of a strap wrench, which will also handle steel pipe of very large diameter. Locking pliers will afford a nonslip grip on nuts. Keep a standard hacksaw for cutting pipe. You should also have a plunger and drain and toilet augers to clear blockages.

High cost by itself does not guarantee quality in a tool. Buy a reputable brand. When in doubt, check with the manager of your hardware or plumbing supply store. In the following pages most of the tools pictured at right are shown in use, with the proper techniques for making specific repairs.

Materials and hardware you should keep on hand include hose and pipe clamps, electrical tape, plastic joint-sealing tape, epoxy adhesive, and self-forming packing. Also keep a variety of O-rings, graphite twist packing, and a supply of all-temperature faucet washers.

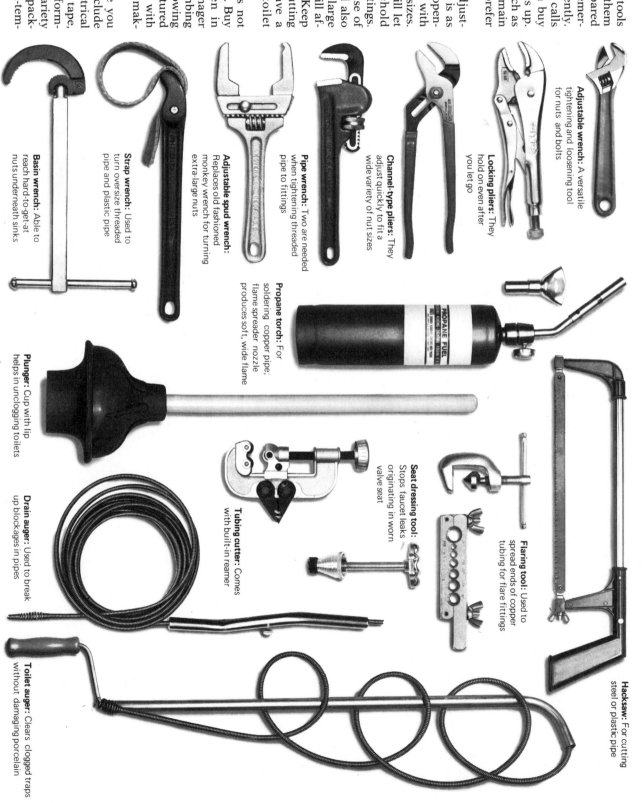

Adjustable wrench: A versatile tightening and loosening tool for nuts and bolts

Locking pliers: They hold on even after you let go

Channel-type pliers: They adjust quickly to fit a wide variety of nut sizes

Pipe wrench: Two are needed when tightening threaded pipe to fittings

Adjustable spud wrench: Replaces old-fashioned monkey wrench for turning extra-large nuts

Propane torch: For soldering copper pipe; flame spreader nozzle produces soft, wide flame

Strap wrench: Used to turn oversize threaded pipe and plastic pipe

Basin wrench: Able to reach hard-to-get-at nuts underneath sinks

Plunger: Cup with lip helps in unclogging toilets

Tubing cutter: Comes with built-in reamer

Seat dressing tool: Stops faucet leaks originating in worn valve seat

Flaring tool: Used to spread ends of copper tubing for flare fittings

Hacksaw: For cutting steel or plastic pipe

Drain auger: Used to break up blockages in pipes

Toilet auger: Clears clogged traps without damaging porcelain

Emergencies

When a pipe leaks, the first step to take is to shut off the water supply to the break. Make it a rule to know where the shutoff valves in your house or apartment are located. Valves are often under or near plumbing fixtures. The hot water supply for the entire house can generally be turned off at the hot water heater. If necessary cut off all water in the house by closing the main water valve, which is usually in the basement near the water meter or on the supply pipe from the well in a well system. Once the water is off, wipe the area around the leak clean and dry before attempting to determine the extent of the damage.

Emergency repairs can range from taking temporary measures, while waiting for the plumber, to making repairs that will last for years. But even minor leaks should be attended to promptly to prevent further damage. Leaks tend to enlarge over a period of time, and dripping water can damage plaster, stain paint and wallpaper, and create an electrical hazard.

Leaks commonly develop at threaded joints. These can frequently be fixed merely by tightening the fitting. But exercise caution; damaged or deteriorated pipe may break when you try to tighten it. Epoxy compound is useful in dealing with such leaks. Electrical tape will seal small cracks or punctures. Before using either to stop a leak, remove any rust or scale from the pipe with steel wool, and make sure that the pipe is clean and dry.

Shutting off the water supply

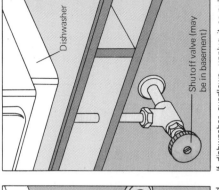

Dishwasher · Shutoff valve (may be in basement)

If dishwasher overflows, unplug it or pull fuse, then turn off water. Shutoff valve may be in basement beneath machine or alongside it under the kitchen sink.

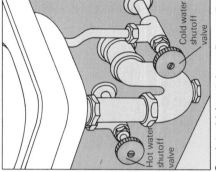

Cold water shutoff valve · Hot water shutoff valve

Supply to sink faucets is usually controlled by valves beneath basin—one for hot water, one for cold. Turn both off when working on single-lever faucets (p.37).

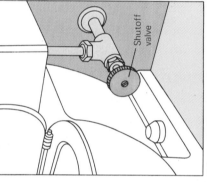

Shutoff valve

Valve controlling water supply to toilet may be under tank. If it is not, trace pipe from tank to find nearest shutoff valve. To clear a clogged toilet, see pp.38–39.

Off · MAIN WATER

Main shutoff is the most important valve. Label it and learn where it is (it is usually near water meter or pump). In an emergency, close it to turn off all water.

Repairing small leaks

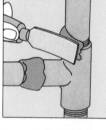

To stop small leak temporarily, shut off water, dry pipe; wrap layers of electrical tape beyond leak on each side.

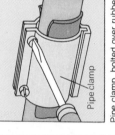

Use epoxy compound to seal leaky fittings. Before applying epoxy, drain water, dry pipe, and clean fitting with steel wool.

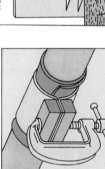

Pipe clamp

Pipe clamp, bolted over rubber pad, can permanently stop a large leak. Be sure clamp is centered directly over leak.

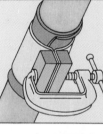

Tin can cut along seam serves as homemade pipe clamp. Use C-clamp and two wood blocks to lock can onto rubber pad.

Hose clamp

Tighten hose clamp around rubber collar to stop a pinhole leak. To avoid future rusting, use stainless steel clamp.

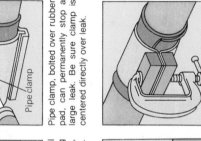

To repair small leak, clamp cloth or rubber strip and wood blocks over hole. Shape blocks with a wood rasp.

Frozen pipes

If heat can be restored to area where pipes are frozen, they will gradually thaw by themselves. Should frozen pipes be in a poorly heated location, such as a cellar or crawl space, they can be thawed with a propane torch, wetproof heating pad, heating cable, household iron, or simply by wrapping rags around the pipe and pouring boiling water over them. No matter which method you use, always open the nearest faucet on frozen line and work back from open faucet to frozen area. This will protect against dangerous pressure buildup by providing an escape passage for water and steam. **Caution: Never heat a pipe so hot you cannot hold it; overheating can produce enough steam pressure to cause an explosion. Be particularly cautious with a propane torch. Use a flame spreader nozzle. Play flame back and forth to keep hot spots from developing and place an asbestos sheet behind the pipe. If pipe has split, leave it frozen until you can get repair materials.**

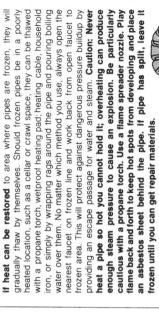
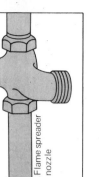

Open · Asbestos sheet · Flame spreader nozzle · Frozen area

Plumbing

Faucets with washers

Every faucet designed on the stem and washer principle has three basic parts: a stem assembly, a flat or bevel-edge seat washer, and a stem sealant. The washer cuts off the flow of water when the stem is screwed in. The stem sealant—either packing or a rubber O-ring—prevents water from seeping out of the faucet at the handle.

Leaky faucets are generally the result of defects in the seat washer, the valve seat against which it presses, or the stem sealant. If the washer or the stem seat is to blame, the leak will be from the spout of the faucet. Problems with the packing or O-ring show up as leaks around the handle shaft or from under the bonnet covering the base of the faucet.

If a faucet drips from its spout after it has been turned off, replace the seat washer. If this does not solve the problem, or if washers wear out frequently, the valve seat is probably rough. The seat is made of soft brass and can be damaged by corrosion or by overtightening the stem in an effort to stop a drip that is really the result of a worn washer. The valve seat can easily be refaced with an inexpensive seat dressing tool, or in certain faucets it can be replaced with a new part.

Leaks around the stem call for replacement of the packing or O-ring. If the faucet is worn beyond repair, you can replace the whole fixture.

Note: When using pliers or a wrench, wrap the jaws with plastic tape to prevent damage to finished surfaces.

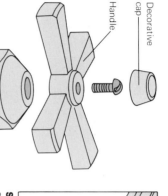

Decorative cap

Handle

Packing nut (may be covered by bonnet)

Stem sealant (packing washer)

Stem

Seat washer

Valve seat

Repairing faucets with dripping spouts

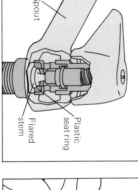

Shut off water and remove faucet handle and bonnet. Unscrew packing nut with wrench, then reattach handle to stem. Screw out stem by turning handle.

Bonnet

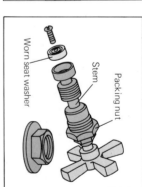

Most faucets have a synthetic, rubber washer at base of stem. If it is worn, faucet will drip. Be sure replacement washer is made for both hot and cold water.

Worn seat washer

Stem

Packing nut

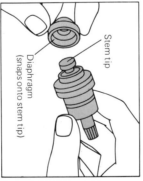

In a reverse pressure faucet, flared metal stem moves up against plastic seat ring to shut off water. To fix leaky spout, take out entire unit and replace seat ring.

Spout

Plastic seat ring

Flared stem

Top hat faucet assembly has a hat-shaped diaphragm in place of conventional washer. To repair it, pull off old diaphragm, snap new one on over circular stem tip.

Stem tip

Diaphragm (snaps onto stem tip)

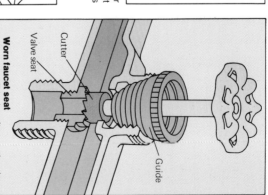

Worn faucet seat. If faucet still leaks after washer is changed, the valve seat probably needs refacing. With stem assembly removed, screw the seat dressing tool into faucet so that cutter is flush against valve seat and guide is snug inside valve. Then, turn handle of tool a few times until it moves smoothly. Let water run briefly to flush away grindings. Install new seat washer before reassembling.

Cutter

Valve seat

Guide

Stopping leaks around handle

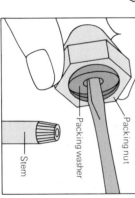

First, try tightening the packing nut (do not overtighten). If this does not work, unscrew nut, exposing packing washer underneath, and replace washer if corroded. If washer is jammed into nut, pry it out.

Stem

Packing washer

Packing nut

Spout

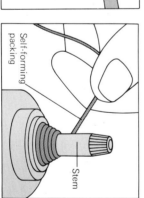

If faucet uses self-forming packing, either add a few turns of new packing or remove old packing and wind enough new packing onto stem to fill nut, then add half as much again. Nut will compress packing.

Self-forming packing

Stem

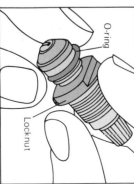

Faucets with locknuts usually have rubber O-rings instead of packing. Remove locknut, lift out stem, and replace O-ring. Be sure new ring is same size as old. Note: Faulty O-rings often appear normal.

O-ring

Locknut

Single-lever faucets

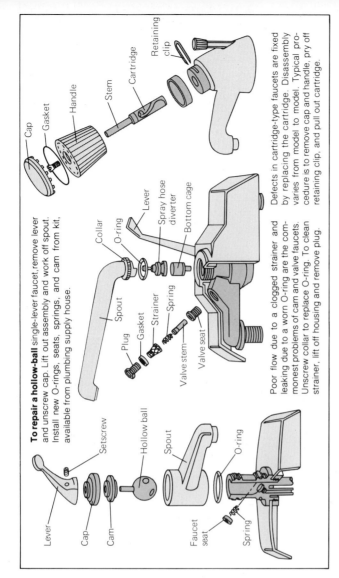

Single-lever faucets combine volume control and temperature control in one handle. Moving the handle from right to left changes the water temperature from cold to hot; pulling the handle forward increases water volume, pushing it to the rear shuts the water off. There are three kinds of single-lever faucets: hollow ball, cam and valve, and cartridge.

The hollow-ball faucet is the simplest. Its key part is a hollow brass ball with three openings, one for the hot water inlet, one for the cold water inlet, and one for the channel to the spout. Moving the handle changes the lineup of each opening with respect to its inlet, varying the proportion of hot and cold water and permitting a greater or lesser flow from the spout.

The cam and valve type is closest to a conventional, two-control faucet. Its handle moves a specially designed cam that presses against the stems of a pair of spring-loaded valves. As the handle is moved from right to left, the cam opens the hot water valve and closes the cold water valve. When the lever is moved forward, the cam opens both valves together without changing the proportion of hot to cold water.

The cartridge-type faucet uses a replaceable cartridge mechanism for volume and temperature control. Hot and cold water are mixed in the cartridge by means of overlapping openings similar to those in hollow-ball faucets. Each type of faucet is prone to certain problems you can repair yourself.

To repair a hollow-ball single-lever faucet, remove lever and unscrew cap. Lift out assembly and work off spout. Install new O-rings, seats, springs, and cam from kit, available from plumbing supply house.

Poor flow due to a clogged strainer and leaking due to a worn O-ring are the commonest problems of cam and valve faucets. Unscrew collar to replace O-ring. To clean strainer, lift off housing and remove plug.

Defects in cartridge-type faucets are fixed by replacing the cartridge. Disassembly varies from model to model. Typical procedure is to remove cap and handle, pry off retaining clip, and pull out cartridge.

Replacing an old faucet

If a faucet is old, you may choose to replace it rather than repair it. Start by turning off water supply. Use basin wrench to undo upper coupling nuts, then unscrew connecting nut that holds faucet supply pipe to valve under fixture, and lift off faucet assembly. If new faucet is same type as old, clean mounting surface with household cleanser and install it. If you are replacing old faucet with single-lever type, you may need to drill a center hole for the supply lines and put in new connections from the shutoff valves. Use compression fittings and soft copper tubing.

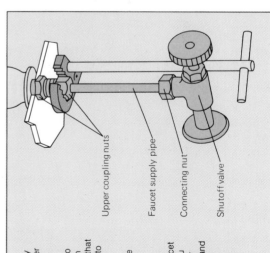

Wall-mounted faucets

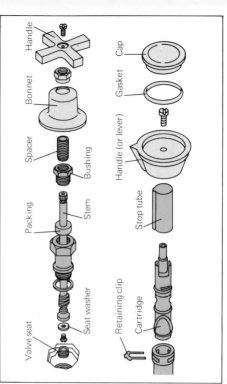

For stem-type faucets (top), replace worn washers and reface valve seats as you would on ordinary sink faucet. If faucet is single-lever type (bottom), disassemble it as if it were a single-lever, cartridge faucet. Take old cartridge to plumbing supply store to insure exact replacement. After reassembling faucet, replace plaster where chipping shows.

A special, deep-bodied socket wrench may be needed to remove a faucet from the wall. Take off handle and cover, then chip plaster away to make room for wrench.

Plumbing

Replacing sink drains and strainers

There are two kinds of strainers, standard and self-tightening. When installing or removing a standard strainer, you will need an assistant to keep the strainer steady while you turn the locknut with a wrench from beneath.

The self-tightening type can be mounted or taken out without a helper. With the strainer body in place, the retainer is positioned from beneath the sink so that its notches line up with the ridges on the neck of the strainer. Tightening the screws draws the assembly together. New strainers usually come with a gasket. Remove the paper from the adhesive surface of the gasket and press the gasket into place under the strainer lip. If no gasket is included, apply a thin bead of a silicone sealant or plumber's putty to the underside of the lip before installing the strainer.

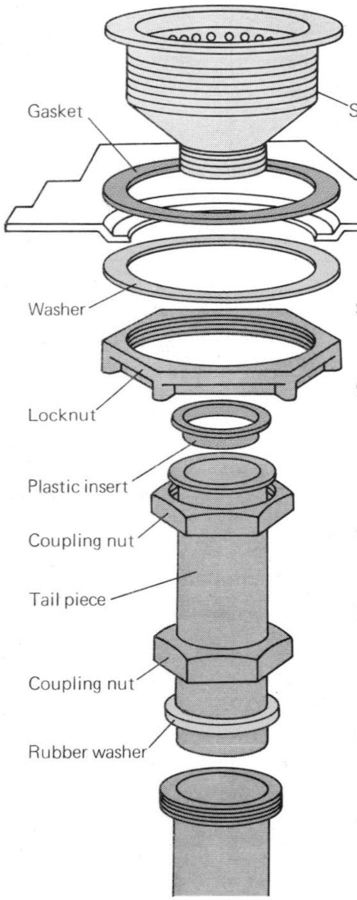

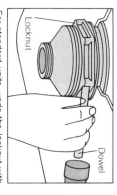

At left, standard sink drain assembly; below, self-tightening drain assembly.

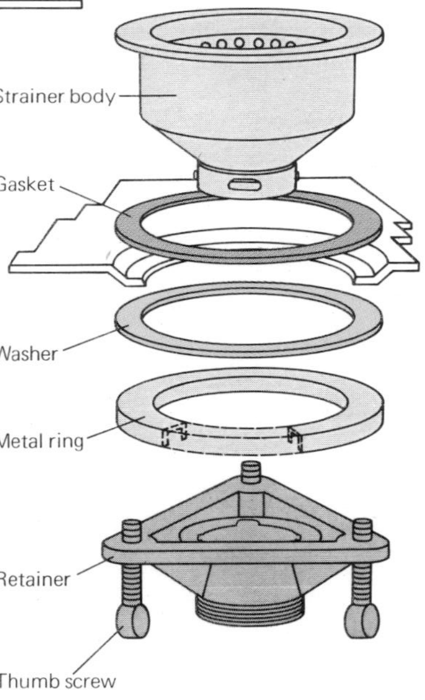

Gasket

Washer

Lock nut

Plastic insert

Coupling nut

Tail piece

Coupling nut

Rubber washer

Strainer body

Gasket

Strainer body

Washer

Metal ring

Retainer

Thumb screw

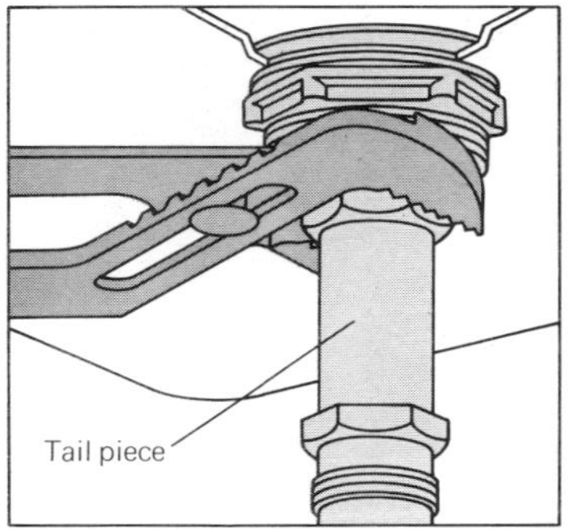

Unclogging drains

Act promptly when you notice a drain emptying slower than usual. A slightly clogged drain is much easier to clear than a totally blocked one. In many cases, flushing the drain with liberal doses of boiling water will restore free flow, but do not use this method on plastic pipes, as they are not made for temperatures over 180°F.

A plunger will often clear a totally blocked drain. Bail out most of the backed-up water, leaving only enough to cover the plunger cup. To increase pressure against the clog, plug the sink overflow opening with a damp rag. With the sink stopper removed, vigorously pump the plunger up and down, timing your strokes rhythmically to reinforce the surge in the pipe.

If the drain remains blocked, abandon the plunger and try a liquid drain opener. They are designed to sink through water, and so are more effective than dry drain chemicals.

Caution: Never use a chemical drain opener in conjunction with a plunger. Splashing onto face could cause serious injury.

Using an auger

Should the above methods fail, a drain auger is called for. Wear glasses and rubber gloves and work with extreme caution if the clog has been treated with drain chemicals, since the trapped water may now be highly caustic. If the auger also fails to work, a main may be clogged. Instructions for unclogging a main appear on page 45.

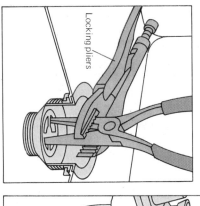

The first step in removing a strainer is to loosen the coupling nuts from both ends of the tail piece. Slide nuts clear of threads and remove tailpiece.

Tail piece

Locking pliers

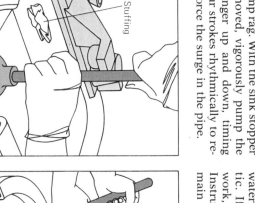

For standard units, undo the locknut with wrench. If nut is ridged, place dowel into ridge and tap with hammer. Remove self-tightening units by undoing bottom screws.

Locknut

Dowel

If strainer turns when nut is rotated and no assistant is available, insert long-nose pliers into strainer holes and clamp on locking pliers to keep strainer steady.

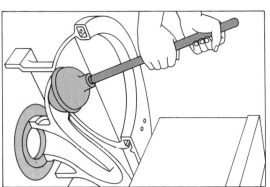

Stuffing

Open and remove drain stopper and stuff up the overflow hole. Leave enough water in basin to cover plunger cup. Before using plunger, tip cup a bit to allow water in.

To unclog toilet, use plunger with fold-out lip that fits snugly into outflow passage. Employ like ordinary plunger. Do not use drain chemicals in toilet.

Using an auger

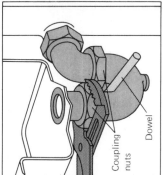

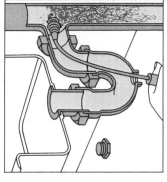

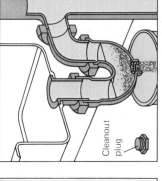

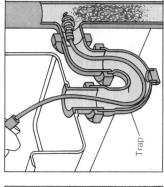

If a pipe has a sharp turn in it, such as a trap, and an auger is to be used to clear it, bend the tip of the auger in the direction of the turn before inserting it.

To clear a basin, insert auger into drain opening until it reaches trap, then rotate it slowly in one direction. Do not push blockage. Try to hook it or break it up.

If you cannot get the auger past the trap, enter pipe through cleanout plug. First, drain water by placing pan under trap, then unscrewing plug with pliers.

Turn handle as you feed auger through pipe. Do not force it; you may worsen the blockage, kink the auger, or damage the pipe. If drain does not clear, remove trap.

To remove trap, unscrew first coupling nut with wrench, while bracing trap with a wood dowel to relieve twisting strain. Support trap while removing second nut.

Coupling nuts — Dowel — Trap — Cleanout plug

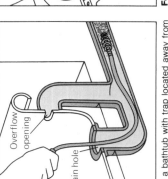

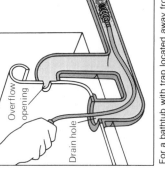

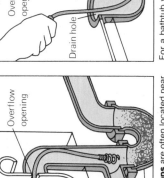

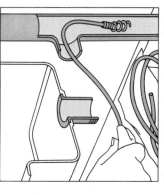

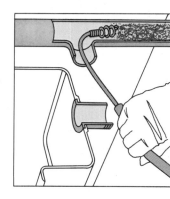

Feed auger in until it hits clog. Then, move auger back and forth, turning it as you crank. Once clog is pierced, continue churning to clear pipe.

Wipe auger clean as you remove it from pipe. Use newspaper or pan to catch sludge. Clean trap before reconnecting it. Flush drain with hot water as a final step.

For a bathtub with trap located away from drain, the easiest entry for auger will probably be through drain hole. Remove stopper before inserting auger.

Bathtub drain traps are often located near the drain hole. In this case, the auger may pass into pipe more easily if inserted into overflow opening rather than drain.

For clogged toilets, use a toilet auger. Position shaft in mouth of outflow passage. Push auger into passage until it hits clog. Turn crank only after blockage is reached.

Overflow opening — Drain hole — Trap — Toilet auger

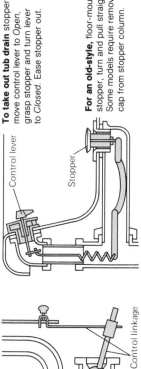

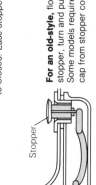

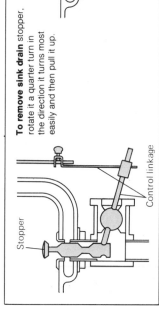

Removing stoppers

To remove sink drain stopper, rotate it a quarter turn in the direction it turns most easily and then pull it up.

To take out tub drain stopper, move control lever to *Open*, grasp stopper and turn lever to *Closed.* Ease stopper out.

For an old-style, floor-mounted stopper, turn and pull straight up. Some models require removing cap from stopper column.

Stopper — Control lever — Control linkage

Flush tanks

To fix a flush tank, it helps to know how it works. The key parts are two control valves: the inlet valve, or ball cock, and the outlet valve, consisting of a stopper ball (or rubber flapper) and a valve seat.

When the flush handle is depressed, a trip lever lifts the stopper ball out of its seat and releases water into the bowl. As the tank empties, two things happen. The stopper ball drops back into the valve seat, plugging the outlet, and the float ball descends, lowering the float arm and opening the inlet valve. Water from the supply pipe then flows through a pair of tubes to refill both the tank and bowl. As the tank fills, the float ball rises, lifting the float arm until the inlet valve is closed, completing the cycle.

Most problems involve the valves. If the inlet valve fails to close, either because it is defective or because the float is incorrectly adjusted, the result is a nonstop trickle of water into the tank and bowl, wasting water and producing noise. If stopper ball does not fit snugly into its seat, the tank will not refill, causing a continual flow of water, and making it impossible to flush the toilet. Repairs and adjustments are illustrated on page 41.

Flush tanks may sweat during warm weather. Sweating can be stopped by fitting an absorbent cover onto the tank, by lining the tank walls with insulating sheets, or by mixing warm water into the tank with a tempering valve, available from a plumbing supplier.

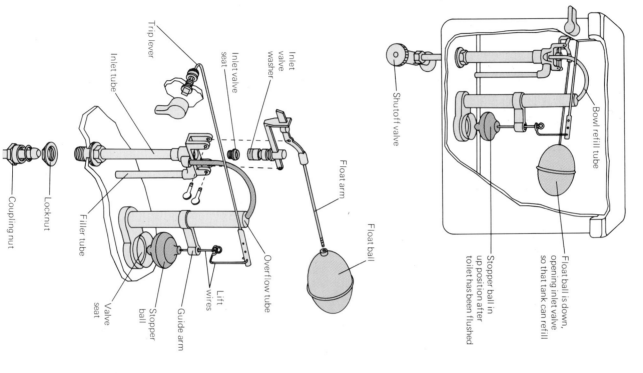

Trip lever

Inlet tube

Inlet valve seat

Inlet valve washer

Inlet valve

Coupling nut

Locknut

Filler tube

Valve seat

Stopper ball

Guide arm

Lift wires

Overflow tube

Float arm

Float ball

Shutoff valve

Bowl refill tube

Float ball is down, opening inlet valve so that tank can refill

Stopper ball in up position after toilet has been flushed

Two modern tank components

Improved ball cock ends most inlet valve malfunctions by replacing conventional washer and packing with diaphragm stopper. Float lever holds diaphragm closed until toilet is flushed; then, lever releases diaphragm, allowing water to flow up shank inlet and down its filler section into tank. Back siphonage is prevented by vacuum seals—pressure drop in shank inlet causes seals to suck closed against filler ports. These new fill valves are available at hardware stores. You can install one yourself to replace an old, noisy ball cock.

Float lever

Diaphragm

Plunger

Shank (filler section)

Shank inlet tube

Bowl refill tube

Combination of float cup and flapper eliminates both stopper and float balls. When toilet is flushed, trip lever lifts flapper, releasing water. As tank empties, flapper returns to its seat and float cup descends, pulling valve lever down and opening inlet valve. Water flows up inlet pipe in center of shank, down filler passage, and out bottom of shank. As tank fills, cup rises, pushing valve lever up to close inlet valve and complete flush cycle.

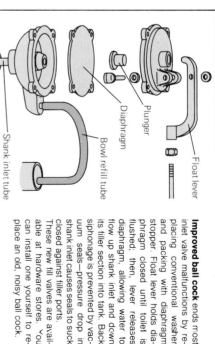

Coupling nut to inlet pipe

Locknut

Gasket

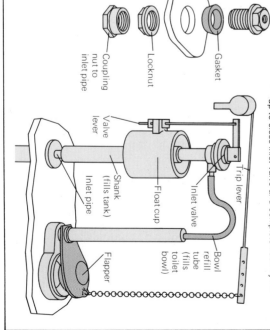

Valve lever

Shank (fills tank)

Inlet pipe

Trip lever

Inlet valve

Float cup

Bowl refill tube (fills toilet bowl)

Flapper

Repairing floats and valves

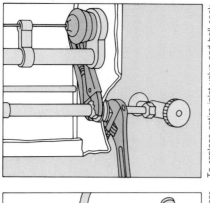

To replace entire inlet-valve and ball-cock assembly, shut off water and empty tank. Unscrew slip and lock nuts under tank and lift out ball cock. Hold hex nut in tank with locking pliers when undoing locknut.

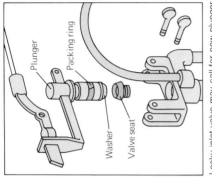

Leaky inlet valve may call for new plunger and packing ring. Shut off water and flush toilet. Remove thumbscrews, lift out float-valve mechanism, and slide plunger off of lever. Replace washer and ring.

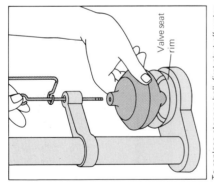

If water keeps running after tank is full, pull up on float. If flow stops, bend float arm downward to increase shut-off pressure on valve. If water still runs, valve is leaky and should be repaired.

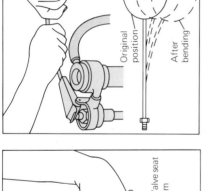

To replace stopper ball, first shut off water and flush toilet. Unscrew ball from lift wire. Clean valve seat rim with steel wool. After installing new ball, open water supply; flush toilet to check alignment.

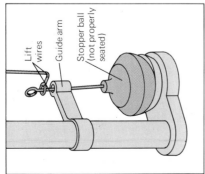

If water enters tank but tank does not refill, check to see if stopper ball is seating properly in valve seat. If it drops in off-center, realign guide arm. Lift wires should be smooth and straight.

Pressure flush valves

Pressure flush valve toilets do away with tanks and save water, but are noisy and require supply pipes of wide diameter. Their flushing mechanisms consist basically of the valve itself and a control stop that meters water pressure and length of flush. There are two standard designs: diaphragm and piston. The piston type is best in hard water areas.

In both types, an adjusting screw in the control stop lets you vary the amount of water per flush. Turn the screw clockwise to cut down the flow, counterclockwise to increase it. If flushing is insufficient when the screw is fully open, the valve section itself may need servicing. Long flushing or no shutoff is often caused by a clogged bypass channel, which can be cleared with a fine wire.

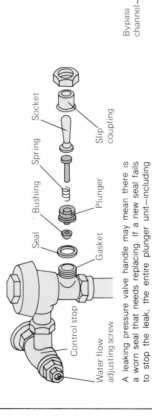

A leaking pressure valve handle may mean there is a worn seal that needs replacing. If a new seal fails to stop the leak, the entire plunger unit—including plunger, spring, bushing, seal, and gasket—should be replaced. Disassemble handle by unscrewing slip coupling, then pull out plunger assembly and unscrew bushing from socket. Clean parts before reassembling.

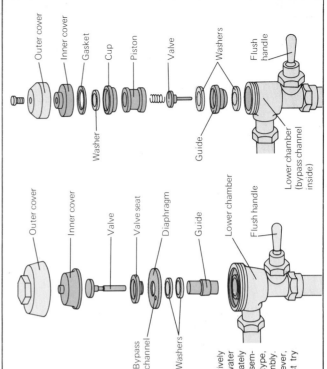

If valve does not shut off completely, or if toilet does not flush effectively even with the stop fully open, repair the valve. First, shut off water supply. On piston valve (far right) only rubber cup is separately replaceable. Remove outer and inner covers, and lift out entire assembly. Cup can be unscrewed from piston. If valve is diaphragm type, unscrew outer and inner covers, then remove diaphragm assembly. It is best to buy a replacement kit and install all new parts. However, to repair valve that flushes too long or does not shut off, first try using a fine wire to clear any blockage in bypass channel.

Plumbing

Galvanized steel pipe

Galvanized steel pipe is durable, strong, and relatively inexpensive. It is available in a large variety of precut, prethreaded sizes or can be cut to order from standard 21-foot lengths. If you buy pipe cut to order, you can have it threaded at the same time. If you wish to cut your own lengths and your own threads, you should buy a hacksaw or pipe cutter, cutting oil, and a reamer. You will also need to rent or buy a stock and die set. Be sure to get the set that is right for the diameter of pipe you plan to thread.

When connecting joints, apply joint-sealing compound or plastic joint-sealing tape to the outside threads of all fittings and pipes. Tighten joints with a pair of wrenches to avoid straining intact pipes.

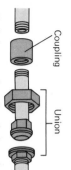

Coupling

Union

Replacing a small section of a long pipe.

Do not overtighten joints. If the fittings and pipe threads are new, the joint will usually be tight enough when about three threads are showing. Old pipes and fittings may need another turn or two, but never screw pipe more than one turn after last thread has disappeared.

Repairing a long run

If a break occurs in a long pipe, you can save money by replacing the damaged section only. Cut out the damaged piece, then connect a new pipe section with a coupling and a union fitting.

Replacing a section of pipe

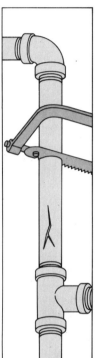

1. After shutting off water supply, cut through pipe with hacksaw. Unscrew pieces from fittings with two pipe wrenches. Use one wrench to steady fitting, other to turn pipe.

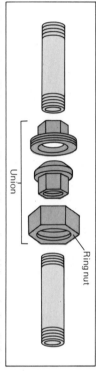

Ring nut

Union

2. Replace pipe with two new lengths joined by a union, which can be bought from a plumbing supplier. When tightened, assembly must equal exact length of old pipe.

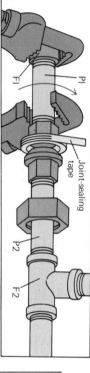

Joint-sealing tape

P1

A

B

C

P2

3. Apply joint-sealing compound or tape to pipe threads. Slip ring nut (C) into position, screw union parts (A, B) onto pipes (P1, P2) with wrenches. Do not tighten.

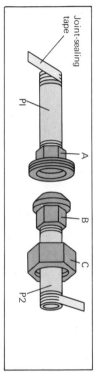

P1

F1

P1

Joint-sealing tape

P2

F2

4. Screw each pipe into its fitting (F1, F2). One wrench steadies the fitting, while the other is used to turn the pipe.

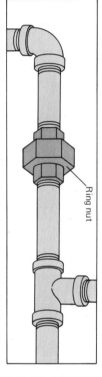

Ring nut

5. After applying joint-sealing compound or tape to exposed threads as shown in Step 4, draw union together by screwing ring nut on tightly with pair of wrenches.

Working with threaded pipes

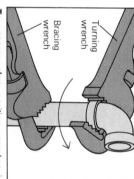

Turning wrench

Bracing wrench

To unscrew pipe, position wrenches in opposing directions; turn free side of connection while bracing other side. Turning force should be toward jaw openings.

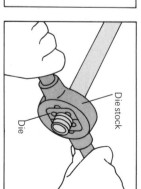

Die stock

Die

When threading pipe, turn die clockwise and back off frequently to remove chips and apply cutting oil. Hold pipe in vise. Match die to pipe diameter.

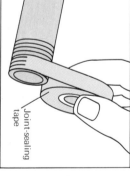

Joint-sealing tape

Apply joint-sealing compound or tape to threads before installing. Wind it clockwise 1½ times around pipe. Pull it tightly enough that pipe threads show through.

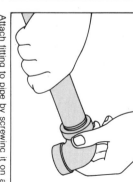

Attach fitting to pipe by screwing it on as far as possible with your hands; finish by tightening with opposed wrenches until only two or three threads are visible.

How to figure pipe length

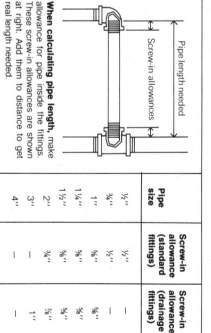

Pipe length needed

Screw-in allowances

When calculating pipe length, make allowance for pipe inside the fittings. These screw-in allowances are shown at right. Add them to distance to get real length needed.

Pipe size	Screw-in allowance (standard fittings)	Screw-in allowance (drainage fittings)
½"	½"	—
¾"	½"	—
1"	⅝"	⅝"
1¼"	⅝"	⅝"
1½"	¾"	⅞"
2"	¾"	1"
3"	—	—
4"	—	—

Copper tubing

Copper pipe, known professionally as copper tubing, is easier to work with, lighter, and more resistant to corrosion than steel pipe. But it costs nearly twice as much per foot.

There are two kinds of copper tubing, flexible (soft temper) and rigid. Soldered connections can be used for either type, but only the flexible copper tubing will accept compression fittings or flare fittings.

Beveled compression ring

Compression fitting before assembly

To make a compression fitting, slide the nut and beveled ring onto the tube, then tighten the nut to the fitting. The soft metal of the compression ring will be pressed against fitting and pipe, forming a watertight and lasting seal.

Soft-temper pipe usually can be shaped by hand. A spring-type bending tool for sharp bends is available from plumbing suppliers, as are the other tools and fittings shown in the illustrations on this page.

If you are using the sweat soldering method to join several fittings and pipe lengths, put the various pieces together, then solder them one after the other. If you solder a joint to a fitting that has other tubing already soldered into it, wrap the finished joints with wet rags to protect them from heat.

Caution: Drain all water from pipe before using torch.

Making a flare fitting

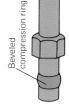
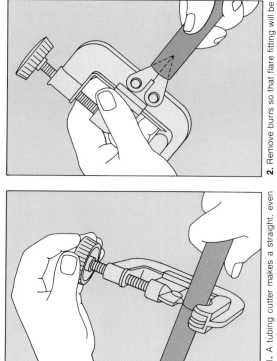

1. A tubing cutter makes a straight, even cut on flexible tubing. Adjust it for a shallow cut on the first turn. Rotate cutter, tightening after each turn, until tube is cut.

2. Remove burrs so that flare fitting will be watertight. Turn cutter's built-in reaming device until lip is smooth. Note: Before taking next step, slip flare nut onto tube.

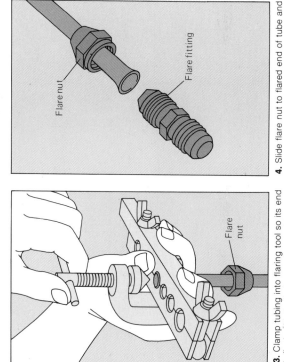

Flare nut

Flare fitting

Flare nut

3. Clamp tubing into flaring tool so its end is flush with tool's face unless tool instructions specify otherwise. Put a few drops of oil on tubing. Screw flaring head in firmly.

4. Slide flare nut to flared end of tube and tighten it onto fitting. Test flare joints under pressure after assembly. They will not leak if carefully made.

Sweat soldering

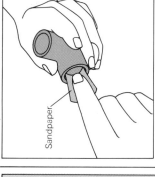

Sandpaper

1. Surfaces to be joined should be clean, smooth, and free of copper oxide film. Use a wire brush or very fine (No. 400) sandpaper to polish the inside of fitting.

Sandpaper

2. Shine end of tube. Use very fine sandpaper and polish gently until metal gleams. Do not use file (it will scar pipe) or steel wool (it leaves shavings).

Soldering flux

3. Immediately after polishing, apply thin coat of paste-type soldering flux to inside of fitting and to end of copper tube. Use a brush to spread the flux.

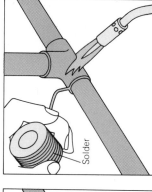

Solder

4. Insert pipe into fitting as far as it will go. Then, give it one complete twist to spread the flux evenly around joint. Wipe off excess flux that squeezes out.

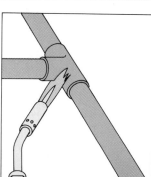

5. Heat pipe and fitting with a torch set for a large, soft flame. Keep flame moving over whole area so that joint heats evenly. Test with solder to avoid overheating.

6. Use solid-core 50/50 solder. Touch it to joint at only one point—it will spread into entire joint by itself. Apply until narrow band of solder appears around fitting.

Plumbing

Plastic pipe

Plastic pipe is lightweight, low in cost, corrosion resistant, and easy to work with. It is available in flexible form for outdoor use and also as rigid pipe. There are three types of rigid plastic pipe—PVC, ABS, and CPVC (the letters refer to their chemical composition.) PVC and ABS are suitable for various cold water applications. For hot water, use CPVC rated at 100 pounds per square inch (psi) at 180°F.

Use solvent cement to join rigid plastic pipe; join flexible tubing with insert fittings. Adapters are available for connecting plastic pipe to metal pipe. Never mix different plastics in the same system. Your supplier will tell you the right cement for each type of plastic.

Before installing a hot water pipe, check the relief valve of the water heater; it should be set at or below 100 psi at 180°F and the thermostat at 180°F or lower. Connect pipe to heater with heat-dissipating fitting.

Solvent-welding

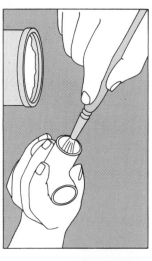

1. For a smooth, even cut, use a miter box and a fine (24-tooth) blade. Ordinary handsaws with coarser blades give a rougher cut.

Miter box

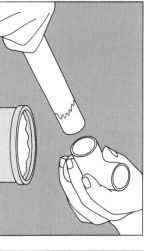

2. Remove burrs from edge with file or sandpaper and rub gloss off mating surfaces of pipe and fitting with medium grit (No. 120) sandpaper. Test-join parts for snug fit.

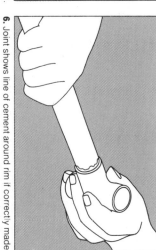

4. Use applicator in lid of can or a natural-bristle brush to apply a generous amount of cement to outside of pipe and a light coating to inside of fitting.

5. Join pieces immediately after applying solvent cement. Twist fitting while pushing it onto pipe. Cement sets quickly, so be sure the fitting is properly oriented.

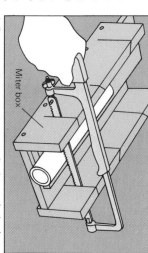

3. Treat pipe and fittings with cleaner-primer to prepare surfaces of pipe for cement. Plastic pipes are joined with special solvent cement, available in hardware stores.

Use rag to apply cleaner-primer

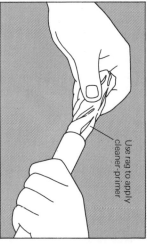

6. Joint shows line of cement around rim if correctly made. Let it set for amount of time specified on label of can. Turn on water and check for watertightness.

Plastic-to-metal adapters

Several kinds of transition fittings are available for connecting plastic pipe to metal pipe. One type has a plastic insert at one end and threads at the other (near right, top). The metal pipe is screwed into the threaded end and plastic pipe is solvent-welded into the insert. A second kind of fitting (far right) uses a plastic transition piece that couples with a brass adapter. Copper pipe is joined to the fitting with solder or a compression ring, and solvent cement is used to bond the plastic pipe. A typical adapter for connecting flexible plastic tubing to a metal pipe or fitting (near right, bottom) is made of galvanized steel or rigid plastic. It has a narrow end that is inserted into the plastic tubing and clamped, and a wider, threaded end that can be coupled to a steel pipe or fitting. Most such pipe connectors have a hexagonal portion to permit tightening with an adjustable wrench. Use only plastic joint-sealing tape on the threads, not liquid pipe sealant. To hold plastic pipe, use a strap wrench—never a pipe wrench. Pipe wrench jaws will damage plastic.

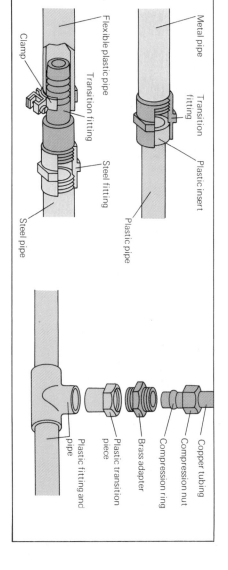

Metal pipe

Transition fitting

Plastic insert

Plastic pipe

Flexible plastic pipe

Transition fitting

Steel fitting

Clamp

Steel pipe

Copper tubing

Compression nut

Compression ring

Brass adapter

Plastic transition piece

Plastic fitting and pipe

Draining the system

There are several reasons for draining the plumbing system. One is to perform major plumbing repairs. Another is to prevent the pipes from freezing if the furnace malfunctions while the house is left untended for long periods in cold weather. Older homes have air chambers that prevent noise and vibration when a faucet is closed. If the air is displaced from these chambers, a hammering noise will develop in the pipes. To cure it, drain the system.

First, turn off the water supply at the main shutoff valve. Then shut off the furnace and the current or gas to the water heater. Next, flush all toilets and open every faucet in the house. If your home is heated by a hot-water system, open all radiator valves (if the radiators have individual valves). Remove the air-escape valve from one or more radiators (baseboard or other types) on the highest floor of the house. Then drain the furnace and water heater.

After the heating system is empty, open the drain valve on the main supply line. If no such spigot exists, determine where the lowest point in your system is and disconnect a fitting there to allow any remaining water to run out of the pipes. If your water supply is from a well, drain both the above-ground pump lines and the tank. Pump lines inside of deep wells seldom freeze, but check with your pump service man to be safe. Be sure to switch the pump off and drain it completely. By that point, all water should have drained out except that in toilet bowls and drain traps. Empty the toilet bowls with a siphon, or by bailing and sponging. Then, pour a mixture of antifreeze and water into all toilet bowls and into the trap of every sink, wash basin, shower stall, and bathtub. Prepare this mixture for the lowest temperature expected in your area, according to the directions on the can.

Unclogging the main drain

If water is backed up in lower floor household fixtures, the main drain in the basement is probably blocked. To locate the clog, begin at the cleanout hole nearest the affected fixtures. Place a bucket beneath the cleanout and partially loosen the plug. If your water drips from the plug, the stoppage is between that cleanout and the sewer. If

water does not drip, check the next plug up the line.

Once the dripping cleanout has been found, loosen its plug gradually and let all the standing water drain into a bucket. Run a drain auger into the pipe until you reach the blockage, then work the auger back and forth vigorously while turning it with the handle to break up the ob-

struction. If you have no auger, and the clog is near, you may be able to clear the line with a makeshift device, such as a straightened-out coat hanger.

If none of your tools will reach the clog, rent a sewer rod from a tool rental agency. Feed it in as you would any auger, but do not rotate it. (This job is better left to professionals.)

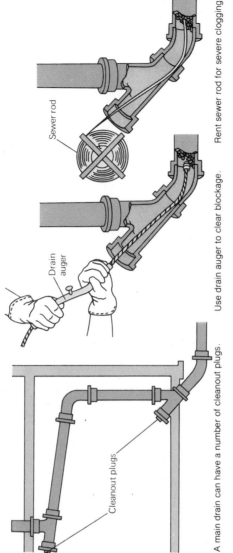

Cleanout plugs

A main drain can have a number of cleanout plugs.

Drain auger

Use drain auger to clear blockage.

Sewer rod

Rent sewer rod for severe clogging.

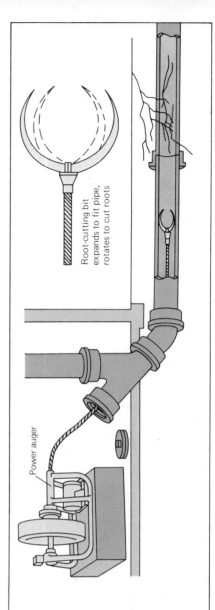

Root-cutting bit expands to fit pipe, rotates to cut roots

Power auger

Removing roots from sewer

Wastelines that have become blocked with roots are best cleared by a professional. But you can do the job by renting a power auger. This machine has a special root-cutting bit. Follow the instructions that come with the tool and work cautiously, otherwise you may damage the sewer line, break the auger's cable, or lose its bit in the pipe. Find where the clog is located and take off the cleanout plug nearest to it before you rent the auger. With the motor turned off insert the auger into the pipe as far as it will go, turn the motor on, and feed the cable through the pipe until it reaches the root blockage (the cable will strain at this point). Feed the cable more slowly until the blades break through, then use a hose to run water into the pipe while continuing to work the auger over the area; this will flush away the debris. If the auger hits a hard obstruction, do not force it—it is probably the main sewer. Withdraw the auger from the pipe slowly, reinstall the cleanout plug, and check out the line by pouring several buckets of water into a toilet bowl.

Scissors, pocketknives, and cutlery

Scissors and shears

The basic whetting, or sharpening, equipment for scissors and shears is an aluminum oxide bench stone, which is generally available at hardware stores. Brown in color, it is coarse on one side and fine on the other. A new stone should be soaked overnight in a pan of light machine oil. Store the stone in a closed box when not using it; otherwise it may clog with dust and become useless. Oil it lightly before each use.

The edges of both scissors and shears should not be honed smooth. They are designed to break through fibers, not to slice them, and the blades should therefore be sharpened only on the coarse face of the stone.

Both scissors and shears are sharpened at a steep angle, as illustrated at right. The blades should meet and bear lightly on one another. If they do not, try tightening the pivot screw, or hammering the pivot down.

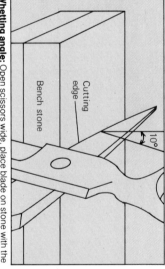

Whetting angle: Open scissors wide, place blade on stone with the inner face vertical; tip it back slightly less than 10°.

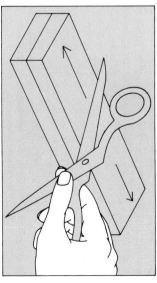

Grip scissors as shown. Rub from side to side on the coarse face of the oiled stone. Work from base to tip. Repeat with second blade.

Pocketknives

Close examination of a new knife blade will show that where the two main faces appear to join there is a secondary pair of narrower bevels; these meet at an angle to form the cutting edge. This sharp edge may feel smooth, but it actually consists of microscopic serrations, or teeth. Dulling results as the teeth bend and splinter. Whetting abrades away the bent and damaged metal, so that the serrated bevels are again aligned at a clean angle along cutting edge. A small knife seldom requires coarse whetting. Use the fine side of a bench stone (see above) or an Arkansas stone—a tool for especially fine honing, available at hardware stores. Put a drop of oil on the stone before using it (and wipe it clean afterward). Press firmly at first, then less so as the edge becomes fine. Finish by lightly stropping both sides of the blade, with the edge trailing, on leather or rouge cloth.

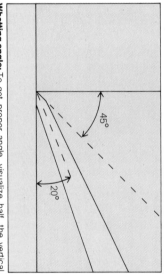

Whetting angle: To get proper angle, visualize half the vertical (45°) and then halve that. You are close to 20°.

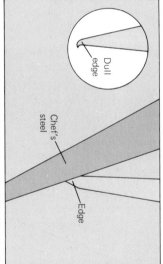

Rub both sides of the blade, using an elliptical motion. Start at the base, raising the handle slightly as you work toward the point.

Cutlery

In the case of carving knives and other unserrated cutlery, the chief cause of dulling is the contact the blade makes with the cutting surface beneath the food. Make a habit of using a cutting board. Ceramic and metal plates and platters, much more so than wood, will bend the fine edge of the cutlery, as shown magnified at right.

If used daily, a chef's steel can keep a good edge on unserrated cutlery for weeks on end. Once the edge has become badly dulled, however, a steel will no longer suffice; sharpen the blade following the procedures described for pocketknives.

A chef's steel simply rubs away the bent lip on the edge of the blade. Move the knife along the steel as illustrated at far right. Other types of motion will not restore the edge.

Note: The use of grinding wheels in sharpening knives and tools is described on page 367.

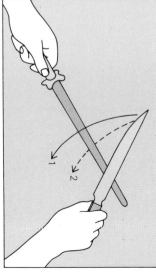

Dull cutlery blade: Contact with a plate or platter turns the edge as seen in the inset. The chef's steel simply wears away the turn.

Stroke downward only, being careful not to cut yourself. Alternate quick strokes from one side of the steel to the other.

Stain removal

Techniques and precautions

The charts below (for auto upholstery, see p.323) are designed to help you select the most effective agent for removing stains from fabrics and from other materials, such as aluminum and marble. Note in fabric chart that different agents may be required for the same type of stain, depending on whether the fabric can be washed or should be drycleaned only, or on whether it is a natural fiber or a synthetic fiber. Where commercial agents are available, their use is recommended in the chart, but no brand names are given. Read all label instructions carefully. Never mix volatile cleaning agents; combining common household chlorine bleach and ammonia, for example, will form a poisonous gas.

Blotting with water or simply pressing a tissue against a fresh stain often removes enough of it so that normal laundering will clean the rest. When using cleaning fluid, place stained fabrics face down on an absorbent pad of paper towels and apply the fluid from above.

Removing fabric stains

Stain	Washable Fabrics	Dryclean Fabrics
Antiperspirant	If stain remains after laundering, apply bleach to it. Sponging with ammonia may restore bleached-out color	Apply bleach as with washables
Beverages (coffee, milk, wine, etc.)	Blot with cool water; spot-clean with solution of 1 oz borax per 1 pt warm water; launder with detergent (soap will set fruit stains). Hardy fabrics: Stretch stained area of fabric over bowl, pour boiling water through stain from height of 2 ft Use cleaning fluid on traces	Blot with cool water, apply cleaning fluid
Cosmetics (lipstick, etc.)	Rub with liquid detergent, rinse; let dry. Repeat procedure until stain disappears	Sponge with cleaning fluid
Glue	Water-base glues: Soak in hottest water possible for fabric; if stain remains, soak hardy fabric in hot white vinegar up to 15 min; launder. Resin glues: Refer to solvents specified in adhesives table, pp.10–12. Use only on natural fibers	Rub liquid detergent into stain, sponge with cold water. Glue is often permanent
Grass	Sponge with rubbing alcohol; rub with liquid detergent; rinse; bleach	Same as for washables
Grease	Rub with liquid detergent; launder. If stain remains, rub with cleaning fluid	Sponge with cleaning fluid
Gum	Rub with ice, scrape with dull knife, rub with cleaning fluid	Use cleaning fluid, pick clean
Ink	Blot immediately; run water through stain to remove loose pigment; apply lemon juice and salt. Launder after 1 hr	Blot, dampen with lemon juice and salt, then dryclean
Liquor	Blot, rinse in cold water, launder	Sponge with solution of 1 tsp white vinegar per 1 pt water
Mildew	Launder, dry in sunlight	Dryclean, air in sunlight
Oil/tar	Rub with liquid detergent; then, rinse, sponge with turpentine, launder	As at left, but dryclean
Paint	Oil: Sponge with turpentine, launder. Latex: Rub with detergent, launder. Lacquer: Dab with acetone, launder. Watercolor: Launder	As at left, but sponge with water instead of laundering
Perspiration	Launder promptly. To restore color, sponge fresh stains with ammonia, old stains with vinegar; rinse. If traces remain, apply cleaning fluid with damp sponge	Dryclean; restore color as for washables
Protein (blood, egg, urine, etc.)	Soak in cold water; launder in warm water and detergent. Remove traces with cleaning fluid. Caution: Heat or hot water will set stains	Sponge with 2 drops ammonia per 1 cup cold water; Let dry, apply cleaning fluid
Scorch	Soak in solution of 1 oz borax per 1 pt cool water. Launder	Dampen with hydrogen peroxide, cover with dry cloth, press with iron set to fabric heat
Vomit/fish oil	Soak in solution of ½ cup salt in 2 qt water, launder	As at left, but dryclean

Removing common household stains

Material	Stain remover and method
Aluminum	Apply commercial metal cleaning powder with steel wool, rubbing in one direction. To remove hard water scale (mineral deposits), boil an equal mixture of water and vinegar in container, let stand overnight; rub with steel wool
Brass, bronze, copper	Apply commercial metal cleaning powder or liquid with cloth. Caution: The green corrosion on copper is poisonous; you can remove it with a cleaning agent or with soapsuds and ammonia. Do not prepare acid foods in pans in which the tinning has been scratched through to the copper
Brick, stone, cement	Scrubbing with detergent and water will remove most stains. Stubborn stains require use of muriatic acid; protect your eyes, face, and hands and follow label instructions. Grease or oil can be soaked up with cat litter, cornmeal, sawdust, or a commercial absorbent
Carpeting	Apply commercial cleaning foam (see p.23). As an alternative, blot the stain with cold water, then sponge outward from center of stain with a solution of 2 cups lukewarm water, 1 tsp white vinegar, and 1 tsp liquid detergent. Spread a paste of cornmeal and cleaning fluid on greasy stains, let it act for several hours, then vacuum. Use ammonia and water on resistant stains
Formica	Use commercial powder or porcelain cleanser. Do not use steel wool
Leather	Clean with saddle soap. Apply rubber cement over a stubborn stain, allow it to dry, rub or peel off. For stains on suede and for grease stains, see Carpeting
Linoleum	Avoid harsh chemical cleaners. Clean in small areas, using hot water and mild soap. Do not allow water to stand; mop or wipe dry immediately
Marble	Apply paste of hydrogen peroxide and powdered chalk (whiting); add a few drops of ammonia, cover with plastic. When bubbling stops, reapply mixture. Polish with tin oxide powder. (Marble cleaning kits are available at many hardware stores or from The Vermont Marble Co., Proctor, Vt.)
Porcelain	If commercial cleaning agents fail to remove stains from porcelain wash basins, sinks, and tubs, try a paste of cream of tartar and hydrogen peroxide, or 5% oxalic acid solution
Silver	Use commercial silver polish. Polish with soft cloth. Rinse thoroughly
Tile	Try chlorine bleach. As alternatives, try white vinegar, ammonia, lighter fluid, alcohol. You can apply a paste of 1 part trisodium phosphate, 1 part sodium perborate, 3 parts powdered talc. Treat as described under Marble
Tin, iron	Remove rust with a raw potato dipped in rottenstone
Wood	See Refinishing, pp.87–103

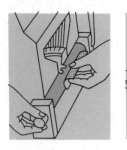 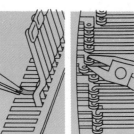 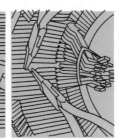 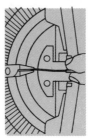 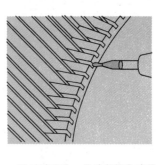

Stiff and sluggish type bars: When you must strike a key with extra force to make the typeface hit the ribbon, the problem is usually a clogged segment slot. The slots fill with erasure dirt and dust.
Action: Regularly clean all slots using a nail file or knife, as shown in Steps 10 to 12 on the opposite page. Insert the blade into the slot as far as it will go and carefully scrape dirt upward and outward. Finally, lubricate each slot with a drop of typewriter oil.

If a type bar remains sluggish, make an ounce of cleaning fluid by mixing equal parts of typewriter oil and nail polish remover or lacquer thinner. Apply this with an eyedropper as shown at left. Let the fluid run down into the slot and then move the type bar by hand to work in the fluid. Test the key after five minutes. If the problem persists, repeat the cleaning procedure until it is corrected.

Type bar sticks in guide: When the type bar sticks in the guide and does not fall back into the rest position, the bar is probably bent.
Action: Examine the type bar while it is stuck in the guide; determine to which side the bar is bent. Bend the bar gently back the other way to straighten it. Grip the bar with pliers, holding the bottom steady, as shown at left. Bend the upper part of the bar. Make a series of small adjustments, testing the bar alignment between each one, until the bar is centered in the guide.

Type bar sticks before reaching type guide; type bar does not move; key action is stiff or impeded: If a type bar sticks before reaching the type guide, the problem may lie with a small object that has lodged under the type bar. The problem may also be caused by a bent or broken type bar link or a bent key lever guide.
Action: Push down the key of the sticking type bar and use your hand to move the bar all the way to a forward position. Depress the remaining keys, gathering them into a bunch in a forward position. Bind them together with a rubber band. This will expose the type bar links; each link is connected to the end of a type bar. With needle-nose pliers or tweezers, remove any foreign object lodged in the links. If there are no such objects, inspect the links themselves. If a link is bent so that it catches on an adjacent link, try to straighten it with needle-nose pliers, as shown. Hold the link steady with one set of pliers, and straighten it with another pair.

Sometimes the type bar will not move at all when you depress a key. This may mean that a type bar link is disconnected. The links are held by rivetlike heads, and one may have come loose. Try squeezing the end of the link back into place with pliers, as illustrated. If you find no faulty links, return all the type bars to their rest position. Place the typewriter on its back, exposing bottom of keyboard. Key levers move between metal guide prongs. If one is bent, causing the lever to stick, straighten it with pliers. Cleaning and lubrication of prongs may also correct key action.

Typewriter ribbon does not reverse: On many machines, the ribbon reverses automatically when the metal rivets at either end of the ribbon trip a reversing arm. On others, the reversing arms are tripped simply by pressure when the ribbon becomes taut, or by a toggle mechanism inside the ribbon spool.
Action: The problem may be merely that the ribbon has become detached from one of the reversing arms. Rethread it through the loops or slots on the metal rivets may have fallen off. If the ribbon is properly threaded, then one of the metal rivets may have fallen off. Look for a hole in the ribbon on the empty spool. To simulate the action of a rivet, tie a small knot, as shown, between the spool and the reversing arm. If a missing rivet is not the cause, try lubricating the mechanisms under the spools.

On some machines, the ribbon is reversed by toggle links located under each ribbon spool. Remove the spools and manipulate the links with your finger. If their movement is sluggish, lubricate them with typewriter oil or aerosol spray lubricant.

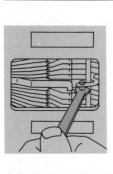 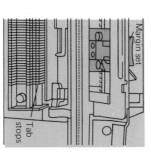 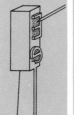 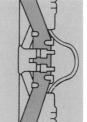 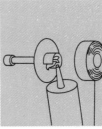 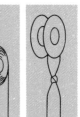

Margin set

Tab stops

Paper slips in platen, causing irregular line spacing: Uneven line spacing is a common problem in old typewriters. The rubber on the roller, or platen, erodes and no longer grips the paper firmly.
Action: With a piece of fine emery cloth, sand the paper along its entire length. To do this, either remove the platen or slowly rotate the platen knob to roughen all the rubber, as illustrated at left. Remove the rubber sandings with a vacuum cleaner. Next, rub down the platen with a lint-free cloth dampened with lacquer thinner or denatured alcohol. This roughing procedure is at best a temporary measure. If the paper still slips, replace the platen.

Print is blurred: While faint print is normally due to a worn ribbon, blurred print commonly results from a dirty typeface.
Action: Replace a worn ribbon. Note how the old one is threaded and thread the new one in the same way.

Clean ink and dirt residue from the typeface. Use either a typewriter brush or an old toothbrush, as shown in Step 3 on the opposite page. Dip the brush into alcohol or lacquer thinner and scrub the typeface with it. Rub the typeface dry with a soft, lint-free cloth. Stubborn deposits can be flicked out with a pin.

If the problem does not lie with the ribbon or typeface, the machine probably requires a professional repairman. The cause may be an old and pitted platen or a carriage that has been loosened by banging or by dropping the machine. Related problems include print that is dark on top and light on bottom, or vice versa, and capitals that print at a different height than lowercase letters.

Margin and tabulator problems: Margin stops and tab keys may not set and release properly on older machines.
Action: Margin and tabulation problems are frequently caused by accumulated dirt. Different typewriters employ different margin setting mechanisms. The easiest to check are the mechanical stops on manual machines, which are set by hand. If they fail to set properly, remove them from the margin bar and soak them in nail polish remover or denatured alcohol to remove any coagulated dirt. Put them back into place; if the margin set remains sluggish, its spring mechanism may be damaged, and should be repaired by a professional. The lever-type margin mechanisms found on electric typewriters should receive professional attention. Work a solution of half nail polish remover and half typewriter oil into stuck tabs

Faulty space bar movement: The carriage movement may be irregular when you press the space bar.
Action: Although faulty space bar movement frequently indicates a problem with the carriage that cannot easily be fixed at home, nothing more may be required than a thorough cleaning and lubrication of the carriage track—as shown in Steps 4 to 6 on the opposite page—or an adjustment of the space bar trip arm. The arm is located beneath the machine. Adjust it, as illustrated at left. By loosening the nut, moving the trip arm, and retightening the nut, you can test the space bar at different adjustments.

Cleaning and lubrication

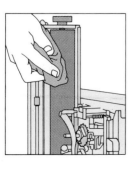

1. Rotate platen, cleaning it with a cloth dampened in alcohol.

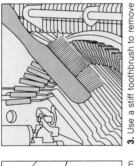

2. Clean all parts accessible from underneath with a soft brush.

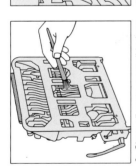

3. Use a stiff toothbrush to remove dirt from the type bars.

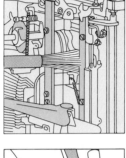

4. Clean the carriage thoroughly with a soft brush.

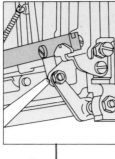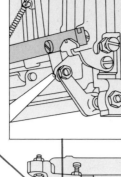

5. Move the carriage to each side and brush along its track.

6. Apply a little thin oil to each end of the carriage track.

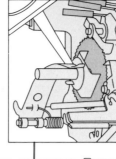

7. Apply the oil to the shift key pivot screws (found on many portables).

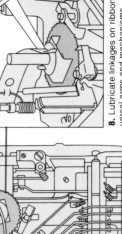

8. Lubricate linkages on ribbon reversal arms and mechanisms.

9. Apply contact cement to any loose key tops and reposition them.

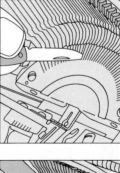

10. Clean dirt from segment slots with a nail file or thin knife blade.

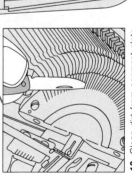

11. Use a soft brush to remove the dirt pried from slots in Step 10.

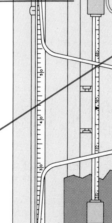

12. Depress keys in large groups and clean beneath the type bars.

13. Lubricate all the nuts and linkages on underside of machine.

49

Window shades and blinds

Venetian blinds

After a number of years, the ladder tapes and cords on a venetian blind will become frayed and may eventually break. Repair kits containing new tape, cord, and knobs are widely available, but be sure the tape is right for your blinds; some blinds have narrow slats and use string instead of tape.

Tapes and cords are attached to the bottom bar in different ways. Most blinds have either a two-piece bar as illustrated at far right, or a one-piece bar with external clips. Tapes on old-style wooden blinds are usually stapled directly to the bar. In general, use the old tapes and cords as guides when you are installing the new ones.

Make sure that the rungs are horizontal when the tilt tube is in the center position and that the rungs on one tape are on a level with those on the other. Once the new pieces are in place, adjust the lift cord so that

Some blinds have one-piece bottom bar, the bottom bar is horizontal, then thread the looped end of the lift cord into the equalizing buckle in order to maintain the adjustment.

Replacing the tape and cord of a venetian blind

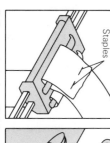

1. Let blind hang to full length, remove end caps, and slide out bottom bar base. This will expose the metal clips that hold the lift cord ends and ladder tapes.

Bottom bar base — Lift cord — Ladder tape — Staples — Clip

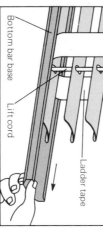

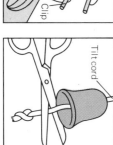

2. Cut off knots to free lift cord from clips. Note that some blinds have a one-piece bottom bar with cord ends fitted into slots or threaded through the bar.

Clip — Lift cord

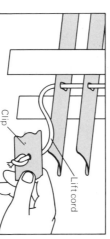

3. Pull lift cord so that its ends come up to the headbox. Knot ends to keep them from passing through, so that you can use the old cord as a guide for the new one.

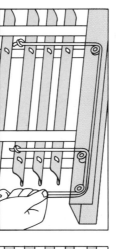

4. Slide out slats. If they are dirty, clean them. Wipe wooden slats with a damp sponge; wash aluminum slats in warm, sudsy water. Do not use abrasive cleansers.

5. Remove tapes from tilt tube and attach new ones. Tape may slide onto hook (left) or be moored with clip. Ends of new tape must be folded and stapled as shown.

Tilt cord

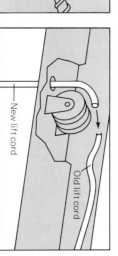

6. Untie or cut bottom knots of tilt cord (left), remove knobs, and pull out cord from above. Cut new cord to same length and thread along path of old one.

Old lift cord — New lift cord

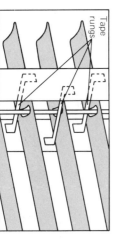

7. Install new lift cord. Free either end of old cord and thread in new one, using old cord as a guide. Leave enough cord on both ends to reach bottom bar.

Tape rungs

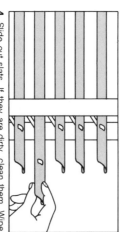

8. Reinsert slats. Pass lift cord ends through slat holes between alternate sides of tape rungs. Knot ends to clips, tuck tapes in, and slide bottom bar back on.

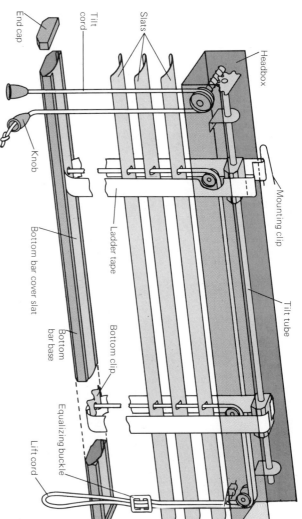

End cap — Tilt cord — Slats — Headbox — Knob — Ladder tape — Mounting clip — Tilt tube — Bottom bar cover slat — Bottom bar base — Bottom clip — Equalizing buckle — Lift cord — Bottom bar base

Repairing a window shade

Sluggish rewinding caused by insufficient spring tension is a common problem with window shades and is easily remedied (see *Increasing spring tension in a shade,* below). Occasionally, the opposite difficulty exists—too much tension. To reduce spring tension, roll the shade all the way up and remove it from the window. Unroll it by hand to about half length and then reinstall it.

If the latching mechanism fails to hold, put a drop of penetrating oil on the pawls. But be sparing with the oil, or it may splatter when the shade rises.

cloth. Remove the roller from the window and unroll the shade. The top end should be squared off and stapled to the roller so that it lines up exactly with the roller's axis.

If the shade rolls up unevenly, make sure the brackets are mounted so that the roller is parallel to the window sill. Uneven rolling may also be due to incorrect mounting of the shade

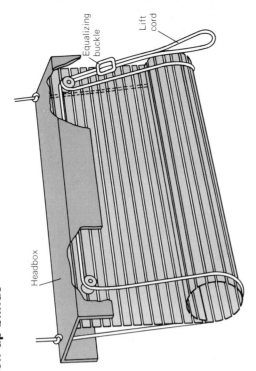

Equalizing buckle

Lift cord

Headbox

Roll-up blinds

Roll-up blinds are a cross between venetian blinds and ordinary window shades. Like venetian blinds, they have slats, a lift cord, and a mechanism to lock the lift cord in place. But like window shades, they can only be raised and lowered, not adjusted, since their slats are not connected to a tilt mechanism.

Restringing the lift cord: The lift cord of a roll-up blind will occasionally break. Any cord suitable for venetian blinds will do as a replacement. Cut off the ends of the old cord and pull it out. Save the equalizing buckle if the new cord does not come with one. When installing the new lift cord, let the blind hang out to its full length. Knot one end of the new cord into the headbox, then take the free end of the new cord and thread it along the path illustrated above. Before securing the second end in the headbox, be sure there is

enough slack in the loop end of the lift cord so that it can be reached comfortably, but preferably not so much that it will drag on the floor when the blind is raised. After both ends are knotted into place, raise the blind halfway and adjust the lift cord loop so that the rolled-up portion of the blind is horizontal. Slip on the equalizing buckle to maintain the cord at its correct alignment.

The slats and their connecting strings: The slats of roll-up blinds are commonly made of plastic or bamboo and are held together by vertical connecting strings that are woven in and out of the slats. If the strings break, retie them, using knots. The blinds should be vacuumed or dusted regularly. Wipe the slats with a damp cloth or sponge for a more thorough cleaning, but avoid using abrasive cleaners or scouring pads.

How the latching mechanism of a shade works

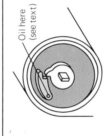

Mounting bracket

Pawl

Rewind spring

Window shade roller and mounting brackets.

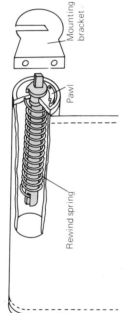

Ratchet tooth

Pawl

Shade is held in position by a small latching device called a pawl, which locks onto ratchet tooth, keeps roller from turning.

When shade is tugged downward, pawl is rotated away from tooth, freeing roller. Shade can then rise under spring tension.

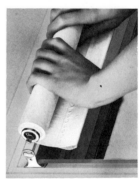

Oil here (see text)

As shade rolls up, centrifugal force keeps pawl pivoted outward, preventing it from engaging ratchet and stopping roller.

When shade is halted at desired point, centrifugal force ceases. Pawl drops down onto ratchet, locks shade in new position.

Increasing spring tension in a shade

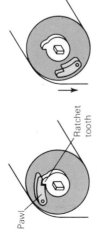

A weak spring will cause the shade to wind sluggishly. To tighten up the spring tension, first roll shade down about 2 ft and remove roller from brackets.

Roll the shade up by hand, then return it to the window brackets. Check it for proper operation by rolling it up and down. If the spring is still weak, repeat the adjustment.

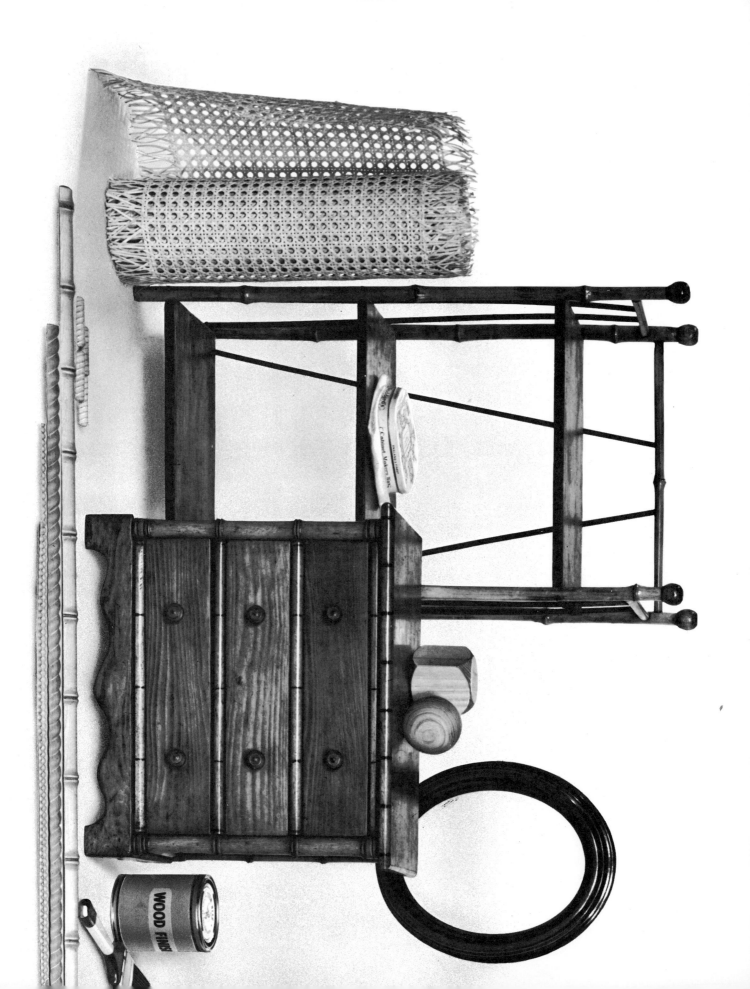

Furniture Repair and Refinishing

If you have failed in your previous attempts to repair furniture, it may have been because you relied solely on nails, screws, brackets, and other hardware to mend breaks in the wood. While hardware has its uses, lasting repairs can usually be achieved only through the application of the artisan's time-tested techniques. This section first introduces a battery of traditional techniques, and then goes on to show these methods being employed to repair different types of furniture. It also presents time-honored approaches to refinishing.

Basic tools

Which tools to buy

Furniture repairs can usually be handled with a few simple handtools and the willingness to improvise in their use. A screwdriver, for instance, can be surprisingly versatile. You will find it handy as a scraper, spreader, prying tool, or lever as well as for driving a screw. Used with care and imagination, the few basic tools shown on this page should equip you to make most of the repairs that are likely to arise in connection with your household furniture.

A workbench with a permanently attached woodworker's vise provides the ideal arrangement for repairing furniture. But, for most purposes, any working surface to which a clamp-on vise can be attached can serve as a workbench. In fact, few jobs absolutely require a vise; in many situations a clamp, masking tape, or cord can be substituted.

You will need a drill for certain tasks (see *Doweling*, pp.65–66) and one or more of the clamps discussed on the opposite page. Modern glues (see *Gluing*, p.61) and dowels minimize the need for screws, nails, and other types of metal fasteners in mending wooden furniture.

Enlarging your tool kit

As you become more involved and more experienced in furniture repair, you may want to add to the basic tools shown here. A practical procedure is to wait until specific jobs require specific tools, then invest in the best tools you can afford. A good tool, properly used and maintained, should last a lifetime.

In the pages that follow, such procedures as gluing and clamping, cabinet-making and refinishing, caning and re-upholstering are discussed in step-by-step detail. The specialized tools and materials needed to make these repairs are also described. Use these pages as a guide when you must add to your tool kit to handle many jobs, from reattaching a chair back to restoring an antique chest.

Clamp-on vise can be attached to any working surface. To protect finishes, insert buffers between the jaws and the furniture.

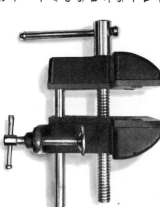

Chisels have many uses, ranging from cutting recessed hinge beds to cutting dowels. Buy a medium or a small chisel.

Rubber mallet is used to tap elements into place or apart. The rubber head helps avoid damage to wooden surfaces.

Claw hammers are available in several different weights. A 16-oz hammer is a good choice for general use.

Screwdriver with small or medium blade will take care of most of your repair needs.

Backsaw is designed for precision work, such as cutting dowels, rungs, tenons, and dovetails. Saw is stiffened along its back with a brass or iron band. Fine teeth allow close control of work.

Pliers are used in most repair jobs. Buy an adjustable pair of the slip-joint type.

Utility knife is a precise cutting tool. The retracting blade is replaceable. Any sharp knife can be used.

Furniture-strength white glue is available in plastic squeeze bottles. The pointed nozzle is convenient for applying the glue directly to joints.

Masking tape is generally useful; it is used to clamp repairs and to hold parts, such as hinges, in position for marking.

Bit brace is a traditional woodworking tool. It requires a custom bit that does not fit other types of drills.

Electric drill is better than a hand drill because it is easier to hold steady and it operates more rapidly.

Hand drill is useful only for small jobs. Heavy work, such as drilling dowel sockets, is better done with an electric drill.

Small block plane shaves down swollen or warped wood and smooths edges and surfaces. You can substitute a standard size jack plane.

Clamps

Most furniture repairs require gluing, and because of this it is essential that you master the use of clamps. Clamps apply even and constant pressure while the glued parts are drying. This insures that the mend will be solid, exact, and long lasting.

Several types of woodworking clamps are illustrated on this page. Each is designed for a specific application, as noted

in the descriptions accompanying the illustrations. However, one type of clamp can often be substituted for another; two small clamps can sometimes substitute for a single large clamp. Frequently, such ordinary household items as twine or masking tape can be used to apply the pressure needed for a good repair. Such improvisations, and the correct techniques for using the clamps shown on

this page, are described in a subsequent section. (See *Clamping,* pp.62–64.)

Clamps of all types are available at most hardware stores. Before buying clamps for a particular job, analyze the job carefully and decide what type or types are called for. If you want to have available a number of clamps that can be used for most jobs, buy the hand-screw type illustrated below. It is the

most versatile, and is especially recommended for working on furniture because its wooden jaws are less likely to damage wood or mar a fine finish.

Clamps are useful for jobs other than gluing, however. A clamp can often be substituted for a vise, for instance, or used as an extra "hand" when you have a repair that must be made and you are working alone on a difficult job.

Types of clamps

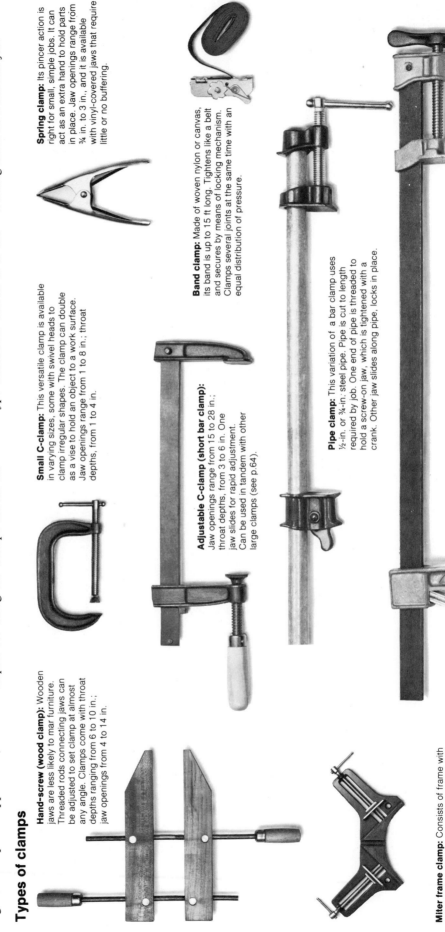

Spring clamp: Its pincer action is right for small, simple jobs. It can act as an extra hand to hold parts in place. Jaw openings range from ¾ in. to 3 in., and it is available with vinyl-covered jaws that require little or no buffering.

Band clamp: Made of woven nylon or canvas, its band is up to 15 ft long. Tightens like a belt and secures by means of locking mechanism. Clamps several joints at the same time with an equal distribution of pressure.

Small C-clamp: This versatile clamp is available in varying sizes, some with swivel heads to clamp irregular shapes. The clamp can double as a vise to hold an object to a work surface. Jaw openings range from 1 to 8 in.; throat depths, from 1 to 4 in.

Adjustable C-clamp (short bar clamp): Jaw openings range from 15 to 28 in.; throat depths, from 3 to 6 in. One jaw slides for rapid adjustment. Can be used in tandem with other large clamps (see p.64).

Pipe clamp: This variation of a bar clamp uses ½-in. or ¾-in. steel pipe. Pipe is cut to length required by job. One end of pipe is threaded to hold a screw-on jaw, which is tightened with a crank. Other jaw slides along pipe, locks in place.

Bar clamp: Flat steel bar has fixed jaw at one end, sliding jaw at other end. Fixed jaw tightens by means of crank. Sliding jaw locks into place. Clamps are designed for big jobs, like a split tabletop. Up to 4 ft in length, they can also be used in tandem with other clamps.

Hand-screw (wood clamp): Wooden jaws are less likely to mar furniture. Threaded rods connecting jaws can be adjusted to set clamp at almost any angle. Clamps come with throat depths ranging from 6 to 10 in.; jaw openings from 4 to 14 in.

Miter frame clamp: Consists of frame with adjustable corner blocks. It is used on picture frames or structures with mitered corners, where it is desirable to clamp all four corners at the same time. Two bar clamps will usually do the job equally well.

Working with wood

Analyzing the job

Before starting a repair, look over the entire piece of furniture closely; the more familiar you are with its construction, the easier it will be to make the repair properly. Pay particular attention to joints, such as those where rails meet legs and where the legs join chair seats or table and desk tops.

Your repair method should always conform to the original construction method. For example, a loose leg that was attached with dowels and glue, or by a mortise and tenon joint, should be reattached using the same techniques and materials. Avoid using nails or other hardware. They are likely to split and weaken the wood.

A second purpose in studying the entire piece is to determine whether the broken element correctly. When separating joints, be especially careful not to break any dowels and tenons. If you do break any, replace them. (See *Doweling*, pp.62–64.) As you disassemble, use a grease pencil (so that marks can easily be cleaned off) to number the parts in the order in which they are removed. Make a sketch of the piece, showing where each part is located. This is particularly important with chair rungs and spindles, which are often graduated in size and must be put back in order.

Dry run: Before regluing or refastening any individual parts, always reassemble the entire piece of furniture in a dry run (see *Gluing*, p.61) to be sure everything fits and to anticipate any hitches.

other structural segments. Be alert to the possibility that the problem you initially noticed may have been caused by another weak or broken element, not apparent at first glance. An unstable chair back, for example, may cause the arms to work loose; one loosened rung may be the reason others fall off completely. When repairing one element, therefore, always check for defects throughout the entire piece of furniture and correct everything at the same time.

Disassembly: It is sometimes necessary to disassemble a large section of a table or chair, or to take a piece completely apart in order to repair a single

Your work area should be clean, and all the tools and materials for the job should be within easy reach and in good working order. Be sure you have enough glue and a damp rag to wipe away any spillage or excess. Place carpeting or towels under the piece to protect its finish. You may also want to cover the floor. The area should be well lighted and well ventilated, especially when using paint remover or any other material that gives off toxic fumes.

Many repairs can be avoided or at least reduced in scope if you examine your furniture regularly for loose joints or other hardware, minor breaks or splits or other signs of developing problems, and take immediate corrective measures.

Wood characteristics

Each wood has certain characteristics that may affect repair procedures. Furthermore, when replacing or patching an element, particularly veneer, you should try to match the original wood.

Most furniture is made of a hardwood, such as mahogany, teak, or oak. But some is made of softwood: Chests and outdoor furniture may be cedar, fir, or redwood; inexpensive furniture is often constructed with pine.

Identifying wood: Color is seldom a reliable guide in identifying wood, since furniture usually has been stained or refinished. The color of an untreated section, such as the underside of a desk, may be helpful, but be sure the entire piece is constructed of the same wood. The best way to identify wood is by its grain, even though the grain pattern of a particular wood can vary, depending on such factors as forest growing conditions, the tree's age, and how the lumber was cut from the log.

Eight woods frequently used in furniture are illustrated at right with their most common grain patterns.

Maple: Cream to light reddish brown. Grain usually straight. Strong, generally has even texture. Easy to work. Glue should be applied generously. Takes high polish. Fir, pine, and spruce are often confused with maple because of similar colors and grains.

American oak: Light tan or light reddish brown. Tan has finer grain than the red. Both have distinctive grain. Heavy, great strength. Holds nails and screws well, but holes must be drilled for screws to prevent the wood from splitting.

Cherry: Varies from light, almost white, to dark reddish brown. Satiny. Usually has straight grain, but sometimes delicately patterned. Moderately hard, medium weight. It resists warping and shrinking better than many other woods.

Rosewood: Varies from a rose-pink to a purplish brown, streaked with lighter or darker stripes. Veneers cut in exotic grain patterns. Finishes to a beautifully smooth, polished surface.

Walnut: Light gray-brown to dark brown. Has medium grain with varied patterns. Medium weight and strength. Sands and glues well. Finishes excellently.

Teak: A tawny yellow to rich dark brown, often with lighter streaks. Moderately hard and strong, but it can be brittle. Much like walnut except wood is oily; resists rot, decay, warping.

Mahogany: Light pink to reddish brown (deep reds result from finishing). Great variety of grain patterns. Heavy, strong. Sands, glues, and finishes well.

Pine: A softwood. Light cream to a light reddish brown. Often characterized by knots. Uniform in texture. Easily worked. Close grained; finishes well. Common softwood for furniture, veneer, plywood.

Preparing the surface

Sanding

Sandpaper is sold in sheets or in packets of small squares. Buying by the sheet is more economical and allows greater flexibility in shaping pieces for specific jobs. Sandpaper consists of a cloth or paper backing and an abrasive mineral coating. To get the best sanding results, make sure you select a sandpaper with the right combination of mineral, backing, grain spacing, and grain size.

Minerals: Flint paper is the cheapest but it cuts slowly and dulls rapidly. Because of its low price, it is a suitable choice for the initial sanding of softwood surfaces that clog paper quickly. Flint paper is available only with paper backing and closed grain spacing.

Garnet paper is durable and is used for smoothing, finishing, and polishing the surface. It is more expensive than flint, but it is the best choice for general sanding. Silicon carbide is excellent for extensive sanding, but it is more expensive than garnet. It wears well; wood dust can easily be knocked out of it, allowing the same piece to be used many times. Aluminum oxide papers are most often used in finishing.

Backings: Coarse sandpapers used for rough carpentry jobs have heavy backings for durability. Fine sandpapers used for finishing have thin, soft backings for flexibility and to reduce scratching. Backings come in three weights: A, C, and D. A is the lightest.

Abrasive spacing: Depending on the spacing between grains, sandpaper, is classified as either open or closed coat. Closed-coat grains completely cover the backing; open-coat grains cover as little as 50 percent of the total surface area.

Open-coat papers cut faster with less pressure. They last longer because they are less likely to clog up, and if they do the dust can easily be shaken out. They are therefore especially suited for use on softwoods and painted surfaces, which clog sandpaper quickly. Aluminum oxide paper is also made with a zinc-stearate coating to reduce clogging.

Grade, or grit: Grade, or grit, numbers refer to the size of the mineral grains. The higher the number, the finer the grains. (See chart at right.) Use the finest grit for the job at hand; for furniture repairs, medium should be the coarsest you will ever need. A rule of thumb is to take more time sanding with finer grades rather than risk damaging a surface with a coarse paper. For small areas, use only one fine grade. For large areas, particularly those to be refinished, start with medium, and go on to finer grades.

Sanding technique: Use straight strokes with a light, even pressure. Move the paper back and forth in a continuous motion. Work over large areas and be sure to sand all parts equally. Always sand with the grain, if possible; sanding across the grain will scratch the surface. On curved areas, sand first in the direction of the curves, but sand the final strokes with the grain. On flat surfaces and edges, use a sanding block or some form of backing other than your hand to avoid producing wavy contours.

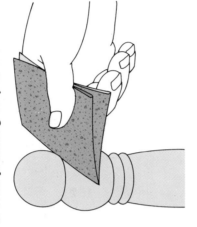

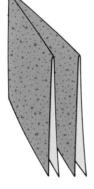

A series of simple folds turns a large sheet of paper into a convenient hand-sized pad with multiple sanding surfaces. To tear into smaller pieces place a crease along a table edge and pull down firmly.

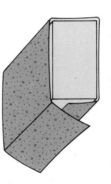

For hard-to-reach edges and crevices, use the fold of a sheet of sandpaper. Do not crease the fold; creasing weakens the backing. Sand gently. Be careful not to slice into the wood.

A sanding block should be used to smooth flat surfaces. Choose a block of wood comfortable to your hand and fold the paper around the block to provide broad working surfaces.

Dowel sockets must be cleaned of all old glue before new glue is applied. This task is sometimes simplified by using a cylindrical sanding block—a strip of sandpaper wound tightly around a pencil or dowel.

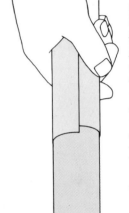

To sand rounded elements, such as dowels, rungs, legs, or spindles, tear off a broad piece of sandpaper. Wrap it around the element and move it up and down or back and forth along the grain.

Sandpaper grades

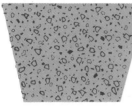

Medium: Coarser papers are rarely necessary for furniture repairs. Except for removing heavy old finishes, you should not require a grade below No. 80.

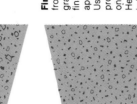

Fine: Grit numbers range from 100 to 180. These grades are used for the final sanding before you apply fillers or paint. Usual A-weight backing provides conformability on curved surfaces. Heavier C-weight backing is best for flat surfaces.

Very fine: Grit numbers range from 220 to 280. Papers have an A-weight backing. These grades are used for sanding between applications of finishing coats. No. 220 is suitable for the final sanding before the refinishing of softwoods; Nos. 220 to 280 are suitable for this same purpose on hardwoods, depending on the hardness of the particular wood.

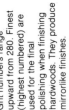

Extra fine, or superfine: Grit numbers range upward from 280. Finest (highest numbered) are used for the final polishing when finishing hardwoods. They produce mirrorlike finishes.

Preparing the surface

Chiseling and planing

A chisel is useful for scraping off old glue or other surface material. Scraping will dull the blade, so use an old chisel. A screwdriver can be used for small jobs. (The use of a chisel to cut a recessed hinge bed is described on p.60.)

A plane is a chisel blade fixed into a metal frame, but it is basically a smoothing rather than a cutting tool. It can be used, for example, to shave down a warped drawer. Use a plane with an adjustable blade so that you can control the thickness of the shavings. Adjust the blade and test it on scrap wood before starting a job.

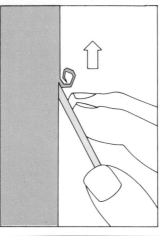

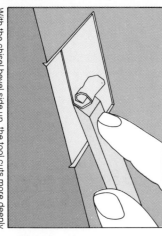

When fine shavings are desired, you must have maximum control over the chisel. Hold it bevel side down and guide the blade by pressing firmly with your fingers close to the cutting edge.

With the chisel bevel side up, the tool cuts more deeply into the wood. Consequently, controlling the amount of wood you cut is much more difficult. Score the area to be removed and work carefully.

Wood putty

Minor defects in a wood surface, from cosmetic repairs, not to fill old holes for driving new screws. A dowel or wedge fixed before proceeding to other repairs. If it is a very shallow blemish, careful sanding may even out the area. The most common and convenient material for filling small holes is wood putty, which is available at hardware stores. You can make your own filler, using a mixture of sawdust and white glue. Put the filler into the hole and let it dry thoroughly. Then, sand the filled area flush with the wood surface. Holes filled with wood putty or sawdust and glue can be finished or painted like ordinary wood.

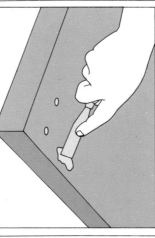

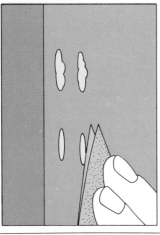

Wood putties contract as they dry; therefore, you should fill the hole slightly higher than the surrounding surface. Two applications may be necessary. Small applications dry in about an hour.

After the wood putty has dried, sand the excess flush with the surface. If repair will show, stain or refinish it to match the piece of furniture. Putties are available in various wood colors.

Dowels and wedges

Wood putty should be used only for cosmetic repairs, not to fill old holes for driving new screws. A dowel or wedge filler is always recommended where a new screw will be inserted in the same position, in order to provide a firm base. Use dowels for round holes, wedges for straight-edged or odd-shaped holes. When a hole is not exactly the right diameter or shape for a dowel, it is usually worth while to drill it out slightly so that a dowel will fit. Be sure to select a drill bit of the same diameter as your dowel. General instructions on doweling techniques appear on pages 65-66.

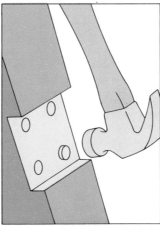

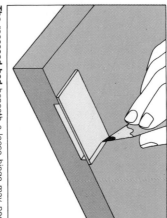

To plug a round hole, cut a length of dowel 1/16 in. longer than the hole. Apply glue to dowel and hole; carefully tap the dowel into the hole. After glue dries, sand the dowel flush with the surface.

If hole is rectilinear or odd shaped, cut wedge of same approximate size and shape from scrap wood. Leave about 1/16 in. protruding and treat it as a dowel: Glue it, tap it into the hole, and sand it flush.

Shimming

It is often necessary to build up a recessed hinge bed that has become worn through constant use, as on a drop-leaf table or an old piece of cabinetry. Similarly, the recessed beds of locks and other types of hardware often require repair. The wood may be so worn or split by screws that it must be chiseled cleanly away and then replaced with new wood. To build up the area and provide a solid base for hardware, use a shim. A shim is a piece of wood either cut from a length of very thin wood or peeled from a block of wood with a chisel. Glue the shim into place; sand the edges flush.

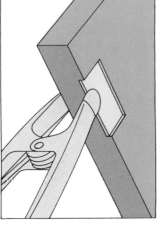

The recessed bed beneath a loose hinge may need to be rebuilt before the hinge can be refastened. Remove any loose wood; fill in old screw holes; glue and clamp splits. Then, cut shim to shape of recess.

Glue recess and underside of shim; Clamp shim into place; let dry overnight. Drill pilot holes in shim and screw down hinge. If necessary, buy a hinge with holes in different positions than old one.

Drill bits, screws, and nails

Drilling

A drill is needed for such furniture repair jobs as installing new dowels and making pilot holes for screws. There are three types of drills: an ordinary hand drill, a ratchet bit brace (see *Basic tools*, p.54), and an electric drill. The hand drill is least expensive, but is convenient only for small jobs. A ratchet brace has greater torque than a hand drill and can also be used to drive screws. The electric drill is the preferred tool: It can be used with one hand, is faster than manually powered drills, and has a variety of attachments to perform many operations.

Bit types: Drill bits that can be used on furniture are available in three types, each sold in a standard range of sizes. Buy odd sizes only as needed for special jobs. The conventional twist bit can be used on materials other than wood. Quick-bore, or woodboring, bits are designed for use only on wood. Because of their sharply pointed tips, these bits seat securely in guide holes and will not shift off center as the drill starts up. Although a twist bit produces a cleaner hole, the quick-bore bit's greater accuracy makes it preferred for creating dowel sockets and pilot holes for screws. The brad-point bit combines the clean boring advantages of the twist bit with the accuracy of the quick-bore; however, many hardware stores do not carry it in stock.

Be sure that the work is firmly supported or braced before you begin drilling. Punch a guide hole with a nail or an awl to center the bit. A special technique is used to make guide holes for sockets (see *Replacing dowels* p.65).

Depth must be carefully controlled in drilling a dowel socket. Depth gauges can be purchased to fit both twist and quick-bore bits. You can save yourself this expense, however, by wrapping a piece of masking tape around the bit to mark the depth, and drilling no deeper.

Screws and nails

A good rule to follow in repairing furniture is never to introduce screws or nails where they were not a part of the original construction. Loose chair backs, wobbly legs, cracked surfaces—and most other problems that develop in furniture—are more durably and esthetically repaired by gluing and clamping. Sometimes the mere introduction of a screw or a nail decreases the market value of furniture—particularly an antique piece.

Pilot holes: When the use of screws is called for in repair—for example, to reattach handles or hinges—choose the smallest size that will do the job properly. Begin by drilling a pilot hole for the screw. Select a drill bit for the pilot hole by matching the bit to the screw's diameter, minus the threads. (Hardware stores usually have charts matching screw size and bit size for the purpose of making pilot holes.) For hardwoods, the size of the pilot hole is especially important. Screwing into too small a hole can split the wood or cause the screw to break off. A hammer and nail, or an awl, can be used to make a pilot hole in softwood. Tighten screws down firmly, but do not enough to hold the screw threads. With softwood, simply drill a small guide hole into each piece.

If you have to remove a nail, pry it out with a claw hammer; for extra lever-

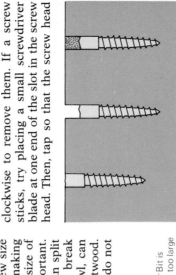

Extra leverage helps in removing old nails and screws.

age, place a block of wood under the hammer head. Turn screws counterclockwise to remove them. If a screw sticks, try placing a small screwdriver blade at one end of the slot in the screw head. Then, tap so that the screw head rotates in a counterclockwise direction. Where the screw slot is too worn to provide a grip for a screwdriver, or the screw head is broken off but the shank still protrudes, use pliers to twist out the shank. If you cannot get a grip to remove a screw or nail shank, you will have to sink it in. Use a nail set (or the tip of a nail) with a diameter less than that of the broken shank. Fill the hole at the top of the shank with wood putty (see *Wood putty*, p.58), sand when dry, and touch up the finish.

Sink broken screw into wood and top with filler.

Bit is too large

Bit is too small

Bit is correct size

Match bit to screw when drilling a pilot hole.

force them. When using screws to bind together two pieces of hardwood, drill a hole into each piece. The entry hole in the first piece should be the same diameter as the screw shank; the anchor hole in the second piece should be small

Twist bit

Brad-point bit

Quick-bore (woodboring) bit

In drilling a hole all the way through a piece of wood, clamp scrap wood firmly underneath. Drill partially into the scrap wood. This approach prevents splintering around the hole at the bottom of the good piece.

To control drilling depth, use either a depth gauge that locks onto the bit, or masking tape. When gauge makes contact with wood, bit cannot go deeper. Or, when mark on tape is even with surface, stop drill.

Common problems

Even a properly installed hinge may strain the wood to which it is attached. Problems are likely to develop with hinges that support heavy weight. Hinges used primarily as pivots, as on the lid of a box, seldom need repair.

Sometimes hinges must be removed to repair other parts of a piece. A problem with the hinges themselves—or the need for a minor adjustment, replacement, or a change in position—may also require their removal. In each case, there are certain procedures to follow, many of which also apply to other kinds of hardware, such as fasteners and handles.

When disassembling a piece of furniture, simply remove the screws from the hinges. But be careful not to damage the hinges themselves or to mar the surface around the hinges. You may discover at this time that the hinge or hinge bed needs repair; otherwise, replace the hinge in exactly the same position.

Hinges that do not pivot smoothly may need a drop of household oil. Screws may require tightening or replacement. If a hinge pin is lost or broken and you cannot cut a close substitute from a nail, replace the entire hinge. When buying

a new hinge, take the old one with you to compare type, style, placement of holes, and other features.

Screws usually work loose because the holes have become enlarged. Substitute screws of a slightly larger size may solve the problem, but there is a risk of splitting the wood and compounding the trouble if you use too large a screw. It is safest to fill in the holes by one of the methods described on page 58, redrill the screw holes in the same places, and insert new screws of the original size. You can also replace the hinge with one having differently spaced holes. Fill in the original holes, then drill new ones to fit the new hinge and install it.

Split hinge bed

Before screwing down a loose hinge, examine the wood underneath. If the hinge bed is split, mend the split with glue, clamp it, and let it dry before replacing the hinge. To provide stronger support for a hinge on a heavy piece, such as a table leaf, reinforce the damaged bed with a shim (see *Shimming*, p.58), in addition to repairing the split. Then, screw the hinge down on top of the shim.

A hinge bed may become so damaged that you must move the hinge to a new position. Since hinges work in sets of two or more, this generally requires moving more than one hinge to maintain symmetry and balanced support. Fill in the old hinge beds and screw holes with wood putty or chips and glue. If the old beds are recessed, they can be leveled by using a shim made of a matching wood, after which the surface should be refinished.

Aligning hinges

When marking the positions for new hinges, you must carefully align the elements being hinged, such as a box and its lid. After deciding on the placement of the hinges, secure them first to one of the hinges, say the lid. Then, line up the lid with the box again and carefully mark the second set of hinge and screw hole positions on the box. Drill pilot holes, and then screw the hinges to the box. Installing a hinge flush with the surface requires an additional step, as illustrated below; first, chisel out a recessed bed, as illustrated below; then, install the hinge.

Installing recessed hinge

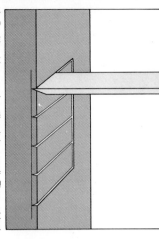

1. Position hinge and outline it in pencil. Then, chisel along inside of outline. Hold chisel straight up and down, bevel side in. Next, make cross-grain cuts within bed to divide it into removable sections.

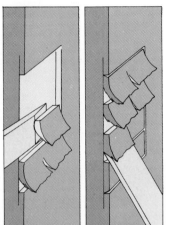

2. Excavate sections in thin layers, holding chisel bevel side down. Be careful not to gouge the wood. Shave the bed to the exact depth of the hinge. Smooth it with sandpaper.

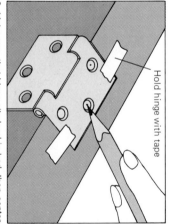

3. Make sure that hinge sits level in bed, then center screw holes on the surface of the bed with a pencil, a nail, or an awl. Remove the hinge, and drill pilot holes for screws (p.59). Screw down one side of hinge.

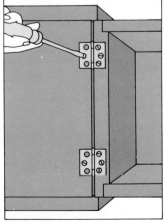

4. When installing more than one hinge, do not completely screw down the second side of any hinge before all hinges have been temporarily secured with one center screw and their alignment verified.

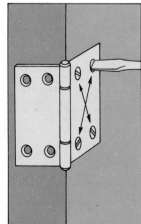

Hold hinge with tape

Best method for installing hinges: Begin by partially tightening down the first screw. Then, continuing in the sequence shown, give a few twists to each screw in turn until all of them are tight.

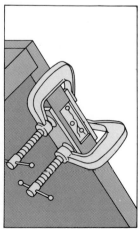

Hinge beds often develop splits along screw lines. Remove hinge and pry split gently apart. Bow out loose splinters. Squeeze glue along length of crack. Work glue in with your fingers. Clamp and let dry.

Gluing

Gluing techniques

Glue is the most durable and reliable fastener for mending furniture. It bonds wood to wood without introducing hardware that might weaken the construction. A nail—and sometimes a screw—may cause splits that later develop into major breaks. But glue, used in combination with clamps (see *Clamping*, pp.62–64), produces strong, long-lasting repairs.

Furniture glues

In the past, furniture manufacturers and repairmen used a hot, animal glue that until recently was the best available adhesive for woods. When repairing an old piece of furniture, you may still find this translucent amber glue in joints and dowel sockets.

Today, the glues most widely used are white polyvinyl resin types and aliphatic resin types. These glues, made especially for furniture, have superior bonding qualities. They are also water soluble, so that excess glue can easily be wiped off the work with a damp cloth; but this must be done quickly, before the unwanted glue dries into a hard crust.

White polyvinyl resin glues are made by a number of manufacturers and are available at hardware and lumber stores. They are usually sold in plastic squeeze bottles for easy application. The same is true of the aliphatic types, but there are fewer brands. If you anticipate a number of repairs, buy the glue in bulk and pour it from the container into a refillable squeeze bottle as needed. For repairing outdoor furniture, use epoxy compound or some other waterproof glue.

Removing old glue

Old glue has a shiny, impervious surface that prevents new glue from penetrating the wood and forming a strong bond. It must be scraped away before new glue is applied. Use a screwdriver blade or an old chisel and work with caution to avoid gouging the wood. Sand away any glue that remains. When working in small openings, such as dowel sockets, you will have to adopt special techniques (see *Sanding*, p.57). In all cases, make sure that the parts to be glued are as free of old glue as possible.

The dry run

Once you have removed all the old glue and have the necessary clamps and dowels at hand, you are ready to make a dry run. Before applying glue to any part, reassemble the entire piece and make sure that all joints fit properly. Most glues are adhesives, not fillers, and cannot compensate for misfitting dowels and sockets. But if the joint is only slightly loose, tighten it by mixing a little sawdust with the glue or by using a gap-filler glue, such as an acrylic or epoxy type. A dry run is a crucial step during which you determine the order of assembly and make sure that pieces are not reversed and that all joints fit. You can also decide on the best choice and the proper placement of clamps.

Applying the glue and drying

Always apply more glue than is needed. Any excess will ooze out of the joint as clamps are tightened, and should be wiped away immediately with a damp cloth. Be sure to coat both elements being joined—the dowel and its socket, or both edges of a break or split. As pressure is applied, the excess glue should squeeze out around the joint. If it does not, the joint probably does not have enough adhesive for a lasting bond. You can quickly detach the elements, add more glue, and reclamp them. Some glue should flow from the joint.

White glue sets in as little as 20 minutes, when the humidity is low. But to ensure a strong repair, you should always keep a glued piece clamped at least overnight before returning it to use or moving on to the next repair step.

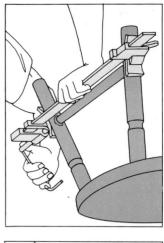

Bits of glue that cannot be easily scraped off are eliminated by buffing the dowel with medium grade sandpaper. Be careful not to alter dowel's shape.

Apply glue evenly to both parts being joined. Begin by drawing nozzle of squeeze bottle over the entire surface area of the dowel. Coat generously.

Once the glued parts have been joined in proper alignment, apply clamp and tighten until glue oozes from joint. Wipe off excess glue with damp cloth.

Regluing a dowel

Old glue must be removed from a dowel before applying new glue. Scrape with screwdriver or chisel. Grip tool low on shank and carefully guide the blade.

Dowel sockets must also be cleaned of old glue. A cylindrical sanding tool can be made with a pencil (see *Sanding*, p.57) and twisted inside the socket.

After coating the dowel with glue, apply adhesive to the walls of the dowel socket; however, do not let the hole completely fill up with glue.

Clamping

Applying clamps

Clamps insure that glued parts bond firmly in exactly the desired position. The illustrations on this page and the following two pages show the best clamps for holding two pieces of wood, and how to use them on various furniture and how to use them on various breaks you are likely to encounter.

Most clamps have one fixed and one movable jaw. While the fixed jaw is held in position, the clamp is tightened by means of a hand screw on the movable jaw. Clamps can damage furniture unless the wood is protected. Always use a piece of scrap wood, rubber, cardboard, folded paper, or cloth as a buffer. Insert it between the jaws of the clamp and their points of contact with the wood.

Clamping pressure should be at exact right angles to the glue line. Sometimes a slight misalignment will result in uneven pressure, which can cause slippage or distortion of the joint. To judge the alignment, imagine a line running straight through the center of the parts being joined. Clamp jaws should make contact with the wood precisely at the opposite ends of this imaginary line.

Once the clamp is correctly positioned, screw the jaws shut until the clamp feels tight. If you have applied glue liberally (see *Gluing*, p.61), some excess will be squeezed out around the joint—a sign that the clamp is tight enough. Do not overtighten; if the fit is accurate, only moderate pressure is needed. Pressure does not help the glue to hold; its basic purpose is to maintain uniform contact between the surfaces being joined while the glue is drying. Too much pressure can warp the wood or cause the repair to break or pop apart.

When two or more clamps are used on the same repair, position them to distribute pressure equally. Be careful that none of your clamps exerts unwanted pressure on some fragile part of the furniture. Repairs should remain clamped at least overnight to allow the glue enough time to dry.

C-clamps

Standard C-clamps are shaped like the letter "C." Adjustable C-clamps, also known as short bar clamps, have an adjustable jaw that slides along a flat metal bar to the desired position. They have a greater spanning capacity and can be tightened rapidly. The clamps are sized according to jaw opening and throat depth. Measure your job requirements carefully before buying the clamps.

C-clamps are useful principally for joining parallel surfaces, such as a strip of veneer to a tabletop. The ball-joint head on the clamping jaw swivels so that work that is not absolutely flat can still be securely held.

Pressure applied by a C-clamp is quite concentrated; be careful not to cause damage by overtightening the clamp. Be sure to insert buffers between the metal jaws and the furniture, as described in the text at left.

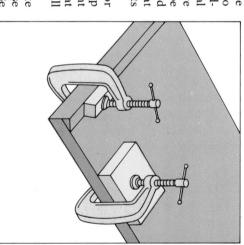

C-clamp is used in combination with a board to hold down a piece of veneer. A second clamp with a swivel head secures ornamental molding.

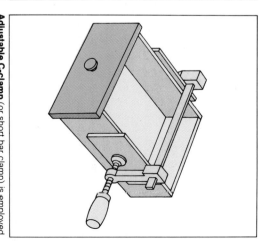

Adjustable C-clamp (or short bar clamp) is employed to clamp sides of a reglued drawer. Scrapwood buffers distribute pressure evenly and protect wood.

Wood (hand-screw) clamps

The wood clamp, commonly known as the hand-screw clamp, is the best all-round woodworking clamp. The design of the two screws and jaws permits the application of parallel gripping pressure throughout the length of the jaws or great pressure at the tips. The steel screws operate through pivots so that the jaws can be set at any required angle to clamp surfaces that are not parallel. The jaws can also be offset.

The jaws of the hand-screw clamp can be set in four basic positions to clamp either parallel or irregular surfaces: (1) To clamp parallel surfaces, open both screws the same distance so that the jaws are parallel. (2) To clamp parallel but offset surfaces (see illustration, far right), set screws so that jaws are parallel, but one jaw extends beyond the other. (3) To clamp irregular contours, open the jaws to the desired angle. (4) To pinch reglued chips or other small elements into place, set the jaws at a more acute angle. Buffering may be necessary to protect finishes.

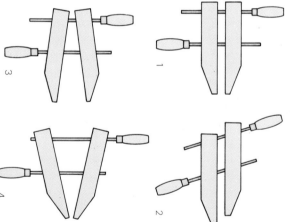

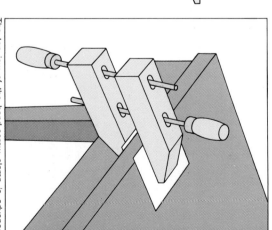

The top jaw of the hand-screw clamp is advanced beyond the bottom jaw, facilitating the clamping of a glued strip of veneer at the edge of a tabletop.

Bar clamps

Bar clamps (also called cabinet, or furniture, clamps) are designed to span large areas beyond the capacity of C-clamps or hand-screw clamps. The jaws are mounted on a flat steel bar, which is usually notched to allow you to adjust and lock the movable jaw (see p.55). The fixed jaw consists of a turnscrew mounted in a head at one end of the bar. The turnscrew has a crank handle to tighten that jaw.

To use the clamp, position the turnscrew jaw against one side of the object being clamped, slide the movable jaw against the other side, and apply final pressure with the crank handle. Be sure that both jaws are buffered and that the pressure is applied along the correct line of force. When using two or more bar clamps on the same surface, place at least one clamp below the surface to counter buckling pressures.

Pipe clamps

The pipe clamp is a variation of the bar clamp. You can make your own in any length. The jaws are available from major hardware suppliers in two sizes—to fit either ½-inch or ¾-inch threaded pipe. The fixed jaw screws onto one end of the pipe; the movable jaw slides over the other end. Final tightening is achieved either by a hand screw, as on a C-clamp, or by a crank handle (see p.55).

The pipe clamp can be extended in length simply by coupling on additional sections of threaded pipe. When needed later for a small area, simply unscrew the extra sections. Pipe clamps are applied in the same way as bar clamps.

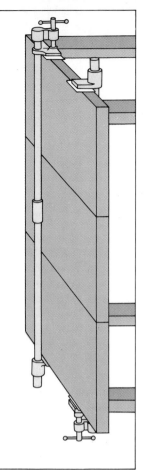

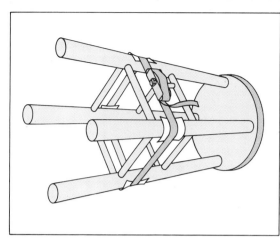

Pipe clamps are ideally suited to a wide, flat surface—here, a tabletop. Where a job requires two such clamps, position one across the top, the other underneath to counter buckling pressures in the wood.

Web clamp placed between cross rails draws together upper and lower sets of rungs simultaneously.

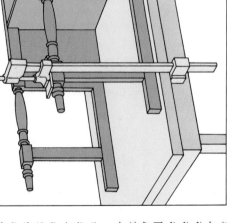

Bar clamp secures glued chair rung. It also braces piece against work surface, acting as a large vise.

Spring clamps

Steel spring clamps, which resemble oversized clothespins, have a maximum jaw opening of 3 inches. Quick and easy to apply, they are a good choice for light-duty clamping. They are perfectly suited to fast-setting glue jobs in which a number of clamps must be applied quickly–split picture frames, cracked chair rails, and other repairs where the glue line is long.

Position these clamps carefully. Some have heavy springs, which can exert considerable pressure. If not correctly placed, so that the pressure is at exact right angles to the glue line, they can push a mend out of alignment or warp or otherwise damage the wood.

Some spring clamps are available with vinyl-covered jaws, and can be applied directly to the piece being glued. Those without covered jaws must be padded with some such material as cardboard or folded cloth to protect the furniture.

Web clamps

A web, or band, clamp is a canvas or nylon belt, up to 15 feet long, with a locking mechanism. One end of the band is attached to the lock; the other end threads through it, like the tip of a belt through a buckle. There are two standard kinds of locking mechanism: One has a built-in crank to tighten the band; the other requires a small ratchet or wrench.

Web clamps are designed to clamp rounded or irregular shapes or to draw several joints together simultaneously–for example, all sides of a drawer, or the legs and rails of a chair. For such jobs, one inexpensive web clamp can take the place of several more costly metal bar clamps. Moreover, the web clamp is much easier to apply. Be sure that the clamping pressure is uniformly distributed and that the band does not slip out of position as the clamp is being tightened. Homemade web clamps are easily improvised (p.64).

A spring clamp is a good choice for clamping a narrow, cylindrical object, such as a chair rail.

63

Clamping

Improvising

Many repairs can be handled satisfactorily by making your own clamping devices from such household items as twine and masking tape—such improvisation can save you the purchase price of conventional clamps.

Improvised clamps, like standard clamps, must be carefully positioned to distribute pressure evenly. Like conventional metal clamps, most clamps made with cord or twine require some form of buffering to keep them from cutting into the wood.

Masking tape is a most convenient, versatile, and inexpensive substitute for many standard clamps. It is the best clamp for a variety of jobs, particularly those involving round, curved, or irregular shapes. The tape may leave a gummy residue, but this can easily be removed. Surfaces to be refinished can be lightly sanded to clean off the residue; finished surfaces can be wiped clean with a rag dampened with a solvent, such as turpentine or mineral spirits.

In using masking tape, first glue the joint or crack; next, press the parts together by hand and wipe off any excess glue. Then, while still holding the repair in place by hand, wrap the tape tightly around it. Overlap the edges of the tape on each turn. Be careful that the glued parts do not slip out of alignment as you work. Allow the glue to dry overnight.

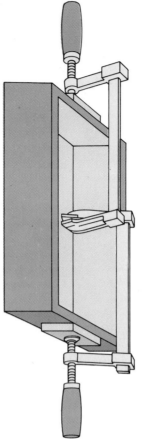

Two short bar clamps substitute for a larger clamp. Hook clamps firmly so that they cannot be jarred apart.

Using twine

Cord is an obvious substitute for a web clamp. It can also do the job of large metal clamps for a broad range of furniture repairs. Cord, twine, or sturdy string can be used. The preferred material is heavy cotton clothesline, because it is soft, strong, and closely woven, and it stretches less than other types of cord and twine. Insert folded cloth or cardboard pads between the cord and the wood of the furniture.

To improvise a substitute web clamp, wrap a double strand of cord around the parts being clamped and tie a secure knot. Apply pressure by inserting a screwdriver, short stick, or similar object between the two strands and twisting, tourniquet-style. Continue twisting until you have reached the desired clamping tension (see *Applying clamps*, p.62), then brace the stick securely against a firm part of the furniture.

In certain clamping situations, rope used in combination with boards can substitute for two or more conventional clamps (see illustration, far right). The boards act as the jaws of the clamp; the rope, as the tightening screw. Check while arranging the boards to be sure they distribute pressure uniformly and that parts remain properly aligned. Tighten the ropes by twisting with sticks.

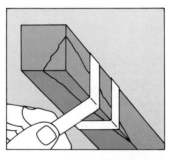

Masking tape applies even pressure over an entire area. It is excellent for replacing chips (left) and veneer (center). It can also be used to secure surfaces in the proper alignment (right) before applying clamps

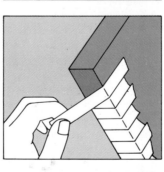

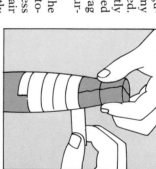

Clamps are interchangeable or can be improvised for most common repairs. A split leg is shown clamped by three alternative methods: with masking tape (left), with a spring clamp, and with a small hand-screw clamp.

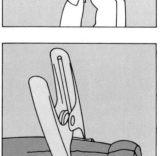

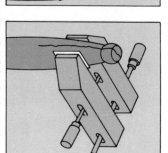

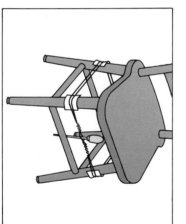

Improvising with cord: Wrap double strand around legs near rails; use screwdriver or slat as a lever to twist cord tight, then lock lever against rail.

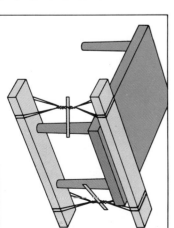

Improvising with boards and cord: Position boards to distribute pressure evenly over elements being clamped, as seen in this stool with reglued legs.

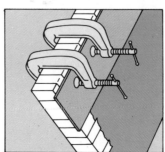

Doweling

The use of dowels

Dowels are wooden pegs that are used in combination with glue in making joints. They are often necessary elements of the joint, not just extra reinforcers, and are almost always preferable to nails, screws, brackets, and other metal fasteners, which are likely to damage the wood. If joint repairs are to be made properly, even the most straightforward jobs—such as tightening a loose table leg or reattaching a broken chair rung—require careful use of dowels.

In making a dowel joint, a pair of aligned sockets are drilled into the surfaces being joined. (The techniques used to attain precision alignment are illustrated on this page.) A single piece of dowel of the correct length and diameter is glued and inserted into sockets as the joint is pulled together.

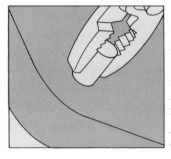

Dowels are embedded within the completed joint.

Old joints often work loose with time, causing such problems as wobbly chair backs and arms. You can try correcting a minor problem simply by squeezing new glue into the dowel holes and clamping the joint until the glue dries. But the presence of old glue in the socket can prevent new glue from penetrating the wood and bonding firmly; durable repairs almost always require disassembling the joint and thoroughly cleaning away the old glue.

Removing a dowel

A worn or broken dowel can often be extracted by twisting and pulling with a pair of pliers. Be careful not to use such force that the dowel breaks off or splinters. And avoid prying with a knife or screwdriver around the dowel, as this may chew up or enlarge the dowel socket.

Broken or tightly lodged dowels should be removed by drilling. Select an appropriate bit matched to the dowel's diameter (see *Drilling*, p.59). Carefully estimate the depth you will need to drill—allowing for the point on the bit—and mark this depth on the bit, with either a strip of masking tape or a commercial depth gauge (p.59). Sometimes a change of resistance as you hit a different wood or a change in the appearance of the wood shavings may tell you when you have reached the end of the old dowel, but you cannot rely on this.

After the dowel has been removed, thoroughly clean the socket of old glue (see *Sanding*, p.57) and remove all traces of sawdust. Be careful not to enlarge or alter the shape of the socket; sand no more than is necessary to remove glue.

Replacing dowels

Dowel rods are sold by most lumber and hardware stores in 36-inch lengths; stock diameters range from ⅛ inch to 1 inch. The diameters most commonly needed for furniture repair are ¼ inch, 5/16 inch, ⅜ inch, and ½ inch. When buying a new dowel, take the old one with you to use in determining the correct diameter. Buy hardwood dowels for hardwood furniture, if available.

Test the new dowel in the hole before proceeding with the gluing, as you may have slightly enlarged the hole by sanding. If the dowel fits loosely you will have to use a filler or get a dowel of slightly larger diameter. Although the dowel should fit snugly, it should nevertheless slide in and out smoothly. It should be cut slightly shorter than the hole; otherwise, when the joint is clamped, the glue pressure will keep the joint apart.

Replacing dowels

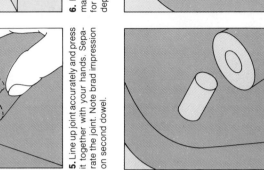

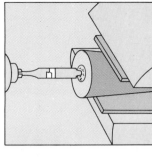

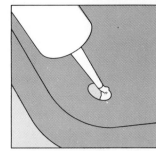

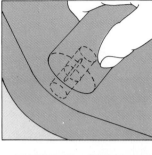

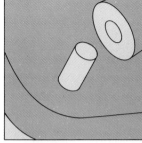

1. An old dowel can often be removed from its socket simply by using pliers. Grip dowel firmly close to its base and twist as you pull.

2. If dowel is broken off in socket, drill it out. Estimate the socket's depth, allowing at least ¼ in. of solid wood beyond end of socket.

3. Mark the depth arrived at in Step 2 on your drill bit, with either a commercial depth gauge or masking tape (see p.59).

4. To align socket holes, tap a brad into center of old dowel. Cut off brad with pliers so that it protrudes only about ¼ in.

5. Line up joint accurately and press it together with your hands. Separate the joint. Note brad impression on second dowel.

6. Remove brad with pliers. Brad marks on both dowels act as centers for your drill bit. Drill to correct depth, as determined above.

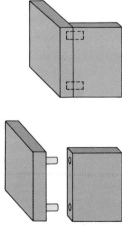

7. After cleaning dust from sockets, measure length for new dowel. This is the combined depth of both sockets. Cut dowel to this size.

8. Before applying glue, make a dry run. Assemble the joint, including dowels. Make any modifications necessary for an accurate fit.

9. Apply glue (see p.61), and reassemble joint with new dowels. Clamp firmly; wipe off glue that squeezes out. Let dry overnight.

Doweling

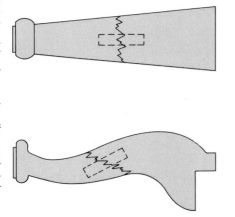

Well-placed dowels may strengthen repairs to legs.

Adding dowels

As a general rule, new dowels should be installed only as replacements for worn or broken dowels already in the piece of furniture being repaired. It is seldom advisable to introduce dowels where they had not initially been used by the manufacturer or cabinetmaker. However, there are exceptions to this rule. You should use your best judgment in determining whether or not the introduction of a new dowel would make a repair stronger than it would be if it were done by gluing and clamping alone.

The basic procedure for adding new dowels is similar to that for replacing dowels, as described on page 65. The main difference is that there are no existing dowels or dowel sockets to guide you in measuring and positioning the respective elements. Always try to center your new dowel sockets, so that as much solid wood as possible will surround the dowel on all sides. Be sure to carefully measure or estimate the depth of a new socket. You must avoid drilling too far through a leg or a supporting element of the frame. If you drill too far, you may weaken the construction.

Where appearance is not crucial, a rung can be repaired without disassembling the chair. Drill a socket through the leg and an inch into the rung.

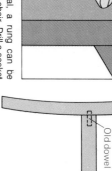

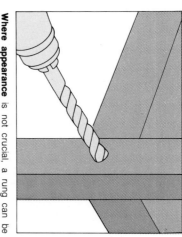

Old dowel

A chair back or leg broken off at a dowel joint can be firmly repaired by installing two new dowels; one to replace the old dowel, if it is badly worn or broken, and one at right angles to the old dowel, as shown in the steps below.

Position the dowels so that they make no contact with each other. Cut dowels and drill center sockets; follow steps for aligning and drilling illustrated on p.65. Before applying glue, insert the dowels and reassemble the joint to be sure that all the parts fit.

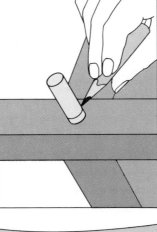

New dowel

Clean out the socket and insert a dowel. Mark and cut the dowel so that nearly ⅛ in. protrudes. Squeeze glue into the socket and insert the dowel.

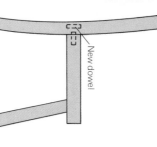

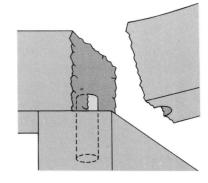

Apply glue to the sockets and dowels and over entire area of break. Fit joint carefully together, clamp, and wipe away any glue that oozes from seams. Let the repair dry overnight. Fill any gouges or splintered edges with wood putty; sand and paint or refinish.

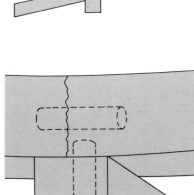

Bar clamp

Tap the dowel firmly into the socket and let it dry overnight. Sand the protruding dowel flush with the surface. Paint or refinish the area.

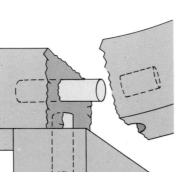

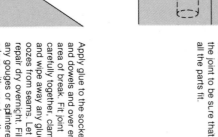

Chairs

Construction and repair

A chair is subject to more stresses and strains than any other piece of furniture. Its interlocking elements—including legs, rungs, back, and seat—must work together to support a person's weight and the additional strains caused by such misuse as leaning back and rocking on only two legs. It is therefore essential to inspect your chairs regularly and repair even minor problems immediately. Each problem, such as a loose rung, will place additional strains on other elements. If repairs are neglected, the entire structure may weaken and the chair may eventually collapse.

Checking the structure: To check a chair that is not obviously broken, sit in it and gently shift your weight around. Then, push on the back and arms; there should be no give. Finally, pick up the chair and examine it from all angles. Familiarize yourself with its construction and note any problems. Mend everything, including chips and small splits—even parts that do not seem to directly affect the chair's construction. Old makeshift repairs—using nails, screws and other hardware—should be put right, even though to do so may involve more work.

Minor problems, if caught in time, will probably not require disassembling the chair. A rung or leg that has worked loose in its socket can often be reglued and clamped without removing the element, providing the problem is noticed and fixed in time. However, if the minor problem is ignored, it is likely to cause a more complex one: A break may develop from a minor split, or several joints may come apart where before only one joint was becoming loose. If a joint is free to shift or move, however slightly, additional strains will be imposed on all the other joints during normal use.

Loose seat frame: If you notice any play in a chair while sitting in it, it may be a sign that the frame or rails are working loose around the base of the

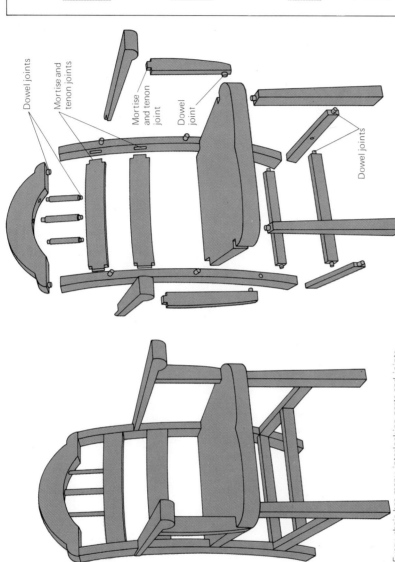

These three shapes of corner braces are cut to fit three different kinds of leg and frame joints.

Every chair has many interlocking parts and joints that must be kept tight.

chair seat. This problem is most common on chairs with upholstered or padded seats, where the legs are joined at the corners of the frame rather than to the bottom, as they are on a chair with a solid wood seat. The looseness must be adjusted before other joints are affected and the whole chair is weakened.

The best method of repairing a loose seat frame entails disassembling the frame and regluing the joints (see p.61). However, you can brace the underside of the seat with corner braces to strengthen the structure.

When corner braces are already a part of the original construction, reinstalling

them with fresh glue and slightly larger wood screws will greatly increase their strength and probably provide the necessary stiffening to the frame. If corner braces are not already in place, they can be added. Cut a block of wood to fit snugly into each corner (see illustrations above). Fitted blocks are best because they provide the maximum surface area for gluing. When possible, corner braces should be at least 1½ inches thick and their sides at least 3 inches long. Position the block in the corner and mark the holes to be drilled (see p.59). The guide hole should extend through the block, and the smaller anchor hole should go

part way into the frame. Drill the holes, glue the adjoining surfaces and the leg joint, then screw the block into place.

Turnbuckle brace: It was once popular to brace loose chair frames by installing screw eyes in each leg just below the base of the seat and threading lengths of heavy picture wire through them. A turnbuckle in the center tightened the wires. This was never a sound method of repair, in part because the screw eyes tend to work loose. You can attempt to make a repair by installing new screw eyes, but the best approach is to throw away the turnbuckle brace and disassemble and reglue the entire chair.

Chairs

Rungs

Chair rungs may work loose or no longer fit snugly in their sockets because the glue has dried out, the wood has shrunk, or a problem in another part of the chair has put a strain on the joint. Simply adding new glue is seldom enough. The glue cannot hold if the joint is no longer tight and if the old glue has not first been scraped off. Therefore, for the best results, you should separate the joint and sand the parts clean before regluing and clamping. These same procedures apply to any similar joints on legs, back rails, and spindles.

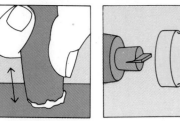
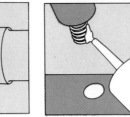
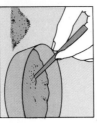

If rung fits snugly in socket but needs regluing, separate the joint, sand clean, reglue, and clamp. To ensure snug fit, you can mix a little sawdust with the glue.

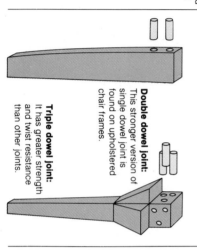

If rung fits loosely in hole, enlarge end of rung. Coat end with small amount of glue and wrap with layer of silk thread. Apply glue over thread and to inside of socket. Insert rung and clamp.

If thread wrap is not adequate, use hardwood wedge. Saw slot across butt end of rung. Tap wedge partway in and glue wedge. Wedge expands as rung is pushed into place.

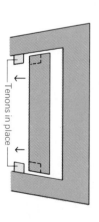

If joint is slightly loose but removal of rung is difficult, squeeze glue into joint. Push rung in and out until glue is worked into socket. Clamp.

Legs

A short leg places unnecessary strains on other legs and joints in the chair. The easiest way to repair one is simply to insert a glide of the right size in its base. However, it may be the floor that is uneven, so first check the chair on a surface you know is level.

A leg that has broken along the grain can simply be glued and clamped. If the break is across the grain, insert a dowel. (See *Adding dowels*, p.66.)

Chair legs are usually attached with a dowel joint, like a rung joint or a joint using separate dowel pins. (Depending on the particular joint, follow repair steps for *Rungs*, at left; *Doweling*, pp.65-66; or *Upholstered chair frames*, p.69.)

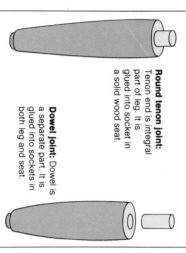

Round tenon joint: Tenon end is integral part of leg. It is glued into socket in a solid wood seat.

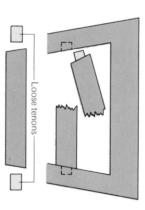

Dowel joint: Dowel is a separate part. It is glued into sockets in both leg and seat.

Double dowel joint: This stronger version of single dowel joint is found on upholstered chair frames.

Triple dowel joint: It has greater strength and twist resistance than other joints.

Replacing rails

Flat back rails and leg stretchers, or slats, are, as a general rule, apart good joints. However, certain repairs will require some disassembly in order to make a strong mend. Examine the chair carefully, consider the repair, and decide which particular joints it would be best to separate. You often have several choices. If possible, take apart those joints that seem to be less firmly bonded together. Be sure to remove any braces, screws, corner blocks, or other supports that may be holding the parts together. Before separating any parts, consider how they must be put back together. You may want to draw a diagram of the chair or just the section; or you may want to number parts—for example, the spindles, which are slightly graduated in size and must therefore be returned to their identical positions.

If break cannot be repaired with a new rail in place, cut two loose tenons to exact width and thickness of mortise but twice its length.

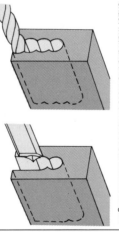

Cut slot in ends of rail to match tenon but to only half its length. Using a bit of desired diameter, first drill out slot, then square off sides with chisel.

Apply glue; insert tenons into mortises. Glue slots in rail; slip rail over both tenons simultaneously. Check that rail is securely in place. Let dry.

Disassembly

As a general rule, try to avoid taking apart good joints. However, certain repairs will require some disassembly in order to make a strong mend. Examine the chair carefully, consider the repair, and decide which particular joints it would be best to separate. You often have several choices. If possible, take apart those joints that seem to be less firmly bonded together. Be sure to remove any braces, screws, corner blocks, or other supports that may be holding the parts together. Before separating any parts, consider how they must be put back together. You may want to draw a diagram of the chair or just the section; or you may want to number parts—for example, the spindles, which are slightly graduated in size and must therefore be returned to their identical positions.

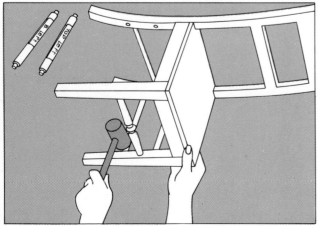

To separate glued dowel joints, grip close to joint and twist firmly. If necessary, gently pound joint with mallet or padded hammer to break old glue bond.

Mending fractures

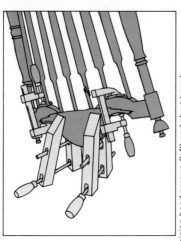

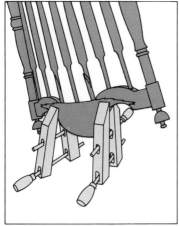

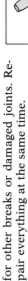

Fractures, where the wood is splintered in several places within the same area, are seldom caused by simple neglect. Such extensive damage is usually the result of rough handling. Fractures can be mended, but if pieces are missing the whole element may have to be replaced. Wherever possible, use the original element as a model in fashioning a replacement part. Before gluing the fractured pieces back together, look over the chair for other breaks or damaged joints. Repair everything at the same time.

Always make a dry run before gluing and clamping a repair. (See *Gluing techniques*, p.61.) Determine in what order to make the repairs, if more than one is involved. Also decide which particular clamps to use and how to position them. Elaborate shapes may interfere with the placing of clamps. You may have to improvise. (See *Clamping*, pp.62–64.)

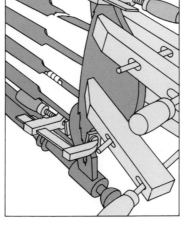

Cross piece: Two-directional pressure is applied by combining hand screws (left) and short bar clamps.

Spindles: Split spindle is clamped with masking tape; broken spindle is clamped with C-clamp and wood blocks.

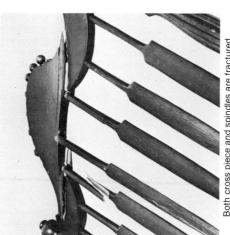

Four types of clamps are combined to make repair.

Both cross piece and spindles are fractured.

Upholstered chair frames

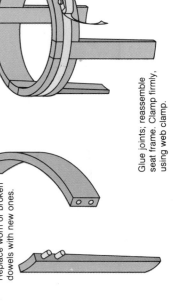

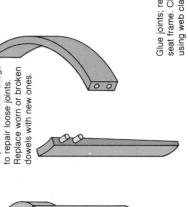

Fully upholstered chairs and chairs with detachable upholstered seats have a different frame construction than chairs with solid wood seats. The legs, instead of being doweled into the base of a solid seat and given further support by rungs, are an integral part of the seat frame. Because the seat is not one solid piece and the legs are without supporting rungs, the seat frame must absorb more counterforces. The joints are therefore especially prone to work loose. Repair an upholstery frame by disassembling it and regluing the joints. (See illustrations at right and *Doweling*, pp.65–66.)

Separate frame and legs to repair loose joints. Replace worn or broken dowels with new ones.

Upholstered seat incorporates legs into the frame structure.

Glue joints; reassemble seat frame. Clamp firmly, using web clamp.

Two bar clamps can be used instead of a web clamp. Position to put pressure on all joints.

Chairs

Armchair

An armchair's structure is more complex than that of other chairs. It has a greater number of interlocking parts and joints, which must be kept tight. Arms reinforce the back and therefore lessen the strain on the joints between the back and seat. However, if the arm joints come loose, this will increase the strain on other elements, which are dependent on the arms for reinforcement. The arms may be separate units, joined to the back and seat, or an integral part of the back, as in the Windsor chair shown on this page.

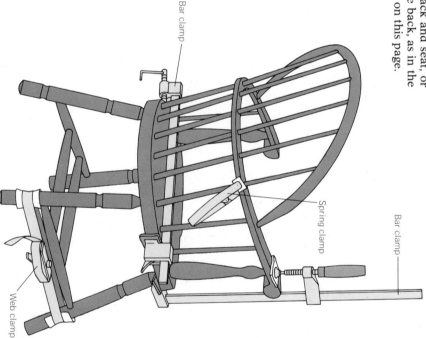

Divided seam

Curved back rail out of socket

Loose arm post and spindle joints

Minor split in arm rail

Leg broken off at base of seat

Rungs out of sockets

Bar clamp

Bar clamp

Spring clamp

Web clamp

A neglected armchair: Seat is made from more than one board; the glue in one of the seams dried out, causing the seat to separate. Rung separated from a front leg, probably because the glue had dried out in the socket; the resulting strain on the back leg caused it to break off near the base of the seat. Strains on other elements caused further damage. The armrest and armpost joint pulled apart allowing the spindles between the armrest and the seat to come loose. The curved back rail was originally secured by wedges in holes in the armrests; one wedge fell out, causing the back rail to separate at one end; then, the back spindles came loose. A minor split developed in the back rail. The photographs starting on this page show the step-by-step repairs that can bring a badly damaged chair back into use.

1. If a seam in a seat begins to open up, pry it slightly apart with a screwdriver, and insert glue.

6. Remove side rung in order to reglue joints. Check all rung joints for looseness, and repair as needed.

11. Curved back rail is loose and separated from spindles. A small wedge is missing from the arm.

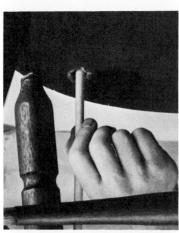

2. Clamp the glued seat firmly. Wipe off any glue that oozes from seam. Be sure seam is properly aligned.

3. Broken leg and rungs must be repaired as part of the same sequence of steps.

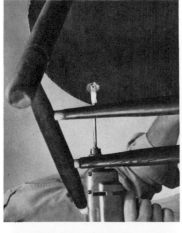

4. Remove leg and drill sockets for dowels both in the leg and the seat. (See *Doweling*, pp.65–66.)

5. Measure dowel for length. Cut to size and sand ends. Insert into joint and check fit with leg.

7. Attach leg to base, applying glue liberally to dowel and socket. Clamp and wipe off excess glue.

8. Tap rung joints with mallet to make them tight. Wipe off any glue that oozes from joints.

9. Clamp rungs securely with web clamp or bar clamp. Let joints dry undisturbed overnight.

10. Armpost and several spindles are separated from armrest. Clean joints of old glue; reglue and clamp.

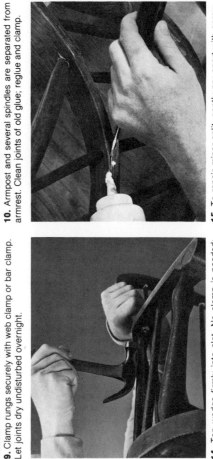

12. Clean spindles and spindle sockets of old glue. Apply fresh glue and insert spindles into sockets.

13. With curved back rail in place, apply glue and insert wedge from underside of arm into slot in rail.

14. Tap wedge firmly into slot. No clamp is needed; wedge and tension of curved back hold joint tight.

15. To repair minor split, gently pry apart with screwdriver. Smear glue under split; clamp; wipe clean.

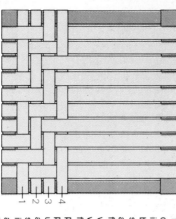

Reseating chairs

Ash splint

Ash splint was perhaps the most common seating material employed by early American furniture makers. The splints were wider than either caning or rushing materials, and were easily obtained by stripping annual rings from the logs of ash trees, a common species in the North American forest. Machine-cut splint is available today, and any diligent person can reseat an ash-splint chair.

Machine-cut ash splint comes in pieces 6 feet long and ⅝ or ¾ inch wide. An ordinary chair seat requires 12 to 15 such splints; a large chair, up to 20 splints; and a stool or child's chair, about 8 to 10 splints. You will also need twine,

heavy short-bladed scissors for cutting the splints, a utility knife and cutting block, a pail for soaking the splints, a brush, and a sealant containing tung oil, such as Danish oil, or boiled linseed oil as a substitute.

Ash splint is soaked in warm water to make it pliable. Soak three or four splints at a time in a pail for about 10 minutes. As you remove one length of splint, put in another. Ash splint has a smooth side and a rough side. It must be worked smooth side out, on both the top and bottom of the seat. Each time you join splints, be sure the new piece is turned smooth side out.

The seat is woven in two stages: First, splints are passed across the seat from front to back for the entire width of the chair; then, a second group is interwoven from side to side with the first set. As the splint dries, it shrinks; therefore, allow enough looseness initially so that you can depress the front-to-rear splints about ½ inch on a small chair and 1 inch on a large chair. When cross weaving is complete, fill in the front corners with individual splints if the seat is splayed—wider at the front than the back. Bring seat to the desired color with diluted stain, then coat both sides of the seat with sealant.

Bend wet splints to determine the smooth and rough sides. The rough side has the small splinters, as seen in the bottom photograph. Always weave with the smooth side out. When you attach a new length of splint (see *Joining splints*, below), be sure that its smooth side will be on the outside.

The weaving pattern

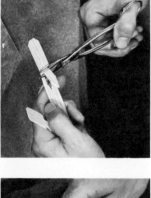

The weaving pattern commonly used in ash splinting is called the diagonal weave because of the way the side-to-side splints are advanced as they are passed through the front-to-back rows. Cross weaving, or side-to-side weaving, begins only when the front-to-back rows are in place. The cross strands are passed over two rows, then under two rows, and so on across the whole width of the seat. However, note in the top illustration that no two adjacent cross strands lock the same pair of front-to-back rows. Rather, each successive cross strand is advanced one row farther along the grid. The bottom drawing shows the final appearance of the weave. Note the variation in the weave along the rails. The pattern repeats itself beginning with the fifth cross row.

Joining splints

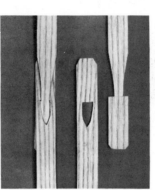

1. Arrow and sheath provide a locking mechanism for joining splints. Arrow is passed through slot in sheath.

2. Hold free end of splint coming from the seat. Cut notches to create a tapered neck, forming a 3-in.-long arrowhead.

3. With a utility knife, cut a triangular slot 3 in. from one end of new splint. Slot is slightly longer than splint's width.

4. Use scissors to complete the cut. Base of slot will lock the arrowhead on the splint previously woven in the chair.

5. Slip arrowhead through slot. Rotate the splints so that they form straight line and arrowhead locks into place (see Step 1).

6. For appearance and strength, all joins are located on the underside of the seat, with the flaps facing upward.

1. The first splint is looped around the front and back rails, and the free outside length is temporarily tied to the side rail with twine.

2. A new length of ash splint is joined onto the first strand (see *Joining splints*, p.72). Add new lengths with the joint on underside of seat.

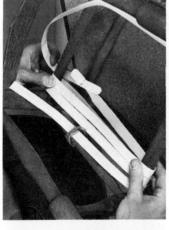

3. When all front-to-back splints are in place, tie the last one under side rail. Splints are tied only temporarily—until cross weaving holds them in.

4. Make sure all splints lie parallel, and perpendicular to front and back rails. Tension should be uniform but loose; splints shrink as they dry.

5. Weave first cross splint (diagrams, p.72). Weave across top of seat; pass short end around side rail; weave it across underside of seat. Tuck in short end.

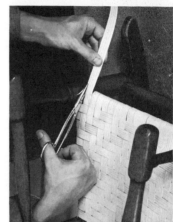

6. Continue weaving pattern shown on p.72. Use short bit of splint to help slide tip of cross strand over and under the tightening front-to-back rows.

7. When it becomes difficult to pass new splints through weave, use a short piece of splint in combination with your finger to push.

8. Splayed chairs are wider along the front rail than along the back rail; therefore, extra lengths of ash splint are added to fill in triangular gaps at the sides.

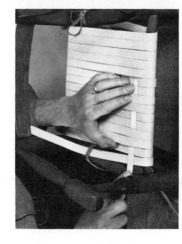

9. Tuck the end of the extra side splint down between the weaving. Then, in the same way, tuck in the other end on the underside of the seat.

10. A second splint may be needed to fill in the gap. It is cut off halfway back and tucked in on both top and bottom (underside is shown here).

11. When working at the corners, it may be necessary to cut a notch in the splint in order to make it fit neatly against the corner post.

12. When seat is fully woven, trim off any rough edges or splinters. Stain seat, if desired; then, preserve with a coat of tung-oil sealant.

Rushing

Reweaving the rush seat of an antique chair is a task that need not be entrusted to a professional artisan. Anyone willing to work patiently can do the job.

Artificial rush—a strong kraft paper twisted into a continuous uniform strand—is easier to work, cheaper, and more readily available than natural rush. About three pounds are required for an average dining room chair, up to five pounds for a large arm chair or rocker, and as little as two pounds for a stool or an antique Shaker chair. The material is available in several sizes and colors, making it possible to match other chairs in a set. Besides the rush itself you will require a hammer and tacks, a smooth piece of wood or a yardstick (called an evener); a sealer containing tung-oil, such as Danish oil, or boiled linseed oil; and corrugated cardboard.

Before starting, carefully study all the illustrations on this and the following two pages. Note that the seat is filled by weaving from the corners toward the middle. And because seat frames are seldom square, the shorter side rails are usually filled first, leaving an unfinished area in the center. The open area is woven in last by means of a series of figure-eight loops passing over front and back rails.

A common splayed seat is wider at the front than at the back. Therefore, you will begin by weaving in the extra width at each front corner. Work until the unwoven area on the front rail is equal to the width of the shorter back rail. Then, start the next stage. Always keep the strands as close together as possible and maintain a uniform tension. Dress the strands with the evener, forcing them tightly into parallel rows.

The illustrations on pages 75 and 76 are for a common splayed seat frame. If the frame on which you are working is rectangular or square, start with continuous weaving (Step 7).

Square knot: Use it to tie on new lengths of cord. Tie the knot on inside of seat.

Clove hitch: Make turns around chair rung; pass cord end under last turn; pull tight.

Half hitch: As weaving is completed, knot the cord securely to an inside strand.

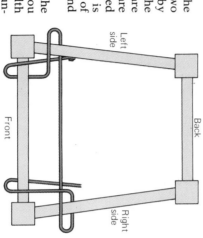

Splayed seat: 1. First, fill in extra width of front rail by weaving around front corners. Tack 3- to 4-ft cord to left rail near front; pass around both front corners; tack to right side rail.

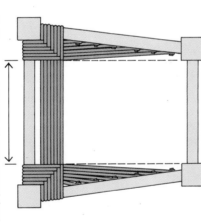

2. Weave short lengths of cord around front corners. Repeat until space between weaving on front rail is equal to width of back rail. Tack ends evenly along side rails.

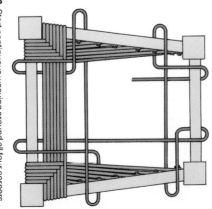

3. Start continuous weaving around all four corners. Using square knots, tie on new lengths of about 15 to 20 ft, as needed. When side rails are filled, weave in central space with figure eights.

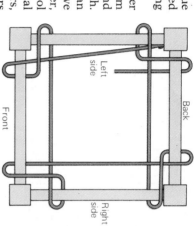

Basic weave: Pass rush over and around front rail, then over and around left side rail. Bring rush across to right side rail and repeat the weaving pattern, progressing around the seat.

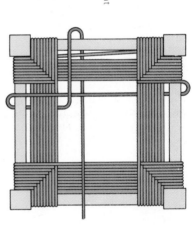

Square seat: Tack cord end to left rail near back post. Weave around four corners consecutively with about 15 to 20 ft of rush. Tie on new lengths with square knots.

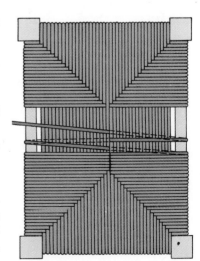

Rectangular seat: Weave as for square seat until side rails are completed. Close center space with figure-eight loops over front and back rails; all loops pass through the same opening between the central cross rows.

1. Cut a 3- to 4-ft length of rush. Tack one end to left rail and loop cord around front rail close to corner post, then around side rail (see diagrams).

2. Bring the cord over to the opposite front corner. Loop over the side rail, then around the front rail, keeping the cord taut and the tension uniform.

3. Tack to the inside of right rail. (Untwist end slightly to insert tack.) Both tacks should be equidistant from front posts. Trim excess cord to ½ in. of tack.

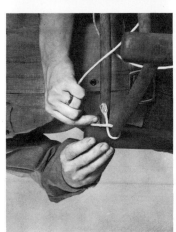

4. Repeat the first three steps with new strands. Cut each cord successively longer to allow for the progressive spacing of tacks along the side rails.

5. After every 5 to 6 rows, compress the strands into each corner with hardwood evener so that the rows lie parallel and close together.

6. Measure space between woven corners on front rail. When this space is equal to width of back rail, start continuous weaving around all four corners.

7. Cut 15- to 20-ft length of rush; tack end to left rail near back post. Weave around front corners as before, then continue to back corner (see diagrams).

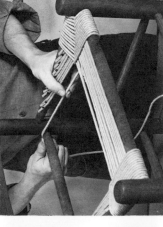

8. Weave around back corner as around front corners. Loop cord over back rail and side rail, keeping tension uniform. Press cord tightly against corner post.

9. Repeat around the opposite back corner. Then, bring the cord up to the front corner again. This completes the first row of continuous weaving.

10. Continue weaving. Attach new cord length with a square knot where strand emerges from the corner weaving. Knot will be woven inside the seat.

11. Dress cord with evener every 5 to 6 rows so that strands lie close together and perpendicular to seat rails. Dress diagonals of weave on both sides of seat.

12. When you want to pause during weaving, tie off cording around rung of chair, using a clove hitch (see diagrams). Be sure cord is taut and securely tied.

13. After completing a few rows of continuous weave, insert padding into front corners. Cut cardboard to corner diagonals. Pieces should meet, not overlap.

14. After further weaving, pad the sides. Padding reduces wear by preventing the cording from rubbing unduly against the rails of the seat.

15. Padding can also be added on the underside. Padded seat should be slightly greater in thickness than the rails. Dress cord with evener after padding.

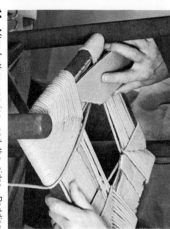

16. The padding will be covered as the weaving progresses. Closely match the color of the cardboard and cord, as the strands may separate slightly.

17. To complete the last cross row, pass the cord around the rail and up through the narrow center opening. Tie on a new length of cord to finish the seat.

18. Weave figure eights over front and back rails (see diagrams, p.74). All loops pass through narrow center opening. Compress loops with evener.

19. To complete the last figure-eight loop, bring cord up through center opening. Then, stretch it over the front rail to underside of seat and turn chair over.

20. Securely tie off cord with several half hitches (see diagrams); pass the cord under the opposite strand, pull the end tight, and proceed to Step 21.

21. With end pulled tight, begin to form the loop seen in Step 22. It is necessary to maintain tension on the cord through all the knotting steps.

22. Pull the half hitch tight. Tie two or three more half hitches, then cut off any excess cord. Push knot down into center to be covered by weave.

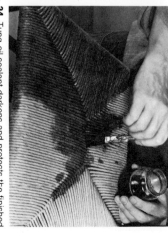

23. Dress the entire seat on both sides. Rub the flat surface of the evener over the loops on the rails so that no strands protrude above the others.

24. Tung-oil sealant darkens and protects the finished seat. Brush onto underside of seat, then top. Let stand 15 minutes and wipe off excess. Let dry overnight.

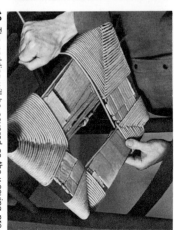

Spline caning

Any cane chair seat with a continuous groove inside the seat opening can be replaced with prewoven cane webbing. The edges of the webbing are forced into the groove and held in place by a tapered spline pressed in on top.

To avoid problems arising from cutting errors at the store, buy a piece of webbing an inch or two larger than the seat in each direction and cut it to size at home. Spline is sold in several thick-

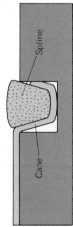

Spline, cane, and groove seen in cross section.

nesses. Measure the width of the groove in your chair seat to determine the correct size, allowing for the thickness of the webbing. Buy a piece several inches longer than the total length of the groove. You will also need white glue; a utility knife; a mallet or padded hammer; a wooden wedging tool, such as half a spring clothespin; a pail for soaking spline and cane; and tung-oil sealant (or boiled linseed oil).

Spline and cane must be worked wet. As the material dries, it will shrink.

1. Cut cane webbing to size, allowing an extra ½-in. margin beyond the groove on all sides. Soak the webbing for 10 minutes in warm water.

2. Squeeze glue generously into groove along its entire length. Position webbing, glossy side up, over seat. Be sure pattern is correctly aligned.

3. At center point on each side, force an inch or two of cane into groove. Do one side, then the opposite side. Keep webbing square, tension uniform.

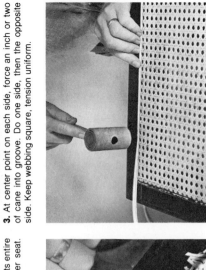

4. Move from the middle outward on each side, pushing cane securely into groove. Work a little at a time on parallel sides to maintain uniform tension.

5. Once all the webbing is securely in the groove around the entire seat, trim off the protruding edges of the cane with a sharp matt knife.

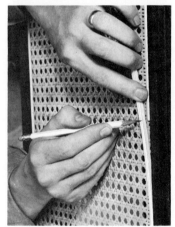

6. Cut more than enough spline to go around the seat. Soak until pliable. Starting at middle of one side, press narrow edge into groove. Tap level with surface.

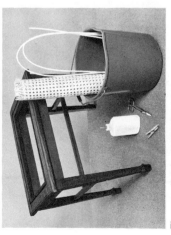

7. Work all the way around groove and back to your starting point. Mark and cut off excess spline. Push end into place and tap down with mallet.

8. Remove bits of frayed cane from webbing before staining and sealing. Either snip off with scissors or singe off with moving flame while cane is still wet.

9. Seat may be darkened with diluted wood stain. Coat underside of the seat first. Wipe away excess. Preserve with tung-oil sealant.

These materials and implements are used in spline caning. If a deep sink is not available, soak materials in pail, but do not bend roll of webbing.

77

Reseating chairs

Cane weaving

Strand cane, as opposed to cane webbing (see *Spline caning*, p.77), is sold in hanks of 1,000 feet, ranging in width from superfine to common. Use the chart to determine the correct width for your chair. Sold with each hank is a wider strand called the binder, which is used to form a border around the seat. About 250 feet of cane are needed for the seat of an average kitchen or dining room chair. Also needed are scissors; caning pegs or golf tees to secure the cane ends temporarily during weaving; an awl to clear the holes; a pail in which to soak the cane; and boiled linseed oil, Danish oil, or some other sealer containing tung oil.

Cane is woven wet to keep it pliable. As the strands dry, they shrink, insuring a taut seat. Begin by separating a few strands from the hank; put aside any defective strands for use in attaching the binder. Coil the strands; fasten each coil with a clothespin and soak it in a bucket of warm water for 15 minutes. As you remove one coil, replace it with another. Periodically, wet the underside of the weaving with a warm, damp towel.

Cane has a rough side and a shiny side. Weave with the shiny side facing up. Keep the tension uniform but loose enough to depress the strands ½ to ¾ inch. When pegging the ends of a strand, allow an extra 4 inches for tying off. As you weave, hold one hand above and one below the seat; move the cane down through one space and up through the next in a continuous motion.

A cane seat is woven in six stages (see illustrations, opposite page). As each step is completed, make sure that no strands are twisted, that the rows are parallel, and that the tension is uniform.

When weaving a splayed seat (see below), it may be necessary to skip holes in order to keep the rows parallel; these will be filled in at a later stage in the weaving. Sometimes the diagonal weave will require that a strand come out of the same hole it entered. When this happens, skip to the next hole, leaving a space in the pattern. On the return weave, fill in the space. Then, skip one hole again and resume the normal sequence.

Once the weaving is completed, singe off any frayed cane with a moving match flame while the cane is wet. Stain, if desired; seal both sides of the seat.

Size of hole	Space between holes	Width of cane
1/8 inch	3/8 inch	Superfine
3/16 inch	1/2 inch	Fine fine
3/16 inch	5/8 inch	Fine
1/4 inch	3/4 inch	Medium
5/16 inch	7/8 inch	Common

Weave pattern: Tracing clockwise around an octagon, each strand should pass under the next strand.

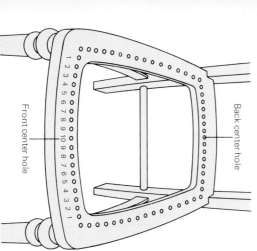

Back center hole

Front center hole

1 2 3 4 5 6 7 8 9 10 10 9 8 7 6 5 4 3 2 1

Begin weaving in center hole at front and back of seat. Mark center holes with pegs. To assure accuracy, count in from each corner hole. On a round-back seat, count around from each front corner hole.

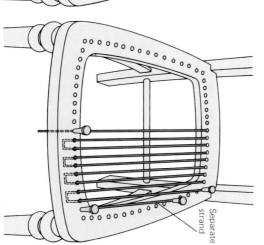

Separate strand

Push strand through front center hole. Leaving 4 in. below, wedge into place with peg. Pass strand down through center back hole and up through hole to right. Continue in parallel rows. Peg end, trim to 4 in.

Splayed seat

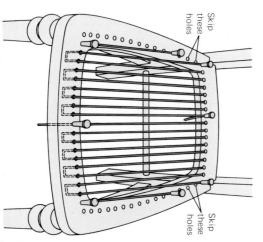

Skip these holes

Skip these holes

Repeat on left side. Peg strand and weave toward left side. On splayed seat (one that is narrower at back than front), skip holes around back corners as required to keep all the rows parallel.

Tying off loose ends

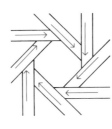

Use an overhand knot to tie off the loose ends under the frame. To do so, first pass the end under the weave.

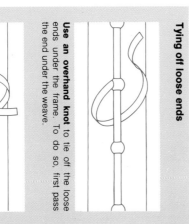

Again, loop the end around and pass it between the first loop and the weave. Finally, pull the end tight and then trim it to 1 in.

Weaving Steps

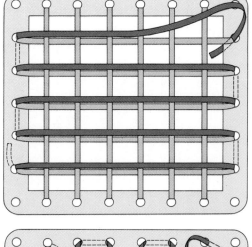

1. As shown in this simplified diagram, seat is first woven from front to back (see diagrams, p.78). For clarity, the pegs used to hold ends in place are not shown here or in the following illustrations.

2. A series of strands is passed from side to side over top of the front-to-back strands. Note that strand is advanced by passing it under the frame (dotted lines) and up through the next nearest hole.

3. Second series of front-to-back rows is woven through same holes as in Step 1 but over top of cross strands. Note: The second front-to-back weave is kept consistently on same side of first weave.

4. This step begins the true weaving. Moving from left to right, strand is passed under front-to-back strands and over those woven in Step 3. Same pattern is followed in bringing strand back from right to left.

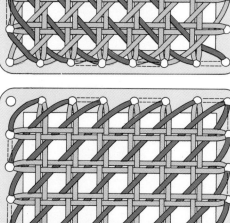

5. First diagonal weave (which can be started at any point) is passed under front-to-back strands and over side-to-side strands. All strands are woven with uniform pressure. Cane is kept wet with a damp towel.

6. Second diagonal weave is at right angles to first. It passes over front-to-back strands and under side-to-side strands. Once weaving is completed, check pattern; tie off ends (see p.78); attach binder.

Applying the binder

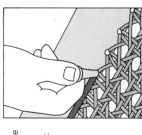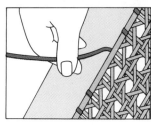
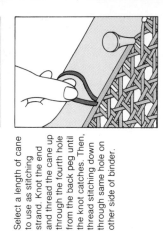

Binder forms a neat border around the edge of the seat. It is held in place by stitching through the holes. Use an awl to separate the strands in the holes enough to allow the stitching through.

Cut the binder a few inches longer than the circumference of the seat. Peg down one end of binder in back center hole. Draw binder tautly over the holes along seat frame as you stitch.

Select a length of cane to use as stitching strand. Knot the end and thread the cane up through the fourth hole from the back peg until the knot catches. Then, thread stitching down through same hole on other side of binder.

Continue stitching from hole to hole all along seat. To finish, remove back peg and put end of binder into starting hole, then stitch past it. Trim loose end. Push peg through octagons to even out pattern.

79

Tables

A table's construction

A table is basically a broad surface supported by legs. Sometimes reinforcing stretchers connect the legs; they are similar to the rungs of a chair. Legs may be fastened directly to the top or attached to wood blocks or cleats, which are secured to the top. The legs may also be attached to a rail, called the apron, that runs along the underside of the tabletop, providing a strong, rigid framework.

Dowel joints and the stronger mortise and tenon joints are the wood joints most commonly used in tables. On some modern furniture, metal fasteners—such as nuts and bolts, screws, metal plates, and brackets—are often used either in place of wood joints or to reinforce them.

Inspect your table periodically for loose joints. Tighten hardware. If necessary, add corner blocks for reinforcement (see *Chairs*, p.67). If joints are only slightly loose you may be able to reinforce them by inserting fresh glue, and clamping them until the glue is dry. Before disassembling a table, mark all the parts and key them to a sketch. When reassembling the table, refer to the sketch to be sure that you return each part to its original position.

Be careful when you separate a table joint. It is often impossible to tell beforehand which type of joint it is. Although a dowel joint can usually be twisted apart without damaging its elements, twisting will break the parts of a mortise and tenon joint. Also, table joints are often reinforced with hidden wedges. Care in working will help avoid complications.

If several leg and rail joints are loose or broken, remove the tabletop and repair the entire supporting structure. Take off any hardware securing the top to the frame; carefully knock out glue blocks with a hammer. If the top still does not lift off, it is probably secured by dowels at each leg. Using a soft-faced mallet, gently tap upwards from the underside of the top to separate the joints.

A damaged tenon can be replaced with a double tenon (see *Chairs*, p.68). Legs or rails that are split or broken along the grain can be repaired by gluing and clamping (see *Clamping*, pp.62–64). If the break is across the grain, insert a dowel. (For instructions on dowel repairs, see *Doweling*, pp.65–66.) Repairs for split or warped tops and for leaf supports are described on the following pages.

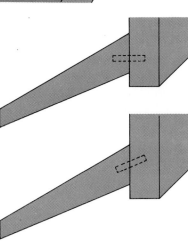

A loose mortise and tenon joint in the frame can be repaired by expanding tenon with a small wedge.

Wedge

Dowel socket at left is easier to align and to drill, but the alignment at right offers stronger support.

Pedestal tables

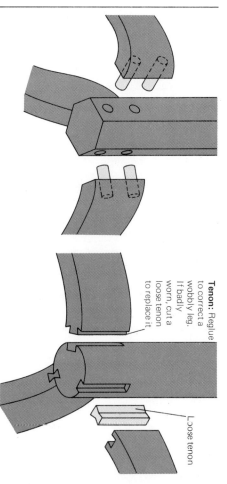

Dowel joints securing leg to central column often work loose. Clean dowels and sockets of old glue, coat with white glue, and clamp. (See *Doweling*, pp.65–66).

Tenon: Reglue to correct a wobbly leg. If badly worn, cut a loose tenon to replace it

Mortise and tenon joint: Replace broken tenon with dovetail-shaped loose tenon (p.68). Cut tenon, chisel out mortise in leg; glue and clamp.

Loose tenon

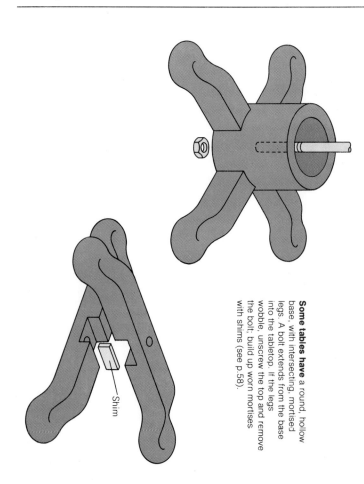

Some tables have a round, hollow base, with intersecting, mortised legs. A bolt extends from the base into the tabletop. If the legs wobble, unscrew the top and remove the bolt; build up worn mortises with shims (see p.58).

Shim

Warping

Wood warps when it is exposed to changes in humidity. Excessive moisture in the air makes wood fibers expand; in the air aridity makes them contract. Warping results from seasonal variations in humidity, from such environmental conditions in the home as steam heating and air conditioning, or from moving furniture from a dry climate to a wet one or vice versa. Broad sections, such as tabletops, that are sealed and finished on one side but not the other are particularly vulnerable to warping. The finished side remains stable while the unsealed side absorbs or loses moisture.

If you suspect seasonal warping, wait for the arrival of the next season and see whether the warp corrects itself. If it does, seal the unfinished surfaces of the furniture with varnish. You can attempt to correct permanently warped plywood by applying cleats, as illustrated below. A solid board should be treated for moisture or dryness and then clamped for at least a day before cleats are applied. If the board curves down, wet the underside with a damp sponge and then clamp it; if it curves up, dry the underside on a radiator or in the sun and apply cleats. Seal the repaired surfaces.

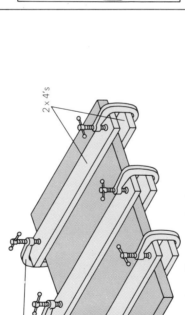

Straightening a warped board: Clamps are formed from pairs of 2 x 4's longer than the width of the warped surface. The 2 x 4's are held by C-clamps. Space pairs of 2 x 4's at 10-in. intervals, tighten C-clamps uniformly. Treat surface for dampness or dryness before clamping (see text, above).

Bracing with cleats: When warp is corrected, brace surface with wooden cleats. Prepare cleats in advance and apply immediately to the newly straightened wood. Drill screw holes through cleats, glue them down, and drive screws. Cleats should run across the grain.

Splits

As they age, tabletops and other broad surfaces may develop splits in the grain, or the glue between planks may dry out, causing separations along seams.

A simple split along the grain is easily repaired by gluing. Pry the split slightly further apart with a screwdriver and squeeze glue into the entire length of the split. Then, clamp the repair (see *Clamping*, pp.62–64). Butterfly patches (see illustrations, below) can be centered across a split to help hold the glued parts in place.

Splits may be so badly splintered that they cannot be glued back together. If this is the case, neatly cut away the damaged section, using a saw or chisel, and then cut a snug patch (see *Patching veneer and wood*, p.86). Be sure that the grain of the patch runs in the same direction as that of the tabletop. Glue the patch in place and refinish the surface (see *Refinishing*, pp.87–103).

Separations along the seams of planks can be repaired by gluing and clamping. Begin by cleaning away dirt and old glue. Apply fresh glue and clamp. Divided seams can be strengthened by replacing worn dowels, if there are any, or by adding dowels (see *Doweling*, pp.65–66).

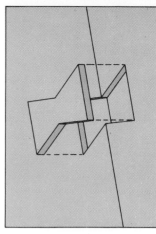

Drill dowel sockets and cut dowels (see *Doweling*, pp. 65–66). Assemble and test the fit before applying glue. Clamp repair overnight.

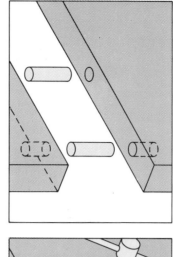

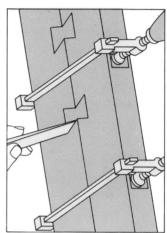

Adding dowels to reinforce seam: Clamp boards back to back and mark lines as shown. Drill dowel sockets at intersection of lines. Space sockets every 6 to 9 in.

Apply thin layer of white glue to bottom and edges of patch; clamp in place. When dry, sand or plane patch flush with surface. Refinish surface.

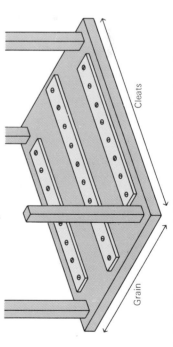

Butterfly patch: Clamp split, and trace an outline of the patch on bottom of planks. Chisel out bed; depth should be slightly less than thickness of patch.

Drop-leaf supports

The most common areas of wear on a drop leaf are the hinges and the support that braces the leaf when it is in use. Keep the hinges tight; if the beds are split or worn, repair them (see *Hinges*, p.60).

Pivot support: The simplest support is a pivot support—a section cut out of the apron that pivots on a dowel secured between the apron and the tabletop. To repair it (see illustration at right), disassemble the top, remove the pivot support, and replace it with a new one of straight-grained hardwood. Use the original support as the cutting pattern.

Hinged support: The hinge itself may break or the metal hinge pin in the knuckle joint may wear the guide hole out of shape, resulting in a loose hinge and wobbly support. The entire support can be replaced either with a new wooden bracket or by substituting a metal hinge. Looseness can be corrected by replacing the metal pin with a dowel of a slightly larger diameter.

Gate leg supports: These swing out like a gate to brace the leaf (see illustration, at right). First, check the support for loose joints, worn or broken parts, and wear at the base of the leg. Then, examine the pivot points of the support for broken dowels or worn sockets.

If leg joints are loose, separate and reglue them. Repair the pivots at the same time. Remove the tabletop and disassemble the frame. Replace the dowels (see *Doweling*, pp.65–66) and glue and clamp the joints. If the joints are solid, and only the pivots need repair, follow the instructions at right.

With continual use, a leaf support can wear a deep groove into the underside of the leaf. Sand or plane smooth any sharp edges on the support that may be cutting into the leaf. Drop leaves usually have a small stop to keep the leaf support in place. If the leaf shows a droop, cut an L-shaped stop to act as a wedge to raise the leaf slightly on its support.

Extension tables

The leaves on one type of extension table are pushed back under the top when not in use. The extended leaves are supported by wooden bearers that slide through notches in the apron. The top lifts slightly as the leaf is being drawn out, then drops back into place.

The bearers may wear or warp. Replace a warped element, using the original as a pattern. If the bearer is simply worn, build it up by gluing on a shim of the correct thickness. Shims can also be used to build up the notches in the frame.

Other extension tables have removable leaves. The main top divides in the middle, the two halves extending outward on rails. Leaves are dropped into place and the tabletop is closed against the leaves. Examine the rails periodically for wear or warping; repair wear with shims. Replace warped rails with rail assemblies, which are sold at builder's supply stores.

Pivot

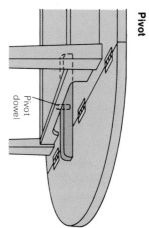

Hinged

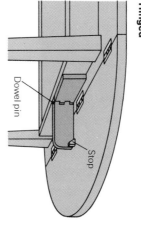

Dowel pin

Stop

Pivot dowel

Gate leg

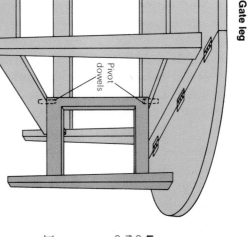

Pivot dowels

Loose hinge support: Replace old hinge pin with a dowel of a larger diameter. Clamp support arm against frame and remove old pin; drill holes to accept the larger dowel pin. Cut dowel insert; glue wedge into place.

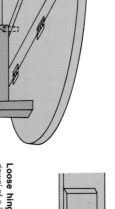

Dowel

Wedge

Loose gate leg: Slip the saw blade between rails and ends of pivot leg and cut through pivot dowels. Remove entire gate-leg assembly. Drill sockets to accept larger dowels. Insert top dowel first. Insert bottom dowel from the underside of the rail and glue wedge in place.

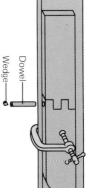

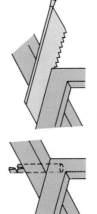

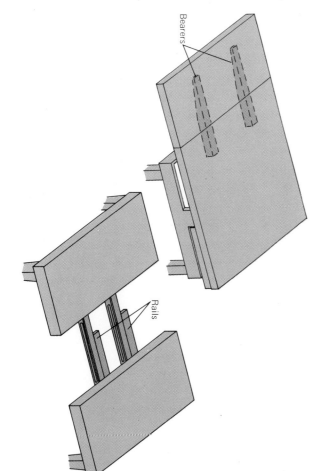

Bearers

Rails

Case furniture

Basic construction

Case furniture includes chests, bureaus, desks, cabinets, and bookshelves. The basic construction is a box; the frame can be solid—usually slabs of hardwood in antique furniture, large sections of plywood in modern furniture—or a skeleton of rails assembled as a framework and covered with thin panels. In the skeleton frame, the rails often provide the structural support while veneered panels give the piece a fine appearance.

Because much of the strength of any box is in its rigidity, it is very important to keep the joints tight. Glue blocks and braces can be added to reinforce joints (see *Chairs*, p.67), or the joints can simply be cleaned and reglued.

Before starting a repair, remove doors, drawers, and detachable shelves. To allow greater accessibility to the interior of the piece, also remove the back panel. This is usually a thin board screwed or nailed into grooves in the frame or the solid sides of the furniture. Because the back adds to the rigidity of the cabinet's structure, a loose or warped panel may cause the piece to shift out of alignment; this in turn may result in other problems, such as sticking doors or drawers and weakened joints. Repair the back (see *Warping*, p.81) or replace it with a piece of ¼-inch plywood.

To remove the top, first examine it from underneath to determine how it is attached to the frame. It is probably attached with screws or glue blocks. If these are not visible, it is more than likely secured with dowels. Remove any screws, then gently tap upward from below with a soft-faced mallet. Dowel joints can also be separated by tapping upward against the underside of the top. If the top is split, repair it as you would a tabletop or any other solid board, and install butterfly patches on the underside for reinforcement (see *Tables*, pp.80–82). Repairs to drawers and rails are covered on the following page.

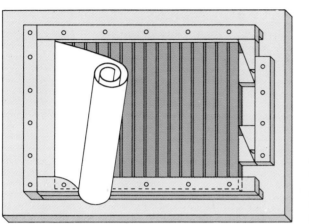

Tambour

Rolltop desk

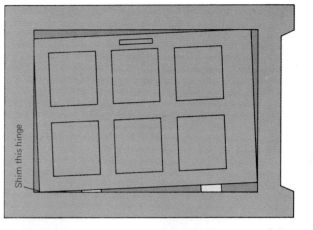

The tambour, or sliding top, on a rolltop desk consists of a row of narrow slats glued to canvas backing. Backings deteriorate with age, and slats come loose. Pry off the top assembly of the desk, and pull the tambour out of its channels. Build a simple, perfectly rectangular frame as shown in the illustration. Wedge tambour firmly into the frame. Wet the canvas to dissolve the old glue and strip the backing from the tambour, using pliers, a putty knife, or a screwdriver blade. Sand away remnants of old glue and canvas. Glue new sheet of canvas over the tambour slats. It should be an inch narrower than the slats on each side.

Cabinet doors

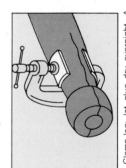

Shim this hinge

Warped cabinet doors can be removed and treated for warping as described on p.81. Other problems with doors may develop if the cabinet is not level. Try shimming the corners of the piece of furniture so that it stands level on the floor. If the door (or doors) stick even though the piece is level, tighten the hinges or install shims behind the hinges to correct the problem (see *Shimming*, p.58; *Hinges*, p.60). Shim the hinge at the corner diagonally opposite the spot where the binding occurs, as illustrated. As a last resort, sand or plane the edge of the door.

Casters

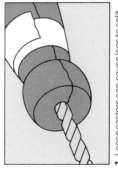

1. Loose casters can cause legs to split. Wrap leg tightly with masking tape; drill socket to larger diameter.

2. Cut a dowel to fit the socket. Remove tape. Apply glue to split and to dowel and socket. Insert dowel.

3. Clamp leg; let glue dry overnight. A glide can be tapped into dowel in place of caster, or caster can be left off.

4. If you want to replace caster, drill a hole in the dowel to take the caster shaft. Fit should be snug.

Case furniture

Drawers

If a drawer does not slide smoothly, examine both the drawer's runners and the rails on which the runners ride (see illustrations at right). High humidity may cause swelling in wood. Before you plane down rails or runners be sure that the sticking is not a temporary condition. Try rubbing the runners, rails, and the sides of the drawer with wax, soap, or talcum powder to reduce the friction.

If you do not want to replace worn rails, you can plane or sand them as smooth as possible and then install plastic slide guides on the rails, or put stem bumpers (plastic buttons) on either the rails or the runners. Both of these products are available at hardware stores.

There may be slides on the bottoms of larger drawers. They fit over guides in the frame and keep the drawer from wobbling as it slides. Worn guides can be built up with shims (see *Shimming*, p.58).

A drawer that is striking the back panel of the cabinet can be repaired by gluing a stop—a small wood block or wedge—at the end of each rail.

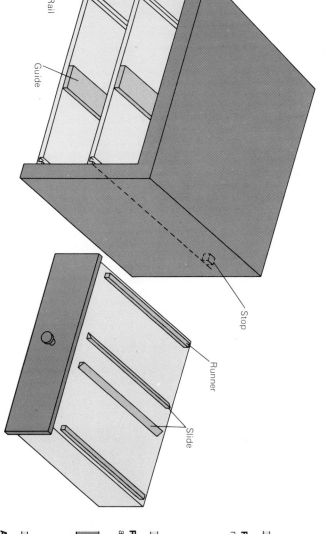

Rail

Guide

Stop

Runner

Slide

Variations in runners

Runner attached to side of drawer rides in groove in the frame.

Runner attached to frame rides in a groove in the drawer.

A hung drawer's runner rides along an elevated rail.

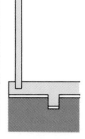

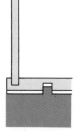

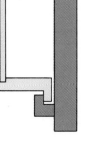

Drawer repairs

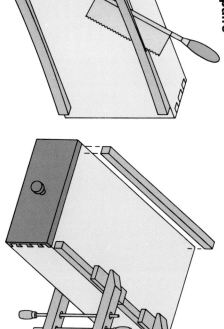

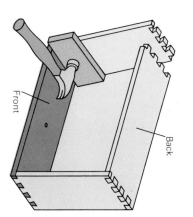

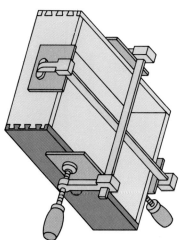

Worn runners: Saw off or plane the runners flush with the bottom of the drawer. Cut new runners of hardwood. The grain should run parallel to the rail. Glue and clamp the new runners to the drawer. Let the glue dry overnight and then sand and wax the runners to help reduce friction.

Front

Back

Rebuilding a drawer: To take the drawer apart, first remove the bottom; some bottoms can be freed by pulling out small anchoring nails. Tap joints open using a wood block to distribute the force. Scrape and sand glue from joints. Apply fresh glue, reassemble and clamp with bottom in place. Check drawer for squareness.

Veneer

Regluing veneer

Veneer is a thin layer of hardwood that is glued in place over the top of plywood or solid wood to create a surface for an attractive finish. Most modern tables, desks, and other pieces with broad, flat surfaces are likely to be made of veneer plywood because plywood is less susceptible to warping and splitting than solid wood, and because the use of solid hardwoods has become very expensive.

Antique veneer may be prone to certain kinds of damage. With time, the glue holding the veneer will dry, causing the edges to lift, normal usage almost insures that something will happen to aggravate the problem; for example, someone may catch a sleeve on the edge and rip a long strip off the base wood. A spilled drink—or simply high humidity—may cause the veneer to blister.

Follow the instructions and illustrations on this page for gluing down loose edges and blisters.

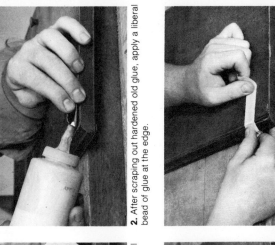

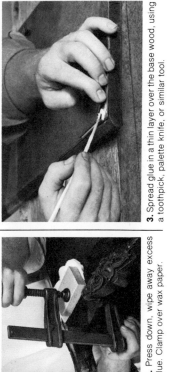

1. With a sharp knife, cut a slit along grain in middle of blister.

2. Depress each side of blister. Put glue under the raised sides.

3. Press down, wipe away excess glue. Clamp over wax paper.

Repairing a loose veneer edge

1. Lift the veneer with a thin screwdriver, being careful not to break the veneer.

2. After scraping out hardened old glue, apply a liberal bead of glue at the edge.

3. Spread glue in a thin layer over the base wood, using a toothpick, palette knife, or similar tool.

4. Press veneer down and wipe away excess glue. Secure with masking tape and let dry overnight.

Clamping veneer

Sandbag conforms to curve to clamp blistered veneer.

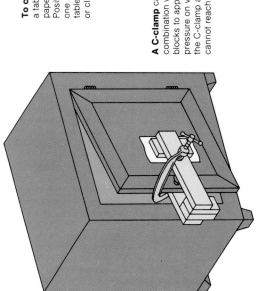

To clamp veneer in middle of a tabletop, cover with wax paper and a wood block. Position two boards, one above and one below the tabletop, and tightly tie or clamp the ends of boards.

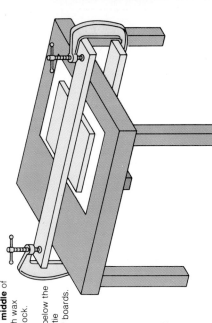

A C-clamp can be used in combination with boards and blocks to apply clamping pressure on veneer at a point the C-clamp alone cannot reach.

Patching veneer and wood

Patching techniques

A tabletop or any other surface can be repaired by cutting out the damaged portion and replacing it with a piece of patch wood. Veneer squares suitable for patching are available from woodworking supply houses and some lumber suppliers.

The most difficult step in patching is fitting the patch exactly to its bed, or grave. To patch veneer, use tracing paper to draw a pattern for the patch, as illustrated below. Cut the patch and the grave simultaneously (Step 3, below), and make the cut on the margins of the pattern, not directly on the outline.

To patch solid wood, begin by drawing and cutting a cardboard template, or pattern. Cut the template large enough to extend beyond the damaged area on all sides. The template should have one of the shapes illustrated at right. First, trace the outline of the template over the damaged surface. Chisel the grave about half an inch deep just inside the outline. (Use the same techniques illustrated for *Installing a recessed hinge*, p.60.) Then, trace the template outline on the patch wood, being sure that the grain will run parallel to that of the surface. Cut the patch with a saw. If it is slightly too large, sand it to fit; if small, cut another patch and glue down. Fill any hairline crevices with wood putty. Refinish the surface.

Tracing and cutting a veneer patch

1. Tape tracing paper over damaged veneer, leaving one side of paper untaped. Trace outline of break.

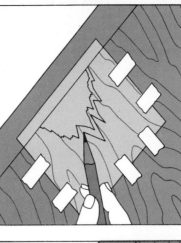

2. Slip a piece of patching veneer under tracing paper as shown, matching its grain to that of the surface.

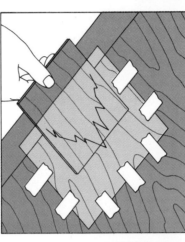

3. Hold piece down; cut through it and the surface underneath it. Cut just outside the traced line.

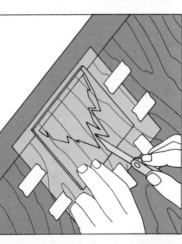

4. Remove tracing paper and patch from bed and sand clean. Test-fit the patch.

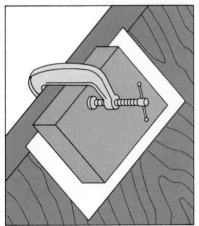

5. Apply a film of glue to the base wood. Dampen the patch so that it will not absorb all the glue.

6. Carefully press patch into place. Cover with wax paper and a wood block, and clamp. Let dry overnight.

Patching solid wood

Grain direction

The best way to repair a large gouge in a solid wood surface is to patch the damaged area with a new piece of matching wood. A template (see *Patching techniques*, this page) is used as a pattern to cut both the patch and the bed, or grave, into which the patch is glued. The fit should be exact, as seen in the top illustration. It is rarely possible to find a piece of patch wood whose grain perfectly matches the surface's grain. Line up the patch so that its grain runs parallel to that of the surface; any dissimilarities are best obscured by angling the ends of the patch into the main grain in one of the ways shown in the illustrations. After the patch is glued in place, strip and refinish the entire surface. (See *Refinishing*, pp.87–103.)

Refinishing

Reviving a finish

An old finish, even if it is dull and scratched, can sometimes be rejuvenated without stripping and refinishing. If it can, you stand to save a great deal of time and energy. Completely refinishing a piece of furniture can be rewarding, but it is time consuming and requires care.

Few hard and fast rules can be given as to whether a particular surface needs refinishing. Qualities that some may find desirable—such as distress marks, stains, and imperfections in an antique rocker—may be unacceptable to others. In the long run, if the topcoat does not have extensive cracks, flakes, or blisters, the decision depends on your own taste.

To establish the condition of the finish, you must clean it thoroughly. Use benzine (not to be confused with benzene, or benzol). Soak a soft, clean cloth in benzine and wipe over the surface. Use fresh cloths and more benzine until the surface is absolutely clean. Then wipe it dry.

Once the dirt has been removed, you may find that the finish is in fine condition, in which case you need only protect it with a good furniture polish. Apply a furniture cleanser-conditioner before using the polish. The conditioner will help restore the natural grain and color of the wood, cover up minor scratches, and condition the furniture against dryness and heat. If the topcoat is shellac, use a conditioner that does not contain water, since water will damage it.

Further restoration

Should cleaning and waxing fail to revive the finish, you will have to take further steps. First, find out whether the topcoat is shellac, varnish, or lacquer.

Testing the finish: Pick an inconspicuous spot and test it with denatured alcohol and lacquer thinner. Use only a drop of each. Alcohol will dissolve shellac; thinner will blister varnish. A lacquer finish will be mildly affected by thinner and not at all by alcohol.

New topcoat: A finish that is worn but adhering well can be beautifully restored with a new topcoat. To get the new coat to adhere well you must remove the gloss on the old finish. Use No. 4/0 steel wool and rub the entire piece gently but thoroughly, always following the grain. This will slightly abrade the surface. Directions for brushing on the new topcoat are given on page 90.

Glazing: The old finish may be in good condition yet look faded and dull. To help revive the color and hide minor blemishes, wipe on a thin glaze of diluted stain (see p.89) before applying a new topcoat. Let the stain dry for at least 24 hours. Apply a sealer coat (see p.89), then a topcoat of clear varnish.

Minor scratches: A small scratch in the finish that does not penetrate the wood can be repaired very easily. After cleaning the area thoroughly and determining the type of finish used, apply a little of the appropriate solvent with a small brush. Move the brush diagonally along the scratch and feather out toward the edges. This will dissolve the finish and allow it to blend over the scratch. Let the area dry thoroughly, then rub with a clean, lint-free cloth. If necessary, wait 24 hours and repeat the procedure. When dry, rub smooth to match the surrounding area (see *Rubbing*, p.91) and buff with wax.

Deep scratches: If a scratch cuts through the finish and into the wood, the piece will probably need restaining. Although you can use commercially available colored wax sticks, you will get better results with oil stain or acrylic artist's paints. First, clean the area with benzine. Then, touch up the scratch to blend it with the surrounding area (see *Stains and staining*, p.89). Let the touch-up stain dry overnight. The next day, apply solvent as described above to blend the finish.

If the scratch is very deep, you will need to build up the finish to make it flush with the surface. Using a fine brush, apply several thin coats of dilute finishing material. Limit the application to the scratch. Let each coat dry before applying the next. Once the scratch has been repaired, clean the entire surface thoroughly and apply a new topcoat to protect the surface to protect the finish and to blend the repair into its surroundings.

Stripping with a chemical remover

If a finish cannot be revived, it must be stripped off and a new finish applied. A chemical remover is the most effective way to remove an old finish without damaging the wood beneath. Sanding is less efficient and may mar the wood.

The best removers contain a high proportion of methylene chloride, a powerful solvent that works well on a wide range of finishes (including most water-based stains and paints). Methylene chloride is also noncombustible.

Three types of strippers are available: water base, oil base, and water rinse. All will do an excellent job. Water can damage veneer and soften glue in joints. So, when using a water-rinse stripper, it is safer not to hose it off, as is sometimes recommended. Instead, remove the finish with steel wool soaked in turpentine. Stripping compounds are available in paste and liquid form. Paste strippers adhere better to vertical surfaces.

Position the work on several layers of newspaper. Remove drawers, doors, and hardware, and strip them separately. If you are not stripping the entire piece, mask off the areas you want preserved.

You will need an ample supply of remover and several old or inexpensive paintbrushes—once a brush is used to apply paint remover, it becomes unfit for any other purpose. Wear rubber gloves. Pour some remover into a coffee can and work from it while keeping the main supply capped.

Strip only a single section at a time, otherwise the mixture of dissolved finish and stripper may dry before you can remove it. Adjust the piece so that the part you are working on is horizontal. Apply a thick coat of remover, ladling it on generously with as few strokes as possible. Do not brush it out. Let the remover work undisturbed for about 15 minutes, then, when the finish is wrinkled and blistered, scrape it off with a putty knife followed by No. 2/0 steel wool. Follow the grain and work carefully, particularly with the putty knife; the wood will be temporarily softened by the stripping chemicals and can easily be scarred. Use a toothbrush or steel wool twisted into a rope to clean corners, joints, and curved surfaces.

Even if some finish remains on the first section, continue stripping the rest of the piece. Then, using fresh remover and clean tools, reattack stubborn sections. If remover drips onto a clean section, quickly wipe it off with gum turpentine.

Caution: Chemicals used in stripping and refinishing can be hazardous. Methylene chloride, benzene (often called benzol), toluene, and xylene are all known or suspected cancer-causing substances. The last three are also highly volatile. Read the manufacturer's instructions and warnings carefully before using them. Heart patients and smokers should avoid breathing the fumes of any of these substances. Others should use them only outdoors or in a room with exhaust ventilation and no access to pilot lights or other ignition sources.

Refinishing

Preparing the surface after stripping

Paint removers leave behind wax and other chemical residues. These deposits must be cleaned away or neutralized before refinishing, otherwise they will obstruct penetration of stains and inhibit adhesion of the new finish.

Gum turpentine is a particularly efficient neutralizing and cleaning agent. Apply the turpentine with the grain, gently with No. 2/0 steel wool, thoroughly washing down all surfaces of the piece of furniture being finished. Pay special attention to crevices and carvings. Leave the turpentine on the surface for a few minutes, then wipe it off with a clean cotton cloth. Let the piece dry overnight.

The wood may retain tinges of color from its original finish, even after it has been meticulously stripped and cleaned. This is not harmful and may contribute to the beauty of the final finish. However, if these traces of color do prove undesirable, they can be removed by sanding.

Once it is completely dry, a stripped surface should be sanded lightly. This enhances the appearance of the finish by smoothing the wood to a fine, silky texture without harming its distinctive patina. Use No. 280 finishing paper (see p.57). Applying straight, even strokes, rub then wait about 20 minutes for the chemical action to take effect. Repeat, if necessary. After bleaching, cleanse the area thoroughly with a 50/50 solution of white vinegar and water. When the surface is dry, lightly sand the treated area with No. 220 finishing Paper to smooth wood fibers raised by the bleaching.

Bleach can also be employed to lighten wood for cosmetic purposes, For example, as an alternative to staining, when dissimilar colored woods have been used in a piece of furniture, the darker parts can be bleached to produce uniform tone. Apply the bleach with a clean cloth, wiping evenly along the grain over the entire surface. Avoid overlapping onto

grain sanding is unavoidable, sand initially with No. 4/0 steel wool, and then give it a light smoothing with finishing paper. On narrow, rounded surfaces, like spindles and carvings, use either finishing paper or No. 4/0 steel wool.

As a final step, check the piece for defects and make necessary repairs (see pp.54–86). Pay special attention to the surface. Examine it carefully for damage and blemishes. Shallow scratches can be feathered out with No. 280 finishing paper, but deeper cuts should be filled with wood putty. Techniques for using wood putty are described on pages 58 and 96.

Bleaching

Water marks, ink stains, and other blemishes can be bleached out once the wood has been stripped and cleaned. Ordinary household bleach or ammonia, used full strength, will succeed in most cases. Apply a little directly to the soiled spot, then wait about 20 minutes for the chemical action to take effect. Repeat, if necessary. After bleaching, cleanse the area

Use bleach on dark wood to match it with light wood.

the sections that have already been bleached. Wait about 20 minutes, repeat the bleach treatment if needed, then neutralize with the vinegar and water solution. After the surface is thoroughly dry, sand it lightly.

More powerful, two-solution bleaching compounds are available at paint stores. Such compounds are difficult to use and could ruin a good piece of furniture if improperly handled. As an alternative to bleaching, you can use a light-colored pigmented wiping stain.

Penetrating resin finishes

Penetrating resins, such as those marketed by Du Pont, Minwax, and Watco, are the easiest finishes to apply and are among the most durable. They seal and preserve the wood, while producing a rich, muted satin finish. Application is practically foolproof; the finish dries dust free and is less likely to be marred by runs, sags, or brush marks.

Unlike conventional finishes (such as shellac, varnish, and lacquer), penetrating resin not only protects the surface but contains chemicals that solidify within the wood fibers. Wood treated with penetrating resin is highly resistant to wear and tear, although it will show dirt if subjected to constant handling. Resin finishes cannot chip, peel, or rub away. Any damage that might occur such as liquid stains and cigarette burns, can be removed with steel wool and treated with more resin to restore the original beauty.

Pour on plenty of resin and spread it thickly.

Wood treated with resin, like wood treated with varnish, resists warping and dimensional distortion, even in unusually damp climates. It is also impervious to wood-boring insects and decay.

Penetrating resin is available clear or in several basic shades. The different colors may be intermixed to produce the desired tone. For a wider range of colors, special quick stains may be applied ahead of time. To refinish a piece with penetrating resin, start by stripping,

cleaning, and sanding it, then vacuum the surface to clear the wood pores. This will allow total penetration of the resin.

Next, read the manufacturer's instructions; details of application vary from one brand to the next. Whenever possible, adjust the piece so that the part you are working on is horizontal Concentrate on a single section at a time. Saturate the wood with a liberal dose of penetrating resin, either by pouring it directly from the container onto the surface or by mopping it on with a rag or a brush.

Let the resin soak in for the time recommended by the manufacturer but keep the surface wet. If dull spots appear, they indicate places where all the resin has been absorbed. Apply more to the area. When the penetration time is up, wipe the surface completely dry. Be thorough. Excess resin left on the surface will dry to an unattractive glaze. Should

this happen, it can usually be corrected by applying additional resin to the affected area, rubbing the spot with 3/0 steel wool, and then wiping it dry. Check the piece as it dries; if small spots of resin rise back to the surface, wipe them away.

Even after the surface is dry, the resin will continue to be absorbed by the wood. Since this may leave insufficient resin at the surface, a second application may be wise, especially if the wood is very porous. In general, do not wait longer than three hours before applying the second coat, or some of the resin may cure, hindering further absorption.

For added luster, the surface can be rubbed. Let it dry overnight. Then, using No. 600 wet/dry sandpaper and a small amount of penetrating resin or paste wax as a lubricant, lightly smooth the surface in the direction of the grain. Wipe dry and polish with a soft cloth.

Wood fillers

Fillers close up the pores of coarse-grained wood and produce a smooth, hard surface on which finishing coats can be applied. The decision whether to use them or not is up to you. Fillers should not be used if a finish with a natural-wood look is desired. Close-grained wood seldom requires a filler; sealer and topcoat are sufficient to pack the small pores, particularly if a pigment stain is used.

A paste filler containing silex (finely powdered quartz) is better than a liquid. The paste will pack the wood grain more tightly and help the topcoat adhere more firmly. In general, the filler should match or be slightly darker than the stain used on the wood. Buy it in the natural tone and tint it with oil pigments. The filler should be applied both with and across the grain either before or after staining. If it is to be applied after, first seal the surface with a coat of thinned shellac.

Sealers

A sealer is a coat of diluted lacquer, shellac, or varnish that is applied over a stain or filler. It prevents bleeding and improves adhesion between the topcoats and undercoats. A sealer may also be used as a primer over bare wood to restrict penetration of a succeeding coat. Shellac is an excellent general choice; it dries fast and provides good adhesion. In the case of wood treated with oil stain, there is no option; only shellac should be used. Thin the shellac by mixing one part shellac with eight parts denatured alcohol. If varnish is to be used as a sealer, mix it with an equal amount of turpentine; if lacquer is to be used, mix it with an equal amount of lacquer thinner.

Before applying a sealing coat, be sure the surface is dry and free of dust. Brush on the sealer with the grain. Let it dry thoroughly, then smooth lightly with No. 3/0 steel wool.

Stains and staining

A stain should reveal and enhance the natural beauty of a wood by improving the color and accenting natural grain patterns. Water, alcohol, and oil stains are all available, but oil stains are best for the home refinisher. They are inexpensive and easily applied.

There are two types of oil stains: pigment and penetrating. Pigment oil stains, the more common, consist of colored powder suspended in a mixture of oil and oleoresin. Penetrating stains are made of aniline dye dissolved in a similar mixture. Pigment stains act like a very thin paint, depositing particles of color within the wood surface. Penetrating stains strike deeper than pigment stains, dying the wood fibers rather than coating them.

Because they soak in less deeply, and dry more slowly, pigment stains are easier to control. However, care must be taken to avoid excessive buildup, since the particles of pigment may clog the wood pores and obscure the grain. In certain cases, this potential to conceal can be used to advantage—for example, to blend dissimilar woods.

Before applying stain, clean and smooth the surface. Using No. 220 or 280 finishing paper (the finer grit should be used on hardwoods, such as oak), sand lightly with the grain. Afterward, remove all dust and wipe with turpentine.

Prior to staining, the more absorbent end grain areas (where the wood is crosscut, as in a chair seat) should be sealed with thinned shellac; otherwise, they will absorb more stain and become much darker than the rest of the piece. Before using a pigment stain, it is good practice to apply a coat of thinned shellac sealer over the entire piece to balance uneven porosity and restrain penetration of the stain. This will make it easier to wipe off excess stain, allowing for more precise color control. Once the color is too dark, it is very hard to lighten, but with the wood sealed, it is an easy matter to make several applications, progressively increasing color intensity until you arrive at the exact shade desired.

Once the wood is prepared, the next step is to test-stain a matching piece of scrap wood. Experiment with penetration time and thinning to produce the desired tone. You might even apply a coat of finish (see p.90) over the test-stain to get a better idea of how the final job will look. When you are ready to stain the piece itself, start with the least conspicuous parts; first do the back, then the sides, then the front, and last of all the top. Whenever possible, adjust the item so that the surface you are working on is horizontal. If you are forced to apply stain to a vertical surface, work from the top down. That way, excess stain will drip onto unstained areas, where it can be wiped away and compensated for as you proceed. Be careful not to splatter or drip onto wood that has already been stained.

Because the degree of darkness is determined by how long the stain is allowed to penetrate before being wiped off, uniform appearance cannot be achieved unless each application receives the same amount of time for penetration. Applying stain over too large an area will make it difficult to keep track of penetration time, and results will be uneven. For this reason, stain only a limited section at a time, one that can be stained and wiped within 15 minutes.

Mix the stain thoroughly and continue stirring frequently during application. This is especially important with pigment stain, because the minute particles of color will settle out of suspension as you work. Use a brush or a clean, lint-free cloth to apply a thin, even coat of stain. Wipe the stain on with long, regular strokes, following the grain. Avoid overlapping areas already stained. While the stain is still wet, check for spots where it is not penetrating and rub them with 3/0 steel wool to work the stain in. You may have to apply more stain to these areas.

Allow the same penetration time that gave you the desired results on your test piece, then remove residual stain with a clean, lint-free cloth or by dry-brushing as explained below. When using a cloth, wipe with the grain. If the stain begins to dry before you start wiping it off, dampen the cloth with turpentine or benzine. This can also be used to blend out streaks or to lighten the stain's color.

The dry-brushing technique permits more precise removal of excess stain. Use a clean, dry brush to stroke the stain off. Follow the grain, blending the stain over the surface and frequently wiping the brush bristles dry on a clean cloth. Dry-brush until all excess stain is removed.

Let the stain dry thoroughly—at least 24 hours. If you are satisfied with the results, brush on a sealer of thinned shellac and let it dry completely.

Glazing: Results that are pale or uneven can be corrected with a glaze of diluted stain. The stain need not be the same color; a complementary tone can enhance the overall effect. First, apply a sealer and let it dry. Next, dilute the stain with gum turpentine to make the glaze. A 50/50 mixture will generally be satisfactory, but if the glaze is only being used to even out the color, thin it more. Wipe on the glaze with a lint-free cloth. Should the results still be disappointing, wipe the glaze off with a cloth dampened in thinner, and try again. When you are satisfied, let the glaze dry completely and seal the surface with thinned shellac.

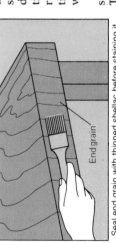

Seal end grain with thinned shellac before staining it.

End grain

Refinishing

Shellac

Shellac was for centuries the traditional finishing material. It is economical and easy to apply and produces a deep, lustrous, smooth coating. Unfortunately, shellac finishes have the drawback of being easily damaged by heat, water, alcohol, and many household chemicals.

Shellac is built up in layers. (One coat is never sufficient.) Each layer dries dust free in half an hour and is ready for the next coat in about four hours. Shellac is sold in its natural orange color or bleached nearly colorless (white shellac). It is common practice to use white shellac on light wood and orange on dark wood, but either color or a mixture can be used on any wood. However, the orange shellac produces a deeper tone.

After about a year on the shelf, shellac begins to undergo chemical decomposition, rendering the product unusable. Accordingly, purchase a brand that has an expiration date printed on the can and get only enough for immediate needs.

Shellac is rarely applied directly from the can. For durability and appearance it is essential to use several well-thinned coats. Dilute the shellac with denatured alcohol to a 1-pound cut (see chart), stirring rather than shaking it. Properly thinned, shellac flows on easily. Do not apply shellac under damp or humid conditions; it may cause the finish to cloud. Room temperature should be 65° or above. A surface must be dry and clean before shellac is applied to it. Whenever possible, adjust the piece so that you are working on a horizontal surface.

Apply the shellac with as little brushing as possible. Follow the grain, flowing the shellac over the surface with long, even strokes. Avoid overlapping already coated areas. Bubbles on the surface indicate excessive or hasty brushwork.

Let the first coat dry a full three hours, then smooth it lightly with No. 220 finishing paper (see p.57) to improve the adhesion of the next coat. Thoroughly dust off the surface and apply the second coat. Allow it to dry longer than the first coat—at least four hours.

Apply a minimum of three coats to the sides and back of a piece and five or more to the top. Sand lightly between coats, being careful not to cut through the finish, especially at edges and turnings.

Let the final coat dry overnight. The finish can be rubbed (see p.91). If it is, wait at least 24 hours before applying wax or furniture polish.

Table shows how much wood alcohol to add per quart of shellac to thin from one cut to another. (Cut is pounds of shellac resin per gallon of wood alcohol.)

Original cut	Alcohol added	Resultant cut
5-pound	1 pint	3-pound
5-pound	1 quart	2-pound
5-pound	⅔ gallon	1-pound
4-pound	½ pint	3-pound
4-pound	¾ pint	2-pound
4-pound	1 quart	2-pound
4-pound	2 quarts	1-pound
3-pound	¼ pint	2-pound
3-pound	½ pint	1-pound
3-pound	3 pints	1-pound

Varnishes

Varnishes are the most durable of the clear finishes. They are long lasting, resistant to abrasion, and are not harmed by water, alcohol, and most household chemicals.

There are various kinds of varnishes, each with different properties. Among the toughest are the synthetic varnishes based on polyurethane, an oil-modified plastic resin. It is a good policy to use the same type of varnish for every coat of finish on a particular piece. Varnish is sold in gloss, satin, or flat. High-gloss varieties tend to be the most durable and are recommended. Moreover, if you do not want a shiny finish, you can rub a gloss coat to produce a satin or matte effect (see *Rubbing*, p.91).

Varnish dries relatively slowly and is thus vulnerable to dust contamination. Conventional oil-base varnishes should generally be left to dry at least 24 hours between coats. Synthetic varnishes are faster. They usually dry dust free in two hours and are ready for recoating in four hours. For the most durable finish, allow more drying time between coats than is recommended by the manufacturer.

The surface should be clean, dry, and free of dust before it is varnished. Wipe it with turpentine, then use a tack rag, available at paint stores, to remove all traces of dust. If oil stain has been applied, the surface must be sealed with shellac to prevent bleeding (see *Sealers*, p.89). To minimize dust problems, choose a draft-free room and vacuum it. Room temperature should be above 65°F.

It is important to use a good varnish brush. Clean the brush with turpentine and then dip it in varnish and sweep the bristles back and forth over clean paper to work the varnish into all the bristles. Stir the varnish well but carefully. Do not shake the can. This will create tiny air bubbles that will unfavorably affect the appearance of the job. Gently pour some varnish into a wide-mouth container and recap the main can so that the volatile solvents do not evaporate. Test the varnish for proper consistency. It should flow easily from the brush. If necessary, thin it with gum turpentine.

Unlike other finishing materials, varnish is first brushed on across the grain, then tipped off by lightly rebrushing along the grain to produce a smooth, even film. When applying varnish, keep the brush full but not so loaded that it drips. Dip the bristles about a third of the way into the varnish and tap them against the inside of the container to release excess varnish. Do not drag the brush across the rim, as that will produce air bubbles.

Flow the varnish on across the grain with long, even strokes and a minimum of brush work. Tip off the coat with an empty brush. Hold the brush almost vertical to the surface so that only its tip touches the wet varnish. Start at one end of the surface and move the brush with the grain to the opposite end in a single continuous motion. Continue parallel sweeps until the entire surface is smooth.

Leave the coat untouched for 24 hours or until completely dry, then lightly rub with steel wool to insure good adhesion for the next coat. For a gloss finish, use No. 4/0 steel wool; for a satin or matte finish, use No. 3/0. Apply a second coat in the same manner as the first. If the piece is to be rubbed, at least three coats should be applied.

Lacquers

Lacquers produce brilliant, clear finishes, but are difficult to work with, primarily because they dry rapidly. The best way to apply them is with a spray gun, but this method requires expensive equipment. Lacquers are also available in spray cans for small jobs and in special brush-on formulas.

The technique of applying lacquer from a spray can is the same as that for applying paint with a spray can. See *Painted furniture*, pp.102-103, for information on using spray cans. If you decide to use a brush-on lacquer, first practice on scrap wood. Even though lacquer dries quickly, allow four hours drying time between coats for optimum results.

Use a shellac sealer (see p.91) before applying lacquer directly to varnish or oil stain; lacquer will blister the varnish and act as a solvent on the stain. A lacquer finish can be rubbed (see p.91) to bring out its gloss even more. Let the final coat dry overnight before rubbing.

Rubbing

No matter how meticulously the topcoat is applied it will not be completely smooth when it dries. Blemishes—such as dust particles, brush marks, and tiny air bubbles—are inevitable. By rubbing the surface with fine abrasive, you can polish out the roughness and get the exact luster you want. Before rubbing, the finish must be absolutely hard. Wait at least 48 hours after applying the final coat.

Any shellac, varnish, or lacquer finish can be rubbed. Surfaces that are to be rubbed should have at least three coats of finish on them, since a shallow finish might wear through to the wood. Edges, corners, and carvings are particularly delicate. It is best to rub only up to them, not actually over them. If it is necessary to rub them, save them for last and be especially gentle. Spots where the finish is accidentally rubbed through should be retouched. Apply a little stain with a fine brush, seal with thinned shellac, then reapply finishing material until the spot is built up flush with its surroundings. Allow drying time between the steps.

Wet/dry sandpaper: This material will produce a finish with a smooth, slightly dull luster known as matte. Use sandpaper only on flat surfaces and work carefully. Sandpaper cuts rapidly, even in the very fine grades used for rubbing.

A lubricant, usually water, must be employed with the paper. Light oil can also be used but it cuts more slowly than water, making the job considerably more laborious. Oil will also leave a film that must be cleaned off with benzine. Water cuts quickly and leaves no residue, but must never be used on shellac. When using water, do not leave it on the surface too long or it may damage the finish.

Begin by soaking a piece of No. 500 wet/dry sandpaper (see p.57) in the lubricant. Wrap the paper around a sanding block and rub over the surface of the furniture, using moderate pressure. Work with the grain and do only one section at a time, inspecting the surface frequently. Keep the paper wet. When the finish is smooth and evenly matte, clean off the residue with a cloth or sponge dampened with clean water, then wipe dry. If oil lubricant was used, wipe the surface with benzine before drying.

Steel wool: Rubbing with steel wool is a simple, effective, and relatively quick way to obtain a smooth, satiny finish. Steel wool is available at most hardware stores in a variety of grades, the finest of which is No. 0000, commonly written as "No. 4/0" (the more zeros in the number, the finer the grade).

Before using steel wool, check the topcoat. If it has serious irregularities, such as runs, sags, or brush marks, smooth them out with wet/dry sandpaper, as described above. When the surface is ready, shape a pad of No. 4/0 steel wool into a loose wad and rub it over the surface, pressing down with the palm of your hand. Move with the grain only and turn the pad periodically to obtain a clean cutting surface. Replace the steel wool as soon as it begins to disintegrate. Once the entire surface has been covered and is free of imperfections, continue rubbing with the grain until you achieve the desired satin sheen, but do not rub more than necessary or you may cut through the finish. Clean the surface by brushing along the grain with a soft cloth. For a smoother, more lustrous finish, dip the steel wool in a light oil or paste wax when you rub. If you use an oil, clean off the residue with benzine.

Rubbing compound: You can get a high gloss finish with the help of rubbing compound. If furniture compound is not available, use a fine grade of white automobile compound instead. Be sure it is pure, without wax or other additives, and avoid harsh, orange compounds.

If the unrubbed topcoat is rough, smooth it before using the compound. No. 600 wet/dry sandpaper is a good choice for this initial rubbing. Next, read the label instructions, clean the surface, and apply the compound.

When you are ready to rub, dampen a clean, lint-free cloth with a little clean water. Scoop up some compound on the cloth and rub the surface, a section at a time, following the grain. Turn the cloth frequently to obtain a clean rubbing surface and scoop up more compound as needed. Wipe the surface clean regularly to inspect your progress. When the surface is completely smooth, wipe it off. Then, take a clean cloth and only a little compound, sprinkle water over the finish, and rub the surface to bring up the polish. Polish until the gloss is uniform and the surface is dry. A light coat of liquid or aerosol wax can be applied for added protection, but paste wax is best. Spread it on with a soft cloth, let it sit a minute or two, then buff with a clean cloth to bring out the full gloss. Do not wait for the wax to dry before you buff.

Selecting a new finish

When you refinish a piece of furniture—either because you want to change its looks or because the old finish has been damaged—you will have to decide what type of finish you want to produce. In most instances, your choice will be a matter simply of personal taste. For example, you may prefer a natural look for an old oak rocker, but a soft satin finish for a pretty cherry dresser. A brilliant lacquer may seem right for an antique picture frame, a subdued matte finish for a walnut desk, and a high gloss for an end table next to an upholstered Victorian couch. However, factors other than taste should also be part of your thinking. Before deciding on the finish for a piece of furniture, ask yourself the questions at right. The techniques used to produce the various finishes are illustrated and discussed on pages 92-101.

Do you like the look of the wood?
If you like the appearance of the natural wood, you may simply want to give it a clear finish, using varnish, wax, or oil. Walnut and teak are often finished by brushing on an oil finish composed of ⅔ boiled linseed oil and ⅓ turpentine, allowing it to penetrate slightly, and then wiping it off. If the wood is pine, maple, beech, or birch, and you desire a more appealing color, you may first want to stain the wood and then finish it with a topcoat of varnish, shellac, or lacquer.

How will the furniture be used?
In choosing a finish you must consider how much and in what way the piece is going to be used, what substances it is likely to come into contact with, and how roughly it will be handled. Pieces likely to be scuffed need a tough topcoat, such as varnish. If alcohol or water will contact the surface, as in the case of a cocktail table, shellac must be avoided. For outdoor furniture an oil paint is generally best. For picture frames or inlaid boxes, a delicate, painstakingly rubbed finish might be in order.

What is the surrounding decor?
Furniture should be compatible with its surroundings. A painted table would look awkward in the midst of natural finished pieces; a glossy cabinet out of place in a subdued room; a chair shaded with a deep-toned stain jarring in a light, airy bedroom.

What is the style of the piece?
Tradition and style influence the selection of finish. Antique mahogany can be filled, shellacked, and rubbed. Contemporary mahogany can be finished simply with penetrating resin. An Early American piece of native pine or cherry can simply be cleaned and waxed; age will deliver its own patina.

How much time do you have available?
Since few people have unlimited time, the choice among finishes can come down to which is quickest to apply. It would be foolish for a person with limited time to strip, sand, stain, varnish, and rub an elaborately carved dresser, when he could get nearly as good a result by merely cleaning the piece with benzine and applying conditioner and wax.

Refinishing

Stripping, glazing, and lacquering a painted picture frame

1. Apply chemical stripper uniformly over the painted frame (see cautions on p.87). Wear gloves.

2. Let the stripper work on the paint for 15 to 20 minutes, or until the finish wrinkles and lifts up.

3. Remove dissolved finish with dull putty knife or No. 2/0 steel wool (p.91). Follow grain; work carefully.

4. Wipe the wood as clean as possible with benzine and a soft cloth or No. 2/0 steel wool.

5. The first application may not remove all the finish. Apply more stripper where necessary.

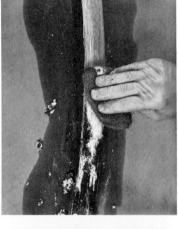

6. Clean to bare wood with No. 2/0 steel wool and benzine. Follow grain, rubbing old finish out of pores.

7. Strippers leave residues that must be removed. Wipe the piece with turpentine. Let it dry for 24 hours.

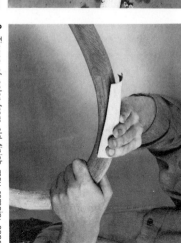

8. Tinges of color from old finish may remain; sand lightly with grain, using No. 280 sandpaper (p.57).

9. Apply glaze of thinned oil stain. Test on scrap wood, then wipe glaze evenly over entire surface.

10. Brush with soft, dry brush to blend the glaze. Do so before glaze penetrates deeply. Let dry 24 hours.

11. Spray on several light coats of lacquer. Hold can 10 inches from surface, and use a slow, even motion.

12. Let lacquer dry 48 hours. For a satin luster, rub finish with No. 4/0 steel wool along the grain.

Stripping, staining, and giving a topcoat to a chair

Chair with old finish that is worn and faded can be stripped and refinished, as shown. See cautions on p.87.

1. Apply stripper to chair seat. Remove dissolved finish with a putty knife. Wear gloves.

2. Apply stripper to rails and remove with No. 2/0 steel wool (p.91). Curves may require more stripper.

3. Remove residue left by stripper with turpentine; apply with No. 2/0 steel wool or rag.

4. Rub chair lightly with very fine sandpaper (see p.57) to remove remaining traces of old finish.

5. Spend extra time sanding joints and curved areas where stains collect. Then, dust chair thoroughly.

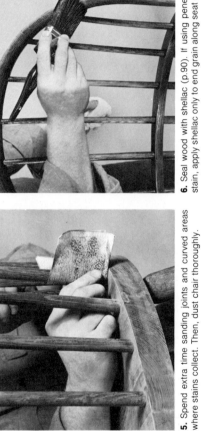

6. Seal wood with shellac (p.90). If using penetrating stain, apply shellac only to end grain along seat edges.

7. For best results when staining, work on complete sections. Test-stain part of underside of chair.

8. Wipe stain over seat with long, even strokes, following the grain. Avoid overlapping already stained areas.

9. On flat areas, even out the applied stain with a dry brush. Clean stain from brush.

10. On rounded elements, wipe on stain with a dry brush. Where stain penetrates, wipe off excess. Let dry 24 hours.

11. Apply three coats of varnish (p.90). Let dry, rub to satin sheen with No. 4/0 steel wool; wax.

93

Refinishing

Unifying a high-gloss finish on dissimilar woods

A special approach is called for to achieve a uniform finish on a desk of dissimilar woods.

1. Remove drawer and apply stripper (see cautions on p.87). After 15 minutes scrape away dissolved finish.

2. Work the dissolved finish out of grooves in drawer with steel wool wrapped around tip of a screwdriver.

3. Use stripper and a small wire brush to remove the finish from carvings in the desk.

4. When working on carved legs, repeat treatment with stripper and steel wool to rid spools of finish.

5. Eliminate wax and other residues by wiping surfaces thoroughly with gum turpentine.

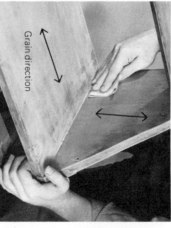

6. To smooth the surface, rub lightly with the grain, using a very fine sandpaper (see p.57).

Grain direction

7. Clean grooves with folded sandpaper. Areas cleaned against grain must later be smoothed with grain.

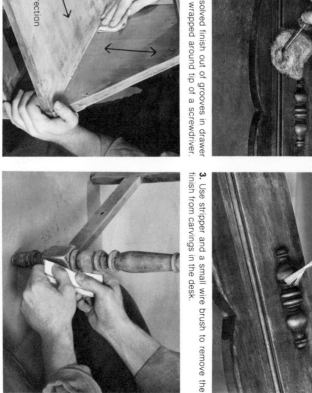

8. Sand carvings using a piece of sandpaper wrapped around the tip of a screwdriver.

9. After carefully vacuuming to get rid of sandpaper dust, apply a sealer coat of thinned shellac (see p.89).

10. Also apply shellac to drawer fronts and dropleaf. (Dropleaf should have been removed at the start.)

11. After the sealer coat has dried, apply stain. Pigmented stains (p.89) are being used in picture.

15. Brush on varnish (see p.90) with the grain and away from the corners. Let it dry for 24 hours.

14. Take care to prevent stain from collecting in carvings and grooves. Allow stain to dry 24 hours.

13. Stains of slightly different hues bring varicolored woods into apparent harmony (see p.89).

12. After wiping on the stain, dry-brush it with the grain to blend it to a uniform tone.

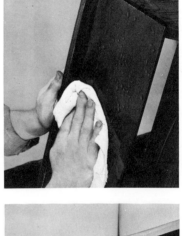

19. Sand carefully with the grain, frequently checking the surface for smoothness. Then, wipe off residue.

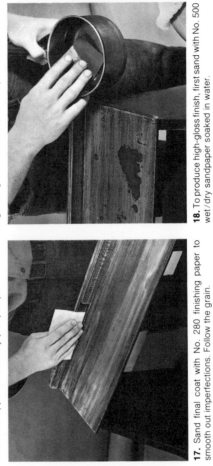

18. To produce high-gloss finish, first sand with No. 500 wet/dry sandpaper soaked in water.

17. Sand final coat with No. 280 finishing paper to smooth out imperfections. Follow the grain.

16. Sand lightly between coats with No. 280 paper. Apply several coats. Let final coat dry 48 hours.

23. Let dry 24 hours. Surface will be highly polished, but apply wax for additional protection.

22. Sprinkle surface with water and, with fresh pad and a little compound, polish surface again.

21. Compound cuts while moist, polishes as it dries in process of rubbing. Continue until surface is smooth.

20. Scoop up rubbing compound (p.91) on damp cloth pad. Rub with straight back and forth motion.

Refinishing

Refinishing a marred and stained surface

A table marred by gouges and food and beverage stains can be given a soft, satiny new finish, as shown here. See cautions on p.87.

1. Wipe off old dirt and wax with benzine so that the stripper will make direct contact with the finish.

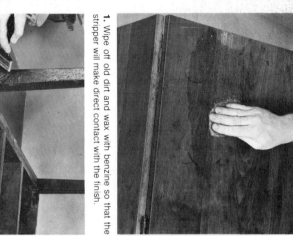

2. Brush paste stripper (p.87) over a small section; be certain to strip all edges of drop leaves and top.

3. Give stripper time to work, then finish with putty knife. Strip grooves with No. 2/0 steel wool (p.91).

4. On stubborn spots, reapply the stripper, let it work, then wipe clean with steel wool and benzine.

5. To facilitate stripping the legs, frame, and underside, turn the table over. Protect top with newspaper.

6. Wipe with gum turpentine to neutralize stripper residues. Wipe again with dry cloth. Dry overnight.

7. Try to smooth away stains and watermarks with very fine sandpaper (p.57). If this fails, use bleach.

8. Smooth out gouges, leaving inside rough for putty to grip. Select a wood putty of neutral color.

9. Pack putty firmly into gouges with fingers. Apply a little too much, since putty shrinks as it dries.

10. To repair chipped corners, apply slightly more than enough putty to replace the missing wood.

11. Reshape the corners with your fingers. The putty will shrink to the right size as it dries overnight.

12. Sand hardened putty flush with surface using a very fine sandpaper (p.57). Sand with the grain.

13. Sand corner square. Work slowly and carefully to avoid pulling hardened putty out of repair.

14. Apply thin wash coat of shellac (p.90) to seal putty. Brush first into grooves, then over top. Let dry.

15. Apply stain (p.89) in sections. First, stain legs and underside of leaves; then, stain top (shown here).

16. Use a dry brush to distribute the applied stain more evenly. Brush with the grain.

17. Seal stain with coat of thinned shellac or spray lacquer (p.90). Let dry thoroughly before proceeding.

18. To touch up repaired gouges, mix oil or acrylic pigments to match stain and apply with fine brush.

19. With No. 4/0 steel wool (p.91), feather out edges of touch-up to blend with grain. Seal with spray lacquer.

20. Touch up corners in same manner. With a good color match, repair should not show through topcoat.

21. Brush on the first coat of varnish and let it dry for 24 hours. A total of three coats should be applied.

Grain direction

22. After each coat of varnish has dried, smooth the surface lightly with No. 3/0 steel wool. Follow grain.

23. Let final topcoat dry 48 hours and then buff with paste wax or furniture polish.

Refinishing

Redoing a high-gloss finish damaged by a cigarette burn

Cigarette burn in wood of a drop-leaf table can be eliminated only by refinishing entire tabletop.

1. Clean table with benzine; examine finish (see cautions, p.87). Mask around work area.

2. First, apply masking tape along top edge of apron, directly against underside of tabletop.

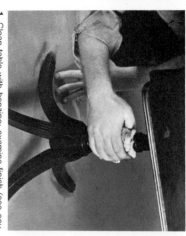

3. Tape several layers of newspaper around apron and legs. Be sure all parts not being stripped are covered.

4. Apply stripper liberally to tabletop and let it work 20 minutes. Carefully scrape off dissolved finish.

5. Apply stripper along edges of leaves and table. Remove dissolved finish with No. 2/0 steel wool (p.91).

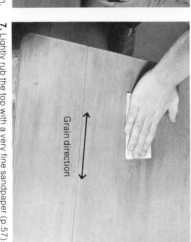

6. Clean off sludge with benzine-wetted cloth. Then, wipe with turpentine and let dry overnight.

7. Lightly rub the top with a very fine sandpaper (p.57). Sand in the direction of the wood grain.

Grain direction

8. Carefully sand burn with No. 280 paper to reduce discoloration. Avoid causing a hollow by oversanding.

9. Vacuum surface to remove all dust. Seal with shellac (p.90); Brush with grain, let dry three hours.

10. Wipe on pigmented oil stain (p.89) with cloth, following grain. Be sure to cover surface, edges evenly.

11. Remove excess stain by dry-brushing along grain. Once desired tone is achieved, let piece dry overnight.

Touching up splits and fractures

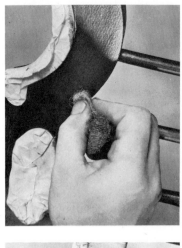

1. Fill crevices with wood putty. Apply liberally and pack down; putty shrinks as it dries.

3. Mask brass with tape. Mix oil stain to match finish; wipe onto putty. Let stain dry, then seal (p. 89).

5. Lightly rub steel wool over touch-up to simulate grain. Let dry and seal with spray lacquer (p.89).

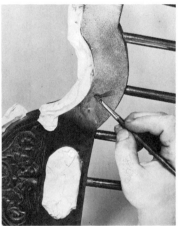

After repairing splits in headrest of rocker with glue (p.69), you can touch up the repairs as follows.

2. After putty has dried 24 hours, sand it flush with surrounding area, using very fine finishing paper (p.57).

4. Using oil colors, touch up putty to make it blend as unnoticeably as possible with surrounding finish.

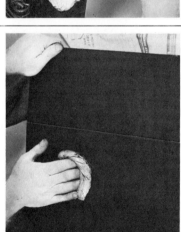

13. Sand lightly with No. 280 paper, rubbing with the grain. Wipe surface clean with a moist cloth.

15. Allow the final coat to dry for 48 hours, then smooth it carefully with No. 280 finishing paper (p.57).

17. Clean off sanding residue. Apply rubbing compound with damp cloth; rub to a high gloss.

12. Seal with shellac (p.90) and let dry three hours. Apply varnish (p.90) and let dry overnight.

14. Apply second coat of varnish. Let dry three hours, then sand lightly. Apply final coat of varnish.

16. Using No. 600 wet/dry sandpaper soaked in water, rub with grain. Rub along edges with special care.

Refinishing

Restoring the finish on an inlaid surface

To preserve patina of age on an inlaid chest, restore finish, rather than stripping it.

4. Blend in touch-ups by gently rubbing with your fingertips. Some unevenness helps simulate grain.

8. Seal glaze with dilute shellac (p.90). Let dry, then apply two more protective coats.

1. Prepare surface for oil paints by cleaning with benzine (p.87). For water colors, use denatured alcohol.

5. Cover surface with wash coat of sealer (pp.89–90). Do not use shellac over acrylic touch-up paint.

9. To reduce surface glare, rub gently over surface with No. 4/0 steel wool (p.91). Rub with the grain.

2. Prepare touch-up paints to match the tone of each veneer inlay. Work with one shade at a time.

6. After sealer dries, lightly smooth surface with No. 280 finishing paper (p.57). Sand with grain, wipe off dust.

10. To bring up soft luster, apply paste or spray furniture wax. Wax gives surface extra protection.

3. Fill in scratches with paint. Daub off excess paint with a clean, dry paintbrush.

7. Wipe on a thin glaze of stain (p.89) to enhance colors and hide scratches. Let dry overnight.

11. Buff well with a clean, soft cloth. Apply more wax for a deeper polish and added protection.

Replacing veneer relief

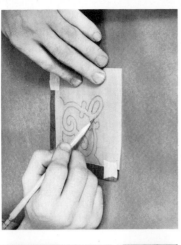

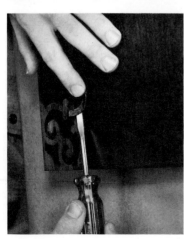

1. Peel off and discard the old relief. It can be replaced with new veneer or built-up coats of paint.

2. Remove glue from imprint left by pattern with No. 280 sandpaper. Sand only within boundaries of design.

3. Make a pattern by taping a piece of tracing paper over imprint and carefully tracing its outline.

4. Tape tracing, penciled side down, on back of new veneer bought from supply store. Retrace outline.

5. Cut veneer precisely on the outline with a sharp utility knife. Hold work down firmly while cutting.

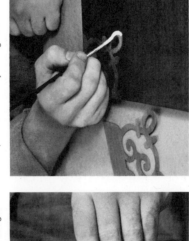

6. Gently smooth the edges of the veneer cutout with No. 280 sandpaper.

7. Brush a thin coat of white glue over old imprint. Do not overlap outline. Let glue dry.

8. Apply fresh glue over imprint. Position veneer and fix in place with masking tape. Let it dry overnight.

9. When glue has dried, turn surface over; carefully trim edges of veneer cutout flush with corner.

10. Stain veneer. When dry, seal it and glaze entire surface (p.89). Apply a protective coat of lacquer.

Sand each coat, when dry, with No. 500 paper. Seal (p.89) and apply topcoat to the entire surface.

If you prefer, fill in imprint (Step 2) with coats of acrylic paint, which build up to simulate relief.

Refinishing

Painted furniture

Enamel paint is the traditional material for producing a colored opaque finish on wood. Strictly defined, an enamel is a varnish to which pigment has been added. In recent years, the conventional enamels have been largely displaced by modern, versatile synthetic resin paints—notably, the alkyd enamels and polyurethane. These have a much shorter drying time, making them less subject to dust contamination than the older formulas. Polyurethane produces one of the most durable finishes of all paints.

Enamels are generally available in gloss, satin, and flat finishes. Gloss is the most durable. If you prefer a duller finish but do not want to sacrifice durability, you can apply a gloss finish and rub it to the exact satin or flat appearance desired (see *Rubbing*, p.91).

Latex enamels and lacquers: Today, the term "enamel" is broadly applied to include certain latex paints and colored lacquers. Latex enamels cannot offer the high gloss of the other enamel paints, but are suitable for use on wood furniture. Although water-based paint will raise the grain of unsealed wood, this minor roughening will be concealed by the thickness of the latex film, providing the paint is not overdiluted. Lacquer enamels are best applied by spraying. Most aerosol enamels are lacquer based. Never apply a lacquer enamel directly over varnish, oil stain, or a nonlacquer paint; lacquer acts as a solvent, and will dissolve them. Protect these materials or any unidentified finish with a sealer coat of shellac (see *Sealers*, p.89).

Primer coats: For the highest quality enamel finish, use an initial wood primer. Enamel wood primers are specially formulated to provide the best surface for the enamel to adhere to. On unfinished wood and wickerwork, a primer is particularly beneficial. It quenches the absorbency of the bare surface, reducing the required number of finishing coats. A

good primer also allows you to apply a heavier topcoat with less danger of developing runs or sags. Primers are usually light in color and could, if the enamel becomes damaged, show through the finish. For this reason, it is worthwhile to tint a primer to the color of the enamel. Be sure to use pigments compatible with the primer.

Do not haphazardly combine primers and topcoats; it is best to use only a primer recommended by the manufacturer of your enamel. For small projects, it may be more convenient to use a thinned coat of the enamel as a primer.

The surface: Careful preparation of the surface is fundamentally important to the success of a painted finish: the surface must be smooth, clean, and dust free (see *Stripping*, p.88). Slight imperfections, which in a clear finish might enhance the natural appearance of the wood, will show up conspicuously under enamel. Scratches, nail holes, and other surface blemishes should be eliminated (see *Preparing the surface*, p.58). Before painting over an old finish, be sure the paint will adhere well. Sand finished surfaces lightly with No. 280 sandpaper (see p.57) to assure adhesion of the enamel.

Preparing to paint: Enamel must be thoroughly mixed to distribute the pigment evenly throughout the paint. Stir it smoothly; do not shake or churn it. Do not allow the paint store to mix your enamel on its paint shaker. Agitation fills the paint with tiny air bubbles, which are harmful to the quality of the final job.

Before starting to paint a piece of furniture, remove easily detachable parts like drawers, doors, and hardware; paint them separately. Mask off any areas that are not to be painted.

First coat: The technique for applying enamels is essentially the same as that for applying varnish (see *Varnishes*, p.90). Begin by painting the hard-to-reach and least visible sections; do the underside of

a piece of furniture first, then the back and sides. Paint the top last. Do not brush lengthwise on narrow cylindrical sections, such as legs; brush with curves.

Aerosol paints are better suited for small projects. Comparatively thin, they perform best when the finish is built up with several light undercoats. Always shake the can well before each application. When spraying, keep the nozzle at a fixed distance from the work (about 12 inches). Sweep back and forth parallel to the surface with smooth, even motions. Swinging the can in an arc causes uneven accumulation, producing sags and runs.

Subsequent coats: Follow manufacturer's instructions regarding the time to wait between coats and the drying time for the final coat. Applying a coat of enamel before the preceding coat has sufficiently cured seriously jeopardizes the appearance, durability, and life span of the finish. Before applying a new coat always smooth the enamel of the preceding coat lightly with No. 280 sandpaper to insure optimum adhesion for the next coat and to reduce blemishes. For a durable, attractive finish and for a finish that is to be rubbed, apply at least one coat of primer and two coats of enamel.

Paintbrushes

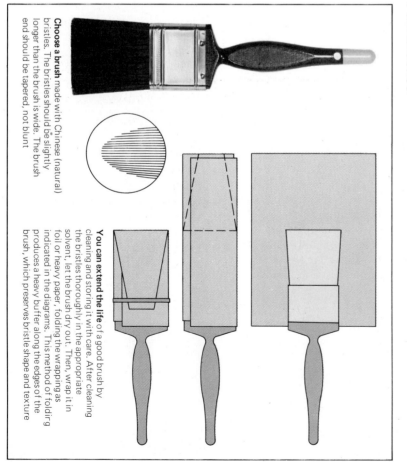

Choose a brush made with Chinese (natural) bristles. The bristles should be slightly longer than the brush is wide. The brush end should be tapered, not blunt

You can extend the life of a good brush by cleaning and storing it with care. After cleaning the bristles thoroughly in the appropriate solvent, let the brush dry out. Then, wrap it in foil or heavy paper, folding the wrapping as indicated in the diagrams. This method of folding produces a heavy buffer along the edges of the brush, which preserves bristle shape and texture

Repairing wicker before spray-painting

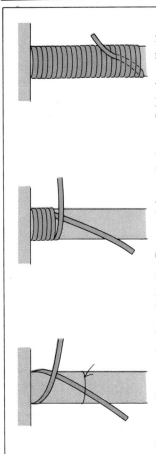

To repair rattan wrapping: Strip off old rattan. Tie one end of new rattan temporarily into place with string; start wrapping other end. Remove string once wrapping holds first end in place. To complete wrapping, tuck second end up through last few rows of wrapping; pull end tight; trim. Secure end with tack. (For pliability, rattan and wicker are woven wet; refer to *Reseating*, pp. 72–79.)

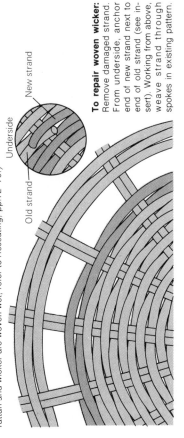

Underside

New strand

Old strand

To repair woven wicker: Remove damaged strand. From underside, anchor end of new strand next to end of old strand (see insert). Working from above, weave strand through spokes in existing pattern.

Classic antique finish

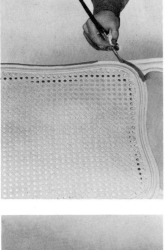

1. A cane chair can be given an antique finish using casein paint. Apply base coat of light pastel color, second of darker shade. Let each coat dry 24 hours.

2. Accent all carved areas and scroll work with a stripe in a third shade. Work freehand, do not be overly concerned about maintaining a clean line.

3. Using a fine sandpaper (see p. 57), sand the frame lightly to make the wood appear worn. Start at an inconspicuous place and follow the line of the frame.

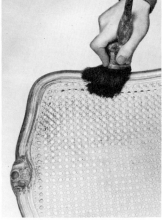

4. Pour dry pigment (and a little powdered rottenstone, if available from your hardware store) onto palette. Dab brush in paste wax, then collect pigment on bristles.

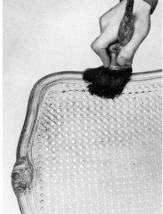

5. Lightly whisk tinted wax over wood and cane. Apply to achieve antique look, according to your taste. Again, follow the line of the frame.

6. With clean, lint-free cloth, rub the wax into the chair and wipe away any excess. Then, buff as you would with ordinary furniture polish.

Painting wicker

Aerosol plastic resin enamel is the best type of paint for wicker. Make a screen (left) to confine spray. Prime the unfinished wicker with a light coat. Spray inside surfaces first, then sides and top. Hold spray can about 12 in. away from work. Apply several more light coats; allow each coat to dry thoroughly.

Reupholstering

Anyone who is willing to work patiently can learn the techniques used by master upholsterers and apply them to reupholster furniture in his home. This section first describes the basic parts of upholstery and then the best techniques for such tasks as estimating the amount of fabric needed for a job, stretching webbing, tying springs, and fitting the cover. These techniques, in turn, are shown as they should be applied, in step by step sequences that illustrate various upholstery repairs.

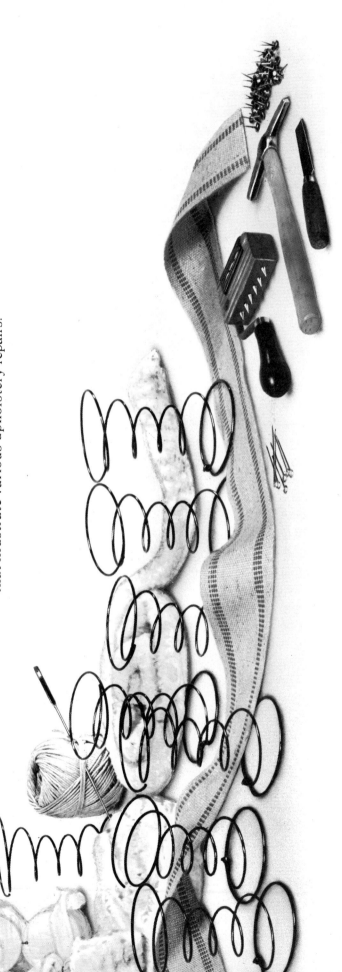

Basics of reupholstery

Materials and techniques

There are three basic types of upholstered furniture: furniture with pad seats, furniture with spring seats, and overstuffed furniture. Pad seats consist of a firm base (either solid or webbed) and a cushion. Spring seats employ a foundation of webbing, which is tacked to the frame to support the springs; the springs are stitched or clipped to the webbing. Overstuffed furniture may have springs in both the seat and back; it may also have springs sewn into the cushions. The above features may be found in a variety of combinations.

If you are replacing only the cover, you will need muslin for the undercover, cotton batting and glazed cotton as stuffing, and a cover fabric. When doing more extensive jobs, save the old materials as you strip them from the furniture. You may be able to use them again; cover pieces will serve as patterns to cut the new pieces. Webbing, burlap, springs, stitching twine, tacks, and stuffing materials—including rubberized hair or foam, loose hair, cotton batting, and glazed cotton—are available at upholstery supply houses and many hardware stores.

A step called baste-tacking is used to temporarily hold a material to the frame. Drive the tacks in only halfway so that they can be easily removed to make adjustments. First, center the material on the frame and secure it with a tack in the middle of each rail. Baste-tack from the middle out to each corner. Once the material is correctly positioned, do the final tacking.

Basic tools

Ripping tool

Upholsterer's magnetic hammer

Regulator

Upholstery needles

Curved needles

Upholsterer's pins

In addition to the tools shown, you will need twine, scissors, chalk, and a tape measure or yardstick; a sewing machine is useful.

Webbing stretcher

Upholstery tack: Use 4-oz tack on light to mediumweight fabric; 6-oz tack on burlap and heavy fabric; 14-oz tack to anchor spring-tying twine.

Webbing tack: This special tack is barbed to provide a strong grip for securing the webbing. Use 8- to 10-oz tacks on hardwoods and fragile frames. Use 12- to 14-oz tacks on other work.

Components of upholstery

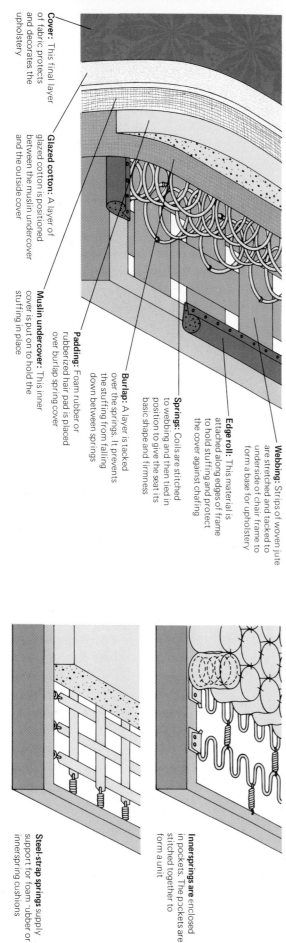

Cover: This final layer of fabric protects and decorates the upholstery

Glazed cotton: A layer of glazed cotton is positioned between the muslin undercover and the outside cover

Muslin undercover: This inner cover is put on to hold the stuffing in place

Padding: Foam rubber or rubberized hair pad is placed over burlap spring cover

Burlap: A layer is tacked over the springs. It prevents the stuffing from falling down between springs

Springs: Coils are stitched to webbing and then tied in position to give the seat its basic shape and firmness

Edge roll: This material is attached along edges of frame to hold stuffing and protect the cover against chafing

Webbing: Strips of woven jute are stretched and tacked to underside of chair frame to form a base for upholstery

Steel-strap springs supply support for foam rubber or innerspring cushions

Innersprings are enclosed in pockets. The pockets are stitched together to form a unit

Foam rubber

Foam rubber is sold in flat sheets and in molded slabs. Both may contain cavities, or cores, which allow air to escape when the foam is compressed. Prefabricated molded foam is the basic material in modern foam furniture.

You can replace worn or damaged foam cushions and seats. When replacing old foam, discuss your requirements with your supplier. Have the foam cut with an extra quarter inch all the way around the seat; foam should be slightly compressed by its cover.

If you have to cut the foam yourself, you will be forced to deal with characteristics of the material that make cutting it difficult. Foam tends to move around, bulge, or compress as it is cut. It also sticks to tools.

Cut foam more than 2 inches thick with an electric carving knife or a bandsaw. If you have neither, use a sharp serrated carving knife, a single-edged razor blade, or well-sharpened scissors. Wet the cutting edge with water and work it back and forth along the line of the cut, penetrating no more than about an inch at a time.

Slab foam can be glued directly to wood, metal, or another piece of foam, using rubber cement (see *Adhesives*, pp.10–13). Molded foam should be attached using a combination of rubber cement and cloth strips—or tacking tape, available from foam suppliers and at hardware stores.

When mounting foam over springs, place cotton wadding over the burlap spring cover.

Fixed pad seat

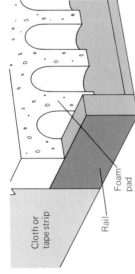

Cloth or tape strip

Foam pad

Rail

Many dining-table chairs have square-edged pad seats of foam mounted on a box base. Cut new foam slightly larger than old pad and to fit edge of frame. Use rubber cement to glue strips of cloth or tacking tape both to the foam and the frame on all sides, as shown. Fold tape under frame and tack to bottom of rail.

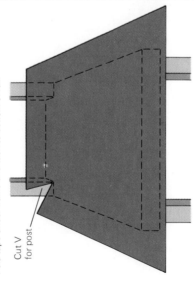

Cut V for post

To fit the cover, measure the dimensions of the top of the seat and the depth of the side rails and foam, allowing an extra inch all around for tacking. Cut V's for corner posts and tuck excess fabric between posts and seat (see p.113).

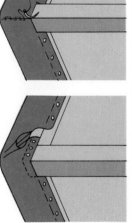

Turn under the raw edge and tack the fabric to the bottom of the rail, keeping the cover taut and smooth. Form pleats at the legs as shown, and hand-stitch the folds neatly.

Stripping the upholstery

A worn cover does not always mean that the upholstery should be stripped to the frame and replaced in its entirety. A well-made foundation on spring seats and overstuffed upholstery will often outlast two to three covers.

You can repair sagging webbing simply by turning the chair upside down, removing the cambric dust cover, and stretching and tacking a new layer of webbing over the old. If a spring comes loose, you may be able to tie it back into place, stripping only the webbing and leaving the padding untouched.

For major repairs, however, all the old upholstery may have to be removed. Position the furniture on a workbench or a pair of saw horses at a comfortable working height. Begin by removing the cambric dust cover and skirt from the underside of the frame. Remove any tacks that will interfere with your work; use a mallet and tack ripper, or pliers, working along the grain to prevent splitting.

Make a sketch of the chair or couch. As you strip each part of the cover, note the rails to which it was attached. Also make notes on how the cover was fitted around posts and corners, and where and how the various cover pieces were joined to one another. Your notes will be a reminder of the order in which you stripped the upholstery; you will reverse this order in recovering the furniture.

Simple repairs to foam rubber seats are covered at left; full-scale reupholstering jobs, on the pages that follow.

Removable pad seat

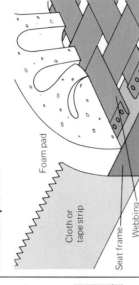

Foam pad

Cloth or tape strip

Seat frame

Webbing

Other dining-table chairs have removable padded seats. The foam is attached to its own frame and may be supported by webbing. To replace the foam, detach the seat frame. Cement cloth strips or tacking tape to the new foam and the seat frame; if curved edges are desired, tape the foam down along the edges, as shown.

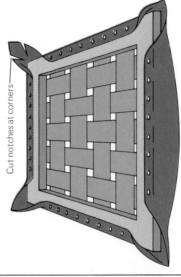

Cut notches at corners

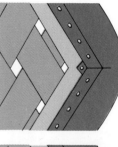

Measure and cut the cover fabric, allowing an extra inch all around for tacking. Fold the raw edges of the fabric under and tack them to the underside of the seat frame, working out from the center on each side. Keep the cover taut, but leave the corners free.

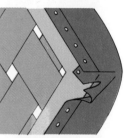

Cut corner notches in the cover fabric as above. Fold under the excess fabric and tack it into place on the seat frame. Attach the covered seat to the chair frame.

Spring seats and padded backs

Basic operations

The seat rests on a foundation of webbing. Webbing is sold by the grade. Use a strong grade on the seat and stretch it taut enough to support the springs without sagging, but not enough to twist or overstress the frame.

Space the webbing so that most of the springs rest on crossovers. Sew the springs to the webbing with stitching twine and tie them with No. 60 six-ply tying twine. Cover the springs with burlap, sew the burlap to the springs, and tack felt edge roll around the frame. Cover the stuffing with a muslin undercover. This will allow you to adjust the seat's shape before attaching the cover.

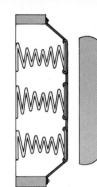

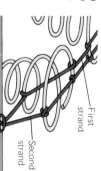

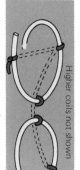

Tacking on edge roll: Drive small tacks (1) through seam to position edge roll on frame. Add larger tacks (2) to hold upright.

Tying springs: Twine used to tie springs is tacked to chair frame as shown.

On the outside springs, tie both the top coil and the next coil down with the first strand of twine. Use loops when tying the first strand. Loops permit you to make adjustments before you firmly secure all the top coils with the second strand of twine.

First strand / Second strand

Shaping the seat: If seat has cushion, tie springs so that their top coils form a flat surface. If seat does not have cushion, tie springs to form a round contour.

Use a clove hitch to tie top coils of all springs with second strand of twine.

Stitching springs to webbing: Secure cord to webbing where first spring will be attached. Tie slip knot. Stitch down through webbing, back up through loop in knot.

Webbing

Higher coils not shown

Sew spring at three points. Draw stitch up through webbing, around bottom coil of spring, and back down through webbing. Draw cord under at point nearest next spring. Finish spring at point nearest next spring.

Stripping and reupholstering the chair

1. After freeing webbing from underside of seat, strip cover, muslin, burlap, and edge roll. Use ripping tool (p.106) to pry out tacks. Note positions of springs, padding, and other materials as you work.

2. Strip the chair down to its frame. Discard all the old stuffing material—except the springs and hair padding, if usable. Turn the chair upside down and tack on new webbing, as shown in the next four steps.

3. Pull webbing off end of roll, tack to underside of rail with five No. 12 tacks. Double end over to prevent tack heads from tearing webbing when chair is in use. Stagger tacks to avoid splitting frame.

4. Brace webbing stretcher against frame at 45° angle. Hook webbing onto stretcher and pull stretcher down until it snaps into horizontal position. Drive in four tacks to hold webbing to frame.

5. Release stretcher and cut webbing, leaving 2 in. excess. Fold webbing over, secure with five tacks. Leave ½ in. of wood around outside to keep webbing from showing and to provide space for tacking dust cover.

6. Interweave webbing, spacing bands evenly and placing them so that springs will rest where bands cross. Bands should be stretched equally and as tautly as possible without straining the webbing or frame.

7. Turn chair right side up. Position all the springs to establish spacing; begin by sewing a rear corner spring to the webbing. Place springs with their sharp sides to the webbing to prevent punctures in the burlap.

8. Finish sewing each spring at point nearest to the next spring. Once all the springs are sewn to the webbing, finish off last stitch with a half hitch or overhand knot underneath the webbing.

9. A common problem is loose springs caused by broken twine. Tie off first and third stitches with overhand knot to secure each spring individually; then, if twine breaks, only one spring will come loose.

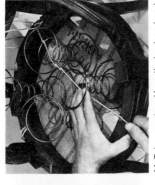

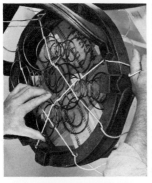

10. Start pair of tacks in line with each row of springs all around frame. Cut pieces of twine three times the distance across frame, double them, and tie off to tacks on back and one side rail (see diagrams).

11. Take one strand from the back and work toward the front of the seat. On springs near the front of the seat, loop strand around the edges of the seat, loop strand around the second coil from the top before looping it around the top coil.

12. After tying the springs with one strand reaching from back of seat to front, tie them in the same way with strand reaching from side to side. Adjust twine so that springs form desired contour (see diagrams).

13. Repeat above steps with second strands, but tie top coils only, using a clove hitch. The first strand positions the springs; the second secures them. Tie off extra twine as shown; hammer tacks down.

14. Finish with two diagonal strands tied around each top coil as shown. At the front edge of the seat tie the extra twine around the strands (as shown in Step 13) to keep them from rubbing against the seat frame.

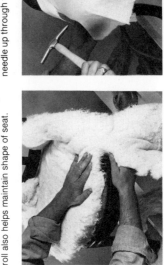

15. Cut a square of burlap 3 in. larger all around than seat. Position it over springs and secure with one tack at center of each rail. Baste-tack (p.106) the burlap snugly over springs all the way around the frame.

16. Once the cover is in position and the tension is evenly distributed, fold in the edges of the burlap and tack them down, using No. 3 tacks. Trim off all the excess material, as shown.

17. With a curved needle and stitching twine, stitch burlap to springs. As you make each stitch, loop twine around itself to form an overhand knot. Sew in the same pattern used to sew springs to webbing.

18. If top of frame is uneven, tack felt edge roll all around to equalize the height of the edge. The thickness of the edge roll can be controlled by the placement of tacks. Edge roll also helps maintain shape of seat.

19. Where more than one layer of edge roll is required, sew layers together. Secure the bottoms of stitches by doubling the twine back around each stitch and drawing the needle up through the loop to make a knot.

20. Cut a piece of rubberized hair padding to the dimensions of the seat. Set it in place and trim the front edge so that it is flush with the edge roll. Pull it down so that it is firmly nested behind the edge roll.

21. Before trimming the back edge, sew the front of the hair mat to the edge roll to hold it in place. If the piece of furniture being reupholstered is larger, cut paper pattern first, then cut stuffing using pattern.

22. Fill crevices with cotton. First, do the front edge, filling in hollows or empty spaces between edge roll and hair mat. Carefully tear and stuff the wads of cotton batting into place, as shown.

23. Cover whole seat with two layers of cotton batting. Cut batting has a hard edge, so trim by pulling excess away with hands, leaving a soft edge and a smooth surface under the cover fabric.

24. Cut undercover from unbleached cotton muslin; allow an extra 3 in. for tacking the sides. Place undercover over stuffing and hold it in place with baste tack at center of each rail. (Continued, next page.)

Spring seats and padded backs

Stripping and reupholstering the chair (continued)

25. Baste-tack muslin along edge of seat. Work from center tack outward on each side, pulling muslin to desired tension. Muslin should hold stuffing firmly, but not compress it so that seat becomes hard.

26. Baste-tack the back of the seat. Mark the spot on the fabric that touches the corner of the back post. Cut the fabric to 1 in. from the mark (see corner post diagrams, p.113).

27. After completing the cut, tuck the edges down between the post and the seat. Use a regulator or a darning needle to help adjust the fit. Continue baste-tacking the muslin, fitting it to each corner post in the chair.

28. After the muslin has been baste-tacked, do the final tacking. As you work, remove the baste tacks and maintain tension to assure a smooth contour. Adjust stuffing by working it carefully through the muslin.

29. Trim the excess muslin along the edge of the seat, pulling the material taut and away from the tacks as you cut. Be careful not to scratch the finish on the frame with the sharp tips of the scissors.

30. Tack webbing into place on back of chair, using tacks and cardboard tacking strip. Webbing should be loose enough to follow back curve but still give support. Cover workbench to protect chair's finish.

31. Cover backrest with burlap. Fold over for strength and tack to frame. Tack top and bottom, then sides, and then fill in—stretching the material to attain desired shape. Trim burlap, leaving a ¾-in. excess.

32. Baste-tack rubberized hair stuffing at top and bottom of frame, then stitch it to burlap with several stitches to hold it in place. Cut it to shape, leaving about ¼ in. around edge for cotton batting.

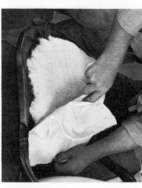

33. Lay cotton batting over the rubberized hair pad and trim and feather the edges by hand as was done for the seat. The cotton should completely cover the hair, but not project over the edge.

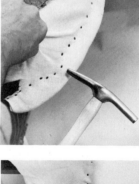

34. Cover with muslin, again emphasizing the stretch from top to bottom. Baste-tack around whole frame, using smallest tacks available. Check padding and curve, then do final tacking and trim, using razor blade.

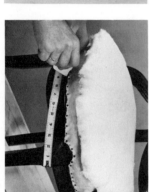

35. Baste-tack burlap over the outside of the chair back. Fold the burlap over at the edges and do final tacking through both layers. Work outward from top and bottom, as shown. Trim away the excess.

36. Measure seat and back exactly, then add 1 in. to each side for stretching and tacking allowance. Cut covering fabric in accordance with measurements. Label each piece and mark top and bottom.

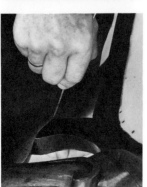

37. Lay sheet of glazed cotton over muslin on seat. Trim it back ½ in. and feather edge. Mark center of front and back rail with chalk, then mark cover fabric by folding pieces in half and cutting small notches.

38. Match notch in cover fabric to mark on chair, tack temporarily. Stretch lightly to back and tack at center. Baste-tack front, as shown, then stretch to sides and hold with tacks. Check the position of fabric.

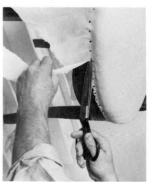

39. Mark where fabric meets rear post. Cut from edge to 1 in. from mark. Fold around post and mark where fabric meets corners, as shown. Cut slits to ½ in. from marks (see diagram, p.113). Tuck fabric in, as shown.

40. If cover fits around post properly, stretch it and tack temporarily. If it does not fit, pull it out, extend the cuts a little closer to the post, and try it again. Be patient and cut only a little at a time.

41. Next, cut around arm post on same side of chair. Mark back of fabric where it meets post, cut in to that point and make angle cuts to ½ in. from where fabric meets post corners (see diagram, p.113). Tuck in.

42. Pull fabric down between posts and baste-tack into place, as shown. Cut and tack fabric around posts on other side of chair. Once all cuts are made and fit is good, begin to stretch fabric.

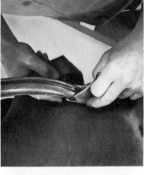

43. Do not stretch fabric so much that it compresses springs; if you do, the cover will wrinkle. Start at front center and baste-tack toward both sides. Stretch fabric front to back, never to one side.

44. Once cover is fully stretched and in position, tack it down close to edge of frame. Trim off the excess with razor blade, being careful not to slash fabric, scratch wood finish, or cut yourself.

45. After covering backrest with glazed cotton, trimmed to about ¼ in. from edge of undercover, lay cover fabric over cotton, baste-tack to center of four sides and then all around; work out from top and bottom.

46. After stretching fabric so that cover conforms to curve of back, check cover for smoothness and evenness of tension; then, tack it down well inside edge of frame and trim close with razor blade, as shown.

47. On outside of back, lay two layers of glazed cotton over burlap. Trim, as shown, to about ¼ in. from edge of burlap; then, feather edge by pulling away tufts so that cover fabric will slope smoothly to frame.

48. Lay cover fabric over cotton and baste-tack at center of each side. Check nap to see that it runs from top to bottom, then baste-tack all around, stretching cover evenly in all directions. Tack down and trim.

49. Cut cambric dust cover to go over webbing on underside of chair. Cut it 2 in. larger than frame. Attach at center of each side. Cut to shape, leaving 1-in. overlap all around. Tuck under overlap and tack down.

50. Gimp is the decorative braid used to conceal the tacks around the edges of the cover. It can either match or accent the cover. Attach it with fancy-headed tacks, as shown, or glue, as in Steps 51–53.

51. After placing glue on end of gimp and baste-tacking it next to back leg, apply glue thinly along several inches and press into place. Baste-tack with large tacks, and continue. Remove tacks after glue dries.

52. To form curve, apply glue to gimp and hold it down at point of curve with pin. Pivot gimp around pin as shown and tap it lightly with a hammer to set it in place. Baste-tack at point of curve.

53. Continue gluing gimp around seat. Where ends meet, trim to fit. Baste-tack ends in place. Use pin, as shown, to push in any frayed threads. Remove tacks when glue dries. Apply gimp wherever needed.

54. Once the gimp is applied, the chair is finished. Before bringing it into your living room, go over it with a brush and vacuum cleaner and touch up the woodwork (see *Refinishing*, pp.87–103).

Cutting the cover

The pattern

To determine how much cover fabric to buy, take measurements on the chair. Add on generous tacking and sewing allowances for each cover piece. To hold down the expense of the job, you may want to sew pull strips, or tacking extensions, of a less costly material around the bottoms and ends of the interior cover pieces. These parts of the fabric are tacked to the frame in such a way as to be hidden in the finished upholstery.

As you strip the old upholstered cover, save each piece to use as a pattern in cutting the new cover. Label each old cover piece "outside of arm," "backrest," "platform cover," and so on. Key the labels to a sketch of the chair; the sketch will show you exactly where each of the new pieces fits on the upholstery.

A muslin seat cover goes over the stuffing (or decking) in the seat and is stitched to the platform cover (the piece of fabric that covers the front of the seat). After the whole chair has been covered with fabric, a cambric dust cover is tacked to the bottom of the chair. The skirt (see *Pleated skirts*, p.117) is the last piece attached to the chair.

Old cover pieces serve as patterns for new covers. Margin is seaming allowance.

Welting

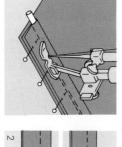

Strips to be used for welting are cut on the bias, at a 45° angle across the fabric.

Welts conceal and reinforce seams. Cut fabric strips 2 in. wide, on the bias. Seam the strips together into one long piece; press the seams open. For single welt, place cord 5/32 in. in diameter in center of strip. Fold one edge over cord. Machine-stitch close to cord with zipper foot attachment. For double welt, strip should be 2½ in. wide. Fold strip over one cord; stitch closed. Wrap other edge around second cord; stitch between two cords.

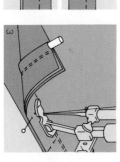

Stitching welting to fabric: 1. Pin welting to the fabric, aligning it with the seam line. Sew the welting to the fabric, stitching close to cord. **2.** Where the ends of the welting meet, remove a few stitches if necessary and cut the cord to butt. Trim the fabric to half an inch and fold under the edge; then, stitch the ends together. **3.** When

Laying out the cover

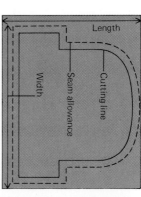

To avoid mismatched patterns and big waste pieces, make a plan of the cover before you begin cutting your material. Use either a very large sheet of brown paper, sketching in the cover pieces at their actual sizes, or draw the plan to scale on graph paper. Begin by stripping off the old cover pieces and measuring them. Check these sizes with a tape measure against chair.

Draw each piece, including tacking and seam allowances, on the paper. Begin with the largest pieces and fit the others—including parts to be used for the skirt and the welting—around them.

Lay out the pieces inside rectangles encompassing their longest and broadest dimensions, as shown here. You can reduce the handling allowances by substituting pull strips and tacking extensions of less expensive fabric, as described in the text. Transfer the final layout onto the right side of the fabric, using a straightedge and tailor's chalk. Mark the top; label each piece of fabric on the back. Cut out the pieces, and do any required trimming or pleating as you attach them to the chair.

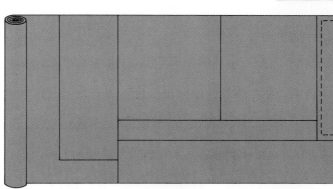

Cushions

Covering a cushion: Cushion's top and bottom cover pieces are cut separately; side panels, called the boxing, are cut as one long strip of material. **1.** Sew welting around cover pieces; then, with fabric turned wrong side out, seam boxing to bottom cover. **2.** Seam top piece, but leave a flap. Turn fabric right side out and insert foam or innersprings wrapped in cotton batting. **3.** Pin flap and blind-stitch it closed.

sewing welting between two cover pieces, first attach the welting to one piece as in Step 1; then, seam both pieces together so that the seaming allowances are hidden on the wrong side of the fabric. When working at corners or curves, make snips in the seam allowance so that the welting will be able to bend.

Attaching the cover

Preparing cover pieces

The cover pieces are usually attached in the following order: first, the seat; second, the inside of the arms and the wings; third, the inside of the back; fourth, the outside of the arms and the wings; and, finally, the outside of the back. To align patterned cover pieces, mark the center of each rail with chalk or a pencil.

Notch the edge of each cover piece at the center. Line up the notch with the mark on the rail. Match the pattern of the cushion to the inside back.

Cutting the cover to fit posts

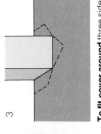

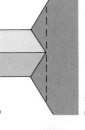

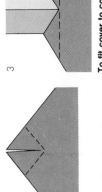

To fit cover to corner of post, cut fabric and fold under along lines shown in Step 1. The fold is seen in Step 2. Slide cover into place, Step 3, and make adjustments in folds.

To fit cover around three sides of post, make cuts and fold under flaps as shown in Steps 1 and 2. Slide the cover into place around the post, Step 3, and adjust folds.

Blind-tacking the cover piece

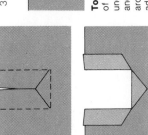

Blind-tacking is a simple means of attaching cover fabric so that unsightly tack heads do not show. **1.** Place the edge of the fabric wrong side out along the rail to which it is to be attached. Baste-tack the piece of fabric into place. **2.** Position a cardboard tacking strip above the baste tacks; tack along the top edge of the strip. **3.** When you pull the attached fabric back into the correct position—right side out—the tacks will be hidden. As an alternative to blind-tacking, tack heads can be concealed by adding welting or gimp. Or you can use tacks with decorative heads.

Fitting the platform cover

Pleats are sewn in the platform cover to fit the front corners of the seat. Begin by centering the cover on the front of the seat (see text), and baste-tack the lower edge to the frame. **1.** Working at one corner, pin the excess fabric into large pleats; then, cut away the excess, leaving a ⅝-in. seam allowance. **2.** Remove the cover and pins. Fold the cover exactly in half and cut matching notches for the other corner. Pin darts in the seam allowance and machinestitch with heavy thread.

Covering a wing chair

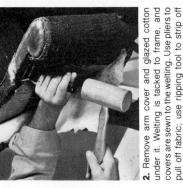

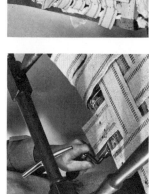

1. Before stripping off the old upholstery, decide on any design changes. Take apart the cushion first, using a razor blade to slit the seams. Save top piece to use as a pattern in cutting a new cushion cover.

2. Remove arm cover and glazed cotton under it. Welting is tacked to frame, and covers are sewn to the welting. Use pliers to pull off fabric; use ripping tool to strip off welting, as shown. Save cover for pattern.

3. Strip cover and burlap from back of chair to expose inner frame. Pull the inside back cover off the rail, then free seat cover, as shown. Pull out any tacks that protrude from the frame.

4. Remove burlap and tacks from arms. Cut front edge of seat cover free from burlap spring cover, as shown. Save seat cover as pattern to cut new cover (Step 9). Remove old cotton and foam padding from seat.

5. If webbing on bottom of chair is intact and springs are firm, instead of replacing these elements (as seen on pp.108–109), simply add another layer of webbing to provide extra support.

6. When webbing supporting back is in poor condition, place layers of cotton and hair padding over it. Stretch new webbing over padding. Trim to edge of frame, as shown. (Continued, next page.)

113

Attaching the cover

Covering a wing chair (continued)

7. Lay the platform cover over the front of the chair. To assure a proper fit, line up the center notch in the fabric (see text, p. 113) with the pencil mark on the center of the rail, as shown.

17. Pull fabric down between arm and seat. Baste-tack to bottom rail (not visible here); cover should conform smoothly to shape of arm. Cut material at angle, then cut notches as shown to fit front of arm.

12. Tacking at legs cannot be done under the rail. Carefully tack the platform cover around top of front legs. As shown here, use a single-edged razor blade to trim off excess close to tacks.

8. Fit the platform cover to front corners. This step requires careful pleating of excess material. Refer to the diagrams on p. 113. Use scissors to make cuts along the folded edges, as seen here.

13. Cover the cotton batting on the seat with a layer of glazed cotton. Push seat cover under back and arms as seen here; pull it all the way through and tack to bottom rail as seen in next photo.

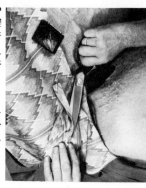

9. Remove the fitted platform cover and machine-stitch it to a new seat cover. Place new cotton batting over burlap spring cover. Then, hand-stitch the joined pieces to the burlap through the seam allowance.

Seat cover folded forward over platform cover

18. Make as many small cuts as necessary to fit the fabric between the front of the arm and the platform. Pull the fabric down between the arm and the leg, then baste-tack the arm cover to the bottom rail.

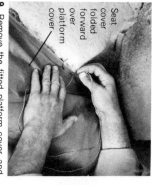

14. Cut seat cover around side posts and pull fabric through. Before baste-tacking, fold under loose edges. Tack through fold to protect fabric against tearing. When seat cover is fully fitted, do final tacking.

19. Continue baste-tacking up behind arm post, but do not stretch fabric too taut or pull marks will show. Tack fabric to top of arm. If it wrinkles at top, stuff a little cotton under it to fill it out.

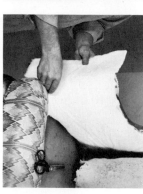

10. Fold back attached platform fabric and cover the platform with glazed cotton. Trim lower edge of cotton ½ in. above edge of frame and feather it by pulling off small tufts with your hand.

15. Lay glazed cotton along inside of arm. Wadding tears easily in one direction but not the other. Place so that you can trim longest edge by tearing. Leave 1-in. overlap at frame. Feather edge cut with scissors.

20. Cut fabric to fit around back posts so that one section goes under the arm and the other under the back. Pull fabric down under arm and back, and baste-tack to the bottom rail of the frame, as in Step 14.

16. Position the inside arm cover and baste-tack it into place. Be sure the stripes in the fabric pattern run vertically. When covering the second arm, carefully match the pattern to that of the first.

11. Pull the platform cover down over the cotton and baste-tack it to the frame. Check centering and smoothness of cover; then, do final tacking underneath the front rail, removing the baste tacks as you work.

21. Working up from bottom, stuff arm cover between wing and back, using a blunt, narrow instrument to push fabric. Then, pull fabric through from back. Adjust the cover so that the pattern is vertical.

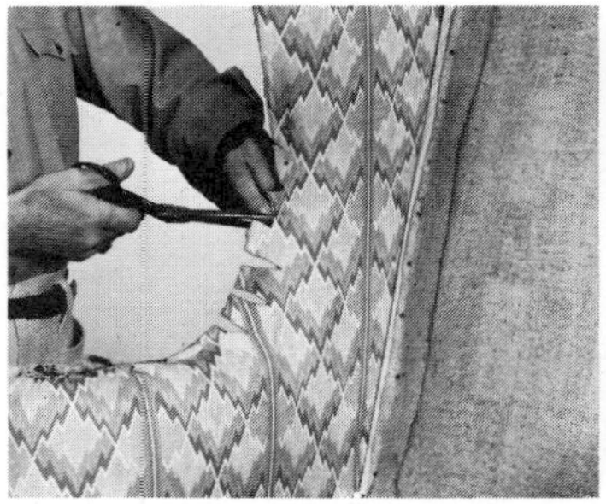

22. Make cuts into the fabric from outside of the arm to fit the cover smoothly over the curve in the wing as shown. Baste-tack in place, recutting and moving tacks to eliminate folds and wrinkles.

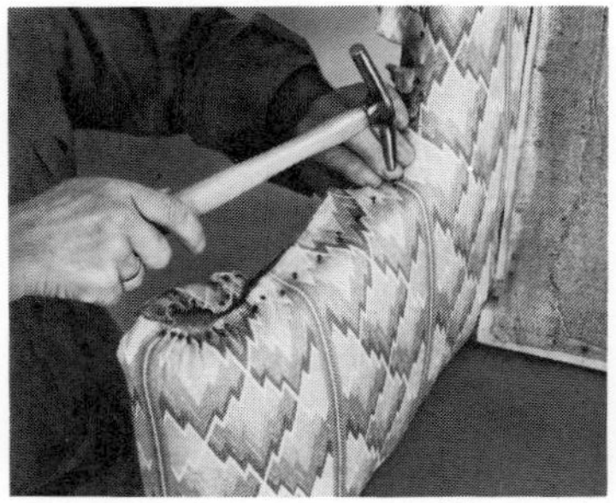

23. Baste-tack the arm cover all the way to the top of the wing, making pleats where necessary to take up excess material. As you work, cut and fit fabric around the top corner of the frame.

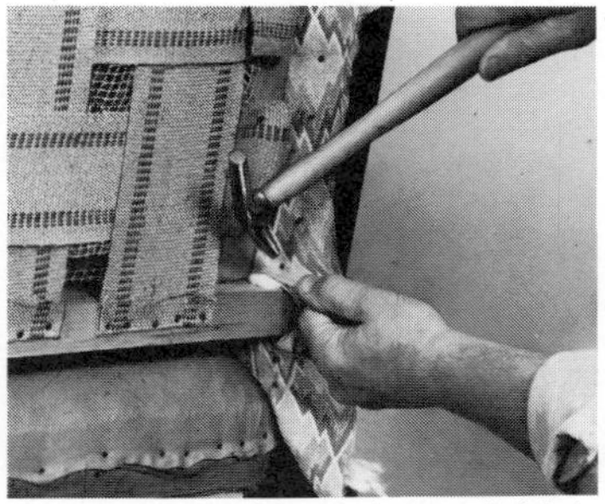

24. At the back of the chair, stretch fabric and baste-tack it to inside of frame. Recheck position of cover on wing to be sure pattern has not been distorted, then tack it down. Trim off excess material.

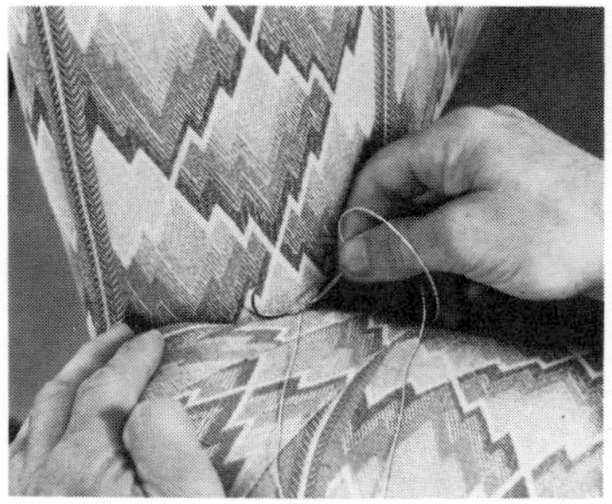

25. At front of arm, use a curved needle and light twine to stitch arm cover to platform cover around inside of arm post. Stitching insures that the rough edge will not be pulled out by a person sitting in the chair.

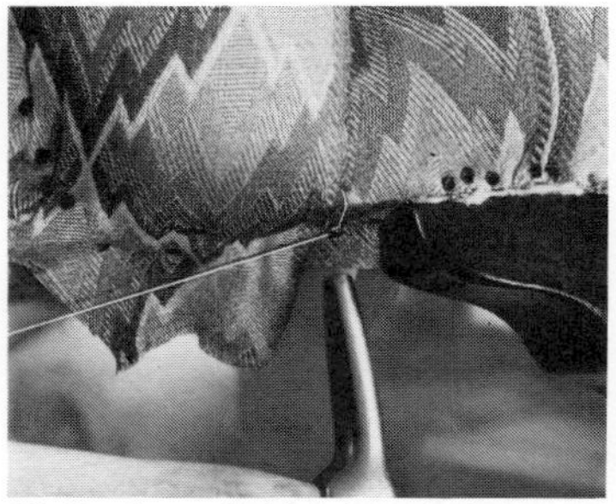

26. Continue stitching down to bottom of front arm post. To secure stitching, drive a tack part way into bottom of frame, wrap the twine around the tack and drive it in. Cut off end. Repeat Steps 15–26 on other arm.

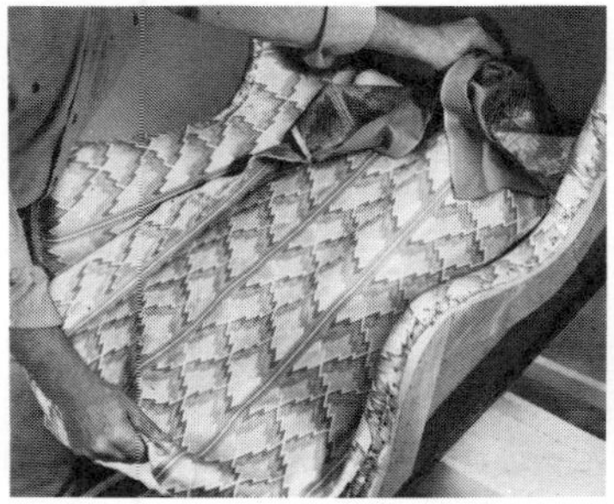

27. Cover the worn top of the chair back with cotton batting. Lay glazed cotton over the backrest and stuff it between the seat and the arms. Cut inside back cover to the old pattern and center it as shown.

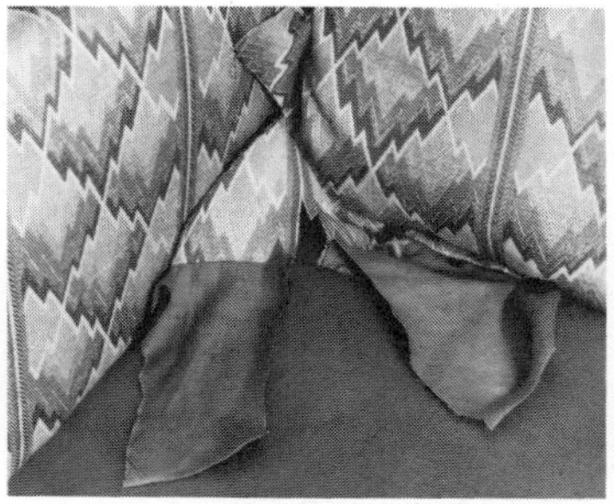

28. Cut fabric to fit around corner post at back of seat, as done with arm cover (Step 20). Note muslin extension sewn to cover. One muslin flap goes under back to rear rail; other goes under arm to side rail.

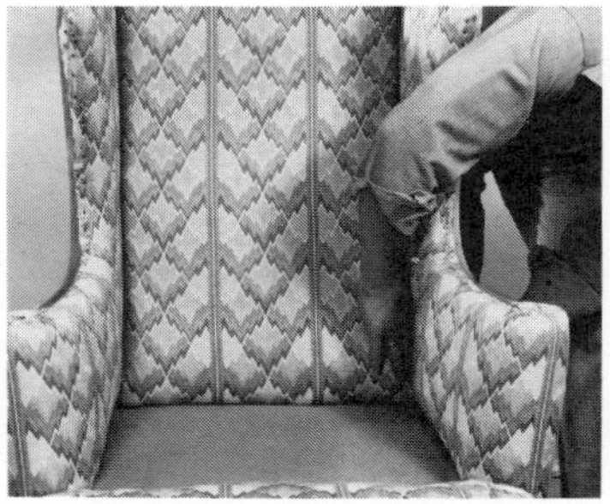

29. Push the cover fabric through on all sides, cutting it to pass around connections in the frame. Pull it through from the back and tack it temporarily to outer frame rail. Take care not to pull pattern out of line.

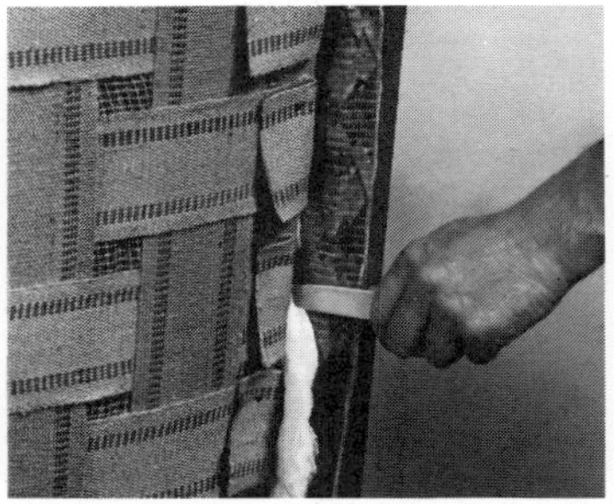

30. Stuff strips of glazed cotton into the back to fill out the edges of the padding that was added in Step 6. Close the crease where the back meets the wing. Use a thin slat or a similar tool, as shown.

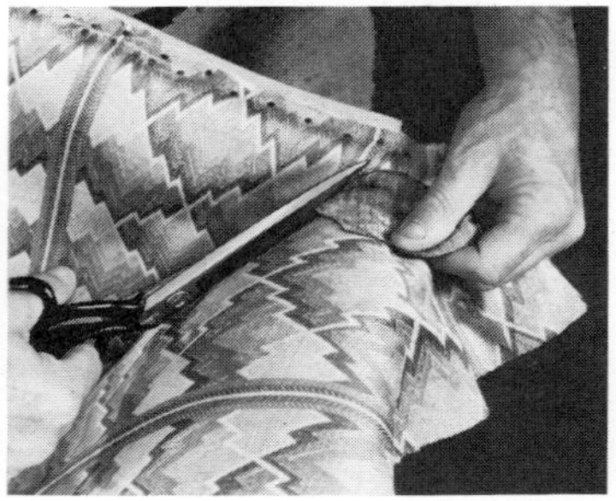

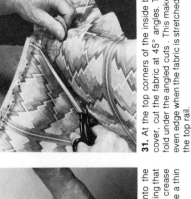

31. At the top corners of the inside back cover, cut the fabric at 45° angles. Then, fold under the angled cuts . This makes an even edge when the fabric is stretched over the top rail.

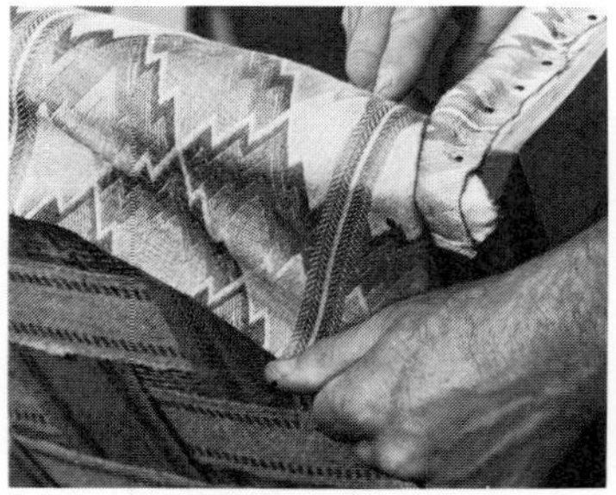

32. At each top corner, fold angled cuts, stretch the fabric over the top rail, and tack temporarily. Stretch and baste-tack the rest of the cover to the top of the frame, starting at center.

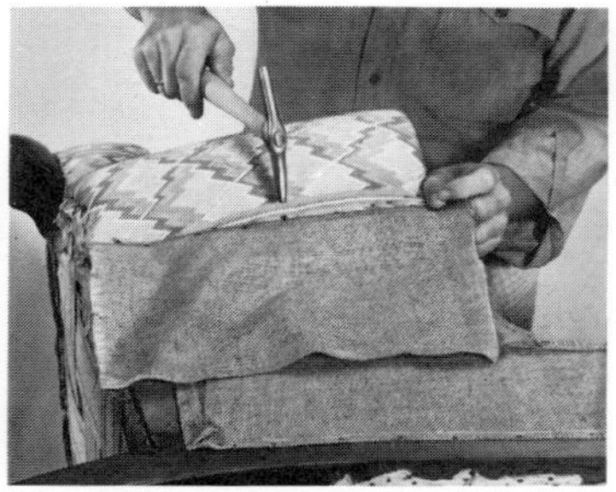

33. Cover the outside of arm with burlap pieces. Save material by using scraps to cover individual sections. Fold burlap over before tacking down, so that tack heads will not tear fabric. Stretch well and trim neatly.

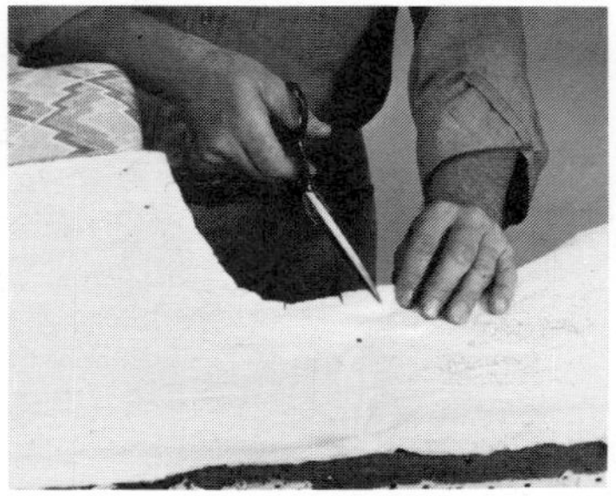

34. After burlap is tacked into place, lay glazed cotton over outside of arm. Hold in place with a few tacks. Trim so that it overlaps the arm, making small cuts along concave curve so that cotton will lie flush.

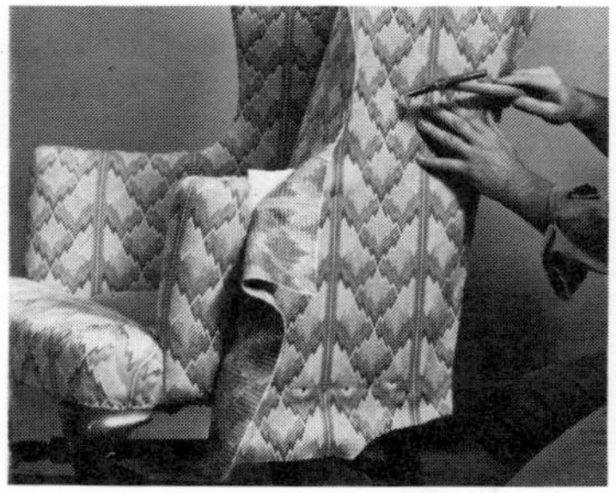

35. Position outside arm cover so that stripes are vertical and pattern matched inside. Hold with a few baste tacks. Stand chair upright to work on it and add baste tacks to top of arm, back, and bottom.

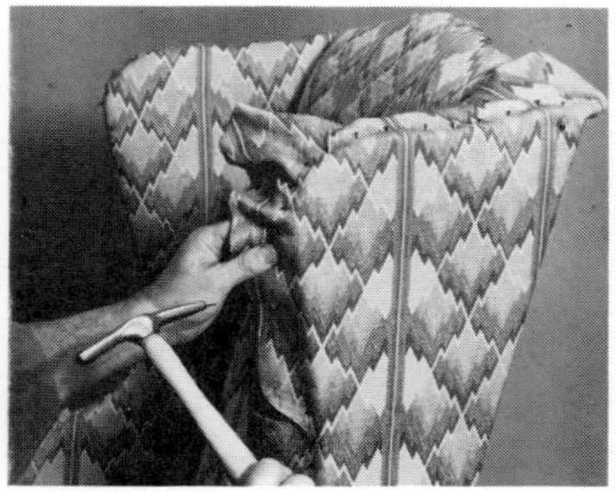

36. As you continue tacking, make cuts into fabric along inside curve of wing so that fabric will lie smoothly over wing. Work up over top of wing, smoothing out folds. Make pleats if necessary.

Attaching the cover

Covering a wing chair (continued)

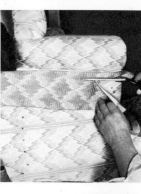

37. Tack cardboard strip along line where covers will be sewn together on outside of arm. (Strip is hidden here.) Mark where cover meets front of tacking strip, and trim it as shown, allowing about ¾ in. for seam.

38. Fold seam allowance under and baste-tack outside arm cover into place. Stitch the back of frame. Cut flaps at rear legs, as you sew, make any minor adjustments needed to line up the patterns in the two pieces.

39. Begin final tacking. Start at top of wing; work down arm, then do bottom rail and back of frame. Cut flaps at rear legs, as shown, and tuck flaps under. Finally, trim off all excess fabric.

40. Lay a strip of fabric over top of arm, with welting along edges. Fold a long strip of glazed cotton in half, tack to arm. Trim as shown and tack on another double layer. Border runs along edge of arm.

41. Remove border piece. Cut it and sew welting along edges. Fold a long strip of glazed cotton in half, tack to arm. Trim as shown and tack on another double layer. Feather edges, cover tacks with tufts.

42. Pin border with attached welting (p. 112) onto arm. Stick pins through welt and into arm beneath border. Stitch welt to arm cover, starting at one side of post and working around it and upward.

43. Inside back and arm covers have been pulled through frame and tacked down; therefore, back webbing (attached in Step 6) can be tacked to main frame. Trim away excess webbing, as shown.

44. Cover outside of back with burlap. Fold edge of burlap over before tacking down. Lay sheet of glazed cotton over burlap, as shown. Trim to size, slightly overlapping the edge of the frame. Tack in place.

45. Align the outside back cover pattern with that of the inside back and mark the outside edge for welting. Trim the cover and sew on the welting (p. 112). Pin the cover to the back of the chair, as shown.

46. Stitch the outside back cover to the adjacent covers along the top and sides, working along the welting, as shown. Stretch the bottom and tack the fabric under the bottom rail of the frame.

47. Tack cover to within a few inches from leg, then cut fabric around leg. Cut in at an angle to about ½ in. from the point at which leg joins frame. Fold inside edge under cover, stretch, and tack underneath frame.

48. Take loose end lying against leg and trim it to ¾ in. from top of leg. Cut away welting and tuck flap under bottom edge of cover, so that it forms a straight, clean edge. Tack it down, as shown.

49. Cut square of cambric for dust cover 2 to 3 in. larger on all sides than bottom of chair. Lay it over webbing, fold edges under and baste-tack it to chair. Then, glue 6- to 8-in. sections. Remove tacks after 24 hours.

50. Start double welting at back of chair, where joint will be least conspicuous. Apply glue to end of welting, as shown, and baste-tack it to chair. Then, glue 6- to 8-in. sections. Remove tacks after 24 hours.

51. The finished chair. Note that the patterns on the covers of the platform, cushion, and back are in alignment, and that patterns on the wings run vertically. The reupholstered chair is full and firm.

Overstuffed upholstery

Tufting

Tufted covers are stitched onto overstuffed upholstery. Twine is stitched to buttons on the cover, through the stuffing, and is anchored to the webbing at the back of the chair. The stitching keeps the tufts in place, maintaining the upholstery's shape.

To strip a tufted cover, first remove all the tacks fastening it to the frame. Then, pull the buttons away from the cover and cut the twine that holds them to the chair. When you remove the cover, you will see that the undercover is also tufted. Leave the undercover in place.

The buttons on the new cover should be in the same positions they were in on the old cover.

of the cover, marking all the button positions accurately on the sketch. Mark these positions lightly with chalk on the wrong side of the new cover. You will attach the buttons one by one, starting from the center, as you put the new cover on the chair. The buttons should be covered with the same fabric you use for the cover. You can have this done at an upholstery supply store or buy a kit from a sewing center and do it yourself.

The proper method for cutting the skirt is illustrated below. Sew the pleats and attach welting (p.112) to the skirt before attaching it, by blind-stitching through the welting.

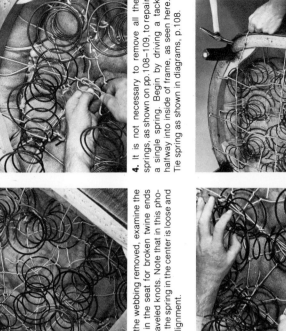

```
        X14        X9
              X7
          X6      X3   X5
      X8    X1
          X2    X10   X11   X13
              X12
                    X15        X4
```

Diagram of button positions, tufted cover.

Spread the old cover wrong side up on a table. Measure the distance between the rows of buttons and between the buttons in the rows. Write down the measurements. Then, make a sketch

Reupholstering an overstuffed chair

1. Examine seat and back to find loose springs poking through the stuffing. Remove the skirt, dust cover, and the outside arm and back covers. Save these cover pieces to use as patterns for the new cover.

2. If the springs are in good condition, you can leave the old webbing in place; merely reinforce the old webbing by stretching new webbing over top of it. Remove webbing to reach loose springs, as shown here.

3. With the webbing removed, examine the springs in the seat for broken twine ends and unraveled knots. Note that in this photograph the spring in the center is loose and out of alignment.

4. It is not necessary to remove all the springs, as shown on pp. 108–109, to repair a single spring. Begin by driving a tack halfway into inside of frame, as seen here. Tie spring as shown in diagrams, p.108.

5. For extra strength, tie the spring with a second length of twine (see p.108 and subsequent pages). Tie the spring to its neighboring coils. Pull the spring tight and tack it down on the inside of the frame.

6. On the bottom of the frame, line up a pair of tacks with each row of springs. Tie the springs together in a series, as shown. Pull the rows flush with the bottom of the frame, tack twine down. (Continued, next page.)

Pleated skirts

Open box pleat

Joined box pleat

Kick pleat

Attaching the skirt is the final step in reupholstering. Hem the bottom or work with a double layer of fabric. Kick pleats and two types of box pleats are illustrated. Kick pleats are formed at the corners of the seat; box pleats along the front, back, and sides. For kick pleats, cut a piece of fabric large enough to go around the seat, plus 6 in. for each corner. For open box pleats, cut fabric to fit 1½ times around seat; for joined box pleats, twice around seat. Then, measure, fold, pin, and sew pleats to the width you desire. Sew the welting along the top of the skirt (p.112) and press the pleats before stitching. You can also attach the skirt by blind-tacking (p.113).

Attaching the buttons

Cut enough twine to be able to pass a double length through stuffing to chair back. Slip twine through button loop; thread both ends through a large needle.

— Webbing
Cotton wadding

Pass the twine through the webbing on the chair back. Knot the twine, inserting cotton wadding to keep the knot from tearing the webbing when the chair is in use. Do not pull the knot tight until all buttons are in place and the tension of each button has been adjusted.

Overstuffed upholstery

Reupholstering an overstuffed chair (continued)

7. Attach new webbing to the bottom of the seat. Double the webbing over at one end and tack that end in place. Then, stretch the webbing at back, as shown. Then, tack the other ends (see p.108, Step 4), and trim the edges.

8. Turn chair right side up. Strip cover, padding, and burlap from front and sides of chair. Sew new burlap to edge roll at front of seat, as shown. Fold and tack burlap along bottom rail. Trim off excess material.

9. Position new hair padding along the front Tuck in the ends, cutting and pleating the material (see diagrams, p.113). Machine-stitch pleats closed, and seam platform to muslin seat cover (see p.114, Steps 8-14).

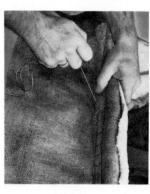

10. Center platform cover over seat front. Tuck in the ends, cutting and pleating the underneath; stitch in place. Then, fold up the platform cover and stuff front panel and a layer of glazed cotton (see p.114, Steps 8-14).

11. Pin platform cover along seam to burlap underneath. Then, fold up the platform cover and stuff front panel and a layer of glazed cotton (see p.114, Steps 3-14).

12. Pull platform cover down over stuffing and baste-tack it to underside of front rail. Use needle to mark point where fabric meets leg and cut nearly to mark, as shown. Stretch fabric around leg; baste-tack.

13. Cover seat with layer of glazed cotton, then smooth muslin seat cover over seat and pull it out under the back and sides of the chair, cutting it to fit around posts. Tack the muslin to the rails, as shown.

14. Tack several new strips of webbing tautly across back of chair. Do not use a stretcher. Cut buttons from cover of backrest and remove the cover. The new buttons will be stitched to the webbing.

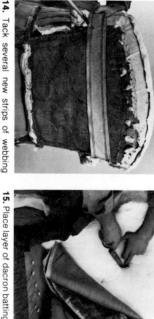

15. Place layer of dacron batting over muslin undercover of backrest. Locate original buttonholes and poke holes in batting at those points. Prepare buttons (see Attaching the buttons, p.117).

16. Attach the backrest cover by stitching buttons through cover and stuffing into webbing as described on p.117. Note that positions of buttonholes have already been marked. Start with center button.

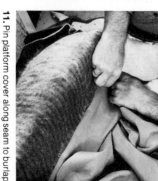

17. Keep the cover smooth as you work. Push the needle through the batting, as shown in Step 16, and out through the webbing at back, as shown here. Knot twine to the webbing as illustrated on p.117.

18. Stitch all the buttons in the middle row before proceeding to the top and bottom rows. Do not knot the button twines tightly; they will be adjusted to attain uniform tension once all are in place.

19. Use a regulator or the blunt end of a letter opener to form pleats along diagonal lines between buttons. Single pleating is sufficient for fine cover fabrics. Heavy fabrics require double pleating.

20. At the back of the chair, tie the ends of the button twines around wads of cotton (see Attaching the buttons, p.117). Adjust the tension on the twines as you do this, until the tufting is uniform on backrest.

21. If the top row of buttons lies close to the frame, tack ends of twine to back of frame instead of tying them off to webbing. Wrap twine around one tack and drive tack in. Secure with second tack.

22. Use enough additional stuffing above the top row of buttons to fill out the backrest into a rounded curve. Then, tack the cover along the frame. Stuffing will be depressed by the finished cover.

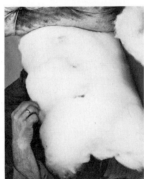

25. Remove old arm cover, leaving muslin in place. Layer with dacron batting. Add dacron between buttonholes. At each button mark on new cover, stitch a small tuck (as shown) as you thread button through.

26. Knot button twines on the outside of the arm, adding cotton wads as was done on the back of the chair. Stretch arm cover around front of arm frame, and tack it to rail, as shown. Use a regulator to form pleats.

31. Lay glazed cotton stuffing over the outside of the arm. Pull the cover down over the cotton and baste-tack the cover to the bottom and back rails. Do not do final tacking until completing Step 32.

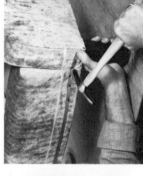

36. Prepare skirt (see *Pleated skirts*, p.117). Pin skirt along sewing line so that ends meet at a back corner. Blind-stitch in place, sewing through welting and cover. Seam at corner. For cushion, see p.112.

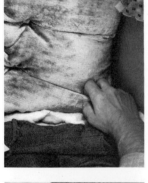

23. Stretch fabric over top of chair, using regulator to form vertical pleats directly above each button of top row. As each pleat is formed, tack fabric temporarily to back. Once cover is adjusted, tack down.

24. Tuck fabric between seat and bottom rail; cut to fit around arm rail and bottom rail. Pull the fabric through the frame at sides. Form pleats, using regulator, at bottom and sides before baste-tacking.

30. Stretch burlap over arm, holding it in place with a few tacks along frame. Fold edges over, tack securely, and trim. Blind-tack (p.113) arm cover as shown, placing tacking strip tightly against arm rest.

35. Skirt is attached ¾ in. above edge of bottom frame rail and hangs to within ½ in. of floor. Mark sewing line all the way around the chair with chalk. Secure platform cover to front rail with tacking strip.

28. Pull cover around front of arm and tack in place. Gather material into small pleats, tacking each pleat down along the underside of the armrest until cover is smoothly stretched. Trim off the excess fabric.

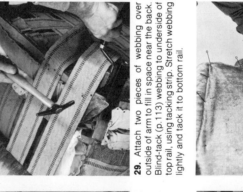

29. Attach two two pieces of webbing over outside of arm to fill in space near the back. Blind-tack (p.113) webbing to underside of top rail, using tacking strip. Stretch webbing lightly and tack it to bottom rail.

34. Baste-tack back cover in place. Pin folded edges to backrest and outside arm covers. Blind-stitch securely in place. Stretch bottom edges and tack them under frame. Tack cambric dust cover to bottom.

27. Turn chair onto its side. Pull bottom of arm cover through frame and tack it to rail. Cut off excess fabric, as shown. Note that a pull strip (see p.112) of less expensive material is sewn to the cover fabric.

33. After stretching and tacking several vertical strips of webbing over back, cover with burlap (as shown). Place the glazed cotton over the burlap, using a few tacks to hold it in position. Trim cotton flush.

32. Pin the front edge of the arm cover in place. Then, using a needle and thread, blind-stitch (p.112) the arm cover neatly to adjoining cover pieces. Do final tacking of arm cover to chair frame.

Electrical Appliances/ Repair Fundamentals

Electrical appliances are easier to fix than most people realize. No deep understanding of electrical theory is required. This section covers principles, procedures, tools, and techniques that will help you handle repair jobs calmly, confidently, and with a minimum of wasted effort. Once you become familiar with these fundamentals, you will be able to solve many problems that might otherwise lead to costly repairs or force you to buy a new appliance.

contents

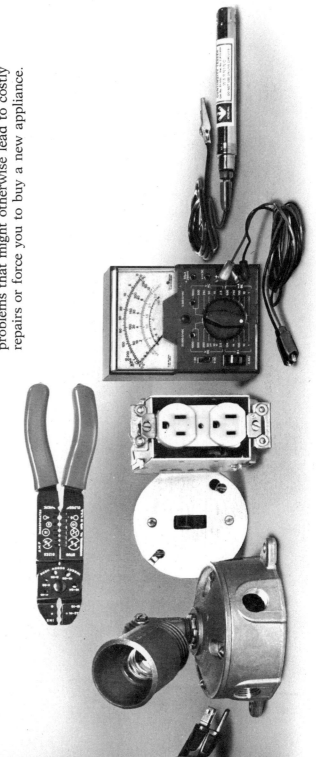

Tools and supplies

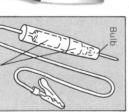

The basic kit

Many of the tools required for appliance repair, including screwdrivers, wrenches, pliers, and a jackknife, are probably already part of your home collection. You can buy more specialized items, such as a soldering iron or a crimping tool, when the need arises. An exception is the volt-ohm meter, an invaluable and modestly priced testing aid that will quickly repay your investment in it.

When buying tools, get good ones even if they cost more; they will wear better, pliers, and be safer to use. Try to purchase tools with insulated grips. The insulation provides a firmer hold and makes the tool safer for electrical jobs.

It is important to get a good set of screwdrivers. There are two types: standard-tip for single-slot screws and Phillips-tip for cross-slot screws. Try to ob-

tain standard-tip models that have non-flared blades (cabinet or electrician's tip). The narrow blades let you reach recessed screws. You can buy screwdrivers in a compact kit that contains a set of nut-drivers as well.

Other implements you will find useful are an adjustable-end wrench and a set of Allen wrenches. One adjustable-end wrench can take the place of an entire set

of open-end wrenches. You will need Allen wrenches (also called hex keys) for working with setscrews.

You should also have slip-joint pliers and long-nose pliers. Slip-joint pliers are among the most versatile light-duty gripping tools. A good pair of long-nose pliers is a must for electrical work. The long, tapered jaws will let you reach into tight spots and shape wires and metal parts.

General purpose tools

Standard-tip screwdriver

Phillips-tip screwdriver

Locking pliers

File

Adjustable-end wrench

Combination box and open-end wrench

Channel-type pliers

Slip-joint pliers

Long-nose pliers

Jackknife

Flashlight

Putty knife

Allen wrenches

All-in-one nutdriver and screwdriver kit

Tools used chiefly for appliance work

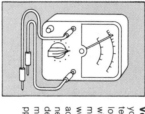

Volt-ohm meter is your most important testing tool. A low-priced model will suffice for most appliance work where extra accuracy is not needed. A full description of the meter is given on pp.124–125.

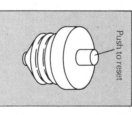

Bulb

Batteries

Continuity tester is simply a small flashlight that lights up when its probe and clip are connected to make a complete circuit. It is used to find open and short circuits but a volt-ohm meter will do the same job better.

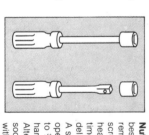

Neon test light glows when electric power is present. It can be used to check wall outlets. If you buy one, be sure it is for range of 120 to 240 volts (some are designed for lower voltages only).

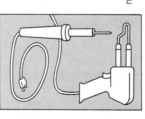

Push to reset

Resettable circuit breaker can save you money when testing a circuit whose fuse has blown. Replace fuse with breaker of same rating. If breaker keeps tripping, find the reason and eliminate the problem. Once you do, go back to using a fuse.

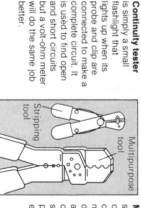

Stripping tool

Multipurpose tool

Multipurpose tool strips insulation, cuts wire, crimps connectors, and measures wire diameters. Stripping and crimping tools can be bought separately. Some persons find them easier to use.

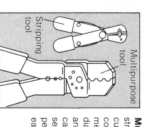

Nutdrivers are the best tools for removing nuts and screws with hexagonal heads. They save time and protect delicate finishes. A set of five, with openings from 3/16 to ⅜ in., will handle most jobs. Alternative choice is socket wrench set with ¼-inch spinner.

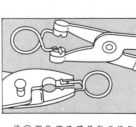

Soldering pencil in 25- to 50-watt range should be used for delicate wires in appliances, radios, TV sets. Soldering gun will heat almost instantly and will handle most medium-duty jobs. See p.131 for more about soldering tools and techniques.

Spring clamp pliers are used to release spring clips from water hoses, such as those in washing machines. Swivel type (top) can reach awkward spots, has ratchet to keep clip compressed. Plain notched type (bottom) is a bit sturdier.

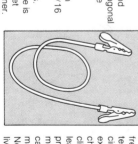

Jumper wire is frequently used in test for open circuit. For example, when checking power cord, clip jumper to cord leads and clip probes of volt-ohm meter to plug. You can buy jumpers or make your own. Never use one on a live appliance.

Supplies you should have on hand

Electrical contact cleaner: This is an extremely pure fluorocarbon solvent that will remove corrosion, dirt, and oxides from electrical components. Often marketed as TV tuner cleaner, it can be used on anything from a blender's pushbutton switch to the controls of a scientific instrument. Unlike other solvents, it will not damage plastic. Use in a place that has adequate ventilation, avoid skin contact, and do not spray on hot surfaces. Some brands contain a light lubricant; all come with a spray tube.

Plastic electrical tape: Also called PVC tape because it is made of polyvinyl chloride, plastic electrical tape has almost totally replaced rubber and friction tape in electrical work. It is neater, stronger, longer lasting, and easier to work with. It is waterproof, resistant to acid, and is safe at temperatures of up to 180°F. At higher temperatures, fiberglass tape should be used.

Rosin core solder: Designed specifically for electrical work, rosin core solder comes as wire wound on a spool. The hollow core of the wire is filled with a rosin flux to help the solder bind to copper parts without harming them as acid flux would. The solder itself should be a 60/40 alloy of tin and lead (60% tin and 40% lead). For more information on solder and flux, see *Electrical soldering*, p.131.

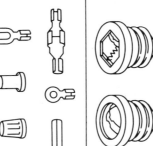

Terminals and connectors: Solderless screw-on and crimp-on terminals and connectors are gradually replacing soldered connections in electrical appliances. Assortments of terminals and connectors are available at radio supply shops and hardware stores. Individual packages of a single kind can also be purchased. Important types to have on hand are: screw-on wire nuts, crimp-on wire nuts, male and female quick connect terminals, sleeve (butt) connectors, spade terminals, and ring terminals.

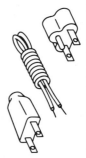

Fuses: Replacement fuses are a must for homes with an entrance panel that uses fuses rather than circuit breakers. Check the amperage rating of your fuses and keep several of each rating on hand. Be sure to get slow-blow (Fusetron) fuses where needed. Do not overlook cartridge fuses inside pull-out blocks. Never replace a fuse with one rated at a higher amperage. If a fuse blows repeatedly, find the cause and correct it.

Cord and plugs: Stock a few feet of standard 18-gauge lamp cord for repairs to small, low-power devices like radios, lamps, and electric clocks. Keep a few extra plugs on hand for the same purpose; quick connect plugs can be used for the light duty applications. If the power cord on an appliance breaks, it is wisest to get a replacement cord from the manufacturer. The size of the cord as well as its insulation and design are tailored to the requirements of the appliance.

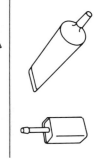

Lubricants: The proper lubricant will not only keep an appliance running trouble free, it can often be used to solve serious problems with minimum effort. Although there are many special-purpose products, some kinds of lubricant are used so frequently that you should have them in the house. These include lightweight machine oil (sewing-machine oil), powdered graphite, penetrating oil (petroleum distillate), multipurpose grease, and white grease (Lubriplate).

Look for the UL label

The terminals, tape, connectors, wires, fuses, and other items you should have on hand for routine electrical repairs will eventually be put into service on appliances and fixtures in your home. It is vital that these supplies be safe and well made, otherwise you risk fire, electrical shock, and damage to valuable equipment. The best way to be sure of the quality and safety of your supplies is to buy only those carrying the label of the Underwriters' Laboratories, Inc.

The UL, as the organization is generally called, is a private, nonprofit corporation that tests materials, equipment, and appliances for compliance with the National Electrical Code. An item can carry the UL label only if it passes the Underwriters' stringent tests. Look for the label whenever you buy an electrical fixture, appliance, or supply. Do not rely on the assurances of a salesman. The

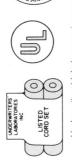

Underwriters' label comes in several forms.

absence of a UL label means the appliance was not UL tested; consequently, there is no assurance as to its safety.

Making a jumper wire

Jumper wire can be any length, but 2 to 3 ft is usually a good choice. Use No. 18 cord or thinner. First step is to strip ½ in. of insulation from either end.

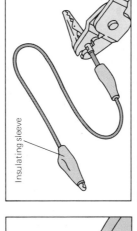

Multipurpose tool

Insulating sleeve

Slip insulating sleeves onto wire, crimp alligator clips to bare ends, and push sleeves over clips. Parts are available at hardware and electrical supply stores.

Using a continuity tester

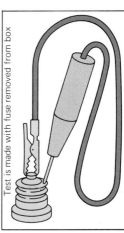

Test is made with fuse removed from box

To check house fuse, apply probe of tester to metal threads, alligator clip to center contact. Tester will light up if fuse is good, stay dark if fuse is blown.

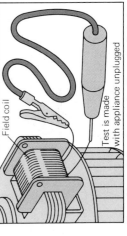

Field coil

Test is made with appliance unplugged

To make partial motor check with continuity tester, apply clip and probe to field leads. If tester glows, coil is OK; if it stays dark, make volt-ohm meter tests.

The volt-ohm meter

Buying and using a volt-ohm meter

The volt-ohm meter, also known as a multimeter or volt-ohm-milliammeter, is a simple, inexpensive, electrical measuring instrument that almost anyone can learn to use in a few minutes. With it you can troubleshoot appliances, test fuses, measure voltages at a wall outlet, check the wires from your roof antenna, find out whether a wall switch is broken, and perform dozens of other household jobs. Almost every radio supply store carries a wide selection of volt-ohm meters. You can get one that will take care of all your household testing needs for about what an electric can opener or drill would cost.

When buying a volt-ohm meter, be sure it can measure from 0 to 250 volts in both alternating current (AC) and direct current (DC). It should also provide accurate readings between zero and 30 ohms. Examine the ohms scale. There should be reasonable space between the 0- and 30-ohm markers, and the scale should not be marked "K ohms" (this would mean it is 1,000 times less accurate than it appears). Also, check the switch positions (or jacks if the meter does not have a switch) for both an RX1 setting and a setting for measuring higher resistances (RX100 or more).

Volt-ohm meters contain batteries that energize the probes when the selector switch is set to an ohms range. When the probes are touched to a motor, heating element, or other appliance part, a small current flows. The size of the current depends on the resistance of the part, and the meter reads accordingly. Since a battery in the meter provides the power, ohm tests are performed with the appliance unplugged. This eliminates any risk of shock and is one of the most important features of volt-ohm meters.

The volt-ohm meter will last indefinitely if you take care of it. Store the meter in a horizontal position and remove its battery if it is not going to be used for a long time. When using the meter, put the selector on the proper setting before you apply the probes, particularly for a voltage test. Test unknown voltages at the highest setting first.

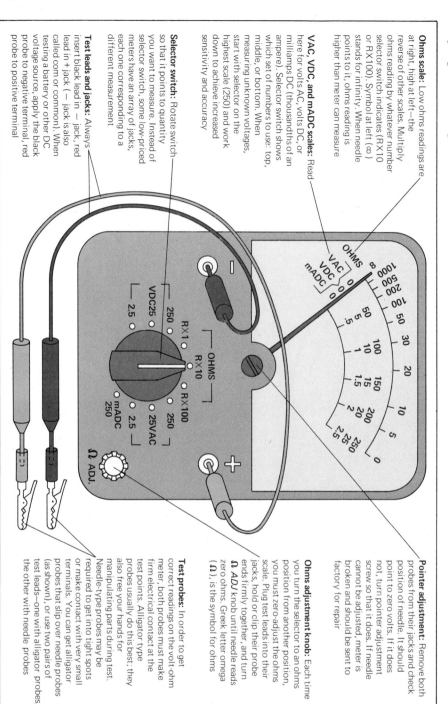

Ohms scale: Low ohms readings are at right, high at left—the reverse of other scales. Multiply ohms reading by whatever number selector switch indicates (RX10 or RX100). Symbol at left (∞) stands for infinity. When needle points to it, ohms reading is higher than meter can measure

VAC, VDC, and mADC scales: Read here for volts AC, volts DC, or milliamps DC (thousandths of an ampere). Selector switch shows which set of numbers to use: top, middle, or bottom. When measuring unknown voltages, start with selector on the highest scale (250) and work down to achieve increased sensitivity and accuracy

Selector switch: Rotate switch so that it points to quantity you want to measure. Instead of selector switch, some low-priced meters have an array of jacks, each one corresponding to a different measurement

Test leads and jacks: Always insert black lead in − jack; red lead in + jack (− jack is also called com or common). When testing a battery or other DC voltage source, apply the black probe to negative terminal, red probe to positive terminal

Pointer adjustment: Remove both probes from their jacks and check position of needle. It should point to zero volts. If it does not, turn pointer adjustment screw so that it does. If needle cannot be adjusted, meter is broken and should be sent to factory for repair

Ohms adjustment knob: Each time you turn the selector to an ohms position from another position, you must zero-adjust the ohms scale. Plug test leads into their jacks, hold or clip their probe ends firmly together, and turn Ω ADJ knob until needle reads zero ohms. Greek letter omega (Ω), is the symbol for ohms

Test probes: In order to get correct readings on the volt-ohm meter, both probes must make firm electrical contact at the test points. Alligator type probes usually do this best; they also free your hands for manipulating parts during test. Needle-type probes may be required to get into tight spots or make contact with very small terminals. You can get alligator probes that slip over needle probes (as shown), or use two pairs of test leads—one with alligator probes, the other with needle probes

Increased sensitivity, greater accuracy, more scales, and a selector switch instead of jacks distinguish middle-of-the-line and high-priced volt-ohm meters (center and right) from budget model (left). Some models may also have overload protection and a switch for reversing test lead polarity. Meter at center is excellent for all-round use but budget model will do.

You can tell that a new battery is needed when you can no longer adjust ohms scale to zero. To replace battery, remove back of meter (usually held on by a small screw). Inexpensive, middle-of-the-line model at left uses only a 1.5-volt AA battery. Middle-of-the-line meter at right uses AA battery plus a 15-volt photo flash battery. Align + and − poles of new battery same way as old one.

Electrical terminology

AC and DC: These initials stand for alternating current and direct current respectively. Electric current that flows in only one direction in a wire is called DC. If the current changes from one direction to the other over and over again, it is called AC. Electricity in the home is 60-cycle (or 60-Hertz) AC, meaning that it changes from one direction to the opposite and back again 60 times each second.

Ampere: One of three fundamental units of electrical measurement (the others are the ohm and the volt). Electric current is measured in amperes (abbreviated amp). The current, or number of amperes of electricity, flowing in a wire is analogous to gallons of water flowing through a pipe per minute.

Ohm: The second fundamental unit of electrical measurement. Electrical resistance is measured in ohms. Even the best electrical conductors, such as copper and silver, resist the flow of current through them in some degree. This occurs in much the same way as the flow of water in a pipe is resisted by friction. The degree of resistance of a wire depends on what it is made of, how long it is, and of what gauge (thickness) it is. The symbol for ohms is Ω (the Greek letter omega).

Volt: The third fundamental unit of electrical measurement. Electrical pressure is measured in volts. Just as water pressure is needed to force water through a pipe, so electrical pressure is needed to force current through a wire. The volt is the electrical equivalent of pounds per square inch of water pressure. Volts, ohms, and amperes are tied together by the equation:

amperes = volts ÷ ohms.

For example, a current of 10 amperes will flow in the 12-ohm heating element of a hot plate when the plate is plugged into a 120-volt outlet (10 amps = 120 volts ÷ 12 ohms).

Watt: A watt represents the same thing horsepower does—power. In fact, one horsepower is the same as 746 watts. The higher the wattage of an appliance, the more power it uses. Watts are equal to volts multiplied by amperes. For example, a 60-watt light bulb will draw ½ ampere when it is in a 120-volt outlet (60 watts = 120 volts × ½ amp).

Watt-hour and kilowatt-hour: If you run a 1-watt appliance for 1 hour, it will consume 1 watt-hour of electric energy. If you use 1,000 watts for an hour, you will have consumed 1,000 watt-hours, or 1 kilowatt-hour, of electric energy. Your monthly bill for electricity is based on the kilowatt-hours of electricity you use, and that depends on the wattage of your appliances, and the amount you use them.

Voltage and current tests

A common test is for voltage at a 120-volt wall outlet. Since any voltage much higher than that of a 12-volt car battery is dangerous, you must be extremely careful. The safest procedure for a beginner is to start by cutting off power to the outlet by removing the fuse (or switching off the circuit breaker) that controls it. Set the volt-ohm meter to the 250 VAC scale and insert its needle probes into the slots of the wall receptacle. To get a reading, activate the outlet by replacing the fuse or throwing the circuit breaker on.

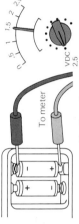

Checking the voltage at an outlet.

A volt-ohm meter can also be used for checking a battery, but the battery should have an electrical load on it during the test. To test a 1.5-volt battery in a hand calculator, set the meter to the 2.5 VDC scale and touch the probes to the battery terminals (red probe to + and black to –). Then, turn the calculator on.

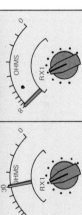

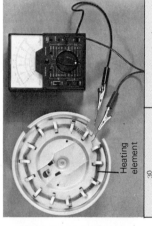

Testing a battery.

If the voltage drops below 1.3 volts, the battery is probably bad.

Most volt-ohm meters can also be used to measure an electric current if it is a direct current (DC) and fairly small (less than ½ ampere). Some meters also permit testing of a small alternating current (AC). Others have a special attachment that allows you to test larger currents. For an example of a DC test, see *The charging unit*, p.137.

Ohm tests for continuity and resistance

The first step in an ohm test is simple but vital: Completely disconnect the appliance or part being checked from any supply of electricity. Remember that turning the appliance off is not enough; its power cord must be pulled from the outlet. If you fail to do this, you are likely to destroy your volt-ohm meter and you risk receiving a serious electric shock.

Next, set the meter's selector switch to one of the ohms positions. The choice of positions depends on what you are looking for. If you are measuring resistance, you will probably use the RX1 scale, since most appliance parts have fairly low resistances. To test for grounding or short circuits, however, you will generally set the meter to the highest position available—RX100 for the meter illustrated on page 124, up to RX1,000,000 on other meters. Once the selector is set, zero-adjust the ohms scale (see p.124).

To make the test, apply the probes of the meter to the electrical terminals of the part being checked—for example, the prongs of a plug, the terminals of a switch, the leads from a motor's field coil, or the ends of a heating element.

There are two types of ohms tests: continuity and resistance. In a continuity test, you simply want to find out whether or not an electrical pathway exists through a particular component. Tests for open circuits, short circuits, and grounding are examples. In a resistance test you are looking for detailed information on the electrical condition of a part by checking its resistance.

For both types of test, it is important that the probes make good contact with the part being tested. They should touch bare wire or metal, not insulation, paint, corrosion, or dirt. Alligator clips give firmer contact than needle probes; use them where possible. Also, it is good practice to manipulate wires especially when you are testing for open circuits, short circuits, and grounding. By twisting, tugging, and pulling on a wire, you will help uncover weak connections.

Typical continuity test is for open circuit in power cord. Set meter to RX1 scale, clip probes to plug, complete circuit with jumper. Zero ohms reading (left) means cord is OK; high ohms indicates an open circuit. Note cord being tugged to uncover loose connections.

Ohms test of corn popper heating element is example of resistance test. Clip meter probes to element and set selector on RX1. Meter should read 20 to 40 ohms. Much higher reading indicates open circuit in element. Much lower reading may mean short circuit.

Electricity in the home

How power is distributed

Power from the local utility is supplied to the house through the entrance panel (either a fuse box or circuit breaker panel). From there it is distributed around the house in branch circuits. Most homes have 120/240-volt service. This means that branch circuits at either voltage can be provided. Exceptions are near large cities, where the supply may be 120/208-volt, and in older homes, which may have 120-volt service only.

Electricity in your home may not be exactly 120 and 240 volts. Typically, a city dweller might have 126 volts at an outlet while a suburbanite receives only 118 volts. Also, outlets at the far end of a branch circuit have lower voltages than those near the entrance panel. (If the difference is more than 4 volts, the wiring in your home is inadequate.) The minimum safe supply is 108 volts; anything lower may damage electrical equipment. For this reason, utilities do not cut back service during a power shortage brown-out by more than 8 percent. Instead, they effect selected local blackouts.

Checking an outlet for ground

Many parts of the home wiring system—including outlet boxes, outlets, switches, the entrance panel, and all neutral (white) wires—are deliberately linked to ground. This is usually done by connecting them to the water main or a special grounding rod driven into the earth. Proper grounding helps protect against shock, fire, and lightning.

Appliances with three-prong plugs are also meant to be grounded when used. Adapters are available that can convert a two-hole outlet for three-prong use, but they will do the job only if the center screw of the outlet plate is itself firmly grounded. Test the adapter as shown at right rather than with a neon test light. Never break off the grounding prong to fit the plug into an outlet.

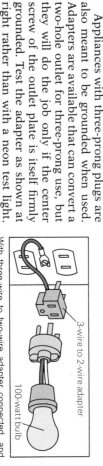

Buy two-wire pigtail socket and three-prong plug at hardware store. Connect white lead to ground terminal (green screw), black lead to hot terminal (brass screw).

Ground terminal

Hot (brass) terminal

Pigtail socket

3-wire to 2-wire adapter

100-watt bulb

With three-wire to two-wire adapter connected, and 100-watt bulb in tester's socket, plug tester in. If bulb lights brightly, outlet is grounded.

Each branch circuit is protected by a fuse or circuit breaker matched to the house wiring in the branch. The diagram at right indicates electrical service in a typical house. From there it is distributed wires entering the house. Note that there are three neutral wire and is grounded. The other two are hot. In the house, wires connected to neutral are sheathed in white insulation; the hot wires are generally sheathed in black. The voltage between the two hot wires is 240 volts; the voltage between the neutral wire and either hot wire is 120 volts.

When an appliance does not operate, check for power at the wall outlet. Barring a power failure, loss of power at an outlet is usually due to a blown fuse or tripped circuit breaker. It is easy to replace a blown fuse or reset a tripped breaker (see p.127), but you should also find out why the device blew or tripped. First, check for an overloaded circuit (p.127). If this is not the problem, an appliance may be short-circuited or there may be trouble in the house wiring.

Branch circuits in the modern home

Type 1: There should be at least five 120-volt, 15- or 20-ampere, general purpose circuits for bedrooms, bathrooms, kitchen, dining room, and living room. These circuits handle light fixtures, table lamps, television sets, radios, and convenience appliances such as shavers, electric knives, electric toothbrushes, clocks, window fans, and hair dryers.

Type 2: There should be two or more 120-volt, 20-ampere, special purpose circuits for kitchen, laundry room, and basement. These circuits handle high-wattage appliances, such as toasters, mixers, blenders, coffeemakers, rotisseries, waffles, refrigerators, freezers, power saws, electric irons, sump pumps, and large power tools.

Type 3: There should be as many 120-volt, 15- or 20-ampere, individual circuits as needed. Each circuit handles one appliance only. A typical modern home will have five. Among the appliances they handle are dishwashers, waste disposers, and washing machines, as well as oil burners, kitchen exhaust fans, and water pumps.

Type 4: There should be as many 240-volt, 20- to 50-ampere, individual circuits as needed. Each circuit handles one appliance only. Among the appliances they handle are kitchen ranges, clothes dryers, central air conditioners, and hot water heaters.

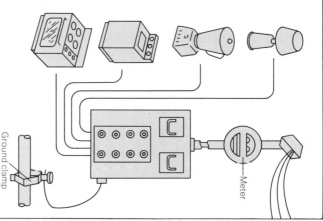

Ground clamp

Meter

Extension and power cords

Inadequate extension and power cords are major causes of fire in the home. A 1,400-watt waffler connected to an 18-gauge extension cord, for example, would cause a definite fire hazard because the cord would overheat, but the fuse (or circuit breaker) guarding the circuit would not cut off power (they are designed only to protect the house wiring). The same threat would exist if an inadequate power cord were installed on the waffler. Safe rules to follow are:

1. Replace a power cord only with a manufacturer's equivalent.
2. Keep the number and lengths of extension cords to a minimum.
3. Be sure to use a grounding-type, three-wire extension cord if the appliance has a three-prong plug.
4. Extension cords should be at least of the same gauge as the power cord. If you are not sure of the gauge, use the following table as a guide:

For 120-volt appliances rated:

	Use:
Up to 6 amps (0–720 watts)	18-gauge cord
6–9 amps (720–1,080 watts)	16-gauge cord
9–14 amps (1,080–1,680 watts)	14-gauge cord
14–18 amps (1,680–2,160 watts)	12-gauge cord

5. Never run an extension cord under a rug or inside an enclosed space.
6. Buy cords with a UL Label (see *Look for the UL label*, p.123). Do not rely on manufacturer's phrases such as "Heavy duty extension cord set" or "Recommended for use with power tools."

Checking for overloads

An overloaded branch circuit is one with too many appliances and lights in it for the wiring to handle. Overloading is the commonest cause of fuses blowing repeatedly or circuit breakers tripping again and again. To check for an overloaded circuit, you must first find out what outlets and fixtures are in it. Remove the fuse that has been blowing (or set breaker to *Off*). Next, turn on all lights in the house and check all the wall outlets with a neon test light or a lamp. The outlets and fixtures in the circuit are the ones that have been inactivated.

Next, add up the wattages of all the lights and all the appliances in the circuit.

Should an appliance be rated in amperes only, multiply the rating by 120 to get its wattage. If an appliance has a volt-amp rating, use that figure in preference to watts. If the circuit has a 15-ampere fuse and the total comes to more than 1,800 watts, the circuit is overloaded; the limit for a 20-ampere fuse is 2,400 watts.

The simplest way to eliminate overloading is to reduce the number of appliances. The alternative is to rewire the house. Repetitive blowing of fuses may be due to other causes too. Refrigerators, room air conditioners, and other devices with large motors should be in circuits using slow blow (Fusetron) fuses.

Leakage current and the GFI

Leakage current—also known as ground fault current because the electricity flows to the ground through any path open to it—can be described as an improper electric current large enough to be felt but not large enough to trigger the action of a fuse or circuit breaker. In recent years, leakage currents, and the potentially lethal shock hazard they represent, have received increased attention.

The usual cause of leakage current is a breakdown of insulation between a current carrying wire and the frame of an electrical device. If the breakdown is severe, it can be detected with a volt-ohm meter, and the condition amounts to improper grounding of a wire. However, a partial breakdown, or one that occurs only when the appliance is turned on, is often impossible to detect without special test equipment.

The GFI, or ground fault interrupter (it is also known as a GFCI, for ground fault circuit interrupter), is a device that affords protection against leakage current and other shock hazards. GFI's are presently required in outdoor installations and new bathrooms. They may soon become mandatory in kitchens and base-

ments of newly constructed homes as well. GFI's respond to currents as low as .005 ampere—slightly above the threshold of sensation—by cutting power off almost immediately. They not only protect against shocks, but also sense ground fault currents in three-wire, grounded appliances and shut down power even though there is no direct threat of shock to the user. Like circuit breakers, GFI's are resettable, but they are meant to supplement breakers or fuses and in no way can replace them.

Typical ground fault interrupters: Permanent model (left) is for outdoor installation. Portable (right) is for indoors; it plugs into three-hole grounded outlets.

Fuses and circuit breakers

If too much current flows in a wire, it can get hot enough to set fire to surrounding materials. Fuses and circuit breakers protect against this possibility by cutting off power to any circuit that is drawing excessive power.

Circuit breakers work like thermostats—when they get too hot, they shut off power. The key element in a fuse is a strip of metal with a low melting point. When too much current flows, the strip melts, or "blows," thereby interrupting power in the circuit. Unlike circuit breakers, which can be reset after they trip, a blown fuse must be replaced. In neither case, however, should the circuit be reactivated until the cause of the problem has been located and fixed.

There are two kinds of fuses: screw-in, for under 30 amperes, and cartridge, for 30 amperes and up. Both are available in slow-blow designs that safely allow temporary overloads. Cartridge fuses often show no sign of having blown. A blown screw-in fuse can generally be spotted by a blackened glass or break in the metal strip. Either type can be checked with a continuity tester (p.123) or a volt-ohm meter (p.124). When using the meter, set it to the RX1 scale and touch its probes to the terminals of the fuse. A reading of zero ohms means the fuse is good.

Left to right: Plug, slow blow, and cartridge fuses.

Fuses and circuit breakers are rated in amperes and are matched to the wiring they protect. Never replace a fuse or breaker with one rated for higher amperage and do not attempt to force a circuit breaker to stay on or to circumvent the operation of a fuse by substituting a penny or a wad of foil.

When replacing a fuse, keep hands and feet dry. If floor is wet, stand on board. For extra safety, open main switch or remove section of panel marked *Main.*

Unscrew blown fuse and replace it with one of same rating and type. Restore power by closing main switch or replacing main panel section.

Cartridge fuses are located in pullout sections. Remove section, pull fuse from spring clips, insert new fuse of same rating, and replace section.

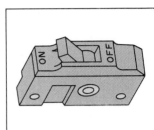

Resetting circuit breaker is easy. Some can be flipped back to *On* like a wall switch. In others, push the handle beyond *Off* to *Reset* before moving it to *On.*

Repair basics

Making the job easier

Before you try to fix a broken appliance, or even start testing it, check to see if it is on warranty; almost all manufacturers provide free service on their products for a year or more after purchase. If it is, let the manufacturer do the work, especially since you may void the warranty if you tinker with the appliance.

Most warranties cover only defective materials and workmanship and rule out damage due to misuse. However, a firm will generally repair or replace a warranty-tied appliance without question. Moreover, many are liberal about providing free repair beyond the nominal cutoff date, particularly if the trouble seems to stem from a defect in the appliance.

In addition to warranties, some large retail chains and manufacturers offer service contracts that pick up where the warranty leaves off. For a fee, you can obtain repair insurance on such appliances as washing machines, dryers, and dishwashers for fixed periods, usually five years. If you do not have the time or inclination to attempt major repair work yourself, one of these contracts may be an excellent alternative. The cost of one service call can easily exceed the total cost of the service contract.

Avoid unnecessary repairs

Experienced service personnel know that the single most frequent reason for customer complaints is the failure of the customer to operate or maintain the appliance properly. Before you assume that one of your appliances is broken, check your owner's manual to make sure that you are following the correct operating procedure. Also, read the manual's use and care information and any instructions on fixing simple operating problems. A few drops of oil on a fan bearing, a quick brushing of a vacuum cleaner's lint filter, or a 10-second bath of a shaving head in the proper cleaner may get an appliance running like new.

Once you determine that an appliance is definitely faulty, start your trouble-shooting with the simple and obvious. Check for a blown house fuse, a closed water valve, a burned out light bulb, or a bad power cord plug before you begin to disassemble the appliance. And when you do begin removing parts, keep the number taken off to a minimum. Unnecessary disassembly and reassembly not only create extra work, but shorten the useful life of a machine. Stripped screw threads, scratched finishes, frayed insulation, grit in moving parts, warped fittings, and broken connections are only some of the difficulties that can be caused by unnecessary disassembly.

In general, you should not tamper with calibrated devices—such as governor springs, gas valves, and thermostats—unless you absolutely establish that the adjustment is needed, that the adjustment procedure is safe, and that no expensive instruments are required. Note that adjustment screws coated with red sealing wax or other sealing substance are factory preset and should not be disturbed.

Service manuals and parts lists

Because they give detailed information on the specific appliance model you own, service manuals and parts lists can help immeasurably in appliance repair work. In some cases (for example, certain steam-spray irons), the manufacturer's service manual is almost essential for successful disassembly and reassembly.

Some companies automatically include parts lists and identifying illustrations in the package with a new appliance; most do not. No manufacturers provide service manuals as part of the purchase; but many will supply them separately, upon request, for a small fee. Letters should be addressed to the Customer Service Department of the particular manufacturer. If you are about to buy a new appliance and intend to do

your own repair work, it would pay you to find out in advance whether or not you will be able to get this repair information.

Keep your service manuals, parts lists, owner's manuals, warranties, and other appliance information in some centralized location, such as a shelf or desk drawer. A simple filing system, with material for each appliance in a separate folder, will help you keep track of the various papers so that the information they contain will be readily available.

Getting parts

Some of the larger manufacturers and retail chains have their own service organizations and parts outlets. More often, a company will authorize a private repair shop to provide parts and service. One such repair shop may represent as many as 50 manufacturers. The yellow pages of your phone book list local parts outlets and service centers.

Be persistent when trying to get a replacement part. If the local factory-authorized parts outlet does not have the item you want, call or write the manufacturer. Explain your problem and specify the part you need. There is an excellent chance that you will get it. When you order a part, give the make, model, model number, and date of manufacture of the appliance. This information is generally printed on a separate plate on the back of major appliances or imprinted directly on the housing bottom or back of small appliances. Describe the part you need as best you can and include the part number if you have a parts list. If you are able to go directly to a parts supplier, take the broken part along. Better still, bring the entire appliance if you can.

It may take time for the factory to ship a particular part so you should order what you need as soon as you can. If you are in a particular hurry for a part, contact the manufacturer's parts department by phone.

Making repairs safely

1. Always disconnect the power cord of any appliance you are working on. If the appliance is permanently connected to the house wiring (for example, a range), remove the house fuse or turn off the circuit breaker control ing it.

2. Do not poke into a heating device, such as a toaster or space heater, with a fork or other metal object. Doing so would very likely short-circuit the appliance or give you a shock.

3. Buy Underwriters' Laboratories (UL) listed appliances only and use only UL listed supplies.

4. Keep several dry-chemical fire extinguishers in strategic locations around the house, particularly in the kitchen, basement, and workshop.

5. Never light a match to investigate a gas or oil appliance, such as a gas heater, stove, dryer, or heating system. If you suspect a gas leak, do not turn on a light. Instead, shut off the supply of gas to the appliance, air the room, and do any checking with a flashlight.

6. If an appliance shocks, disconnect it immediately from the wall outlet. Do not use it again until the cause of the shocking has been found and eliminated. In some instances, an appliance will shock intermittently. This may occur because there is an intermittent connection, because the shocking can be felt only on humid days or when the appliance is damp, or because the shock depends on which way the power cord plug is inserted into the wall socket.

7. Do not try to move a heavy appliance such as a washing machine or freezer, without assistance. Be sure the appliance is unplugged and empty, and disconnect any water lines leading to it. If the appliance must be tilted, lean it against a wall and prop it up firmly. Never move an appliance that is connected to a gas line.

8. Do not circumvent built-in safety devices, even for a test. On occasion, you may have seen service personnel using a jumper wire to bypass a thermostat or a lid safety switch. Leave tests of this nature to the specialists. Improperly performed, they may cause shock, damage to the appliance, and fire.

9. Even though power is off, there may still be a shock hazard. Some devices—for example, television sets, air conditioners, and air cleaners—have components that store charge. Discharge them before you work on them.

Taking it apart

Before you do any kind of work on an appliance, be absolutely certain it is disconnected from the electrical power supply. You should also make sure that the appliance can be disassembled. Microwave ovens, for example, should be repaired only by professionals and are deliberately designed to discourage disassembly. Other appliances are permanently sealed, either for safety's sake (electrical toothbrushes) or to permit them to be washed in a sink (electric percolators and frying pans).

When you take an appliance apart, work slowly and be gentle. Take time to put tape on the jaws of your pliers to avoid scratching a delicate finish. Use penetrating oil and patience rather than brute force to free a rusted screw. If you need a special tool (such as a soldering iron, hose clamp pliers, or a nut driver), go out and buy it. When you improvise, you risk damaging an expensive part.

Assembly is generally the reverse of disassembly, so observe the order in which you remove components. Pay close attention to details, particularly to the orientation of parts—which end of a control shaft is up and which down, which side of a bearing faces front and which back, whether an insulator goes under or over an assembly, whether a spacing washer goes on before or after a spring washer. It helps to sketch the parts in their proper positions. Making a light scribe mark across the junction of mating components is also helpful.

Small, separate items should be kept in a saucer or other container until you are ready for reassembly. Whenever there is a chance of confusion, label matching parts or make a written note of which part goes where. Some home repairmen go so far as to take polaroid pictures at key points in the disassembly process to show how parts fit together. Another trick is to lay out parts on a strip of masking tape in the order of their removal.

The following disassembly techniques are particularly useful. Make it a point to become familiar with them.

Self-locking terminal: This type of terminal will lock onto any wire inserted into it to provide a sound electrical connection. To free the wire, insert a straightened-out paper clip and pull the wire out.

Quick connect terminals: Push the female terminal off with a screwdriver. Pulling it off is likely to damage the wire.

Metal to plastic connections: When a metal part is force-fitted into plastic, it helps to warm the metal with a soldering iron in order to free it.

Control knobs: A good trick for pulling off a tight-fitting control knob without damaging it is to slip a clean rag behind the knob, then pull evenly on the rag.

Terminals and leads: When replacing an electrical component, remove leads from the terminals of the old part and attach them to the new part one by one.

Dials and adjustment screws: Do not move dials, adjustment screws, or control cams unless you must.

Left-hand threads: Nuts and bolts on rotating parts may have left-hand threads. Forcing them the wrong way will strip the threads.

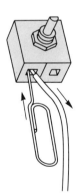

Insert clip to free wire from self-locking terminal.

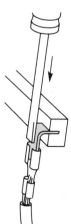

Push quick connect terminals off with screwdriver.

Hidden screws and trick connections

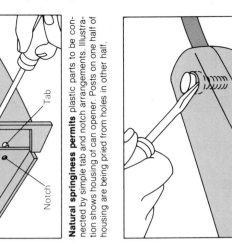

Tab

Notch

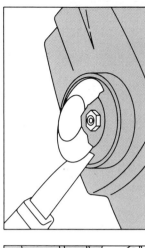

Natural springiness permits plastic parts to be connected by simple tab and notch arrangements. Illustration shows housing of can opener. Posts on one half of housing are being pried from holes in other half.

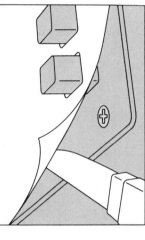

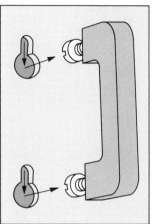

Screws are often concealed under decorative metal facings. Press facing with finger to locate screws, then pry facing up with knife. Work carefully to minimize creasing. Use strong contact cement to reglue.

To separate parts held together by keyhole and bolt method, slide one part horizontally with respect to the other, then pull the two apart. Sharp rap may help if parts are stuck. Bolts are adjustable for tighter fit.

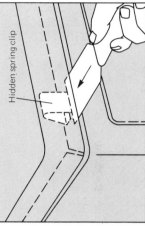

Plastic plug in housing of appliance is almost sure to have assembly screw beneath it. Pry plug out with strong, sharp instrument. Some marring of finish is inevitable no matter how carefully you work.

Hidden spring clip

Top of clothes dryer may be held by hidden spring clips. To release top, insert putty knife under it, push knife against clip, and pull up on top. Pair of clips 2 in. from each end are usually used.

Metal cap must be pried off to reach both main assembly nut and thermostat adjustment screw of this fryer control. Nut can be removed with hollow shank nut driver. Adjustment screw is in center of control shaft.

Repair basics

Putting it together

Before you reassemble an appliance, be as sure as you can that whatever was wrong with it has been fixed. Note that it is not only important to repair a broken part, but to make sure that something else did not cause the damage or that the broken component did not result in damage to other parts.

Reassembly is largely a matter of working backward from the last disassembly step to the first. Accordingly, put the appliance back together as soon as you can. The steps will be fresh in your mind and the parts less likely to be misplaced. Work slowly and carefully. Do not overtighten screws and nuts or try to force parts together.

All new parts should be the equivalent of the old. Quick connect terminals in a cooking appliance, for example, should be heat resistant. Wire nuts in motorized appliances, such as vacuum cleaners, should be the crimp-on type; vibration loosens screw-on wire nuts.

Make sure all electrical connections are tight and neat, with no frayed ends or loose strands jutting out. It is a good practice to tin the ends of stranded wires with solder (see p.131) before attaching them to a screw terminal or inserting them into a self-locking terminal. This prevents loose strands and improves electrical contact. When putting parts

Strands of wire should not protrude from under screw.

together, take care that no electrical leads are pinched by the housing or other parts and that all are clipped in place where called for or in their proper channels. The insulation on a pinched or rubbing wire will soon wear through; a short circuit or ground may result.

Keep in mind that most appliances are carefully engineered, that every part has a purpose, and that every tab, hole, bend, or marking has a reason for being there. Notches and irregularities in shape may indicate proper alignment or may be used to keep a part, such as a motor bearing, from rotating.

On occasion, a trick or special tool can help in reassembly. A bit of chewing gum on the tip of a screwdriver will hold a screw long enough to start it in an inaccessible hole. Screwdrivers with special screwholding tips are also available for the same purpose. Crimp-on connectors and terminals should be put on with a crimping tool, not pliers, in order to guarantee connections that are sound both electrically and mechanically. At various stages in the assembly process you should turn moving parts by hand—for example, the rotor of an electric motor—to make sure they move freely without hitting or rubbing other parts.

When everything is assembled, test the appliance cautiously. If it is noisy or overheats, turn it off and find out what is wrong. Be aware, however, that new parts may take a while to break in. A new

Bearing has notch to prevent rotation.

switch may be stiff, a new heating element may smoke a bit the first few times it is used, or new motor brushes may create more than normal static until they wear down to fit the commutator.

Joining wires

Easiest way to join wires is with a wire nut. Twist leads together in clockwise spiral, then screw on wire nut in clockwise direction.

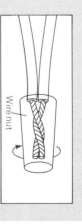

Crimp-on wire nuts are used in appliances that vibrate. To install, twist leads together, squeeze nut over them with crimping tool.

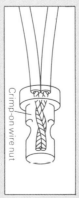

To splice wires, strip inch of insulation from each, twist together, reinsulate with several layers of tape wound in overlapping fashion.

Working with wires and plugs

To install plug, strip ½ in. insulation from wires, tie Underwriters' knot as shown. Tighten knot and pull it into plug recess. Knot acts as strain relief device.

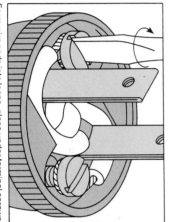

Form wire ends into loops, place under terminal screws, and tighten screws firmly. Note that direction of loops should follow screw direction as it is tightened.

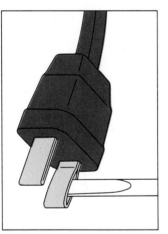

Plugs that fit loosely in wall outlets make poor contact and may fall out. Prongs can sometimes be spread with screwdriver to improve fit. Do not bend the prongs.

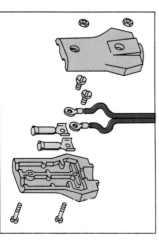

To remove female plug of detachable power cord, take out nuts and bolts, separate the halves, undo terminal screws. If plug is molded, replace entire power cord.

Tinning and other soldering techniques

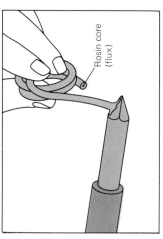

Rosin core (flux)

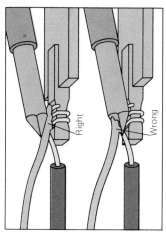

Plug iron in and hold solder to tip. Flux must flow before solder melts, so never tin with tip at full heat. Remove excess solder with clean rag rather than by shaking.

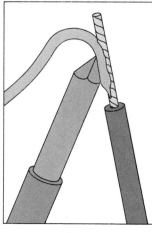

Right Wrong

Wrap wire around terminal post, hold solder to it, and apply tip of soldering iron to the solder. Note that solder is applied to the work, not to the iron.

Tinning of parts produces better connections, keeps wires from unraveling. To tin, clean part, then hold solder to it as you heat to insure proper fluxing.

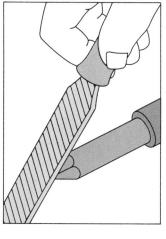

Keep tip of soldering iron tinned with silvery coat of solder. To tin, unplug iron, file or sand tip to bare metal. Next, break open solder to expose core.

First step in soldering parts together is cleaning. Use sandpaper, emery paper, knife blade, file, or wire brush to scrape metal down to bare, shiny copper.

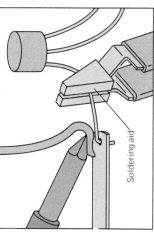

Soldering aid

Soldering aid with self-closing jaws holds work steady, bleeds off heat before it reaches delicate parts. Jaws are nickel plated so that solder will not stick.

Electrical soldering

To make a soldered connection that is mechanically sound and provides good electrical contact, you need the correct kind of soldering iron, high quality solder, and the proper flux. You must also carefully prepare the parts.

The type of soldering iron you should use depends on the work you are doing. For delicate parts and wiring like that found in blenders, radios, shavers, electric knives, and TV sets, a 25- to 50-watt soldering pencil is best. It is easy to handle, has a small tip that will reach into tight spaces, and is not likely to damage parts by overheating. A low-wattage soldering gun can be used as an alternative. It will put out more heat and is heavier, but will heat up almost instantly and can produce excellent results if handled carefully. Some guns have high and low heat settings for greater versatility.

Whatever iron you use, its tip must be kept tinned (covered with a coating of solder) at all times. Tinning aids heat transfer and prevents pitting, corrosion, and the formation of oxides (tarnish). Even though it is tinned, wipe the tip occasionally with a damp cellulose sponge to remove oxides. This should be done while the iron is hot. When the iron is not being used, turn it off or unplug it; prolonged hot idling will accelerate erosion and pitting.

The solder used for electrical work should be a mixture of 60% tin and 40% lead. Solders with less tin and more lead are available and cost less, but they produce weaker joints and are more difficult to work with.

A material called flux must always be used in conjunction with solder. There are two kinds of flux: acid and rosin. Only rosin can be used in electrical work since acid will corrode copper parts. The purpose of flux is to remove tarnish, prevent further tarnish from developing, and act as a wetting agent to help the molten solder spread and penetrate.

Rosin core solder, in the form of wire wound on a spool, is universally used in electrical work. The hollow core is filled with the required rosin flux. When this solder is used correctly, there is no need for a separate application of flux.

Just before you solder, clean the parts to be joined down to the base metal. Steel wool, emery paper, sandpaper, or a sharp knife can be used. Note that the windings of electric motors are coated with a nonconducting lacquer that must be thoroughly scraped off before a motor lead can be soldered to a terminal or to another wire.

Parts to be soldered should have a secure mechanical connection before the solder is applied. In electrical work, this usually means that wires must be twisted together or a lead must be twisted around or crimped inside its terminal. It helps if the parts are tinned beforehand.

For a sound joint, the parts being joined must be heated as well as the solder. When applying the soldering iron's tip to a joint, use a flat surface of the tip to maximize the area that touches the work. This will improve heat contact and help the solder penetrate the whole joint rather than a small part of it.

Hold the solder against the joint rather than against the tip of the iron. That way, the solder will penetrate completely and bind the parts together. Moreover, if rosin core solder is held to the tip of the iron rather than to the joint, the flux will run out over the hot tip and burn up before it reaches the joint. Tarnish will form as a result, and the solder will not bind properly. A generally satisfactory technique is to hold the solder to the work and apply the tip of the soldering iron to the solder. The flux will coat the joint before oxidation takes place and the molten solder will transfer heat to the parts being joined much more efficiently than if the iron had been applied directly to the work.

Universal motors

The electric motor

When current flows through a wire, it creates a magnetic field. By regulating the direction and intensity of the field, a cylindrical metal rotor can be made to turn. This principle—using an electromagnetic field to turn a rotor—is basic to all electric motors.

The universal motor is one of the most widely used types. It is called universal because it will work on either alternating current (AC) or direct current (DC). Appliances using universal motors include vacuum cleaners, electric drills, blenders, and mixers.

All electric motors—including the small, permanent magnet, DC motors used in cordless appliances (see pp.136–137) and the induction-type motors described on page 135—have a stationary component (the stator, or field) and a rotating component (the rotor) that turns inside the field. A distinguishing characteristic of universal motors is that they have coils or windings for both the field and the rotor (a wound rotor is sometimes called an armature). In contrast, permanent magnet DC motors have rotor coils but no field coils, and induction motors have field coils but no rotor coils.

In addition to having both rotor and field windings, universal motors have a commutator and a pair of brushes. The commutator consists of a number of brass bars attached to the rotor and wired to the rotor coils. The brushes, mounted on the frame of the motor, press against the commutator. As the rotor and commutator turn, the brushes conduct current to the rotor coils through the brass bars. As each rotor coil is activated, it sets up a magnetic field that interacts with the magnetic field of the stator to produce rotation. Brushes in modern motors are made of carbon particles bonded into rectangular or cylindrical rods. Formerly, brushes were bundles of fine wire or metal strips that brushed against the commutator.

Troubleshooting checklist

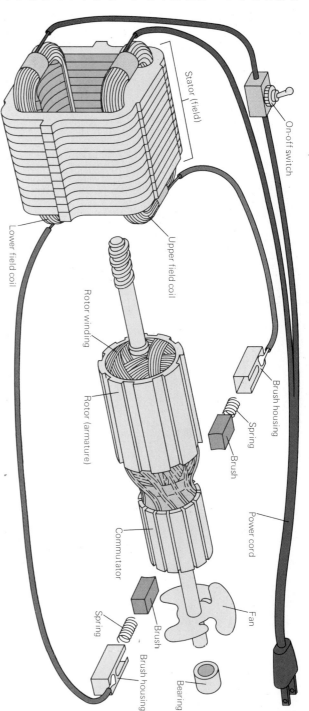

Stator (field)

On-off switch

Lower field coil

Upper field coil

Rotor winding

Rotor (armature)

Brush housing

Spring

Brush

Power cord

Commutator

Fan

Spring

Brush

Bearing

Brush housing

PROBLEM	POSSIBLE CAUSE	ACTION
Motor does not run	No power at wall outlet	Test outlet with a lamp you know is working. If there is no power, replace fuse or reset circuit breaker (p.127). If fuse keeps blowing or breaker keeps tripping, check for overload (p.127) or shorted field coil (p.133). Reduce appliance load in circuit to eliminate overload. Shorted field coil must be replaced
	Open circuit in power cord or motor	Test power cord, motor leads, field coil, and motor switch; replace if defective. See p.133
	Dirty commutator	Clean commutator (p.133) to see if this clears up the trouble
	Brushes not contacting commutator bars	Check brushes, brush springs, and brush housings; look for stickiness, bad springs, worn brushes (p.133)
	Motor jammed (may hum and try to start)	Unplug power cord, try to turn motor by hand. If you cannot, look for jammed gears, rotor striking field, frozen bearings. Replace broken parts; lubricate bearings. Note: Condition may be due to excess load on motor
	Open circuit or short circuit in rotor winding (motor may hum and try to start)	Try bar-to-bar test of rotor windings (p.133). If open or short circuit is indicated, replace rotor. If bar-to-bar resistance is very low for all bars, special test equipment may be required in order to spot a short circuit
	Defective speed control device	See Speed control devices for universal motors, p.134
Motor vibrates, is noisy	Worn bearings	Disassemble motor. Check for play of rotor shaft in bearings. Replace bearing if shaft is loose
	Loose or worn parts	Tighten all screws, nuts, bolts. Replace worn rubber mounts. Make sure fan is on tightly. Remove rotor and clean any debris from air gap. Check commutator bars; if any are loose, replace rotor
	Short circuit in rotor winding	Make bar-to-bar test of rotor windings (p.133). Replace rotor if a winding is shorted. If bar-to-bar resistance is very low for all bars, special test equipment may be required
Excessive TV or radio interference; sparking from brushes	Rough commutator	Remove rotor, examine commutator for loose bars, high mica between bars, pitting. File high mica with hacksaw blade. Polish commutator with very fine (No. 400) sandpaper if pitted. Replace rotor if bars are loose

Electrical problems

The power cord and the brushes are the likeliest sources of electrical trouble in a universal motor, although the field and rotor coils or the commutator may also be to blame. The volt-ohm meter checks shown at right will help pinpoint the trouble. Be sure to unplug the motor from the wall outlet before conducting the tests. For information on using a volt-ohm meter, see pages 124–125.

After you determine that a particular part is defective, replace it with a new one from the manufacturer. In the case of an open-circuited field coil or broken rotor winding, you may have to buy a new motor or even a new appliance.

Visual inspection of parts can also provide repair clues. Examine the commutator of a motor that is running roughly. Look for burned spots, variations in color along the strip where the brushes rub, and loose or unevenly spaced bars.

Brush replacement is a common repair chore. Although a brush will operate satisfactorily until it is just about worn away, it is best to replace it before this happens, otherwise the commutator may get damaged. As a rule of thumb, replace brushes when they are shorter than they are wide. Always replace both brushes.

Besides wearing out, brushes may stick in the housing. Remove both brush housings (the brushes are spring loaded and will jump out if you are not careful). Examine the brushes, springs, and housings. A brush should move freely in its housing, and the spring should press it firmly against your finger. A weak spring should be replaced. If the housings are dirty, spray them and the brushes with electrical contact cleaner (p.123). The ends of brushes are curved to fit the curve of the commutator; be sure to align them correctly when installing them. Brushes on most appliances will last a number of years before they wear out. Frequent brush replacement may indicate a rough commutator.

Volt-ohm meter tests

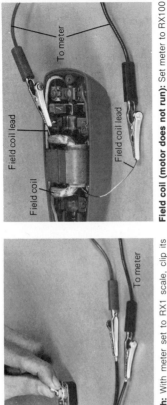

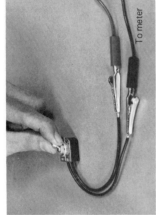

Power cord: Set meter to RX1 scale and clip its probes to plug. Attach jumper to power cord leads. Bend and twist cord during test. If meter reads zero ohms, cord is OK; if high, there is an open circuit in the cord.

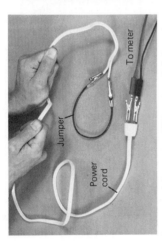

Field coil (motor shocks): Set meter to RX100 scale. Clip one probe to field coil lead, other to motor frame. If meter reads low. coil is grounded. If meter reads high, leakage current (p.127) may be causing shock.

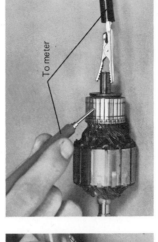

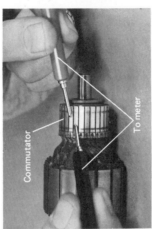

On-off switch: With meter set to RX1 scale, clip its probes to switch terminals. Turn switch on and off. If switch is OK, meter needle will jump from zero ohms to high ohms as switch goes from on to off.

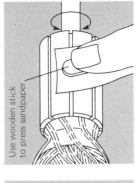

Field coil (motor does not run): Set meter to RX100 scale. Attach probes to field coil leads. High reading indicates open circuit. If there are several leads from field coil, motor has tapped field (p.134).

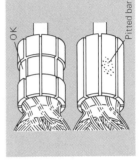

Rotor test (motor shocks): Set meter to RX100 scale. Clip one probe to shaft, touch other to each commutator bar in turn. Low reading may mean grounded coil. High reading may mean leakage current.

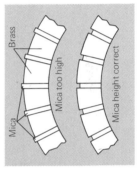

Bar-to-bar commutator check: Set meter to RX1 scale, touch probes to adjacent bars all around commutator. All should read about the same. High reading means open circuit, zero ohms means short.

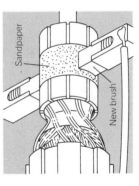

Polish a rough commutator by holding sandpaper to it as you turn rotor shaft. Also, replace brushes; they may have caused roughness.

Commutator with shiny ring is OK even if groove is deeply worn. A single shiny, pitted, or dark bar indicates short circuit or open circuit in a rotor coil.

Brass bars on commutator are separated by mica insulation. If mica protrudes, scrape it carefully with knife so that it is just below brass level.

Brushes and commutator

If new brushes are not precurved, wrap sandpaper strip (not emery cloth) around commutator, turn rotor a few times to grind brush to shape.

Mechanical problems

In addition to the electrical malfunctions described on page 133, motors may suffer from a number of purely mechanical troubles. Chief among these are difficulties with the bearings, fan, and rotor.

Bearings support the rotor shaft while allowing it to turn freely. Most small appliance bearings are made of bronze or other soft metal and fit like sleeves over the rotor shaft. A little light machine oil should be applied occasionally to the bearings or the felt pads built into them or near them. Use a minimum of oil to avoid contaminating the commutator and brushes. Ball bearings are occasionally found in electrical appliances. Sealed ball bearings are permanently greased and should never be opened. Other types should be repacked every two years.

Noise, overheating, loss of power, or outright stoppage of the motor are all symptoms of bearing troubles. With the appliance unplugged and the motor accessible, try turning the motor shaft by hand. It should move easily and smoothly in the bearings. At the same time, the rotor shaft should fit snugly, with no up and down play. Tight bearings can sometimes be cured by lubrication. But if the bearings are badly worn or if they have seized so that the rotor cannot turn, they must be replaced. Examine the rotor shaft any time you are replacing bearings. If it is scored, or if the bearings are frozen onto it, the rotor, too, must be replaced. The expense of replacing both the rotor and the bearings may be high enough to warrant the purchase of a new motor or new appliance. To avoid damage to the rotor shaft, check out any symptoms of bearing trouble thoroughly before you use the appliance again.

A universal motor usually has a fan attached to its rotor shaft to keep the motor cool. If the blades of the fan are broken or distorted, or if the fan is loose on the shaft, noise and vibration will result. The fan may be attached to the shaft by a setscrew, nut, or C-clip, it may simply screw onto the shaft, or it may be permanently pressed or welded in place. Loose fans must be tightened or replaced. Sometimes a bent fan can be straightened by bending the distorted blades so that they are aligned with the others (it will help to remove the fan and lay it on a flat surface when realigning the blades). A badly warped fan or one with chipped blades must be replaced or it will eventually damage other parts of the motor. If the fan is pressed onto the rotor shaft, you may have to buy a new rotor, but check with a repairman first.

There must be a small air gap between the rotor and the interior of the field frame for proper operation of an electric motor. If the rotor is out of line, it may rub against the field resulting in noise, overheating, damage to the motor, and inefficient operation. Once you have determined that the bearings are good, check for rotor misalignment by turning the rotor manually (be sure the power cord is unplugged). Difficulty in turning may indicate misalignment. Next, remove the rotor from the field frame and examine it and the inside of the field for signs of wear. Look for a worn or shiny strip on the rotor and a worn or shiny spot on the field frame. A warped motor frame or appliance housing may be responsible for the misalignment, in which case replacing the appliance is probably the only solution. A more likely cause, however, is incorrect installation of one or both bearings or their retainers. Check the bearings and their retainers carefully. Small cutouts in the outside of the bearings, projections on the retainers or the bearing seats, and asymmetry in the shape of the bearings are there for a purpose. Failure to mate the bearings, bearing retainers, and bearing seats properly will cause the rotor shaft to be misaligned and will eventually destroy the motor.

Speed control devices for universal motors

Tapped field speed control, in which one of the rotor's field windings has several leads, or taps, coming from it, is commonly used for varying speed. The control shown at left has three taps; some blender motors have as many as six. The selector switch permits power to be applied to any tap. Motor speeds are lowest when current flows through the entire coil, highest when current flows through the smallest segment. (This is because a short wire has less resistance, allowing more current to flow.) To 'est tapped field control, unplug the power cord, set a volt-ohm mreter to the RX1 scale, and clip one meter probe to the low speed terminal. Apply the second probe to each of the other terminals in turn. Ohms readings should increase gradually as higher speed taps are touched, but should never reach the high end of the scale. If the meter does not read high, the motor should be replaced.

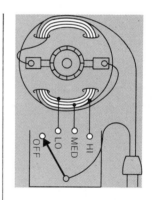

Governor-type speed controls provide variation from nearly zero up to maximum free-running speed, while maintaining constant torque (turning force). The illustration shows one type of governor. In it, a scissorlike device with weights is attached to the motor shaft. When the shaft spins, centrifugal force pulls the weights outward, causing the scissors to close. As they do, the actuator pin is pushed against the contact arm. When the force is sufficient, electrical contact is interrupted and the motor begins to slow down. This permits the scissors to open, reestablishing electrical contact and turning the motor on again. By means of such constant on-off action, a governor can maintain a precise motor speed. Speeds are varied by adjusting contact arm tension (higher tension gives more speed). Problems in a governor control may include a melted actuator tip, fused contacts, and a dirty actuator shaft.

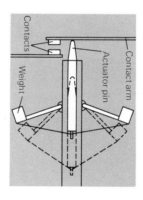

Contacts
Weight
Actuator pin
Contact arm

A solid state control is an electronic version of a governor. The key part is a silicon controlled rectifier (SCR) that gates current according to a control voltage that is impressed on it. SCR circuits vary, but all use the same principle. Altering the control voltage changes speed by metering the power flow to the motor. If an SCR control fails, the motor may run at high speed only or not run at all. Usually the entire control unit must be replaced, but let a repairman decide. SCR solid state controls are often used on drills, blenders, and mixers. Certain appliances working on the tapped field principle have a small solid state device known as a diode to double the number of speeds available. For advertising purposes, manufacturers often describe these as solid state controls. Lamp dimmers also use SCR's, but do not attach appliances to them, or you may burn out a motor or overload the dimmer.

Older appliances may have rheostats for controlling speed. Rheostats are simple and reliable, but waste energy by heating up, and do not provide constant torque. A rheostat is basically a wire coil that can be tapped at any point by means of a sliding contact. When a rheostat is wired into a motor circuit, it provides a means of varying resistance by moving the sliding contact. If the resistance is high, current drops, and so does motor speed. Movable brushes are used on some early mixers. To decrease speed, the brushes are shifted away from the optimum center position on the commutator. In addition to speed controls, some universal motors have reversing switches, which make it possible to change the rotational direction of the rotor. Typical reversing switches work by interchanging the electrical connections between field windings and brushes. They are often found on hand-held power drills.

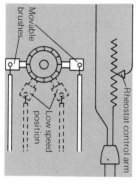

Movable brushes
Rheostat control arm
Low speed position

Other electric motors

Induction motors

With the exception of universal motors, induction motors are the ones most frequently found in the home. There are two common types: split phase and shaded pole. Split phase motors are used in washing machines, dishwashers, oil burners, refrigerators, and air conditioners—wherever an efficient, heavy-duty, single-speed drive is needed. Shaded pole motors are used in can openers, rotisseries, clocks, fans, and bonnet-type hair dryers. They are inexpensive and durable, but are relatively inefficient. Like all induction motors, split phase and shaded pole motors have no brushes or rotor windings, work only on alternating current, and require special means for starting them up.

Split phase motors use a separate start winding. When the motor reaches 75 percent of full speed, a centrifugal switch cuts off power to the winding to keep it from burning up. Split phase motors also have a thermal overload protector that will shut the motor down if it overheats. Should this happen, wait several minutes for the motor to cool before restarting it. Some overload protectors must be reset manually after they trip; there will be a reset button on the motor housing if this is the case. Split phase motors often have an electrical device known as a capacitor in their starting circuit to provide greater start-up force. The capacitor is usually mounted on the motor housing. Most difficulties with split phase

motors are similar to those in universal motors: frozen or worn bearings, open-circuited windings, damaged power cord, and the like. The starting circuitry, however, leads to some special problems. A split phase motor that hums but does not turn may be the result of a faulty centrifugal switch. If the motor is accessible, try spinning the rotor shaft by hand. If it starts up, it means the switch is stuck in the open position or broken. The switch may also stick in the closed position. In this case, the motor will shut down a second or two after it starts. Cleaning the switch contacts and lubricating the mechanism may solve either problem, otherwise replace the switch. Weak starting of a motor may be caused

by a short circuit in the capacitor; a motor that hums but does not turn may have a capacitor with an open circuit. Test the capacitor with a volt-ohm meter and replace it if either defect shows up.

Shaded pole motors can be recognized by a copper band that circles, or shades, a portion of each field pole. The purpose of the bands is to create an electromagnetic asymmetry that gives the rotor its initial twist. Unlike the start winding in a split phase motor, the bands are not deactivated after the motor reaches speed, a fact that decreases efficiency but makes for increased reliability. As a result, shaded pole motors seldom break in normal use, and when they do, it is usually wisest to replace the entire motor.

To meter

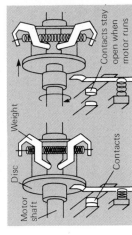

To check capacitor, set volt-ohm meter (p.124) to RX100 scale and touch its probes to capacitor terminals. If capacitor is OK, needle will jump to zero ohms, drift back to high. Steady zero ohms means a short circuit, steady high ohms means an open circuit.

Centrifugal switch of split phase motor has weights that move outward as motor speeds up, pulling disc with them. This lets switch contacts open, shutting down power to start winding. Dirty or fused contacts, sticky mechanism, or broken springs may cause trouble.

Contacts stay open when motor runs

Weight

Disc

Contacts

Motor shaft

Shaded pole motor

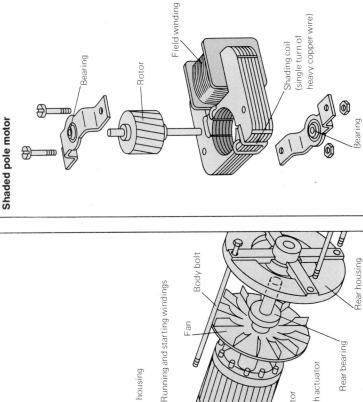

Bearing

Rotor

Field winding

Shading coil (single turn of heavy copper wire)

Bearing

Split phase motor

Capacitor cover

Front housing

Capacitor

Main housing

Running and starting windings

Fan

Body bolt

Rear housing

Rotor

Centrifugal switch actuator

Rear bearing

Centrifugal switch contact arm

Front bearing

On-off switch

Power cord

Cordless appliances

General troubleshooting procedures

Cordless appliances consist of two units: a power handle and a charger. The power handle contains the motor, gears, and other working components as well as a battery—generally called a power pack—that supplies power for the motor. The charging unit plugs into a wall outlet and converts house current into a form suitable for recharging the energy cells of the power pack. The power handle is generally kept seated in the charger when it is not in use (the power pack cells are of a type that cannot be overcharged).

Most of the problems associated with cordless appliances are the same as those for appliances that work directly from a wall outlet. Such difficulties as worn or frozen bearings, stripped gears, a broken on-off switch, worn motor brushes, loose parts, and mechanical overloads produce the same symptoms and require the same repairs for either kind of appliance. Special testing procedures must be followed only when there is a fault in the charging unit or power pack. These are described on the next page and outlined in *Troubleshooting checklist* at right.

Cordless appliance motors

The motors of cordless appliances closely resemble universal motors (see pp.132-134). Both kinds of motor have a wound rotor, a pair of carbon brushes, and a commutator. The chief difference is in the field. Motors of cordless appliances use permanent magnets instead of windings. As a result, they are smaller and more efficient, but have less power and run on direct current only. Aside from there being no field coils to burn out, short circuit, or become grounded, repair and troubleshooting are the same as for universal motors. In particular, the brushes will eventually have to be replaced. Because of their small size, permanent magnet DC motors are sometimes used even on cord-type appliances such as hair styler-dryers.

Troubleshooting checklist

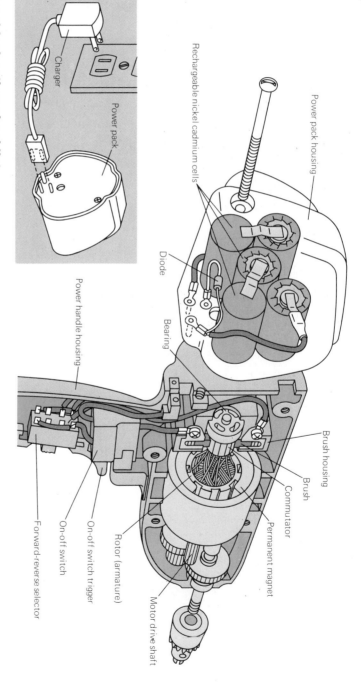

Charger

Power pack

Rechargeable nickel cadmium cells

Power pack housing

Diode

Power handle housing

Bearing

Rotor (armature)

On-off switch

On-off switch trigger

Forward-reverse selector

Motor drive shaft

Permanent magnet

Commutator

Brush

Brush housing

PROBLEM	POSSIBLE CAUSE	ACTION
Motor does not turn, lacks power, or does not run long enough	Poor electrical contact between charger and power handle	Check wall outlet with a lamp you know is working. Also be sure that outlet is not wired into wall switch or light switch (for example, on a medicine cabinet); charger must be on continuously in order to keep battery charged
	Defective charging unit	Clean contacts. Use very fine (No. 400) sandpaper. If contacts are difficult to reach, spray with electrical contact cleaner (p.123). Rotate and slide power handle in and out of charger well several times
	Bad cells in power pack	Test charger and power cord (See p.137). Replace power cord if bad. Replace charger if test results are negative
	Defective diode rectifier	One or more cells in power pack may have open circuit or short circuit. Open up power handle if possible. Look for sticky substance (electrolyte) leaking from battery, corroded terminals, bad leads. Test battery cells and replace any that are defective. If power handle is sealed, continue with next troubleshooting step before taking appliance to repair shop
		If test of charger terminals shows an AC voltage but the indirect diode test shows no charging current, the diode rectifier is bad. Diode may be in charging unit or handle. If it is accessible, check it again according to the direct diode test and replace it if it is broken
	On-off switch faulty, brushes worn, motor jammed, commutator dirty, short circuit or open circuit in rotor winding, brushes not contacting commutator	See *Universal motors*, pp.132-134, or refer to section on particular appliance involved. Tests and repairs for these difficulties are the same for both cord and cordless appliances
Motor vibrates, is noisy	Worn bearings, loose or worn parts	See *Universal motors*, pp.132-134, or refer to section on particular appliance involved. Tests and repairs for these difficulties are the same for both cord and cordless appliances

The power pack and charging unit

The power pack consists of one or more nickel cadmium cells, each of which provides direct current at about 1.2 volts (about the same as one of the AA penlight batteries they superficially resemble). The length of time that a fully charged power pack will run a cordless appliance depends on how many cells it has and the amount of power the appliance consumes. Typical figures are 10 minutes running time for an electric toothbrush and ½ hour for an electric drill. If the battery has been completely discharged, it takes about 14 hours to recharge it to maximum strength. Charging voltages must be about 1 volt higher than the total output voltage of the power pack. To find the power pack voltage, open up the power handle, count the number of nickel cadmium cells inside, and multiply this number by 1.2. Thus, a 4-cell power pack puts out about 5 volts and charges at about 6 volts.

In most cordless appliances, contacts in the well of the charging unit mate with matching contacts on the power handle to provide the charging current. In some models, however, there is no metal-to-metal contact. Instead, the charger sets up an alternating electromagnetic field, similar to the fields in electric motors. When the power handle is seated in the charger well, a current is induced in the power handle that is strong enough to recharge the battery.

Home electricity is in the form of alternating current (AC) at about 120 volts. The power pack requires direct current (DC) at a much lower voltage in order to recharge. Two devices, a transformer and a diode rectifier, accomplish this change. The transformer does the job of stepping the voltage down; the diode changes the alternating current to direct current. The diode is a small solid state device that is usually sealed, together with the larger and heavier transformer, inside the charging unit. In some cases the diode is

in the power handle and can be tested with a volt-ohm meter (see p.124).

Although nickel cadmium cells can be charged and discharged hundreds of times, they eventually break down and must be replaced. In cases where the power handle is permanently sealed, as in electric toothbrushes, direct testing of the cells is impossible. However, if tests show that the charger is working properly, yet the appliance does not run or runs feebly, there is probably a bad cell. But before replacing a cell, clean the charger and power handle contacts with fine sandpaper or electrical contact cleaner to see if this solves the problem.

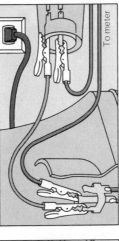

Attach other probe to remaining handle contact. Plug charger into outlet. If meter reads zero, reverse probes. Reading of about 50 mA or higher either time means charger is OK. Zero readings, combined with earlier AC volt reading, indicate shorted diode.

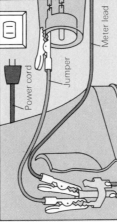

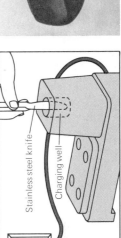

Power pack cells can be tested with volt-ohm meter. Set meter to 2.5 VDC scale, touch red probe to + terminal of battery, black to – terminal. Turn on appliance. If reading dips below 1 volt, cell is probably bad. Make test with power handle removed from charger.

To make indirect diode test, set volt-ohm meter to read milliamperes (mA). Use 250 mA scale (1mA = .001 amp). Clip jumper between one charger contact and corresponding contact of power handle, then attach one probe of meter to other charger contact.

If reading was zero volts both times in first test, next step is to test for AC volts. Set meter to 25 VAC scale and touch its probes to charger contacts. If AC voltage reading is obtained, check the diode. If reading is still zero, check the power cord.

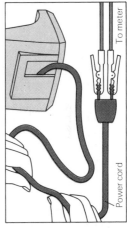

Some charging units have no contacts; they work by induction. Plug in power cord, hold stainless steel blade against side of charging well. If unit is OK, blade will vibrate; otherwise, unit is broken. Diode and battery are sealed into handle in these appliances.

Testing a cordless appliance

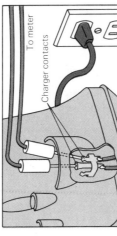

First step is to check charging unit for DC volts. Set volt-ohm meter to 25 VDC scale, plug charger into outlet, touch meter probes to charger contacts. If meter reads zero, reverse probes. Proper reading either time (1 volt more than power pack) means charger is OK.

Charger may have power cord or may plug directly into wall outlet. In either case, set meter to RX100 scale and clip its probes to prongs of plug. Meter should read between 500 to 1,000 ohms. If it reads high or zero ohms, power cord or transformer is faulty.

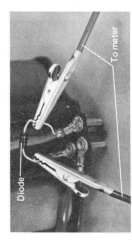

Direct diode test can be made if diode is accessible (it may be in handle or charger). Unplug power cord, set meter to RX1 scale, touch probes to diode leads. Reverse probes. If meter reads high one way, low the other, diode is OK. Zero readings mean a short.

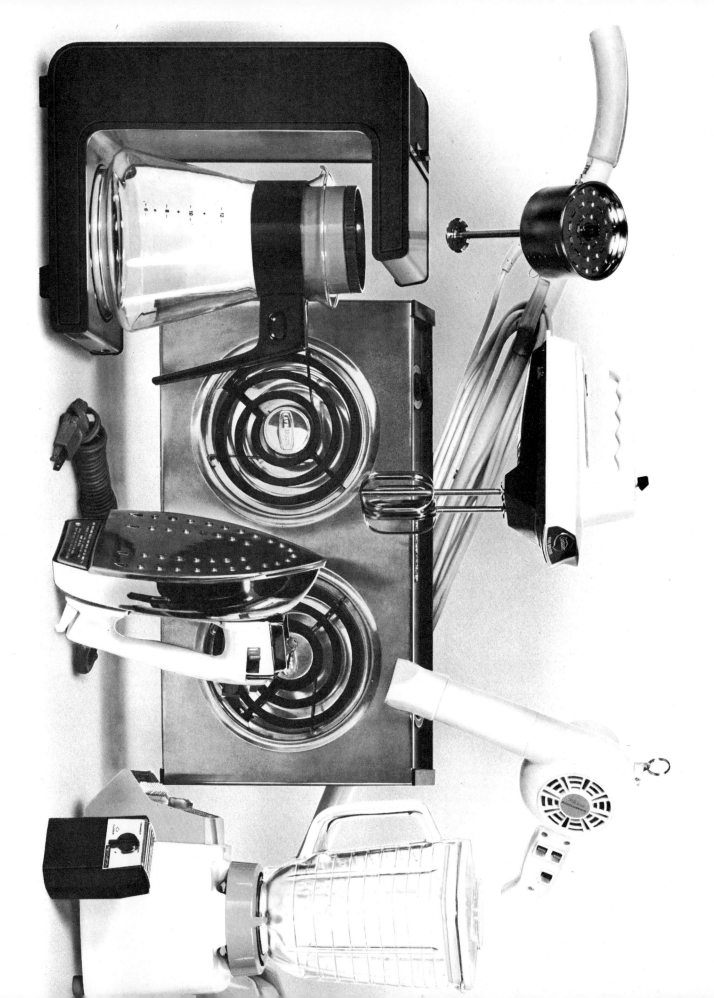

Small Appliances

Once you gain a little experience, you will find that fixing small appliances can be surprisingly easy. When trying to pinpoint the cause of a malfunction in an appliance, make the simplest and most obvious checks first. Resort to more complicated tests, or ones that require you to disassemble the appliance, only when other tests fail to locate the problem. The charts in this section are designed to help you do just that. Each chart contains a series of questions dealing with a problem in a particular appliance. Under each such question is a test that enables you to answer the question yes or no. If the answer is yes, follow the arrow marked "YES" to the instructions that tell you how to fix the appliance. If the answer is no, follow the arrow marked "NO" to the next question, and the next, until you arrive at a question that gives you a yes answer. Symbols under the repair instructions indicate whether the repair is simple or difficult.

Blankets

Blanket does not heat

If blanket fails to heat, it means current is not flowing through heating elements. The cause is determined through step-by-step testing, starting with the wall outlet and continuing with the various parts of the blanket. Repairs range from changing a house fuse to replacing blanket or temperature control unit.

Power off at outlet?

NO ←

TEST: Unplug power cord and check wall outlet with a lamp you know is working.

YES →
FIX: Replace fuse or reset circuit breaker. See p.127. If fuse keeps blowing, see *Blanket blows fuses*, p.142.
△

Heating element broken?

NO ←

TEST: With blanket unplugged, disconnect control cord. Set volt-ohm meter (p.124) to RX1 scale. Clip its probes to the pins of blanket plug, and twist and squeeze blanket. If heating element is OK, meter will read a steady 80 to 200 ohms. If needle jumps around or reads high ohms, heating element is broken.

YES →
FIX: Replace blanket or take it to an authorized repairman. Do not try to fix the heating element yourself. Repairs are difficult and pose potential shock and burn hazards and should be done incorrectly. If you buy a new blanket, be sure it is designed to work with your old control.
△△△

Power cord broken?

NO ←

TEST: Unplug power cord and examine it for fraying and the plug for loose or distorted prongs. Remove back cover of control unit. Attach jumper wire across power cord leads inside unit. Set volt-ohm meter to RX1 scale and clip its probes to the prongs of the plug. Bend and pull power cord. If cord is OK, meter will read zero ohms; if bad, needle will jump or read high.

YES →
FIX: Replace power cord. Disassemble control unit so that old power cord leads are accessible. Pry open crimp-on terminals and disconnect old leads. Use pliers to crimp the leads from new wire into place. If necessary, repair cord temporarily by replacing a broken plug with a standard appliance plug or by cutting away damaged portions of wire, then splicing the wires back together.
△△

Control cord broken?

NO ←

TEST: With power cord unplugged from outlet, examine control cord for fraying. Disassemble control unit so control cord leads are accessible and attach jumper wire across leads. Set volt-ohm meter to RX1 scale and clip its probes to terminals of control cord plug. Bend and pull cord. If cord is OK, meter will read zero ohms; if bad, needle will jump around or read high.

YES →
FIX: Replace control cord. Pry open crimp-on terminals and disconnect control cord leads. Use pliers to crimp new leads into place. If necessary, you can repair cord temporarily by cutting away damaged portions of wire, then splicing the wires back together.
△△

Dirty contacts on switch or thermostat?

TEST: Disassemble control unit completely. Clean switch contacts and thermostat contacts (see **Fix**). Reassemble and operate blanket to see if problem is solved.

YES →
FIX: Clean contacts. Polish both sets of contacts with very fine (No. 400) sandpaper. Blow away filings from contacts. Note: When reassembling control unit, reset dial according to thermostat adjustment procedure in *Blanket is too hot or too cold*, p.142.
△△

Ease of fix: △ simple △△ average △△△ difficult

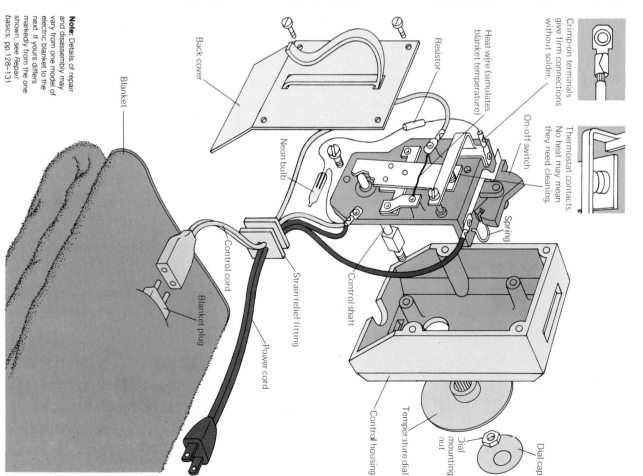

Crimp-on terminals give firm connections without solder.

Thermostat contacts: No heat may mean they need cleaning.

Heat wire (simulates blanket temperature)

Resistor

On-off switch

Neon bulb

Back cover

Spring

Control shaft

Control cord

Blanket plug

Blanket

Strain relief fitting

Power cord

Control housing

Temperature dial

Dial mounting nut

Dial cap

Note: Details of repair and disassembly may vary from one model of electric blanket to the next. If yours differs markedly from the one shown, see *Repair basics*, pp.128–131.

Use and care

When the blanket is on, do not lie on it, put things on it, or tuck in wired portions. (You can feel the wires inside the blanket.)

Do not place the control near the radiator or window sill, or where it will be shielded from the normal room air flow. Blankets can usually be laundered by hand or machine but not drycleaned. Use lukewarm water with mild soap. Check the blanket's label before you wash it. To set warmth, start by turning heat control to *High*, then lower it slowly to a temperature you find comfortable. Electric blankets are mothproof. Do not store them with moth balls.

Disassembling the control unit

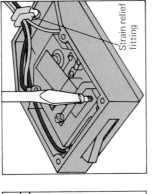
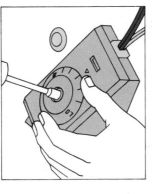
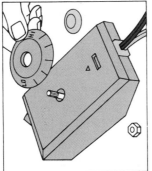
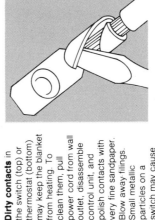

Strain relief fitting

1. With blanket unplugged from wall outlet, remove screws holding back cover onto control housing and take cover off.

2. To remove temperature dial, first pry up the small center cap to expose the mounting nut. (The cap is glued on.)

3. Unscrew mounting nut with nut driver. Put nut and other small parts in envelope or container to keep from losing them.

4. Lift temperature dial off control shaft. After reassembly, glue center cap back in place with dab of household cement.

5. Undo mounting screws and lift control unit from housing along with power cord, control cord, and strain relief fitting.

Testing for open circuits

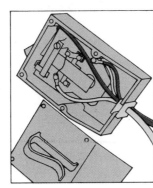
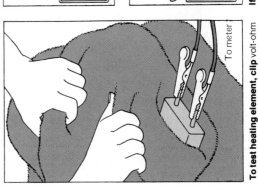

To meter

To test heating element, clip volt-ohm meter probes to the heating element terminal pins on the blanket. Ruffle the blanket during test to help find intermittent connections. Replace blanket or take it to repairman if it is broken.

 Set meter to RX1 scale for all three tests at left. When testing either power cord or control cord, meter will read zero ohms if part is OK, high ohms if there is an open circuit. When checking heating element, meter will read 80 to 200 ohms if element is OK, high ohms if there is an open circuit.

Jumper wire · To meter · Power cord

Jumper wire · Control cord · To meter

If there is an open circuit in the power cord (top) or control cord (bottom), the blanket will not heat. Test the cords separately with the volt-ohm meter. In each case, attach a jumper wire across the terminals of the cord being checked and clip the meter probes to its plug.

Cleaning contacts

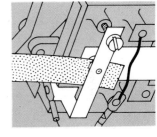
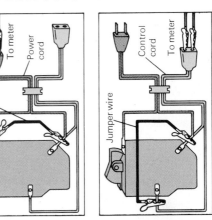

Dirty contacts in the switch (top) or thermostat (bottom) may keep the blanket from heating. To clean them, pull power cord from wall outlet, disassemble control unit, and polish contacts with very fine sandpaper. Blow away filings. Small metallic particles on a switch may cause it to fail.

Installing new cords

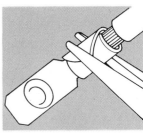

Most difficult step in replacing power or control cords is prying open crimp-on terminals. Use a strong, sharp tool like an awl. Crimp them closed with pliers. If you cannot open them, cut off old wire and solder new wire into place or splice new wire to the stub of the old wire and insulate it with electrical tape. See *Repair Basics*, pp. 128–131.

Blankets

Blanket is too hot or too cold

Temperature problems are generally caused by trouble in the thermostat, either because it is broken or because it is out of calibration. If adjustment fails to correct the difficulty, the entire control unit, including the power cord and control cord, should be replaced with a manufacturer's equivalent.

Thermostat out of adjustment?

NO →

TEST: Unplug control unit from both wall outlet and blanket. Clip jumper wire across terminals of female plug. Set volt-ohm meter (p.124) to RX1 scale and clip its probes to the prongs of the power cord plug. Turn temperature dial to Low and set control switch to On position. Slowly move dial from Low to High and back again while watching meter. If thermostat is properly adjusted, meter needle will jump from high to zero ohms about midway between the low and high temperature settings and back to high ohms when the control dial is returned to the low temperature setting. If the needle does not jump at all or jumps well before or beyond the midpoint on the temperature dial, then the thermostat is either broken or out of adjustment. Note: Be sure to conduct this test at normal room temperature.

YES → **FIX: Adjust or replace thermostat.** Leave volt-ohm meter set up as in the test. Remove dial from control (see p.141. *Disassembling the control unit,* steps 2 and 3). *Disassembling* stem clockwise to the point where volt-ohm meter needle jumps from high to zero ohms, then remount dial on stem so that the dial reads slightly lower than the exact middle temperature setting. Screw on dial nut and tighten. Check adjustment by turning temperature dial toward Low. Needle on volt-ohm meter should jump from zero ohms to high before dial comes to full stop (lowest temperature setting). If this does not happen, repeat adjustment, setting the temperature control dial somewhat higher than before. △△

Thermostat broken?

If repeated attempts to adjust the thermostat fail, the thermostat must be broken and you should replace the entire control unit, including power cord and control cord, with a manufacturer's equivalent. First be sure, however, that you have been using the blanket correctly, as it is a widely misunderstood appliance. Consult *Use and care* (p.141) and your owner's manual.

Ease of fix: △ simple △△ average △△△ difficult

Testing and adjusting the thermostat

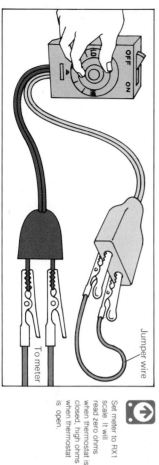

Set meter to RX1 scale. It will read zero ohms when thermostat is closed, high ohms when thermostat is open.

Jumper wire

To meter

Clip volt-ohm meter probes to power cord plug and attach jumper wire across control cord plug. Turn switch to On and rotate heat dial. Reading should jump to zero when dial is near midtemperature. To adjust, remount dial so that reading jumps at midpoint.

Blanket blows fuses

When a fuse blows or circuit breaker trips, it means there is either an electrical overload or a short circuit. Overloads are fixed by reducing the number of appliances in the circuit. Short circuits are located by inspection and testing. Parts found to be shorted must be repaired or replaced.

Circuit overloaded?

TEST: To check for overloads, see p.127. Too many appliances in a circuit is the commonest cause of blown fuses.

YES → **FIX: Reduce number of appliances in the circuit. Caution: Never replace a fuse or breaker with one having a larger capacity.** △

Short circuit in blanket?

TEST: Disconnect control cord from blanket. Set volt-ohm meter (p.124) to RX1 scale and clip its probes to the pins of the blanket plug. (See *Testing for open circuits,* p.141.) Twist and squeeze blanket. If blanket is OK, meter will read 80 to 200 ohms; if needle jumps around or reads zero ohms, heating element is shorted.

YES → **FIX: Replace blanket or take it to an authorized repairman.** Do not try to fix the heating element yourself. Repairs are difficult and pose potential shock and burn hazards and should the work be done incorrectly. If you buy a new blanket, be sure it is designed to work with your old control. △

Short circuit in cords or control unit?

TEST: Disconnect power cord from wall outlet. Examine power cord, control cord, and plugs for bare wires and burn marks. Turn switch to On and heat control to High. Set volt-ohm meter to RX100 scale and clip its probes to the prongs of power cord plug. Bend and pull power and control cords. If cords are OK, meter will read high; if shorted, needle will jump around or read zero ohms.

YES → **FIX: Repair or replace control unit** (p.141). Separate any wires that appear to be touching and mend broken or cracked insulation with plastic electrical tape. If there is extensive damage, replace the entire control unit, including the power cord and control cord, with a manufacturer's equivalent. △△

Checking for a short circuit

Set meter to RX1 scale. It will read high ohms if part is OK, zero ohms if there is a short circuit.

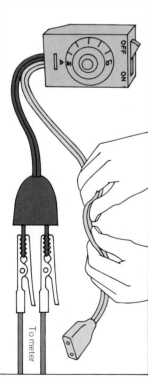

To meter

Blown fuses often mean a short circuit in an appliance. To test control unit and cords for shorts, unplug blanket, turn switch on, set heat control to High, and clip volt-ohm meter probes to prongs of plug. Bend cords during test to help disclose loose wiring.

Blanket shocks user

A frayed power cord or control cord or improper electrical contact with wiring inside the blanket—often caused by the insertion of a safety pin or other metal object into the blanket—will cause shocking. The hazard is cured by replacing defective cord or removing the cause of electrical contact.

Power cord or control cord frayed?

TEST: Receiving a shock from power cord or control cord is sufficient evidence that it needs repair.

 FIX: Replace power or control cord. Disassemble control unit so that cord leads are accessible (p.143). Pry open crimp-on terminals and disconnect cord leads (see *Installing new cords*, p.141). ▲▲

Blanket shocks through material?

TEST: Look for safety pin or similar object stuck in blanket. Note: It is normal for a blanket to cause a "tingle" if a sensitive part of the body contacts a nearby grounded object or another person under blanket.

 FIX: Remove pin. Metal touching a heating element will cause a shock. Note: If two blankets are near each other, the "tingle" effect may be heightened. It may help to reverse one of the plugs at the wall outlet. ▲

Ease of fix: △ Simple △△ average △△△ difficult

Blankets with two controls

Electric blankets are available with either one or two controls. Dual control models, usually found in double bed and larger sizes, are basically a pair of single control blankets sewn together with one control for each half. In addition to a two-wire power cord, which goes into one of the control units, and a three-wire control cord, which comes out of the other, there is also a three-wire connecting cord linking the two controls.

Like models with only one control, dual control blankets have small neon bulbs in each control unit that remain lit whenever the power cord is plugged in and the switches are in the *On* position

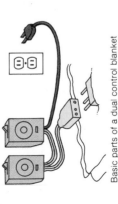

Basic parts of a dual control blanket

(they do not go on and off with the on-off cycling of the thermostats). As explained elsewhere on this page, the operation of the two neon lamps, along with a few, simple volt-ohm meter tests, can be used to uncover the causes of many problems you may be having with your blanket without the necessity of disassembling any of your dual control blanket's electrical components.

The control cord plug is designed so it will fit on the blanket in only one way. This prevents accidental reversal of the cord and insures that the control units govern the temperatures of the correct halves of the blanket. Care must be taken when setting the blanket up, however, to make sure the control units are on the proper sides of the bed. Look at the bottoms of the controls. One will be marked with a message such as: "This unit controls label side." In other words, there is a cloth label sewn on the side of the blanket whose temperature is controlled by this unit, while the other half is governed by the second unit.

Checking dual heating elements

There are three, rather than two, terminals on dual control blankets and they must be checked out in pairs. Set volt-ohm meter (p.124) to RX1 scale and clip one of its probes to the middle pin of the blanket plug and the other to either of the outside pins. Observe meter while squeezing the blanket in various places.

First volt-ohm meter test

Repeat this procedure twice more, once with the probes clipped to the middle pin and the other outside pin and once with the probes attached to the two outside pins. In each test, if the heating element is OK, the meter will read a steady 50 to 200 ohms. If the needle jumps around or reads zero for any pair of pins, there is a short circuit, or reads high for any pair of pins, there is an open circuit. If the needle jumps around or reads zero for any pair of pins, there is a short circuit. In case of either an open or short circuit, take the blanket to a repairman to determine whether it should be fixed or replaced. Be sure the probes are firmly attached to the terminal pins during all tests.

Second and third volt-ohm meter tests

Testing a dual control blanket

What the signal lamps can tell you: Much of the troubleshooting for blankets with two controls can be handled without disassembling anything. Set up the blanket for normal use, turn both heat controls to *High* and both switches to the *On* position, plug in the power cord, and observe the signal lamps.

If neither control bulb lights and neither side of the blanket heats:
Then there is no power at the wall outlet or the power cord is broken. For repair information, see *Blanket does not heat*, p.140.

If one bulb lights but neither side of the blanket heats:
Then the connecting cord is broken. It is advisable to replace the entire assembly—including control units and all cords—with manufacturer's parts.

If one bulb lights and only one side of the blanket heats:
Then the switch contacts on the control with the unlit bulb may be dirty. Clean contacts (p.141). If problem remains, replace both control units, including cords.

If both bulbs light but neither side of the blanket heats:
Then test for a broken heating element (see below, *Checking dual heating elements*). If the elements are OK, replace both control units, including cords.

If both bulbs light but only one side of the blanket heats:
Then test for a broken heating element (see below, *Checking dual heating elements*). If the elements are OK, clean the thermostat contacts in both control units as shown on p.141. If problem persists, replace both control units.

Blenders

Motor does not run or runs sluggishly

Jammed parts or too heavy a load can slow down a blender, sometimes to the point where it stalls. If power is on at the wall outlet and cleaning has not solved the problem, the blender's power cord, on-off switch, or motor may be broken. Repairs range from changing a house fuse to replacing motor parts.

Power off at outlet?

 TEST: Unplug power cord and check wall outlet with a lamp you know is working.

YES→ FIX: Replace fuse or reset circuit breaker. See p.127. If fuse keeps blowing see *Blender blows fuses,* p.147. △△

Blender jammed?

 TEST: Operate blender with container in place and with container removed. If motor does not run properly, even with container off, then the power cord, on-off switch, or motor is broken. If motor runs much faster when container is off than when it is on, the blade assembly is jamming.

YES→ FIX: Clean blade assembly. Unscrew jar bottom and remove blade assembly. Undo cap nut, take off washers and blades, and push out drive shaft. Clean shaft and housing with steel wool. Wash all parts in hot, sudsy water. Note: On some models blade assembly is riveted together and cannot be disassembled. In this case replace the entire assembly. △△

Power cord broken?

 TEST: Unplug blender from wall outlet and examine the power cord for fraying and the plug for loose or distorted prongs. Remove bottom plate and slip collar off motor. Unscrew wire nut. Pull power cord lead away from other wires and attach jumper wire from it to terminal of other power cord lead. Set volt-ohm meter (p.124) to RX1 scale and clip its probes to the prongs of the plug. Bend and pull power cord. If power cord is Ok, meter will read zero ohms; if power cord is broken, needle will jump around or read high.

YES→ FIX: Replace power cord. Undo nut holding fan to motor shaft and remove fan. Locate brush housing to which lead from power cord is attached and pry off spring clip that holds housing to motor mount. Lift brush housing from its seat (a concealed spring may cause the brush to pop out) and pull cord terminal out of the housing. Squeeze strain relief device with pliers, rotate it a quarter turn, pull it from hole in baseplate, and remove power cord. Note: New cord should be factory equivalent of old one. △△

On-off switch broken?

 TEST: With blender unplugged, pull control housing away from body so that on-off switch is accessible. Set volt-ohm meter to RX1 scale, clip its probes to each of the leads from the switch, and set switch in *On* position. If switch is broken, meter will read high; if it is OK, meter will read zero ohms.

YES→ FIX: Replace on-off switch. Pull off knob, unscrew nut holding switch to base, and remove switch from its seat. Insert a straightened-out paper clip or very small screwdriver into each switch terminal alongside the wires leading into them and pull on the wires. This will enable you to free the wires and remove the switch. △△

Motor faulty?

If the above tests fail to locate the problem, the trouble lies in the motor. Poor lubrication, worn brushes, a damaged bearing, or a bad wire in either the field coil or armature winding may be to blame. See the section on *Universal motors,* pp.132–134, for information on testing and repairs. **Caution: if motor hums but does not turn, shut it off immediately to prevent damage.**

Ease of fix: △ simple △△ average △△△ difficult

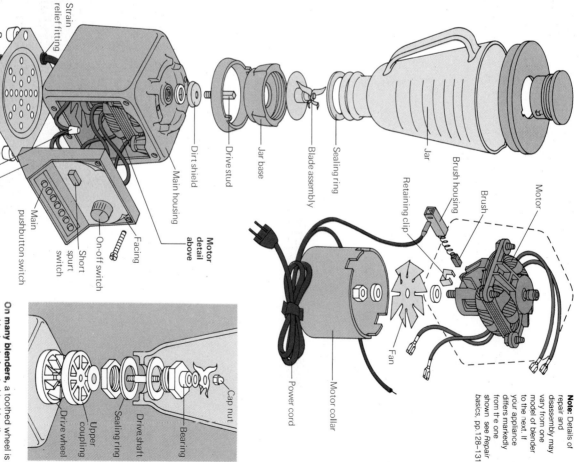

Strain
relief fitting

Power cord

Baseplate
(bottom plate)

Wire nut

Control housing

Main
pushbutton switch

On-off switch

Short
spurt
switch

Facing

Main housing

**Motor
detail
above**

Dirt shield

Drive stud

Jar base

Blade assembly

Sealing ring

Jar

Brush housing

Retaining clip

Brush

Motor

Fan

Power cord

Motor collar

Cap nut

Bearing

Drive wheel

Upper
coupling

Sealing ring

Drive shaft

Note: Details of repair and disassembly may vary from one model of blender to the next. If your appliance differs markedly from the one shown see *Repair basics,* pp.128–131.

On many blenders, a toothed wheel is used instead of a stud to drive the agitator. The upper coupling looks like a spoked wheel and is usually made of plastic. In order to replace it, unscrew it from the agitator shaft.

Disassembling the blender

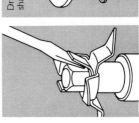

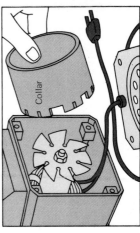

Collar

1. Be sure blender is disconnected from wall outlet. Unscrew feet and pull baseplate away from base. Remove protective plastic motor collar.

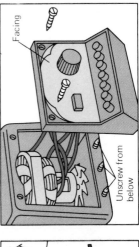

Facing

Unscrew from below

2. In a two-piece base, the control housing is fastened by screws. Peel back facing with knife to get at top screws. Reach others from inside.

Spring

Lead

Lead

4. Trace power cord lead to the brush housing. Pry off clip (left), remove housing, and pull out cord lead (right). Note: spring is concealed in housing.

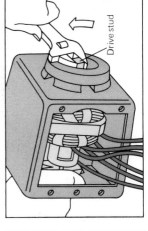

Drive stud

3. Grasp fan to keep the motor shaft from turning. Unscrew drive stud and remove dirt shield and washers. Take off fan by unscrewing fan nut.

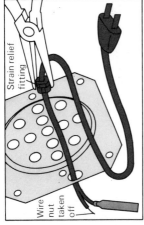

Strain relief fitting

Wire nut taken off

5. Unscrew wire nut and separate power cord lead from other wires. Squeeze strain relief fitting, rotate it a quarter turn, and remove power cord.

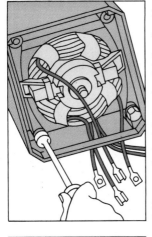

6. After removing leads from main switch (see *Repairing short spurt and main pushbutton switches*, p. 146), unscrew mounting screws and remove motor.

Unjamming the blade assembly

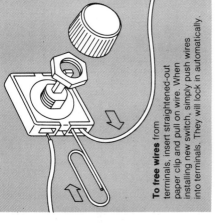

Drive shaft

Jammed blade unit is disassembled for cleaning. If there are tabs (left), pry them down before unscrewing nut. To free stuck shaft, rap unit on board (right).

Use and care

1. Clean the blender after each use. Fill the container half full with warm water, add a little liquid detergent, cover, and blend at low speed for 5 seconds. Rinse and dry thoroughly. To clean the base, wipe it with a damp sponge. Never immerse the base in water.

2. Every few weeks, disassemble the container unit (jar, jar bottom, sealing ring, blade assembly, and lid) and wash the parts in warm, soapy water. Do not use scouring powder or pads. The glass jar may be washed in a dishwasher but not the other parts.

3. Do not store food overnight in the glass container.

4. To keep from damaging the blades, do not insert any utensils into the jar while the blender is in operation.

5. Do not add ice cubes to the blender without first putting at least 1 cup of liquid into the container.

6. The agitator blades can be razor sharp. Keep your hands away when the blender is running; handle with care when the blender is off.

7. If the motor labors when processing a heavy mixture, switch the blender to the next higher speed. If the blender ever stalls, for whatever reason, turn it off immediately to prevent any possible damage to the motor.

Replacing the on-off switch

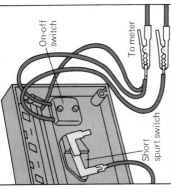

To free wires from terminals, insert straightened-out paper clip and pull on wire. When installing new switch, simply push wires into terminals. They will lock in automatically.

Testing for open circuits when blender does not run

Set meter to RX1 scale for both tests.

Test 1: Meter will read zero ohms if cord is OK. Needle will jump around or read high if cord is broken.

Test 2: Meter will read zero ohms if switch is OK. high if it is broken.

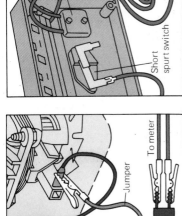

On-off switch

To meter

Short spurt switch

2. On-off switch: Put switch in *On* position and clip volt-ohm meter probes to each of the wires coming from the switch.

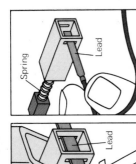

Jumper

To meter

1. Power cord: Attach volt-ohm meter probes to prongs of plug, clip jumper wire across leads of power cord. Bend and twist cord.

Blenders

Blender operates at some speeds but not others

The trouble may go beyond a broken switch. Some of the terminals or switch contacts may be dirty, or motor may be defective. If problem can be traced to a particular switch, its contacts can be cleaned or the entire switch replaced. Otherwise, blender must be taken to qualified repairman.

Short spurt switch broken?

TEST: Unplug blender from wall outlet. Disassemble base of blender so that control housing can be pulled away from base (p. 145) and examine short spurt switch. Its contacts should be clean and should close firmly when short spurt button is pressed.

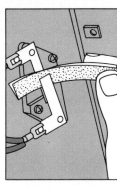

YES ➡ FIX: Repair or replace short spurt switch. Polish contacts with very fine (No. 400) sandpaper. If contacts do not close as button is pressed, bend contact arm until they do. If contact arm or pushrod is broken, replace switch. Remove leads from terminal posts and take out screws that hold switch to the control housing. Lift out old switch. △△

⬅ NO

Broken wiring inside base?

TEST: With blender unplugged and the control housing pulled away from the base of blender, examine wires leading to terminals on back of switch. Look for burn marks and broken wires.

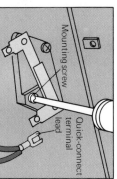

YES ➡ FIX: Repair broken wires. Strip off ½ inch of insulation on each side of break, splice ends together, and wrap with plastic electrical tape. If break is adjacent to terminal, discard old terminal, strip ¼ inch of insulation from wire, crimp on new terminal. △△

⬅ NO

Contacts on main pushbutton switch dirty?

TEST: With blender unplugged and disassembled, spray-clean interior of switch and terminal posts at back of switch (see **Fix**). Reassemble blender and operate it to see if the difficulty has been cleared up.

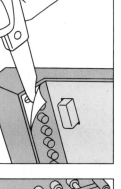

YES ➡ FIX: Clean contacts. Peel facing from lower corners of control housing. Remove screws and pull main pushbutton switch out of its seat. Spray electrical contact cleaner (p. 123) into button slots and openings in back of switch and onto terminals. △△

If previous tests have failed to pinpoint the cause of the problem, either the motor or main pushbutton switch may be broken. The switch is probably to blame if the blender works in the lowest speed setting but not in one or more of the other speed settings. However, it is best to take the blender to a qualified repairman. A complete checkout is complicated and requires a wiring diagram.

Repairing short spurt and main pushbutton switches

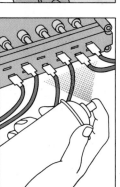

Mounting screw

Quick-connect terminal lead

To replace short spurt switch, remove quick-connect terminals (be gentle, they are fragile), then take out mounting screws.

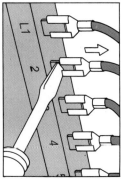

Mounting screws for pushbutton switch are usually hidden under facing strip. Peel back corners of strip to reach screws.

Polish contacts of short spurt switch with sandpaper, not emery cloth or metallic abrasive. Blow away filings.

Blender makes excessive noise while operating

Noisy operation is usually due to a loose part. Repairs consist of tightening or replacing components. Bad motor bearings, broken wiring in the motor, chipped blades, or a worn drive stud will also cause noise. The blades and drive stud can be replaced. Problems with the motor are covered on pp. 132–134.

Loose or broken components in base?

TEST: Run blender at several speeds without jar. If it is noisy, the trouble lies in the base unit rather than the jar or blade assembly. Perform repairs indicated in **Fix**, reassemble blender, and operate it to see if problem has been cleared up. If trouble persists, the motor bearings may be worn or there may be a defect in motor's wiring. (See *Universal motors,* pp. 132–134.) Note: Make sure sealing ring is in place and jar bottom is seated correctly and screwed on tightly.

YES ➡ FIX: Repair or replace loose and damaged parts. Unplug blender. Tighten all knobs and screws on exterior of base. Remove bottom plate and check fan. If it is loose on shaft, tighten the nut. If fan blades are bent or strike plastic collar, undo nut, remove fan, replace with a new one. If blender still runs noisily, remove control housing and tighten screws and nuts holding the various switches in place. Refer to illustrations on p. 145, *Disassembling the blender.* △△

Blades broken or deformed?

TEST: Operate blender briefly with and without jar. If it is noisy only when jar is attached, remove jar from blender and unscrew bottom. Examine agitator unit. If blades are chipped, broken, or bent, they may vibrate excessively and cause noise.

YES ➡ FIX: Replace blades (p. 145). Unscrew cap nut and remove blades (p. 145). If blades are riveted to shaft, replace entire blade assembly. △

Drive stud worn?

TEST: Remove container and inspect stud. If its edges are rounded off rather than square, it may slip in the drive socket and make noise when the blender is heavily loaded.

YES ➡ FIX: Replace drive stud. Turn blender on for a moment to determine which direction motor rotates. Unplug blender and remove bottom plate (p. 145). Hold fan so motor shaft cannot turn and remove drive stud by turning it in same direction motor rotates (c. 145). △

Ease of fix: △ simple △△ average △△△ difficult

146

Blender leaks

The leak may be between the bottom of the jar and the agitator assembly or through the agitator drive shaft itself. A visual check will tell if the jar opening is chipped or the sealing ring defective. If both are OK, the agitator shaft may be loose. Any broken parts should be replaced.

Poor seal between jar and jar bottom?

TEST: Screw bottom off jar and remove agitator unit and sealing ring. Examine bottom of glass container for chipping; inspect sealing ring for splits and cracking.

YES→ FIX: Replace jar or sealing ring. When reassembling container, set jar upside down, lay sealing ring in place, insert blade unit, and screw bottom on firmly. Be sure threads engage properly. △

Loose agitator shaft?

TEST: If jar and sealing ring are OK, then agitator shaft or its bearing must be worn.

YES→ FIX: Replace agitator blade assembly. Either shaft, bearing, or both may be faulty, so it is best to replace unit. △

Blender shocks user

A frayed power cord, an electrically live component grounded to (touching) a metal part, or leakage current due to faulty insulation will cause shocking. In the case of a frayed cord or grounding, the part can be fixed or replaced. If leakage current is suspected, the blender should be taken to an authorized repairman.

Power cord frayed?

TEST: Receiving a shock from power cord is sufficient evidence it needs repair.

YES→ FIX: Replace power cord. Follow instructions in Motor does not run or runs sluggishly, p.144, and in illustrations on p.145. △△△

Leakage current present?

TEST: If exposed metal part causes shocks, unplug blender. Set volt-ohm meter (p.124) to RX100 scale and attach one probe to metal part, the other to either prong of the plug. Turn on-off switch to On and push each speed control button. If meter reads at or near high ohms for all speed settings, leakage current (p.127) is indicated.

YES→ FIX: Take blender to an authorized repairman. Eliminating leakage current requires special equipment. Note: It is possible that the shock is not caused by leakage current but by a wire that becomes grounded only when the blender is turned on. To investigate this, proceed with the tests before taking the blender to a repair shop. △△△

Wiring inside base grounded to metal part?

TEST: Unplug blender, disassemble base (p.145), and examine wires for bare spots. Set volt-ohm meter to RX100 scale and clip one probe to drive stud, the other to a prong of the plug. Turn on-off switch to On and set speed to Low. Bend and pull wires. If needle jumps when a wire is handled, that wire is grounded.

YES→ FIX: Repair or replace faulty insulation. Insulate bare spots on wire with plastic electrical tape. If wire at a terminal is frayed, cut off terminal and install a new one. If cause of grounding cannot be found or if repairs fail to cure problem, grounded wire may be inside motor. See Universal motors, pp.132–134, for tests and repairs. △△

Blender blows fuses

When a fuse blows or circuit breaker trips, it means there is either an electrical overload or a short circuit. Overloads are fixed by reducing the number of appliances in the circuit. Short circuits are located by inspection and testing. Parts found to be shorted must be repaired or replaced.

Circuit overloaded?

TEST: To check for overloads, see p.127. Too many appliances in a circuit is the commonest cause of blown fuses.

YES→ FIX: Reduce number of appliances in the circuit. Caution: Never replace a fuse or breaker with one having a larger capacity. △

Short circuit in power cord or plug?

TEST: Unplug blender and remove bottom plate (See Disassembling the blender, p.145). Examine power cord and plug for bare wires and burn marks. Unscrew wire nut and pull away lead coming from power cord. Set volt-ohm meter (p.124) to RX100 scale and clip to plug. Bend and pull cord. If OK, meter will read high; if shorted, needle will jump around or read zero.

YES→ FIX: Replace power cord. Undo nut holding fan to motor shaft and remove fan. Locate brush housing to which the lead coming from power cord is attached. Then pry off spring clip that holds housing to motor mounting. Next, lift brush housing from its seat (a concealed spring may cause the brush to pop out when you do this) and pull the cord terminal out of the housing. Detach strain relief fitting and cord (See p.145). △△△

Short circuit in motor?

If the above tests fail to locate the problem, there is probably a short circuit in the wiring of the motor. See Universal motors, pp.132–134, for information on testing and repairs.

Ease of fix: △ simple △△ average △△△ difficult

Testing for short circuits and grounding

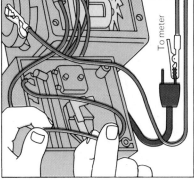

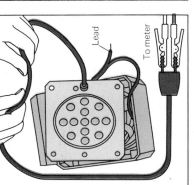

Lead

To meter

To meter

1. To check power cord for short circuit, disconnect one lead, clip volt-ohm meter probes to plug. Bend cord during test.

2. Grounded wires cause shocks. To test, set on-off switch to On, clip one probe to plug, one to drive stud, and tug on wires.

Set meter to RX100 scale for tests.

Test 1: If needle reads high ohms, power cord is OK; if it jumps around or reads zero ohms, cord is shorted.

Test 2: If needle reads high ohms there may be leakage current (see p.127); if it jumps around when a particular wire is handled, that wire is grounded.

Can openers

Motor does not run or runs sluggishly

Jammed parts will cause stalling or sluggish operation. If motor fails completely, it may be due to a blown fuse, a tripped overload protector on the motor, or a broken power cord, switch, or field coil. Repairs include replacing field assembly, freeing jammed components, and installing new cord.

Power off at outlet?

← NO

TEST: Unplug power cord and check wall outlet with a lamp you know is working.

YES →

FIX: Replace fuse or reset circuit breaker. See p.127. If fuse keeps blowing, see *Can opener blows fuses*, p.151.
▷

Motor, gears, or grinding wheel jammed?

← NO

TEST: Run opener without can. If motor runs normally, the can may have been irregular. If motor does not run and is silent, continue testing below for broken power cord, broken switch, etc. If motor runs sluggishly or hums without turning, opener is jammed. Unplug power cord and remove housing. Examine gears and sharpener guides for objects jammed in them. Remove motor. Try turning motor shaft and primary gear by hand. If either fails to turn freely, it is jammed.

YES →

FIX: Remove obstructions; clean and lubricate moving parts. With opener unplugged, complete disassembly of machine, including gears. Pull rotor out of field assembly and remove grinding wheel. Buff-clean both ends of the rotor shaft with silver polish or automobile polishing compound. Wipe dirt from bearings and gears with a clean, lint-free cloth. Lubricate gears, bearings, and motor shaft with petroleum jelly or a commercial lubricant such as Lubriplate. If gears are worn (p.150), replace them. If rotor is rusted or stuck, take opener to a repairman.
▷▷

Power cord broken?

← NO

TEST: Unplug opener. Remove housing and examine power cord for fraying and the plug for loose or distorted prongs. Unscrew wire nut and pull away lead coming from power cord. Attach jumper wire across power cord leads. Set volt-ohm meter (p.124) to RX1 scale and clip its probes to the prongs of the plug. Bend and pull power cord. If cord is OK, meter will read zero ohms; if broken, needle will jump around or read high.

YES →

FIX: Replace power cord. Disconnect power cord lead that is attached to switch. If there is a cover on the switch, first remove screw and take it off. If power cord lead is soldered to switch terminal, try to pry out terminal and leaf contact as a unit from switch. New power cord from manufacturer will come with a leaf contact attached to it. If leaf contact cannot be pried out, use a soldering iron to disconnect power cord lead from terminal.
▷▷

Overload protector tripped?

← NO

TEST: If motor stops after extended use of knife sharpening wheel or will not start again after motor has stalled, the motor's overload protector has probably tripped.

YES →

FIX: Let motor cool down. Can opener motors have a built-in protective device to prevent overheating. Once the device has tripped, it takes about 10 minutes to cool off.
▷

Switch broken?

← NO

TEST: With opener unplugged and disassembled, set volt-ohm meter to RX1 scale, clip its probes to the switch terminals, and close switch. If switch is OK, meter will read zero ohms; if bad, it will read high.

YES →

FIX: Repair switch. If there is a cover over the switch, remove screw and take it off. Polish switch contacts with very fine (No.400) sandpaper. If necessary, bend switch contacts with a pair of long-nose pliers so that they are about 1/16 inch apart.
▷▷

Field coil in motor faulty?

← NO

TEST: With opener unplugged and disassembled, set volt-ohm meter to RX1 scale and clip a probe to each field coil lead. If motor is OK, meter will read 5 to 12 ohms; if faulty, meter will read high.

YES →

FIX: Replace field assembly. Continue disassembly of can opener until you have removed the rotor out of the field. Pull the rotor out of the field. The defective field assembly can then be replaced with a new one.
▷▷

Ease of fix: △ simple △△ average △△△ difficult

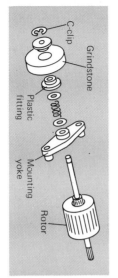

C-clip
Grindstone
Plastic fitting
Mounting yoke
Rotor

Most can openers have a grindstone for sharpening knives attached directly to the motor shaft. The sharpener should produce clean, sharp, even edges. If it does not, either the grindstone is dirty or it has developed a wobble. Replace stone by prying off C-clip, slipping old stone off shaft, and slipping new one on.

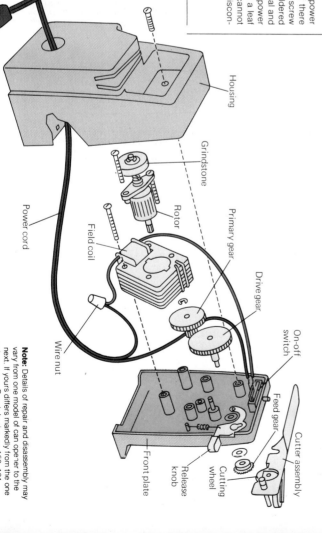

Housing
Grindstone
Power cord
Rotor
Field coil
Primary gear
Wire nut
Drive gear
On-off switch
Feed gear
Cutter assembly
Cutting wheel
Release knob
Front plate

Note: Details of repair and disassembly may vary from one model of can opener to the next. If yours differs markedly from the one shown, see *Repair basics*, pp.128-131.

Disassembling the can opener

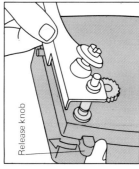

1. Be sure can opener is disconnected from wall outlet. Lift release knob on side and remove cutter assembly.

Release knob

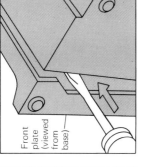

2. Remove the screws that hold the housing to the front plate and gently pry the housing from the plate.

Front plate (viewed from base)

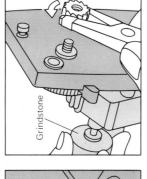

3. Tape pliers to protect feed gear. Hold grindstone to keep motor from turning. Unscrew feed gear with pliers.

Grindstone

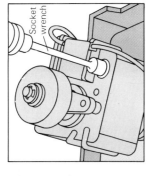

4. Remove motor screws with screwdriver or socket wrench, depending on type of screw, and lift out motor.

Socket wrench

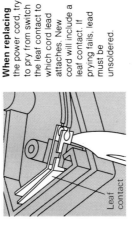

5. Pry off C-clip with small screwdriver; lift out primary gear, then the drive gear. Gears made of nylon may wear out, requiring replacement.

Primary gear

Testing for open circuits

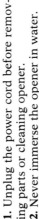

Set meter to RX1 scale for all tests. **Test 1:** If cord is OK, meter will read zero ohms. If meter reads high, or needle jumps, there is an open circuit. **Tests 2 and 3:** If switch and motor are OK, meter will read zero and 5–12 ohms.

Jumper

To meter

1. If can opener does not run, problem may be a broken power cord. To test, unplug the cord and attach a jumper wire across terminals of cord. Clip volt-ohm meter probes onto prongs of plug. Bend the cord to help disclose loose connections.

Leaf contacts

To meter

2. To test switch, clip meter probes onto leaf contacts. Turn switch on and off several times, by pushing button, to be sure switch is making good contact.

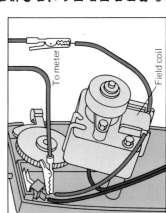

To meter

Field coil

3. Check motor by clipping probes of volt-ohm meter to both leads from the field coil. If the field coil is broken, replace the entire field assembly.

Cord and switch repairs

Leaf contact

When replacing the power cord, try to pry from switch the leaf contact to which cord lead attaches. New cord will include a leaf contact. If prying fails, lead must be unsoldered.

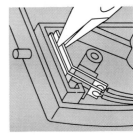

Polish switch contacts with very fine sandpaper. Do not let metal filings fall into motor. If switch contacts are difficult to reach, clean them with electrical contact cleaner.

Bend leaf contacts of switch with a pair of pliers so firm contact is made between leaves when switch is pressed. Do not bend them so close that there is no gap between them when switch is open.

Use and care

1. Unplug the power cord before removing parts or cleaning opener.
2. Never immerse the opener in water.
3. Clean the cutting wheel (or cutting blade) and its shaft regularly in hot, sudsy water. Do not use scouring pads or cleansers with abrasives. Be careful when handling the cutting wheel; it may be quite sharp.
4. A can with a heavy rim may cause the opener to stall. Should this happen, grasp the can and rotate it counterclockwise to help the cutting action. If there is a large dent in the rim, open the can at the other end or start cutting just beyond the dent.
5. Do not open aerosol-type cans.
6. Knives should be clean and dry before they are sharpened.
7. The can opener's motor is designed with built-in protection against overheating. If you have been sharpening a number of knives and the motor suddenly stops, it indicates you are overworking the sharpener. Allow the motor to cool for 10 minutes.
8. Do not sharpen blades with scalloped or serrated edges.
9. If you use the sharpener frequently, take off the housing periodically and clean out metal filings.

Can openers

Blade-type cutters and automatic openers

The standard can opener has a wheel-type cutter and does not operate automatically. The user must depress the cutting lever to initiate cutting action and must continue to hold the lever down until the lid is off. There are two important variations from this basic design. One is the use of a straight-edged cutting blade, sometimes called a plow, rather than a cutting wheel. The other is the incorporation of a mechanism that makes the opener fully automatic. With the automatic can opener, once the cutting action has started, the opener will complete the job and shut itself off without any further effort on the part of the user.

Straight-edged cutting blades: Troubleshooting procedures for blade-type openers are virtually the same as for openers with wheel cutters. In both cases, proper operation depends on correct spacing between cutter and feed gear (.005 to .012 inch for the wheel and .015 to .030 inch for the blade) so that the can will not fall out of the opener or ride up on the feed gear. As with the cutting wheel, the blade should be cleaned regularly. It should not be sharpened, however, since its straight-edged blades are designed to be dull.

Recognizing worn gears

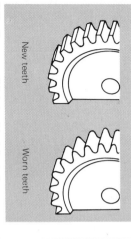

New teeth   Worn teeth

Reduction gear: If it is hard to tell whether a gear is worn, hold one gear steady and try to turn the other by hand. Worn gear teeth do not mesh compactly with one another and will slip under pressure.

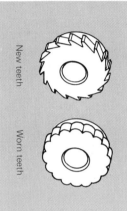

New teeth   Worn teeth

Feed gear: The teeth on the feed gear are designed to bite into the rim of a can. They should be sharp and abrasive to the touch. When replacing the gear, be sure teeth point in the direction that gear turns.

Automatic openers

Automatic can openers: These models permit hands-off operation; once a can is started they run until the lid is removed, then shut themselves off. In a typical design, the sideways pressure to-

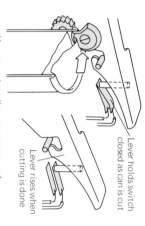

How an automatic can opener works

Lever holds switch closed as can is cut

Lever rises when cutting is done

ward the left from the can pushing against the cutter will lock the cutter assembly lever in the down position, keeping the opener going. Once the lid is cut all the way around, the sideways pressure drops, allowing the spring action of the switch's leaf contact to open the switch and shut the motor off. Should the opener fail to turn itself off, food residue is probably jamming the cutter. Clean the cutter assembly in hot, sudsy water, dry it thoroughly, then lubricate it with mineral oil.

Motor runs but opener does not cut can

If the feed gear turns normally but the opener fails to cut the lid, the cutter may need replacement, the teeth on the feed gear may be worn or dirty, or the gap between the feed gear and cutter may be too large. If the feed gear does not turn, speed reduction gears inside opener may be broken.

Cutting wheel worn?

NO ➡

TEST: If can rotates but opener does not cut properly, the cutting wheel is worn.

YES ➡ **FIX: Replace cutting wheel.** With opener unplugged, unscrew cutting wheel and pull cutter off shaft.
△

Worn or dirty feed gear?

NO ➡

TEST: Operate opener with a can in it. If feed gear rotates but fails to turn can, its teeth are either worn or clogged with dirt. Remove can and examine teeth of feed gear. They should be sharp and clean.

YES ➡ **FIX: Clean or replace feed gear.** With opener unplugged, remove housing. Hold motor shaft to keep it from turning and unscrew feed gear (p.149). If feed gear is dirty, scrape out packed-in residue with a knife and wash thoroughly with detergent. If it is worn, replace with a new one.
△

Too much space between cutter and feed gear?

NO ➡

TEST: Unplug the opener and insert a can. The cutting wheel should bite cleanly into the lid when the lever is depressed. Pull on the can. It should be tight against the feed gear. Now plug opener in and allow it to run. If can falls off or rides up, or if opener stops prematurely (on models with automatic shut off), the gap between the cutter and feed gear is excessive.

YES ➡ **FIX: Tighten cutting wheel screw and shim up feed gear.** Unplug opener. Before tightening cutting screw, clean cutting assembly (see Use and care, p.149). To shim up feed gear, remove housing (p.149), hold motor shaft steady, and unscrew feed gear. Add spacing washers (available from parts suppliers) to feed gear shaft one at a time. Replace feed gear and test opener after each addition to see if it operates properly.
△△

Worn or stripped gears?

NO ➡

TEST: Operate opener with a can in it. If the feed gear does not turn, one of the reduction gears is broken. This may also cause the opener to be noisy.

YES ➡ **FIX: Replace damaged gears.** Unplug can opener and disassemble it (p.149). Examine reduction gears carefully for broken teeth and signs of wear. If there is any question about the condition of either gear, replace both. Lubricate with a commercial lubricant such as Lubriplate after installation of new parts.
△△

Ease of fix: △ simple △△ average △△△ difficult

Disassembling cutters

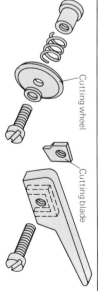

Cutting wheel

Cutting blade

Install cutting wheel so that slanted side faces in toward can opener. Mount for blade-type cutter (right) is notched to receive blades.

Can opener blows fuses

When a fuse blows or circuit breaker trips, it means there is either an electrical overload or a short circuit. Overloads are fixed by reducing the number of appliances in the circuit. Short circuits are located by inspection and testing. Parts found to be shorted must be repaired or replaced.

Circuit overloaded?

NO →

TEST: To check for overloads, see p.127. Too many appliances in a circuit is the commonest cause of blown fuses.

YES → FIX: Reduce number of appliances in the circuit. Caution: Never replace a fuse or breaker with one having a larger capacity. △

Short circuit in power cord or plug?

NO →

TEST: Unplug opener and remove housing (p.149). Unscrew wire nut and pull away power cord lead. Set volt-ohm meter (p.124) to RX100 scale and clip its probes to prongs of plug. Bend and pull cord. If it is OK, meter will read high; if it is bad, needle will jump or read zero ohms.

YES → FIX: Replace power cord. With opener unplugged and disassembled, follow instructions given in *Motor does not run or runs sluggishly*, p.148. △ △

Short circuit in motor?

NO →

TEST: Unplug opener. Set volt-ohm meter to RX1 scale, clip its probes to motor leads. If motor is OK, meter will read 5 to 12 ohms; if it reads zero, motor is shorted.

YES → FIX: Replace field assembly of motor. Continue disassembly of the unplugged can opener until motor is removed (p.149), then pull rotor out of field. Defective field assembly can then be replaced with new one. △ △

Short circuit in other internal wiring?

TEST: With opener unplugged and apart, examine wiring for burns, bare spots.

YES → FIX: Replace or repair broken parts. Separate any wires that touch, mend insulation with electrical tape. △ △

Can opener shocks user

A frayed power cord, an electrically live component grounded to (touching) a metal part, or leakage current due to faulty insulation will cause shocking. In the case of a frayed cord or grounding, the part must be fixed or replaced. If leakage current is suspected, appliance should be taken to a repairman.

Power cord frayed?

NO →

TEST: Receiving a shock from power cord is sufficient evidence it needs repair.

YES → FIX: Replace power cord. Follow instructions given in *Motor does not run or runs sluggishly*, p.148, and in illustrations on p.149. △ △

Leakage current present?

NO →

TEST: If metal part on outside of opener shocks, unplug opener and set volt-ohm meter (p.124) to RX100 scale. Attach one probe to the part, the other to either prong of the plug. Press lever. If meter reads high, leakage current (p.127) is indicated.

YES → FIX: Take can opener to authorized repairman. Eliminating leakage current requires special equipment. Note: It is possible the shock is not caused by leakage current but by a wire that becomes grounded only when the opener is on. To investigate this, proceed with tests before taking opener to shop. △ △ △

Internal wiring grounded to metal part?

NO →

TEST: With power cord unplugged, remove housing (p.149) and examine wires for bare spots and loose strands.

YES → FIX: Repair or replace faulty insulation. Reinsulate bare spots on wires with electrical tape. Make sure wire nut is on securely and completely encloses bare wire. △ △

Field coil grounded to metal part?

TEST: Unplug can opener and free a motor lead. Set volt-ohm meter to RX100 scale; clip one probe to metal, the other to lead. If meter reads below maximum, coil is grounded.

YES → FIX: Replace field assembly of motor. Continue disassembly of can opener until you have removed the motor (p.149), then pull rotor out of field. Defective field assembly can then be replaced with new one. △ △

Ease of fix: △ simple △ △ average △ △ △ difficult

Testing for short circuits

1. To check power cord, unscrew wire nut, pull away power cord lead, and clip volt-ohm meter probes to prongs of plug. Bend and pull cord.

2. Test for short in motor by attaching volt-ohm meter probes to each lead from the field coil.

Test 1: Set meter to RX100 scale. If it reads high, cord is OK; if needle jumps or reads zero ohms, cord is bad. **Test 2:** Set meter to RX1 scale. If it reads 5 to 12 ohms, motor is OK; if it reads zero ohms, motor is shorted.

Testing for shock hazards

1. To find out if leakage current or grounding is causing shock, attach one volt-ohm meter probe to part that shocks, the other to a prong of the plug.

2. Field coil may be grounded. Clip one probe of meter to coil lead, other to motor.

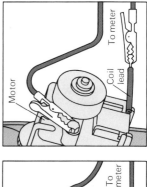

Set meter to RX100 scale. **Test 1:** Close switch by pushing lever. If meter reads high, leakage current (p.127) is indicated. **Test 2:** Any reading lower than maximum means field coil is grounded.

Clocks and timers

Clock does not run

If the clock fails to run, it means current is not flowing through motor, or gear assembly is defective. The cause is determined through step-by-step testing, starting with the wall outlet and continuing with the various parts of the clock. Repairs range from changing a house fuse to replacing clock parts.

Power off at outlet?
TEST: Unplug power cord and check wall outlet with a lamp you know is working.

YES→ **FIX: Replace fuse or reset circuit breaker.** See p.127. If fuse keeps blowing, see *About clocks in general,* p. 153.

NO↓

Power cord broken?
TEST: Unplug clock, take movement out of case, and examine power cord for fraying and the plug for loose or distorted prongs. Attach jumper wire across power cord leads; then set volt-ohm meter (p.124) to RX1 scale and clip its probes to the prongs of the plug. Bend and pull power cord. If OK, meter will read zero; if broken, needle will jump around or read high.

YES→ **FIX: Replace power cord.** Use a soldering iron or soldering gun to remove power cord leads from the motor terminals. A new cord may be purchased from manufacturer's parts outlet or you can make your own with a standard appliance plug and 3 to 4 feet of No. 18 zip cord, the common electrical wire used for lamps, extension cords, and small appliances. △ △

NO↓

Field coil in motor faulty?
TEST: Unplug clock, set volt-ohm meter to RX100 scale and clip its probes to motor terminals. If field coil is OK, meter will read in the neighborhood of 500 to 2,000 ohms. If coil is broken, meter will read high.

YES→ **FIX: Replace field coil assembly.** Use a soldering iron or soldering gun to remove the power cord leads from motor terminals, then undo mounting screws and lift field assembly out of movement. △ △

NO↓

Rotor unit broken?
TEST: Remove motor and set it on table with rotor unit still in place and the small pinion gear facing upward. Plug power cord into wall outlet. If pinion gear turns slowly (4 revolutions per minute), unit is OK. If gear does not turn, unit is broken. **Do not touch motor while cord is plugged in. Unplug immediately after test.**

YES→ **FIX: Replace rotor unit.** Replacement involves a simple interchange of a new rotor unit for the old one. If the rotor in your clock is permanently bonded to the field, the entire motor must be replaced. In that case, use a soldering iron or soldering gun to remove power cord leads from motor terminals. △ △

NO↓

Broken or dirty gears in gear assembly?
TEST: If previous tests have not pinpointed the cause of the problem, the difficulty is probably with the gears—they may be dirty, jammed, or broken. With the clock unplugged and disassembled, check them by spinning the time set shaft by hand. (Be sure the motor is separated from the gears.) All gears should turn freely. All clock hands, including sweep second hand, should move as you spin the shaft.

YES→ **FIX: Clean gears.** If necessary, replace gear assembly. Spray gears with electrical contact cleaner (p.123) or other cleaner designed for electrical equipment. Turn the time set shaft to work cleaner in. If you still cannot get gears to turn freely, remove dial and clock hands and replace entire gear assembly. △ △

Ease of fix: △ simple △△ average △△△ difficult

Clock dial and hands may be replaced if damaged. Unplug clock and take out crystal. Pry off hands carefully with a knife or screwdriver, then remove dial face. When reassembling, put the alarm hand on first. Press it onto stem so that it is snugly seated. Next, set alarm shut-off lever to *On* and rotate the alarm set shaft until alarm clicks. Press hour hand onto stem directly over alarm hand. Turn the time set shaft so that hour hand reads 12 o'clock before attaching minute hand and then second hand directly over it.

Household timer (see p.154) turns an electric outlet on instead of an alarm.

Diagram labels: Dial, Movement, Motor assembly, Switch, Power wire, Power cord, Outlet

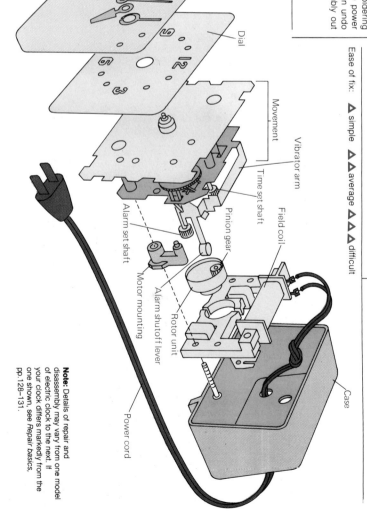

Exploded diagram labels: Crystal, Dial, Movement, Vibrator arm, Time set shaft, Field coil, Pinion gear, Alarm set shaft, Motor mounting, Alarm shutoff lever, Rotor unit, Case, Power cord

Note: Details of repair and disassembly may vary from one model of electric clock to the next. If your clock differs markedly from the one shown, see *Repair basics,* pp.128-131.

Disassembling a clock

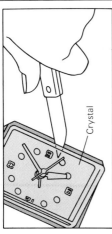

1. Be sure clock is disconnected from wall outlet. Pry out crystal with blade of knife. Clock hands are fragile; be careful with them during disassembly.

Crystal

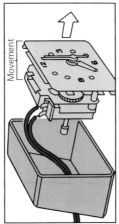

2. Remove screws in back of clock and slip movement out front of case. On some models, movement must be pried from case with screwdriver.

Movement

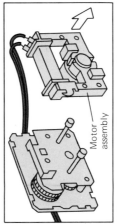

3. Remove screws and lift motor assembly from rest of movement. Motor mounting and alarm shut-off lever (not shown in this view) will slip out.

Motor assembly

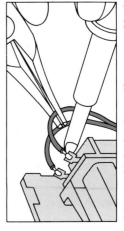

4. Use a soldering iron to unsolder power cord leads from terminals on field coil of motor. Untie knot in power cord and slip cord out of case.

Clock is noisy

Excessive noise in a clock is caused by loose parts and vibration. Often, cushioning the clock by placing it on a soft surface, such as a cloth, will solve the problem. Otherwise, it is necessary to identify and tighten loose parts or to replace a noisy rotor assembly or the complete motor.

Loose parts in clock?

TEST: Unplug clock from wall outlet and take movement out of case. Prop up movement on cushioned surface and plug power cord into wall outlet. **Caution: Do not touch movement while cord is plugged in. Unplug immediately after test.** If movement runs quietly, one of the case screws or the crystal may have been loose or you may have been operating the clock on a surface that echoes sound. If movement runs noisily, follow repairs in **Fix.**

 FIX: **Tighten loose parts; put grease at metal-to-metal contact points.** If movement ran quietly in test, reassemble clock making sure case screws are tight. If crystal is loose, wedge a bit of aluminum foil between it and the case. If surface where clock is placed is hard, use a piece of cloth under it to cushion sound. If movement ran noisily in test, tighten motor mounting screws and knobs of alarm set and time set shafts. Dab small amounts of petroleum jelly at points where alarm lever, alarm set shaft, and time set shaft contact metal plates. ▲▲

Rotor unit noisy?

TEST: Unplug power cord from wall outlet and remove motor. With rotor unit still in place, prop up motor on cushioned surface and plug power cord into wall outlet. If motor runs noisily, rotor unit is the cause. **Caution: Do not touch motor while cord is plugged in. Unplug after test.**

 FIX: **Replace rotor unit.** Replacement involves a simple interchange of a new rotor unit for the old one. If the rotor in your clock is permanently bonded to the field, the entire motor must be replaced. In that case, use a soldering iron or soldering gun to remove power cord leads from motor terminals. ▲▲

Ease of fix: △ simple △△ average △△△ difficult

Testing for open circuits

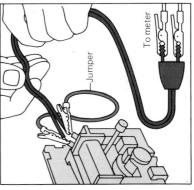

Jumper

To meter

1. Power cord can be tested for open circuit by clipping jumper wire across its terminals and clipping volt-ohm meter probes to plug.

To meter

Test 1: Set meter to RX1 scale. If it reads zero ohms, power cord is OK. If needle reads high or jumps, cord is broken.

Test 2: Set meter to RX100 scale. If it reads about 500 to 1,000 ohms, motor is OK. If meter reads high, field coil is bad.

2. Broken field coil will keep clock from working. Test by touching volt-ohm meter probes to the motor terminals.

About clocks in general

Electric clocks give relatively little trouble to their owners. Since their accuracy is based on the 60-cycle-per-second house current supplied by the utility, they are usually good to within a few seconds a day. On occasion, an electric clock will keep the wrong time because of worn or broken gear teeth (see *Checking and cleaning gears*, above). A more likely cause is a loose hand. Tighten a loose hand to the stem by gently squeezing its hub with pliers.

Shocking is seldom a problem. If it does occur, the power cord's insulation is probably cracked. The same is true of a clock that appears to blow fuses or trip a circuit breaker repeatedly: It is probably due to a broken power cord or plug. In either case, the power cord and plug should be replaced. To make this repair, follow the procedure that is described in *Clock does not run*, p.152.

Checking and cleaning gears

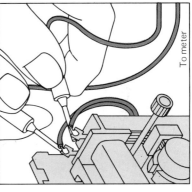

To test for stuck or broken gears, separate the motor from the gear assembly and spin the time set shaft. Clock hands and gears should move freely and easily.

If gears are stiff, spray them with electrical contact cleaner (p.123). Spin time set shaft to help cleaner penetrate. Relubricate with light machine oil.

Clocks and timers

Alarm does not operate satisfactorily

The alarm may sound at a time different from that set for it, or at any time regardless of setting; or it may sound poorly or not at all. These problems are solved by adjusting alarm hand to the correct time or by changing the gap between vibrator arm and laminated metal core of the field assembly.

NO → **Alarm hand out of adjustment?**
TEST: Set alarm for 6 o'clock. Plug clock into outlet and slowly turn clock hands until alarm goes off. Alarm should sound within 5 minutes either way of setting.

YES → **FIX: Adjust alarm hand.** Pull alarm lever out and turn clock hands until alarm goes off. Unplug power cord, pry off crystal, and nudge alarm hand sideways until it reads correctly. △

NO → **Alarm mechanism dirty or broken?**
TEST: If alarm does not ring, rings whenever alarm lever is pulled out, or has a poor tone, the mechanism may be dirty or broken. Unplug clock. Set time to 6 o'clock and take movement out of case. (See *Disassembling a clock*, p.153.) Pull alarm lever out and turn alarm set knob. Observe free end of vibrator arm. If alarm mechanism is OK, arm will release as alarm hand reaches 6 o'clock, then lock again as hand moves past. If it does not, the mechanism is broken or dirty.

YES → **FIX: Clean alarm mechanism or, if necessary, replace gear assembly.** Spray area around alarm mechanism with electrical contact cleaner (p.123). Move alarm lever in and out and turn alarm set knob to work cleaner in. If alarm mechanism still does not work, replace entire gear assembly. △△

Vibrator arm greasy or out of adjustment?
TEST: If previous test indicates alarm mechanism is OK, the trouble is either oil contamination or an incorrect gap between vibrator and field assembly.

YES → **FIX: Clean and adjust vibrator arm.** Spray vibrator and field assembly with electrical contact cleaner (p.123). Set alarm to sound and plug in power cord. If tone is not satisfactory, unplug cord and bend vibrator to adjust gap. Repeat testing and adjustment until tone is satisfactory. **Caution: Do not touch motor while power cord is plugged in.** △△

Ease of fix: △ simple △△ average △△△ difficult

How to check and adjust the alarm

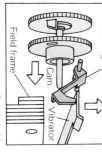
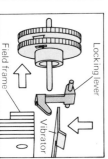

Locking lever — Cam — Vibrator — Field frame — Locking lever — Field frame — Locking lever — Vibrator

Before alarm goes off, cam holds locking lever in up position, preventing vibrator from buzzing.

At proper time, cam releases locking lever, freeing vibrator to strike magnetized field frame.

To adjust timing of alarm, move alarm hand on shaft to agree with time when alarm sounds.

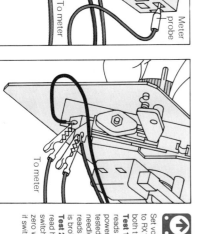

Meter clip — Power wire — To meter — Meter probe — To meter

Repairing your household timer

The instructions in *Clock does not run*, p.152, and in *Clock is noisy*, p.152, may be used to fix household timers as well as clocks. But a timer does not include an alarm mechanism; instead, it switches current on and off at its own built-in electric outlet. The timer's power wires and its switch may therefore need to be checked with a volt-ohm meter to determine the cause of defective operation. The tests are described in the following paragraphs.

1. Testing the power wires. Two heavy gauge wires—one black, the other white—carry power to the timer's outlet. If the outlet does not operate, check both wires for open circuits. The test is illustrated below. Unplug the power cord from the wall outlet and disconnect one of the timer's internal power wires from the power cord at the wire nut. Set the volt-ohm meter (p.124) to RX1 scale and clip one of its probes to the end of the connected wire. Insert its other probe into the outlet slot to which the wire goes, then bend and pull the wire. If the wire is OK, meter will read zero ohms. If it is broken, the needle of the meter will jump around or read toward the high end of the ohms scale. Test the other power wire the same way. If either wire is broken, replace it.

2. Testing the switch. Unplug power cord from wall outlet and set volt-ohm meter to RX1 scale. Clip the meter's probes to the terminals of switch (as illustrated below) and rotate timer dial clockwise so that switch opens and closes. If switch is in working order, volt-ohm meter will read zero ohms when it is closed and high ohms when it is open. If meter always reads zero ohms, switch contacts are probably fused and switch must be replaced.

If meter reads at or near high end of the ohms scale even when switch is closed, switch contacts are dirty or bent out of shape. Polish them with very fine (No. 400) sandpaper. If that does not clear up the difficulty, examine switch contacts when switch is closed. If they are not making firm contact, bend contact arms with a pair of long-nose pliers until switch closes firmly. (When switch is open, there should be a clearly visible gap of about 1/16 inch.)

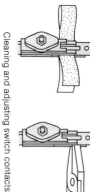

Cleaning and adjusting switch contacts

Set volt-ohm meter to RX1 scale for both tests.
Test 1: If meter reads zero ohms, power wire being tested is OK; if needle jumps or reads high, wire is broken.
Test 2: Meter will read high when switch is open, zero when closed if switch is good.

Coffeemakers/drip type

Two systems: pump and gravity

Coffeemakers of the drip type brew coffee by passing hot water through a container of ground coffee beans. Unlike percolators, which recirculate the water, drip systems pass water through the grounds only once, a technique that experts say produces a better cup of coffee. Drip coffeemakers fall into two categories: pump feed and gravity feed. The pump type (right) heats the water

in its base and forces it up to a spout on top of the coffeemaker so that it drips into the basket. The gravity-feed type (below) heats the water in the top unit and lets it drip by force of gravity into the container.

Both types include a keep-warm element in the base that either turns on automatically after brewing or is controlled by a switch.

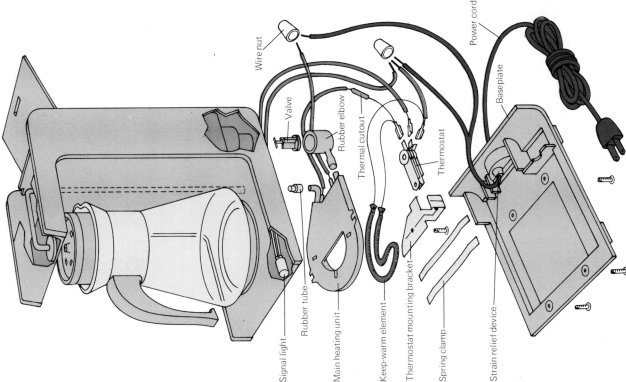

Wire nut · Valve · Rubber elbow · Power cord · Baseplate · Thermal cutout · Thermostat · Signal light · Rubber tube · Main heating unit · Keep-warm element · Thermostat mounting bracket · Spring clamp · Strain relief device

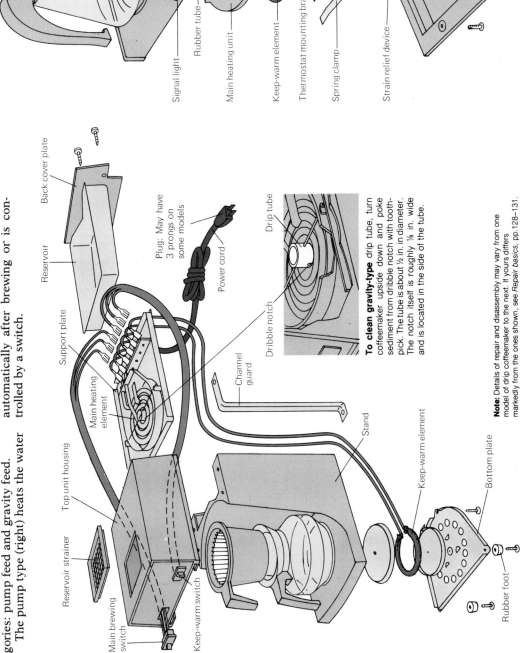

Back cover plate · Reservoir · Support plate · Main heating element · Top unit housing · Reservoir strainer · Main brewing switch · Keep-warm switch · Plug: May have 3 prongs on some models · Power cord · Channel guard · Stand · Drip tube · Dribble notch · Keep-warm element · Bottom plate · Rubber foot

To clean gravity-type drip tube, turn coffeemaker upside down and poke sediment from dribble notch with toothpick. The tube is about ½ in. in diameter. The notch itself is roughly ⅛ in. wide and is located in the side of the tube.

Note: Details of repair and disassembly may vary from one model of drip coffeemaker to the next. If yours differs markedly from the ones shown, see *Repair basics*, pp.128–131.

Coffeemakers/drip type

Disassembly of gravity-feed coffeemaker

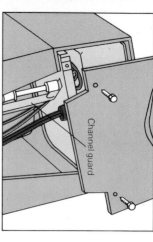

1. After unplugging unit and snapping out reservoir strainer, unscrew and remove back cover plate. Next, loosen channel guard over keep-warm element wires.

Reservoir

Support plate

Channel guard

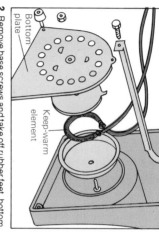

2. Remove base screws and take off rubber feet, bottom plate, and channel guard. Undo center nut and separate the keep-warm element from the bottom plate.

Bottom plate

Keep-warm element

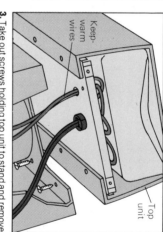

3. Take out screws holding top unit to stand and remove unit. Be careful not to damage keep-warm element—it hangs from the top unit by its lead wires.

Keep-warm wires

Top unit

Strain relief devices

Strain relief device protects power cord from wear and tear. One kind is bondec to the cord and must be forced out with screwdriver.

Two-piece strain relief device is removed by compressing it with pliers, turning it a quarter turn, and pulling it straight out.

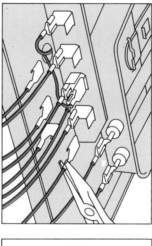

4. Bend sides of top unit outward with your thumbs to loosen support plate so that its back edge drops an inch or so; then, remove reservoir.

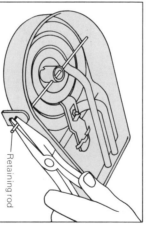

5. Use long-nose pliers to disconnect lead wires of front-mounted switches from rear terminal board. Make a note of which wire belongs to which terminal.

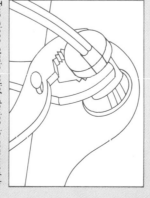

6. Slide out main element support plate from top unit. Grip retaining rod of main heating element with pliers, pull out rod, and lift off pan and element.

Retaining rod

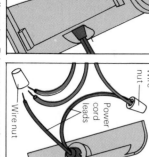

Wire nut

Power cord leads

Wire nut

Disassembly of pump-type coffeemaker

1. Unplug coffeemaker. Take out screws and remove baseplate. Unscrew wire nuts and separate the power cord leads from leads going to internal parts.

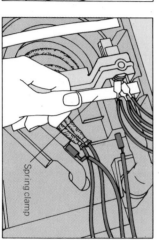

2. Release the two spring clamps that hold heating unit in place. Work carefully; the clamps are stiff and considerable strength is required to remove them.

Spring clamp

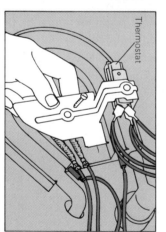

3. Undo screw and lift off thermostat mounting bracket along with thermostat. Bracket may catch under heating unit and need some jiggling to remove.

Thermostat

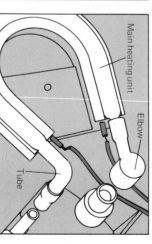

4. Pull rubber elbow and tube from pipes and remove main heating unit. Note that the entire unit must be replaced if any part of it is defective.

Main heating unit

Elbow

Tube

Hot water does not flow from spout

If hot water does not flow from spout, it means current is not passing through main heating element or the flow of water is blocked. Electrical repairs range from changing a house fuse to replacing heating element. The water flow problem is solved by cleaning spout or reservoir, or fixing pump valve.

Power off at outlet?

TEST: Unplug power cord and check wall outlet with a lamp you know is working.

Spout or reservoir clogged?

TEST: Clean coffeemaker (see **Fix**), then operate it to see if hot water flows down into the basket properly. Note: Clogging is usually the result of mineral accumulation and is more likely to occur in hard water areas.

Pump valve jammed or broken?

TEST: If your coffeemaker is the pump type, water will not rise to the spout if the valve is broken or stuck. Unplug coffeemaker and empty out water. Remove baseplate and pull rubber tube from reservoir outlet. Examine valve for dirt and mineral deposits that may be jamming it open. Push valve up. It should move freely.

Power cord faulty?

TEST: Unplug power cord from wall outlet and disassemble coffeemaker so that cord leads are accessible. Attach jumper wire across leads. Set volt-ohm meter (p.124) to RX1 scale and clip its probes to the prongs of the plug. Bend and pull power cord. If cord is OK, meter will read zero ohms; if broken, needle will jump or read high.

Main brewing switch broken?

TEST: If coffeemaker has a main brewing switch (some do not), unplug and disassemble coffeemaker and turn main brewing switch on. Set volt-ohm meter to RX1 scale and touch its probes to the leads of the switch. If switch is OK, meter will read zero ohms; if broken, meter will read high.

Part of the heating unit broken?

TEST: Unplug and disassemble coffeemaker. Set volt-ohm meter to RX1 scale and touch its probes, first, to terminals of main heating element; second, to leads of thermal cutout; and, third, to terminals of thermostat. If parts are OK, meter will read 7 to 15 ohms in test of heating element, zero ohms in cutout and thermostat tests.

Ease of fix: △ simple △△ average △△△ difficult

YES → FIX: Replace power cord. Disconnect power cord leads from any wire nuts, terminals, and connecting wires. Remove strain relief device from its seat in the housing either by prying it out with a screwdriver if it is bonded on the cord, or by compressing it with pliers and rotating it a quarter turn if it is a separate, hard plastic, two-piece unit. △△

YES → FIX: Replace main brewing switch. Press spring clamps together and push switch out of housing. (See *Signal lights and switches*, p.158.) New switch comes with leads installed. Note: If switch has a built-in signal light, there will be three leads coming from it instead of two. △△

YES → FIX: Replace broken components or entire heating unit. On some coffeemakers, the entire heating assembly, including heating element, thermal cutout, thermostat, and keep-warm element, must be replaced as a unit. On other models, one or more of the components may be replaced separately. A part is usually available separately if it is attached by quick-connect terminals, but not if it is soldered or riveted into place. △△△

NO → FIX: Replace fuse or reset circuit breaker. See p.127. If fuse keeps blowing, see *Coffeemaker blows fuses*, p.159. △

NO → FIX: Clean coffeemaker. Unplug coffeemaker and empty it of water. If coffeemaker is gravity feed type, clean reservoir outlet by carefully poking out residue with a needle. For either type of coffeemaker, turn appliance upside down and clean drip tube with a toothpick. (See illustration on p.155 for location of dribble notch on gravity models.) Run coffeemaker through brewing cycle with a half water, half vinegar mixture, then twice more with clean water. △

NO → FIX: Clean or replace valve. Pry valve out from the bottom with a knife or push it out from above by reaching down through reservoir. Remove dirt, foreign objects, and mineral deposits from the valve and valve seat. If valve is broken, replace it. After cleaning, reassemble coffeemaker and flush it out with a vinegar and water mixture as described in the previous **Fix.** △△

Cleaning the valve

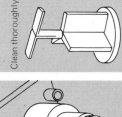

Clean thoroughly

If a stuck valve prevents water flow in pump-type coffeemaker, pry it from tube and clean it. Valve should move easily when pushed up and down.

Testing for open circuits

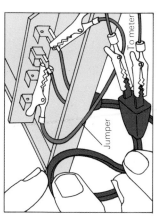

1. To test power cord, clip jumper wire across its terminals and clip volt-ohm meter probes to its terminals and plug. Bending cord shows up loose wires.

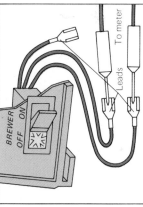

2. If coffeemaker has main brewing switch, check it for open circuit. Disassemble appliance; touch probes to switch leads two at a time.

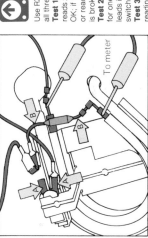

Use RX1 scale for all three tests.
Test 1: If meter reads zero, cord is OK; if needle jumps or reads high, cord is broken.
Test 2: Zero ohms for one pair of leads indicates switch is OK.
Test 3: 7–15 ohm reading means unit is OK; high ohms means it is broken.

3. Test entire heating unit. Probes are shown applied to heating element terminals. Also check thermostat (A) and thermal cutout (B).

157

Coffeemakers/drip type

Brewed coffee does not keep warm

If coffee, after brewing is completed, does not keep warm in the pot—with pot still in place in the coffeemaker—the keep-warm element is not operating. Either being clogged by a buildup of mineral deposits. Repairs consist of replacing either the switch or the element.

Keep-warm switch broken?

TEST: If coffeemaker has a separate keep-warm switch, unplug and disassemble coffeemaker (refer to illustrations on p.156). Turn keep-warm switch to *On*. Set volt-ohm meter (p.124) to RX1 scale and touch its probes to each lead of keep-warm switch. If the switch is OK, the meter will read zero ohms; if the switch is broken, meter will read high. Note: If switch has a built-in signal light, there will be three leads coming from it instead of two.

NO

YES → **FIX: Replace keep-warm switch.** Press spring clamps together and push switch out of housing. New switch comes with leads installed. Note: Many drip coffeemakers go into the keep-warm mode automatically. These models generally have a signal light to show that the keep-warm element is on. If light does not go on but coffeemaker is operating correctly otherwise, the light is broken and must be replaced. To reach it, remove baseplate, disconnect leads, and push light out front of housing. ▲▲

Keep-warm element broken?

TEST: With the coffeemaker disassembled, disconnect one terminal of keep-warm element lead from terminal post. Set volt-ohm meter to RX1 scale and touch its probes to the terminals of keep-warm element. If element is OK, meter will read 100 to 300 ohms; if element is broken, meter will read high.

YES → **FIX: Replace keep-warm element or entire heating unit.** On some models, the entire heating assembly—including heating element, thermal cutout, thermostat, and keep-warm element—must be replaced as a unit. On others, the keep-warm element may be obtained separately. Check with the manufacturer. Be sure to specify model number when you do. ▲▲▲

Checking the keep-warm system

Set meter to RX1 scale for both tests.

Test 1: If switch is OK, meter will read zero ohms; if broken, meter will read high.

Test 2: If keep-warm element is OK, meter will read 100–300 ohms; if broken, meter will read high.

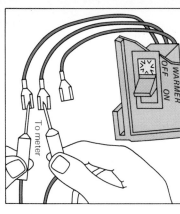

1. To check keep-warm switch, unplug coffeemaker, turn switch on, touch volt-ohm meter probes to leads. Test leads two at a time.

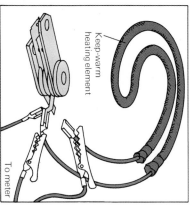

Keep-warm heating element

To meter

2. To test heating element, disassemble coffeemaker. Take one terminal of element lead off post. Touch meter probes to terminals.

Coffeemaker sputters, leaks, or steams

If coffeemaker sputters, leaks, or steams, it will be due either to a leak in the rubber tubing used to join heating unit to reservoir and outlet tube, or to the water passages still in place in the coffeemaker—the keep-warm switch does not work. Repair consists of replacing rubber tubing or cleaning coffeemaker.

Leak in rubber tubing?

TEST: If your coffeemaker is a pump type, leaks are probably due to defects in rubber tube connectors in base. Unplug appliance and remove baseplate (p.156). Inspect rubber elbow and tube for cracks. Fill reservoir with water, watch to see if water leaks from either elbow or tube.

NO

YES → **FIX: Replace rubber parts.** Disassemble coffeemaker to gain access to rubber tubing. Pull both rubber elbow and tube free from water intake and outlet of main heating assembly. Before installing new rubber parts, clean all of the surfaces to which the rubber will connect. ▲▲

Water passages clogged?

TEST: Built-up mineral deposits will cause coffeemaker to sputter or steam excessively. Test by cleaning coffeemaker according to directions in **Fix**, then operating it to see if problem is cleared up. Note: Mineral accumulation occurs more rapidly in hard water areas.

YES → **FIX: Clean coffeemaker.** Unplug coffeemaker and empty it of water. If it is gravity type, clean reservoir outlet by carefully poking out residue with a needle. For either style, turn appliance upside down and clean drip tube with toothpick. Gravity-feed models have a small cutout in the side of the drip tube called a dribble notch (see illustration on p.155). Clean with toothpick. Run coffeemaker through brewing cycle once with mixture of half water and half vinegar, then twice with clean water. ▲

Ease of fix: △ simple △△ average △△△ difficult

Signal lights and switches

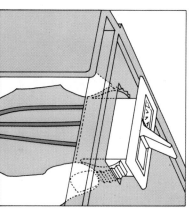

To remove either keep-warm or main brewing switch of gravity-feed coffeemaker, compress holders, push switch through opening.

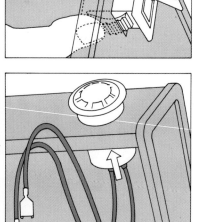

Signal light tells when coffee is ready. To replace one, disconnect its leads from terminals inside base and push light out of hole.

Coffeemaker shocks user

A frayed power cord, an electrically live component grounded to a metal part, or leakage current due to faulty insulation will cause shocking. In the case of a frayed cord or grounding, the part can be fixed or replaced. If leakage current is suspected, the coffeemaker should be taken to a repairman.

Power cord frayed?

 TEST: Receiving a shock from power cord is sufficient evidence it needs repair.

YES→ FIX: Replace cord. Follow instructions given in *Hot water does not flow from spout*, p.157, and in illustrations, p.156. ▲▲

Leakage current present?

TEST: If you receive a shock from touching an exposed metal part, unplug coffeemaker and turn whatever switches it has to *On* position. Set volt-ohm meter (p.124) to RX100 scale and attach one probe to metal part, the other to either prong of the power cord plug. If meter reads at or near high ohms, leakage current (p.127) is indicated.

YES→ FIX: Take coffeemaker to authorized repairman. Eliminating leakage current requires special equipment. Note: It is possible the shock is not caused by leakage current but by a wire that becomes grounded only when the coffeemaker is on. To investigate this, proceed with next test before taking coffeemaker to a repair shop. ▲▲▲

Internal wiring grounded to metal parts?

TEST: Unplug and disassemble coffeemaker. Examine wires for bare spots and loose strands. With volt-ohm meter set to RX100 scale, clip one probe to an exposed metal part, the other to a prong of the plug. Turn whatever switches your coffeemaker has to *On* and bend and pull each wire. If needle jumps when a particular wire is handled, that wire is grounded.

YES→ FIX: Repair or replace faulty insulation. Insulate bare spots on wires with plastic electrical tape. Make sure all wire nuts are on securely and completely enclose bare wire. If wire at a terminal is frayed, cut off terminal and install a new one. If the cause of the grounding cannot be found, or if repairs fail to stop the shocking, take appliance to an authorized repairman. ▲▲

Coffeemaker blows fuses

When a fuse blows or circuit breaker trips, it means there is either an electrical overload or a short circuit. Overloads are fixed by reducing the number of appliances in the circuit. Short circuits are located by inspection and testing. Parts found to be shorted must be repaired or replaced.

Circuit overloaded?

NO→ TEST: To check for overloads, see p.127. Too many appliances in a circuit is the commonest cause of blown fuses.

YES→ FIX: Reduce number of appliances in the circuit. Caution: Never replace a fuse or breaker with one having a larger capacity. ▲

Short circuit in power cord or plug?

NO→ TEST: Unplug and disassemble coffeemaker so that power cord leads are accessible (p.156). Examine wires and plug for bare wires and burns. Disconnect power cord leads. Set volt-ohm meter (p.124) to RX100 scale and clip its probes to prongs of plug. Bend and pull power cord. If cord is OK, meter will read high; if shorted, needle will jump around or read zero ohms.

YES→ FIX: Replace power cord. Follow instructions given in *Hot water does not flow from spout*, p. 157, and illustrations on p.156. Note: Some coffeemakers have a power cord with a three-prong plug to safeguard the user against shock hazards. It is possible that a short circuit between internal wiring and ground may cause fuse to blow. Check for grounding by following instructions in *Coffeemaker shocks user* (left). ▲▲

Short circuit in internal wiring?

TEST: With coffeemaker unplugged and disassembled, examine all interior wiring and parts. Look for burn marks, broken insulation, loose wires. A short will occur wherever two wires cross and the insulation between them is either worn or absent.

YES→ FIX: Replace or repair broken parts. With coffeemaker unplugged and disassembled, separate any wires that appear to be touching. Mend any broken insulation you find with plastic electrical tape. ▲▲

Ease of fix: ▲ simple ▲▲ average ▲▲▲ difficult

Use and care

1. Use cold, fresh water and the coffee bean grind recommended by manufacturer. (Artificially softened water may make coffee taste bitter.)
2. Do not reheat coffee by placing container on a stove.
3. Coffeemaker should never be immersed in water. To clean housing, wipe it with a damp sponge, dry with a towel.
4. Every three to six months, depending on how hard the water is in your area, operate coffeemaker with a mixture of half vinegar, half water to flush out mineral deposits. Brew with water alone to clean out any residual vinegar.

Testing for shock hazards and short circuits

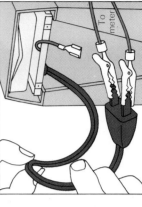

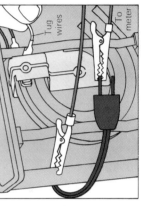

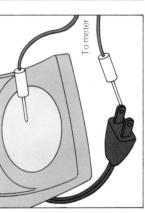

Use RX100 scale for all three tests. **Test 1:** If meter reads high, then leakage current is indicated. **Test 2:** If needle jumps when wire is handled, that wire is grounded. **Test 3:** If cord is OK, meter will read high; if not, needle will jump or read zero.

1. Shock may be caused by a leakage current. Check by touching one probe of volt-ohm meter to part that shocks, other to plug.

2. Bad wire can cause shock. Unplug appliance, turn switches on, touch one probe to part that shocks, other to plug. Tug wires during test.

3. To check for short in power cord, disconnect one of cord's leads, clip meter probes to plug. Bend cord to help disclose loose wires.

Coffeemakers/perk type

Coffeemakers does not heat

If the coffeemaker fails to heat, it means current is not flowing through the heating elements. The cause is determined through step-by-step testing, starting with the wall outlet and continuing with various parts of the coffeemaker. Repairs range from changing a house fuse to replacing main heating element.

Power off at outlet?

TEST: Unplug power cord and check wall outlet with a lamp you know is working.

YES → FIX: Replace fuse or reset circuit breaker. See p.127. If fuse keeps blowing, see *Coffeemaker blows fuses,* p.163.

Power cord broken?

NO

TEST: With power cord unplugged, examine it for fraying and the plugs for loose or broken terminals. Clip jumper wire across terminals of female plug. Set volt-ohm meter (p.124) to RX1 scale, clip probes to prongs of male plug. Bend, pull cord. If OK, meter will read zero ohms; if broken, needle will jump or read high.

YES → FIX: Replace power cord. If necessary, you can repair cord temporarily by replacing a broken plug with an equivalent plug or by cutting away damaged portions of wire, then splicing the wires back together.

Dirty terminals on power cord or at base?

NO

TEST: Clean terminals (see **Fix**), then operate coffeemaker to see if the problem has been solved.

YES → FIX: Clean terminals. Polish terminal pins on base with extra-fine steel wool. Spray female terminals of power cord with electrical contact cleaner (p.123).

Dirty terminals inside coffeemaker?

NO

TEST: Unplug coffeemaker and unscrew baseplate from base. Clean terminals inside base (see **Fix**), then operate coffeemaker to see if it is working properly.

YES → FIX: Clean internal terminals. Loosen terminal contact screws, then spray terminals with electrical contact cleaner (p.123). Before reassembling, loosen and tighten each screw a few times to ensure good contact.

Main heating element broken?

NO

TEST: With coffeemaker unplugged and baseplate removed, set volt-ohm meter to RX1 scale and touch its probes to terminals of main heating element. If element is OK, meter will read from 10 to 35 ohms; if element is broken, meter will read high.

YES → FIX: Replace main heating element. Take coffeemaker to authorized repairman. A special tool is needed to remove the heating element. In addition, great care must be taken when tightening the nut so that gaskets are not damaged but coffeemaker does not leak.

Ease of fix: △ simple △△ average △△△ difficult

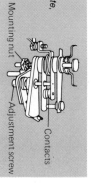

The thermostat determines how long the coffee brews. If the coffeemaker does not perk (*Water heats but does not percolate,* p.161) or does not shut off (*Coffee is too strong,* p.162), the thermostat may be defective. Polishing its contacts with fine sandpaper may help; usually it must be replaced.

Mounting nut

Contacts

Adjustment screw

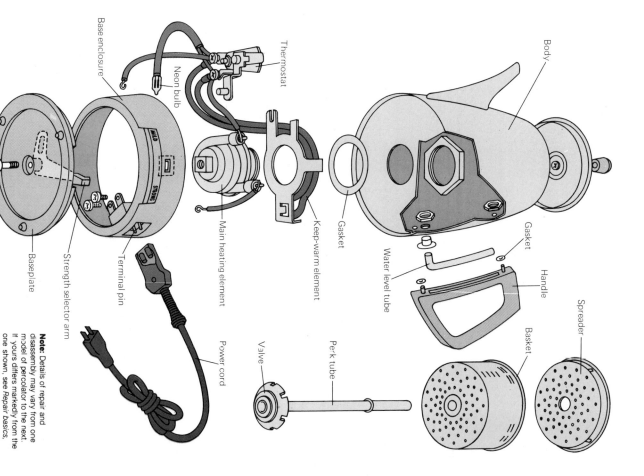

Base enclosure

Neon bulb

Thermostat

Body

Baseplate

Strength selector arm

Terminal pin

Main heating element

Keep-warm element

Gasket

Water level tube

Gasket

Handle

Basket

Spreader

Power cord

Valve

Perk tube

Note: Details of repair and disassembly may vary from one model of percolator to the next. If yours differs markedly from the one shown, see *Repair basics,* pp.128–131.

Disassembling a coffeemaker

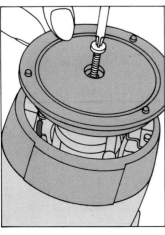

1. Remove screw in center of base and pull off base-plate. Note that on some models, the base is in one piece rather than two separate parts as shown here.

Neon bulb

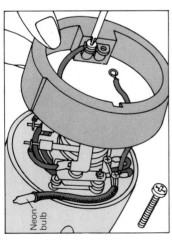

2. Undo screws and detach lead wires from terminals on base enclosure, then pull neon signal bulb from its mounting and remove enclosure from coffeemaker.

Tab

Keep-warm element

Main heating element

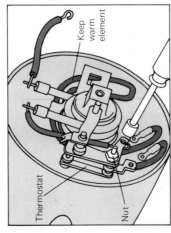

3. After removing screws and detaching leads from thermostat terminals, unscrew nut that holds thermostat to its mount inside base. Lift out thermostat.

Keep warm element

Thermostat

Nut

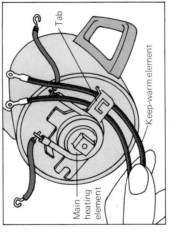

4. A metal tab holds the keep-warm element wire in place. Pry it up, then slide the keep-warm wire around coil of the main heating element and pull it out.

Water heats but does not percolate

If water in the coffeemaker heats but does not percolate, the perk tube may be clogged. The problem may also be due to a defective thermostat that prevents the main heating element from turning on, or a broken heating element. Repairs include cleaning the perk tube and replacing faulty parts.

Perk tube clogged?

TEST: Shake the perk tube. If it is OK, the valve washer will rattle. If washer does not rattle, the space between it and the valve cover may be clogged by coffee residue, or the tube may be defective.

YES → FIX: Clean or replace perk tube. (See illustrations on p.162.) Use a toothpick to remove coffee grounds and any accumulated matter from holes in valve cover. Use a knife with a thin blade to clean the space between the valve washer and valve cover. If the problem remains, replace the perk tube. △

Thermostat broken?

TEST: Unplug coffeemaker. Set coffee strength selector to *Strong*. Unscrew the baseplate from base. Set volt-ohm meter (p.124) to RX1 scale, touch probes to terminals of thermostat. If it is OK, meter will read zero ohms; if thermostat is broken, meter will read above 50 ohms.

YES → FIX: Replace thermostat. Complete the disassembly of coffeemaker's base. Note: Some thermostats require calibration after installation. Take coffeemaker to authorized repairman. Adjusting thermostat requires special equipment. △△

Main heating element broken?

TEST: With coffeemaker unplugged, set volt-ohm meter to RX1 scale and touch its probes to terminals of main heating element. If element is OK, meter will read from 10 to 35 ohms; if broken, meter will read high.

YES → FIX: Replace main heating element. Take coffeemaker to an authorized repairman. A special tool, similar to an oversized socket wrench, is needed to remove the large nut that holds the heating element in place. In addition, it is difficult to reinstall the nut properly. It must be tight enough so that the coffeemaker does not leak, but not so tight as to damage the heating element gaskets. △△△

Ease of fix: △ simple △△ average △△△ difficult

Cleaning dirty terminals

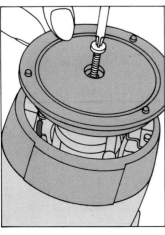

Remove baseplate and loosen terminal screws. Spray terminals with electrical contact cleaner, then tighten and loosen screws several times to aid cleaning.

Three tests for open circuits

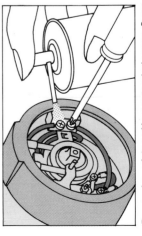

1. To check power cord, clip jumper wire across female plug, attach volt-ohm meter probes to male plug. Bend cord while testing.

Jumper wire

To meter

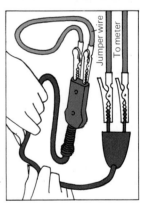

2. Remove baseplate and touch meter probes to terminals of heating element when testing it. Let shop put in new element if needed.

To meter

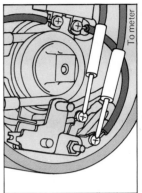

3. Baseplate must be removed to test thermostat. Set strength selector arm to *Strong* and touch meter probes to terminals.

To meter

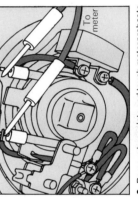

Set meter to RX1 scale for all three tests.
Test 1: Needle will jump or read high if cord is broken.
Test 2: If meter reads high, heating element is open.
Test 3: Reading over 50 ohms means thermostat is bad.

Coffee is too weak

Adequate coffee strength depends on keeping the basket and perk tube free of obstructions, taking care to fill coffeemaker with cold water only at start of brewing, and proper functioning of the thermostat. Repairs include cleaning the basket and perk tube, and replacing defective parts.

Warm water used to fill coffeemaker?

TEST: Check whether the tap water with which you are brewing coffee is cold enough. It should be between 40°F and 50°F. Use 1½ tablespoons of coffee for each 6-ounce cup you wish to brew.

[NO]

YES→ FIX: Use cold tap water. Electric percolators are designed to function properly only if used in this manner. If they are filled with warm water, the brewed coffee will be too weak.

△

Basket clogged?

TEST: Hold basket up to light. All holes should be open and clear of obstruction.

YES→ FIX: Clean basket. Use commercial coffeemaker cleaner (available at supermarkets). Clean clogged holes with toothpick or needle.

△

Perk tube partially clogged?

[NO]

TEST: Shake tube. If it is OK, valve washer will rattle. If it does not, space between valve washer and cover is clogged by coffee residue or tube is defective.

YES→ FIX: Clean or replace perk tube. Use toothpick to remove coffee grounds and accumulated matter from holes in valve and in space between washer and cover. If problem remains, replace perk tube.

△△

Thermostat out of adjustment?

[NO]

TEST: Brewing time for perk-type coffeemakers varies from as little as 7 minutes to as long as 18 minutes. If coffee is weak and the coffeemaker stops perking in less than 10 minutes, the thermostat is either out of adjustment or broken.

YES→ FIX: Have thermostat adjusted. Take coffeemaker to authorized repairman. The thermostat should shut off main heating element when coffee temperature is just below boiling. Proper adjustment requires the use of special temperature-sensing devices.

△△△

Cleaning perk tube and basket

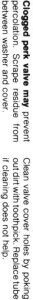

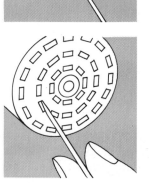

Clogged perk valve may prevent percolation. Scrape residue from between washer and cover.

Clean valve cover holes by poking out dirt with toothpick. Replace tube if cleaning does not help.

To clear badly clogged basket, use needle or toothpick to poke residue out of each hole.

Coffee is too strong

If coffee is too strong, it means either the thermostat or keep-warm element is broken. A defective thermostat will fail to turn off the main heating element when brewing is complete. A broken keep-warm element will let the coffeemaker repercolate. Repairs consist of replacing the defective part.

Percolation lasts too long?

TEST: Percolation should not last more than 20 minutes. If it does, thermostat is broken. Note: A coffeemaker with a signal light will signal when percolation stops. If percolation stops but the light does not go on, then the light is broken. Although this will not interfere with the functioning of the coffeemaker, you may want to replace the light for convenience.

YES→ FIX: Replace thermostat. Unplug coffeemaker from wall outlet and disassemble base (see *Disassembling a coffeemaker*, p.161). Some thermostats require calibration after installation. If yours does, take coffeemaker to authorized repairman, since calibration requires special equipment. (If your signal light is broken and you want to replace it, remove its leads from thermostat terminals and slip it from base.)

△△

Coffeemaker repercolates?

TEST: If percolation stops as it should but begins again a few minutes later, the keep-warm element is broken.

YES→ FIX: Replace keep-warm element. To do so, unplug coffeemaker from wall outlet and disassemble base (p.161).

△△

Ease of fix: △ simple △△ average △△△ difficult

Use and care

1. Do not plug an empty coffeemaker into wall outlet.
2. Be sure perk tube is well seated inside coffeemaker, otherwise coffeemaker may not percolate.
3. Use either a filter or a grind that is coarse enough that grounds do not slip through holes in basket.
4. When pouring coffee grounds into basket, place finger over top of perk tube to keep grounds from pouring down it.
5. If coffee is bitter, percolate a mixture of two teaspoons of baking soda in eight cups of water for one complete cycle to remove coffee residue. In hard water areas, repeat with a mixture of half water, half white vinegar to remove mineral deposits.
6. Do not immerse coffeemaker in water if not specifically designed for this.
7. Wipe outside with a damp cloth and polish with a clean dry cloth. Do not use steel wool or abrasive cleaners.

Repairing leaks

Leaks occur in two places: where the handle is attached to the body and around the main heating element in the base. In time, the gaskets used at these points deteriorate. To repair leaks at the handle, unscrew nuts and remove handle.

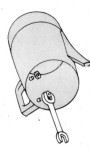

Remove nuts to take off handle

Replace gaskets at the handle screws and water-level tube. (Refer to exploded view on p.160 for location of gaskets.) If water leaks from the base, take coffeemaker to an authorized repairman. Removal and reinstallation of heating element requires a special set of tools.

Coffeemaker shocks user

A frayed power cord, an electrically live component grounded to a metal part, or leakage current due to faulty insulation will cause shocking. In the case of a frayed cord or grounding, the part can be fixed or replaced. If leakage current is suspected, the coffeemaker should be taken to a repairman.

Power cord frayed?

 TEST: Receiving a shock from power cord is sufficient evidence it needs repair.

 FIX: Replace power cord. Use manufacturer's replacement. ◢

Leakage current present?

TEST: Unplug power cord from wall outlet but not from coffeemaker. Set volt-ohm meter (p.124) to RX100 scale and attach one probe to body shell, the other to either prong of the power cord's plug. Set coffee strength selector to *Strong*. If meter reads high, leakage current (p.127) is indicated.

FIX: Take coffeemaker to authorized repairman. Eliminating leakage current requires special equipment. Note: It is possible that the shock is not caused by leakage current but by a wire that becomes grounded only when the coffeemaker is on. To investigate this, proceed with next test before taking coffeemaker to repair shop. ◢◢◢

Wiring inside coffeemaker grounded to shell?

TEST: Unplug coffeemaker and disassemble base (p.161). Examine wires for bare spots. Put strength selector on *Strong*. Set volt-ohm meter to RX100 scale, clip one of its probes to body shell, the other to a heating element terminal. Bend and pull wires. If needle jumps when a particular wire is handled, wire is grounded.

FIX: Repair or replace damaged parts. Use high-temperature (fiberglass) tape to reinsulate wires with loose strands or damaged insulation. Straighten out bent terminals. If a wire or other part must be replaced, use manufacturer's replacement or the equivalent. ◢◢

Coffeemaker blows fuses

When a fuse blows or circuit breaker trips, it means there is either an electrical overload or a short circuit. Overloads are fixed by reducing the number of appliances in the circuit. Short circuits are located by inspection and testing. Parts found to be shorted must be repaired or replaced.

Circuit overloaded?

 **TEST:** To check for overloads, see p.127. Too many appliances in a circuit is the commonest cause of blown fuses.

FIX: Reduce number of appliances in the circuit. Caution: Never replace a fuse or breaker with one having a larger capacity. ◢

Short circuit in power cord or plug?

TEST: Unplug power cord from wall outlet and examine cord, both plugs, and coffeemaker for bare wires and burn marks. Set volt-ohm meter (p.124) to RX100 scale and clip its probes to the prongs of male power cord plug. Bend and pull cord. If it is OK, meter will read high; if cord is shorted, needle will wobble or read zero.

FIX: Replace power cord. If necessary, you can repair cord temporarily by replacing a broken plug with an equivalent plug or by cutting away damaged portions of wire, then splicing the wires back together. ◢

Short circuit in coffeemaker?

TEST: Disassemble base of coffeemaker (see *Disassembling a coffeemaker*, p.161) and examine interior parts. Look for burn marks, distorted terminal posts, broken insulation, loose wires.

FIX: Repair or replace damaged parts. Use high-temperature (fiberglass) tape to reinsulate wires with loose strands or damaged insulation. Straighten out bent terminals. If a wire or other part must be replaced, use manufacturer's replacement or the equivalent. ◢◢

Ease of fix: ◢ simple ◢◢ average ◢◢◢ difficult

Testing for shock hazards and short circuits

1. To find out if shock is due to leakage current, clip one probe of volt-ohm meter to body shell, the other to power cord plug.

2. An internal ground may cause shocks. Unplug coffeemaker, remove baseplate. Clip probes to body, heating element; tug wires.

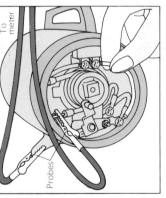

3. Short circuit in power cord will blow fuses. With cord disconnected, clip meter probes to male plug. Bend and pull on cord during test.

Immersible coffeemakers

Many electric percolators are now designed to be immersible in water. Since the base assemblies of these models are permanently sealed, no internal repairs can be made. However, leaks at the handle and problems with the power cord can be fixed the same way you would fix a conventional percolator.

Manufacturers provide service for most other repairs by replacing a broken coffeemaker with a new one. It is wise to examine your immersible coffeemaker periodically. Look for burn marks, cracks, and looseness at the terminal area, cracks in the base, and defects in the base of the body seal.

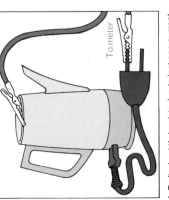

Set meter to RX100 scale for all three tests.
Test 1: If meter reads high ohms, leakage current is indicated.
Test 2: If needle jumps, wire being handled is faulty.
Test 3: Meter will read high if power cord is OK. Needle will jump or read zero ohms if cord is broken.

Fans

Motor does not run at all or runs sluggishly

If the fan does not run at all and the motor does not hum, look for a blown house fuse, broken power cord, or defective motor to be the cause. Replacement of the fuse, power cord, or motor is called for. If the motor is stalled or sluggish, try lubricating it; the motor bearings may be dry.

Power off at outlet?

TEST: Unplug power cord and check wall outlet with a lamp you know is working.

 NO

 YES **FIX: Replace fuse or reset circuit breaker.** See p.127. If fuse keeps blowing, see *Fan blows fuses*, p.166.

Power cord broken?

TEST: Unplug fan. Examine power cord for fraying and the plug for loose or distorted prongs. Take off rear grille and remove switch from its mount. Free the ends of both power cord leads (see **Fix**) and twist the bare wires together. Set volt-ohm meter (p.124) to RX1 scale and clip its probes to the prongs of the plug. Bend and pull power cord. If cord is OK, meter will read zero ohms; if cord is broken, needle will jump around or read high.

NO ←

YES → **FIX: Replace power cord.** Remove power cord lead from insulated wire connector by squeezing connector open with locking pliers. Free other lead by inserting a straightened-out paper clip into the switch terminal to which it is attached and pulling on lead. Complete the removal of power cord by squeezing strain relief device with pliers, rotating it a quarter turn, and pulling it out of mounting hole. When installing new cord, strip ⅜ inch of insulation from each lead. Insert one lead into switch terminal with aid of paper clip. Join other wire to lead from motor and crimp them together with a new insulated connector. ▲▲▲

Motor faulty?

TEST: Unplug fan and turn switch to *Off*. The motor of a three-speed fan has four leads coming from it. Free the ends of all four leads (see **Fix**). Set volt-ohm meter to RX1 scale. Clip one probe to motor lead formerly attached to power cord lead, the other to each of the other motor wires in turn. If motor is OK, meter will read from 5 to 100 ohms all three times; if meter reads high, the motor is broken.

NO ←

YES → **FIX: Replace motor.** One of the four motor leads will already be free as the result of removing the insulated wire connector in the previous test. To release the ends of the other three motor leads, push a straightened-out paper clip into the switch terminals to which they are attached and pull out leads. No record of which wire goes into which switch terminal, so that leads from new motor can be installed correctly. To complete removal, see *Disassembling the fan*, p.165. ▲▲

Motor bearings dry?

TEST: If motor hums but does not turn or runs sluggishly, bearings may be dry. Lubricate them (see **Fix**), then operate fan to see if the difficulty has been cleared up.

YES → **FIX: Lubricate bearings.** Unplug fan from wall outlet. Lubricate bearings according to instructions in *Lubricating your fan*, p.167. ▲

Ease of fix: ▲ simple ▲▲ average ▲▲▲ difficult

Getting the most from a fan

There are two kinds of fans, circulators and ventilators. A circulating fan moves the air around within a room. A ventilating fan changes the air in a room, either by exhausting it outward or by drawing outside air in. The most effective fan for the overall cooling of a home is a ventilating type installed at a window and set on *Exhaust* (blowing outward). It will pull air through the house from open windows in other rooms. Enclosing the fan with panels will greatly improve its efficiency. It is nearly as effective, however, to put a fan on a table top about two feet from a raised window.

Open windows only in rooms you wish to cool. To ventilate a single room that has only one window, install fan on sill and press both sashes down on it; air will be drawn in through the top.

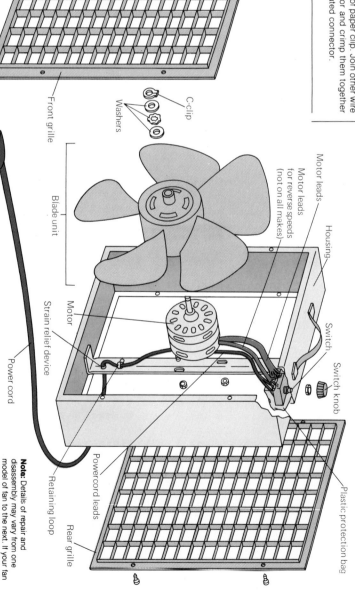

Front grille

Washers

C-clip

Blade unit

Motor leads for reverse speeds (not on all makes)

Motor leads

Housing

Switch

Switch knob

Plastic protection bag

Rear grille

Retaining loop

Powercord leads

Power cord

Strain relief device

Motor

Note: Details of repair and disassembly may vary from one model of fan to the next. If your fan differs markedly from the one shown, see *Repair basics*, pp.128–131.

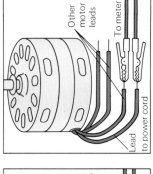

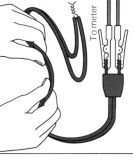

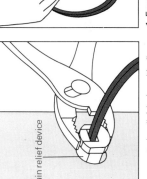

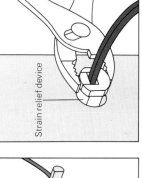

Fan operates in some speeds but not others

If the fan operates at some speeds but not all, it means either that some of the switch contacts are dirty or that the wiring inside the motor is faulty. If the problem is in the switch, cleaning the contacts may solve it. Otherwise, the switch or the motor must be replaced.

Switch dirty or broken?

TEST: Unplug fan. Take off rear grille. Clean switch contacts (see **Fix**), then operate fan to see if the difficulty has been cleared up. If it has not, the switch is broken and should be replaced.

NO →

YES → **FIX: Clean or replace switch.** Spray electrical contact cleaner (p.123) into switch terminals and turn switch knob back and forth several times to help improve contact. If problem persists, replace the switch. Remove rear grille, pull off switch knob, and undo mounting nut. Pull out switch and take off plastic protection bag. Insert straightened-out paper clip into switch terminals, and pull out leads. Note: Keep a record of which wire goes into which terminal. △△

Motor faulty?

TEST: Unplug fan and turn switch to *Off*. The motor of a three-speed fan has four leads coming from it. One connects to one of the power cord leads, the three others go to switch. Free ends of all four leads (see **Fix**). Set the volt-ohm meter (p. 124) to RX1 scale and clip one of its probes to the motor wire that was attached to the power cord lead. Clip the other probe to each of the other motor leads in turn. If the motor is OK, meter will read from 5 to 100 ohms all three times; if meter reads high, motor is broken.

YES → **FIX: Replace motor.** Squeeze insulated wire connector open with locking pliers to free motor lead that is attached to power cord. The three other motor leads go to the switch. Remove the switch from its mount, then insert a straightened-out paper clip into the switch terminals and pull the leads out. Keep a record of which wire goes into which terminal so that leads from new motor can be attached correctly. To complete removal of motor, see *Disassembling the fan*, at left. △△

Ease of fix: △ simple △△ average △△△ difficult

Testing for open circuits

Set meter to RX1 scale for both tests. **Test 1:** Meter will read zero ohms if cord is OK; needle will jump around if there is an open circuit. **Test 2:** Meter will read 5 to 100 ohms if motor is OK, high ohms if motor is broken.

Other motor leads — To meter — Lead to power cord

2. To check motor, clip one probe to wire formerly attached to power cord, the other to each motor lead in turn.

To meter

1. Free the power cord leads, twist bare ends together, clip volt-ohm meter probes to plug. Bend cord during test.

Disassembling the fan

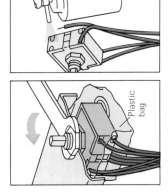

Allen screw

Allen wrench

C-clip

1. Unplug fan and remove front and rear grilles. Take off C-clip (left) or Allen screw (right) by which blade unit is attached to motor, and remove blades.

Plastic bag

2. Pull off switch knob. Undo nut, slip out switch, and remove plastic protection bag. At right, terminals are being cleaned with electrical contact cleaner.

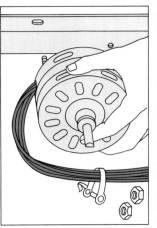

Retaining loop

Strain relief device

3. Disengage the various retaining loops on the frame that hold wires in place by prying plug of each out of its socket with the blade of a screwdriver.

4. Hold motor to relieve strain and unscrew nuts that secure it to mounting bracket. Pull the motor out. Its leads will still be attached to power cord and switch.

Removing the power cord

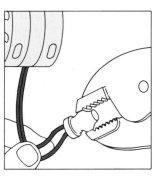

Strain relief device

Compress strain relief device with pliers, rotate it a quarter turn, and remove it from its seat. Pull out cord.

Free the other cord lead from switch by inserting straightened-out paper clip into terminal and pulling on lead.

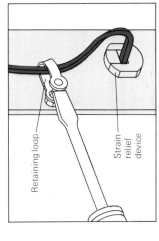

Separate the power cord lead from the motor lead by squeezing open insulated connector with locking pliers.

Fans

Excessive noise while operating

Noisy operation may be due to loose parts in the fan, vibrations from the surface where the fan is located, bent blades, or dry bearings. After finding the cause, repairs include tightening nuts and screws, jamming cardboard into the window sash, straightening or replacing the blades, and lubricating the motor.

Fan causing window or table to vibrate?

TEST: Operate fan on a cushioned surface. If it runs quietly, the problem is probably due to surface or window vibrations.

 YES ► **FIX: Cushion fan with pad; insert wedge into window shaft.** Jam cardboard wedge between window frame and sash. Also make sure window panes are firmly installed.

▷

Loose parts in fan?

TEST: While fan is operating, listen and look for vibrating parts. Items to check include grilles, exterior screws, carrying handle, and switch. If you think a particular part may be loose, hold your hand against it to see if noise ceases.

 YES ► **FIX: Tighten loose parts.** Unplug fan and remove switch knob and front and rear grilles. (See *Disassembling the fan,* p.165.) Tighten mounting nuts of switch and motor. Tighten blade assembly set screw if there is one. When reassembling fan, tighten screws firmly; make sure none are missing.

▷

One or more fan blades bent?

TEST: Unplug fan. Insert pencil through front grille until point just grazes the front of one of the blades, then use another pencil to rotate the blades. If blades are straight, pencil point will graze each one as it passes by; any blade out of line by more than a quarter inch should be straightened.

 YES ► **FIX: Straighten blade or replace blade assembly.** With fan unplugged, remove front grille and blade assembly. (See *Disassembling the fan,* p.165.) Place the assembly on a table and carefully bend misaligned blades so that all blades are at the same distance from table top (or are all touching it). If any blade is severely misshapen, replace entire blade unit.

▷▷

Motor bearings dry?

TEST: Lubricate bearings (see **Fix**), then operate fan to see if the difficulty has been cleared up.

YES ► **FIX: Lubricate bearings.** Unplug fan from wall outlet. Lubricate bearings according to instructions in *Lubricating your fan,* p.167.

▷

Checking and aligning blades

With fan unplugged, insert pencil through front grille until point just touches edge of one blade. Rotate blades slowly. If they are straight, pencil will graze each as it passes.

If a blade is out of line by more than ¼ in., straighten it. Remove blade assembly (see *Disassembling the fan,* p.165) and lay it on table. Carefully bend blades so that each tip touches surface.

Fan blows fuses

When a fuse blows or a circuit breaker trips, it means there is either an electrical overload or a short circuit. Overloads are fixed by reducing the number of appliances in a circuit. Short circuits are located by inspection and testing. Parts found to be shorted must be replaced.

Circuit overloaded?

TEST: To check for overloads, see p.127. Too many appliances in a circuit is the commonest cause of blown fuses.

 YES ► **FIX: Reduce number of appliances in the circuit. Caution: Never replace a fuse or breaker with one having a larger capacity.**

▷

Short circuit in power cord or plug?

TEST: Unplug fan and remove rear grille. Check power cord and plug for bare wires, burns. Insert straightened-out paper clip into switch terminal and pull out cord lead. Set volt-ohm meter (p.124) to RX100 scale and clip its probes to prongs of plug. Bend and pull power cord. If cord is OK, meter will read high; if shorted, needle will jump around or read zero ohms.

 YES ► **FIX: Replace power cord.** Follow instructions in *Motor does not run or runs sluggishly,* p.164, and in *Removing the power cord,* p.165.

▷▷

Short circuit in motor?

TEST: Unplug fan and turn switch to *Off.* Free the ends of the four motor leads (see **Fix**). Set volt-ohm meter to RX1 scale. Clip one probe to the motor lead formerly attached to power cord lead, the other to each of the other motor wires in turn. If motor is OK, meter will read from 5 to 100 ohms all three times; if meter reads zero ohms, motor is faulty. (See *Testing for open circuits,* p.165, for illustration of test set-up.)

YES ► **FIX: Replace motor.** Squeeze insulated wire connector open with locking pliers to free motor lead that is attached to power cord. The three other motor leads go to the switch. Remove the switch from its mount, then insert a straightened-out paper clip into the switch terminals and pull the leads out. Keep a record of which wire goes into which terminal so that leads from new motor can be attached correctly. To complete removal of motor, see *Disassembling the fan,* p.165.

▷▷

Ease of fix: △ simple △△ average △△△ difficult

Testing for short circuits

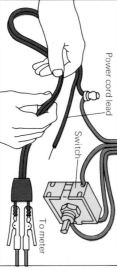

Power cord lead

Switch

To meter

Set meter to RX100 scale. If meter reads high, power cord is OK. If needle jumps zero, cord is shorted.

Unplug fan and remove switch from its mount. Free power cord lead from switch terminal, then clip volt-ohm meter probes to the plug. Bend cord during test to help disclose loose connections.

Fan shocks when touched

A frayed power cord, an electrically live component grounded to a metal part, or leakage current due to faulty insulation will cause shocking. In the case of a frayed cord or grounding, the part can be fixed or replaced. If leakage current is suspected, the fan should be taken to a repairman.

Power cord frayed?

TEST: Receiving a shock from power cord is sufficient evidence it needs repair.

FIX: Replace power cord. Follow instructions given in *Fan blows fuses*, p.166, and *Removing the power cord*, p.165.
△△

Leakage current present?

TEST: Unplug fan from wall outlet. Set volt-ohm meter to RX100 scale. Clip one of its probes to frame, the other to either prong of the power cord plug. Turn switch to *Low*, then *Medium*, then *High*. If needle reads at or near high for all settings, leakage current (p.127) is indicated.

FIX: Take fan to authorized repairman. Eliminating leakage current requires special equipment. Note: It is possible that the shock is not caused by leakage current but by a wire that becomes grounded only when the fan is on. To investigate this, proceed with remainder of tests before taking fan to shop.
△△△

Internal wiring grounded to frame?

TEST: Unplug fan and remove grille. Check all wires for bare spots and loose strands. Set volt-ohm meter to RX100 scale. Clip one probe to frame, the other to either prong of the plug. Turn switch to *Low* and bend and twist wires. Repeat with switch on *Medium* and *High*. If needle jumps when a wire is handled, that wire is grounded.

FIX: Repair or replace faulty power cord or wiring. Reinsulate bare spots on wires with plastic electrical tape. To replace power cord, follow instructions given in *Motor does not run or runs sluggishly*, p.164, and in *Removing the power cord*, p.165.
△△

Motor wiring grounded?

TEST: Unplug fan and remove motor. (See *Disassembling the fan*, p.165.) Set volt-ohm meter to RX100 scale and clip one probe to motor housing, the other to any motor lead. If meter reads high, motor is OK; anything lower means motor wiring is grounded.

FIX: Replace motor. The motor has already been removed as part of the test. When installing new motor, be sure to connect wires to switch the same way as in old motor.
△△

Ease of fix: △ simple   △△ average   △△△ difficult

Cleaning instructions

The exposed parts of a fan require periodic cleaning. First, remove the grilles and blades. On some fans the grilles snap out and the blade assembly can be simply pulled off of the motor shaft. On other fans the grilles or blades or both must first be unscrewed. (See *Disassembling the fan*, p.165.)

Testing for shock hazard with volt-ohm meter

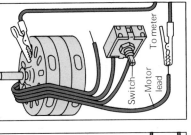

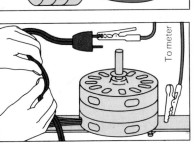

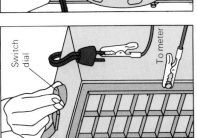

Switch dial

To meter

Switch

Motor lead

To meter

To meter

1. For leakage current test, clip one meter probe to frame, other to plug. Turn switch to all settings.

2. To see if internal wiring is grounded, attach meter probes to frame and plug, and tug on wires.

3. Check motor for ground by removing it from fan. Clip one probe to housing, other to any lead.

Set meter to RX100 scale for all three tests.

Test 1: If meter reads high for all speed settings, leakage current is indicated. **Test 2:** If needle jumps when a wire is handled, that wire is grounded. **Test 3:** If meter reads high, motor is OK; if it reads anything lower, the motor wiring is grounded.

Lubricating your fan

Unless your owner's manual advises you not to, your fan motor should be lubricated periodically. Even those designed to run for an extended period without it, will eventually need lubrication. As a rule, you should oil a fan motor before each cooling season.

To lubricate fan motor, look for an oil

Oil hole

Use spray lubricant if motor has no oil hole.

hole or tube in the motor housing. You may have to disassemble the fan to gain access to it. Clean the hole with a straightened-out paper clip and apply two or three drops of light machine oil. Run the fan for a few minutes to help spread the oil around the bearings.

If the motor appears sluggish and gummed up, but there is no oil hole, spray a penetrating-type lubricant onto the motor shaft where it enters the housing. Run the motor a few minutes to allow oil to work in. Penetrating oil dissolves dirt, then vaporizes, leaving a light film of lubricant. Since this lubricant will not last long, it is wise to follow up with a more thorough lubrication (described below) or else spray the motor shaft once a month, particularly if the fan is heavily used. Do not use penetrating lubricant if motor has ball bearings, sometimes found in large fans.

For longer lasting lubrication, disassemble motor and add two or three drops of oil directly to each bearing or to the adjacent cloth wicks. When reassembling motor, be sure its shaft is correctly seated. Tighten housing bolts with fingers, then run motor a few seconds to align shaft before tightening them with a wrench. If the motor labors, loosen the bolts slightly.

Wash the blade unit and both grilles in a solution of warm water and mild detergent. If it is too difficult to remove the blade assembly, leave it on and wipe the blades with a cloth dampened in the solution. Clean the motor housing and frame with a damp cloth, but be sure to keep the motor dry.

Fryers and cookers/detachable control type

Appliance does not heat

If your cooker fails to heat, current is not flowing through the heating element. Step-by-step testing will determine the cause. Start with the wall outlet and continue by checking the various parts of the cooker. Repairs range from changing a house fuse to replacing all or part of the appliance.

Power off at outlet?

 NO

TEST: Unplug power cord and check wall outlet with a lamp you know is working.

 NO

 YES **FIX: Replace fuse or reset circuit breaker.** See p.127. If fuse keeps blowing, see *Appliance blows fuses*, p.170.

△

Heating element broken?

 NO

TEST: Detach probe control. Set volt-ohm meter (p.124) to RX1 scale and clip its probes to terminal pins of pan. If heating element is OK, meter will read 10 to 15 ohms; if it is broken, meter will read high.

YES **FIX: Replace body unit of appliance.** The heating element is permanently embedded in the unit and cannot be repaired.

△

Dirty terminals on body unit or probe control?

NO

TEST: Unplug power cord and clean all terminals (see **Fix**), then operate appliance to see if difficulty has been cleared up.

YES **FIX: Clean terminals.** Polish terminal pins on body unit with extra-fine steel wool. Spray female terminals of probe control with electrical contact cleaner (p.123). Push the probe control unit in and out of body unit several times to improve electrical contact. Note: Terminal pins of some cookers can be replaced, but do not try to take them off unless you are sure they are removable. If you break one, you will have to buy a new body unit.

△△

Power cord broken?

NO

TEST: Unplug power cord from wall outlet. Examine it for fraying and the plug for loose or distorted prongs. Remove bottom cover of probe control. Set volt-ohm meter to RX1 scale. Attach jumper wire across power cord leads and clip meter probes to prongs of power cord plug. Bend and pull power cord. If cord is OK, meter will read zero ohms; if cord is broken, needle will jump or read high.

YES **FIX: Replace power cord.** If power cord leads are crimped to terminals inside the probe control, pry terminal sleeves open with a small screwdriver. Use long-nose pliers to crimp new cord leads back onto terminals. If you cannot free power cord from its terminals inside probe control, slip leads off, leaving ⅜-inch stubs, and install new power cord by connecting its leads to the stubs with solderless sleeve connectors.

△△

Thermostat broken?

NO

TEST: Unplug power cord from wall outlet and remove bottom cover of probe control. Turn temperature dial to *High*. Set volt-ohm meter to RX1 scale and touch its probes to thermostat terminals. If thermostat is OK, meter will read zero; if it is broken, the meter will read high.

YES **FIX: Replace probe control.** Repairs to control units are not likely to stand up, particularly if control is old or has been misused by immersing it in water or dropping it. Take old control with you when you buy new one to be sure you get correct replacement as well as for possible trade-in.

△

Ease of fix: △ simple △△ average △△△ difficult

On some cookers, the thermostat may be built into the body rather than part of a detachable probe control unit. Among such appliances are most models of deep-fat fryers, wafflers, crock pots, slow cookers, and corn poppers. For repair information on these cookers, see *Wafflers, corn poppers, and slow cookers,* pp.226–229. Also note that the probe controls of many probe-type appliances cannot be disassembled and the entire control must be replaced if it is broken.

Note: Details of repair and disassembly may vary from one model of probe control cooker to the next. If your appliance differs markedly from the one shown here, see *Repair basics,* pp.128–131.

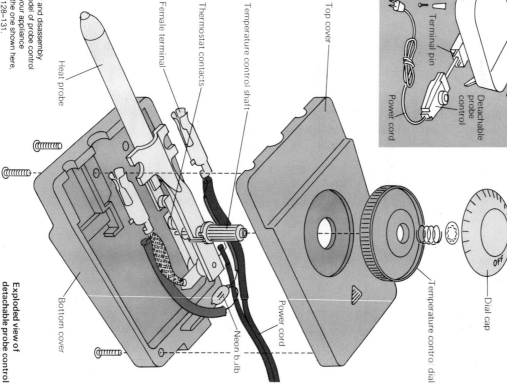

Body unit
Terminal pin
Power cord
Detachable probe control
Top cover
Temperature control shaft
Power cord
Temperature control dial
Dial cap
Temperature control dial
Thermostat contacts
Female terminal
Heat probe
Neon bulb
Bottom cover

Exploded view of detachable probe control

Improper temperature

If the cooker heats but does not operate at the correct temperature, it is safe to assume that the problem is with the thermostat—it may either be broken or out of calibration. If several attempts at adjustment fail to correct the difficulty, the entire probe control unit should be replaced with a new one.

Thermostat out of adjustment?

TEST: Fill pan 1 inch deep with water and attach probe control. Set temperature dial to 212°F (start of simmer range) and plug power cord into wall outlet. If thermostat is adjusted correctly, water will repeatedly come to a simmer, then stop, then come to a simmer again, then stop again. If water does not heat to simmer point, thermostat is set too low; if it simmers or boils continuously, thermostat is set too high.

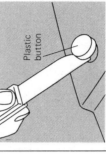 **YES→** **FIX: Adjust thermostat.** Unplug probe control from wall unit, and detach it from pan. If control has a plastic button on the bottom, pry it out with a knife—the thermostat adjusting screw can be reached through the opening where the button was. If the control does not have such a button, pry off the dial plate with a knife—the adjusting screw is in the center of the dial shaft. To adjust thermostat, turn screw a quarter turn counterclockwise if the thermostat is set too low, or a quarter turn clockwise if the thermostat is set too high, then test it out. Adjust again if necessary. If repeated adjustments fail to solve problem, the thermostat is broken and the entire probe control should be replaced. Be sure new control is correct one for your cooker. △△

Ease of fix: △ simple   △△ average   △△△ difficult

Cleaning terminals

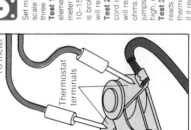

Polishing terminal pins on body with steel wool may improve the cooker's heating performance.

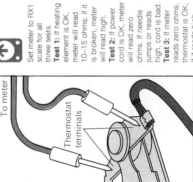

Spray female terminals of probe with electrical contact cleaner to remove accumulated residue.

How to adjust the thermostat

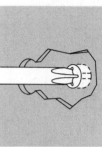

Dial cap

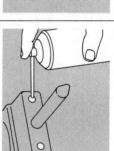

Plastic button

On some probe controls, access to thermostat adjustment screw is gained by prying out small plastic button on underside of probe (left). Other models require prying off dial cap (right) to reach screw.

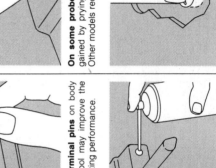

Turn adjustment screw clockwise if cooker is overheating, counterclockwise if underheating. Screws may be Phillips (left) or standard (right). Standard screw is shown in center of control shaft—a common location.

Replacing the power cord

Terminal sleeve

Sleeve connector

Crimping tool

If power cord leads are crimped to terminals inside probe control, try prying sleeves open.

Attach new cord to old terminals by crimping terminal sleeves over old lead leaving ⅜-in. stub. Attach new lead with sleeve connector.

If sleeve cannot be opened, cut off old lead leaving ⅜-in. stub. Attach new lead with sleeve connector.

Use and care

1. Clean probe control by wiping it with a damp cloth. Never immerse the probe in water. If it becomes wet accidentally, dry it by removing bottom cover, then playing warm air over the interior with a blower-type hair dryer or similar device until all the moisture evaporates.
2. The pan is made so that it can be washed in a sink, though not in a dishwasher. Use hot sudsy water (avoid harsh cleansers). Dry around the terminal pin area carefully before using the cooker.

If you employ a scouring pad, be sure no steel particles remain near terminals.
3. Never run cold water into a hot pan. It may warp the aluminum body.
4. When using the cooker, attach the probe control unit to the pan before plugging in the power cord. To disconnect the pan, first turn the dial to *Off,* then unplug power cord.
5. Do not store the pan in the drawer of an oven. The high temperatures from the broiler will damage plastic parts.

Checking for open circuits

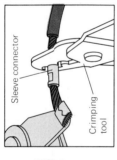

Terminal pins

To meter

1. Check heating element by clipping volt-ohm meter probes to terminal pins.

Jumper

Power cord leads

To meter

2. For power cord test, use jumper across leads and clip probes to plug. Tug on cord.

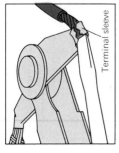

To meter

Thermostat terminals

3. To test thermostat, touch probes to its terminals. Set temperature dial to *High.*

 Set meter to RX1 scale for all three tests.
Test 1: If heating element is OK, meter will read 10–15 ohms; if it is broken, meter will read high.
Test 2: If power cord is OK, meter will read zero ohms. If needle jumps or reads high, cord is bad.
Test 3: If meter reads zero ohms, thermostat is OK; if it reads high, thermostat is bad.

Fryers and cookers/detachable control type

Appliance shocks user

A frayed power cord or an electrically live component grounded to either the heat probe or the body unit may be causing the shock. If tests show this to be the case, replace the defective part. If the tests are negative, leakage current is probably present. Take the cooker to an authorized repairman.

Power cord frayed?
TEST: Receiving a shock from power cord is sufficient evidence it needs repair.

 YES→ FIX: Replace power cord. Follow instructions given in *Appliance does not heat*, p. 168, and in *Replacing the power cord*, p. 169.
▷▷

 NO

Live component grounded to heat probe?
TEST: Detach probe control from pan and wall outlet. Turn temperature control to *High*. Set volt-ohm meter (p.124) to RX100 scale and touch one of its probes to heat probe, the other to each female terminal in turn. If meter reads low for either terminal, a live component is grounded to heat probe.

YES→ FIX: Replace probe control. Repairs to control units are not likely to stand up, particularly if control is old or has been misused by immersing it in water or dropping it. Take old control with you when you buy new one to be sure you get correct replacement as well as for possible trade-in.
▷

NO

Wiring inside cooking pan grounded?
TEST: Detach probe control from pan. Immerse pan in warm water for several minutes, then dry it thoroughly with a towel. Set volt-ohm meter to RX100 scale and clip one of its probes to metal of pan, the other to either terminal pin. If wiring is OK, meter will read high; anything lower means wiring is grounded.

YES→ FIX: Replace cooking pan. The entire cooking unit of a probe control appliance is sealed so that it can be immersed in water. There is no practical way to repair damage to the wiring inside it.
▷

Leakage current present?
If previous tests have **failed to locate** the cause of the shocking, it is probably due to leakage current (p.127). Take the appliance to a dealer. Eliminating leakage current requires special equipment.

Testing for shock hazards

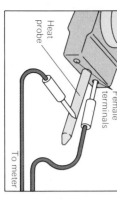
Heat probe
Female terminals
To meter

1. To test wires in probe control for grounding, touch one probe of volt-ohm meter to heat probe, other to each female terminal.

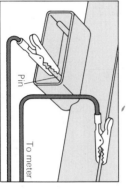
Pin
To meter

 Set meter to RX100 scale. If it does not read high, there is a grounded wire in the part tested. If meter reads high, part is OK. If neither test shows grounding, leakage current (p.127) is likely.

2. Heat element inside pan may be grounded. Check by clipping one meter probe to body of pan, the other to either terminal pin.

Appliance blows fuses

When a fuse blows or circuit breaker trips, it is caused by either an electrical overload or a short circuit. First, look for a possible overload and reduce the number of appliances in the circuit. Check for short circuits by testing the parts of the cooker. Parts found to be shorted must be replaced.

Circuit overloaded?
TEST: To check for overloads, see p.127. Too many appliances in a circuit is the commonest cause of blown fuses and tripped breakers.

YES→ FIX: Reduce number of appliances in the circuit. Caution: Never replace a fuse or breaker with one having a larger capacity.
▷

NO

Short circuit in power cord or plug?
TEST: Unplug power cord from wall outlet and detach probe control from pan. Examine power cord, plug, and control unit for bare wires and burn marks. Set volt-ohm meter (p.124) to RX100 scale and clip its probes to the prongs of the power cord plug. Turn temperature dial to *Off*. Bend and pull power cord. If cord is OK, meter will read high; if cord is shorted, needle will jump around or read zero ohms.

 YES→ FIX: Replace power cord. If power cord leads are crimped to terminals inside the probe control, pry terminal sleeves open with a small screwdriver. Use long-nose pliers to crimp new cord leads back onto terminals. If you cannot free power cord from its terminals inside probe control, slip leads off, leaving ⅜-inch stubs, and install new power cord by connecting its leads to the stubs with solderless sleeve connectors. (see *Replacing the power cord*, p.169.)
▷▷

 NO

Short circuit inside probe control?
TEST: Unplug power cord from wall outlet and detach probe control from pan. Set volt-ohm meter to RX100 scale and clip its probes to the female terminals of the probe control. Turn temperature dial through its entire range. If meter reads low or zero ohms at any time while turning, there is a short circuit inside probe control.

YES→ FIX: Replace probe control. Repairs to control units are not likely to stand up, particularly if control is old or has been misused by immersing it in water or dropping it. Take old control with you when you buy new one to be sure you get correct replacement as well as for possible trade-in.
▷

Ease of fix: ▷ simple ▷▷ average ▷▷▷ difficult

Testing for short circuits

To meter

1. Blown fuses may be due to short in power cord. To check, clip volt-ohm meter probes to plug, set dial to *Off*, and bend cord.

 Use RX100 scale for both tests.
Test 1: If cord is OK, meter will read high; if shorted, needle will wobble or read zero ohms.
Test 2: If meter reads low or zero ohms while you are turning dial, probe control has a short.

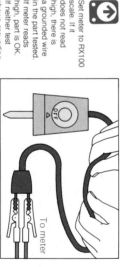
Female terminals
To meter

2. Test for trouble inside control unit by clipping meter probes to female terminals and moving dial through entire temperature range.

Hair curlers

Curler does not heat

If the curler fails to heat, it means that no current is flowing through the heating elements. Step-by-step testing of wall outlet, power cord, swivel contacts, and heating unit will determine the cause of the failure. Repairs range from a simple change of a house fuse to replacing the heating unit.

Power off at outlet?

NO →

TEST: Unplug power cord and check wall outlet with a lamp you know is working.

YES → **FIX: Replace fuse or reset circuit breaker.** See p.127. ▲

Power cord broken?

NO →

TEST: Unplug power cord and examine it for fraying and the plug for loose or distorted prongs. Disassemble curler and attach jumper wire across prongs of plug. Set volt-ohm meter (p.124) to RX1 scale. Use one hand to hold meter's probes firmly in the two small holes in the cord swivel where pins and springs were seated. With other hand, bend and twist cord. If cord is OK, meter will read zero ohms; if cord is broken, needle will jump around or read at high end of dial.

YES → **FIX: Replace power cord.** Note: Before attempting to replace power cord—or any other curler component—make sure the part is available. Some manufacturers stock only the water reservoir as a supply part and take care of other problems by exchanging a broken curler for a new one. ▲▲

Dirty contacts on swivel mechanism?

NO →

TEST: Unplug power cord, disassemble curler, and clean all terminals (see **Fix**). After cleaning, operate curler to see if difficulty has been cleared up.

YES → **FIX: Clean contacts.** Lightly polish surfaces of pins, springs, and central and outside swivel contacts with extra-fine sandpaper. Spray electrical contact cleaner (p.123) into small holes in cord swivel where pins were seated. Scratch cord contacts lightly with a small screwdriver. ▲▲

Heating unit broken?

TEST: With power cord unplugged and curler disassembled, set volt-ohm meter to RX100 scale and touch its probes to central and outside swivel contacts. If unit is OK, meter will read between 300 and 750 ohms; if it is broken, meter will read high.

YES → **FIX: Replace heating unit.** With curler disassembled, unscrew plastic tip from end of curling wand and replace entire heating assembly. New unit will include swivel contacts, neon bulb, and built-in heating element and thermostat. ▲▲

Ease of fix: ▲ simple ▲▲ average ▲▲▲ difficult

Use and care

1. Never use curler while bathing, showering, standing in water, or while your hands are wet.

2. Do not immerse curler in water.

3. Unplug curler before filling reservoir with water.

4. To prevent sputtering of hot water from steam vents, do not use curler until it has reached operating temperature; an indicator light will tell you it is ready. Sputtering can also be caused by operating the mist button too rapidly.

5. Hold the curler horizontally when using it.

6. Apply hair spray after curling, not before; it will clog the steam vents.

7. The curler can be used on wigs made of human hair, but not on synthetics.

8. For best results, use curler only in nonhumid environments. Avoid using the appliance in such places as the bathroom after taking a shower or a bath, or washing stockings or undergarments.

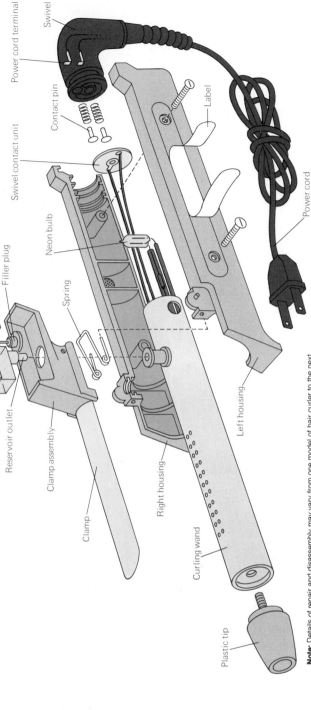

Swivel
Power cord terminal
Contact pin
Label
Swivel contact unit
Neon bulb
Filler plug
Reservoir
Power cord
Spring
Steam button
Reservoir outlet
Clamp assembly
Right housing
Left housing
Clamp
Curling wand
Plastic tip

Note: Details of repair and disassembly may vary from one model of hair curler to the next. If your appliance differs markedly from the one shown here, see *Repair basics*, pp.128–131.

Hair curlers

Disassembling the curler

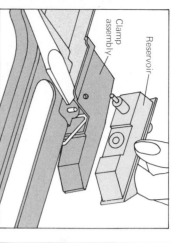

Clamp assembly

Reservoir

1. The clamp assembly pivots on two small pegs on housing. With curler unplugged, lift out reservoir, then gently but firmly pry off clamp. Remove metal spring.

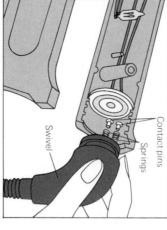

Contact pins

Springs

Swivel

2. Peel label from side of housing to expose screws that hold the two sections of the housing together. Remove screws and separate the housing sections.

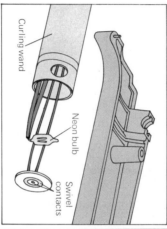

Curling wand

Neon bulb

Swivel contacts

3. Note how the cord swivel is seated in the housing, then lift it out. Be careful not to lose the contact pins and springs that are located in the swivel.

4. Remove entire heating unit from housing, including swivel contacts, neon bulb, curling wand, and associated wiring. Unscrew plastic tip from wand.

Testing for open circuits

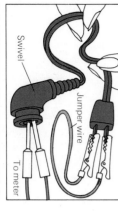

Swivel

Jumper wire

To meter

1. A broken power cord may appear good. To check, clip jumper wire across plug, press volt-ohm meter probes into swivel holes; bend cord.

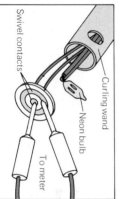

Swivel contacts

Curling wand

Neon bulb

To meter

Test 1: Use RX1 scale. If needle reads zero ohms, cord is OK; if it jumps or reads high, cord is bad.
Test 2: Use RX100 scale. If meter reads 300–750 ohms, unit is OK; if it reads high, unit is broken.

2. To test heating unit for open circuit, unplug and disassemble curler. Touch volt-ohm meter probes to central and outside swivel contacts.

Cleaning vents and contacts

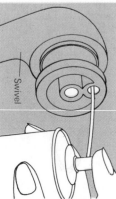

To improve steaming, poke sediment from vents, water inlet, and reservoir outlet, then operate curler with vinegar and water solution.

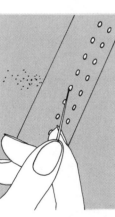
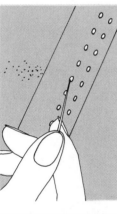

Swivel

Failure to heat may mean dirty contacts. Spray contact cleaner into swivel holes; polish pins and swivel contacts with extra-fine sandpaper.

Improper temperature or steaming action

Improper steaming, especially insufficient steam, is probably due to clogged water vents or steam passages. These should be cleaned. Underheating, overheating, and sputtering indicate temperature troubles stemming from dirty electrical contacts or a faulty heating element. Clean or replace defective parts.

Clogged water passages or steam vents?

NO ←

TEST: If curler does not steam, unplug power cord and wait for curler to cool. Clean water and steam channels (see **Fix**), then run appliance to see if difficulty has been cleared up. Note: Hold curler in horizontal position for proper mist action.

YES → **FIX: Clean water passages and steam vents.** Poke sediment out of steam vents, reservoir outlet, and water inlet with needle. Rinse out reservoir. Fill reservoir with mixture of half vinegar and half water, then run curler until it is empty. Flush by operating curler with water. △

Dirty contacts on swivel mechanism?

NO ←

TEST: If the temperature of curler is low, swivel contacts may be dirty. Clean them (see **Fix**), then operate curler to see if problem has been cleared up. (Temperature is low if curler does not steam or if it takes much longer than 30 seconds to set a curl.)

YES → **FIX: Unplug and disassemble curler.** Lightly polish surfaces of pins, springs, and central and outside swivel contacts with steel wool. Spray electrical contact cleaner (p.123) into small holes in cord swivel where pins were seated. Scratch cord contacts lightly with screwdriver. △△

Heating unit broken?

TEST: If curler is underheating or overheating, and previous tests have not isolated the cause, then heating unit is broken. (You can tell if curler is too hot by clamping tissue paper into the wand and operating the curler. The paper should not scorch.) Other signs of temperature problems are scorched hair—the curler should never damage your hair—and sputtering during mist operation.

YES → **FIX: Replace heating unit.** Unplug and disassemble curler. Unscrew plastic tip from end of curling wand and replace entire heating unit. Note: Before attempting to replace heating unit—or any other curler component—make sure the part is available. Some manufacturers stock only the water reservoir as a supply part; any other problems are handled by replacing the curler. △△

Ease of fix: △ simple △△ average △△△ difficult

Curler shocks user

A frayed power cord, an electrically live component grounded to a metal part, or leakage current due to faulty insulation will cause shocking. In the case of a frayed cord or grounding, the part usually can be replaced. If leakage current is suspected, take the hair curler to an authorized repairman.

Power cord frayed?

TEST: Receiving a shock from power cord is sufficient evidence it needs repair.

YES→ FIX: Replace power cord. (See *Disassembling the curler*, p.172.) △△

Leakage current present?

TEST: If you receive a shock from touching an exposed metal part of curler, set volt-ohm meter (p.124) to RX100 scale. Clip one of its probes to metal part and the other to either prong of the plug. If meter reads at or near high ohms, leakage current (p.127) is indicated.

YES→ FIX: Take curler to authorized repairman. Eliminating leakage current requires special equipment. Note: It is possible the shock is not caused by leakage current but by a wire that becomes grounded only when the appliance is on. To investigate this, continue testing before taking curler to repair shop. △△△

Internal wiring grounded to metal part?

TEST: Unplug power cord and wait for curler to cool. Disassemble curler (see *Disassembling the curler*, p.172) so that interior swivel contacts are accessible. Set volt-ohm meter to RX100 scale. Clip one probe to metal part and touch other probe to central and outside swivel contacts in turn. Bend and pull wires during each test. If needle jumps around or reads anything less than high ohms, a wire is grounded.

YES→ FIX: Replace heating unit. With curler disassembled, unscrew plastic tip from end of curling wand and replace entire heating assembly. New unit will include swivel contacts, neon bulb, and built-in heating element and thermostat. Note: Before attempting to replace heating unit—or any other curler component—make sure the part is available. Some manufacturers stock only the water reservoir as a supply part; any other problems are handled by replacing the curler. △△

Curler blows fuses

If the curler blows fuses or trips a circuit breaker repeatedly, there is a short circuit in its wiring. The short may be due to moisture inside the curler or to a defect in the power cord or heating unit. Use a blower-type hair dryer to dry out the curler. If a part is found to be shorted, it must be replaced.

Moisture in wiring?

TEST: If curler has gotten wet, its interior wiring may be shorted.

YES→ FIX: Dry out interior of curler. Open up curler's housing (see *Disassembling the curler*, p.172) and play warm air over all parts with blower-type hair dryer. △△

Short circuit in power cord or plug?

TEST: Unplug power cord and wait for curler to cool. Remove cord from curler (see *Disassembling the curler*, p.172). Set volt-ohm meter (p.124) to RX100 scale and clip its probes to the prongs of the plug. Bend and pull cord. If cord is OK, meter will read high; if cord is shorted, needle will jump around or read zero ohms.

YES→ FIX: Replace power cord. (See *Disassembling the curler*, p.172.) Note: Before attempting to replace power cord—or any other curler component—make sure the part is available. Some manufacturers stock only the water reservoir as a supply part; any other problems are handled by replacing the curler. △△

Short circuit in heating unit?

TEST: With curler unplugged and disassembled, set volt-ohm meter to RX100 scale and touch its probes to central and outside swivel contacts. If unit is OK, meter will read between 300 and 750 ohms; if unit is broken, meter will read zero ohms. See *Testing for shorts*, below.

YES→ FIX: Replace heating unit. With curler disassembled, unscrew plastic tip from end of curling wand and replace entire heating assembly. New unit will include swivel contacts, neon bulb, and built-in heating element and thermostat. △△

Ease of fix: △ simple △△ average △△△ difficult

Testing for shock hazards

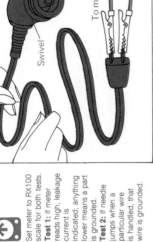

1. If touching body of curler causes shock, clip one volt-ohm meter probe to metal body part, other to prong of power cord plug.

Clamp — Curling wand — To meter

2. To test for grounded internal wiring, clip one probe to metal, touch other to central and outside swivel contacts in turn.

Curling wand — Neon bulb — To meter — Swivel contacts

Set meter to RX100 scale for both tests. **Test 1:** If meter reads high, leakage current is indicated; anything lower means a part is grounded. **Test 2:** If needle jumps when a particular wire is handled, that wire is grounded.

Testing for shorts

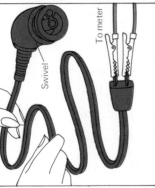

1. Blown fuses may mean short in power cord. Remove cord and swivel from housing, clip volt-ohm meter probes to plug, bend cord.

Swivel — To meter

2. To check heating unit for a short, disassemble curler, touch meter probes to central and outside swivel contacts.

Curling wand — Neon bulb — To meter — Swivel contacts

Set meter to RX100 scale for both tests. **Test 1:** If power cord is OK, meter will read high; if it is shorted, needle will jump or read zero ohms. **Test 2:** If heating unit is good, meter will read 300–750 ohms; if it is shorted, meter will read zero ohms.

Hair dryers/bonnet type

Motor does not run

If motor fails to run, the motor is jammed or current is not flowing through it. The cause of the problem is determined through step-by-step testing, starting with the wall outlet and continuing with the various parts of the hair dryer. Repairs range from changing a house fuse to replacing dryer parts.

Power off at outlet?

TEST: Unplug power cord and check wall outlet with a lamp you know is working.

 FIX: Replace fuse or reset circuit breaker. See p.127. If fuse keeps blowing see *Hair dryer blows fuses,* p.176.
△

Power cord broken?

TEST: Unplug power cord. Remove mounting screws and separate upper housing from lower housing. Examine the cord for fraying and the plug for loose or distorted prongs. Separate the power cord leads from terminals and clip jumper wire across them. Set volt-ohm meter (p.124) to RX1 scale and clip its probes to the prongs of the plug. Bend and pull cord. If cord is Ok, meter will read zero ohms; if cord is broken, needle will jump around or read at high end of dial.

 FIX: Replace power cord. Use a manufacturer's replacement. Terminals of cord have already been freed during test. Cordset can simply be lifted out.
△△

Switch faulty?

TEST: With dryer unplugged and opened, set control knob to *Cool* and remove heat control switch from its seat. Locate switch terminals to which power cord lead and motor lead are attached. Set volt-ohm meter to RX1 scale and insert its probes into these terminals. If switch is OK, meter will read zero; if faulty, meter will read high.

FIX: Clean switch contacts or replace switch. Spray electrical contact cleaner (p.123) into switch terminals and move knob of switch back and forth several times to work cleaner in. If problem remains, replace switch. Remove leads, pull off control knob, and take out switch. Mark leads with tags so that they may be inserted correctly in new switch.
△△

Motor or blower jammed?

TEST: With hair dryer unplugged and housing opened up, try spinning the blower fan by hand. It should turn easily with very little friction.

FIX: Remove obstructions. Take blower and motor unit out of case. Look for objects like bobby pins jammed in blower. Vacuum out hair or other debris from case and blower.
△△

Motor faulty?

TEST: With dryer unplugged, remove motor unit and switch from housing. Separate motor leads from their terminals. Set volt-ohm meter to RX1 scale and clip its probes to the motor leads. If motor is Ok, meter will read between 10 and 30 ohms; if motor is faulty, meter will read high.

FIX: Replace motor. Undo screws and remove fan and heating unit from motor assembly. Note: On some models these parts may be riveted or pressed together, making replacement of the motor impractical. If this is the case with your dryer, take it to an authorized repairman.
△△

Ease of fix: △ simple △△ average △△△ difficult

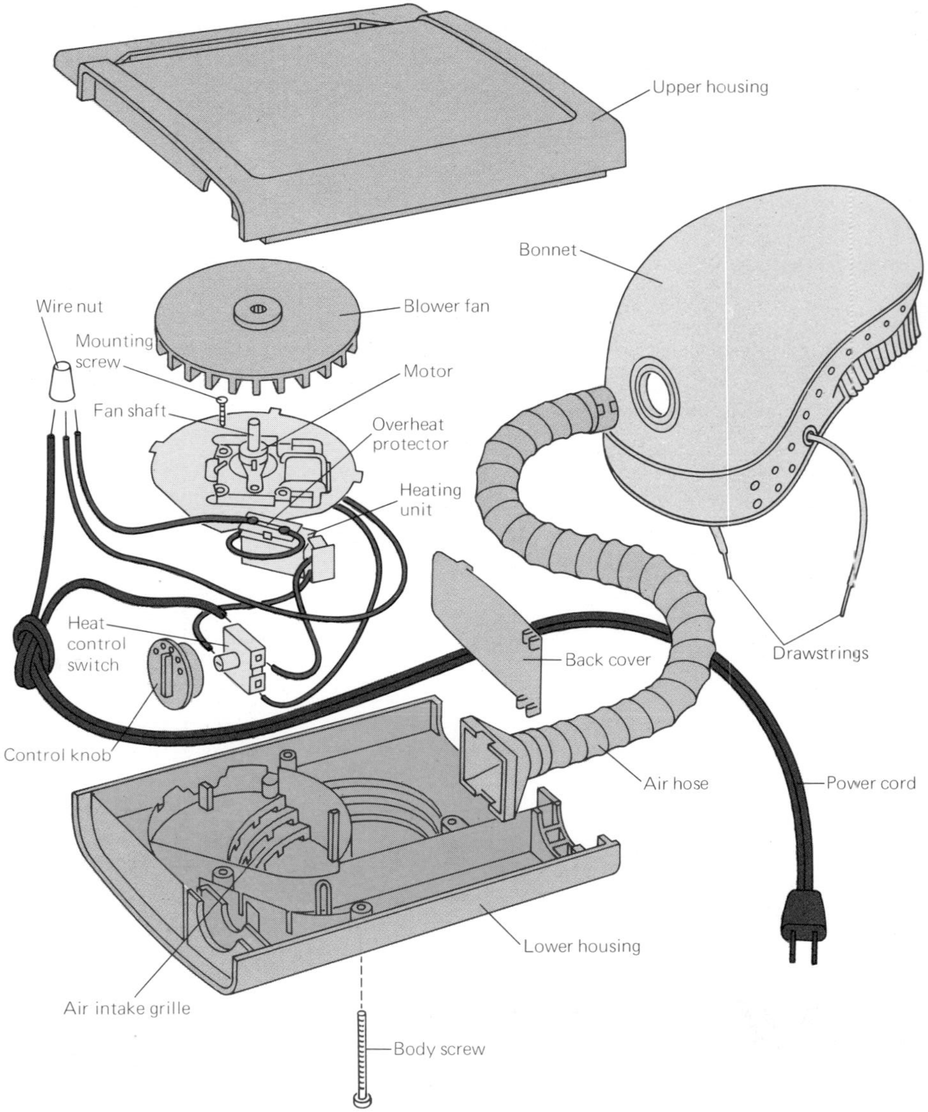

Wire nut

Mounting screw

Fan shaft

Heat control switch

Control knob

Air intake grille

Body screw

Lower housing

Back cover

Heating unit

Overheat protector

Motor

Blower fan

Bonnet

Upper housing

Air hose

Drawstrings

Power cord

Note: Details of repair and disassembly may vary from one or e model of hair dryer to the next. It yours differs markedly from the one shown, see *Repair basics,* pp.128-131.

Motor runs but dryer does not heat at one or more settings

If motor runs but there is no heat at one or more switch settings, the overload protector may be tripped or broken, the switch contacts may be dirty or the switch broken, or one or both heating elements may be faulty. Correct these problems by repairing or replacing the defective component.

Overheat protector tripped or broken?

TEST: If hair dryer goes off while in use, let it cool for 30 minutes, then try it again. If it works, the overheat protector has tripped and then reset. If dryer does not go on after 30 minutes, or if it does not work even when cool, the protector may be blown or broken. In that case, unplug power cord and open up housing by removing screws. Turn control to *Off* and set volt-ohm meter (p.124) to RX1 scale. Touch its probes to terminals of overheat protector. If protector is OK, meter will read zero ohms; if it is blown or broken, meter will read high. Note: Overheat protector may have tripped or blown because air passages are blocked or because motor has ceased functioning. For information on troubleshooting the motor, see *Motor does not run*, p.174.

YES→ FIX: Clean hair dryer; replace heating unit if necessary. Remove any bobby pins, hair, or other debris that is clogging air passages or jamming motor or fan. If overheat protector is broken, replace entire heating unit. Unscrew wire nut and separate the overheat protector lead from line cord lead. Insert straightened-out paper clip into switch terminals and pull out heating unit leads. File head off rivet and lift out heating unit. When installing new unit, replace rivet with screw, nut, and lock washer. Note: On some hair dryers you may be able to slide overheat protector out of heating unit and replace it separately. ▲▲▲

Switch faulty?

TEST: With dryer unplugged and opened, locate switch terminals to which leads from power cord and heating unit are attached. Set volt-ohm meter to RX1 scale. Insert one probe into terminal holding power cord lead, the other into one of the terminals holding a heating unit lead. Turn control knob to *Low*, *Medium*, and *High*. Repeat with probe in terminal holding the other heating unit lead. In both tests, if switch is OK, meter will read zero ohms in two of three control knob positions, high ohms in the other position. If the volt-ohm meter readings in either set of tests differ from those described, then the switch is faulty.

YES→ FIX: Clean switch contacts or replace switch. Spray electrical contact cleaner (p.123) into switch terminals and work knob of switch back and forth several times to improve electrical contact. If problem persists, replace switch. Remove leads, pull off switch knob, and take out switch. Mark leads with tags so that they may be inserted into correct terminals in new switch. ▲▲

Heating element faulty?

TEST: With dryer unplugged and opened, use a straightened-out paper clip to remove heating unit leads from switch. Set volt-ohm meter to RX1 scale and clip its probes to the heater leads. If heating elements are OK, meter will read between 80 and 200 ohms; if either element is open, meter will read at high end of dial.

YES→ FIX: Replace entire heating unit. Procedure is described above in the first **Fix**. Do not try to repair a broken heating element. Such repairs seldom last long and may be destructive since they may cause hot spots to develop in the element that can result in damage to other parts. ▲▲▲

Ease of fix: ▲ simple ▲▲ average ▲▲▲ difficult

Disassembling the hair dryer

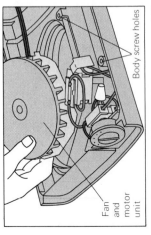

Fan and motor unit
Body screw holes

1. Unplug power cord, take out body screws, and lift off upper housing. Remove mounting screw and take out motor, fan, and heater out of housing as one unit.

Lead
Lead
Lead
Paper clip
Heat control switch
Wire nut

2. Unscrew wire nut. Part wires. Insert straightened-out paper clip into switch terminals, pull out power cord and motor leads. Note which goes to which terminal.

Volt-ohm meter tests when the motor does not work

Jumper
To meter

1. Power cord: Clip jumper across leads; clip meter probes to plug. Bend cord.

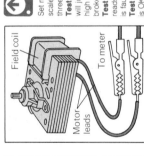

Probe
Probe
To meter

2. Switch: Insert probes into terminals containing power cord and motor leads.

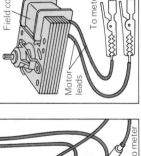

Field coil
Motor leads
To meter

3. Motor: Disconnect both motor leads and clip meter probes to them.

← Set meter to RX1 scale for all three tests.
Test 1: Needle will jump or read high if cord is broken.
Test 2: If meter reads high, switch is faulty.
Test 3: If motor is OK, meter will read 10–30 ohms; high reading means motor is broken.

Checking for heating problems

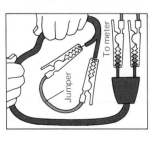

Overheat protector
Meter probes
To meter

1. Overheat protector: Touch the volt-ohm meter probes to its terminals.

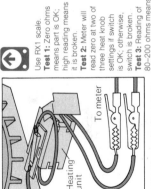

A
B
C
Power cord lead
To meter

2. Switch: Insert a probe at A, another at B, then C. Turn knob during test.

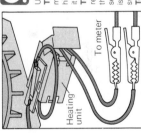

Heating unit
To meter

3. Heating unit: Clip meter probes to the heating element leads.

← Use RX1 scale.
Test 1: Zero ohms means part is OK; high reading means it is broken.
Test 2: Meter will read zero at two of three heat knob settings if switch is OK; otherwise, switch is broken.
Test 3: Reading of 80–200 ohms means part is OK; high reading means it is broken.

Hair dryer blows fuses

When a fuse blows or a circuit breaker trips, it means there is either an electrical overload or a short circuit. Overloads are fixed by reducing the number of appliances in the circuit. Short circuits are located by inspection and testing. Parts found to be shorted must be repaired or replaced.

Circuit overloaded?
TEST: To check for overloads, see p.127. Too many appliances in a circuit is the commonest cause of blown fuses and tripped circuit breakers.

YES→ **FIX: Reduce number of appliances in the circuit. Caution: Never replace a fuse or breaker with one having a larger capacity.** △

NO→

Short circuit in power cord or plug?
TEST: Unplug power cord and open up housing (see *Disassembling the hair dryer*, p.175). Examine cord, plug, and adjacent parts for bare wires and burn marks. Unscrew wire nut and separate the power cord lead from other wires. Set the volt-ohm meter (p.124) to RX100 scale and clip its probes to the prongs of the plug. Bend and pull cord. If cord is OK, needle will read high; if cord is shorted, needle will jump around or read zero ohms.

YES→ **FIX: Replace power cord.** One power cord lead was already freed during test. Insert straightened-out paper clip into switch terminal holding other cord lead and pull lead from terminal. Power cord can then be lifted out. (See *Disassembling the hair dryer*, p.175.) Use a manufacturer's replacement. △△

NO→

Short circuit in heating unit?
TEST: With dryer unplugged and housing opened up, separate the overheat protector lead from other wires. Remove heating unit leads from switch terminals (mark them to insure correct reassembly). Set volt-ohm meter to RX1 scale and clip one probe to overheat protector lead, the other to each of the heating unit leads in turn. If heater is OK, meter will read between 30 and 80 ohms for one heating unit lead, about twice that for the other heating unit lead. If heater is shorted, meter will read zero ohms during one or both tests.

YES→ **FIX: Replace entire heater assembly.** The lead from the overheat protector has already been freed as part of the test, and the two heater leads have also been freed from the switch terminals with the aid of a straightened-out paper clip. File head off rivet and lift out heater assembly. When installing new unit, replace rivet with screw, nut, and lock washer. △△△

Short circuit in motor?
TEST: With power cord unplugged and housing opened up, remove motor unit and control switch from case. Detach one motor lead from wire nut connection, the other from switch terminal. Set volt-ohm meter to RX1 scale and clip its probes to the motor leads. If motor is OK, meter will read between 10 and 30 ohms; if motor is faulty, meter will read zero ohms.

YES→ **FIX: Replace motor.** Undo screws and remove fan and heating unit from motor assembly. Note: On some models, these parts may be riveted or pressed together, making replacement of the motor impractical. If that is the case with your dryer, take it to an authorized repairman. △△

Testing for short circuits

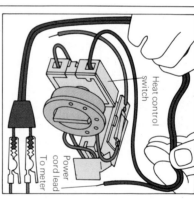

Heat control switch
Power cord lead
To meter

1. Separate the power cord lead from wire nut connection and clip volt-ohm meter one probe to plug. Bend cord during test.

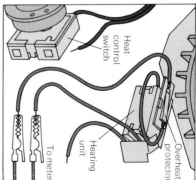

Heat control switch
Overheat protector
Heating unit
To meter

2. Detach leads from switch terminals. Clip one probe to overheat protector lead, the other to each heating unit lead in turn.

Test 1: Set meter to RX100 scale. If meter reads high, power cord is OK. If needle jumps or reads zero ohms, cord is broken.

Test 2: Set meter to RX1 scale. If meter will read 30-160 ohms for either heating unit lead if heating unit is OK, meter will read zero ohms either heating unit lead. If meter reads zero ohms either time, heating unit is shorted.

Keeping the dryer running well

Your hair dryer will work at top efficiency if its air passages are free of obstructions and leaks. When using the dryer, make sure that nothing blocks the air intake grille. Also, be sure the air hose is round, clean, and free of leaks. If it has been accidentally flattened, air flow will be restricted and drying time will be lengthened. Fix it by inserting a broom handle in the hose and working it with your fingers to restore the hose to its original shape. Take care not to pull the

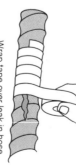

Use broom handle to reshape squashed hose.

A leak in the hose can be detected by running your hand along the hose while the dryer is operating. The leak can be repaired with ordinary plastic or cloth tape obtainable in stationery, hardware, and variety stores. Wrap the tape parallel to the spirals. Use it sparingly so that the compressibility of the hose will not be

reduced by the wrappings.

If the blower seems weak, even when the air passages are clear and free of leaks, the fan may be slipping on its shaft.

Unplug the dryer and open its housing. (See *Disassembling the hair dryer*, p.175.) Try turning the fan while holding the rotor of the motor stationary. If the fan slips, tighten the setscrew holding it to the shaft. If there is no setscrew, the fan

Wrap tape over leak in hose.

Tighten setscrew so that fan does not slip.

Allen wrench

is simply pressed onto the shaft. Try pushing it further onto the shaft. If it is still loose after you have taken these steps, replace the fan.

Air flow in hood of salon dryer

Power cord

Control knob

Mounting strap

Hood cover

Motor

Blower fan

Heat control switch

Housing

Mist chamber

Wire nut

Heating unit

Baseplate

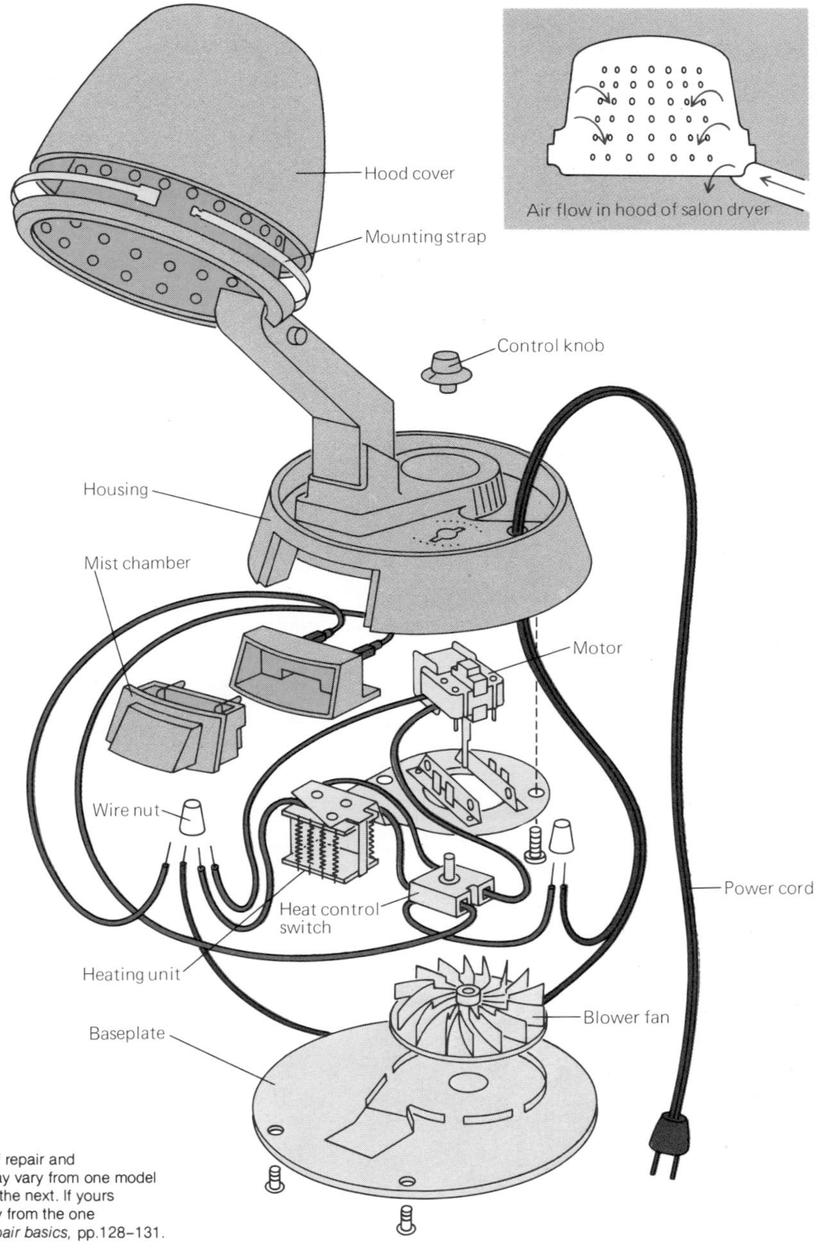

Note: Details of repair and disassembly may vary from one model of hair dryer to the next. If yours differs markedly from the one shown, see *Repair basics*, pp.128–131.

Salon-type hair dryers

Salon dryers are consumer versions of the professional dryers commonly found in beauty parlors. They are more expensive than bonnet dryers, put out more heat, take up more space, and consume more electricity. Other than the difference in the design of the dryer hood, however, the basic working parts—heating unit, motor, blower fan, and control switch—are almost identical to those found in bonnet dryers. By following the troubleshooting instructions and repair information given on the preceding pages for bonnet-type hair dryers, you should be able to repair your salon dryer too.

An exploded view of a salon dryer, with its important parts labeled, appears at right. Refer to it when disassembling, testing, or fixing a salon dryer. In general, there will be more screws to take off and more body parts to remove than for a bonnet dryer. If the air flow seems inadequate or if the dryer is noisy, see *Keeping the dryer running well*, p.176.

Misting action

Some salon dryers—for example, the one shown in the exploded view—have a mist-making feature for setting dry hair. The control switch on such models has an extra (*Mist*) position and five wires leading into it instead of four.

There are two misting systems: electrolytic and boiling water. You can tell which kind is used on your dryer from the manufacturer's instruction booklet. If the booklet suggests adding a little salt or baking soda to the water to improve

mist performance, then the dryer is the electrolytic type. If no mention is made of this, the steam is provided by simply boiling the water.

If you have an electrolytic model and you live in an area with soft water (water low in minerals), the amount of mist may be insufficient. When you fill the misting chamber, add a sprinkle of baking soda. That should give you more than enough mist. If it does not, take the dryer to an authorized repairman.

If the mist unit is the boiling water type, you can check it out with a volt-ohm meter. Set the meter to the RX1 scale and touch its probes to the leads from the mist unit's heater. If the meter reads high ohms, the heater is broken and the unit should be replaced.

With either mist system, it is a good idea to clean the mist chamber of accumulated mineral deposits periodically. Fill the chamber with warm vinegar and let it stand for 15 minutes, then flush with tap water.

Remote control switch

On some salon dryers, the switch is wired to a cord to permit remote operation. In that case, there will be more wires making connections inside the dryer than are described in the preceding instructions. Should this added complexity make you uncertain about whether you are testing the right part, take the dryer to a repair shop. Otherwise, you may draw inaccurate conclusions and replace a part that is actually in good working order.

Using bonnet and salon dryers safely

The housings of most home hair dryers, whether bonnet or salon, are made of plastic, reducing the chances of shock to a minimum. However, if a dryer gets wet the danger of shock is greatly increased. For this reason, never use a hair dryer while taking a bath, never immerse any

part of the dryer (other than the mist chamber) in water, and avoid using the dryer in the bathroom. It is also possible for a frayed or split power cord to present a shock hazard. If the power cord causes a shock, even a slight tingle, replace it. (See *Disassembling the hair dryer*, p.175.)

Hair styler-dryers

Styler neither heats nor blows air at any setting

Failure to heat or blow air means current is not flowing through the motor or heating elements. A blown house fuse, broken power cord, or tripped or blown overheat protector may be to blame. Cleaning the styler will stop the protector from tripping. In all other cases, replacement of parts is required.

Power off at outlet?

TEST: Unplug power cord and check wall outlet with a lamp you know is working.

NO →

Power cord broken?

TEST: Unplug power cord and open up housing. Examine the cord for fraying and the plug for loose or distorted prongs. Unscrew wire nut and clip a jumper wire across the power cord leads. Set volt-ohm meter (p.124) to RX1 scale and clip its probes to the prongs of the plug. Bend and pull power cord. If cord is OK, meter will read zero ohms; if cord is broken, needle will jump around or read high.

NO →

Overheat protector tripped or broken?

TEST: If styler goes off while in use, let it cool for 30 minutes, then try it again. If it works, the overheat protector has tripped and then reset. If styler does not work even when cool, the protector may be broken. In that case, unplug power cord and open housing. Set volt-ohm meter to RX1 scale and touch its probes to terminals of overheat protector. If protector is OK, meter will read zero ohms; if it is blown, meter will read high. Note: On some styler-dryers, the motor will not run if one of the heating elements is broken. To check out this possibility, see *Styler heats but blower works poorly or not at all,* p.180, and follow the instructions given there.

YES → FIX: Replace fuse or reset circuit breaker. See p.127. If fuse keeps blowing, see *Hair styler blows fuses,* p.181.
△

YES → FIX: Replace power cord. Unsolder one power cord lead from switch terminal and pull other lead away from wires to which it is joined. Power cord can then be lifted out. Use manufacturer's replacement; it will come with strain relief device attached.
△ △

YES → FIX: Clean styler; replace overheat protector if necessary. Whether the overheat protector blew or merely tripped, the cause of overheating was probably hair and dust accumulated in the styler. Open up housing and clean styler, taking care to remove dirt blocking the air inlet and hair wound around blower shaft. Add a pinpoint drop of light oil to shaft bearing. If protector is broken (see **Test**), replace it by disconnecting its leads and installing manufacturer's replacement. Note: On some models, entire heating unit must be replaced.
△ △

Ease of fix: △simple △△average △△△difficult

Overheat protectors

The overheat protector on most stylers is a small thermostat like the one in the exploded view at right. It shuts off power

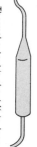

Thermal cutout is about ½ in. long

to the appliance if the temperature goes too high (due to a blocked air intake grille, for example) and resets itself when the dryer cools. Some styler-dryers also have a fuselike backup device called a thermal cutout. Cutouts are one-shot devices; if they blow, replace them.

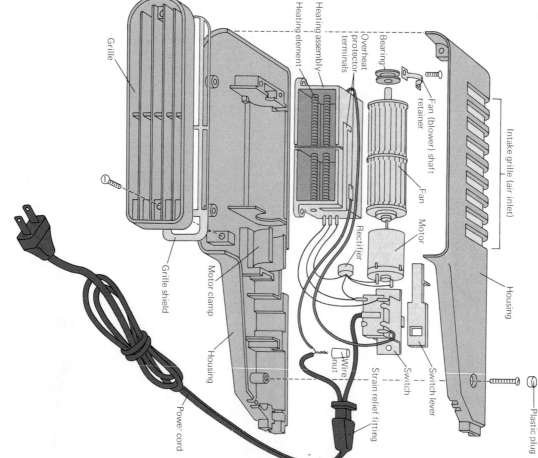

Intake grille (air inlet)

Heating element

Heating assembly

Overheat protector terminals

Bearing

Fan (blower) shaft retainer

Fan

Motor

Housing

Plastic plug

Rectifier

Strain relief fitting

Switch

Switch lever

Wire nut

Grille

Grille shield

Motor clamp

Housing

Power cord

Note: Details of repair and disassembly may vary from one model of styler-dryer to the next. If yours differs markedly from the one shown, see *Repair basics,* pp.128–131.

Disassembling the styler-dryer

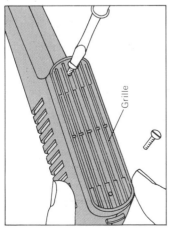

1. Unplug power cord, remove grille screws, and pull off grille and grille shield. Note orientation and location of all parts. Mark with pencil if necessary.

Grille

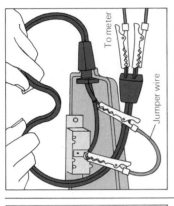

2. Pry out plastic plug at rear of styler, undo main body screw, and separate the housing halves. Removing plug is difficult and scratching is unavoidable.

Plastic plug

Testing for open circuits

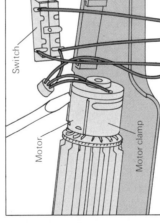

To meter

Jumper wire

1. Power cord: Unscrew wire nut and clip jumper across cord leads. Attach volt-ohm meter probes to plug and bend and pull wire.

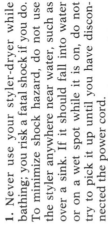

Overheat protector terminals

To meter

Set meter to RX1 scale for both tests. **Test 1:** If power cord is OK, meter will read zero ohms; if it is broken, needle will jump around or read high. **Test 2:** If overheat protector is OK, meter will read zero ohms; if it is broken, meter will read high.

2. Overheat protector: Unplug styler and pry open housing. Touch meter probes to terminals of overheat protector.

Use and care

1. Never use your styler-dryer while bathing; you risk a fatal shock if you do. To minimize shock hazard, do not use the styler anywhere near water, such as over a sink. If it should fall into water or on a wet spot while it is on, do not try to pick it up until you have disconnected the power cord.

2. Styler-dryers should never be immersed in water or other liquids, even when they are unplugged.

3. Children should be closely supervised when they are operating a dryer.

4. Do not use your dryer for heavy-duty tasks for which it was not designed, such as defrosting the freezer compartment of a refrigerator. If you are using it for anything other than styling and drying hair, be careful not to operate it for too long a time.

5. The heating elements are electrically live. Do not insert any object into the front grille, especially when appliance is running.

6. Do not operate styler-dryer where aerosol products are being used.

7. Keep air intake clean of hair and lint. Do not block intake or outlet or lay styler down when it is running.

Disassembling the styler-dryer

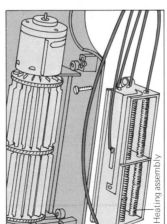

Switch

Motor

Motor clamp

3. Undo screws that hold heating assembly in place and maneuver assembly out of housing. Its leads will still be connected to switch and power cord.

4. Take off fan shaft retainer and remove bearing from fan shaft. Pry motor from clamp with screwdriver. Lift out fan, motor, switch, and power cord.

Heating assembly

Cleaning and lubrication

Hair blocking intake grille or wrapped around fan shaft is major cause of trouble with styler-dryers. Use toothbrush to keep intake grille clean. Never use water.

Overheat protector will shut down blower if hair is wound around fan shaft. To clean, unplug styler, open up housing, and pull hair from shaft with tweezers.

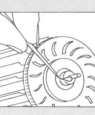

Add a pinpoint drop of light machine oil to end of fan shaft before reassembling the dryer. Do not oil near the motor.

Disassembling the styler-dryer

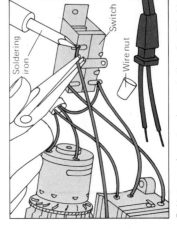

Soldering iron

Switch

Wire nut

5. Unscrew wire nut and separate the wires it holds. Remove heating assembly and power cord by unsoldering their leads from the switch.

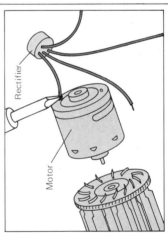

Rectifier

Motor

6. Unsolder rectifier from motor and remove motor and fan. On some stylers, the motor can be separated by prying out rubber fitting from fan.

Hair styler-dryers

Styler heats but blower works poorly or not at all

If the styler heats but the blower runs sluggishly or does not work at all, the fan may be jammed, the air intake may be clogged, or the motor may not be running because of an internal defect or a broken heating element in its external circuit. Repairs include replacing parts and cleaning the styler.

Fan shaft dirty or stuck?

TEST: Unplug power cord and open housing. Spin fan by hand. It should turn easily. Look for hair wrapped around ends of fan shaft. It is common for hair to be sucked into the air intake and become wrapped around fan shaft.

YES→ **FIX: Clean and lubricate fan.** Remove motor and fan (see *Disassembling the styler-dryer,* p.179). Pull off hair from front of shaft and at rear, near motor. Clean dust and hair from other parts of styler, then add a pinpoint drop of light oil to fan shaft. (See *Cleaning and lubrication,* p.179.) △△

Heating element in motor circuit broken?

TEST: Turn switch off, unplug styler, and remove the heating assembly (see *Disassembling the styler-dryer,* p.179). Set volt-ohm meter (p.124) to RX1 scale and hold probes across each heating element. If element is OK, meter will read 15 to 50 ohms; if element is broken, meter will read at high end of dial.

YES→ **FIX: Replace heating assembly.** Unplug power cord and disassemble styler. (See *Disassembling the hair styler-dryer,* p.179.) Unscrew wire nut and pull apart leads. Unsolder leads connected to heating assembly and remove assembly. Keep track of which wires go to which terminals so that you will be able to reassemble styler correctly. △△△

Motor faulty?

TEST: Unplug power cord and open up housing. Unsolder one of the leads to motor. Set volt-ohm meter to RX1 scale and touch its probes to terminals of motor. If motor is OK, meter will read between 5 and 50 ohms; if motor is broken, meter will read at high end of dial.

YES→ **FIX: Replace motor.** Unsolder leads from motor and remove motor and fan from housing (see *Disassembling the styler-dryer,* p.179). Pry out rubber fitting holding motor shaft to fan and remove motor. If the fitting does not come out easily, replace motor and fan as a unit. Note: Most stylers use small, DC motors, but some use larger, universal-type motors with replaceable carbon brushes. See *Universal motors,* pp.132-134, for information on repairing these motors. △△△

Rectifier broken?

Most styler-dryers use small, low-voltage DC motors to run their fans. A device called a rectifier changes house current into the 12 volts DC needed by these motors. If previous tests fail to locate the cause of the problem, the rectifier may be broken. Take styler to authorized repairman.

If the styler shocks

The plastic housings of styler-dryers greatly reduce the likelihood of your receiving a shock from any part other than the power cord. If the power cord shocks you (even if it gives you only a slight tingle), it should be replaced. Unplug the styler and open up the housing. Free one power cord lead by unscrewing the wire nut. Release the other by unsoldering it from the switch terminal. (See *Disassembling the styler-dryer,* p.179, and *Fundamentals of Appliance Repair,* pp.121-138.)

Blower works but styler heats poorly or not at all

If the blower is working properly at all switch settings, but the styler does not heat properly at one or more settings, the trouble probably lies in the switch itself or else in the heating assembly. Cleaning the switch contacts may solve the difficulty. If it does not, the heating assembly must be replaced.

Switch contacts dirty?

TEST: Unplug power cord and open up the housing (See *Disassembling the styler-dryer,* p.179.) Clean switch contacts (see **Fix**), then reassemble dryer and run it to see if difficulty has been cleared up.

YES→ **FIX: Clean switch contacts.** Lift out switch from housing and spray contacts with electrical contact cleaner (p.123). Work switch control back and forth a number of times to help work the spray cleaner in. See *Fixing the switch,* p.181. △△

Heating element open?

TEST: If heat is the same on Style and Dry, a heating element is probably broken. Turn switch off, unplug power cord, and take out heating assembly. (See *Disassembling the styler-dryer,* p.179.) Look for open wire in a heating element. Set volt-ohm meter (p.124) to RX1 scale and hold probes across each heating element. If element is OK, meter will read 15 to 50 ohms; if element is broken, meter will read high.

YES→ **FIX: Replace heating assembly.** With power cord unplugged and heating unit removed from housing, unscrew wire nut and pull apart leads. Unsolder leads connected to heater assembly and remove assembly. Keep track of which wires go to which terminals so that you will later be able to reassemble styler correctly. See *Disassembling the styler-dryer,* p.179. △△△

Ease of fix: △ simple △△ average △△△ difficult

Checking the motor and heating element

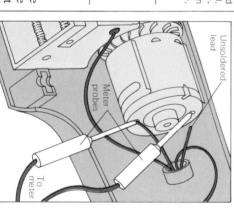

Unsoldered lead
Meter probes
To meter

1. To test motor, first isolate it by unsoldering one of its leads, then touch volt-ohm meter probes to the motor terminals.

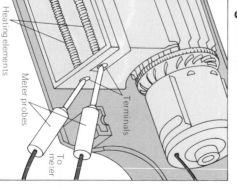

Heating elements
Meter probes
Terminals
To meter

2. Remove heating assembly from housing when checking it. Set switch to *Off*. Test terminals of each element.

Set meter to RX1 scale for both tests.
Test 1: If motor is OK, meter will read 5-50 ohms; if motor is broken, meter will read high.
Test 2: If heating element is OK, meter will read 15-50 ohms; if element is broken, meter will read high.

Hair styler blows fuses

If your styler-dryer causes a fuse to blow or a circuit breaker to trip, there is either an electrical overload or a short circuit. Overloads are fixed by reducing the number of appliances in the circuit. The only styler component likely to short is the power cord. Replace it if testing shows it is broken.

Circuit overloaded?

TEST: To check for overloads, see p.127. Too many appliances in a circuit is the commonest cause of blown fuses and tripped circuit breakers.

NO →

YES → **FIX: Reduce number of appliances in the circuit. Caution: Never replace a fuse or breaker with one having a greater capacity.** △

Short circuit in power cord or plug?

TEST: Unplug power cord and open up the housing. (See *Disassembling the styler-dryer*, p.179.) Examine power cord, plug, and adjacent parts for bare wires and burn marks. Unscrew wire nut and separate the power cord lead from other wires. Set volt-ohm meter (p.124) to RX100 scale. Clip its probes to the prongs of the plug and bend and pull power cord. If cord is OK, meter will read high; if cord is shorted, needle will jump around or read zero ohms.

YES → **FIX: Replace power cord.** Unsolder power cord lead from switch terminal. Other lead was separated from wire nut during test. Power cord can then be lifted out. Use manufacturer's replacement; it will come with strain relief device attached. (See *Disassembling the styler-dryer*, p.179.) △△

Ease of fix: △ simple △△ average △△△ difficult

Fixing the switch

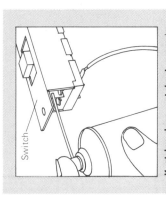

If styler does not heat properly, switch contacts may be dirty. Spray electrical contact cleaner (p.123) into switch and move control several times to work cleaner in. If problem persists and other tests fail to solve it, switch may be broken. Checking it is complicated, so take appliance to authorized manufacturer's service center.

Switch

Testing for a short

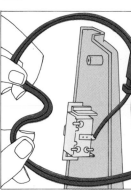

 Set meter to RX100 scale. If power cord is OK, meter will read high; if power cord is shorted, needle will jump around or read zero ohms.

Power cord lead

Wire nut

Power cord plug

To meter

Unscrew wire nut, separate power cord lead from other wires, and clip volt-ohm meter probes to plug. Bend cord during test.

Pro-type dryers

Right housing

Power cord

Heating assembly

Motor brush unit

Fan

Air barrel

Motor

Switches

Left housing

Strain relief fitting

Pro-type hair dryers do the same job as styler-dryers but they put out more heat, use more electricity, and may not come with such accessories as teasing combs or brushes. Since the key parts of both kinds of appliances are the same—heating elements, fan, motor, switch, and power cord—the same repair instructions can be used. The main differences are in the location of parts and disassembly procedure.

The motor in a pro-type dryer is more powerful and does not need a rectifier. To test and repair these motors, see *Universal motors*, pp.132–134. The most common problem is that the motor will not run because the brushes are worn. Always replace both brushes. Simply unscrew the caps that hold them inside the brush assembly and install identical new brushes purchased from the manufacturer or an authorized dealer.

Some pro-type dryers use a slide switch. Others, like the one in the exploded view, have several separate switches—one for the motor, the others for individual heating elements. Separate switches make troubleshooting easier. For example, if the dryer does not heat when a particular switch is on, you know that the switch or heating element connected to it is faulty.

Heaters

Heater does not heat

If the heater fails to heat, it means current is not flowing through the heating elements. The cause is determined through step-by-step testing of the wall outlet, power cord, thermostat, and heating elements themselves. Repairs range from replacing a house fuse to installing a new heating unit.

Power off at outlet?

NO →

TEST: Unplug power cord and check wall outlet with a lamp you know is working.

YES →

FIX: Replace fuse or reset circuit breaker. See p.127. If fuse keeps blowing, see *Heater blows fuses*, p.184.

Power cord broken?

NO →

TEST: Unplug power cord. Examine cord for fraying and the plug for loose or distorted prongs. Remove side panel near power cord. Unscrew wire nut and clip jumper wire across cord leads. Set volt-ohm-meter (p.124) to RX1 scale and clip its probes to the prongs of the plug. Bend and pull cord. If power cord is OK, meter will read zero ohms; if it is broken, needle will jump around or read high.

YES →

FIX: Replace power cord. Pull apart leads attached by wire nut and pry quick-connect terminal of cord off the thermostat. Squeeze strain relief device with pliers, rotate it a quarter turn, and remove power cord. **Caution: Use a manufacturer's replacement cord. Portable heaters are high-power appliances, and an inadequate power cord is a severe fire hazard.**

Thermostat contacts open or dirty?

NO →

TEST: Turn heater switch to *High*. With heater unplugged and side panel removed, push tip-over weight with your finger. It should rotate freely, opening and closing thermostat contacts. Next, clean thermostat contacts (see **Fix**), reassemble heater, and operate it to see if the problem has been cleared up.

YES →

FIX: Clean contacts or replace thermostat. Polish thermostat contacts with very fine (No. 400) sandpaper and make sure tip-over weight rotates freely. If problem remains, replace thermostat. Pry off quick-connect terminals and remove thermostat assembly. Note: On some models the tip-over switch is separate from the thermostat; if it is in working order, it need not be replaced.

Heating element broken?

NO →

TEST: With heater unplugged and side panel nearest the power cord removed, pry off one of the quick-connect terminals from heating element. Set volt-ohm meter to RX1 scale and touch its probes to terminals of heating element. If element is OK, meter will read 5 to 30 ohms; if element is broken, meter will read high.

YES →

FIX: Replace heating unit. Pry off the second quick-connect terminal from the heating element. Remove the other side panel and undo the screws holding the heating unit. The heating unit, including element and reflector, can then be removed from the housing.

Ease of fix: △ simple △△ average △△△ difficult

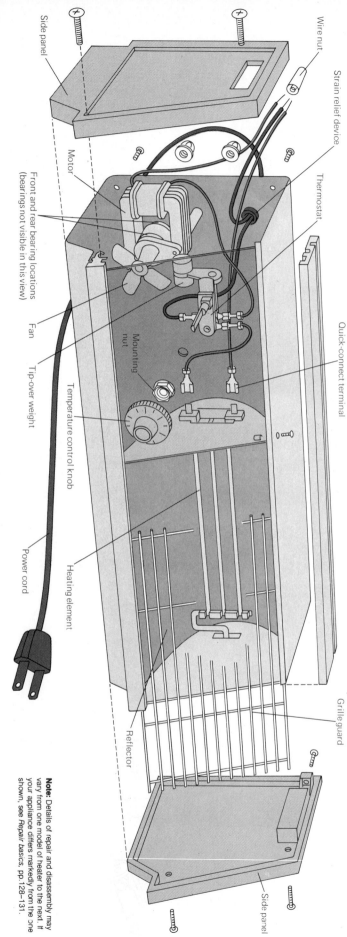

Diagram labels:
- Side panel
- Wire nut
- Strain relief device
- Motor
- Thermostat
- Quick-connect terminal
- Mounting nut
- Temperature control knob
- Fan
- Front and rear bearing locations (bearings not visible in this view)
- Heating element
- Power cord
- Reflector
- Tip-over weight
- Grille guard
- Side panel

Note: Details of repair and disassembly may vary from one model of heater to the next. If your appliance differs markedly from the one shown, see *Repair basics*, pp.128-131.

Heater warms but motor does not run

When the heating elements work but the fan motor fails to operate, the problem is either a jammed motor or an electrical fault in the motor. If the motor is jammed, it should be cleaned and lightly lubricated. If the volt-ohm meter shows that the motor's field coil is open, a new motor must be installed.

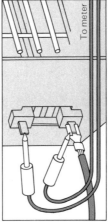

Motor jammed or binding?

TEST: Unplug power cord and remove side panel near cord. Examine fan blades to see if they are obstructed by wiring, dirt, or foreign objects. Spin blades by hand. If fan does not turn easily, motor is binding.

YES → FIX: Remove obstacles, clean motor, lubricate bearings. Remove objects and wires blocking fan. Take out motor and wipe off dirt with cloth. Spray bearings with penetrating-type lubricant, then put a drop of light-weight machine oil on each bearing. Do not overoil. △△

Field coil open?

TEST: With heater unplugged and panel off, undo wire nut and pull apart leads. Set volt-ohm meter (p.124) to RX1 scale and touch probes to motor leads. If field coil is OK, meter will read 5 to 25 ohms; if broken, meter will read at the high end of the dial.

YES → FIX: Replace motor. One motor lead has already been freed during the test. Remove the other one by prying off quick-connect terminal from thermostat. Unscrew mounting nuts and take out motor. △△

Ease of fix: △ simple △△ average △△△ difficult

Testing for open circuits

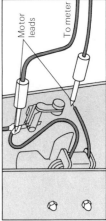

Set meter to RX1 scale for all three tests.
Test 1: If power cord is OK, meter will read zero ohms; if cord is broken, needle will jump around or read high.
Test 2: If heating element is OK, meter will read 5–30 ohms; if it is broken, meter will read high.
Test 3: If motor is OK, meter will read 5–25 ohms; if field coil is open, meter will read high.

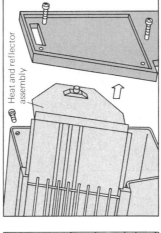

1. To test power cord, clip jumper across its leads, clip volt-ohm meter probes to plug, and bend cord.

Power cord leads — Jumper wire — To meter

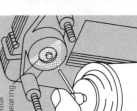

2. Failure to heat may be due to open circuit in heating element. Check by prying lead wire off one terminal, touching meter probes to both terminals.

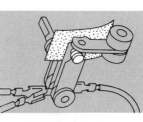

3. When motor does not run, its field coil may be broken. Undo wire nut, separate the motor lead from other wires, and apply meter probes to motor leads.

Motor leads — To meter

Disassembling the heater

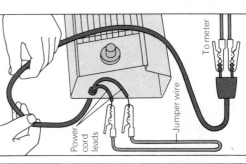

Control knob — Strain relief device — Nut — Quick connect terminal — Thermostat — Wire nut — Leads

1. Unplug power cord from wall outlet. Remove screws that are near power cord at side and back, and pull off the side panel adjacent to temperature control.

2. Squeeze and rotate strain relief device, then pull it out. Pry off control knob, undo mounting nut, and slide thermostat out. Remove wire nut; free leads.

Heat and reflector assembly

3. Pull off quick-connect terminals from thermostat. Take out power cord through rear. Undo motor mounting nuts and remove motor and fan unit.

Fan — Motor and fan unit — Rear bearing

4. Remove screws at side and back and pull off second side panel. Undo reflector mounting screws; slide out heat and reflector assembly and grill guard.

Helping the heater to work properly

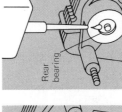

Lubrication: Apply small drop of light oil to each bearing after spraying.

Rear bearing

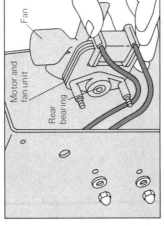

Motor: If the motor jams, spray bearings with penetrating oil.

Rear bearing

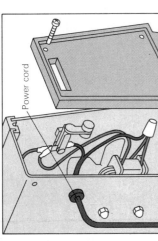

Thermostat: Polish contacts with very fine sandpaper to remove dirt.

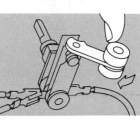

Tip-over switch: Check by pushing with finger. It should rotate freely.

Heaters

A frayed power cord, an electrically live component grounded to (touching) a metal part, or leakage current due to faulty insulation will cause shocking. In the case of a frayed cord or grounding, the part can be fixed or replaced. If leakage current is suspected, take the heater to a repairman.

Heater shocks user

Power cord frayed?

TEST: Receiving a shock from power cord is sufficient evidence it needs repair.

YES→ FIX: Replace power cord. Follow instructions given in *Heater does not heat*, p.182, and in *Disassembling the heater*, p.183.

△△

Leakage current present?

TEST: If you receive a shock from an exposed metal part of heater, unplug power cord, set volt-ohm meter (p.124) to RX100 scale, and turn switch to *High*. Clip one meter probe to shell, other to either prong of the plug. If meter reads high, leakage current (p.127) is indicated.

YES→ FIX: Take heater to authorized repairman. Eliminating leakage current requires special equipment. Note: It is possible the shock is not caused by leakage current, but by a wire that becomes grounded only when the heater is on. To investigate this, proceed with tests before taking heater to repair shop.

△△△

Heating element or internal wiring grounded?

TEST: With heater operating, look through grille to see if heating element touches grille or heat reflector. Unplug power cord and remove side panel near control knob. (See *Disassembling the heater*, p.183.) Examine wiring for bare spots and loose strands. With volt-ohm meter set to RX100 scale, clip one of its probes to shell, the other to either prong of the plug. Turn temperature control to *High* and bend and twist each of the wires inside heater. If needle jumps around when a particular wire is handled, that wire is grounded.

YES→ FIX: Repair or replace faulty parts and insulation. Unplug heater. If heating element touches grille or reflector, use bent paper clip to hook heating element and gently draw it away from grille or reflector surface. Using plastic electrical tape, insulate bare spots on all wires, except leads having asbestos insulation. Those leads, which are recognizable by their thick matte finish, should be replaced with manufacturer's equivalents if they are damaged. Unscrew wire nut and pull apart burn marks. Unscrew wire nut and pull apart leads. Set volt-ohm meter (p.124) to RX100 scale and clip its probes to the prongs of the plug. Bend and pull power cord. If cord is OK, meter will read high; if cord is broken, replace it. Follow instructions given in *Heater does not run*, p.182, and in *Disassembling the heater*, p.183.

△△

Testing for short circuits and shock hazards

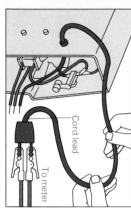

Cord lead

To meter

1. To check power cord for short, undo wire nut, free cord lead, and clip volt-ohm meter probes to plug. Bend and pull cord during test.

To meter

2. If unit shocks, check for leakage current. Set fan switch to *High*, clip one meter probe to metal body part, the other to prong of plug.

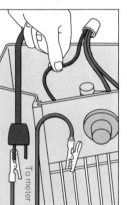

To meter

3. Grounded wire may be causing shock. With side panel off, clip one probe to grille, other to prong of plug, then tug each wire in heater.

When a fuse blows or a circuit breaker trips, it means there is either an electrical overload or a short circuit. An overload is fixed by reducing the number of appliances in a circuit. A short circuit is located by inspection and testing. Parts found to be shorted must be replaced.

Heater blows fuses

Circuit overloaded?

TEST: To check for overloads, see p.127. Too many appliances in a circuit is the commonest cause of blown fuses and tripped circuit breakers.

YES→ FIX: Reduce number of appliances in the circuit. Caution: Never replace a fuse or breaker with one having a larger capacity.

△

Short circuit in power cord or plug?

TEST: Unplug power cord and remove the side panel near the control knob. (See *Disassembling the heater*, p.183.) Examine power cord and plug for bare wires and burn marks. Unscrew wire nut and pull apart leads. Set volt-ohm meter (p.124) to RX100 scale and clip its probes to the prongs of the plug. Bend and pull power cord. If cord is OK, meter will read high; if cord is shorted, needle will read zero.

YES→ FIX: Replace power cord. Pull apart leads attached by wire nut and pry quick-connect terminal of cord off the thermostat. Squeeze strain relief device with pliers, rotate it a quarter turn, and remove power cord. (See *Disassembling the heater*, p.183.) Use a manufacturer's replacement power cord. Portable heaters are high-power appliances, and an inadequate power cord is a severe fire hazard.

△△

Short circuit in motor?

TEST: With heater unplugged and side panel nearest control knob off, unscrew wire nut and pull apart leads. Set volt-ohm meter to RX1 scale and touch its probes to the motor leads. If motor is OK, meter will read between 5 and 25 ohms; if it is shorted, meter will read zero ohms.

YES→ FIX: Replace motor. One motor lead has already been freed during the test. Remove the other one by prying its quick-connect terminal off the thermostat. Unscrew mounting nuts and take out motor. (See *Disassembling the heater*, p.183.)

△△

Ease of fix: △ simple △△ average △△△ difficult

Fixing a grounded element

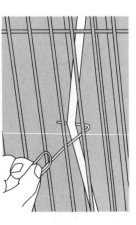

Heating element touching reflector will cause shocks. Unplug heater, hook element with paper clip, gently draw it away from reflector.

Use RX100 scale for all tests.
Test 1: Cord is OK if meter reads high; it is shorted if needle jumps or reads zero ohms.
Test 2: If meter reads zero ohms, current is likely.
Test 3: Needle will jump if grounded wire is handled.

Heating pads

If heating pad fails to heat, current is not flowing through heating elements. The cause is determined through step-by-step testing, starting with the wall outlet and continuing with the various parts of the heating pad. Repairs range from changing a house fuse to replacing a switch spring or power cord.

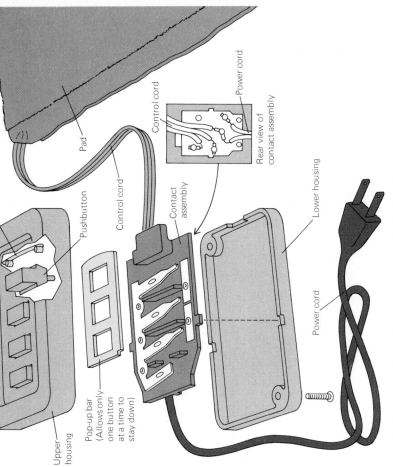

Pop-up spring

Pushbutton

Control cord

Upper housing

Pop-up bar (Allows only one button at a time to stay down)

Contact assembly

Pad

Control cord

Power cord

Rear view of contact assembly

Lower housing

Power cord

Note: Details of repair and disassembly may vary from one model of heating pad to the next. If your appliance differs markedly from the one shown, see *Repair basics*, pp. 128–131.

Heating pad does not heat

Power off at outlet?

TEST: Unplug power cord and check wall outlet with a lamp you know is working.

NO

FIX: Replace fuse or reset circuit breaker. See p.127. If fuse keeps blowing, see *Heating pad blows fuses*, p.186. △

YES

Switch spring broken?

TEST: Unplug heating pad. If the pad's temperature control switch has several buttons, none of which stay depressed when pushed, the switch spring is broken.

NO

FIX: Replace switch spring. See *Disassembling the temperature control switch*, p.186. Note: Pressure of spring makes reassembly tricky. Work carefully and observe what part goes where as you take switch apart. △△

YES

Power cord broken?

TEST: Unplug power cord. Examine the cord for fraying and the plug for loose or distorted prongs. Disassemble temperature control switch and clip jumper wire across power cord terminals. Set volt-ohm meter (p.124) to RX1 scale and clip its probes to the plug. Bend and pull cord. If power cord is OK, meter will read zero ohms; if it is broken, needle will jump around or read at high end of dial.

NO

FIX: Replace power cord. If power cord leads are crimped to terminals, pry terminal sleeves open with a small screwdriver. Use long-nose pliers to crimp new cord leads back on. If you cannot open the terminals, snip leads off, leaving ⅜-inch stubs, and install new power cord by connecting its leads to the stubs with solderless sleeve connectors. △△

YES

Switch contacts dirty?

TEST: Clean contacts (see **Fix**), then operate heating pad to see if difficulty has been cleared up.

FIX: Clean contacts. With switch disassembled, polish contacts with very fine (No. 400) sandpaper. (See *Temperature check and repair*, p.186.) If problem persists, the control cord or heating element may be broken. Take pad to repairman or replace it. △△

YES

Ease of fix: △ simple △△ average △△△ difficult

Replacing the power cord.

Terminal sleeve

If power cord leads are crimped to terminals, try prying open terminal sleeves with screwdriver.

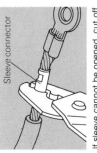

Install new cord by recrimping the old terminal sleeves onto the new leads. Use long-nose pliers.

Sleeve connector

If sleeve cannot be opened, cut off old lead, leaving ⅜-in. stub. Attach new lead with sleeve connector.

Use and care

1. Only pads marked "Wetproof" should be used for wet or moist applications.
2. Never insert pins into a heating pad. The pin might contact a live element or rupture the waterproof lining, creating an additional shock hazard.
3. Heating pads can cause burns if used carelessly. Do not lie on a pad or make sharp folds in it. Never use a pad on a child or a sleeping person.
4. Examine the waterproof inner cover of the heating pad before each use. If it is worn or cracked, discard the pad. A wet heating element is a serious shock hazard.
5. There is a waterproof seal where the control cord enters the heating pad. It is essential to avoid damaging the seal, so never put tension on the control or power cords.

Heating pads

Disassembling the temperature control switch

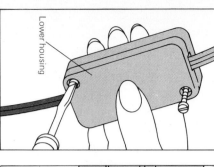

Lower housing

1. Unplug pad. Undo screws while holding the upper and lower halves of switch housing firmly together.

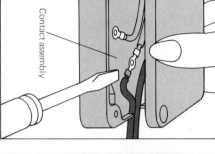

Contact assembly

2. Insert screwdriver to keep contact assembly from springing out as you remove lower switch housing.

Pushbuttons

Pop-up bar

3. Lift out contact assembly. Note exact arrangement of pushbuttons and pop-up bar before removing.

Testing power cord for open and short circuits

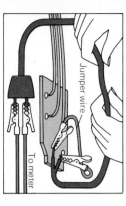

Jumper wire

To meter

1. Open circuit test: Clip jumper wire across terminals of power cord, attach volt-ohm meter probes to plug. Bend cord during test.

 Test 1: Use RX1 scale. If cord is OK, meter will read zero. If open, needle will jump or read high.

To meter

2. Short circuit test: Contacts of switch must be open. Clip probes of meter to plug. Bend and pull on cord while testing.

 Test 2: Use RX100 scale. If cord is OK, meter will read high; if bad, needle will jump or read zero.

Temperature check and repair

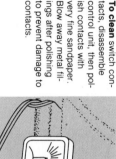

1. Open circuit test: Clip jumper wire across terminals of power cord, attach volt-ohm meter probes to plug. Bend cord during test.

To clean switch contacts, disassemble control unit, then polish contacts with very fine sandpaper. Blow away metal filings after polishing to prevent damage to contacts.

Test for correct heat by folding pad over shaft of meat thermometer. After 20 minutes on *High*, thermometer should read near 155°F for late model pads. Pads made before June 1971 may read up to 180°F.

Heating pad is too hot or too cold

Temperature problems in a heating pad may be caused by dirty switch contacts in the temperature control unit or by defective circuitry inside the pad itself. First, clean the switch contacts with very fine sandpaper. If the problem persists, use a meat thermometer to check the heating pad's temperature.

Switch contacts dirty?

TEST: If the pad does not heat in one or more heat settings, switch contacts may be dirty. Clean contacts (see **Fix**), then operate heating pad to see if difficulty has been cleared up.

YES **FIX: Clean switch contacts.** Disassemble the temperature control switch. Polish contacts with very fine (No. 400) sandpaper. Blow away metal residue from contacts after polishing them. △

NO **Defective circuitry in pad?**

TEST: Fold heating pad in half over a meat thermometer and operate pad at its highest setting for 20 minutes. Pads manufactured after June 1971 should read close to a maximum of 155°F. Pads manufactured before that date may read as high as 180°F.

YES **FIX: Replace heating pad in most instances.** Repairs to the wiring in the pad require cutting and resewing. The effort is seldom worth while. △△△

Heating pad blows fuses

When a heating pad repeatedly blows house fuses (or trips circuit breakers), it means there is a short circuit in its power cord, temperature switch, control cord, or heating element. It is possible to fix the power cord or control switch if they are broken, but other repairs are beyond the scope of home repair.

Short circuit in power cord or plug?

TEST: Unplug pad and examine power cord and plug for bare wires and burn marks. Disassemble temperature control switch and lift out contact assembly. All contacts should be open. Set volt-ohm meter to RX100 scale and clip its probes to the prongs of the plug. Bend and pull power cord. If cord is OK, meter will read high; if shorted, needle will wobble or read zero.

YES **FIX: Replace power cord.** If power cord leads are crimped to terminals, use long-nose pliers to crimp new cord leads back on. If you cannot open the terminals, snip leads off, leaving ⅜-inch stubs, and install new power cord by connecting its leads to the stubs with solderless sleeve connectors. (See *Replacing the power cord*, p.185.) △△

Short circuit in switch?

TEST: With power cord unplugged and switch disassembled, examine parts. Look for burn marks, distorted terminals, broken insulation, or loose wires.

YES **FIX: Insulate and align parts.** Spread apart wires that touch. Reinsulate, where necessary, with plastic electrical tape. If the problem remains, the trouble lies in the control cord or heating element. Take the pad to an authorized repairman or replace pad with a new one. Repairs on either part are generally not worth the trouble. △△

Ease of fix: △ simple △△ average △△△ difficult

Hot plates

Burner does not heat

If one of the burners fails to heat, it means current is not flowing through its heating elements. The cause is determined by testing the wall outlet, then the various components of the hot plate. Repairs may be as simple as replacing a house fuse or cleaning terminal contacts, or may require replacement of parts.

Power off at outlet?

TEST: Unplug power cord and check wall outlet with a lamp you know is working.

YES → **FIX: Replace fuse or reset circuit breaker.** See p.127. If fuse keeps blowing, see *Hot plate blows fuses*, p.188. △

Power cord broken?

TEST: Unplug power cord. Examine cord for fraying and the plug for loose or distorted prongs. Remove top deck (See *Disassembling the hot plate*, p.188.) Unscrew porcelain wire nuts, and clip jumper wire across power cord leads. (See *Testing for open circuits*, p.189.) Set volt-ohm meter (p.124) to RX1 scale, clip its probes to the plug, and bend and pull cord. If cord is OK, meter will read zero ohms; if cord is broken, needle will jump or read high.

YES → **FIX: Replace power cord.** Pull away cord leads from wires to which they are attached (they had been held in place by the porcelain wire nuts). Squeeze strain relief device with pliers, rotate it a quarter turn, and pull it out of seat in rear panel along with power cord. △△

Terminals dirty or heating element broken?

NO →

TEST: With power cord unplugged and top deck off, set volt-ohm meter to RX1 scale and clip its probes to terminals of heating element. (See *Testing for open circuits*, p.189.) If element is OK, meter will read below 35 ohms; if element is broken or terminals are dirty, meter will read high. Clean terminals (see **Fix**). If problem persists, element is broken.

YES → **FIX: Clean terminals; replace heating element if necessary.** Loosen screws and spray terminals with electrical contact cleaner (p.123). Tighten and loosen terminal screws several times each to improve contact. If problem remains, the heating element is broken and should be replaced. Remove terminal screws and disconnect lead wires. Pull out and tilt up element from top deck, remove screw that fastens drip pan, and snap out pan. Remove element from above. △△

Thermostat broken?

TEST: With hot plate unplugged and top deck removed, turn control knob of burner that is not working to its hottest setting. Set volt-ohm meter to RX1 scale and touch its probes to the thermostat terminals. If thermostat is OK, meter will read zero ohms; if thermostat is broken, meter will read high.

YES → **FIX: Replace thermostat.** Pull control knob off stem, remove felt washer, and undo thermostat mounting screw. Lift out thermostat and detach leads from its terminals. After installing new thermostat, adjust control knob and thermostat as described in *Improper temperature*, p.188. △△

Ease of fix: △ simple △△ average △△△ difficult

Use and care

1. Do not use an extension cord with a hot plate. It should always be plugged directly into the wall outlet.

2. For best results, use flat-bottomed, medium-weight, aluminum or copper-bottom cookware. Both metals conduct and transfer heat quickly and evenly.

3. Select a pan size that best fits the burner; small pans for a small burner, large pans for a large one.

4. Never immerse the hot plate in water or allow water to drip inside. The drip pans are the parts that get the dirtiest. Take them off and clean them separately in detergent and water. Do not use cleaners with abrasives or bleach; corrosion will result.

5. Clean other parts of hot plate by wiping with damp cloth or sponge. Be sure the hot plate is unplugged and cool before you start cleaning.

6. Clean spills immediately. Once baked on, they are much harder to remove.

Note: Details of repair and disassembly may vary from one model of hot plate to the next. If yours differs markedly from the one shown, see *Repair basics*, pp.128–130

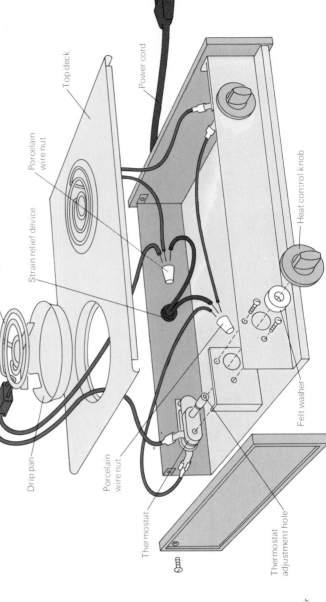

Top deck

Power cord

Porcelain wire nut

Strain relief device

Heating element

Drip pan

Porcelain wire nut

Thermostat

Heat control knob

Felt washer

Thermostat adjustment hole

Hot plates

Disassembling the hot plate

1. Unplug hot plate and remove screws in rear and above control knobs. Lift off top deck along with drip pans and burners.

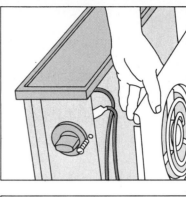

2. Peel off fiberglass tape and unscrew both wire nuts inside the housing, then free power cord leads from all other wires.

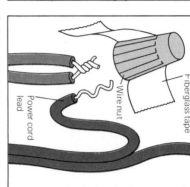

Fiberglass tape — Wire nut — Power cord lead

3. Squeeze strain relief fitting with pliers, rotate it a quarter turn, and pull it out of housing along with power cord.

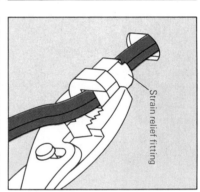

Strain relief fitting

4. Remove leads from heating element terminals, pop element out from above, and snap out drip pan after removing screw.

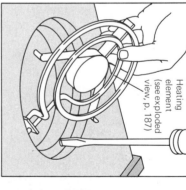

Heating element (see exploded view, p. 187)

5. Pull control knob and felt washer from stem. Undo thermostat mounting screw, disconnect leads, and remove thermostat.

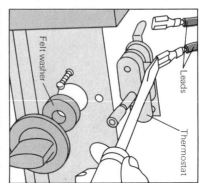

Felt washer — Leads — Thermostat

Improper temperature

The simplest cause of a hot plate running too hot or too cold is that one of the control knobs is incorrectly positioned on its stem. Try adjusting it. If that does not work, the next step is to attempt to adjust the thermostat itself. If the problem persists, the thermostat should be replaced with a new one.

Control knob out of position?

TEST: Turn knob toward low heat as far as it will go. In that position it should read Off. If it does not, it is out of position.

 NO

FIX: Reposition control knob. With hot plate unplugged, pull control knob off of stem. Turn stem toward low heat as far as it will go and reattach knob so that it reads Off.

YES → △

Thermostat out of adjustment?

TEST: First, check burner by setting it to maximum heat and heating a quart of water in a saucepan that just fits the burner. Medium burner should bring water to a low boil in 15 to 20 minutes. High burner should bring water to a rolling boil in 8 to 12 minutes. If either burner fails this check, try adjusting the thermostat (see **Fix**). If adjustment proves impossible, the thermostat is broken and should be replaced.

FIX: Adjust thermostat; replace if necessary. Unplug hot plate; allow it to cool. Set volt-ohm meter (p.124) to RX1 scale and clip its probes to the prongs of the plug. With other burner off, set control knob of defective burner half way between Off and Low. Pull knob off without turning stem. Turn adjustment screw in center of stem clockwise until needle of meter jumps from low to high ohms. After adjustment, reposition control knob as described above. If adjustment fails, replace the thermostat. Remove screws in back of hot plate and above each control knob and lift off top deck. Pull control knob off stem, remove felt washer, and undo thermostat mounting screw. Lift out thermostat and detach leads from its terminals. After installing new thermostat, adjust it and its knob.

YES →

Hot plate blows fuses

When a fuse blows or circuit breaker trips, it means there is either an electrical overload or a short circuit. Overloads are fixed by reducing the number of appliances in the circuit. Short circuits are located by inspection and testing. Parts found to be shorted must be repaired or replaced.

Circuit overloaded?

TEST: To check for overloads, see p.127. Too many appliances in a circuit is the commonest cause of blown fuses and tripped circuit breakers.

FIX: Reduce number of appliances in the circuit. Caution: Never replace a fuse or breaker with one having a larger capacity.

YES → △ △

Short circuit in power cord or plug?

TEST: Unplug hot plate and remove top deck. Unscrew porcelain wire nuts and free both power cord leads from other wires. Set volt-ohm meter (p.124) to RX100 scale and clip its probes to the prongs of the plug. Bend and pull power cord. If cord is OK, meter will read high; if cord is shorted, needle will jump around or read zero ohms.

 NO

FIX: Replace power cord. Power cord leads have already been separated from wires to which they were attached (formerly held in place with porcelain wire nuts) as part of the test. Squeeze strain relief device with pliers, rotate it a quarter turn, and pull it out of seat in rear panel along with power cord.

YES → △ △

Short circuit inside hot plate?

TEST: With hot plate unplugged and disassembled, check interior wiring for burn marks, broken insulation, loose wires.

FIX: Repair or replace broken parts. If insulation is damaged, replace (special high-temperature insulation is required).Bend distorted terminals back into shape.

YES → △ △

Ease of fix: △ simple   △△ average   △△△ difficult

Hot plate shocks user

A frayed power cord, an electrically live component grounded to (touching) a metal part, or leakage current due to faulty insulation will cause shocking. In the case of a frayed cord or grounding, the part can be fixed or replaced. If leakage current is suspected, the blender should be taken to a repairman.

Power cord frayed?

 NO→ TEST: Receiving a shock from power cord is sufficient evidence it needs repair.

YES→ FIX: Replace power cord. Follow instructions given in *Burner does not heat*, p.187, and disassembly instructions on p.188. △△

Leakage current present?

NO→ TEST: If you receive a shock from touching an exposed metal part of hot plate, unplug power cord. Set volt-ohm meter (p.124) to RX100 scale and turn both control knobs to *High*. Clip one meter probe to body of hot plate, the other to either prong of the plug. If meter reads at or near high, leakage current (p.127) is indicated.

YES→ FIX: Take hot plate to authorized repairman. Eliminating leakage current requires special equipment. Note: It is possible that the shock is not caused by leakage current, but by a wire that becomes grounded only when the hot plate is operating. To investigate this, proceed with tests before taking appliance to a repair shop. △△△

Internal wiring grounded?

TEST: Unplug power cord from wall outlet and remove top deck of hot plate. (See *Disassembling the hot plate*, p.188.) Examine internal wires for bare spots and loose strands. With volt-ohm meter set to RX100 scale, clip one of its probes to body of hot plate, the other to either prong of the plug. Turn both control knobs to *High* and bend and twist each wire inside hot plate. If needle jumps when a particular wire is handled, that wire is grounded.

YES→ FIX: Repair or replace faulty parts and insulation. Insulate any bare spots on wires with high-temperature tape (available from manufacturer) or replace wires with manufacturer's replacement. △△

Ease of fix: △ simple △△ average △△△ difficult

Testing for shock hazard

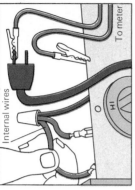
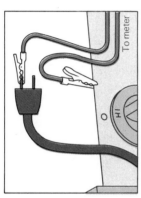

Set meter to RX100 scale.
Test 1: If meter reads at or near high, leakage current is indicated.
Test 2: If needle jumps when a particular wire is handled, that wire is grounded.

Internal wires — To meter

2. To test for grounded wiring, lift off top deck, set controls to *High*. Clip meter probes to body and plug, then tug on internal wires.

1. If hot plate shocks, unplug cord, turn controls to *High*. Clip one volt-ohm meter probe to metal body, other to prong of plug.

Cleaning and adjustments

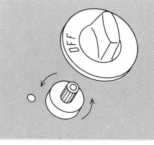
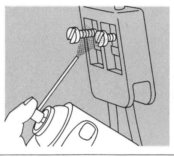

To adjust thermostat, set volt-ohm meter to RX1. Needle should jump as knob is moved from *Off* to *Low*.

Reposition heat control knob if it does not read *Off* when it is turned down as far as it will go.

To clean terminals, loosen heating element terminal screws. Spray with electrical contact cleaner.

Testing for short circuits

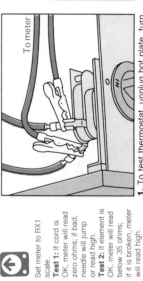

Test 1: Set meter to RX1 scale. If thermostat is OK, meter will read zero ohms; if bad, it will read high.
Test 2: Set meter to RX100 scale. If cord is OK, meter will read high; if shorted, needle will jump or read zero ohms.

To meter

Wire nut — To meter

2. Check power cord by undoing porcelain wire nuts, freeing the cord leads, and clipping meter probes to plug. Bend cord during test.

1. To test thermostat, unplug hot plate, turn control knob to highest setting. Clip volt-ohm meter probes to thermostat terminals.

Testing for open circuits

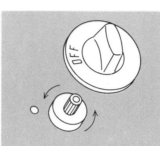
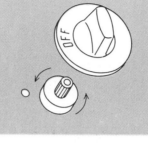

Set meter to RX1 scale.
Test 1: If cord is OK, meter will read zero ohms; if bad, needle will jump or read high.
Test 2: If element is OK, meter will read below 35 ohms; if it is broken, meter will read high.

Heating element terminals and leads — To meter

To meter

1. To test power cord, unscrew porcelain wire nuts. Clip jumper wire across cord leads and clip volt-ohm meter probes to plug.

2. Open circuit in heating element will cause burner to fail. To check, unplug power cord, clip meter probes to terminals of element.

Irons

Iron does not heat or heats slowly

If the iron is a travel model and it is heating slowly, it may be that it is set for overseas operation. Total lack of heat means current is not flowing through the heating element. The cause may be a blown fuse, broken power cord, bad heating element, or broken thermostat. Test these parts and replace the broken ones.

Iron set for overseas operation?

TEST: If iron is a travel model, be sure that voltage switch is set for 120 volts, not 220 volts. An incorrect setting will cause iron to heat very slowly.

FIX: Set voltage switch to 120 volts. If the iron still fails to heat quickly, the contacts on the switch may be fused. If so, the switch should be replaced.

▷

Power off at outlet?

TEST: Unplug power cord and check wall outlet with a lamp you know is working.

FIX: Replace fuse or reset circuit breaker. See p.127. If fuse keeps blowing, see *Iron blows fuses*, p.195.

▷

Power cord broken?

TEST: Unplug power cord. Examine cord for fraying and the plug for loose or distorted prongs. Remove rear cover plate and clip jumper wire across power cord leads. Set volt-ohm meter (p.124) to RX1 scale and clip its probes to the prongs of the plug. Bend and pull power cord. If cord is Ok, meter will read zero ohms; if broken, needle will jump around or read high.

FIX: Replace power cord. Disconnect power cord leads from terminals and withdraw power cord. Use a manufacturer's replacement; ordinary appliance cord is not suitable for use in an appliance, such as an iron, that operates at high temperatures and draws considerable current.

▷

Heating element broken?

TEST: With power cord unplugged, disassemble iron so that heating element terminals are accessible. Set volt-ohm meter to RX1 scale and touch its probes to the heating element terminals. If element is Ok, meter will read a steady 10 to 25 ohms; if element is broken, meter will read high.

FIX: Replace soleplate. Since fused contacts in the thermostat may have caused the heating element to fail, continue testing before starting repairs. To put in new soleplate, complete disassembly of iron. When reassembling, apply silicone sealant (available from manufacturer) to mating surfaces of steam chamber and cover. (See *Repairing the steam chamber*, p.195) Note: Some companies do not supply replacement plates.

△△△

Thermostat broken?

TEST: With power cord unplugged and iron partially disassembled, set volt-ohm meter to RX1 scale. Clip probes of meter to thermostat terminals and open and close thermostat contacts (push on thermostat arm or turn temperature control). Needle should jump from high to zero ohms when contacts close. Steady high reading means an open circuit; steady low, fused contacts.

FIX: Replace thermostat. Continue disassembly of iron until thermostat is removed. After reassembly, adjust thermostat, as described in *Improper temperature*, p.193. If thermostat lead wire is soldered to the heating element, high temperature solder must be used when installing new thermostat.

△△△

Ease of fix: △ simple △△ average △△△ difficult

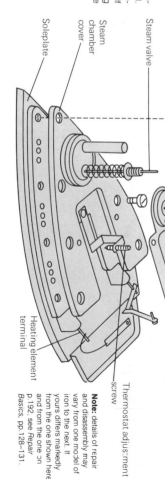

Labels: Temperature control lever · Spring support · Spring · Dial plate · Spring · Spray knob · Handle · Sprayer nut · Sprayer cover · Steam button · Rubber gasket · Spray nozzle · Spray lever · Water level tube · Mounting screw · Mounting clamp · Saddle plate · Rear cover plate · Power cord · Spray tube · Shell · Water tank · Temperature shaft · Thermostat · Tank holddown · Tank holddown screw · Steam valve · Steam chamber cover · Soleplate · Heating element terminal · Thermostat screw · Thermostat adjustment screw

Note: details of repair and disassembly may vary from one model of iron to the next. If yours differs markedly from the one shown here and from the one on p.192, see *Repair Basics*, pp.128–131.

Disassembly problems

Modern steam-spray irons (many incorporating special features, such as "burst of steam," "shot of steam," or "self-cleaning" devices) are probably the most difficult home appliances to disassemble or reassemble. Not only are there a large number of models to contend with, but the component parts of an iron must be taken apart and put together in precise order. In addition, these parts are often delicate and easily damaged.

If your iron does not resemble the model illustrated on page 190 or the one illustrated on page 192, you are advised not to undertake any disassembly beyond the most basic steps, such as removing the power cord and lifting off the saddle plate. Send to the manufacturer for service instructions if you wish to go further. Even when you have information on disassembly, as you remove parts, be sure to keep careful track of their proper orientation and of their relationship to other parts. Taking polaroid pictures at various stages of disassembly would be a help. Scribing lines to indicate how one part fits into another or the direction a particular part should face would also help. Keep in mind, especially when you are putting the iron together, that parts should fit without forcing.

Disassembling an iron: type 1

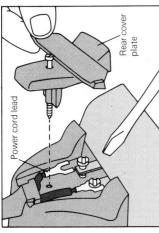

Power cord lead
Rear cover plate

1. Unplug iron from wall outlet, remove rear cover plate, and disconnect power cord leads from terminals. Power cord may then be withdrawn from iron.

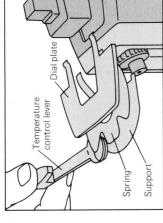

Temperature control lever
Dial plate
Spring
Support

2. Turn temperature control lever from center position to maximum heat while pressing down on dial plate. This will free dial plate, lever, spring, and support.

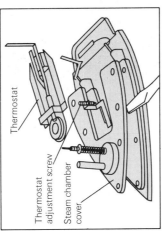

Sprayer cover
Spray nozzle
Sprayer nut

3. Use long-nose pliers with tape on jaws to remove sprayer nut. Then, carefully pry up edge of sprayer cover with a knife and pull cover off front of handle.

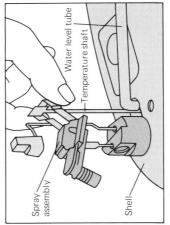

Spray knob
Mounting screw
Mounting clamp
Saddle plate

4. Pry off saddle plate, remove mounting screw and clamp, and lift off handle. (Tilt spray assembly when lifting handle, to disengage spray lever.)

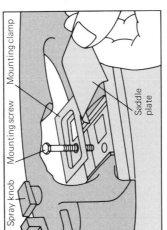

Water level tube
Temperature shaft
Spray assembly
Shell

5. Pull out spray assembly and water level tube and lift off shell. Remove water tank by taking out the tank holddown screw and pulling off the holddown.

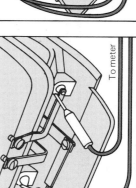

Thermostat
Thermostat adjustment screw
Steam chamber cover

6. Remove bolts and heating element lead, and slide out thermostat. Undo all other bolts and pry off steam chamber cover (considerable force is required).

Testing for open circuits

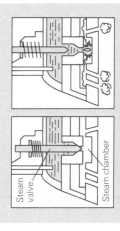

Jumper
Power cord
To meter

1. Check power cord with jumper wire across its leads. Clip volt-ohm meter probes to prongs of plug and bend and pull cord during test.

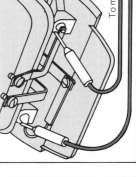

To meter

2. For heating element test, disassemble iron, touch meter probes to terminals of element. If it is broken, soleplate must be replaced.

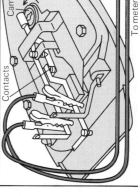

Contacts
Cam
To meter

3. To check thermostat, clip meter probes to its terminals. Then, open and close its contacts by pressing its arm or turning cam (illustrated).

Use RX1 scale for all three tests. **Test 1:** Needle will jump or read high if cord is broken. **Test 2:** Meter will read high if element is broken. **Test 3:** Needle should jump from high to low when contacts close. If it does not, thermostat is bad.

How a steam iron works

Steam valve
Steam chamber

With valve closed (left), water does not enter steam chamber, iron operates dry. When valve is up (right), water drips into heated steam chamber, pours out vents in soleplate as steam.

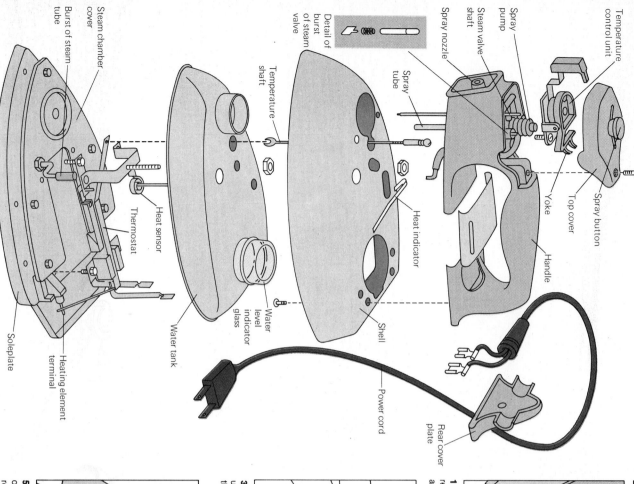

Temperature control unit
Spray pump
Steam valve shaft
Spray nozzle
Spray tube
Steam valve shaft
Spray button
Top cover
Yoke
Handle
Temperature shaft
Detail of burst of steam valve
Steam chamber cover
Burst of steam tube
Steam chamber cover
Thermostat
Heat sensor
Soleplate
Heating element terminal
Water tank
Water level indicator glass
Temperature shaft
Heat indicator
Shell
Power cord
Rear cover plate

Disassembling an iron: type 2

1. With iron unplugged, take out screw and remove rear cover plate. Pull power cord leads from terminals and withdraw power cord from back of iron.

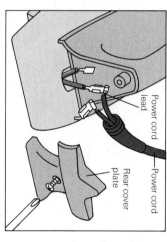

Power cord lead
Power cord
Rear cover plate

2. Take off screw on top of handle and lift off top cover along with spray button and selector dial for spray or "burst of steam" operation.

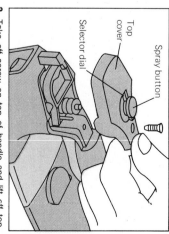

Spray button
Top cover
Selector dial

3. Remove screws and take out temperature control unit by slipping its yoke out from under the head of the temperature shaft. Do not pull on the shaft.

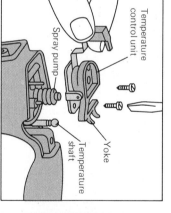

Temperature control unit
Spray pump
Yoke
Temperature shaft

4. Pry saddle plate off with knife and remove heat indicator by squeezing it together where it attaches to the shaft. Tape pliers to prevent scratching.

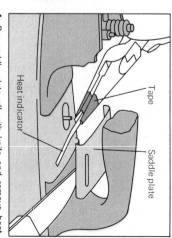

Heat indicator
Tape
Saddle plate

5. Pull tube from rubber hose, unscrew nut, and lift off handle and shell as unit. To take off water tank, remove nut in center of tank.

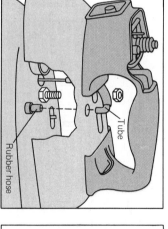

Tube
Rubber hose

6. Take out remaining bolts and pry up steam chamber cover (considerable force is required). If thermostat lead is soldered in place, do not remove it.

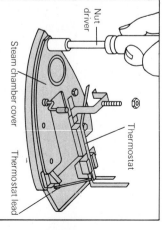

Nut driver
Steam chamber cover
Thermostat
Thermostat lead

Improper temperature

A damaged or incorrectly adjusted thermostat is the likely cause of an iron operating at too high or too low a temperature. A simple test with an oven thermometer will show whether or not the iron has a temperature problem. Should that fail, replace the thermostat.

Thermostat out of adjustment?

TEST: Unplug iron from wall outlet and drain all water from it. Set temperature control to start of steam range. Suspend iron upside down on rim of a pot. Place oven thermometer on the soleplate and cover with a can. Plug power cord into outlet. After five minutes, remove can. (It will be hot, so use a pot holder.) If thermometer reads between 220°F and 280°F, thermostat is OK. If it reads above or below these values it is out of adjustment or broken.

FIX: Adjust thermostat. Remove saddle plate (*Type 1 iron*, p.191) or top cover (*Type 2 iron*, p.192) to reach thermostat adjustment screw. Rotate screw a quarter turn at a time and recheck temperature after each adjustment. On most irons, turning screw clockwise raises temperature. Repeat adjustments and checks until iron is within proper temperature range, or it becomes clear that it cannot be adjusted. After adjustment, check highest and lowest settings. At high, temperature should be between 450°F and 550°F. At low, iron should not heat at all. △△

Thermostat broken?

TEST: Unplug power cord and disassemble iron so that thermostat terminals are accessible (*Type 1 iron*, p.191; *Type 2 iron*, p.192). Set volt-ohm meter (p.124) to RX1 scale and clip its probes to the thermostat terminals. Open and close the thermostat contacts either by pushing on the thermostat arm or by turning temperature control cam. If thermostat is OK, needle will jump from high to zero ohms when contacts close. Steady high reading means an open circuit; steady low means thermostat's contacts are fused. Set up test as in final illustration in *Testing for open circuits*, p.191.

FIX: Replace thermostat. Continue disassembly of iron until thermostat is removed. After reassembly, adjust thermostat as described above. If thermostat lead wire is soldered to the heating element, high temperature solder and a propane torch must be used to install new thermostat. △△△

Iron does not slide smoothly

If an iron sticks, grabs, or snags, its soleplate may be rough or dirty or the temperature may be wrong for the material. Changing the iron's temperature setting often solves the problem. Clean a dirty soleplate with detergent and water. A scratched metal soleplate can be buffed smooth with polishing compound.

Incorrect temperature?

TEST: A sticky iron—one that does not slide smoothly or that causes material to bunch up and wrinkle—is often caused by incorrect operating temperature. Try adjusting the temperature (see **Fix**).

FIX: Use different temperature setting. For example, if iron sticks on *Nylon*, move temperature control lower, toward *Dacron*. If that does not work, move control lever higher, toward *Wool*. If problem remains, see *Improper temperature*, at left. △

Soleplate dirty?

TEST: Buildup of starch and other debris may cause iron to stick and drag. With power cord unplugged, clean soleplate (see **Fix**) to see if it clears up the difficulty.

FIX: Clean soleplate. Scrub soleplate with a mild liquid detergent or baking soda. Use a damp, clean sponge to apply cleanser. Do not immerse iron in water or use cleaners with harsh abrasives. △

Soleplate rough or scratched?

TEST: Small burrs raised by scratches cause an iron to grab and pull. Although difficult to see or feel, burrs can be detected by lightly rubbing a wad of cheesecloth over the soleplate. If they are present, they will snag the cloth.

FIX: Buff soleplate (metal only). If soleplate is aluminum or stainless steel, put a small amount of an automobile polishing compound on a soft, clean, dampened pad and buff soleplate gently with a back and forth, tip it to heel motion. If plate is badly gouged, polish it with extra-fine steel wool before buffing. After buffing, clean plate with damp sponge and clear residual compound from steam ports with paper clip. Operate iron on steam for several minutes to get rid of any remaining compound. **Caution: Do not buff nonstick soleplates.** △

Ease of fix: △ simple △△ average △△△ difficult

Use and care

1. Use only distilled or soft water in the iron. Hard water, even if processed through a home softener, can leave harmful mineral deposits.

2. Do not iron over buttons, zippers, fasteners, or other abrasive objects, particularly if the soleplate is aluminum or is coated with a nonstick finish.

3. Empty the iron immediately after using it, while it is still hot. Unplug iron from wall outlet, put steam button in the *Off* position, and tip iron so that opening is down. Rock iron back and forth until all water is drained out of it.

4. Keep iron on its heel rest with steam button in the *Off* position when it is not in use. Be sure the iron is cool before putting it into a cabinet.

5. If you wrap the cord around the iron, keep it loose to avoid damage to the wires or outer braid.

6. Never keep the iron in its carton. Residual moisture can contact the cardboard and damage the soleplate. If the iron is to be stored, dry it thoroughly by running it on *Steam* for 45 minutes.

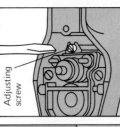

Adjusting screw

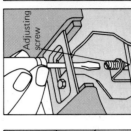

Adjusting screw

Temperature in test should be 220°F–280°F. Correct it by turning thermostat adjustment screw. Screw may be under saddle plate (left) or top cover (right).

Testing and adjusting temperature

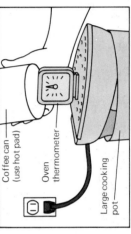
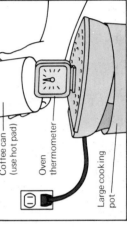

Coffee can (use hot pad)

Oven thermometer

Large cooking pot

To check heat, drain iron, set temperature control to start of steam range. Place oven thermometer on soleplate and operate iron. Can helps keep heat in.

Irons

Water or steam leak

Water leaks may be the result of a defective steam valve or a leaky water tank. Be sure the leak is not due to sloppy filling or moisture condensing inside the shell after the tank has been filled with cold water. If steam leaks from under the shell, the steam chamber is cracked or needs to be resealed.

Broken steam valve?

TEST: If water or steam leaks from steam vents during nonsteam operation, make sure that steam button is in *Off* position. If it is, steam valve is probably broken.

FIX: Replace valve stem or valve seat. Disassemble iron (*Type 1 iron*, p.191; *Type 2 iron*, p.192) and examine steam valve components. Look for crack in valve seat or broken pin on valve stem.
▷▷

Leaky water tank?

TEST: Water leaking from beneath shell may be due to leaky tank but make sure leak is not due to careless filling or condensation. To check tank, unplug power cord, empty water from iron, and disassemble it. Fill tank and look for leaks.

FIX: Replace tank and tank gaskets. Completely disassemble and remove tank and gaskets. If silicone seal has been used on any of the gaskets, be sure to apply it when installing new tank and gaskets.
▷▷

Leaky steam chamber?

TEST: If steam leaks from beneath shell when iron is operated on *Steam* setting, the steam chamber cover is cracked or the seal between it and the soleplate is defective.

FIX: Reseal or replace steam chamber cover. Disassemble iron (*Type 1 iron*, p.191; *Type 2 iron*, p.192) until steam chamber cover is off. If chamber is cracked, replace it. Scrape off old silicone sealant, apply new with roller, let dry 15 minutes before reassembly. (See *Repairing the steam chamber*, p.195).
▷▷▷

Improper steam or spray

Steam and spray troubles may be due to clogged passages, broken components, or improper temperature. A vinegar and water flush will often improve steam performance. Other fixes include cleaning orifices with a needle, pipe cleaner, or straightened-out paper clip; adjusting the temperature; and replacing parts.

Insufficient spray?

TEST: Clean spray passages (see **Fix**) and test to see if the difficulty is cleared up. If it is not, the spray unit is broken and should be replaced. Note: Some spray units work by pump action but others, called power sprays, tap the iron's steam pressure to provide a continuous spray. If your iron has a power spray, the iron must be operating in the *Steam* range for the spray to work.

FIX: Clean spray passages; replace spray unit if necessary. First, clean the hole in the spray nozzle with a fine wire or needle. Take care not to enlarge the hole when cleaning. If spray still fails to work properly, disassemble iron and remove spray unit (*Type 1 iron*, p.191; *Type 2 iron*, p.192). Clean spray tube with a pipe cleaner and check to see if it works. (If your iron has a power spray, you will have to reassemble the iron to do this. If problem persists, replace spray unit if it is the pump type or take iron to an authorized repairman if it is power spray.
▷▷

Iron spits or drips during steam operation?

TEST: Be sure controls are set for *Steam*. If they are, try adjusting the temperature (see **Fix**) to see if it solves the problem.

FIX: Adjust temperature control. If there is no steam but water drips from vents, set control to higher reading. If water and steam spit from vents, set control lower. If problem persists, see *Improper temperature*, p.193.
▷▷

Poor steam performance?

TEST: To check steam, unplug iron from wall outlet and fill with water. Place it in normal operating position on a rack over a broiling pan. Set iron for steam operation, plug in power cord, and check the total length of time the iron steams. If it steams more than 45 minutes, steaming rate is low. Clean the steam chamber (see **Fix**), then test iron to see if problem has been solved. If it has not, steam valve opening may be clogged or valve spring may be broken.

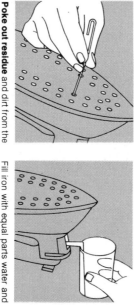

FIX: Flush steam chamber; clean valve or replace spring if necessary. Unplug iron and clean vents with straightened-out paper clip. Fill iron with mixture of half water, half vinegar and set it on a rack over a broiling pan. Allow a minute for water to drip into steam chamber, then operate the iron on *Steam*. After iron stops steaming, set temperature to maximum and let it run 30 minutes more. If problem persists, unplug iron and disassemble it. Clean steam valve opening with needle. If valve spring is broken, replace it.
▷▷

Ease of fix: △ simple △△ average △△△ difficult

Clearing water and steam passages

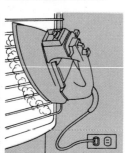

Poke out residue and dirt from the steam vents with a straightened-out paper clip or stiff wire.

Steam valve opening

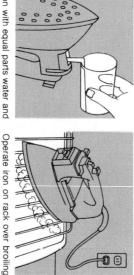

Fill iron with equal parts water and white vinegar. Wait 60 seconds for mixture to fill steam chamber.

Spray nozzle

Operate iron on rack over broiling pan until it stops steaming, then run it another half hour.

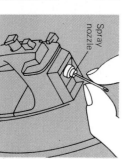

Poor steaming may mean a clogged or broken steam valve. Use needle to poke out mineral residue.

Spray tube

To clean spray nozzle, push fine needle into opening. Be careful not to enlarge the opening.

Pipe cleaner

Spray unit

If spray is still defective, remove unit from iron, insert pipe cleaner into tube to clear blockage.

Iron shocks user

A frayed power cord, an electrically live component grounded to (touching) a metal part, or leakage current due to faulty insulation will cause shocking. In the case of a frayed cord or grounding, the part can be fixed or replaced. If leakage current is suspected, take the iron to a repairman—special equipment is needed.

Power cord frayed?

 TEST: Receiving a shock from touching power cord means cord needs repair.

FIX: Replace power cord. Take off rear cover plate and remove power cord leads from terminals. (*Type 1 iron*, p.191; *Type 2*, p.192.) △

Leakage current present?

TEST: Unplug power cord. Set volt-ohm meter (p.124) to RX100 scale and turn temperature control to *High*. Touch one probe to shell, the other to either prong of the plug. If meter reads high, leakage current (p.127) is indicated.

FIX: Take iron to authorized repairman. Eliminating leakage current requires special equipment. Note: It is possible the shock is not caused by leakage current, but by a part that becomes grounded only when the iron is operating. To investigate this, continue testing before taking appliance to repair shop. △△△

Internal wiring grounded?

TEST: Unplug and disassemble iron. Check for loose wires, bent terminals.

FIX: Repair damaged parts. Use high-temperature (fiberglass) tape to reinsulate wires with loose strands. Straighten bent terminals. △△

Heating element grounded?

TEST: With iron unplugged and disassembled, turn temperature control to *Off* position. Set volt-ohm meter to RX100 scale and touch one probe to bottom of soleplate, the other to each terminal of heating element in turn. If meter reads below highest point on ohms scale, heating element is grounded.

FIX: Replace soleplate. Complete disassembly of iron (*Type 1*, p.191; *Type 2*, p.192). When reassembling, apply silicone sealant (available from manufacturer) to mating surfaces of steam chamber and cover. Note: Some manufacturers do not supply soleplates as replacement parts. △△△

Iron blows fuses

When a fuse blows or a circuit breaker trips, it means there is either an electrical overload or a short circuit in the appliance. An overload is fixed by reducing the number of appliances in a circuit. A short circuit must be located by inspection and testing. Parts found to be shorted must be repaired or replaced.

Circuit overloaded?

 TEST: To check for overloads, see p.127. Too many appliances in a circuit is the commonest cause of blown fuses and tripped circuit breakers.

FIX: Reduce number of appliances in the circuit. Caution: Never replace a fuse or breaker with one having a larger capacity. △

Short circuit in power cord or plug?

TEST: Unplug iron from wall outlet and remove power cord (see *Disassembling an iron: type 1*, p.191; *Disassembling an iron: type 2*, p.192). Examine power cord and plug for bare wires and burn marks. Check the plug for loose prongs. Set volt-ohm meter (p.124) to RX100 scale and clip its probes to the prongs of the plug. Bend and pull power cord. If power cord is OK, meter will read high; if power cord is shorted, needle will jump around or read zero ohms.

FIX: Replace power cord. Power cord has already been removed from iron during test. Replace it with a manufacturer's equivalent. Ordinary appliance cord is not suitable for use in an appliance, such as an iron, that operates at high temperatures and draws considerable current. △

Short circuit in iron?

TEST: Unplug power cord and disassemble iron. (See *Disassembling an iron: type 1*, p.191, or *Disassembling an iron: type 2*, p.192.) Examine all parts. Look for burn marks, distorted terminal posts, broken insulation, loose wires, fused metal.

FIX: Replace or repair broken parts. Use high-temperature (fiberglass) tape to insulate bare wires. Straighten out bent terminals. If cause of short circuiting cannot be found, take iron to authorized repairman. △△

Ease of fix: △ simple △△ average △△△ difficult

Tests for shocks and shorts

Shell
Power cord
To meter

1. Touch one volt-ohm meter probe to shell, the other to plug, for leakage current test.

Heating element terminal
To meter

2. Check for grounded heating element by touching probes to soleplate, element terminal.

Power cord
To meter

3. To test power cord for short, clip probes to plug, bend and pull on cord.

Use RX100 scale for all tests.
Test 1: High reading means leakage current.
Test 2: If meter reads below maximum, element is grounded.
Test 3: If needle jumps or reads zero ohms, power cord is shorted.

Repairing the steam chamber

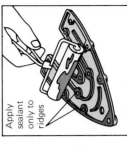

Scraper
Steam chamber cover

1. Scrape off old sealant from both cover and steam chamber. Be careful not to damage metal.

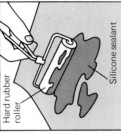

Hard rubber roller
Silicone sealant

2. Use a hard rubber roller to spread silicone sealant evenly on a clean piece of paper.

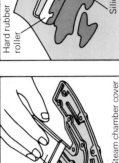

Apply sealant only to ridges

3. Apply thin coat of sealant to steam chamber, wait 15 minutes, then bolt cover on.

Knives

Motor does not run or runs sluggishly

Current must reach the motor in order for it to operate. A blown house fuse, a break in the power cord, or a dirty or broken on-off switch can interrupt the current flow. In addition, moving parts may be jammed by dirt, or the motor itself may be faulty. Repairs include changing a fuse, replacing parts, and lubricating parts.

Power off at outlet?

NO ←

TEST: Unplug power cord and check wall outlet with a lamp you know is working.

YES → **FIX: Replace fuse or reset circuit breaker.** See p.127. If fuse keeps blowing, see *Shock hazards and short circuits,* p.197.
△

Power cord broken?

NO ←

TEST: Unplug power cord from wall outlet. Set volt-ohm meter (p.124) to RX1 scale and clip its probes to the prongs of the plug. If cord is separate from knife, clip jumper wire across terminals of its female plug. If cord is built into knife, open up housing, remove wire nut, and clip jumper wire across cord's leads. Bend and pull power cord. If cord is OK, meter will read zero ohms; if cord is broken, needle will jump or read high.

YES → **FIX: Replace power cord.** If the cord is separate, buy a manufacturer's replacement. If it is built in, remove one of its leads from brush housing, the other from beneath wire nut. Squeeze strain relief device with pliers, rotate it a quarter turn, and withdraw power cord.
△ △

On-off switch dirty or broken?

NO ←

TEST: Unplug knife and open housing. If switch is in handle, remove wire nuts from its leads. If switch is in lower housing, remove driver assembly. Set volt-ohm meter to RX1 scale and clip its probes to the switch leads. If switch is OK, meter will read zero ohms when switch is in the *On* position; if switch is faulty, meter will read high.

YES → **FIX: Clean or replace switch.** If switch is in handle, try spraying electrical contact cleaner (p.123) into it. If problem persists, replace handle (upper housing) including switch. If switch is in lower housing, and be dirty from food residues. Clean switch by spraying it with electrical contact cleaner, then polish contacts with very fine (No. 400) sandpaper.
△ △

Motor or driver assembly jammed?

NO ←

TEST: With power cord unplugged and housing open, try turning the motor by hand by pushing on the fan blades. Motor should offer only slight resistance to turning (a certain amount of stiffness is normal). If motor shaft is difficult to turn, clean and lubricate the driver assembly and bearings (see **Fix**), then test again to see if difficulty has been cleared up.

YES → **FIX: Clean and lubricate driver assembly bearings.** Remove driver assembly from lower housing and clean out debris and dirt from upper and lower housings. Apply multipurpose grease to worm screw and worm wheel. Add a pinpoint of light machine oil to front and rear bearings. Be careful not to get lubricant in the motor.
△ △

Motor faulty?

If the above tests fail to isolate the problem, the trouble lies in the motor. Poor lubrication, worn brushes, a damaged bearing, or a bad wire in either the field coil or armature winding may be to blame. See *Universal motors,* pp.132-134, for information on testing and repairs. **Caution: If the motor hums but does not turn, shut knife off immediately to prevent damage.**

Ease of fix: △ simple △△ average △△△ difficult

Note: Details of repair and disassembly may vary from one model of electric knife to the next. If your appliance differs markedly from the one shown, see *Repair basics,* pp.128-131. Some electric knives are of cordless design. If yours is that type and you trace a problem with it to the motor, see *Cordless appliances,* p.136-137, for further information.

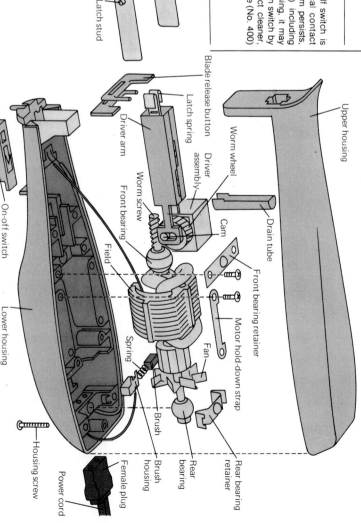

Front blade rivet

Blade

Grease guard

Latch stud

Upper housing

Blade release button

Latch spring

Driver arm

Driver assembly

Worm wheel

Worm screw

Front screw

Front bearing

Cam

Field

Drain tube

Front bearing retainer

Motor hold-down strap

Spring

Fan

Brush

Rear bearing

Rear bearing retainer

Brush housing

Female plug

Power cord

Housing screw

Lower housing

On-off switch

built into knife, be sure to free one of its leads before testing it.

If the power cord shows no signs of a short but the knife keeps blowing fuses,

Removing strain relief fitting.

the problem may be with the motor. Either take the knife to an authorized repairman or try troubleshooting the motor according to instructions in *Universal motors*, pp.132–134.

In the case of a knife that shocks when the power cord is touched, no further testing is needed; the power cord should be replaced. If the cord is built into the handle, open the housing, free both its leads, then remove cord by squeezing strain relief fitting with pliers, rotating it a quarter turn, and withdrawing it from its seat. (See *Disassembling the knife*, at left, and exploded view, p.196.)

Freeing jammed parts

Motor and drive arms should move with only slight resistance when you push on fan. If they do not, disassemble knife, clean out all dirt, lubricate moving parts.

Fan

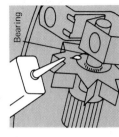

Lubricate driver assembly with a multipurpose grease or a grease that is recommended by the manufacturer. Add drop of light machine oil to each bearing. Be careful not to get lubricant into motor.

Bearing

Disassembling the knife

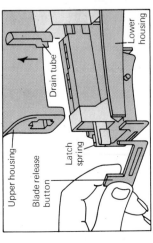

Upper housing
Brush housing
Blade release button
Latch spring
Brush
Spring
Drain tube
Lower housing

1. With power cord unplugged from knife and wall outlet, remove housing screws, separate the upper and lower housings. Slip blade release buttons from latch springs and remove drain tube by pulling it up.

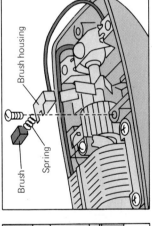

Rear bearing retainer
Rear bearing
Front bearing
Rotor
Worm screw

2. Undo screws and lift both brush housings from their seats. Springs may cause the brushes to fly out. If drive arms are attached by plastic welds, cut welds off, drill holes, and use small screws when reassembling.

Front bearing retainer
Driver assembly
Field
Motor hold-down strap

3. Remove screws holding driver assembly and front bearing retainer. Pull out driver assembly. (On some knives the drive arms can be removed separately.) Undo screws and lift out motor hold-down straps.

4. Pry out rear bearing retainer and pull rotor assembly (fan, rotor, worm screw, and bearings) out from rear. To remove field, both leads must be unsoldered. This is a delicate job and is not advised.

Testing for open circuits

Jumper wire
Female plug
To meter

1. Unplug power cord and clip volt-ohm meter probes to plug. Clip jumper to female plug. Bend cord during test. (For built-in cords, clip jumper across leads inside knife.)

Set meter to RX1 scale for both tests.
Test 1: Meter will read zero ohms if power cord is OK; needle will jump or read high if cord is broken.
Test 2: Zero ohms when switch is closed means switch is OK.

Switch terminals

To meter

2. To test switch, clip meter probes to switch terminals and close switch. If switch is in lower housing, remove driver assembly. If switch is in handle, free its leads.

Shock hazards and short circuits

Because electric knives run on very little electric current (about the same as a light bulb), they are not likely to blow fuses or trip circuit breakers. In addition, their plastic housings reduce the probability of the user being shocked. If either of these problems does occur, the cause is apt to be a defect in the power cord.

To test the power cord for a possible short circuit that may be causing fuses to blow, use a volt-ohm meter set to its RX100 scale. Clip the meter's probes to the prongs of the plug and bend and twist the cord. If there is a short, the needle will read zero ohms or jump when cord

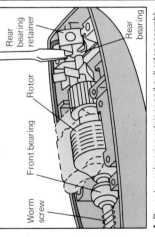

To meter

Checking power cord for short.

is twisted. If the cord is OK, the meter will read high. Note: If power cord is

Use and care

1. Unplug power cord from wall outlet before inserting or removing blades.

2. Never use the knife with only one blade in place. Be sure that the blades are joined at the tip by the front rivet and that both are securely latched into the latch springs before using knife.

3. Let the knife do the cutting. Do not press down on it or use a back-and-forth sawing motion.

4. Do not use the knife to cut through frozen foods, bones, or other hard materials.

5. Do not attempt to resharpen blades. Replace both blades even if only one seems worn.

6. To clean housing, wipe it with a damp cloth and dry thoroughly. Never immerse housing in water or other liquid.

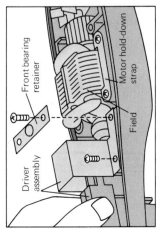

Knives

Motor runs but blades do not cut properly

If the cutting performance of the knife is poor but the motor runs properly, look for worn blades, a faulty latching mechanism, or a stripped gear in the knife. In the case of double slicing, there is probably too much space between the blades. Replacing defective parts is the suggested repair for all these problems.

Blades worn or dull?

TEST: If the knife is operating correctly but cutting is poor, the blades are probably worn. With blades inserted in handle, examine the edges. The points of both blades should be the same height.

YES ▶ FIX: Replace blades. Do not attempt to sharpen the blades, it will only make them worse. Blade wear may be due to incorrect use (cutting through bone or frozen food) or accidentally contacting a metal pan.
△

Too much space between blades?

TEST: If the knife occasionally makes a double cut (an extra slice emerges between the blades), the blade gap is probably excessive. Test by inserting a strip of paper between the blades with the knife unplugged. The paper should fit snugly. If it moves easily, the gap between blades is too large. If the paper is tight, the user putting too much pressure on the knife when cutting.

YES ▶ FIX: Replace blades. The excess space may be the result of a worn blade rivet or bent or distorted blades. Repairs are difficult and not worth the trouble.
△

Latching mechanism faulty?

TEST: Run knife with and without blades. If one of the blades does not move but both driver arms move, the latching mechanism is bad (but be sure you have inserted both blades firmly). Unplug knife, insert blades, and tug on each by pulling on the grease guard. If one comes out, it indicates latching mechanism is defective. Remove blades and compare their drive studs; both should be the same shape and thickness, and the edges should not be rounded off or scored. If the studs are OK, the trouble is in the latch springs on the driver arms.

YES ▶ FIX: Replace blades or driver arms. If latch studs on blades are worn, replace both blades. To replace driver arms, see *Disassembling the knife*, p.197. For the knife illustrated there and in the exploded view on p.196, the entire driver assembly, including driver arms, cams, and gear, must be replaced as a unit. On other models, the driver arms can be slipped off and replaced once the driver assembly has been removed from the housing.
△△

Stripped worm wheel

TEST: If the blades latch firmly but do not work properly when used for cutting, the worm wheel's teeth may be stripped. Unplug power cord, take out blades, and remove upper housing. Hold driver arms firmly with one hand and turn motor by pushing on fan blades. If you can keep the driver arms from moving as you turn the motor shaft, the worm wheel is stripped.

YES ▶ FIX: Replace worm wheel. Refer to *Disassembling the knife*, p.197. For the knife illustrated there and in the exploded view on p.196, the entire driver assembly must be replaced as a unit. On other models, the wheel can be replaced separately after the driver assembly has been taken out of the housing.
△△

Knife vibrates excessively or is noisy

Bent blades, a noisy motor, loose screws, or worn holes where the blades connect to the latch springs, are among possible causes of noisy operation. Tightening the grease guards may stop blade noise, otherwise the blades must be replaced. Other repairs include tightening screws and installing new driver arms or bearings.

Faulty blade assembly?

TEST: Run knife with and without blades. If noise stops when blades are off, latching mechanism or blades are faulty. Look for bent blades, loose grease guards, worn drive studs, or an overly tight front rivet.

YES ▶ FIX: Repair or replace blades. If the grease guards are loose and they are held on by screws, tighten the screws. Other faults require replacement of the blades.
△

Worn latch hole?

TEST: If knife makes noise only when blades are inserted but there are no apparent defects in the blades, unplug the knife and remove the driver assembly (see *Disassembling an electric knife*, p.197). Examine holes in latch springs for wear.

NO ◀

YES ▶ FIX: Replace driver arms. The driver assembly has already been removed as part of the test. For the knife illustrated in the exploded view on p.196, the entire driver assembly must be replaced as a unit. On other models, the driver arms can be slipped off the assembly and replaced separately.
△△

Noisy motor, fan, or bearings?

TEST: Tighten all screws in knife and reassemble it. If it is still noisy, even with the blades removed, the problem is due to a moving part inside the knife. Unplug knife and remove upper housing (see *Disassembling the knife*, p.197). Turn motor by pushing on fan blade. Listen for rotor rubbing against field. Pull up on motor shaft. If it is loose, the bearings are worn.

YES ▶ FIX: Repair or replace worn or broken parts. Pull damaged wiring away from fan and reinsulate it with plastic electrical tape. Replace damaged bearings. If rotor is rubbing against field, take appliance to a repair shop to see if repairs are worth while.
△△

Ease of fix: △ simple △△ average △△△ difficult

Troubleshooting a knife that slices poorly

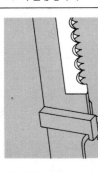

The blades will stay sharp if used properly. Do not try to sharpen them. Blades should be replaced if tooth height on both is not the same.

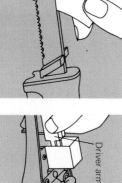

If knife double slices, you may be pressing too hard or blade gap may be excessive. Paper should fit snugly if inserted between blades.

Driver arm

Worn gear teeth will cause weak cutting. To test, hold driver arm. If you can turn motor shaft by hand, teeth on worm wheel are stripped.

Mixers

Motor does not run or runs sluggishly

If the mixer does not run at all, look for a blown house fuse, broken power cord, or faulty on-off switch as the cause. Sluggish operation may be due to a food mixture too thick for the mixer to handle. The motor or speed control mechanism may also be responsible. These parts are covered in *Universal motors*, pp.132–134.

Food mixture too thick?

TEST: Remove bowl and operate mixer over its entire speed range. If it runs normally, the food mixture in the bowl may have been too thick. Note: If beaters interfere with each other because they are bent or because the slots in the gear shafts are misaligned, see *Mixer makes excessive noise*, p.201.

YES→ FIX: Use higher speed setting and thin out mixture. Caution: If motor hums but does not run, shut mixer off immediately to prevent motor damage. △

Power off at outlet?

TEST: Unplug power cord and check wall outlet with a lamp you know is working.

YES→ FIX: Replace fuse or reset circuit breaker. See p.127. If fuse keeps blowing, see *Mixer blows fuses*, p.202. △

Power cord broken?

TEST: Unplug power cord, remove screws in baseplate, and lift off housing. Undo wire nuts and clip jumper wire across power cord leads. Set volt-ohm meter (p.124) to RX1 scale and clip its probes to the prongs of the plug. Bend and pull power cord (see *Testing for open circuits*, p.200). If cord is OK, meter will read zero ohms; if broken, needle will jump around or read high.

YES→ FIX: Replace power cord. Use a manufacturer's replacement. Be sure wire nuts are on firmly and cord is seated on strain relief fitting when reassembling. △△

On-off switch dirty or broken?

TEST: If mixer has a separate on-off switch inside housing (as in model shown in the exploded view), unplug power cord and remove housing. Turn the speed cam to *High* position. With volt-ohm meter on RX1 scale, clip its probes across on-off switch terminals (see *Testing for open circuits*, p.200). If switch is OK, meter will read zero; if broken or dirty, meter will read high.

YES→ FIX: Clean contacts or replace switch. Polish contacts of on-off switch with very fine (No. 400) sandpaper. If problem persists, replace switch. On model illustrated, switch is built into the gear cover and entire cover must be replaced. △△

Motor or speed regulator faulty?

If the above tests fail to isolate the problem, the trouble lies in the motor or speed regulator. Worn brushes or a bad wire in the motor's field coil or rotor may be to blame. Problems with the speed regulator depend on the type used in your mixer (governor, silicon controlled rectifier, or tapped field). See *Universal motors*, pp.132–134, for information on testing and repairing the motor and speed regulator or else take the appliance to an authorized repair shop.

Ease of fix: △ simple △△ average △△△ difficult

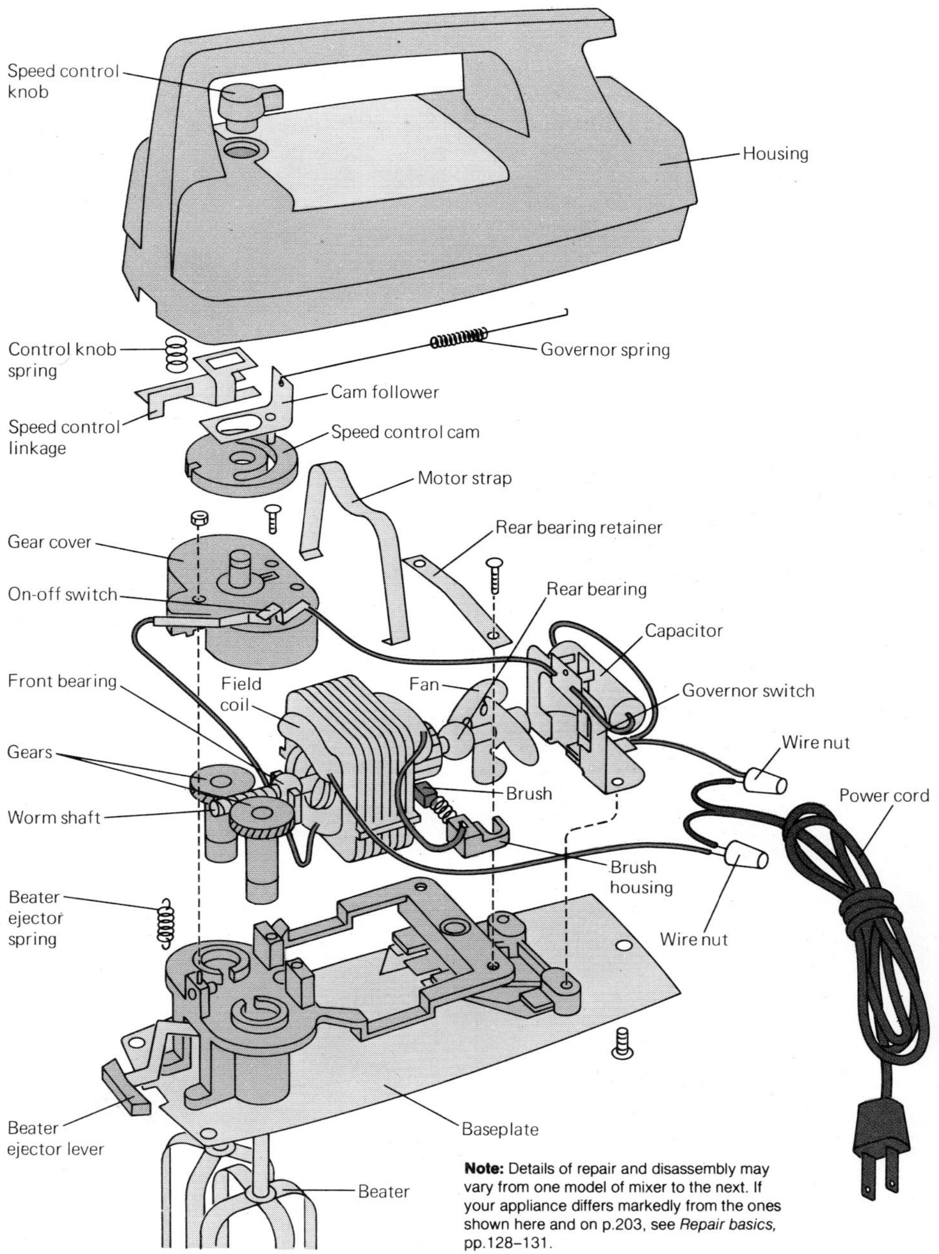

Housing
Governor spring
Speed control knob
Cam follower
Speed control cam
Control knob spring
Speed control linkage
Motor strap
Rear bearing retainer
Rear bearing
Capacitor
Governor switch
Wire nut
Wire nut
Power cord
Brush
Brush housing
Fan
Gear cover
On-off switch
Field coil
Front bearing
Gears
Worm shaft
Beater ejector spring
Baseplate
Beater
Beater ejector lever

Note: Details of repair and disassembly may vary from one model of mixer to the next. If your appliance differs markedly from the ones shown here and on p.203, see *Repair basics*, pp.128–131.

Mixers

Disassembling the mixer

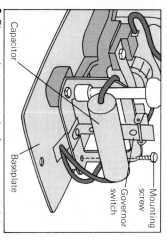

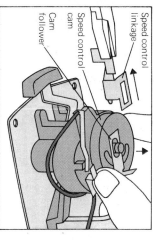

1. Unplug power cord from wall outlet and remove mixer from stand. Eject beaters. Take out screws from baseplate and lift off housing along with speed control knob. Undo both wire nuts and remove power cord.

Speed control linkage

Speed control cam

Cam follower

3. Compress the control knob spring and withdraw it from speed control linkage. Disconnect governor spring from cam follower, pull off speed control linkage, and remove cam follower, and speed cam.

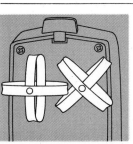

Capacitor

Mounting screw

Governor switch

Baseplate

5. Disconnect governor spring from governor switch, remove the switch's mounting screws, and lift it from baseplate. To free governor switch completely, unsolder its lead from the on-off switch.

---

2. Take out screws and remove rear bearing retainer. This will free the brush assemblies, which should also be removed. Ease brush assemblies and springs from jumping out.

Power cord

Wire nuts

Housing

Brush

Bearing retainer

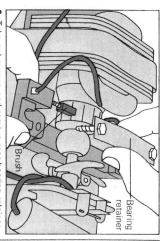

Gear

4. Disconnect ejector spring from gear cover. Remove screws and nut holding gear cover in place and take out cover. Pull out gears from above. See *Reassembly tips,* at right, when reinstalling the gears.

Gear cover

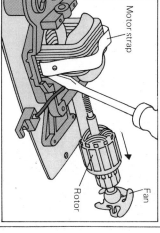

Motor strap

Rotor

Fan

6. Pry off motor strap (force is required) and lift off motor assembly (field, rotor, fan, and bearings). Pull out rotor and fan from rear. To free field, unsolder its lead from the on-off switch.

Testing for open circuits

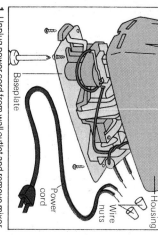

Power cord

Jumper

To meter

1. Test power cord by unplugging mixer, freeing power cord leads. Clip jumper across leads and attach volt-ohm meter probes to prongs of plug. Bend cord during test.

Speed control cam

On-off switch

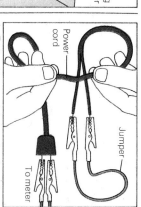

2. Clip meter probes to terminals of on-off switch and turn speed control cam to *High.* If switch is built into gear cover, cover must be replaced too if switch is broken.

Use RX1 scale for both tests.
Test 1: Meter will read zero ohms if power cord is OK; needle will jump or read high if cord is broken.
Test 2: Zero ohms means switch is OK; high ohms means it is broken or dirty.

Reassembly tips

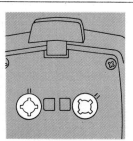

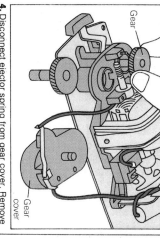

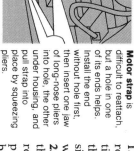

Motor strap is difficult to reattach, but a hole in one of its ends helps. Install the end without hole first, then insert one jaw of long-nose pliers into hole, the other under housing, and pull strap into place by squeezing pliers.

Motor strap

Proper alignment of gears is vital. They should also be put back into the same holes they came from. Sometimes marks on baseplate show how slots in gear shafts should align. Gears on some mixers are marked on top.

If mixer lacks any notches or marks to help align gears, use the beaters. Simply insert beaters into gear shafts and adjust position of gears so that blade of one beater bisects angle formed by blades of other beater.

Use and care

1. The bowl of a stand mixer should rotate slowly when the mixer is in operation. If it does not, clean and lubricate the turntable's pivot pin and the hole it sits in. Clean with detergent and fine steel wool. Lubricate with mineral oil.

2. The beaters should just clear or graze the bottom of the bowl if the bowl is to rotate properly. See *Height adjustment,* p.201, for information on correcting beater height.

3. Turn speed control off and unplug the mixer whenever you are attaching or removing the beaters, taking the mixer off the stand, or putting it on the stand.

4. Be sure mixer is unplugged when you clean it. Wipe the housing and baseplate with a damp cloth. Never immerse the mixer in water. A mild, nonabrasive cleaner can be used for stubborn spots. The beaters and bowl can be cleaned in a dishwasher or in the sink. Clogged air vents on the housing may cause the motor to overheat. Clean out dirt with a pipe cleaner. If necessary, remove housing; wash in warm, sudsy water.

5. If you need to scrape the sides of the mixing bowl during operation to help the mixing process, use a rubber spatula. Do not use metal or wooden implements and be sure to keep your hands away from the beaters while the mixer is running.

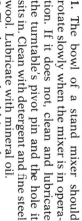

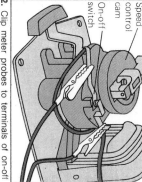

Motor runs but beaters do not turn

The beater gears or the beaters themselves are responsible if the motor runs but the beaters do not turn. The beaters may be slipping in their shafts, their blades may be clashing, or the gears may be stripped. Fixes include replacing the beaters and cleaning, realigning, or replacing the beater gears.

Beaters not locked into gear shafts?

NO→ TEST: Operate mixer without beaters. If gear shafts turn normally, shut off mixer, unplug power cord, and insert beaters. The fins on beater shafts should snap firmly into the matching slots in gear shafts. Twist the beaters. They should not slip in the gear shafts. If they do, gear shafts may be clogged or beater fins may be worn.

YES→ FIX: Clean gear shafts; replace beaters if necessary. If fins are worn, replace beaters. If gear shafts are clogged, unplug mixer and remove gears (see *Disassembling the mixer*, p.200). Poke out dirt with toothpick, then thoroughly clean gears in warm, sudsy water. When reassembling, lubricate gears with multipurpose grease. △△

Blades of beaters clashing?

NO→ TEST: If mixer runs normally with blades removed but not when they are in, the beaters may be clashing. Remove beaters and pulse mixer on and off until slots of one gear shaft are perpendicular to sides of housing. If the gears are properly aligned, the slots of the other gear should make a 45° angle with housing sides.

YES→ FIX: Realign beater gears. Unplug mixer and remove gear cover (see *Disassembling the mixer*, p.200). Disengage gears from worm gear and shift them to proper alignment. The baseplate or the gears may be marked to aid in alignment. If there are no markings, use blades of beaters as guides. When fully inserted, the blades of one beater should split the angle made by the blades of the other. △△

Stripped teeth on beater gears?

TEST: Unplug mixer. Insert one beater and try turning it. If beater turns, gears are stripped. Note: Apply firm pressure to beater but do not use excessive force. Repeat the test with the beater in the other opening.

YES→ FIX: Replace beater gears. Always replace both even though only one appears bad. Remove gear cover and lift out gears (see *Disassembling the mixer*, p.200). Lubricate gears with multipurpose grease when reassembling and be sure to align them correctly. △△

Mixer makes excessive noise

Noisy operation may be due to something as simple as the beaters hitting the bowl. It may also be the result of incorrectly aligned gears that cause the beater blades to clash, loose parts in the mixer, or problems with the motor or bearings. Repairs include tightening screws and realigning or replacing parts.

Beater hits bowl?

NO→ TEST: The beaters of stand mixers should just clear the bottom of the bowl.

YES→ FIX: Adjust height. Unplug mixer and remove it from stand. Lift up hinge and turn screw to raise or lower the hinge. △

Beaters striking each other?

NO→ TEST: Run mixer at lowest speed while watching beaters to see if they strike each other. Also check the beater shafts. They should spin straight, with hardly any wobble. Next, check gear alignment. If the gears are properly aligned, the blade of one beater should split the angle formed by the blades of the other beater.

YES→ FIX: Replace bent beaters or adjust gears. If beaters are damaged or wobble when they run, they should be replaced. If the gears are misaligned, unplug mixer, remove gear cover (see *Disassembling the mixer*, p.200), and realign gears. The baseplate or the gears themselves may be marked to aid in alignment. If there are no markings, insert the beaters into the gear shafts and use the beater blades as a guide, as in the test. △△

Loose parts on mixer?

NO→ TEST: Touch various parts of mixer while it is running to see if you can find source of noise. Tighten screws inside and outside mixer to see if this solves the problem.

YES→ FIX: Tighten loose parts. Unplug mixer and remove housing (see *Disassembling the mixer*, p.200). Tighten all screws. Reassemble mixer, tighten body screws, and make sure all knobs are snug. △△

Defect in drive train?

If the above tests fail to isolate the problem, the source of the noise is probably in the drive train. See *Universal motors*, pp.132–134, or take mixer to authorized repairman.

Ease of fix: △ simple △△ average △△△ difficult

Gear test

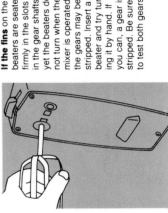

If the fins on the beaters are seated firmly in the slots in the gear shafts yet the beaters do not turn when the mixer is operated, the gears may be stripped. Insert a beater and try turning it by hand. If you can, a gear is stripped. Be sure to test both gears.

Height Adjustment

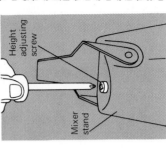

Height adjusting screw

Mixer stand

The height of stand mixers should generally be set so that the beaters are just above or just grazing the bottom of the bowl when the mixer is not running. The adjustment screw may be in the stand, as shown in the illustration, or on the mixer itself. See your owner's manual if in doubt.

Troubleshooting the capacitor

Mixers with governor-type speed controls, like the one shown in the exploded view on page 199, use an electrical device called a capacitor to reduce sparking at the contacts of the governor switch. A short circuit in the capacitor will cause the mixer to run at high speed only. An open circuit in the capacitor will result in excessive radio and television interference. The volt-ohm meter (p.124) can be used to test the capacitor if the meter has a setting of RX10,000 or greater. To make the test, set the meter to this scale, prop open the contacts of the governor switch, and touch the meter probes to the capacitor's leads. If the capacitor is OK, the needle of the meter will dip toward the low end of the ohms scale and then climb back to the high end. (The lower the resistance scale, the quicker this will happen.) A steady reading of zero ohms means the capacitor is shorted. A reading that stays steadily high means there is an open circuit. Double check your result by reversing the meter probes and testing the capacitor again.

Mixers

Mixer shocks user

A frayed power cord, an electrically live component grounded to (touching) a metal part, or leakage current due to faulty insulation will cause shocking. In the case of a frayed cord or grounding, the part can be fixed or replaced. If leakage current is suspected, the mixer should be taken to a repairman.

Power cord frayed?

TEST: Receiving a shock from power cord is sufficient evidence it needs repair.

 FIX: Replace power cord. Unplug mixer and remove housing. Undo wire nuts and withdraw power cord. (See *Disassembling the mixer*, p.200.) Be sure power cord is seated on strain relief device when reassembling.

Leakage current present?

TEST: If you receive a shock from an exposed metal part of the mixer, unplug power cord, set volt-ohm meter (p.124) to RX100 scale, and turn speed control switch to *High*. Clip one meter probe to a metal body part of mixer, the other to either prong of the plug. If meter reads high, leakage current is indicated.

 FIX: Take mixer to authorized repairman. Eliminating leakage current requires special equipment. Note: It is possible the shock is not caused by leakage current, but by a wire that becomes grounded only when the mixer is on. To investigate this, proceed with tests before taking mixer to repair shop.

Internal wiring grounded to exposed metal part?

TEST: Unplug power cord and remove mixer's housing (see *Disassembling the mixer*, p.200). With volt-ohm meter set to RX100 scale, clip one probe to baseplate, the other to a prong of the plug. Turn speed switch to *High* and bend and pull wires in mixer. If needle of meter jumps when a wire is handled, that wire is grounded.

 FIX: Repair grounded wires. Reinsulate bare spots on wires with plastic electrical tape. If problem remains (or if the test failed to turn up a bad wire), the motor's field winding or rotor winding may be grounded. See *Universal motors*, pp.132–134, for information on troubleshooting and repair.

Mixer blows fuses

When a fuse blows or circuit breaker trips, it means there is either an electrical overload or a short circuit. Reducing the number of appliances in the circuit will eliminate the overload. If tests show the power cord is short-circuited, replace the cord. To check the motor for shorts, see *Universal motors*, pp.132–134.

Circuit overloaded?

TEST: To check for overloads, see p.127. Too many appliances in a circuit is the commonest cause of blown fuses or tripped circuit breakers.

FIX: Reduce number of appliances in the circuit. Caution: Never replace a fuse or breaker with one having a larger capacity.

Short circuit in power cord or plug?

TEST: Unplug power cord and remove mixer housing (see *Disassembling the mixer*, p.200). Examine power cord, plug, and adjacent parts for bare wires and burn marks. Unscrew both wire nuts and disconnect the power cord leads from the wires they are attached to. Set volt-ohm meter (p.124) to RX100 scale and clip its probes to the prongs of the plug. Bend and pull power cord during test. If power cord is OK, meter will read high; if broken, needle will jump around or read zero.

 **FIX: Replace power cord.** Use manufacturer's replacement. Be sure power cord is seated correctly on strain relief device and corresponding notch in housing when reassembling.

Short circuit in motor?

If the above tests fail to locate the trouble, there is probably a short circuit in the motor or the wiring associated with it. See *Universal motors*, pp.132–134, for information on testing and repairs or take appliance to an authorized repair shop.

Ease of fix: △ simple   △△ average   △△△ difficult

Testing for shock hazards and short circuits

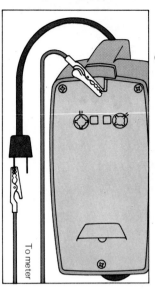

1. To test mixer for leakage current, clip one probe of the volt-ohm meter to either prong of the plug, the other probe to the metal baseplate, and turn speed control knob to *High*.

To meter

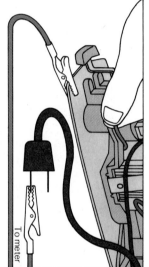

2. Check for grounded internal wiring with power cord unplugged and housing removed. Clip probes of meter to baseplate and plug, set speed cam to *High* position, and tug on individual wires.

To meter

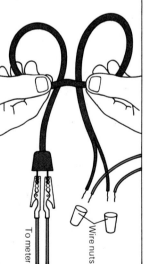

3. Short circuit in power cord is likely cause of blown fuses. Unplug mixer, open housing, and free power cord leads from other wires. Clip volt-ohm meter probes to plug; bend cord during test.

To meter

Wire nuts

 Use RX100 scale for all tests.
Test 1: If meter reads high, leakage current is present.
Test 2: If needle jumps when a wire is handled, wire is grounded.
Test 3: If meter reads high, power cord is OK; if needle jumps or reads zero ohms, cord is shorted.

Differences in mixer design

Whatever differences there are between hand-held and stand mixers have to do with the need to make hand-held mixers lighter in weight. This means that they have smaller motors, more compact housings, and, usually, fewer speed settings. Otherwise, the two types are much the same and the troubleshooting information in this section applies as well to one as to the other.

The area of major variation between one make and model of electric mixer and another, whether it is a hand-held or a stand mixer, is the kind of mechanism used to regulate motor speed. Three systems are in use: governor control, tapped field, and silicon controlled rectifier (SCR). Unplug the mixer and rotate the speed control knob. If it moves smoothly, your mixer probably uses a governor or SCR control. If the knob has click stops at the various speed settings or if speed control is by pushbutton, the mixer is probably a tapped field model.

Governor controls

Governors are mechanical devices that keep the mixer at a preselected speed. They cut off power to the motor if the mixer starts going too fast and turn the power back on if the mixer is going too slowly. The exploded view on page 199 shows a mixer with a governor control.

In operation, the actuator, a sleevelike device at the end of the motor shaft, is pushed against the arm of the governor switch when the motor is running. The force of the push increases as motor speed rises. Depending on the amount of tension exerted by the governor spring, the actuator maintains a constant motor speed by opening and shutting the contacts of the governor switch. Although all governors operate on the same principle (a switch that is opened or closed depending on motor speed), their designs differ in details. (One common type uses a scissorlike actuator; the scissors close as the speed increases, and this movement is used to turn the governor switch off.) If your mixer has a governor and the motor surges when in use, the actuator may be sticky or broken. Unplug the power cord and remove the rotor assembly (see Disassembling the mixer, p.200). The actuator should move freely on the motor shaft. If it does not, polish the shaft with crocus cloth. Also, check the small button at the end of the actuator—it sometimes melts off. If there are signs of damage, replace the actuator.

Tapped field controls

Tapped field mixers can be spotted easily because they have several wire leads going from the motor's field coil to the speed control switch (at least three, often as many as six). If the mixer fails to operate at some speeds, one of the field windings may be bad, the speed control switch may be dirty or broken, or some of the connections between the motor and switch may be bad. Try spraying the switch with electrical contact cleaner (p.123) as a first fix. If the problem persists, refer to the Universal motors section (pp.132–134) or take the mixer to a qualified repairman.

SCR controls

Silicon controlled rectifiers (SCR's) are solid state (transistor) devices and troubleshooting is difficult. If the mixer's motor does not operate at all, and other possible causes have been eliminated, there is a good chance that the SCR is at fault. Replacing it on that basis alone, however, is a gamble. In most instances it is wiser to take the mixer to an authorized repairman.

Mixers with separate power cords

In addition to differences in switches and speed regulation systems, there are relatively minor brand-to-brand variations in power cords. Quite a few are detachable rather than built in (the mixer in the exploded view on page 199 has a built-in power cord). Troubleshoot a separate cord just as you would a built-in cord except for one thing: The jumper wire should be attached across the female terminals rather than across the cord leads as shown in the test for open circuits on page 200.

If there is a partial or total loss of power in a mixer with a separate power cord, the terminals on the cord or mixer may be dirty or corroded. Clean the male terminals on the cord with steel wool. Spray the female terminals on the cord with electrical contact cleaner (p.123) and work the plug on and off several times to rub away corrosion.

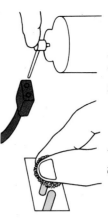

Open circuit test for separate power cord.

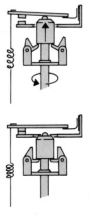

Cleaning power cord terminals.

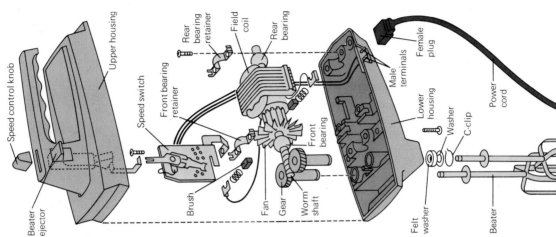

Speed control knob · Upper housing · Rear bearing retainer · Field coil · Rear bearing · Speed switch · Front bearing retainer · Front bearing · Male terminals · Female plug · Lower housing · Washer · C-clip · Power cord · Felt washer · Beater · Beater ejector · Brush · Fan · Gear · Worm shaft

Governor: Switch closed (left) and open (right).

Appliance does not heat at one or more switch settings

In the case of a rotisserie that does not heat at all and whose spit does not turn, look for a blown house fuse or broken power cord. If the spit is working or if the appliance is a broiler-oven, possible causes of the trouble also include a broken heating element, switch, or thermostat, as well as defective wiring.

Power off at outlet?

TEST: Unplug power cord and check wall outlet with a lamp you know is working.

NO →

YES → **FIX: Replace fuse or reset circuit breaker.** See p.127. If fuse keeps blowing, see *Appliance blows fuses,* p.207.
▷

Heating element broken?

TEST: Unplug power cord and remove heating element. Set volt-ohm meter (p.124) to RX1 scale and clip its probes to terminals of heating element. If element is OK, meter will read between 10 and 20 ohms; if element is broken, meter will read high. Note: (1) If appliance has motor, the spit will turn even though heating element is broken. (2) If there are two heating elements, it is unlikely both will fail together.

NO →

YES → **FIX: Replace heating element.** Note: If heating element is not of plug-in type, it will be necessary to disassemble appliance in order to replace it (as well as to test it). In some cases, leads to heating element must be cut and soldered onto new element with high-temperature (silver) solder.
▷

Power cord broken?

TEST: Unplug power cord and remove back panel and control panel. Clip jumper wire across power cord leads. Set volt-ohm meter to RX1 scale and attach its probes to the prongs of the plug. Bend and pull power cord. If cord is OK, meter will read high; if cord is broken, needle will jump around or read zero ohms.

NO →

YES → **FIX: Replace power cord.** One power cord lead was freed during the test. Remove the relief device with pliers, rotate it a quarter turn, and withdraw it and the power cord from control panel. Save heat insulating sleeves and install them on new power cord from manufacturer.
▷▷

Bad wiring or corroded terminals?

TEST: With appliance unplugged and disassembled, examine wires for obvious breaks. Pull on wires near terminals to make sure they are strong. Clean dirty terminals and repair broken wires (see **Fix**), then reassemble appliance and operate it to see if it is working properly.

NO →

YES → **FIX: Clean terminals; replace broken wiring.** Spray terminals with electrical contact cleaner (p.123), then take them off and put them on again several times to break up corrosion. (If terminals are screw-on type, work screws in and out.) Replace broken wires with new ones from manufacturer.
▷▷

Thermostat broken?

TEST: Unplug power cord and remove control panel from oven body. Turn temperature control knob to highest position and set volt-ohm meter to RX1 scale. Touch probes of meter to terminals of thermostat. If thermostat is OK, meter will read zero ohms; if it is broken, meter will read high.

YES → **FIX: Replace thermostat.** Remove leads from thermostat terminals. Carefully pry off temperature control knob with screwdriver and undo nut securing thermostat to panel face. Lift off thermostat from inside control panel.
▷▷

Switch broken?

TEST: Unplug power cord and separate the control panel from oven body. Set volt-ohm meter to RX1 scale and clip one probe to switch terminal holding power cord lead, the other probe to each of the other switch terminals in turn. Each time run switch through all settings. For each test, the meter should read zero ohms at one or more switch settings. If it does not, the switch is broken.

YES → **FIX: Replace switch.** Make a record of which lead goes to which switch terminal. Remove leads from switch. Peel back faceplate with a knife so that switch mounting screws can be reached, undo screws, and pull switch from panel. Apply firm, even pressure on knife when peeling back faceplate, taking care not to cut yourself or damage faceplate. If switch is riveted in place, file off rivet heads and use machine screws, nuts, and lock washers when installing new switch.
▷▷▷

Ease of fix: ▷ simple   ▷▷ average   ▷▷▷ difficult

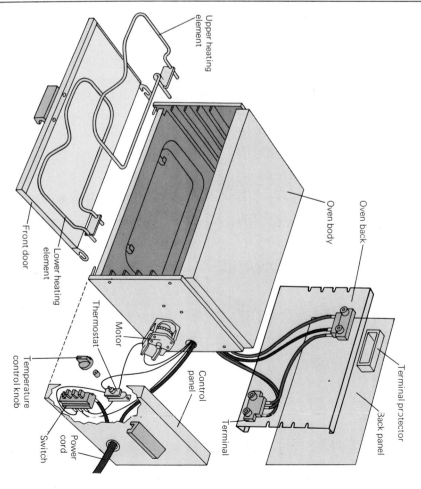

Upper heating element

Oven body

Oven back

Terminal protector

Back panel

Terminal

Lower heating element

Thermostat

Motor

Temperature control knob

Front door

Control panel

Switch

Power cord

Note: Details of repair and disassembly may vary from one model of rotisserie or broiler-oven to the next. If your appliance differs markedly from the ones discussed and illustrated in this section, see *Repair basics,* pp.128–131.

Disassembling a rotisserie

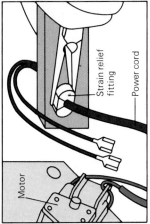
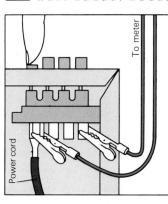

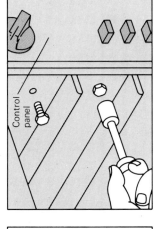
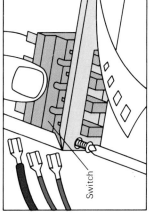

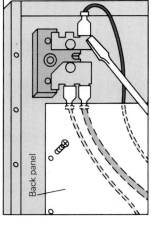
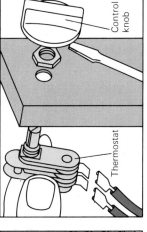

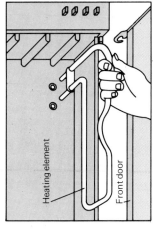
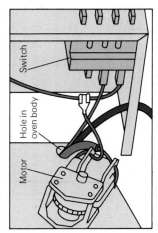

1. Unplug power cord and let appliance cool off. Take out spit, grill, and baking tray and lift off front door. Pull out both upper and lower heating elements.

Heating element; Front door

2. Remove screws and take off back panel and terminal protectors. Label the various leads and the terminals to which they attach, then disconnect the leads.

Back panel

3. Remove screws holding control panel to oven (they are inside oven) and pull away control panel. Do not take out motor mounting screws (the ones near spit).

Control panel

4. Trace power cord lead to the switch, label its terminal there, and pull off lead. Squeeze strain relief fitting, rotate it a quarter turn, and remove cord.

Strain relief fitting; Power cord; Motor

5. Label the switch terminal to which motor lead attaches and remove lead. Free the control panel from oven body by feeding out leads through hole in side.

Switch; Motor; Hole in oven body

6. Remove leads from thermostat terminals, pry off temperature control knob, undo mounting nut, and pull out thermostat from control panel face.

Control knob; Thermostat

7. Pull off remaining leads to switch after labeling terminals. Peel up facing, remove screws, and take out switch. (If rivet is used, file off its head.)

Switch

8. Feed second motor lead out through hole in oven body, remove motor mounting screws from inside oven, and take off motor unit including gears.

Motor and gears; Motor mounting screws

Testing heating element and power cord for open circuits

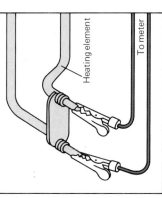

1. Unplug power cord and remove heating element that is not heating. Clip probes of volt-ohm meter to terminals of element.

Heating element; To meter

Set meter to RX1 scale for both tests.
Test 1: If element is OK, meter will read 10 to 20 ohms; if element is broken, meter will read high.
Test 2: If cord is OK, meter will read zero ohms; if cord is broken, needle will jump or read high.

2. If power cord is broken, appliance will not work at all. Clip jumper to cord leads, attach probes to plug, bend and pull cord.

Jumper; To meter

Testing thermostat and switch for open circuits

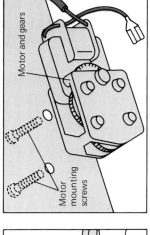
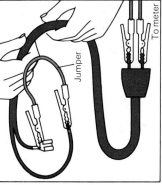

1. To check thermostat, unplug power cord and turn control to *High*. Touch volt-ohm meter probes to thermostat terminals.

Temperature control knob; Thermostat; To meter

Set meter to RX1 scale for both tests.
Test 1: If meter reads zero ohms, thermostat is OK; if it reads high, thermostat is faulty.
Test 2: If switch is OK, meter will read zero ohms at least one switch setting for each test. If it does not, switch is broken.

2. Clip one probe to terminal holding power cord, second to each other terminal in turn. Run switch through all settings each time.

Power cord; To meter

Rotisserie heats but spit does not turn

Since the appliance heats, the power cord and wall outlet must be OK and the trouble has to lie in a defective switch, bad wiring, corroded terminals, or a problem with the motor unit (including gears and spit). Corroded terminals can be cleaned. Other difficulties require replacement of the faulty part with a new one.

Switch broken?

TEST: Unplug power cord and separate control panel from oven body (see *Disassembling a rotisserie,* p.205). Set volt-ohm meter (p.124) to RX1 scale and clip one probe to switch terminal with power cord lead, the other to switch terminal with motor lead. Set switch to *Rotisserie.* If switch is OK, meter will read zero ohms; if it does not, switch is broken.

FIX: Replace switch. Make a record of which lead goes to which switch terminal. Remove leads from switch. Peel back faceplate with a knife, undo screws, and pull switch from panel. Apply firm, even pressure on knife when peeling back faceplate, taking care not to cut yourself or damage faceplate. If switch is riveted in place, file off rivet heads. Use machine screws, nuts, and lock washers when installing new switch.

Bad wiring or corroded terminals?

TEST: With appliance unplugged and control panel removed, examine motor leads for breaks. Clean terminals and repair wires (see **Fix**), then reassemble rotisserie and operate it to see if it is working properly.

FIX: Clean terminals; replace broken wiring. Spray terminals with electrical contact cleaner (p.123), then push them on and off several times. (If terminals are screwed on, work several screws in and out.) Replace broken wires with new ones from manufacturer.

Motor unit broken?

TEST: With power cord unplugged, remove motor and gear unit (see *Disassembling a rotisserie,* p.205). Spin rotor by hand. If it does not turn easily, it is jammed. Spin one large gear near the rotor. The rotor should turn rapidly and the spit should turn slowly. If they do not, a gear may be stripped. Finally, check field coil for possible open circuit. Separate leads of coil from their terminals. Set volt-ohm meter to RX1 scale and clip its probes to the leads. If coil is OK, the volt-ohm meter will read 40 to 100 ohms; if the coil is bad, volt-ohm meter will read high.

FIX: Replace motor. Replace motor and gear train as a unit. New motor assembly will include gear train and leads. Save heat insulating sleeve from old motor and install it on the new unit. Be sure to note terminals to which motor leads are attached.

Testing the motor

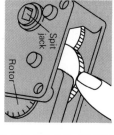

Field coil

To meter

Set meter to RX1 scale. If field coil of motor is OK, meter will read between 40 and 100 ohms. If coil is broken, meter will read high.

If spit does not turn, unplug and disassemble rotisserie, clip probes of volt-ohm meter to the leads of the motor's field coil.

Checking the gears

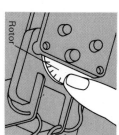

Rotor

Spit jack

Rotor

Jammed parts may prevent the spit from turning. Try spinning rotor by hand. If it is hard to turn, the rotor or its gears are jammed or sticking. It may be necessary to replace the motor unit.

Spin the large gear nearest the rotor by hand. The rotor should spin rapidly when the gear does, and the spit should revolve slowly. If it does not, one of the gears may be stripped.

Improper temperature

Should the oven seem to run too hot or too cold, try repositioning the control knob. If that does not work, ascertain how far wrong the temperature is. For small errors, compensate by setting the control knob higher or lower. Otherwise, replace the thermostat. Note that the temperature control may work only on *Bake.*

Thermostat or control knob incorrectly mounted?

TEST: With appliance unplugged, turn temperature control knob as far as it will go in either direction. It should line up with the highest and lowest temperature readings at its extreme positions. If it does not, the knob is incorrectly positioned.

FIX: Reposition temperature control knob. Pry knob from thermostat shaft with screwdriver and replace it so that it indicates highest and lowest temperatures at its extreme positions. If knob is keyed to thermostat shaft so that it cannot be repositioned, loosen thermostat mounting nut and rotate thermostat so that knob reads correctly.

Thermostat broken?

TEST: Place an oven thermometer on rack inside appliance. Set switch to *Bake* and temperature to 350°F and operate appliance for 30 minutes. If thermostat is OK, thermometer will read between 325°F and 375°F. If it reads over 400°F or under 300°F, thermostat is broken and should be replaced. If the reading is only slightly out of correct range, compensate by simply setting temperature control knob somewhat higher or lower when cooking.

FIX: Replace thermostat. Unplug appliance and wait for it to cool down. Separate the control panel from the oven body (see *Disassembling a rotisserie,* p.205) and remove leads from thermostat terminals. Carefully pry off temperature control knob with screwdriver and undo nut securing thermostat to panel. Lift off thermostat from inside control panel.

Built-in timers

An increasing number of rotisseries and broiler-ovens come equipped with built-in timers. The user sets the cooking time and the timer shuts off the appliance automatically when the time is up. Some models also have a timed outlet that allows the rotisserie or broiler-oven to double as a household timer.

If the timer on your appliance is not working properly, see *Clocks and timers,* pp.152–154. Note that the high temperature of the oven may damage the leads to the timer over a period of time. Food residue may also gum up the timer's switch contacts. Spraying with electrical contact cleaner (p.123) may help.

Ease of fix: △ simple △△ average △△△ difficult

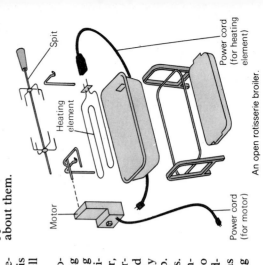

An open rotisserie broiler.

Test 1: Set meter to RX100 scale. If meter reads high, power cord is OK; if meter reads zero ohms or the needle jumps when wire is handled, cord is shorted.

Test 2: Set meter to RX1 scale. If coil is OK, meter will read between 40 and 100 ohms; if coil is shorted, meter will read zero ohms.

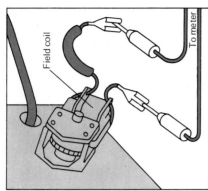

Field coil · To meter

2. Short circuit in field coil of motor may cause fuses to blow. Check by touching probes of volt-ohm meter to leads of coil.

Testing for short circuits

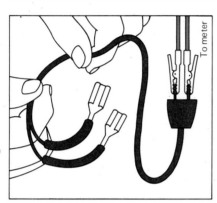

To meter

1. Unplug power cord and free its leads. Clip volt-ohm meter probes to prongs of plug. Bend and pull cord while testing it.

Different styles and models

Two sorts of rotisserie are on the market today: enclosed cabinet models, like the one shown in the exploded view on page 204, and open models, like the one illustrated at right. Both have the same operating parts (heating elements, motor units, and power cords), and the troubleshooting and repair information in this section applies to open rotisseries as well as it does to cabinet types.

In addition to the two varieties of rotisserie, there are broiling and baking appliances that do not have rotating spits. These are usually enclosed or semi-enclosed models and tend to be smaller, lighter, and less expensive than rotisseries. Some come with both upper and lower heating elements, others with only a single element on the bottom or top. There are also a few vertical broilers. These are constructed like oversized, single-slice toasters. One kind uses two heating elements with the meat suspended in a rack between them. Another has a single element and the meat is hung vertically on either side.

Other than differences in disassembly procedure, the instructions in this section apply to all these various models. Toaster ovens are an exception. These are difficult appliances to repair. See *Toasters,* pp.213–218, for additional information about them.

Appliance blows fuses

When a fuse blows or a circuit breaker trips, it means there is either an electrical overload or a short circuit. Reducing the number of appliances in the circuit will eliminate the overload. If tests show the power cord or motor is short-circuited, the cord or motor unit should be replaced with a manufacturer's equivalent.

Circuit overloaded?

TEST: To check for overloads, see p.127. Too many appliances in a circuit is the commonest cause of blown fuses and tripped breakers.

NO → FIX: Reduce number of appliances in the circuit. Caution: Never replace a fuse or breaker with one having a larger capacity. △

Short circuit in power cord or plug?

TEST: Unplug power cord and separate the control panel from the oven body (see *Disassembling a rotisserie,* p.205). Examine power cord and plug for bare wires and burn marks. Free the power cord leads from their terminals. Set volt-ohm meter (p.124) to RX100 scale and clip its probes to the prongs of the plug. Bend and pull cord. If power cord is OK, meter will read high; if cord is shorted, needle will jump around or read zero ohms.

NO → FIX: Replace power cord. Both power cord leads were freed during test. Squeeze strain relief device with pliers, rotate it a quarter turn, and withdraw it and the power cord from control panel. Save heat insulating sleeves and install them on new power cord from manufacturer. △△

Short circuit in motor?

TEST: With power cord unplugged and side panel removed, free both motor leads from their terminals. Set volt-ohm meter to RX1 scale and touch its probes to motor coil leads. If motor is OK, meter will read between 40 and 100 ohms; if motor is shorted, meter will read zero ohms.

YES → FIX: Replace motor. Both motor leads have been freed during test. Remove motor mounting screws from inside oven and remove motor and gear train unit (see *Disassembling a rotisserie,* p.205). New motor assembly will include gear train and leads. Save heat insulating sleeve from old motor and install it on the new unit. Be sure to note terminals to which motor leads are attached. △△

Ease of fix: △ simple △△ average △△△ difficult

Checking the oven temperature

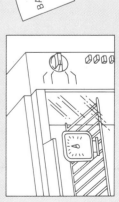

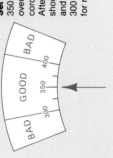

BAD · GOOD · BAD · 300 · 350 · 400

Set temperature control to 350°F, place thermometer on oven shelf, plug in power cord, and put switch to *Bake.* After 30 minutes, thermometer should read between 325°F and 375°F. A reading below 300°F or above 400°F calls for replacing the thermostat.

Rotisseries and broiler-ovens

Appliance shocks user

A frayed power cord, an electrically live component grounded to (touching) a metal part, or leakage current due to faulty insulation will cause shocks. If leakage current is suspected, take the appliance to an authorized repairman. A frayed power cord or grounded wire in the motor or elsewhere should be replaced.

Power cord frayed?

NO ←

TEST: Receiving a shock from power cord is sufficient evidence it needs repair.

YES →

FIX: Replace power cord. Follow instructions given in *Appliance does not heat at one or more switch settings*, p.204, and in *Disassembling a rotisserie*, p.205. △△

Leakage current present?

NO ←

TEST: If you receive a shock when you touch an exposed metal part of the rotisserie or broiler-oven while it is in operation, there is either a grounded wire in the appliance or leakage of current due to defective insulation. To check, unplug power cord and set appliance controls to the position they were at when shock occurred. Set volt-ohm meter (p.124) to RX100 scale and clip one of its probes to metal shell of appliance, the other to either prong of the plug. If meter reads high, leakage current (p.127) is present; otherwise, wiring is grounded.

YES →

FIX: Take appliance to authorized repairman. Eliminating leakage current requires special equipment. Note: It is possible the shock is not caused by leakage current, but by a wire that becomes grounded only when the appliance is running. To investigate this, proceed with tests before going to repair shop. △△△

Internal wiring grounded to shell?

NO ←

TEST: Unplug power cord and disassemble appliance so that control panel and backplate are free from oven body (see *Disassembling a rotisserie*, p.205). Examine wiring for bare spots and loose strands. With volt-ohm meter set to RX100 scale, clip one of its probes to metal shell of oven, the other to either prong of the plug. Be sure appliance switch is in position where shock occurred. Twist and pull each of the wires inside the appliance. If needle jumps when a wire is handled, that wire is grounded.

YES →

FIX: Replace faulty wires. Install a manufacturer's equivalent in place of any wire that is defective or shows signs of damage. Do not try to repair faulty insulation with plastic electrical tape; the wiring inside rotisseries and broiler-ovens is sheathed in asbestos or other high-temperature insulation because of the heat generated by the appliance, and ordinary electrical tape will not stand up. If leads from the power cord are damaged, replace the power cord. △△

Motor wiring grounded?

NO ←

TEST: With power cord unplugged and control panel separated from oven body, remove both motor leads from their terminals. Set volt-ohm meter to RX100 scale and clip one probe to a lead, the other to motor frame. If motor is OK, meter will read high; otherwise, wiring is grounded.

YES →

FIX: Replace motor. Both motor leads were freed during test. Undo motor mounting screws from inside oven and remove motor and gear train unit (see *Disassembling a rotisserie*, p.205). New motor assembly will include gear train and leads. Save heat insulating sleeve from old motor and install it on the new unit. Be sure to note terminals to which motor leads are attached. △△

Ease of fix: △ simple △△ average △△△ difficult

Testing for grounded wires

Use RX100 scale for all tests.
Test 1: High reading means leakage current.
Test 2: If needle jumps when a wire is handled, wire is grounded.
Test 3: If meter reads less than high ohms, field coil is grounded.

1. If rotisserie or broiler-oven shocks when a metal part is touched, it may be due to leakage current or grounding. Clip one probe of volt-ohm meter to prong of plug, the other to metal frame of appliance. Controls should be set as they were when shock occurred.

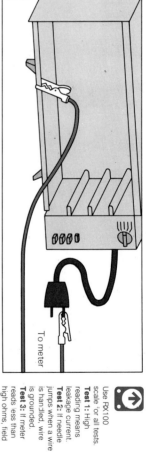

To meter

2. Test internal wires for grounding by clipping meter probes to plug and frame. Set appliance controls as they were when shock occurred. Tug each wire in turn.

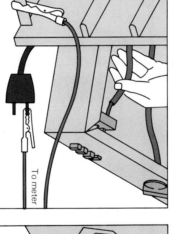

To meter

3. To test motor for possible ground in its field coil, free both of the coil's leads, clip one volt-ohm meter probe to one lead, other to motor frame.

Motor frame
Field coil
Lead from field coil
To meter

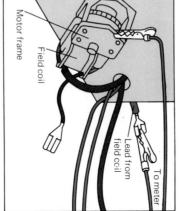

Use and care

1. The spit of a rotisserie will turn more smoothly if the food on it is balanced. Be sure the square end of the spit is fully inserted into the matching hole in the spit jack and that the other end of the spit is in its holder on the oven wall.

2. Unplug power cord from wall outlet and let oven cool before removing heating elements or cleaning the appliance.

3. Do not immerse the heating elements or oven in water. Make sure the oven door is cool before washing it. Clean the door in hot, sudsy water but do not soak it or wash it in a dishwasher.

4. The bottom surface of the oven should shine to reflect heat upward. Clean it with a detergent and a plastic pad. If it is dull, polish it with very fine steel wool. Be sure no metal strands remain near electrical terminals when you are done. Do not use steel wool, scouring pads, or cleaners with harsh abrasives on the exterior shell.

5. If appliance has continuous clean coating on oven, wash it with a soft cloth or sponge, but never clean it with an abrasive, with a caustic cleaner, or with a scouring pad.

Shavers

Motors and shaving heads: the various types

Electric shavers differ from one another in the design of their shaving heads (flat, rotary, flexible curved, and rigid curved) and in the kind of motor they use (rotary or vibrator). The exploded views illustrate two basic designs. The shaver at right uses a rotary motor to drive three rotary heads. The model at the far right has a vibrator motor and a flat shaving head. The heads on both these shavers can be taken apart for cleaning. When reassembling them, be sure to return the

blades to the same heads they came from. Between the exploded views, two curved-head styles are shown. The upper one uses a thin, flexible screen. Its cutter is driven back and forth by the same type of vibrator motor as the flathead model. Below it is the shaving head of a rigid screen model. Its blades are made to oscillate by a connecting rod driven by a rotary motor.

Vibrator motors are extremely simple and seldom need repair. In operation, the vibrator section is pulled back and forth as the field changes polarity at the 60-cycle-per-second rate of the house current. The action is similar to the buzzer of an electric alarm clock.

Rotary motors in shavers are always of the type known as universal. Repairs and troubleshooting are covered in *Universal motors*, pp.132–134. The bearings of these motors occasionally need lubrication. If the brushes have to be replaced, see *How to remove motor brushes*, p.212, as well as *Universal motors*.

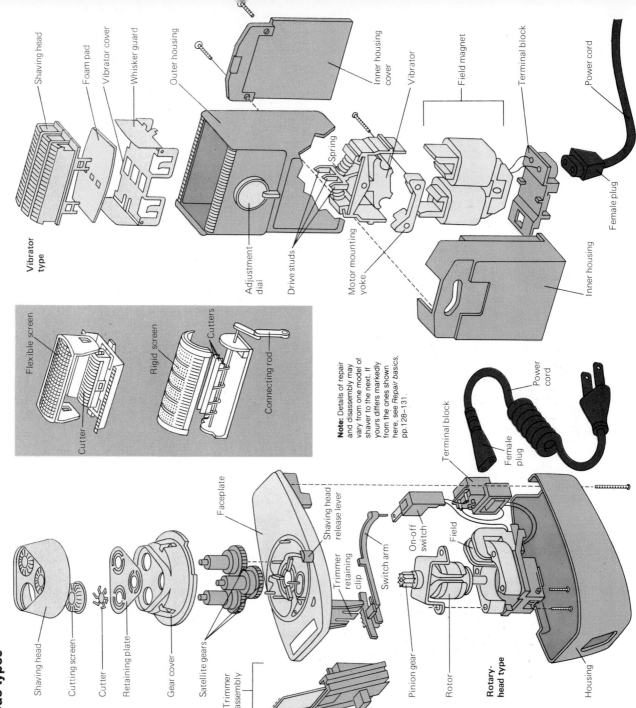

Vibrator type

Shaving head
Foam pad
Vibrator cover
Whisker guard
Outer housing
Inner housing cover
Vibrator
Field magnet
Terminal block
Power cord
Female plug
Spring
Adjustment dial
Drive studs
Motor mounting yoke
Inner housing

Note: Details of repair and disassembly may vary from one model of shaver to the next. If yours differs markedly from the ones shown here, see *Repair basics*, pp.128–131.

Flexible screen
Cutter
Rigid screen
Cutters
Connecting rod

Shaving head
Cutting screen
Cutter
Retaining plate
Gear cover
Satellite gears
Trimmer assembly
Faceplate
Shaving head release lever
Trimmer retaining clip
Switch arm
On-off switch
Field
Pinion gear
Rotor
Power cord
Female plug
Terminal block
Rotary-head type
Housing

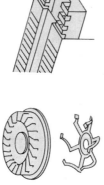

Rotary head cutting unit (left) and flat head (right).

209

Shavers

Disassembling a rotary-head shaver

1. Unplug power cord and remove shaving head as you would for ordinary cleaning, then undo screws in back of shaver and pull off housing.

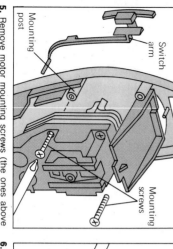

Housing

Faceplate

Shaving head

2. Trimmer assembly can be removed as a unit. Press down on plastic retaining clip at its rear, and slide trimmer out backwards from shaver.

Retaining clip

Trimmer

3. Remove screws in back of faceplate and lift off gear cover. Note: When reinstalling cover, be sure cutout portion is over the shaving head release.

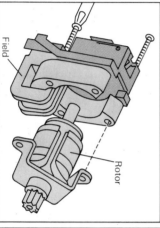

Gear cover

Mounting screws

4. Satellite gears and central pinion gear are now exposed. Pinion gear is permanently attached to motor shaft. Satellite gears can be lifted off.

Satellite gears

Pinion gear

5. Remove motor mounting screws (the ones above the mounting posts). Snap on-off switch from its seat; remove motor, switch, switch arm, terminal block.

Switch arm

Mounting post

Mounting screws

6. Take out brushes (see *How to remove motor brushes*, p.212). Make scratches on bearing support and field (for proper reassembly), unbolt and remove rotor.

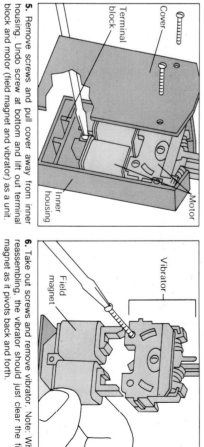

Field

Rotor

Disassembling a shaver with a vibrator motor

1. With power cord unplugged, set adjustment dial to *Clean* and pull off shaving head and foam pad. Next, turn dial to fully retracted position.

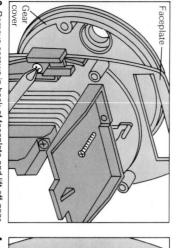

Foam pad

Shaving head

CLEAN

2. Pry apart inner and outer housings with a broad-bladed screwdriver inserted near the adjustment dial so that stud on dial disengages from slot in housing.

Outer housing

Adjustment dial stud

3. After the dial stud is fully disengaged from the inner housing, slide the entire inner body of the shaver out the bottom of the outer housing.

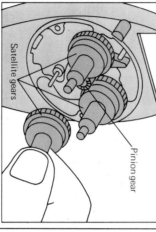

Inner body of shaver

Outer housing

4. Use a penknife to pry sides of vibrator cover off protuberances on inner housing and remove vibrator cover. Do not disturb whisker guards.

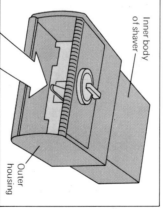

Whisker guards

Vibrator cover

5. Remove screws and pull cover away from inner housing. Undo screw at bottom and lift out terminal block and motor (field magnet and vibrator) as a unit.

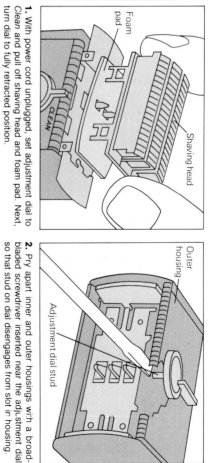

Cover

Terminal block

Motor

Inner housing

6. Take out screws and remove vibrator. Note: When reassembling, the vibrator should just clear the field magnet as it pivots back and forth.

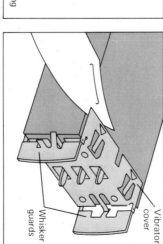

Field magnet

Vibrator

Motor does not run or runs sluggishly

If a shaver motor runs sluggishly or does not operate at all, the problem may be the result of an incorrectly set overseas switch, a blown house fuse, an open circuit in the shaver's power cord or on-off switch, or trouble with the motor itself. Repairs include lubrication, cleaning, and replacement of defective parts.

Shaver set for overseas operation?

TEST: If shaver has a switch to permit using it overseas, check to see whether it is set to the 110-volt or 220-volt position.

FIX: **Set switch to 110 for domestic operation.** Domestic electric service is about 110 volts. Shaver will not run or will run poorly if switch is set for 220-volt operation.

Power off at outlet?

TEST: Unplug power cord and check wall outlet with a lamp you know is working.

FIX: **Replace fuse or reset circuit breaker.** See p.127.

Power cord broken?

Test: With power cord unplugged from both shaver and wall outlet, clip jumper wire across the prongs of its male plug—the plug normally inserted into wall outlet. Set volt-ohm meter (p.124) to RX1 scale and insert its probes into terminals of power cord's female plug—the plug normally pushed onto the terminal pins on shaver. Bend and pull power cord during the test. If power cord is OK, meter will read zero ohms; if power cord is broken, needle of meter will jump around or read high.

FIX: **Replace power cord.** Use a manufacturer's replacement. Note: It is possible that the terminal pins on the shaver or matching female terminals on power cord are dirty. Try cleaning them with electrical contact cleaner (p.123) to see if that solves the problem. Do not try bending the terminal pins on the shaver even if the female plug seems to fit loosely. They are fragile and easily damaged.

On-off switch broken?

TEST: Not all shavers have an on-off switch. If yours does, unplug power cord and disassemble shaver so that switch is accessible. Set volt-ohm meter to RX1 scale and touch its probes to the terminals of the switch. Turn switch to On. If switch is OK, meter will read zero ohms; if it is broken, meter will read high.

FIX: **Replace on-off switch.** Continue disassembly so that motor, drive assembly, switch, and terminal block are out of housing. Remove leads from switch and withdraw switch. Note: On some shavers, the leads can simply be pulled out of the switch terminals; on others, they must be unsoldered. If unsoldering is necessary, use soldering iron as briefly as possible to avoid damage to delicate wiring. △△

Shaving head, motor, or drive assembly jammed?

TEST: If motor hums but does not run, a moving part may be jammed. Try operating shaver with shaving head removed. If it runs normally, the shaving head is damaged. Otherwise, the trouble is in motor or drive unit. Unplug power cord and disassemble shaver. If shaver uses rotary (universal) motor, try turning rotor by hand. If it does not move easily, it is jammed.

FIX: **Clean and lubricate shaver; replace broken parts.** If shaving head is damaged, replace it. Brush hair and other material from shaver. Lubricate drive gears with a commercial gear lubricant, such as Lubriplate. Apply a drop of lightweight machine oil to pivot points in cutter (if any) and to motor bearings. Do not use too much lubricant. If cleaning and lubrication fail to free jammed part, replace it with a new one. △△

Motor faulty?

If previous tests have failed to solve the problem, the trouble is in the motor. If shaver uses a rotary motor, worn brushes, bad bearings, or an open circuit in the field or armature may be to blame. See *Universal motors*, pp.132–134, for information on testing and repairs. To find out how to check the wiring of shavers with vibrator motors, see *Testing for open circuits*, below.

Ease of fix: △ simple △△ average △△△ difficult

Unjamming the motor

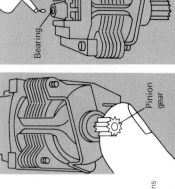

Try spinning rotary motor by hand (left) to see if it is jammed. Lubricating its bearings with light machine oil (right) may improve performance.

Bearing · Pinion gear

Testing for open circuits

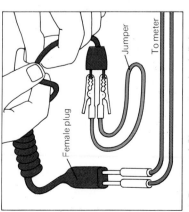

Use RX1 scale for all three tests.
Test 1: If meter reads zero ohms, cord is OK; if needle jumps or reads high, cord is broken.
Test 2: Meter will read zero ohms if switch is OK.
Test 3: Reading of 100–200 ohms means coil is OK. Reading at high end of ohms scale indicates an open circuit.

1. Power cord: Disconnect cord and clip jumper wire to prongs of its male plug. Insert volt-ohm meter probes into female plug and bend cord.

Female plug · Jumper · To meter

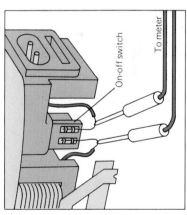

2. On-off switch: Unplug shaver, remove housing, and touch probes of volt-ohm meter to terminals of switch. Switch must be in On position.

On-off switch · To meter

3. Field coil: To check field coil of vibrator motor, remove motor from housing, then touch meter probes to the coil's terminals.

Field coil · Terminal block

Shavers

Shocks, short circuits, and other special problems

An electric shaver that shocks is particularly dangerous since it is normally used in the bathroom, near water. If the power cord shocks, replace it. If a metal body part shocks, use a volt-ohm meter set to the RX100 scale to test the shaver. Unplug the power cord and disassemble the shaver (see p.210). Clip one probe of the meter to a terminal pin of the power cord and the other to a metal body part. Set the shaver's switch to *On* and pull on the various internal wires. If the volt-ohm meter needle jumps when a wire is handled, the wire is grounded. If you cannot find the cause of the shocking, take the shaver to a repairman.

Since shavers are low-power devices, an overloaded circuit is not likely to be the reason that a shaver blows house fuses. The most likely source of the trouble is the power cord. Disconnect it completely and check it with a volt-ohm meter set to the RX100 scale. Clip the meter's probes to the prongs of the power cord's wall plug and bend and pull the cord while testing it. If the cord is shorted, the meter's needle will jump around or read zero ohms.

Worn blades and screens

Worn cutting screens are obvious; they will have holes or missing teeth. Spotting a worn blade is harder. Use a magnifying glass to examine the blade. The blade contacts the screen should be smooth and the blade profile, except with vibrator-head models, should be wider at the cutting edge.

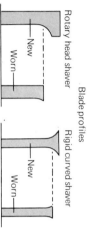

Profiles of new blades (top) and worn blades (bottom).

Rotary head shaver — Blade profiles — Rigid curved shaver
New / Worn

Cordless shavers

A number of shavers are capable of operating on self-contained, rechargeable batteries, called power packs, as well as on house current. In addition to the problems that affect other shavers, cordless models may develop defects in their power packs or charging units. (See *Cordless appliances*, pp.136–137.)

Use and care

There are many shaver models, each with its own special maintenance procedures. Follow your user's manual. Blow out whiskers after every use and then for a thorough cleaning. If you use a shaver cleaner, choose one that will not damage the plastic parts of your shaver.

How to remove motor brushes

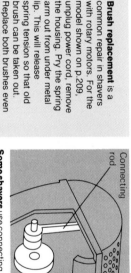

Retaining spring arm
Metal lip
Brush

Brush replacement is a common repair in shavers with rotary motors. For the model shown on p.209, unplug power cord, remove the housing. Pry the spring arm out from under metal lip. This will release spring tension so that old brush can be taken out. Replace both brushes even if only one is worn.

Motor runs but shaver cuts poorly or is noisy

Noisy operation and poor cutting are usually traceable to worn blades or cutting screens. Other causes of the trouble vary, depending on the type of shaver. Shavers with vibrator motors may have a broken drive stud or misaligned vibrator section. If the shaver has a rotary motor, look for a broken gear or connecting rod.

Worn blades or cutting screen?
TEST: Pulse shaver on and off while observing the shaving head. If the blades move properly but shaver pinches, pulls, or does not cut well, the blades or cutting screen are probably worn. Disassemble shaving head. Examine blades for wear; check cutting screen for holes.

 NO

YES FIX: Replace worn parts or entire shaving head. On shavers with multiple blades or cutting screens, replace all blades if one is worn; replace all screens if one is worn. △

Broken drive unit?
TEST: For shavers of vibrator type, remove shaving head and check drive studs. For shavers with rotary (universal) motors, disassemble (p.210) and examine gears. If shaver has curved heads, look for broken connecting rod between motor and blades.

 NO

YES FIX: Replace broken parts. If a drive stud on the vibrator section is broken, replace entire section. When installing, be sure vibrator section just clears body of magnet as it pivots. For shavers with rotary motors, replace gears or drive arms, depending on model. △△

Vibrator or rotor striking field?
TEST: Unplug and disassemble shaver (see p.210). If shaver is vibrator type, be sure that vibrator section just clears field magnet. Blades will not cut if adjustment is poor. Also, if vibrator hits field, shaver will be noisy. For shavers with rotary motor, try spinning rotor by hand. If it is hard to turn or if it scrapes, rotor may be striking field, or bearings may be bad.

 YES FIX: Readjust parts; oil bearings. Adjust vibrator section of vibrator-type shaver so that it just clears field magnet as it pivots. For rotary motors, try lubricating bearings with a drop of light machine oil. If this does not clear up the problem, take the shaver to an authorized repairman. △△

Ease of fix: △ simple △△ average △△△ difficult

Shavers with connecting rods

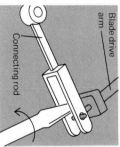

Connecting rod

Some shavers use connecting rods to drive the blades. If rod breaks, shaver will not cut.

Blade drive arm
Connecting rod

Connecting rod of one model has a forked end. Spread it apart to get it off drive arm of blades.

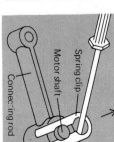

Spring clip
Motor shaft
Connecting rod

Earlier design uses spring clip to hold rod on motor shaft. Pull off clip with small screwdriver.

Toasters

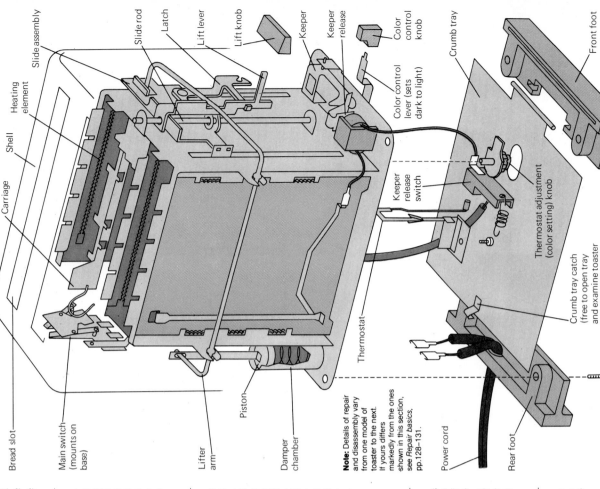

Slide assembly
Slide rod
Latch
Lift lever
Lift knob
Keeper
Keeper release
Color control knob
Crumb tray
Front foot
Heating element
Shell
Carriage
Color control lever (sets dark to light)
Keeper release switch
Thermostat adjustment (color setting) knob
Bread slot
Main switch (mounts on base)
Lifter arm
Piston
Damper chamber
Thermostat
Crumb tray catch (free to open tray and examine toaster from below)
Power cord
Rear foot

Note: Details of repair and disassembly vary from one model of toaster to the next. If yours differs markedly from the ones shown in this section, see *Repair basics,* pp.128–131.

Bread carriage does not stay down

A defect in the locking mechanism will prevent the carriage from staying down when the lift lever is pressed. Burnt toast jamming the carriage or trouble in the thermostat, latch, keeper, or keeper release switch may be to blame. Repairs include adjustment, cleaning, and replacement of defective parts.

Bread carriage obstructed?

TEST: Unplug toaster and press down lift knob. The carriage should lower easily until it locks. If it does not, look through bread slots to see if a broken piece of toast or some other object is blocking it. Open crumb tray and repeat examination from below. If you cannot find what is causing the trouble, remove shell of toaster and check moving parts for obstructions.

YES→ FIX: Clean and lubricate toaster. With toaster unplugged, shake out crumbs, first with toaster upright, then upside down. Brush away crumbs and dirt, especially around moving parts. Clean moving parts and areas that rub together with electrical contact cleaner (p.123) or other nonflammable cleaner designed for electrical work. Lubricate keeper and keeper release with small amounts of graphite. △△

Thermostat or keeper release switch faulty?

TEST: If toaster has a mechanical release, go to next test. If it has a magnetic release, unplug toaster and press down lift knob. If carriage locks, plug toaster into wall outlet. If carriage rises immediately, the thermostat or keeper release switch is faulty. Unplug toaster, open crumb tray, and check gap between switch contact and thermostat tip. (See *Checking the thermostat and keeper release switch,* p.215.) It should be about 3/16 inch. If it is, disconnect lead of keeper release switch from metal strip. Set volt-ohm meter (p.124) to RX100 scale and clip one probe to terminal of release switch, other to lead that has been freed. If meter reads at high end of ohms scale, switch is OK; if it reads low or zero ohms, it is broken.

YES→ FIX: Adjust thermostat or replace keeper release switch. Unplug power cord, turn toaster upside down, and open crumb tray. To adjust thermostat, try turning thermostat adjustment knob so that thermostat's tip is about 3/16 inch from keeper release switch contact. If this cannot be done, set adjustment knob and color control lever to center position, loosen thermostat mounting screw, and shift thermostat so that tip is at proper distance from switch contact. If volt-ohm meter test shows that keeper release switch is defective, replace it with new one (see *Disassembling a toaster with a magnetic release,* p.214). △△

Latch slips from keeper?

TEST: With toaster unplugged and shell removed, press lift lever down until latch mates with keeper, then release lever slowly while watching keeper. If keeper rises to free the latch, push lift lever down again and check to see if keeper release is pressing into notch on keeper. If it is not, the keeper release is broken.

YES→ FIX: Replace keeper release. If release is magnetic type, free magnet's leads from thermostat and heating element. File head off mounting rivet and pull out keeper release unit. When installing new release, use nut, bolt, and lock washer instead of rivet. If release is mechanical, replace entire color control unit. (See *Disassembling a toaster with a mechanical release,* p.214.) △△△

Defective keeper or latch?

TEST: Repeat previous test. If keeper does not rise but latch slips off of it, either part may be worn or bent.

YES→ FIX: Repair keeper or latch. If latch is worn, file it so that it hooks securely onto keeper. If either part is bent, straighten it with pliers so that it mates properly. △△

Ease of fix: △ simple △△ average △△△ difficult

213

Toasters

Disassembling a toaster with a magnetic release

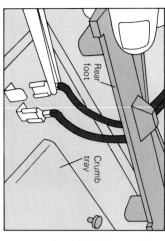

1. Unplug power cord and remove screws from front and rear feet. Lift off front foot and crumb tray. Work power cord leads off terminals and remove rear foot.

Rear foot — Crumb tray

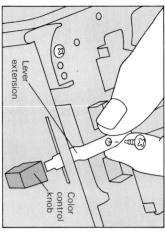

2. Pull strain relief fitting from its seat in rear foot. Pry fitting apart with screwdriver, slip insulating sleeves off of power cord leads, and remove cord.

Power cord — Strain relief fitting

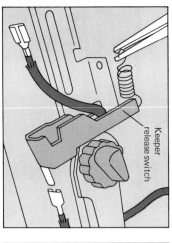

3. Pull knobs from lift lever and color control lever. Take screw out of color control lever and remove lever extension. Toaster shell can then be lifted from body.

Lever extension — Keeper release switch — Color control knob

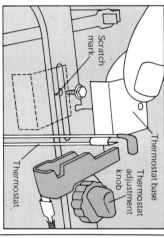

4. Scratch frame to show position of thermostat mounting screw, then remove screw. Maneuver thermostat from between bread guides and heating element.

Scratch mark — Thermostat base — Thermostat adjustment knob — Thermostat

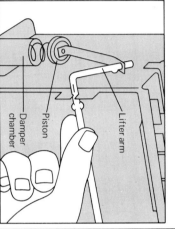

5. Remove lead going to keeper release switch and pull switch's own lead from terminal holding it. Free end of spring and remove switch.

6. Pull end of lifter arm out of slot in slide assembly. Rotate arm to release piston and spring from damper chamber and remove piston from end of lifter arm.

Piston — Damper chamber — Lifter arm

Disassembling a toaster with a mechanical release

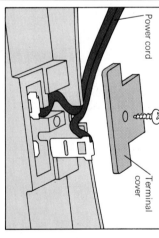

1. Unplug toaster, remove screws, and take off front off crumb tray. To remove rear foot, undo screws, pry off terminal cover, and free power cord leads.

Power cord — Terminal cover

2. Take out remaining screws from toaster bottom. Lift off crumb tray. Turn toaster upright, pull off lift knob, and remove shell. Remove bread guides from above.

Bread guides

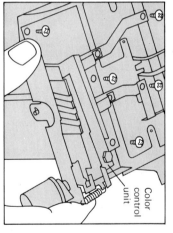

3. With toaster upside down, remove screws holding color control unit to body and pull off unit. (Two of the screws are attached to current carrying strips.)

Color control unit

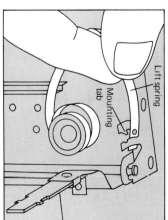

4. To take off lift spring, bend it so that the hole in the top of it disengages from mounting tab, then slide spring out and remove it from drum.

Lift spring — Mounting tab

How a magnetic pop-up mechanism works

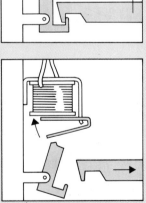

Keeper release — Keeper — Latch — Magnet

Mechanism is shown with carriage down (left) just before pop-up has started. Sequence begins when the thermostat closes keeper release switch. This sends current into magnet, which pulls keeper release out of niche in keeper. With keeper no longer held down, latch slides off, carriage rises, and toast pops up.

Checking the thermostat and keeper release switch

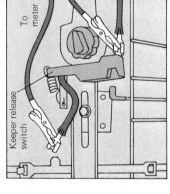

To meter

Keeper release switch

Set meter to RX100 scale. If meter reads at high end of ohms scale, switch is OK; if meter reads low or zero ohms, switch is faulty.

Tip of thermostat

If carriage does not stay down, check gap between keeper release switch and tip of thermostat. It should be about 3/16 in.

To test keeper release switch, unplug toaster, disconnect switch lead, and clip volt-ohm meter probes to lead and switch terminal.

Use and care

1. Unplug toaster before cleaning it. Empty crumb tray regularly and shake toaster over sink to remove particles (particularly raisins) that may interfere with moving parts. Clean the shell with a damp rag. Do not use abrasive cleaners and never immerse the toaster in water.
2. If the toaster has a magnetic release, it will have a slot marked "One slice." Be sure to toast single slice in that slot, otherwise the toast will burn.

Problems with the damper

Most toasters have a damper to keep the toast from rising too rapidly. After extended use, it may lose its effectiveness so that the toast is thrown out.

The most common damper design is the piston and cylinder type shown in the exploded view on page 213. Air in the cylinder serves to cushion the carriage as it rises. The piston must fit snugly in the chamber for the damping effect to work. To repair this kind of damper, simply replace the piston.

Another cushioning mechanism uses a flywheel to slow the carriage. If your

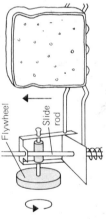

Some toasters use a flywheel to slow upward motion.

Flywheel

Slide rod

toaster has this sort of damper and the toast is being thrown out, try cleaning the slide rod and rubber sleeve of the flywheel with alcohol. Should the problem persist, take the toaster to a repair shop. Replacement is difficult.

Replacing a keeper release

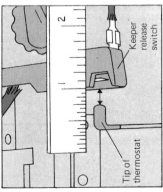

Magnet

Rivet

Release consists of magnet and U-shaped metal piece. To remove unit, free both magnet leads and file off rivet. Use nut and bolt when installing new unit.

Toaster-ovens

Toaster-ovens operate on the same principles as conventional toasters but, since they are made to double as small broiler-ovens, they are vastly different in design. Repairs that can be performed on them at home are limited. Problems arise from the way in which toaster-ovens are constructed—many parts are welded, riveted, or soldered on with high temperature solder—and many repairs require the use of special thermometers.

Toaster-oven repairs that are within the capability of most home repairmen include cleaning and lubricating moving parts; replacing the power cord, main spring, and damper chamber; and cleaning the inside of the shell. On some models, heating elements can be replaced. Although provision is made for adjusting the thermostat (in the model shown below, the right-hand hole in the control cover provides access to the thermostat adjustment screw), it is suggested that you do not attempt this adjustment, since the balance between the appliance's function as a toaster and as an oven could be upset. For best results, keep the interior clean and bright. Be sure to unplug the power cord before doing any work on the toaster-oven.

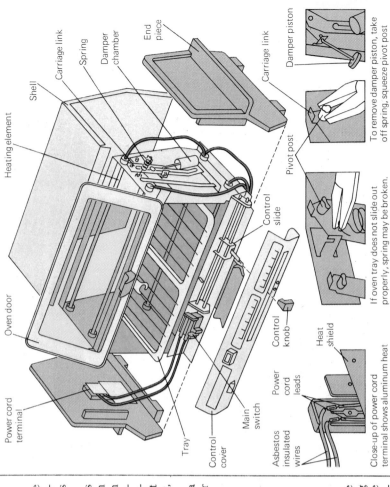

Shell

Carriage link

Spring

Damper chamber

End piece

Carriage link

Damper piston

Heating element

Oven door

Power cord terminal

Control slide

Pivot post

Control knob

Heat shield

Main switch

Control cover

Tray

Power cord leads

Asbestos insulated wires

Close-up of power cord terminal shows aluminum heat shield that protects power cord. Note asbestos insulation on wires going to main switch.

To remove damper piston, take off spring, squeeze pivot post with pliers to free carriage link. Raise oven door, slip link off post, remove piston

If oven tray does not slide out properly, spring may be broken. To replace spring, pull its end off notched tab. There is a second spring on other side

Toasters

Carriage stays down but toaster does not heat

When the carriage is fully depressed, the toaster should turn on. If it does not, power is not reaching the heating elements. Possible causes are a blown house fuse, broken power cord, and faulty main switch. A broken power cord should be replaced. The switch may be repairable, otherwise it must be replaced.

Power off at outlet?

TEST: Unplug toaster and check wall outlet with a lamp you know is working.

YES ► **FIX: Replace fuse or reset circuit breaker.** See p.127. If fuse keeps blowing, see *Toaster blows fuses*, p.218.
△

Power cord broken?

◄ NO

TEST: Unplug power cord and examine it for fraying and the plug for loose or distorted prongs. Disassemble toaster (p.214) so that power cord terminals are accessible. Attach jumper wire across cord terminals. Set volt-ohm meter (p.124) to RX1 scale and clip its probes to the prongs of the plug. Bend and pull power cord. If cord is OK, meter will read zero ohms; if broken, needle will jump or read high.

YES ► **FIX: Replace power cord.** Refer to disassembly sequences, p.214. Be sure to use a manufacturer's replacement power cord to be certain cord is properly insulated against heat and that it has sufficient current carrying capacity.
△△

Main switch broken?

◄ NO

TEST: Unplug toaster and remove shell. Press lift lever down until carriage locks, then check main switch to see that actuator is pressing both contact arms closed. Attach jumper wire across leads (they may be metal strips) coming from switch. Set volt-ohm meter to RX1 scale and clip its probes to power cord terminals. If main switch is OK, meter will read zero ohms; if switch is broken, meter will read high.

YES ► **FIX: Repair or replace switch.** Bend contact arms of switch so that it closes when carriage is down, or bend switch actuator so as to make switch open and close properly. If problem persists, replace switch. Remove any screws and file off any rivets that hold switch to toaster. Replace rivets with nuts, bolts, and lockwashers when installing new switch.
△△△

Bread does not toast to desired color

Poor color due to undertoasting, overtoasting, or uneven toasting may be the result of a faulty thermostat, stains inside the shell, variations in bread moisture, or a broken heating element. Repairs include adjusting the thermostat and cleaning the shell. A broken heating element usually calls for replacing the toaster.

Thermostat broken or out of adjustment?

◄ NO

TEST: With color control set to center position, a fresh slice of bread should toast to a medium gold brown. If toast is consistently too light or too dark or successive slices become lighter or darker, try adjusting the thermostat (see **FIX**). If problem persists, thermostat is broken.

YES ► **FIX: Adjust or replace thermostat.** Unplug toaster and remove shell. Refer to disassembly sequences, p.214. Set color control to middle position and try adjusting thermostat adjustment knob or screw so that toast color is correct. Make adjustments a little at a time and test after each adjustment. If adjustment proves impossible, replace the thermostat (magnetic release models) or entire color control unit (mechanical release models). Refer to disassembly sequences, p.214.
△△

Interior of shell stained?

◄ NO

TEST: If parts of toast are much lighter or darker than other parts, unplug toaster and remove shell (see disassembly instructions, p.214). Check inside of shell for dirt and discoloration; they will cause variations in reflected heat. Note: If problem is occasional, the trouble may be due to uneven moisture content in the bread.

YES ► **FIX: Clean inside of shell.** Use bicarbonate of soda or a mild detergent or a clean, damp rag. Do not use steel wool, scouring pads, or any compound containing an abrasive. Rinse shell thoroughly and dry it before reassembling.
△△

Broken heating element?

TEST: If bread toasts on one side only, one of the heating elements is broken.

YES ► **FIX: Replace toaster in most cases.** Replacing a heating element usually must be done at a repair shop and is seldom worth the cost.
△

Ease of fix: △ simple △△ average △△△ difficult

Testing for open circuits

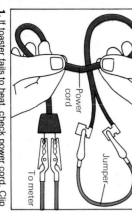

Power cord
Jumper
To meter

1. If toaster fails to heat, check power cord. Clip jumper to its leads and attach probes of volt-ohm meter to its plug. Bend cord during test.

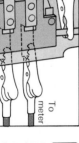

Jumper
Main switch
To meter

Use RX1 scale for both tests.

Test 1: If meter reads zero ohms, cord is OK; if needle jumps, or reads high, cord is broken.

Test 2: Switch is OK if meter reads zero ohms; high reading means it is broken.

2. Check main switch with carriage down. Attach jumper to inner terminals of switch; clip meter probes to terminals that held power cord leads.

Main switch repairs

Main switch

On many toasters, a wire loop actuates the main switch when the carriage is down. If the switch does not close, bend the loop so that it does.

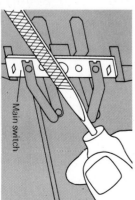

Main switch

Replacing a main switch may involve filing off rivets as well as removing screws and leads. Replace rivets with nuts and bolts.

Toast burns or does not pop up

The toast will burn if it does not pop up or if the main switch fails to turn off the heat when it does pop up. On toasters with a slot marked "One slice," a broken heating element may cause the toast to burn on one side. Replacement of the main switch, lift spring, or parts of the pop-up mechanism, are among the repairs.

Heating element broken?

TEST: If a bread slot is marked "One slice" or "Single slice" and toast in this slot burns while not toasting on the other, a heating element is broken.

YES→ FIX: Replace toaster in most cases. Replacing a heating element usually must be done at a repair shop and is seldom worth the cost. △△△

Main switch broken?

TEST: If toast pops up but heat stays on, burning lower part of toast, main switch is defective (its contacts may be fused or its contact arms may be badly bent or may have lost their spring).

YES→ FIX: Replace main switch. Unplug toaster and remove its shell (see disassembly information, p.214). Remove any screws and file off any rivets that hold switch to toaster. Replace rivets with nuts, bolts, and lockwashers when installing new switch. △△△

Thermostat blocked, broken, or out of adjustment?

TEST: If toaster has a magnetic keeper release, set toaster up between two piles of books and open crumb tray so that you can see thermostat arm. Insert toast, plug toaster into wall outlet, and depress carriage. If thermostat is OK, you will be able to see its arm bend slowly until its ceramic tip presses the keeper release switch closed. If it does not, thermostat is blocked, broken, or out of adjustment.

YES→ FIX: Clean, readjust, or replace thermostat. Unplug toaster and remove its shell (see *Disassembling a toaster with a magnetic release*, p.214). Brush away and shake out any pieces of toast or other obstruction blocking the thermostat. Tip of thermostat should be about 3/16 inch from keeper release switch contact when toaster is cool. Adjust it with the trim knob or by loosening the thermostat mounting screw and sliding thermostat closer to contact. Reassemble and test toaster again. If problem persists, replace the thermostat by removing the mounting screw and pulling the thermostat out. △△

Lift spring broken?

TEST: Press carriage down until it locks, then push lift lever up slightly to release carriage. If carriage does not rise by itself, the lift spring is probably broken.

YES→ FIX: Replace spring. Refer to disassembly sequences, p.214. On some models, spring may be mounted on front of toaster frame. Before replacing spring, make sure it has not merely slipped out of its seat. Also check lifter arm and piston (if present) for proper alignment. △△

Color control unit faulty?

TEST: If toaster has a mechanical keeper release and the previous test indicated spring mechanism is functioning properly, the color control unit is defective. (If toaster has a magnetic keeper release, go on to the next test.)

YES→ FIX: Replace color control unit. See *Disassembling a toaster with a mechanical release,* p.214. △△

Keeper release magnet or switch faulty?

TEST: If toaster has a magnetic keeper release, unplug power cord and take off shell. Free the lead of the magnet coil from its terminal on the keeper release switch. Set volt-ohm meter (p.124) to RX100 scale and clip its probes to the leads of the magnet coil. If meter reads close to zero ohms, coil is OK; if it reads high, coil is broken. Clip one meter probe to terminal of keeper release switch, the other to the end of the lead coming from keeper release switch, and press the thermostat arm so that switch closes. If keeper release switch is OK, meter will read zero ohms.

YES→ FIX: Replace keeper release or keeper release switch. If test indicated coil was bad, replace keeper release. Free other lead coming from magnet coil. File off mounting rivet and pull out keeper release unit. When installing new release, use a small nut, bolt, and lockwasher instead of a rivet. If keeper release switch is broken, free its lead from the terminal to which it is attached, release one end of spring on switch, and remove switch. Refer to *Disassembling a toaster with a magnetic release,* p.214. △△△

Ease of fix: △ simple △△ average △△△ difficult

The thermostat in operation

You can check thermostat in operation if toaster has a magnetic release. Open the crumb tray, prop toaster between piles of books as shown, and start it. If the thermostat is working properly, you will be able to see its ceramic tip bend slowly toward keeper release switch. When switch closes, carriage should rise.

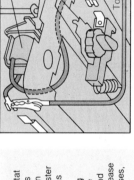

Keeper release switch

Ceramic tip of thermostat

Volt-ohm meter tests for toaster that burns toast

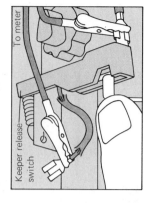

Magnet

To meter

Keeper release switch

To meter

1. Keeper release magnet: Unplug toaster and remove shell. Free both magnet leads, then attach volt-ohm meter probes to them.

2. Keeper release switch: Clip one probe to switch's lead, the other to its terminal. Push thermostat tip to close switch.

Use RX100 scale for both tests. **Test 1:** If meter reads high, coil is broken. **Test 2:** If switch is OK, meter will drop from high to zero ohms when switch is closed.

Toasters

A frayed power cord, an electrically live component grounded to (touching) a metal part, or leakage current due to faulty insulation will cause shocks. If leakage current is suspected, take the toaster to an authorized repairman. A frayed power cord or wire should be replaced. Remove metal objects and repair bent parts.

Toaster shocks user

Power cord frayed?

TEST: Receiving a shock from power cord is sufficient evidence it needs repair.

YES→ **FIX: Replace power cord.** Refer to illustrated disassembly sequences, p.214. Use a manufacturer's replacement power cord.

△△

Leakage current present?

TEST: If you receive a shock when you touch metal shell of toaster, unplug power cord and push lift lever down until it locks. Set volt-ohm meter (p.124) to RX100 scale and clip one of its probes to shell, the other to either prong of the plug. If meter reads high, leakage current (p.127) is indicated.

YES→ **FIX: Take appliance to authorized repairman.** Eliminating leakage current requires special equipment. Note: It is possible the shock is not caused by leakage current, but by a wire that becomes grounded only when the appliance is in operation. To investigate this, proceed with next test before taking toaster to a repair shop.

△△△

Toaster circuitry grounded to body frame?

TEST: Unplug toaster and remove its shell (see disassembly sequences, p.214). With volt-ohm meter set to RX100 scale, clip one probe to toaster frame, the other to a terminal of main switch. Depress lift lever so that carriage locks. If meter reads low or zero ohms, toaster circuitry is grounded. Look for current-carrying element bent against frame or bread guide touching heating element. Examine wiring for bare spots.

YES→ **FIX: Repair broken parts; remove metal objects.** Bend current carrying metal strips away from body frame. Replace poorly insulated wires with manufacturer's parts. (Do not reinsulate wires with ordinary electrical tape; it cannot withstand the high temperatures in toaster.) Bend bread guides away from heating elements.

△△

Checking for grounded wires and short circuits

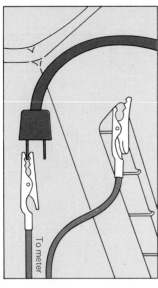

To meter

1. Shock may be due to leakage current. Check by unplugging power cord, clipping volt-ohm meter probes to either prong of plug and to metal shell of toaster.

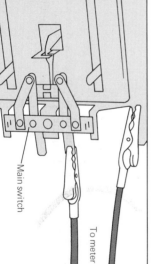

Main switch

To meter

2. To test for grounded wiring inside toaster, push carriage down. Clip one meter probe to frame, other to terminal of main switch. If test is positive, look for bent wires or bent bread guides.

Toaster blows fuses

When a fuse blows or circuit breaker trips, it means there is either an electrical overload or a short circuit. Reducing the number of appliances in the circuit will eliminate the overload. If the power cord is short-circuited, replace it. Also, check for metal objects that may have fallen into the toaster.

Circuit overloaded?

TEST: To check for overloads, see p.127. Too many appliances in a circuit is the commonest cause of blown fuses and tripped breakers.

YES→ **FIX: Reduce number of appliances in the circuit. Caution: Never replace a fuse or breaker with one having a larger capacity.**

△

Short circuit in power cord or plug?

TEST: Unplug toaster and remove power cord. (See disassembly illustrations, p.214.) Examine cord and plug for bare wires and burn marks. Set volt-ohm meter (p.124) to RX100 scale and clip its probes to the prongs of the plug. Bend and pull cord. If power cord is OK, meter will read high; if cord is shorted, needle will jump around or read zero ohms.

YES→ **FIX: Replace power cord.** If cord is still attached to rear foot of toaster, free it by pulling out strain relief fitting. Use manufacturer's replacement cord and plug to be certain they are properly insulated against heat, as well as electrical breakdown, and that they have enough current carrying capacity.

△△

Short circuit inside toaster?

TEST: Unplug toaster and remove its shell. Check interior parts for burn marks, bent terminal posts, broken insulation, loose wires. Look for small metal objects, such as skewers or safety pins, that may have fallen into toaster.

YES→ **FIX: Repair broken parts; remove metal objects.** Bend distorted terminals back into shape. If insulation on wire is damaged, replace wire with manufacturer's part. Ordinary electrical tape cannot be used because of high temperatures in toaster.

△△

Ease of fix: △ simple △△ average △△△ difficult

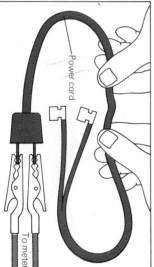

Power cord

To meter

3. Blown fuses may be due to short circuit in power cord. Remove power cord from toaster and attach volt-ohm meter probes to its plug. Bend and pull on power cord while testing.

Use RX100 scale for all tests.

Test 1: High meter reading indicates leakage current.

Test 2: If meter reads low or zero ohms, wiring is grounded.

Test 3: If needle jumps or reads zero ohms, cord has a short; high reading means cord is OK.

Toothbrushes

Details of construction

Electric toothbrushes are made in both cord and cordless models. A rechargeable nickel cadmium battery in the power handle energizes the motor of the cordless type. The power handle is kept in a charging unit when not in use.

Both cord and cordless brushes use a small direct current (DC) motor to move the toothbrush shaft from side to side or back and forth, depending on model. The power handle is permanently sealed. Since breaking this seal on a cord-type brush will expose the user to the danger of a lethal shock, no internal repairs on the power handle should be attempted. However, a limited number of repairs are possible on the charging unit.

Note: Details of repair and disassembly may vary from one model of electric toothbrush to the next. If yours differs markedly from the one shown, see *Repair basics,* pp.128–131.

Toothbrush shaft

Eccentric drive (gives shaft reciprocating motion)

Power handle (sealed unit)

Motor

Nickel cadmium battery

On-off switch

Diode (changes AC to DC for charging battery)

Power handle charge contacts

Charging well

Power cord

Upper charger housing

Charger contacts

Lower charger housing

Transformer (reduces voltage from wall outlet)

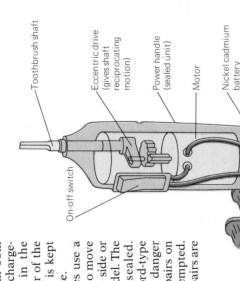

Toothbrush does not run or runs poorly

Repairs to electric toothbrushes are limited because power handle is permanently sealed. If trouble is not due to external conditions (blown house fuse, bathroom outlet that is not always activated), repairs usually consist of replacing handle or charging unit. See *Cordless appliances,* pp.136–137 for more information.

Bathroom outlet controlled by light switch?

NO →

TEST: Some bathroom outlets—for example, those on a medicine cabinet—may be wired so that they are on only when the light is on. Use lamp to check outlet into which toothbrush charger is plugged to see if it goes off when bathroom light does.

YES → **FIX: Use different outlet or rewire fixture.** Charger must be on continuously and power handle should be kept in it to insure that batteries are maintained at full charge. (It takes about 16 hours for drained batteries to reach full charge.) △

Power off at outlet?

NO →

TEST: Unplug power cord and check outlet with a lamp you know is working.

YES → **FIX: Replace fuse or reset circuit breaker.** See p.127. △

Gears stripped or out of mesh?

NO →

TEST: Try to stall toothbrush motor by turning motor on, then grasping brush and pushing it firmly toward handle (see illustration). If you can hold the brush still while motor continues to run at full speed, gears are stripped or out of mesh.

YES → **FIX: Replace power handle.** Handle unit of toothbrush is sealed and no repairs are possible. Return handle to dealer for replacement. △

Charger or power handle faulty?

If the above tests fail to locate the problem, the trouble is in the charging unit or one of the electrical parts in the handle. See *Cordless appliances,* pp.136–137, for information on repair.

Ease of fix: △ simple △△ average △△△ difficult

Testing the gears

Check for stripped gears inside power handle by attaching toothbrush to handle, turning switch on, and pushing down firmly on brush. Motor should slow down while you hold brush. If you can hold brush steady while motor keeps running, gears are stripped. Replace handle.

Use and care

1. Never try to disassemble the power handle; it is permanently sealed. If the seal is broken, take the handle to an authorized service shop.

2. Even though the power handle is sealed, do not immerse it in water unless the owner's manual says you can.

3. Keep the base of the handle and the well of the charger clean. An accumulation of toothpaste or other matter will interfere with charging. Disconnect the power cord before cleaning the charger.

4. Do not try to lubricate the power handle; it is permanently lubricated.

Vacuum cleaners

Canister and upright: the two basic designs

The most typical vacuum cleaner designs are the upright (right) and canister (below). Each uses a motor-driven fan to force dirty air through a porous bag that filters out dust and debris. The fan in a canister vacuum cleaner is isolated from the incoming air by a filter screen. The fan of an upright lies directly in the path of the dirty air, and so is more susceptible to damage. Many of the test and repair instructions that follow can be used for both types of vacuum. Others—for example, those dealing with problems with the hose in a canister or the power brush in an upright—apply to only one.

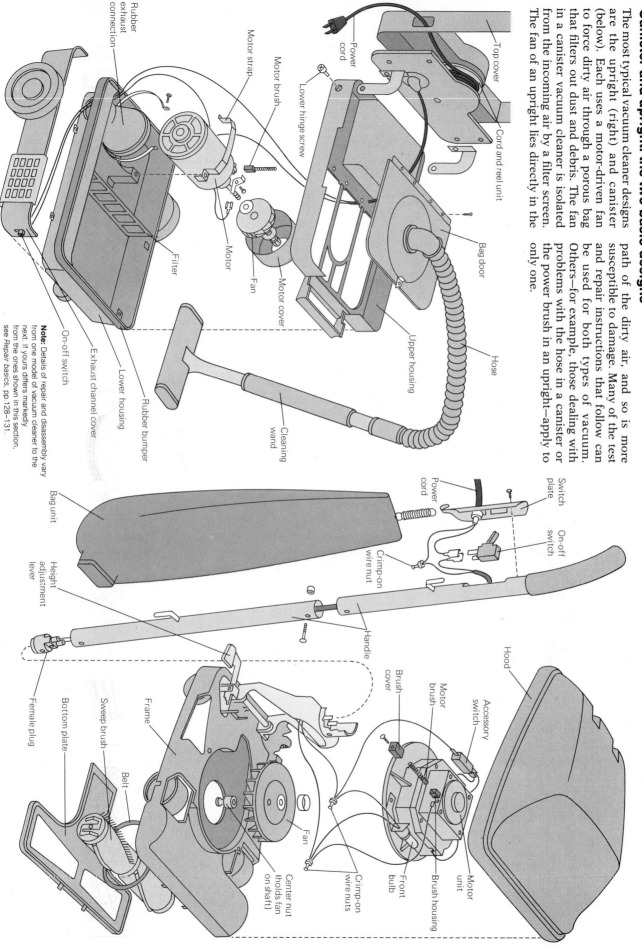

Power cord

Top cover

Cord and reel unit

Bag door

Rubber exhaust connection

Motor strap

Motor brush

Lower hinge screw

Motor

Fan

Motor cover

Filter

On-off switch

Exhaust channel cover

Lower housing

Rubber bumper

Upper housing

Hose

Cleaning wand

Note: Details of repair and disassembly vary from one model of vacuum cleaner to the next. If yours differs markedly from the ones shown in this section, see *Repair basics*, pp. 128-131.

Bag unit

Height adjustment lever

Female plug

Bottom plate

Sweep brush

Frame

Belt

Power cord

Switch plate

On-off switch

Crimp-on wire nut

Handle

Hood

Brush cover

Motor brush

Accessory switch

Fan

Center nut (holds fan on shaft)

Crimp-on wire nuts

Front bulb

Brush housing

Motor unit

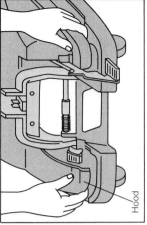

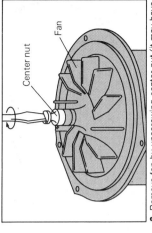

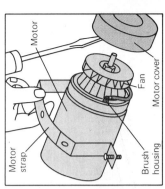

Disassembling an upright

1. Unplug vacuum and remove bag unit and handle (see your owner's manual). Open clamp levers and remove bottom plate. Slip belt off and pull out brush.

Bottom plate · Clamp lever · Belt · Brush

2. Undo screws and remove switch plate. Pull both leads off switch, free power cord lead by squeezing crimp-on wire nut with locking pliers, and remove cord.

On-off switch · Switch plate · Strain relief fitting · Crimp-on wire nut

3. Remove switch. Pull strain relief fitting out of handle and remove fitting from cord. Pry female plug from handle bottom and pull out both plug and wire.

Female plug · Handle bottom

4. Turn vacuum upside down, locate mounting posts in hood, and remove mounting screws. Take hood off from above (prying and bending may be necessary).

Hood

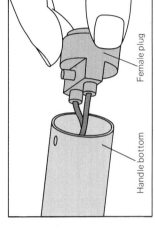

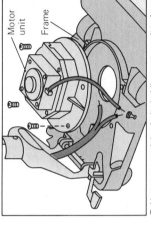

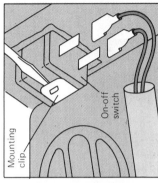

5. To remove brush, undo housing screw, take off brush cover, and pull terminal from brush housing. Use your finger to keep spring from flying out.

Brush cover · Brush housing · Motor brush · Terminal · Housing screw

6. Remove both front bulb unit and accessory switch if your vacuum has one. (Switch increases motor speed when accessories are used.)

Accessory switch · Accessory switch actuator

7. Unscrew remaining bolts holding motor unit to frame and lift out motor unit. To remove unit completely, free any wiring that holds it to rest of vacuum.

Motor unit · Frame

8. Remove fan by unscrewing center nut (it may have left-hand thread). On some cleaners fan is held on by a setscrew or is screwed directly onto motor shaft.

Fan · Center nut

5. Undo motor strap screws and lift out motor unit. Pry off motor cover, unscrew nut, and remove fan. Take out brushes by undoing screws in terminal pieces.

Motor · Fan · Brush housing · Motor cover · Motor strap

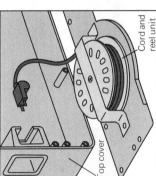

4. Remove both leads from on-off switch. Pry apart mounting clip and remove switch from exhaust channel cover. Note orientation of switch for proper reassembly.

On-off switch · Mounting clip

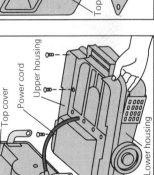

3. Take out screws along perimeter of top cover and remove cord and reel unit. Undo screws at bottom of lower housing and pull off exhaust channel cover.

Cord and reel unit · Top cover

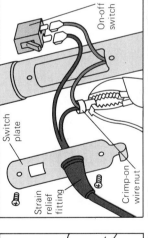

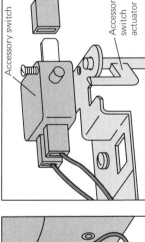

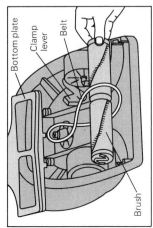

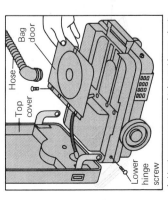

Disassembling a canister

1. Unplug vacuum and take out hose, dustbag, and filter. Undo screws in upper housing, slip off bag door, and take out lower hinge screws to release top cover.

Top cover · Hose · Bag door · Lower hinge screw

2. Remove remaining screws from upper housing, pry up bumper, separate upper and lower housings. Squeeze crimp-on nuts with pliers to free power cord leads.

Top cover · Power cord · Upper housing · Lower housing · Bumper

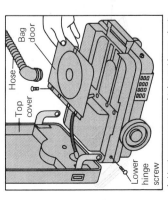

221

Vacuum cleaners

Motor does not run

If the motor does not run, there may be no power at the outlet, the power cord may be broken, the fan may be jammed, or there may be a defect in the on-off switch, the handle cord, or the motor itself. Repairs range from replacing the house fuse to installing a new power cord reel or motor unit.

Power off at outlet?

TEST: Unplug power cord and check wall outlet with a lamp you know is working.

NO →

YES → **FIX: Replace fuse or reset circuit breaker.** See p.127. If fuse keeps blowing, see *Vacuum cleaner blows fuses*, p.224.

▷

Power cord broken?

TEST: Unplug vacuum cleaner. Unwind power cord and examine it for fraying and the plug for loose or distorted prongs. Disassemble cleaner so that power cord leads are accessible (see p.221) and free leads from other wiring. Attach jumper wire across power cord leads. Set volt-ohm meter (p.124) to RX1 scale and clip its probes to the prongs of the power cord's plug. Bend and pull power cord. If cord is OK, meter will read zero ohms; if cord is broken, needle will jump or read high.

NO →

YES → **FIX: Replace power cord.** It may be necessary to detach a strain relief fitting that mounts the cord to the vacuum cleaner. One type of fitting has a metal clip that can be pulled out; another type can be squeezed with pliers, rotated a quarter turn, and pulled out. If the power cord is on a reel, the easiest procedure is to replace the entire cord and reel assembly. Refer to appropriate disassembly sequence on p.221.

▷▷

Fan jammed by foreign object?

TEST: If vacuum cleaner does not run, but the motor hums when it is turned on, unplug and disassemble the cleaner (see p.221), and check fan for objects stuck in it.

NO →

YES → **FIX: Remove jamming object.** Note: This problem is more likely to occur in uprights.

▷▷

Testing the power cord and switch

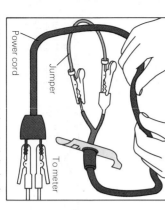

Power cord · Jumper · Power cord · To meter

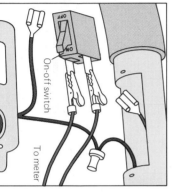

On-off switch · To meter

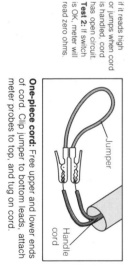

Set meter to RX1 scale for both tests.

Test 1: If meter reads zero ohms, power cord is OK; if it reads high or jumps when cord is handled, cord has open circuit.

Test 2: If switch is OK, meter will read zero ohms.

1. Unplug power cord, free both its leads, and clip jumper to them. Attach volt-ohm meter probes to plug. Bend cord during test.

2. Remove switch plate and take leads off terminals of on-off switch. Turn switch to On, and clip meter probes to its terminals.

Switch-to-motor cord broken?

TEST: Upright vacuums have a handle cord connected to the on-off switch. To test it, unplug power cord, remove switch plate, and take off upper housing (see *Disassembling an upright*, p.221). Separate the cord leads from motor and switch, and attach jumper wire to leads that went to motor. Set volt-ohm meter to RX1 scale and clip its probes to leads that went to switch. If cord is OK, meter will read zero ohms; if cord is broken, meter will read high.

NO →

YES → **FIX: Repair or replace cord.** If cord is in two parts connected by a plug and socket, polish prongs of plug with fine steel wool. Spray electrical contact cleaner (p.123) into contacts in socket. Push plug in and out of socket several times to improve electrical contact. To remove cord, take out any clamps and strain relief fittings that hold cord in place and thread cord out through handle. (See *Disassembling an upright*, p.221.)

▷▷

On-off switch broken?

TEST: Unplug power cord and disassemble vacuum cleaner so that on-off switch is accessible (see p.221). Turn switch to On. Set volt-ohm meter to RX1 scale and touch its probes to the switch terminals. If switch is OK, meter will read zero ohms; if switch is broken, meter will read high.

NO →

YES → **FIX: Replace switch.** Disconnect leads attached to switch. Pry off retaining clips or remove screws that hold switch to housing. (In some cases, switch may be removed by pressing together spring clamps along sides of switch and pushing it out through housing.)

▷▷

Motor faulty?

If the above tests fail to locate the problem, the trouble lies in the motor. Poor lubrication, worn brushes, a damaged bearing, or a bad wire in either the field coil or armature winding may be to blame. See *Universal motors*, pp.132–134, for information on testing and repairing motors. **Caution: If the motor hums but does not turn, shut it off immediately to prevent damage.**

Ease of fix: ▷ simple   ▷▷ average   ▷▷▷ difficult

Testing the handle cord

Handle cord · To meter

Handle cord

One-piece cord: Free upper and lower ends of cord. Clip jumper to bottom leads, attach meter probes to top, and tug on cord.

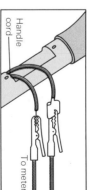

Handle cord · Female plug · Jumper · To meter

Two-piece cord: Test segments separately using jumper at one end and meter probes at other in each case. Tug cords while testing.

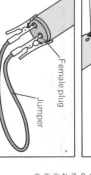

Set meter to RX1 scale for all tests. For one-piece cord or either segment of two-piece cord, meter will read zero ohms if cord is OK, high ohms if cord has an open circuit.

Motor runs but suction is poor

Poor suction may be the result of a broken hose, obstructions, leaks, or a loose or jammed fan. If the hose is broken, replace it. Other difficulties can generally be fixed by cleaning and tightening parts. A sluggish motor can also cause poor suction. Motor problems are covered in *Universal motors*, pp.132–134.

Obstruction in air passages?

TEST: First, be sure problem is not simply due to an overfull dustbag. Next, examine intake (on upright) or nozzle and attachments (on canister) for objects blocking the flow of air. In upright cleaner, also check port where dustbag is attached. In canister cleaner, check intake and exhaust ports for blockage due to accumulated dust. Clean out hose (see **Fix**) and retest operation.

FIX: Clean parts and replace filter. Brush dirt from air passages. Clean attachments by vacuuming them with the cleaner's own hose. To clear the hose, connect it to exhaust port and run vacuum until obstruction is blown out of hose. If that does not work, disconnect hose and push a broom handle through it from one end to the other. Note: If hose clogs repeatedly, it is probably damaged and should be replaced (see next **Fix**). △

Leaks in attachments, hose, or housing?

TEST: On canister vacuum cleaners, the entire air passage from nozzle to exhaust must be airtight for the cleaner to function properly. Examine the air passage step by step. First, look for breaks in the hose—it is the most likely spot for a leak. Next, check for loose or less-than-snug connections between hose, attachments, and intake port. Also, examine housing for leaky gaskets and loose or missing screws (a single open screw hole will significantly reduce suction).

FIX: Repair or replace leaking part. Replace missing screws, leaky gaskets, and faulty attachments. To replace the hose, remove fittings at each end. If they are rubber, they can be twisted off. If they are metal or plastic, look to see if the hose can simply be unplugged from the fitting (raised tabs on hose that lock into fitting indicate that it can). If not, cut the hose with a knife about 2 inches from each fitting and pull out the remaining wire and material with pliers. When installing new hose, brush white glue on hose and fitting before joining them. In some cases, the hose is attached with a sleeve and collar; get new ones when you buy the hose and use them when you install it. △△

Fan Loose or obstructed?

TEST: Unplug and disassemble vacuum (see p.221) so that fan can be inspected. Check for dust accumulations that might interfere with rotation. Test fan to see if it is snug on motor shaft by holding shaft and turning fan. Next, check for a leak. Fan problems are more likely in an upright than a canister unless the canister's filter is torn so that dust can get into the fan and motor.

FIX: Clean area around fan; tighten fan on shaft. To clean thoroughly, take fan off of motor shaft (it may be threaded onto shaft or held on by a nut or setscrew). Reattach fan firmly on shaft when reassembling. △△

Motor faulty?

If the above tests fail to locate the problem, the trouble is probably with the motor. Poor lubrication, worn brushes, a binding rotor, a dirty commutator, or a shorted wire in either the field or armature may be to blame. See *Universal motors*, pp.132–134.

Ease of fix: △ simple △△ average △△△ difficult

Replacing the hose

Pull back collar and scrape old glue from fitting. Coat end of fitting liberally with quickset epoxy compound or rubber-base glue; push or screw new hose onto it.

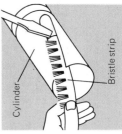
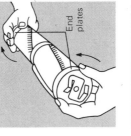
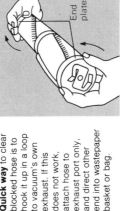

Some hoses are mounted with metal insert and plastic collar. Attach insert and collar to hose end and push hose onto fitting so that pegs and holes mate.

Do not tape a broken hose; replace it. Twist old hose off fitting or else cut it near fitting with wire cutter. Pull out remaining wire and material with pliers.

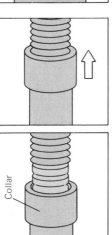

Apply some glue to portion of hose that will be under the collar (left) and push collar over hose (right). Let glue dry overnight before using vacuum.

Fixing the power brush

Keep brush clean, check that bristles reach below bottom plate, and remove brush cylinder to see if it spins easily. If bristles are worn, replace them. Twist end plates in opposite directions until one plate unscrews.

Pull off end plates and shaft and pry out bearing unit from end of roller. Bristle strips can then be pushed out of their channels with screwdriver. If strips are bonded on, replace entire cylinder.

Clearing the hose

Quick way to clear blocked hose is to hook it up in a loop to vacuum's own exhaust. If this does not work, attach hose to exhaust port only, and direct other end into wastepaper basket or bag.

If stoppage remains, push broom handle through hose. This may require removal of fittings if they are curved. Alternately, use drain auger. Tape one end of auger to prevent damage to hose.

223

Vacuum cleaners

Vacuum cleaner blows fuses

When a fuse blows or circuit breaker trips, it means there is either an electrical overload or a short circuit. Reducing the number of appliances in the circuit will eliminate the overload. If tests show the power cord or handle cord is short-circuited, replace it. To check the motor, see *Universal motors*, pp.132–134.

Circuit overloaded?

NO → **TEST:** To check for overloads, see p.127. Too many appliances in a circuit is the commonest cause of blown fuses.

YES → **FIX: Reduce number of appliances in the circuit. Caution: Never replace a fuse or breaker with one having a larger capacity.** △

Short circuit in power cord or plug?

NO → **TEST:** Unplug power cord and examine cord and plug for bare wires and burn marks. Disassemble cleaner so that power cord leads are accessible (see p.221), and free one lead from other wiring. Set volt-ohm meter (p.124) to RX100 scale and clip its probes to the plug. Bend and pull cord. If cord is Ok, meter will read high; if it is shorted, needle will jump or read zero ohms.

YES → **FIX: Replace power cord.** It may be necessary to detach a strain relief fitting that mounts the cord to the vacuum cleaner. One type of fitting has a metal clip that can be pulled out; another type can be squeezed with pliers, rotated a quarter turn, and pulled out. If the power cord is on a reel, the easiest procedure is to replace entire cord and reel assembly. △△

Short circuit in switch-to-motor cord?

NO → **TEST:** Uprights have a handle cord leading to the on-off switch. To test it, unplug power cord, remove switch plate, and take off upper housing (see *Disassembling an upright*, p.221). Separate cord leads from motor and switch. Set volt-ohm meter to RX100 scale and clip its probes to leads that went to switch. If cord is Ok, meter will read high. If cord is in two parts, test each.

YES → **FIX: Repair or replace cord.** Take screws out of clamps that hold cord in place and thread cord out through handle. △△

Short circuit in motor?
If the above tests fail to locate the problem, there is probably a short circuit in the motor wiring. See *Universal motors*, pp.132–134, for information on testing and repairs.

Ease of fix: △ simple △△ average △△△ difficult

Use and care

1. Never use the vacuum outdoors or for sucking up water unless it is specifically designed for those jobs. If cleaning fluid was used on a rug, let it dry thoroughly before vacuuming.
2. Unplug vacuum before removing dustbag or doing any other work on it. Be sure to replace disposable dustbags when they become three-quarters full of dust.
3. Keep brush bristles and hoses clean.
4. Canister vacuums have a filter to keep dirt out of the motor. It should be kept clean. Some filters can be washed or vacuumed, others must be replaced when they become clogged. Follow instructions in your owner's manual.

Other kinds of vacuums

All vacuum cleaners work in a similar way: A motor-driven fan pulls dust-laden air into the cleaner, passes it through a dustbag to filter out the dirt, and forces the cleaned air out an exhaust port. Differences between models have to do with (1) location of motor, fan, and dustbag; (2) shape of the housing; and (3) available accessories, such as a power brush. A standard upright and a canister are shown on page 220. Other common models are shown below.

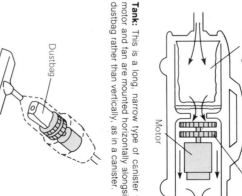

Shop vacuum: Motor is mounted on top to isolate wires from water that may be sucked in. There is no dustbag and motor is bigger than on standard canister.

Filters
Dustbin

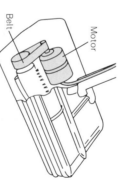

Tank: This is a long, narrow type of canister whose motor and fan are mounted horizontally alongside the dustbag rather than vertically, as in a canister.

Dustbag
Motor
Fan

Power nozzle: Some tanks and canisters come with a power brush attachment to improve effectiveness on rugs. Brush includes built-in power cord and motor.

Motor
Belt

Lightweight: Also known as electric brooms, lightweight cleaners are really tank cleaners mounted on a handle. Repairs are the same as for canisters.

Dustbag

Testing for a short circuit

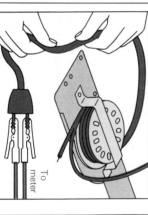

1. Unplug power cord and free one lead when testing cord for short. Clip volt-ohm meter probes to plug, bend cord while testing.

To meter

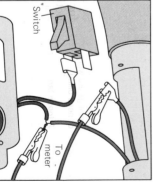

2. To check handle cord, remove switch cover, free switch lead, remove crimp-on connector. Clip meter probes across leads.

Switch
To meter

Use RX100 scale for both tests.
Test 1: If cord is Ok, meter will read high; if it is shorted, needle will jump or read zero ohms.
Test 2: If cord is Ok, meter will read high. Reading of zero ohms means cord is shorted.

Vacuum cleaner is noisy

Excessive operating noise means that a moving part is out of balance or hitting other parts. The power brush and blower fan are common sources of noise and can be adjusted or, if necessary, replaced. Motor problems such as worn bearings may also be to blame. They are covered in *Universal motors*, pp.132–134.

Power brush noisy?

TEST: Tilt vacuum cleaner up so that you can look at the brush, then pulse vacuum on and off for a moment. Watch brush to see if it strikes bottom plate as it spins. Unplug power cord and check to see if plate and brush are mounted incorrectly or either one is bent. Next, take off bottom plate and remove brush. By hand, try spinning brush to see if it turns easily on its shaft. If it does not, the bearings are worn or dry.

FIX: **Adjust or replace parts; lubricate bearings.** Remount brush and bottom plate in correct position if they were misaligned. Replace either if it is bent. If bearings are dry, lubricate them with grease recommended by manufacturer or multipurpose grease. If brush is still noisy, replace it. ▲▲

Fan loose or fan blades broken?

TEST: Disassemble cleaner so that fan is accessible (see p.221). Inspect fan for chipped or broken blades. Hold motor shaft with one hand and wiggle fan with the other. If there is up-and-down or side-to-side play of fan on motor shaft, fan is loose.

FIX: **Tighten or replace fan.** Fan may be threaded onto shaft or held on by a nut or setscrew. Tighten the appropriate part. If fan blade is chipped or broken, replace fan. Even a very small chip can put the fan out of balance enough to create an obvious noise. Correct it before a major fault develops. ▲▲

Motor noisy?

If the above tests fail to locate the problem, the trouble lies in the motor (or the fan enclosed with the motor). Poor lubrication, loose or worn bearings, imbalance in armature and fan assembly causing vibration or interference, dirt in the motor, or a shorted wire in the motor may be to blame. See *Universal motors*, pp.132–134, for information on testing and repairs.

Vacuum cleaner shocks user

A frayed power cord, an electrically live component grounded to (touching) a metal part, or leakage current due to faulty insulation will cause shocking. In the case of a frayed cord or grounding, the part can be fixed or replaced. If leakage current is suspected, the vacuum should be taken to a repairman.

Power cord frayed?

TEST: Receiving a shock from touching cord is sufficient evidence it needs repair.

FIX: **Replace power cord.** Follow instructions given in *Motor does not run*, p.222, and in disassembly sequences, p.221. ▲▲▲

Leakage current present?

TEST: If you receive a shock from an exposed metal part of vacuum cleaner, unplug cleaner. Set volt-ohm meter (p.124) to RX100 scale and attach one probe to metal part, the other to a prong of the plug. Turn switch to On. If meter reads high, leakage current (p.127) is indicated.

FIX: **Take vacuum cleaner to authorized repairman.** Eliminating leakage current requires special equipment. Note: It is possible the shock is not caused by leakage current but by a wire that becomes grounded only when the vacuum cleaner is on. To investigate this, proceed with next test before taking vacuum cleaner to repair shop. ▲▲▲

Wiring inside cleaner grounded to metal part?

TEST: Unplug vacuum cleaner and disassemble it so that internal wiring is accessible (see p.221 for disassembly information). Examine wires for bare spots and loose strands. Set volt-ohm meter to RX100 scale. Clip one of its probes to metal part that shocks, the other to either prong of the plug. Turn switch to On, and bend and twist various wires. If needle jumps when a wire is handled, wire is grounded.

FIX: **Repair or replace faulty wiring.** Reinsulate bare spots on wires with plastic electrical tape. If the cause of the grounding cannot be found or if repairs fail to eliminate the problem, the grounded wire may be in the motor. See *Universal motors*, pp.132–134, for tests and repairs. ▲▲

Ease of fix: ▲ simple ▲▲ average ▲▲▲ difficult

Testing for shock hazards

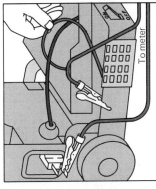

Set meter to RX100 scale for both tests.

Test 1: If meter reads high, leakage current is indicated.

Test 2: If needle jumps when a wire is handled, that wire is grounded.

To meter

1. To check for leakage current, unplug vacuum and turn switch to On. Clip volt-ohm meter probes to metal housing and to plug.

2. Grounded wire may cause shock. With meter and vacuum set up as in first test, open up housing and twist and bend various wires.

Noise sources

Power brush may cause noise. Check for brush hitting bottom plate. Next, remove brush and spin it by hand. If hard to turn, brush bearings are worn or need oiling.

Chipped blades

A loose fan or one that has a damaged blade will produce excessive noise. Be sure fan is snug on shaft. If it is broken, replace it to prevent further damage.

Radio interference

It is normal for the motor of a vacuum cleaner to interfere somewhat with radio and television reception, especially if the machine is being operated in the same room as the radio or television set. However, if, after using the vacuum cleaner for some weeks or months, there is a noticeable increase in interference when you are vacuuming, there is probably a fault in the cleaner's motor. Worn or sticking motor brushes, a defective commutator, or a damaged armature may be to blame. Refer to *Universal motors*, pp.132–134, for information on testing and repairs.

Wafflers, corn poppers, and slow cookers

Cooking appliances with built-in thermostats

There are a number of common electric cooking devices that share the characteristic of having a built-in thermostat rather than one located in a detachable control. In addition to wafflers, corn poppers, and slow cookers, such appliances include fondue pots, crock pots, deep fryers, egg warmers, and kettles.

The waffler (below, left) is among the most sophisticated of these appliances. It has two separate heating elements and a temperature control, and it can be used as a griddle for pancakes, meat, and sandwiches. A view hole in the upper shell serves as a signal light by showing whether the heating element is on.

The corn popper (below, right) is a simpler type of electric cooker, amounting to nothing more than an enclosed heating element and a thermostat that turns the popper off when the corn is done. Slow cookers have single strand heating elements rather than coils, and their thermostats can be set for different cooking temperatures. They use less power and operate at lower temperatures than corn poppers, but in other respects are almost identical in construction.

Waffler

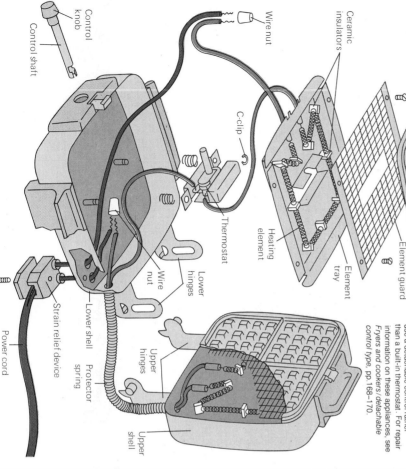

Control knob — **Control shaft** — **Wire nut** — **Ceramic insulators** — **C-clip** — **Thermostat** — **Wire nut** — **Lower hinges** — **Heating element** — **Element tray** — **Element guard** — **Grill** — **Upper hinges** — **Protector spring** — **Upper shell** — **Lower shell** — **Strain relief device** — **Power cord**

Note: Details of repair and disassembly may vary from one model of waffler, corn popper, or slow cooker to the next. If your appliance differs markedly from the ones shown here, see *Repair basics*, pp. 128–131. Also note that many cooking appliances use a detachable control rather than a built-in thermostat. For repair information on these appliances, see *Fryers and cookers/detachable control type*, pp. 168–170.

Replacing a heating element

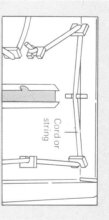

Cord or string

New heating element coil must be stretched to fit. To find correct length, knot one end of piece of cord, run cord through ceramic insulators along pathway of old element.

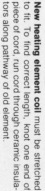

New heating element

Stretch coil by pulling ends apart slowly and steadily. When tension is released, length should be same as cord. Allow extra wires at ends if needed for attaching to terminals.

Start at midpoint when installing new heating element. If element needs additional stretching, remove it and stretch it from ends. There should be no sag after installation.

Corn popper

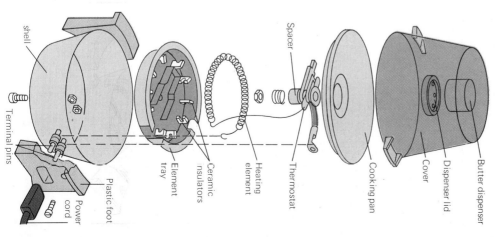

shell — **Terminal pins** — **Plastic foot** — **Power cord** — **Element tray** — **Ceramic insulators** — **Heating element** — **Thermostat** — **Spacer** — **Cooking pan** — **Cover** — **Dispenser lid** — **Butter dispenser**

Disassembling a waffler

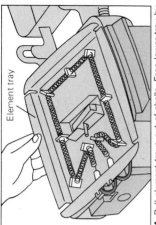

4. Pull element trays out of shells. Free lower tray by tilting thermostat. Note that heating element leads will still be attached to terminals inside waffler.

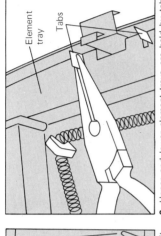

3. Upper and lower element trays are held by tabs protruding from upper and lower shells. Straighten tabs with pliers so that they align with slots in trays.

Element tray
Tabs

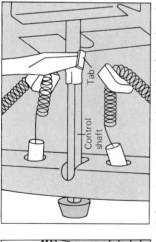

2. Spread apart end tabs of control shaft to release it from thermostat shaft. Withdraw the control shaft and control knob as a unit.

Control shaft
Tab

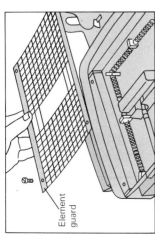

1. Unplug power cord from outlet and remove both waffle grilles. Undo screws holding upper and lower element guards to element trays, and lift off guards.

Element guard

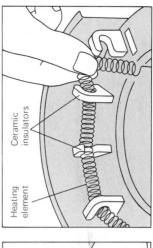

8. Remove C-clips from mounting posts and take out thermostat. Clips can be pried off posts by inserting screwdriver blade in cutout portion of each clip.

Thermostat
C-clips

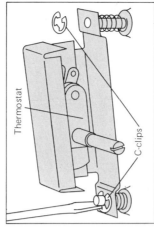

7. Pry off end of protector spring from grommet in lower shell. Spread lower hinges far enough apart to free upper hinges and separate the two halves of the waffler.

Upper hinge
Protector spring
Lower hinge
Grommet

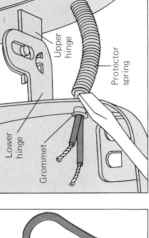

6. Free leads to thermostat by removing screws holding them to thermostat terminals. Element trays along with heating elements can then be completely withdrawn.

Thermostat terminals

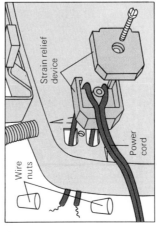

5. To remove power cord, unscrew two ceramic wire nuts attached to its leads. Undo screws holding strain relief device in place, and withdraw power cord.

Strain relief device
Power cord
Wire nuts

Disassembling a corn popper

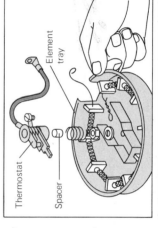

4. Slip heating element out of ceramic insulators and lift out insulators individually. Note how insulators alternate directions along path of element.

Ceramic insulators
Heating element

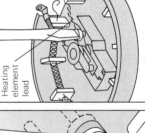

3. After taking out center screw from bottom of body shell, pull off thermostat along with spacer and spring. Then, lift off element tray.

Element tray
Thermostat
Spacer

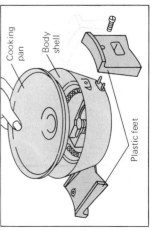

2. Free leads to terminal pins by undoing nuts that hold them (left). Also free heating element lead by removing screw from thermostat terminal (right).

Heating element lead

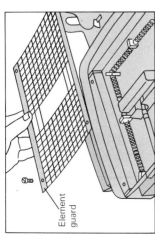

1. Disconnect power cord from both wall outlet and corn popper. Remove mounting screws, take off plastic feet, and lift cooking pan from body shell.

Cooking pan
Body shell
Plastic feet

Wafflers, corn poppers, and slow cookers

Appliance does not heat

When a waffler or other cooking appliance does not heat at all, it means that current is not flowing through its heating elements. Test the wall outlet, then the power cord. If these are good, the trouble may be in the thermostat or internal wiring. Repairs range from replacing a house fuse to installing a new thermostat.

Power off at outlet?

TEST: Unplug power cord and check wall outlet with a lamp you know is working.

 FIX: Replace fuse or reset circuit breaker. See p.127. If fuse keeps blowing, see *Appliance blows fuses*, p.229. △

Power cord faulty?

TEST: Unplug power cord from wall outlet. If cord is built in, disassemble appliance (p.227) so that cord leads are accessible, and clip jumper wire across them. If power cord is separate, clip jumper wire across terminals of female plug. Set volt-ohm meter to RX1 scale and clip its probes to the two ends of the element. If element is OK, meter will read zero ohms; if cord is broken, needle will jump or read high.

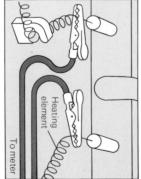 **FIX: Replace power cord.** Replace a separate cord as a unit, including male and female plugs. To remove built-in power cord, separate its leads from other wiring and withdraw cord from lower shell. Use a manufacturer's replacement for either type of cord. Note: If appliance has separate power cord, trouble may be due to dirty cooking (slow cooker), over-cooking (corn popper), over-cooking (slow cooker), and overheating. Polish terminal pins on body with steel wool; spray terminals of female plug with electrical contact cleaner (p.123). △△

Heating element broken?

TEST: Unplug appliance and disassemble it (see p.227). Examine element for breaks. Set volt-ohm meter to RX1 scale and clip probes to the two ends of the element. If element is OK, meter will read between 5 and 20 ohms for waffler, 20 and 40 ohms for corn popper, 50 and 200 ohms for slow cooker. If element is broken, meter will read high.

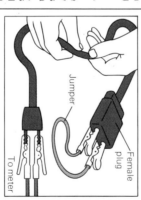 **FIX: Replace heating element.** Remove heating element (see disassembly sequences on p.227). Use manufacturer's replacement element in a hardware store, be sure it is rated for the same wattage as old element. Most heating elements are coil type and must be stretched to proper length before installation (see *Replacing a heating element*, p.226). △△

Thermostat broken?

TEST: Unplug power cord and disassemble appliance (see p.227) so that thermostat is accessible. If there is a temperature control shaft, turn it all the way toward *High*. Set volt-ohm meter to RX1 scale and clip its probes to terminals of thermostat. If thermostat is OK, meter will read zero ohms; if thermostat is broken, meter will read high.

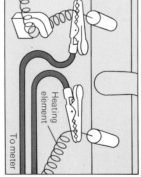 **FIX: Replace thermostat.** Remove terminal screws on thermostat and detach leads that they were holding. Pry off C-clips (waffler) or undo thermostat mounting screw (corn popper, slow cooker) and lift out thermostat. Refer to disassembly sequences on p.227. △△

Broken or corroded wiring?

TEST: With appliance unplugged and disassembled, examine all interior wiring and terminals. Look for broken wires and evidence of corrosion at terminals.

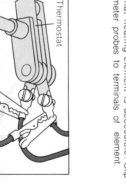 **FIX: Clean terminals; replace broken wires.** Spray terminals with electrical contact cleaner (p.123). Replace damaged wires with manufacturer's parts. △△

Ease of fix: △ simple △△ average △△△ difficult

228

Problems with the thermostat

Depending on the appliance, a thermostat may act as a timer or a temperature control. Symptoms of thermostat trouble include failure of the appliance to shut off automatically (corn popper), over-cooking (slow cooker), and overheating of plastic parts (waffler).

The thermostat is generally held tightly against the cooking surface by a spring. A weak or broken spring will result in overheating. Rather than trying to tighten a defective spring, replace it.

In most instances, the thermostat should be replaced if it is out of calibration. One model, however, has a pair of metal tabs that permit adjustments.

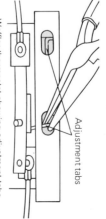

Waffler thermostat showing adjustment tabs.

Checking for an open circuit

1. Clip probes of volt-ohm meter to prongs of plugged-in power cord plug. If cord is detachable, clip jumper to female terminals. If cord is built in, attach jumper across cord leads.

2. Check heating element with appliance unplugged and cool. Disassemble appliance so that heating element is accessible. Clip meter probes to terminals or element.

Use RX1 scale for both tests.

Test 1: If cord is OK, meter will read zero ohms; if it is bad, needle will jump or read high.

Test 2: High reading means bad element. Good readings are 5–20 ohms for waffler, 20–40 for corn popper, 50–200 for slow cooker.

Testing the thermostat

Corn popper thermostat has no control shaft, maintains a fixed temperature. To test it, remove pan from body shell, clip volt-ohm meter probes to thermostat terminals.

Slow cookers and wafflers have adjustable thermostats. When testing, turn temperature control shaft to *High*. Clip meter probes to thermostat terminals.

Set volt-ohm meter to RX1 scale. If meter reads zero ohms, thermostat is OK; if meter reads high ohms, thermostat is broken. Note: This test does not show whether or not the thermostat is out of adjustment.

Appliance shocks user

A frayed power cord, an electrically live component grounded to (touching) a metal part, or leakage current due to faulty insulation will cause shocks. If leakage current is indicated by the tests, take the appliance to an authorized repairman. A frayed power cord or a grounded wire inside the appliance should be replaced.

Power cord frayed?

TEST: Receiving a shock from power cord is sufficient evidence it needs repair.

YES FIX: **Replace power cord.** See disassembly sequences on p.227. Use manufacturer's replacement power cord. ▲▲

Leakage current present?

TEST: If you receive a shock when you touch an exposed metal part of the appliance, there is either a grounded wire or leakage current. Leave control knob as it was when shock occurred. Unplug power cord from wall outlet. Set volt-ohm meter (p.124) to RX100 scale and clip one probe to metal shell of appliance, the other to a prong of the plug. If meter reads high, leakage current (p.127) is indicated.

YES FIX: **Take appliance to authorized repairman.** Eliminating leakage current requires special equipment. Note: It is possible the shock is not caused by leakage current but by a wire that becomes grounded only when the appliance is in operation. To investigate this, proceed with next test before taking appliance to repair shop. ▲▲▲

Internal wiring grounded to shell?

TEST: Unplug appliance and disassemble it so that internal wiring is accessible (p.227). Check wires for bare spots. Examine heating element to see that it is not touching element tray. Set volt-ohm meter to RX100 scale and clip one probe to metal shell of appliance, the other to either prong of power cord plug. Pull each wire in appliance. If needle jumps when a wire is handled, that wire is grounded.

YES FIX: **Repair or replace faulty wiring.** Pull heating element away from points where it may be touching shell. If necessary, tighten up coil-type element by gently squeezing several loops slightly closer together with long-nose pliers. Replace damaged wires with manufacturer's replacements. Do not try to repair faulty insulation with standard electrical tape; wafflers and other cooking devices operate at high temperatures and their wiring requires special insulation. ▲▲

Appliance blows fuses

When a fuse blows or a circuit breaker trips, it means there is either an electrical overload or a short circuit. Reducing the number of appliances in the circuit will eliminate the overload. If tests show the power cord or one of the interior wires is short-circuited, the defective part must be replaced.

Circuit overloaded?

TEST: To check for overloads, see p.127. Too many appliances in a circuit is the commonest cause of blown fuses.

YES FIX: **Reduce number of appliances in the circuit. Caution: Never replace a fuse or breaker with one having a larger capacity.** ▲

Short circuit in power cord or plug?

TEST: Unplug power cord from wall outlet. If cord is separate, unplug it from appliance. If cord is built in, disassemble appliance so that cord leads are accessible (see *Disassembling a waffler*, p.227), then free cord leads. Examine power cord for bare wires and burn marks and the plug for loose or distorted prongs. Set volt-ohm meter (p.124) to RX100 scale and clip its probes to the plug. Bend and pull cord. If power cord is OK, meter will read high; if cord is shorted, needle will jump or read zero ohms.

YES FIX: **Replace power cord.** Replace a separate cord as a unit, including male and female plugs. If cord is built in, withdraw it from lower shell. Use a manufacturer's replacement for either type of cord. ▲▲

Short circuit in internal wiring?

TEST: Unplug and disassemble appliance (see p.227). Examine all interior parts and wires. Look for burn marks on insulation and metal, distorted terminals, broken insulation, loose wires.

YES FIX: **Repair or replace broken parts.** Replace damaged wiring with manufacturer's replacements. Do not repair faulty wiring with standard electrical tape; most cooking appliances operate at high temperatures and their wiring requires special insulation. ▲▲

Ease of fix: ▲ simple ▲▲ average ▲▲▲ difficult

Testing for shocks and short circuits

1. Leakage current may cause shock. Unplug appliance, clip one volt-ohm meter probe to shell. If cord is separate, clip other probe to terminal pin (left). Otherwise, clip it to plug (right).

To meter   To meter

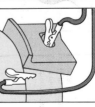

2. Another source of shock may be defective internal wiring. Leave meter set up as in first test. Open appliance housing so that wiring is accessible, and tug wires individually.

To meter

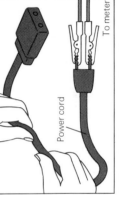

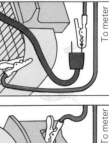

Power cord

To meter

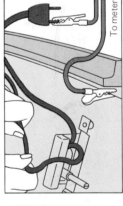

Use RX100 scale for all tests.
Test 1: High meter reading indicates leakage current.
Test 2: If needle jumps when a wire is handled, wire is grounded.
Test 3: If needle reads zero ohms or jumps, power cord is shorted.

3. Short circuit in power cord may blow fuses or trip circuit breakers. Disconnect cord (or free its leads if it is built in). Clip meter probes to plug. Twist and pull cord during test.

Use and care

1. No part of any of the appliances, other than the removable grilles of the waffler, should be immersed in water.

2. Clean a nonstick finish with soapy water and a sponge. Do not use scouring pads or abrasive cleansers. If the surface is aluminum, a scouring pad can be used to remove stubborn spots.

3. Cooking surfaces should be conditioned after each cleaning by brushing on a light coat of nonsmoking vegetable oil. Wipe off excess oil with a paper towel before using the appliance.

Large Appliances

Large appliances are relatively simple for their size. If you hesitate to tackle one, keep in mind that its defects are probably mechanical. The demanding aspect of most jobs is the number of steps involved in taking the appliance apart to inspect it, and all you need for that is time. This section is organized to help you do this as easily and as quickly as possible.

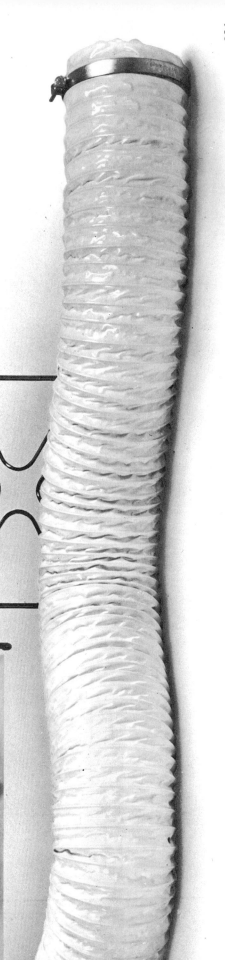

Air conditioners

Air conditioner problems

PROBLEM	POSSIBLE CAUSE	ACTION
Air conditioner does not turn on	No power at wall outlet	Check outlet with a lamp you know is working. If lamp does not turn on, replace fuse or reset breaker (p.127). If fuse keeps blowing, reduce number of appliances in circuit ●
	Open circuit in power cord or selector switch	Test power cord and switch and replace either one if defective (p.234) ●●■
Fan runs but cooling system does not.	Voltage at wall outlet incorrect	Measure voltage at wall outlet (p.234). (For 240-volt outlet, call a repairman.) ●●■
	Defective thermostat	Test thermostat and replace if defective (p.235) ●●■
	Open compressor overload protector	Test overload protector and replace if defective (p.236) ●●■
	Condenser fins clogged by dust	Clean condenser fins (p.236) ●●
	Faulty compressor motor	Call an appliance repairman to service the compressor motor ●●●
Cooling system runs, but fan does not	Defective selector switch	Check selector switch and replace if defective (p.234) ●●
	Capacitor faulty	Test capacitor and replace if defective (p.235) ●●■
	If motor hums but fan does not turn, the fan may be loose or obstructed or the motor shaft or bearings may be binding	Examine fan and restore it to working order (p.237) ●●
	If there is no humming, the fan motor itself may be defective	Test fan motor and replace if defective (p.237) ●●■
Fan and cooling system run, but unit cools poorly	Wrong sized air conditioner for room	Use an air conditioner with the correct cooling capacity (p.233) ●
	Air leaking into room from outdoors	Seal air gaps that occur between air conditioner and window ●
	Voltage at wall outlet incorrect	Measure voltage at outlet (p.234). (For 240-volt outlet, call a repairman.) ●●■
	Filter clogged by dust	Wash or replace filter (p.233) ●
	Ventilator stuck in open position or broken	The ventilator door controls the flow of air from outdoors into the room. Use a spray lubricant to free sticking parts. If any part is broken, replace the part ●●
	Bent evaporator fins	Straighten evaporator fins (p.236) ●
	Evaporator fan loose on motor shaft or clogged by dust	Tighten fan to shaft; clean fan (p.237) ●
	Loss of refrigerant	Call an appliance repairman to check for refrigerant leak ●●●
Cooling system cycles on and off over short time intervals	Thermostat on air conditioner set too warm	Reset thermostat ●
	Overload protector actuated	If compressor (cooling system) is started very soon after it is turned off, the protector will turn it off again. Wait two minutes before restarting cooling system ●
	Voltage at wall outlet incorrect	Measure outlet voltage (p.234). (For 240-volt outlet, call a repairman.) ●●■
	Capacitor faulty	Test capacitor and replace it if defective (p.235) ●●■
Air conditioner is noisy	Screws, trim, or exterior panels, rattling or vibrating	Tighten screws on trim and exterior panels ●
	Window, mounting supports, and paneling around air conditioner vibrate	Secure mounting supports or add more supports. If a window rattles, insert wooden wedges or pieces of folded cardboard between window and window jamb ●
	Fan loose on motor shaft. (A loose fan is usually indicated by a metallic rattle that changes when you change the fan speed.)	Tighten fan to shaft (p.237) ●●
	Bent evaporator fins. (Bent fins will be indicated by a whistling noise.)	Straighten evaporator fins (p.236) ●
	Chafing refrigerant tubes. (Chafing will be indicated by a ticking sound.)	Disassemble air conditioner (p.236) to gain access to refrigerant tubes (p.233). Bend tubing just enough to keep it from rubbing against adjacent parts ●●
	Old, hardened rubber in compressor mounts	Replace compressor mounts (p.236) ●●
Air conditioner frosts up	Low outdoor air temperature.	Avoid using air conditioner when temperature outdoors drops below 70°F ●
	Filter or evaporator fins clogged by dust	Wash or replace filter; clean evaporator fins (p.233) ●
Moisture drips into room	Cabinet not set at proper angle	Position unit so that its outdoor side is ¼ inch lower than its indoor side ●
	Bent evaporator fins	Straighten evaporator fins (p.236) ●
Air conditioner has a bad odor	If unit has a musty odor, a drain hole is clogged	Unclog drain hole in base pan (p.234) ●
	If odor is of oil or tobacco, evaporator fins are dirty	Vacuum evaporator fins, or spray them with deodorant. If problem is severe, take unit to an appliance or automobile repair shop to be steam cleaned ●

Ease of fix: ● simple ●● average ●●● difficult ■ Volt-ohm meter required for this step (see p.124)

How air conditioners work

Air conditioners work by circulating a refrigerant through two sets of coils in one continuous loop. One set, the evaporator coils, cools the room; the other set, the condenser coils, gives off heat to the outdoors. Between them, to keep the two parts from working against each other, is a barrier. Near the barrier—and as part of the refrigerant loop—is the compressor, which circulates the refrigerant and compresses it. The system works on the principle that a liquid (the refrigerant) absorbs heat (cools the room) when it expands into a gas, then gives off heat (to the outdoors) when it is compressed into a liquid again. The two fans help transfer the heat from the air to the coils to the outside air.

Cooling capacity of air conditioners

An air conditioner should have a cooling capacity adequate for the room it is intended to cool. If the unit is too small, it will run too long and not cool well; if it is too large, it may not stay on long enough to reduce the humidity to a comfortable level.

Here is a rough guide for fitting an air conditioner to a room: Measure the room's volume by multiplying its width by its length by its height in feet. Multiply the result by an exposure factor: 16 if the longest outside wall faces north; 17 if it faces east; 18, if south; 20, if west. Divide this result by an insulation factor: 6 if the room is well insulated, 4 if it is poorly insulated or has a lot of windows, 5 if your estimate lies somewhere in between. The resulting figure will be the approximate number of British thermal units (Btu's) per hour your air conditioner should be rated at for adequate cooling. To make a more accurate estimate, write The Association of Home Appliance Manufacturers, 20 N. Wacker Dr., Chicago, Illinois, 60606, for a copy of their Cooling-load Estimate Form for home air conditioners.

Cleaning the filter: The filter is located at the air intake on the room side of the air conditioner. This is usually at the front of the unit (as in the view below), although it can be at the sides. On some models the filter can simply be lifted out. With others you must first remove a front panel or filter retainer (as in the illustration) by prying or by pressing the panel or retainer away from the edge of the unit and pulling. Other retainers are attached by screws. Clean the filter, if it is the reusable type, by agitating it in a basin of detergent and water. Otherwise, replace it. If the filter has torn, dust has probably accumulated on the evaporator fins. Remove the dust with a vacuum cleaner.

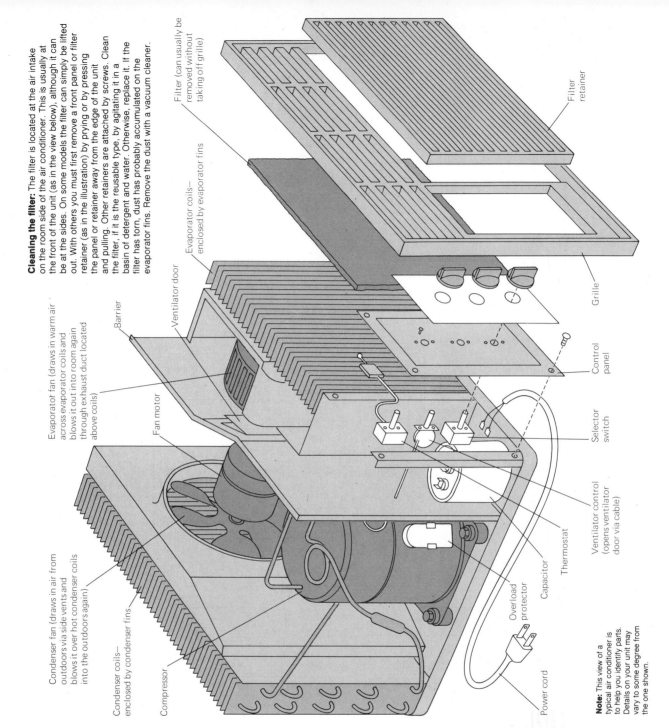

Filter retainer

Filter (can usually be removed without taking off grille)

Evaporator coils— enclosed by evaporator fins

Grille

Barrier

Ventilator door

Evaporator fan (draws in warm air across evaporator coils and blows it out into room again through exhaust duct located above coils)

Fan motor

Control panel

Selector switch

Ventilator control (opens ventilator door via cable)

Thermostat

Capacitor

Condenser fan (draws in air from outdoors via side vents and blows it over hot condenser coils into the outdoors again)

Condenser coils— enclosed by condenser fins

Compressor

Overload protector

Power cord

Note: This view of a typical air conditioner is to help you identify parts. Details on your unit may vary to some degree from the one shown.

Checking voltage at a 120-volt wall outlet

First test: Unit not plugged in.

Turn off the power at the service panel. Set a volt-ohm meter (p.124) to the 250 VAC scale and insert its probes into the outlet. Turn on the power. If the meter now reads less than 108 volts, report this to your power company. If the voltage is normal (108 to 130 volts), make a second voltage test as shown at right.

Second test: Unit plugged in.

Turn off the power. Plug the air conditioner into one receptacle and insert an adjacent receptacle. Then turn on the unit. If the power and the unit, turn on the power. If the voltage drops to below 108 volts, and the drop is 10 volts or more from the first reading, wiring is too poor to sustain a heavy operating load. Consult an electrician.

Clearing the drain holes

When an air conditioner is being operated, water collects in the evaporator side of the unit. The water exits through a chassis part way or all the way out of the drain passage into the condenser side; there it is picked up by the condenser fan and sprayed against the condenser coils. The drain passage is frequently just a hole or space under the barrier separating the evaporator from the condenser. It should be kept clear.

On some models the evaporator pan and drain passage will be readily visible after the front grille has been removed. The grille may be attached to the unit by one or more screws hidden from view by the filter retainer, so remove the retainer to look for screws before trying to take off the grille. If the passage cannot be reached from the front, take the cabinet to gain access to it (See *Gaining access to the interior of the air conditioner*, p.236). When you have exposed the drain passage, remove any debris that is clogging it.

Some air conditioners have an additional drain hole in the back of the unit, facing outdoors, which permits water that has not been picked up and sprayed by the condenser fan to flow off. Clear this hole if it is clogged by debris, otherwise some water may back up into the evaporator pan. The hole is easy to locate without disassembling the unit.

By simply removing the front grille from certain models, you gain access to the drain hole. Take out any retaining screws, pry out the grille or pull it down and out, or up and out, to remove it.

Water collected under the fan is a sure sign that the drain hole is clogged. Push a stiff wire, such as a straightened-out clothes hanger, down the drain hole to remove any debris that is clogging it.

If the evaporator coils block access from the front, unclog the drain hole from the side. To do this, pull the chassis part way from the cabinet or remove the chassis entirely (see p.236).

Safety precaution: Discharge capacitor

Before doing any work on the inside of the air conditioner, discharge the capacitor to avoid shock, or damage to a volt-ohm meter. Capacitors (you may find more than one) are located in the recessed area behind the control panel or near the compressor or fan motor. Purchase a 20,000-ohm, 2-watt resistor (for about 50 cents) at an electrical supply store and discharge the capacitor by connecting the resistor leads to its terminals. If there are three terminals, connect each of the outer ones to the center terminal.

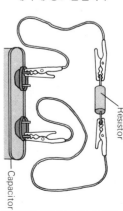

Resistor — Capacitor

Checking and replacing the power cord and selector switch

The power cord terminates behind the control panel. Unplug the cord, then remove the grille and lift off the panel to gain access to the cord leads. Test the power cord with a volt-ohm meter (p.124) set to RX1; pull the leads free and replace the cord if it is defective.

Without disassembling the air conditioner or performing any electrical tests, you may be able to diagnose a faulty selector switch by means of the following simple observations. Turn the air conditioner on. Rotate the selector knob (or push the buttons on a pushbutton switch) through all settings and observe which part of the unit works at each setting:

1. If neither the fan nor the compressor runs at any switch setting, the switch is defective. Replace the switch (see below).

2. If the fan does not run but the compressor runs when the selector switch is set to *Cool*, the fan motor is at fault. Replace the fan motor (p.237).

3. If the fan runs at one speed setting but not at another, examine leads connected to the switch. If a terminal is burned or insulation is discolored, repair the lead (pp.128-131) and replace switch.

If these approaches have not disclosed anything, you must make electrical tests. Unless you are an experienced electrician and have the required circuit diagram, call an appliance repairman.

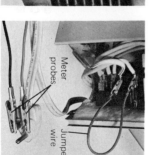

To gain access to the power cord and selector switch terminals, take out retaining screws and pull the control panel away from unit. Disconnect the control panel. **Caution: Remember to discharge the capacitor (see above).**

To test power cord, set volt-ohm meter to RX1 scale and clip its probes to plug. Attach jumper wire across cord leads; bend and pull cord. If needle jumps around or reads high, cord is defective.

Meter probes — Jumper wire

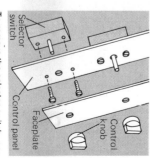

To remove the selector switch, pry control knobs off control panel with a knife and remove faceplate. Disconnect leads from switch terminals and take out screws holding switch to control panel.

Selector switch — Faceplate — Control knob — Control panel

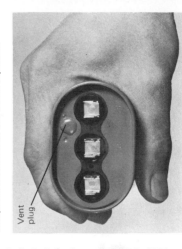

To remove capacitor, take out clamp screw and remove clamp. Disconnect leads and lift out capacitor.

Vent plug

Some capacitors have a third terminal, labeled "C." The vent plug is found on all capacitors.

Testing and replacing the thermostat

The thermostat responds to variations in room temperature as measured by the sensing bulb; the bulb is mounted on the evaporator coils and is in turn controlled by a dial on the control panel. The thermostat switches the compressor on or off when the temperature goes above or below that on the dial setting.

To test the thermostat, unplug the air conditioner and remove the front grille. Take out retaining screws and pull the control panel away from the unit to make the thermostat terminals accessible. Test the thermostat with a volt-ohm meter (p.124) and replace the thermostat if it is defective. Some thermostats have more than two leads connected to them. In such cases, unless you are an experienced electrician and have the circuit diagram for your unit, call a repairman.

Caution: Be sure to discharge capacitor as illustrated on the opposite page.

Testing and replacing the capacitor

A short or open circuit in the capacitor will stop the compressor—and the fan motor also, in units where the fan motor is part of the capacitor circuit. Usually there is only one capacitor, but there may be two of them.

To reach the capacitor, unplug the unit and remove the front grille. Take out retaining screws and lift off the control panel. If the capacitor is not there, remove the chassis from the cabinet (see *Gaining access to the interior of the air conditioner*, p.236) and look for it next to the compressor or the fan motor.

Examine the capacitor. If it bulges, or if its vent plug is blown off and it leaks oil, the capacitor is defective and you should replace it. If nothing is visibly wrong, test the capacitor with a volt-ohm meter (p.124). Disconnect one of the leads to the capacitor. Set meter to the RX100 scale and touch its probes to the capacitor terminals. If the needle of the meter jumps toward zero ohms, then slowly returns to high ohms, the capacitor is OK. If the needle jumps and remains at zero ohms—or if it does not move at all—the capacitor is faulty. Replace it. To double-check, reverse the meter probes and repeat the test.

Some capacitors (those with three terminals) are designed to work in conjunction with the fan motor as well as the compressor. They incorporate two capacitors in one and should be tested twice with the volt-ohm meter. Touch one probe to the terminal labeled "C" (for common), the other probe to each of the other terminals in turn.

When replacing the capacitor, obtain a new one with the same rated capacitance and peak voltage as that indicated on the case of the old one. Remember to label the leads before disconnecting them from the old capacitor. Connect them to the new one in the same order.

Caution: Discharge the capacitor before handling it (see opposite page).

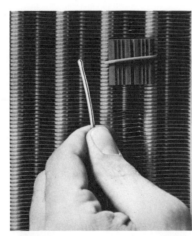

To replace thermostat, first remove thermostat sensing bulb from its mount. The mount is located near the evaporator fins, but the exact location will depend on the model of air conditioner.

Test capacitor with a volt-ohm meter. Do it after you have discharged capacitor to avoid damage to meter.

Sensing bulb — Tube

Control knob

Control panel

Faceplate

Thermostat

To remove thermostat, pry control knobs off panel and take off faceplate. Disconnect leads from terminals and take out screws holding thermostat to panel. Remove thermostat control, sensing bulb, and tube.

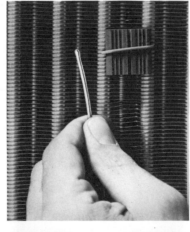

Meter probes

To test thermostat, turn temperature control dial to coldest setting. Set volt-ohm meter to RX1 scale and clip its probes to thermostat terminals. If meter reads zero, thermostat is OK; if high, it is defective.

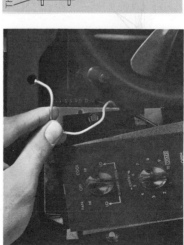

On some models, the sensing bulb tube traces a winding path. When replacing the bulb, thread tube backwards along the same path followed in removing it. Install the new bulb in the old location.

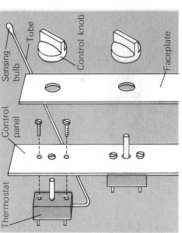

Air conditioners

Straightening evaporator fins and cleaning condenser fins

Fins are found on both the evaporator and the condenser coils. They serve to transfer heat from the air to the evaporator coils, and from the condenser coils to the air, more efficiently. The fins are fragile and only a small amount of distortion in them can cause whistling and

water drip. Generally, this will become a problem only at the evaporator side. Unplug the air conditioner, remove the front grille, and carefully straighten the evaporator fins.

Dirt on the condenser fins can disable the compressor. After unplugging the

unit, remove the chassis from the cabinet (see *Gaining access to the interior of the air conditioner,* below). Clean the condenser fins and the cabinet interior. If necessary, wash the interior.

Caution: Discharge capacitor after removing chassis from cabinet (p.234).

Some units have spine fins. Despite their contorted appearance, do not attempt to straighten them.

Use a putty knife to restore the space between fins. No two fins should touch one another.

Clean the condenser fins and the inside of the cabinet adjacent to fins with a vacuum cleaner.

Gaining access to the interior of the air conditioner

Some units are built so that you may gain access to more deeply located parts without removing the air conditioner from the window. In particular, look for the pull-out type you may simply lift out the chassis itself, otherwise you must lift the entire air conditioner out

the chassis part way out of the cabinet, allowing access from the sides and top.

For other repairs, however, you must remove the chassis from the window. If it is the pull-out type you may simply lift out the chassis itself, otherwise you must lift the entire air conditioner out

of the window and then the chassis out of the cabinet. Since these units are heavy, find someone to help you. Place a sturdy table of approximately the same height as the window sill alongside the air conditioner and maneuver the air conditioner onto it.

The chassis of some air conditioners can be pulled from the cabinet after the front grille has been removed. When the chassis is more than halfway out, its weight must be supported from below.

The cabinet on some units can be lifted off after removing the air conditioner from the window and taking out the screws holding the cabinet to the chassis. It may also be necessary to remove the accordion slides.

On other models you will be able to slide

On some lightweight units, the chassis lifts out of cabinet. First, remove screws, accordion slides, and any covers. Do not attempt to turn unit upside down and lift cabinet from chassis; parts may come loose.

The compressor mounts

Compressor

Rubber mount

The sound of the compressor will become excessively loud after the rubber mounts age and lose their cushioning effect. Unplug the air conditioner and remove the chassis from the cabinet. Reach in and feel the mounts. If they have become hard and cracked, replace them. Take off the mounting nuts and lift the compressor slightly to remove the mounts. **Caution: Moving the compressor too far out of position may damage refrigerant tubes.**

The overload protector

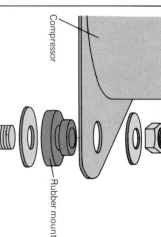

To meter

The overload protector is mounted on the compressor and turns the compressor off if it overheats. A protector that does not close again after a two-minute cooling period, permitting the compressor to come back on, may be defective. Unplug the air conditioner and remove the chassis from the cabinet. Take off the overload protector cover after prying off the clamp that holds the cover in place. Take off the overload protector with a volt-ohm meter (p.124) set to RX1 scale. If the meter reads zero ohms, the protector is OK. If it reads high, replace the overload protector.

236

Solving problems with the fans

There are two fans, generally run by one motor. The evaporator fan takes air from the room and moves it through the evaporator coils and back into the room as cooled air; the condenser fan moves air from outdoors through the condenser coils and back outdoors as heated air.

Unplug the air conditioner and take off the front grille to reach the fan. If the evaporator coils block access to the evaporator fan, slide the chassis out of the cabinet part way or remove the chassis

(see *Gaining access to the interior of the air conditioner*, opposite). Then, turn the fan by hand:

If the fan feels loose on the motor shaft, tighten it. If the fan is the push-on type that does not have a setscrew, the rubber hub by which the fan should grip the motor shaft may have hardened and cracked. Replace the hub, then press the fan securely onto the motor shaft. Replace the fan if any of its blades are broken (to stop excessive vibration).

If the fan is a squirrel cage type, you will need a special setscrew wrench with a long arm to tighten it. Vacuum any dust accumulated on the fan vanes. Dust inhibits air flow in a squirrel cage fan.

If the fan is difficult to turn by hand, the motor shaft is out of alignment or its bearings need oil. (To solve these problems you will in most instances need to remove the chassis from the cabinet.) Lubricate the motor. If this does not help the fan turn more easily, loosen the

motor mounting nuts. If the motor shaft then moves freely, the problem was caused by poor motor alignment. To correct the alignment, first tighten all the mounting nuts a couple of turns and turn the fan, then tighten each nut another few turns and try the fan again; it should remain easy to turn. Repeat this procedure until all the nuts are tight. If the fan is noisy, the fan motor mounting nuts may simply need tightening.

Caution: Discharge capacitor (p.234).

Secure fan to motor shaft by tightening the setscrew on the hub with either a screwdriver or a setscrew wrench.

Squirrel cage type fan has gap through which long-armed setscrew wrench must be inserted to reach screw on motor shaft.

To lubricate the motor, add one or two drops of SAE #10 oil to the oil holes or tubes on either end of the motor.

Adjust the fan motor's mounting nuts if the motor is binding. Tighten the nuts if the motor is noisy.

Motor mounting nuts on some models can be tightened from the front of the unit. First, remove the front grille and fan.

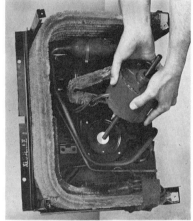

Motor is removable only after fans have been detached and motor mounting nuts are unscrewed. Disconnect motor leads from their terminals on control panel or capacitor and loosen lead clamps if there are any. Thread leads out of unit after removing motor.

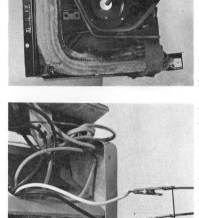

On some models, you cannot remove the fan motor without first unscrewing and shifting the condenser coils and associated housing out of the way. However, be careful not to bend the refrigerant tubes between the compressor and condenser coils excessively.

Testing and replacing the fan motor

The fan motor turns both the evaporator and condenser fans. To test the motor, unplug the air conditioner and remove the chassis from the cabinet (see opposite page). Turn the selector knob to (or set the push button switch at) *Off* and measure the resistance of the motor wiring with a volt-ohm meter (p.124). If there are more than two motor leads, test from the white (common) lead to each of the other leads in turn.

Replace the motor if it is defective. If motor leads follow a tortuous path through the unit, tie a string to each when removing them. Then, tie the strings to the new motor leads and use the strings to pull the leads back to the terminals to which they are to be connected.

Caution: Discharge capacitor (p.234).

To test fan motor, unplug unit and trace motor leads to where they terminate on control panel or capacitor and clip probes of volt-ohm meter to them. Set meter to RX1 scale. If meter reads between 2 and 30 ohms, motor is OK; if zero or high, it is defective.

To meter

Dehumidifier problems

PROBLEM	POSSIBLE CAUSE	ACTION
Dehumidifier does not turn on	No power at wall outlet	Check outlet with a lamp you know is working. If lamp does not turn on, replace fuse or reset circuit breaker (p.127). If fuse keeps blowing, reduce number of appliances in circuit ●
	Open circuit in power cord	Test power cord and replace if defective (see Air conditioners, p.234) ●● ■
	Faulty overflow prevention switch	Test overflow prevention switch and replace it if defective (see below) ●● ■
	Faulty humidistat	Test humidistat and replace it if defective (see below) ●●● ■
Unit runs, but dehumidifies poorly	Unit too small	Close doors or partition the area, and dehumidify a section of it at a time ●
	Condenser fins clogged by dust	Unplug unit, remove cabinet, and clean the fins with a vacuum cleaner ●●
	Fan loose on motor shaft	Tighten fan to shaft (see opposite page) ●●
	Fan motor bearings dry	Lubricate fan motor bearings (see opposite page) ●●
	Fan motor defective	Test motor and replace it if defective (see opposite page) ●●● ■
	Faulty compressor motor	Call an appliance repairman to service compressor motor ●●●
Dehumidifier is noisy	Screws, trim, or exterior panels rattling or vibrating	Tighten screws on trim and exterior panels ●
	If the noise is a metallic rattle, the fan may be loose on its motor shaft	Tighten fan to shaft (see opposite page) ●●
	Old, hardened rubber in compressor mounts	Replace compressor mounts (see Air conditioners, p.236) ●●●
Dehumidifier frosts up	Air temperature too low	Do not operate dehumidifier when room temperature is below 65°F ●
	Air circulation obstructed	Move the dehumidifier away from wall and curtains ●
	Condenser fins clogged by dust	Unplug unit and remove cabinet. Clean the fins with a vacuum cleaner ●●
Dehumidifier leaks water	Drip pan not emptied (in units that do not have an overflow prevention switch)	Empty drip pan ●
	Kinks in drain hose (if a hose is used instead of the drip pan)	Remove kinks from hose ●
	Overflow prevention switch defective	Test overflow prevention switch and replace it if defective (see below) ●●● ■
Dehumidifier has a bad odor	If unit has a musty odor, stagnant water has collected in its base	Unplug the unit and remove the cabinet. Wipe away water collected in the base of the unit under the fan and compressor ●●● ■
	If odor is of oil or tobacco, condenser fins are dirty	Vacuum condenser fins or spray them with room deodorant. If problem is severe, take unit to an appliance or automobile repair shop to be steam cleaned ●

Ease of fix: ● simple   ●● average   ●●● difficult   ■ Volt-ohm meter required for this step (see p.124)

The humidistat

The humidistat operates like a thermostat, but unlike the thermostat it responds to the amount of water vapor in the air rather than to the air temperature. After you have set the control knob the humidistat will periodically switch the unit on and off to maintain the level of humidity you desire.

A humidistat will be unable to turn the unit on or off if it is defective. To check it, unplug the unit and remove the cabinet. Dismount the humidistat from the cabinet, remove its leads, and test it with a volt-ohm meter (p.124). If the humidistat is defective, replace it.

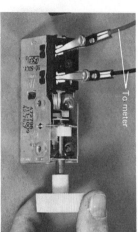

To test humidistat, set volt-ohm meter to RX1 scale and clip its probes to humidistat terminals. Turn knob through its entire range. If meter reads zero ohms during a portion of range, the humidistat is OK; if it reads zero or high during all of range, it is faulty.

The overflow prevention switch

The overflow prevention switch has a rubber tube that reaches down into the drip pan. When air trapped inside the tube is compressed by water rising in the pan, the air trips the switch, and the unit turns off.

A faulty switch will let the drip pan overflow or keep the unit from turning on. To check the switch, first unplug and disassemble the dehumidifier. Remove the switch and disconnect its leads. Test the switch with a volt-ohm meter (p.124). Set the meter to the RX1 scale and clip its probes to the switch terminals. Replace a faulty switch.

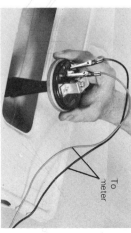

Test switch with drip pan filled with water. Initially, meter should read zero ohms. After switch has been lowered into water to about level at which it is mounted over pan in unit, needle of meter should jump to high. A different reading in either case means switch is faulty.

How dehumidifiers work

A dehumidifier works very much like an air conditioner (see *How air conditioners work*, p.233). It uses the same parts, but the parts are assembled in a way that cancels the air cooling one expects from an air conditioner.

On a warm day, anything cool, such as a glass of iced tea, will collect and condense water vapor. In the same way, water collects on the dehumidifier's moisture collecting coils (called evapora-

tor coils in the air conditioner) and eventually trickles down into the drip pan. Air conditioners collect water too; but the water is sprayed onto hot condenser coils, which expel it outdoors as vapor.

Dehumidifiers do not cool like air conditioners because the condenser coils give off their heat inside the dehumidifier, not to the outdoors. Air cooled by the moisture-collecting coils is thus immediately made warm again.

Solving problems with the fan and fan motor

The fan circulates air from the room, through the dehumidifier, and back into the room again. Inside the unit the air becomes dehumidified when blown over the moisture collecting coils. When the fan does not work, the unit loses most of its ability to transfer dry air back into the room. You may not know immediately when this has happened, because the noise of the still running compressor inside the dehumidifier can mask the cessation of fan noise.

Unplug the dehumidifier, then disassemble it to gain access to the fan. Turn the fan by hand and tighten it if it feels loose or wobbly on the motor shaft. The fan may be a push-on type that does not have a set screw; in this case, the rubber

hub by which the fan should grip the motor shaft may have become hardened and cracked. Replace the hub, then press the fan securely back into position on the motor shaft.

If any of the fan blades are broken, replace them, otherwise they will cause excessive vibration. Other noise may be due to loose motor mounting nuts. Correct the problem by tightening them. If the fan is difficult to turn on its shaft, the fan motor bearings probably need oil. Lubricate the bearings, but avoid overlubricating them.

The fan motor should be tested with a volt-ohm meter (p.124) set to the RX1 scale. Replace the motor if the test indicates it is defective.

To test fan motor, clip probes of meter to motor leads after disconnecting leads from relay. If meter reads between 2 and 30 ohms, motor is OK; if high, it is faulty.

To lubricate the motor, add one or two drops of SAE #10 oil to the oil holes or tubes. These will be found at either end of the motor, sometimes with plastic caps on them.

Secure fan to motor shaft by tightening the setscrew on the fan hub. Depending on the type of screw, you will need either a screwdriver or a setscrew wrench to do this.

Note: This view of a typical dehumidifier is to help you identify its parts. Details on your unit may vary to some degree from the one shown. Since the appliance closely resembles an air conditioner, many of the repairs given under *Air conditioners*, p.232–237, can be adapted to a dehumidifier.

Humidistat

Fan

Fan motor

Relay

Overflow prevention switch

Compressor

Condenser coils

Moisture collecting coils

Drip pan

Power cord

(Cabinet not shown)

Dishwashers

Dishwasher problems

PROBLEM	POSSIBLE CAUSE	ACTION
Dishwasher does not run	No power at wall outlet	Replace fuse or reset circuit breaker ●
	Door switch defective	Test door switch and replace it if defective (p.243) ●●■
	Selector switch or timer faulty	Check selector switch and timer and replace either one if defective (p.243) ●●
Dishwasher does not fill	Float on float switch jammed upward	Remove obstruction from under float on float switch (p.244) ●
	Inlet valve screen clogged	Clean or replace inlet valve screen (p.245) ●●
	Inlet valve solenoid defective	Test inlet valve solenoid and replace it if defective (p.245) ●●■
	Selector switch or timer faulty	Check selector switch and timer and replace either one if defective (p.243) ●●
	If water drains from the dishwasher during fill, the drain valve is stuck open	Replace the drain valve (p.245) ●●
Dishwasher does not drain	Pressure switch defective	Test pressure switch and replace it if defective (p.245) ●●■
	Strainer clogged	Clean strainer (p.242) ●
	Pump impeller clogged	Remove clogging matter from pump (p.244) ●●
	Drain valve solenoid defective	Test drain valve solenoid and replace it if defective (p.245) ●●■
	Drain valve clogged	Clean drain valve (p.245) ●●
	Motor faulty	Call an appliance repairman to service the motor ●●●
Dishwasher does not wash well	Water not hot enough	Run hot water from kitchen faucet over a thermometer for two minutes. It should read between 140°F and 160°F. Correct your hot water supply to lie within this range ●
	Sprayer and strainer clogged	Clean sprayer and strainer (p.242) ●
	Detergent dispenser not dumping	Check operation of detergent dispenser and repair any defective part (p.242) ●
	Pump impellers clogged	Remove clogging matter from pump (p.244) ●●
	If unit stays on wash cycle, cycle extender switch may be defective	Test cycle extender switch and replace it if defective (p.243) ●●●
	Selector switch or timer faulty.	Check selector switch and timer and replace either one if defective (p.243) ●●
	Motor faulty	Call an appliance repairman to service the motor ●●●
Dishes do not dry well. Dishes come out spotty	Water not hot enough	Run hot water from kitchen faucet over a thermometer for two minutes. It should read between 140°F and 160°F. Correct your hot water supply to lie within this range ●
	Wetting agent dispenser empty	Refill dispenser ●
	Heater defective	Check the heater and replace any part that is defective (p.244) ●●
Dishwasher leaks	If water leaks from door vent, dishes may have been improperly loaded	Reposition dishes in racks to avoid accidental deflection of water through door vent ●
	If leaks are from the bottom of the door, the unit may be oversudsing	Use only a detergent recommended for dishwashers. Do not prewash dishes with a liquid detergent before putting them into the dishwasher ●
	If the door leaks, the door gasket may be defective	Replace defective door gasket (p.242) ●●
	If dishwasher overfills (water continues to rise during fill beyond door sill), the timer may be faulty	Check timer and replace it if defective (p.243) ●●
	If dishwasher overfills, inlet valve may be stuck open	Replace stuck inlet valve (p.245) ●●
	If leak is from under the tub, a hose clamp may be loose or a hose hardened and split	Turn off power, remove lower access panel (p.243). Adjust clamps or replace hose ●●
	If leak is at the junction of pump and tub bottom, pump seal may be defective	Call an appliance repairman to replace pump seal ●●●
Dishwasher is noisy	Dishes poorly loaded	Load dishes in the way your owner's manual recommends. The sprayer must be able to turn freely without striking whatever you put into the tub ●
	Low water level in tub—caused by low water pressure or a clogged inlet valve screen	Avoid using house water supply while dishwasher is running. Check inlet valve screen and clean or replace it if clogged (p.245) ●
	If there is a chatter or knocking sound during fill, the inlet valve is defective	Replace the inlet valve (p.245) ●●
Door or dish rack does not work properly	Door not latching	Adjust the door strike or replace the latch (p.242) ●
	Door dropping hard when opened	Adjust or replace the door spring (p.242) ●●
	Racks binding	Repair or replace the dish rack (p.242) ●

Ease of fix: ● simple ●● average ●●● difficult ■ Volt-ohm meter required for this step (See p.124).

Spots, marks, stains and film

If any of the following occur, take the steps indicated:

Spotting and filming (removable)

1. Increase the amount of detergent. Be certain to use only those detergents that are specially manufactured for use in automatic dishwashers.

2. Make sure temperature of hot water supply is at least 140°F.

3. Reduce the load of dishes you place on the rack.

4. Refill wetting agent dispenser. If unit does not have a dispenser, hang a bar rinse conditioner on the top rack.

5. Try another brand of detergent.

Note: to remove the spots or film, set a bowl containing two cups of white vinegar on the bottom rack after the wash and rinse cycles have been completed. Repeat wash and rinse cycles.

Etching (filming that cannot be removed; most noticeable on glass)

1. Decrease the amount of detergent.

2. Reduce the load of dishes on the racks.

3. If water pressure is low, do not use house water for other purposes while the dishwasher is running.

Black marks on china

These are caused by utensils rubbing against china during wash. Separate china and utensils when loading.

Dishes (and the interior of the dishwasher) stained yellow or brown

1. Temporary solution: After the unit fills for wash, stop it and add ¼ cup of citric acid crystals. Then, complete the full wash and rinse cycle.

2. Permanent solution: Install an iron filter in the water supply.

Darkening of aluminum

Try another dishwasher detergent. To remove the darkening, scour the utensil with steel wool.

Small, dark spots on silverware

Rinse the silverware before putting it into the machine if it is to stand for several hours before washing. To remove the spots, use silver polish.

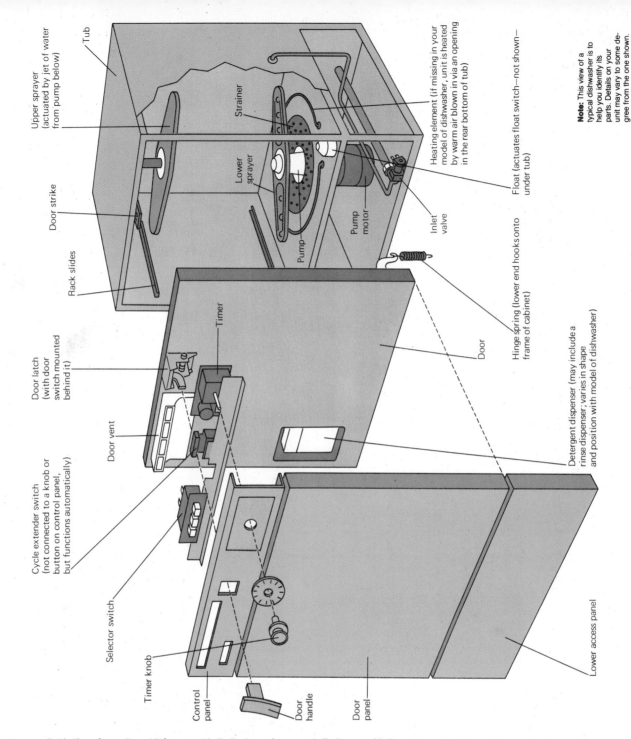

Tub

Upper sprayer (actuated by jet of water from pump below)

Strainer

Heating element (if missing in your model of dishwasher, unit is heated by warm air blown in via an opening in the rear bottom of tub)

Door strike

Lower sprayer

Float (actuates float switch—not shown—under tub)

Rack slides

Pump

Pump motor

Inlet valve

Timer

Door

Hinge spring (lower end hooks onto frame of cabinet)

Door latch (with door switch mounted behind it)

Door vent

Cycle extender switch (not connected to a knob or button on control panel, but functions automatically)

Detergent dispenser (may include a rinse dispenser; varies in shape and position with model of dishwasher)

Door panel

Selector switch

Lower access panel

Timer knob

Control panel

Door handle

Note: This view of a typical dishwasher is to help you identify its parts. Details on your unit may vary to some degree from the one shown.

Dishwashers

Cleaning the sprayer and strainer

During the wash and rinse cycles the sprayer sprays water on the dishes with considerable force. The water then drips to the tub bottom, to be filtered by the strainer and circulated by the pump back through the sprayer.

Dishes do not wash well when the holes in the sprayer or strainer are clogged. One way to check for clogging is to listen to the sprayer during wash. If you cannot

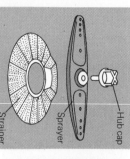

Sprayer   Strainer   Hub cap

Remove sprayer and strainer from tub. Unscrew hub cap, lift sprayer, then disengage clips, if any, to lift strainer out of tub bottom.

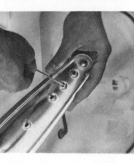

Use a stiff wire to unclog the holes in the sprayer. If the unit has a second sprayer mounted under the upper dish rack, clean it too.

Unclog the holes in the upper tub spray if the dishes in the upper rack clean poorly. Note: Only a few washers use an upper tub spray.

hear it turn at about 40 swishes per minute, the sprayer has slowed or halted. This occurs when the spray holes, which point horizontally to make the sprayer turn, clog with food particles.

Remove the sprayer and strainer from the dishwasher to clean them. Flush both under a running faucet. Scrub strainer with a stiff brush to remove heavy accumulations of food and debris.

Adjusting and repairing the door

The door must latch securely, otherwise the door switch will not close and the place will not start. Check the position of the door strike as you close the door and adjust the strike until proper latching is accomplished. If that does not correct the problem, replace the latch.

Weak or broken hinge springs will cause the door to drop abruptly when opened. These springs are usually located

The door strike (or the catch) on many units can be repositioned. Loosen screws, slide the strike inward or out, then retighten screws.

Remove the door latch after lifting off control panel (see opposite page). Take out the retaining screws at top edge and inner side of door.

The door springs are hooked onto the door and to the cabinet frame underneath tub. Remove panel (see opposite page) to replace them.

under the front corners of the tub. Replace bad springs. Note: The cabinet frame sometimes has a series of holes adjacent to the pair on which the springs hook. They permit you to change the spring tension. Select a different hole and hook the spring to it.

After long use, the inner door panel may become scratched. Clean scratches and patch them with epoxy compound.

The dish racks

A dish rack may stick when you try to pull it out because the rollers do not turn or because the rack or the rack slides are bent. Replace the part that causes the problem.

To remove a dish rack, take out pins that hold it to the rack slides. Note: The racks in some units can be lifted out simply by pulling and tilting them.

The rollers on some dish racks clip on and can be removed simply by pulling. If rollers do not loosen, replace entire rack. Note: Replace rack that has chipped.

The detergent dispenser

The detergent dispenser opens automatically during the wash cycle to add detergent to the water in the tub. Some dispensers open in two stages, separated by a time interval.

Occasionally a large dish or the handle of a utensil obstructs the dispenser cup as it opens and prevents much or all of the detergent from dumping out. To ascertain if that is what is happening, relocate the dishes in the rack adjacent to the dispenser cup and repeat cycle.

If the problem persists, check the dispenser mechanism for a broken spring or lever, or binding due to corrosion. To make a thorough inspection, you may need to remove the front panel (see Gaining access to parts inside the door and under the dishwasher, opposite.) Replace broken or corroded parts.

Replacing the door gasket

The door gasket maintains a watertight seal between the door and the cabinet, and may be mounted on either of them. When the rubber in the gasket becomes hard and cracked it loses its effectiveness, and the door leaks.

Replace a defective gasket. On some units the gasket is not held by retaining screws; it may be unclipped and removed or simply pried out. If you buy a replacement that has crimps in it, lay the gasket in a sink filled with warm water for a few minutes to remove the crimps before installing it.

After installing a new gasket, check the door for proper latching (see Adjusting and repairing the door, above). A snug fit is sufficient; do not let the door press the gasket too tightly or it may damage the rubber and cause leaking.

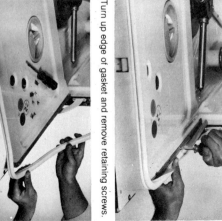

Turn up edge of gasket and remove retaining screws.

Lift off the gasket after all screws have been removed.

The door switch

The door switch is a protective device that keeps the dryer from running unless the door is closed. You can spot it easily. It is a button or lever mounted on the cabinet that the door actuates as it closes. When the switch is faulty the dryer cannot run at all.

To check the switch, first unplug the dryer and lift the dryer top (see *Gaining access to interior parts*, at right). Test the door switch with a volt-ohm meter set to the RX1 scale (see p.124). Replace it if it is defective.

To meter

To test door switch, clip probes of volt-ohm meter to switch terminals after disconnecting the leads to the terminals. Close switch with your finger. If meter reads zero ohms, switch is OK; if high, it is faulty.

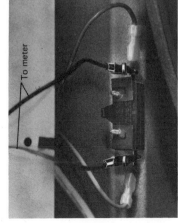

CAUTION:
Dry ... fabrics cleaned in water.
Do ... ly items containing foam

To replace door switch, disconnect leads, take out screws that mount switch to dryer, then push switch through mounting hole. On some models you may also need to depress spring clips on switch.

Gaining access to interior parts

To remove control panel: Take out the panel retaining screws, and lift off the panel. On some panels you may first have to remove the control knobs; some knobs unscrew, others can be removed by slipping a piece of cloth behind the knob around the knob shaft and pulling on the cloth.

To lift the top: First, take out the top retaining screws, if there are any. On the dryer shown here, the retaining screws are adjacent to the lint screen slot.

Insert a putty knife under the top and rap it with the palm of your hand to open the spring clips that moor the top to the cabinet at each of its corners. Raise the top.

To remove lower access panel: Pull the panel away from the bottom of the dryer. Note: On some dryers you must first depress a spring tab on the cabinet above the center of the panel with a screwdriver.

To lift off front panel: First, unhook the door springs located inside the cabinet. There are two of them, one under each corner of the panel.

To remove control panel:

Take out the screws that moor the panel to the cabinet and lift off the panel. **Caution: On some models the drum is supported by the front panel. Place a block of wood underneath the drum to hold it up after removing the panel.**

To remove the back panel: Take out the panel retaining screws and lift the panel away from the cabinet.

To remove air outlet duct: Take out the duct retaining screws and lift the duct out through the top of the cabinet. Note: Before being able to do this, you may have to remove the drum (see p.252).

249

Dryers

Solving problems with the thermostat, start switch, and timer

The thermostat, start switch, and timer are mounted behind the control panel. All three govern the selection and duration of drying cycles made available to you in your model of dryer.

To check and replace any of the parts, first unplug the dryer and remove the control panel (see *Gaining access to interior parts*, p.249). Look for burnt terminals (see below) and test each part with a volt-ohm meter set to the RX1 scale (p.124). If a part has more than two terminals, select for the test that pair of terminals to which leads made of heavy

wire are connected. Replace any part you find to be defective. When testing the thermostat, turn it to any setting except *Fluff-dry*. If you install a new unit, avoid kinking the bulb tube.

Note: On some models the parts behind the control panel are combined, or they are mounted together with an array of switches that perform special functions. The parts are therefore difficult to distinguish and separate for testing. Unless you are an experienced electrician and have the required circuit diagram to help you, call an appliance repairman.

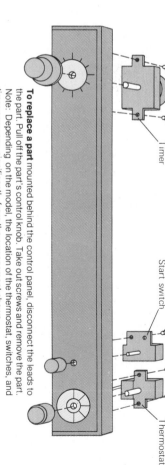

To replace a part mounted behind the control panel, disconnect the leads to the part. Pull off the part's control knob. Take out screws and remove the part. Note: Depending on the model, the location of the thermostat, switches, and timer can vary significantly from the arrangement shown.

Timer

Start switch

Thermostat

To test thermostat, clip meter probes to terminals after disconnecting leads. Place lighted match under sensing bulb (right) for no longer than a moment. If needle of meter jumps, thermostat is OK; if not, unit is faulty.

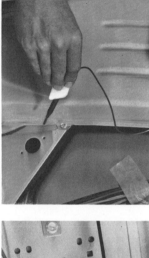

To remove thermostat, first take out the thermostat sensing bulb located in the back of the dryer. Pry sensing bulb from its mount in exhaust duct and thread the bulb and the bulb tube up and out of the dryer.

To test start switch, disconnect those leads to it made of heavy wire and clip volt-ohm meter probes to switch terminals. Press the switch button. If meter reads zero ohms, the switch is OK; if high, it is defective.

To test timer, disconnect one of the leads to it and clip meter probes to timer terminals. Turn timer knob to *Normal Dry*. If meter reads zero ohms, the timer is OK; if high, it is defective.

The power cord and terminal block

The power cord in 240-volt units usually connects to a terminal block at the rear of the dryer. The connections can in time deteriorate. Unplug the dryer, remove the access plate, and check the block for burnt terminals (see right). Replace the block as indicated.

If the terminal block is OK, test the power cord with a volt-ohm meter set to the RX1 scale (p.124). Attach a jumper wire to the cord terminals and bend and pull the cord when making the test. Replace the cord if it is defective. Note: If the cord has three wires, test the outer two. The middle wire is a ground.

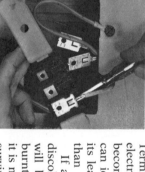

Take out the retaining screws at the back of the dryer and lift off the metal access plate covering the terminal block.

To test power cord, clip volt-ohm meter probes to cord plug. If meter reads zero, cord is OK; if needle jumps or reads high, cord is faulty.

Jumper wire

To meter

Disconnect leads to terminal block and take out screws that mount the block. Remove the block, check for burnt terminals.

Checking for burnt terminals

Terminals that carry large amounts of electric current tend after some time to become hot, then corrode and burn. You can identify a high-current terminal by its lead, which is made of heavier wire than that used elsewhere in appliance.

If a terminal is burned it will appear discolored and the lead connected to it will be charred. Wherever you find a burnt terminal, replace the part on which it is mounted. It is unlikely that the part survived the build-up of heat without internal damage. Repair the lead by cutting off the charred part and attaching a new connector (see pp.128-131).

Testing and replacing the heater (electric dryers)

The heater is located in the back of the dryer inside a duct through which air is forced to circulate. When the heater is defective, the air will not get hot enough or will not heat at all, and clothes will take too long to dry, or will remain wet.

To check the heater, unplug the dryer and remove the back panel (see *Gaining access to interior parts*, p.249). Examine the heater terminals for burns (see opposite page). Test the heater twice with a volt-ohm meter (p.124), once for an open circuit, and once for grounding to the heater duct. If the tests indicate grounding or an open circuit, replace the heater with a new one from the manufacturer.

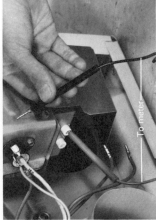

To test heater for an open circuit, disconnect the leads to it and insert volt-ohm meter probes into heater terminals. If the meter reads between 8 and 20 ohms, the heater is OK; if high, it is defective.

To test heater for grounding, disconnect its leads. Insert one meter probe into a heater terminal, and touch the other to heater duct. If meter reads high, heater is OK; if needle swings toward low, heater is grounded.

To remove the heater, first remove the heater duct. Take out duct retaining screws. Note: It may be necessary to lift the top in order to reach the screws that secure the duct to the upper edge of the dryer cabinet.

Remove duct cover and heater retaining screw and slide heater out of duct. **Caution: To avoid grounding between heater coils and heater duct, be careful not to bend the coils when installing a new heater.**

The overheat protector (electric dryers)

The overheat protector is mounted on the heater and works like a thermostat to turn the heater off whenever a certain temperature is exceeded. To check the protector, unplug the dryer and remove the back panel (see *Gaining access to interior parts*, p.249). Test the protector with a volt-ohm meter set to the RX1 scale (p.124). Replace it if it is defective. Note: If the protector has three terminals, test it across the outer two. A second protector may be on the air outlet duct. Check all the protectors you can find, if the dryer is not heating.

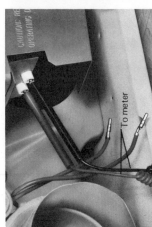

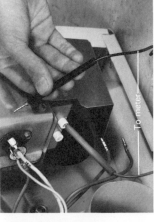

To test protector, disconnect one of the leads to it and clip volt-ohm meter probes to its terminals. If meter reads zero ohms, protector is OK; if high, it is faulty.

To remove the protector, take out the protector retaining screws and lift the protector out of its mount on the heater duct or air outlet duct.

Repairing the gas burner (gas dryers)

The gas burner is generally located at the bottom of the gas dryer. If the dryer heats poorly, remove the lower access panel and examine the burner flame while the dryer is operating. The flame burns a mixture of gas and air. A very light blue flame making a roaring sound indicates too much air in the mixture; a flame with yellow tips indicates too little air. These improper mixtures lead to poor combustion and inefficient heating. To correct the mixtures, adjust the air shutter in the burner so that the flame appears light blue yet does not roar. Note: To check the flame or reach the air shutter in some models, you may have to unplug the dryer, lift the top, and remove the front panel and drum (see *Gaining access to interior parts*, p.249, and *Removing the drum*, p.252).

If the dryer continues to heat poorly and the rest of the machine works, call an appliance repairman. Due to the complexity of gas burners, it is better not to attempt further repairs.

Adjust the air shutter by loosening the thumbscrew and moving the shutter so that the proper amount of air can enter. Tighten the screw when done.

Gas dryer precautions

If you smell gas near the dryer, turn off the gas shut-off valve and call an appliance repairman. In general, when you work on a gas dryer:
1. Turn off the gas shut-off valve.
2. Do not smoke or use a lighted match around the dryer.
3. Call an appliance repairman if a part is so inaccessible that the dryer must be moved.

Checking and replacing the drum belt

Most dryer drums are turned by a motor-driven belt that wraps completely around the drum. The belt can wear and sometimes break.

A worn belt will make a thumping noise while the dryer is running; a broken one will result in the drum not turning at all. To check the belt, open the dryer door, reach in, and turn the drum by hand. If you hear a slow thump that varies with the speed at which you turn the drum, the belt is responsible for the noise. If the drum turns very easily, the belt is broken.

Replace a belt that is worn or broken. Unplug the dryer, then lift the top and remove the front panel to provide space to remove the belt (see *Gaining access to interior parts*, p.249). Lift the drum slightly and slide the belt off of it. Install the new belt so that its ribbed side is against the drum. Note: The new belt should be the manufacturer's replacement. Another belt may cause the drum to turn at a speed for which the dryer was not designed, resulting in poor tumbling action and causing vibration that may damage mechanical parts.

If dryer has drum support slides, take out the screws that secure them to the cabinet and remove the slides.

To remove the drum belt, first disengage it from its pulleys. Push the idler arm forward to allow the belt to slip free of the drive shaft and idler pulley.

Slide the belt forward off the dryer drum. Note the block of wood placed under this type of drum to keep it from sagging after removal of front panel (see p.249).

Removing the drum support slides and the drum

The drum can be removed after you have lifted the top, removed the front panel (see *Gaining access to interior parts*, p.249), and removed the drum belt (see above). Some units are constructed so that the drum is then free to be simply lifted forward and out. In other units you must first remove the drum support slides located at the front of the dryer cabinet. In addition, the drum may be moored by its shaft to a bearing located in the back of the cabinet. Remove the bearing access plate to free the shaft, then lift out the drum.

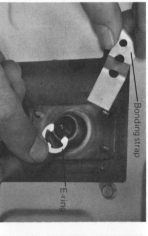

Free drum shaft from rear bearing by unscrewing and removing bonding strap and prying off E-ring.

Free the drum of its supports and lift it forward and out of the dryer cabinet.

Replacing a support roller or idler pulley

A support roller or idler pulley can make objectionable noise if worn. Both parts are located under the drum; the support rollers support the drum, the idler pulley engages the drum belt and keeps the belt under tension.

Check the support rollers by opening the dryer door, reaching in, and turning the drum by hand. If you hear the machine thump at a rate much faster than one thump for each revolution of the drum as you turn it, a worn support roller is causing the noise.

To reach the rollers, unplug the dryer,

lift the top, and remove the front panel and drum (see *Gaining access to interior parts*, p.249, and *Removing the drum*, above). Look at the support rollers and replace any that are broken or worn flat on one side.

An idler pulley makes a rattle or metallic noise when it is worn. To gain access to the idler pulley, remove the lower access panel (see p.249). Replace the pulley if it is broken or if it wobbles on its shaft when you move it with your hand. But be sure that the wobble is not merely side play in the pulley.

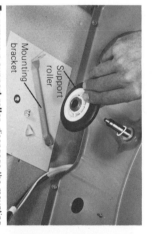

To remove a support roller, disengage the mounting bracket by taking out the screw that holds the bracket to the bottom of the cabinet. Pry off retaining clips and slide the support roller off its shaft.

To remove the idler pulley, reach under the drum and pry the pulley mounting bracket together with the pulley off the bottom of the cabinet. The pulley can then be pried loose from the bracket.

Solving problems with the motor

The motor is located at the bottom of the cabinet and is usually mounted so that the motor shaft turns the drum at one end and the blower at the other end. Before proceeding to repair the motor, unplug the dryer. Check for the following symptoms and take the indicated steps:

Motor hums but does not start

First, remove the lower access panel and check the belt to make sure it is not broken and is still engaged by the motor pulley. Otherwise, you may mistake the unloaded running sound of the motor for motor hum. Next, turn the dryer back on. With the door open, press the door switch with one hand and rotate the drum with your other hand. If the dryer begins to run, either the motor or its centrifugal switch is defective and one or both must be replaced.

To replace switch or motor, unplug the dryer, lift the top, and remove the front panel and the drum. On many motors the centrifugal switch is externally mounted. Check the switch terminals for burns (see p.250) and replace the switch if necessary. Otherwise, detach the blower from the motor shaft and remove the motor. Take the motor to an appliance repair shop where someone will be able to test the motor and its centrifugal switch for faults. Replace the part that is faulty.

Motor neither hums nor starts

Lift the top and remove the front panel and the drum. Test the motor overload protector with a volt-ohm meter (p.124) set to the RX1 scale. Replace the protector if it is defective. Also, check the centrifugal switch. If it has burnt terminals (p.250) and if it is externally mounted, replace it. (See exploded view, p.247, and the illustration below.)

Heater does not turn on

This can be caused by a defective centrifugal switch. Lift the top and remove the front panel and the drum. Check the switch for burnt terminals (see p.250) and replace it as indicated.

If the dryer did not start running as you rotated the drum by hand with the door switch on, check the motor bearings. After gaining access to the motor, turn the motor pulley by hand. If the pulley cannot turn without your applying force to it, the bearings need lubrication. Most dryer motors are permanently lubricated by the manufacturer and do not include oil holes or ports. You may try to lubricate the bearings nonetheless by putting several drops of SAE #20 oil around the motor shaft wherever it is possible to reach it. If this does not succeed, remove the motor and take it to your dealer for overhaul or replacement.

To test overload protector, disconnect a lead to the part and clip volt-ohm meter probes to terminals. If meter reads zero ohms, part is OK; if not, it is faulty.

To remove overload protector, disconnect leads to it and pry it off motor housing with a screwdriver. Note: On some models protector is inside motor and inaccessible.

To remove centrifugal switch, disconnect leads to it, take out screws, and lift it off motor. Note: On some models the switch is inside motor and inaccessible.

Mounting clamp

To remove motor, disconnect the leads to it, pry off motor mounting clamp, and lift out the motor. Note: On some models you may need to remove retaining screws as well.

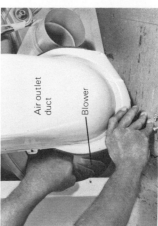

Blower hub — Motor shaft

To detach blower from motor shaft, turn blower hub with one wrench, motor shaft with another wrench. Rotate shaft opposite to the direction in which motor turns.

Use a setscrew wrench or a screwdriver to tighten a blower hub moored to a motor shaft by a screw.

Cleaning and tightening the blower

The blower moves air past the heater and through the dryer. It is usually located in back of the unit inside the air outlet duct. When the blower becomes clogged with lint, or when it becomes loose on the motor shaft, the air flow diminishes or stops and the dryer dries poorly or takes too long to dry.

To check the blower, unplug the dryer, remove the rear panel (see *Gaining access to interior parts,* p.249), and loosen the air outlet duct. Reach behind the duct with your hand to feel how badly the lint has collected. Remove the lint with your hand

or a vacuum cleaner. Also check to see if the blower is loose on the motor shaft by turning it with your hand. If it spins very freely, chances are it has become loose. Lift the top and remove the drum. Examine the motor shaft where it joins the blower in the back of the unit. Tighten the blower to the shaft; turn it by hand until it locks tightly on the threads of the motor shaft. Note: In some cases a setscrew secures the blower to the motor shaft; tighten this screw. (See *Solving problems with the motor,* above, and consult the exploded view, p.247.)

Air outlet duct — Blower

Remove lint from inside the air outlet duct and from around the blower with your hand or a vacuum.

Humidifiers

Humidifier problems

PROBLEM	POSSIBLE CAUSE	ACTION
Humidifier does not turn on	No power at wall outlet	Check outlet with a lamp you know is working. If lamp does not turn on, replace fuse or reset circuit breaker (p.127). If fuse keeps blowing, reduce number of appliances in circuit ●
	Open circuit in power cord	Test power cord and replace it if defective (below) ●
	Faulty lid switch (if the humidifier has one)	Test lid switch and replace it if defective (facing page) ●●
	Defective float switch	Test float switch and replace it if defective (facing page) ●●■
	Faulty humidistat	Test humidistat and replace it if defective (facing page) ●●■
	Defective fan motor (drum-type humidifiers only)	Check fan motor and replace it if defective (below) ●●■
Humidifier runs but does not humidify	Water in reservoir low	Refill humidifier reservoir ●
	Belt (or drum) clogged by residue	Clean belt with a mixture of half white vinegar and half water or replace belt ●
	Faulty belt motor	Test belt motor and replace it if defective (below) ●●■
	Loose fan or defective fan motor	Check fan and fan motor. Repair or replace defective part (below) ●●■
	Exterior walls of your house lack a vapor barrier	Short of installing a vapor barrier in your house, there is nothing you can do ●
	Belt (or drum) drive mechanism clogged by residue	Clean drive mechanism with a mixture of half white vinegar and half water ●
Humidifier is noisy	Fan motor bearings dry	Lubricate fan motor bearings (below) ●

Ease of fix: ● simple ●● average ●●● difficult ■ Volt-ohm meter required for this step (see p.124)

The power cord

To check the power cord, unplug the humidifier, disassemble the unit, and locate the terminals to which the cord leads are connected. Test the cord with a volt-ohm meter set to the RX1 scale (p.124). Clip the meter probes to the cord plug and connect a jumper wire to the cord leads. If the meter reads zero ohms, the cord is OK. Replace the power cord if it is defective.

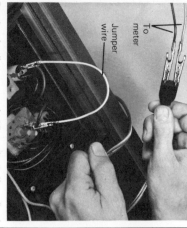

To meter

Jumper wire

Bend and pull power cord while testing it. If needle of meter jumps around or reads high, cord is faulty.

The belt motor

The belt motor rotates the belt. To check the belt motor, unplug the humidifier, lift the lid, and disconnect the leads to the motor. Then, take out any retaining screws and lift the motor out of the unit. With the probes of a volt-ohm meter clipped to the motor leads, test the motor with the meter set to the RX1 scale (p.124). If the motor is defective, replace it with a new one from your dealer.

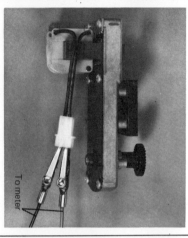

To meter

If volt-ohm meter reads between 25 and 100 ohms, it is OK; if high motor is faulty.

Solving problems with the fan

The fan vaporizes the water lifted by the belt from the reservoir and blows the vaporized water out into the room. To check the fan, first unplug the humidifier and lift the lid. By hand, pull the fan blades away from the fan motor to see if the fan hub is loose on the motor shaft. If it is, tighten it with spring clamp pliers (see p.122). Rotate the fan by hand. If it does not spin easily, lubricate the motor bearings with nondetergent SAE #20 oil. Note: Noisy operation of the fan is often an early indication that the motor bearings are dry and in need of lubrication.

If the fan motor is a single-speed model, test the motor in the same way you would test the belt motor (see left). Call an appliance repairman to test a multispeed motor.

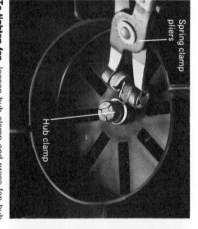

Spring clamp pliers

Hub clamp

To tighten fan, loosen hub clamp and press fan hub farther onto the motor shaft before releasing clamp.

Lubricate fan motor with two or three drops of oil in each oil tube or hole at the opposite ends of motor.

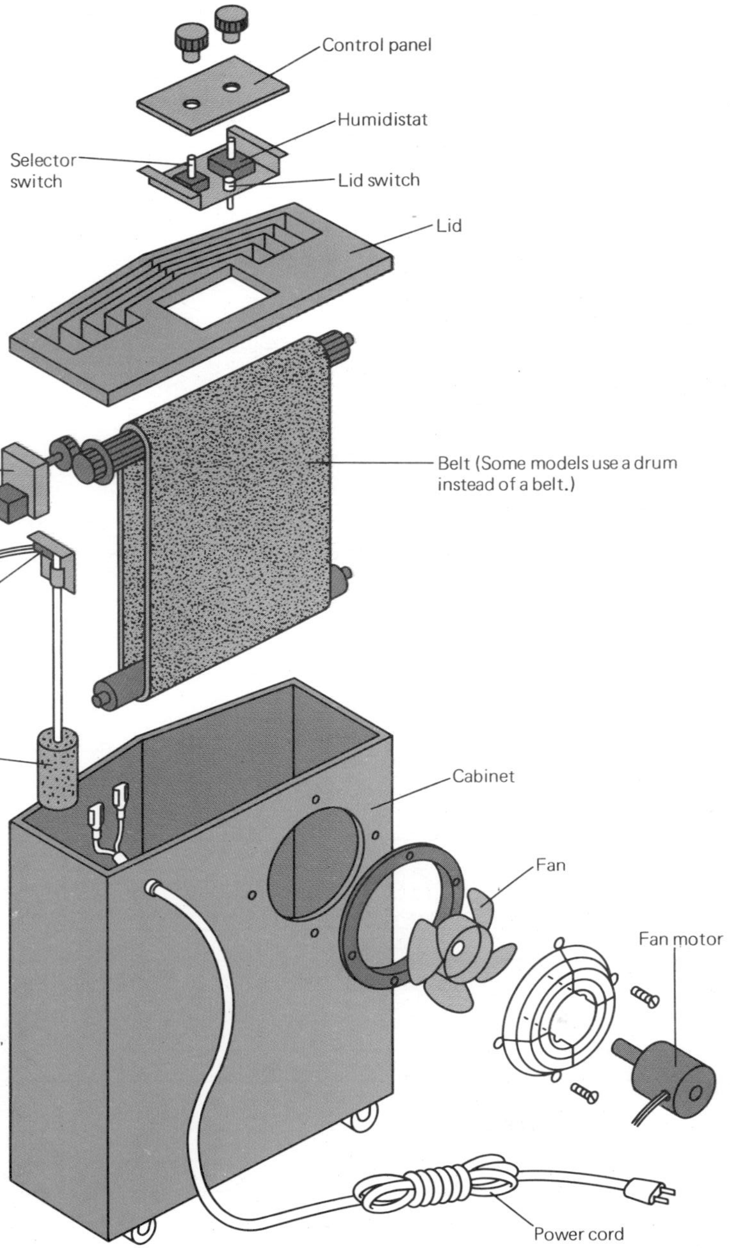

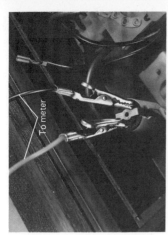

When testing lid switch, meter should read zero ohms with humidifier lid closed; if high, switch is faulty.

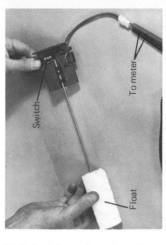

When testing float switch, meter should read zero ohms with switch closed; if not, switch is faulty.

When testing humidistat, meter should read zero ohms with humidistat set to maximum humidity.

Testing and replacing the lid switch

When you raise the lid on the humidifier, the lid switch releases and turns off the unit. To check the switch, unplug the humidifier and remove the control panel to expose the leads to the switch.

Test the switch with a volt-ohm meter (p.124) set to the RX1 scale. Disconnect a lead to one of the switch terminals, clip the meter probes to the terminals, and close the lid. If the switch is faulty, replace it. Disconnect the remaining lead, press in the retaining clamps or take out the retaining screws, and remove the switch from the appliance.

Testing and replacing the float switch

The float switch is connected to a long shaft, at the lower end of which is the float. When the water in the reservoir drops below a set level, the float descends and releases the switch, which turns off the unit.

To check the switch, unplug the humidifier and raise the lid. Test the switch with a volt-ohm meter (p.124) set to the RX1 scale. After lifting out the switch, disconnect its leads and clip the meter probes to the switch terminals. Then, push the float up until the switch closes. If the switch is faulty, replace it.

Testing and replacing the humidistat

To check the humidistat, unplug the humidifier and remove the control panel. Test the part with a volt-ohm meter (p.124) set to the RX1 scale. Disconnect one of the leads to the humidistat terminals and clip the meter probes to the terminals. Then, turn the humidistat from *High* all the way to *Low*. The meter should start at zero ohms and jump to high ohms at some point as you turn down the humidistat. If it does not, the part is faulty and should be replaced. Disconnect the remaining lead, take out the screws, and remove the humidistat.

Control panel

Humidistat

Lid switch

Lid

Selector switch

Belt (Some models use a drum instead of a belt.)

Belt motor

Float switch

Float

Cabinet

Fan

Fan motor

Power cord

Note: This view of a typical humidifier is to help you identify its parts. Details on your unit may vary from the one shown. For example, you may have a drum-type humidifier, which resembles the belt-type shown here, except that a rotating drum is used in place of the moving belt. The drum-type humidifier sometimes uses one motor to turn both the fan and the drum, instead of using two motors, as in the belt type.

Ranges and ovens

Range and oven problems

PROBLEM	POSSIBLE CAUSE	ACTION
Range does not operate at all	No power to unit	Replace fuse or reset circuit breaker (p.127) ●
	Faulty terminal block	Check terminal block and replace it if defective (p.259) ●●
Surface heating element does not heat, or it heats poorly (electric ranges)	Wrong pot	Use a pot that lies flat on the heating element coils. Remove dents from the pot, if there are any ●
	Defective surface element	Check surface heating element and its terminals for burns, and test the element with a volt-ohm meter (p.260). Replace it if defective ●■
	Defective heating element leads	Test element leads and replace them if defective (p.260) ●●■
	Faulty heating control	Check element heating control for burnt terminals and replace it if faulty (p.261) ●●●
One or both oven heating elements do not heat (electric ranges)	Defective selector switch	Check bake-broil selector switch and replace it if defective (p.261) ●●
	Defective oven heating element	Test oven heating element and replace it if defective (p.260) ●●●■
	Defective thermostat	Check oven thermostat and replace it if defective (p.261) ●●●■
Surface burner does not light, or it operates poorly (gas ranges)	Clogged burner	Clean surface burner (p.262) ●
	Gas supply turned off	Check other surface burners, the oven burner, then other gas appliances in your house to see if they are operating. If they are not, call the utility company ●
	Pilot out	Relight pilot on surface burner (p.262). If the range is located in a drafty part of your kitchen, find a way to reduce the draft and keep it from blowing out the pilot flame ●
	Improper gas-air mixture causing poor heating	Check condition of flame on surface burner and adjust air shutter on burner's gas line if necessary (p.262) ●
Surface burner does not simmer (gas ranges)	Simmer out of adjustment	Adjust simmer on surface burner (p.262) ●
Soot forms on bottom of utensils (gas ranges)	Improper gas-air mixture	Adjust air shutter on surface burner's gas line (p.262) ●
Oven does not light, or it heats poorly (gas ranges)	Gas supply turned off	Check surface burners, then other gas appliances in your house to see if they are operating. If they are not, call the utility company ●
	Pilot out	Relight oven burner pilot (p.263) ●
	Pilot flame too low	Adjust height of oven burner pilot flame (p.263) ●●
	Faulty flame switch	Test flame switch in oven burner assembly, and replace it if defective (p.263) ●●●■
	Defective ignition system (if not any of above)	Call appliance repairman ●●●
Baked goods burn	Dark utensils	Use bright utensils for baking ●
	Utensils too large	Use utensil just large enough to hold the food being cooked ●
	Blocked exhaust vent	Clear oven exhaust vent of obstructions (p.258) ●
Baked goods turn out soggy	Oven not hot enough	Reset oven thermostat control. Recalibrate thermostat, if necessary (p.261) ●
Oven bakes unevenly	Defective gasket	Check oven door gasket and replace it if worn or cracked (p.258) ●●
	Faulty thermostat	Check oven temperature and adjust or replace thermostat if faulty (p.261) ●●
Oven temperature too low or too high	Oven not preheated	Preheat oven with door open ●
	Oven temperature too high	Reset oven thermostat control. Recalibrate thermostat if necessary (p.261) ●
	Blocked exhaust vent	Clear oven exhaust vent of obstructions (p.258) ●
Oven sweats or drips water	Defective gasket	Check oven door gasket and replace it if worn or cracked (p.258) ●
Panel light does not turn on	Light burned out	Replace panel light (p.258) ●●
Outlet on range does not operate	Appliance plugged into outlet not functioning, fuse blown, or circuit breaker tripped	Check appliance outlet with a lamp you know is working. If lamp does not turn on, replace fuse or reset circuit breaker inside the range (p.258) ●
Timer does not work	Burnt terminals on timer	Check timer and replace it if defective (p.258) ●●
Microwave oven works poorly	Improper cooking procedure	Follow rules for the correct operation of a microwave oven (p.263) ●
	Defective electrical or mechanical part	Call appliance repairman ●●●

Ease of fix: ● simple   ●● average   ●●● difficult   ■ Volt-ohm meter required for this step (see p.124)

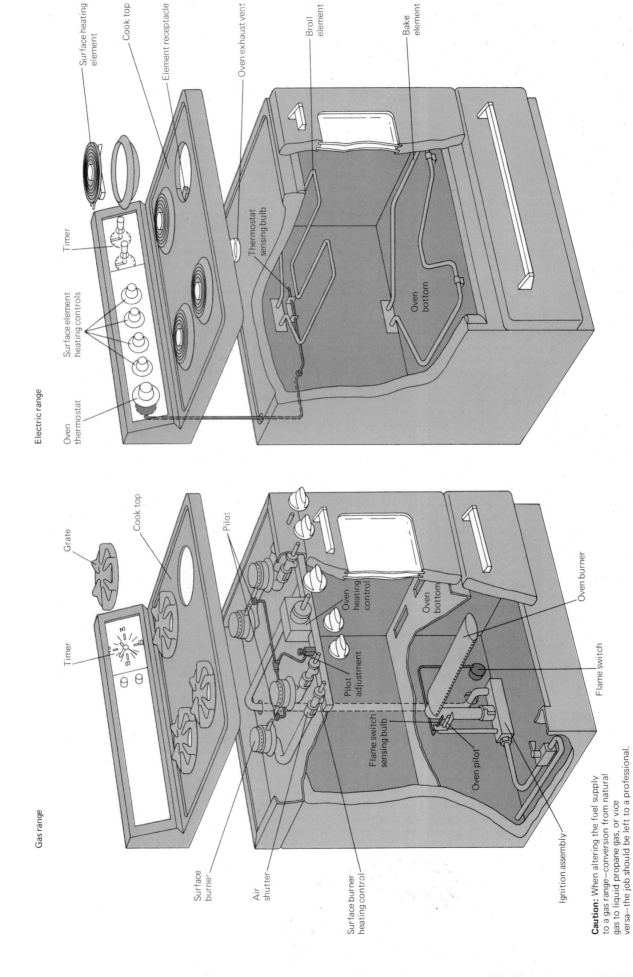

Surface heating element

Cook top

Element receptacle

Oven exhaust vent

Broil element

Bake element

Timer

Electric range

Surface element heating controls

Thermostat sensing bulb

Oven thermostat

Oven bottom

Grate

Cook top

Pilot

Timer

Gas range

B 3

Oven heating control

Oven bottom

Oven burner

Pilot adjustment

Flame switch

Surface burner

Air shutter

Flame switch sensing bulb

Oven pilot

Surface burner heating control

Ignition assembly

Caution: When altering the fuel supply to a gas range—conversion from natural gas to liquid propane gas, or vice versa—the job should be left to a professional.

Note: These views of a typical electric range and gas range are to help you identify their parts. Details on your unit may vary to some degree from the ones shown.

257

Ranges and ovens

The oven exhaust vent and door gasket

The oven has vents to assure an even distribution of temperature during baking and to remove excess moisture. Air passes through a gap (usually at the bottom of the oven door), is heated, then rises out of a port at the top rear of the oven or under the surface burners.

Check the oven exhaust vent and clear it of obstructions. If you are putting aluminum foil underneath the surface heating elements of your electric range, be careful not to block the vent. Also be careful when using aluminum foil in the oven not to cover the oven bottom or ventilation gaps with it.

A door gasket, usually running along the side edges and the top edge of the door, helps maintain the proper air flow. Replace the gasket if it becomes worn and cracked.

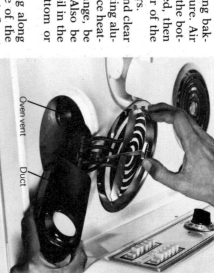

The oven vent in this model is located beneath a rear surface heating element. Raise element, lift out reflector pan, then the duct, and clean both duct and vent.

To replace a door gasket, pull off the old gasket and clip on a new one. Note: These gaskets are usually designed with a gap at the door bottom for ventilation.

Checking for burnt terminals

Terminals that carry large amounts of electric current tend after some time to become hot, then corrode and burn, and lose their ability to conduct electricity. You can usually identify them by the heavy wire used in the leads connected to them. Carefully check such terminals—on any part that you investigate—for corrosion or burn marks.

Look for discoloration of the terminal, or charred insulation on the lead connected to the terminal. The appearance of either indicates that the part to which the terminal is joined has suffered internal heat damage and should be replaced. The charred lead should also be replaced with an equivalent new wire or be repaired by cutting it off an inch beyond the charred portion and attaching a new connector (see p.123).

The panel light, timer, and appliance outlet

The panel light can be a small light that shows when the range is turned on, or a larger light that serves as a signal and illuminates the cook top. If the range operates but the light does not glow, replace the light. Turn off the power to the range (see p.261) and remove the back or front of the control panel (see p.259) to reach the bulb.

The timer and the appliance outlet usually have a special fuse or circuit breaker wired into their circuit inside the range. Sometimes the fuse or breaker is mounted on the control panel. More frequently it is located under the cook top. Occasionally, especially in gas ranges, it is at the bottom of the cabinet. Whenever the timer or the appliance outlet does not operate, check the fuse or circuit breaker inside the range, and replace or reset it as necessary.

If the fuse or breaker is OK, check the timer for burnt terminals (see above) and replace as indicated. You should not attempt any further tests unless you are an experienced electrician and have a circuit diagram. Instead, remove the timer and take it to an appliance repair shop.

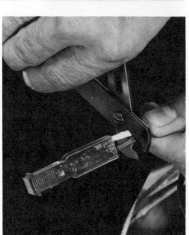

The panel lights on this model can be reached by taking off the front of the control panel. These lights can be replaced with ordinary light bulbs.

On some models the panel light is clamped behind the control panel. Cut the leads to the light and splice a new light onto the cut wires (see pp.128–131).

The timer can usually be removed by disconnecting its leads, from back, then pressing in spring clamps that hold it to panel and pushing it forward out of panel.

The fuse is most often located under the cook top and can be reached by lifting the top. Do not replace the fuse with one rated higher than 15 amperes.

To remove access cover to terminal block at the back of the range, first take out cover retaining screws.

The terminal block can be removed after disconnecting the leads to it and taking out retaining screws.

The terminal block

The terminal block is simply a part on which the power cord and the leads from inside the unit terminate. The block is found in electric ranges, usually at the back of the range. When the connections at the block corrode and become burnt, power ceases to flow and neither the surface burners nor the oven operate.

To check the terminal block, turn off the power to the range (see p.261), remove the access cover, and examine the block for burnt terminals (see facing page). If any damage is apparent, replace the terminal block and repair injured leads (see p.128).

Back of control panel can be removed after taking out retaining screws along edge of panel.

The door on late models can be removed by simply pulling it straight off the door hinges.

To lift out a broiler drawer, first take out the screws that hold the drawer to the support slides.

Gaining access to interior parts

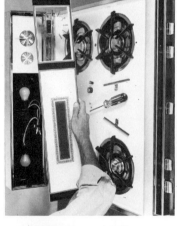

Front of accessory panel on this gas range can be lifted off after removing retaining screws and knobs.

To remove the control trim on a gas range, pull off knobs, take out retaining screws, and lift trim off.

The heat baffle is under the oven bottom and lifts up and out. Unscrew retaining nut, if there is one.

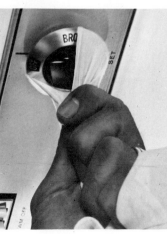

Pry knobs off control panel by slipping thin cloth beneath knob around shaft and pulling forward.

The cook top is easy to lift. On some models you may first have to push it toward the rear.

The bottom of the oven in a gas range can be lifted out after getting a grip along one of its edges.

Testing and replacing an electric surface heating element

The surface heating elements on an electric range consist of either a single coil or a double coil. Heating of the single-coil element is usually regulated by a variable heat control that works like a thermostat, turning the element on and off periodically to assure a relatively uniform temperature. A coil in a double-coil element, on the other hand, stays on until you turn it off. For a selection of heat settings, the surface indicates that the element is de-

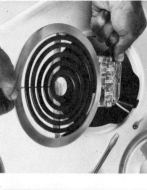

more complicated switching circuitry. If there is no visible damage, turn off the power to the range (see facing page) and check the element for burnt terminals (see p.258). Some elements can be unplugged from their receptacle without lifting the cook top, but you may have to lift the top to examine the receptacle itself.

A further test may be made with a volt-ohm meter (p.124) set to the RX1

The surface heating elements on an electric range consist of either a single coil or which employs combinations of voltages with one or the other coil, or with both coils simultaneously.

To check a heating element, set its heating control to *High*. If the element does not glow within seconds, or if only one coil of a double-coil element glows, turn off the range and examine the dead coil. A hole or burn marks in the coil

fective; replace it with a new element.

scale. Since there are four terminals on a double-coil element, visually trace the spiral path of the coil you wish to test and clip the probes of the volt-ohm meter to each of its terminals.

If you find nothing wrong with the heating element, the leads that connect the element to its heating control may be defective. Test them with the volt-ohm meter set to the RX1 scale, and replace them if they are defective.

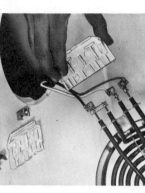

To remove a surface heating element, take off reflector pan, unscrew element, and pull the element up and out of the cook top opening.

To test the element, first pry off clips and remove the glass (or ceramic) insulating block. Disconnect one of the leads to the terminal pair being tested.

To
meter

Clip volt-ohm meter probes to the terminal pair being tested. If the meter reads between 40 and 120 ohms, the heating coil is OK; if high, the coil is defective.

To
meter

Clip volt-ohm meter probes to the terminal pair being tested. If the meter reads between 40 and 120 ohms, the heating coil is OK; if high, the coil is defective.

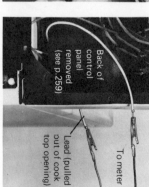

To examine receptacle of a surface element that unplugs, take out receptacle retaining screw and lift cook top. You will then be able to reach the receptacle.

Back of
control
panel
removed
(see p.259)

Lead (pulled
out of cook
top opening)

To meter

To test a heating element lead, clip the probes of a volt-ohm meter to each end of the lead. If the meter reads zero ohms, lead is OK; if high, lead is defective.

Testing and replacing an electric oven heating element

The oven contains two heating elements, the bake element mounted in the oven bottom and the broil element mounted in the oven top. Check the oven by turning it to *Bake*, then turning it to *Broil*. If neither the bake nor the broil element glows after being turned on, the trouble probably lies elsewhere. Check the thermostat and the bake-broil selector switch (see *Testing and replacing the oven thermostat and The heating controls*, facing page).

If one of the elements glows but the other does not, test the one that does not glow with a volt-ohm meter (p.124) set to the RX1 scale. Turn off the power to the range, then remove the element to be tested. Replace a defective element with a new part from the manufacturer.

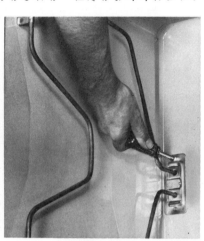

To remove a broil or bake heating element, first take out the screws that secure the element to its mount on the back panel inside the oven.

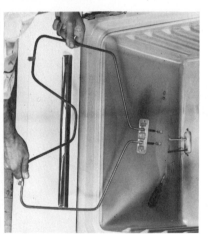

Pull the oven element several inches forward out of its mount and disconnect the leads from the element terminals, then lift out the element.

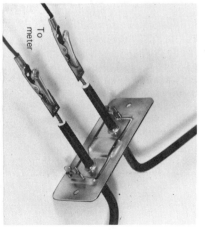

To test either heating element, clip volt-ohm meter probes to element terminals. If meter reads 15 to 30 ohms, element is OK; if high, element is defective.

Testing and replacing the oven thermostat

The oven thermostat is located on the control panel and regulates the temperature inside the oven. If the oven shows any of the following symptoms, take the action indicated:

Oven does not turn on

Turn off the power to the range (see right) and check the thermostat for burnt terminals (see p.258). If no damage is visible, test the thermostat with a volt-ohm meter (p.124) set to the RX1 scale. If the

thermostat is defective, replace it along with its sensing bulb and tube. Note: If the thermostat has more than two terminals and you have no means of judging which pair of terminals should be tested, call an appliance repairman.

Oven overheats (does not cycle off)

Turn off the power to the range and replace the thermostat, including the thermostat sensing bulb and tube, with new parts from the manufacturer.

Incorrect operating temperature

Place an oven thermometer inside the oven and run the oven for 20 minutes with the thermostat set at 350°F. If at the end of the period the oven temperature differs from 350°F by more than 25°F, pull off the thermostat knob (see p.259) and recalibrate the thermostat. Most thermostats can be reset by adjusting a disc in the knob or a screw inside the thermostat shaft.

Caution: Turn off the power

Whenever working on the inside of a range, turn off the power to it before beginning. A permanently installed unit will be connected as a separate circuit to the service panel in your house. To turn it off, remove the fuses or trip the circuit breaker (see p.127). If the unit is a gas range, and it has an electrical power cord, unplug it from the wall outlet.

The heating controls

If a surface heating element on an electric range does not heat, examine its control for burnt terminals (see p.258). Turn off the power to the range and remove the back of the control panel. Replace the control and repair the leads if they are defective. Check the bake-broil selector switch in the same way.

If there is no visible damage, test the part with a volt-ohm meter (see p.124). For range heating controls the procedure is complex. Unless you are an experienced electrician and have the required circuit diagram to help you, call an appliance repairman.

Note: To remove a control on some models you first have to remove all the control knobs and the faceplate.

To replace a control, first take off the control knob (see p.259), then disconnect leads, and remove screws that hold the control to the control panel.

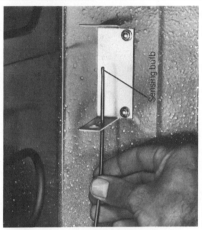

Sensing bulb

3. Slide thermostat sensing bulb from its mount inside oven. Note: If necessary, push thermostat down to create slack in the tube leading to the sensing bulb.

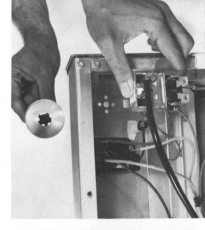

2. To replace thermostat, first detach leads connected to its terminals and pry off control knob. Take out screws and lift thermostat away from control panel.

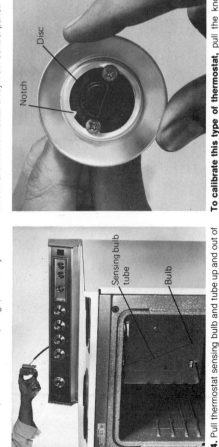

Notch

Disc

To calibrate this type of thermostat, turn screw inside hollow control shaft. Give it an eighth of a turn counterclockwise to raise oven temperature 25°F.

To calibrate this type of thermostat, pull the knob from the control panel, loosen screws, and change the notch setting on the disc located underneath knob.

Back of control panel removed (see p. 259)

To meter

1. To test thermostat, disconnect a lead to it and clip volt-ohm meter probes to thermostat terminals. If meter reads zero, thermostat is OK; if high, it is faulty.

Sensing bulb tube

Bulb

4. Pull thermostat sensing bulb and tube up and out of the back of the oven. Note: Be careful not to kink the tube when reinstalling.

Solving problems with a gas range surface burner

If a surface burner does not light, lift the cook top (see p.259) and check to see if the pilot has gone out. If it has, relight it and adjust it.

If the burner does not light when the water and household ammonia. If the pilot is on, but you are able to light the burner with a match, the burner ignition

holes have become clogged with dirt or spilled food. Uneven flame height at the cone with a light blue flame tip. If the burner roars and the flame lifts off the burner, too much air is being mixed with the gas; if the flame is part yellow and causing soot to collect under the pot, too little air is being mixed with the gas. In

A burner flame should have a blue flame. Uneven flame indicates clogging also. Remove the burner and wash it in hot, sudsy burner indicates clogging also. Remove the burner has narrow slots instead of holes, use a razor blade to clean them.

both cases, the burner will heat poorly. To correct the air-gas mixture, adjust the air shutter on the burner.

Note: On some models it is possible to make a simmer adjustment. Do this under draft-free conditions, and set the flame so that it barely stays lit.

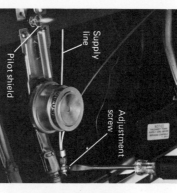

To adjust pilot, turn adjustment screw on the pilot supply line so that the tip of the flame is ⅜ in. above pilot shield.

To remove a surface burner, take out the burner retaining screw and lift the burner from its support.

Clean the ignition holes in the side of the burner head with a toothpick or with a straightened-out paper clip.

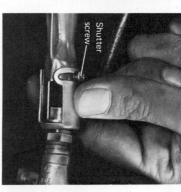

To adjust the air shutter, loosen the shutter screw and open or close the shutter by twisting it; then, tighten screw.

To adjust simmer, remove the control knob and use a small screwdriver to turn screw inside shaft of burner control.

Gas range precautions

If you smell gas near a gas range, first check to see if all of its pilots are lit. If they are, turn off all of the gas shut-off valve immediately and call an appliance repairman. A gas range, as any gas appliance, can explode if it has been leaking gas. Note: Do not turn on anything electrical, such as the kitchen wall switch, until the gas leak has been located and fixed. Ventilate the house.

In general, when attempting to repair the gas range, follow these rules:
1. Do not smoke near the range.
2. When looking into dark corners of the appliance, use a flashlight, not a lighted match.
3. Call an appliance repairman if a part is so inaccessible that the range must be moved away from the wall in order to reach the part.

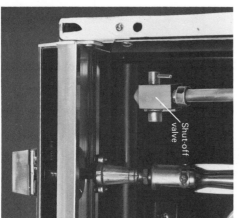

The gas shut-off valve in this model is located under the range cook top. The valve is shown open.

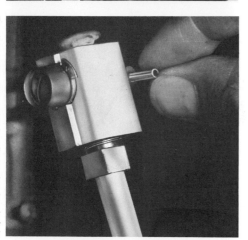

To close valve, turn valve handle so that its shaft is perpendicular to gas line to which valve is attached.

Shut-off valve in this range is under cabinet bottom. You may need to remove a broiler drawer to reach it.

Solving problems with a gas range oven burner

Most ovens use a pilot. It is underneath the oven and frequently located to the rear of the unit. Pull out the oven drawer and relight the pilot if it is out. To reach the pilot you may have to remove the oven bottom and oven baffle (see *Gaining access to interior parts, p.259*).

The oven may not light because the pilot flame, though burning, is too low. Remove the oven bottom and baffle and turn the adjustment screw on the ignition assembly to increase or decrease the height of the flame.

The flame switch, found in a number of

ovens, should be checked when the oven does not ignite—even though the pilot flame happens to be lit. With the power to the range turned off (see p.261) and the oven bottom and baffle removed, test the flame switch with a volt-ohm meter (p.124) set to the RX1 scale. To test, the

pilot flame must be out, or the flame switch bulb must be pulled away from the flame and be cool. Replace the switch, including the flame switch bulb, if the switch is defective.

Note: To check other kinds of ignition systems, call an appliance repairman.

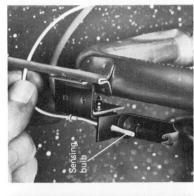

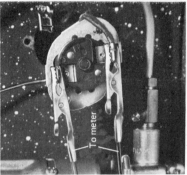

To remove flame switch sensing bulb, pry it loose from its mount and slip it out. Note: Loosen burner assembly, if in way.

Clip volt-ohm meter probes to flame switch terminals. If the meter reads zero ohms, switch is OK; if high, switch is faulty.

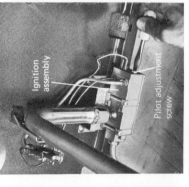

To test a flame switch, first take out retaining screws and remove switch. Disconnect the leads attached to its terminals.

The pilot flame on this type of oven ignition system can be adjusted by turning a screw on the ignition assembly.

The pilot on most models resembles the one here being lit by a match. Small tube above pilot orifice senses the flame.

Microwave ovens

For safety reasons, the microwave oven is built in such a way as to discourage the user from disassembling and repairing it. In addition, a manufacturer will usually void his warranty to repair the appliance if the oven has been disassembled.

Microwave radiation is similar to the heat produced by an oven heating element, except that, because the radiation has a different wavelength, the surface of your skin cannot feel warmth when exposed to it. To avoid the danger of becoming exposed to it without your knowing, be sure the oven door is closed at all times whenever the oven is on. Call an appliance repairman if a door gasket is damaged, or if any of the safety interlocks built into the door-latching mechanisms of more recent models are broken.

Also, observe these rules when using the oven:

1. Do not block the flow of air around the back of the unit in such a way that the air exhaust vent there becomes obstructed.

2. Do not operate the microwave oven when it is empty.

3. Do not cook with anything made partly or wholly of metal inside the unit. This includes metal cookware, metal handles on glass cookware, aluminum foil, meat thermometers, and wire ties.

4. Do not cook any food that is airtight without first opening it or puncturing it with a fork. Examples are eggs, tomatoes, potatoes, apples, and plastic bags containing food. This is to prevent steam from building up and causing the food to burst and splatter inside the oven.

Cleaning the range

Turn off the range and let it cool before proceeding to clean it. When you clean food from around and under the surface heating elements and burners, use mild soap and water. Avoid using abrasives and oven cleaners. Heating elements for the most part clean themselves during operation, but if they do need attention, use an implement made of plastic, not of metal, to scrape the dirt or charred matter off the element.

Clean the inner surface of a continuous-clean oven with soap and a nylon pad. Do not scour the surface or use an abrasive pad on it. The oven bottom, however, will not have a continuous-clean coating, so that these cleaning restrictions do not apply to it. Use an oven cleaner recommended by the manufacturer of the range.

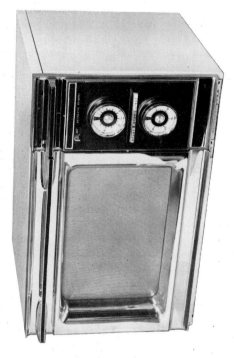

Refrigerators and freezers

Refrigerator and freezer problems

PROBLEM	POSSIBLE CAUSE	ACTION
Refrigerator does not run or make a sound	No power at wall outlet	Check outlet with a lamp you know is working. If lamp does not turn on, replace fuse or reset circuit breaker (p.127). If fuse keeps blowing, reduce number of appliances in circuit ●
	Faulty power cord	Test power cord and replace it if defective (p.268) ●●■
	Faulty temperature control	Test temperature control and replace it if defective (p.267) ●●■
	Defective compressor motor relay	Check compressor relay and replace it if defective (p.271) ●●
Refrigerator does not run but makes a clicking sound at intervals	Voltage at outlet incorrect	Call power company. Voltage at wall outlet should be between 108 and 130 volts AC ●
	Condenser coils clogged by dust	Clean condenser coils (p.271) ●
	Obstructed or defective condenser fan (frost-free refrigerators)	Check condenser fan. Clear fan of obstructions, or replace it if defective (p.271) ●●■
	Defective compressor motor	Call an appliance repairman ●●●
Refrigerator cools poorly or runs continuously (Note: If the unit is cooling properly, a thermometer placed in liquid that has been standing in the refrigerator for 24 hours should read between 35°F and 40°F, though on a hot day and with heavy usage this figure may climb to 50°F.)	Weather hot and humid	No repair if unit runs continuously but cools well. Refrigerator is operating normally
	Refrigerator not defrosted	Defrost the refrigerator. If unit is an automatic defrost model and heavy frost collects, see *Refrigerator does not defrost or frosts too quickly, below* ●
	Refrigerator door sags or does not close by itself	Adjust door to correct the sag, and tilt refrigerator so that door closes by itself (p.266) ●
	Leaking door gasket	Replace door gasket (p.266) ●●
	Condenser coils clogged by dust	Clean condenser coils (p.271) ●
	Refrigerator light on when door closed, caused by faulty door switch	Test door switch and replace it if defective (p.266) ●●■
	Wet insulation inside refrigerator walls and door	On a dry day, turn off refrigerator and leave refrigerator door open for 24 hours, then replace cracked jamb strips (p.267) and tape over cracks on inner door panel ●●
	Obstructed or defective condenser fan (frost-free refrigerators)	Check condenser fan. Clear fan of obstructions, or replace it if defective (p.271) ●●■
	Faulty evaporator fan (frost-free refrigerators)	Test evaporator fan and replace it if defective (p.268) ●●■
	Defective heater on all the time, due to faulty defrost timer (frost-free refrigerators)	Test defrost timer and replace it if defective (p.268) ●●■
	Loss of refrigerant	Call an appliance repairman to check for refrigerant leak ●●●
Refrigerator does not defrost or frosts too quickly	Food not carefully covered	Wrap food so that the moisture it contains does not evaporate inside the refrigerator ●
	Refrigerator door open too much of the time (frost appears snowy, rakes off easily)	Open refrigerator door only when necessary ●
	Refrigerator door sags or does not close by itself (frost appears snowy, rakes off easily)	Adjust door to correct sag, and tilt refrigerator so that door closes by itself (p.266) ●
	Leaking door gasket (frost appears snowy, rakes off easily)	Replace door gasket (p.266) ●●
	Wax from cartons or oily fingerprints on evaporator plate (coils)	Wash evaporator with water and a detergent that will not harm aluminum ●
	Clogged drain (frost-free refrigerators)	Clear the drain in the freezer compartment (p.270) ●
	Defective defrost timer (frost-free refrigerators)	Test defrost timer and replace it if defective (p.268) ●●■
	Faulty defrost heater (frost-free and cycle defrost refrigerators)	Test defrost heater and replace it if defective (p.269) ●●■
	Faulty limit switch (frost-free refrigerators)	Replace the defrost limit switch if you cannot find any other defect (p.269) ●●
Refrigerator is noisy	Rattling drain pan	Reposition the drain pan (p.270) ●
	Fan blades striking an interfering object (frost-free refrigerators)	Check condenser fan (p.271) and evaporator fan (p.268); remove any obstructions ●●
	Old, hardened rubber in compressor mounts	Replace compressor mounts (p.271) ●●
Water leaks inside and under refrigerator	Clogged drains	Clear drains inside the refrigerator (p.270) ●
	Cracked drain hose or drain pan	Replace drain pan or drain hose (p.270) ●
	Water dripping from cabinet seams	Empty refrigerator and let it defrost for a day or two ●
Refrigerator has odors	Dirty drain pan	Clean drain pan under the refrigerator ●
	Clogged drains	Clear drains (p.270), and flush drain system with a solution of baking soda and water ●
Freezer operates improperly	Freezer door lock broken	Replace door lock (p.270) ●●
	Mechanical and electrical defects in freezer	Freezer problems differ very little from refrigerator problems; check chart above

Ease of fix: ● simple   ●● average   ●●● difficult   ■ Volt-ohm meter required for this step (see p.124)

How refrigerators work

The refrigerator compressor circulates refrigerant through two sets of coils in one continuous loop. One set, the evaporator coils, cools the refrigerator; the other set, the condenser coils, is located under or in back of the refrigerator and gives off heat to the kitchen. The system works on the principle that a liquid (the refrigerant) absorbs heat (cools the interior of the refrigerator) when it evaporates into a gas, then gives off this heat to the room when it is condensed.

from one area to re-form in the colder area. As a result, frost is never seen inside the freezer and refrigerator compartments; it collects only in the area of the evaporator/defrost heater. There it is removed by the heater, which operates periodically when actuated by a defrost timer under the refrigerator. A special feature of the frost-free system is the evaporator fan, which is needed to circulate the air between the hidden evaporator coils and the food compartments.

Defrosting the refrigerator

Some refrigerators must be defrosted manually by turning the control dial to *Defrost*. Both the cycle defrost system and the frost-free system discussed below are automatic in operation.

Cycle defrost system: It uses a defrost heater inside the refrigerator compartment. The heater is turned on and off by the temperature control inside the unit. When the temperature at the evaporator plate drops below a point set by you on

the control, the compressor stops and the defrost heater turns on. The heater does not turn off until it raises the compartment temperature to about 35°F, melting any frost collected in the refrigerator.

Frost-free system: It hides the defrost heater, together with the evaporator coils, inside the panel that separates the freezer and refrigerator compartments. Frost always collects first at the coldest spot in the refrigerator—in a process called sublimation, it will even disappear

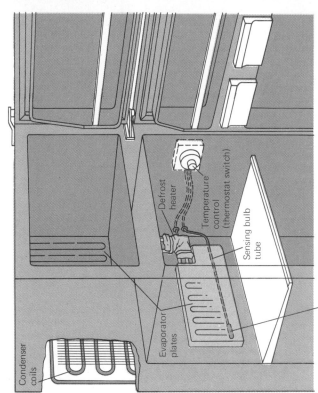

Defrost heater

Temperature control (thermostat switch)

Sensing bulb tube

Evaporator plates

Condenser coils

Temperature sensing bulb: It is usually attached behind evaporator plate by one or more clamps. Clamps are held tight by screws visible on front of plate. Tube follows different paths on different model refrigerators. Locate the clamps by feeling behind edges of plate with your fingers; then, loosen screws on front of plate to free tube. New sensing bulb tube that comes with manufacturer's thermostat replacement kit must be repositioned in the clamps exactly as the old one.

Cycle defrost refrigerator

Note: These views of typical, late-model refrigerators are to help you identify parts. Details on your unit may vary to some degree from the ones shown. Not all refrigerators defrost automatically. Non-automatic models must be defrosted by manually turning the temperature control to *Defrost*. Automatic defrosters of older models use a special timer to activate the defrost sequence—a system similar to that used in later frost-free models.

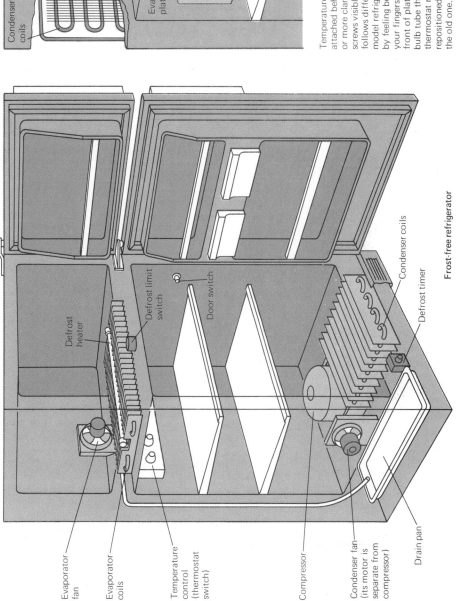

Evaporator fan

Evaporator coils

Temperature control (thermostat switch)

Compressor

Condenser fan (its motor is separate from compressor)

Drain pan

Defrost heater

Defrost limit switch

Door switch

Condenser coils

Defrost timer

Frost-free refrigerator

Replacing a door gasket

A leaking door gasket will cause frost to collect on the evaporator plate, and extend refrigerator running time. On refrigerator doors that latch, test the gasket by placing a dollar bill between the gasket and the doorjamb and pulling on it. On refrigerator doors that latch magnetically, look at the gasket to be sure it touches the doorjamb at all points around the door.

If a leak is apparent, first check the door for warping. If the door is warped, it is probably causing the leak. Realign it as described below. If there is no warp, re-

place the gasket. Most gaskets can be pulled off without taking out screws. When installing, push the new gasket's bead under the retainer with your fingers.

Refrigerator doors tend to warp when the gasket retainer screws are loosened. To correct this, realign the door by hand after installing the new gasket. Close the door to check the realignment. Repeat as often as necessary, then tighten the gasket screws.

Note: If the new gasket has crimps, remove them by laying it for a few minutes in a sink filled with warm water.

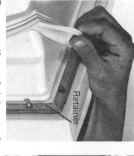

To check the condition of the door gasket, close the door on a dollar bill and pull on it. If gasket is OK, you will feel tension.

To remove the gasket, loosen all the retainer screws and pull it out from behind the gasket retainer. *Note:* Do not remove the screws.

Retainer

Straighten a warped door by pulling at the bottom and pushing at the top, or pushing at the bottom and pulling at the top.

Adjusting the doors

The refrigerator door should shut slowly by itself when left open at an angle of 45° or less. If the door does not do this, lean the refrigerator slightly backward and prop up the front with a cap or a block of wood.

To correct this, realign the door by adjustment. Repeat this step until the door closes properly.

If a door sags so that it cannot close completely, adjust the door hinges to reposition the door. A sagging door is not

the same as a warped door (see *Replacing a door gasket,* at left).

On some models the hinges are covered by a cap that you must pry off in order to reach the hinge screws. If the refrigerator has a separate freezer door, you may have to open the freezer door to reach the upper hinge screws on the refrigerator door. Remove the motor compartment grille (see p.268) to reach the lower hinge screws.

Note: To reach the refrigerator door screws on some models, you have to move the freezer door entirely.

Adjust the tilt of the refrigerator cabinet by turning the leveling legs under the front corners of the unit to move the legs up or down.

A sagging door is one whose sides and top do not quite line up parallel to the sides and top of the refrigerator cabinet.

To correct the sag in a door, loosen the hinge screws at the top of the door, then reposition the door and tighten the screws.

Testing and replacing a door switch

When you close a refrigerator door, the door pushes a button in the doorjamb, switching off the light bulb inside the refrigerator. If the switch fails to turn the light off, the bulb may generate enough heat to cause the refrigerator to run continuously and frost to collect.

To check a door switch, operate the switch with your finger to see whether the bulb turns on and off as it should. If it does not, check the bulb by screwing it into another lamp socket in your house or test the door switch itself.

Unplug the refrigerator and pull the switch out of the doorjamb. Test the switch with a volt-ohm meter (p.124) set

to the RX1 scale. If the switch is OK, the meter should read high when you press the switch button with your finger and zero ohms when you release the button. A different result indicates a defect; disconnect the leads, if you have not already done so, and replace the switch.

Note: In some frost-free refrigerators the evaporator fan is also turned on and off by a door switch, though in an opposite sense when compared to the light bulb. Test the fan switch with a volt-ohm meter set to the RX1 scale. If the switch is OK, the meter should read zero ohms when you press the switch button and high when you release the button.

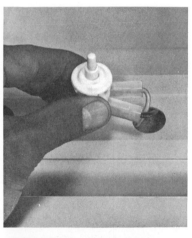

To test the door switch, first pry the switch out of the doorjamb to gain access to the switch terminals.

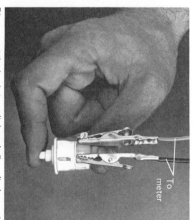

To
meter

Disconnect the leads to switch and clip volt-ohm meter probes to the switch terminals.

Testing and replacing the temperature control

A temperature sensing bulb in the refrigerator compartment is connected by a tube to the temperature control. The control responds hydrostatically to the bulb, causing the refrigerating system to turn on and off and maintain the desired temperature inside the unit.

To check the temperature control, unplug the refrigerator and test the control with a volt-ohm meter (p.124) set to the RX1 scale. If the meter reads zero ohms with the control at its coldest setting, the control is OK. If the meter reads high, the control is defective and should

be replaced, together with its sensing bulb and tube, with equivalent new parts from the manufacturer.

The type of temperature control used, and its location, depend on the type of refrigerator. In a frost-free model, the control is usually simple to disassemble and replace. In a cycle defrost unit, however, replacing the control can become involved. The sensing bulb may be threaded behind the compartment liner and you must take care not to kink the tube when rethreading a manufacturer's new bulb and tube into place.

Jamb strips and shelf supports

Cracks in a jamb strip permit moisture to enter and wet the insulation between the cabinet wall and compartment liner. This reduces the quality of insulation and degrades the unit's performance.

If the crack has been there for some time, it may help to unplug the unit on a dry day and leave its door open for the day to help dry the insulation. Replace the cracked strip afterward.

Shelf supports attach to the compartment liner by screws, by twisting on, or by clipping on. They are usually easy to replace if broken.

Notes: 1. When you tie a string to the end of the old sensing bulb tube, for rethreading purposes, wrap tape around the knot to keep it from catching.

2. If the old sensing bulb tube is sheathed in plastic, see that its replacement is sheathed in plastic.

3. The replacement tube may come from your parts supplier coiled. To straighten the coils, slide the shaft of a screwdriver along the tube.

4. When installing the sensing bulb, place it in the refrigerator exactly where you found the old bulb (see p. 265).

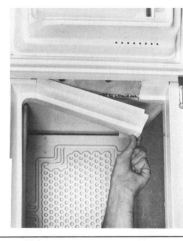

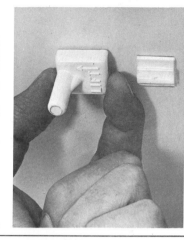

Jamb strips in refrigerator and freezer compartments can be removed by prying and pulling the strips off with your hands. New strips simply snap into place.

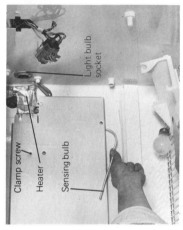

Light bulb socket

Clamp screw

Heater

Sensing bulb

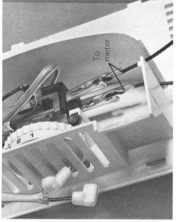

To meter

To remove temperature control, unscrew light bulb, pry off heater cover. Loosen sensing bulb clamp screws and pull bulb from behind evaporator plate.

Disconnect leads to the frost-free temperature control and clip the probes of a volt-ohm meter to the control terminals. Turn the control to its coldest setting.

The shelf support in this model of refrigerator can be removed by simply lifting the support up and off. Note: On other units method of attachment may differ.

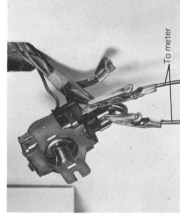

To meter

To test the temperature control, first pry off the control knob and take out the retaining screws, then pull the control from its opening inside the cabinet.

Disconnect a lead to the control and clip the probes of the volt-ohm meter to the control terminals. Turn the control to its coldest setting.

To test the temperature control in a frost-free refrigerator, take out retaining screws, if any, pry tabs loose, and lower the control assembly housing.

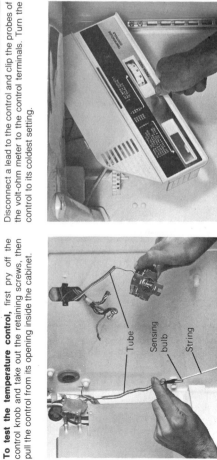

Tube

Sensing bulb

String

Thread sensing bulb and tube out from behind compartment wall. Note: Tie a string to bulb before threading, and use string as a guide to rethread new bulb.

Refrigerators and freezers

The frost-free refrigerator evaporator fan

The evaporator fan circulates air between the evaporator coils and the freezer and refrigerator compartments. Failure of the fan will result in poor cooling in the refrigerator compartment and will prevent the frost-free mechanism of the unit from operating properly.

The fan is switched on either by a door switch or in conjunction with the compressor motor. To check the fan, first open the freezer and refrigerator compartment doors. Wait for the compressor motor to turn on, if it is not already on (you will notice this by the low throbbing noise it makes at the bottom of the refrigerator). With one hand, press any switch you can find in the doorjamb (see p.267). Place your other hand over the fan duct in the freezer compartment and feel whether air is blowing through the duct. (For an illustration of a fan duct, see *Gaining access to the evaporator fan and defrost heater*, facing page.) If you can feel no draft, check the fan blade for obstructions and remove any you find. If the blades are free, unplug the refrigerator, disassemble the parts enclosing the fan (see facing page), and test the fan motor with a volt-ohm meter (p.124) set to the RX1 scale. If the motor is defective, replace it with an equivalent model from the manufacturer.

To test motor, disconnect the leads to it and clip volt-ohm meter probes to its terminals. If meter reads 50 to 200 ohms, motor is OK; if high, it is faulty.

To separate the fan motor from its bracket and fan blades, first disconnect its leads, take out screws, and remove fan assembly from freezer compartment.

The frost-free refrigerator defrost timer

The defrost timer turns the defrost heater, and in many cases the evaporator fan, on and off. When functioning properly, the timer keeps the freezer from accumulating frost.

To check the timer, first unplug the refrigerator and test both the timer mechanism and the timer motor with a volt-ohm meter (see p.124).

When testing the timer mechanism, set the meter to the RX1 scale. Turn the timer movement until you hear a click. If the needle of the meter jumps from high to zero ohms when the part clicks, the timer is OK. If the needle does not move, the timer mechanism is defective.

When testing the timer motor, set the meter to the RX100 scale. Clip meter probes to terminals No. 1 and No. 3. If the timer reads between 500 and 3,000 ohms, the timer motor is OK; if it reads higher than 3,000 ohms, it is defective.

Replace the timer if either the mechanism or the motor is defective. To remove the timer, take off the mechanism or the motor.

Note: If the timer terminals are not numbered, and you do not have a circuit diagram for the refrigerator to help you determine which terminals to clip the meter probes to, call an appliance repairman.

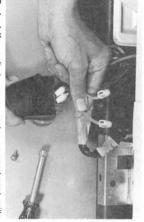
To test timer, first remove motor compartment grille (see below, left), take out screw, and pull out timer. Disconnect leads from terminals No. 2 and No. 3.

Test timer mechanism with probes of volt-ohm meter clipped to terminals No. 2 and No. 3 on timer. Turn timer movement with a coin inserted into the time-set slot.

Gaining access to parts under the refrigerator

Remove the motor compartment grille by pulling or prying it away from the bottom of the refrigerator.

Remove the rear lower access cover, take out cover retaining screws and lift off the cover.

Testing and replacing the power cord

The power cord is connected in back of the unit either to a terminal block or directly to refrigerator leads.

To check the cord, unplug it from the wall outlet and move the unit away from the kitchen wall. Remove the rear lower access cover (left), and pull out the terminal block or cord lead ends. Connect a jumper wire across the cord terminals and test the cord with a volt-ohm meter (p.124) set to the RX1 scale.

Replace the cord if defective. If splices or connectors were used, reconnect the new power cord with wire nuts, either the screw-on or the crimp-on type (p.123).

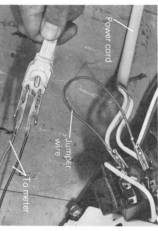
To test power cord, clip meter probes to cord plug and bend and pull cord. Meter should read zero ohms. If its needle jumps around or reads high, cord is faulty.

Testing and replacing the defrost heater

The defrost heater, located adjacent to the evaporator plate, melts the frost accumulated in the refrigerator. When checking the heater, first examine the frost on the evaporator plate (or coils). If one side is heavy with frost but the other is not, there is either a refrigerant leak or an obstruction in the refrigerant system. Call an appliance repairman.

If the frost on the plate is evenly distributed and feels hard, remove the frost before checking the heater. Use a canister vacuum cleaner run in reverse to blow warm air from the room onto the frost; this both hastens the melting time and blows ice from the crevices.

To check the defrost heater, unplug the refrigerator and disassemble it sufficiently to gain access to the heater (see below). Test the heater with a volt-ohm meter (p.124) set to the RX1 scale. Replace the heater if it is defective.

Note: The leads of the heater in a cycle defrost unit may be most easily tested at the point where they terminate on the temperature control. Pry off the control knobs, remove the control, and take out the screws. Clip the meter probes to the leads that are the same color as those at the heater.

Temperature control

Heater leads

To meter

To test heater, disconnect heater leads from temperature control terminals and clip meter probes to the leads. If meter reads between 200 and 1,000 ohms, the heater is OK; if high, it is defective.

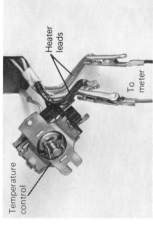

To remove heater, peel any tape from heater leads and cut the leads. Note: When installing new heater, reconnect leads with crimp-on wire nuts (see p.123) and fill nuts with silicone sealer to keep out moisture.

The defrost limit switch

The defrost limit switch is found on frost-free refrigerators. It operates like a thermostat to keep the defrost heater from heating above a certain temperature. When the switch is defective, the freezer compartment will frost up.

It is difficult to test a defrost limit switch. Make sure that the other parts—the evaporator fan, defrost timer, and defrost heater—are working, then assume that the trouble lies with the switch and replace it with a new one.

If you feel this assumption is too uncertain for you to rely on, call an appliance repairman.

Switch

To replace the defrost limit switch, take out switch retaining screws, cut leads, and lift out switch. Note: Connect the new switch leads with wire nuts (see p.123) and fill the nuts with silicone sealer.

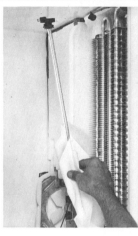

Heater (recessed)

Evaporator coils

To meter

To test the heater in this frost-free unit, disconnect heater leads and clip meter probes to heater terminals. If meter reads between 15 and 100 ohms, heater is OK; if meter reads high, heater is defective.

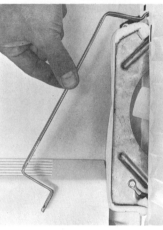

To remove heater from frost-free unit, lift heater cover, then heater, out of bottom of freezer compartment. Use a paper towel when grasping heater, to avoid corrosive effects of fingerprints on its surface.

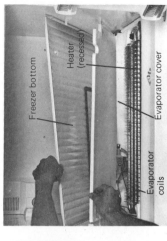

Freezer bottom

Heater (recessed)

Evaporator coils

Evaporator cover

Take out bottom retaining screws and remove the freezer bottom and the evaporator cover.

Gaining access to the evaporator fan and defrost heater in frost-free refrigerators

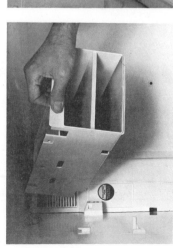

To reach fan and heater, first take out any retaining screws and lift out ice cube unit (or ice cube maker).

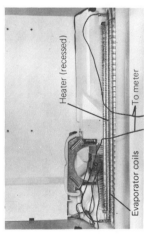

Duct assembly

Take out the freezer duct retaining screws and remove the duct assembly from the compartment.

After taking out the screws that moor it in position, lift off the fan shroud hold-down.

Refrigerators and freezers

Clearing the drains

Both the freezer and refrigerator compartments have drains for the removal of melted frost during a defrost cycle. If a drain becomes clogged, water will collect at the bottom of the compartment and leak or spill onto the floor when the door is opened. In addition, a clogged freezer compartment drain in a frost-free unit will create a frost problem. Unclog any drain that causes these difficulties.

Note: The freezer compartment drain on some frost-free models is located under the defrost heater inside the panel that encloses the evaporator coils. It can be reached only after considerable disassembly (see *Gaining access to the evaporator fan and defrost heater*, p.269).

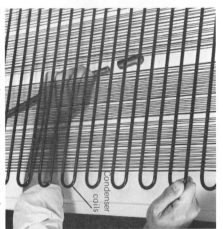

Reposition the drain pan underneath the refrigerator to stop the pan from rattling.

The drain pan and drain hose

The drain pan is located underneath the refrigerator. It collects the water that drains from inside the refrigerator during the defrost cycle. In the pan, the water slowly evaporates and goes into the air as vapor. If the pan rattles, reposition it.

On a number of refrigerators the melted frost goes to the drain pan through a drain hose in back of the unit. An old hose, if it is made of rubber rather than metal tubing, can become cracked and leak water onto the floor. Pull the refrigerator away from the wall to examine the hose. Replace it if it is defective.

Note: A cracked pan can sometimes cause leaks as well. Replace the pan if it presents this problem.

Condenser coils

To remove drain hose, take out screws to loosen condenser coils, unclamp hose, pull from outlet tube.

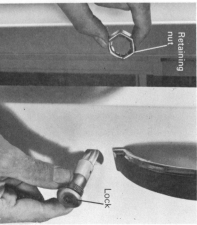

Lock assembly

To reach the lock assembly, first take out the panel retaining screws and remove the inner door panel.

Replacing the freezer door lock

Freezer door locks are intentionally made fragile to guard against a child's being accidentally locked inside. The lock is easy to break, so that the door can be pushed open from inside.

To replace a broken lock, first remove the door gasket (see p.266). Take out the panel (gasket) retaining screws and lift the inner door panel off the door. Re-move the lock mechanism from the door.

Note: Some gaskets are asymmetrical. Before removing the gasket, mark both it and the door with a pencil so that you can reinstall it in the same position. When reinstalling the gasket, check the door for warping (see p.266). Use tape to hold loose fiberglass insulation in place when putting the door back together.

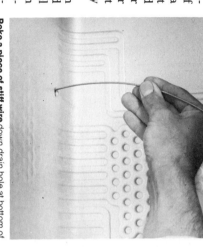

Poke a piece of stiff wire down drain hole at bottom of either compartment to unclog that drain.

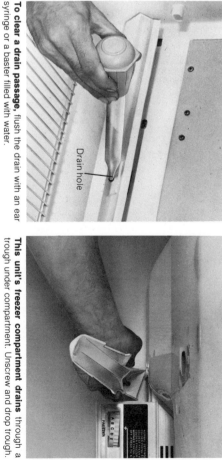

Drain hole

To clear a drain passage, flush the drain with an ear syringe or a baster filled with water.

This unit's freezer compartment drains through a trough under compartment. Unscrew and drop trough.

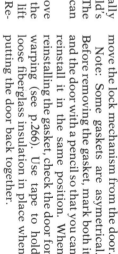

Retaining nut

Lock

Take off the lock retaining nut with pliers and remove the lock from the door.

Solving problems with the condenser fan in frost-free refrigerators

The condenser fan, located underneath the refrigerator, blows air over the condenser coils to cool them. With failure of the fan, the refrigerator will cool poorly or run continuously. In some cases, the unit will cease to run entirely.

Try cleaning the condenser coils to correct the problem (see below, right), and wait eight hours. If the difficulty has not cleared up, with the motor compartment grille at the bottom of the refrigerator removed, look at the condenser fan with the help of a flashlight to see if the blades are turning while the compressor motor is on. You can tell when the motor is on from the low throbbing noise it makes; if necessary, open the refrigerator doors to warm the refrigerator, and thereby start the compressor.

The fan blades may be obstructed. Sometimes you may hear a ticking sound, caused by paper hitting the blades. Unplug the unit and use a stick to clear away the obstruction, taking care not to distort the blades with the stick.

If the fan still does not turn when the refrigerator is running, unplug the refrigerator and pull it away from the wall. Remove the rear lower access cover (see p.268) and check the blades on the fan motor shaft for tightness. If the blades are OK, test the fan motor with a volt-ohm meter (p.124) set to the RX1 scale. Replace the motor if it is defective.

To remove fan motor, unscrew motor mounting nuts, lift out the motor, then take off the hub screw and remove the fan blades from the motor shaft.

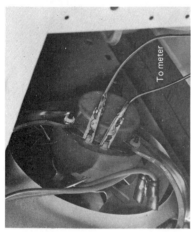

To test fan motor, disconnect the leads to it and clip volt-ohm meter probes to its terminals. If meter reads 50 to 200 ohms, motor is OK; if high, it is faulty.

Solving problems with the compressor

The compressor, in conjunction with the condenser and evaporator coils, cools the refrigerator. The part is located underneath, where it makes a low throbbing sound when working properly. If the refrigerator does not turn on, but you hear a click, there may be a problem with the compressor.

To check the compressor, unplug the refrigerator and pull it away from the wall. Remove the rear lower access cover (see p.268) and take off the motor relay cover on the compressor. Examine the terminals on the relay for discoloration due to burns, and the leads connected to the terminals for charred insulation. Take a look also at the terminals and leads at the other end, where the relay leads may connect to a power cord terminal block (see p.268).

Replace the compressor motor relay and the overload protector if you find evidence of burning in that area. If you find evidence of burning at the other end, replace the cord terminal block. Repair the charred leads (see p.123). If you find no evidence of burning, call an appliance repairman to check the compressor.

The rubber mounts that support the compressor sometimes become hard and cracked with age; this leads to excessive vibration in the refrigerator. Prop up the compressor with a lever and replace hardened mounts. Work with one mount at a time so as to disturb the position of the compressor as little as possible.

The condenser coils

The condenser coils are mounted on the back of the refrigerator, or under it in frost-free models. When they become clogged by dust, the refrigerator cools poorly or stays on continuously, and the unit fails to defrost. If the condition is severe, the refrigerator will stop running entirely. Clean the coils when this happens. Pull the refrigerator from the wall to reach coils that are in back. To reach coils that are under the unit, remove the motor compartment grille (see p.268).

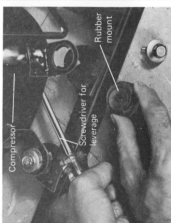

Clean the dust from condenser coils that are located in back of a refrigerator with a brush or a vacuum cleaner.

Use a wand of a vacuum cleaner to reach the dust around condenser coils that are located underneath a refrigerator.

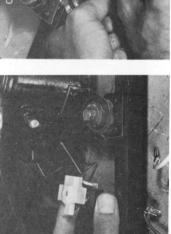

To remove a rubber motor mount, take out the mounting screw and slip the mount out.

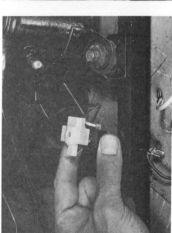

To remove the relay, unplug it from the compressor and disconnect the leads to the relay.

To check the motor relay, first slip off the cover clamp and remove the relay cover.

Sewing machines

Sewing machine problems

PROBLEM	POSSIBLE CAUSE	ACTION
Motor does not turn on	No power at wall outlet	Check wall outlet with a lamp you know is working. If lamp does not turn on, replace fuse or reset circuit breaker. If fuse keeps blowing, reduce number of appliances on circuit ●
	Open circuit in power cord or foot switch	Check power cord and foot switch and replace either part if it is defective (>275) ●●
Motor hums but machine does not operate	Machine needs oil	Lubricate the sewing machine (facing page) ●
	Bobbin or take-up assembly jammed	Clear the bobbin and the take-up assembly (p.274) ●●
	Motor defective	Check the motor and replace it if it is defective (>275) ●●
Motor runs but machine does not operate	Clutch slipping	Tighten clutch at the hand wheel ●
	Machine set to wind bobbin	Release bobbin wind control ●
	Drive belt too tight, too loose, worn, or broken	Adjust drive belt, or replace it if it is worn or broken (p.275) ●
	Machine needs oil	Lubricate the sewing machine (facing page) ●
Needle thread breaks	Machine not threaded correctly	Thread the machine correctly. See owner's manual ●
	If the spool is on a vertical spool pin, thread may be catching on spool notch	Turn spool upside down so that notch is at bottom of spool ●
	Needle inserted into needle clamp incorrectly	Reposition needle. Usually, flat part of needle shank should face away from last thread guide. See owner's manual ●
	Needle is of wrong size or is bent or burred	Use a needle of correct size and be sure it is not bent or burred at the tip ●
	Thread tension too high	Decrease needle thread tension (p.275) ●
	Path of needle thread has burrs or rough edges	Smooth edges with emery cloth or replace the rough part (p.275) ●
	Feed dog clogged by lint or thread	Unplug the machine, remove needle plate, and clean the feed dog with a small brush ●
Needle breaks	Wrong needle	Use needle of proper size. See owner's manual ●
	Bent needle	Replace needle ●
	Needle inserted in needle clamp incorrectly	Reposition needle. Usually, flat part of needle shank should face away from last thread guide. See owner's manual ●
	Presser foot or needle plate loose, or of wrong type	Use the correct presser foot and needle plate. Be sure they are tight. See owner's manual ●
	Bobbin case inserted incorrectly	Insert bobbin case correctly ●
Bobbin thread breaks	Burred edges on hole in needle plate	Smooth edge of hole with emery cloth or replace needle plate (p.275) ●
	Bobbin wound poorly	Wind thread on bobbin correctly (p.274) ●
	Bobbin case entangled by lint or thread	Clean area around bobbin case (p.274) ●
	Thread tension too high	Decrease bobbin thread tension (p.275) ●
	Burrs or rough edges on bobbin case or bobbin tension spring	Smooth edges of bobbin case with emery cloth or replace bobbin tension spring (p.275) ●●
Thread loops or bunches	Thread tension incorrectly set	Adjust needle thread tension. If problem persists, adjust bobbin thread tension (p.275) ●
	Lint clogging thread path	Clean lint from needle thread tension discs and bobbin area (facing page) ●
	Needle bent or burred	Replace needle ●
	Bobbin not wound correctly	Rewind bobbin (p.274) ●
Machine does not stitch or it skips stitches	Wrong or bent needle	Use needle of proper size (see owner's manual), or replace needle ●
	Needle inserted into needle clamp incorrectly	Reposition needle. Usually, flat part of needle shank should face away from last thread guide ●
Machine feeds fabric poorly or not in a straight line	Wrong type of presser foot	Use the correct presser foot for the job. See owner's manual ●
	Presser foot not in line	Adjust the presser foot ●●
	Feed dog clogged by lint or thread	Unplug the machine, remove needle plate, and clean the feed dog with a small brush ●
	Teeth on feed dog dull	Replace feed dog (p.274) ●
Bobbin winds incorrectly, or does not wind	Bobbin thread guide incorrectly positioned	Adjust bobbin thread pre-tension guide (p.274) ●
	Worn friction wheel	Replace friction wheel or rubber rim on friction wheel (p.274) ●

Ease of fix: ● simple   ●● average   ●●● difficult

Cleaning and lubricating

From time to time you should clean and lubricate the sewing machine. How often you should do so depends on how often it is used. Failure to do so eventually causes the machine to operate sluggishly and erratically.

To clean the machine, first unplug it. Then, with a soft piece of cloth or a small brush, remove all the lint that has accumulated between the tension discs; around the take-up lever, thread guides, presser foot, and needle bar; and under the slide plate and the needle plate.

Lubricate the machine with the oil recommended or sold by the manufacturer. Do not overoil. As a rule, place one drop of oil in each oil hole adjacent to a rotating shaft or moving part. Your owner's manual is the best guide to which parts of the machine should be lubricated.

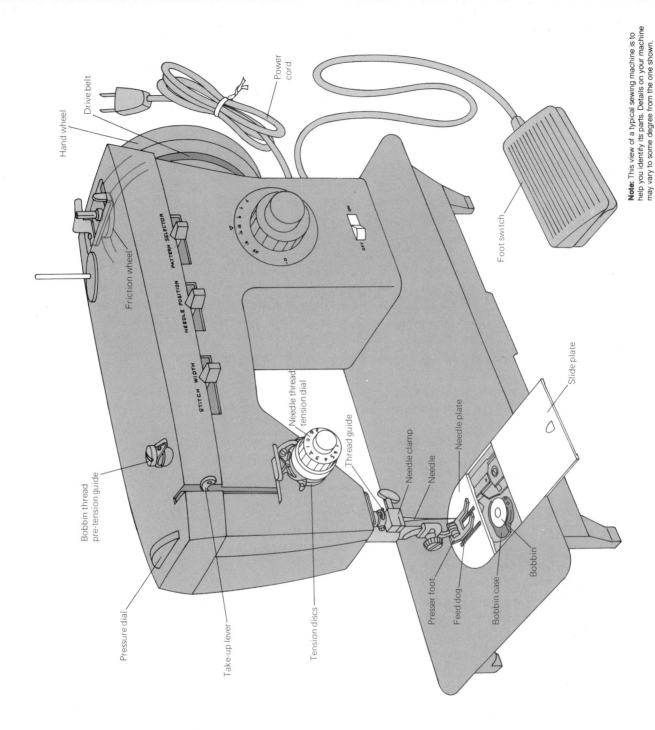

Hand wheel

Drive belt

Power cord

Friction wheel

PATTERN SELECTOR

NEEDLE POSITION

STITCH WIDTH

OFF ON

Foot switch

Bobbin thread pre-tension guide

Pressure dial

Take-up lever

Tension discs

Needle thread tension dial

Thread guide

Needle clamp

Needle

Needle plate

Presser foot

Feed dog

Bobbin case

Bobbin

Slide plate

Note: This view of a typical sewing machine is to help you identify its parts. Details on your machine may vary to some degree from the one shown.

Hand wheel

Drive shaft

Oil hole

Oil holes, such as this one leading to a drive shaft, can be reached after lifting top (see p.274).

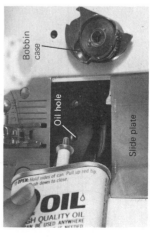

Bobbin case

Oil hole

Slide plate

This oil hole is located in the bobbin area. It can be reached after lifting out the bobbin case (see p.274).

Sewing machines

Clearing the bobbin and the take-up assembly

When thread becomes tangled in the bobbin area, either the needle thread or the bobbin thread will break. If the condition is severe, the sewing machine will jam and be unable to start. To remove tangled thread, first unplug the machine, remove the needle and the presser foot, and lift or pry off the slide plate and the needle plate. After untangling the thread, remove all lint from the area with a brush. If the bobbin thread has become tangled under the bobbin case tension spring, loosen the spring with a screwdriver, clear the thread, then retighten and adjust the spring (see facing page). Note: The bobbin assembly on your machine may differ substantially from the one illustrated here. If you cannot disassemble it, refer to your owner's manual.

Jamming of the machine can also occur if some object, such as a pin, accidentally falls through the slot behind the take-up lever into the take-up and needle bar assembly. If this happens, unplug the unit, disassemble it (see below), and remove the object.

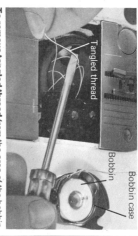

To remove tangled thread from the area of the bobbin case, first remove the bobbin, and lift and push the bobbin case holder to right to remove the case.

Remove any object that may have slipped into the space around the take-up lever and needle bar assembly; it may prevent parts from moving up and down.

Disassembling the sewing machine

Procedures for disassembling sewing machines vary greatly with the different models. Most of the time, however, the problems you will have with the machine will not require that you take much of it apart. On a number of models, inside parts that should be checked occasionally can be reached simply by lifting off the top or swinging open the faceplate. To take off the front or the back of a machine like the one illustrated here, take out the retaining screws and lift it off. Pry off any dials that interfere with removal of the front.

To remove the top from this model of sewing machine, take out screws that secure top and lift it off.

To remove the front and back, take out the screws that secure them to the machine and lift it off.

The bobbin thread guide and friction wheel

A bobbin is wound properly when the thread on it is uniform rather than bunched toward one side.

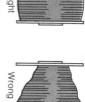

Winding the bobbin.

You can correct poor winding of the bobbin by adjusting the bobbin thread pre-tension guide. Continue making adjustments until the problem is solved.

If the bobbin does not wind at all when the machine is set for winding it, the friction wheel that turns the bobbin is probably worn. To check the wheel, unplug the machine and disassemble it so that the wheel is accessible (see below, left). If the rubber rim on the wheel is worn, take out the mounting screws and replace the wheel assembly, or simply replace the rubber rim if you are able to separate it from the wheel.

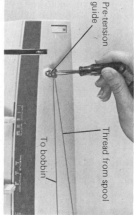

The rubber rim of the friction wheel on this model of sewing machine can be separated from the wheel by simply prying the rim off.

Turn the screw on the bobbin thread pre-tension guide to adjust the height of the guide. Note: On many models, guide is located near base of machine.

Checking and replacing the feed dog

The feed dog is a part—usually with jagged saw-toothed edges—that pushes fabric through the sewing machine. If the teeth of the feed dog are dull from long use or if the feed dog is improperly positioned, fabric will not move properly through the machine. Inspect the teeth.

If they are worn, unplug the sewing machine and replace the feed dog. To check the position of the feed dog, place a needle next to it so that the flat side of the needle's shank lies face down. Turn the hand wheel. If the feed dog rises higher than the needle, call a repairman.

To replace feed dog, remove needle, presser foot, and needle plate. Take out screws and lift out feed dog.

The feed dog in its raised position should not reach higher than thickness of a needle placed next to it.

Adjusting the tension

The tension on the needle and the bobbin threads must balance for the machine to stitch correctly. If the balance is off, the stitching will show loops, either on top or underneath the fabric.

Needle thread too tight (bobbin thread too loose).

Needle thread too loose (bobbin thread too tight).

Needle and bobbin thread tension balanced.

To balance the tension, turn the needle thread tension dial. This will adjust the needle thread tension and is normally sufficient. If, however, the dial's range of adjustment is not great enough, adjust the bobbin thread tension also. Turn the screw on the bobbin case very slightly—clockwise to tighten the bobbin thread, counterclockwise to loosen it.

Lint will collect between the needle thread tension discs, making the stitching erratic and the needle thread tension difficult to adjust. Clean the lint from between the discs with a piece of cloth.

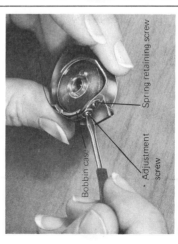

Turn the adjustment screw on the bobbin case to increase or decrease bobbin thread tension.

Burrs and rough edges

The needle thread will break if there are any burrs or rough edges on any part the thread passes along its route through the sewing machine. These parts include the thread guides, the presser foot, the needle, and the needle plate. The bobbin thread may break if the hole in the needle plate is burred or rough. To check each of the parts, feel their edges with your fingers, or examine the parts with a magnifying glass. Rub the parts with emery cloth to smooth out any burrs or roughness. If the problem persists, replace the part that causes it.

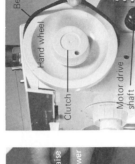

To remove the thread guide above the needle, take out the screw that secures guide to needle clamp.

The power cord and foot switch

Foot switches vary in design and are wired to the power cord and the sewing machine in different ways. Some use solid state circuits. If you are an experienced electrician, you may test and repair the foot switch and cord(p.125) after examining their wiring. If you are not, take the switch and cord assembly to a sewing machine repair shop and ask them to plug the assembly into a working machine and wall outlet to ascertain whether or not the cord and switch work. Replace any part that does not work.

Solving problems with the motor and the drive belt

The machinery in most sewing machines is run by a drive belt driven in turn by the motor. If the motor runs but the machine fails to operate, the belt may be slipping because it is loose or worn, or it may be broken. The machine may also operate sluggishly because the belt is too tight. To alter the tension in the belt, unplug the sewing machine and reposition the motor. Tighten the belt just enough to run the machine. Besides making the machine run sluggishly, overtightening increases wear in the belt and the motor. If the belt is broken, replace it.

The motor may hum but not run as you turn on the machine. If this happens, disengage the motor from the machinery by opening the clutch on the hand wheel. If the motor runs by itself, some other part of the machine is jammed (see *Clearing the bobbin and the take-up assembly*, facing page). If the motor still fails to run, it is defective. Replace it.

Note: On many sewing machines the motor is inside the machine housing. Before removing the motor, you must disassemble the housing (see *Disassembling the sewing machine*, facing page).

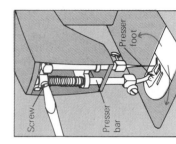

To remove the motor, take out the motor bracket screw and lift out. If the motor is wired to a switch or a lamp, also unscrew and remove the switch or lamp from the machine.

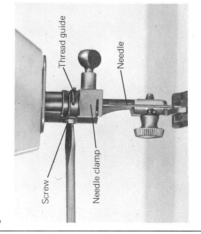

To remove the belt, loosen the motor bracket screw and raise the motor bracket screw and raise the motor. Then, slip the belt off the motor drive shaft and from around the hand wheel.

To tighten the belt, loosen the motor bracket screw, lower the motor, then retighten the screw. To loosen the belt, raise the motor instead of lowering it.

Adjusting the presser foot

If fabric does not feed through the sewing machine in a straight line, the presser foot may be positioned incorrectly. You can check this visually by sighting along the edge of the foot to observe whether or not it lines up parallel to the normal direction of feed travel. If the foot lies at an angle, unplug the sewing machine and disassemble it so that you can reach the adjustment screw on the presser bar with the blade of a screwdriver (see *Disassembling the sewing machine*, facing page). Adjust the angle of the presser foot.

To adjust the presser foot, loosen the screw on the presser bar, twist the bar until the foot is properly lined up, then retighten the screw. Note: This adjustment may alter the pressure of the presser foot on fabric. If it does, the adjustment should be made at a repair shop.

Washing machines

Washing machine problems

PROBLEM	POSSIBLE CAUSE	ACTION
Tub does not fill with water	No power at wall outlet	Replace fuse or reset circuit breaker. If fuse keeps blowing or breaker keeps tripping, test the motor for a short circuit and replace it if it is defective (p.282) ●● ■
	Water inlet hoses kinked	Reposition the hoses. If the kinks are hardened and set, replace the hoses ●
	Inlet valve screens clogged	Clean the water inlet valve screens or replace them ●
	Power cord defective	Test the power cord and replace it if it is defective (p.279) ●●● ■
	Timer or selector switch faulty	Check timer and temperature selector switch and replace either one if defective (p.278) ●●
Water does not shut off	Air hose on water level switch fallen off	Reattach air hose on water level switch (p.278) ●●
	Inlet valve defective	Check water inlet valves and replace any part that is defective (p.279) ●●● ■
Water is at the wrong temperature	Faucets connected to water inlet valves improperly adjusted or hot water supply exhausted	Turn hot and cold water faucets down or up. Check hot water supply to house ●
	Inlet valve screen clogged or inlet valve solenoid defective	Clean water inlet valve screens or replace any defective inlet valve part (p.279) ●●● ■
Tub fills normally but motor does not start	Lid safety switch out of adjustment or defective	Adjust lid safety switch; replace it it if is defective (p.278) ●●
	Overload protector tripped or defective	Reduce wash load in tub and wait 15 minutes for overload protector to reset. If protector does not reset, test it and replace it if it is defective (p.282) ●●● ■
	If the motor hums, the motor may be faulty	Check the motor and replace it if it is defective (p.282) ●●●
	If the motor hums, the drain pump may be jammed	Unjam the drain pump or replace it if it is defective (p.283) ●●
Motor runs but washing machine does not agitate or spin	Drive belt slipping, loose, or broken	Tighten drive belt or replace it if it is broken (p.282) ●●
	Pulley on motor shaft loose	Tighten or replace motor pulley (p.282) ●●
	Agitator solenoid defective	Test agitator solenoid and replace it if it is defective (p.283) ●●● ■
Washing machine agitates but does not spin, stops on spin, or spins lazily	Wash load unbalanced or tub overloaded	Redistribute wash load evenly in tub. If problem persists, reduce amount of wash in tub ●
	Lid safety switch out of adjustment or defective	Adjust lid safety switch; replace it if it is defective (p.278) ●●
	Drive belt slipping, loose, or broken	Tighten drive belt or replace it if it is broken (p.282) ●●
	Basket jammed by clothing caught underneath it	Remove clothing caught around the tub shaft under the basket (p.281) ●●
	Spin solenoid faulty	Test spin solenoid and replace it if it is defective (p.283) ●●● ■
	Washing machine draining poorly	See *Washing machine spins but water does not drain*, below
	Timer defective	Check the timer and replace it if it is defective (p.278) ●●
Washing machine spins but water does not drain	Water inlet hoses kinked	Reposition the hoses. If the kinks are hardened and set, replace the hoses ●
	Oversudsing in washtub, causing machine to spin slowly	Add cold water and ½ cup of white vinegar to reduce suds. After emptying, rinse tub ●
	If drain hose is connected to a closed drain on the house plumbing, the house drain may be clogged	Remove drain hose from plumbing and run the machine with the hose in a bucket. If water then drains easily, the house drain is clogged. Clear the drain ●●
	Drain pump jammed	Unjam the drain pump or replace it if it is defective (p.283) ●●
	Washtub oversudsing	Add cold water and ½ cup of white vinegar to washtub to reduce suds ●
	Part in the washing machine poorly sealed or cracked	Locate leak and repair or replace the part that causes the leak (p.280) ●●
Washing machine leaks	Washtub oversudsing	Add cold water and ½ cup of white vinegar to washtub to reduce suds ●
	Wash load unbalanced or tub overloaded	Redistribute wash load evenly in tub. If problem persists, reduce amount of wash in tub ●
Washing machine vibrates or makes excessive noise	Washtub oversudsing	Add cold water and ½ cup of white vinegar to washtub to reduce suds ●
	Washing machine stands on three legs	Adjust washing machine legs (p.279) ●
	Basket hold-down nut loose or basket support worn	Tighten basket or replace worn basket support ●●
	Snubber not working properly	Repair snubber assembly or replace defective part in the assembly (p.281) ●●
Washing machine tears clothes	Only white clothes tearing in the washing machine indicates bleach damage; the tears appear as holes	Use less bleach. If washing machine does not have a bleach dispenser, dilute bleach in a quart jar with water. Add mixture to clothes only when they are fully immersed in water ●
	Clothing abrading and snagging; the tears appear as gashes or are L-shaped	Reduce size of wash load and length of time used to wash. Raise the water level in unit if it is low. Close zippers and turn clothing with hooks inside out ●
	Agitator vane broken or wash basket surface rough	Replace agitator or basket (p.281) ●●

Ease of fix: ● simple ●● average ●●● difficult ■ Volt-ohm meter required for this step (see p.124)

Lint, dingy clothing, stains

Clothing commonly washes poorly because an inappropriate wash procedure is used. Save yourself from unnecessary searches for nonexistent defects in your washing machine by consulting your owner's manual. If any of the following occur, take the steps indicated:

Lint on clothing

1. Wash those items that give off lint, such as bath towels, separately from items that attract lint, such as permanent press and synthetic fiber clothing.

2. Use more detergent.

3. Be sure you are not overloading the machine; select the right amount of water for the size of load being washed.

Grey, dingy clothing

1. Sort white clothes, colorfast clothes, and noncolorfast clothes and wash them as three separate loads.

2. Wash with water that is above 140°F.

3. Use more detergent. If you use a high suds detergent and increasing the amount causes too much suds, switch to a low suds detergent. Note: Some parts of the country ban phosphate detergents. Nonphosphate products, however, can cause fading and streaking and may clog filters and other parts in your unit. Follow manufacturer's directions exactly when using a nonphosphate detergent, and consider installing a water softening system in your home if you live in a hard water area where the problem is severe.

Stains from body oils on clothing

Make sure the water is at least 140°F, that you use enough detergent, and that the unit runs through a full wash cycle.

Clothing stains yellow or brown

1. If the stains are caused by iron in your water pipes or heater, run the hot water for a few minutes before starting the machine. Occasionally drain the heater.

2. If the stains are caused by iron or manganese in the water supply, add a nonprecipitating water conditioner during the wash and deep rinse cycles. Also, install an iron filter.

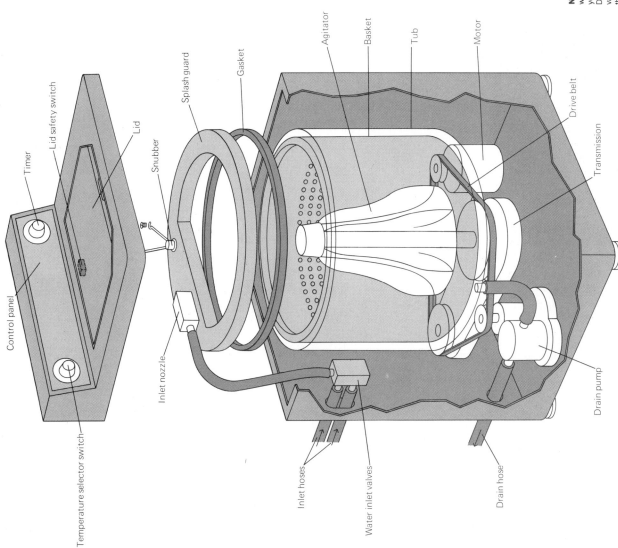

Control panel

Timer

Lid safety switch

Temperature selector switch

Lid

Snubber

Splash guard

Gasket

Inlet nozzle

Inlet hoses

Water inlet valves

Agitator

Basket

Tub

Motor

Drive belt

Transmission

Drain pump

Drain hose

Note: This view of a typical washing machine is to help you identify its parts. Details on your unit may vary to some degree from the one shown.

277

Washing machines

Adjusting or replacing the lid safety switch

The lid safety switch protects you by turning off the motor every time you raise the lid. The switch is mounted under the top. In time, the switch may change position so that when you close the lid the switch fails to start. Or the motor fails to start. Or the motor starts, but vibration, particularly during the spin mode, causes the lid or the switch to shift out of position enough to cause the switch to open and the motor to stop.

If the motor does not start, raise the lid, then close it. If the motor still fails to start, adjust the position of the switch again to reposition the switch. Use the meter to indicate when the lid is tripping the top (see p.280).

The switch itself may be defective. To check it, remove the spray shield and test the switch with a volt-ohm meter (p.124) set to the RX1 scale. The test may be performed by closing the lid, or by pressing the switch lever or button with your finger. Checking with the lid indicates whether or not the switch is in a correct working position relative to the lid; checking with your finger indicates whether or not the switch is broken.

If the switch is broken, replace it. If it is not, put the spray shield back on and try again to reposition the switch. Use the meter to indicate when the lid is tripping the switch properly.

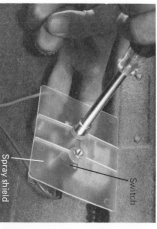

Loosen the mounting screws on the lid safety switch with a nutdriver or screwdriver. Reach under the spray shield and adjust the position of the switch. Tighten the screws after you have made the adjustment.

Spray shield / Switch

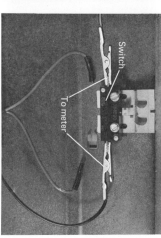

To test the switch, disconnect its leads and clip the probes of a volt-ohm meter to its terminals. Close the lid. If the meter reads zero ohms, the switch is OK; if it reads high, the switch is not working.

Switch / To meter

The timer, temperature selector switch, and water level switch

The timer, temperature selector switch, and water level switch are mounted behind the control panel. The timer regulates the sequence of fill, drain, agitate, and spin modes. In tandem with the temperature selector switch it also opens the hot and cold water inlet valves during fill to provide water at the desired temperature. The water level switch turns off the valves to keep the machine from overflowing. To check any of these parts, unplug the unit and remove the back of the control panel (see p.280).

Defects in the timer can cause a variety of problems, including the following:

1. The timer mechanism may not advance when you start the washing machine. As a positive check, start the unit with the timer knob turned to a setting at which the machine should spin.

2. The machine does not fill or it fills with hot water but not cold or vice versa.

3. The water does not shut off when the machine is full. This occurs only in units that do not use a water level switch.

4. The unit agitates but does not spin.

In each instance, without special knowledge you cannot do much with the timer except check the condition of its terminals and cam teeth. Pry the connectors off the timer terminals one by one and check each connector and terminal for corrosion. Polish the connectors and terminals with very fine sandpaper to remove any corrosion, then reconnect them. To check the cam teeth, dismount the timer from the control panel. If they have become rounded from wear, replace the timer.

If the machine fails to fill, or fills at the wrong water temperature, the trouble may be in either the temperature selector switch or the timer. Check the terminals on the selector switch for corrosion.

Failure of the machine to shut off after filling with water may be due to the air hose having slipped off the water level switch. Reattach the hose.

Test for other faults in the timer and the water temperature selector switch only if you are an experienced electrician and have a circuit diagram for your unit. Otherwise, call an appliance repairman or take the suspected part or parts to an appliance repair shop for checking or replacement. Take both the timer and selector switch if you have a fill problem. For other problems, take the timer only.

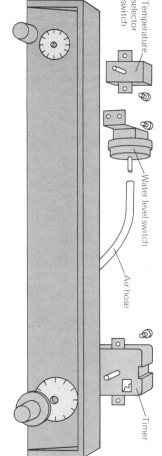

Temperature selector switch

Water level switch

Air hose

Timer

To replace the timer or one of the switches, disconnect the leads to the part, take out retaining screws, and remove it. Note: Depending on the model, the location of the timer and switches can vary substantially from the arrangement shown here.

Connector

To disconnect a lead from any part mounted behind the control panel, pry the connector from the terminal with a screwdriver.

Cam teeth / Timer control knob

After screwing the timer control knob back on, turn it and look through opening in side of timer to check cam teeth for wear.

Water level switch / Air hose connection

Cut off about 1 in. of air hose from the end of the hose before reattaching it to the hose connection on the water level switch.

Solving problems with the water inlet valves

The water inlet valves are mounted in the back of the washing machine cabinet and are connected by a pair of inlet hoses to your water supply. A defective valve can create several problems. If any of the following occur, take the steps indicated:

Machine fills too slowly or not at all First, make sure that the faucets to which the inlet hoses are connected are open and water is in the system. Then, check the inlet valve screens after turning off the faucets and disconnecting the hoses from the valves. Remove the screens from both valves and examine them for clogging. If clogged, clean the screens under an open faucet with a brush, or replace them. If the clogging occurs fre-

quently, install an additional pair of screens at the other end of the hoses, where they are attached to the faucets.

Fill water is at the wrong temperature Set the water temperature selector to *Hot*. If no water flows, set the selector to *Warm*. If only cold water flows, the hot water valve is probably defective. To check the cold water valve, use this procedure in reverse, substituting *Cold* for *Hot*. Clean the screen of the valve that seems to be defective as described in the preceding paragraphs. If cleaning does not correct the problem, unplug the machine, lift the top (see p.280), and remove the inlet valve assembly from the unit. Disconnect a lead to one of the valve's

solenoid terminals and test the solenoid with a volt-ohm meter (p.124) set to the RX100 scale. Replace the valve if it is defective.

Water still runs after machine is full Unplug the unit. If the water stops, the defect is electrical (see *The timer, temperature selector switch, and water level switch,* facing page). If the water still flows, a valve plunger is stuck open. Turn off both faucets, lift the top, and remove the inlet valve assembly from the unit. Take the assembly apart and replace the diaphragm, plunger, spring, and valve guide in both valves. Note: In some models, you cannot take the valve assembly apart; replace it as a unit.

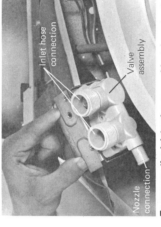

Inlet hose connection

Valve assembly

Nozzle connection

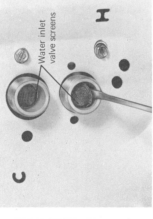

Water inlet valve screens

To remove a screen, pry it out with a small screwdriver. Note: When reinstalling screen, use tubing of roughly the same diameter to push screen into place.

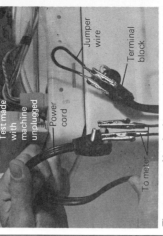

Test made with machine unplugged

Jumper wire

Terminal block

Power cord

To meter

The power cord

The power cord is wired to a terminal block inside the washing machine. To test the cord, set a volt-ohm meter (p.124) to the RX1 scale and clip the meter probes to the cord plug. Attach a jumper wire to the cord leads where they connect to the block. Take out a mounting screw and pull the block a short way out of the unit, if necessary, to attach the jumper wire. Bend and pull the power cord. If the meter reads zero ohms, the cord is OK. If the needle of the meter jumps around or reads high, the cord is defective and should be replaced. Note: On some models the cord plugs into a receptacle mounted on the back of the machine. Attach the jumper wire across the plug connectors at the end of the cord that plugs into the receptacle.

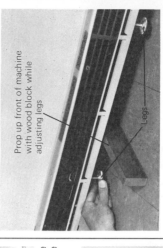

Prop up front of machine with wood block while adjusting legs

Legs

Adjusting the legs

Improperly adjusted legs on the washing machine result in excessive vibration, particularly during spin. To check the legs, place your hands on diagonally opposite corners of the top and try to make the cabinet rock. Eliminate any rocking motion by adjusting one leg or the other by loosening the locknut and turning the leg. Retighten the locknut. Note: After adjusting, place a spirit level on top of the unit to make sure that you have adjusted the legs in such a way that the machine remains level from front to back.

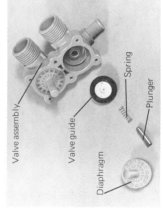

Valve assembly

Spring

Valve guide

Plunger

Diaphragm

To remove the inlet valve assembly, take out valve retaining screws, disconnect nozzle hose, and lift the assembly out from inside the washing machine.

Remove the diaphragm, plunger, spring, and valve guide from the valve assembly after lifting off the side plate and solenoids.

To meter

Solenoid

Inlet valve assembly

Test made with machine unplugged

Valve assembly

Solenoids

To remove the inlet hoses from the water inlet valves in back of the washing machine, unscrew the hose couplings with a wrench.

To remove a solenoid from the inlet valve assembly, take out the solenoid retaining screws. Note: On some assemblies, both solenoids remove as a unit.

To test a solenoid, clip probes of volt-ohm meter to solenoid terminals. If meter reads between 250 and 1,000 ohms, the solenoid is OK; if high, it is faulty.

Washing machines

Locating and repairing leaks in the washing machine

If the washing machine leaks water while it is filling, pull it away from the wall and see if water drips from the inlet hoses or valves as the unit fills. If it does, tighten the faucet packing nuts. Then, inspect the hoses and replace them if they have become cracked. Also look for cracks in the casing of the inlet valves. Unplug the unit and lift the top (see *Gaining access to parts inside and under the washing machine*, below) to better inspect the valves. Replace any valves that are cracked (see

Solving problems with the water inlet valves, p.279). Note: Valves usually crack during the wash sequence other than when the machine is filling with water, unplug the unit, remove the back panel (see below), and examine the parts under the machine. You can make a closer inspection by tipping the unit over onto its front or side. Tighten hose clamps that have become loose. If water is leaking from the pump, replace the pump (see *Solving problems with the drain pump*, p.283).

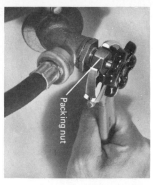

Packing nut

If the leaking occurs at some time during the wash sequence other than when the machine is filling with water, unplug the unit, remove the back panel (see below), and examine the parts under the machine. You can make a closer inspection by tipping the unit over onto its front or side. Tighten hose clamps that have become loose. If water is leaking from the pump, replace the pump (see *Solving problems with the drain pump*, p.283).

place the nozzle if you find cracks in it.

A cracked inlet nozzle can leak during fill. The leaking water will drip down the outside of the tub and collect under the unit. Be sure that the hose connected to the inlet nozzle is tightly clamped. Re-

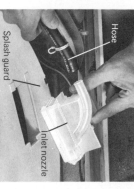

Hose
Splash guard
Inlet nozzle

The gasket between the tub and the splash guard may wear out and leak. To check the gasket, lift the top and remove the snubber and splash guard (see p.281). Replace a worn gasket.

A hole can develop in the bottom of the tub. If the hole is less than ¼ inch in diameter, remove the agitator and basket (see facing page) and seal the hole as illustrated below. If the hole is larger, call a repairman to replace the tub, or replace the washing machine.

If a faucet packing nut leaks water, which runs down the inlet hose, tighten the nut with a smooth-jawed wrench (see p. 36).

To remove inlet nozzle, disconnect hose and pry nozzle loose from splash guard. On some models, first take out screws.

To tighten clamp, try loosening and shifting the clamp to a slightly different position on the end of the hose.

Tub rim
Gasket

The gasket between the tub and the splash guard can be removed by simply lifting the gasket off the rim of the tub.

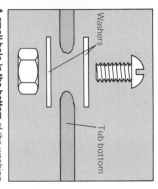

Washers
Tub bottom

A small hole in the bottom of the washing machine tub can be sealed with a screw, a nut, and washers of appropriate size.

Gaining access to parts inside and under the washing machine

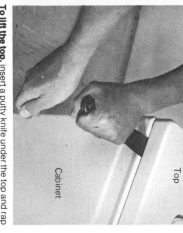

Top
Cabinet

To lift the top, insert a putty knife under the top and rap on the knife with the palm of your hand to open the spring clips that moor the top to the cabinet at each of its corners. Raise the top.

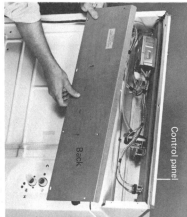

Back
Control panel

To reach parts mounted behind the control panel, take out retaining screws and lift off back of panel. Note: On some models you may have to remove the panel front and perhaps even the sides to reach parts.

To remove the lower access panel in back of the washing machine, first take out retaining screws, then lift off the panel. Note: The location of the panel varies with different models.

Blanket

To reach parts under the washing machine, empty the washtub of water and have someone help you tip the machine over onto its front or side. Place a blanket under the unit to protect its finish.

Solving problems with the agitator, snubber, basket, and tub

The washtub assembly includes the basket, which spins the clothes; the agitator, which swishes the clothes back and forth; and the snubber, which holds the tub assembly in position inside the machine yet lets the tub move back and forth to absorb any shaking or vibration while the unit is operating. Defects in any of these parts can create problems. If any of the following occur, unplug the unit and take the steps indicated:

The machine tears clothes
Check the agitator and replace it if any of its vanes are broken. The agitator is sometimes difficult to remove. Half fill the tub with hot water, wait 10 minutes, and try to loosen the agitator. Then, try rapping it with a hammer. If neither method works, drive wooden wedges under the base of the agitator to loosen it.

Clothes may be torn by a rough surface inside the basket. Roughness can be caused by water or by cleaning or conditioning agents interacting chemically with the surface. If you can feel a roughness in the basket with your fingers, replace the basket.

Machine vibrates or is excessively noisy
Inspect the snubber for a loose or broken suspension spring. Tighten or replace the spring if it is defective. Clean the friction pad with emery cloth if the snubber sticks to its surface. Note: Snubber design varies greatly between models. Some units use a set of friction pads and damping fins in the tub suspension assembly located between tub and cabinet.

Move the basket back and forth by hand. If it moves excessively, tighten the basket hold-down nut (or the hold-down bolts at the bottom of the basket). If the problem persists, the basket support is worn. Replace the support.

The machine stops during spin
Rotate the basket by hand. If it is hard to turn, clothing may be caught around the tub shaft under the basket. Lift out the basket and remove any caught clothing.

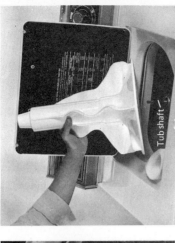

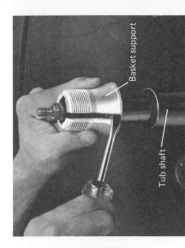

After loosening the agitator from the tub shaft, simply lift it off of the shaft and out of the tub.

To remove basket, first loosen hold-down nut with hammer. (Use block of wood to protect nut.)

To remove a worn basket support, pry it from beneath with a screwdriver to expand it, then pull it up.

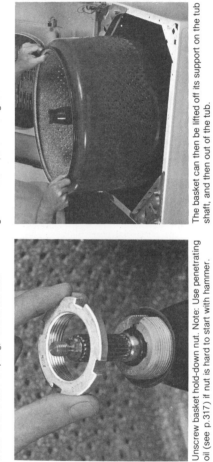

If agitator is tight, loosen it with a hammer. Use a block of wood, as shown, to protect agitator from damage.

To remove splash guard, detach springs that clip guard to tub rim, then lift off guard.

The basket can then be lifted off its support on the tub shaft, and then out of the tub.

To remove the agitator, first lift off softener dispenser and unscrew or lift off agitator cap.

To remove this type of snubber, lift the spring and pull it out. To take out the spring, remove the bolt.

Unscrew basket hold-down nut. Note: Use penetrating oil (see p.317) if nut is hard to start with hammer.

Washing machines

Tightening or replacing the drive belt

The motor uses a drive belt to operate the drain pump and the transmission. When the belt is loose, it may yet provide enough friction for the motor to drive the agitator and the pump, but may slip during the spin mode so that the machine spins lazily or stops spinning before the spin cycle is complete. If the belt is very loose or if it is broken, the machine will not agitate or spin at all.

To check the belt, unplug the unit, pull it away from the wall, and remove the access panel at the bottom of the ma-

Checking tension in drive belt.

chine (see *Gaining access to parts inside and under the washing machine*, p.280). Tighten the belt if it is loose; replace it if it is broken. You can tell when the belt is properly tightened by pressing it firmly inward—it should deflect ¾ inch from the straight line it makes when it is tight between pulleys.

In some machines you can remove the belt easily after loosening and lifting it off the pulleys. In others, to free the belt from the machine you must first loosen or disconnect one or more mounting brackets, hoses, or parts.

Note: If there is a leak in some part of the unit, particularly in the drain pump, the leaking water may drip onto the drive belt and cause it to slip and behave like a belt that is too loose. Repair the leak (see p.280).

Solving problems with the motor

The washing machine is run by a motor that is located under the tub. To check the motor, first unplug the unit and pull it away from the wall. Remove the access panel at the bottom of the unit (see 280).

If the machine repeatedly blows fuses or trips a circuit breaker, test for a short circuit between the housing and the internal wiring of the motor with a volt-

ohm meter (p.124) set to the RX100 scale. Replace the motor if there is a short.

To check the operation of the motor, first loosen and disengage the drive belt from the motor pulley (see above). Set the timer dial to *Spin*, and plug in and run the machine for a few seconds to listen to the motor. Then, if any of the following occur, take the steps indicated:

The motor does not run and is silent Test the overload protector with a volt-ohm meter set to the RX1 scale. Replace the protector if it is defective.

The motor hums but does not run Check the motor terminals and tighten any loose connectors. If there is an odor of burning in the motor, replace the motor. Otherwise, call an appliance re-

pairman to check the motor and its associated wiring, or remove the motor and take it to a repair shop. (See also p.135)

The motor runs but the machine does not operate when the belt is engaged Turn the motor pulley with your hand. If the pulley is loose on the motor shaft, tighten the setscrew on the pulley hub. If that does not help, replace the pulley.

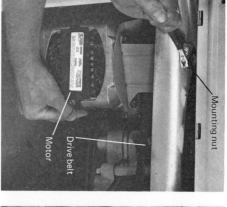

To tighten a loose drive belt, loosen the motor mounting nut with a wrench, shift the motor's position to increase belt tension, and retighten the nut.

Mounting nut / Motor / Drive belt

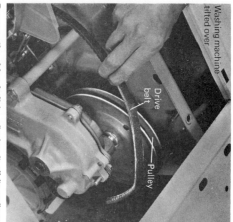

Remove the drive belt by slipping it off its pulleys. Note: The belt is made specifically for your model of machine. Replace it with an identical part.

Washing machine tilted over / Drive belt / Pulley

Motor housing / Motor lead / To meter

To test motor for a short, clip one volt-ohm meter probe to any motor lead, the other to motor housing. If meter reads high, motor is OK; if it reads low or zero ohms, motor is shorted.

Motor pulley (behind bracket) / Mounting nuts / Drive belt

To remove the motor, loosen the mounting nut to put slack in the drive belt, and slip the belt off the motor pulley. Disconnect the leads to the motor, take out the motor mounting nuts, and lift out the motor.

Motor / Overload protector / To meter

To test the overload protector, disconnect a lead to the part and clip volt-ohm meter probes to protector terminals. If the meter reads zero ohms, the protector is OK; if it reads high, protector is faulty (see p.135).

Clips / Overload protector / Motor housing

To remove the overload protector, disconnect the remaining lead from the part and use the blade of a small screwdriver to pry the protector off the motor housing where it clips to the motor housing.

Solving problems with the drain pump

The drain pump is mounted under the washing machine tub. It empties the tub and pumps the tub water into a drain hose. The pump tends to become clogged by stray bits of clothing or extraneous objects not removed from the pockets of clothing before loading. The machine then cannot drain. In addition, the pulley on the pump impeller shaft stops turning. Because the drive belt engages the pump pulley, the stuck pulley slows or stops the belt so that the machine spins sluggishly or is unable to agitate or spin at all.

To check the pump, first unplug the unit and empty the tub. The tub (or the machine itself) is very difficult to lift or move when it is full of water. If the drain hose from the machine to the sink connects at the bottom of the machine you can lower the end of the hose to the floor to let the water run out into a pail. If the drain hose connects at the top of the machine, siphon or bail the water out of the tub with a pot. Next, pull the unit away from the wall and remove the access panel at the bottom of the machine (see *Gaining access to parts inside and under the washing machine*, p.280). Disengage the drive belt from the pump pulley (see facing page). Turn the pulley by hand. If it turns easily, the clogging may be at the tub drain rather than inside the pump. Remove the basket from the tub (see p.281), check the tub drain, and remove any obstructing material from it. If the pulley does not turn easily, the pump is jammed. Remove the pump, disassemble it if necessary, and remove any obstructing material you find in it. If you find little or no obstruction, the pump impeller may have seized. Unscrew the pump pulley and remove the impeller. Check the impeller shaft. If it is pitted, polish it until it is smooth again, then lubricate the pump. Reassemble the washing machine. If the pump continues to jam, replace it.

If the pump pulley is turning easily and the tub drain is obstructed, the pulley may be stripped. Disassemble the pump and check the pulley. If it turns freely on the impeller shaft when you hold the impeller stationary with your hand, it is stripped. Replace the pump.

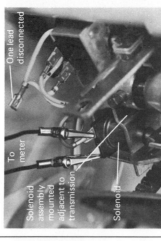

Hose

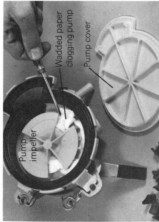

Pump impeller — Wadded paper clogging pump — Pump cover

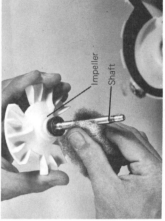

Solenoid assembly mounted adjacent to transmission — To meter — One lead disconnected — Solenoid

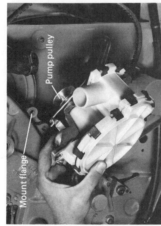

Mount flange — Pump pulley

Impeller — Shaft

To clear material from around pump impeller, pry off clips, lift off pump cover, remove obstructions.

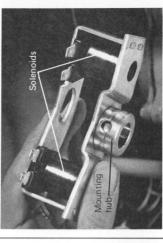

Solenoids — Mounting hub

Test solenoid with volt-ohm meter. If it reads 250 to 1,000 ohms, solenoid is OK; if high, part is faulty.

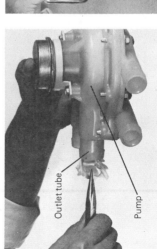

Pump mounting bolts — Drain pump

To remove the drain pump, first disconnect the hoses from the pump with a pair of spring clamp pliers.

Felt

Take out the pump mounting bolts and remove the pump from the bottom of the washing machine.

Outlet tube — Pump

On some models, you can remove clogging material from inside the pump with pliers via the outlet tube.

To lubricate the pump, place a few drops of SAE # 20 oil on the felt that encircles the impeller shaft.

Polish the bearing surface on the pump impeller shaft with very fine emery cloth or steel wool.

The agitator and spin solenoids

The agitator and spin solenoids are mounted under the tub. When actuated electrically, they shift the transmission into gear. A defect in one or the other will result in the machine being unable to agitate, or unable to spin.

To check the solenoids, first unplug the unit and pull it away from the wall. Remove the access panel at the bottom of the machine (see p.280) and test each solenoid with a volt-ohm meter (p.124) set to the RX100 scale. Disconnect a lead to a solenoid and clip the meter probes to each terminal of the solenoid. Replace the solenoids if either is defective.

Note: In some models agitate and spin are controlled by the motor; there are no agitate and spin solenoids.

To remove solenoid assembly, disconnect other lead, take out retaining screws, and lift out assembly.

283

Waste disposers

Waste disposer problems

PROBLEM	POSSIBLE CAUSE	ACTION
Disposer does not run and motor makes no sound	No power (disposer plugs into a wall outlet)	Check outlet with a lamp you know is working. If lamp does not turn on, replace fuse or reset circuit breaker. If fuse keeps blowing, reduce number of appliances on circuit ●
	No power (disposer is wired directly to house wiring)	Check fuse or circuit breaker. Replace defective fuse or reset breaker ●
	Overload protector tripped	Press reset button, or wait for overload protector to turn on automatically (see below) ●
	Wall switch faulty (continuous feed disposers only)	Test wall switch and replace it if it is defective (p.286) ● ● ■
	Stopper switch faulty (batch feed disposers only)	Test stopper switch and replace it if it is defective (p.286) ● ● ■
	Motor defective	Call appliance repairman to service motor ● ● ●
Disposer starts, but stops when stopper is released	Worn cam on stopper switch (batch feed disposers only)	Replace cam on stopper switch (p.286) ●
Motor hums but disposer does not run	Flywheel jammed	Free the flywheel by jogging it with a broom handle (see below) ●
Note: Overload protector may trip after a few seconds	Motor defective	Call appliance repairman to service motor ● ● ●
Disposer grinds too slowly	Insufficient water flow	Open cold water faucet more when operating the disposer ●
	Improper waste material put into disposer	Put into the disposer only waste material that it can grind easily (see facing page) ●
	Flyweight on flywheel broken or shredder ring dull	Replace flywheel or shredder ring (p.287) ● ●
Disposer drains poorly	Insufficient water flow	Open cold water faucet more when operating the disposer ●
	Drain line clogged	Clear the drain line (see *Plumbing,* pp.34–45) ● ●
	Flyweight on flywheel broken or shredder ring dull	Replace flywheel or shredder ring (p.287) ● ●
Disposer leaks water	Loose flange on drain gasket	Tighten drain gasket screws (p.287) ●
	Poor seal at sink gasket	Tighten sink gasket screws; apply plumber's putty to gasket if necessary (p.287) ● ●
	Poor seal between hopper and shredder housing	Replace shredder housing gasket (p.287) ● ●
Disposer is noisy	Silverware or other foreign object in disposer	Remove foreign object from disposer with a pair of pliers or forceps (see below) ●
	Loose mounting screws	Tighten mounting screws that secure disposer to support flange under sink (p.286) ●
	Broken flyweight on flywheel	Replace flywheel (p.287) ● ●
	Motor defective	Call appliance repairman to service motor ● ● ●
Trash compactor works poorly	Improper usage	Follow rules for the operation of a trash compactor (see facing page) ●
	Defective electrical or mechanical part	Call appliance repairman to service compactor ● ● ●

Ease of fix: ● simple   ● ● average   ● ● ● difficult   ■ Volt-ohm meter required for this step (see p.124)

Freeing the flywheel and resetting the overload protector

The waste disposer may jam, particularly if you put material into it that cannot be ground easily, such as metal waste. When this happens, the disposer motor stops and hums. The hum lasts for perhaps half a minute, then the overload protector in the motor cuts off the motor.

If the disposer jams, free the flywheel in the disposer. On some units you can free it by switching on the disposer so that it runs in reverse. On others, turn off the power to the unit (see facing page) and free the flywheel with a broom handle. If the problem persists, remove the handle. If the problem persists, remove the handle, and free the flywheel with pliers or a similar jamming material with pliers or a similar

tool. Do not insert your hand into the opening under any circumstances.

If the overload protector cuts off the motor, wait 15 minutes for the motor to cool, then reset the protector. Some disposers do not have a protector reset button. If your disposer is one of them, its protector should eventually turn on automatically. If it does not, the protector is defective. Since the motor is a sealed unit, you must then replace the entire motor assembly or the disposer itself.

Note: After unjamming the unit, drop a handful of ice cubes into it to help remove any residue of jamming material.

Flywheel is inside disposer under sink (see facing page)

Stopper

To free a jammed flywheel, jog the flywheel with the end of a broom handle.

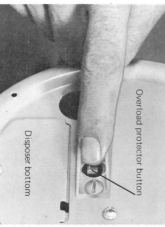

Overload protector button

Disposer bottom

To reset the overload protector, press the button at the bottom of the disposer.

Trash compactors

Trash compactors help to dispose of waste that cannot be ground, such as empty cans and bottles. The units crush the refuse into compact bundles that are easy to carry or store in garbage cans. Tremendous force is exerted by the compactor when crushing. This makes the unit somewhat dangerous, particularly if children can come near it. To alleviate the danger, manufacturers build in safety devices and make the disposer difficult to disassemble for servicing.

You can avoid some of the problems that arise with trash compactors if you follow these rules:

1. Lay glass bottles flat in the compactor. Do not let them stand straight up.

2. Do not put in aerosol cans or cans or bottles containing flammable fluids, insecticides, or other strong chemicals.

3. Hold the filled compactor bag only at the top when emptying the compactor, to avoid being cut by glass that has pierced the sides of the bag.

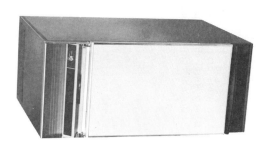

Power screws inside the compactor, when turned on, slowly drive the compactor ram downward. When the ram attains a force of about 2,000 pounds, the motor stalls and automatically reverses, and the ram lifts.

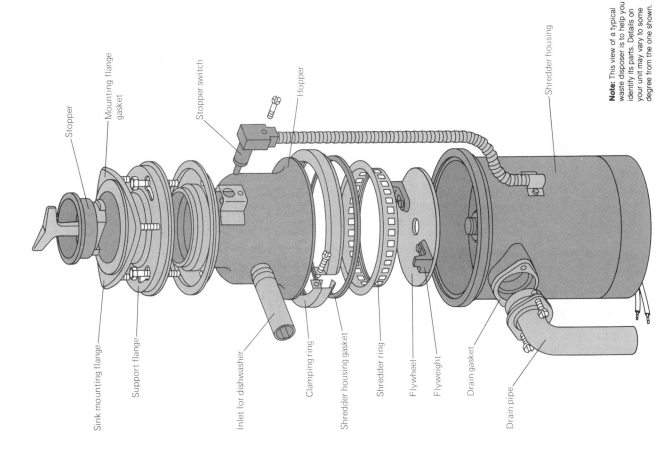

Stopper

Mounting flange gasket

Stopper switch

Hopper

Sink mounting flange

Support flange

Inlet for dishwasher

Clamping ring

Shredder housing gasket

Shredder ring

Flywheel

Flyweight

Drain gasket

Drain pipe

Shredder housing

Note: This view of a typical waste disposer is to help you identify its parts. Details on your unit may vary to some degree from the one shown.

Caution: Turn off the power

Whenever working on parts inside the disposer, unplug its power cord from the wall outlet before beginning. If the unit does not use a power cord but is wired directly to the house wiring, turn the disposer off at the service panel by removing the fuse or tripping the circuit breaker that protects the circuit to which the disposer is connected (see p.127).

Batch feed and continuous feed

The exploded view on the right illustrates a batch feed disposer. The unit is turned on by a switch located in the neck, actuated by the stopper when the stopper is inserted and rotated until it locks. A continuous feed disposer does not have this switch. Instead the unit is wired to a wall switch, which when left on permits you to drop waste material continuously into the disposer as it grinds.

Using a waste disposer correctly

To avoid frequent jamming of the disposer, follow these rules:

1. Do not pack waste material down into the disposer.

2. Do not put in material that is partly or wholly made of metal, china, glass, rubber, cloth, or leather unless your owner's manual indicates that the disposer will accept such materials.

3. Use a strong flow of cold water when flushing material into the disposer. The low temperature congeals grease, which aids in the removal of the grease.

4. After grinding is completed and you have turned off the disposer, let the water run for a minute to clear the drain line.

In addition, take these precautions:

1. Do not add chemical drain cleaners to the waste disposer. They can cause serious damage.

2. Do not insert your hand into the disposer, even when it is not operating. Someone may accidentally turn it on.

Waste disposers

Disassembling the disposer

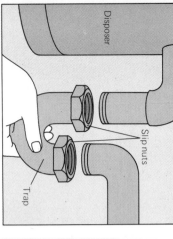

Disposer

Slip nuts

Trap

1. Loosen slip nuts and drop the sink trap to separate the disposer from the house plumbing.

Shell

2. Loosen mounting screws, rotate disposer slightly, and drop it from the support flange.

Stopper switch

3. Pry open clips and remove the sound insulating shell if your disposer has one.

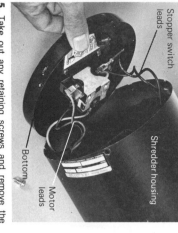

Stopper switch leads

Bottom

Motor leads

Shredder housing

4. Take out mounting screw and pull the stopper switch away from the disposer (batch feed models only).

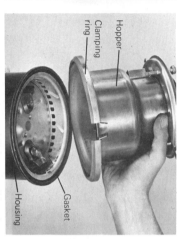

Hopper

Clamping ring

Gasket

Housing

5. Take out any retaining screws and remove the bottom from the disposer.

6. Loosen clamping ring and lift hopper off housing. Note: Replace housing gasket each time you do this.

The stopper switch in batch feed disposers

Batch feed disposers are turned on by a switch in the neck of the disposer. The switch is actuated by a cam on the stopper as you insert the stopper and rotate it. After some time the cam may wear to a degree that the unit stops when you lift your hand from the stopper. Replace the cam when this happens.

If the disposer does not turn on at all when you insert and rotate the stopper, the switch itself may be defective. To check the switch, turn off the power to the unit (see p.285) and disassemble the disposer sufficiently to gain access to the switch (see *Disassembling the disposer*, at left). Test the switch with a volt-ohm meter (p.124) set to the RX1 scale. Remove the disposer bottom and clip the meter probes to the two leads coming from the switch where they emerge from under the motor. (Before clipping them on, disconnect the two leads from the terminals to which they are connected.) Replace the switch if it is defective.

Note: When removing the switch, tie a string to the lead ends before pulling the switch leads out of the disposer. The string will make it easy for you to tie on and pull through the leads of the new switch when you install it.

Ball bearings

Switch cam

Stopper

To separate the switch cam from the stopper, take out the screw that holds the parts together. Note: The stopper assembly may include ball bearings. Do not leave them out when reassembling.

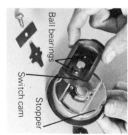

Leads from switch

Switch

To meter

When testing the stopper switch, press the switch button. The volt-ohm meter reads zero ohms when the button s pressed, the swich is OK; if the meter reads high, th e switch is defective.

Switch leads

Switch

To remove the stopper switch, take off any retaining screws or clamps and pull it, along with its leads, out of the disposer.

The wall switch of continuous feed disposers

Continuous feed disposers are turned on by a wall switch. After much use, the mechanical parts of the switch sometimes break. The defect shows up as looseness in the switch toggle when you turn the switch on and off.

To test the wall switch, first turn off the power to the disposer (see p.285). Take out the faceplate screws and remove the faceplate. Take out the switch mounting screws and pull the switch from its box in the wall. Then, disconnect the leads to the switch and test the switch with a volt-ohm meter (p.124) set to the RX1 scale. Replace the switch if it is defective.

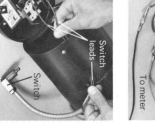

Wall faceplate

Switch

To meter

To test switch, clip volt-ohm meter probes to switch terminals and turn on switch. If meter reads zero ohms, switch is OK; if high, switch is defective.

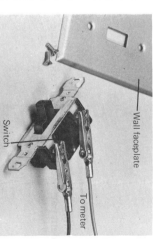

The flywheel and the shredder ring

The disposer uses a flywheel and a shredder ring to grind waste material rapidly into small particles. The flywheel is turned by the motor and flings the material outward against the ring, which is perforated with sharp-edged holes. The edges of these holes, and the flyweights, which are bolted loosely to the surface of the flywheel, work together to slice the material into fine bits. The flyweights (which on early models were tight) are deliberately made to swing freely to keep them from becoming jammed or prematurely broken.

After prolonged, heavy use, the shredder ring may wear or the flyweights break. A broken flyweight usually unbalances the flywheel enough to create a noticeable vibration in the unit and in the sink. Determine whether or not any flyweights are broken by simply looking at each of them in the disposer hopper. If any are broken, turn off the power to the disposer (see p.285), disassemble the disposer to gain access to the flywheel (see facing page), and replace the flywheel.

Dull edges on the shredder ring holes will become noticeable gradually: The disposer will take more and more time to grind the same amount of waste material. Some disposers are made reversible to help prolong the sharpness of the edges. If it becomes apparent to you that the unit does not grind as quickly as it used to, remove and examine the shredder ring after disassembling the unit. You may have difficulty in judging how worn the part is. In this case, take the ring to an appliance repair shop and compare its cutting edges with those on a replacement part. Replace a worn shredder ring.

The bearings in the motor can also become worn, causing the flywheel to turn more slowly than when new. The motor however is factory sealed so that you cannot examine or lubricate it. If replacing the shredder ring fails to clear up the difficulty, replace the disposer.

Repairing the seals

Gaskets are used as seals to prevent water from leaking onto the kitchen floor while the unit is operating. There are three gaskets—one between the sink bottom and the sink mounting flange, another where the disposer drain pipe is connected to the shredder housing, and the third at the junction between the hopper and the shredder housing. Check each of these seals in turn if you see water dripping down the sides of the unit.

If the water seems to come from the drain gasket seal, tighten the drain gasket screws. Similarly, tighten the sink gasket screws if the water appears near it. To reach the sink gasket screws, first turn off the power to the unit (see p.285), then drop the sink trap, loosen the mounting screws on the support flange, and lower the disposer (see facing page). After tightening, insert a stopper and run water into the sink to see whether or not you have eliminated the leak. If not, loosen the gasket screws, apply plumber's putty between the mounting flange and the sink, and retighten the screws.

To stop a leak at the junction between the hopper and the shredder housing, separate the hopper from the housing and replace the housing gasket.

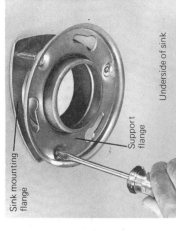

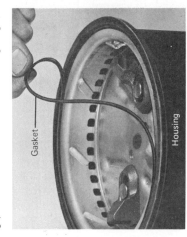

Underside of sink

Sink mounting flange

Support flange

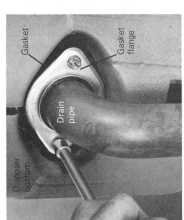

Gasket

Gasket flange

Drain pipe

Disposer bottom

Tighten the screws on the disposer drain gasket if water is dripping from the gasket area.

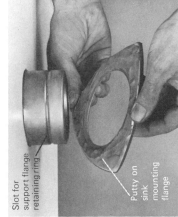

Gasket

Housing

Tighten the sink gasket screws to prevent leaks at the gap between the sink and the sink mounting flange.

Slot for support flange retaining ring

Putty on sink mounting flange

If the leak does not stop apply plumber's putty to the sink mounting flange.

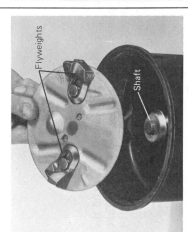

Flyweights

Shaft

Lift flywheel from housing. Note: Some shafts have a screwdriver slot to help when loosening flywheel.

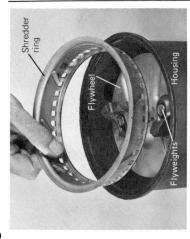

Shredder ring

Flywheel

Housing

Flyweights

To remove the flywheel, first lift the shredder ring out of the shredder housing.

Flywheel shaft

Flywheel

Rap the flywheel loose from its shaft with a hammer and a piece of wood. Use sharp, quick blows.

To remove the shredder housing gasket, simply lift the gasket off the housing rim.

Audio and Visual

Despite the technical complexity of TV sets, radios, hi-fi, and photographic equipment, there are numerous simple adjustments and repairs you can make yourself. In fact, many of the problems you may have with your equipment should require only such simple attention, because interior parts are being made more and more trouble free.

Still cameras

Taking care of your camera

Cameras are precision instruments. If you expect one to perform well over the years, use it carefully and maintain it properly. Tighten the camera's body screws occasionally, particularly after a car trip or an airplane flight where it may have been subjected to vibration. Lenses are especially subject to damage. To minimize the chance of scratching the lens, keep it capped except when taking pictures. It is also a good idea to keep a neutral filter on the lens at all times. Above all, never touch the lens surface with anything other than the cleaning materials described on page 292.

Sand in a camera can be extremely destructive. Do not open the camera on the beach if the wind is blowing. If sand does get into your camera the parts will jam or make a grinding sound when manipulated. If this happens, make no further attempt to use the camera. Instead, take it in for repairs with a note attached explaining that sand has gotten into the works. When you use a camera in dusty conditions, blow out the

interior with an ear syringe whenever you reload. Do not expose a camera to temperature extremes. For example, do not leave it in the glove compartment or trunk of a car. When a camera is to be brought indoors after being used in very cold weather, put it in a plastic bag, squeeze out most of the air, and close the bag tight. Then, take the camera indoors and let it warm up gradually.

Do everything you can to keep the camera dry. Moisture can be very damaging, either by causing rust on the high carbon steel parts used in most cameras, or by facilitating the growth of molds and fungi. If sea spray gets on the camera, wipe it off immediately. If your camera should become immersed in salt water, remove the film and flush the camera in several changes of clear, fresh water. Then, dry it thoroughly in an oven at low heat (130°F or less) and get it to a repair shop quickly. Even this may not save your camera, but it will improve the odds. Fungi and molds flourish in humid weather and attack paint, leather, shutter curtains, and even the

lens. If mold or fungus gets into your camera, take the camera to a repair shop.

Be sure to keep the lens clean (see p.292), and the inside of the camera clean and free of dust. This is especially important for reflex cameras with lenses that are often interchanged, since removing the lens exposes the interior to contamination. Do not blow into the camera to get rid of dust; breath has a high moisture content. Instead, use an ear syringe (sold at drug stores) or a blower brush (available at photo shops). Whisk away dust from the pressure plate, shutter curtains, diaphragm, and lens mount with a camel's-hair brush. The pressure plate should also be cleaned periodically with a cotton swab and a little lens cleaning fluid. Wipe it dry with lens tissue. If the diaphragm gets dirty (the leaves will become difficult to move), take the camera to a repair shop for cleaning. In any case, a camera should be completely cleaned and checked by a professional every few years—particularly if it is an expensive one.

Single lens reflex cameras

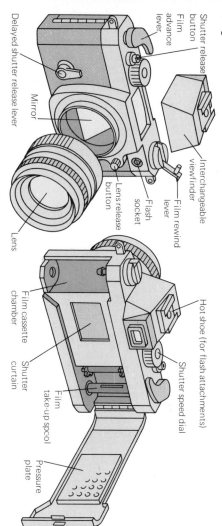

Shutter release button

Film advance lever

Delayed shutter release lever

Mirror

Interchangeable viewfinder

Film rewind lever

Flash socket

Lens release button

Lens

Hot shoe (for flash attachments)

Shutter speed dial

Film cassette chamber

Film take-up spool

Pressure plate

Shutter curtain

Among better cameras, single lens reflex (SLR) models account for the vast majority of sales. They feature interchangeable lenses and a viewfinder/rangefinder that lets the user see almost the exact picture he will take. Most are heavy, complex, and expensive. Consequently, they require more than ordinary care in use and storage. Since their lenses are removable, it is important to clean the rear surface as well as the front surface of a lens (p.292). When not in use, lenses should be kept in cases with lens caps on both front and rear. When you remove a lens, you expose a delicate mirror mechanism in the camera.

Never touch the mirror but clean it occasionally by holding the lens opening facing downward and blowing air from an ear syringe into the opening. The viewfinder prism on some SLR's is removable (see p.292). Clean the prism eyepiece and bottom prism surface of these models occasionally, just as you would clean a lens (see p.292). Exposure timing is controlled by a pair of shutter curtains that slide between lens and film. Clean these curtains occasionally by whisking them very gently with an extremely soft camel's-hair brush.

Rangefinder cameras

These cameras are usually lighter and cheaper than SLR's, but seldom have interchangeable lenses. They generally have double image rangefinders in which a pair of images appears in the viewing window; the photographer adjusts the lens until the images merge or align. To test rangefinder accuracy, first focus on an object at least ¼ mile away. The lens should indicate infinity (∞). Next, focus on an object a few feet away and measure its distance from the film plane. The lens reading and measurement should agree within inches.

Cartridge cameras

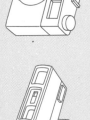

No film threading is required. Instead, a film cartridge is dropped into the camera and removed when exposed. The lowest priced models use plastic lenses with a fixed focus and have only a single shutter speed. This means that they give acceptable pictures only when there is fairly bright daylight and the subject is more than 12 ft from the camera. Most cartridge cameras have a flash attachment, which lessens the lighting limitation. Higher priced models incorporate features found in other types of cameras.

Instant-picture cameras

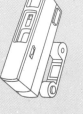

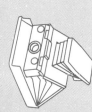

In the latest models, the film emerges and develops by itself. Older designs required separating the picture from an emulsion strip, then coating the picture with a fixative solution. The film pack for one brand has a battery to power the camera. If you wait too long before using the pack, the battery may become depleted. Photos taken with another brand are sensitive to light. It is wise to store pictures made by the instant method in a dark place. If you display them in the open, sunlight may eventually fade them.

Flashguns and strobes

If your flash unit is giving you trouble, first check the owner's manual for your camera to be sure you are following the proper procedure. For example, shutter speeds of 1/60 second or slower are usually required when using a strobe on an SLR camera.

When a flashgun fails to go off, try replacing the bulb. If that does not work, replace the battery. Also, make sure that the electrical contacts between the bulb and the socket and between the flash cord and the camera are clean (this is important for strobes as well). Spray the contacts with electrical contact cleaner (p.123) and connect and disconnect the parts several times. Other tests are shown at right.

If you have a strobe with a rechargeable power pack, the charging unit or pack may be faulty. If your unit is the kind that requires an overnight charge, see *Cordless appliances*, pp.136–137, for information on repair and testing. If the problem persists or you have a fast-charge model, take the strobe to a repair shop.

Testing flash equipment

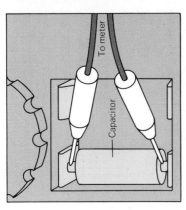

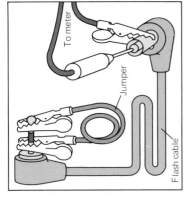

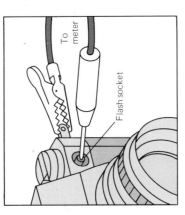

To check camera's flash socket, set volt-ohm meter (p.124) to RX1 scale. Clip one probe to metal part of camera, touch other probe to center of flash socket. Cock and release shutter. If meter reading dips to zero momentarily, camera is OK. Otherwise, it is broken.

Broken flash cable is a common problem. To test it, clip jumper across terminals of one jack. Set volt-ohm meter to RX1 scale, clip one probe to outer contact of other jack, touch second probe to inner contact. Zero ohms means cord is good. High ohms indicates open wire.

Check flashgun capacitor by setting meter to RX100 scale, touching probes to both ends of capacitor. Meter needle will jump toward low ohms and slowly come back if capacitor is OK. Steady high or low ohms reading means capacitor is faulty. To repeat test, reverse probes.

What to do about battery corrosion

The leakage of chemicals from old batteries is one of the most common, and easily prevented, sources of trouble in photographic equipment. Check the batteries in your camera regularly. Many cameras have built-in battery testing devices specifically for this purpose. Remove batteries at the first sign of weakness. Never leave batteries in equipment that is being stored for a month or longer. Some experts also recommend removing the batteries used to operate the built-in exposure meters found in some cameras (they are much smaller than the AA penlite batteries used to power flash attachments or automatic exposure systems). These, however, should be changed periodically according to the instructions in your owner's manual, or once a year if you are not sure.

Once the battery compartment of a camera has become contaminated by acid from a leaking battery, it must be thoroughly cleaned. Spray electrical contact cleaner (p.123) over corroded parts and scrape away accumulated debris with a cotton swab or a thin piece of wood, such as a matchstick. The cleaner, often sold as TV tuner cleaner, will dissolve the battery residues without damaging delicate electrical contacts. It will not, however, remove rust. If the contacts are rusty you may have to scrape them gently with a knife blade or nail file. If they are severely corroded, take the camera to a repair shop.

Exposure meters

There are two main types of exposure meters: those using a selenium photoelectric cell and those using a cadmium sulfide (CdS) cell. The latter type contains a small mercury battery and is the kind most frequently used in cameras with built-in meters. There are also two different light measuring systems: reflected light and incident light. Reflected-light meters measure the light coming from a scene; incident-light meters measure the light impinging on a scene.

Photoelectric meter.   Cadmium sulfide meter.   Incident light meter.

There is usually a small zero-adjust screw in the back of hand-held exposure meters. Turn it with a small screwdriver so that the meter reads zero when no light is entering it. When a CdS meter is grossly inaccurate, it may mean that the battery is bad. (The meter will generally indicate less light than is actually present, resulting in overexposed pictures.) Repairs other than zero-adjusting and battery replacement should be done by a trained technician.

To check the remainder of the scale, test it against a meter that you know is working properly, or use your meter as an exposure guide for taking pictures with a camera that is in good operating condition. (If you have been getting poor results with the camera you have been using, choose a different one.) Experiment with a variety of scenes and lighting conditions for both kinds of checks, but avoid extremes such as a brilliant sky, gleaming white surfaces, direct sunlight, or sunlight mirrored into the camera. If you are checking against another meter, note that both must be measuring the same light. For this reason, choose a broad area of essentially even illumination and get close enough to prevent extraneous light from entering the meters. A

Turning the zero-adjust screw.

quick check can also be made by comparing the exposure indicated by your meter with the instructions that accompany the film.

Still cameras

Cleaning photographic lenses

Camera lenses should be kept clean, but it is a mistake to clean them too often; the marginal improvement in picture quality is not worth the risk of lens damage. You will need the following equipment to do a good lens cleaning job:

1. A rubber ear syringe or a can of pressurized air. Pressurized air is sold under such names as Whisk-O-Way and Dust-Off.

2. A camel's-hair brush.

3. Photographic lens tissue. Do not use eyeglass tissues; they may be impregnated with chemicals that will damage the lens.

4. Lens cleaning fluid.

5. Cotton swabs such as Q-Tips.

The swabs and ear syringe are available in drug stores. The other items are sold in camera shops.

When you clean a lens, be sure to start by blowing or brushing away loose dirt. Never touch a lens surface with anything other than a clean lens tissue, cotton swab, or lens brush, and never try to dismantle a lens in order to clean an inner element. Should an interior lens surface become fogged, take the camera to a repair shop. You can check a lens for fogging by shining a flashlight beam through the back of the lens.

1. Use a clean camel's-hair brush to whisk dust from surface of lens. If lens is removable (as on a camera with interchangeable lenses), take it off camera and brush rear lens surface as well as front. Be careful not to rub sand or grit across the lens.

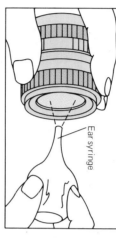

Ear syringe

2. Use an ear syringe or pressurized air to blow away remaining dust and dirt, especially particles that might be caught at the edges. It is best not to breathe on the lens. The moisture in your breath could cause some of the dirt to stick and induce corrosion.

Lens cleaner

3. Moisten the tip of a cotton swab with a drop of lens cleaning fluid and gently swirl the tip over the lens surface. Work in a limited circular area (about half the diameter of the lens) and gradually shift the circle until the whole lens has been covered.

Lens tissue

4. Tear a piece of lens tissue in two, roll one half into a small cylinder, and dry off the lens by gently brushing its surface with the frayed end of the tissue. Move the tissue in the same swirling motion used with the cotton. Never use a lens tissue more than once.

Improving the pictures you take

The appearance of your finished prints can provide a great deal of information about what is wrong with your camera or the way that you are using it.

Static electricity and dust produce distinct defects in a picture. Light-colored branching marks on prints or transparencies are generally caused by static electricity, which may be produced when the film is rewound. Static electricity is more common when the air is cold and dry. Avoid the problem by rewinding more slowly. Small, dark, sharply defined areas on pictures are the result of dust on the exposed film. Clean out the interior of the camera (see p.290).

A lightening effect at the edges of finished pictures means light was getting into the cassette, cartridge, or roll of film before or after exposure. In the case of roll film, wrap the exposed film roll in aluminum foil or other light-tight material after removing it from the camera. The same problem with a cartridge or cassette indicates a manufacturing defect. Ask for a free replacement.

On occasion, the camera itself may have a light leak. This will show up on a finished picture as a lightened area or an overall fogging. To test for a light leak, load the camera with a relatively fast film (one that has an exposure rating of more than ASA 160 and is therefore quite sensitive to light). Advance the film and cock the shutter so that the camera is ready to shoot, then suspend it by a string from a tree limb or other object, in bright sunlight. After an hour or two, rewind the film and have it developed. All prints should be jet black (negatives completely transparent). Anything else indicates a light leak.

Lines parallel to the length of the film roll probably mean the film is being scratched in the camera. Grit in the cassette or on the pressure plate is a possible cause. Clean the pressure plate with a lens tissue moistened in lens cleaning fluid. On instant cameras, particularly those using peel-apart film, the rollers may become gummed with chemicals. The result will be streaked prints. Use a cloth dampened in warm water to clean the rollers. Do not scrape them with a knife.

Most picture problems stem from incorrect camera operation. Blurring due to camera movement, subject movement, or incorrect range setting are examples. Other common problems are color distortion because the wrong film was used (daylight film used in artificial light), prints that are too dark or too light because the wrong exposure was used, and double exposures due to failure to advance the film. However, some of these same troubles may be due to camera malfunction. Incorrect exposure could be the fault of the exposure meter, a sticky shutter, or the automatic diaphragm used in single-lens reflex cameras. Similarly, a broken rangefinder will cause out of focus prints.

Old film, or film that has been improperly stored, is responsible for many photo defects. To store film, wrap it in several layers of plastic wrap and place it in the main food compartment of your refrigerator. Let it warm to room temperature before loading it into the camera, or moisture will condense in the camera.

Once a roll of film has been exposed, have it processed as quickly as possible; this is especially true for color film. Keep your prints, slides, and movie film at room temperature in a dry, dark location. Stored properly, a black and white print will last indefinitely. Color prints tend to fade over the years, particularly if they are constantly in the light. Transparencies tend to lose their color eventually, no matter how carefully they are handled and stored.

Slide projectors

Basic care and repair

Almost all slide projectors sold today are automatic. The chief difference between brands is the kind of slide tray they use: circular, straight, or slide cube. Slide projectors have two sets of lenses. The front set focuses the picture on the screen. The other set, called the condenser, is inside the projector. It concentrates the light from the projection bulb to provide uniform illumination of the slide. Both sets of lenses should be cleaned periodically (see p.292).

Automatic projectors jam occasionally, usually because of a bent or frayed slide. If the slide is badly damaged (or even slightly misshapen in the case of a slide cube), remount it in a new frame. Cardboard, plastic, and plastic and glass slide mounts are sold in most camera shops. Repeated jamming of projectors with vertically mounted circular trays can sometimes be fixed by bending the slide tray's mounting taps slightly inward. This will lock the magazine more firmly into the matching slots on the projector.

New projectors often have an automatic focus feature that maintains the sharpness of the projected picture after the initial slide is focused manually. To check the auto focus mechanism, load one slide in the tray with the emulsion, or dull, side toward the front, and a second slide with the emulsion side toward the rear.

Focus on the first slide and run the projector. You should be able to observe the second slide come into focus and the focusing knob move.

On some projectors the power cord is removable, on others it is permanently attached. Wind up a permanently attached cord by folding it back and forth. Winding it in a circular fashion will twist it so that the cord or its connections will eventually break.

If the projected image appears consistently dim, the problem may be a poor screen or you may be placing the projector too far from the screen. Lenticular screens, rather than matte or beaded, are generally preferred. They provide a bright image even in rooms that are not totally dark and viewers can sit at a considerable angle to the screen and still see an acceptable image.

Bend tray tabs inward to keep this projector's slides from jamming.

Focus knob

Height adjustment

Front focusing lens

Motor

Cooling fan

Built-in slide changing controls

Remote control

Power cord

Slide changing mechanism

Condenser lenses

Projection bulb

Slide tray

Plastic insert (to keep slides in place)

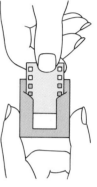

Some projectors have straight slide trays. As in circular (carousel) models, each slide is inserted in a separate slot

Slide cube projectors use small, cubical trays in which up to 40 slides can be stacked, one on top of the other

Two electrical tests

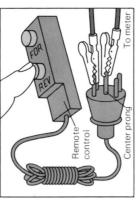

Jumper

Power cord

To meter

To check power cord, set volt-ohm meter (p.124) to RX1 scale and clip its probes to the plug. Clip jumper to female terminals (removable power cord) or interior terminals (built-in cord). Bend and pull cord. Zero ohms means cord is OK. High ohms means it is broken.

FOR

REV

Remote control

Center prong

To meter

For remote control test, set meter to RX1 scale. Clip one probe to plug's center prong, second probe to an outside prong. Press *Forward* and *Reverse*. Repeat for all outside prongs. One outside prong should give a zero ohms reading for *Forward*, another for *Reverse*.

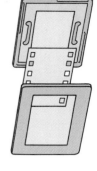

Plastic mounts are sturdy and easy to use. Insert transparency under tabs, and snap two halves of mount together by pressing firmly.

Remounting a damaged slide

Remove transparency from old slide by slitting cardboard open with razor blade. Be careful not to touch picture area of slide.

Simplest mount is a cardboard sandwich, much like original mount, but with widened opening into which transparency can be slid.

Motion picture cameras

Care and repair of 8-mm cameras

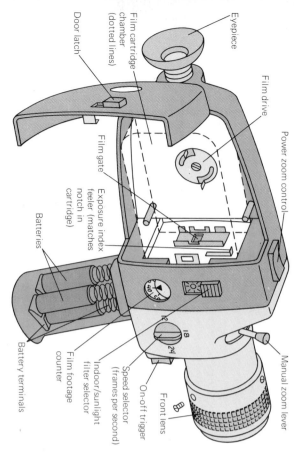

- Eyepiece
- Film drive
- Power zoom control
- Film cartridge chamber (dotted lines)
- Door latch
- Film gate
- Film cartridge feeler (matches notch in cartridge)
- Exposure index notch in cartridge)
- Batteries
- Manual zoom lever
- Battery terminals
- Film footage counter
- Front lens
- On-off trigger
- Indoor/sunlight filter selector
- Speed selector (frames per second)

Film of old-style, regular 8-mm camera is threaded through gate, onto take-up reel, onto take-up reel. If the film jams inside the camera, open it up in a dark place, such as a closet. Lift out take-up reel and wind any jammed, loose film onto it, then reseat reel on take-up shaft. Make sure the film is fitted smoothly in the gate. Note. Do not leave unused film in the camera for more than a week; it may warp away from gate and not run when the trigger is pressed.

Pressure plate

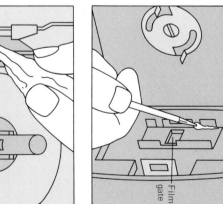

Film gate

Almost all home motion picture cameras now sold use super-8 film cartridges. However, many older regular 8-mm cameras are still in use, as are some 16-mm models. Picture frames on super-8 film are considerably larger than on regular 8-mm film. Unlike super-8 cameras, film must be threaded manually in regular 8-mm cameras and in 16-mm cameras.

Even more than other photographic equipment, the lens and interior of a movie camera should be kept clean. Follow the lens cleaning instructions given on page 192. Never attempt to dismantle the lens or remove it from the camera. To clean the interior, whisk out dust with a camel's-hair brush and blow away remaining particles with an ear syringe (not with your breath). You should regularly clean built-up dust, dirt, and film emulsion from the gate (see the top two illustrations at right).

Although there are still some old-fashioned wind-up cameras in use, new movie cameras have motor driven film advances powered by several AA, 1.5-volt penlite batteries. In addition, all but the lowest priced models have battery powered, cadmium sulfide exposure systems (see *Exposure meters*, p.291). The exposure mechanism usually shares the same batteries as the film drive, although sometimes there is a separate battery.

It is extremely important to keep the penlite batteries fresh and not to leave them in the camera for extended periods of time. If left in, they will eventually leak, leading to corrosion damage. This problem is particularly common in motion picture cameras since there is a tendency to use them only on special occasions, and let them sit on a shelf the rest of the time. The only safe procedure is to remove the batteries whenever the camera is put away.

If corrosion does occur, follow the cleaning advice in *What to do about battery corrosion*, p.291. Note, too, that it is important to keep the battery terminals free of oxides or other films even when there has been no battery leakage. Occasionally spray the terminals with electrical contact cleaner (p.123) and scrape them lightly with very fine (No. 400) sandpaper.

The focus ring on the front of an adjustable lens is usually held in place by several very small setscrews. Over a period of time, these may work loose, letting the ring shift from its correct position. To realign the ring, loosen the setscrews with a jeweler's screwdriver that just fits them and remove the ring. Focus the lens on an object at least ¼ mile away, replace the focus ring so that the infinity symbol (∞) is opposite the indicator line, and retighten the screws.

Dirt and film emulsion in the gate area may cause film to jam, particularly in a regular 8-mm camera. Scrape emulsion deposits away with a pointed stick, such as a sharpened match.

Use a little lighter fluid or rubber cement thinner to complete cleaning job. Apply it with a clean, lint-free cloth. Reach difficult spots, such as the pressure plate of a regular 8-mm camera, by wrapping cloth around a pointed stick.

If super-8 film cartridge jams, remove it from camera but do not attempt to open it. Try winding up film jammed inside cartridge by turning center shaft of cartridge clockwise with tweezers. If shaft does not turn, return cartridge to manufacturer.

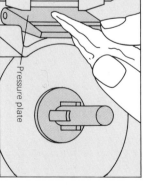

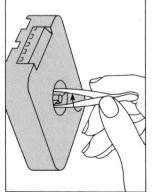

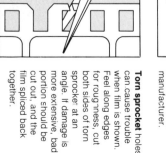

Torn sprocket holes can cause trouble when film is shown. Feel along edges for roughness, cut both sides of torn sprocket at an angle. If damage is more extensive, bad portion should be cut out, and the film spliced back together.

Motion picture projectors

Care and repair of 8-mm projectors

Projectors usually have condenser lenses as well as front focusing lenses. The condenser concentrates light onto the film. The focusing lens projects the image onto the screen. There is also a mirror behind the projection bulb to maximize light intensity. Focusing lenses can be withdrawn for cleaning. Rotate the lens forward as far as it will go, then pull it out. (In some projectors, you must press back on the lens while rotating a focus knob forward in order to remove the lens.)

The focus lens should be cleaned regularly; the condenser and mirror, once or twice a year (see *Cleaning photographic lenses*, p.292). It is vital to keep the gate and pressure plate clean. One piece of grit can scar a film from one end to the other. Clean before every showing, using the techniques described on page 294 for movie cameras.

When a bulb goes dead, let it cool before taking it out. Leave the cover on the new one until you have seated it; oil from your skin will damage its quartz envelope. If you do touch it, clean it with a cloth moistened in alcohol. Check the bulb now and then. A bulge indicates it could explode and must be replaced.

To gain access to the interior of a projector, look for a screw, knob, or slide catch holding the projector's shell to the frame. The projector shown below has two screws in its carrying handle; once they are removed, the entire shell can be lifted off from above. Always unplug the power cord before working on a projector and avoid removing screws in the base or frame.

In the event your projector does not operate, check the wall outlet with a lamp and replace the house fuse if the outlet is dead. Also, test the projector's power cord as shown below. Buy a manufacturer's replacement if it is broken. With the power cord unplugged and the shell removed, examine the wiring. Look for broken wires and burn marks. Spray electrical contact cleaner (p.123) into the switch and work each button a number of times. Also spray cleaner on all electrical terminals and pull the connections off and push them back on several times. If one of the quick connect terminals is loose, squeeze it with pliers to tighten it.

It is a good idea to clean the interior of the projector while the shell is off. Hold the nozzle of a vacuum cleaner a few inches away and brush dust and dirt into it with a soft, dry, new paint brush. A dab of white grease or general purpose grease on the gears will quiet down a noisy projector, but use only a little, and be careful not to get any on other parts.

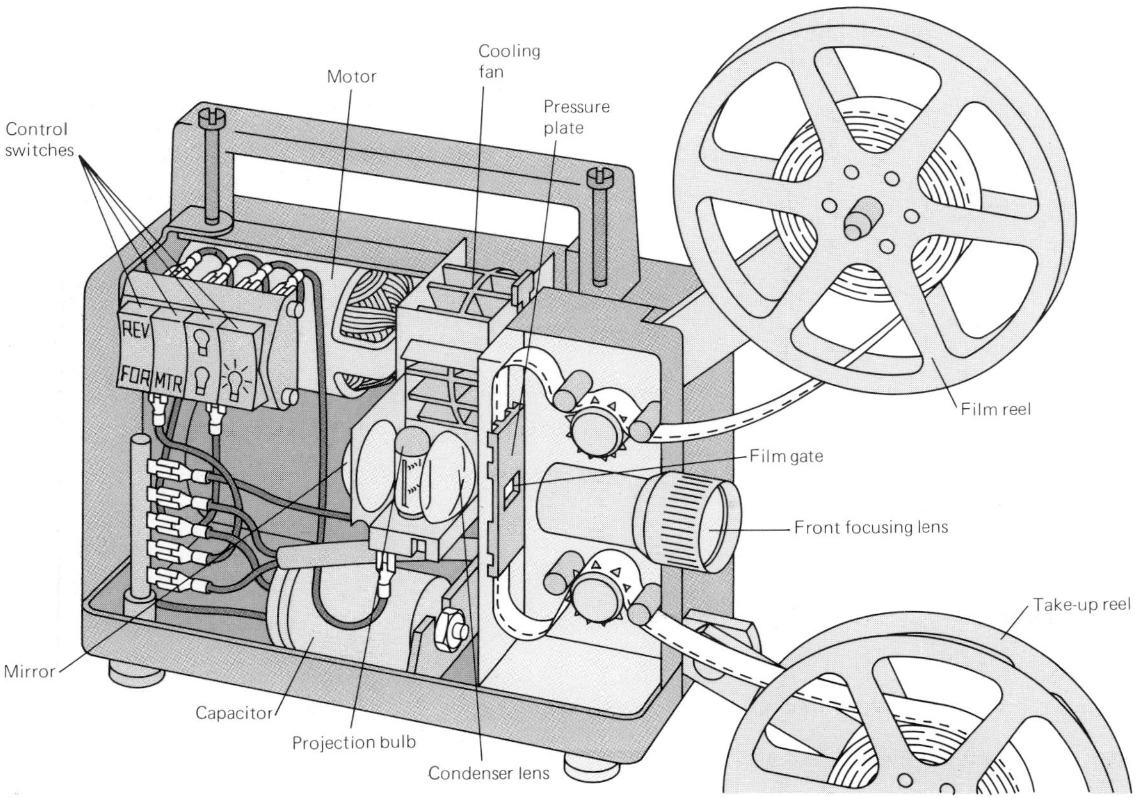

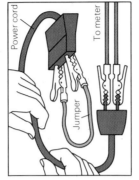

When checking power cord, set volt-ohm meter (p.124) to RX1 scale. Clip jumper wire to female terminals and attach meter probes to prongs of the plug. Bend and pull cord during test to help show up loose wires. If meter reads zero ohms, cord is good. High ohms means it is broken.

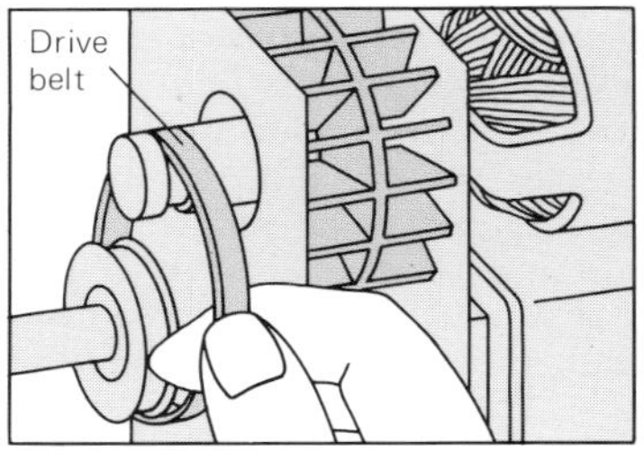

Power cord

Jumper

To meter

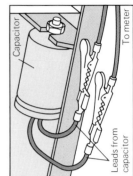

Slipping drive belt will cause slow or erratic film speed. Broken belt will result in no film movement at all. To change drive belt, unplug power cord, pull old belt off pulleys, and clean pulley surfaces with cloth moistened in rubber cement thinner or alcohol. Replace with new belt from manufacturer.

Drive belt

Motor will not run if capacitor is broken. Disconnect capacitor leads from terminals, set volt-ohm meter to RX100 scale, and clip probes to leads. If capacitor is OK, needle will jump toward low ohms, slowly come back. Steady high or low reading means it is broken. To repeat test, reverse probes.

Capacitor

Leads from capacitor

To meter

Film reel

Take-up reel

Film gate

Front focusing lens

Cooling fan

Pressure plate

Condenser lens

Motor

Projection bulb

Capacitor

Control switches

REV

FOR MTR

Mirror

Hi-fi, radios, phonographs, and tape recorders

Isolating the defective component in hi-fi equipment

By rearranging the way the components of a hi-fi stereo system are connected to each other you can usually determine which of them is defective.

For example, in a system with two loudspeakers, one of the speakers may stop working. When this happens, disconnect the one that works and connect in its place the one that failed. If the substituted speaker still does not work, you know then that that speaker is defective. If, on the other hand, it acts normally, the defect must then exist somewhere else in the channel to which the speaker was originally connected. This procedure may then be repeated with other components in the non-working channel until you have eliminated every component that still works one by one and found the one that does not work.

You can use this approach in many ways. For each problem, think the approach through in advance, particularly if the defect appears to be elusive, as would be the case with a poor connection between the plug of a connecting cable and the jack in which it terminates. Were you to do nothing more, this effort could still save you trouble. A small part such as a cable is easy to replace, and a major component is generally light enough to take to a repair shop. Otherwise you may be stuck with transporting an entire system to the shop or paying the added cost of a house call.

For additional insight into the procedure, consider this example. Suppose the sound you hear from the equipment is weak or distorted when the record player is in use. Turn the function selector switch on the receiver from *Phono* to *FM*. Is the sound—now FM sound—still weak or distorted? If it is not, the trouble must lie either in the record player or in the cables connecting the record player to the receiver. If the sound remains weak and distorted, the defect must be in the receiver, the loudspeakers, or the wires connecting these components.

Take the first case, and suppose the poor sound is coming only through one channel, while the sound coming through the other channel is normal. Pull out the cables from the record player where they plug into the back of the receiver, reverse them, and plug them in again so that the left goes to the right channel and the right goes to the left channel. Has the weak or distorted sound transferred from one channel to the other? If not, the plug in the affected channel must be making poor contact with its jack (see *Insuring good connections between hi-fi components,* facing page). If it has, the

defect once again lies somewhere else—in this case in wires connecting them. Again go through the system substituting one part for another and studying the consequences. For example, reverse the wires of the left speaker with those of the right speaker where they connect at the receiver terminals to see if the poor sound transfers from one speaker to the other.

It may be that both channels remain weak or distorted. In that case, to make a useful substitution, find or borrow a third speaker to connect to each of the channels of the receiver. If you cannot get another speaker, plug in a set of headphones and, one way or the other, narrow the trouble down to either the receiver or the loudspeakers.

Note: You can usually assume that two components will not go bad simultaneously. But loudspeakers provide an exception to this rule. A receiver may drive a pair of speakers at too high a power and burn them both out at the same time (see *Minimizing distortion,* p.299).

As before, repeat the procedure. This time, manipulate the four wires that connect to the phonograph cartridge in the record player tone arm. Reverse the pair that connect to the left channel with the pair that connect to the right channel, taking care to identify which of the wires belongs where. If the poor sound does not transfer to the other channel, the connectors are faulty. If it does transfer after reversing the wires, the connections are OK and the cartridge itself is defective (see *Keeping records free of noise and wow,* p.298).

What should you do if both channels are weak and distorted? In this case, less suspicion falls on the cables, since it is unlikely that both would simultaneously fail to work well. Instead you should check the cartridge first. Perhaps the trouble is caused by nothing more than a buildup of lint around the stylus.

If the cartridge and needle are OK, then there is a problem with the receiver, the loudspeakers, or the record player wiring or the phonograph cartridge.

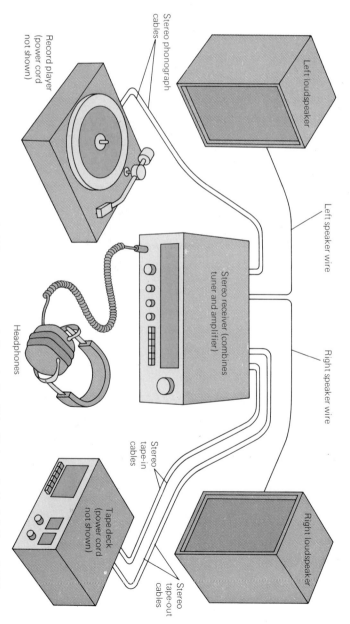

Left loudspeaker

Left speaker wire

Right speaker wire

Stereo phonograph cables

Record player
(power cord
not shown)

Stereo receiver (combines
tuner and amplifier)

Headphones

Stereo
tape-in
cables

Stereo
tape-out
cables

Tape deck
(power cord
not shown)

Right loudspeaker

Become familiar with how the components of a hi-fi system are connected to each other. This will help you find faults in the equipment.

Insuring good connections at jacks and terminals

Poor electrical connections at jacks and terminals are a quite common source of trouble. The junctions at these points are purely mechanical. Mechanical contacts are made of metal normally oxidize over time and can collect dirt as well. The oxide and dirt act like electrical resistance at the contact surfaces, and heat up when current passes through them. The heat accelerates the oxidation until so much oxide has built up that the current ceases to flow.

To avoid this problem, periodically clean all plugs, jacks, lugs, connectors, and terminals. Note that the larger the area of clean metal contact at each junction, and the firmer the pressure at each mating surface, the longer the connection will remain trouble free.

If a defect develops in a hi-fi system, or in a radio or tape recorder that has equipment such as headphones or microphones plugged into it, you may, as an alternative to looking for the defect, clean all connections first. In this way you stand a fair chance of correcting the defect without having to go to the trouble of finding it.

The easiest way to clean connections is to spray them with TV tuner cleaner. Or you may clean them, where they are accessible, with a pencil eraser, or scrape them with fine sandpaper. Pull all the plugs out of their jacks and push them back in several times. Loosen and tighten the screw terminals and do anything else that scrapes and tightens the contacts.

Also, check to make sure there are no short circuits between adjacent terminals. When stranded wire is hooked to a screw terminal without being soldered, it may leave a stray strand or two. Clip off the stray strands to keep them from bridging the gap to an adjacent terminal.

Note: You should scrape new stranded wire before hooking it to a terminal, since the wire is coated by the manufacturer. A better method, however, for connecting stranded wire to a screw terminal is to first scrape and add solder to the wire end, or attach a lug to it.

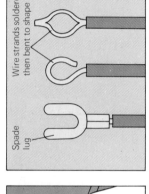

Squeeze the outer connector of this type of plug with a pair of pliers so that the plug grips tightly when inserted into the jack.

Jack
Plug
Metal outer connector

To clean the jack terminals, spray them with TV tuner cleaner, then slide the plug in and out of the jack several times.

Jack
Plug
TV tuner cleaner

Spade lug

Wire strands soldered, then bent to shape

Speaker connections are more reliable if proper terminals—spade lugs or soldered wire ends—are used at each end of speaker wires.

ANT: AM FM
PHONO AUX TAPE MON
RIGHT
LEFT
GND

Jacks for record player cables
Jacks for tape deck cables
AM antenna
Stereo speaker terminals
Ground terminal
TAPE TAPE IN OUT
RIGHT
LEFT
SPEAKER FUSES
A SPEAKERS RIGHT LEFT + −
B SPEAKERS RIGHT LEFT + −
Terminals for extra pair of speakers
FUSE

You can plug record player and tape deck power cords into these outlets
The terminals, jacks, fuses, and power cord outlets in the back of a receiver are usually well labeled.

Repairing headphones

Most headphones are simply a pair of tiny loudspeakers in roughly hemispherical housings. To check them, set a volt-ohm meter (p.124) to the RX1 scale and touch its probes to the contacts on the headphone plug; if you hear a click from both speakers in the headphone set, the headphones are OK.

Stereo headphones are slightly more complicated. They require three meter checks at the headphone plug, as shown below. In the course of testing, you should hear a click in first one speaker, then the other.

Note: This volt-ohm meter test works only for electromagnetic headphones. Some headphones of higher quality are electrostatic and will not click when tested with a volt-ohm meter.

If one or both headphone speakers do not appear to work, there is probably a bad connection in the headphone cordset—either in the cord wiring or at the junction where the wiring is connected to the plug. Resolder the bad connection, or replace the cordset.

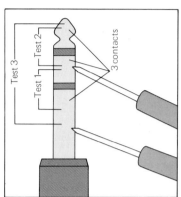

To check headphones, touch the volt-ohm meter probes to the contacts on the plug. On stereo headphone plugs, there are three contacts and three ways to touch the probes to them pair by pair. Touch all three pairs and listen for the headphones to click.

Test 3
Test 2
Test 1
3 contacts

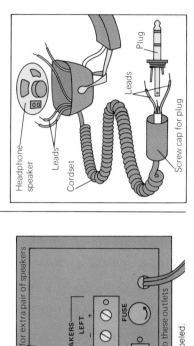

To remove headphone cordset, or just the plug on the cordset, pry off the headphone cover and unsolder cordset leads from headphone terminals. Or unsolder the plug from the cordset.

Headphone speaker
Leads
Cordset
Plug
Leads
Screw cap for plug

Hi-fi, radios, phonographs, and tape recorders

Improving the sound quality of loudspeaker systems

The sound quality of a high fidelity system, particularly the stereo effect, depends very much on where the loudspeakers are placed in the room. In general, the stereo pair should be separated about 8 feet, with the listening area centered in front of them. This rule however is not strict, because the perception of quality in sound is highly subject to individual preference.

If your loudspeakers are housed in one cabinet, as those in a stereo console, there is not much you can do to alter their location. To improve the quality of the system, you may want to buy a separate pair of speakers and hook them into the system, but you should take into account the fact that manufacturers when they build consoles pay greater attention to the cabinet than to the sound equipment; these units do not have a high reputation for quality.

The sound quality of a system depends on the acoustics of the room in which the system is placed. A room

In a rectangular room it is usually preferable to place stereo loudspeakers along one of the shorter walls.

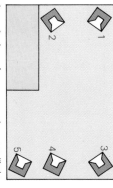

In an L-shaped room; speakers are likely to sound better at positions 1 and 2, or 3 and 4, than at 1 and 3, or 3 and 5.

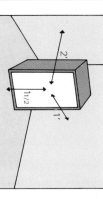

For a smoother bass response from a speaker, locate the speaker at unequal distances from the floor and each wall.

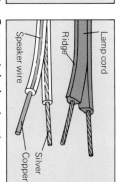

When a pair of stereo loudspeakers is out of phase, the sound from one speaker tends to cancel the sound from the other.

may be "live," one that is uncluttered and has large areas of hard reflecting surfaces; or it may be "dead," one that is not being in phase with each other. The with sound absorbing fabrics and drapes. If you prefer the room that houses your hi-fi to be more live, or more dead, try changing the furnishings in the room. In addition, the quality of the sound will depend on the shape and size of the room and where inside the room the sound is coming from. As a rule, unequal dimensions are better than equal dimensions. A room that is a cube will tend to resonate, giving undue prominence to certain frequencies. Similar resonances may occur if a loudspeaker is placed at an equal distance from the floor and each wall. Ultimately, you must use your own judgment. Not enough is known about acoustics; modern concert halls are still being gutted and rebuilt because architects continue to misjudge and build them with bad sound.

Loudspeakers should be in phase with each other. The effect of their not being in phase is not always noticeable, but you can check it easily. Switch the receiver from *Stereo* to *Mono* and listen to a recording with extensive bass passages. Disconnect the wires to one of the speakers, either at the speaker end or the receiver end, reverse the wires, then reconnect them. The connection that gives you richer bass sound (before reversing or after) is the connection that establishes the proper phase between the two speakers.

If the system does not play loud enough to your taste, there is a slight possibility that the wires connecting the loudspeakers to the receiver are not heavy enough. What is sold as "speaker wire" in some stores tends to be too thin for connections over distances greater than 10 feet; it will heat up and dissipate much of the power that should be going to the speakers. Ordinary lamp cord of the proper size works well as speaker wire.

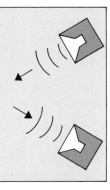

For correct phasing of speakers, connect the ridged, or copper, wire to the plus terminals on the receiver and speaker.

Keeping records free of noise and wow

Clean your phonograph records periodically to keep dust and lint from creating noise and distortion when the records are played. Handle the records at their edges; fingerprints degrade the record surface. If the records rapidly become noisy with use, check the weight of the stylus on the record. Cartridge manufacturers recommend the weight best suited for their product. If the weight of your stylus is heavier or lighter than that recommended, adjust the weight.

A warp in a record slightly changes the speed at which the stylus travels over the warped portion of the record. This produces a change in frequency at the loudspeaker, an effect called wow. To keep records from becoming warped, store them vertically, not on their sides, and store them in a cool place.

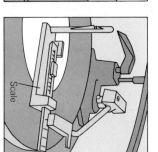

To clean records, wipe them with a soft brush. Note: Do not clean them on a running turntable; you will damage the turntable drive wheel.

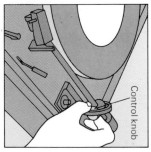

To measure the weight of a phonograph stylus on a record, use a scale made for the purpose. The scale is not expensive.

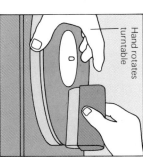

Adjust stylus weight on this model of record player by turning the stylus pressure control knob on the tone arm support.

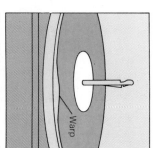

Warped phonograph records cause wow. Records become warped when they are left lying in the sun or exposed to excessive heat.

Minimizing distortion

Distortion of sound is a quality that listeners often tolerate in their sets, particularly if the set is an inexpensive AM radio or phonograph. In some listening experiences the quality is even looked for, as in certain types of rock music where the performers drive their electronically amplified instruments into an overload condition that makes the rock music raspy, even harsh. But for most music, particularly when the music is reproduced with equipment that has an excellent frequency response and negligible hiss, distortion is disagreeable and tiresome to listen to over a period of time, even if the effect at any given moment is so slight you may hardly think about it.

There are other causes of distortion than those that are inherent in the design of your equipment. Multipath distortion results when a delayed version of an FM signal adds to the same signal at the receiver antenna. It makes FM program material sound slightly or noticeably fuzzy. If the sound comes and goes, it may be caused by reflections from aircraft passing overhead. The effect is similar to the ghosts you may sometimes see on a TV screen, and is eliminated—as TV ghosts are—by repositioning the antenna so that the reflected secondary signal, whether fixed or changing, is not picked up by it. It is sometimes better to have an FM antenna that is easy to adjust, such as the kind of rabbit ear antenna often used for television sets or just a floppy piece of wire.

If you hear distortion only when the record player is on, the cause may simply be lint and dust that has collected around the phonograph stylus. Remove the lint and dust with a small brush and clean your records periodically (see *Keeping records free of noise and wow*, facing page). Note: Do not clean the records on a running turntable.

If the distortion you hear is permanent, you may have damaged loudspeakers. The enclosed loudspeakers in hi-fi systems can be damaged if they are connected to amplifiers with enough power to overload the speakers. The damage usually occurs when you turn up the receiver volume control to the overload level and leave it there for several minutes or more. Both speakers must be replaced when this happens.

A loudspeaker inside a radio, phonograph, or tape recorder may be damaged by a child poking an object, such as a pencil, through the speaker grille and tearing the speaker cone. Unplug the set, remove its back, and examine the speaker. Replace speaker if its cone is torn.

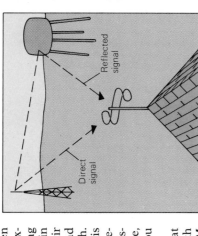

A signal that reflects off of the metal structure of a water tower or a nearby building takes longer to arrive at the antenna than a direct signal. The delayed signal interferes with and distorts the direct signal.

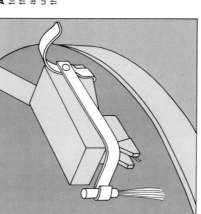

A tiny brush attached to the tone arm of the phonograph automatically picks up lint and dust as the phonograph plays.

The cone of the loudspeaker in this portable tape recorder can easily be inspected for damage after removing the back cover of the set. To replace the speaker, unsolder the leads connected to it, take out the speaker retaining screws, and remove the speaker.

Reducing hiss

Hiss is the background noise inherent in all systems. Every electronics part contributes some hiss, and were the contribution at all possible to eliminate, we would still pick up hiss from the atmosphere and from the stars.

However, you can reduce hiss in some ways. If you hear too much of it in your FM receiver, install an antenna with greater sensitivity, obtainable at electronics supply stores. You can select from a wide range of FM antennas, from a simple wire that you hang from an antenna terminal to a sophisticated, motor-driven, roof-top array. But before discarding your present antenna make sure the problem is not caused by a poor connection of the antenna leads to their respective terminals (see *Insuring good connections at jacks and terminals*, p.297). In addition, hiss may originate at the radio station itself; check this by switching to a different station.

Hiss may also be coming from your tapes (see *Maintaining tape recorders at peak performance*, p.304) or your records (see *Keeping records free of noise and wow*, p.298).

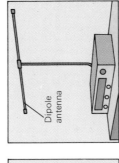

Dipole antenna

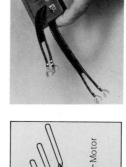

The dipole is a more effective FM antenna. You can tape it to a wall or under a portion of the rug not stepped on.

This TV/FM splitter lets you use an existing TV antenna for FM reception. Note: Some TV antennas are made to block FM signals.

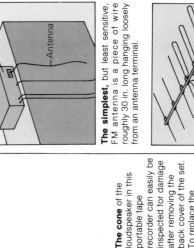

Receiver

Antenna

The simplest, but least sensitive, FM antenna is a piece of wire roughly 30 in. long hanging loosely from an antenna terminal.

Motor

A roof-top antenna is the best type for FM. Mount it on a remotely controlled motor to use its directional characteristics.

Screws

Lead

Speaker cone

Reducing interference

Interference can come from many sources, and can sometimes enter audio equipment in a very peculiar way that is difficult to isolate. Some of it can be blocked only by protective circuits, which may or may not be designed into your equipment. But there are steps that you can take.

Interference can come from a nearby commercial radio or TV station, a ham or citizens band transmitter, or police or fire units. The interference may occur at only one point on your radio dial. If it is from a station very near in frequency to the one you are listening to, you can sometimes block it by orienting the antenna or the receiver in some other direction. If the receiver is operating on AM, you may have to rotate the radio set itself, since the AM antenna is often inside it. An external AM antenna is usually adjustable without your having to move the set.

If rotating the antenna fails to work, or if the interference enters the equipment at some other point, there are several things you can try. First, tighten all plugs and screw terminals in the system (see *Insuring good connections at jacks and terminals*, p.297). A poor electrical connection sometimes acts like a crude crystal radio set, which picks up and rectifies the interfering signal. Next, rearrange the components of the hi-fi system by rotating or relocating them. Next, substitute cables with better shielding for those used to connect the record player or tape recorder to the receiver. Also, use shorter cables, if they have much slack or if the components can be placed nearer to each other. If you can, shorten the power cord also. As a further alternative, you may try to get in touch with the operator of the equipment (commercial radio, ham, or CB) that is transmitting the interference your set is picking up. He may have some suggestions. Finally, do not be surprised if after these efforts you have failed to solve the problem. It is one that can be very tricky, and may equally defeat a specialist in electronics repair.

Interference can come from fluorescent lights, dimmer switches, and appliances in the home that use motors. Such interference makes a steady, unpleasant noise. It will be on during only a portion of the day, as compared to the behavior of noise that originates inside the set, which is not likely to turn on and off in this manner. The noise is usually transmitted to your equipment through the house wiring. To reduce this type of interference, try plugging your radio or hi-fi set into another wall outlet or into an outlet that is not wired to the circuit into which the offending appliance is plugged. If this does not work, purchase a low-frequency interference filter (less than $10) from an electronics supply store and connect it to the receiver in such a way that current from the wall outlet must pass through the filter to reach the receiver.

Intermittent faults and scratchy controls

Intermittent faults are a nuisance, particularly when you try to repair them at a moment when the set is working well and the fault is not in evidence. Either you can sit and wait, or you can try to make the fault reappear by jiggling wires and cables and rapping the equipment with your hand.

Aside from defective transistors, the usual problem is a wire or cable that makes intermittent contact at its terminals. Clean and tighten all terminals, plugs, and jacks (see *Insuring good connections at jacks and terminals*, p.297). Sometimes a cable wire is broken at the solder junction inside its plug. If a plug and jack appear to be making good contact, yet cause sound from the speakers to jump in and out as you jiggle the plug with your hand, disassemble the plug and resolder any broken wire that you find (see *Repairing headphones*, p.297). If the fault appears to be inside the set or hi-fi component, take the unit to a repair shop.

After a period of time, the contacts inside the switches and controls on a receiver or tape deck may become dirty or corroded. This makes them sound scratchy when you operate them. If the condition is severe, they work only intermittently. Clean the contacts when this happens. If the contacts cannot be reached by spraying them from the outside, unplug the unit and disassemble it to gain access to them from the inside.

Braided wire shields

C B A

Shielded cable (B) is less likely to pick up unwanted interference than is unshielded cable (A). For the best protection, use shielded cable with three conductors (C), and ground the shield conductor to the receiver.

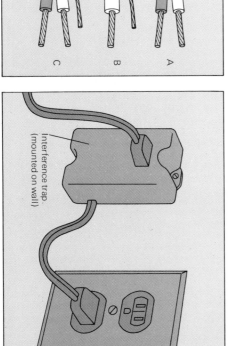

Interference trap (mounted on wall)

This interference trap blocks low-frequency disturbances, such as those caused by dimmer switches and electric motors. Plug the power cord of your set into the trap, and the trap into the wall outlet.

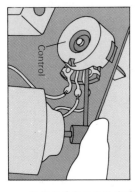

Control

When cleaning a control from inside the set, direct the spray into any hole or gap you can find in the housing of the control. On those controls without a housing, reaching the contacts should not be a problem.

To clean the controls, spray TV tuner cleaner into them. Operate the controls to help work the spray solution onto the electrical contacts. Do this until the scratchy sound s cleared up.

Eliminating howl and vibration

The shelf on which a loudspeaker is placed, and anything standing on the shelf with the speaker, may vibrate whenever the loudspeaker sounds certain notes. To eliminate these vibrations, acoustically isolate the loudspeaker from the vibrating object, or put the speaker in another location. Note: Make sure that all speaker wire connections are tight.

If a record player is on the same shelf as a loudspeaker, the shelf may transmit sound from the speaker to the phonograph cartridge in the record player. If the cartridge then tends to act like a microphone, it can pass the speaker sound on to the receiver where it will be amplified in feedback fashion to a loud howl. To stop the howl, acoustically isolate the speaker from the record player.

Isolation may not be sufficient, however. Other sounds in the room can trigger a cartridge that behaves like a microphone into causing howl. If you cannot solve the problem, replace the cartridge. But before doing so, make sure it is the cartridge and not some other part in your system, say a vacuum tube in the receiver, that is acting like a microphone. Rap the receiver with your hand to check whether or not the blow induces an echoing sound in the speakers. If it does, take the receiver to a repair shop to locate and replace the microphonic part inside it.

Note: You may confuse a very loud hum with howl. The hum is usually caused by a poorly connected cartridge or cable (see *Minimizing hum and turntable rumble*, below).

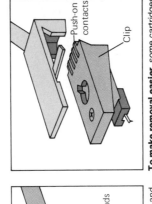

Loose objects—such as shelves that are not rigid, vases or other objects standing on the shelf, and windows—may vibrate or rattle if they are in the vicinity or in contact with a loudspeaker.

Loudspeaker

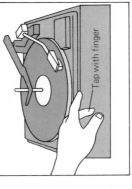

To acoustically isolate a record player from a speaker, place the components on separate shelves, or put a sound-dampening pad under the speaker or record player or between the turntable and the records.

Sound dampening pads

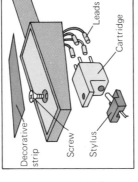

To check whether or not a cartridge acts like a microphone, rest the tone arm on a record and tap the record player lightly. A microphonic cartridge will produce an echoing sound in the speakers.

Tap with finger

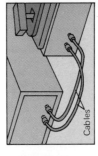

To replace a cartridge, remove stylus and disconnect cartridge leads. Then, take out any mounting screws and remove cartridge from arm. Note: Screw may be hidden under a decorative strip that peels off.

Decorative strip · Screw · Stylus · Leads · Cartridge

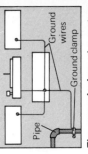

To make removal easier, some cartridges are mounted on a clip that you can slip off the tone arm. Note: The clip has push-on contacts; they must connect firmly when you remount the clip.

Push-on contacts · Clip

Minimizing hum and turntable rumble

Hum and turntable rumble are continuous, low frequency sounds. If you are not sure whether your set exhibits one or the other, switch off the turntable; turntable rumble will stop. In the event the sound occurs while you are listening to the radio, check whether or not the sound is originating at the station by turning the dial to another station.

Hum usually comes from the AC power line. There are several things you can try to reduce its effect in your equipment. Although it rarely works, try reversing the set's power cord or cords in the wall outlet. If a cord from one of the components plugs into the back of the receiver, reverse that cord's plug also.

Next, if the hum is very loud, check the phonograph cartridge terminals to make sure the leads connected to them are tight. Similarly, check the cables between the record player or tape recorder and the receiver to make sure they plug in tightly (see *Insuring good connections at jacks and terminals*, p.297).

If the hum is low, try shortening the cables. One way to do this is to place the components closer to each other. Keep the cables separate from the power cord or cords. Also, keep a fair distance between tape recorder heads and the receiver, which usually contains a power transformer surrounded by a magnetic field that may transmit hum to the heads.

In addition, ground hi-fi components to the receiver, and the receiver to a house ground—a bare water pipe, for example. Finally, do not plug an inexpensive AM radio or a TV set into hi-fi equipment.

Turntable rumble is acoustically transmitted from the turntable motor to the record stylus. You can reduce it by placing a foam rubber pad on the turntable under the record. You may also try to replace the rubber mounts between the motor and turntable chassis if the rubber has become hard; finding replacements may be a problem, however. To gain access to the motor mounts, unplug the record player, then remove the bottom and the turntable (see *Repairing mechanical defects inside record players and tape recorders*, p.305).

A sometimes effective way to reduce hum is to reverse the power cord plug in the wall outlet.

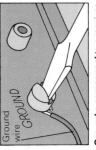

Ground wire · GROUND

Ground a component to a receiver by connecting a wire between their ground terminals.

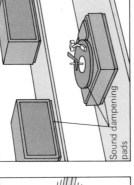

Cables

There is less chance of hum if cables between record player, tape deck, and receiver are kept short.

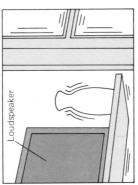

Ground wires · Ground clamp · Pipe

The ground wires of a system should trace a loopless path, like the branches of a tree.

Hi-fi, radios, phonographs, and tape recorders

Locating and repairing defects inside the receiver

If you spend 15 minutes or more carefully looking at every part inside a defective receiver, you stand a fair chance of finding out what is wrong. Unplug the receiver before proceeding to disassemble it.

Frequently, the trouble is a broken or disconnected wire, or a part, such as a vacuum tube, that is loose in its socket. Or you may notice one wire crossing and accidentally making metal-to-metal contact with another wire. Or a bare wire may accidentally touch the chassis or the metal exterior of some neighboring part. To repair, simply separate the touching parts with your fingers, and tighten loose parts. Reconnect broken or disconnected wires. If the wire must be resoldered, use a soldering iron with a small tip and avoid heating transistors that may be wired into or near the circuit that you are soldering.

In addition, look for burnt parts and charred or frayed insulation on wires. An odor of burning when you disassemble the receiver quickly indicates that a burnt part is what you should look for. If the burn is at a terminal, or where parts such as wires have accidentally touched and burned through their insulation, you may be able to solve the problem by separating the shorted parts or repairing the terminal. But do not replace a part such as a burnt resistor unless you can determine what caused the resistor to burn. Instead, take the receiver to a repair shop, point out the part to the repairman, and let him handle it.

Vacuum tubes may be tested with one of the tube testers set up in radio supply stores for customers' use. When replacing tubes, be sure to replace any shields or covers that had been on them.

Note: When replacing tubes, be sure to replace any shields or covers that had been on them.

To disassemble a receiver, unplug it and take out its cabinet mounting screws. Then, remove the receiver chassis from the cabinet. Note: Mounting screws may be hidden behind the control knobs.

Chassis

Cabinet

This burnt resistor cracked into halves, and the burn left a trail of soot on the side of the capacitor. Note: You simply replace the resistor if you simply replace the resistor without making further tests.

Resistor

Capacitor

Repairing an inaccurate or jammed dial, or a broken dial cord

A dial pointer in a radio receiver may become loose and read inaccurately, the pointer may not move as you turn the tuning knob, the knob may stick before the end of the receiver scale is reached, or you may not be able to tune the receiver at all. To solve these problems, first unplug the receiver and disassemble it (see *Locating and repairing defects inside the receiver*, above).

If the dial pointer jams somewhere along the scale, examine the dial cord assembly to see how it works or should work. Part of the cord or perhaps the dial pointer itself may be catching on some protruding object. Remove or bend back the object.

An inaccurate dial is sometimes due to a loosening of the dial pointer on the dial cord; reset the pointer and tighten it to the cord. If the pointer is secure, however, and the dial cord is tight, leave them alone; have the receiver's alignment checked at a repair shop. If there is no movement at all in the cord as you turn the tuning knob, the cord has probably become glazed through use and is slipping on the tuning knob shaft; apply a small amount of belt dressing (no-slip compound) to the shaft, or replace the cord.

Also replace the cord if it is broken and preventing the receiver from being tuned at all. When replacing the cord, study the shafts and pulleys that make up the tuning assembly to find out how to string the cord around and through them. You may be able to see how to do it. Otherwise, you will have to obtain the information from the manufacturer or a radio repair shop.

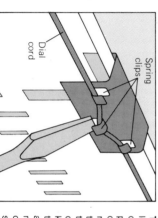

Dial cord

Spring clips

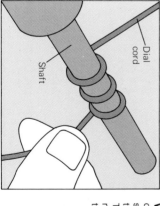

Dial cord

Shaft

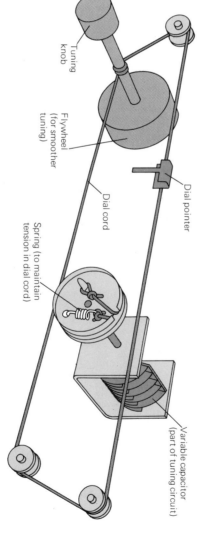

Tuning knob

Flywheel (for smoother tuning)

Dial pointer

Dial cord

Spring (to maintain tension in dial cord)

Variable capacitor (part of tuning circuit)

To reset a dial pointer, loosen the spring clips, slip the pointer along the dial cord until it reads correctly on the receiver scale, then tighten the clips. Turn the tuning knob to check the travel of the pointer across the scale, to make sure the pointer does not catch on some part.

When stringing a dial cord, wrap the cord several times around the tuning knob shaft. This will insure a nonslip contact with the shaft.

Actions to take when there is no sound, or the set does not turn on

In the back of a hi-fi receiver you can usually find a circuit breaker or a fuse. If the receiver stops working, reset the circuit breaker, or replace the fuse if it is blown. The fuse has a transparent case and you should not find it difficult to judge from its appearance whether or not it is blown; the wire element will have burnt through and left a smudge on the glass. In the event the new fuse blows, or the circuit breaker trips again, something is wrong inside the receiver; repair it (see *Locating and repairing defects inside the receiver*, facing page), or take the receiver to a repair shop for servicing.

In some cases the receiver may also have its own fuses, usually located in back of the receiver, to protect any loudspeakers that are connected to it. If the sound goes out but the panel or dial lights on the receiver remain on, check the speaker fuses also. Replace all fuses with fuses of the same type and rating. Do not use slow-blow fuses unless they are called for.

If the set does not turn on, there may be no power at the wall outlet. Check the outlet with a lamp you know is working. If the lamp does not light, check the service panel in your house for a blown fuse or tripped circuit breaker. Replace the fuse or reset the circuit breaker (see p.127).

Perhaps the power cord to the set is not working. Test the cord with a volt-ohm meter (see p.124) set to the RX1 scale. To gain access to the cord leads where they terminate inside the receiver, unplug the receiver and disassemble it. Replace a defective power cord.

If the set is a portable radio or tape recorder that is battery operated, the batteries may be making poor electrical contact or they may be dead. Clean the battery terminals and their mating terminals inside the set and see if the trouble has been cleared up. If not, check the batteries by substituting new batteries, or batteries you know to be in good condition, in place of the old ones.

Portable sets sometimes have a jack into which you can plug headphones for private listening. The jack switches off the loudspeaker in the set whenever a plug is inserted into it. The jack on occasion may cease to function; when you pull out the plug the contacts in the jack that are part of the speaker circuit fail to close because they have become bent or corroded. Unplug set (if it has a power cord) and disassemble it to gain access to the jack. A jack of this type has three or four metal contacts; by inserting and removing the plug, you should be able to discern from its action which two contacts of the three or four should close when the plug is pulled out. Clean the jack contacts and bend them if necessary, so that they make good electrical contact after the plug is removed. Note: A hi-fi receiver may have a loudspeaker cut-off feature too, but more usually, the loudspeakers are cut off by the function selector switch.

A circuit breaker is mounted in the back of this receiver. It can be reset by simply pressing the button. The button is usually colored red.

To test the power cord, clip the volt-ohm meter probes to the cord plug and connect a jumper wire across the cord lead terminations inside the receiver. Bend and pull the power cord. If the meter reads zero ohms, the cord is OK; if the needle of the meter jumps around or reads high, the cord is defective.

To meter

Jumper wire

Power cord

A set of fuses may be used in a receiver to protect its circuitry: a main fuse that cuts off the power to the set and a fuse for each loudspeaker. The type of fuse used in each case is designated on the panel under each fuse holder. *Slow Blow* means a type of fuse that takes a few seconds to blow, rather than reacting instantaneously.

Clean the battery terminals inside the set with a cotton swab dipped in trichloroethylene to remove corrosion from them. If you do not have a cleaning solution handy, rub the terminals with a pencil or typewriter eraser.

Terminals

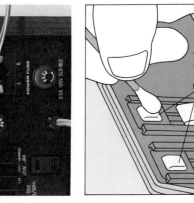

To check the fuse in a receiver panel, push in and twist, or unscrew the fuse cap and lift it away from the fuse holder. The fuse usually will come out along with the cap when you withdraw it.

Holder

Fuse

Cap

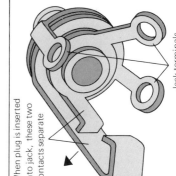

On this type of jack, two of the contacts are designed to close when the plug is pulled out of the jack. Note: Miniature versions of this jack can also be found.

When plug is inserted into jack, these two contacts separate

Jack terminals

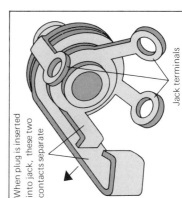

Hi-fi, radios, phonographs, and tape recorders

Maintaining tape recorders at peak performance

Tape recorders and tape playback units gradually lose their fidelity with use if they are not properly maintained. Several problems can arise. As tape plays through the machine, an oxide coating rubs off of the tape onto the tape heads and guides, building up a layer on the heads that prevents the tape from keeping intimate contact with them; the result is a noticeable loss of high frequencies, and sometimes a sudden drop in volume. The same buildup occurs at the capstan and the pinch roller; this affects the uniformity of speed with which these parts draw the tape through the machine, producing wow and flutter in the sound output. Also, the magnetized particles in a recorded tape tend to magnetize the tape heads and anything else made of metal that the tape touches as it travels; the accumulated magnetism degrades the tape and tape head performance.

To prevent these problems, clean the heads, tape guides, and the tape transport mechanism periodically, perhaps every month or so, or after every 30 hours of recording and listening time. Head cleaning equipment is available at any electronics supply store; the equipment should include a cleaning solution and cotton swabs. Do not use rubbing alcohol or alcohol that has oil or perfume in it. As an alternative, you can get a special tape that automatically cleans the tape heads when it is played through the machine.

At the same time, demagnetize the tape heads and other metal parts touched by the moving tape. For this you need a head demagnetizer (costing less than $10), obtainable at the same stores that supply head cleaning equipment. When using the demagnetizer, keep tapes several feet away from it, or they may be partly erased. Unplug the tape recorder and turn the demagnetizer on when it is 2 feet away from the recorder. Do not turn the demagnetizer off until you have moved it again 2 feet away from the recorder.

Note: In some units, as in cartridge players, the tape heads are deeply recessed; the cotton swabs and head demagnetizer that you purchase must be long and slim enough to reach them.

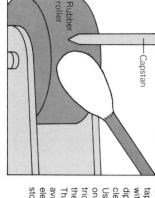

Rubber roller

Capstan

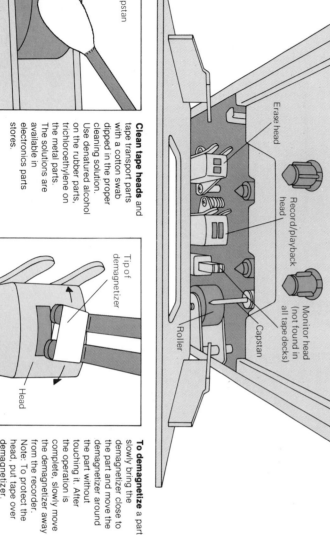

Erase head

Record/playback head

Monitor head (not found in all tape decks)

Capstan

Roller

Clean tape heads and tape transport parts with a cotton swab dipped in the proper cleaning solution. Use denatured alcohol on the rubber parts, trichloroethylene on the metal parts. The solutions are available in electronics parts stores.

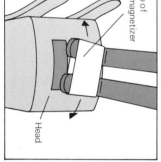

Tip of demagnetizer

Head

To demagnetize a part, slowly bring the demagnetizer close to the part and move the demagnetizer around the part without touching it. After the operation is complete, slowly move the demagnetizer away from the recorder. Note: To protect the head, put tape over demagnetizer.

Repairing cassette and cartridge tape

Tape inside cassettes and cartridges sometimes tangles, jams, or breaks. You will find it easier to correct these problems if you can avoid taking the cassette or cartridge apart. When the tape jams inside the cassette (or cartridge), try holding the cassette in the palm of your hand and slapping it firmly against a tabletop to jar the tape loose. If the tape is broken, try to fish out the two broken ends in order to splice them. Wands with a sticky surface at one end are available for this purpose.

If these approaches fail, take the cassette (or cartridge) apart. Some may be simply unscrewed. When unscrewing, place the cassette on a table so that it lies flat, remove the screws, and carefully lift off the top half of the case. Those that do not have screws must be pried apart along the weld that joins the top and bottom shells. Prying ruins the case; when putting the assembly back together, you must substitute a replacement case (complete with interior parts without tape), obtainable at electronics stores. After prying the case loose, practice the same care in separating the top half from the bottom half as you would with a screwed cassette, to prevent the parts inside from falling out. With the cassette open, you can then untangle or unjam the tape with your fingers or a toothpick.

For splicing a broken tape, there are several kits available. You need a splicing block, adhesive splicing tape, and an instrument to cut the tape and trim the splice. Follow the instructions that accompany the splicing kit.

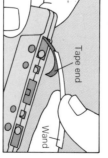

Tape end

Wand

If the parts inside the cassette should accidentally fall out as you open the cassette, use this illustration as a guide to putting them back properly.

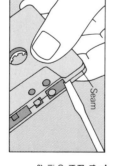

Seam

To open a cassette that is welded shut, pry apart the two halves of the cassette case along its welded seam with a screwdriver.

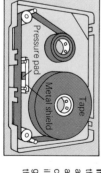

Pressure pad

Metal shield

Tape

Some tape splicing kits include a thin, flexible plastic wand with a sticky end that enables you to fish for the broken tape ends inside a cassette.

Repairing mechanical defects inside record players and tape recorders

A variety of mechanical malfunctions can occur in record players and tape recorders. A tape may not rewind, a tone arm may not lift, or a turntable may not turn. Some of these problems cannot be solved without a major overhaul; others are caused by no more than a sticking or bent part, or a loose or broken spring.

To check a record player or tape recorder, unplug the unit and disassemble it so that the interior mechanisms are open to view. On a record player, you may have to lift off the turntable as well as unscrew the bottom to gain access to all the parts. Inspect every mechanical linkage, lever, pulley, gear, spring, and screw. Try to figure out what may be wrong by actuating transport levers one by one and observing how each part in the mechanism does or should do its job. If you can, repair the part that is causing the trouble, or replace it.

A common fault is that rubber drive rollers and wheels become so hard with age that their surface slips rather than grips the part that they should be driving. As a result, tape fails to advance, and turntables fail to turn; or if they do advance or turn, they do so at a slower or inconstant speed. As a temporary solution, you can try to soften the rubber surface of the wheel by scraping it with a knife or applying a rubber-softening solution to it. Otherwise, replace the part.

Note: Before assuming that something is wrong with the transport mechanism in a cassette or cartridge tape machine, check whether or not the malfunction is caused by a defect inside the cassette or the cartridge by substituting another cassette or cartridge.

To disassemble a tape deck, unplug the deck and take out its cabinet retaining screws. Then, lift the cabinet off the chassis.

Cabinet

Chassis

This turntable spring has become detached from the hole in the turntable base to which the spring was hooked. As a result, the turntable does not rotate when you turn the record player on.

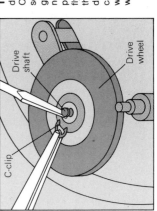

Spring

Spring mounting hole

To remove a rubber drive wheel, pry off C-clip with a small screwdriver while grasping the clip with needle-nose pliers to prevent the clip from flying off. Then, pull the wheel off of the drive shaft. Note: Be careful to replace any washers that come off with the wheel.

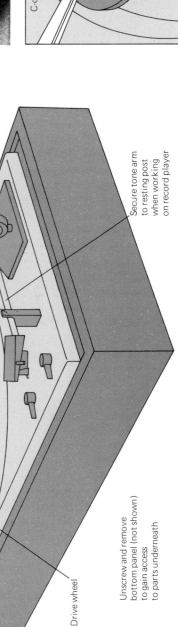

Drive shaft

Drive wheel

C-clip

To lift off turntable, first pull out spindle and pry off C-clip

Post

Secure tone arm to resting post when working on record player

Spindle

C-clip

Turntable

Drive wheel

Unscrew and remove bottom panel (not shown) to gain access to parts underneath

Car radios

Gaining access to and removing car radios

The functioning parts of a car radio are the receiver, mounted in or beneath the dashboard; the loudspeaker or speakers, which can be anywhere inside the passenger compartment but are usually found above the dashboard; and the antenna, mounted somewhere on the outside of the car or in the windshield. These are connected to each other by cables and wires. The car battery supplies the power that runs the radio; the body and frame of the car serve as a common ground.

The exact arrangement of the radio parts and the cables connecting them varies significantly with different car models. A characteristic they tend to have in common is that the parts can be quite difficult to reach in order to check and repair them, and even more difficult at times to remove.

To remove a car radio, first pry off the control knobs, disconnect the speaker wires and cables in back of the receiver, and take out the screws and nuts that mount the unit to the dashboard. Next, remove all parts behind the dashboard that may interfere with the radio as it is being removed. This may include the heater and air conditioner ducts, and in some cases parts of the instrument panel as well. When the way is clear, drop the radio back and out from under the dashboard. To do all of this you may have to push the front seat to the rear and lie on your back on the seat.

Note: In some foreign cars, the radio as installed by the manufacturer may be removed by simply taking out its mounting screws and nuts and pulling it from the front of the dashboard.

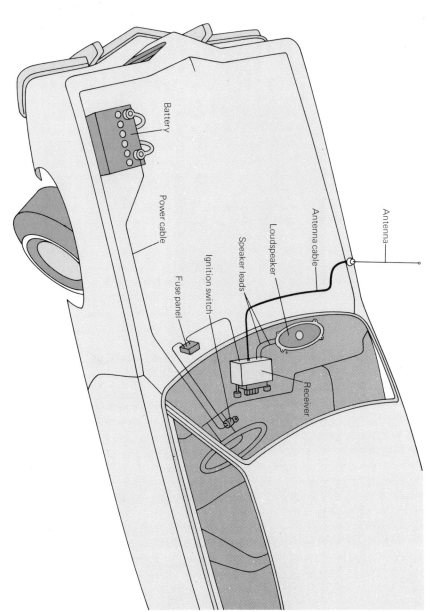

Antenna
Antenna cable
Loudspeaker
Speaker leads
Ignition switch
Receiver
Fuse panel
Power cable
Battery

Grounding a car radio

A car radio cannot function when it is not properly grounded. The ground runs from the radio chassis, through the car mounting brackets to the car body, then on through the car frame and engine to the ground terminal of the battery. If the connection is poor at any point in this sequence, the radio will sound scratchy, play intermittently, or cease to work at all. If this happens, first tighten all the screws and bolts that mount the radio to the dashboard. Then, see if there is a wire that serves as a back-up ground—it would be connected from the metal casing on the car radio to the car frame. If you find one, clean and tighten its terminals at both ends. You may check the results of these efforts with a volt-ohm meter (p.124) set to the RX1 scale. Clip one meter probe to the radio chassis, the other to a bare metal part of the car body—such as a bolt that connects the body to the frame—as far from the radio as the meter probe can reach. If the meter reads zero ohms, the ground is OK; if it reads high, the ground is faulty. Attach an additional back-up ground wire, if necessary.

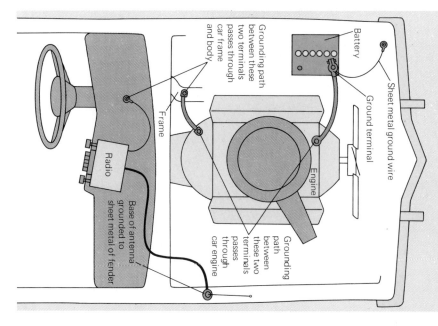

Grounding path between these two terminals passes through car frame and body
Frame
Radio
Battery
Sheet metal ground wire
Ground terminal
Engine
Grounding path between these two terminals passes through car engine
Base of antenna grounded to sheet metal of fender

What to do when the set does not receive any stations or does not turn on

If you cannot receive any stations on the radio, but the radio makes a thumping in the loudspeaker as you turn it on, or a slight scratchy noise as you turn the volume control, there is probably a defective connection between the radio and the antenna. To make sure, pull the antenna cable plug from its jack in the back of the receiver and insert a makeshift antenna into the jack. If the radio then picks up stations, albeit poorly, it is likely that the radio is OK and the antenna is at fault. As an added check, you may test the antenna with a volt-ohm meter (p.124) set to the RX1 scale. Replace the antenna if it is defective.

If you hear no sound at all when you turn on the radio, check the fuse in the power line from the battery. You can find it on the fuse panel of the car, which is usually under the dashboard. Replace the fuse if it is defective. Next, examine the leads to the loudspeaker to be sure they are making good electrical connections at their terminals. In addition, test the loudspeaker with the volt-ohm meter. Disconnect the speaker leads from the radio and clip the meter probes to them. You should hear a click in the speaker as you clip on the probes. Replace the speaker if it is defective. (Take out the speaker retaining screws to remove the speaker.) Finally, make sure the radio and antenna are properly grounded (see *Grounding a car radio,* facing page).

If the foregoing procedures do not solve the problem, the receiver itself is probably defective. Remove the receiver (see *Gaining access to and removing car radios,* facing page) and take it to a repair shop for servicing.

A short piece of wire plugged into the antenna jack in back of the radio serves as a makeshift antenna. Note: Do not let a bare part of the wire touch the outer conductor part of the jack.

Antenna jack / Wire / Outer conductor

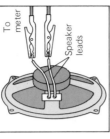

To test the antenna, clip one probe of the volt-ohm meter to the center conductor of the antenna cable jack, the other to the antenna. If the meter reads zero ohms, the antenna is OK.

Antenna / To meter / Antenna cable (unplugged from receiver)

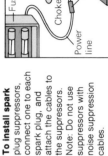

To test the speaker, clip volt-ohm meter probes to each speaker lead after disconnecting the leads from the radio. Set meter to RX1 scale. If you hear a click in speaker as its leads are touched, it is OK.

To meter / Speaker leads

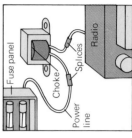

To remove a fender mounted antenna, loosen the securing nut, then lift the antenna up and out, together with its base trim, clamps, and gaskets. Pull the antenna cable through the mounting hole also.

Nut / Gasket / Top clamp / Bottom clamp / Cable

Eliminating engine noise in the radio

A car engine is an inherent source of electrical noise because of the sparks it generates. The hood and fenders of the car are used to shield the car antenna from the interference caused by these sparks. However, the hood will not shield effectively unless there is a good electrical connection between it and the car body. The connection is made by a braided, flexible strap or by a spring contact on the body that the hood pushes against as you close it. If you hear interference on the radio when the car engine is running, check the condition of this connection, and clean and tighten the part where necessary. Replace the strap or spring contact if it is broken. A poor ground between the radio or antenna and the battery may also contribute noise. Check the grounding and repair it if it is defective (see *Grounding a car radio,* facing page).

If the problem persists, listen to determine the type of noise being made. A high pitched whine that goes up in frequency as the engine is accelerated is caused by the alternator; a steady ticking or snapping sound, whose ticking rate varies with engine speed, is ignition noise.

If you hear ignition noise on the radio, look at the engine in the dark while it is running. Sparks arcing from the spark plug cables to a grounded part, such as the engine, indicate that the cables are defective and should be replaced. In any case, replace the cables if they are more than several years old. In addition, the ignition coil capacitor may be defective. The easiest way to check the capacitor is to replace it with a new one and see if this clears up the interference.

Note: If the car radio was not installed by the manufacturer but at some later time by the owner, the car may not have an ignition coil capacitor or spark suppression cables as original equipment. You must then add the capacitor, or substitute suppression cables, if either of them is needed. Or, in place of noise suppression cables, add a set of spark plug suppressors.

If the interference is alternator noise, splice a choke into the power line from the battery, where it connects to the radio. The choke, as well as the capacitor and the spark plug suppressors mentioned above, can be obtained in most electronic supply stores.

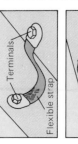

The terminals of a flexible strap connection should be clear of corrosion and tight. If the ground is through a spring contact, the contact should be free of dirt and grease.

Terminals / Flexible strap / Spring contact

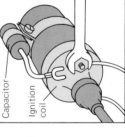

When installing an ignition coil capacitor, follow the instructions that come with the part.

Capacitor / Ignition coil

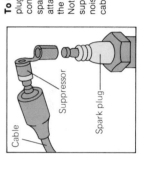

To install spark plug suppressors, connect one to each spark plug, and attach the cables to the suppressors. Note: Do not use suppressors with noise suppression cables.

Cable / Suppressor / Spark plug

To splice a choke into the power line, cut the line and solder the leads from the choke to each of the cut ends. Wrap each splice with insulating tape.

Fuse panel / Choke / Splices / Radio / Power line

Television sets

What to do when your set starts giving trouble

When your television picture or sound is not what it should be, make some simple checks before calling a repairman or engaging in extensive troubleshooting. Start by switching to different channels or waiting an hour or two to be sure the trouble is in the set rather than the broadcast or antenna (if you have another set, that should tell you). Examine controls, front and rear, to determine if they are set properly. Most sets, for example, have a service switch in the rear (see p.310) that must be set on *Normal* in order to get reception.

Check connections and wires. Unplug the power cord and examine it for signs of broken insulation, burn marks, and loose prongs at the plug. Loosen and then retighten the antenna lead-in connections to be certain they are firm. There may also be a break in the lead-in line. If you get better reception when only one lead is connected, then the line is broken. The lead-in can also be checked with a volt-ohm meter (p.124). Set the meter to the RX1 scale and clip its probes to the two leads. If the meter reads zero ohms, the lead-in is good. However,

a high reading does not necessarily mean it is broken. To check further, clip a jumper wire across the lead-in line at the point where it connects to the antenna. A continued high reading indicates a break. In this event, replace the lead-in (see p.311).

Should the set not come on at all, test the wall outlet for power by plugging in a lamp you know is working. If there is no power, replace the house fuse or reset the house circuit breaker (p.127). Repeated fuse blowing may indicate an overloaded house circuit, trouble in the house wiring, or a short circuit in the TV.

Although safety considerations dictate that only qualified personnel examine the interior of a receiver, there are still many jobs that the homeowner can handle himself—jobs for which most people would ordinarily turn to a repairman. Many of these are in the nature of adjustments and are described on page 310. Others relate to antennas and antenna accessories (p.311). An overall guide showing picture problems and the steps you can take to alleviate them, is provided on page 309.

Four common types of interference

Appliances and auto ignition.

Diathermy equipment.

CB and other radio signals.

Cochannel.

Cochannel interference pattern means set is picking up signal from channel other than the one tuned to. A more directional antenna is best cure. Other three types of interference can often be remedied by attaching filter trap at the antenna terminals of set.

How television works

The picture on the screen of a television set is produced by an electron beam striking a phosphorescent coating on the inner face of the picture tube. At any instant, the beam illuminates only a small dot on the screen. To achieve a picture, the beam is made to sweep out a series of horizontal lines, one beneath the next, until the entire screen has been covered. The beam then starts at the top again and repeats the process to form another picture. Like a motion picture projected on a movie screen, the rapid sequence of picture frames gives the illusion of a single, continuous picture.

Tones and shadings are produced by variations in intensity of the electron beam in response to the broadcast signal picked up by the home antenna. When the beam is strong, the phosphor glows brightly; when the beam is weaker, darker tones result. In black and white television sets a single, uniform, phosphor coating translates the beam variations into shades of gray. Color sets have separate red, green, and blue phosphors. In the most common arrangement, dots of each color phosphor are arranged in triplets over the tube's face; three separate electron beams—one for red, one for green, and one for blue—activate their respective dots. The resulting combination of the three colors appears to the eye as a single, realistic color picture.

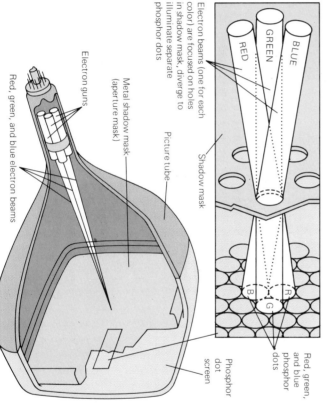

Electron beams (one for each color) are focused on holes in shadow mask, diverge to illuminate separate phosphor dots

RED
GREEN
BLUE

Shadow mask

Metal shadow mask (aperture mask)

Picture tube

Electron guns

Red, green, and blue electron beams

Red, green, and blue phosphor dots

Phosphor dot screen

Safety precautions

1. Never remove the back cover of your television set or perform internal repairs. An error in reassembly could result in dangerous X-radiation as well as shock and fire hazards. Moreover, touching parts inside the set might cause a shock, since the picture tube and other elements sometimes have residual charges on them even with the power cord unplugged.

2. The power cord plug of some sets has one prong with a widened tip. The wide prong is meant to fit only the wide, or neutral, slot of the wall receptacle. Never try to defeat the purpose of such a plug by filing the wide prong down or by plugging it into an extension cord or cube tap rather than the outlet.

3. Do not block the ventilation slots in the cabinet or place the set near a radiator or in a small, enclosed space.

4. If the cabinet has been damaged, there may be a shock hazard. Have a trained technician examine the set. Similarly, if you get a shock from a metal part, have the set checked.

5. Turn the set off before cleaning the tube face.

Picture problems and how to solve them

Snow in picture (colored or black and white specks): 1. Check for bad connections at antenna lead-ins. 2. If set has an AGC delay adjustment (see p.310), turn set to weak channel and adjust AGC delay control until snow is minimized. 3. There may be a switch near antenna lead-ins; set it to 300 ohms for twin-wire lead-in, or to 75 ohms for coaxial cable. 4. If snow appears only in rainy weather, the antenna lead-in is bad. 5. More powerful antenna may be needed (see p.311).

Screen lights up, no snow is present but picture is weak, or there is no picture: 1. If there is sound, perform the AGC adjustment (p.310). 2. If there is no sound, look for a switch on the back of the set that is labeled *Normal*, *Raster*, and *Service* and check it to see whether someone has accidentally set it to *Raster*. (If it is on *Raster*, the screen will light up without a picture.) Set the switch on *Normal* to get the picture back.

Vertical roll (picture frames move continuously upward or downward): 1. Adjust vertical hold. Control is usually a knob or screw on side or rear of set (see p.310). 2. A picture that is vertically stretched will tend to roll. Adjust vertical height and linearity (p.310). 3. If picture not only rolls, but also slips diagonally or breaks into diagonal segments that roll, try adjusting the automatic gain control (AGC) as described on p.310. Note: Do not confuse AGC control with the AGC delay control.

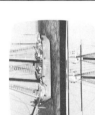

Vertical distortion: 1. If the screen shows only a single line (no height at all), reduce brightness to prevent tube damage due to burnt phosphor. 2. Look for service switch on back of set (see p.310). It will have *Service*, *Normal*, and, possibly, *Raster* positions. Check to be sure it is set on *Normal*. 3. Perform vertical height and linearity adjustment (see p.310). 4. Try cleaning vertical height, linearity, hold, and centering controls by spraying TV tuner cleaner into openings nearest to them.

Picture breaks into fixed bars tilted left or right: 1. Adjust horizontal hold control—usually a knob on side or back of set (see p.310). Turn control in direction that causes fewer bars. Should bars change direction of tilt, you have gone past correct adjustment. 2. On some sets, screen will show picture with horizontal bars as warning against X-ray danger when the picture tube voltage goes too high (more than 30,000 volts). Turn set off and take it to a repair shop if you cannot get rid of the bars.

Black screen, no picture, no light: 1. Make sure set is plugged in. 2. Test wall outlet with a lamp you know is working; replace house fuse or reset house circuit breaker if outlet is dead. 3. Most sets have built-in circuit breaker in back. Try resetting it. (It will click if it was open.) 4. Many portables and table models with vacuum tubes are wired so that all tubes will go out if the filament of one tube goes bad. Take set to a repair shop and ask to have the tubes checked.

Bright areas of picture look silvery; features are indistinct: This problem is caused by a defective picture tube. When brightness is turned to a low level, picture will appear normal but dull. With brightness up, detail in white areas is lost, faces look silvery, features disappear. If set has been off for a long period, picture may improve after set operates an hour or more. Picture tube booster, also known as picture tube brightener, will not help. Tube replacement will eventually be required.

Blotches of color (usually due to magnetization of metal parts of picture tube): 1. Most sets have a built-in device for demagnetizing. Turn set on for 60 seconds, then off. Repeat several times at half hour intervals. 2. Demagnetize tube manually with a purifier (also called a degaussing coil), available at radio supply stores. Plug purifier into an outlet, move it slowly over top, sides, bottom, and front of picture tube. Then, slowly move coil from set as far as you can and unplug it.

Poor color; black and white picture may have color tint: 1. If black and white picture has a tint, perform gray scale tracking adjustment (p.310). 2. If it does not have a tint, turn the drive controls (p.310) fully clockwise; then, back down gradually to achieve good color quality. 3. If color is poor only when automatic color control (ACC) is on, adjust ACC controls. They may be in back of set, inside a panel, or inside the color, tint, brightness, and contrast shafts.

No color: 1. Turn up color control. 2. Push automatic color control (ACC) button to *Off*. Adjust fine tuning until weavy pattern appears. Back up control just enough to clear picture. 3. Turn color killer control (p.310) counterclockwise until color comes on. (For complete color killer adjustment, see p.310.) 4. More powerful antenna may be needed (see p.311).

Poor focus: 1. Tune in strong channel, set controls for best picture, and adjust focus control (p.310) for sharpest picture. 2. Adjust sharpness control (p.310) to obtain crisper picture. 3. Reduce brightness. If results are still not satisfactory, turn brightness to maximum and adjust brightness limiter control (p.310) until picture images just begin to bloom (spread out). Then, reduce brightness control to normal. 4. Perform gray scale tracking adjustment (p.310).

Ghosts (one or more faint, duplicate images of picture alongside true picture): 1. Push automatic color control (ACC) button to *Off*. Adjust fine tuning until weavy pattern appears on screen, then back up control just enough to clear picture. 2. Experiment with different antenna orientations. 3. Change location of antenna. 4. A directional antenna may be required (one that receives from only one direction). See p. 311 for information on antennas.

Television sets

Adjusting for the best possible picture

All adjustments are made with the set on and fully warmed up. Except where indicated, fine tuning, contrast, color, tint, and brightness should be adjusted for the best possible picture. The procedures described and the control layout at the bottom of this page are for a typical set. Controls and their locations will vary from model to model. Since the set is plugged in while it is being adjusted, be sure to use a screwdriver with an insulated handle.

Color killer adjustment

Color sets have a special circuit, called a color killer, to keep color snow out during black and white programs. Adjust the color killer control as follows:

1. Tune the set to a blank channel.
2. Turn the color control to maximum.
3. Turn the color killer control fully counterclockwise. When snow appears on the screen, turn the control clockwise until the snow just vanishes.
4. Check all channels. If color is missing from one, turn the color killer control a bit more clockwise.

Automatic gain control (AGC) adjustment

The AGC circuit maintains stable picture and sound levels despite variations in broadcast strength.

1. Tune the set to the strongest channel and set contrast to maximum.

2. Turn the AGC control so that the contrast is a little too strong.
3. Readjust the contrast control for the best picture.
4. If your set has an AGC delay control, adjust it by tuning the receiver to a weak channel and turning the AGC delay control until color snow just disappears from the screen or until it is at a minimum.

Vertical height and linearity adjustment

The picture should fill the screen from top to bottom without stretching or compressing. Note that the vertical linearity control has most effects on the top of the picture while the reverse is true for the vertical height control.

1. Adjust the linearity control so that the individual scanning lines on the screen are equally spaced.
2. Adjust the vertical height control so that the picture just fills the screen.
3. Since the two controls interact, repeat the two adjustments, going back and forth until the picture is satisfactory. In the course of this procedure, you will probably have to turn the vertical hold control as well; changes in height and linearity generally cause the picture to roll.

Gray scale tracking adjustment

The gray scale tracking adjustment is also known as a color temperature adjustment or black and white setup adjustment. Its purpose is to achieve a picture that is as bright as possible during color reception while still maintaining the proper shades of gray during black and white broadcasts.

1. Tune to a strong channel, set the brightness and contrast controls for normal viewing, and put the automatic color control button in the *Off* position.
2. Turn the three screen controls all the way counterclockwise. Turn the drive controls (there are usually two or three of them) all the way clockwise.
3. Throw the service switch to the *Service* position.
4. Turn the red screen control clockwise until a single red line barely appears on the screen.
5. Turn the green screen control clockwise until a green line barely appears on the screen or, if the two colors overlap, until the combination is yellow.
6. Turn the blue screen control clockwise until a blue line barely appears on the screen or, if the three colors overlap, until the combination is white.
7. Return the service switch to the *Normal* position so that the set is receiving a picture. Turn the color control clockwise to get a black and white picture or get the same effect by detuning the fine tuning.
8. Adjust the drive controls to remove any hint of color other than a faint bluish or greenish cast. Check overall black and white tracking by turning the contrast and brightness controls over their entire range.

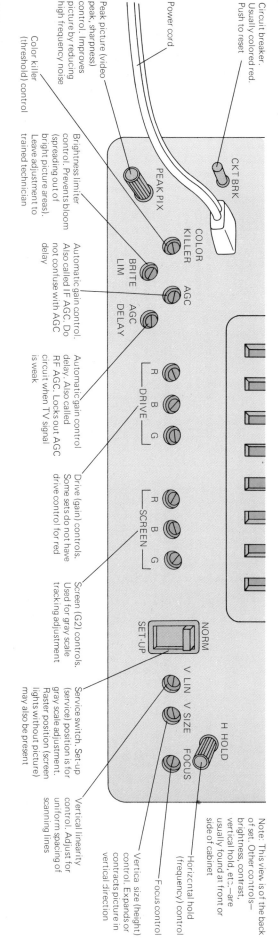

Circuit breaker. Usually colored red. Push to reset

Power cord

Peak picture (video peak, sharpness) control. Improves picture by reducing high frequency noise

Color killer (threshold) control. Leave adjustment to trained technician

Brightness limiter control. Prevents bloom (spreading out of bright picture areas). Also called IF AGC. Do not confuse with AGC

Automatic gain control. Also called RF AGC. Locks out AGC circuit when TV signal is weak

Automatic gain control delay. Also called delay

Drive (gain) controls. Some sets do not have drive control for red

Screen (G2) controls. Used for gray scale tracking adjustment

Service switch, Set-up (service) position is for gray scale adjustment. Raster position (screen lights without picture) may also be present

Vertical size (height) control. Expands or contracts picture in vertical direction

Vertical linearity control. Adjust for uniform spacing of scanning lines

Focus control

Horizontal hold (frequency) control

Note: This view is of the back of set. Other controls— brightness, contrast, vertical hold, etc.—are usually found at front or side of cabinet.

Television antennas

Installing a rooftop television antenna

The proper antenna, correctly installed, can improve television reception dramatically. To get the most out of any antenna, mount it as high as possible—this means the roof usually. Typical mounting sites are the chimney, the side of the house where the roof peaks, and directly on top of the roof along the ridge.

Installing an outside antenna can be hazardous. Roof work carries with it the danger of a fall, and there is a risk of shock as well. Never let the antenna or lead-in come close to a power line. It is also important that the finished structure be sturdy and durable enough to withstand high winds, icing, and corrosion.

Two types of antenna lead-ins are in general use: flat twin-wire and coaxial cable. Cable is more durable, more weatherproof, and less prone to pick up interference. Twin-wire is much less expensive and conducts the television signal from antenna to set with considerably less loss than cable (except during rain). Shielded twin-wire and foam insulated twin-wire combine the advantages of twin-wire lead-in with some of those of coaxial cable. However, they cost more than regular twin-lead. Some television sets have a switch marked 300 ohms (for twin-wire) and 75 ohms (for cable) near the antenna lead-in terminals. A special coupling transformer must be used for a cable lead-in on sets lacking this provision.

Install the lead-in line as directly as possible. Do not let it lie on the roof where it can be buried in ice, snow, or water, and avoid long horizontal runs. Use standoffs to keep the lead-in line away from gutters, drain pipes, and other metal objects. A minimum standoff distance of 7½ inches is safe. Never run the line inside a drain pipe. Feed the line into the house through an upward slanting hole drilled into its side rather than through a window, particularly an aluminum storm window.

Attach the lead-in to the antenna through a strain relief device before you raise the mast into position. Leave slack at the top if you have an antenna rotator. To avoid roof leaks, be sure the base of the mast does not press on the roof and try to place mounting screws so that they penetrate beams rather than unsupported roofing. Caulk all screw holes and mounting plates with asbestos cement.

Once the mast is up, the antenna must be aligned for optimum reception (usually pointing to the direction of broadcast) before it is locked in position. You can do this by having someone watch the set while you adjust the antenna, or else, hook up a portable TV nearby.

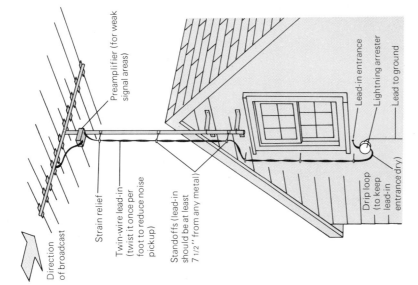

Direction of broadcast

Preamplifier (for weak signal areas)

Strain relief

Twin-wire lead-in (twist it once per foot to reduce noise pickup)

Standoffs (lead-in should be at least 7 1/2" from any metal)

Lead-in entrance

Lightning arrester

Lead to ground

Drip loop (to keep lead-in entrance dry)

Considerations in choosing an antenna

The practical limit on television reception is about 125 miles (75 miles for UHF). Within that limit, reception can be grouped into deep fringe (100–125 miles), fringe (50–100 miles), suburban (20–50 miles), and local (less than 20 miles). Rabbit ears may be sufficient for local reception. Far fringe may call for a stacked array (several high gain antennas arranged on top of one another). Not only distance, but topography, station location, and broadcast frequency (you need a special antenna for UHF) affect the choice of an antenna. It is wisest to check with a professional before you buy. Note, too, that a larger antenna may hurt, rather than help. For example, a directional antenna will sometimes enhance one channel at the expense of others.

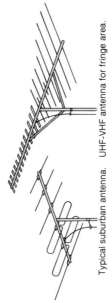

Typical suburban antenna.   UHF-VHF antenna for fringe area.

Antenna accessories for better reception

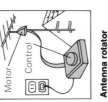

Motor   Control

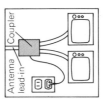

Antenna lead-in   Coupler

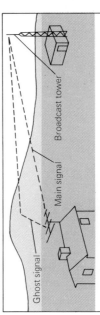

VHF   UHF   Splitter   Antenna lead-in

Antenna rotator solves dilemma of reception in fringe areas where broadcasts come from many different directions. Rotator has mast-mounted motor unit that turns antenna as dial on remote control unit is turned. Device permits high gain, directional antenna to be aimed at whatever broadcast is wanted.

Couplers permit two or more television sets to be hooked up to the same antenna. Simplest type has a circuit that divides the signal from the antenna into two parts, each somewhat less than half as strong as the original. In fringe areas, or if more sets are involved, more expensive couplers with built-in amplifiers must be used.

Signal splitter, like a coupler, divides up the antenna signal. Difference is that it separates signal into its components: VHF, UHF, and, sometimes, FM. It is used when one antenna provides reception for several frequencies. After splitting, the signals are fed into the appropriate terminals of TV set or FM receiver.

Ghosts and their elimination

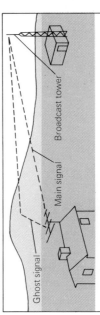

Ghost signal   Main signal   Broadcast tower

The illustration shows the reason why double images, called ghosts, appear on television screens. A ghost signal is one that has been reflected from a large object such as a building or mountainside. Since it travels farther than the main signal, it arrives later. On the screen it shows up as a faint duplicate slightly to the right of the main image. Ghosts can usually be eliminated by installing a directional antenna—one that accepts television signals from only one direction. When the antenna is aimed at the broadcast tower, it receives only the main signal.

The Automobile

contents

Many of the professionals who work on your car—even those who work on the brakes—are not highly trained mechanics. They are often merely apprentices or technicians, who have been taught to perform only a limited number of jobs. Such practitioners may or may not be familiar with the specific details, quirks, and foibles of your particular car. Like these technicians, you can quickly learn the basics of auto maintenance and repair without mastering the theory of how and why every component on a car works the way it does. This section shows how to perform nearly all the routine maintenance jobs that the average car requires. It also describes in detail repairs that can easily be made in your driveway or garage without high-priced special tools.

You as the mechanic

Fixing it yourself

You can save money by doing routine maintenance and minor repair work on your car yourself. Professional mechanics are expensive and in short supply. The labor charge at a repair shop or garage pays not only the mechanic's salary but also such overhead items as rent, heating, equipment, insurance, and—in some cases—franchise fees. Labor rates have risen steadily over the past decade, and the trend seems likely to continue. You can save these substantial charges, and pay only for parts, by doing the work yourself.

Many otherwise handy people are afraid to work on their cars. This is a natural reaction to the confusing maze of hoses and wires to be found under the hood of a modern car. The average car today has more than 15,000 parts. Fortunately, only a small percentage of these parts regularly wear out or need adjustment. Some can be fixed only by a professional mechanic, using special tools and expensive instruments. Others can easily be adjusted or repaired by anyone with the time and the knowledge of how to do so. It is the intention of this chapter to provide that knowledge and to give tips on when to take the car to a repair shop. The contents are arranged alphabetically, with troubleshooting charts for all the major systems of the car: brakes, cooling, engine, suspension, steering, and transmission.

Working on your own car is mainly a matter of self-confidence. Once you have performed a few jobs successfully, you will want to do more. When attempting a particular job for the first time, many novice mechanics prefer to have some coaching from a neighbor or friend who regularly works on his own car.

Where to buy parts

Today you can buy auto parts at many drug stores and supermarkets, as well as at more traditional outlets. Where you buy the parts will determine their price and, to some extent, their quality. Here are your choices:

The parts department of a new-car dealership that handles your make of car should have (or should be able to order) most mechanical parts for cars up to 10 years old. They will be duplicates or improved versions of the parts that were on the car when it was new. They will also be relatively expensive.

Professional auto parts stores carry an extensive selection of parts made by the so-called aftermarket manufacturers. These are the parts you would get if you took the car to a gas station or garage for repair instead

of to the service department of a new-car dealership. The auto parts store also handles rebuilt parts, such as alternators, carburetors, and starters, which have been refurbished by firms specializing in such work. These are less expensive than new parts and are sometimes of even higher quality, because they are inspected more thoroughly both during and after manufacture.

Auto parts stores are open to the general public, and offer discounts of 25 to 40 percent off list price to anyone who walks in the door. The staff is usually highly knowledgeable and used to helping do-it-yourselfers.

Discount chains, department stores, supermarkets, and even some drug stores carry a limited stock of the most popular auto parts and supplies (usually filters,

spark plugs, ignition points, and oil). Their prices can be very low, but the quality of the merchandise can also be low if it does not carry familiar brand names. The sales staff may be unable to answer technical questions.

Wrecking yards are a good source of parts that are hard to get elsewhere (including body panels, trim, instruments, and seats). Modern auto dismantlers subscribe to a teletype service that can track down parts within reasonable shipping distance. Reputable yards offer a guarantee that all parts sold are in good working condition, although you may have to install the part first to determine its fitness. A wrecking yard is a good place to buy used but still serviceable wheels, tires, alternators, steering pumps, and batteries for an older car.

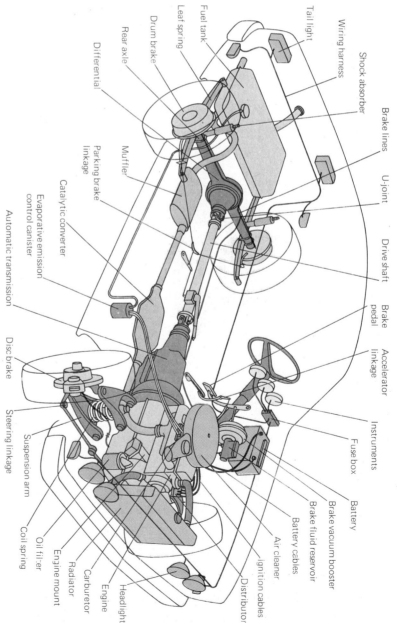

Tail light
Wiring harness
Shock absorber
Brake lines
U-joint
Drive shaft
Accelerator linkage
Brake pedal
Instruments
Fuse box
Battery
Brake vacuum booster
Battery cables
Brake fluid reservoir
Ignition cables
Distributor
Air cleaner
Headlight
Engine
Carburetor
Radiator
Engine mount
Oil filter
Coil spring
Suspension arm
Steering linkage
Disc brake
Automatic transmission
Evaporative emission control canister
Catalytic converter
Parking brake linkage
Muffler
Drum brake
Rear axle
Differential
Leaf spring
Fuel tank

Choosing a repair shop

Often you simply cannot fix the car yourself. When this happens you must take it to one of the many shops that specialize in auto repairs. The various facilities are listed below. Your choice will affect the price and, perhaps, the success of the repair. Many shops specialize in very limited areas, such as brakes, transmissions, air conditioning, and mufflers. Shops with a specialty may attempt other work, but in many cases they are most competent only within the limited area in which they specialize.

The auto dealer's service department should be able to fix anything on your car, if the parts are still available from the factory. However, dealers often charge the highest prices around, and they are usually closed evenings and on weekends.

The corner gas station or service station may take on a wide variety of work, but it is usually best for many of the fast, routine jobs that you can easily do yourself—changing oil and filters, lubrication, tuneups, replacing mufflers and shock absorbers. Many of the workers are best described as apprentices, rather than full-fledged mechanics. The service station may farm out brake, radiator, transmission, and major engine work to a specialty shop, and then add a markup to the specialty shop's fee.

An independent garage is often hard to distinguish from a service station. The key is usually the amount of gasoline they sell. A garage will sell gasoline as a sideline. It will have perhaps two or three pumps. Most service stations have six or more pumps, and gasoline sales are a major part of their business. The garage employs experienced mechanics who can diagnose and solve out-of-the-ordinary problems that may baffle the "grease monkeys" at a gas station. The garage will have more elaborate instruments and equipment, and will be able to tackle more complex engine, transmission, electrical, and brake problems than a gas station. It will also pay its mechanics more, so the labor charge at a garage may be higher than at a service station, although it will usually be lower than at a new-car dealer.

Chain stores, discount stores, department stores, and tire stores often have car repair facilities. As a rule, they do the same type and quality of work as a gas station, although the prices for parts and labor may be lower, especially during seasonal sales.

Specialty shops deal exclusively in the replacement or repair of mufflers, radiators, transmissions, bodywork, auto glass, upholstery, brakes, air conditioners, suspension components, or tires. Since they seldom see a customer more than once every few years, they tend to rely on low prices or heavy advertising to attract sales, rather than on repeat business from satisfied clients. This, of course, can lead to abuses. It is best to use such shops only when you are absolutely certain that you need the services they offer. If you cannot determine this for yourself, it is often worth paying the markup to a service station or garage that you trust, to confirm that the work is actually needed. As a general rule, prices are higher at specialty shops that belong to nationwide chains than they are at local, unaffiliated shops. The costs of large franchise fees and heavy advertising budgets are passed along to the consumer.

Dealing with a mechanic

Once you have chosen a shop, you must then deal with the mechanics in that shop. In most establishments, you can explain your problem directly to the mechanic who will do the work, or to his immediate boss, who is a highly trained mechanic. In other places, such as new-car dealerships, you will be speaking to a service writer, a man whose talent is in selling work. He may receive a commission on the amount of work he sells. He generally will not be a trained mechanic. In such cases, the normal problems of communication between layman and mechanic are compounded.

When dealing with a professional repairman, it is usually best to simply describe the symptoms in detail, and not venture a diagnosis of your own. This is especially true when dealing with a service writer. Most mechanics will do whatever the service writer has instructed them to do, whether that is the actual cause of the problem or not. Always tell the mechanic or service writer the following things:

Exactly what is happening. Do not just say, "The brakes are bad." Report all pertinent information. Is the car pulling to one side? Does the pedal sink to the floor? Do the brakes emit unusual noises or odors?

When it happens. All the time? Only in the rain? Only when the engine is cold? Only when the engine is hot?

How long the condition has existed. Did it just start today? Has it been going on for weeks? Does it happen all the time? Does it come and go?

Periodic maintenance

Regular maintenance is the key to long car life. The following service procedures are compiled from car-makers' recommendations for cars manufactured during the early and mid-1970s. Cars built earlier may require more frequent service, those built later may need less frequent service. Always check your owner's manual or with the car dealer to determine the exact service intervals for your car model and year. List all the jobs you do in a service diary for your car.

Every other week	Check the engine oil level (p.353); check bodywork for chips, scratches, and rust (p.319)
Every month	Check air pressure in all five tires (p.356); check battery fluid level (p.335); check the level of the fluid in the power steering reservoir (p.354)
Every 3 months (or 3,000 miles)*	Change engine oil† (p.353); check exhaust system for leaks (p.351); lubricate the chassis† (p.352); check fluid, oil levels in transmission and differential (pp.357–358); check radiator coolant level (p.330); check condition of all drive belts (p.334)
Every 6 months (or 6,000 miles)*	Change engine oil filter† (p.353); check cooling system (pp.329–330); check brake fluid level (p.324); rotate the tires (p.356); have headlight aim checked at a garage; check air conditioner sight glass (p.331); check clutch play (p.359); lubricate locks and hinges (p.352)
Every 12 months (or 12,000 miles)*	Inspect brakes (pp.324–327); tune up engine† (p.348); have wheel bearings repacked at a garage; check air cleaner filter (p.339)
Every 2 years (or 24,000 miles)*	Replace brake fluid (pp.326–327); replace antifreeze† (pp.330–331); replace automatic transmission fluid (pp.357–358); replace oil in differential and manual transmission (p.358); replace cooling system hoses† (p.329); replace PCV valve† (p.343)
Every 3 years (or 36,000 miles)*	Replace ignition cables (p.346)

*Whichever occurs first
†See your owner's manual; intervals vary from car to car

Tools and techniques

Stocking your toolbox

Many of the tools used in auto repair are the ordinary wrenches, pliers, and screwdrivers already found in the toolboxes of most homeowners, but there are some specialized instruments and devices needed (see *The engine*, p.348). In addition, the crowded working conditions under the hood may force the purchase of specialized tools for working in cramped quarters. Start out with the basic array of auto tools shown below. Purchase the specialized tools (below, right) one at a time, when and if they are needed.

Wrenches will be your biggest expense. For some jobs, an open-end wrench is the only type that will fit. For others, you will prefer the surer grip of a box wrench. A set of 10 or 12 combination open-end/box wrenches ranging from ¼ to 15/16 inch will cover most of the nuts and bolts on American cars. A ⅜-inch drive ratchet wrench, with a set of sockets from ⅜ to ¾ inch, will reduce the time needed to remove and replace nuts and bolts. Accessories for the ratchet should include: a spark plug socket with rubber insert (13/16- or ⅝-inch size, as needed for the plugs on your car); 3-, 6-, and 10-inch extensions; and a U-joint.

The nuts and bolts used on most imported cars are in metric sizes. To work on such a car, you will need a full set of metric-size wrenches from 6 to 19 millimeters. U.S. carmakers are slowly adopting metric measurements for the cars they build in North America. Every new design—be it an engine, transmission, or a completely new car—will use metric fasteners. Consequently, many newer American cars use both metric and inch fasteners. Since auto tools receive hard use, it is best to invest in high-quality tools that will not break. Some brands carry a lifetime guarantee against breakage.

Basic tools *Carry in car at all times

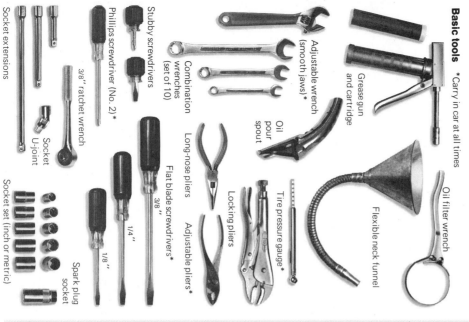

Socket extensions

Phillips screwdriver (No. 2) *

Stubby screwdrivers

Adjustable wrench (smooth jaws) *

Grease gun and cartridge

Oil pour spout

Combination wrenches (set of 10)

Long-nose pliers

Locking pliers

Tire pressure gauge *

Flexible neck funnel

Oil filter wrench

⅜ " ratchet wrench

Socket U-joint

Flat blade screwdrivers ⅜ "

Adjustable pliers *

¼ "

⅛ "

Spark plug socket

Socket set (inch or metric)

Specialized tools

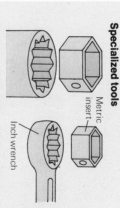

Metric insert

Inch wrench

Metric inserts convert inch-size sockets and box wrenches to fit metric fasteners. Sleeves fit 11 standard inch wrenches.

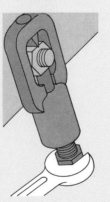

A nut splitter will destroy a badly corroded or damaged nut that cannot be removed any other way, but it will not damage the bolt.

Twist and pull

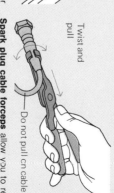

Do not pull on cable

Spark plug cable forceps allow you to remove and replace cables properly (by pulling on their boots) in cramped quarters.

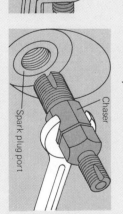

Allen wrench

GM gap adjuster

Allen wrenches fit the hexagonal recesses in the heads of Allen bolts. You need one to set breaker point gap on General Motors cars.

Use a gasket scraper to remove stuck-on gasket material. A chisel or screwdriver will score the machined gasket mating surfaces.

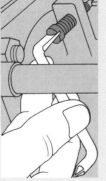

An offset screwdriver with one flat and one Phillips blade can often reach screws that even a stubby screwdriver cannot reach.

Adapter compensates for the wider gap created by ring

Feeler and adapter

Cam

Ring

A distributor cam ring and special feeler gauge allow you to set breaker point gap without loosening the distributor (p.345).

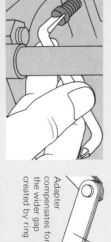

Chaser

Spark plug port

If spark plugs are difficult to install by hand, clean the carbon deposits from each spark plug port with a thread chaser.

You can open spring-type hose clamps with adjustable pliers (left), but hose-clamp pliers (right) are easier to work with.

How to remove a broken bolt

Bolts and studs that thread into blind holes on the engine, transmission, and differential can be broken off flush with the surface by excessive tightening or by attempts to remove a bolt that is frozen in place and weakened by corrosion. If possible, first remove the entire manifold, valve cover, oil pan, or whatever component the bolt held in place before it was broken. If the broken bolt protrudes far enough, file a groove into it, and remove it with a screwdriver. Otherwise, buy a stud extractor that has a diameter slightly greater than half the diameter of the broken bolt. Remove the bolt fragment as shown at right, using penetrating oil if needed. Clean the hole's threads with penetrating oil and the proper size tap before installing a new bolt.

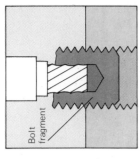

Dimple the exact center of the broken bolt, using a punch and hammer. This will keep the drill from wandering off center.

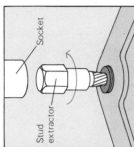

Drill a hole down the center of the broken bolt, using a variable-speed electric drill and a bit half the diameter of the bolt.

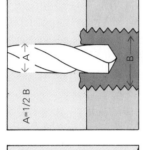

Apply penetrating oil around bolt. Place the extractor into the hole and turn it counterclockwise with socket until it wedges firmly.

Continue to turn the extractor counterclockwise, and the bolt fragment will unscrew. Clean threads in hole if they are corroded.

How to repair stripped threads

The external threads on bolts, studs, and spark plugs—and the internal threads on the nuts, holes, and ports they engage—can be stripped by excessive tightening, by assembling gritty components, or by forcing parts whose threads are not properly engaged (called cross threading). Nuts, bolts, studs, and spark plugs are inexpensive and easy to replace if they are damaged. A major engine or transmission component with stripped threads is another matter; its threads must be repaired. The most practical way is with a spring-type thread insert kit, sold in auto parts stores. The inserts have a diamond cross section that duplicates the stripped threads. Inserts are available for spark plug ports and bolt holes in common inch and metric sizes.

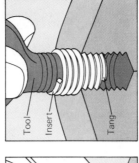

Use a thread gauge (see p.364) to determine the exact size and pitch of the threads on an undamaged bolt. Buy proper insert kit.

Gauge tells number of threads per inch

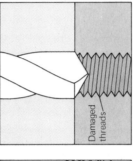

Drill out the damaged threads to the bottom of blind holes, using the drill size specified on the kit. Clean out all metal chips.

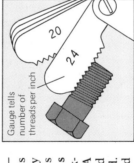

Use tap supplied with kit to cut threads that will accept insert. Keep tap perpendicular and well oiled. Remove chips.

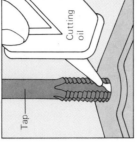

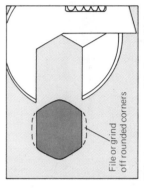

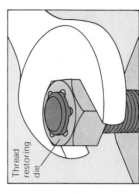

Use tool in kit to screw insert into hole until it is half a turn below the surface. Break driving tang off insert and install bolt.

How to remove damaged or corroded parts

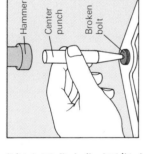

Soak rusted or overtightened fasteners with penetrating oil. Tap parts gently to set up vibrations and let oil soak in. Use several applications on stubborn cases.

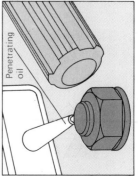

To get a good grip on odd-sized bolts, or fasteners whose corners have been rounded off, force a screwdriver between a flat edge of the bolt and one jaw of wrench.

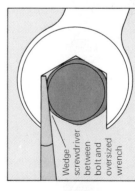

You can often remove an Allen screw with a damaged recess by hammering a screwdriver into the recess, and then turning screwdriver with a wrench.

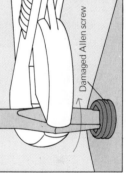

If the corners on a nut, bolt, or drain plug are rounded off, file two parallel flat surfaces on the part and remove it with an adjustable wrench. Replace the part.

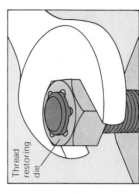

The threads on shock absorber and suspension bolts and studs may be clogged with built-up grit and rust. Clean with a die and large amount of penetrating oil.

Tools and techniques

Special-purpose wrenches

Use a torque wrench to tighten fasteners and spark plugs to the carmaker's exact specifications. Buy a model that indicates 0-150 ft-lb and fits your sockets and extensions (½- or ⅜-in. drive).

A ratchet box wrench can open fasteners in areas with very tight clearances. All you need is room to slip the wrench over the nut or bolt head and swing it through an extremely small arc.

An offset or starter wrench is needed to reach the nuts and bolts on some starters and exhaust manifolds. Box ends in 9/16- and ⅝-in. sizes fit most common starter and manifold bolts.

An impact driver is struck with a hammer to loosen, frozen or over-tightened nuts, bolts, and screws. It has flat and Phillips screwdriver tips and a shaft that fits ½-in. socket sets. Use adaptor for ⅜-in. sockets.

The brake bleeder valves on some cars are positioned at an angle that makes them awkward to turn with an ordinary wrench. Special offset brake bleeder wrenches are sold for use on these models.

Ignition wrench sets are designed for use on the tiny, hard-to-reach nuts inside the distributor. The short, thin wrenches have the same span at each end, but the jaws are at different angles.

How to raise the car

Never work under a car that is supported only by the tire-changing jack—a rickety device designed more for economy of manufacture than sturdiness. The car can easily be pushed off the jack by a passerby or even by the person working under the car. Jack up the car and place the stands under the jacking points illustrated below. Then, lower the car onto the stands. Before raising the front of the car, put an automatic transmission into *Park* or a manual transmission into *Reverse* and set the parking brake. Before raising the rear of the car, block the front wheels with stones or lengths of 4- by 4-inch lumber. These procedures will prevent the car from rolling off the jack or stands. If the job does not require that the wheels hang free, you can raise the car simply by driving it up onto a pair of ramps. You can buy steel ramps or make your own ramps out of pieces of 2- by 12-inch lumber, cut to the proper shape and bolted together. Use the transmission and parking brake to keep the car from rolling off the ramps.

Jacking points

Caution: Park on level ground

○ Standard front-engine, rear-drive cars can be supported at the rear axle, differential housing, suspension arms, or front chassis cross member (if any).

△ Cars equipped with bumper jacks can also be supported at the bumpers or bumper brackets.

□ Cars equipped with side-mounted jacks can also be supported at their side jacking points. Cars with separate body and frame construction can be supported at almost any point along the frame.

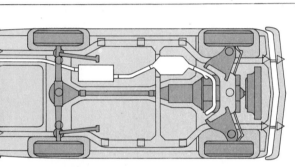

Never work under a car that is supported only by the tire-changing jack. Buy two to four jack stands with at least a 1½-ton capacity. Jack up the car and place the stands under the jacking points illustrated below. Then, lower the car onto the stands. Before raising the front of the car...

If you need to raise only one end of the car, and the job does not require that the wheels hang free (oil change, radiator drain, etc.), position ramps so that the wheels are parallel and touch the tires. Have a helper direct you to make certain you do not drive off the ramps

When the wheels must hang free (to remove wheels, to check for brake drag, etc.) or when you want to raise both ends of the car, jack up one end at a time, position jack stands, and lower car onto them. Use 1½-ton stands for light cars, 2½-ton stands for big cars, 5-ton stands for campers.

Scissors jack with geared crank will lift car more easily and safely than bumper jack. Low-priced hydraulic jacks do not fit under many cars, or do not raise car enough to use jack stands.

A mechanic's creeper is a platform with casters and a headrest. It makes moving around under a car cleaner and easier, but it requires at least 3 in. of extra clearance under the raised car.

Body and interior

Paint touchup

Mechanically sound cars are often junked because their bodies have rusted out. To prevent rust, wash the car often, wax it at least twice a year, and repair all chips, scratches, and dents before rust can set in. Two types of paint can be used on cars: lacquer and enamel. They cannot be mixed or they will crinkle (see illustration at right). General Motors cars are generally finished with lacquer; most others, with enamel. Touchup paints are sold in aerosol cans marked with the carmaker's color code number. These numbers are found on a plate mounted under the hood or on the door post of your car. If the paint on your car is an enamel, use enamel primer; if it is lacquer, use a lacquer primer.

Before sanding or painting, clean the area with a commercial wax remover (available at body shops) or rubbing alcohol. Always use wet-or-dry type sandpaper and keep it thoroughly soaked with water. Use small pieces and plunge them into a bucket frequently. They cannot be too wet. Minor paint stains and imperfections can be buffed out with polishing compound, a white abrasive paste. This may dull the surface, but waxing will restore the shine. Orange-colored rubbing compound should be used only on pre-1964 cars. Follow instructions on fillers and paints. Do not wax new paint for two to three weeks. Note: Regularly hose mud, snow, and salt build-up from wheel wells and underbody.

Apply paint in quick, horizontal strokes. If applied too heavily, paint will run (left). Sand away runs with wet No. 400 sandpaper, and repaint. If lacquer and enamel are mixed, they will crinkle (right). Sand crinkled paint down to the metal and begin again.

Small chips, scratches

1. Scrape away loose paint particles with a penknife. If you cannot scrape away all traces of rust, you must sand them off (see *Deep chips*, at right). Clean with alcohol.

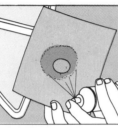

2. Spray some aerosol touchup paint into a paper cup. Dip an artist's brush into the paint and dab it onto the surface. Let the paint flow from the loaded brush into the chip.

Deep chips

Hold paper this way

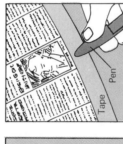

1. Remove all the rust and feather the edges of surrounding paint with *Very Fine (No. 240) wet-or-dry* sandpaper. Keep paper and repair area soaked with water.

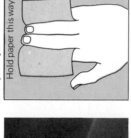

Tape
Pen

2. Cover adjoining panels with masking tape and several layers of newspaper. Cover chrome trim with masking tape. Use top of a pen to press tape down firmly.

3. If scratch is small, cut a hole to shape of damaged area in a piece of shirt cardboard. Hold cardboard an inch from the car and spray the primer through the hole.

Minor dents

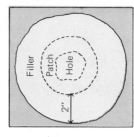

1. Round, shallow dents can sometimes be pounded out with your fist. If you cannot reach the back of the panel, wet a plunger, press it to the body and pull out sharply.

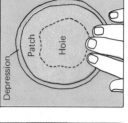

2. If Step 1 fails, drill a series of holes in the dent and insert sheet metal screws. Pull dent out with a claw hammer, using slow, steady pressure against a hardwood block.

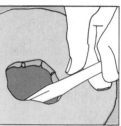

3. Remove screws. Sand with No. 40 sandpaper. Fill in low areas with auto body filler, let it cure, and sand with No. 80 sandpaper. Then follow directions for *Deep chips*, above.

4. Let primer dry 30 minutes, then sand smooth with No. 400 sandpaper soaked in water. Clean area with rubbing alcohol. Apply color coat in same manner as primer.

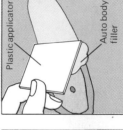

5. Do not try to cover large areas with one heavy coat, or paint will run. Use several quick, light coats. Let paint dry for three days, then rub with polishing compound.

Rustouts

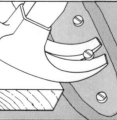

Plastic applicator
Auto body filler

1. Sand damaged area with a coarse (No. 40) sanding disc. Cut away all the rusted areas and sand back to the bare metal. Rusted area may be larger than appears.

Depression
Patch
Hole

2. Crimp back weakened metal using a screwdriver and, if necessary, a ball peen hammer. Hammer a slight depression in the area surrounding the hole.

Filler
Patch
Hole
2"

3. Cut a piece of fiberglass auto body patch or aluminum tape big enough to span the hole but smaller than the depression. Apply according to manufacturer's directions.

4. Apply auto body filler over the patch, overlapping it 2 in. into surrounding metal. Let filler cure, and sand with No. 80 sandpaper. Then follow directions for *Deep chips.*

Body and interior

Windshield wiper maintenance

Windshield wipers deteriorate after 6 to 12 months of exposure to the elements and should be replaced. Most of the time, only the rubber squeegee (called a refill) needs replacing. If the swivels in the blade assembly are worn or corroded, the entire unit must be replaced. Rubber covered snow blades keep ice out of the blade assembly. Occasionally, the arm must be replaced; the usual cause of arm failure is a rusted tension spring. Some common wiper defects are shown at right. Replacement blades have installation instructions. Getting the old blade off is the first step (below). Take the old blade along when you buy a new one. Wash away grime from the windshield and squeegees periodically with a mild soap and warm water.

Common wiper problems

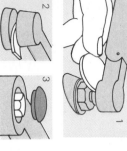

A dirty or worn wiper will streak and smear. Clean or replace the rubber squeegee.

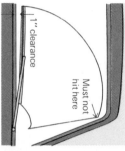

A brittle squeegee or twisted arm will chatter. Replace squeegee or straighten arm.

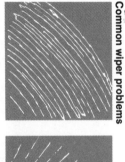

Blade assembly

Connector

Rubber squeegee (refill)

Wiper arm

Tension spring

Knurled spindle

Wiper arm replacement

1" clearance

Must not hit here

Position new arm on shaft so that engine when wiper is at midstroke. it does not hit windshield frame when in use, and rests about 1 in. from cowl when not in use.

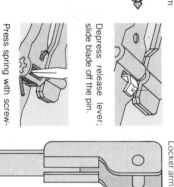

1. Pry wiper arm off with a coin or screwdriver. **2.** Pivot release latch on cars so equipped. **3.** On some imports, arm is held by a nut.

Squeegee replacement

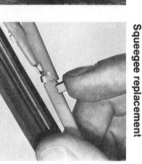

To fix a chattering blade, turn off remove link, and pull out squeegee. Twist arm until it stays parallel to glass. Otherwise, replace arm.

On Anco blades, push red button, remove link, and pull out squeegee. Thread refill through both links. Snap loose link back into place.

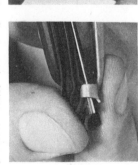

On Trico blades, squeeze ends of metal clip together and pull out squeegee. Thread refill back into blade assembly and push clip home.

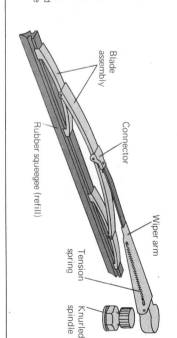

Squeeze ends of VW squeegee and twist free of retaining clips. Slide the squeegee out of the clips and save steel strips for use with refill.

How to remove various blade assemblies

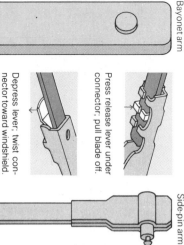

Bayonet arm

Depress lever; twist connector toward windshield.

Press release lever under connector; pull blade off.

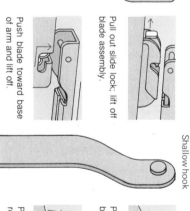

Side-pin arm

Depress release lever; slide blade off the pin.

Press spring with screwdriver; slide off.

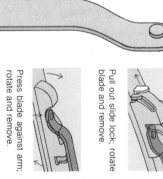

Locker arm

Pull out slide lock; lift off blade assembly.

Push blade toward base of arm and lift off.

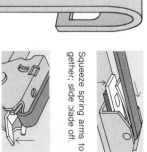

Shallow hook

Pull out slide lock; rotate blade and remove.

Press blade against arm; rotate and remove.

Shepherd's crook

Squeeze spring arms together; slide blade off.

Push lever down until arm unlocks; slide blade off.

Windshield washer care

A windshield washer system is now required on all cars sold in the U.S. Special windshield washer antifreeze (not engine antifreeze!) should be added to the water in the reservoir in winter. In summer, dilute this cleaner/antifreeze to prevent streaking the paintwork (see instructions on container). Most washer problems are caused by blocked nozzles, filters, valves, or by leaking tubes. When tubes get old and brittle they may no longer form a watertight seal. Replace them. In an emergency, cut ½ inch off the end of any plastic tubing that has become brittle, and soften the ends of what is left by holding a match under it briefly. Replacement pumps are sold in auto parts stores, but first check the switch and wiring for faults (see p.332).

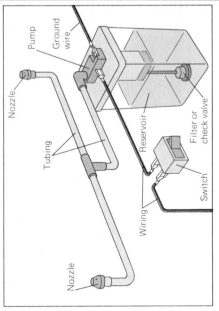

Nozzle

Nozzle

Tubing

Pump

Ground wire

Reservoir

Wiring

Switch

Filter or check valve

Check hoses and pump for filters or valves that may be blocked. Clear blocked valves by flushing system, using a syringe and warm water.

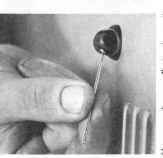

Use a sewing needle to clear grit blocking spray nozzle. On most cars you can aim the spray by using a needle to swivel the spherical jet.

Adjusting doors and lids

The hinges and latches for the hood, trunk, and doors are mounted with bolts that run through oblong holes. When the bolts are loosened, the parts can be repositioned to correct rattles or misalignment. A door or lid that closes too tightly will crush the weather stripping, causing it to lose resiliency and to leak. The door may

also be hard to close properly. A loose-fitting door may rattle or leak, and will not align with the rest of the bodywork. Misaligned doors may also cause excessive wear on the latches. Periodically lubricate the hinges, latches, and locks with white grease (see p.352) to prevent their binding and being damaged.

Some hoods have support bumpers at the outer edges. To adjust bumper (and hood) height, loosen the locknut under the bumper, screw bumper in or out as needed, tighten locknut.

To fix a sagging door, slightly loosen the bolts or screws on the hinge and force the door upward with a hydraulic jack, then retighten the bolts or screws. Check alignment again.

Place a lump of modeling clay on striker plate and lower hood just enough to make a dimple in the clay. If the dimple is off center, loosen bolts and center striker. Retighten bolts.

To adjust trunk lid, loosen bolts holding the U-shaped locking bolt and reposition it as needed; retighten bolts. Adjust hinges and striker plate in the same way as those on hood.

To replace a worn striker or plate, remove all screws but one and swivel old plate out of the way. Attach new plate with one screw, then remove old plate. Fit all screws; adjust plate.

If hood is hard to close (too tight) or if it rattles (too loose), adjust locking bolt. Open locknut with a wrench and screw bolt in or out until hood closes properly. Retighten locknut.

A misaligned hood is adjusted at the hinge. Draw a line around the hinge in case you must return it to its original position, then loosen nuts and shift hood position. Retighten nuts.

If door lifts or drops as it is closed, striker plate is askew. Hold crayon against inside of door above plate; close door slowly. If line is not parallel to top of plate, reposition plate.

If door does not close flush with the bodywork, loosen the striker and move it in or out. Post type of striker in Ford products can be loosened with pliers. Tighten after adjustment.

Body and interior

Locating leaks

Water leaks can ruin carpeting and cause rust. Wind leaks make annoying noises. A wind leak in a protected area (such as the upper edge of a door) will leak air but not rain. It may let water in at the carwash, though. To fix a leak, you must first locate it, then mark it with chalk. Weather stripping that does not seal tightly enough will leak; stripping that is compressed too tightly will deteriorate in time. The paper test (Test 1, below) is difficult to perform (trunk, lower doors), try Test 2, below, using soft carpenter's or artist's chalk, not hard blackboard chalk. For windshields and rear windows, only the water test (Test 3) will work. If you use the water test on doors, start at the bottom and work up. Mark each leak as you find it. Wind noise can be located with tape (Test 4). When looking for a water leak in the trunk, check around the taillight housings and rear window, as well as around the trunk lid.

1. Close the door on a 2-in.-wide strip of paper. If paper is easy to pull out, seal is too loose. If paper tears, seal is too tight.

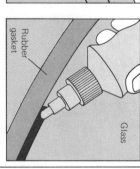

2. Rub soft chalk along entire sealing edge of weather stripping, then close trunk. Gaps in transferred chalk line indicate low spots.

3. With a helper inside the car, run a gentle stream of water over windshield gasket. Move hose slowly. Stop when water appears inside.

4. To locate a wind leak, seal suspect area with masking tape. Test-drive car and have a helper peel off tape until noise reoccurs.

Fixing leaks

Once you have located the leak, check the weather stripping for obvious damage. Check the alignment of the doors and trunk to be sure they are closing properly (p.321). Before you replace undamaged weather stripping, try removing and repositioning it. You will need auto weather-stripping adhesive and adhesive release agent (or solvent), sold by car dealers or auto parts stores. You can shim up ill-fitting auto weather stripping with thin slices of self-adhesive household weather stripping, sold in hardware stores. Remove the auto stripping, add the household stripping, then reglue auto stripping. Weather stripping that is being crushed can be pared down from the bottom with a razor blade, then reglued. Or, you can fix irregularities in the metal area that the stripping contacts. Windshield and rear window gaskets can be sealed with a special auto window gasket sealant, or with black silicone calking compound, sold in hardware stores.

Aerosol snorkel

1. Use weather stripping release agent to remove faulty weather stripping. Reglue with auto weather stripping adhesive.

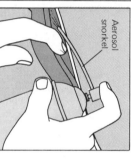

2. If weather stripping contacts a high spot or weld, grind it down with a sander or file, then prime and paint damaged area (see p.319).

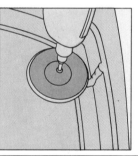
Glass
Rubber gasket

3. If the surface the weather stripping contacts has a hole or depression in it, fill it with auto body filler; sand and repaint (p.319).

4. Pull windshield gasket away from glass in area of leak (if you can) and apply window gasket sealant or black silicone calking compound.

Vinyl roof care

Vinyl roofs and convertible tops should be washed only with mild soaps and water. Special vinyl top cleaners, dyes, and dressings are sold in auto parts stores to cure the damage done by weathering and detergents. Physical damage can be repaired with a vinyl repair kit (see opposite page) or by melting the vinyl (see below). Auto trim cement, sold by dealers and in auto parts stores, is best for regluing tops that have started to peel. In some cases, the old glue can be reused by melting it with a heat lamp or hair dryer.

Melt vinyl with the tip of a household iron to repair cuts that do not extend into cloth backing. Set temperature at the low end of the *Permanent Press* range. When the iron cools, clean it with a nylon scouring pad.

If cut extends through the cloth backing, glue backing into place with trim adhesive first, then melt surface of vinyl as shown above. Do not get glue onto the surface of the vinyl; solvents that remove the adhesive will also mar the top.

Cover a bubble with masking tape, then pierce it a few times with a needle. Heat it with a 250-watt infrared lamp held 3 to 5 in. from the top. Press vinyl to roof with wood block until glue rehardens. Remove tape and excess glue.

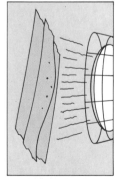

If bubble will not stay down, leave masking tape in place and inject more adhesive with a hypodermic needle, or cut an X through vinyl with a razor and repair as shown above. Keep car out of hot sun for 24 hours.

Repairing vinyl upholstery

Do not simply glue torn vinyl upholstery back in place; the adhesive will destroy the foam padding underneath. Make a vinyl patch from excess seat material. If there is not enough, buy matching or similar material from an auto upholstery shop or car dealer. Use an automotive vinyl or trim adhesive.

1. Cut a piece of vinyl larger than the tear from the excess material tucked up under the edges of the seat. For big tears, try to buy a matching or similar material.

2. Fold the patch and push it under the tear in the upholstery. Open it up and spread it out evenly under the tear with the finished side facing up, the backing facing down.

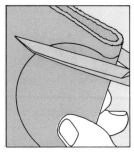

3. Carefully lift the torn piece of upholstery and apply vinyl adhesive all around the underside of the tear. Apply adhesive to the surface of the patch material as well.

4. Press the flap gently into place, keeping the edges as close together as possible. Do not press too hard or edges will part. If a gap remains, use repair kit (right) to fill it.

How to fix split piping

You can fix split seat piping with a thin wooden matchstick or piece of doweling and contact cement. Remove match head. Apply cement to one end of wood and insert it part way into split piping. Apply cement to protruding end of stick and work other piece of piping onto it. Let cement set thoroughly before using seat.

Piping

Wood

Vinyl repair kit

Cuts, tears, or cigarette burns in vinyl (or leather) roofs and upholstery can be mended so that they are invisible, if you use a vinyl repair kit sold by specialty mail-order houses. The kit contains patching compound in several colors, graining sheets, and a material for making your own graining sheets to match odd patterns.

1. Mix patching compound to match color of upholstery (or roof).

2. Trim threads from edge of hole and apply compound with spatula.

3. Place textured graining sheet over patch and heat with an iron.

4. Let repair cool, then peel off graining paper. Patch is invisible.

Fixing carpet burns

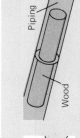

1. Cut away charred pile with curved cuticle scissors. Cut a few undamaged loops of carpeting from under the seats, behind a piece of molding, or up under the dash.

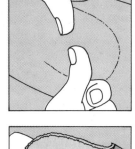

2. Fill the charred depression with a clear-drying glue. Insert the undamaged loops into the glue with tweezers. Make sure loops remain fairly upright and let glue set.

Cleaning cloth upholstery

Cloth upholstery is usually nylon or rayon that has been chemically treated to resist the spread of flame. It reacts differently to stains and to cleaning agents than household upholstery does. Some stains cannot be removed; attempts to do so may cause further damage. Auto manufacturers' suggestions appear below.

STAIN	TREATMENT
Coffee, fruit, ice cream, liquor, milk, soda, wine	Wipe with cloth soaked in cold water. If needed, rub lightly with cleaning fluid. Do not use soap and water; it may set the stain.
Candy	Use cloth soaked in lukewarm water for chocolate. Flush other candies with lukewarm water; allow to dry. If needed, rub lightly with cleaning fluid.
Chewing gum	Harden gum with ice cube, then scrape off with a dull knife blade. Moisten with cleaning fluid and scrape again if necessary.
Catsup	Wipe with cloth soaked in cool water. Use mild detergent if more cleaning is needed.
Butter, crayon, oil, grease, margarine	Scrape off excess with a dull knife blade. Use cleaning fluid sparingly.
Shoe polish (paste)	Use cleaning fluid sparingly.
Tar	Scrape off excess with a dull knife blade; moisten with cleaning fluid; scrape again; rub lightly with more cleaning fluid.
Ball-point ink	Use rubbing alcohol. If stain remains after repeated applications, do not try anything else.
Lipstick	Cleaning fluid works on some brands. If stain remains, do not try anything else.
Mustard	Rub with a warm, dampened sponge; then, rub mild detergent on dampened stain and work into fabric. Rinse with clean, damp cloth. Repeat several times.
Blood	Wipe with a cloth and cold water. Do not use soap.
Urine	Sponge with lukewarm soapsuds from a mild soap; rinse with clean cloth soaked in cold water. Soak a cloth in a solution of one part ammonia to five parts water. Hold it on stain for one minute. Rinse with a clean, wet cloth.
Vomit	Sponge with a clean cloth dipped in clean, cold water. Wash lightly with lukewarm water and mild soap. If odor persists, treat area with a solution of 1 teaspoon baking soda to 1 cup warm water.

Brakes

How they work

Two types of brakes are used on modern cars, disc brakes and drum brakes (see drawings below). Both work by forcing a friction material—called the brake lining—against a rotating metal surface that is bolted directly to the wheel. When you step on the brake pedal, a hydraulic system of steel tubing and flexible hoses transfers fluid pressure from a master cylinder-mounted under the hood at the rear of the engine compartment—to smaller cylinders at the four wheels. Pistons in these cylinders push the brake linings into contact with the spinning drums or discs. A leak anywhere in the system will cause the brakes to fail. Since 1967 all cars sold in America have had dual brake systems—one for the front wheels and one for the rear wheels. Failure of either circuit will still leave you with

two operating brakes. A red warning light on the dash indicates that something is wrong. If the front brakes fail, you'll know immediately—they provide two-thirds of a car's stopping power. If the rear brakes fail, you may not even notice. If the warning light comes on, you may still be able to drive very slowly and carefully to a nearby garage for repairs.

Caution: Brake fluid is poisonous and should be stored in a safe place, out of the reach of children. Glass containers used when bleeding the brakes should be disposed of after use. The fluid will damage painted surfaces. Be careful not to spill any onto the bodywork of your car. It will also deteriorate in time, and should be replaced every two years (see *How to bleed the brakes*, p.326).

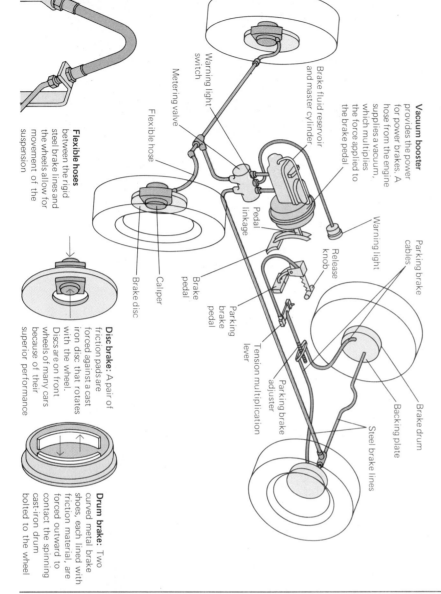

Vacuum booster
provides the power
for power brakes. A
hose from the engine
supplies a vacuum,
which multiplies
the force applied to
the brake pedal.

Warning light switch

Metering valve

Flexible hose

Brake fluid reservoir
and master cylinder

Pedal linkage

Warning light

Release knob

Parking brake cables

Brake drum

Backing plate

Steel brake lines

Parking brake adjuster

Tension multiplication lever

Parking brake pedal

Brake pedal

Caliper

Brake disc

Flexible hoses
between the rigid
steel brake lines and
the wheels allow for
movement of the
suspension

Disc brake: A pair of
friction pads are
forced against a cast
iron disc that rotates
with the wheel.
Discs are on front
wheels of many cars
because of their
superior performance

Drum brake: Two
curved metal brake
shoes, each lined with
friction material, are
forced outward to
contact the spinning
cast-iron drum
bolted to the wheel

Checking brake fluid

At least twice a year, and before taking long trips, check the level of the brake fluid in the fluid reservoir. It should be filled to within half an inch of the top with brake fluid labeled "meets MVSS No. 116, DOT 4 specifications." Be sure the car is parked on level ground when you check the fluid. Brake fluid attracts and absorbs moisture, which can cause corrosion and failure of the brake system. Buy it only in pint cans, keep it tightly closed, and discard it no later than one year after the seal on the can is first opened.

The brake fluid reservoir is located at the rear of the engine compartment, on the driver's side. The cover is held in place with a spring clamp that can be pried off with a screwdriver or by hand. Clean the cover with a rag before removing it.

Be careful that no dirt, water, or oil gets into the fluid. Contaminated fluid must be replaced (see *Checking the brake system*, p.326). There are two separate chambers in the reservoir (one for each of the two brake circuits) and each should be filled to within ½ in. of the top with fluid.

Some imported cars have one or more cylindrical reservoirs with screw-on tops. When checking the fluid, clean the vent hole in the center of the top with a straight pin. On some older U.S. cars, the top is held on by a bolt that runs through the center of the reservoir.

Newer imports have clear plastic reservoirs. Fluid should be kept between the *Full* and *Add* marks. If the fluid level is allowed to drop below the bottom of the reservoir in any car, air will be drawn into the system and it must be bled (see p.326).

Analyzing brake troubles

Problems in the brake system tend to develop slowly over hundreds of miles and may go unnoticed. A spongy pedal or brakes that pull slightly to one side are easy to get used to and ignore. Make a conscious effort to evaluate the performance of your brakes each time you drive, looking for the problems below. Some people feel that the brakes are too vital a system to be adjusted or repaired by an amateur, but millions of careful, knowledgeable owners successfully do their own brake work. Only you can decide if you are skilled enough to work on your car brakes, but this section should allow you to spot brake problems sooner than the average driver so that you can take the car to a professional for repairs.

What can go wrong

HOW TO USE THIS CHART

Find problem at top of chart. Look down columns to locate possible causes. First, check out things you can fix yourself; then, things you may be able to fix yourself. If problem is still not cured, consult a competent mechanic.

o You can fix it yourself.
● You may be able to make complete repair.
■ You need a mechanic.

Adjusting drum brakes

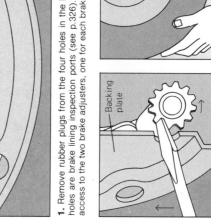

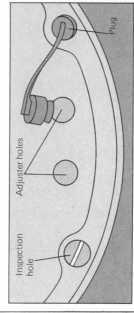

Plug
Adjuster holes
Inspection hole

For the last 15 years all manufacturers have used drum brakes with self-adjusters. Each time a car is braked to a halt in reverse, the self-adjuster automatically takes up any play between the brake shoe and drum. If the brake pedal travels more than an inch before the brakes start to catch, the self-adjusting mechanism may be corroded. It can sometimes be broken free by making a sharp stop in reverse, then driving forward and backward repeatedly to take up the pedal play. Use the brakes, not the transmission, to stop the car before changing direction. If this does not work, see a mechanic.

To adjust Volkswagen brakes, raise the car (p.318) and release the parking brake. Press brake pedal firmly several times to center the shoes in the drums, then follow the steps illustrated below. Repeat Steps 1 to 3 on both adjusters for all four wheels, then road-test the car to check pedal travel. Always replace the rubber plugs in the backing plate to prevent brake corrosion. Use saliva or brake fluid to ease plugs in if they have become inflexible.

Backing plate

1. Remove rubber plugs from the four holes in the backing plate (see p.326). Outer holes are brake lining inspection ports (see p.326). Inner holes provide access to the two brake adjusters, one for each brake shoe.

2. The brakes are adjusted by using a screwdriver to turn the serrated knobs behind the backing plate.

3. Turn adjuster until wheel drags when spun, then loosen the adjustment until wheel just spins freely.

POSSIBLE CAUSE	Play in pedal	Pedal feels hard	Pedal feels spongy	Pedal sinks to floor	Pedal pulsates	Brakes grab	Brakes drag	Erratic brake performance	Brakes noisy	Brakes do not work	Parking brake not holding	CURE
Low fluid level	o		o	o						o		Add fluid (p.324), check for leaks (p.326)
Air in hydraulic system	o		o	o						o		Bleed brakes (p.326)
Brakes need adjustment	●						●	●		●	●	Adjust main brakes (p.325) or parking brake (p.327)
Brake fade due to overheating		o						■		o		Shift to lower gear, coast to stop, let brakes cool
Grease or fluid on linings or pads						■	■	■				Have pads or linings replaced
Pads or linings glazed						■			■			Have pads or linings replaced
Brakes wet with rainwater						o		o				Dry brakes by applying light pedal pressure as you drive
Faulty vacuum booster or hose		●								●		Repair or replace booster or hose (p.326)
Linkage binding at pedal or brake		●					●			●		Lubricate pedal linkage (p.352); have brakes checked
Weak flexible hoses			●				●	●				Replace hoses; bleed brakes (p.326)
Loose or worn wheel bearings					■	■			■			Have bearings tightened or replaced
Loose or worn front end parts					●	●		●				Tighten or replace front end parts (p.354)
Front wheels out of alignment						■		■				Have wheels aligned (p.354)
Warped brake disc					■	■			■			Have disc machined or replaced
Out-of-round brake drum					■	■			■			Have drum machined or replaced
Faulty wheel cylinder or caliper						■	■			■		Have cylinder or caliper repaired or replaced
Faulty master cylinder				■						■		Have master cylinder repaired or replaced
Weak or broken retracting springs							■		■			Have springs replaced
Scored brake drums or discs					■	■			■			Have parts machined or replaced
Dirt in brake mechanism						●	●		●			Have brakes inspected and cleaned
Kinked brake hose or line		●					●			●		Have hose or line replaced
Dirt clogging hydraulic system		●					●			●		Bleed brakes (p.326), if possible
Cable stuck, kinked, or broken							●				●	Lubricate, repair, or replace cable (p.327)
Brake linings or pads worn						■	■		■	■		Have linings or pads replaced

Checking the brake system

Replacing the brake linings is a job for an experienced mechanic. When the lining thickness on any wheel gets down to about ⅛ inch, both wheels on that axle should be relined. On some cars this can be checked by a simple visual inspection (see Step 1 below). On others, a mechanic must remove the brake drum to inspect the linings. This should be done every 12,000 miles, at which point the mechanic can give you an estimate of how many miles of use are left. A scraping noise when you apply the brakes indicates the brake linings are completely worn out, which will damage the brake drums and discs. If the brakes pull to one side in dry weather, you should see a professional mechanic.

Every 12,000 miles, perform the following tests in your driveway: If you have power brakes, start the engine first. Press hard on the brake pedal for 30 seconds. It should remain firm. If it slowly sinks to the floor, check the system for leaks at the wheels and as shown in Steps 2 to 5 below. Pump the pedal. If it feels spongy or bouncy, the vent in the fluid reservoir may be clogged (see p.324). If it is not, one of the hoses may be soft or there may be air in the system.

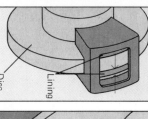

Disc / Lining

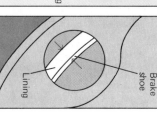

Lining / Brake shoe

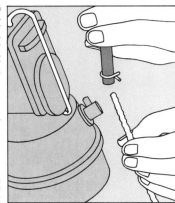

1. Remove the wheel to check the thickness of the lining material on a disc brake (between the arrows, left hand drawing). On Volkswagens, you can inspect the lining on the brake shoes through a hole in the backing plate (right).

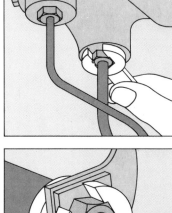

2. Periodically check all the connections in the brake system for leaks. Start at the master cylinder. A special flare wrench prevents damage to soft fittings by grasping them more surely than an open-end wrench.

3. Tighten connections between rigid tubing and flexible hoses with two flare wrenches. (Nuts tighten in opposite directions.) Have a helper push hard on brake pedal; check again for leaks. If a leak persists, see a mechanic.

4. Check connections at the wheel, too. Flex the hose and look for cracks and brittleness. If hose feels soft, have a helper press hard on the brakes. If hose swells, it is defective. Install a duplicate hose and bleed the brakes.

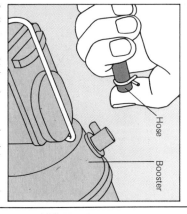

Hose

Booster

5. A leak inside the vacuum booster can pull fluid into the engine with no external sign. To check, remove the vacuum hose at the booster and insert a pipe cleaner. If it comes out wet, have booster rebuilt or replaced.

6. If power brakes become hard to operate, remove vacuum hose at booster and, with the engine running, check for suction. No suction means hose is leaking. Replace it. If there is suction, booster is faulty. See a mechanic.

How to bleed the brakes

Air trapped in brake lines due to leaks or the replacement of parts will make the pedal feel spongy and reduce the force with which the linings are pressed against the drums or discs. This air must be forced out through bleed valves at each wheel.

If your car has power brakes, begin by pumping the brake pedal 10 times, with the engine off, to use up any vacuum in the booster. Raise the car (see p.318) and attach a length of clean vacuum hose to one of the bleed valves. Insert the other end of the hose into a jar partly filled with fresh brake fluid. Use a wrench to open the valve three-quarters of a turn. Have a helper apply the brakes slowly but steadily. When the pedal reaches the floor, close the valve; then, have your helper let the pedal slowly return to its normal position. Repeat this procedure until air bubbles stop coming out of the hose. Keep adding fresh fluid to the reservoir so that it will not run dry. To replace all the fluid in the system, bleed each wheel until old fluid runs clear.

On some disc/drum systems, a metering valve (found under the master cylinder) may prevent fluid from being pumped out of the front disc brakes. In that case, you must hold the metering valve open.

When you have finished bleeding the brakes, the brake warning light on the dash will be lit. To turn it out on late model cars, turn the ignition switch to the *Acc* or *On* position and apply the brakes once.

On older models, you must center the metering valve housing to shut off the light. To do this, open a bleed valve in the circuit opposite the one that was bled last (at a rear wheel, for example, if you bled the front wheels last). Have your helper press the brake pedal slowly just until the light goes out. Close the bleed valve immediately. If the light goes on again, you have overshot the center of the switch and must repeat the procedure at the opposite end of the car. You can avoid this tedious procedure by replacing the light switch with a small threaded stud—sold in auto parts stores—before bleeding the brakes. If you have a 1974 or earlier American Motors car, unscrew the brake warning light switch from the metering valve before you begin. Replace it when you are through.

Before driving the car, start the engine and pump the brakes to test for a firm pedal. If the pedal feels spongy, there is still air in the system. The following cars must be power bled by a mechanic: all Chrysler Corporation cars from 1969 onward, 1969 Lincolns, and 1970-72 Fords, Lincolns, and Mercurys.

Adjusting the parking brake

The parking brake is often mistakenly called an "emergency" brake. It operates the rear brakes only, using a system of cables and levers rather than the main hydraulic system. Should the entire hydraulic system fail, the parking brake is worth a try, but it will not do much good unless you are traveling quite slowly in a relatively light car.

As the cable stretches from use, you must engage the parking brake farther and farther before it takes hold. This slack should be taken up whenever the brake requires six or more clicks to engage. If the main brakes must be adjusted manually (see p.325) or if the system requires bleeding, do that first. Then, raise the car (see p.318) and check the parking brake system for sticking and crimped or frayed cables. Using white grease, lubricate the tension multiplying lever and all brackets that the cable rubs against. A sticking cable will cause excessive wear of the brake lining. Frayed or crimped cables should be replaced by a mechanic. If the adjuster is corroded, spray it with penetrating oil.

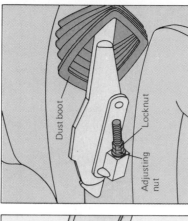

Dust boot — Locknut — Adjusting nut

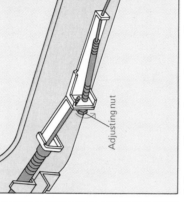

Adjusting nut

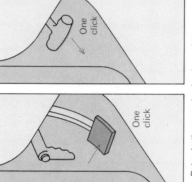

One click — One click

1. Raise both rear wheels clear of the ground. Apply parking brake until it clicks once. Locate the adjuster mechanism—a threaded rod with one or two nuts on it—under the car.

Locknut — Adjusting nut

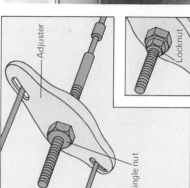

Adjuster — Single nut — Locknut

2. On some Chrysler Corporation cars (Chrysler, Dodge, Plymouth), the adjuster nut is located at the end of a stamped steel housing. It is adjusted like the single-nut unit in Step 5.

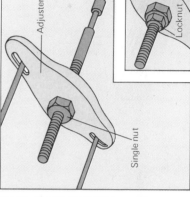

Locknut — Adjusting nut

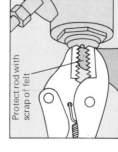

3. On some cars with bucket seats, the adjuster is located inside the car at the base of the parking brake handle. You must unscrew or pry off the rubber dust boot to get at it.

4. Volkswagens have two inside adjusters, one for each wheel. Hold a screwdriver in slotted rod to keep it from turning, then loosen locknut before making adjustment. Adjust both wheels.

5. Hold adjuster steady and tighten nut a little at a time until rear wheel just begins to drag when it is spun. On twin-nut adjusters, loosen locknut first. Retighten it when adjustment is done.

6. Tighten adjuster until the rear wheels start to drag when spun by hand. With the brake fully released, there should be no drag at all. If there is, back off adjustment until drag stops.

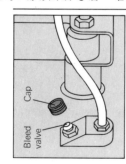

Switch — Metering valve

1. Replace warning light switch on older cars with special stud. Ask parts dealer if your car needs this.

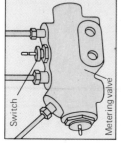

Cap — Bleed valve

2. Remove dust cap (if any) and clean off bleed valve. It is on the backing plate of drum brakes.

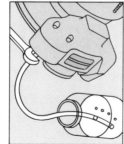

Hose

3. Bleed valve is found on calipers of disc brakes. Put box wrench over valve, then force on hose.

4. Have helper pump brakes until bubbles stop or darkened old fluid is displaced. Keep hose submerged.

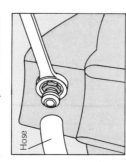

Protect rod with scrap of felt

5. If discs cannot be bled, apply brakes, hold metering-valve rod in open position with locking pliers.

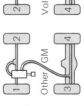

6. Check reservoir every four to five pumps. Refill it to within ¼ in. of the top and replace cover.

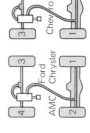

AMC Ford Chrysler — Chevrolet — Other GM — Volkswagen

7. Bleed the brakes in the sequence recommended by the manufacturer of your car (above). If the master cylinder has a bleed valve, bleed it before any of the wheels. If the reservoir is allowed to run dry, air will enter the system and you must start the bleeding sequence all over.

Cooling system

How it works

Gasoline exploding inside the cylinders of an engine produces temperatures of over 4,500°F. To keep the lubricating oil from burning up and the engine parts from melting, some of this heat must be carried off by the cooling system. On most cars this is done by circulating a mixture of water and antifreeze through passages in the engine block, where heat is absorbed, then through a radiator, where heat is given up to the atmosphere. This liquid, called coolant, is kept in circulation by the water pump, which is located at the front of the engine and driven by a rubber V-belt. A fan is attached to the front of the water pump pulley, and it keeps air moving through the radiator when the car is stuck in traffic. A temperature-controlled valve, called the thermostat, blocks the flow of coolant to the radiator when the engine is cold.

So-called antifreeze not only lowers the freezing point of the coolant mixture, but raises its boiling point as well. Modern engines need antifreeze winter and sum-

mer. A spring-loaded radiator cap keeps the entire system under about 14 pounds of pressure, which raises the boiling point of a 50/50 mixture of water and antifreeze from 226°F to 263°F. The freezing point of the same mixture would be −34°F. Antifreeze concentrations of up to 70 percent can be used, and they will produce boiling and freezing points of +274° and −85°F in a 14-pound pressurized system. More than 70 percent antifreeze will begin to raise the freezing point.

Today's engines run with a coolant temperature of about 220°F. The coolant warning light does not come on below 245°F, so you must have both a working radiator pressure cap and at least a 50 percent antifreeze mix to prevent boilover. The owner's manual should list the capacity of your car's cooling system in quarts. Antifreeze containers have charts showing how many quarts are needed for various freezing and boiling points. Do not add hard water to the radiator; its minerals can clog the system. Use distilled water.

Overheating

There are two basic causes of overheating: a mechanical fault that interferes with the operation of the cooling system, or simply too much heat for the cooling system to handle. The various mechanical faults are detailed in the troubleshooting chart on the opposite page. The service checks on the following pages tell how to find and fix these faults.

Sometimes an engine overheats simply because there is too much heat for it to dispose of. This usually happens during stop-and-go driving in hot weather. A temperature gauge can give you advance warning if you notice it creeping up from its normal level toward the danger zone. A warning light often will not go on until the radiator has already begun to boil over. If you are stuck in traffic, and other cars are boiling over, too, you are probably close to the danger point. Here is what to do to prevent overheating:

1. Shift into neutral and rev the engine at two to three times idle speed so that the fan will pull a greater volume of air through the radiator.

2. Leave at least 10 feet between your car and the one in front, so that its hot exhaust does not flow directly into your radiator.

3. Turn off the air conditioner. It pumps extra heat into the engine compartment.

4. As a last resort, turn the heater on *High*. It acts as a second radiator and will cool off the engine somewhat, though it may be a bit hard on you.

5. If possible, get off the crowded highway and onto a freely moving back route. If you can keep the car moving at moderate speed, it is unlikely to overheat.

6. *Do not* stop and shut off the engine. When you do that, the water pump stops operating but the engine continues to reject built-up heat, and it will almost certainly boil over. Drive until the engine cools somewhat before shutting it off.

If the engine does boil over, pull off the road and turn off the ignition. If you can open the hood without getting burned, do so. Wait 15 to 20 minutes, until the engine cools down. Being careful not to get burned, check for leaks, burst hoses, broken fan belts, or other obvious mechanical faults (see table opposite). If you find none, carefully open the radiator cap and check the coolant level. Refill the radiator with a 50/50 mixture of water and antifreeze, if available. If you must use plain water, check the mixture with a hydrometer as soon as possible and adjust it accordingly (see *Checking the system*, p.330).

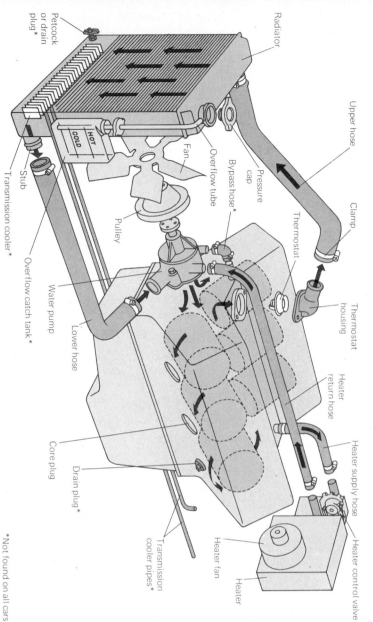

Radiator

Upper hose

Clamp

Thermostat

Thermostat housing

Heater return hose

Heater supply hose

Heater control valve

Heater fan

Heater

Transmission cooler pipes*

Drain plug*

Core plug

Lower hose

Water pump

Overflow catch tank*

Transmission cooler*

Stub

Petcock or drain plug*

Pulley

Bypass hose*

Overflow tube

Pressure cap

Fan

COLD HOT

*Not found on all cars

Types of clamps

Worm/screw clamp is the type carried by most auto parts stores. Vibration can loosen it in time.

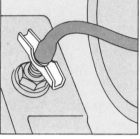
Screw/tower clamp is hard to remove without damage. Can be replaced by same size worm/screw clamp.

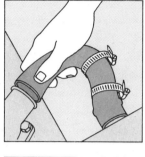
Spring clamp requires special pliers to remove and install. It may lose tension over the years.

Twin-wire screw clamp needs periodic tightening, but overtightening can cut into hose—be careful.

Replacing a hose

There are at least four hoses in every cooling system: two to the radiator and two to the heater. Some water pumps also have a short external bypass hose, and some heater hoses take a detour to a coolant-operated carburetor choke. All of these hoses should be checked at least twice a year for cracks, brittleness, swelling, or mushiness. If any of these conditions exist, replace the hose with one designed for your car make and model. Take along the old hose when buying a new one. Some carmakers recommend replacing all hoses every two years to avoid the severe overheating and possible engine damage that a burst hose can cause. Check your owner's manual.

Drain radiator to below the level of the hose to be replaced. If coolant is clean and less than two years old, you can save and reuse it. Put a length of clean vacuum hose over radiator petcock and drain coolant into a clean basin.

Check hose by squeezing it firmly. It should be flexible but resilient. Replace brittle or mushy hose. Flex hose and look for hidden cracks. Check for leaks at hose clamps. Tighten or replace loose or damaged clamps.

Open the clamps and pull off the damaged hose. If it is stuck, slit the hose at several points, using a utility knife or hacksaw blade. Twist or peel the hose off gently to avoid damaging soft brass radiator tubes or soldered joints.

Clean metal pipes with emery cloth. Slip clamps onto hose before installing it. If hose is a tight fit, lubricate it with water or antifreeze only. Push hose home, position clamps ¼ in. from hose ends, and tighten. Replace coolant.

What can go wrong

HOW TO USE THIS CHART

Find problem at top of chart. Look down columns to locate possible causes. First, check out things you can fix yourself; then, things you may be able to fix yourself. If problem is still not cured, consult a competent mechanic.

○ You can fix it yourself.
● You may be able to make complete repair.
■ You need a mechanic.

Engine overheats	Repeated coolant loss	Engine warms up slowly	Heater does not work	Poor air conditioning	POSSIBLE CAUSE	CURE
○					Low coolant level	Check for leaks and refill system (p.330)
●					Cooling system clogged	Drain and flush (p.330) or have radiator repaired
○					Loose or broken fan belt	Tighten or replace belt (p.334)
●					Thermostat stuck closed	Check, replace thermostat (p.331)
		●	●		Thermostat stuck open	Check, replace thermostat (p.331)
		●	●		Thermostat missing	Install proper thermostat (p.331)
○					Insufficient antifreeze	Adjust antifreeze concentration (p.330)
○					Debris on radiator	Hose off debris (p.330)
■					Faulty water pump	Have water pump replaced
■					Collapsed water hose	Locate and replace hose (pp. 329, 330)
■					Leaking cylinder head gasket	Have gasket replaced
○					Late ignition timing	Adjust timing to specifications
○					Exhaust system blocked	Replace damaged parts (p.351)
●					Oil or grease in coolant	Flush system (p.331); have oil leak traced
○					Carburetor mixture too lean	Adjust carburetor to specifications
○					Pre-ignition, or pinging	Use higher octane gasoline
	○				Faulty or incorrect radiator cap	Check, replace with proper cap (p.329)
	○				Leak in radiator, hose, or block	Find and fix leak (p.330), refill system
			●		Clogged heater core	Drain and flush (p.331) or replace core
			■		Faulty heater control valve	Have heater control valve checked
				●	Low refrigerant charge	Recharge system, check for leaks (p.331)
				○	Loose or broken belt	Tighten or replace compressor belt (p.334)

How the radiator cap works

Expanding coolant is allowed to escape at a preset pressure by spring-loaded outlet valve. When coolant contracts, air (or liquid from overflow tank) is drawn back through inlet valve.

Pressure rating · Inlet valve · Outlet valve · CLOSE

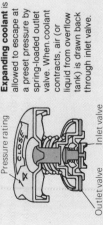
Hold rag over a hot cap and turn 45° to first stop. Let steam run out of overflow tube. Press cap down, open to next stop, and remove. Replace with a cap listed for your car model.

Overflow tube

Checking the system

At least twice a year, and before going on long trips, check the cooling system. Also inspect it if the engine has overheated or if the temperature gauge is running abnormally high. First, check the coolant level in the radiator. If it is low, add a 50/50 mixture of antifreeze and water. If you must use water only, check the concentration later with a hydrometer (Step 2), and adjust it by draining some coolant from the radiator and replacing it with straight antifreeze. Run the engine to mix the coolant, then recheck the concentration. Check hoses and clamps as shown on page 329. Leaks are easy to spot because antifreeze is brightly colored.

Caution: Antifreeze is sweet tasting but poisonous. Keep it well out of the reach of children. Funnels, hoses, and containers used to handle antifreeze should never be used for anything else.

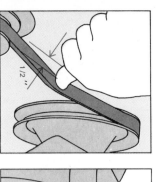

1. Overflow tank shows safe coolant level if the overflow tube is not blocked. Best way to check level is to open cap. Liquid should cover tubes inside or reach level marked.

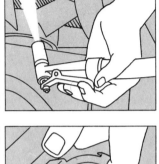

2. Check antifreeze protection with dicate a leak. Stop-leak compound hydrometer and add more if needed. Some hydrometers use floating balls to show freezing point. Others use a floating degree scale.

3. White deposits on radiator indicate a leak. Stop-leak compound (sold at gas stations) may temporarily cure a minor leak until you can have the radiator fixed.

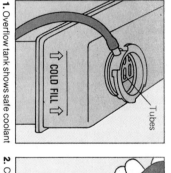

4. Check for leaks or the engine block wherever two components are bolted together. Also check core plugs near the bottom of the engine. Have a mechanic fix such leaks.

5. Check fan belt for cracks and for proper tension. Press belt; if it flexes more than ½ inch, it is loose and may be slipping. Tighten or replace belt (p.334).

6. Check radiator to be sure it is not clogged with insects, leaves, or paper. If it is, clean it off by spraying it from the back, using a garden hose at high pressure.

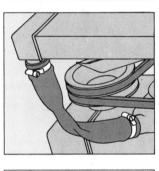

7. Remove radiator cap and run a finger around the inside of the filler neck. If it is covered with rust or greasy deposits, the cooling system needs flushing (p.331).

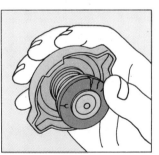

8. Replace the cap and run the engine at a fairly high speed. If the lower radiator hose flattens out, the spring inside it has collapsed, and the hose must be replaced.

9. Stop the engine and open radiator cap (p.329). If there is no gush of air, or if the rubber gasket is cracked, replace the cap with a new one designed for your car model.

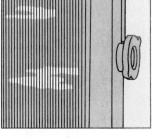

10. Run a finger under the water pump housing, behind fan, to check for leaks. A small amount of seepage is normal, but a steady leak means pump must be replaced.

How to change antifreeze

Drain the cooling system every two years, flush it, and add enough antifreeze to give a 50/50 mixture (see your owner's manual for cooling system capacity). On most cars the engine drain plugs are inaccessible, and you will be able to drain only the radiator. Some cars have no radiator petcock or drain plug; remove lower hose to drain radiator on these models. Before starting, set the heater to *Hot*. After adding fresh antifreeze and water, run the engine until the thermostat opens (the upper radiator hose will become warm to the touch). Shut off the engine, carefully open the radiator cap, and check the coolant level. Refill as needed.

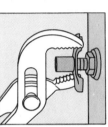
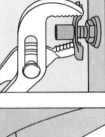

1. Remove radiator cap, then drain the radiator by opening the petcock or drain plug at the bottom.

2. If you can, remove the engine block drain plug. Replace it before flushing or adding antifreeze.

3. Remove heater supply hose and insert a garden hose. Flush until clear water runs from radiator.

Heater supply hose — Garden hose

4. Drain water, close petcock, replace hose, and add enough antifreeze to make a 50/50 mixture.

Funnel

5. Squeeze upper radiator hose to force out air. Fill radiator, install cap, run engine to mix coolant.

Installing and using a flushing T

On most cars, the engine drain plug cannot be opened and you must force the old coolant out of the engine by backflushing. Fitting a flushing T to the heater supply hose makes this job easier. The heater supply hose is the one that runs to the engine block or carburetor manifold, not the one that runs to the water pump. The T should be placed so that water escaping from it cannot soak the alternator. Flushing with fresh water alone may not remove heavy buildups of grease or corrosion. In such cases, use a one-step, fast-flushing agent, sold in auto parts stores. Then, replace the anti-freeze. On most cars, you cannot drain 50 percent of the coolant without opening the cap on the flushing T. Leave the cap off as you add antifreeze.

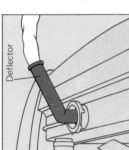

Cap T when water turns color.

Drain water from radiator. Close petcock and add antifreeze. It will force enough water out the T to allow a 50/50 mixture in most cars.

Garden hose

Heater supply hose

Install deflector. Run water until it exits deflector clear (about five minutes). Run engine while flushing air conditioned car; then, shut off.

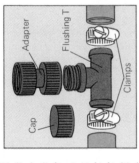

Adapter

Flushing T

Cap

Clamps

To flush system, attach garden hose to T, using adapter. Set heater controls inside car to *Hot*. Remove radiator cap and open petcock.

Flushing T's come in three sizes, to match inside diameters of heater hoses. To find yours, measure outside diameter and subtract ⅜ in.

How to test and replace a thermostat

On most cars, the thermostat is located inside a cast-iron housing where the upper radiator hose meets the engine block. (On the Ford V-6, it is at the engine end of the lower radiator hose.) Your thermostat is designed to open at a specific temperature, which is marked on it. If a thermostat gets stuck in the closed position, the engine will overheat. If it sticks while open, the engine will warm up slowly and the heater will not provide much warmth. Test a thermostat you believe defective before discarding it. You will need a candy thermometer, sold in housewares stores. Replace a bad thermostat with one that has the same temperature rating. First, drain about half the coolant from the radiator and save it if it can be used again. (For instructions on saving and reusing coolant, see *Replacing a hose*, p.329.)

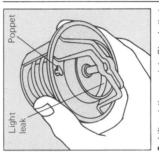

Poppet

Light leak

2. Lift out thermostat. Check that bleed poppet is free to jiggle. Hold thermostat to a bright light. No light must show past closed valve.

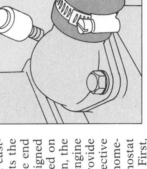

Suspend in water

Candy thermometer

3. Test thermostat on kitchen stove. Valve should start to open within 5° of temperature marked on it. If not, replace the thermostat.

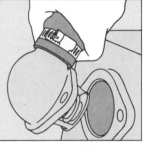

1. Remove the bolts holding the thermostat housing to the engine. If it sticks in place, tap the housing with hammer; do not pry under it.

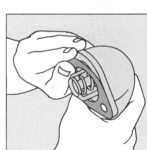

4. Remove any bits of old gasket from engine, housing, and recessed lip. Use a putty knife; a screwdriver or chisel will damage the surface.

Air conditioner recharge kits

The air conditioner contains compressed freon gas. Some freon will escape in time, and the air conditioner will lose its effectiveness. You can replace lost freon with a recharge kit, but only if the leak is not too bad. Check the freon level at the sight glass—a metal block with a small window in it. It is often found at the top of the dryer, but it may be located at a hose junction elsewhere in the system. (Some late model systems do not have sight glasses.) Clean off the sight glass, start the engine, and set the air conditioner to *Maximum Cold*. If you see nothing in the sight glass after 10 minutes, the system is either full or completely empty. (If it is empty, it will not cool at all.) Light foaming means you can use the kit, but if more than one can of freon is needed the leak is bad enough to require professional attention. Heavy foam or nothing but oil streaks indicate a major leak—see a mechanic.

How different freon levels appear in the sight glass:

Light foam, minor leak.

No bubbles, system OK.

Oil streaks, system empty.

Heavy foam, major leak.

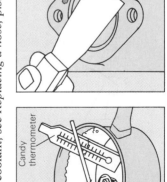

Compressor

Radiator

Hose to passenger compartment

Sight glass

Dryer

Condenser

5. Place thermostat in housing. Hold it in place with a self-adhesive gasket. Line up holes in housing and gasket, then press down firmly.

6. Refit the housing. The end of the thermostat with the springs goes into the engine. Some thermostats have one edge marked *Front*.

Electrical system

How it works

Your home has a double-wire electrical system. Current flows out to lights and appliances through one wire and returns through a second, making the complete circuit needed for electricity to flow. Your car uses a single wire system to supply current from the battery to the various lights and accessories. One terminal of the battery is connected, or grounded, to the car body, and each bulb or accessory is grounded, to the body as well. So the car body serves as the return wire for the entire electrical system.

A burned-out bulb, motor, or fuse; a faulty switch; or any loose connection will result in an incomplete circuit, and the component served by that circuit will not work. Chafed or loose wires may cause a short circuit in which the electricity returns to the battery via the car body before it can reach the bulb or accessory. A blown fuse is often the sign of a short elsewhere in the circuit, in which case new fuses will blow as soon as they are installed. You can check electrical circuits with a simple test light, as shown at the right. The various wires are bundled into a protective harness, but they are color coded so that you can pick out the same wire at either end of the harness. A schematic wiring diagram—available from the car dealer or manufacturer—shows every wire in the car, its color, where it comes from, and where it goes.

What can go wrong

	Alternator warning light on	Taillights or headlights very dim	One light not working	Turn signals flash on one side only	Turn signals do not flash at all	Windshield wipers do not work	Windshield washers do not work	Brake lights do not work	Brake lights stay on	Clock does not work	Taillights or headlights flicker	POSSIBLE CAUSE	CURE
		○	○									Lights dirty	Wash with soap and water
	○	○										Battery discharged	Test battery; recharge or replace (pp.334–335)
	○	○										Alternator belt slipping	Check and adjust belt tension (p.334)
	●	●										Alternator belt broken	Replace broken or missing belt (p.334)
	●	●										Defective voltage regulator	Have regulator tested, repaired, or replaced
	●	●										Defective alternator	Have alternator tested, repaired, or replaced
			●	●				●			●	Bulb burned out	Replace bulb (p.333)
	●	●	●	●	●	●	●	●	●	●	●	Faulty wiring	Test and repair wiring (pp.332–333)
	○		○		○	○	○	○		○		Fuse blown	Replace fuse (pp.332–333)
				■	■							Faulty flasher unit	Test, replace flasher unit (pp.332–333)
			■		■	■	■	■	■			Defective switch	Test, replace switch (pp.332–333)
						●	●					Faulty electric motor	Test, replace motor or entire unit (pp.332–333)
							●					Clogged lines; faulty pump	Unclog lines or replace pump (p.321)

HOW TO USE THIS CHART

Find problem at top of chart. Look down columns to locate possible causes. First, check out things you can fix yourself; then, things you may be able to fix yourself. If problem is still not cured, consult a competent mechanic.

○ You can fix it yourself.
● You may be able to make complete repair.
■ You need a mechanic.

Typical single-wire circuit

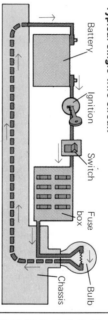

Battery · Ignition · Switch · Fuse box · Bulb · Chassis

Tracing electrical faults

When a light or electrical accessory fails to work, the cause may be a burned-out bulb or motor, a melted fuse, a short or bad connection in the wiring, or a faulty switch. If the battery has gone dead, none of the car's electrical equipment will work, including the starter. If the starter works but nothing else will, a fusible link has melted because of a massive overload. Have it fixed by a car dealer or by a shop that specializes in auto electrical systems.

If only one component does not work, check the fuse box, located under the dashboard or the hood. Replace any blown fuses. If the fuses are OK, check any bulbs or flasher units involved. The turn signals and hazard warning lights each have their own flasher units. They may be located under the dash or under the hood. It is a good idea to locate yours before it goes bad by turning on the flasher and tracking down its clicking noise. Remove a suspect flasher and perform Circuit test 1 (p.333). Flashers, light bulbs, and fuses all have model numbers or amp ratings marked on them. Use only exact duplicates as replacements.

Next, turn on the ignition switch but do not start the engine. Remove the wires from the back of the switch that controls the nonworking unit and touch them together (Circuit tests 2 and 3). If the unit then works, the switch is bad. Replace it with a duplicate, available from your car dealer or a junkyard.

If the bulbs, fuses, and switches are good, check the wiring with a 12-volt circuit tester. Attach the tester's clip to a good, clean ground on the chassis or engine. Switch on the ignition and the unit being tested, then proceed with Circuit tests 4 to 7. If there is no current at the supply line, trace back as much of the supply wiring as possible. Look for chafing where the wire passes through metal clips and holes in the bodywork. Wrap chafed wiring in electrical tape. Test at both sides of all plugs and connectors. If a connector is not passing current, open it and clean its contacts with emery cloth. Cut out any length of wire that will not pass current, and solder in a new length.

If there is power at the unit, disassemble and clean all ground connections between the unit and the chassis, including the sockets on bulbs. Some units are grounded internally, through their mounting bolts. Remove the unit and clean corrosion from all mounting holes, then refit the unit and test it again.

If no fault can be found, it is likely that the unit itself is bad and must be repaired or replaced.

Types of fuses

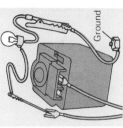

Glass tube fuses | Ceramic fuses | New GM plug-in fuse

Good Blown Blown

Good Blown

Good

Replacing a fuse

Ceramic fuses are easily replaced by hand, but you need a fuse puller for the glass tube type. Do not pry fuses out with a screwdriver; it may cause a short. If replacement fuse blows, test wiring for a short circuit.

North American cars use glass tube fuses; some imports use ceramic fuses. If all circuits go dead, a fusible link has melted. To replace the type shown, you must replace the entire battery cable.

Fusible link

Cable

How to make a test light

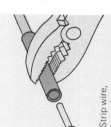

Solder here

You can buy an automotive circuit tester or make one from a 12-volt single filament auto bulb and holder, two 12-in. lengths of auto wire, an alligator clip, and a straight pin. Connect the clip to the center of the bulb holder. Solder the second wire to the outside of the holder and to the pin.

How to replace a bulb

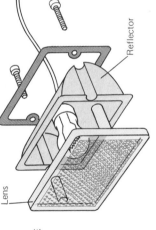

Reflector

Lens

Two wires

Twin filament bulb

Gasket

Lens

Offset locking tabs engage slots in socket

If there are bolts through the lens, remove bolts, lens, and gasket. Push in bulb, turn counterclockwise, re-move. Buy a new bulb (model number is on base); push it in; rotate clockwise to lock; install lens, gasket.

To reach some bulbs, you must remove the entire light unit. Unbolt unit from rear (reach behind fender or inside trunk), pull unit out, separate lens from reflector, and replace bulb as shown in previous step.

Headlight replacement

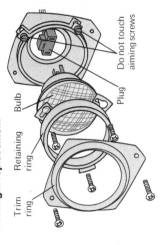

Trim ring

Retaining ring

Bulb

Plug

Do not touch aiming screws

Reflector

Single filament bulb

Holder

Socket

Parallel locking tabs

Single wire

Remove the trim ring, then loosen the three screws that hold the retaining ring. Do not touch the two aiming screws or the lights will have to be adjusted at a garage. Unplug faulty light and install a new one.

On some models, the bulb holder can be pulled from the back of the light assembly. Push on holder, turn it counterclockwise, and pull it out. Replace bulb and reinstall holder. Always clean corrosion from sockets.

Circuit tests

Plug

Test wire

Flasher

1. Unplug flasher and insert a U-shaped wire into plug. With ignition on, try the turn signals both ways. If all bulbs light, replace bad flasher.

2. To test a switch, find and remove the wires behind the dash that lead to it. Touch wires together. If unit then works, replace bad switch.

Plug

3. Test switches with plug-in connectors as shown in Test No. 1. If you cannot reach the back of the switch, it may pull out of the dash from the front.

Test wire

Ground

4. With the inoperative unit switched on, pull off the power supply wire and check it with the tester. If tester does not light, check the wiring.

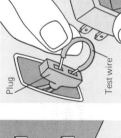

Wiring harness

5. Trace the wire back from faulty unit. Pierce it before and after every connector. If tester lights on one side only, open and clean connector.

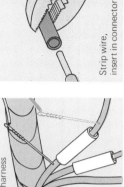

Strip wire, insert in connector

6. If the cleaned connector still will not pass current, cut it out and splice the wires with a crimp-on connector or by soldering them.

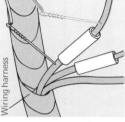

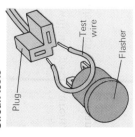

Ground

7. If the nonworking unit has a separate ground wire, check it as shown. If the tester does not light, clean ground connection and test again.

Electrical system

How to adjust and replace drive belts

The rubber drive belts on an engine operate the fan, water pump, power steering pump, air conditioning compressor, and air injection pump. One or more belts may be used for these various accessories. Check the belts every few months. If they are cracked, brittle, or stained with grease, replace them with exact duplicates. If they are loose, tighten them. Accessories are generally secured by bolts that pass through elongated holes. By loosening the bolts and repositioning the accessories, you can change the belt tension. A belt that is too tight will cause rapid wear of the accessory bearings. A belt that is too loose will slip, and the accessory will not work properly. A loose belt may also squeal. A slipping or broken alternator/fan belt will lead to a dead battery and engine overheating. To replace a belt, move its accessory toward the engine and force the belt over the pulleys. To replace the belt nearest the engine, you must first remove any other belts in front of it. Any time a belt is installed, its tension must be adjusted. Make all checks and adjustments with the engine off.

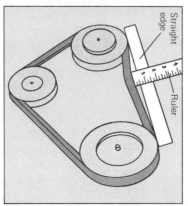

Straight edge — Ruler

Mechanics use special tools to measure belt tension, but you can make a rough judgment by pressing down on the belt midway on its longest span between pulleys. If the belt deflects more than ½ in., it is too loose.

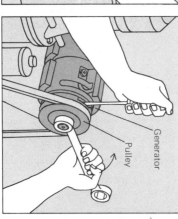

Loosen inboard bolts

Check the belt condition by twisting it and inspecting its underside. If it is cracked, glazed, or grease stained, replace it. If the belt has not stretched, it will help to bring it along when buying a replacement.

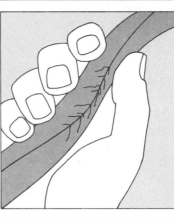

To adjust belt tension, loosen the bolts that hold the accessory and pry it away from the engine with a jack handle. When the tension is correct, tighten the bolts while you continue to apply pressure to the accessory.

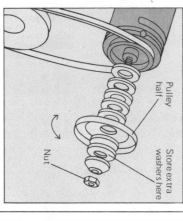

Generator / Pulley

To adjust belt tension on Volkswagen Beetles, remove some washers from between the pulley halves to increase belt tension; add washers to lessen tension. Replace belt, outer pulley half, and extra washers. Then, replace and tighten center nut. Recheck tension.

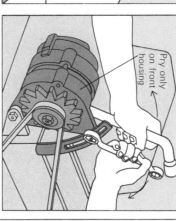

Pry only on front housing

To adjust belt tension on Volkswagen Beetles, add or remove washers between the halves of the split pulley. Turn engine over until slot in pulley is at the top. Wedge a screwdriver into the slot to hold pulley still, and remove nut.

Pulley half / Store extra washers here / Nut

Some accessories may have right-angle mounting brackets. To tighten the belt, loosen the inboard bolts and tighten the outer nut to draw the accessory outward. When belt tension is correct, tighten the inboard bolts.

Battery maintenance

A car battery converts chemical action into electrical current. It is recharged by the alternator, whenever the engine is running. A device called a voltage regulator keeps the battery from being overcharged. A battery that seems to be completely dead can often be recharged at a gas station in an hour, or overnight at home with a trickle charger (p.335). A hydrometer test (p.335) will tell you if the battery can be recharged.

When replacing a battery, always buy one at least as powerful as the one that came with your car. In cold areas, you may want a more powerful model. At 0°F a battery has less than half the cranking power it would have at 80°F. A battery too weak to start a car on a cold morning may recover later in the day.

Caution: Batteries can be dangerous to handle or work on. They are filled with sulfuric acid, which can eat through clothing and burn flesh. In use, they may produce explosive hydrogen gas. Never smoke or cause a spark near an auto battery. Always wear heavy outer garments, rubber gloves, and industrial safety goggles when working on a car battery. If battery acid gets on your skin or into your eyes, flush with cold water for 15 minutes. Get medical attention immediately.

How to replace the battery

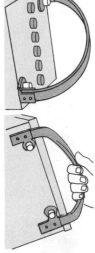

The safest way to move a heavy car battery is with a lifting strap, designed for batteries with terminals on top (left) or on the side (right). Use strap to remove old battery, and install new one. Replace clamps, cables, and fusible links (if any).

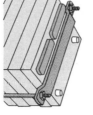

Remove hold-down clamps that keep the battery from bouncing around. Before you can open them you may have to remove rust with a wire brush and apply penetrating oil. If they are badly corroded, buy replacements. Tighten and clean clamps periodically.

Battery maintenance procedures

Types of terminal clamps

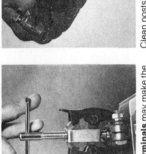

The battery supplies electricity to the car through heavy cables that are clamped to its terminals. Most cars have soft lead bolt-on clamps.

Cables of newer General Motors cars are bolted into terminals on the side of the battery. Remove them with a wrench.

Cleaning terminals and clamps

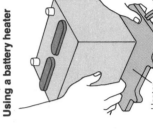

Older General Motors cars use squeeze-type terminal clamps. To remove battery cables, squeeze lugs with pliers, twist, and lift off.

You need not replace the cable if only its clamp is damaged. Cut off clamp, strip off ¾ in. of insulation, and bolt on a replacement clamp.

Corroded terminals may make the engine hard to start. Remove clamp to clean it. You may need a special puller for badly corroded clamps.

Clean posts and clamps with a wire brush until they shine. Refit clamps and coat them with white grease or petroleum jelly to stop corrosion.

Checking battery condition with a hydrometer

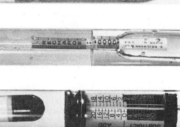

A battery hydrometer measures the specific gravity of the acid and water solution inside a car battery. Squeeze the bulb and draw up enough fluid to float the scale inside. Return the fluid to the same cell it was drawn into. Test all six cells and write down the results. A fully charged battery will read 1.265, a half-charged battery 1.220, and a dead battery 1.180. If the readings between any two cells vary by more than .050, replace the battery. If the readings are closer than .050, the battery can be recharged.

Read the hydrometer scale at the point where the fluid meets the float. Do not let acid drip on you or the car. The best hydrometers have a built-in thermometer for temperature corrections (far left). Less accurate types are marked *Full Charge, Half Charge,* and *Dead* (center). They do not allow cell-to-cell comparison of specific gravity. The least expensive models indicate the state of charge with a number of floating colored balls (right).

How to recharge a battery

A dead battery that passes the hydrometer test (left) can be recharged overnight with a trickle charger. Add water to the battery if needed (see *Checking fluid level,* below). Leave the vent caps off and connect the red charger wire to the positive battery terminal (the fatter of the two—it may be marked + or *Pos*) and the black wire to the negative terminal. Then, plug in the charger and switch it on. Charge until the meter reading drops to 1 amp. You must calculate charging time for models without meters (see instructions). Unplug charger before removing clips to avoid sparks. Replace vent caps.

Checking fluid level

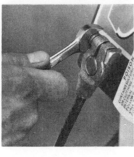

Once a month, check the level of fluid in all six battery cells. It should cover the metal plates inside and come to within ¼ in. of the bottom of the filler hole. Use a pocket mirror for cells you cannot otherwise see into.

Add distilled water to battery cells that are low. Use a small funnel or the special dispenser shown. Do not add water in freezing weather unless car will be driven a few miles afterwards. Wipe top of battery dry after filling.

Cleaning the battery

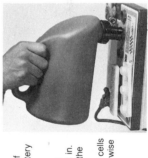

Dirt and water on the battery top can let current trickle away. Plug vent holes with tape or toothpicks, then scrub the battery with a mixture of baking soda and water. Rinse well and wipe dry. Unplug vent holes.

Using a battery heater

Heater

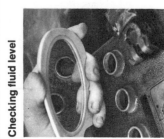

A battery heater may give a weakened battery enough power to start the engine on a cold morning. Place the heater under the battery and plug it into an electrical outlet overnight. A 100-watt droplight can do the same job.

Engine

How it works

It is not necessary to understand exactly how a complex automobile engine works in order to make simple repairs on it or to do routine tuneup work. The theory and practice of internal combustion engines is beyond the scope of this book. Essentially, an automobile engine operates like a multicylinder version of the single-cylinder lawn mower engine; see *The four-cycle (four-stroke) engine*, p.370. The carburetor mixes air and gasoline in the proper proportions, the mixture is drawn into the cylinders by the pumplike action of the pistons, and is then ignited by spark plugs. The resulting explosive combustion forces one piston at a time down its cylinder bore and turns the crankshaft. Other pistons, also connected to the crankshaft, are moved up and down their cylinders in turn. Details vary from car to car, but the major parts of a typical V-8 engine are shown in the illustration at right.

Modern automobile engines have from 4 to 12 cylinders, depending on how much power they are designed to produce. The arrangement of these cylinders determines the placement of accessories, such as carburetors, exhaust manifolds, distributors, and spark plugs. Five popular arrangements are shown below. Other versions, such as the V-4, V-12, and in-line 5-cylinder engines, do exist, but they are not common.

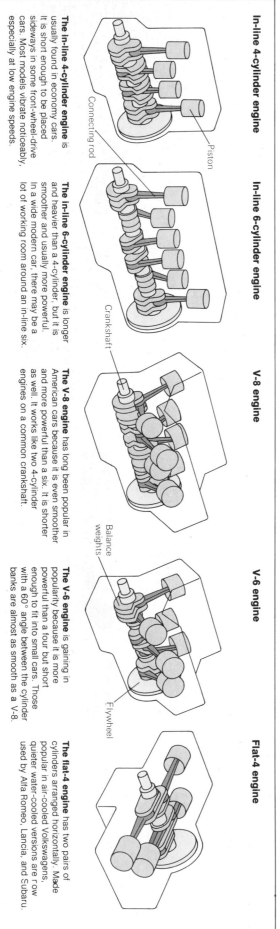

In-line 4-cylinder engine

Piston

Connecting rod

The in-line 4-cylinder engine is usually found in economy cars. It is short enough to be placed sideways in some front-wheel-drive cars. Most models vibrate noticeably, especially at low engine speeds.

In-line 6-cylinder engine

Crankshaft

The in-line 6-cylinder engine is longer and heavier than a 4-cylinder, but it is smoother and usually more powerful. In a wide modern car, there may be a lot of working room around an in-line six.

V-8 engine

Balance weights

The V-8 engine has long been popular in American cars because it is even smoother and more powerful than a six. It is shorter with a 90° angle between the cylinder banks are almost as smooth as a V-8.

V-6 engine

Flywheel

The V-6 engine is gaining in popularity because it is more powerful than a four but short enough to fit into small cars. Those with a 60° angle between the cylinder banks are almost as smooth as a V-8.

Flat-4 engine

The flat-4 engine has two pairs of cylinders arranged horizontally. Made popular in air-cooled Volkswagens, quieter water-cooled versions are now used by Alfa Romeo, Lancia, and Subaru.

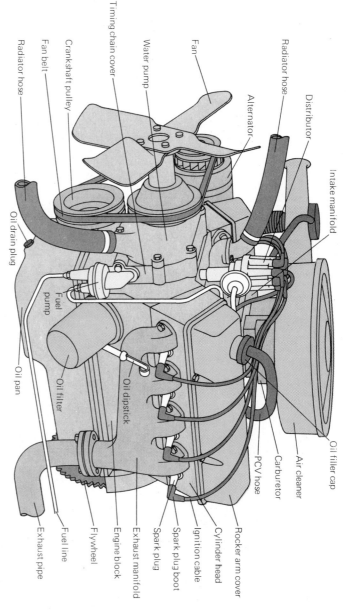

Radiator hose

Fan belt

Crankshaft pulley

Timing chain cover

Water pump

Fan

Alternator

Radiator hose

Distributor

Intake manifold

Oil filler cap

Air cleaner

Carburetor

PCV hose

Cylinder head

Rocker arm cover

Spark plug boot

Spark plug

Ignition cable

Engine block

Exhaust manifold

Flywheel

Exhaust pipe

Fuel line

Oil pan

Oil dipstick

Oil filter

Fuel pump

Oil drain plug

What can go wrong

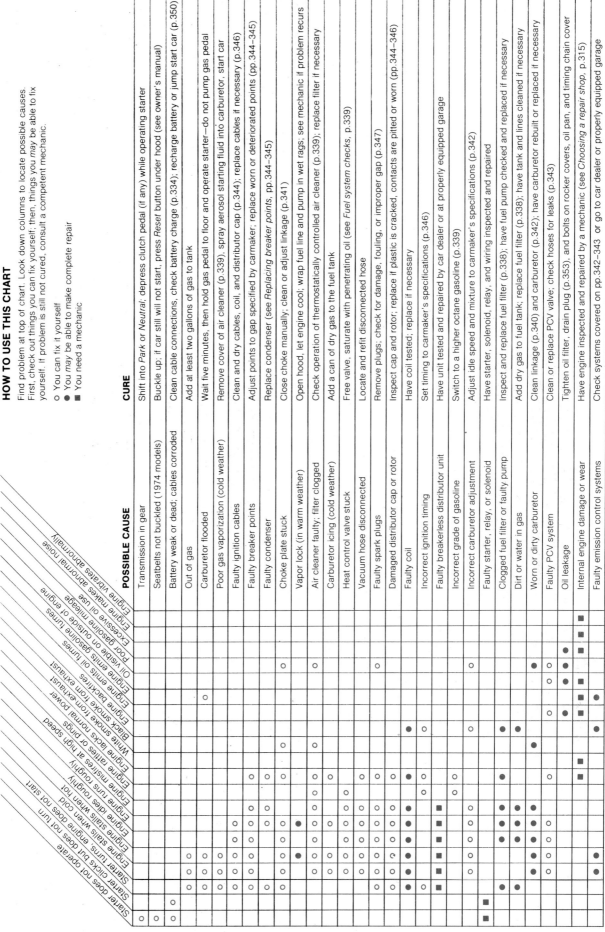

HOW TO USE THIS CHART

Find problem at top of chart. Look down columns to locate possible causes. First, check out things you can fix yourself; then, things you *may* be able to fix yourself. If problem is still not cured, consult a competent mechanic.

- o You can fix it yourself
- ● You *may* be able to make complete repair
- ■ You need a mechanic

POSSIBLE CAUSE	CURE	Starter does not operate	Starter clicks but engine does not turn	Starter turns, engine does not start	Engine stalls when cold	Engine idles roughly when hot	Engine runs roughly	Engine misfires roughly	Engine rattles or pings	Engine lacks normal power	White smoke from exhaust	Black smoke from exhaust	Engine backfires	Engine emits oil fumes	Oil visible on outside of engine	Poor gasoline mileage	Excessive oil use	Engine makes abnormal noise	Engine vibrates abnormally
Transmission in gear	Shift into *Park* or *Neutral*; depress clutch pedal (if any) while operating starter	o																	
Seatbelts not buckled (1974 models)	Buckle up; if car still will not start, press *Reset* button under hood (see owner's manual)	o																	
Battery weak or dead; cables corroded	Clean cable connections, check battery charge (p.334); recharge battery or jump start car (p.350)	o	o	o															
Out of gas	Add at least two gallons of gas to tank			o															
Carburetor flooded	Wait five minutes, then hold gas pedal to floor and operate starter—do not pump gas pedal			o									o						
Poor gas vaporization (cold weather)	Remove cover of air cleaner (p.339), spray aerosol starting fluid into carburetor, start car			o	o														
Faulty ignition cables	Clean and dry cables, coil, and distributor cap (p.344); replace cables if necessary (p.346)			o		o	o	o											
Faulty breaker points	Adjust points to gap specified by carmaker; replace worn or deteriorated points (pp.344–345)			o		o	o	o											
Faulty condenser	Replace condenser (see *Replacing breaker points*, pp.344–345)			o			o	o											
Choke plate stuck	Close choke manually; clean or adjust linkage (p.341)				o	o	o	o				o							
Vapor lock (in warm weather)	Open hood, let engine cool; wrap fuel line and pump in wet rags; see mechanic if problem recurs			o			●	●											
Air cleaner faulty; filter clogged	Check operation of thermostatically controlled air cleaner (p.339); replace filter if necessary					o	o	o		o		o				o			
Carburetor icing (cold weather)	Add a can of dry gas to the fuel tank				o		o	o											
Heat control valve stuck	Free valve, saturate with penetrating oil (see *Fuel system checks*, p.339)					o	o	o											
Vacuum hose disconnected	Locate and refit disconnected hose					o	o	o								o			
Faulty spark plugs	Remove plugs; check for damage, fouling, or improper gap (p.347)					o	o	o	o										
Damaged distributor cap or rotor	Inspect cap and rotor; replace if plastic is cracked, contacts are pitted or worn (pp.344–346)					●	●	●											
Faulty coil	Have coil tested; replace if necessary						●	●		●									
Incorrect ignition timing	Set timing to carmaker's specifications (p.346)			o			o	o	o	o			o						
Faulty breakerless distributor unit	Have unit tested and repaired by car dealer or at properly equipped garage			■			■	■											
Incorrect grade of gasoline	Switch to a higher octane gasoline (p.339)								o										
Incorrect carburetor adjustment	Adjust idle speed and mixture to carmaker's specifications (p.342)				o	o	o			o		o				o			
Faulty starter, relay, or solenoid	Have starter, solenoid, relay, and wiring inspected and repaired	■	■																
Clogged fuel filter or faulty fuel pump	Inspect and replace fuel filter (p.338); have fuel pump checked and replaced if necessary			●			●	●		●						●			
Dirt or water in gas	Add dry gas to fuel tank; replace fuel filter (p.338); have tank and lines cleaned if necessary			●			●	●		●						●			
Worn or dirty carburetor	Clean linkage (p.340) and carburetor (p.342); have carburetor rebuilt or replaced if necessary					●				●		●				●			
Faulty PCV system	Clean or replace PCV valve; check hoses for leaks (p.343)					o	o				o			o			●		
Oil leakage	Tighten oil filter, drain plug (p.353), and bolts on rocker covers, oil pan, and timing chain cover														●		●		
Internal engine damage or wear	Have engine inspected and repaired by a mechanic (see *Choosing a repair shop*, p.315)								■	■	■			■			■	■	
Faulty emission control systems	Check systems covered on pp.342–343 or go to car dealer or properly equipped garage									●		●				●			●

337

Engine

The fuel system

The fuel system consists of the carburetor, the fuel tank, the fuel pump, the lines connecting them, and filters for fuel and air. On cars built since 1971, there is also an evaporative emission control system consisting of a charcoal filter and a canister that stores gasoline vapors. Hoses lead from it to the fuel tank and carburetor. Some have filters that should be changed every 12,000 miles. On other models (notably Ford), the entire canister is scheduled for replacement every 25,000 miles, but since it is an expensive part (nearly $50), you probably would not replace the canister unless it were completely clogged and emitting strong gasoline odors. Also, check the canister hoses for cracks and deterioration.

Fuel and air filters should be checked once a year and replaced if they are clogged. A clogged fuel filter can cause stalling, hard starting, and misfiring. A clogged air filter can cause stalling, hard starting, less than normal gas mileage, and, in extreme cases, black smoke emission from the exhaust.

A worn fuel pump may cause the engine to miss at high speeds or to backfire. If the pump fails, the engine will not run. Very hot weather may cause the fuel to vaporize in the fuel lines or pump, leading to stalling, hard starting, and rough running. To correct the problem, allow the engine to cool down, or apply wet rags to the pump and lines until the engine can be started.

Caution: Allow the engine to cool completely before disconnecting any fuel or vapor line. Do not spray solvents, starting fluid, or other flammable chemicals at or near a hot engine. Never smoke or cause an electrical spark while working on the fuel system. Never work in an enclosed area without ample ventilation. Gasoline vapors are highly explosive; exhaust fumes are poisonous. Keep doors between the garage and living quarters or furnace room closed. If gasoline gets onto your skin, wash it off as soon as possible

Changing fuel filters

All modern fuel systems are equipped with a filter. It may be a fine screen built into the carburetor or the fuel pump, or a pleated paper filter housed in a canister in the fuel line or fuel pump. The in-line filter is easiest to spot; look for it in the engine compartment, between the fuel pump and carburetor. If there is no in-line filter, and the fuel line is attached to the carburetor by a large nut, there may be a filter or screen behind the nut. If a screen clogs often, discard it and splice a larger capacity paper filter into the fuel line (kits are sold in auto parts stores). If the filter is not in the carburetor or fuel line, it is in the fuel pump. Volkswagen pumps have an internal screen. Others have spin-on filter canisters.

In-line filters are replaced as a unit. Use hose-clamp pliers to open the spring clamps, then pull filter out of hose. Push new filter canister into hose ends and reposition the clamps. Some filters are marked to show installation position.

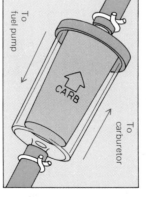

Use an open-end wrench to loosen the nut that holds the fuel line to the carburetor. Save all washers, gaskets, and springs not supplied with the replacement filter. Reinstall all components in their original order.

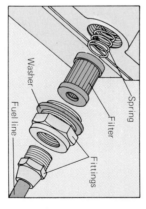

Older-model cars have a screen or paper filter in the fuel pump itself. Clamp fuel line (or lines) closed near pump, then remove housing and replace filter. You need a special strap wrench to remove spin-on filter cartridges.

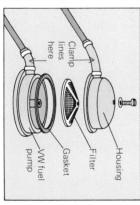

Labels (diagram, clockwise)

Vapor separator

Fuel filler and cap

Access plate to fuel gauge sending unit

Vapor return line

Vapor collection lines

Charcoal canister stores fuel vapors until engine is started, then returns them to the intake manifold. Vapors are drawn into the engine and burned

Do not allow vapor lines to sag, or liquid fuel may condense in the low spots. This may lead to a strong gasoline odor when starting the engine or to difficult starting when the engine is hot

Fuel line

Fuel tank

Engine

Fuel pump

Air cleaner

Carburetor

Fuel filter

Intake manifold

Exhaust manifold

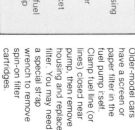

Clamp lines here

Housing

Filter

Gasket

VW fuel pump

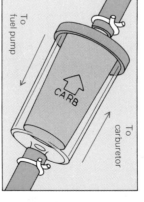

To fuel pump

CARB

To carburetor

Washer

Spring

Filter

Fuel line

Fittings

Air cleaner service

The air cleaner is not the simple bolt-on filter it once was. On today's smog-controlled cars, it is a complex housing containing two filters plus thermostatically and vacuum-controlled valves. The major filter is the circular air filter. Replace it as recommended in your owner's manual (usually every two years), or whenever it becomes so blackened that you cannot see light through it when a droplet is held against its inner surface. A clogged air filter can cause hard starting, stalling, low gasoline mileage, and black smoke from the exhaust. You can dislodge some dirt from a clogged filter by striking it sharply against a flat surface. Replace the PCV filter and check hoses annually.

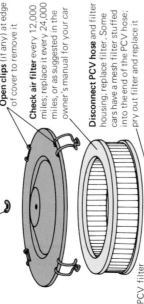

Open wing nut for access to air filter; do not overtighten wing nut

Open clips (if any) at edge of cover to remove it

Check air filter every 12,000 miles; replace it every 24,000 miles, or as suggested in the owner's manual for your car

Disconnect PCV hose and filter housing; replace filter. Some cars have a mesh filter stuffed into the end of the PCV hose; pry out filter and replace it

A cold heat sensing valve should open slightly when heated with a hair dryer; if it does not open, replace it

Open clamp (if any) to pull heat hose from metal duct atop exhaust manifold

Heat hose

Damper flap should close when a cold engine is first started, then open slowly as engine warms up; if it binds, free it with carburetor and choke solvent.

PCV filter and housing

PCV hose

Replace vacuum hoses that have cracked, split, or deteriorated.

Vacuum motor should close damper flap when a cold engine is started, open flap when vacuum hose is disconnected. If flap does not move, check hoses for blocks or leaks. Replace motor if hoses are OK.

To remove entire air cleaner, open wingnut and disconnect all hoses.

Fuel system checks

Not all fuel system problems are caused by the carburetor itself. Tighten the carburetor hold-down bolts periodically. If they loosen repeatedly, remove them one at a time, apply a liquid thread-locking compound, and reinstall them. Heat-control valves often stick open or shut. A closed valve can overheat both the engine and spark plugs (see p.347); an open valve will waste fuel and cause slow engine warmup, carburetor icing, and spark plug fouling. If the valve shaft will not turn, free it with solvent. On vacuum-controlled models, also check for vacuum before and after the control switch. Start engine, open hose connections, and feel for suction. Replace defective hoses, diaphragm, or switch.

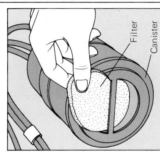

Filter

Canister

Replace the filter in the evaporative emission control canister every 12,000 miles. Replace leaking hoses or a clogged canister if a strong gasoline odor develops.

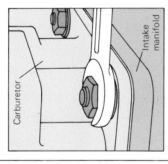

Carburetor

Intake manifold

If the engine runs roughly and idles hesitantly, check the carburetor hold-down bolts. Loose bolts will let in excess air and upset the air-fuel mixture; tighten bolts.

Gasoline, octane, and pinging

Although the combustion that occurs inside an engine is said to be explosive, the gasoline vapors do not really explode; they should burn rapidly but smoothly. Abnormal combustion may cause the engine to rattle or ping. There are three causes of pinging. On rare occasions, a hot carbon deposit will ignite the gas vapors before the spark plug fires; add a chemical upper cylinder cleaner to the gasoline. If the pinging does not stop, the cylinder head must be removed and the carbon deposits scraped away.

More often, pinging results from incorrect ignition timing or the use of gasoline that has too low an octane rating. It often occurs only when the car is accelerating or climbing a steep hill.

If your engine is pinging, check the ignition timing first (p.346). If it is correct, check the octane ratings of various brands and try a higher octane gasoline, if one is available for your car. This may be difficult for cars restricted to nonleaded gasoline. If you cannot buy a higher octane gas, retard the timing 1 degree at a time until the pinging disappears. This will also lower the car's performance.

There are two systems for measuring gasoline octane: the Research Method and the Motor Method. Your owner's manual will probably specify a certain Research Octane Number (RON) gasoline for your car. Federal law requires that an average of the Research and Motor ratings be posted on all gasoline pumps in the U.S. This average number is about four points lower than the Research number, and can be confusing. The table below compares the two systems. As a car gets older, deposits inside the cylinders may, at first, raise the compression ratio of the engine and, therefore, its octane requirement. As time passes and the engine parts wear, the compression and octane requirement may drop, allowing you to use lower octane gasoline.

If neither adjusting the timing nor switching to a higher octane gasoline eliminates the pinging, try a chemical upper cylinder cleaner. If that fails, see a mechanic. Do not continue to drive a car that pings—engine damage may result.

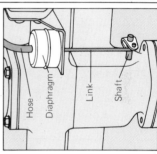

Hose

Diaphragm

Link

Shaft

Some heat control valves have an external link to a vacuum diaphragm. Check link for movement when engine is started; check vacuum hose for leaks; free valve shaft.

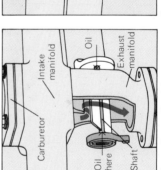

Intake manifold

Oil

Exhaust manifold

Carburetor

Oil here

Shaft

On self-contained heat control valves, free a sticking shaft by soaking it with penetrating oil when engine is cold and tapping lightly on manifold and shaft with a hammer.

Octane rating systems

Federal octane	87	88	89	90	91	92	93	94	95	96
Research octane	91	92	93	94	95	96	97	98	99	100

Engine

The carburetor

The carburetor mixes air and gasoline in the needed proportions for different driving conditions. Starting up on a cold morning may call for a mixture as rich as 7 parts of air for each part of gasoline; cruising at a slow, steady speed may call for a mixture as lean as 18 parts of air for each part of gasoline. To do all this and still not violate current antipollution laws, the carburetor must be an extremely complex apparatus. Although it is complex, the carburetor is also comparatively durable. Its parts do not wear out as quickly, or need adjustment as often as those in the ignition system. When the engine runs poorly or refuses to start, the fault is probably in the ignition system, not in the carburetor. Therefore, you should check the ignition system thoroughly (see pp.344-347) before attempting to make any carburetor adjustments.

Specifications for the various carburetor settings are printed on a decal located in the engine compartment of every new car sold in the U.S. since 1970 (see p.348). More detailed specifications and instructions are printed in shop service manuals (available from auto dealers) or in specialized mechanic's repair manuals (often available in public libraries). Professional auto parts stores should also be able to supply tuneup and adjustment specifications for your car.

Over the years, moving parts on the carburetor become worn, passages become blocked by sediment, and gaskets and diaphragms deteriorate. When these things happen, the carburetor can no longer be properly adjusted; it must be cleaned and rebuilt, or replaced.

One barrel carburetor

Two barrel carburetor

Four barrel carburetor

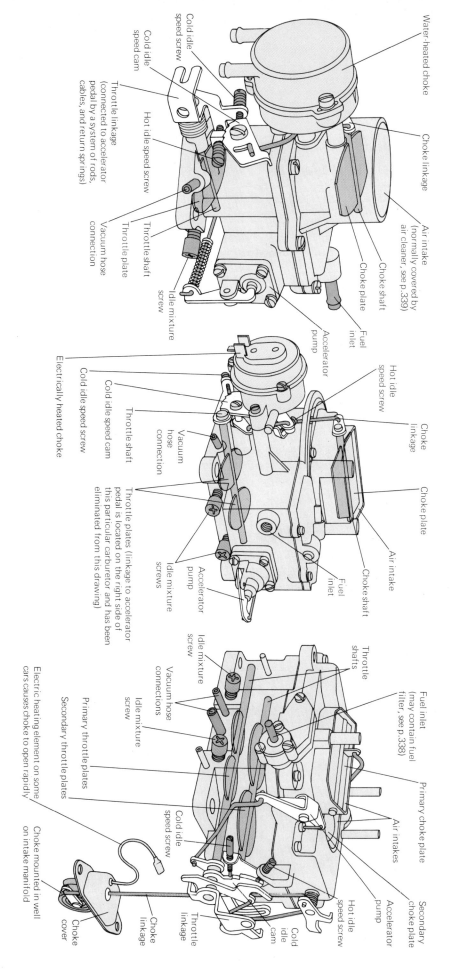

One barrel carburetor:
- Water-heated choke
- Choke linkage
- Cold idle speed screw
- Cold idle speed screw
- Cold idle speed cam
- Hot idle speed screw
- Throttle linkage (connected to accelerator pedal by a system of rods, cables, and return springs)
- Vacuum hose connection
- Throttle plate
- Throttle shaft
- Idle mixture screw
- Air intake (normally covered by air cleaner, see p.339)
- Choke shaft
- Choke plate
- Fuel inlet
- Accelerator pump

Two barrel carburetor:
- Hot idle speed screw
- Choke linkage
- Choke plate
- Air intake
- Choke shaft
- Fuel inlet
- Accelerator pump
- Idle mixture screws
- Throttle plates (linkage to accelerator pedal is located on the right side of this particular carburetor and has been eliminated from this drawing)
- Throttle shaft
- Vacuum hose connection
- Cold idle speed cam
- Cold idle speed screw
- Electrically heated choke

Four barrel carburetor:
- Idle mixture screw
- Vacuum hose connections
- Idle mixture screw
- Primary throttle plates
- Secondary throttle plates
- Electric heating element on some cars causes choke to open rapidly
- Choke mounted in well on intake manifold
- Choke cover
- Choke linkage
- Throttle linkage
- Cold idle cam
- Cold idle speed screw
- Hot idle speed screw
- Accelerator pump
- Air intakes
- Secondary choke plate
- Primary choke plate
- Fuel inlet (may contain fuel filter, see p.338)
- Throttle shafts

Adjusting the choke

Most cars have an automatic choke, which slowly opens as the engine warms up. Tap the accelerator pedal when the engine is cold; the choke should close up completely. When the engine is started, the choke should open just a crack. After from one to five minutes of engine operation, it should be completely open (vertical). A sticking choke plate or linkage is a common cause of hard starting; you can free them with an aerosol carburetor and choke solvent. The choke plate is operated by a bimetallic spring that responds to temperature changes by either curling up or unwinding. The tension of this spring can be adjusted, and this adjustment determines to what extent the choke plate opens or closes. The adjusting mechanism has a series of index marks labeled *Rich* and *Lean* (or *R* and *L*). The carmaker's choke-setting specifications may say "Index" (the center mark), or "Two Notches Lean" (two marks off center toward the side marked *L*), etc. As the bimetallic spring weakens with age, you may have to ignore the index marks and adjust the spring so that the choke closes completely when the engine is cold.

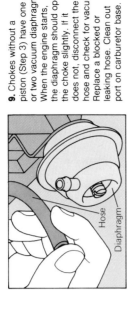

Choke plate
Linkage

1. Remove the air cleaner (p.339) to observe choke operation. With the engine cold (after sitting overnight), tap the gas pedal once. The choke plate should close fully. If it does not, spray choke linkage and shaft with solvent until they can be moved freely.

Pointer
Index marks

5. Rotate the choke housing to the proper index mark. Jiggle the throttle to engage the fast idle cam. Choke plate should close tight. Rotate the housing until plate closes, then tighten three screws. If plate will not close, replace spring/housing unit.

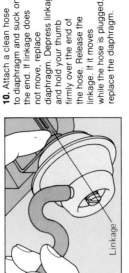

Hose
Diaphragm

9. Chokes without a piston (Step 3) have one or two vacuum diaphragms. When the engine starts, the diaphragm should open the choke slightly. If it does not, disconnect the hose and check for vacuum. Replace a blocked or leaking hose. Clean out port on carburetor base.

Housing
Gasket
Heat tube

2. Loosen the three screws on a carburetor-mounted choke; remove the bimetallic spring housing. If there are carbon deposits inside the housing, replace the cover gasket and check the heat tube for exhaust leaks. Replace a suspect heat tube.

Link
Cover
Choke well

6. If there is no obvious choke mounted on the carburetor, wiggle the choke plate to identify its linkage. Follow the long link down to its well on the intake manifold. Open the bolts so that the bimetallic spring can be lifted from its well.

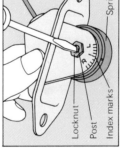

Linkage

10. Attach a clean hose to diaphragm and suck on the end. If linkage does not move, replace diaphragm. Depress linkage and hold your thumb firmly over the end of the hose. Release the linkage. If it moves while the hose is plugged, replace the diaphragm.

Cylinder
Arm
Piston

3. If the arm that the bimetallic spring engages is attached to a vacuum-operated piston, be sure the piston moves freely. If not, remove the arm and piston. Clean the piston and its cylinder thoroughly with solvent. Reinstall arm and piston; recheck for binding.

Spring
Locknut
Post
Index marks

7. Lift the choke from its well and clean the spring with solvent. Loosen the locknut and turn the post with a screwdriver until the index marks are set to the carmaker's specs. Tighten locknut and reinstall choke in well.

Look for spark here

11. Some chokes have an electrically heated element. To test them, start the engine, pull off the wire, and touch it to the contact. If it does not spark, trace wiring for shorts (p.332). If wiring is sound but choke does not open within four minutes, replace unit.

Arm
Spring

4. Clean the bimetallic spring with solvent and reassemble choke. If there is more than one slot on the control arm, engage the spring in whichever slot will close the choke plate completely when the choke housing is set to the proper index mark.

Bend link to change its length

8. If the choke plate does not close tight when the engine is cold, open the well and reset the choke. If you run out of adjustment, try to close the choke by bending the connecting link. If the link then scrapes the well cover, replace choke unit and link.

Water hoses

12. Some chokes have a water-heated element. When the three retaining screws are loosened, the entire element can be cleaned and adjusted like any other carburetor-mounted choke (Steps 2–5). Check that water hoses are not kinked, blocked, or damaged (p.329).

Engine

Adjusting idle speed

Once the choke is operating properly (p.341), you can adjust the carburetor to the carmaker's specifications for hot and cold idle speed. Both are adjusted by spring-loaded screws in the throttle linkage, near the base of the carburetor. With the engine warmed up and the choke completely open, attach a tachometer and adjust the hot idle speed against the hot idle speed screw according to the instructions (p.348) and set the hot idle speed. Some manufacturers ask that idle speed be set with the transmission in gear, the air conditioner on, etc. Check with a service manual. Set the cold idle speed after positioning the cold idle screw against the proper step on the cold idle cam. (Note: Some manuals refer to cold idle speed as "fast idle speed," and to hot idle speed as "slow idle speed" or "curb idle speed.")

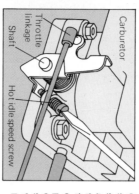

Carburetor · Throttle linkage · Shaft · Hot idle speed screw

On most cars, hot idle speed is adjusted by a screw that bears against a flange on the swiveling throttle shaft. Turning the screw in or out opens or closes the throttle plate slightly, thereby changing engine idle speed. It should be done with the air cleaner in place.

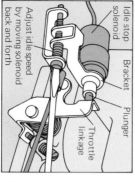

Idle stop solenoid · Bracket · Plunger · Throttle linkage

Many newer cars have an idle stop solenoid (see *Correcting dieseling,* p.343). On such cars, idle speed is adjusted by moving the solenoid back and forth on its bracket, or by adjusting a nut at the tip of the plunger. Fords may have separate idle speed and solenoid adjuster screws.

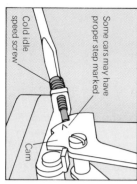

Cold idle speed screw · Cam · Some cars may have proper step marked

Remove air cleaner, pull back the throttle linkage, close the choke plate by hand, and place the cold idle speed screw against the step on the cold idle cam that is specified in shop manual. Turn screw until engine idles at specified cold idle speed (sometimes called fast idle speed).

Adjusting idle mixture

It is seldom necessary to adjust the idle mixture, unless the engine will not idle smoothly at the specified hot engine idle speed. Cars built since 1968 have plastic caps over the fuel mixture screws to limit their movement. These caps also help to identify the idle mixture screws. Single barrel carburetors have one screw; two and four barrel carburetors have two screws. Adjust them until the engine idles as smoothly as possible. Then, replace the air cleaner and recheck the hot idle speed. Reset it if necessary. Mixture adjustment on some late model cars requires sophisticated equipment and procedures, and should only be attempted by a professional mechanic who has the proper equipment. See the shop manual for your car.

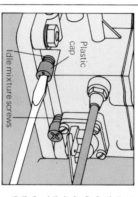

Plastic cap · Idle mixture screws

Locate the idle mixture screws, which are at the very bottom of the carburetor and covered by colored plastic caps. Adjust the screws one at a time to achieve the smoothest idle possible. This adjustment may change the hot idle speed, so recheck it with the tachometer.

Emission controls

Since 1963, new cars sold in the U.S. have been equipped with a growing array of devices designed to reduce the emission of various air pollutants. These devices vary from car to car and from year to year, as the antipollution laws have become progressively stricter. Some of these devices are built into the engine to prevent tampering. Others are external, and must be checked or adjusted periodically to keep the engine in proper tune. Those listed here can be checked, at least partially, by the car owner—if they are found on his car. Others require special tools and instruments to make adjustments and should only be serviced by a trained mechanic. Most pollution controls tend to make routine servicing more challenging than it used to be.

Carburetor cleaning

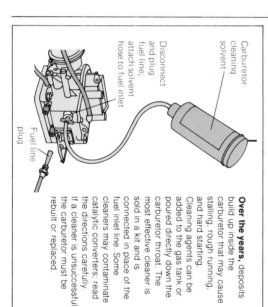

Carburetor cleaning solvent · Disconnect and plug fuel line; attach solvent hose to fuel inlet · Fuel line plug

Over the years, deposits build up inside the carburetor that may cause stalling, rough running, and hard starting. Cleaning agents can be added to the gas tank or poured directly down the carburetor throat. The most effective cleaner is sold in a kit and is connected in place of the fuel inlet line. Some cleaners may contaminate catalytic converters; read the directions carefully. If a cleaner is unsuccessful, the carburetor must be rebuilt or replaced.

EGR valve service

An exhaust gas recirculation (EGR) system is used on many cars built since 1973. It has a vacuum-controlled valve that feeds small amounts of exhaust gas into the intake manifold. The gas lowers the temperature of the combustion inside the cylinder and reduces the emission of nitrogen oxide. Locate the EGR valve and check its operation every 12,000 miles. If the EGR valve sticks open, poor performance and fuel waste will result. If it sticks shut, it is not doing its intended job. On many EGR valves, the stem is exposed and you can check it to see if it is free. If the stem cannot be moved, unbolt the valve from the engine and clean the valve stem and seat with a wire brush. If the stem still cannot be freed, then replace the valve itself.

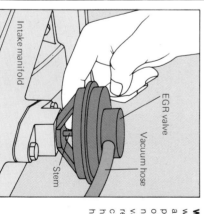

Intake manifold · EGR valve · Vacuum hose · Stem

With the engine warm and idling, have a helper tap the gas pedal. If the stem of the EGR valve does not move, unbolt valve and clean or replace it. Also, check all vacuum hoses for cracks, holes, or blockage.

Correcting dieseling

An engine that continues to run and stumble after the ignition is turned off is said to diesel. To prevent this problem, some cars have an idle-stop solenoid incorporated into the throttle linkage (see *Adjusting idle speed*, p.342). Not every solenoid mounted on a carburetor is an idle-stop solenoid. To determine if a solenoid is indeed an idle-stop model, have a helper hold the gas pedal to the floor and turn the ignition switch on and off (he need not start the engine). If the solenoid's plunger extends and retracts, it is an idle-stop unit. If the plunger does not move, the solenoid serves some other purpose.

To check the operation of an idle-stop solenoid, have a helper start the engine, then depress the gas pedal slightly. The solenoid plunger should extend to touch the throttle linkage. At idle, the plunger should remain in contact with the linkage. Shut off the engine: The plunger should retract, allowing the throttle to close a bit more and causing the engine to stall. If the idle speed is properly set and the solenoid does not stall the engine, replace the solenoid. Dieseling can also be caused by overheating, the use of low octane gasoline, carbon deposits in the cylinders, or incorrect timing or dwell settings (see pp.345–347).

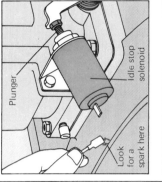

To check solenoid action, observe the solenoid while a helper turns the engine on and off. The solenoid plunger should operate as described above. With the ignition on, pull off the solenoid wire and touch it to the engine block. If it does not spark, trace wiring for a short (p.332).

Plunger — Look for a spark here — Idle stop solenoid

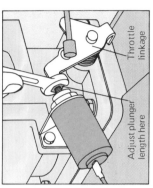

Once the solenoid plunger is operating, adjust its length to achieve the correct hot idle speed (see opposite page). If plunger operates erratically and the wiring is OK, replace the solenoid. Adjust idle speed after replacing solenoid.

Throttle linkage — Adjust plunger length here

PCV system service

The positive crankcase ventilation (PCV) system first appeared on 1961 models sold in California and on 1963 models sold elsewhere. It collects exhaust gases that have escaped past the pistons and into the crankcase, and routes them back to the intake manifold, where they are sucked back into the cylinders and burned. The system has a valve that may become clogged, causing a slow or rough idle, oil dilution, stalling, and loss of power. Check the PCV valve, filter (p.339), and hoses at least twice a year. Most manufacturers recommend replacing the PCV valve at every tuneup. A clogged valve can be freed with special solvent, but replacing it is faster. The valve is located in a hose that runs from the rocker cover or oil filler to the intake manifold.

PCV filter is inside air cleaner — Air inlet hose — Breather cap — Air cleaner — Carburetor base — Rocker covers — PCV hose — PCV valve — Mount — Intake manifold

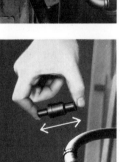

1. Start engine and let it warm up. Pull PCV valve from its mount. If valve and hose are working properly, you may hear a hissing sound and will feel moderate suction at the valve inlet.

2. If there is no noise or suction, remove the valve and shake it; a good valve will click, a clogged one will not. If there is no suction at the hose end, check the hose for blockage or leaks.

3. Reassemble PCV system. Remove air inlet hose and hold a 3- x 5-in. index card to opening. If card is not pulled against hose opening after a few minutes, either the hose or breather cap is clogged.

4. Remove oil breather cap and oil filler from the engine and inspect them carefully. If they contain filters, wash them with a petroleum base solvent and shake dry. Reinstall caps and hoses.

Antistall dashpot adjustment

Cars with automatic transmissions have been equipped with antistall dashpots since the 1950's. Although the dashpot looks a bit like a vacuum diaphragm (see p.341–Step 9), it is a self-contained unit with no hoses attached. It has a plunger that bears against a flange in the throttle linkage and prevents the throttle from snapping shut suddenly if the accelerator pedal is released after wide-open operation. If your car stalls when it comes to a halt after high speed driving or a burst of acceleration, suspect the dashpot. With the engine warmed up and idling at the specified speed, push the dashpot plunger against its spring until it stops. It should clear the throttle linkage by about 1/16 (.062) inch. If stalling continues, reduce clearance to about 1/32 (.032) inch. If the throttle takes a dangerously long time to close, increase clearance to 3/32 (.094) inch.

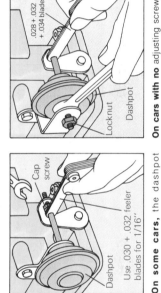

.028 + .032 + .034 blades — Locknut — Dashpot

On cars with no adjusting screw, the entire dashpot is moved back and forth. Open locknut and turn the dashpot on its threaded mounting shaft. When adjustment is correct, retighten locknut.

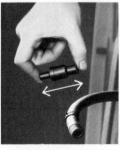

Cap screw — Use .030 + .032 feeler blades for 1/16" — Dashpot

On some cars, the dashpot plunger bears against a cap screw in the throttle linkage. Open locknut (if any) and adjust clearance by threading screw in or out. Tighten locknut when job is done.

Engine

The ignition system

The ignition system supplies high voltage to the spark plugs at the proper moment (when the piston is near the top of its compression stroke—see p.370) to explode the air-fuel mixture in each cylinder. The heart of the system is the distributor. Each time the breaker points in the distributor are opened, the 12-volt electricity flowing through the coil is stepped up to 20,000 volts or more. This high voltage is returned to the center of the distributor cap by a heavy cable. A rotor, spinning just under the cap, distributes this current, in proper sequence, to a series of heavy cables. One cable leads to each spark plug. When the current reaches the plug, it jumps a gap between two small prongs (see p.347), igniting the fuel mixture in the cylinder. The current then returns to the battery through the engine block and frame, completing the circuit. This high voltage will seek the path of least resistance back to the battery. If the ignition cables, distributor cap, or coil are cracked, wet, or dirty, current may leak out of them, causing a weak spark or no spark at all. Loose or corroded connections in the system will have the same effect. If you experience starting or stalling problems, clean and dry all the cables and spray them with a waterproofing silicone aerosol. Pull each cable from its terminal (one at a time, to prevent mixups), use a penknife or wire brush to remove any corrosion, then push the cables firmly home. If the system becomes soaked with rainwater, it may not work. Dry the cables, the top of the coil, and the inside of the distributor cap with a dry, lint-free towel or a special water-repelling spray made for this purpose and sold in auto parts stores.

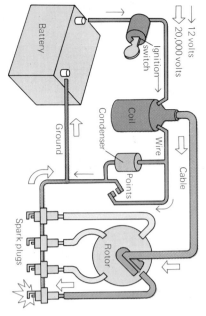

12 volts
20,000 volts

Battery
Ignition switch
Ground
Coil
Condenser
Wire
Points
Cable
Spark plugs
Rotor

Checking the distributor

Remove dirt, moisture, and corrosion from distributor cap, inside and outside. Replace cap if it is cracked or has carbon tracks between metal contacts

Replace cap if metal contacts inside are badly pitted, eroded, or burned (black or blue color)

Replace cap if carbon contact at its center is worn flush with the rest of the cap

Replace rotor if metal contact is badly burned. Push up spring so that it touches carbon contact

Replace condenser and points if metal has transferred between the points to form a small mound and crater

Replace point set if the breaker points are worn or burned. Clean, file, and regap discolored points

Rotate baseplate assembly in the direction opposite to shaft rotation, then release it. If plate does not snap back to its original position, replace vacuum advance diaphragm

Remove vacuum hose with the engine running and check for suction; clean hose if it is blocked, replace it if it is leaking

Low tension wire to coil

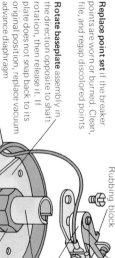

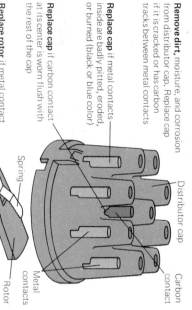

Distributor cap
Carbon contact
Spring
Rotor
Metal contacts
Condenser
Breaker points
Rubbing block
Leaf spring
Nut
Pivot
Base plate
Cam
Shaft
Housing
Spring clip
Vacuum advance diaphragm
Drive gear
Shaft

Replacing breaker points

American cars built since 1975 have an all-electronic ignition system with no breaker points to adjust or replace (Chrysler Corporation has used such a system since 1972). There are few adjustments you can make on breakerless distributors. You must go to your car dealer or a properly equipped garage for ignition work.

On a conventional breaker point ignition system, the points deteriorate with use. As the rubbing block wears, the critical point gap becomes smaller. Both conditions can lead to hard starting, stalling, rough running, loss of power, and increased fuel consumption. Bad or maladjusted points are the most common cause of starting trouble. Because the condenser is difficult to test, it is usually replaced at the same time as the points (every 12 months or 12,000 miles, or as recommended in your owner's manual). Specifications for the breaker point gap (Step 9) and dwell angle (Step 12) appear on the tuneup decal under the hood, and in service manuals. If the gap is correct, the dwell angle should be, too. If it does not meet specifications, shut off the engine and readjust the gap until the dwell reading is correct. The dwell angle is more important than the actual gap measurement. On General Motors cars, you can adjust the points only with the aid of a dwell meter (far right).

Combination point sets

GM "Uni-Set"
Chip
Chrysler "Sure Set"

Chrysler and General Motors now make all-in-one breaker point and condenser sets. The Chrysler set uses a ceramic chip instead of the traditional condenser and is available for many makes of car.

How to use a feeler gauge

Because the blades or wires of a feeler gauge differ by only thousandths of an inch, it is hard to tell when you have reached the specified gap. Mechanics use a go/no-go method. When the desired feeler blade or wire will slide into the gap with a light drag, but the next larger size will not fit without forcing, the gap is correct.

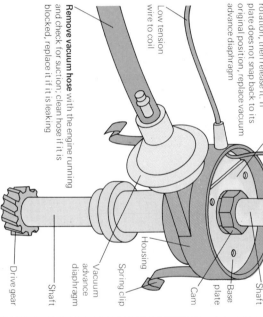

Replacing General Motors points

1. General Motors distributors are different from all others. Except for the steps shown here, the procedure is similar to that used on other cars. To remove General Motors distributor cap, press and turn spring-loaded clips. *Clip*

2. Inspect rotor spring and contact as you would any other (See Step 2 at left). To remove rotor, take out screws on either side.

3. Point set is held by two screws with lock washers. Coil and condenser wires fit between leaf spring and plastic clip. Points are preset to nearly correct gap. *Screwdriver* *Clip*

4. Skip Steps 8, 9, and 11 at left. Lubricate cam, refit cap, and attach dwell meter. Start engine, open window on cap, adjust dwell with an Allen wrench or special tool made for General Motors cars. Close window to keep out dirt, water. *GM tool*

---

4. Use a small wrench to remove the nuts that hold the condenser wire, coil wire, and leaf spring in place. Lay out all nuts and washers in order.

8. Mark a line on the distributor and engine, loosen the clamp bolt, and rotate the distributor until rubbing block rests on a high point of the cam. *Offset wrench* *Clamp bolt* *Chalk line*

12. Attach dwell/tachometer according to directions and read dwell angle. If it does not match specifications, readjust point gap until it does.

3. Open the points and inspect their mating surfaces. If they are pitted, discolored, or worn away, replace them. Pitting indicates a defective condenser. *Crater* *Pit*

7. Install new point set in the same manner as the old one. Do not tighten hold-down screw all the way. Attach leaf spring, coil, and condenser wires. *Fixed point* *Moving point*

11. If cam has a lubricating pad, do not grease cam; replace pad. Put two drops of oil onto other pad (if any) in center of shaft. Reinstall rotor and cap. *Pad* *Pad*

2. If cap is cracked or its contacts are burned, replace it (p.346). Pull rotor straight up to remove it. Replace it if spring is weak or contact is pitted.

6. Remove the screw that holds the condenser in place and use it to install new condenser. Use of an all-in-one point set will eliminate this step. *Screwdriver*

10. Reposition distributor so chalk marks are aligned, and tighten clamp bolt. Place a thin coat of grease (supplied with some points) on cam.

1. Open the clips on the sides of the distributor and lift off the cap. Twist it up and out of the way. Do not kink or remove the cables.

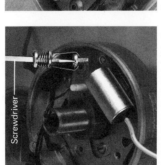

5. Remove the screw (or screws) holding breaker points in place and lift out the point set. Do not drop the screws; they may lodge in the distributor. *Point set*

9. Position the fixed point so that the specified feeler gauge can slide between the points with just a slight drag. Tighten hold-down screw. *Pry here to move fixed point*

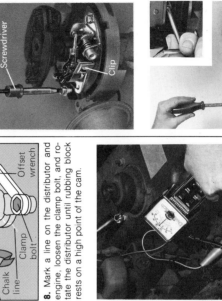

Engine

Setting ignition timing

Ignition timing determines exactly when the spark plug will fire. In most engines, it fires just before the piston reaches the top of its stroke. The correct timing is specified in degrees of crankshaft rotation *Before Top Dead Center* (a typical specification may read: 12° BTDC). Increasing this figure is called advancing the timing, and decreasing it is called retarding the timing. Although the timing figure is listed on the tuneup decal under the hood, it is wise to check with your dealer; specifications are sometimes changed after a car is sold. Use a timing light that is powered by the car battery, not household current; it is easier to use (see p.348). Timing that is too advanced may cause pinging. Retarded timing will cause a loss of power and overheating.

A common problem when using a timing light is parallax error—a faulty reading caused by not holding the light properly. The light must be in the same plane as the pulley, not ahead of it or behind it.

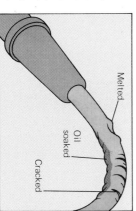

1. Attach timing light according to directions. Most are attached to both battery terminals and to an adapter placed between the distributor cap and No. 1 plug cable.

Adapter

2. Remove vacuum hose from diaphragm on the distributor, and plug the end with a blunt pencil or golf tee. Plug both hoses on distributors with two diaphragms.

Diaphragm

Hose

3. Locate the timing marks on the crankshaft pulley, low on the front of the engine. Draw a line in bright chalk along the pointer and the specified degree mark.

4. Attach a tachometer according to directions, start the engine, and let it warm up. If it does not idle at the specified speed, adjust the hot idle speed (p.342).

5. Aim the timing light at the crankshaft pulley and sight along it as you would a pistol. The chalk marks should appear stationary and should line up with one another.

Light

6. If the marks do not line up, loosen clamp bolt (use an offset wrench, if necessary) and rotate the distributor until the marks do line up. Retighten clamp bolt.

Typical timing marks

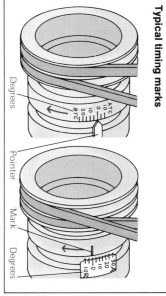

Degrees
Pointer
Mark
Degrees

The timing marks are found on the crankshaft pulley at the front of the engine. Several systems are used: The degrees may be marked on the pulley, and the engine block will have a mark or pointer; or the degree marks will be on the block with a mark or notch in the pulley. The degree numbers may be labeled *BTC* and *ATC* (Before and After Top Dead Center) or *A* and *R* (Advance and Retard). A zero means Top Dead Center.

How to find the No. 1 cylinder

In-line engines

Ford V-8's

AMC, Chrysler, most GM V-8's

The timing light should be attached to the No. 1 cylinder. This varies from car to car, and can be looked up in a shop manual. On some distributor caps, the cable leading to the No. 1 cylinder is marked "1." On 4- and 6-cylinder engines it is the forward cylinder on the passenger side of the car; on Ford V-8 engines it is the first cylinder on the driver's side.

Replacing the distributor cap and ignition cables

The trick to replacing a distributor cap is to transfer the ignition cables from the old to the new cap one at a time. Handle ignition cables carefully; if they are pulled or bent sharply, internal damage may occur. If you are replacing both the cables and the cap, install the new cap first and transfer the old cables to it. Then, replace the cables one at a time. The cables in the replacement set should be at least as long as those in the original. Lay out the new set and pick out the shortest cable. Remove the cable that seems to be the shortest from the engine. Put the new cable in its place. Repeat the process until all the cables have been replaced. If the engine backfires or runs very roughly, the cables have been mixed up; see a mechanic or a shop manual.

Melted
Oil soaked
Cracked

Inspect cables periodically. Replace them all if any one is cracked, burned, or oil soaked. Replace all cables every three years, in any case. Newer cars use radio-suppressed silicone cable.

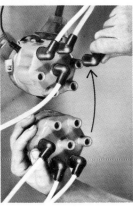

Replace cables one at a time to avoid mixups. Grasp the cable by the boot and pull it off with a slow, twisting action. Do not pull on or twist the cable itself, if it will be reused.

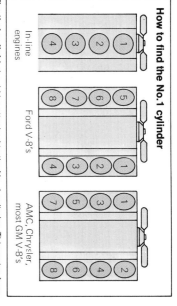

When replacing distributor caps, gently twist the old one out of the way and install the new one (most caps fit only one way). Transfer one cable at a time to its former position on cap.

Spark plug service

The spark plugs should be inspected and cleaned or replaced once a year. Cars that run on unleaded gas may get over 30,000 miles on a set of spark plugs. Cars using leaded gas may get only 10,000 to 15,000 miles. Inspect the plugs before buying replacements. Label the plug cables to prevent a mixup, or remove and reinstall one plug at a time. Pull cables only by their boots. The new plugs should be the same brand and model as those originally supplied with the car, or an equivalent model from a well-known manufacturer.

Constant high speed or stop-and-go driving may cause the plugs specified for your car to overheat or acquire deposits. If your plugs overheat, switch to a plug with a lower heat range. If your plugs acquire deposits, switch to a hotter plug. Engine malfunctions can cause the plug conditions shown below.

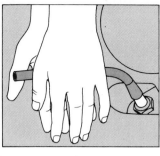

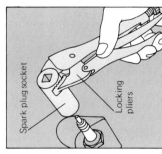

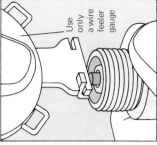

Cylinder head

Gasket

Tapered seat

Square seat

4. Slip a length of old ignition cable over plug and spin between palms to remove plug. Reverse the procedure to replace plug.

8. Screw plugs in by hand until they seat. Tighten plugs with gaskets an additional ¼ turn, tapered seat plugs 1/16 turn, using wrench.

Spark plug socket

Locking pliers

3. If plug is hard to reach, slip socket over plug first (remove rubber insert for added clearance), then loosen with locking pliers.

Use only a wire feeler gauge

7. Check the gap with a wire feeler gauge (see pp. 344, 382, 396). Bend outer electrode with tang on gauge to change the gap.

Ratchet wrench

Extension

U-joint

Spark plug socket

2. Use a ratchet wrench, a U-joint, and a spark plug socket with appropriate extensions (up to 18 in. long) to remove plugs.

Square off electrodes

6. When plugs dry, carefully open their side electrodes. File electrodes until surfaces are flat and edges sharp. Use a plug file.

Clothespins

1. Label the plug cables to prevent confusion. Number them from front to back; mark driver's side "D" and passenger's side "P."

Scrub off all deposits

5. If plugs can be reused, wash them with auto parts solvent and a stiff bristle brush (do not use a wire brush). Let plugs dry.

Terminal

Resistor

Metal shell

Gasket

Ceramic insulator

Center electrode

Side electrode

How to read spark plug condition

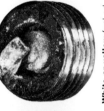

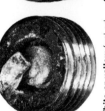

Melted electrodes result from pinging, intake manifold deposits, or crossed ignition cables. Fix car before driving.

Spots come from combustion chamber deposits that have melted and splashed plugs. Plugs may be cleaned, reused.

White or yellow fuel additive deposits are not as bad as they look. Scrape, clean, file, gap, and reuse such plugs.

Eroded electrodes and a dark, pitted insulator mark the end of a plug's useful life. They are the results of normal wear.

Eroded electrodes and blistered insulator result from overheating, faulty timing, lean fuel mixture, too high a heat range.

Dry black deposits are caused by too rich a fuel mixture, a clogged air cleaner, or plugs that are too cold for slow driving.

Oily black deposits may come from internal engine wear, or a leaking brake booster or transmission modulator.

Normal plug has brown to grayish-tan deposits and only slight electrode wear. It can be cleaned, gapped, and reused.

Engine

Tuneup procedures

Most cars need a tuneup once a year to keep them running smoothly and economically. The makers of some new models that have breakerless ignition systems and use unleaded gasoline claim their cars need tuneups only every 20,000 to 30,000 miles. Use your owner's manual and your common sense as a guide. If your car's engine runs roughly and is hard to start, and it has gone more than 12,000 miles since its last tuneup, it is probably due for another.

The definition of a tuneup varies from mechanic to mechanic. A good annual tuneup should include the following jobs, done in the order listed:

Check and clean or replace spark plugs (p.347).
Replace and adjust breaker points (p.344).
Replace condenser (p.345).
Check distributor for deterioration (p.344).
Check ignition cables for deterioration (p.346).
Check and adjust ignition timing (p.346).
Inspect and replace air filter (p.339).
Check air cleaner operation (p.339).
Replace PCV valve (p.343) and filter (p.339).
Replace fuel filter (p.339).
Check choke operation (p.341).
Check idle speed (p.342).
Check emission control components (pp.342-343).

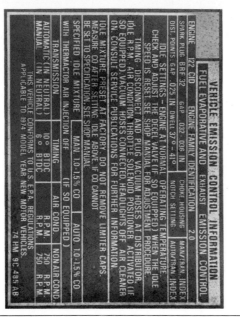

VEHICLE EMISSION CONTROL INFORMATION

ENGINE 12Z CID
SPARK PLUG BRF 32 GAP .032-.036 IN
DIST. POINTS 6AP .025 IN DWELL 37°-41°

FUEL EVAPORATIVE AND EXHAUST EMISSION CONTROL
ENGINE FAMILY IDENTIFICATION 2.0

CHOKE HOUSING NOTCH SETTING
MAN./TRANS. INDEX
AUTO./TRANS. INDEX

TRANSMISSION	TIMING	MAN. 1.0-1.5% CO AUTO. 1.0-1.5% CO (IF SO EQUIPPED)	R.P.M. AIR COND.	NON AIR COND.
AUTOMATIC (IN NEUTRAL)	10° BTDC		750 R.P.M.	750 R.P.M.
MANUAL (IN NEUTRAL)	10° BTDC			

IDLE SETTINGS - ENGINE AT NORMAL OPERATING TEMPERATURE (IF SO EQUIPPED) WHEN THE IDLE SPEED IS RESET SEE SHOP MANUAL FOR ADJUSTMENT PROCEDURE.

TIMING - DISCONNECT AND PLUG VACUUM HOSES AT DISTRIBUTOR. IF SO EQUIPPED. VACUUM HOSES CONNECTED, HEADLIGHTS OFF, AIR CLEANER ON. CONSULT SERVICE PUBLICATIONS FOR FURTHER INFORMATION.

IDLE R.P.M. - PRESET AT FACTORY, DO NOT REMOVE LIMITER CAPS.

IDLE MIXTURE - PRESET AT FACTORY. DO NOT REMOVE LIMITER CAPS. MEASURE CO AFTER SETTING IDLE ABOVE. IF CO CANNOT BE SET TO SPECIFICATION, SEE SHOP MANUAL.

SPECIFIED IDLE MIXTURE WITH THERMACTOR AIR INJECTION OFF

THIS VEHICLE CONFORMS TO U.S. EPA. REGULATIONS APPLICABLE TO 1974 MODEL YEAR NEW MOTOR VEHICLES.
'74 HM 9C 485 AB

Basic tuneup specifications are found on a plate or decal in the engine compartment of all cars sold in America since 1970. More detailed specifications and instructions are printed in service and repair manuals, which are available for reference in libraries or auto parts stores, and may also be purchased from the parts department of your car dealer.

Basic tuneup tools

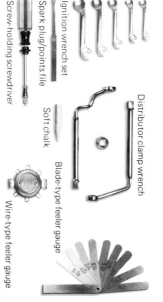

Screw-holding screwdriver · Ignition wrench set · Spark plug/points file · Distributor clamp wrench · Soft chalk · Blade-type feeler gauge · Wire-type feeler gauge · Dwell/tachometer · Timing light

How to use a dwell/tachometer

A combination dwell meter and tachometer is a basic tuneup instrument. Today's complex emission-controlled engines can no longer be tuned by ear. An accurate gauge is needed, but it need not be an expensive professional model built to take years of daily use. Check consumer publications for brand-by-brand tests of dwell/tachometers for accuracy and ease of use. The dwell/tachometer is hooked up as shown below. Get one that works on 8-, 6-, and 4-cylinder cars.

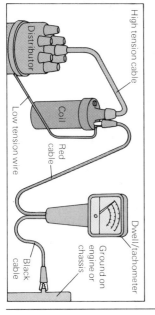

Distributor · Coil · High tension cable · Low tension wire · Red cable · Black cable · Dwell/tachometer · Ground on engine or chassis

How to use a timing light

There are two types of DC timing lights available. The least expensive is called a neon or stroboscopic light. It is connected directly to the Number 1 spark plug cable (see *Setting ignition timing*, p.346) and to a ground. It produces a fairly weak light, and you may not be able to see it unless you are working in a darkened garage. The xenon or powered timing light is more expensive, but it produces a strong flash that can be seen even in bright sunlight. It can also be had with a convenient inductive pickup that simply clamps around the spark plug cable.

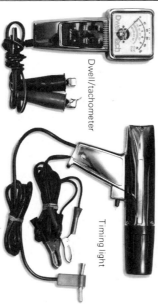

Fan · Timing marks · No. 1 plug cable · Distributor

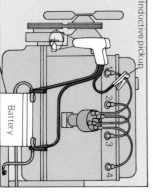

Battery

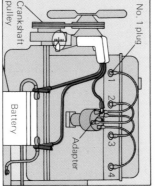

Crankshaft pulley · No. 1 plug · Adapter · Battery

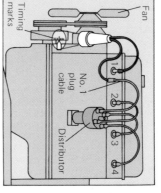

Inductive pickup · Battery

Neon timing light is attached to the No. 1 spark plug and to its cable, as shown. Hold it even with the crankshaft pulley and sight along its outer shell, as with a pistol.

Powered light is connected to both battery terminals and to the No. 1 spark plug by an adapter that fits between the cable and distributor cap. Never pierce the cable with a pin or blade; buy the correct adapter.

The latest advance in timing lights is the inductive pickup, which clamps around the No. 1 plug cable and picks up fluctuations in the magnetic field. It eliminates the need to remove the cable but it is very expensive ($40-$50).

How to use a compression gauge

A compression test will tell you if the valves and piston rings are making airtight seals, as they were intended to do, or if they are worn and leaking enough to require replacement—an expensive job. If the spark plugs are not easily accessible, you will not want to perform this test at every tuneup. You should perform it on any used car you intend to buy, or when a tuneup fails to restore normal power to your present car.

A compression test should be performed on a hot engine, but if the plugs are hard to reach and there is a danger of being burned, do it on a cold engine. First, label the spark plug cables and remove all of the plugs (p.347). Then, remove the air cleaner (p.339). If the engine is cold, hold the choke plate open. Disconnect the cable from the center of the coil. Use a compression gauge with an adapter that screws into the spark plug port. Screw the gauge into one port, hold the gas pedal to the floor, operate the starter for 5 to 10 seconds, then write down the reading. Do this for each cylinder. Compare these readings to the carmaker's compression specifications for your engine. The readings should all be at least 100 pounds per square inch (psi). If they vary by more than 25 psi, or any of them are 25 percent below the specifications, the valves or rings are worn, or the cylinder head gasket is leaking.

Screw compression tester into one spark plug port, open the throttle and choke plates, and operate the starter. Write down the reading, reset gauge to zero, and move on to next cylinder.

If readings are not acceptable, squirt some engine oil into faulty cylinders and repeat the test. If readings stay low, the valves or the head gasket are leaking. If the readings improve, the rings are worn.

How to use a vacuum gauge

Vacuum or fuel economy gauges can tell you a lot about the internal condition of an engine. While you need not use one at every tuneup, the vacuum gauge will help to diagnose unusual engine behavior or to check out the engine of a used car you are considering buying. Vacuum gauges are calibrated in inches of mercury (in.-Hg.), usually ranging from 0 to 30. Some are also marked with colored bands to indicate engine condition or fuel consumption. They record the difference in air pressure between the outside atmosphere and the engine's intake manifold. Vacuum gauges can be purchased for use under the hood as diagnostic instruments, or in kits for mounting in the dash.

The vacuum reading with the engine warmed up and running at idle speed should be a steady 17 to 22 inches (usually a green band). Fluctuating, low, or high readings at idle indicate the problems illustrated at the right. At driving speeds, the gauge should read 10 to 18 inches (yellow to green bands); the higher the reading, the better the fuel economy.

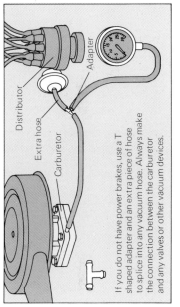

Brake booster

Carburetor

Adapter

Buy adapters at an auto parts store if they were not supplied with your gauge. Use straight adapter to connect gauge to a hose that does not affect engine operation, such as power brake vacuum booster hose. After test, reconnect booster hose firmly.

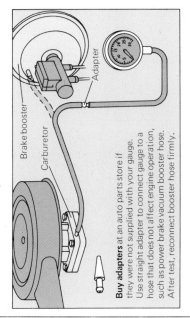

Distributor

Extra hose

Carburetor

Adapter

If you do not have power brakes, use a T shaped adapter and a vacuum hose. Always make the connection between the carburetor and any valves or other vacuum devices.

What the readings mean

Steady reading below 5 in.-Hg. indicates a leaking intake manifold or carburetor gasket, or a disconnected vacuum hose.

A steady reading between 8 and 14 in.-Hg. indicates incorrect ignition timing (see *Setting ignition timing*, p.346).

A steady reading above 21 in.-Hg. may mean clogged air filter (see *Air cleaner service*, p.339), or stuck choke, (p.341).

A fast, vibrating reading between 14 and 19 in.-Hg. indicates that the valve guides are worn. See a mechanic.

A reading that periodically drops 2 to 6 in.-Hg. from normal means worn breaker points (p.344) or a sticking valve.

If the needle drifts back and forth over a range of 4 to 5 in.-Hg. in normal range, check carburetor adjustments.

Rev the engine. If reading drops to near zero, then rises to something below 17 in.-Hg., exhaust system is restricted.

Press steadily on accelerator. If needle swings back and forth erratically, the valve springs are weak. See a mechanic.

How to jump start a car

If your car will not start because the starter does not operate or barely turns over, suspect a dead battery. Remove and clean the battery cables (see *Battery maintenance*, p.334); reconnect them and try again. If your headlights do not work, or grow very dim when the starter is operated, you can be almost certain that the problem is a dead battery. If the lights shine brightly when the starter is in use, the trouble is in the starter or its wiring, and you need a mechanic.

A car with a dead battery can be started with a set of jumper cables and a second car that is operating. Be sure both cars have 12-volt batteries, which have six filler holes (6-volt batteries have three filler holes). Always wear safety goggles when jump starting a car. See precautions and first-aid instructions in *Battery maintenance*, p.334.

1. If possible, bring both cars nose to nose and open their hoods. (Some imported cars have their batteries in the trunk or under the rear seat; position these cars so that their batteries are as close to one another as possible.) Do not allow the cars to touch.

2. Set both parking brakes. Put automatic transmissions into *Park*, manuals into *Neutral*. Turn off both ignitions and all electrical accessories.

3. Remove the vent caps from both batteries and allow any built-up gases to escape. Then, cover the vent holes with clean rags.

4. Determine which of the battery posts in each car is the positive terminal. The positive post is generally fatter than the negative post. It may be marked with a plus sign or "POS." Except in English cars, it is the one that is connected to the starter.

5. Attach the red booster cable to the positive terminals of both batteries.

6. The other battery post in each car is the negative one. If the posts have different diameters, the negative one will be smaller. It may be marked with a minus sign or "NEG." Except in English cars, it is the one grounded to the car's chassis or body.

7. Attach one end of the black cable to the negative terminal of the good battery. Attach the other end to a good ground on the second car, such as an unpainted bolt or flange on the engine, chassis, or body.

8. Make sure all hands and cables are clear of the fans and other moving parts on both cars, then start the engine of the car with the good battery and have a helper rev it moderately.

9. Start the second engine. If it still will not start, check for additional problems in the ignition and fuel systems (see *What can go wrong*, p.337).

10. Keep the formerly stalled car running and carefully remove the cables in the opposite order from which they were attached—black cable from the dead car, then from the booster car; red cable from the dead car, then from the booster car.

11. Replace the vent caps and discard the rags.

12. Drive the formerly stalled car for at least 30 minutes to recharge its battery.

Push starting

A car with a manual transmission may also be started by pushing it if its battery goes dead. This requires a second, operative car with bumpers that match the stalled car in size and height. Bring the working car up behind the stalled one until the two cars touch. Check the bumpers to be sure they are compatible and will not override one another. Turn the ignition key in the stalled car to the *On* position, release the parking brake, and put the transmission into *Neutral*. Have your helper gently push your car with his until your speed reaches 10–15 mph. Then, your helper should apply his brakes, let you coast ahead, and beep his horn. When you hear the horn, shift into *Second* and ease in the clutch. This should spin the engine over fast enough to start it. Drive the car for at least 30 minutes to recharge its battery.

Correct jumper cable connections

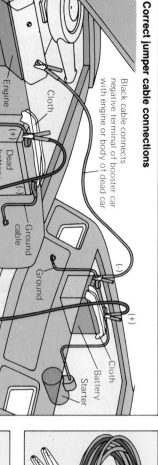

- Starter relay
- Starter
- Engine
- Cloth
- (+)
- Dead battery
- (−)
- Ground cable
- Ground
- Cloth
- Battery
- Starter
- Booster car
- (−)
- (+)
- Black cable connects negative terminal of booster car with engine or body of dead car
- Red cable connects positive terminals

Jumper cables should be made of four-gauge wire so that they will pass current easily. Cables 16 ft long will reach from one battery to another even if cars cannot be positioned nose to nose. Be sure cables are color coded.

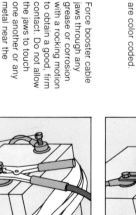

Force booster cable jaws through any grease or corrosion with a rocking motion to obtain a good, firm contact. Do not allow even if cars cannot the jaws to touch one another or any metal near the batteries. This could cause a spark and a battery explosion.

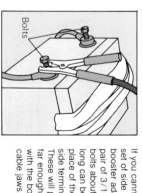

Cover vent holes with a cloth

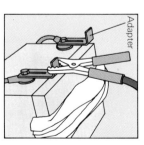

Bolts

Adapter

If you cannot find a set of side terminal booster adapters, a pair of 3/16-in bolts about 2 in. long can be used in place of the original side terminal bolts. These will protrude far enough to grip with the booster cable jaws.

It is difficult to get a firm grip on General Motors side terminal batteries with the booster cable jaws. Auto parts stores sell special adapters for use with side terminal batteries.

Exhaust system

How it works

The exhaust system consists of the manifold (which collects the exhaust gas), one or more mufflers (which silence the noise of explosive combustion from the engine), and the pipes connecting them. Many new cars also use an antipollution device called a catalytic converter. Flexible hangers let the system absorb engine vibrations. A leaking exhaust can allow carbon monoxide gas to enter the car. This colorless, odorless gas causes headaches, nausea, impaired vision, sleepiness, slowed reflexes, unconsciousness, and death.

Hissing, rumbling, or rattling from under the car indicates a leaking or deteriorating exhaust system. Small leaks may not cause much noise, but they still release poisonous gas. Acid in the exhaust gases eats away at the system from the inside, especially during short trips when the system does not warm up enough to vaporize them. The muffler and tail pipe usually rust out first; the manifold and exhaust pipe rarely do.

Whenever you are under the car, check the system for leaks and faulty hangers. Poke at rusty spots with a screwdriver to see if they are ready to give out. Replace damaged parts as shown below and at the right.

Always wear goggles when working on a rusty exhaust system. Replace only the parts that are rusted through. Buy the replacement parts before you start, and make sure they match the parts on the car. Soak nuts, bolts, and joints overnight with penetrating oil before trying to open them. Cut away parts that cannot be loosened. During reassembly, tighten clamps until snug; do not overtighten them and distort pipes.

To check for exhaust leaks, raise car (p.318), start the engine, and have a helper hold a wad of rags over the tail pipe. A hissing noise or puffs of escaping gas indicate a leak. Turn off engine. Tighten bolts between manifold and engine to cure a leak there. Open the manifold-to-exhaust pipe flange and replace the gasket if it is leaking. At pipe joints, loosen clamp and joint, coat parts with muffler sealer, reassemble parts, and retighten clamp. If a leak cannot be cured by tightening bolts and clamps, replace the parts involved.

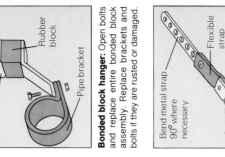
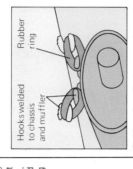

Manifold bolt
Exhaust manifold
Gasket
Manifold flange
Exhaust pipe
Joint
Clamp
Catalytic converter*
Exhaust extension*
Muffler
Hangers
Connecting pipe*
Resonator*
Hanger
Tail pipe
Crossover pipe*

*Not found on all cars

Replacing hangers

A broken exhaust hanger will weaken nearby joints and allow parts of the system to rattle against the chassis. Buy replacements from a new-car dealer. If replacements are no longer available for your car, you will have to improvise with universal hangers, which are sold in auto parts stores.

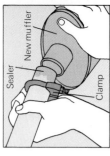

Rubber block
Chassis bracket
Pipe bracket

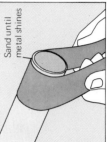

Chassis bracket
Flexible strap
Pipe bracket

Bonded block hanger: Open bolts and replace entire bonded block assembly. Replace rubber and bolts if they are rusted or damaged.

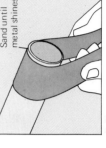

Bend metal strap 90° where necessary
Flexible strap
Pipe bracket

Universal hanger: Bolt strap to chassis through hole that will allow proper hanging height. Tighten clamp around pipe.

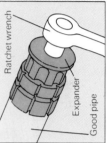

Rubber ring
Hooks welded to chassis and muffler

Flexible strap hanger: Open bolts at chassis and at pipe. Replace rubber and fabric strap. Replace brackets and bolts if necessary.

Rubber ring: Push up on pipe and slip off old ring. Stretch new ring to fit, using a long screwdriver as a lever if necessary.

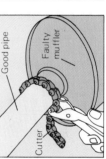

Sand until metal shines

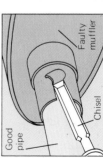

Ratchet wrench
Expander
Good pipe

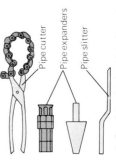

Sealer
New muffler
Clamp

4. Use pipe expander to round out end of old pipe remaining on the car. This assures a snug, leak-free fit with new pipe or muffler.

5. Clean a 1½-in. area at the end of any old pipe remaining on the car before fitting new sections. Use emery cloth or sandpaper.

6. Install new parts, working from front to rear. Coat all joints with muffler sealer. Reuse sound clamps, but replace all hangers.

Replacing exhaust components

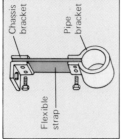

Pipe cutter
Pipe expanders
Pipe slitter

1. Specialized exhaust tools cost more than $30 but make the job easier. Some stores that sell exhaust parts will rent or lend them.

Good pipe
Faulty muffler
Chisel

2. To remove rusted-out parts, open clamps at joints, then cut away outer pipe with pipe slitter or an old carpenter's chisel.

Good pipe
Faulty muffler
Cutter

3. Do not open every joint. Use pipe cutter or hacksaw to remove sections of pipe to be discarded. Cut next to welds, not through them.

Lubrication

Periodic lubrication points

Metal parts that rub against one another would soon wear out without periodic lubrication. In some cases, only a little grease is needed. Inside the engine, fast moving parts must actually float on a film of quality oil that will not break down under high temperatures or pressures. This oil is slowly contaminated in use and must be replaced.

Every 3,000 miles or three months, whichever comes first, change the engine oil. Change the oil filter at every second oil change (6,000 miles or six months). Some carmakers recommend longer oil change periods under certain driving conditions. Read your owner's manual carefully; there will probably be two suggested oil change intervals, depending on how you drive. If in doubt, change at the earlier interval.

Use the weight and quality of oil suggested in the manual. Most call for 10W-30 weight oil, with 10W-40 or 10W-50 recommended if you drive at high speeds in hot weather or use your car to tow a trailer. As for quality, the oil should be marked: "For API Service SE" and "Exceeds all auto makers' warranty specifications."

Getting rid of the old oil can be a problem. The Environmental Protection Agency estimates that 370 million gallons of crankcase drainings are dumped down sewers or leach into the water table every year. Some service stations sell their used oil to recycling firms. You might convince such a station owner to take your old oil. Otherwise, funnel it into a leakproof jug and put it out with the garbage.

Twice a year, lubricate all hinges, locks, linkages, and other items shown in the illustration above. Also, check the lubricant levels in the differential, transmission (p.358), and power steering pump (p.354) or manual steering gearbox. Some steering boxes are sealed; others have a filler plug similar to the one on the differential. Open the plug, add gear oil until it overflows, then replace the plug. Do not confuse the slotted adjusting screw, found on some steering boxes, with the hexagonal filler plug. Grease the chassis at every engine oil change, or as recommended in your owner's manual.

Labels

Trunk weather stripping 6
Lock cylinder 5
Differential 7
U-joints 4
Lock cylinders 5
Parking brake linkage 1
Door strikers and latches 1
Door hinges and stops 1
Wheel bearings 4
Door and window weather stripping 6
Trunk hinges 1
Seatback hinges 2
Seat rails 1
Hood hinges 1
Pedal linkages 1
Shift linkage 1
Hood latch and release 1
Distributor pads 3
Manual steering box 7
Engine oil dipstick 3
Steering and suspension joints 4
Manual transmission 7

Lubricants: 1. Nonstaining, waterproof white grease. 2. Household oil; 3. Motor oil; 4. Multipurpose chassis grease. 5. Graphite. 6. Silicone spray. 7. Gear oil.

How to grease the chassis

Bearings in the steering, suspension, and drive train should be greased at every engine oil change. Some cars have no grease fittings, others have more than 20. Check with your dealer or a service manual to locate all the fittings on your car—do not overlook even one of them. You will need a hand-operated grease gun, a cartridge of multipurpose chassis grease, and—for late model cars—a selection of grease nipples. Raise the car (p.318) and clean encrusted dirt from the nipples or plugs before applying grease. If a nipple will not accept any grease, unscrew it and clean it in solvent. If it still does not work, replace it with a new nipple.

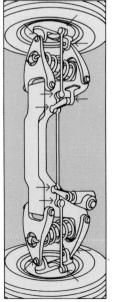

Grease nipples or plugs may be located at some or all of the joints in the steering linkage and front suspension (arrows).

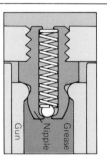

1. A grease nipple is a one-way valve. It may be straight or angled. Force tip of gun over nipple and squeeze the trigger. Grease should flow into nipple, not around it.

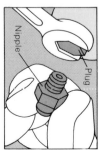

2. Use a wrench to remove grease plugs on late model cars, then in-stall nipples. After greasing, you can reinstall the plugs or leave the nipples in place.

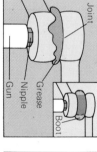

3. Slowly squeeze trigger of gun until old grease starts to ooze out of joint in bearing. Apply grease to a sealed bearing until the rubber boot begins to swell (inset).

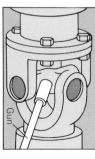

4. U-joints may have grease nipples on their center sections. Rotate each joint and look for a nipple. Apply grease until it is forced out the seals at all four bearings.

How to change the engine oil and filter

To change the oil, you will need a basin, an oil filter wrench, and an oil pour spout. There are many types of filter wrench (see Steps 3 and 4). Your car dealer or a helpful auto parts salesman should be able to tell you which type you need. You can use a can opener and a clean funnel instead of the pour spout. On cars with hard-to-reach oil filler caps, a funnel with a flexible neck may be needed. Check your owner's manual to see how much oil the engine holds, and deduct one quart if you are not changing the filter. Raise the front of the car (p.318) and locate the oil drain plug. Do not confuse it with drain plugs for the radiator or transmission. If the engine is warm, the old oil will drain more completely, but some parts may be too hot to handle comfortably. If the engine is cold, let the old oil drain for at least 20 to 30 minutes. Add about half a quart of oil to the new filter before you install it; this will help get oil to the bearings faster when you start the engine.

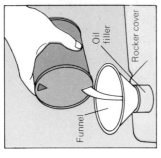

Rocker cover
Oil filler
Funnel

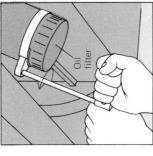

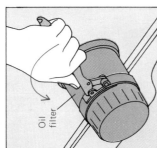

Oil filter

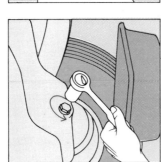

Oil filter

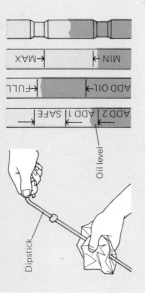

Gasket

1. Position an old basin with at least a 6-quart capacity under the drain plug. Loosen drain plug with a wrench, then remove it by hand. Let old oil drain into basin.

2. Clean drain plug with paper towel. Some plugs are magnetized to trap metal particles. Wipe off all metal and grit. Clean washer (it may be in the basin), and replace plug.

3. Locate the oil filter (at the side or bottom of the engine) and move the basin under it. Loosen the filter with a special oil filter wrench and remove it by hand.

4. In some engine compartments, there is no room to swing a conventional filter wrench. Use offset band wrench. Make sure gasket is removed with filter.

5. Apply a film of oil to the new filter's gasket. Spin filter onto pipe until it stops. Tighten by hand another half turn. Do not use the wrench; it will damage filter.

6. Locate oil filler and add the amount of oil listed in the owner's manual. Start engine and check for leaks at drain plug and filter. Check oil level; adjust if needed.

Drain plug repair kit

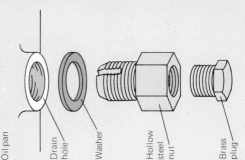

Oil pan
Drain hole
Washer
Hollow steel nut
Brass plug

When replacing the oil drain plug (or any threaded fastener), always align the threads carefully and tighten the plug as far as you can by hand. If the plug will not turn smoothly, the threads are dirty or misaligned. If you force the plug with a wrench, you will strip the threads. Rather than replacing an oil pan that has stripped threads, you can use one of several drain plug repair kits. With the type shown, a self-tapping steel nut is forced into the pan; oil is then drained by opening the small brass plug. Other kits use less durable rubber stoppers.

How to check engine oil level

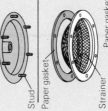

Dipstick
Oil level

MAX / MIN
FULL / ADD OIL
ADD 2 / ADD 1 / SAFE

Shut off the engine if it is running, wait at least three minutes, then remove the engine oil dipstick. Do not confuse the oil dipstick with the transmission dipstick on cars with automatic transmissions (see p.358). Wipe the dipstick clean and reinsert it all the way into its tube. Pull it out again and observe the level of the oil clinging to the blade. Most dipsticks are marked *Full* and *Add*. The *Add* mark means the engine is one quart low. If you add oil before the level is down to the *Add* mark, the engine will be overfilled. This will lead to churning and foaming of the oil, which can lower its lubricating properties. When checking the oil, park the car on level ground.

Volkswagen oil change

Air-cooled Volkswagens do not have oil filters; they have a wire strainer that must be removed and cleaned in solvent at every oil change. Cars built after 1972 do not have a drain plug; loosen the retaining plate to drain the oil. All the gaskets must be replaced; do not reuse them. Gasket kits are sold in auto parts stores.

Drain oil and remove all six nuts. Remove and clean strainer. Dry strainer thoroughly, then install gaskets, strainer, and retaining plate. Tighten nuts carefully by hand. Tighten them a bit more with a short-handled wrench. They are very easy to strip. Replace drain plug and add about 2½ quarts of oil. If you strip the threads on one of the nuts, the drain plug, or the retaining plate, buy replacements from a dealer. If you strip one of the studs, it must be replaced by a mechanic.

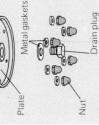

Engine
Stud
Paper gasket
Strainer
Paper gasket
Plate
Metal gaskets
Nut
Drain plug

Steering and suspension systems

How they work

The steering and suspension systems are as important to driving safety as the brakes. Both systems are interrelated. If one or more parts in either system are bent, damaged, too loose, or too tight, both steering and handling can be affected.

The front suspension can be adjusted to change the angle at which the tires meet the road. These settings—collectively called wheel alignment—affect the way the car handles in turns, its stability in a straight line, and the rate and pattern of tire wear (see p.356). Wheel alignment should be adjusted only by a competent repairman, using sophisticated equipment.

Ball joints are swiveling links in the front suspension that allow the wheels to move up and down and steer at the same time. They should be lubricated periodically (p.352). As they wear, play develops in the ball joints

and steering becomes imprecise. On most cars, more than ¼ inch of play is considered dangerous, and the ball joints should be replaced by a mechanic.

There are two popular steering systems (shown below): Pitman and the simpler rack and pinion. Both can be power assisted. The Pitman arrangement has seven arms bolted together. The Pitman arms should be checked periodically for tightness. If they have grease fittings or plugs, they should also be lubricated. The rubber boots on a rack and pinion system contain lubricant. If they are leaking, have them replaced and have the boots checked for damage. If your car has power steering, check the fluid level every few weeks, as shown below. A dipstick is built into the cap on the power steering pump, which is driven by a rubber V-belt and is usually mounted on the driver's side of the

engine. There are several types of power steering fluid. Use only the kind specified in your owner's manual.

No tire is precisely round, no wheel completely uniform. At high speeds these minor imperfections become major vibrations—felt as a shimmy through the steering wheel—unless the wheels and tires are properly balanced. There are two methods of balancing: static and dynamic. Only dynamic balancing, in which both the wheel and tire are spun up to high speed on a special machine, is worth while. A shop that can spin and balance the wheels on the car will do the best job.

The front wheel bearings should be disassembled, inspected, and repacked with grease every two years. Any gas station can do this job. Shimmy in the steering or squeaking noises from the wheels may be caused by wheel bearings that need greasing or adjusting.

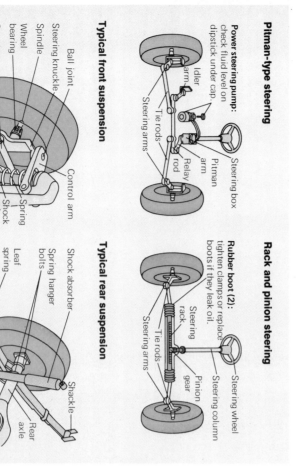

Pitman-type steering

Power steering pump: check fluid level on dipstick under cap.

Steering box — Idler arm — Pitman arm — Relay rod — Steering arms — Tie rods

Rack and pinion steering

Rubber boot (2): tighten clamps or replace boots if they leak oil.

Steering wheel — Steering column — Pinion gear — Steering rack — Tie rods — Steering arms

Typical front suspension

Ball joint — Steering knuckle — Spindle — Wheel bearing — Steering arm — Ball joint — Control arm — Control arm — Spring — Shock

Typical rear suspension

Shock absorber — Spring hanger bolts — Leaf spring — Spring eye — Differential — Rear axle — Shackle

Test shock absorbers periodically (opposite page). The lower ends of the shocks are bolted to the suspension; their upper ends, to brackets inside or under the car. Some upper brackets can be reached from under the hood, inside the trunk, or—in some station wagons—through access panels in the floor.

What can go wrong

HOW TO USE THIS CHART

Find problem at top of chart. Look down columns to locate possible causes. First, check out things you can fix yourself; then things you *may* be able to fix yourself. If problem is still not cured, consult a competent mechanic.

○ You can fix it yourself.
● You *may* be able to make complete repair.
■ You need a mechanic.

POSSIBLE CAUSE	Car difficult to steer	Car pulls to one side	Car wanders from side to side	Uneven tire wear (see p.356)	Steering wheel shimmy	Car vibrates at high speeds	Car is not level	Heavy thumps on rough roads	Play or looseness in steering	Loud squeal in steering	Grinding noise in steering	CURE
Improper tire pressure	○	○	○	○								Adjust tire pressure (p.356)
Steering linkage dry	○								■	○		Lubricate linkage (p.352)
Front end misaligned	■	■	■	■								Have alignment checked
Suspension arms damaged	■	■	■		■			■				Check, repair suspension
Ball joints binding	●	●										Check (p.353) or replace joints
Springs broken or sagging			●	●			■	●				Install new or helper springs
Power steering belt slips	■									■		Tighten or replace belt (p.334)
Power steering fluid low	○									○		Add power steering fluid (p.354)
Faulty power steering pump	●									●		Have pump tested and repaired
Loose front wheel bearings			■		■			■	■		■	Tighten, replace bearings
Worn ball joints			●	●	●			●	●			Have ball joints replaced
Loose steering linkage		■	■		■			■	■			Tighten steering linkage
Maladjusted steering gear	●				●				●			Have steering gear adjusted
Worn shock absorbers			●	●	●	●		●				Replace shock absorbers
Wheel out of balance				■	■	■						Have wheels balanced

Replacing shock absorbers

If the suspension of your car bottoms out with a loud thunk at railroad crossings, if the front end dives sharply on quick stops, if the wheels skitter across rough roads, or if the car wallows up and down for a long while after a bump, the shock absorbers are probably worn. Few original equipment shocks last more than 25,000 miles. You can buy shocks on sale and save them until they are needed.

For balanced handling, shocks should always be replaced in pairs (both fronts or both rears), even if only one is damaged. Buy shocks specifically designed for your car make and model. Heavy-duty shocks last longer and give greater stability than standard types. Some adjustable shocks can be used for 25,000 miles, then adjusted to a firmer setting and reinstalled.

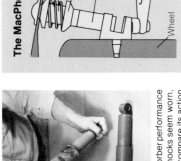

Check shock absorber performance while driving. If shocks seem worn, remove one and compare its action to that of a new shock.

Periodically check the shocks for oil leaks, bad dents, and scratched or pitted piston rods. If you find such damage, replace the shock.

Shock absorber mounts

Ring with rubber bushing.

Ring with metal sleeve insert.

Ring with two-bolt crossbar.

Ring with right-angle stud.

Two-bolt plate.

Stud mount with rubber bushings.

Types of replacement shocks

Standard shocks have a thin bore, give softest ride but least control and service life.

Heavy duty shocks give firmer ride and better control, and have longer life than standards.

Adjustable shocks can be set for a relatively soft ride or for maximum control, but not for both.

Air adjustable shocks are pumped up to restore ride height of a heavily loaded car.

Overload shocks have helper springs to increase trailer towing or cargo capacity of a car.

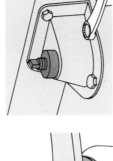

The MacPherson strut

Spring — Shock — Flange — Strut — A-arm — Wheel

Replacing shock absorbers is a simple job, except on those imported cars that have a MacPherson strut suspension—identifiable by a heavy tubular strut attached to the wheel assembly. The shock absorber is inside this strut. To replace it, you must dismantle part of the suspension. Leave this job to the car dealer or to a repairman who specializes in foreign cars.

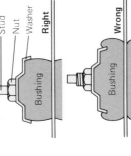

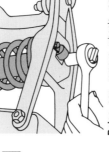

Removing worn shocks

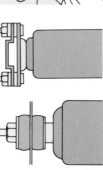

Raise car, remove wheels, and soak all mounting bolts with penetrating oil. Unbolt old shocks.

Stud mounts require two wrenches, one for the mounting nut and a second to keep shock from turning.

Fitting new shocks

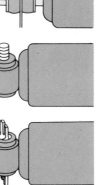

Most adjustable shocks must be set for a firm or a soft ride before installation. This is usually done by compressing, then twisting the shock. Follow the instructions.

On some cars, you may have to unbolt and remove a mounting plate in order to gain access to the shock.

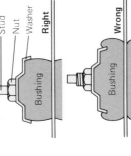

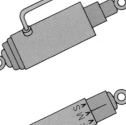

Stud — Nut — Washer — **Right** — Bushing

Bushing — **Wrong**

Bolt new shocks into place. You may have to raise the suspension slightly with a jack to do so. On stud mounts, tighten bolts until rubber bushings just begin to swell.

Make sure all bushings, washers, and nuts are installed in their original order. Protect threads from rust with rubber caps (if supplied) or with white silicone caulking compound.

Tires

Maintenance and replacement

Once a month check the air pressure in all tires, including the spare. An underinflated tire can affect steering, wears out faster than a properly inflated tire, and lessens the load you can safely carry. The recommended tire pressures for your car are printed in the owner's manual or on a sticker inside the glove compartment. Check the pressure when the tires are cold (in the morning, before you have driven too far). When the tires get hot from driving, the pressure of the air inside them goes up. If you adjust the pressure when the tires are hot, they will be underinflated when they cool off. Also check for excess or abnormal tread wear (shown below, right). Replace tires that have bumps or bulges in the rubber, deep cuts that expose the fabric plies, or tread less than 1/16 inch deep. Pry out pebbles or pieces of glass with a screwdriver. Always buy new tires that are at least as big as the old ones. Tires one or two sizes wider may be OK if they fit the wheels and fender wells of your car (have the dealer check). Smaller tires will be dangerously overloaded when the car is full. Tire sidewalls contain the following data:

Tire size: P means passenger car tire, R is radial, B is belted bias, D is bias ply. First number is tire width in millimeters; second is ratio of tire height to width; third is wheel diameter in inches

Load range runs from B (former 4-ply rating) to D (8-ply rating). Maximum load per wheel and maximum inflation pressure are also indicated

Materials used in the tire, plus "tubeless" or "tube-type" must be shown

Identification code indicates tiremaker plus date and place of manufacture

TUBELESS RADIAL

SIDEWALL 2 PLIES POLYESTER
TREAD 4 PLIES (2 PLIES STEELCORD)

P205/75R15
LOAD RANGE B
MAX. LOAD 1620 LBS. @ 32PSI MAX. PRESS

DOT VCUS CX3728

Construction

Radial ply tires

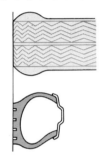

There are three kinds of tires: radial ply, bias ply, and belted bias. The radial tire has a very stiff reinforced tread and fairly flexible sidewalls. A properly inflated radial bulges noticeably where it meets the road and may look soft. In turning a corner, its sidewalls flex but the stiff tread stays flat on the road.

Bias ply tires

A fully inflated bias ply tire bulges less than a radial. Its stiff sidewalls can pull part of the flexible tread from the road in a tight turn. The belted bias tire is a compromise design with stiff sidewalls and a stiff, reinforced tread. It handles nearly as well as a radial but rides harder than a bias ply.

Proper rotation

Radial ply tires

For maximum tread life, rotate the tires every 6,000 miles. Radial tires should always revolve in the same direction: Switch them from front to back on each side of the car.

Bias ply tires

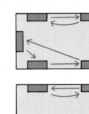

Bias ply and belted bias tires are cross switched, as shown. Include the spare in your rotation pattern if it is in usable shape. Readjust tire pressures after rotation.

Tightening sequence

Tighten the wheel nuts in the order shown above to prevent stress buildup, which can crack the wheels.

Periodic checks

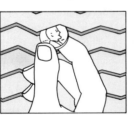

1. Once a month, check the air pressure in all five tires. Use a good pocket gauge, which is much more accurate than the gauges on service station airhoses.

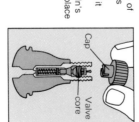

2. A tread depth of 1/16 inch or less is illegal in most states. Measure it with a penny. If the top of Lincoln's head shows, replace the tire.

 Cap

Valve core

3. Remove cap and wet the valve stem. Bubbles indicate a leak. Unscrew the leaking valve core at a gas station and replace it. Tire will then be flat. Reinflate the tire.

 Bubbles

Causes of tread wear

1. Normal wear: Replace tire when smooth strips appear across tread.

2. Chronic overinflation causes center of tread to wear out first.

3. Chronic underinflation causes edges of tread to wear out first.

4. Out-of-balance wheel causes uneven wear at one or more spots.

5. Feathering at one edge of tread is caused by bad wheel alignment.

6. Incorrect camber wears out one edge only; have wheels aligned.

7. Flat spot at one point is caused by a long skid on dry pavement.

8. Car's worn suspension parts can cause scalloping at even intervals.

Transmission and drive train

How it works

The transmission and drive train connect the engine to the driving wheels of the car. A manual transmission requires a device to disconnect the engine and transmission temporarily so that the gears can be shifted smoothly. This is the clutch, which is operated by a foot pedal next to the brake. With an automatic transmission, a fluid turbine device does the job of the clutch. The gears are shifted by a complicated system of hydraulic control valves, triggered by vacuum signals from the engine and by road speed signals from the accelerator pedal and the transmission itself.

Manual transmissions are filled with heavy lubricating oil; automatic transmissions, with a special fluid. The levels of both should be checked, and topped up, if necessary, every time you change the oil in your car's engine. The differential also contains heavy oil, and it should be checked at the same time. Frequent refills indicate a leak, which should be found and fixed, either by tightening loose bolts and fittings or by replacing faulty gaskets (a job for a mechanic). Change the fluid and oil every two years or 24,000 miles (especially if you tow a trailer). The bands on an automatic transmission should be adjusted every 24,000 miles for those models that have provisions for such adjustments.

Automatic transmission fluid is cooled in a small chamber built into the bottom of the radiator on most cars. A leak in this chamber or in its fittings will contaminate the transmission fluid with antifreeze and vice versa. Antifreeze globules on the transmission dipstick signify an internal leak. Some 1972–1975 cars were plagued by this problem. A transmission fluid additive may prevent the corrosion that causes these leaks. If you have the original fluid in your car, drain it and replace it with new fluid plus Automatic Transmission Conditioner. There are several types of transmission fluid. Use the one listed in your owner's manual.

As the clutch wears on a manually shifted car, less pedal travel is needed before the clutch begins to disengage. At a certain point, the clutch will start to disengage, or slip, when there is no pressure on the pedal at all. Long before this happens, you should adjust the linkage to restore proper pedal play (p.359).

The transmission and differential are connected by a driveshaft and two or more swiveling universal joints, or U-joints. U-joints can break and drop the driveshaft to the road, but they generally give you a warning by rattling or making a clunking sound during acceleration for some time before they actually fail.

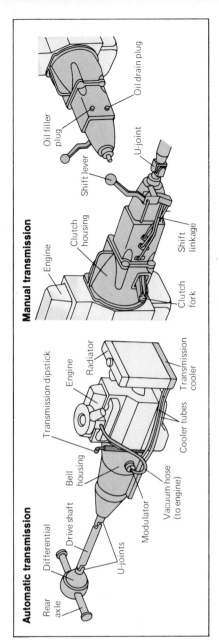

Automatic transmission — Transmission dipstick, Engine, Radiator, Transmission cooler, Cooler tubes, Modulator, Vacuum hose (to engine), U-joints, Drive shaft, Differential, Rear axle, Bell housing

Manual transmission — Oil filler plug, Oil drain plug, U-joint, Shift lever, Engine, Clutch housing, Shift linkage, Clutch fork

What can go wrong

HOW TO USE THIS CHART

Find problem at top of chart. Look down columns to locate possible causes. First, check out things you can fix yourself; then, things you may be able to fix yourself. If problem is still not cured, consult a competent mechanic.

- o You can fix it yourself
- ● You may be able to make complete repair
- ■ You need a mechanic

Clutch slips	Gear shift hard to operate	Clashing noise when shifting	No drive transmitted to wheels	Automatic transmission slips	Transmission not shifting properly	Rough gear engagement	Heavy rattle at low speed	Vibration at high speed	Whine from rear axle	POSSIBLE CAUSE	CURE
o	o									Clutch needs adjustment	Adjust clutch free play (p.359)
■		o								Clutch disc worn; springs weak	Have disc and springs inspected, replaced
	o	o								Transmission low on lubricant	Check lubricant level, add if needed (p.358)
	o	o								Incorrect grade of lubricant	Drain and refill transmission (p.358)
	■									Shift linkage out of adjustment	Have linkage adjusted
				●		■				Bands need adjustment (some cars)	Have bands adjusted if car has that provision
			●	●	●					Modulator, shift controls sticking	Replace modulator (p.358); have controls checked
				■	■	■				Antifreeze in transmission fluid	Go to radiator shop or car dealer (p.357)
					■					Faulty throttle linkage adjustment	Have linkage adjusted
				■						Leaking seals or gaskets	Have seals or gaskets replaced
			■			■				Internal transmission damage	Have damage repaired or transmission replaced
			■				■			Worn or broken U-joints	Have U-joints inspected, replaced
							■	■		Unbalanced driveshaft or tires	Have driveshaft, tire balance checked
									o	Differential oil level low	Add oil to differential (p.358)
									■	Worn gears or bearings	Have differential gears, axle bearings checked
									o	Tire noise	May be normal; check tire pressure(p.356)

Automatic transmissions

Check the level of the transmission fluid every few months. Fluid clinging to the dipstick indicates the level inside the transmission. Every two years or 24,000 miles (whichever comes first) drain the transmission, clean its screen or replace its filter, and add fresh fluid. Always use the type of fluid recommended in your owner's manual. At this point you should also replace

the modulator, if the transmission on your car has one. The modulator is a small can at the side of the transmission. It controls shifting. One or two vacuum hoses run from it to the engine. A clogged or leaking hose, or a faulty modulator, will cause rough or erratic shifting. So will a vacuum hose that has vibrated loose. Reconnect any hoses that have come loose.

Checking and adding fluid

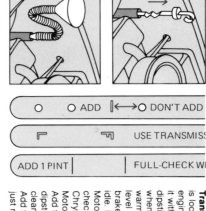

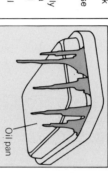

Transmission dipstick is located behind the engine. Do not confuse it with the engine oil dipstick. Check fluid when the engine is fully warmed up. Park on a level spot, set parking brake, and let engine idle. Ford and General Motors cars must be checked in *Park*; Chrysler and American Motors cars, in *Neutral*. Add fluid through the dipstick hole, using a clean flex-neck funnel. Add fluid until it just reaches *Full* mark.

Changing fluid and filter

Raise car (p.318). Loosen transmission oil pan bolts, starting at one end, and let fluid drain into a large basin. Remove oil pan.

Remove the screws or clips that hold the filter inside the transmission, then remove the filter by pulling it straight down.

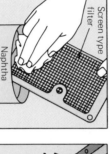

Metal screens are cleaned in naphtha, dried, and reused. Filters must be replaced. Take old unit to parts store; buy same kind.

Scrape old gasket material from transmission housing and oil pan. Use a putty knife or gasket scraper, not a screwdriver or chisel.

Modulator replacement

If the transmission shifts erratically, check the modulator hoses for cracks or holes. Trace them all the way back to the engine. Replace faulty hoses. Pull the hose off the modulator; if it is wet inside, the modulator is leaking and must be replaced. Drain the transmission fluid, then remove the modulator by unscrewing it. Some modulators are held on by a metal fork. Unbolt it and pull modulator out. Save metal pin (if any) and rubber O-ring. Buy a replacement modulator. Install pin, ring, and modulator. Reattach hoses.

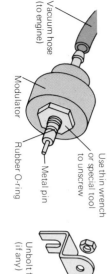

Vacuum hose (to engine)

Modulator

Rubber O-ring

Metal pin

Use thin wrench or special tool to unscrew

Unbolt fork (if any)

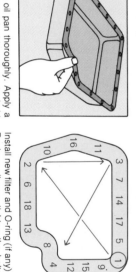

Clean oil pan thoroughly. Apply a thin coat of white grease to hold gasket in place. Use a new gasket whenever the oil pan is removed.

Install new filter and O-ring (if any). Replace oil pan; tighten the bolts in a crisscross sequence, following order shown. Add new fluid.

Manual transmissions

Check the level of the oil in the transmission, and in the differential, every time you change the engine oil. Every 24,000 miles, drain and replace it. Use only the type and weight of gear oil recommended in your owner's manual (usually SAE 80 or 90 weight). There is seldom enough clearance under the car to pour in new oil, but it can be forced in with a special mechanic's syringe or a clean plastic squeeze bottle and a length of tubing. Some brands are sold in squeeze bottles.

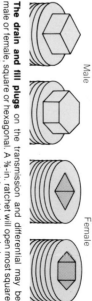

The drain and fill plugs on the transmission and differential may be male or female, square or hexagonal. A ⅜-in. ratchet will open most square female plugs. Special wrenches are needed for odd-shaped plugs.

Male

Female

Remove the upper (filler) plug and insert a finger to check oil level. Transmission should be filled up to opening. If not, add more oil. Bottom plug is for draining the lubricant.

Oil level

Some transmissions have only one plug; the oil (and lubricant must be siphoned out if you want to change it. Use a mechanic's syringe, or a cheap plastic bellows pump.

Oil

Checking differential lubricant

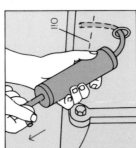

Most differentials have a single plug, similar to those on transmissions. Check the oil level with your finger, as shown above. Add oil until it overflows. A clean household squeeze bottle and a length of aquarium hose can be used. Limited slip differentials use special oil (check your owner's manual). Old oil must be siphoned off; there is no drain plug.

Adjusting clutch play on various makes of car

The linkage that operates the clutch must be adjusted periodically to maintain the proper amount of free play or slack in the system. There are two common types of linkage: rod operated and cable operated (see below). Both are adjusted under the car, via a threaded rod and one or more nuts. A tension spring must often be removed temporarily to make the adjustment. The adjusting mechanism varies from one make of car to another, as shown below. If in doubt about how to make the adjustment on your car, turn the adjuster a few times and check its effect on the pedal play. On some cars, free play is increased by shortening the linkage; on others, it is increased by lengthening the linkage.

Twice a year measure the clutch play. If there is too little, raise the car (p.318) and turn the adjuster until you achieve the proper free play. Loosen the locknut (if there is one) before making the adjustment; tighten it afterwards to hold the adjusting nut in place.

Measure clutch play by placing ruler alongside the pedal and depressing the pedal until you feel resistance. If you cannot feel it, unhook tension spring (see illustrations below), make measurement, then reattach the spring. On Ford products, play is measured with engine running. One inch of play is usually right; check owner's manual.

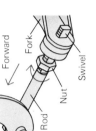

Rod-operated clutches

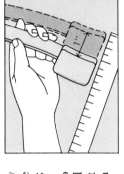

Pedal return spring
Clutch pedal
Opening in clutch housing
Clutch operating fork
Tension spring
Adjuster

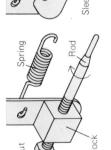

General Motors (V-8 engines): Unhook tension spring, loosen locknut. Screw adjusting rod into block to increase free play. When 1-in. play is achieved, tighten locknut, hook up spring.

Spring
Rod
Nut
Block

General Motors (6-cylinder engines): Unhook the tension spring, back off locknut. Screw rod into outer sleeve. When 1-in. free play is achieved, tighten locknut and reattach spring.

Spring
Sleeve
Nut
Rod

Fords: Unhook spring, loosen nuts. Push rod and fork back until resistance is felt. Use feeler to set nuts 0.2 in. from sleeve. Attach spring. Pedal play at fast idle must be 1 in.

Spring
Adjuster nut
Locknut
0.2"
Sleeve

American Motors: Loosen the locknut and turn the adjuster nut so as to shorten the length of the threaded rod. Pedal play should be ⅞ to 1⅛ in., with 1⅛ in. preferred.

Adjuster nut
Rod
Locknut

Chrysler cars: Loosen self-locking adjuster nut on threaded rod so that the fork moves forward. If nut binds, tap swivel with wrench to free it. Correct pedal play is 1 in.

Forward
Fork
Nut
Rod
Swivel

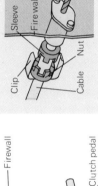

Cable-operated clutches

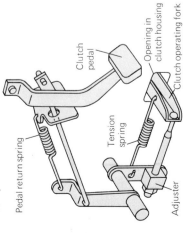

Firewall
Fender bracket
Opening in clutch housing
Clutch pedal
Pivot point
Yoke
Pedal return spring
Clutch fork

Pintos: Pull away rubber boot (if any) and loosen all nuts. Pull cable forward until resistance is felt, then position adjuster nut ¼ in. from metal flange. Retighten locknuts.

Rubber boot
Cable
Flange
Adjuster nut
Forward

Imports usually have one or two nuts at the clutch operating fork. Loosen locknut (if any) and turn the adjuster nut so as to increase free play at pedal.

Cable
Rubber boot
Fork
Nuts
Front

Volkswagen clutches

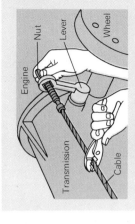

Engine
Nut
Lever
Wheel
Transmission
Cable

Air-cooled Volkswagens use cable to operate a lever at the top of the transmission. To reach it, raise the rear of the car (p.318) and remove the left rear wheel and heater hose. Reach up past the axle and grasp the clutch cable with pliers, to keep it from twisting. With your other hand, loosen the wingnut until pedal play is between ⅝ and ¾ in. After adjustment is made, rotate wingnut to horizontal position so that it engages lever.

Mustang: Open clip and unbolt fender bracket. Pull cable all the way forward. Adjust nut to barely touch sleeve. Replace clip and bracket. Pedal play should be 1½ in.

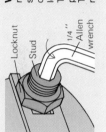

Clip
Sleeve
Fire wall
Cable
Nut

Vega: Adjustment is made on passenger side. Remove dust cap (if any) and loosen locknut. Turn stud until pedal play is 1 in. Tighten locknut and replace dust cap.

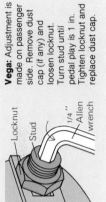

Locknut
Stud
¼" Allen wrench

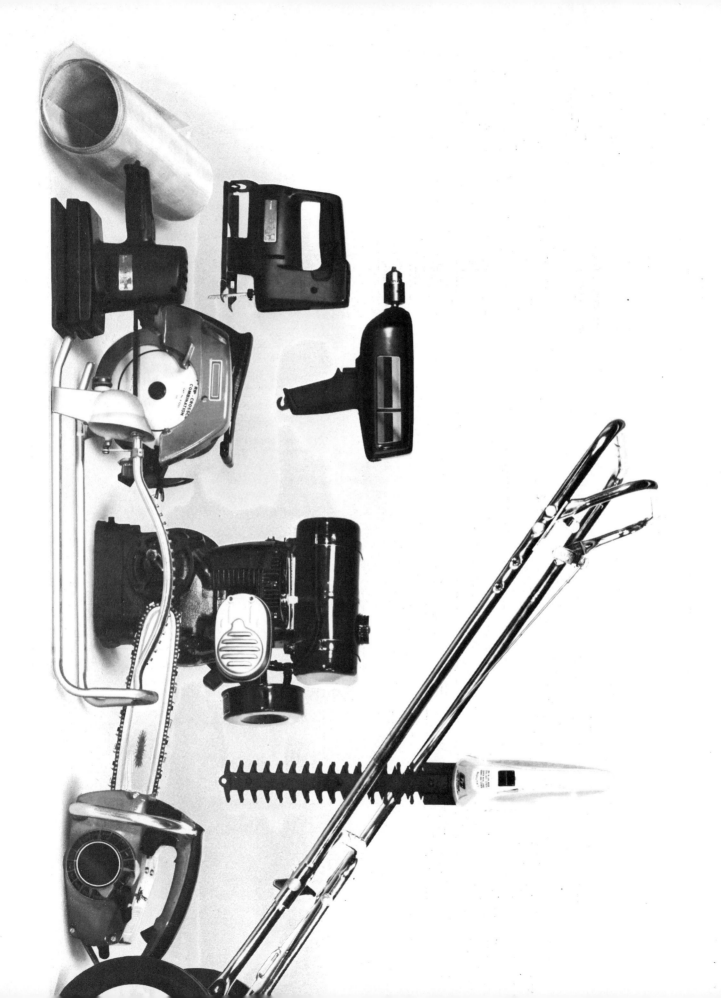

Lawn, Basement, Garage, and Garden

Many of the hidden costs of owning a home arise from the need to purchase and maintain a variety of equipment, including lawn mowers, garden tools, and water heaters. It can be expensive to have this equipment repaired professionally. Moreover, such items as hoses and lawn sprinklers must be repaired by the homeowner himself or else discarded, as it is difficult to find any repairman willing to do such work. This section deals with repairs the homeowner can easily and inexpensively make himself. The sections on tools, pests, screens, and thermostats may be of interest to apartment dwellers as well.

contents

Basic tools

To be well prepared to fix things and handle emergencies around your home, there are a number of hand and power tools you should own and keep in good working condition. Besides the garage and basement workshop tools shown on this and the following pages, various types of tools are covered in other sections of this book: Plumbing tools, p.34; furniture repair tools, pp.54-55; upholstery tools, p.106; appliance repair tools, pp.122-123; and car repair tools, pp.316-318. Also see *Adhesives*, pp.10-13.

The key to buying tools is to get quality tools. A good tool can last a lifetime and, just as important, it can make a job safer, faster, and easier. It is generally a mistake to buy bargain basement tools. Poor tools may make a job much more diffi-

cult, especially for a beginner. In the long run, a good but expensive tool that will do a given job more quickly and easily than you could do it with ordinary hand stand up to years of use will be less expensive than two or three replacements for a cheap tool that does not last.

An apartment dweller may well get by with a claw hammer and small crosscut saw, flat and crossblade screwdrivers, a pair of combination pliers, an adjustable wrench, a steel tape measure, utility knife, a level, an awl, a small vise that will clamp onto the kitchen table, and perhaps an electric drill. These can easily be stored in a closet or deep drawer. A homeowner will have the room (and the need) for many if not all of the tools shown here and on the following pages. A tool box with a lift-out tray is useful for carrying selected tools to and from a job.

Unusual tools

Often a specialized tool will allow you to do a given job more quickly and easily than you could do it with ordinary hand tools. However, these tools are often expensive and would seldom be needed again. In such cases it makes sense to rent the tool from a tool rental agency (listed in the Yellow Pages under *Rental Service Stores* or *Tools-Renting*). Tools offered for rental are usually in good repair and are industrial models that can withstand heavy use better than consumer versions of the same tool. The dealer should be able to give you detailed operating instructions and safety precautions for any tool you rent.

Tools that are commonly rented include: steam carpet cleaners, floor polishers and sanders, wallpaper steamers,

moving equipment, paint sprayers, paint strippers, plumber's tools, generators, power post-hole diggers, power saws, rug shampooers, vacuums, and ladders.

Mail-order firms specializing in unusual and hard-to-find tools are often the only source of exotic, special-purpose tools. One typical catalog contains, among many others, the following tools: flexible drill extensions, ear plugs, a glue injector, saw sharpeners, soldering jigs, cabinetmaker's screwdrivers, thread restorers, plane and chisel sharpeners, stud extractors, 24-inch-long drill bits, offset pliers and screwdrivers, thread pitch gauges, internal pipe wrenches, sharpening stones, a vinyl repair kit, gear and bearing pullers, flexible files, an offset funnel, and a nut splitter.

Tools for measuring and aligning

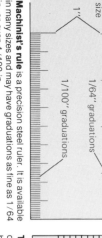

Housing

Tape

Hook

Pull tape

Push tape

Flexible steel tape measures are available in lengths up to 100 ft. A 12-ft model is a reasonable choice. The hook at the end of the tape should slide back and forth a distance equal to its thickness for accurate inside or outside measurements. On some models, you can replace a broken tape without buying a new housing.

1"

Twice actual size

1/64" graduations

1/100" graduations

Machinist's rule is a precision steel ruler. It is available in many sizes and may have graduations as fine as 1/64 in. or even 1/100 in.

45° vial

Level

Horizontal vial

Vertical vial

Centering marks

Bubble

Vial

Fluid

Torpedo level is relatively short and has tapered ends; it will fit into places a carpenter's level will not. When bubble is centered in vial, item being checked is level. Many levels have extra vials for checking surfaces that are vertical or at a 45° angle. Vials should be visible from top and sides of level.

Ruler

90°

Handle

45°

90°

45°

A

B

A=B

Try square is used to measure and mark 90° angles for cutting and fitting lumber. You can measure a 45° angle by marking off the same distance on both arms.

Eight tools in one

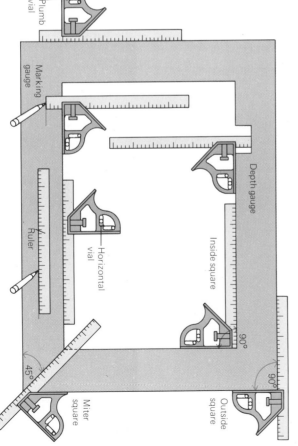

Plumb vial

Marking gauge

Horizontal vial

Depth gauge

Inside square

Ruler

90°

90°

45°

90°

Miter square

Outside square

Combination square contains a ruler, 45° and 90° angles, and two levels. The ruler can be separated from the remainder of the tool. In various configurations, this square can be used as eight different tools, including a vertical (plumb) or horizontal level, a depth gauge, and a marking gauge for cutting lumber.

Screwdrivers

The best known screwdrivers are the flat blade and cross blade (or Phillips), both available in a number of sizes to fit different sized screws. There are a number of other patented screw-driving systems, and they require special drivers, should you ever come across such screws. The most common of these is the Reed & Prince, which is easily confused with the Phillips system. Due to subtle differences in shape, a Phillips driver cannot be used on a Reed & Prince screw, or vice versa, without damaging the screw.

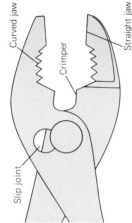

Long shank
Medium
Stubby
Too small
Too wide

Use the right size screwdriver. Too wide a blade will damage the work surface; too small a blade may slip and damage the screw.

Flat blade driver should be same width as screw head and fit slot snugly.

Phillips driver has a blunt tip; screw slots curve at junction.

Reed & Prince driver has a pointed tip; screw slots meet at right angle.

Allen screw, or setscrew, is driven by hexagonal key or driver (p.365).

Wedging action grips screw slot

Before attempting to drive a screw into wood, make a pilot hole with a drill or an awl (shown).

Awl

Screw-holding tips prevent loss of screws in hard-to-reach spots. Type on left needs less clearance.

Blade — Clamp

Posidrive® screws look like Phillips screws with a square drive added.

Clutch head, or butterfly, screws are used on some automobile assemblies.

Scrulox® system uses a square drive similar to ratchet and socket sets.

Torx® system is used in some auto seatbelt and door lock systems.

Straight shank

A gimlet makes a wider pilot hole than an awl (good for screws up to No. 8 size).

Gimlet or screw starter

Offset screwdrivers (made with or without ratcheting action) work best in cramped spaces.

Offset

Ratcheting offset

Cabinetmaker's screwdriver has no flanges on blade; fits into deep recesses and other confined areas.

Direction control

Spiral ratchet screwdriver twists blade in preset direction when handle is pushed toward screw.

Pliers

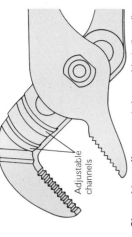

Curved jaw
Straight jaw
Crimper
Slip joint

Slip-joint pliers adjust to two or more positions for different-sized work. Combination jaws grip flat or curved objects. Some models include a crimper.

Lineman's pliers have straight jaws and a cutter; can be used to twist and cut wire, but not nails.

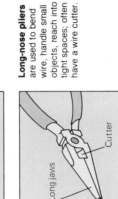

Straight jaw
Cutter

Long-nose pliers are used to bend wire, handle small objects, reach into tight spaces; often have a wire cutter.

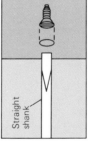

Long jaws
Cutter

Adjustable channels

Channel-type pliers can grip larger objects than slip-joint pliers; they are also less likely to slip out of adjustment as you squeeze the handles.

Bent long-nose pliers are used in cramped areas or in spaces where straight-in access is blocked.

Return spring on some pliers keeps jaws open and ready to use and greatly simplifies one-handed operation of pliers.

Spring

Locking pliers can be used as pliers or as a clamp, a vise, or a wrench. They are available with straight, curved, C-clamp, bending, or adjustable chain wrench jaws. Some include a powerful cutter that may be used on wire, nails, and small bolts.

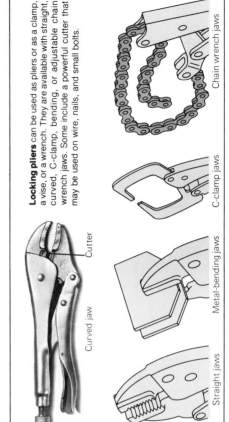

Cutter
Curved jaw

Chain wrench jaws

C-clamp jaws

Metal-bending jaws

Straight jaws

Tools and techniques

Cutting tools

Cutting pliers are used to cut the soft copper or aluminum wire found in household electrical systems, TV antenna systems, model train and auto racing sets.

Cutter

Tin snips are used to cut sheet metal of 20 gauge or lighter. Never use them to cut wire, nails, or hardened steel; if you do, you will ruin the blades.

Single pivot

Nail nippers are used for pulling or cutting nails. Long handles give extra leverage for extracting nails. Cutter pinches off nail heads to remove shingles, etc.

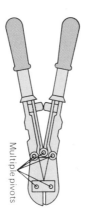

Lock

Multiple pivots

Aviation snips have multiple leverage for cutting heavy gauge sheet metal, vinyl tile, air conditioning ducts. Separate snips are needed for straight and curved cuts.

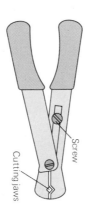

Screw

Cutting jaws

Bolt cutters have multiple leverage and heavy blades for cutting through bolts, padlock hasps, chain-link fencing, and other heavy materials.

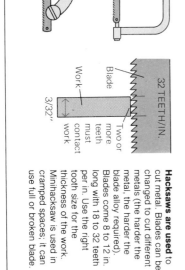

Multiple pivots

Adjustable wire stripper removes insulation from wire of various gauges without damaging metal. Position of movable screw determines jaw opening.

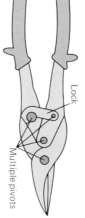

Screw

Hacksaws

Handle

Frame

Blade

Minihacksaw

Hacksaws are used to cut metal. Blades can be changed to cut different metals (the harder the metal, the harder the blade alloy required). Blades come 8 to 12 in. long with 18 to 32 teeth per in. Use the right tooth size for the thickness of the work. Minihacksaw is used in cramped spaces; it can use full or broken blade.

32 TEETH/IN.

Blade

Work

3/32"

Two or more teeth must contact work

Vises

Metal jaws

Bolt hole

Anvil

Machinist's vise has a built-in anvil for metalwork; bolts to workbench. Smaller models have clamp-on or suction cup base for temporary use in apartments or homes without workshops. Woodworking vise (right) has wooden jaws that hold lumber without marring it.

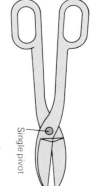

Clamp

Wooden jaws

Bench-sized vise combines the functions of a bench, vise, clamp, and sawhorse. Folds flat so that it can be hung behind a closet door for storage.

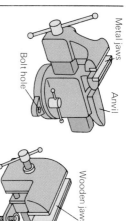

Open

Folded

Staplers

Stapler (left) forces heavyweight wire staples into paneling, insulation, upholstery, and screens. Electric stapler (right) is the preferred tool for lengthy and heavy stapling jobs.

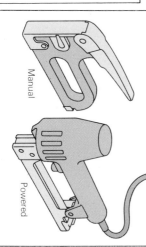

Manual

Powered

Fasteners

When replacing damaged or lost fasteners, always use nuts and bolts of the same size and strength as the originals. Bolt heads are marked to indicate their tensile strength. Never use hardware bolts on automobiles or machinery.

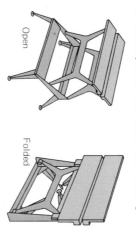

Bolt marking	Quality or grade	Tensile strength
	Hardware grade	74,000 psi**
	S.A.E.* 3	100,000 psi**
	S.A.E.* 5	120,000 psi**
	S.A.E.* 6	133,000 psi**
	S.A.E.* 7	133,000 psi**
	S.A.E.* 8	150,000 psi**
	Setscrew	212,000 psi**

*Society of Automotive Engineers. **Pounds per square inch

Measure bolt diameter with an accurate steel ruler (left). Measure number of threads per inch with a thread gauge. Marking at right indicates metric threads.

Gauge

20

9.8

Thread-restoring file has teeth that fit eight common thread sizes exactly. It is used to remove rust and grit from bolts or studs without damaging the threads.

Wrenches

Open-end wrenches

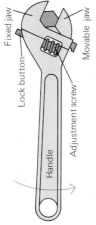

Open-end wrenches have fixed jaws. Better quality wrenches are made of chrome valadium steel and are machined to accurate tolerances for a proper fit. The standard open-end wrench has its jaws offset 15° from the handle. Wrenches with no offset are of limited use in tight quarters. Wrenches with greater than normal off-set are made for working in tight areas.

Using the offset feature to tighten a bolt with limited access

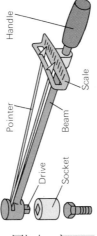

Place wrench on bolt at best possible angle. Come in from right.

Rotate the bolt until wrench hits obstruction, then remove wrench.

Turn wrench over and approach bolt from best angle on right.

Rotate the bolt again, remove wrench, turn it over, repeat sequence.

Adjustable wrenches

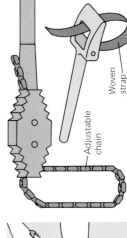

Adjustable wrench is a basic, general purpose tool. It will fit nuts and bolts up to the maximum opening of its jaws. Buy a model with a locking feature; it will prevent jaws from jiggling out of adjustment while wrench is in use. Whenever possible, turn wrench so that the load is applied to the fixed jaw—the fixed jaw can withstand more pressure than the movable jaw.

Box wrenches

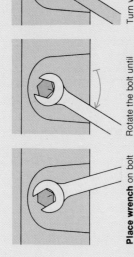

Box wrenches surround a nut or bolt and apply pressure to all its corners; they are less likely to ruin a fastener than an open-end wrench, which bears on only two corners. A six-point box wrench bears against all six faces of a hexagonal fastener, further dissipating stress. A 12-point wrench bears only against the corners, but it will fit both hexagonal and square nuts.

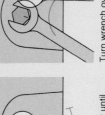

The head of a box wrench should be set at an angle to its handle to allow clearance between the wrench and adjacent fasteners, and between the hand of the user and the equipment being serviced. Some box wrenches have no offset.

Allen wrenches

Allen wrenches are L-shaped keys (left) that fit the hexagonal recesses in the heads of Allen screws, or setscrews. Ball-point Allen driver (right) works at an angle when access to the Allen screw is limited or blocked.

Torque wrenches

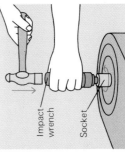

A torque wrench measures the tightening force applied to fasteners. The unit of measure is the foot-pound. The square drive at the end of the wrench is attached to a socket or extension. Torque is read on the scale as the beam bends and the pointer remains straight. Manufacturers of some machinery specify tightening torque for specific nuts and bolts.

Nut drivers

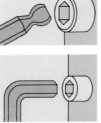

Nut drivers have handles like screwdrivers, and socket ends for use on square or hexagonal nuts and bolts. They are sold in sets of graduated sizes, or as a single handle with interchangeable sockets. They work faster than wrenches.

Socket sets

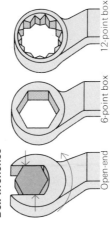

Sockets can be driven by a ratcheting handle, a breaker bar, a torque wrench, or an impact wrench. They are sold in graduated sets to fit square or hexagonal fasteners, and have 4 to 12 internal corners.

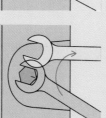

A ratcheting handle can be set to turn a fastener in one direction, then ratchet on the backswing. It is much faster than a wrench.

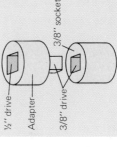

The drive end of the socket may be ¼, ⅜, or ½ in. square. You can buy adapters that let you use a ½-in. drive with smaller sockets.

Chain and strap wrenches

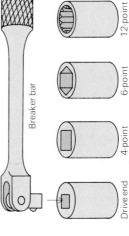

A chain wrench (top) can be used on large pipes and fittings in cramped quarters where an adjustable pipe wrench or monkey wrench will not fit. Use a strap wrench (below) to avoid marring soft or plated pipe.

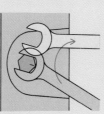

An impact wrench is used with a socket to free stubborn nuts and bolts; it transforms the blow of a hammer into a twisting force.

Tools and techniques

Electric drill

The electric drill is usually the first power tool acquired by a do-it-yourselfer. It is a versatile tool that can drill holes in metal, wood, plastics, and concrete (with special bits) and can take dozens of accessories for sanding, grinding, shaping, stripping, buffing, sharpening, and cutting holes.

A drill is classified by the largest bit its chuck will accept—¼, ⅜, ½, or ¾ inch (the last two sizes are used mainly by professional masons and carpenters). A ⅜-in. drill with an infinitely variable speed feature and a trigger lock (which may work at only the highest speed) is the most useful for the homeowner. If you will be using a screwdriver bit often, you may want a reversible motor. Double insulated models with plastic housings and two-prong plugs will fit any 120-volt outlet without an adapter. Rechargeable, battery-powered drills are now available in many sizes and models (variable speed, reversible). Although expensive, they are quite convenient for anyone who does not drill many holes or use sanding and grinding accessories. They are handy for use out of doors or in attics, basements, or garages where electrical outlets are unavailable. Many drill more than 100 holes on an overnight charge.

Standard twist bits have a cutting edge with a 59 degree angle, which is perfect for drilling mild steel but less than ideal for some other materials. You can regrind a standard twist bit to any desired angle if you will be doing much work with especially hard or soft metals (see *Sharpening drill bits*, p.367). Inexpensive bits are made of carbon steel. More expensive bits, designed to cut harder metals, are made of a material usually called high-speed alloy steel.

Electric drill attachments

Drill

Standard twist bits are sold singly or in packaged sets

Oversize bit with step-down shank

Spade bit drills large holes in wood

Paint stirrer

12" bit extender

Wire brush removes rust from metal

Stripping wheel removes paint from wood

Disc sander

Drum sander

Hole saw with interchangeable blades

Rotary rasp shapes wood

Sabre saw attachment

Chipping wheel removes paint from cement

Mower blade sharpener

Rotary file

Lamb's-wool buffing wheel

Muslin buffing wheel

Felt polishing drum

Bit points for drilling various materials

Masonry bit is made of carbide steel for use on brick, cement, stone.

67½°

Blunt point is best for very hard metals, such as heat-treated steel.

50°

Medium point is used on fiber, hard rubber, cast iron, and copper.

30°

Extra-sharp point is for hardwoods, hard rubber, and fiber board.

42°

Sharp point works best on wood, thermoplastics, high-silicon aluminum.

59°

Standard point suits materials such as mild steel and some plastic.

Pilot bit drills screw pilot holes and countersinks in one operation

Carbide bit drills holes in brick, concrete, and masonry

Straight-fluke bit cuts clean holes in soft metals

Screwdriver bit speeds cabinetry and furniture construction

Drill bit sharpeners work in much the same way as pencil sharpeners to grind a standard 59° point on ⅛- to ⅜ in. twist bits. This model is powered by the drill itself; more costly models have built-in motors.

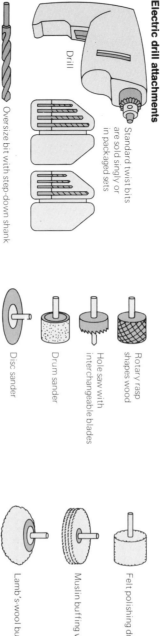

To drill a hole in a dimly lit area or in cramped quarters where the drill itself casts a shadow on the work, attach a battery-powered penlight to the drill housing with easily removed electrical tape.

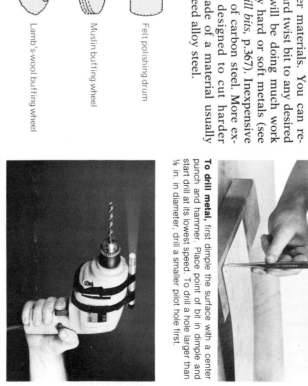

To drill metal, first dimple the surface with a center punch and hammer. Place point of bit in dimple and start drill at its lowest speed. To drill a hole larger than ⅛ in. in diameter, drill a smaller pilot hole first.

Electric grinder

A powered grinder can be fitted with coarse or fine stone wheels for sharpening tools, with fiber or wire brushes for cleaning and polishing, and with lamb's wool or felt discs for buffing. Good grinders turn at more than 3,000 revolu-

tions per minute (rpm) and can be dangerous. Always wear safety goggles when working at a grinder, even if it has transparent eye shields. Be sure the metal wheel guard is in place to protect you in case the wheel shatters.

Remove stone wheels periodically to test their soundness. To test a wheel, support it with a screwdriver shank and tap it gently with a tool handle at several points around its flat side. A vitrified or silicate wheel should make a ringing

sound. If it does not, discard it. If the wheel has rubber or organic bonding agents in it, it will not ring: inspect it and discard it if it is chipped or cracked. A replacement wheel must fit snugly and have the same rpm rating as the grinder.

If your grinder does not have a swiveling tool rest, fashion a stop for it. Make a clamp from two mending plates and a pair of bolts with wing nuts. Position clamp so that edge of tool meets the wheel at desired sharpening angle.

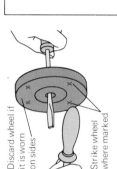

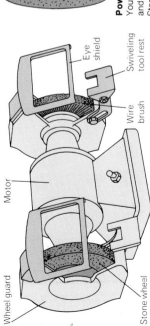

Eye shield
Swiveling tool rest
Wire brush
Motor
Wheel guard
Stone wheel

Power grinder has two wheels. You can mount a stone on one side and a wire brush or buffer on other. Stones come in many shapes.

Discard wheel if it is worn on sides
Strike wheel where marked

To test a wheel, support it by its mounting hole and strike it as indicated above. Discard the wheel if it does not make a ringing sound.

Making a stop

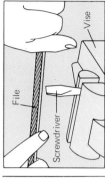

Wing nuts
Mending plate
Wheel
Tool rest
Tool

Sharpening chisels and planes

Chisels and plane irons are first hollow-ground to a 25° angle on the grinding wheel, then sharpened to a flat 30° bevel using a whetstone and light oil.

Position the adjustable tool rest so that the blade meets the wheel at the level of its mounting shaft and forms a 25° angle with the surface of the wheel. Then, grind.

Hold hollow-ground blade at 30° angle to whetstone; hone by hand to achieve flat, even bevel. Honing jig assures accuracy. Remove the burr that forms on the back of the blade by turning it over and honing its flat side lightly on whetstone.

Whetstone
Wheel
30°

Blade
Wheel
25°
Rest

Dull blade
Hollow
25°

Blade
Jig
30°
Burr
Whetstone
Stone

Sharpening drill bits

Common twist bits have an angle of 59° at the cutting (straight) edge of the point. The heel (curved) edge is 12° to 15° less. Measure it with a drill point gauge, sold by power tool dealers.

Make a drill grinding jig by clamping a scrap of wood to tool rest. Position a wooden guide at a 59° angle to the side of the wheel, and draw a series of parallel straight lines at a 44° to 47° angle to the wheel. (Set up other angles for extra sharp or blunt points; see p.366).

Hold cutting edge of bit against wheel and guide. Grind until proper angle is achieved, then swing and rotate bit simultaneously until heel of bit is against wheel and the bit itself is parallel to the pencil lines. Grind both sides evenly.

Gauge
59°
12°
59°

Wheel
45°
59°
Guide
Jig
Pencil lines on scrap wood

Swing and twist
Push bit

Restoring screwdrivers

A screwdriver tip that has become rounded will slip out of screw slots. Square off the end with a hand file or by holding tip against side of grinding wheel. Dip tip in water often to keep it from overheating and losing its temper.

After being squared off, the tip will be wider than it was originally. Restore its original width by grinding both edges lightly. Taper should be gradual and symmetrical. Measure your progress by holding the tip up to a screw head.

After completing the above two steps, the blade will be shorter and thicker than it was originally. Grind the first ¼ in. of the blade on both sides to form a hollow-ground tip whose edges are nearly parallel. Stop when tip fits screw snugly.

File
Screwdriver

Tip
Vise

Wheel
Tool rest

Screw
Tip

Wheel
Hollow ground
¼"
Tip
Tool rest

Tools and techniques

Soldering

Soldering is a relatively simple and inexpensive method for joining metal pipes (see p.43), wiring (p.131), and sheets. Although a well soldered joint should last indefinitely, it can be opened without damage to its parts by heating it to the solder's melting point (360°F to 460°F). This cannot be done with welded joints. The tools required for soldering are: a soldering iron, pencil, or gun; a stand to keep the hot tool from burning the work surface; and cleaning tools, such as emery cloth, steel wool, a file, or a wire brush. The two secrets of soldering are to clean the joint thoroughly and to heat the work, not just the solder. The choice of the proper solder and flux is also important (see table). Common solder is a mixture of tin and lead. A 60/40 solder (60 percent tin, 40 percent lead) is the most expensive, but it makes the strongest bond and is easiest to work with, due to its low melting point. A 40/60 solder is more difficult to work with. A 50/50 solder is a good compromise between cost and ease of use.

Flux is used to clean the metal surfaces to be joined, to prevent oxidation of the metal when it is heated, and to lower the surface tension of the molten solder so that it spreads and penetrates more readily. Several types of flux are available in liquid or paste form (see table). Flux-core solders are also available, and they eliminate a separate fluxing step when soldering small objects. Acid flux is highly corrosive; avoid contact with the skin and eyes, and clean any residue from the work with alcohol or commercial cleaners.

Successful soldering requires just enough heat to melt the solder. The work should be held by wooden clamps, clothes pins, or vise jaws. A metal vise or tabletop may draw too much heat away from the work, resulting in a poor job. If you must work on a metal surface, insulate the work with scraps of lumber. Too much heat causes the solder to form a ball that will not spread.

Use a soldering iron that is big and powerful enough to heat the work quickly and completely. A multirange soldering iron or gun of 240/325 watts will handle most household soldering jobs. For detailed instructions on soldering household appliances, see *Electrical soldering*, p.131. For complete information on soldering silver, see *Soldering silver links* and *Pickling*, p.31.

1. The tip of the soldering iron or gun must first be tinned to assure proper heat transfer. File tip to remove all pits and black corrosion. When bright copper is exposed, clean with steel wool. It cannot be too clean.

2. Heat iron until new flux-core solder will just melt, then coat tip with solder. Wipe off excess solder with a wad of dry rags: a smooth silver coating should remain. If iron overheats, coating will turn black and require retinning.

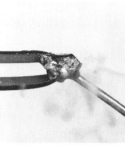

3. Use steel wool, emery cloth, and alcohol or cleaning solvent to remove all corrosion and film from areas to be soldered. Do not touch cleaned areas with your fingers; they will leave oily deposits that will weaken the solder bond.

4. Make sure parts fit snugly; loose fits result in weak soldered joints. Apply the proper flux to the cleaned areas with a brush or swab (do not use your fingers). Skip this step when using a flux-core solder. Heat iron to working temperature.

5. Hold tip flat against work for maximum heat transfer. Feed solder under tip and move slowly along joint. (If solder forms a ball that will not spread, work is too hot.) Let work cool. Wash off flux residue with warm water.

6. Large joints should be sweat soldered. Clean and flux areas to be joined, then apply a thin coat of solder to each piece and let it cool. Clamp pieces together and heat until solder remelts. Protect bench with an asbestos pad.

Propane torch

Choosing the right solder and flux

METAL	SOLDER	FLUX
Aluminum	Special aluminum solder	Special aluminum flux
Brass, bronze	60/40 or 50/50	Rosin or acid
Copper	60/40 or 50/50	Rosin or acid
Electrical wiring	60/40	Rosin
Galvanized metal	60/40 or 50/50	Acid
High temperature applications	Silver solder	Silver brazing flux
Silver	Silver solder	Rosin or silver flux
Steel, tin, zinc	60/40 or 50/50	Acid
Stainless steel	60/40 or 50/50	Stainless steel flux

How to replace soldering gun tips

1. When tip becomes worn down from repeated filing and tinning, or soft due to heat fatigue, open the retaining nuts and remove tip. Keep nuts and discard tip.

2. Place nuts over prongs on new tip. Insert prongs about ¼ in. into small holes on sides of gun barrels. Bend tip downward to form two 90° bends simultaneously.

3. Remove tip from side of gun and insert its prongs down the center of the barrels in such a way that the 90° bends poke through the holes. Tighten retaining nuts.

Riveting

Riveting produces a stronger joint than soldering, although the process is more tedious. Pop rivets are the easiest to install, but solid rivets of iron, brass, copper, or aluminum make the strongest joints. Pop rivets can be used even when you have access to only one side of the work (such as patching over a rusted-out panel on an old car or truck). Solid rivets require access to both sides of the work, plus a ball-peen hammer and a special steel tool called a rivet set.

First, clamp together the pieces that are to be joined; then, drill a series of holes for the rivets. The holes must be slightly larger than the diameter of the rivet shank. Pop rivets are sold in three sizes for joining work that is ⅛, ¼, and ⅜ inch thick. Solid rivets are sold in a wide variety of shapes and sizes. Choose one that will project from the work a distance equal to 1½ times its diameter—this will provide enough material to form the head. A solid rivet that is too long can be cut shorter.

Remove the clamps, separate the pieces, and file off any burrs caused by the drilling, so that the pieces can make close contact. Align and firmly clamp the pieces once more, then install the rivets.

Welding

Welding makes the strongest metal-to-metal joints by actually melting the parts, then allowing the molten metal to cool and solidify. Additional material, in the form of metal rods, is added to the molten pool to act as a filler, and preserve the original dimensions of the pieces being welded. Welding provides such a strong bond that it is often possible to join two pieces with a series of small spot welds instead of one continuous weld.

Three methods of welding are feasible for home use: electrical arc welding, oxy-acetylene welding, and oxy-propane welding. The last two methods burn a gas (acetylene and propane, respectively) in the presence of pure oxygen. They require the use of highly compressed gases, which are stored in steel cylinders. The most common, industrial sized cylinders are unwieldy and potentially dangerous.

In arc welding, the heat is generated by an electric arc of high amperage (supplied by a transformer) that jumps a gap between the welding rod and the work. Arc welding outfits of 30 to 300 amps are available for home use. Those of less than 180 amps are not suitable for joining thick metals, and are difficult to use in any case.

Some homes will require special wiring for a 180-amp welder. Such wiring should be installed by a licensed electrician, and the welding unit should be approved by the Underwriter's Laboratory.

Welding is a skill that is difficult to learn without expert instruction and supervision. Although it is a popular offering in adult education courses, you would need to do a lot of welding to pay for the cost of welding courses and equipment. Most people will find it more economical to take an occasional welding job to a welding shop (listed in the Yellow Pages of your phone book).

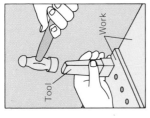

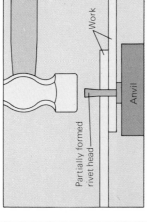

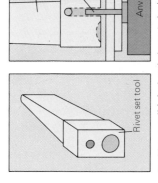

Position a solid rivet and pieces to be joined on an anvil or other hard surface. Position deep hole of rivet set over the rivet shank, then strike rivet set sharply with a ball-peen hammer.

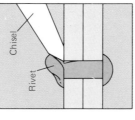

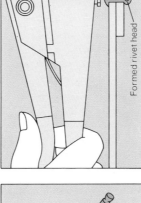

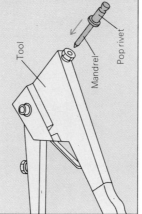

Remove the rivet set and strike top of rivet with hammer. This will flatten head slightly and cause rivet shank to expand for a tight fit. Be sure metal pieces are held tightly together.

Insert rivet into hole and press tool firmly against work. Squeeze handles together until rivet head is formed and mandrel breaks off. Release pressure on handles, remove tool, discard mandrel.

Position shallow depression in the rivet set over the rivet and strike with hammer until head is rounded off. If rivet was too short, head will be narrow; if rivet was too long, head will be misshapen.

To remove a rivet, grind, file, or chisel off its head, then drive it out of hole with a hammer and punch. If rivet head is countersunk, score it with a punch, then drill through head and shank.

Select the proper pop rivet for the thickness of the pieces to be joined (see text) and insert it into riveting tool. Squeeze tool handles together just enough to keep rivet from falling out.

One lightweight home welding outfit uses small tanks of oxygen and propane. It will weld, braze, solder, and cut steel plate up to ¼ in. thick.

The four-cycle (four-stroke) engine

Small gasoline engines power a wide variety of lawn and garden equipment. Although this section deals mainly with lawn mower, lawn tractor, and chain saw engines, the information given applies to small engines used on most other machinery. Specific engine repair jobs are cross-indexed in the troubleshooting table on page 373.

Maintenance and repair procedures that do not concern the engine are given for the following types of equipment under separate headings: chain saws (pp. 388–391), lawn mowers (pp. 394–401), lawn tractors (pp. 402–403), snow throwers (p. 420), and tillers (p. 424).

The four-cycle engine is similar in design to the standard automobile engine; but it is considerably smaller, is cooled by air (not water), and generally has only one cylinder. It is also known as the four-stroke engine.

As in the automobile engine, power is produced by the explosive combustion of gasoline vapors inside the cylinder. A carburetor mixes gasoline and air to supply these vapors, and a spark plug sets off the combustion. The high pressures generated by this combustion force a piston down the cylinder bore. The piston transfers its power to the crankshaft by means of the connecting rod. The interaction of the connecting rod and crankshaft changes the up and down motion of the piston into rotary motion, just as a bicycle's pedals transform the up and down motion of the rider's legs into the rotary motion of the bicycle wheels.

This sequence of events is shown on p. 371. For clarity, the two cams have been shown on opposite sides of the cylinder, although they actually share a common shaft on one side of it. The camshaft is geared to turn at half the speed of the crankshaft. In the four-cycle engine there is one power stroke for every four up or down strokes of the piston.

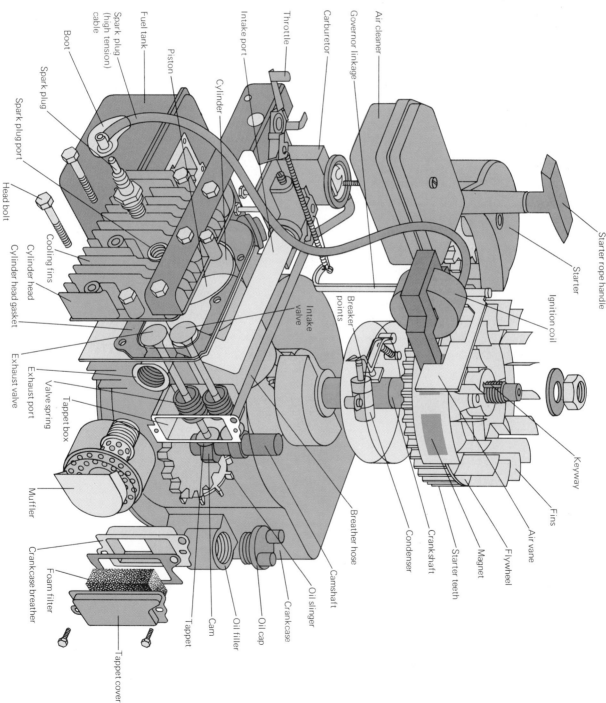

Starter rope handle
Starter
Ignition coil
Keyway
Fins
Air vane
Flywheel
Magnet
Starter teeth
Crankshaft
Condenser
Breather hose
Camshaft
Oil slinger
Crankcase
Oil cap
Oil filler
Cam
Tappet
Crankcase breather
Tappet cover
Foam filter
Muffler
Exhaust valve
Valve spring
Tappet box
Exhaust port
Cylinder head gasket
Cylinder head
Cooling fins
Head bolt
Spark plug port
Spark plug
Boot
Fuel tank
Spark plug (high tension) cable
Piston
Cylinder
Intake port
Intake valve
Breaker points
Throttle
Carburetor
Governor linkage
Air cleaner

How a two-cycle engine works

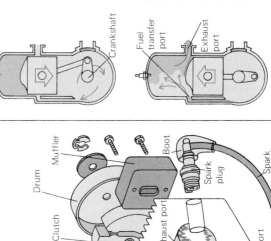

1. On upward stroke, fuel mixture already in cylinder is compressed. Vacuum formed in airtight crankcase by rising piston draws more mixture from the carburetor and past the reed valve.

Labels: Cylinder, Piston, Reed valve, Crankcase

2. At top of stroke, pressure stabilizes in the crankcase and the reed valve springs shut. The spark plug fires and starts the power (downward) stroke.

Labels: Spark plug, Connecting rod

3. On downward stroke, power is transmitted to the crankshaft, and the fuel-air mixture in the crankcase is compressed by the descending piston.

Labels: Crankshaft

4. Near the bottom of the stroke, the piston uncovers the ports and the pressurized fuel-air mixture rushes into the cylinder, forcing the burned gases out the exhaust port.

Labels: Fuel transfer port, Exhaust port

The two-cycle (two-stroke) engine

In the two-cycle engine, there is one power stroke for every second stroke of the piston. It occurs, of course, on each downward stroke. Because there is no exhaust stroke, the exhaust gases must be released from the cylinder when the piston completes its power stroke. This is accomplished when the piston uncovers ports (or holes) in the walls of the cylinder during its downward movement. (See sequence illustrated at right.)

The ports of a two-cycle engine serve the same purpose as the valves in a four-cycle engine. Some designs use a reed valve—a flexible strip of metal or plastic that serves as a one-way gate—between the carburetor and the airtight crankcase. To distinguish between these two kinds of valves, the mushroom-shaped valves of a four-cycle engine are technically known as poppet valves.

The underside of the piston acts as a pump on the two-cycle engine, drawing the fuel-air mixture into the crankcase, then forcing it up into the cylinder.

The spark plug is fired by a magnetic ignition. Magnets in the flywheel generate an electrical current in a coil of wire every time they pass it. When the breaker points are opened, this current jumps as high as 20,000 volts and is transferred to the spark plug.

Because it has fewer parts, and gives twice as many power strokes per engine revolution, the two-cycle engine is lighter and more powerful than a four-cycle engine of the same size. But because it uses more fuel than a four-cycle engine, the two-cycle is generally used only on machines that need an especially small or lightweight power plant, such as chain saws. To determine if an engine is a two-cycle or a four-cycle model, look for oil fill or drain plugs on the crankcase. Oil is mixed with the gasoline on two-cycle engines, so they have no oil plugs. Two-cycle engines are also known as two-stroke engines.

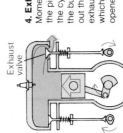

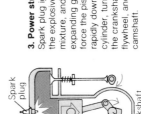

Labels: Air filter, Filter housing, Carburetor, Vaporized fuel, Gasket, Reed valve, Connecting rod, Gasket, Liquid fuel, Fuel tank (mix oil with gas), Chain oil tank (on chain saws only), Crankcase, Magnet, Flywheel, Ignition coil, Crankshaft, Piston, Fuel transfer port, Exhaust port, Spark plug, Boot, Drum, Muffler, Clutch, Spark plug cable

How a four-cycle engine works

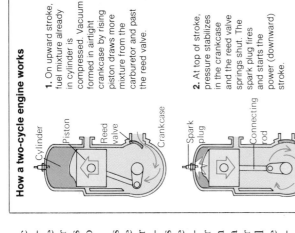

1. Intake stroke: Egg-shaped cam on rotating camshaft forces intake valve open. The piston moving down the cylinder draws in fuel-air mixture from the carburetor.

Labels: Intake valve, Cylinder, Piston, Cam, Cam

2. Compression stroke: Camshaft rotation allows the spring to close the valve. The piston moves back up the cylinder, and compresses the fuel and air mixture near the top.

Labels: Spring, Connecting rod

3. Power stroke: Spark plug ignites the explosive mixture, and the expanding gases force the piston rapidly down the cylinder, turning the crankshaft, flywheel, and camshaft.

Labels: Spark plug, Crankshaft

4. Exhaust stroke: Momentum carries the piston back up the cylinder, forcing the burned gases out through the exhaust valve, which has been opened by the cam.

Labels: Exhaust valve, Crankcase

Periodic maintenance

You can avoid many mechanical problems with a piece of equipment by maintaining its engine. Most engine trouble can be avoided by keeping the engine clean, inside and out. Dirt blocking the cooling fins and air cleaner will cause the engine to overheat, which can lead to serious damage. It is also important to change a four-cycle engine's oil periodically. Combustion byproducts eventually work their way into the oil and reduce its lubricating properties.

At regular intervals, certain steps should be taken to properly maintain a small engine. These steps are illustrated at right. The intervals may differ for different makes of engines. Check your owner's manual.

To keep track of an engine's operating hours, place a piece of adhesive tape somewhere on the machine and keep a running tally on it in ink. If you prefer not to keep such a close account, estimate your yearly use of the machine and mark its service dates on a calendar. Equipment that is used seasonally, such as a lawn mower or snow thrower, should be checked and cleaned at the beginning or end of each season and again at midseason if the machine is used often (see pp. 395–396).

An engine that has been in storage for a long time may be hard to start because the gasoline has evaporated from the entire fuel system. Such an engine must be primed. Some models have a priming button that will pump fuel into the carburetor. On simpler models, attempting to start several times with the choke closed will draw fuel into the carburetor. A short squirt of starting fluid into the carburetor should get a sound but reluctant engine going. (Remove the air cleaner to gain access to the carburetor.) Starting fluid is sold at auto parts stores. If an engine fires several times at full choke but will not keep running, it will probably start and run at half choke.

Before each use

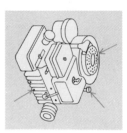

Clean the cooling air intake screen (usually visible at the top of the flywheel), the engine cooling fins, and the oil filler area (see pp. 370–371) to prevent dirt buildup.

Every 25 operating hours

Change the oil in a four-cycle engine. Use separate drain plug, if your engine has one. Otherwise, tip machine of filler hole. Refill with type and amount of oil listed in manual.

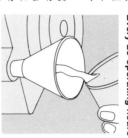

Check the oil level on four-cycle engines. Use the dipstick, if your engine has one. Otherwise, open the oil filler plug and make sure that the oil is up to the opening (see p. 395).

Every 50 operating hours

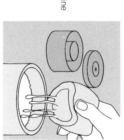

Remove spark plug. Clean and regap it, or replace it if necessary (p. 382).

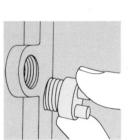

Change the oil and wash the filter on oil bath air cleaners (p. 374).

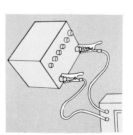

Clean or replace dry-type air filters (p. 374, 395). Check owner's manual for replacement intervals under various operating conditions.

Every 150 operating hours

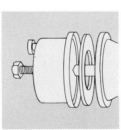

Check the ignition timing and adjust it if necessary (see p. 382).

Examine the breaker points and reset points and replace the gap, or replace the points and condenser (p. 375).

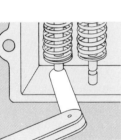

If your electric starter uses a wet cell battery, check the fluid level in each battery cell. Charge the battery if it needs it (see pp. 383, 334–335).

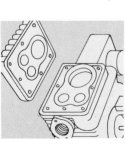

Check the ignition timing and adjust it if necessary (see p. 382).

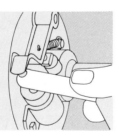

Check clearance between valve stems and tappets (see p. 387).

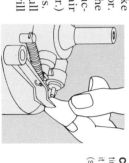

If carburetor has a fuel sediment bowl, remove it, clean it, and reinstall it (see p. 376).

Clean carbon from cylinder head and valves. Install a new head gasket (see p. 380).

Troubleshooting common small engine problems

The table at the right can be used to solve operating problems on both two- and four-cycle engines. There may be several possible causes listed for a specific problem. For example, under "Engine dies during use" you will find 16 possible causes. These are listed in order, from the most easily checked to the most difficult. If the engine has also been overheating and smoking, skip the nine possible causes for stalling that do not also cause overheating or smoking and concentrate first on the seven that do.

You can prevent serious engine damage by recognizing when your engine is running abnormally. Many of the problems listed in the table are a matter of degree—an engine that suddenly produces more heat, smoke, noise, or vibration than usual. In order to recognize an abnormal amount of heat, smoke, noise, or vibration, you must note how much the engine normally produces.

Overheating may be hardest to judge. Now and then, note how much heat radiates from the engine after about 20 minutes of normal operation by holding your hand near the cooling fins (do not touch them!). In the future, if the engine runs unevenly, stalls, or is hard to restart you will be able to tell whether or not the engine is giving off an abnormal amount.

When an engine will not start, the problem is usually in the ignition or the fuel system. To avoid checking through both, first see if the spark plug is working. Make a test plug by breaking off the side electrode of an old plug.

Remove spark plug (p.382). Attach test plug to cable and hold against engine. Operate starter. If spark jumps gap on test plug, ignition is OK. Repeat test on normal plug to see if it is defective.

POSSIBLE CAUSE	Starter does not turn engine	Engine turns, will not start	Engine starts, then stalls	Engine stalls unevenly, lacks power	Engine dies during use	Engine will not stop	Engine vibrates excessively	Engine overheats	Engine smokes profusely	Engine backfires	Engine is extra noisy or quiet
Starter rope jammed (p.383)	●										
Starter spring or pawls worn or broken (p.383)	●										
Electric starter battery low (pp.332–334, 383, 401)	●										
Electric starter connections loose or corroded (p.383)	●										
Fuel tank empty		●	●		●						
For two-cycle, fuel mixture incorrect (p.388)		●	●	●					●		
Fuel cap breather hole(s) blocked (p.381)		●	●		●						
Insufficient oil in crankcase								●			
Water in fuel (p.381)		●	●	●	●						
Air filter blocked with dirt (p.374)				●					●		
Spark plug fouled or broken (p.382)		●	●	●							
High tension cable loose or damaged (p.382)		●	●	●	●						
Choke in wrong position (p.379)		●	●								
Broken flywheel fins; replace flywheel (p.397)							●				
Muffler damaged or clogged (p.381)				●				●			
Cooling fins covered with debris								●			
For two-cycle, obstructed exhaust ports (p.381)				●				●			
Compression low (p.379)		●		●							
Fuel line obstructed, pinched, or broken (p.381)			●	●	●						
Idle speed adjustment wrong (pp.376–378)			●	●							
Overheated; allow to cool, then restart engine					●			●			
Carburetor fouled or badly adjusted (pp.376–378)		●	●	●					●		
Crankshaft bent; replace engine							●				
Flywheel key bent, broken, or worn (p.397)		●		●							
Ignition points dirty or poorly set (p.375)		●		●						●	
Poppet valves sticking or burned (pp.386–387)				●						●	
Governor linkage broken or out of adjustment (p.381)				●			●				
Loose engine mounting bolts							●				
Loose or bent machinery attachments							●				
Faulty clutch (pp.384–385)											●
Transmission belts slipping, gears jammed (p.384)											●
For two-cycle, faulty reed valve (p.386)				●						●	

Safety precautions

Before working on an engine, disconnect the spark plug cable to prevent the engine from accidentally starting. Do not allow the cable to dangle free. Pull back the rubber boot (if there is one) to expose the connector and attach it securely to an engine cooling fin or to the special grounding clip found on some engines.

If you place the engine on its side for repairs, keep the oil fill hole and fuel tank cap facing upward to prevent oil or gas from spilling.

After refueling the engine, move it at least 10 feet from the refueling spot before starting it. Spilled fuel and lingering fumes are then less likely to be ignited.

Whenever possible, allow the engine to cool off before working on it. This will protect you from burns and eliminate the possibility of hot engine parts igniting any fuel that may spill.

Small engines

Air cleaners

The air cleaner filters dust and grit from the air entering the carburetor. It prevents dirt from getting into the engine, where it could cause excessive wear of the moving parts. The cleaner contains one or more filter elements that must be cleaned or replaced periodically. Check your owner's manual for the service interval recommended by the manufacturer of your engine. Most manufacturers suggest cleaning or replacing the filter after every 25 to 50 hours of engine operation. If the engine is operated in an unusually dusty or sandy area, service the air cleaner at even shorter intervals.

The most common types of air cleaners are illustrated below. They are usually located toward the top of the engine, attached directly to the carburetor or connected to it by a short hose. To clean a paper filter, remove it and tap it lightly on a hard surface to dislodge loose dirt. Replace the filter if it still appears dirty.

A clogged air filter may make an engine difficult to start. It may also cause it to stall, run hesitantly, or overheat. Chain saw filters can clog after less than 10 hour's use.

Oil bath filter

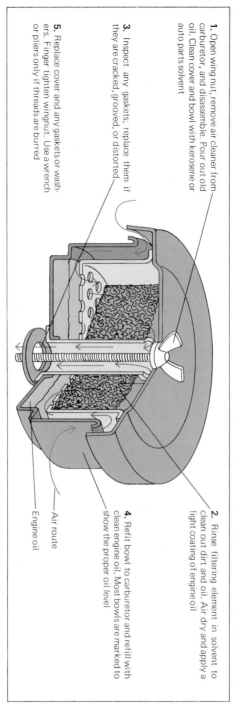

1. Open wing nut, remove air cleaner from carburetor, and disassemble. Pour out old oil. Clean cover and bowl with kerosene or auto parts solvent

2. Rinse filtering element in solvent to clean out dirt and oil. Air dry and apply a light coating of engine oil

3. Inspect any gaskets; replace them if they are cracked, grooved, or distorted

4. Refit bowl to carburetor and refill with clean engine oil. Most bowls are marked to show the proper oil level

5. Replace cover and any gaskets or washers. Finger tighten wingnut. Use a wrench or pliers only if threads are burred

Air route

Engine oil

Foam filter

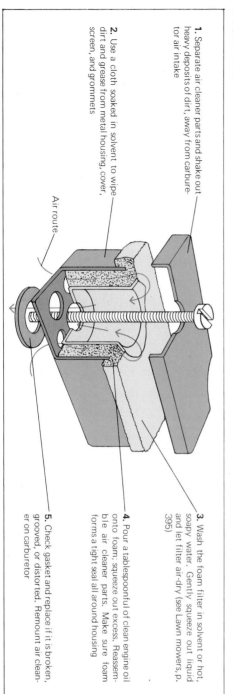

1. Separate air cleaner parts and shake out heavy deposits of dirt, away from carburetor air intake

2. Use a cloth soaked in solvent to wipe dirt and grease from metal housing, cover, screen, and grommets

3. Wash the foam filter in solvent or hot, soapy water. Gently squeeze out liquid and let filter air-dry (see Lawn mowers, p. 395)

4. Pour a tablespoonful of clean engine oil onto foam; squeeze out excess. Reassemble air cleaner parts. Make sure foam forms a tight seal all around housing

5. Check gasket and replace if it is broken, grooved, or distorted. Remount air cleaner on carburetor

Air route

Pleated paper filters

1. Open wing nut and remove air cleaner cover and filtering element(s)

2. Wash the foam sleeve (if any) in soap and water; gently squeeze dry. Some should be coated with oil (check owner's manual)

3. Tap paper element lightly on a flat surface to dislodge loose dirt. Do not wash or oil

4. Replace gaskets that are cracked or distorted

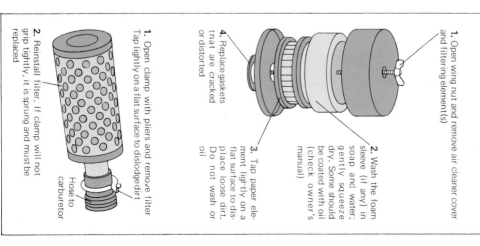

1. Open clamp with pliers and remove filter. Tap lightly on a flat surface to dislodge dirt

2. Reinstall filter. If clamp will not grip tightly, it is sprung and must be replaced

Hose to carburetor

Servicing breaker points and condenser

The breaker points act as a switch that sends current to the spark plug at the right moment. They should be adjusted or replaced periodically, using a kit available at most hardware stores.

You must remove the flywheel (see p.397) to reach the points on most engines. On a few models the points are reached through an access panel on the block; check your owner's manual. To work properly, the gap between the fully opened points must be set at a specified distance, measured to within 1/1000 inch. This is done with a feeler gauge—a set of metal blades of precise thickness, sold in auto parts stores. (See below and also *How to use a feeler gauge*, p.344.) The condenser is customarily replaced at the same time as the points.

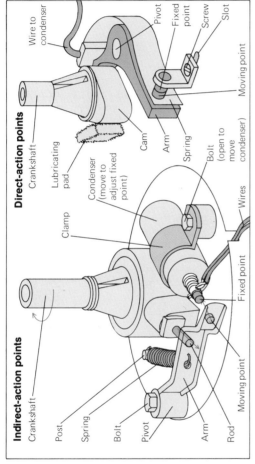

Indirect-action points

- Crankshaft
- Post
- Spring
- Bolt
- Pivot
- Arm
- Rod
- Moving point
- Fixed point
- Wires
- Clamp
- Condenser (move to adjust fixed point)
- Lubricating pad

Direct-action points

- Crankshaft
- Wire to condenser
- Pivot
- Fixed point
- Screw
- Slot
- Moving point
- Spring
- Arm
- Cam
- Bolt (open to move condenser)

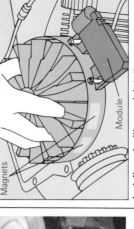

Remove flywheel (p.397) and clean loose dirt from breaker point housing. Open bolts and remove housing cover.

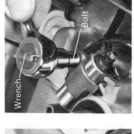

Remove pivot, bolt, arm, and spring. If points are burned or pitted, replace them. If dirty, clean with solvent.

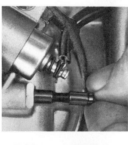

Pull rod from its housing and clean. If rod (or V-shaped arm on direct-action points) has been worn by cam, replace it.

Open clamp to remove condenser. Wire is held by a spring on indirect-action points (shown) or by a nut.

Use the plastic tool from kit to compress condenser spring. Push wire into hole; release spring. Install new condenser.

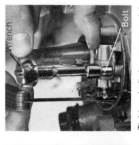

Test crankshaft for play. If it wobbles, the gap cannot be set accurately. Replace short block assembly or entire engine.

Insert rod into housing with grooved end outward. Fit arm into groove on pivot, bolt firmly into place. Attach spring.

Remove spark plug and turn saw chain or mower blade by hand (wear a heavy glove) until points open as wide as possible.

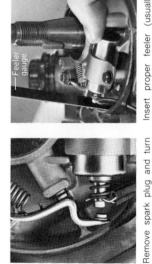

Insert proper feeler (usually .020 in.—see owner's manual). Position fixed point so feeler can be removed with light drag.

Tighten bolt to secure point. Place a few drops of oil on lubricating pad (if any). Install housing cover, flywheel.

Electronic ignition

A growing number of engine manufacturers are replacing the points and condenser with an electronic module mounted next to the flywheel. Few adjustments are possible with such a setup; if the module malfunctions, it is replaced as a unit. Buy the replacement before removing the faulty unit, if possible. Then, install and connect the replacement in the same manner as the original. Some engines have a single module, others have two. There must be a specified air gap between the ignition module and the flywheel, but it is not as critical as the breaker point gap. Usually, it is simply listed as more than a certain figure (.014 inch is common). You can set this with a feeler gauge or a post card. Ask your parts dealer for the correct gap.

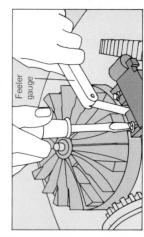

Module

Magnets

Install new ignition module in the same manner as the old one. Tighten screws only part way, so that module is free to move in its elongated mounting slots. Rotate the flywheel until its magnets are facing the module.

Feeler gauge

Place feeler blade or post card on top of the magnets and push the module gently toward the flywheel. The magnets should draw the module toward your gauge and hold it in position while you tighten the screws.

Small engines

How to adjust and service the carburetor

Several types of carburetors are used on small engines. It is not necessary to understand exactly how each works in order to adjust, clean, or rebuild it. You need only recognize the type used.

The carburetor settings seldom need adjustment. If an engine that worked well suddenly runs poorly, the problem is not likely to be the carburetor. Use the troubleshooting table (p.373) to look for trouble elsewhere. Make adjustments only after cleaning or rebuilding the carburetor or if an inspection of the spark plugs shows that the engine has been running too rich or too lean (p.382).

Check your owner's manual for adjustment procedures on your engine.

There are three basic carburetor adjustments: the choke (p.379), the idle speed, and the fuel mixture. Idle speed is adjusted by a screw that bears against the throttle linkage. It keeps the engine idling fast enough to prevent stalling and to provide proper lubrication. The fuel mixture is adjusted by one or two needle jets, which look like screws emerging from the carburetor. The smaller of two screws is for low speed mixture, the larger one is for high speed mixture.

Usually, you must turn the mixture screws all the way in (clockwise) until they just touch bottom (do not over-tighten) and back them out one full turn. Back out the idle speed screw until it just clears the throttle linkage, then tighten it one full turn. Set the choke and start the engine. After a three-minute warmup, that are subject to wear. To use it, disassemble and clean the carburetor, then substitute all the parts found in the kit.

smoothly and without stumbling both at idle and under load.

An old carburetor may be gummed up. Disassemble it and clean it with automotive carburetor solvent. Do not clean nonmetallic parts. Whenever the carburetor is disassembled, replace all gaskets. A rebuild kit (available from dealers and repair shops) contains new gaskets, needles, springs, diaphragms and other parts make fine adjustments an eighth of a turn at a time, until the engine runs

Float carburetors

This type of carburetor uses a float to regulate the flow of fuel. When fuel is low in the bowl, the float drops and opens a needle valve, allowing gasoline to enter. The rising fuel level pushes the float up, closing the valve. This action assures a consistent supply of fuel at the carburetor, regardless of fluctuations in fuel pump performance or gravity feed.

Before you remove any carburetor for cleaning, sketch or take a snapshot of the various control linkages so that you can reconnect levers on the carburetor to their proper cables and springs. Do not stretch the springs. Check the gasket flanges for warping before you reattach the carburetor (see *How to check mating surfaces*, opposite page). Also make sure that the throttle and choke plates move freely, without binding (see p.379).

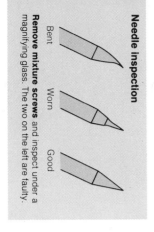

Needle inspection

Bent   Worn   Good

Remove mixture screws and inspect under a magnifying glass. The two on the left are faulty.

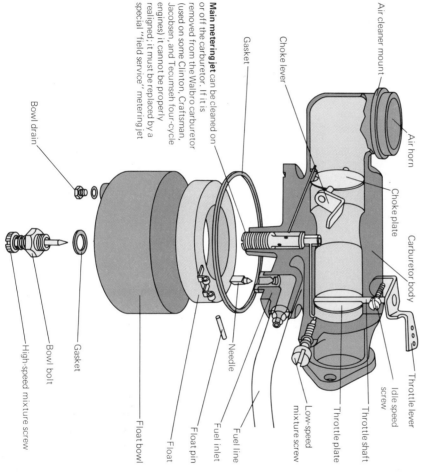

Air cleaner mount

Air horn

Choke plate

Choke lever

Carburetor body

Gasket

Throttle lever

Idle speed screw

Throttle plate

Throttle shaft

Low-speed mixture screw

Needle

Fuel line

Fuel inlet

Float pin

Float

Float bowl

Bowl drain

Gasket

Bowl bolt

High-speed mixture screw

Main metering jet can be cleaned on or off the carburetor. If it is removed from the carburetor. If it is removed from the Walbro carburetor (used on some Clinton, Craftsman, Jacobsen, and Tecumseh four-cycle engines) it cannot be properly realigned; it must be replaced by a special "field service" metering jet

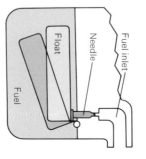

Fuel inlet

Needle

Float

Fuel

Remove float and shake it. If there is fuel inside, float has sprung a leak and must be replaced. A float with a leak will slowly sink

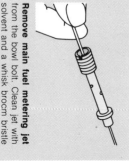

Remove main fuel metering jet from the bowl bolt. Clean jet with solvent and a whisk broom bristle (not a wire) or compressed air.

Hold diaphragm to light, inspect for pinholes. Hold metal pin in center, gently try to rotate diaphragm. If it turns, there is a leak; replace it.

Pry out filter screen with a needle or awl. Use a punch that conforms to screen curvature to press the replacement firmly into place.

Pierce old Welch plug with an awl and pry it out. Flatten replacement plug slightly with a blunt punch to install. Coat edges with nail polish.

Diaphragm carburetors

This kind of carburetor is used on equipment that must operate in many positions, such as a chain saw. It contains one or more pulsating diaphragms, which act as pumps to supply fuel to the carburetor jets. Unlike floats, diaphragms are not affected by gravity.

Remove the carburetor from the engine for cleaning or rebuilding. Gaskets, diaphragms, and nylon parts can be damaged by strong cleaning solvents. Remove them all from the carburetor body before cleaning it. Lay the pieces out in the order in which they are removed and make a sketch or take a Polaroid picture of them to be sure you can reassemble all the pieces properly. If you prefer, you can buy a parts list with an exploded-view drawing from the dealer or manufacturer.

If your carburetor has plastic jets (check with the parts dealer when buying gaskets or solvent), soak it in solvent for no more than 20 minutes, agitating it every 5 minutes. If you have an all-metal model, soak it for an hour, agitating it every 15 minutes. Blow passages dry with compressed air (available in aerosol cans at photo supply stores). Clean springs, adjustment screws, and other metal parts that will not be replaced. Check the gasket mating surfaces for warping.

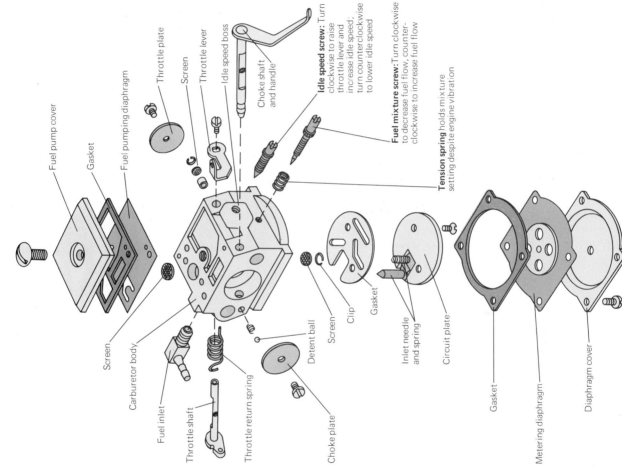

Idle speed screw: Turn clockwise to raise throttle lever and increase idle speed; turn counterclockwise to lower idle speed

Fuel mixture screw: Turn clockwise to decrease fuel flow, counterclockwise to increase fuel flow

Tension spring holds mixture setting despite engine vibration

Fuel pump cover · Gasket · Fuel pumping diaphragm · Throttle plate · Screen · Throttle lever · Idle speed boss · Choke shaft and handle · Screen · Carburetor body · Fuel inlet · Throttle shaft · Throttle return spring · Choke plate · Detent ball · Screen · Clip · Gasket · Inlet needle and spring · Circuit plate · Gasket · Metering diaphragm · Diaphragm cover

How to check mating surfaces

Check the gasket mating surfaces on the carburetor and engine with a straightedge. If you can slip a .002-in. feeler gauge under it, the surface is badly warped. Use two gaskets or a nonhardening liquid gasket for reassembly.

Small engines

Suction lift carburetors

The simple suction lift carburetor is mounted on top of the gas tank. Air rushing through the air horn forms a partial vacuum that draws fuel up a pipe to the carburetor, where it is atomized. The principle is identical to the one used in perfume atomizers. The carburetor has one or two fuel pipes. Those with two have a simple diaphragm fuel pump at the top of the longer pipe.

Some of these diaphragms have flaps that act as one-way valves to control fuel flow. Others use fiber discs or balls for the same purpose. Hold the carburetor so that the diaphragm is on top and level; then, remove it carefully to prevent the tiny balls from falling out before you have a chance to note where they belong.

The rebuild kit for these carburetors contains new fuel pipes. Nylon pipes are simply unscrewed; metal pipes must be pried out (see illustrations at right). Before you pry out a metal pipe, measure its length from the bottom to the point where it enters the carburetor body. The replacement pipe must be pressed into the body exactly the same distance. Use small sockets and screwdrivers when working on the carburetor to prevent damaging delicate parts.

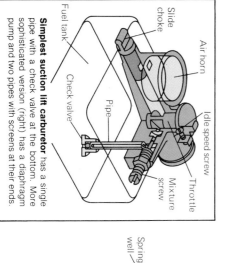

Simplest suction lift carburetor has a single pipe with a check valve at the bottom. More sophisticated version (right) has a diaphragm pump and two pipes with screens at their ends.

- Slide choke
- Air horn
- Idle speed screw
- Throttle screw
- Mixture screw
- Pipe
- Check valve
- Fuel tank

Remove cover to replace choke link

Check diaphragm for holes, creases, or worn spots. Replace it if necessary

- Spring well
- Fuel pipe
- Choke link
- Choke plate
- Air horn
- Throttle lever
- Idle speed screw
- Throttle plate
- Mixture screw
- Fuel pipe

Check spring length against manufacturer's specifications. If it is too short or long, replace diaphragm and spring

Check mating surface for warpage (p.377)

Check automatic choke operation. Remove air cleaner and replace stud. Set speed control on Stop. Pull starter rope rapidly. Choke plate should open and close alternately. If plate binds, clean link, plate, and air horn with solvent. If choke still does not work, replace link, spring, and diaphragm

- Fuel tank

To test a ball check valve, remove pipe and shake it. If ball does not rattle, dip valve briefly in solvent. Replace pipe if ball will not move. Use a small socket wrench on nylon pipes; do not force or strip threads.

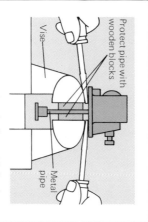

Measure the exact length of a metal pipe (see text), then remove it by mounting it in a vise and prying against the carburetor with two screwdrivers. Insert new pipe same distance.

- Vise
- Protect pipe with wooden blocks
- Metal pipe

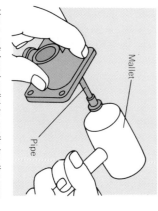

Use a soft-faced mallet to gently tap the new pipe into the carburetor body, or press it in using the jaws of the vise. Measure the length of the pipe often as you install it.

- Mallet
- Pipe

Chokes

The choke is a part of the carburetor that limits the amount of air that can enter the engine. When the engine is cold, this simple device makes starting easier by, in effect, increasing the amount of gasoline in the air-fuel mixture.

There are two types of chokes. One is a swiveling plate mounted across the air intake of the carburetor. The other type, called a slide choke, consists of a pair of cylinders that slide one inside the other; when the holes in the two cylinders are aligned, the choke is fully open.

On some engines (especially chain saw engines) the choke is operated by a handle attached directly to the swiveling shaft. There may be detents on the shaft, to indicate the fully open, half open, and fully closed positions. Other engines have a remotely located choke control, which is attached to the carburetor by a cable or other linkage. Some chokes are simply labeled *Start* and *Run*; others, *In* (open) or *Out* (closed). The choke may be connected to the throttle by a second linkage or it may be attached to a diaphragm fuel pump and operate automatically.

Make sure that the choke plates are tight and the shafts swivel smoothly. If a shaft sticks, drip some solvent at the point where it enters the carburetor body. If it still sticks, disassemble and clean the carburetor. Be sure that the holes in the choke plate are clear. Remove burrs in the carburetor air horn with automobile polishing compound.

Remotely operated choke

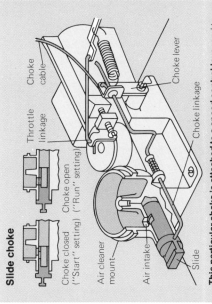

This choke plate is operated by a short lever, which is connected to a cable. The plate has a gap at the bottom to allow some air to pass, even when it is fully closed. To remove choke, open screws, remove plate, and pull shaft out of body. Do not lose spring-loaded detent ball (if any) in shaft housing. Remove any burrs; reassemble choke. Depress ball with a small screwdriver to reinsert shaft.

Directly operated choke

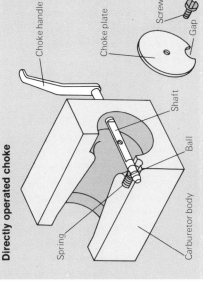

This choke plate is operated by a long handle attached to the swiveling shaft. To disassemble choke, remove screw and center plate and pull shaft out of body. Do not lose spring-loaded detent ball (if any) in shaft housing. Remove any burrs, and reassemble choke. Shaft's tapered end can be reinserted through carburetor body without first depressing detent ball.

Slide choke

This particular choke is attached to a speed control lever and to the throttle so that both move to the proper positions automatically when the lever is placed in the *Start* or *Run* position. Set the control to *Start* and see if the slide is fully closed. If it is not, use pliers to bend the linkage until it closes. Replace any slide when it wears so much that it moves with no resistance.

Checking compression

Low compression results in loss of power, hard starting, and stalling. The most common causes are a loose spark plug, a cracked cylinder head gasket, burned or worn valves, and worn piston rings. If the engine exhibits signs of low compression, make sure that the spark plug is tight and that the metal gasket under the plug has not been removed. Check compression in one of three ways:

1. Disconnect the spark plug cable and turn the flywheel by hand. Judge if the amount of resistance you feel is normal.

2. Remove the spark plug and hold your thumb over the hole. Have a helper operate the starter. You should feel a distinct alternating suction and pressure.

3. For the most accurate check, insert an automotive compression gauge into the spark plug hole and operate the starter three or four times. A new engine should have a reading of 50 to 60 pounds per square inch (psi). One with a compression release feature for easier starting should read 40 to 45 psi. Normal wear will reduce readings by 25 percent.

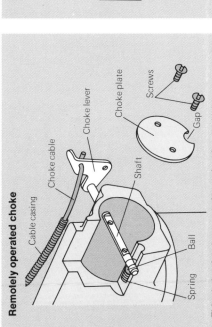

Insert compression gauge into spark plug hole and operate starter. If reading is low, remove gauge and squirt in some engine oil. Test again. If readings improve, the piston rings are worn. If readings remain low, remove cylinder head and inspect gasket and valves.

A less accurate method is to remove the spark plug and hold your thumb over the hole. Operate starter and feel for alternating suction and pressure. (Test the engine when it is new, using either method, so that you can spot low compression if it develops.)

Controls

The engine and transmission on gasoline-powered machinery are often controlled by several levers, knobs, or handles and connecting cables or rods. These parts should be cleaned and lubricated every time you change the engine oil to assure smooth operation. If the engine begins to run poorly, check the controls. The problem may be simply a loose cable or a slipping knob. Some typical control repairs are shown at right. When checking the controls, do not forget the small choke and governor linkages on the engine itself (see pp.379, 381).

Cylinder head and gasket

If your engine shows signs of low compression (see p.379), check the tightness of the cylinder head bolts. If none are loose, remove the cylinder head and check the condition of the gasket. If it has cracked, a new gasket should restore proper compression, provided the valves and piston rings are not damaged.

To remove and replace the head, you will need a socket wrench, a torque wrench (see *Tools and techniques,* p.318), and a new head gasket. Never reuse an old gasket; it will usually leak. Use the socket wrench to remove the head bolts. Do not be surprised if the bolts make a cracking sound as they are first loosened; this is normal. Keep the head bolts in order, so that you can reinsert each one into its original hole.

While you have the head off, check it and the mating surface of the engine for warping. If a .003 feeler gauge will fit between the ruler and the gasket surface, the gasket surface is warped enough to leak. Have it resurfaced at a machine shop. If a great deal of metal must be removed at the machine shop, you may have to use a thicker than normal head gasket (or two normal gaskets) to restore the original cylinder volume.

Engine manufacturers specify a tightening sequence and a specific tightening torque for the head bolts. If you cannot get this information from the dealer or manufacturer, tighten the bolts on aluminum engines to 12 foot-pounds, and cast-iron engines to 15 foot-pounds. (Use a magnet to determine which material your engine is made of.) For engines of more than 5 horsepower, add 2 or 3 foot-pounds per bolt. Tighten head bolts in three steps. If you are tightening to 15 foot-pounds, tighten each bolt (following the criss-cross sequence) to 5 foot-pounds. Then, follow the sequence again and tighten to 10 foot-pounds. Finally, go through the sequence again, bringing each bolt up to 15 foot-pounds.

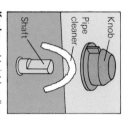

Knobs and twist handles may loosen on their shafts. Replace worn part or tighten by wedging a length of pipe cleaner between knob and shaft.

Levers can part from their cables. If a replacement is not available, get some cable from a bicycle or hardware shop. Tie or clamp it to lever.

Turnbuckles can be kept from vibrating loose by adding locknuts or lock washers. Check them for tightness often or use a locking compound.

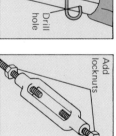

Cable brackets can loosen and let casing slip, which may change control adjustment. Apply locking compound and retighten bolts.

Cable casings may get kinked or gummed up. Replace kinked casing. Remove dirty cable, clean in kerosene, lubricate with oil or graphite.

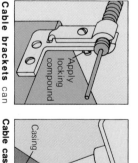

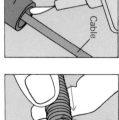

Springs and rods that have come loose or broken must be replaced. Twist spring as shown, then, push it over lever until it snaps into hole.

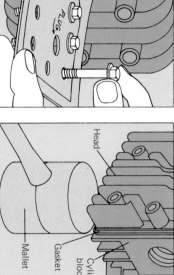

Remove spark plug and take out cylinder head bolts. Each bolt must be put back into its original hole. Make a cardboard pattern of the head and place bolts in it. This will keep them in proper order.

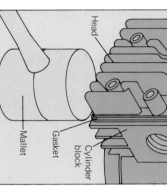

In order to free the cylinder head to lift it off, you may have to push gently against the gasket with a screwdriver or tap the head with a wooden or buffered mallet. Do not pry against the cylinder or head.

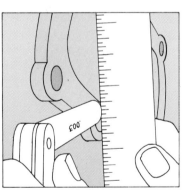

Scrape carbon deposits from the head, valves, and piston with an ice cream stick or copper coin. Turn the crankshaft to raise each valve in turn and scrape carbon from their undersides, stems, and seats.

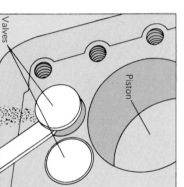

Check the gasket mating surfaces on the head and engine with a metal straightedge. If you can slip a .003-in. feeler gauge under the ruler at any point, the part is warped. Have it trued by a machine shop.

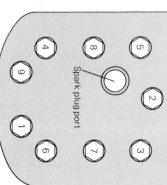

Replace gasket and tighten head bolts in a criss-cross sequence. Tightening bolts on one side first could warp the head. If you do not know the enginemaker's recommended tightening sequence, use the one shown.

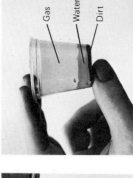

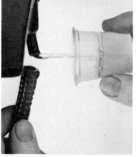

Gas
Water
Dirt

Wait several minutes, then hold glass to light. The colored gasoline or gas-oil mixture will float above any water. Dirt and gum will settle to bottom.

If your carburetor has no drain, pull the fuel line from its connection. Pinch line to stop flow of fuel when glass is nearly full. Reconnect fuel line.

To check fuel condition, drain some into a small glass. If your carburetor has a drain, push up on button and gasoline will flow out. Wash hands immediately.

Clean breather holes in the gas cap with a fine wire. If cap is metal, you can clean it in carburetor cleaning solvent after removing cork or rubber gasket.

Fuel lines and tank

Condensation will cause water to collect inside the fuel tank. This may lead to carburetor icing, loss of power, and frequent stalling. If the engine has been stored for a long period with fuel in the tank, gummy deposits will form in the tank, fuel lines, and carburetor. To check the condition of the fuel, drain some into a small, clear glass and inspect it. Remove gummed fuel lines and clear them with pipe cleaners. Replace any that are cracked, pinched, or broken. Flush tank and lines with fresh fuel mixed with dry gas (sold in auto parts stores).

Crankshaft
Yoke
Collar
Arm
Spring
Speed control lever
Throttle plate
Throttle lever
Weights

Centrifugal governor

As engine speeds up, weights pivot outward, forcing yoke, collar, and arm downward, which closes throttle. As engine slows, weights drop and throttle is opened. Speed control changes tension on arm.

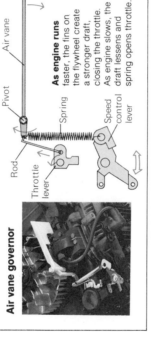

Air vane
Pivot
Rod
Throttle lever
Spring
Speed control lever

As engine runs faster, the fins on the flywheel create a stronger draft, closing the throttle. As engine slows, the draft lessens and spring opens throttle.

Air vane governor

Governors

The governor keeps the engine running at a fairly constant speed despite changing loads. It also keeps the engine from running too fast when the load is removed. It is a complex apparatus vital to safe engine operation and should not be tampered with. Clean the linkages with auto solvent. Do not oil. If any linkage becomes disconnected, the engine may stall, run poorly, or race too fast. Make a sketch or take a snapshot of the linkage so that you can reconnect it properly.

Ice cream stick

To clean exhaust port on a two-cycle engine, remove muffler and move piston until it covers port (to keep carbon out of cylinder). Scrape off carbon with a wooden or plastic tool; do not use metal. Blow particles from port.

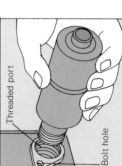

Threaded port
Bolt hole

The one-piece muffler on four-cycle engines is either held by a flange and two bolts or it screws into the exhaust port. Some engines have both features; if their flange bolts break or strip, replace muffler with a screw-in type.

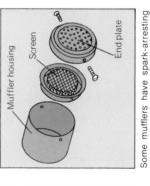

Muffler housing
Screen
End plate

Some mufflers have spark-arresting screens approved for use in wooded areas by the U.S. Forestry Department. The screen catches burning carbon particles. It should be cleaned every 25 hours. Replace screen if it is damaged.

Screws
Bracket
Cover
Bolt
Baffle
Base
Gasket

Typical two-cycle muffler from a chain saw consists of a few simple baffles held together by a small bolt. Disassemble the parts and scrape off carbon deposits. Replace any parts that are damaged or cannot be unblocked.

Mufflers and exhaust port

The muffler lowers the noise level of the engine. If the muffler is loose or deteriorates from the corrosive action of the exhaust gases, engine noise may reach annoying or painful levels and cause permanent hearing damage. Much heat leaves the engine along with the exhaust gases. A blocked exhaust port or muffler may cause the engine to overheat or to lose power and run erratically. Small engine mufflers are quite simple in design and are usually attached with one or two bolts. Always allow the engine to cool before touching the muffler. Clean the exhaust ports regularly, especially on two-cycle engines.

Small engines

Spark plug and high tension cable

Check the spark plug every 50 operating hours. If the electrodes are not worn, clean the plug with solvent and a stiff bristle brush. If the electrodes are rounded, replace the plug. Check and adjust the electrode gap before installing the plug. The condition of the spark plug may indicate the cause of a poorly running engine (see illustrations below).

Before attempting to remove the spark plug, make sure that the engine is not hot. Then, slip off the clip at the end of the high tension cable. On some models, it may be covered by a rubber boot. Un-

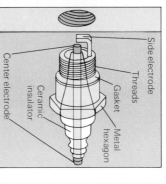

Side electrode
Threads
Gasket
Center electrode
Ceramic insulator
Metal hexagon

screw the plug, using an inexpensive plug wrench or a ratchet wrench with an automotive spark plug socket.

Replace the spark plug with the same brand and model as the original, if possible (see owner's manual for plug specifications). Supposed equivalents may vary in performance from the original. If you must use a substitute, be sure the metal parts closely match those on the original plug. The threads should be the same size and length, and the electrodes should extend no farther into the engine than the old ones did.

Use a round wire feeler gauge to check the spark plug gap. The gauge has a magnetic coil are bolted into place and cannot be moved in such a way that will change the ignition timing. However, the notched metal tab for bending the side electrode in order to change the gap. Most engines call for a .025-inch gap; Briggs & Stratton engines call for a .030-inch gap. Check your owner's manual.

Tighten the plug by hand as far as it will go, making sure that the threads engage smoothly. If it has a metal gasket, tighten it an extra quarter turn with the wrench. If it has a tapered seat and no gasket, give it only 1/32 to 1/16 of a turn with the wrench.

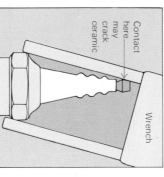

Contact here may crack ceramic

Wrench

Keep the plug wrench square on the metal hexagon or you may crack the ceramic insulator. A cracked insulator will leak current, leading to misfiring and uneven engine performance.

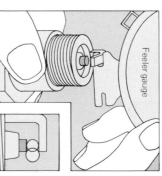

Feeler gauge

Bend the side electrode until the specified feeler wire slips between the electrodes with only slight drag (see inset). Wire of the next larger size should not fit into the gap (inset).

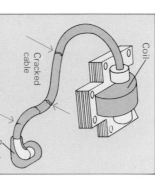

Coil
Cracked cable
Boot

Check high tension cable for cracks, which can leak current. Replace a cracked cable. Some are permanently attached to the magnetic coil, in which case the coil must be replaced too.

Analyzing spark plug condition

The spark plug carries electricity down its center electrode, which is insulated by a ceramic collar. The current jumps the small gap between electrodes, creating the spark that ignites the fuel.

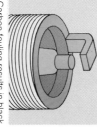

Light brown, dustlike deposits and only moderate wear of the electrodes indicate that the engine is running properly. This plug can be cleaned with a stiff bristle brush and reused. Do not use a wire brush.

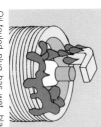

Carbon fouling results in black, powdery deposits that can short-circuit the plug. It can be caused by an overly rich fuel-air mixture in a two-cycle engine or by worn piston rings, clogged air filter, or idle speed set too high in a four-cycle engine.

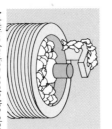

Oil-fouled plug has wet, black deposits on the electrodes. It is caused by wrong fuel-oil mixture in a two-cycle engine or by engine miss under heavy loads at high speeds. It is caused by clogged exhaust ports or muffler or by high-test gas.

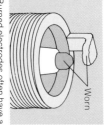

Additive fouling coats the electrodes with brown, yellow, or white deposits. It will make the plug also show excessive wear. Burning is caused by clogged cooling fins, too lean a fuel-air mixture, incorrect timing, or improper spark plug installation.

Burned electrodes often have a white, blistered look. They may also show excessive wear. Burning is caused by clogged cooling fins, too lean a fuel-air mixture, incorrect timing, or improper spark plug installation.

Worn

Timing adjustments

On most small engines, the flywheel and magnetic coil are bolted into place and cannot be moved in such a way that will change the ignition timing. However, the breaker points may be attached to a moveable housing or plate, and its position relative to the crankshaft will affect the time at which the spark plug fires.

To make a rough check of the timing, remove the spark plug and set the breaker points to their correct gap (p.375). Position the engine so that the spark plug hole faces up and slide a dowel into the hole. Turn the crankshaft until the piston is at its highest point, as indicated by the upward movement of the dowel. Place a small scrap of paper between the opened points. (If the points have not opened, you are on the exhaust stroke; rotate the piston through one more up-and-down stroke.)

Turn the crankshaft backward until the dowel drops 1/16 to 1/8 inch. Loosen the proper bolts and rotate the breaker point housing or plate until the points just begin to open (see illustration, below). Tighten the housing or plate bolts. Recheck the point gap and reset it if necessary (see p.375). Replace the flywheel and spark plug.

You can make a more accurate check with a special gauge that screws into the spark plug hole.

When points loosen their grip on scrap of paper, they have just begun to open; tighten housing bolts.

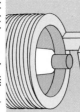

Electric starters

Special equipment is needed to diagnose problems in the electric starter itself; but if the starter fails to move when you press the button, it may be due to more easily traced outside problems. First, make sure the battery cables are clean and firmly connected to the battery and starter. Check the battery charge on wet cell batteries (see *Electrical system*, pp.334–335, and *Electric starters*, p.401). Some garden tractors have safety switches that cut out the starter unless the accessories are properly fastened and the operator is on the seat.

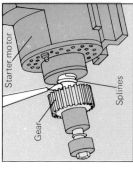
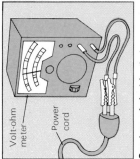

Ignition switch · Stop switch · Starter · Motor · Battery · Power cord · Charger unit

Corroded battery cable connections will result in hard starting. Disconnect cables and clean all posts, plugs, and receptacles (arrows) inside and out with a wire brush. A nickel cadmium battery of the type shown will be completely drained by 40 to 60 starts. It must be recharged overnight to restore full power.

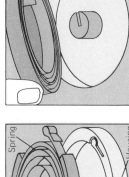

Volt-ohm meter · Power cord

One type of electric starter operates on house current. A damaged power cord is a common fault. Test cord with a volt-ohm meter. (p.124).

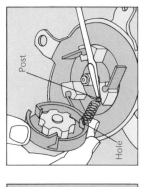

Starter motor · Gear · Splines

Unbolt and remove the starter after every 100 operating hours. Turn the small gear to expose the splines and apply light oil. Reinstall the starter.

Impulse starters

The impulse starter is a wind-up mechanism that uses a strong steel spring to turn the engine. Removing and replacing this spring can be dangerous, and is best left to an experienced mechanic. The wind-up starter pawls, which can become jammed with debris, and the pawl housing spring, which can break, can easily be serviced at home. On many models you can simply remove the wind-up starter unit from the engine, and clean and reinstall the pawls and the housing spring without even seeing the large impulse spring.

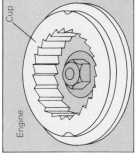

Pawls · Housing spring

Lift off housing and clean dirt from pawls. Use solvent to remove gum. Pawls must move freely. Replace housing spring if stretched or broken.

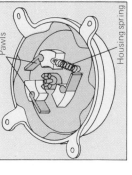

Cup · Engine

Check the teeth inside the starter cup (on top of engine). If teeth are worn, pawls will slip. Replace a worn cup with the manufacturer's recommended part.

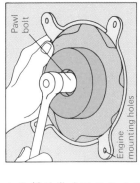

Pawl bolt · Engine mounting holes

Release tension from the large spring by pushing the *Start* lever. Unbolt and remove starter from engine. Turn the starter over and remove pawl bolt.

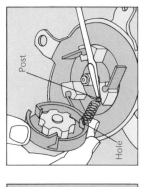

Post · Hole

Replace worn or damaged pawls. Hook spring onto post on one pawl holder, then through hole in housing. Refit housing and bolt. Install starter.

Recoil starters

This pull-rope starter is the type most often found on small engines. The most common faults are a broken starter rope or spring. For instructions on replacing a broken starter rope, see page 389. Procedures for replacing various types of springs are illustrated at right.

Remove the cover plate from the front of the starter to gain access to the spring. If the cover plate does not unbolt, remove the entire starter from the engine; access to the starter is from under the engine. Use an impact wrench, if needed, to remove the spring housing.

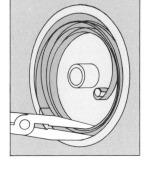

Unbolt starter from engine and lift off. Release spring tension as much as possible by freeing rope from pulley. Grasp spring with pliers and pull out.

Clip · Post

Fasten the outer end of the new spring to its clip on the housing. Coil up spring, starting from the outside and working in. Place inner hook over post.

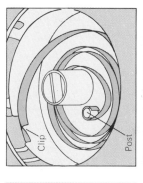

Spring · Clip · Housing

Some starter springs are sold in a retaining clip. After removing the old spring, hold the clip up to the housing and carefully push coils into place.

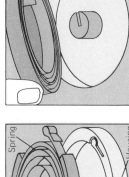

Still other springs are sealed in a separate housing. Lift out the entire assembly and buy a replacement. Fit new assembly into place. Reinstall cover.

Small engines

Transmission and clutch service

The power generated by a small engine must be passed on to the machinery—lawn mower, chain saw, or whatever the engine is running. The transmission system that conveys this power may be a simple shaft, as on a rotary push mower, or a complex system of belts, pulleys, or

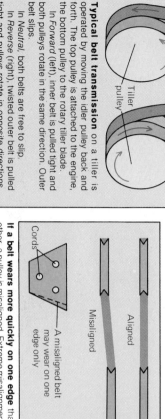

Engine pulley

Tiller pulley

Idler pulley

Typical belt transmission on a tiller is operated by moving the idler pulley back and forth. The top pulley is attached to the engine, the bottom pulley to the rotary tiller blade. In *Forward* (left), inner belt is pulled tight and both pulleys rotate in the same direction. In *Neutral*, both belts are free to slip. In *Reverse* (right), twisted outer belt is pulled tight and pulleys rotate in opposite directions. Outer belt slips.

ratios, as does an automobile transmission.

In most cases, the small engine transmission does not provide a choice of gear

gears, as on a self-propelled mower. Some transmissions—used on machinery ranging from chain saws to snow throwers—also employ a clutch.

In most cases, the small engine transmission does not provide a choice of gear ratios, as does an automobile transmis-

Belts and idler pulley

Belt transmissions use an idler pulley—a clutching device that simply moves away from a V-belt (for *Neutral*), or against the belt (for *Drive*). Proper belt tension is critical. When a belt squeals, it is slipping. Most often the problem is incorrect tension, but some squealing is caused by

worn pulleys. Slipping belts should be adjusted promptly to avoid rapid wear and strain on the engine.

Belt arrangements can be quite complex. There may be two or three belts, and if one should break, you must know exactly what twists and turns it made in

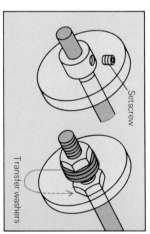

Cords

Aligned

Misaligned

A misaligned belt may wear on one edge only

If a belt wears more quickly on one edge than the other, a pulley is misaligned. Extreme misalignment may twist belt inside out and break its internal reinforcing cords. Align pulleys and replace belt.

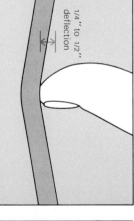

Belt

Tension spring

Pulley

Bracket

Some idler pulley systems depend on spring tension to maintain correct belt tension. As the spring ages, it may lose tension, allowing the belt to slip or override the pulleys. If this happens, replace the spring.

order to install a new one properly. A good way to record this information is to take photographs or draw a diagram of the belt arrangements when you first buy a piece of equipment.

A replacement belt should match the original one in width, length, and mate-

sion, but provides simple stop or go functioning. The purpose is to allow the engine to achieve some speed between the time it is started and the time it takes gears at least every 50 operating hours. Chains can be cleaned, oiled, and replaced in much the same manner as bicycle chains (see *Bicycles*, p.438).

Much transmission difficulty can be prevented by keeping the unit clean and by lubricating the pulleys, chains, and

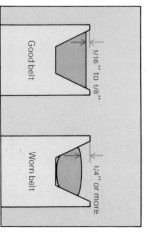

Setscrew

Transfer washers

To align most pulleys, you must loosen the setscrew that holds the pulley on the shaft, then move the pulley in or out, as required. On some models, you must transfer washers from one side of the pulley to another.

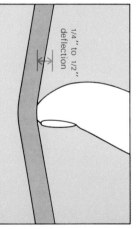

1/4" to 1/2" deflection

A correctly tensioned belt will deflect ¼ to ½ in. under moderate thumb pressure midway between pulleys. Another test is to slap the belt. A properly tensioned belt will give a lively bounce, not feel stiff or limp.

rial. Compare the new belt with the old one, remembering that the old one has probably stretched half an inch or so. You may be able to compare the code numbers of the belts if you buy the same brand. There is no standardization of codes among manufacturers.

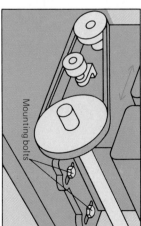

Mounting bolts

1/16" to 1/8"

Good belt

Worn belt

1/4" or more

V-belts depend on a wedging action of the belt between the pulley walls for traction. The belt should ride 1/16 to ⅛ in. below the rim of the pulley for full contact. A worn belt will ride ¼ in. or more below rim.

On some mowers, belt tension is adjusted by moving the engine. Loosen the two to four engine mounting bolts, position engine for proper belt tension, retighten the bolts. Larger mowers have a tension knob.

Centrifugal clutches

The average clutch is a durable device and seldom causes trouble. However, if your engine is running well but the machinery runs poorly or not at all, you should examine the clutch for slipping.

The centrifugal clutch operates the machine when its friction hub presses against a drum. The hub sections are held against a central shaft by springs, and will not engage the drum until engine speed flings them outward. This allows the engine a satisfactory start before taking on the equipment load.

Before dismantling the clutch, remove the spark plug from the engine and rotate the crankshaft to lower the piston. Stuff the upper end of the cylinder with clothesline; it will act as a shock absorber when you knock the clutch loose. Make a large knot in the end of the clothesline to keep the entire length from falling into the engine.

Use a feeler gauge to assure that the clearance between the drum and the friction hub is equal all around.

When removing the clutch from the shaft, note that the clutch invariably has reverse threading and must be loosened by being turned clockwise. Otherwise, it would unscrew in normal operation.

If friction hub is visible, check its clearance from drum before removing clutch from crankshaft. Turn the shaft and watch the hub for irregular movement.

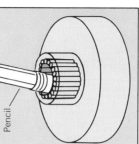

Gap should remain even

On some engines, drum will be on outside of hub, usually held by a spring clip. Pry off the clip and remove the drum. Spin the hub and check for wobbling.

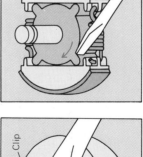

Clip

To remove hub, pack the cylinder with clothesline (see text), then force hub to turn clockwise, using a hammer and a punch or a dulled old screwdriver.

Spring clutches

While the centrifugal clutch engages automatically, the spring clutch must be shifted manually. It consists of a square-section spring surrounding the driven shaft. When engaged, the spring winds tightly around the shaft. The clutch housing and sprocket, or pulley, then rotate as a unit. It is a very durable component; the most likely failure is a broken spring. If the spring breaks, you will be able to rotate the sprocket freely in both directions. You cannot disassemble this machine-pressed unit, but must replace the entire assembly.

How a centrifugal clutch works

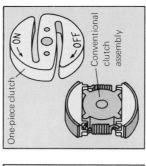

Engine off

Engine running

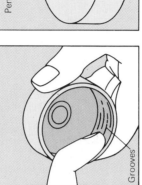

Camshaft
Friction material
Hub
Spring
Drum
Roller bearing
Spring clip

Examine inner surfaces of drum for scoring. Normal friction marks will not snag a fingernail drawn across them. If nail catches in grooves, replace the drum.

Grooves
Pencil

Turn bearing by hand to detect any roughness in action. Listen for noise. Look for blue tinge of heat damage. If these symptoms exist, replace bearing.

One-piece clutch

ON   OFF

Conventional clutch assembly

If hub movement is irregular or if springs are too weak to keep hub clearance even when engine is stopped, replace hub and springs, usually sold in sets.

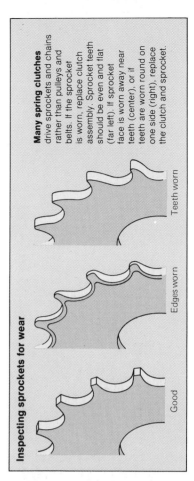

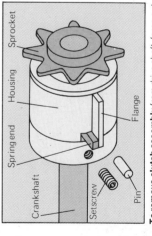

Crankshaft
Setscrew
Pin
Flange
Spring end
Housing
Sprocket

To remove clutch assembly from drive shaft, force out pin with a hammer and punch. Some clutches may use a setscrew instead of a pin; if so, unscrew it.

Inspecting sprockets for wear

Many spring clutches drive sprockets and chains rather than pulleys and belts. If the sprocket is worn, replace clutch assembly. Sprocket teeth should be even and flat (far left). If sprocket face is worn away near teeth (center), or if teeth are worn round on one side (right), replace the clutch and sprocket.

Good   Edges worn   Teeth worn

Small engines

Two-cycle reed valves

The reed valve controls the flow of the fuel-air mixture into a two-cycle engine. Made of spring steel, the reed remains closed until the suction of the rising piston pulls it open, allowing fuel to enter the crankcase (see p.371).

The reed valve is located between the carburetor and the crankcase. It is necessary to remove the carburetor to service the valve. Check linkages carefully before removing the carburetor, so that you can replace them.

If a reed is bent, replace it. The tempered steel of the reed cannot be straightened. Always buy the manufacturer's recommended part; its spring action is calibrated so that the valve will open at a specified crankcase vacuum. If the engine will not run, perform the paper test by operating the starter.

Remove air cleaner and open choke. Hold white paper about an inch from air intake and run engine. If paper becomes spotted with fuel, reed is leaking.

Remove air cleaner and open choke. Hold white paper about an inch from air intake and run engine. If paper becomes spotted with fuel, reed is leaking.

To reach valve, remove carburetor. On some engines a reed holder will come off with carburetor. When reassembling, replace gaskets on both sides of holder.

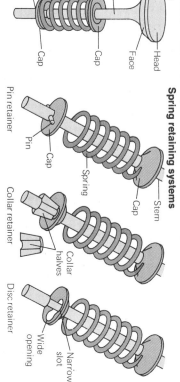

Examine reeds for bends or breaks. Check for proper seating; there should be no clearance. If you can slide a sheet of paper between reed and its seat, replace reed.

On some valves, only the spring steel reed need be replaced. Simpler reeds come as a single unit, with holder and stop. Entire unit can be replaced cheaply.

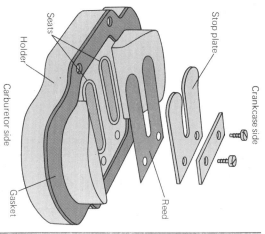

Seats
Holder
Stop plate
Crankcase side
Carburetor side
Gasket
Reed

Four-cycle poppet valves

Poppet valves are held closed by springs until the camshaft pushes them open. When closed, the valves must form a tight seal to maintain compression in the engine. Therefore, if the valve faces are worn or if the springs are weak, compression is reduced and the engine will run poorly. Remove the cylinder head (p.380) to check and clean the valves.

Manufacturers usually give different clearance specifications for the intake and exhaust valves (the larger one is the intake valve). Ask your engine parts supplier for these specifications.

Special suction-cup devices (some models fit onto a drill) are sold for valve grinding, but you can do the job with a child's toy arrow or dart.

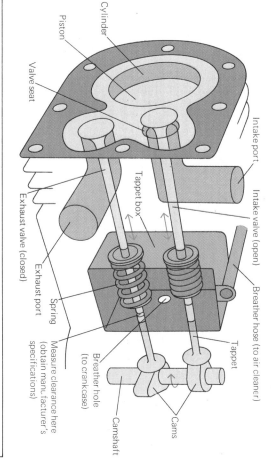

Cylinder
Piston
Valve seat
Intake port
Intake valve (open)
Breather hose (to air cleaner)
Tappet box
Spring
Exhaust port
Exhaust valve (closed)
Measure clearance here (obtain manufacturer's specifications)
Breather hole (to crankcase)
Tappet
Cams
Camshaft

Valve parts

Margin
Stem
Spring
Retainer fits here
Cap
Cap
Face
Head

Both valves are the same shape. Intake valve may be larger than exhaust valve.

Spring retaining systems

Pin retainer
Pin
Cap
Spring
Stem
Cap

Collar retainer
Collar halves

Disc retainer
Wide opening
Narrow slot

Poppet valves are closed by coil springs. Each spring has a cap at its top and bottom. The spring retainer bears against these caps, except for the design at right, which uses the cap itself as a retainer.

How to check and replace poppet valves

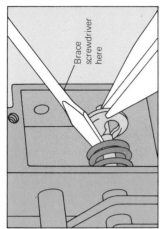

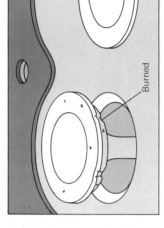

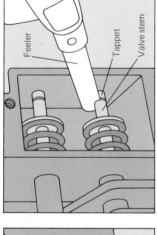

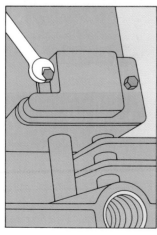

1. If the engine has a breather hose attached to the tappet cover, disconnect it. Most tappet covers are held in place with two screws; open screws with a wrench or screwdriver. Remove tappet cover; buy a new gasket.

2. Disconnect spark plug and turn crankshaft until both valves close. Check clearance between valves and tappets with a feeler gauge. If clearance is too great, replace valve; if clearance is too small, see Step 9.

3. Remove cylinder head and check both valve faces for pitting and burning. If metal is missing from the valve circumference, the valve is said to be burned. Replace burned or pitted valves with enginemaker's parts only.

4. Remove spring retainers by compressing spring with a screwdriver and pulling off retainer with needle-nose pliers. Pull valves out of engine. Use a screwdriver, if necessary, to pry springs out of tappet box.

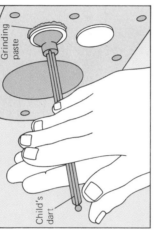

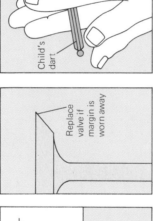

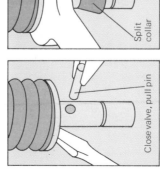

Margin: 1/32" OK, 1/64" minimum — Face

Replace valve if margin is worn away

Child's dart — Grinding paste

Close valve, pull pin — Split collar

Right — Wrong

5. Turn crankshaft to open valves with pin retainers. Twist valves until pins face front. Pry up spring and pull out pin (left). On valves with collar retainers, pry up spring and separate collar halves (right).

6. Measure the valve margin with a machinist's ruler or a caliper to be sure it is thick enough to allow reasonable wear. Margin should be between 1/32 and 1/64 in. If it is less than 1/64 in., replace valve.

7. Smear some automotive grinding compound onto the valve face and attach valve to grinding stick. Press valve lightly against seat and twirl stick between palms. Lift valve occasionally; give it a quarter turn, grind again.

8. Clean paste from valves and seats. Reinstall the valves without springs. Rotate crankshaft until both valves close. Press each valve tightly closed and check clearance; on a new valve it may be too small.

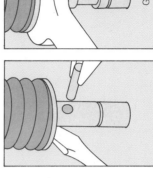

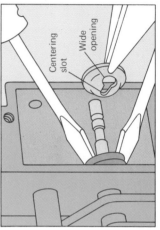

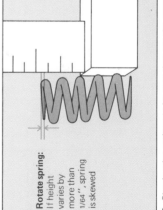

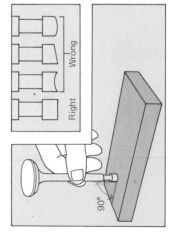

Grease — Centering slot — Wide opening

Rotate spring: If height varies by more than 1/64", spring is skewed

90°

9. To increase clearance, remove valve and grind some metal off the end of the stem with an oil stone or a grinding wheel. Ends of valves must be ground square, not hollow or at an angle (inset).

10. Check valve springs to be sure they are the same length. Hold spring ends against a try square to see if they are square. Replace springs that are pitted, cracked, skewed, or unequal in length.

11. Install valves, springs, and spring caps. Have a helper pry up the spring with one or two screwdrivers. Lift valve slightly and install retainer. Slip valve stem through wide opening; center retainer on stem.

12. On valves with pin retainers, lift spring and insert pin (left). On collar retainers, lift spring with screwdrivers or wrench (right). Coat insides of collar halves with grease so that they stick to valve. Install tappet cover, gasket.

Brace screwdriver here

Burned

Feeler — Tappet — Valve stem

Chain saws

Maintenance and service

Chain saws are powered by either electric motors or gasoline engines. Electric saws are sharpened and adjusted in the same way as gasoline saws.

Oiling: All saws have either automatic or manual oilers, which lubricate the chain. Both types of oiler must be refilled frequently with the grade of oil specified in the owner's manual. With a manual oiler, push the oiling button about once every minute while cutting. Otherwise the chain will be damaged from over-heating.

Oil-gas mix: Most chain saws are powered by two-cycle gasoline engines. The oil used to lubricate two-cycle engines (entirely different from the oil used to lubricate the chain) is mixed with the gasoline. Check the manufacturer's instructions for the proper oil-to-gas ratio for your saw. If instructions are unavailable, try 16 parts gas to 1 part oil. If the engine smokes heavily, reduce the amount of oil. Always mix the oil and gasoline in a separate container and then pour the mixture into the fuel tank.

Cleaning: Keep your chain saw free of accumulated sawdust. Use a wire or head to force the wood apart and free oil used to lubricate two-cycle engines small screwdriver to clean the oil holes in the guide-bar and the guide-bar slot. Brush all vents around the engine housing and muffler, so that air can cool the engine. Always wipe spilled fuel or oil from the engine housing to avoid fire hazards and possible fouling of the starter, the engine ignition points, or the carburetor.

Pinched bar: Never use the bar on a saw as a lever. If the saw becomes pinched in a log, use wedges or an ax head to force the wood apart and free the bar. Do not twist the saw free, or you may bend the crankshaft and bar beyond repair. If you support a log at each end and cut it in the middle, it will buckle inward and pinch the bar. Support the log so that the cut portion falls away from the saw. If this is not possible, stop sawing before the log buckles and drive a wedge into the cut to prevent the log from pinching the saw. Then, continue to cut through log.

Engine and drive elements

On gasoline-powered saws, the fuel-air mixture and idle speed are controlled by adjusting screws. If your engine stalls often, or if the chain moves rapidly along the bar as the engine idles, adjust the idle speed. On most saws, the idle speed is decreased by turning the idle screw counterclockwise and is increased by turning it clockwise. (See *Small engines*, pp. 370–387.)

Watch for signs of a faulty clutch. If the engine of your saw runs normally at full throttle, but the chain does not, the clutch is probably slipping. Should the clutch fail to disengage at the proper idle speed, immediately stop the saw to avoid serious damage. (Clutch problems are covered in *Small engines*, pp.370–387.)

The major drive element of a saw is the drive sprocket. Check it for wear at least every 40 or 50 operating hours. If the rails show wear or if the sprocket teeth are worn down by more than one-third their thickness, take the saw to a dealer for repair.

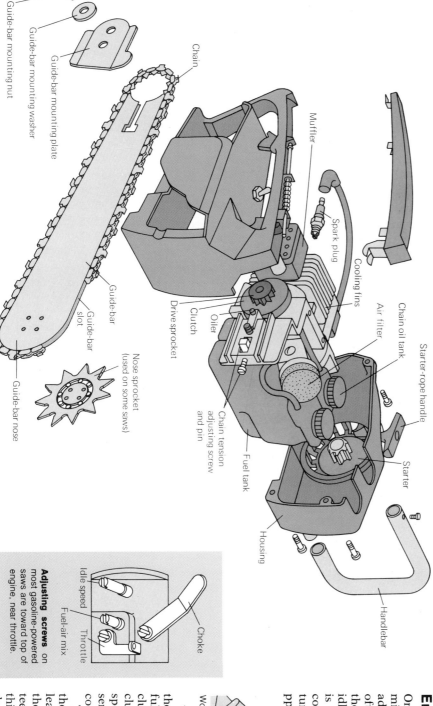

Muffler

Spark plug

Cooling fins

Oiler

Clutch

Drive sprocket

Chain

Guide-bar slot

Guide-bar slot

Guide-bar mounting plate

Guide-bar mounting washer

Guide-bar mounting nut

Guide-bar nose

Nose sprocket (used on some saws)

Air filter

Chain oil tank

Chain tension adjusting screw and pin

Fuel tank

Starter-rope handle

Starter

Housing

Handlebar

Adjusting screws on most gasoline-powered saws are toward top of engine, near throttle.

Idle speed

Fuel-air mix

Throttle

Choke

Worn sprocket: Replace it

New drive sprocket

Safety precautions

Always start chain before making contact with the wood to prevent the saw from kicking out of control.

Be sure that the saw is free of obstruction. Kickback from surrounding tree limbs, earth, rocks, and other obstacles causes many injuries.

After refueling, move at least 10 ft from the spot before starting engine. Spilled gasoline can easily ignite.

When using a gasoline saw for long periods, it is wise to wear earplugs to protect your hearing. Work gloves are always advisable.

Serious accidents result from bad work habits. Do not use saw in semidarkness or when fatigue, intoxication, or illness may impair your coordination. Never let children use a saw unsupervised.

Starter

Gasoline saws employ recoil starters, whose ropes and recoil springs are susceptible to breakage. To reach the starter for repairs, first remove the housing and handlebar screws, then separate the halves of the housing.

Caution: To prevent the spring from ejecting violently from the starter, release the tension before removing the reel (see illustrations below).

Starter rope

When buying a replacement rope or spring, be sure it is designed for your model saw. A rope that does not fit precisely may jam the mechanism.

After reinstalling the starter rope, check the handle on the starter rope before putting the engine housing back together. The handle should stand tightly against the housing without dangling. If it is loose, take up the slack by turning the reel clockwise, making sure that the rope remains in the notch. Do not put more tension on the spring than is necessary to keep the handle safely in place.

Frequent breaking of the starter rope may be a sign that your starting technique is incorrect or that the rope is too short. In starting the saw, pull the rope straight out to avoid rubbing the housing. You should not be pulling too far. Be sure

that the rope is long enough so that ignition occurs before the rope yanks to a halt. Jerking may cause the knot in the rope to pop out of the reel, requiring you to disassemble the starter to reinsert it.

Symptom of engine trouble

Most often, however, the repeated breaking of the rope indicates engine trouble. For example, the engine may be hard to start because of fouled spark plugs or the wrong fuel mixture. So if your rope breaks often, do some troubleshooting on the saw's engine and try to get to the root of the problem. (See *Small engines*, pp.370–387.)

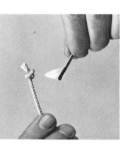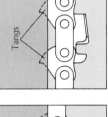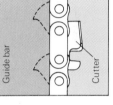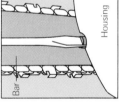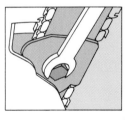

1. To replace the starter rope, release spring tension by lining up rope with notch on reel and turning reel counterclockwise. Stop turning as soon as the spring loses tension.

2. With a large screwdriver remove the mounting bolt and washer from the center of the starter reel. If washer sticks, lift it out with pliers. The starter reel will remain in place.

3. Lift the reel from the unit, exposing the recoil spring. If spring is broken, remove it carefully with a needle-nose pliers. To install new spring, see *Recoil starters*, p.383.

4. Remove old rope. Knot one end of new rope. Insert knot into slot in reel and wind rope on reel. Thread loose end of rope through housing and handle; knot free end.

5. To keep nylon starter rope knots from unravelling, sear with flame. Clothesline is less prone to unravelling, but a dealer's nylon cords are often stronger and thinner in cross section.

Adjusting chain tension

Proper chain tension is a key to safe and efficient cutting. The tension changes due to heating during operation, stretching, and wear, and should be checked whenever you refuel the saw. Adjust the tension before operating the saw, when the chain and bar are cool. If you must adjust the chain in the middle of a job, let the saw cool until you can press your hand against the bar for about half a minute without discomfort. Before adjusting the chain tension, loosen the bar-mounting nut or nuts.

Loosen the guide-bar nut or nuts. Retighten them after you have completed adjusting chain tension.

Hold the saw so that the guide bar points upward; turn the adjusting screw clockwise to tighten chain.

On a cool chain that is properly adjusted, tangs do not show below bottom edge of the guide bar.

On a warm chain that is properly adjusted, tangs should always show to about half of their depth.

Chain saws

Replacing chain, bar, and nose sprocket

Although both the chain and guide bar are replaceable, the chain will require changing far more often than the bar. The chain is a series of links, with every other one acting as a cutter. If just one or two cutters are damaged in a good chain, these can be purchased separately and replaced.

You will get two components when you buy a new cutter—the cutter itself and its connecting link. The cutter is a single piece of metal. One end is the sawtooth and the other is the depth gauge, which controls the depth of the tooth's bite into the wood as the chain is running.

The whole chain should be replaced when its cutters have been worn thin by repeated sharpening, or when they can no longer be sharpened to produce a straight saw cut. Replace the bar when the chain tangs begin to show wear from contact with the bar groove, or if the bar becomes bent or distorted.

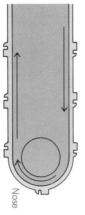

Nose

When replacing or reversing bar, reposition chain so that cutters on top of the bar face the nose.

Most guide bars are reversible. To equalize the wear along the top and bottom edges of the bar, reverse the bar after every five hours of use. After turning the bar over, make sure that the chain oiler hole is still fed by the oiler. If not, put the bar back into its original position. Burrs can be removed from the bar by careful filing with a flat file. The sprocket nose that is a feature on many newer model saws is replaceable, and can be changed as illustrated at right. When buying replacements, it is best to take the old parts along to the store to assure a perfect matchup. Buy only the manufacturer's spare parts for your model.

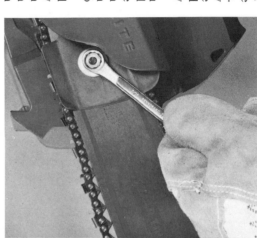

1. To replace the chain or guide bar, first take off the guide bar by removing the guide-bar nut. Larger saws have more than one nut. Also remove any washers and plates that accompany the nuts.

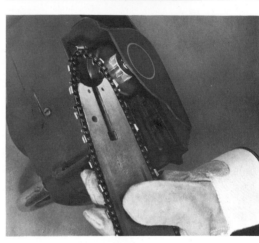

2. Lay the saw on its side. Lift the chain from the drive sprocket and the bar from the adjusting pin. If the bar sticks, turn the tension adjusting screw counterclockwise to ease tension on the adjusting pin.

3. Hold the bar upright and hang new chain over nose; then, slip the chain tangs into the guide-bar slot. Cutters on top of bar should face away from engine when bar is on saw (see drawing in text at left).

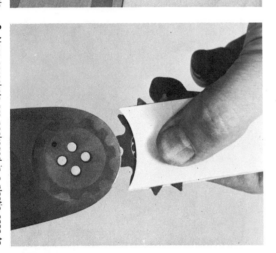

1. To replace the nose sprocket, grind off rivet heads using a power drill with a small carborundum grinding wheel attachment. Then, drive the rivets out with a punch and hammer; sprocket will fall from bar.

2. Nose sprockets are packaged in a plastic case to keep bearings in place. Do not remove from case. Hold curved side of case against bar nose and slide new sprocket directly from case into position in bar.

3. New rivets are supplied with replacement nose sprockets. Place rivets into sprocket holes. Then, lay bar on an anvil or other hard surface and flatten rivet ends by striking them with a small hammer.

Sharpening

Dull cutters are the cause of most chain saw malfunctions. They result in overheating and excessive wear, and may cause accidents. Sharpening at home will save money and is easy to do with the special set of files and gauges available from dealers.

Chains should be resharpened after every three to four hours of normal use; this figure will vary depending on the type of wood being cut. For example, oak is much harder than pine and will dull the chain faster, as will wood that is frozen. If the chain strikes nails or other obstructions it will need immediate sharpening. A properly sharpened chain cuts fast, smoothly, and straight, with little exertion by the operator. When the sawdust from your cuts turns from chips to a fine powder, it is a sure sign that the chain needs sharpening.

Round file and holder

To best achieve the uniformity needed in sharpening, use a round file and file holder. File the cutters from the inside toward the outside at the angle specified by the manufacturer for your type chain. Hold file handle level or slightly tilted, according to manufacturer's instructions. As cutters wear, change to a file of smaller diameter. For example, on a new 4-inch pitch chain use a file 5/32 inch in diameter. When about half the original tooth has been filed away, switch to a file 1/8 inch in diameter.

Ideally you should use a chain-filing vise to hold the cutters steady during filing, but you can do a satisfactory job without a vise if you tighten chain tension on the bar until the chain cannot wobble. Do all filing at the midpoint of the bar, loosening the chain in order to bring dull cutters to the midbar position and then retightening the chain. Use two or three firm strokes of the file on every cutter. First, file all the cutters on one side of the chain; then, those on the other side. Occasionally rotate the file in the holder to equalize wear on files.

Depth gauge tool

File down the depth gauges every second or third time you sharpen the cutters. Use a depth gauge tool as a template to equalize the height of the cutters. If you replace cutters, file the new ones and their depth gauges to the same height as those in the rest of the chain. If the gauges are too high, the teeth will not bite deeply enough and will cut slowly; if too low, the teeth will bite too deeply and grab. If some gauges are left higher than others, the chain will cut off line.

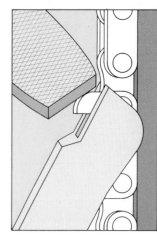

1. Sharpen at center of bar. Relax chain tension (p. 389) and turn chain by hand, moving dull cutters to center. Reset tension before filing. File all cutters on one side of chain; turn saw around and file others.

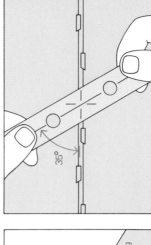

2. Use the degree marks on file holder to determine filing angle. For standard chains, the angle is 35°. File from inside of cutter toward outside. Give each cutter two or three light strokes with the file.

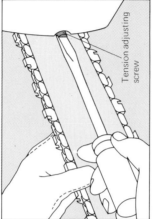

3. After every two or three sharpenings, depth gauges will be too tall in relation to filed cutters. Use a depth-gauge tool and a flat file to cut protruding gauges to a uniform height.

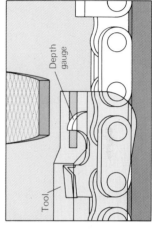

4. After you file down a depth gauge, its front surface will be square and tend to drag, creating excessive friction and heat. To correct, round off all the corners with a flat file.

Parts of the chain

Tie strap

Depth gauge | Side plate | Top plate

Left-hand cutter

Drive links

Tie strap

Right-hand cutter

Your owner's literature should show the proper sharpening silhouette for your particular chain.

Sharpening tools

File holder

Round file

Flat file

Depth gauge tool

Some typical sharpening mistakes that crop up in all types of chains are shown below.

Correcting common filing errors

Hook shape results from use of a file that is too small and is held with handle too high. A cutter with this shape dulls rapidly.

Too large a file with handle held too low while filing produced this sloping cutter. It will cut slowly, requiring much exertion.

Depth gauge is not filed down to conform to cutter height. Making cuts with this chain will be hard, slow work.

Because this depth gauge is filed down too far, cutter will bite too deeply. Chain will strain engine and give a very rough cut.

The gullet in this cutter has not been filed. Chips will lodge inside cut. File gullet using round file without holder.

Gullet

Cutters are not filed at uniform angles. This chain will not cut straight. It will bind and be hard to control. Links wear quickly.

Garden tools and hoses

Tool care

High quality garden tools will last a life-time with proper care. The steel heads on wooden handles with a mixture of half hoes, shovels, rakes, spades, trowels, and picks should be kept clean, sharp, and rust free. Clean all mud and dirt from tools after each use, and store them in a dry place. Occasionally give them a light coat of oil to prevent rust. Always oil tools before putting them away for the season. Apply oil with a brush or rag for the removing chemical, then coat with oil. by the technique shown at right. If rust has already accumulated, remove it with a wire brush, sandpaper, or a rust-

Coat unpainted, or unvarnished wooden handles with a mixture of half turpentine and half linseed oil. Apply mixture generously, then wipe off the excess with a clean rag to prevent gummy deposits from forming. If a han-dle is already badly weathered, sand it smooth, then apply the turpentine and linseed oil mixture. If a handle is broken, replace it or fix it as shown below. Buy only hardwood replacement handles—ash, hickory, or oak. Keep cutting and digging edges sharp to prevent the need for excess pressure on tool handles.

(see *Riveting*, p.369)

To sharpen digging tools, place tool in a vise and use a coarse 10-in. file to restore the original edge (usually a 45° bevel). Sharpen the corners as well as the cutting edges on hoes and shovels.

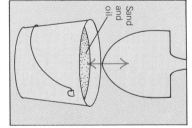

To clean and oil a tool in one easy operation, fill a 5-gal. can with sand, then add old oil drained from the crankcase of your lawn mower or car. Thrust tool into the oil-soaked sand several times. Blade will emerge clean and oily.

How to fix a broken handle

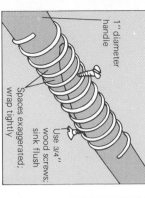

1" diameter handle

Spaces exaggerated; wrap tightly

Use 3/4" wood screws; sink flush

Glue a long split with epoxy adhesive. Add short wood screws to thick handles, as shown. Soak heavy twine in adhesive and wrap it around handle for added strength.

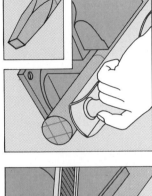

Hold the new handle in a vise with its socket end upward. Hold the old stub in the center of the new handle and mark its thickness with four lines, as shown.

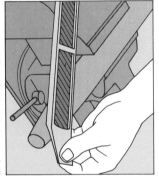

Use a plane to taper the new handle from the squared taper to match the tool socket. To insure a tight fit, occasionally test-fit the handle in the socket as you file.

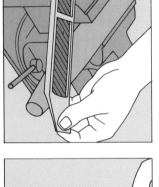

Use a wood file or Surform tool, round off socket line around its circumference to the squared taper to match the tool socket. To insure a tight fit, occasionally test-fit the handle in the socket.

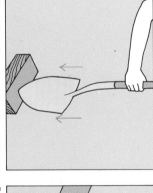

Using a wood file or Surform tool, round off the tool socket. line around its circumference to socket are snug and parallel, strike tool on a wooden block to drive handle home.

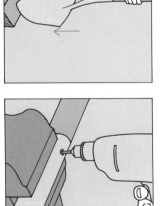

Drill a pilot hole and insert a new retaining rivet (see *Riveting*, p.369) or a round-headed wood screw that is slightly shorter than the diameter of the socket.

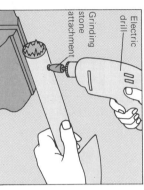

Electric drill

Grinding stone attachment

Replace or shorten handle if break runs straight across it. Grind off head of retaining rivet; drive rivet out of tool socket with a punch and hammer.

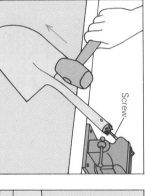

Insert a 6-in. wood screw into the broken stub until threads disappear. Clamp the head of the screw tightly in a vise and hit tool with a mallet to extract stub.

Screw

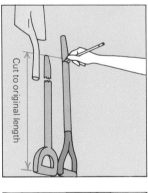

Lay out the pieces of the old handle and cut the new one to the same length. (You may be able to shorten and reuse the straight handles on rakes and hoes.)

Cut to original length

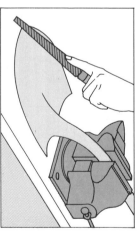

Lay the new handle next to the tool head and mark the position of the socket top on the handle. On most tools, the handle will have to be tapered to fit the socket.

When taper is correct, handle will fit into socket up to the line. When handle and socket are snug and parallel, strike tool on a wooden block to drive handle home.

Fixing loose grips

Remove a loose wooden grip from tang and shake out any wood or glue particles. Clean the inside of the ferrule with emery cloth.

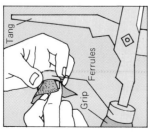

If the metal tang tapers toward its end instead of flaring out, file a series of sawtooth notches into the tang so that the adhesive will have something to grip.

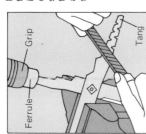

Clean the tang with emery cloth and place the ferrule over it, open end facing the tang. Mix and apply epoxy adhesive to the tang, ferrule, and hole in the grip.

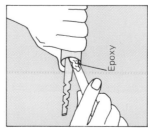

Push the grip over the tang. Be sure it seats in the ferrule. Tap it home with a mallet if necessary.

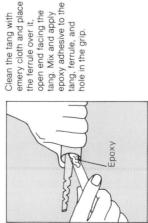

How to repair a leaking hose

A hose left on the ground for days on end will soon deteriorate. Drain and wind up hose after each use. Do not allow water to freeze in a hose. Bring hose indoors for the winter, but do not store it in a room where electric motors are used—the ozone produced by electric motors attacks rubber. Store hose on a reel or coiled on the floor; do not hang it from a nail. Straighten out kinks and creases as soon as you discover them—a pinched hose will soon crack. Several types of repair kits (right) are sold in hardware stores, but if a hose has several leaks it has probably deteriorated so badly that it is not really worth fixing.

Types of hose repair kits

Clamp-type mender

Insert coupling nut

Crimp coupling set

Crimp-type hose mender

To fix a rubber hose, cut away damaged section with a razor blade or sharp knife. If cuts are not perpendicular to length of hose, trim away ends of hose until they are.

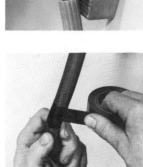

You can temporarily repair a small leak with electrical tape. Clean and dry hose. Overlap and stretch tape as you apply it. Do not stretch first and last three or four turns of the tape.

Place hose on a metal anvil or wooden block and hammer down the prongs gently and gradually until they grip the hose tightly all around. Repeat this procedure on the second piece of hose.

Buy a crimp-type hose mender, or male and female coupling set, to join the two remaining lengths of hose. Insert corrugated tube into hose end until it seats. Wet hose if tube is a tight fit.

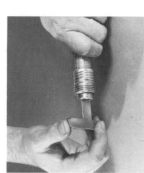

Insert the tapered, threaded bushing into the end of the hose by hand to keep hose from flattening out. Push coupling over hose until hose seats against shoulder inside coupling.

To fix a plastic hose, use an insert-type male and female coupling set. Cut away the leaking portion of the hose as shown above. Dip cut hose end into hot water to soften it.

Screw the male and female couplings together to complete the repair. Save the key; this coupling can be removed and saved for future use when the hose is eventually discarded.

Fit special key (included in kit) into notches inside bushing. Turn key clockwise until top of bushing is flush with end of hose. Repeat this operation on second piece of hose.

Lawn mowers

Maintenance

The storage, maintenance, and start-of-season procedures on these pages apply to all gasoline-powered mowers, whether with rotary or reel blades. Combustion engine repairs are dealt with in a separate section on two-cycle and four-cycle engines. (See *Small engines*, pp.370–387.) Two special sections on electrical motors (pp.132–135) cover the types of power units found in electrically operated mowers. The sharpening, lubricating, and cleaning procedures described for power reel mowers (pp.400–401) also apply to manual reel mowers.

At the start of the mowing season, three critical items should be checked in all gasoline-powered mowers: the oil, the air filter, and the fuel. If you have a four-cycle engine, make sure the crankcase oil is at the full mark. Next, clean the air filter; instructions for cleaning appear on page 395. Finally, check the fuel. Because gasoline evaporates, leaving behind a gummy residue that fouls the fuel line and carburetor, never store your mower over the winter with fuel in the tank. If you have stored it this way, drain the old fuel and refill the tank with a fresh supply before starting the engine. Do not use gas left over from last season. (See *Off-season storage*, p.396.)

A two-cycle engine must be fueled with the correct mixture of gasoline and oil. Anyone who has lost his owner's manual, and cannot get the needed information from a dealer or manufacturer, can determine the right fuel mixture in the following way: Start with 16 parts gasoline to 1 part oil; should the engine smoke profusely, reduce the amount of oil—to a mixture of, say, 1 to 18—and try again; if the engine continues smoking badly, further reduce the proportion of oil.

Remove all dirt from the engine cooling fins as a precaution against overheating. A rag soaked in kerosene and wrapped around a screwdriver is an excellent tool for such cleaning jobs.

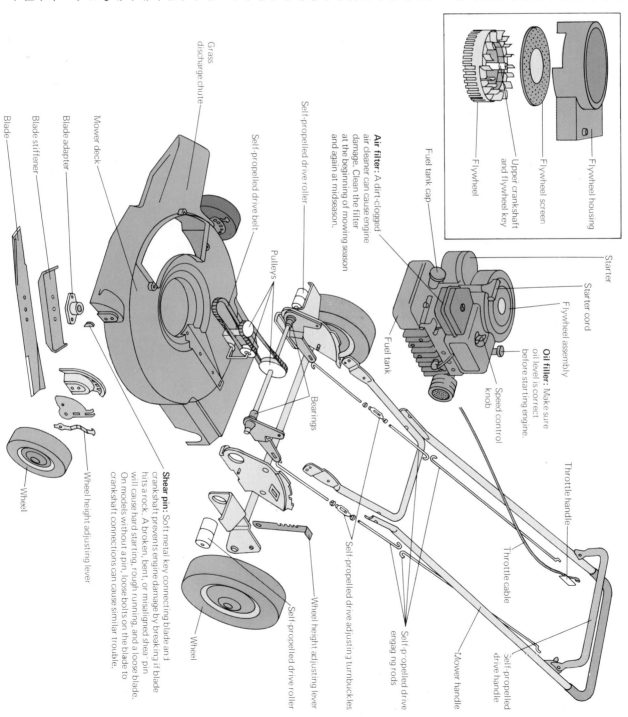

Flywheel housing

Flywheel screen

Upper crankshaft and flywheel key

Flywheel

Fuel tank cap

Air filter: A dirt-clogged air cleaner can cause engine damage. Clean the filter at the beginning of mowing season and again at midseason.

Starter

Starter cord

Flywheel assembly

Oil filler: Make sure oil level is correct before starting engine.

Fuel tank

Speed control knob

Throttle handle

Throttle cable

Grass discharge chute

Self-propelled drive roller

Self-propelled drive belt

Mower deck

Pulleys

Bearings

Self-propelled drive adjusting turnbuckles

Self-propelled drive roller

Wheel height adjusting lever

Self-propelled drive engaging rods

Self-propelled drive handle

Mower handle

Blade

Blade stiffener

Blade adapter

Wheel

Wheel height adjusting lever

Wheel

Shear pin: Soft metal key connecting blade and crankshaft prevents engine damage by breaking if blade hits a rock. A broken, bent, or misaligned shear pin will cause hard starting, rough running, and a loose blade. On models without a pin, loose bolts on the blade to crankshaft connections can cause similar trouble.

Blade

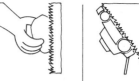

Safety precautions

When repairing a mower, always disconnect the spark plug wire to prevent engine from accidentally starting. Do not allow spark plug wire to dangle. Pull rubber insulator back, expose the connector, and ground it by attaching it securely to an engine-cooling fin or to a special grounding clip found on some mowers. Or, remove spark plug entirely.

When turning mower on its side to make a repair, place it so that the oil fill hole is higher than the crankcase. This will prevent oil from running out.

When mowing, always wear heavy shoes to protect your feet and toes. The best protection is that afforded by steel-tipped safety shoes.

Before starting to mow, clear the lawn of all foreign objects, such as sticks, stones, and toys. This prevents injury from objects thrown by blade.

When mowing on slopes, always mow uphill and downhill, never across the slope. Uphill and downhill mowing reduces the chances of slipping and overturning the mower.

Start of the season

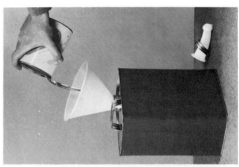

1. At start of season and before every mowing, check to see that the crankcase in a four-cycle engine is filled with an oil recommended by the engine manufacturer. If the oil-filler plug sticks, use a screwdriver to loosen it.

2. Next, remove and service the filter in the air cleaner. The fastener that releases the air cleaner cover, usually a long screw, also releases the entire air cleaner unit from the engine air intake assembly. Remove the entire unit.

3. Separate the air cleaner parts. Shake out heavy accumulations of dust and grass clippings. Use a solvent, such as kerosene, to wipe away grease or dirt from the metal parts of the air cleaner, especially air-intake vents and holes.

4. Wash foam or metal filters in a solvent such as kerosene. Squeeze solvent from filter and let the filter dry before reassembling. If solvent is not available, substitute hot, soapy water. Dirty paper filters cannot be cleaned; replace them.

5. Before assembling air cleaner, pour a tablespoon of motor oil over the filter. Make sure edge of foam forms a seal all the way around the filter housing, or dirt will get through. (A few mower engines have oil-bath filters; see p.374.)

6. Check air filter gasket for breaks and wear. Damaged gasket allows dirt to leak into engine. Replace worn or broken part with manufacturer's recommended gasket, then reinstall air cleaner. Start long screw by hand.

7. With the spark plug disconnected, wiggle blade to test for looseness. (Wear gloves.) Tightening bolts may not help; you may have to remove the blade and replace a damaged shear pin (see exploded view, p.394).

8. Fill fuel tank. For two-cycle engines, mix oil and gasoline in a separate container, then pour mixture into fuel tank. Never use fuel tank as the mixing receptacle, because poorly mixed fuel will quickly clog a fuel line.

Lawn mowers

Off-season storage

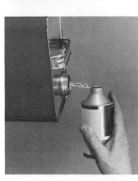

1. Evaporating fuel will gum fuel lines. To prepare mower for storage, first drain the fuel tank. Instead of tilting mower, use syringe or siphon to prevent spillage. Then, run engine until it stalls in order to drain fuel line and carburetor.

2. If you choose to store fuel for use next season, add a fuel stabilizer, available at garden and hardware stores. This prevents gasoline, which is a relatively unstable mixture, from separating into its component parts.

3. Four-cycle engine: While the engine is still warm, after Step 1, drain out all oil. The oil drain plug is located on the bottom or side of the engine. Some engines have no plug, and the oil must be drained through the filler hole.

4. Remove the spark plug with a spark plug wrench. This is an opportune moment to give the spark plug a quick analysis for carbon fouling and other clear symptoms of engine and carburetor problems. (See *Engines*, at right.)

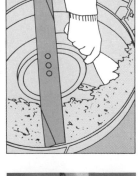

5. Clean plug electrodes with kerosene and stiff brush. Use spark plug gauge to check gap against manufacturer's recommendations; adjust gap by bending the side electrode to the proper distance from the center electrode.

6. Pour about 2 tablespoons of fresh engine oil into the spark plug hole. Crease a paper cup to form a pouring spout. This step is recommended for two-cycle as well as four-cycle engines. It prevents corrosion during storage.

7. Next, use starter cord to turn the engine over about six times so that oil will spread throughout cylinder and coat the wall and rings. If you have an electric starter, use it to turn engine over before charging battery for storage.

8. Replace spark plug, turning it by hand to be sure threads engage properly. Then, tighten firmly with wrench; but be careful not to overtighten plug, which could strip the cylinder-head threads, requiring a major engine repair.

9. With a screwdriver blade wrapped in cloth, to keep it from scratching painted areas, and with a stiff brush, thoroughly clean engine and lawn mower. Remove all caked grass and mud from engine-cooling fins.

10. With spark plug still unconnected, use stiff wire brush and putty knife to clean blade and underside of deck. Caked material may throw blade out of balance. Blade should be sharpened (p.399) before start of the season.

11. To prevent rusting, spray all bare metal parts, particularly where paint has worn from the underside, with a waterproof protective coating or with paint. Manufacturers sell matching spray paint through dealers and service centers.

12. Refill crankcase with clean engine oil. This should be your last procedure prior to winter storage. Do not refill crankcase immediately after draining (Step 3): oil may spill when mower is turned over to clean its underside.

Engines

The care and repair of engines are fully covered in other sections of this book. Two-cycle and four-cycle engines are discussed in *Small engines*, pp.370–387. Electrical power units are dealt with in the sections on electrical motors, pp.132–135. These are the sections to turn to when you want to troubleshoot a lawn mower engine that operates poorly or fails to start.

Sometimes, replacing an old spark plug—or simply cleaning and tightening the plug's connection—will be enough to make the lawn mower start up and run properly. But should the replacement plug quickly foul up, then this is a symptom of engine problems that must be corrected.

The illustration below shows four typical spark plug conditions that indicate engine problems.

1. Carbon-fouled plug caused by too rich a fuel mixture.
2. Oil fouling caused by crankcase oil within cylinder.
3. Combustion deposits mean clogged muffler, air filter, or dirty oil.
4. Burned insulator electrode results from clogged fins, air cleaner.

To check the spark plug, you will need a spark plug wrench and a gap gauge. These are available at hardware and automotive supply stores.

Gap gauges come in many styles, and you need not buy the most expensive to work on your mower. Get a gauge with a notched section for bending the side electrode when you need to change the gap on your plug.

Handle spark plugs carefully to avoid cracking the porcelain insulator or breaking the electrodes. Always adjust the side electrode to change the spark gap. Never attempt to bend the center electrode.

Engine flywheel key

A displaced flywheel key is a common problem of rotary mowers. If the blade hits a rock, the impact may break the key—particularly in mowers lacking a shear pin. With the key broken, the flywheel may slide around the crankshaft so that its magnets are out of synchronization and the spark plug does not fire correctly. (See *Small engines*, pp.370-387.)

If the engine runs poorly after the blade receives a severe jolt, check the key. Disconnect the spark plug. (See *Safety precautions*, p.395.) Then remove the flywheel and inspect the key. If it is damaged, replace it. A tool called a flywheel puller is used to remove the flywheel, and dealers sell the proper size pullers for their engines. Some handymen rig makeshift pullers, employing bolts and a 2 x 4. But flywheels are expensive and easily broken, so it is advisable to buy the standard-make tool, rather than improvise your own.

Always replace the flywheel key with the manufacturer's recommended part. Never buy or make a substitute. The correct part is designed to break under stress, so that the crankshaft will not.

1. Remove starter. Most starters are secured to engine by bolts. You may need a socket wrench to reach some bolts that are recessed. When all bolts are removed, you can simply lift the starter unit from its mountings.

2. Once the starter is off, remove bolts holding flywheel housing and lift off housing. If there is a control linkage between the housing and the carburetor, disconnect it by carefully unhooking the end of the bent rod.

3. Loosen bolts and remove flywheel protective screen. (Mower in illustration has bolts around edge of screen; some mowers have only a single bolt in the center.) Lay out all the bolts in the order of removal to make reassembly easier.

4. Remove the flywheel nut and washer. The nut may be extremely difficult to loosen, but do it carefully so as not to break any of the fan blades on the flywheel. Locking pliers (shown here) and penetrating oil may be required to loosen nut.

5. Fasten puller onto flywheel. (Some pullers hook under edge of flywheel; others bolt to the top.) Turn center bolt of puller to slowly force flywheel from shaft. A puller is highly recommended. Without one you can break the flywheel.

6. When flywheel is removed, the key may fall out. Here it is shown in proper position and condition. A broken, sheared, or bent key must be replaced only with the engine manufacturer's recommended part, never with a steel key.

Troubleshooting guide

Problem	Action
Mower scalps lawn in spots; may cut grooves in lawn.	Clean caked mud or clippings from blade. Check blade balance. If rotary blade is badly chipped, file to balance (p.399). Check wheel height; may be too low. On reel mower, check level of cutting bar (pp.400-401).
Growing grass looks brown the day after mowing.	Blades are probably dull. Dull blades tear grass rather than cutting it. Sharpen rotary blade (p.399); backlap reel mower (p.401).
Engine will not start.	Is fuel tank empty? For two-cycle engine, is fuel mixture correct (p.394)? Is fuel line or fuel strainer obstructed, pinched, or broken (p.381)? Check air filter for dirt. If blocked, clean (p.395). Check spark plug. Is it fouled or dirty (p.396)? Is high-tension lead cracked or broken (p.382)? Check flywheel key. Is it bent or broken (left)? Check carburetor, compression, and points (pp.375-379).
Engine runs unevenly and lacks power.	Check high-tension lead clip. Is it loose or dirty (p.382)? Check spark plug. Dirty or incorrect gap (p.396)? Is air filter element clean (p.395)? Is there water in fuel? Drain tank, fuel filter, and carburetor (p.381). Check fuel flow at carburetor. Clean needle valve (pp.376-378). Check flywheel key. If damaged, replace (left). Check compression and ignition points (pp.375-379).
Runaway engine (runs with controls on *Stop*).	Check idle speed adjustment screw. Engine may idle too fast (pp.376-378). Check the clutching mechanism. Do the drive rollers touch the wheels in the *Stop* position (p.398)?
Engine dies in use.	Check fuel tank. Check crankcase oil in four-cycle engine. Refill if empty. If mower runs very noisily after refill, overhaul may be needed (p.372). Check spark plug. Is it fouled (p.396)? Is it making firm contact with lead (382)? Check carburetor. If very hot, it may have vapor lock. Let cool, then restart. If it still will not start, check for dirty carburetor (pp.376-378). Is fuel line obstructed or kinked? Check fuel-cap breather hole (p.381). On two-cycle engines, check for excessive carbon on exhaust ports. Look for oily deposits on muffler (p.381). Check governor linkage for breaks or bad adjustment (p.381). Has blade just hit a rock or heavy clump of grass? Check flywheel key (left). Check compression. If weak, engine may need overhaul (p.379). Check ignition. Are contact points pitted? Is their gap correct (p.375)?
Unusually harsh vibration.	Check all nuts and bolts, especially engine bolts, for tightness. Check rotary blade for balance (p.399).
Engine runs, but mower stands still.	Check transmission belts, pulleys, clutch adjustment. Check drive rollers (p.398).

Self-propelled mowers

Most self-propelled mowers have V-shaped ridges on drive rollers that propel the mower by pressing against the wheels. When replacing these rollers, be sure the V's point toward the engine as viewed from behind the mower.

Drive roller maintenance

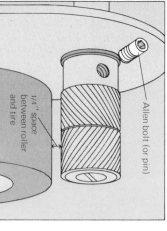

Allen bolt (or pin)

¼" space between roller and tire

Many clutch devices simply move the rollers on or off of the tires. For a mower to run straight, both rollers must touch the tires with equal pressure at the same instant. When the clutch handle is in *Neutral* the rollers should be ¼ inch from

the tires. Whenever you change the mower wheel height, adjust this clearance.

Belts, chains, or gears power the drive port. Then, the procedure is similar to that for a top belt. If there is no port, have the work done by your dealer.

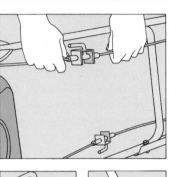

Engaging rods are adjusted with clamps or turnbuckles. First, put clutch in *Neutral* and loosen clamps; adjust so that both rollers touch tires when clutch is engaged, and clearance in neutral is ¼ in.

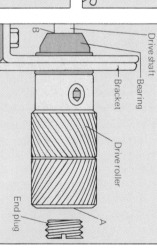

Drive shaft
Bearing
Bracket
Drive roller
End plug
A
B

Twice each season, grease the drive-roller bearings by removing plug and applying axle grease at "A." Then, tighten plug until snug. Repeat this process until grease shows at "B."

Upper drive belt replacement

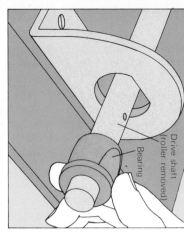

Bearing
Drive shaft (roller removed)

If engine runs well but mower does not move, first check Allen bolts or pins that hold drive rollers. If they are loose, rollers will slip. Tighten bolts or replace pins. If rollers are snug, check clearance at wheels.

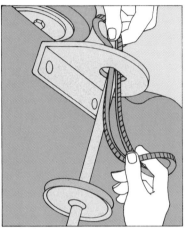

Position new belt so that its V-shape fits into pulley grooves. Do not allow it to twist unnecessarily, as this will cause extra wear and possible jamming of belt. Slide new belt through opening in the housing and under the drive shaft. Then, seat lower loop of drive belt into groove of drive-shaft pulley.

To replace an upper belt, first, remove pin or loosen Allen bolt on left roller. Remove roller, washer, and sleeve. Many mowers have a lower belt around a pulley below the engine. Unless there is an access plate for this pulley, the engine may have to be lifted to replace the belt (a shop job).

Pulley and gear lubrication

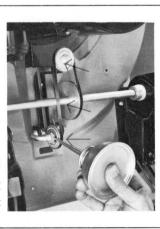

Two or three times each season, it is advisable to clean accumulated grass clippings from the pulleys and belt of a self-propelled mower. Remove drive-system housing; clean drive parts with brush and screwdriver wrapped with cloth. Place a drop of fine oil on each pulley bearing (see arrows).

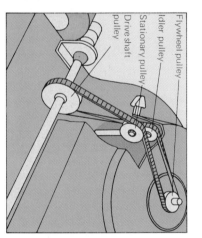

Flywheel pulley
Idler pulley
Stationary pulley
Drive shaft pulley

Bring belt up to top of engine. Place belt over stationary pulley and flywheel pulley. Depress idler pulley and slide belt on. The drive-shaft pulley and idler pulley usually have setscrews for adjusting. Run mower briefly, then check belt for abrasion. Adjust pulleys as needed to change belt alignment and eliminate abrasions.

Once each season, lubricate gear drives using light grease, not oil. First, clean debris from gear case; then, remove cover and apply grease directly to gears with finger. If bearings have automotive-type grease fittings (arrows), use a grease gun to inject grease at "A" until it oozes from seam at "B."

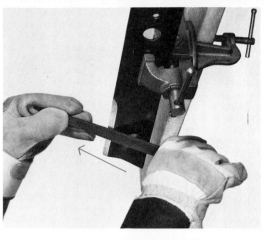

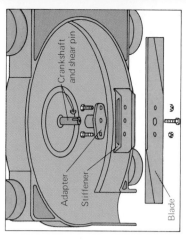

Sharpen with medium-rough flat file along original angle of cutting edge. File in one direction only—toward the edge. Electric drill sharpening attachment, available at hardware stores, is as good as a file.

Crankshaft and shear pin

Adapter

Stiffener

Blade

Cutting edge

Lift

Blade cross section

Put sharpened and balanced blade back on mower. Make sure the lifts point upward, toward the deck, when mower is right side up. This assures that blades will draw grass up for proper cutting and discharge.

Remove blade and check stiffener for cracks or bends. Replace defective stiffener only with a manufacturer's recommended part. A bent or homemade part can cause vibration that will damage the engine.

If the same end of the blade drops consistently, file some metal from heavy end, avoiding the cutting edge. This lightens blade without ruining newly sharpened edge. Check blade balance again.

Sharpening

Many problems of rotary lawn mowers are avoidable if blades are kept sharpened and balanced. Check your blade for the symptoms illustrated below.

Always replace a badly bent or partly broken blade. The vibrations of a deformed or unbalanced blade may cause serious engine damage. Sharpen the blade using the methods illustrated at right. Sharpen twice a season, or at least frequently enough to retain the original cutting-edge angle. Once this angle is lost, attempts to sharpen the blade will be unsuccessful.

After disconnecting spark plug (see *Safety precautions*, p.395), grasp blade in gloved hand or with heavy cloth and loosen blade's securing nuts or bolts. If the bolts stick, tap the wrench with a hammer.

Blade in good condition provides plenty of lift.

Dull blade will tear grass instead of cutting it and will also strain engine.

Twisted blade will make a very ragged cut and probably scalp lawn in spots.

Badly nicked blade will likely lose balance and cause vibration during operation.

Use screwdriver or knife as pivot on which to balance blade. Check balance one way, then flip blade over and check again. If balanced both ways, reinstall blade on mower (see illustration at far right).

Blade with no lift will not pick up grass and will cut the lawn unevenly.

399

Lawn mowers

Reel mowers

Because the cutting mechanism of the reel mower is more complicated than that of the rotary, it is not possible for the homeowner to do a complete sharpening job. Special and expensive sharpening machinery is required. However, much can be done to maintain a reel mower, whether power or manual, and keep it cutting well.

A procedure called backlapping (p.401) will keep the cutting edges honed and eliminate the need for frequent sharpening. Slightly bent blades can usually be straightened at home (p.401). But if the reel becomes badly bent and out of balance, it is better to take it to a service center for replacement. Avoid having an old reel repaired or rebalanced. Either is expensive, and reconditioned reels often do not perform satisfactorily. Buy a new reel from the manufacturer if the part is still available.

If yours is a powered reel mower, most of the problems will be related to the engine. (See *Small engines*, pp.370–387.) Keep the engine clean and properly fueled and oiled, and you will eliminate many troubles before they start.

Adjusting height of cut

The cutting height on both power and manual reel mowers is set by adjusting the rear roller. On most mowers the two ends of the roller are adjusted separately. It is important to make sure the roller is level after resetting it. If it is not, the cutter bar may scrape the ground, damaging both lawn and cutting surfaces of the mower.

When grass has grown very high, do not try to mow it with a single cutting. Mow twice. Make the first cut with the roller lowered all the way, which raises the cutter bar. Then, mow again with cutter bar at desired grass height.

To cut grass short with a reel mower, raise rear roller (left). This moves cutting bar closer to ground. Lower the roller (right) to raise the bar to a higher level for a longer cut.

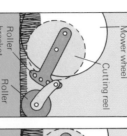

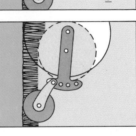

Mower wheel

Cutting reel

Roller bracket

Roller

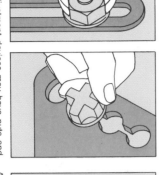

Roller height adjustment devices may have nuts and bolts at each end (left), or wing nuts. Others have knobs (right) with pins that slip into higher or lower notches, allowing for roller adjustment.

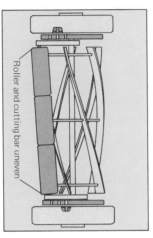

A roller that is not level causes the cutting bar to scrape the lawn. Loosen and adjust each end of the roller to the same desired height, then retighten fasteners and test mower. Readjust if necessary.

Roller and cutting bar uneven

(See *Safety precautions*, p.395.)

Caution: Before doing maintenance work on your power reel mower, disconnect spark plug.

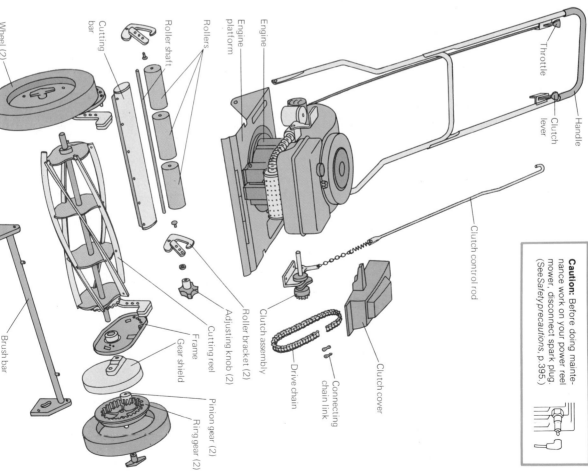

Wheel (2)

Cutting bar

Roller shaft

Rollers

Engine platform

Engine

Throttle

Clutch lever

Handle

Clutch control rod

Clutch cover

Connecting chain link

Clutch assembly

Roller bracket (2)

Drive chain

Adjusting knob (2)

Cutting reel

Frame

Gear shield

Pinion gear (2)

Ring gear (2)

Brush bar

Straightening reel blades

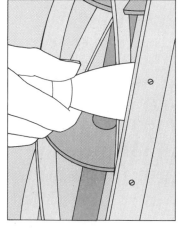

Even minor bends in blades will cause the reel to skip over parts of the cutting bar, making mower cut unevenly. Check blades with a straightedge.

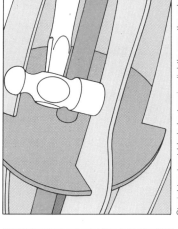

Straighten bent blade by tapping lightly near the edge with a hammer. To avoid dulling blade, be careful not to strike directly on the cutting edge.

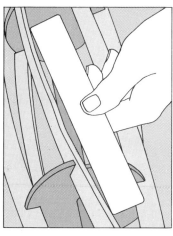

Straight blades should pass at a uniform, close distance to the bar. Turn blade slowly by hand, using thin knife blade as a gauge to test distance.

Backlapping and adjusting bar

1. With a smooth-cut flat file, remove burrs from the upper and lower surfaces of the blades. Take care not to file directly on the cutting edges. Also use a flat file to eliminate any burrs that have appeared on the reel mower's strike bar. **Caution:** Before starting work on a power mower, be sure that the spark plug is disconnected.

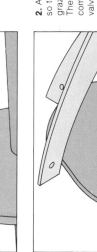

2. Adjust the strike bar so that the blades just graze it as they turn. Then, apply a grinding compound—an automobile valve-grinding paste will do the job well—and rotate the reel backwards. This action sharpens the bar and the blades simultaneously.

3. After wiping all metal surfaces clean of the grinding paste, adjust the bar so that it grazes the blades lightly along their full length as the reel rotates. Power mowers are adjusted so that the blades make firmer contact, as indicated by Step 4.

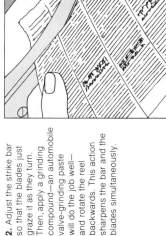

4. Power-mower blades should cleanly cut a single sheet of newspaper along the full length of the strike bar. Manual-mower blades should cut cleanly through a sheaf of newspaper that is three sheets in thickness.

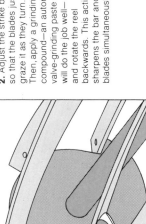

Electric starters

Lawn mowers with electric starters are turned on by key, much as an automobile is started. The electric starter's commonest problem is a dead battery. Thus, be sure to recharge your battery according to the manufacturer's schedule and instructions. If you cannot obtain information from manufacturer or dealer, charge your battery according to the following general rules:

Dry battery—Charge for 48 hours both at the beginning and the end of the mowing season. Throughout the season, charge for 24 hours once a month.

Wet battery—Be sure battery is kept properly filled with distilled water. Charge the battery to full charge once a month all year round. Check the charge with a hydrometer (see p.335).

Failure to start is not always the result of a dead battery. As covered earlier in these pages, the problem may lie with the spark plug or in the engine. The trouble may also be in the connection between the starter motor and the engine. The connecting belt employed by some mowers may be loose or broken. It should be tight enough so that it gives only about ⅛ inch when pressed lightly in the center.

Connection to starter switch

Pinion gear spring

On some mowers, the starter connects to the engine by a spring-protected pinion that engages the flywheel gear when the starter operates. Sometimes the spring breaks and the engine does not start. The pinion spring is easy to replace, though you must first remove the starter motor to do it.

Lawn tractors

General maintenance

Tractors vary in detail from one manufacturer to another. Most popular designs have a single-cylinder engine, pneumatic tires, a multispeed transmission, a single brake-clutch pedal, and rotary grass-cutting blades. On most units, the blades and transmission are driven by rubber V-belts. Power is passed to the rear axle by a chain.

Safety interlock switches will prevent the engine from starting if the driver is not in the seat, the clutch is engaged, the brake is not on, or accessories are not properly attached. Check your owner's manual for the proper starting procedure; if it is being followed and the engine still will not start, check the interlock wiring and the individual interlock switches for faults.

After every 25 hours of use, oil all the drive chains, steering gears, front wheel bearings and spindles, pulley bushings, and all linkage and control pivots. Use a multiweight motor oil.

Note: Interlock (safety or lockout) switches may be located near brake-clutch pedal, idler pulley, and transmission pulley

Troubleshooting guide

PROBLEM	ACTION
Engine will not start	Check battery condition (pp.334–335); add water to battery or recharge if necessary
	Check interlock switches and wiring (pp.332–333); replace faulty switches or wiring
	Check starter connections and operation (pp.383, 401); clean connections; oil starter
	Make sure throttle is in *Choke* or *Fast* position (see owner's manual)
	Check engine for possible mechanical problems (p.373); repair as shown on pp.370–387
Excessively rapid belt wear	Check pulleys for dents, cracks, gouges, or rough spots; repair or replace damaged pulleys
	On mowers with a belt brake, make sure brake clears belts when unit is running; adjust clearance if necessary or replace broken brake cables (p.380)
	Check all belt guides; they should not rub belt when it is engaged; set clearance at 1/16 in. (p.403)
	Check to see if foreign objects are interfering with belt; remove any you find
Vibration when mower or clutch is engaged	Check for grass accumulations under mowing deck; scrape away dried grass
	Check to see if mower blades are damaged or out of balance (p.399)
	Replace any damaged pulleys, bearings, pivots, or brackets in belt drive system
	Check belts for flat spots or other irregularities; replace faulty belts
	Check for proper belt tension (p.384); adjust tension if necessary
	Check sprockets and chain for proper alignment and possible wear (pp.384–385, 438)

PROBLEM	ACTION
Mower cuts grass poorly or unevenly	Check blades for dullness or other damage (p.399); sharpen or replace if necessary
	Check for grass accumulations under mowing deck; scrape away dried grass
	Check mower deck height and level settings (see owner's manual) and readjust
	Analyze grass condition: tall or wet grass may need a second mowing
	Operate tractor in the proper gear; engine should run between ¾ and full throttle
Mower is hard to shift or does not move when clutch is engaged	Check owner's manual for proper shifting technique
	Check brake-clutch synchronization adjustment (p.403); readjust if necessary
	Check for proper belt tension (p.384); adjust tension if necessary (p.403)
	Check transmission and differential units for damaged gears; have dealer repair it
	Check drive pulleys and sprockets for a bent or missing key; replace a damaged key
	Check chain tension; adjust tension (p.403); replace worn or damaged chain (p.438)
V-belts slip or come off in use	Analyze grass condition; tall or wet grass may cause belts to slip
	Check for proper belt tension (p.384); adjust tension if necessary (p.403)
	Check belt condition; if it is worn, replace it with the mower manufacturer's part
	Check idler pulley spring tension; if spring is stretched or damaged, replace it
	Check pulley alignment (p.384); realign pulleys if necessary
	Check pulleys for cracks, gouges, or other damage; replace any damaged pulleys
	Check belt guides (p.403); they should be 1/16 in. from the engaged belt
Belts squeal when brake is applied	Check brake-clutch synchronization adjustment (p.403); readjust if necessary
	Check for proper belt tension (p.384); adjust tension if necessary (p.403)

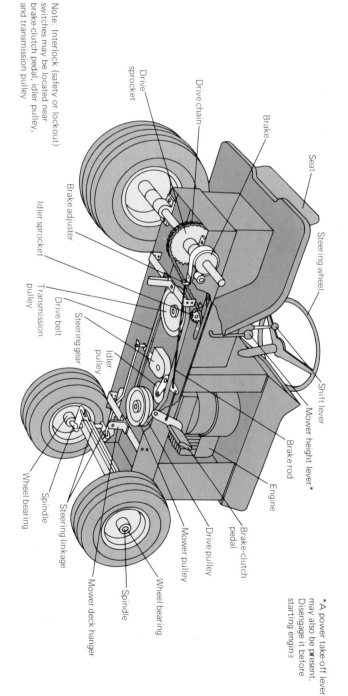

Steering wheel

Shift lever

Mower height lever*

Brake rod

Engine

Brake-clutch pedal

Drive pulley

Mower pulley

Wheel bearing

Spindle

Steering linkage

Mower deck hanger

Wheel bearing

Spindle

Steering gear

Idler pulley

Steering gear

Drive belt

Transmission pulley

Idler sprocket

Brake adjuster

Brake

Seat

Drive chain

Drive sprocket

*A power take-off lever may also be present. Disengage it before starting engine.

How to remove the mower deck

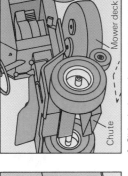

4. Slide deck out from under the right side of tractor. On mowers with a rear grass discharge, you will have to raise the right rear wheel of the tractor to clear the discharge chute.

Mower deck · Chute

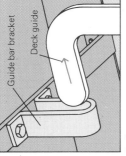

3. Slide the deck farther forward to disengage the rear deck guide from its guide bar bracket. The deck is now disengaged from the tractor. Reverse procedure to reinstall deck.

Guide bar bracket · Deck guide

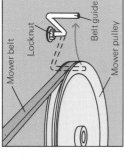

2. Note the position of the mower belt guides, loosen their locking nuts, and swing them out of the way. Slide deck forward and remove the belt from the mower pulley.

Mower belt · Locknut · Belt guide · Mower pulley

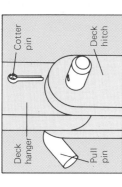

1. Remove the cotter pin from the pull pin at the front of the deck, then remove the pull pin. If the cotter pin breaks or feels mushy from repeated bending, buy a replacement.

Cotter pin · Deck hitch · Deck hanger · Pull pin

The mower deck shields the blades and prevents stones and other missiles from being thrown at bystanders. On many mowers, it must be removed in order to replace a V-belt or make belt adjustments. You must also remove a warped or dented deck in order to repair it.

Start by placing the mower height adjustment lever (if any) in the lowest grass cutting position. If the tractor has a mower interlock switch, unplug the interlock wire. The engine cannot then be started until the deck is reinstalled and the interlock reconnected.

Belt and chain adjustments

When the chain cannot be tightened any further, replace it (p.438). To open the type of connecting link shown here, insert a screwdriver between the side plates and twist sharply.

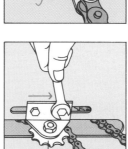

2. Separate side plates

1. Find master link

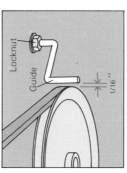

Move sprocket to tighten chain

The chain may have an idler sprocket; if so, adjust it as you would an idler pulley. To tighten a chain without an idler, loosen axle mounting bolts, move axle backwards, and retighten bolts.

Locknut · Guide · 1/16"

If belt cannot be tightened sufficiently, replace it. Guides keep belts from jumping off the pulleys. Open locknuts to position guides within 1/16 in. of engaged belts. Retighten locknuts.

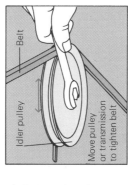

Idler pulley · Belt · Move pulley or transmission to tighten belt

To tighten a belt, loosen the bolt that holds the idler pulley and press the pulley against the belt. Retighten bolt. Make adjustments only when the engine is off but the belt is engaged.

The belts and chains used in your lawn tractor stretch and wear with use. Up to a point, they can be adjusted to take up any slack. A V-belt should deflect only 1/4 to 1/2 in. when pressed midway between its pulleys (see p.384). Some tractors have an idler pulley that can be adjusted to increase tension. On others, the driven component is moved to take up slack. To replace a belt, relax its tension as far as possible, pull off the worn belt, and roll the new belt onto the pulleys. Tractor chains are replaced in the same way as bicycle chains (p.438).

Brake-clutch adjustments

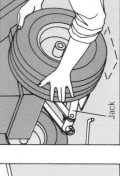

4. Raise rear of tractor with a scissors jack (p.318). With brake-clutch pedal depressed, you should not be able to turn the rear wheels by hand. If you can, readjust the brake (Step 1).

Jack

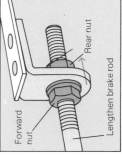

3. If idler does not let V-belt slip on the drive pulley before the brake takes hold, tighten the forward nut on the brake rod and loosen rear nut until synchronization is correct.

Rear nut · Forward nut · Lengthen brake rod

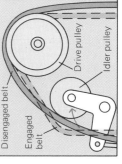

2. With transmission in *Neutral*, press brake-clutch pedal all the way down by hand. Idler pulley must relax belt tension enough for the drive belt to slip freely around the drive pulley.

Disengaged belt · Engaged belt · Drive pulley · Idler pulley

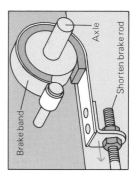

1. To adjust an ineffectual brake, turn adjusting mechanism until brake band nearly touches the axle, or brake pads nearly contact the disc when there is no pressure on brake pedal.

Brake band · Axle · Shorten brake rod

Most tractors have a combination brake-clutch pedal. When you push the pedal partway down, the drive belt is disengaged from its pulley. When you push the pedal all the way down, the brake is applied. The brake-clutch adjustment must be synchronized so that the brake does not begin to grab before the belt is disengaged. If the belt is fully disengaged but the brake does not stop the tractor, the brake linkage needs adjusting. Adjust the brake linkage and the tension on all belts before attempting to adjust the brake-clutch synchronization.

Rats, mice, and other mammals

The most effective method of controlling rats, mice, and other mammalian pests is to prevent them from entering your home. The traps and poison baits described further down this page provide only short-term solutions to rat and mouse infestations. Unless pest prevention measures are undertaken in conjunction with exterminating traps and poisons, infestations will recur.

Denying rodents a food supply

Rats and mice are attracted to our homes because they feed on many of the foods that make up a normal human diet. Therefore, both cleanliness and the proper storage of foods are critical to controlling these domestic pests.

Cleanliness: Be particularly meticulous in cleaning under and behind stoves, refrigerators, sinks, kitchen counters, and other places where food scraps may fall and accumulate. Mop floors with special care along walls and baseboards, since the favored runways of rats and mice lie alongside and inside walls. Do not allow dirty dishes to stand on the dinner table overnight. If you intend to leave dishes stacked in the sink or in an automatic dishwasher, scrape and thoroughly rinse them. More than one housewife has been astonished to find mice in her dishwasher. The creatures are equally adept at climbing down under the burners of gas stoves and through the heat vents into the ovens of both gas and electric ranges. An infrequently cleaned oven and range are often thus prime sources of food for rodents. Food that has spilled and hardened on a highchair or playpen will attract rats.

Garbage bags should be tied and kept in a metal garbage can with a secure clamp-down lid. The state of the grounds around your home is important, as rats attracted to the area may come inside.

Food storage: Sugar and flour should be stored in metal, glass, or crockery containers with tight lids; bread should be stored in a breadbox or the refrigerator. Noodles, macaroni, spaghetti, dried fruits, breakfast cereals, and other packaged foods should be kept in similar containers. Soap—a favorite food of rats—should be kept in a closed soap dish or high off the floor in a recessed wall dish, not on the rim of the tub or wash basin. Soap flakes should be kept in jars. Potatoes, squash, carrots, and other vegetables should be stored in rat-proofed bins.

Rat-proofing: Rats, mice, squirrels, and other rodents are not easy to keep out of a house—particularly an older house, where subsidence, weathering, and neglect often combine to create many openings. Inspect the basement and the attic (where squirrels and the roof rat often nest) for openings.

Rat-proofing of windows, foundation and attic vents, coal chutes, and ventilating fans should be done with heavy screening or metal hardware cloth with mesh openings no larger than ½ inch. Pipes and wires running up outside walls can be rat-proofed with commercial rat guards. Protect wooden doorjambs and door bottoms with sheet metal.

Holes in foundations and masonry walls should be filled with cement. Holes

in plaster walls should be packed with steel wool before being plastered over. Holes in wooden walls should be covered with sheet metal or hardware cloth.

All basement drains should be covered with heavy metal drain plates. The openings around water pipes where they pass up from the basement should be packed with steel wool and caulking compound, or asbestos insulation.

No trapping or baiting campaign can succeed unless you carry out a rat-proofing program. Your strongest weapon is your own intelligence. Try to identify and block off every possible access route rats might follow into your home.

Poisons and traps: Poison bait is the favored rat extermination method of professional exterminators, since rats are especially wary of traps. Modern anticoagulant rodenticides—sold under such names as Warfarin, PMP, Pivalyl, Fumarin, and Diphacinone—are recommended. They are far less toxic to human beings than older rat poisons, and almost exclusively in industrial rat-control programs. These new rodenticides cause the animals to die from internal bleeding; they become thirsty and leave favored rat runways to seek water, and thus usually die in moist basements or

out of doors where their decaying bodies create no odor problem.

The poisons are mixed with water or with such baits as corn meal, peanut oil, peanut butter, sugar, molasses, or dried cheese. Both liquid and solid baits should be set out in small paper cups or plates, for easy disposal later. The baits should be located along known or suspected rat runways close to basement, garage, or attic walls; on beams; and near doorways. The rooms should be closed off to pets and children. Place a long board, bricks, or boxes along a wall to create a narrow corridor; then, place poison or traps inside the corridor.

Although mouse poisons are widely available, traps are recommended for mice. Conventional snap-back traps should be positioned with the trigger end touching the baseboards along which the mice usually travel. Use up to a dozen traps in one room, as the mice are likely to overlook just two or three. Cheese is a poor choice of bait for mice. Sardines, gum drops, hard candy, bacon, nuts, and peanut butter are the best mouse baits. Tie solid bait to the trigger mechanism.

Automatic live mousetraps are now available. These traps are very effective, and do not require baits. They trap up to 20 mice at one setting. The mice can later be drowned inside the trap by dipping it into water.

Squirrels should be taken out of doors and then released out of doors. Afterwards, screen off attic vents and other openings to upper floors.

A bat can usually be coaxed out of the house at night by brightly lighting the room where you find it and opening a door or window onto the night. Close off the doors to other rooms.

All these pests are potential carriers of disease, including rabies. Their bites may be infective. Avoid handling them if you trap them live, and call your physician immediately if you are bitten.

Norway rat, also known as the grey rat, brown rat, or sewer rat: This is the most common domestic intruder. The adult may attain the size of a cat; the young Norway differs from an adult mouse in its thick tail and a head and feet that are larger in proportion to its body.

Roof rat, or black rat: Its subspecies include the white-bellied roof rat. All are more slender than Norway, and their tails are longer in proportion to their bodies. Rats gnaw big, rough holes, leave large droppings, and leave dark grease spots on wood.

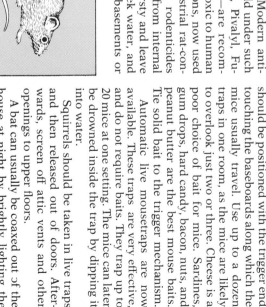

House mouse: It is tiny, delicate in appearance, and darting in movement compared even to a young rat. The house mouse chews neat, rounded holes that contrast markedly to rat holes. Its sounds in walls are slight compared to the gnawing and traffic of the heavy-footed rat.

Pesticides

Before using any pesticide, carefully read the instructions and precautions on the container's label. Use the pesticide only as directed. Failure to do so could cause serious injury. Do not let a pesticide get on food or eating and cooking utensils or surfaces. Be careful not to inhale it or get it on your skin or in your eyes. Wash your hands and face thoroughly after use.

Never use a spray near an open flame, such as a pilot light or furnace; do not smoke when handling a spray. Leave the room as soon as you have used an aerosol spray; keep the room closed and stay out of it for at least half an hour—or longer when the label instructions so advise. Then, ventilate the room. Do not hang a chemically treated pest strip in rooms where people will be present for prolonged periods, particularly infants or sick or elderly people; do not use a pest strip where food is prepared or served. Do not let children touch surfaces where residual sprays have been used.

Store pesticides in a cool, dry place out of reach of children and pets, and never near food. Dispose of pesticides in such a way that they cannot contaminate water or wildlife; do not flush down toilets, sinks, or sewers. Do not use pesticide containers or mixing receptacles for any other purpose. If you swallow a pesticide, follow the antidote instructions on the label, call a doctor immediately, and bring the container to him. The Ortho Division of Chevron Chemicals has a national emergency phone number for use by physicians. It is: (415) 233-3737.

Some pesticides, such as DDT and chlordane, leave residues in the soil for years, and should not be employed where they will pollute streams, ground water, or artesian wells. Several powerful chemicals indicated on the chart are likely to be removed from the market in coming years as the result of federal regulation. Their use may subject the user to fine and imprisonment.

How to read a pesticide label

ACTIVE INGREDIENTS:
....
....
....
....

BRAND NAME
FORMULATION
TYPE OR PURPOSE

DIRECTIONS ....

NET WEIGHT   EPA NO. 000

CAUTION:
....
....
....
....

By law, **pesticide labels must carry** certain information, including brand name, formulation (powder, liquid, aerosol); uses for pesticide; active ingredients; directions for use; amount in container; Environmental Protection Agency number; and an indication of how hazardous the pesticide is to man and wildlife, using the key words "CAUTION" (relatively safe to use), "WARNING" (moderately toxic), or "DANGER" (highly toxic).

Properties of commonly used pesticides

Common chemical name (Trade names are marked ®)	Uses	Length of potency**	Toxicity to mammals***
Aldrin*	Soil insects	Long	High
Allethrin	Broad spectrum insecticide	Short	Low
Baygon®	Crawling insects	Very long	Moderate
Carbaryl (Sevin®)	Broad spectrum insecticide	Moderate	Low
Chlorobenzilate®	Mites and spiders	Moderate	Low
Chlordane*	Broad spectrum insecticide	Very long	Moderate
Coumaphos (Co-Ral®)	Rodents, other mammals	Moderate	High
DDT*	Broad spectrum insecticide	Very long	Moderate
Diazinon	Broad spectrum insecticide	Long	Moderate
Dichlorvos (DDVP, Vapona®)	Parasites, household pests	Short	High
Dicofol (Kelthane®)	Mites	Long	Moderate
Dieldrin*	Broad spectrum insecticide	Long	High
Dimethoate	Flies, vegetable parasites	Long	Moderate
Dioxathion (Delnav®)	Insects, mites	Moderate	High
Endosulfan (Thiodan®)	Broad spectrum insecticide	Moderate	High
Fenthion (Baytex®, Entex®)	Flies, mosquitoes	Moderate	Moderate
Heptachlor*	Soil insects	Long	High
Kepone** (Decachlorooctahydro-1,3,4-metheno-2H-cyclobuta(cd)pentalen-2-one)	Ants, crawling insects	Very long	Moderate
Lindane*	Broad spectrum insecticide	Long	High
Malathion	Broad spectrum insecticide	Moderate	Low
Metaldehyde	Slugs, snails	Long	High
Methoxychlor (Marlate®)	Broad spectrum insecticide	Moderate	Low
Mirex*	Ants, crawling insects	Long	Low
Naled (Dibrom®)	Broad spectrum insecticide	Short	Low
Petroleum oils	Insects and eggs	Long	High
Ovex	Mites	Long	Low
Pyrethrins	Broad spectrum insecticide	Short	Low
Ronnel (Korlan®)	Parasites, household pests	Moderate	Low
Rotenone	Broad spectrum insecticide	Moderate	Low
Sulfur	Mites	Long	Nontoxic
TDE	Broad spectrum insecticide	Long	Low
Tetradifon (Tedion®)	Mites	Long	Low
Toxaphene	Broad spectrum insecticide	Long	High
Trichlorfon (Dipterex®)	Broad spectrum insecticide	Long	Low

*These products are currently banned or may soon be banned from public sale by the EPA. Check with your pesticide dealer for current local and federal restrictions and possible substitutes.

**Based on recommended application intervals on label instructions: Short—up to 3 days; Moderate—up to 14 days; Long—up to 35 days; Very long—over 35 days (may last months or years).

***Hazard level when swallowed by humans, pets, livestock, or wildlife.

405

Pests and rot

Household insect control

INSECT	DESCRIPTION (Where found)	CONTROL
Ant 	Many species are pests, ranging from tiny thief, pharaoh, little fire, and little black ants to ½-inch-long carpenter ants (see below). Most ants nest outside in mounds or burrows, under slabs and stones, in cracks in cement, or in dead wood. Some nest indoors under flooring, inside walls, under papers, or in remote corners of the house, basement, or garage.	Trace ants to where you see them entering or leaving, as under a baseboard, at a doorsill. Cover area with film of residual insecticide containing chlordane, dieldrin, diazinon, lindane, or malathion. Pastes, baits, or traps containing Kepone are an alternative; poison is carried back to kill ants in nest. If you find nest, treat with insecticide dust.
Carpenter ant 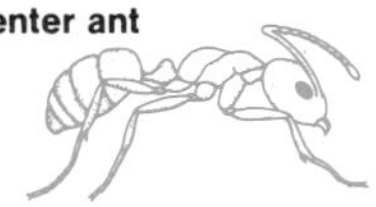	These black or brownish ants may reach more than ½ in. in length. They excavate moist wood for purpose of nesting. Unexplained sawdust on ground, wall, or floor is clue to their presence. Porches, roofs, columns, or any wood exposed to wetness is vulnerable. Galleries (holes in wood) are distinguished from termite damage by polished appearance, absence of debris.	Do not try drowning ants by flooding the galleries with water, as this leads to further complications. Enlarge gallery entrances and blow in pesticide dust containing chlordane, dieldrin, or heptachlor. Drill small holes at intervals above entrance and along gallery and blow in more dust. Correct leaks, sweaty pipes, or improper drainage.
Cockroach 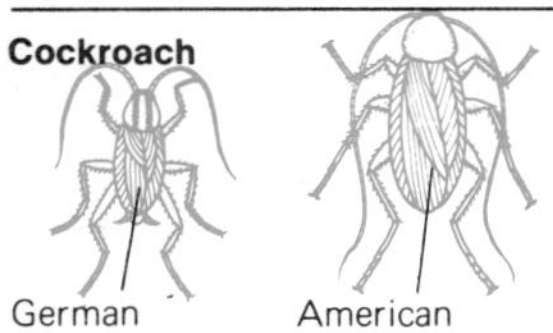 German American	Five species of roaches are house pests. Adults range from about ½ in. to 1 in. in length and from yellowish or reddish brown to black in color. The tiny German roach poses a special problem because of its resistance to many pesticides. Adult German roaches are about ⅝ in. long; they are light brown with black stripes. All species tend to be active only at night or in the absence of light. They nest and hide in dark, sheltered spaces. Females lay eggs in capsules which form at the ends of their bodies. They feed on human food and garbage, scattered crumbs, soiled clothing, and the glue in book bindings.	Good housekeeping is crucial; deny roaches access to garbage, crumbs, and stored food. Pesticides containing diazinon, malathion, or ronnel should kill all species—though German roaches are becoming resistant to diazinon. Fight heavy infestations by using a spray, then a commercial boric acid dust. Apply where roaches are likely to nest or hide, including baseboard cracks, bookcases, behind loose molding, wall clocks, window and door frames, where pipes and ducts pass through walls, under shelf paper, around and beneath sinks, and in cupboards and cabinets (especially the upper corners of cabinets).
Carpenter bee 	The common eastern species closely resembles the bumblebee, being a large black bee with areas of yellow. Other species vary from black to green or purplish in color, with white, yellow, or red markings. The females excavate their egg galleries by boring into clapboards, wooden shingles, eaves, porch columns, and other external wooden elements.	Females often reuse and enlarge old galleries in the same structure where they hatched as young. If uncontrolled, a community can grow large and seriously damage a structure. Galleries continue inward, then turn to run parallel to grain of wood. Force a broad-spectrum insecticidal dust into gallery entrance; drill small holes along grain and force in more dust.
Wasp Yellow jacket Paper wasp 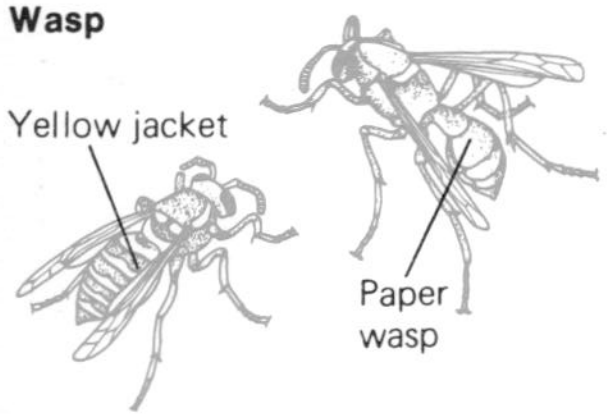	The name "wasp" is commonly given to five closely related flying insects: yellow jackets and cicada killers, which nest in the ground, and hornets, mud daubers, and a species known as the paper wasp or polistes, which nest above the ground. Hornets and polistes nest in shrubbery and trees, as well as under the eaves of a house or high on the wall under the roof of an attic, garage, or outbuilding. Mud daubers nest under eaves, porch roofs, behind shutters. A hornet nest is grayish, shaped like a football, and has a papery shell. Polistes build nests with many open, circular cells. Mud daubers make mud formations with a number of side-by-side tubes. In the fall, hornets and polistes leave their nests and do not reuse them. Mud daubers winter over as larvae in the nest. All wasps are distinguishable from bees by their slender waists and long, slim bodies.	To people who are allergic to their venom, the sting of wasps can be fatal; therefore wasp nests close to human habitats should be destroyed. On nests above ground, use a spray containing chlordane, carbaryl, Baygon, or malathion; bombs are available that have enough force to direct a stream of insecticide at the nest from a great distance. Ask hardware clerk for a wasp bomb. To further lessen risk of being stung, spray at dusk or night when all wasps have returned to the nest and are inactive. Wear protective garments, including gloves, hat, cheesecloth veil, and long sleeves. Button and turn up collar. For nests in the ground, direct insecticidal dust into opening with a duster; throw a shovelful of damp earth over the hole. If you see wasps coming and going through a crack or knothole in a wall, force dust into opening. Passing wasps will carry poison back to nest.
Bedbug 	Adults are flattish, brown insects up to ⅜ in. in length; after biting a human being they swell up with blood and have a dull red hue. Because they avoid light, they are not often seen. Bites on the skin and blackish or brownish spots on mattresses, in mattress seams, on pillows, or on bed linen are evidence of their presence.	Fumigate with spray containing pyrethrins, malathion, ronnel, or lindane. Cover (but do not soak) mattress completely. Spray seams, tufts, bed frame, slats, springs, bedroom baseboards, cracks in walls and between flooring, and closets. **Caution: Never use concentration of more than 0.1 percent lindane or 1 percent malathion on a mattress. Dry mattress before use.**
Millipede and centipede 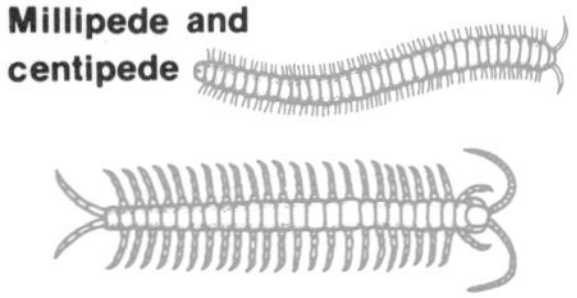	Centipedes and millipedes normally inhabit damp places out of doors, such as piles of decaying leaves, rotting boards, the undersides of rocks, tree bark, mulch, and compost heaps. Centipedes frequently wander into houses; if injured they may bite. Although the bite generally is not serious, pain and swelling may result from it. Use an antiseptic on the bite and call your family physician.	Residual films or wettable powders containing malathion, chlordane, or lindane should be applied to doorsills, windowsills, or other places where centipedes or millipedes are entering the house, such as ventilating fan ports and points where pipes pass up through flooring from a crawl space. Occasionally millipedes will migrate inside in large numbers. Apply pesticide to all the areas infested by the creatures, then clear the grounds around the house, crawl spaces, garage, and basement of decaying leaves, rotting wood, and all other decomposing vegetable matter. Relocate compost further from the house.
Carpet beetle and moth 	Adult clothes moths are buff or yellowish in color and have a wingspan of about ½ in. Females lay eggs in clothes and other fabrics; larvae hatch from the eggs and feed on the fabric. It is the larva, not the adult moths, that do the damage. Fully grown larvae are ½-in. long white worms with dark heads. Black carpet beetles have black bodies and brown legs. Again, it is the larvae that do the damage; they are about ½ in. long and yellowish to brown in color. Other species are varicolored; their larvae have bristles and attain ½ in. in length.	Because larvae feed in clothing, blankets, rugs, carpets, drapes, pillows, mattresses, brushes, and upholstery, good housekeeping is a key to control. The vacuum cleaner bag should be emptied of dirt promptly after use; it may contain eggs, larvae, or adult beetles or moths. Carpet beetle larvae feed under furniture where they are protected from room traffic and light; rotate carpets and furniture frequently. Spray infested carpet with insecticide containing methoxychlor, Perthane, or Strobane. Clothes can be decontaminated by drycleaning; store in plastic bags and use mothballs in closets.

INSECT	DESCRIPTION (Where found)	CONTROL
Cricket	Both the house cricket and the field cricket normally live outdoors but may invade households in large numbers in late summer or during cricket plagues. Crickets eat everything from woolens, silks, and paper to fruits and vegetables. House crickets are nocturnal creatures, and are usually inactive during the day. A single cricket is merely a nuisance, because of its nighttime chirping. An infestation requires action.	Use a residual, broad-spectrum insecticide to spray behind and under furniture, in closets, under baseboards, the folds of drapes and curtains, windowshades, lampshades, and the edges of carpets. Also treat points of possible entry into the house, such as around fireplaces, doors, windows, ventilating fans, hot-air registers, attic and cellar windows and vents, cellar doors, crawl spaces, and cracks between flooring. Tight-fitting screening is a must, both on windows and around pipes leading to an unused basement or crawl space.
Earwig	These insects are easily recognized by their prominent rear forceps. Adults may attain an inch in length. They have wings but are poor flyers. Recently their infestations have reached epidemic proportions in some parts of the southern United States, where they nest primarily in lawns. However, they are becoming increasingly common everywhere, and may enter houses in large numbers. They are omnivorous.	Programs to fight neighborhood epidemics should be undertaken only in cooperation with local conservation authorities. Call your county agent. Householders can combat limited infestations with dusts or wettable powders containing carbaryl, chlordane, or dieldrin. Besides lawns, treat likely breeding places; these include moist, sheltered areas, such as cracks in foundations, the hollow tubing of lawn furniture, and damp sills, baseboards, and flooring.
Housefly	The common housefly's relatives include the larger face and stable (horse, dog, or beach) flies, cluster flies, and the smaller latrine and little houseflies. All lay eggs in garbage, excrement, and other decaying organic matter, or in contaminated ground. Maggots hatch out in from 12 hours to 3 days, depending on species and temperature. Face and cluster flies winter over in house walls. Flies spread disease, and many bite.	Well maintained screening and good sanitation are the main requirements for control. Screens should have at least 14 meshes to the inch. Do not leave foods exposed to flies. If you have a pet dog, clean its excrement from the lawn every day and dispose of it as garbage. Seal garbage in plastic bags and keep cans covered. Fight infestations—face and cluster flies in early spring, houseflies in late summer or fall—with commercial flying-insect aerosol space sprays.
Mosquito	More than 100 species are pests in North America. After mating, the females of most species need a blood meal to nourish their developing eggs, and it is the females that bite. Inside the house, females will usually light on a ceiling or an upper wall area to digest the blood meal. They lay their eggs in quiet water, such as a pond, a marshy place, puddles, or water trapped in artificial containers or the crooks of house and garden plants.	Kerosene or an emulsifiable insecticide can be used to kill larvae in rain gutters, puddles, and other areas of stagnant water. Do not treat any body with an outlet to a stream without the approval and guidance of local conservation authorities. Call your county agent. Screens with 18 meshes to the inch will keep all species out of your home. Use residual sprays to film upper walls and ceilings; use space sprays for heavy infestations.
Scorpion	Scorpions are common creatures throughout the southern United States. Most species are no more poisonous than bees or wasps; however, two species found in southern Arizona, New Mexico, southern California, and Texas inject a venom that may be fatal. Report a scorpion sting to a physician immediately; the first few hours are crucial to effective treatment.	Clear the grounds around your house of woodpiles, loose boards, and debris in which scorpions hide. (Wear protective garments.) Use residual insecticide containing chlordane, lindane, or dieldrin to create a film on doorsills, windowsills, vents, fan ports, and other points where scorpions enter. Force insecticidal dust into cracks in flooring, under baseboards, around plumbing, and into closets. Spread dust outside doorways and windows.
Silverfish and firebrat	Silverfish and firebrats are similar insects. The most common silverfish is silvery, but other species may be marked with black lines or have a gun-metal look. Firebrats sport markings that give their backs a mottled appearance. Both firebrats and silverfish feed on a broad diet of glue, paste, fabrics, flour, cereals, dried scraps of meat, sugar, and paper. Silverfish can go a long time without food. Eggs are deposited in out-of-the-way crevices, as in baseboards, drawers, and bookcases. Firebrats prefer hot temperatures, as around ovens, and are common pests in bakeries and boiler rooms.	Apply a residual spray or a dust containing chlordane, lindane, ronnel, diazinon, or malathion to crevices in baseboards, window and door casings, portals where pipes and ducts pass through walls or floors, crevices in basement walls and floors, clothes closets, cupboards, partitions, and under and behind kitchen stoves, cabinets, counters, and sinks.
Spider Black widow Brown recluse	All spiders inject venom when they bite. But just two North American spiders are consistently dangerous to man. The brown recluse is found in Kansas, Missouri, and the southwestern United States. The black widow is common only to the warm southern tier of the country. The former is identifiable by a distinctive violin-shaped mark on the top of its head (technically, the cephalothorax). The venomous female black widow—males are not dangerous—has an hourglass design of red or yellow on the underside of its black abdomen. Report spider bites to a physician immediately.	Any structures where the brown recluse or black widow has been observed should be treated promptly with a residual oil spray containing lindane, chlordane, or malathion. Spray liberally in dark corners. If you find the web, do not attempt to knock it down; spray the web with the residual insecticide. Ordinary house spiders can be controlled by spraying or dusting their preferred habitats, ranging from casement windows to basements and crawl spaces. Remove webs after spiders are dead.
Tick Normal Engorged	Ticks carry such diseases as Rocky Mountain spotted fever, relapsing fever, Texas cattle fever, and a condition known as tick paralysis, which quickly disappears after the tick has been removed. The only tick that commonly establishes itself in a home is the brown dog tick, which carries no diseases. A blood-filled adult tick drops off the dog and seeks the protection of an upholstery seam, the wool of a carpet, or a crevice in a baseboard. Young ticks hatch out and develop in these hidden places.	You can remove a tick from skin by holding a lit cigarette close to its protruding end—or by applying a heavy concentration of moist salt, kerosene, or alcohol. The tick will withdraw without breaking off its head, which is important to prevent infection. Let the vet detick a badly afflicted pet, while you rid the house of the hidden brood of ticks. Burn the pet's bedding. Spray with an insecticide containing malathion or diazinon wherever the pet sleeps—rugs, upholstered furniture—and in all likely breeding crevices.

Note: Changing government regulations may result in the removal from pesticides of many of the above-named active ingredients. Check with your dealer for newly introduced substitutes that meet present standards.

Termite control

Termites are a problem for many home-owners, but termite damage should not cause undue alarm. If handled properly, termites can easily be eliminated.

Termite-proofing is a job for a professional. The information that follows will familiarize you with the insect and help you to make an informed choice in selecting a professional exterminator.

There are three major species of termites: dry-wood, damp-wood, and subterranean. The subterranean termite is the most common.

Subterranean termites live in colonies deep within the ground. They have been discovered at depths of 25 feet. Within each colony there are various castes of termites, each performing a certain function. The winged termites reproduce. Soldiers defend the colony against intruders, such as ants. Worker termites, the most numerous, feed the colony. The workers do the damage in a house.

Winged termites are often mistaken for ants, but there are two distinct differences: Ants have a pinched-in waist and have front wings slightly longer than the hind wings; termites have a thick waist and their wings are of equal size.

Termites work their way up through the soil from their nest and enter any wood they can. This may be wood in direct contact with the ground, such as stair supports, piers, and porch posts, or wood in close proximity to the ground, such as structural members on concrete or block foundations. Termites gain entrance by crawling up the sides of foundations, building mud shelter tubes to shield them from light. They may also go up hollow sections in block foundations or up cracks inside poured concrete foundations.

Termites feed on the softer parts of wood and are hard to detect because they do their damage inside the wood, leaving exterior surfaces undisturbed. Normally, they attack the bottom portions of studs and walls; it is rare to find them higher. The time it takes termites to do extensive damage to a house varies. Sometimes it is only a couple of years; sometimes 10 or more years.

For the layman, finding termites is extremely difficult. Their mud tunnels are hard to detect. The winged termites do swarm, but this occurs only once a year for a few hours. It is a good idea to get your house inspected by a professional exterminator, but choose one carefully.

Unfortunately, it is possible for incompetent and unscrupulous operators to enter the termite exterminating field. You can check on an exterminator through your local Chamber of Commerce or Better Business Bureau. Beware of those who:

• Quote a charge based on gallons of supplies, lives and breeds in dry wood; it materials to be used. The chemical is relatively cheap in relation to the labor.

• Profess to have a secret formula or ingredient for termite control.

• Have no listed telephone number.

• Show up unexpectedly and use "evidence" of termites in trees outside your house to inspect your home and sell an exterminating job.

Before work is begun you should ask the operator for references—and check them. Get a written statement of work to be done and an estimate of cost. Seek an estimate by more than one firm.

A reputable operator will offer a written guarantee, up to five years. He will agree to come back and treat for termites again if any show up within that time.

Every 48 hours or so termites must return to the soil to get moisture or they will die. The professional sets up a barrier of chemicals in the soil that the termites cannot pass through.

To do this, he injects a diluted chemical (usually chlordane) into the soil through a tubelike device with holes on the end. It is driven into the earth every 18 inches, around the entire house.

Termite identification

The same procedure must also be followed inside the house. Holes are drilled next to foundation walls every 18 inches, and the chemical injected. If floors are tiled, carpeted, or the like, professional exterminators have equipment to remove and replace floor coverings without causing permanent damage.

The job described would be expensive even if finished flooring need not be repaired. The U.S. Forest Service is now experimenting with poisoned termite baits that can wipe out whole colonies with very little work or expense.

The dry-wood termite, as its name implies, lives and breeds in dry wood; it does not need to return to the soil. In the United States these termites are found in a narrow strip from Cape Henry, Virginia, to Florida, and along the Gulf of Mexico and the California coast. Dry-wood termites are a threat to any dry wood, including furniture. After boring their way into wood, they plug the holes behind them with a brownish material.

Damp-wood termites are very large, often 1 inch long with 2-inch wings. They do not require soil moisture, but live in wood with high moisture content.

The powder-post beetle is technically not a termite, but it is often considered one. It lives in dry wood, entering through tiny openings and boring galleries throughout. Smaller than the dry-wood termite, the powder-post beetle is especially damaging to furniture.

Elimination of dry- and damp-wood termites is a job for professionals. The treatment is to fumigate the entire house with a toxic gas or dust. Residents and pets must move out of the house during treatment. Powder-post beetles can be eliminated by injecting chemicals into the galleries they eat in furniture.

It may be that only part of a house is infested. Still, the entire house must be termite-proofed or the termites in the soil may migrate to untreated parts.

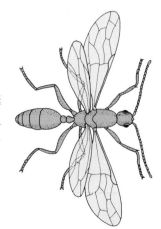

Winged ant.

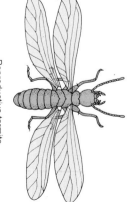

Reproductive termite.

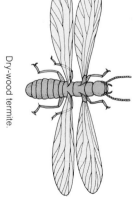

Dry-wood termite.

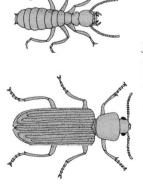

Worker termite.

Powder-post beetle.

Decaying wood

Certain kinds of fungi attack wood under the right conditions—mainly when the proper amount of moisture and temperature (70°F to 85°F.) are present. The resultant weakening of the wood is variously known as wet rot, dry rot (a misnomer), or simply decay. No matter what the name, the cause is the same—a fungus feeding on the wood.

Depending on the fungus and the stage of the condition, rotting wood may look brown and crumbly. At earlier stages the wood may be white and spongy to the touch. These conditions may not appear on the surface of the wood for some time. Wood with interior rot may sound hollow if you tap it or feel spongy when pressed. When the surrounding atmosphere is very damp, the fungi may grow out on the surface of the wood, appearing as mottled white or brown growths in patches, strands, or vinelike structures.

The way to prevent rot, or at least slow its progress once it is present, is to keep affected or potential decay sites dry and cool. Adequate ventilation is a must, and keeping the area as dry as possible is also important. This is not always possible without elaborate drainage and ventila-

tion arrangements, which are best built into a structure when it is first constructed. If you find advanced rot in structural members of a house, boat, or camper, the affected parts must be replaced. This, of course, can be expensive.

If the rot is confined to small areas that do not bear weight—window and door sills, floors and walls adjacent to sweating toilet fixtures—or very small spots on posts and beams, you can treat it with a thin epoxy resin designed to arrest the spread of rot and repair some of the damage it has caused. Several brands are available at boating supply stores. The compound is sold in two containers, the contents of which must be mixed together before use. Pour the mixture into holes drilled into the rotted portions of the wood. The material seeps into the wood pores and, when dry, forms a solid plastic filler that can arrest the spread of the fungus for years. These products come with detailed directions for use in various situations. The resin takes several days to work; more can be added to the damaged area as the original application finds its way down into various small voids.

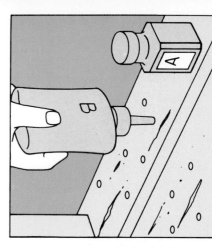

Mix resin according to directions and pour it slowly down the holes. Add more as resin soaks in.

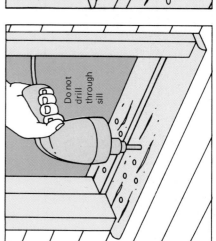

Do not drill through sill

To inject epoxy resin into decaying wood, drill a series of ¼-in. holes well into the rotted area.

Holes must be made through flooring and concrete slabs every 18'' along inside of foundation

Mud tubes shield termites from the light and allow access to soil. They are rounded and cementlike in appearance

Access routes may be located inside cracks or hollow cement blocks in the foundation. These are impossible to see

Injection sites for chlordane are series of holes 18'' apart. If there are walks or patios next to house, they must be drilled through

Termite nests are underground. The insects work their way up in search of wood to feed on

Chlordane barrier must extend under entire foundation. Check location of water supply before treatment. Do not allow chlordane to be injected near an artesian well

The only effective treatment for termites is to saturate the ground beneath the foundation with a dilute solution of chlordane. This creates a barrier that prevents the termites from returning to the soil for life-giving moisture. In the illustration, the termite nest is shown close to the bottom of the foundation, but nests have been found as deep as 25 ft into the ground. The chlordane must be pumped in from both sides of the foundation. Holes for injecting the insecticide must be close to the foundation and about 18 in. apart. Skilled termite control operators have special equipment that allows them to remove small segments of flooring and drill through concrete slabs, then return these materials to their original spots without visible damage. Properly done, termite-proofing lasts for years.

Electric drill

The electric drill is the most widely owned power tool. A common fault is a parted power cord, caused by carrying the tool by its cord instead of its handle or by improperly disconnecting the cord from an electrical outlet (see *Safety precautions*, opposite page). If the drill will not run, lock the trigger switch in the *On* position and wiggle the cord back and forth, both where it enters the drill and at the plug. If the drill then runs in inter-mittent spurts, one of the power cord wires has broken. If it is broken near the plug, you can cut the cord beyond the damaged area, strip back the insulation, and attach a new plug (see p.130). If it is broken where the cord enters the drill, you may have to replace the entire cord; many cords have a molded-on rubber cushion where the cord meets the tool, and cannot be shortened easily.

Other common problems are a rotor, a commutator, or brushes that are burned as a result of overloading the tool. Any power tool—drill, saw, or sander—should be allowed to work at its own pace. Do not bear down on the tool with excessive pressure. Do not use dull bits or blades. And do not use a bigger bit or blade than the tool was designed to accept. Burned or worn brushes are easily replaced (see p.412). To repair other motor faults, see pages 132–137.

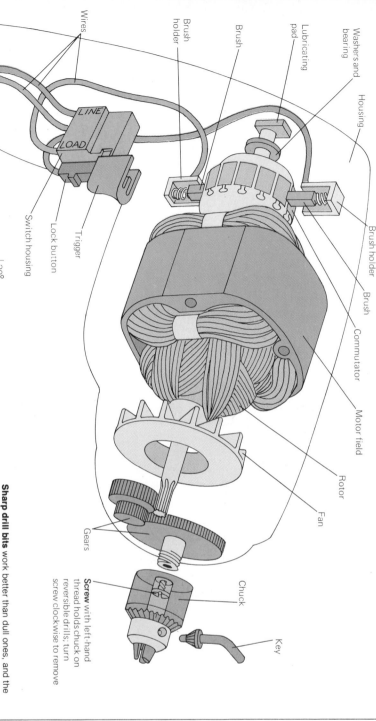

Wires

Brush holder

Brush

Lubricating pad

Washers and bearing

Housing

Brush holder

Brush

Commutator

Motor field

Rotor

Fan

Chuck

Key

Power cord cushion

Switch housing

Lock button

Trigger

LINE

LOAD

Gears

Screw with left-hand thread holds chuck on reversible drills; turn screw clockwise to remove

Extra-sharp bit

30°

Standard bit

59°

Masonry bit

Sharp drill bits work better than dull ones, and the drill user is therefore less likely to bear down on the tool and overload the motor. A sharp twist bit cuts curlicue shavings from wood and metal; a dull bit scrapes away small chips. An extra-dull bit produces a lot of heat and may cause wood to smolder. Dull twist bits should be sharpened (see p.367) or replaced. The bit can be sharpened at various angles to make it more suitable for drilling different materials (p.366). Use special masonry bits on brick or cement.

Disassembly

To remove the chuck from a nonreversing drill, open jaws fully, then strike key with hammer to free threads. Spin chuck counterclockwise. On a reversible drill, first close jaws and strike key to turn chuck clockwise. Then, open jaws and remove chuck screw by turning it clockwise. Strike Key to unscrew chuck.

Stacked housing

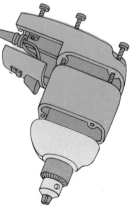

Remove long screws from rear of housing to disassemble drill. Lay out all washers, shims, and springs in order of removal.

Clamshell housing

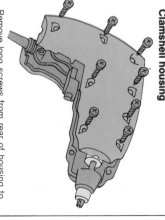

Remove long screws from rear of housing to disassemble drill. Lay out all washers, shims, and springs in order of removal.

Troubleshooting

Problem	Action
Motor does not run	Check for current at outlet with a lamp you know is working. If there is no power, check fuses or circuit breakers (p.127) and house wiring Check power cord for fraying or bent prongs (p.130) With switch locked in *On* position, twist cord near tool and plug; if tool runs in spurts, cord has a broken wire (see *Electric drill*, facing page) Test cord with a volt-ohm meter (Step 4, at right) With tool unplugged, turn fan or motor through several rotations by hand (Step 1, at right). If tool then runs, one rotor or commutator segment is faulty (p.132). You may use tool temporarily, but should repair motor as soon as possible Inspect brushes for wear or sticky action (pp.412,133). Replace worn or pitted brushes; free sticking brushes Spray commutator with electrical contact cleaner (p.123) Test switch with a volt-ohm meter (p.133); replace if necessary
Motor hums but does not run	With tool unplugged, turn fan or motor through several rotations by hand (Step 1). If it cannot be turned, disassemble tool and motor, looking for jammed gears, rotor striking field, a bent fan, or frozen bearings (p.134). If motor can be turned, then runs when plugged in, a rotor or commutator segment is faulty (p.132) Remove tool from work. If it then operates, tool was overloaded. Allow tool to reach operating speed before applying it to work. Work more slowly, and do not apply as much pressure. Make sure bit or blade is not too big for tool
Tool is noisy, vibrates	Tighten bit or blade if loose. If tight, remove and reposition bit or blade. Replace a warped or broken bit or blade. Open housing and tighten all screws, nuts, bolts. Replace worn rubber mounts. Be sure fan is on tightly. Clean debris from rotor and field. Replace rotor if commutator bars are loose. Check bearings for wear (p.134)
Tool dropped into water	Turn off power at fuse box, shake water out of tool, allow to dry in a warm, dry place such as a furnace room. Disassemble and clean tool if it was submerged in muddy water. If it was submerged in salt water, flush with tap water and dry.

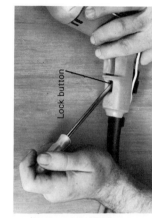

1. If motor hums but drill will not run, unplug tool and rotate fan a quarter turn. If the drill then works, one of the rotor windings or commutator segments is bad (see p.132). If it still hums, the fan, gears, rotor, or bearings are jammed (p.134).

3. Use a straightened-out paper clip to release the retaining springs that hold the wires in the switch housing. Note that the wires from the motor are marked *Load*; wires from the power cord are marked *Line*. These markings aid reassembly.

Lock button

2. Disassemble housing as shown on opposite page. Rubber cushions may cause parts to stick; pry gently apart with a screwdriver. Squeeze trigger and push out lockbutton with the screwdriver. Slide trigger control switch out of handle.

4. Attach volt-ohm meter to each prong of the plug (p.125). Clip together the bare wires at the other end of the cord. Flex cord along its entire length. If meter remains on zero, cord is OK; if reading is high, a wire is broken. Fix or replace cord.

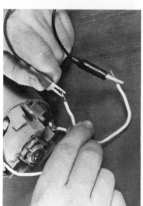

5. Attach volt-ohm meter to motor (brush) leads. Meter needle should move toward zero as the second connection is made. If not, the motor is faulty or the commutator is dirty (pp.132–133). If the motor and power cord are OK, the switch is bad.

6. Open gear housing and scrape away the grease. Inspect gears for wear, jamming, or missing teeth. Replace damaged gears with factory parts. Apply nonstaining white grease to gears, and reassemble drill. Keep wires in channels and clear of screws.

Safety precautions

Always wear shatterproof safety glasses when operating any power tool. Safety goggles fit over prescription eyeglasses. Wear a face mask when using tools that produce a lot of sawdust.

Always connect a tool with a three-pronged, grounded plug to a grounded, three-hole outlet (see p.126). Use it only with a three-wire extension cord. If you use a plug adapter, place it between the extension cord and the outlet, not between the power cord and the extension cord. Double insulated tools have plastic housings and two-prong plugs; they can be used safely in two-hole outlets.

Do not use power tools while standing in water or wet grass, or on a damp basement, garage, or workshop floor.

Do not carry a power tool by its cord; use the handle. Do not pull on the cord to unplug the tool; pull only on the plug itself. Improper handling may break the wires inside the power cord.

When repairing any power tool, use only factory replacement parts. Be sure to reassemble tool correctly, following the manufacturer's exploded-view drawings. Otherwise, a serious shock hazard will result.

Power tools

Replacing brushes

The brushes in a power tool used only for light hobby work may last the life of the tool. The brushes in a tool that receives prolonged use (such as a saw or sander used by a professional carpenter) may need yearly replacement.

The brushes are blocks of a soft carbon material much like pencil lead, which are held against the rotating commutator by small springs (see *Universal motors*, pp.132–134). The brushes should be replaced before their length is worn down to equal their width. Wear beyond this point may cause a brush to wedge sideways in its housing. If the brush wears away completely, the spring will come into contact with the commutator and damage it. Always replace both brushes.

To reach the brushes you must usually disassemble the tool housing. On a tool with a clamshell housing, the brushes are easy to reach: You need only lift off half the housing to replace them. On tools with a stacked housing, you may have to clamp the tool in a vise to keep the rotor and commutator in place as you install the brushes. On some professional models, the brushes can be withdrawn through screw-on ports in the housing.

Reassembly: Clean dirt, carbon, or sawdust accumulations from the housing recesses before reassembling the tool. Use warm water and a mild liquid dishwashing soap only. Do not use detergents, kerosene, or other solvents—they may damage the plastic used in some housings. Let the housing air dry, then reassemble it. The tool dealer or manufacturer can supply a parts list and exploded view of your particular tool. Consult one to be sure you get all the washers, spacers, bearings, and springs assembled in the right order. Fit wiring and plugs into their original channels. You may have to force rubber cushions into place, but the self-tapping screws should twist smoothly into their threads without undue pressure.

On a Skil drill

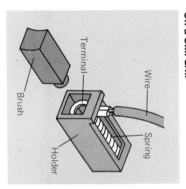

1. Open clamshell housing and lift off upper half. Pivot brush holders back and lift out of recesses.

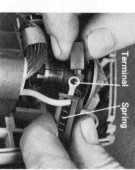

2. Remove each old brush if it does not spring out by itself. Note arrangement of wire terminal and brush spring.

3. Place wire through side of holder, put cylindrical end of brush through terminal and into spring. Install holder.

On a Black & Decker drill

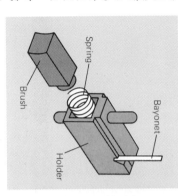

1. Place drill in a vise and remove handle and trigger assemblies. Pry out brush holders and remove brushes.

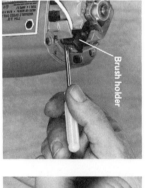

2. Place new brushes into holders. If bayonet connector was bent when holder was removed, straighten it.

3. Push brush back into holder with a thin knife blade or bent paper clip. Insert bayonet and press holder home.

On a Craftsman cordless drill

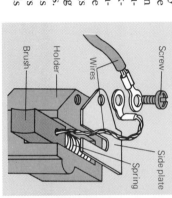

1. Open clamshell housing and lift off upper half. Remove screws that hold wires and holder side plates in place.

2. Remove holder plate, brush, and spring. Spring may pop out and stick to magnets in motor; do not lose it.

3. Place new brush in holder, force spring behind it, reattach the side plate and both wires with screw.

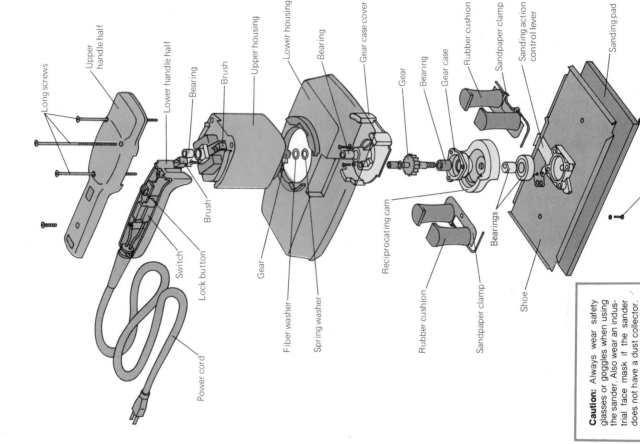

To reach the brushes on a power sander, remove the screws from the top of the tool and lift off the upper half of the handle. Brushes will then be accessible at the top of the motor. Replace as shown on facing page for drills. Manufacturers generally use the same design for brushes and holders throughout their tool lines.

To reach the gearcase without disturbing the brushes, remove the three long screws only. Turn the sander upside down, and pull off the sanding pad and lower part of the housing.

Remove pad screws and lift off lower housing. Remove gearcase screws, open case, and inspect and lubricate single gear inside. Reassemble unit and replace long screws before turning it right side up.

Long screws

Upper handle half

Lower handle half

Bearing

Brush

Upper housing

Lower housing

Bearing

Brush

Gear

Gear case cover

Gear

Bearing

Gear case

Reciprocating cam

Rubber cushion

Sandpaper clamp

Sanding action control lever

Fiber washer

Spring washer

Bearings

Sanding pad

Rubber cushion

Shoe

Sandpaper clamp

Pad screws

Switch

Lock button

Power cord

Caution: Always wear safety glasses or goggles when using the sander. Also wear an industrial face mask if the sander does not have a dust collector.

Sander

Orbital, in-line, or dual-action sanders greatly speed tedious sanding projects. Common faults include a parted power cord (see *Electric Drill*, p.410) and worn brushes (see pp.410–412). Other problems may be caused by improper use of the tool or improper choice of sandpapers.

Always hold the sander off the work before turning it on or off. Allow the tool to reach its full operating speed before bringing it into contact with the work. Keep the sander moving over the work; do not allow it to remain in one place for too long or it will create a depression. Let the sander work at its own pace with little or no downward pressure. Excessive downward pressure will cause overheating and possible motor damage. Be sure the sandpaper is tightly secured to the sanding pad; tight paper lasts longer and does a better job.

Use only aluminum oxide, silicon oxide, or other synthetic abrasives for power sanding. Natural abrasives, such as flint or garnet, wear too quickly and are not economical for power sanding. To remove the greatest amount of material, use a coarse (50-grit) paper, then proceed to a medium (80-grit) and fine (120-grit) paper. On dual-action sanders, use the orbital action for fastest sanding. Use in-line action only with fine paper for final finish, moving with the grain.

After each use, wipe any oil or grease from the sander's cord and clean its air vents with a small brush. Periodically add a few drops of SAE #20 oil to the felt wick under the oiling hole (if any). At least once a year, you should: Open the housing and inspect the brushes; clean out accumulated sawdust with mild soap and warm water; clean the gears and relubricate them with white, stainless grease; and test the switch, motor, and power cord for electrical faults (see pp.132–137, 411–412). Follow this same procedure if the motor stops or sparks excessively.

413

Power tools

Circular saw

Every 6 to 12 months (or if the motor stops, smokes, or sparks excessively): Inspect the brushes; disassemble the housing and clean out accumulated sawdust with mild soap and warm water; clean the gears and relubricate them with white, stainless grease; and test the switch, motor, and power cord for electrical faults (pp.132–137, 411–412). After each use: Unplug the saw; clean sawdust from its air vents with a small brush; and

wipe any oil or grease from the cord to prevent deterioration. Occasionally add a few drops of SAE #20 oil to any oiling holes or lubricating pads.

Always use the right size blade for your saw. The size required is printed on the nameplate of every saw. (Diameters of cost little more than professional sharp-from 5¼ to 8½ inches are common.) Position the saw on the work with the blade just clear. Let the motor reach operating speed before bringing the blade into con-

tact with the work. Never force a saw; use light, continuous pressure only to guide it. A dull blade will cause slow cutting and may burn the lumber or overload the motor. Keep extra blades on hand to replace dull ones. Inexpensive blades cost little more than professional sharpening. Gum on the blade will also slow cutting. Remove the blade from the saw to prevent damaging the plastic case and clean it with kerosene or turpentine.

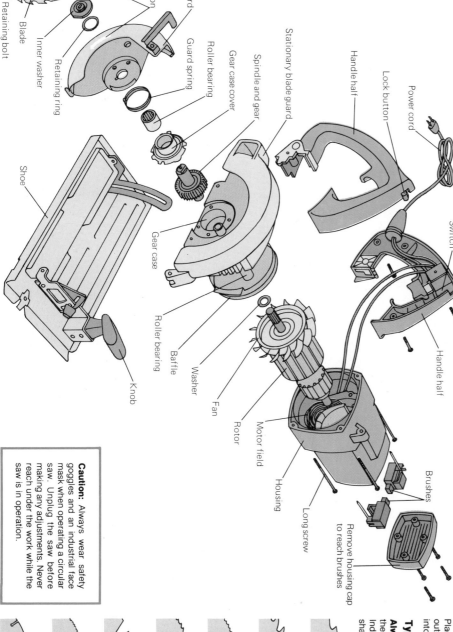

Outer washer
Retaining bolt
Blade
Inner washer
Retaining ring
Arrows indicate direction of rotation
Movable blade guard
Guard spring
Roller bearing
Gear case cover
Spindle and gear
Stationary blade guard
Handle half
Lock button
Power cord
Switch
Handle half
Shoe
Gear case
Baffle
Washer
Fan
Rotor
Motor field
Housing
Knob
Roller bearing
Brushes
Long screw
Remove housing cap to reach brushes

Caution: Always wear safety goggles and an industrial face mask when operating a circular saw. Unplug the saw before making any adjustments. Never reach under the work while the saw is in operation.

Blade replacement

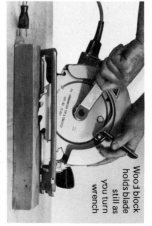

Wood block holds blade still as you turn wrench

Unplug saw, pull back blade guard, then press saw teeth into a piece of scrap lumber. Open retaining bolt. Place new blade over inner washer and spindle, add outer washer, then hand-tighten bolt. Press saw teeth into lumber for final tightening with wrench.

Types of blades

Always use a blade with the correct tooth design for the material being cut or you may overload the motor. Industrial chrome-plated blades cost the most but stay sharp longer and resist gum buildup and rust.

Combination chisel-tooth blade is for general rip and cross cutting where finish or smoothness are not important.

Framing/rip blade gives fast cuts both with and across the grain; gives smooth finish when cutting with the grain.

Crosscut blade gives a smooth finish when cutting across the grain of hard or soft wood. Use to rip-cut very hard woods.

Planer blade gives very smooth cuts both with and across the grain of hard or soft wood. Used for cabinetwork.

Carbide-tipped blade with only eight teeth cuts hardboard and laminates, such as asbestos, Formica, and Masonite.

Plywood blade gives a very smooth cut with a minimum of splintering on plywood. Can also be used for cabinetwork.

Friction action blade is made especially for cutting sheet or corrugated steel, wrought iron, and furnace pipe.

Sabre saw

About once a year (depending on how much use the saw gets): Inspect the brushes; disassemble the housing and clean out sawdust accumulations with mild soap and warm water; and check and relubricate the gears. Do not clean the housing with detergents that contain ammonia; they will damage the plastic. After every 15 hours of running time, add a few drops of SAE #20 oil to the lubricating hole or pad, if any (see owner's manual). After every use, unplug the saw, clean sawdust from its air vents, and clean any grease or oil from the cord. If the motor stops or smokes or sparks excessively, first check the brushes, then test the switch, motor, and power cord for electrical faults (see pp.132–137, 411–412). Always let the blade reach its operating speed before bringing it into contact with the work. Never force the saw; you may overload the motor.

Choosing a blade

The choice of the correct blade is very important, both for proper cutting and to the life of the tool. The wrong blade, or a dull blade, will cut slowly, tempting you to force the tool along and consequently overloading the motor. A dull blade may also stick in the work and stall the motor, which may damage it. Sabre saw blades are too inexpensive to make resharpening worth while; discard dull blades. Saw blades are made in various alloys for cutting many materials, from wood to slate; the smoother the finish desired, the more teeth per inch you need.

Coarse wood cutting blade gives a rough cut; use at highest speed.

Fine wood cutting blade gives a medium cut; use at medium speed.

Hollow-ground blade gives a smooth cut on hardwoods.

Hollow-ground blade with 10 teeth per in. cuts wood and Formica.

Plywood blade gives a medium cut; use it at fast saw speed.

Plaster cutting blade gives fast, rough cuts on plaster, plastic.

Fleam-ground blade makes smooth cuts on wet or green wood.

Scroll blade gives an extra-fine cut on plastic, softwoods, hardwoods.

Metal cutting blade has 14 teeth per inch. Makes extra-smooth cuts.

Knife blade makes fast, smooth cuts in rubber, leather, vinyl tile.

Double-edged blade can cut intricate, pointed patterns in wood.

Extra-long blade is for cutting wood or plastic up to 4 in. thick.

Extension cord requirements

When using an extension cord, be sure it can pass enough power to run the tool properly. An undersized cord will cause a drop in voltage, which can overheat the motor. The table below shows the proper size wire (from 2 to 18 gauge), depending on its length and the amperage rating of the tool, which is printed on the nameplate. The heavier the wire, the lower the gauge number.

Length of cord (feet)	Gauge of wire required								
	25	50	100	150	200	250	300	400	500
0-2 amps	18	18	18	16	16	14	14	12	12
2-3 amps	18	18	16	14	14	12	12	10	10
3-4 amps	18	18	16	14	12	12	10	10	8
4-5 amps	18	18	14	12	12	10	10	8	8
5-6 amps	18	16	14	12	10	10	8	8	6
6-8 amps	18	16	12	10	10	8	8	6	6
8-10 amps	18	14	12	10	8	8	6	6	4
10-12 amps	16	14	10	8	8	6	6	4	4
12-14 amps	16	12	10	8	6	6	4	4	2
14-16 amps	16	12	10	8	6	6	4	4	2
16-18 amps	14	12	8	8	6	4	2	2	2
18-20 amps	14	12	8	6	6	4	4	2	2

Amperage rating (115-volt tools)

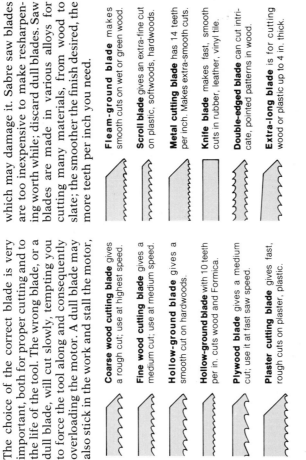

Remove long screws and housing cap to reach brushes · Housing cap · Brush · Housing · Motor field · Baffle · Bearing · Brush · Washer · Rotor · Fan · Gear · Gear · Power cord · Switch · Button · Handle half · Handle half · Shoe locking screw · Shoe · Gear case · Shaft · Shaft bearing · Blade holding screw · Oil pad · Bearing clamp · Blade clamp

Caution: Be sure switch is in the *Off* position before plugging in the saw. Always wear safety glasses when using the saw. Wear an industrial face mask if working conditions are dusty. Always unplug saw to change blades or make adjustments.

Pumps

General maintenance

Centrifugal pumps are used in swimming pool filters, basement drain sumps, and some hot water heating systems. The pump's impeller is driven by an electric motor. The impeller, housing, and pipe may be of either metal or plastic construction. The most common problems are a worn or damaged impeller or shaft seal. The seal keeps water from leaking out of the impeller housing. On some pumps, a worn shaft seal will let water seep back into the motor and damage it. To repair the motor and its bearings, see *Universal motors*, pp.132-134. Most pumps must be primed (the housing filled with water) before they will work. Water acts as a coolant and lubricant for the shaft seal. If the pump is run without first being primed, the seal will quickly

wear out. A leak anywhere in the suction or delivery lines may cause the pump to lose its prime. Periodically tighten all nuts, bolts, pipe fittings, and the packing nuts on valves (p.36). Follow the manufacturer's instructions for priming the pump before operating it. So-called self-priming pumps lift water only a few feet at most. When installing a centrifugal pump or using a portable centrifugal pump, make sure you are not trying to lift water over a greater distance than the pumpmaker recommends. Keep any air vents on the motor bearings as recommended by the manufacturer. Periodically clean any strainers or filters in the suction or delivery lines. Replace the motor brushes (p.133) and shaft seal when worn.

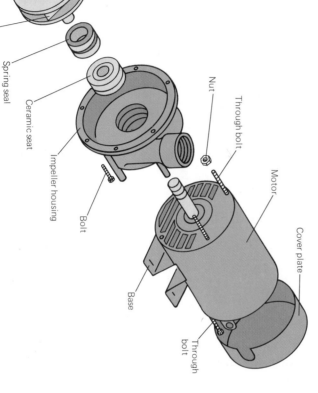

Nut
Washer
Gasket
Impeller
Housing cover
Impeller blades
Spring seal
Ceramic seat
Impeller housing
Bolt
Nut
Through bolt
Motor
Cover plate
Base
Through bolt

Troubleshooting guide

PROBLEM	ACTION
Motor will not start or cuts out	Check for loose connections, open switches, or blown fuses or circuit breakers Manually rotate motor shaft; if shaft binds, check for burned bearings (p.134)
Pump will not self-prime	Make sure suction pipe is filled with water at least as far as suction valve Check that suction and discharge valves are open and unobstructed Check any strainers or filters in suction line; clean them out if they are blocked Check and tighten all bolts on pump and all fittings on suction line Open pump housing; check for obstructed passages, worn or clogged impeller, worn or leaking shaft seal; replace worn or leaking parts
Pump delivers little or no water	Check for closed valves, clogged strainers, filters, or pipes Check for air leaks, loose fittings, or faulty gaskets in suction pipe Open pump housing; check for worn or clogged impeller; replace impeller if worn
Pump is noisy	Tighten fittings and bolts on suction pipe; an air leak will cause rumbling Check pump, motor, and pipe mountings; tighten if necessary Check for restricted suction pipe or partially closed suction valve—these cause cavitation; clear pipe or close discharge valve until cavitation stops Open pump housing; check for sticks, pebbles, or foreign matter in impeller Check motor bearings for excessive wear, burning, or rust (p.134)

Cavitation: a partly closed suction valve or an obstructed suction pipe will result in the formation of partial vacuums within the moving water. This condition is known as cavitation. Not only does it make a pump run noisily, but the repeated collapse of the vacuums will eventually pit or wear away the impeller and other parts and surfaces inside the system

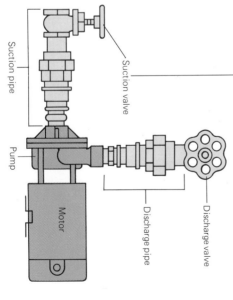

Suction valve
Suction pipe
Pump
Motor
Discharge pipe
Discharge valve

How to replace the impeller and shaft seal

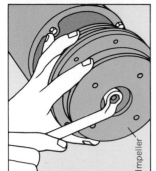

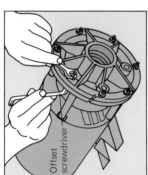

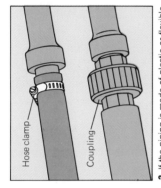

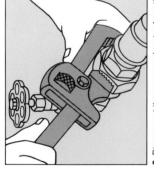

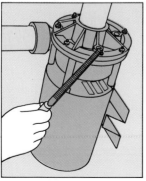

1. Turn off the pump motor and shut the suction and discharge valves. Use a file to make a mark across both halves of the impeller housing; use this mark to align the halves properly during reassembly.

2. Disconnect the pump and motor from the suction and delivery pipes. If the piping is metal, use a wrench to unscrew the unions or fittings (see *Plumbing*, pp.38 and 42, for details of metal pipe connections).

3. If the piping is made of plastic or flexible hose (common on swimming pool pumps), it will be attached to the pump by hose clamps (see p.329) or by plastic couplings that can be unscrewed by hand.

Hose clamp — Coupling

4. Remove the bolts that hold the halves of the impeller housing together. Use two wrenches on hexagonal bolts, a screwdriver and wrench on slotted bolts. Open housing and carefully remove the gasket.

Offset screwdriver

5. If the impeller has a nut in its center, remove the nut and pull the impeller off the shaft. If there is a locating key on the shaft, save it. If the impeller or key is bent or worn, replace with pumpmaker's part only.

Impeller

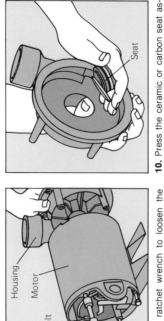

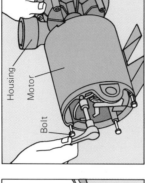

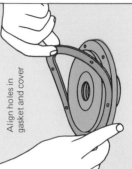

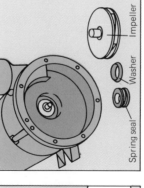

Seat

6. If there's no nut, the impeller is screwed onto a threaded shaft. Insert a screwdriver into a ventilating slot on the motor to keep the fan from turning, then unscrew impeller by hand or by levering against blades.

Impeller — Slot

7. As you withdraw the impeller, note the position of the various springs and washers in the spring seal assembly. Remove the assembly and lay out the parts in order. Buy replacements for worn or damaged parts.

Impeller — Washer — Spring seal

8. Separate the pump from its motor. To do so on the model shown here, loosen the two screws at the back of the motor and remove the rear cover plate. This will give you access to the four long through-bolts.

Cover plate

9. Use a ratchet wrench to loosen the through-bolts until the impeller housing can be pulled clear of the motor. You need not remove the bolts from the motor, nor the nuts that fit between motor and housing.

Housing — Motor — Bolt

10. Press the ceramic or carbon seat assembly out of the recess in the impeller housing. If it sticks, tap it lightly with a screwdriver handle. Inspect all parts and replace worn parts, damaged O-rings.

Tighten bolts in order shown
Notch
1 2 3 4 5 6 7

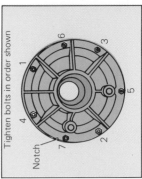

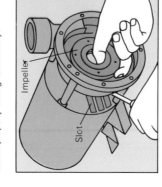

11. Clean the motor shaft and housing recess with kerosene and let dry. Grease shaft and recess with petroleum jelly and press new seat assembly into place. Be sure all the parts are in their original order.

12. Hold the impeller housing up to the motor and tighten the through-bolts to draw them together. Be sure nuts, bolts, and housing are drawn tightly together, with no space or play between them.

13. Wipe the polished face of the ceramic seat clean with a dry cotton cloth. Then, place spring seal over boss on impeller, being sure that all parts are in original order and facing the right direction.

Seal — Boss — Impeller

14. Reinstall the impeller and spring seal assembly. Hold fan to keep shaft from turning. Be sure to reinstall the locating key on pumps that use them. Clean gasket; replace it if it is cracked or stretched.

Align holes in gasket and cover

15. Align the marks on the halves of the impeller housing, then secure housing and gasket with nuts and bolts. Tighten bolts in a criss-cross pattern. Reconnect piping and prime the pump before starting it.

Pruning and trimming tools

Restoring the cutting edge

Cutting tools work best when kept sharp, properly adjusted, clean, and lubricated. Low-carbon steel blades can be sharpened with a file. Use an oiled sharpening stone or a nearly new, good quality file on hardened steel blades. Sharpen tools often; if they get very dull or nicked, the blade must be reshaped on a grinding wheel before it can be sharpened. Use the file or stone to restore the original bevel angle on the blade. Then, rub the stone along the flat back of a blade to remove metal that curls under during sharpening. Oil, then tighten the pivot bolt until a slight drag is felt when shears and clippers are used.

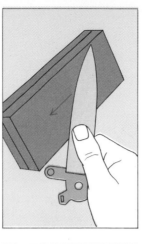

Pruning shears have a rounded cutting blade with a bevel of about 25° and a curved hook or cutting bar with a square edge. If possible, remove the pivot bolt and clamp the cutting blade in a vise for sharpening with a file or stone.

Vise

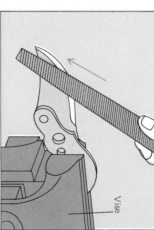

If you cannot separate the blades, open shears as wide as possible and plant handles firmly in the ground. File toward cutting edge, moving file from throat of shears toward tip of blade in a single motion. Do not file unless it is burred.

Hook — Blade — 25°

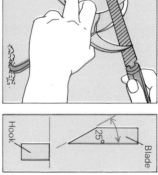

Sickles have a bevel of 25° to 35° on one side of the blade only. Unless blade is badly nicked or burred, use a stone with an oval cross-section, not a file. Sharpen away from the cutting edge, with long strokes. Use flat side of stone on the back of the blade.

25°

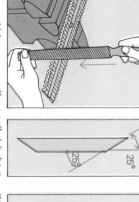

Grass shears should be disassembled and each blade sharpened separately on a flat stone, as scissors are sharpened separately on a flat stone (see p. 46). When reassembling shears, tighten pivot bolt until blades close with slight drag. If bolt has a spring, tighten bolt until best cutting is achieved.

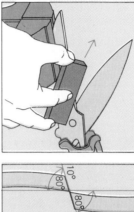

If shears are riveted and therefore cannot be disassembled, restore the original bevel with a thin file or stone. Grip one blade at a time in a vise and sharpen away from the cutting edge at an angle of 80°. Wipe off grinding grit, then oil pivot.

80° 10° 80°

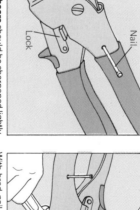

Anvil-type pruning shears should be sharpened lightly and infrequently; if you reduce the height of the blade, it will no longer contact the anvil. To disassemble the shears, first lock them closed and insert a brad nail through the holes in the handle.

Anvil — Blade — Lock — Nail

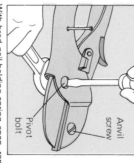

With brad nail holding spring open, remove pivot bolt, disassemble shears, and sharpen blade with a fine stone. Remove screw on lower jaw to replace soft metal anvil. Reassemble shears and remove nail. Make sure blade contacts entire length of anvil.

Pivot bolt — Anvil screw — Blade Anvil 45°

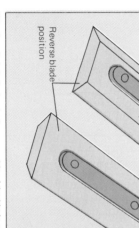

Grass whips, which are swung like a golf club, have either straight or serrated blades with a single, simple bevel of about 25° (the bevel does not run down into the valleys between serrations). Clamp the tool handle in a vise and sharpen blade with a file.

Reverse blade position

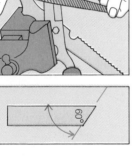

If the handle is bolted onto the same side of the blade as its bevel, it may interfere with the file. Unbolt the blade, turn it upside down, and bolt it back onto the handle, then sharpen as shown at left. You may reverse the blade again, or use it as is.

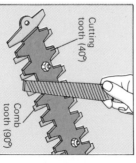

Manual hedge clippers need not be disassembled; a file can be used to restore the bevel—usually 60°. A rough edge with tiny nicks is best; it will dig into twigs and not let them slide along the blade. Some clippers have two cutting blades; others only one.

60°

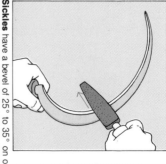

Power hedge clippers must be unplugged before sharpening. By moving the cutters back and forth manually and using a thin file, you can restore the bevel on the cutting teeth without disassembling the cutter. Do not file 90° comb teeth unless they are worn.

Cutting tooth (40°) — Comb tooth (90°) — 90° 40°

Screens and storm windows

How to replace screening

Aluminum and nylon screening is sold by the foot in hardware stores. Although nylon screening will not corrode, aluminum is easier for the beginner to work with. You will need enough screening to cover the frame, with at least a 2-inch overhang at all edges. Also buy a screen installing tool (Step 4).

1. Pry the old spline from the frame and pull it free. Save it for reuse if it is sound. If it is in one continuous length, cut it into four pieces to match the four sides of the frame.

2. Remove old screening. If it is not badly corroded, save it for patching. Clamp metal frame to a workbench or four pieces of shelving lumber so that it is slightly bowed in the center.

3. Center screening over frame and hold it taut with spring clamps or locking pliers. Using scissors, make a diagonal cut in each corner of the screening, just up to the spline channel.

4. Gently press screening down into channel with convex wheel of installing tool. Make several passes, shaping the screening a little at a time. Do not press too hard or screening will tear.

5. When screening is pressed all the way to bottom of channel, use concave wheel of tool to insert spline. Make several careful passes; if tool slips it will damage the new screening.

6. Pull screening taut and clamp it at the opposite end of the frame. Install spline as before. Remove clamps and two shelving pieces. Install spline on the long edges of the frame.

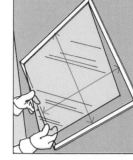

7. Use a blunt screwdriver to press spline home at the corners. Carefully trim off excess screening with a sharp utility knife. Save scrap pieces more than 4 in. wide to use as patches.

On wooden frames, stretch screening taut and clamp it to the frame or tack it to the work surface. Staple screening to frame, then trim it. Do not bend a wooden frame; it may split.

Patching a screen

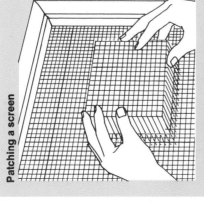

Cut a piece of aluminum screening at least 2 in. larger than the rip or hole. Remove four strands of wire from each edge of the patch. Bend protruding wires 90° (as shown) and push them through the damaged screen. Bend wires flush to hold patch in place.

How to replace a storm window pane

Cutting glass is tricky, and mistakes can be costly. Buy glass cut to your specifications from a glazier. Bring along a fragment of the broken pane so that the glazier can measure its thickness. It is easy to replace a pane in a drop-in frame, which has a rubber spline on only one side of the glass. If your window has a spline on both the inside and outside, the frame must be marked, disassembled, and carefully reassembled to replace the pane. Such work requires special tools and skills; you would do best to leave it to an experienced glazier.

Spline   Frame

1. Carefully pull spline from window frame. Do not cut yourself on broken glass. If spline is sound, save it for reuse; if it has deteriorated, buy new spline of the same shape.

Wear gloves

2. Wear heavy gloves to pull broken glass from frame. If glass was glued to frame, brush on paint remover to free it. Run a small screwdriver around frame to clear out bits of glass.

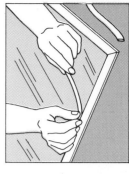

3. Measure the distances between the inner edges of the frame channels carefully. (If you use a tape, pull it taut). Order new glass 1/32 in. smaller. Lay it into the frame gently. Wear gloves.

4. Remove gloves and press the spline under the frame lip with your fingers. Start at a corner and work around the frame. If old spline appears too short, stretch it as you install it.

Snow throwers

Troubleshooting the snow thrower

Many snow thrower problems are caused by careless maintenance and storage. Follow the general maintenance and storage procedures for lawn mowers (see pp.394–396). Lubricate all control linkages, bearings, and chains with light-weight motor oil after every 10 hours of use. Check and adjust tension on all drive belts (see p.384). Service drive chains in the same way as bicycle chains (p.438). If your unit has grease nipples on the axle shafts or chain housings, service them in the same way as you would grease nipples on automobiles (p.352). Always stop the engine and disconnect the spark plug cable before making any repair.

PROBLEM	ACTION
Engine is hard to start, or runs unevenly	Disengage all clutches and other safety interlocks (see your owner's manual) Check for engine malfunctions (see *Small engines*, p.373)
Excessive vibration	Tighten all bolts and subassemblies on unit; see p.373 if engine vibrates
Auger or impeller turns sluggishly or sticks	Adjust tension on drive belts; replace worn belts (see p.384) Check for ice in auger and impeller housings; bring unit indoors; chip out ice
Unit does not discharge snow	Check discharge chute for ice; chip out ice. If snow is wet, run engine at a higher speed, set deflector for maximum height, and put transmission into a lower gear Adjust tension on auger and impeller belts; replace worn belts (p.384) Check auger shear bolts; replace only with manufacturer's parts Check oil level in auger gear case; replace leaking oil seals; replace worn gears
Wheels do not turn when unit is in gear	Check and adjust shift control rods and clutch cables Adjust tension on drive belts or chains; replace worn belts or chains (pp.384–385, 438) Check oil level in transmission gear case; refill if needed; replace worn belts or chains Check and adjust drive disc clearance; clean any grease or oil from disc with solvent Check drive pins at wheels; replace broken or missing pins with manufacturer's parts

Adjustments and repairs

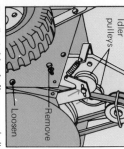

To adjust drive belts remove belt guard, remove bolts at top of auger housing, loosen bolts at bottom, and pivot housing forward. Loosen locknuts (arrows) and move idler pulleys to tighten belts.

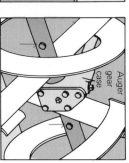

Auger shear bolts (arrows) may snap if the auger hits a branch or stone. Keep spares handy and re-place only with the manufacturer's recommended part; a stronger bolt is a safety hazard.

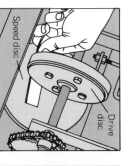

To check drive disc clearance, snap if the auger hits a branch or remove plate from back of unit. A piece of cardboard about ⅛ in. thick should fit between the drive and speed discs with no drag when shift lever is in *Neutral.*

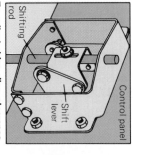

To adjust drive disc clearance, loosen nut between shift lever and shifting rod. Shorten rod's length to increase clearance. Increase rod's length if discs do not touch when unit is in gear.

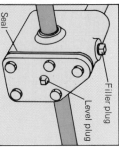

Auger gear case connects the auger and impeller. Remove both plugs. Add No. 30 motor oil to filler hole until it runs out oil level hole. Replace plugs. Tighten gear case bolts or replace seals to stop leaks.

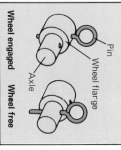

Drive pins on wheels allow option of freewheeling. If pins are broken or missing, engine will not drive wheels. On axles with two holes, unit will freewheel when pin is in outer hole.

Idler pulleys

Loosen

Remove

Auger gear case

Speed disc

Drive disc

Shifting rod

Shift lever

Control panel

Seal

Filler plug

Level plug

Pin

Wheel flange

Axle

Wheel engaged   Wheel free

Clutch control

Control panel

Shifting rod

Gas tank

Engine

Drive belts

Caution: use tire chains

Impeller

Caution: Set auger height skids as high as possible to clear a gravel drive

Auger gear case

Auger

Auger shaft

Impeller shaft

Discharge chute

Deflector angle determines height snow is thrown

Belt guard

Throttle lever

Shift lever

Auger housing

Sprinklers

General Maintenance

Most lawn sprinklers are variations of the revolving and oscillating models shown here. Revolving sprinklers are quite simple and have few parts. If kept clean and rust free, they should last indefinitely. Oscillating sprinklers have many moving parts, which are subject to wear, and tiny orifices, which may become blocked by grit or dirt in the water supply or by hard water deposits. Always drain the sprinkler after each use and store it indoors. Do not allow water to freeze inside the sprinkler, or it may bulge or crack the motor housing. If the unit is not equipped with a filter-washer, buy one in a hardware store. Remove it periodically and flush off accumulated dirt. If an individual nozzle becomes clogged, ream it out with a straight pin. If the spray tube fails to oscillate or does so erratically, disassemble the motor housing and clean its internal parts with kerosene. Do not use strong solvents on plastic or nylon parts; such solvents may damage them. Replace worn or damaged parts. Replacement parts are generally available by mail from the sprinkler manufacturer. A parts list and exploded view drawing of your particular sprinkler probably came with it when it was new. If you have lost this material, obtain the manufacturer's address from a store that carries your brand of sprinkler, and write for a new parts list and drawing; it will help you reassemble the unit correctly.

Oscillating sprinkler service

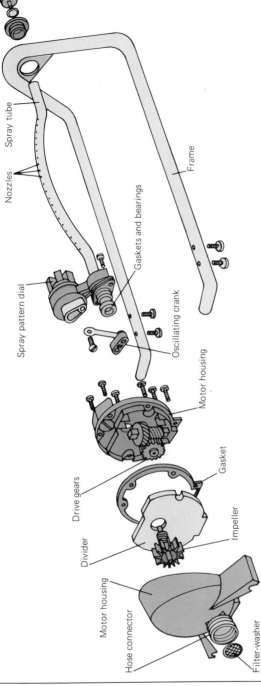

Plug

Spray tube

Nozzles

Frame

Gaskets and bearings

Spray pattern dial

Oscillating crank

Motor housing

Drive gears

Gasket

Divider

Impeller

Motor housing

Hose connector

Filter-washer

Revolving sprinkler

Nozzle

Rotating arm

Bearing assembly

Washer

Hose connection

Base

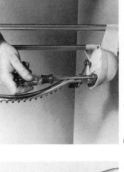
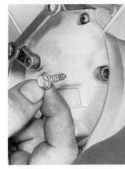

Remove the screws that hold the halves of the motor housing together. If they are corroded in place, use penetrating oil or drill them out.

If the screw holes in the motor housing were stripped during disassembly, replace the original screws with self-tapping screws one size larger.

If the unit does not oscillate properly, it must be disassembled. Start by unscrewing the plug that holds the spray tube to the frame assembly.

If the spray pattern does not match its description on the dial, loosen the setscrew on the dial arm and turn the tube until pattern is correct. Tighten screw.

Apply a thin coat of white, waterproof grease (unless special grease is required by the manufacturer) to all gears, and reassemble the unit.

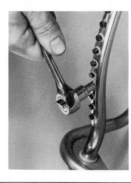

If a single nozzle clogs, unscrew it from the oscillating tube with a small wrench (if possible), ream it out with a sewing needle, then reinstall it.

Carefully remove all gaskets, O-rings, and nylon washers. Clean and inspect them. Replace any that are worn, cracked, stretched, or deteriorated.

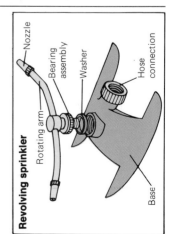

Open the motor housing, remove the impeller and gears, and clean them in kerosene. Inspect the parts and replace any that are worn or damaged.

Thermostats

Troubleshooting common problems

A thermostat is a temperature-activated switch that turns a furnace on and off in order to maintain a preset temperature in the home. Most thermostat malfunctions result from improper location, maintenance, or use of the device. To work properly, the thermostat must be mounted on an inside wall, away from doors and windows, so that it will not be affected by the outside temperature or by drafts. Do not place lamps, appliances, TV sets, or heaters under the thermostat—their heat will affect furnace operation. Mercury switch thermostats must be level in order to work accurately.

If an accurate thermometer (*not* the switch that turns on the thermostat) shows that the preset temperature is not turning on the furnace in one on the thermostat) shows that the furnace is not turning on within 5°F of after cleaning, the thermostat still will not turn on the furnace within 5°F of the preset temperature, check the furnace first (see opposite page).

If the furnace has both power and fuel, move the thermostat's system switch (if any) to *Heat*, then move the temperature dial to the highest possible setting. If the furnace does not go on, remove the thermostat cover and connect the *R* and *W* terminals with an insulated jumper wire. If the furnace still will not turn on, the furnace or its relays are defective; call a repairman. If the furnace does go on

when you jump the terminals, clean and adjust the thermostat (opposite page). If, and the word *Shorter* or *Longer*. Set the pointer to the number stamped on the gas control valve, oil furnace control box, or relay. If the room gets too cold between cycles, have a serviceman repair or replace the thermostat. Never tamper with the bimetallic coil yourself.

Heat continues to come out of the system for some time after the furnace shuts off. To compensate for this overrun, a small electrical heating element called an anticipator is built into many thermostats. It causes the thermostat to shut off the furnace before the room temperature actually reaches the preset level. The an-

ticipator scale has a series of numbers and the word *Shorter* or *Longer*. Set the pointer to the number stamped on the gas control valve, oil furnace control box, or relay. If the room gets too cold between cycles, set the anticipator to a *Longer* value. If the room gets too hot when the furnace runs, then cools down to a comfortable level, set the anticipator to a *Shorter* value. If the room is always either too hot or too cold, adjust the anticipator, not the thermostat. Allow 48 hours between each anticipator adjustment to let temperatures throughout the system reach equilibrium.

Single-range thermostat

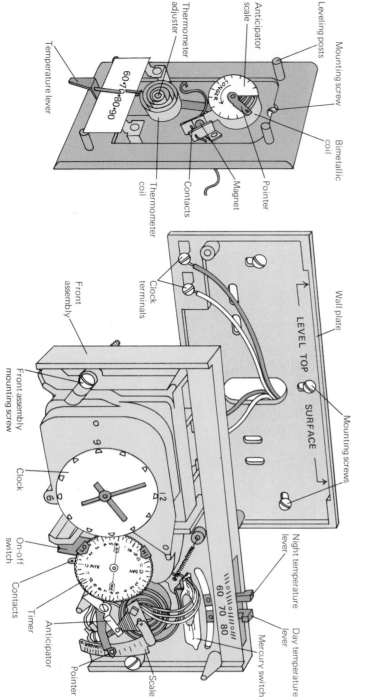

- Mounting screw
- Leveling posts
- Anticipator scale
- Thermometer adjuster
- Temperature lever
- Bimetallic coil
- Thermometer coil
- Contacts
- Magnet
- Pointer
- 60 70 80 90

Dual-range clock thermostat

- Wall plate
- LEVEL TOP
- SURFACE
- Mounting screws
- Clock terminals
- Front assembly
- Front assembly mounting screw
- Clock
- On-off switch
- Timer
- Anticipator
- Pointer
- Scale
- Contacts
- Mercury switch
- Day temperature lever
- Night temperature lever
- 60 70 80

How it works

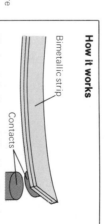

Bimetallic strip

Contacts

The heart of a thermostat is a bimetallic strip—a sandwich of two metals that expand at different rates when heated. Because the pieces are joined together, the strip must flex in order to allow both pieces to expand. The flexing movement of the strip is used to make and break electrical contact. When the straight strip above is heated, the contacts separate and the furnace shuts off. When the strip cools, the contacts meet and the furnace starts.

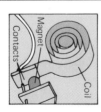

Coil

Contacts

Magnet

Modern thermostats use a coiled bimetallic strip in order to save space. A magnet makes the contacts snap quickly open or shut to lessen electrical arcing.

Wires

Mercury

A sealed tube and mercury can be used instead of contacts. When coil tips tube, mercury completes the circuit. When tube tips other way, circuit is opened.

If the furnace will not start

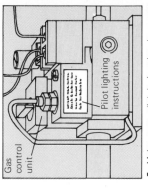

Tripped circuit

1. Turn on several lights to be sure the house has power. Check for blown fuses or tripped circuit breakers on furnace circuit. Replace blown fuse; reset circuit breaker.

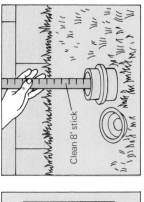

Wall switch · Furnace switch · OIL BURNER ON OFF · ON OFF

2. Make sure emergency switch has not been accidentally turned off. Some units have two switches—one on the furnace, the other at basement entrance. Check both.

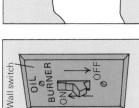

RESET

3. If the furnace control box or blower has a reset switch, press it once, but only once. If furnace starts up, then immediately shuts down, call a repairman.

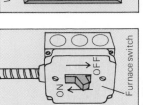

Clean 8' stick

4. If you have an oil burner, check the fuel level in the tank. If tank has no gauge, dip a long stick into the filler pipe to check for the presence of oil.

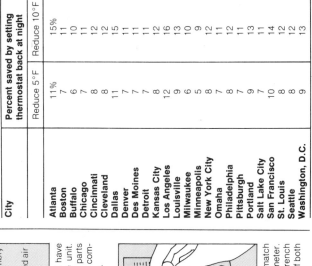

Gas control unit · Pilot lighting instructions

5. Make sure pilot is burning in a gas furnace. If room smells of gas, air it out thoroughly before trying to relight pilot; then, follow instructions on unit.

Thermostat cleaning and adjustment

Front assembly mounting screw

1. Remove thermostat cover by pulling on it gently. If you cannot see the leveling device or the red and white furnace terminals, they are on the wall plate. Remove the front assembly.

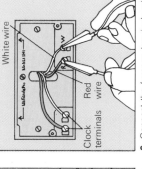

White wire · Red wire · Clock terminals

2. Connect the furnace terminals with insulated jumper wire (p.123). If furnace does not start up (and you have made the checks shown above), have a repairman check the furnace and relays.

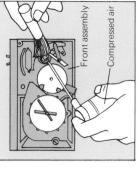

Spirit level

3. If furnace starts, remove jumper and shut off furnace emergency switch. Place a spirit level atop leveling pins or mark. If unit is not level, loosen mounting bolts and adjust it. Retighten bolts.

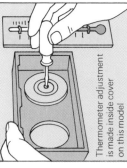

Front assembly · Compressed air

4. Reinstall front assembly if you have not already done so to level the unit. Clean all moving and electrical parts with a small brush and can of compressed air (sold in photo shops).

Clean all metal contacts on unit

5. Turn temperature selector switch so as to close metal contacts. Clean contacts by sliding a strip of heavy bond paper between them. Be careful not to damage delicate bimetallic strip.

Rating (in amps)

6. Find the anticipator rating on your furnace. It may be called *Low Voltage Circuit Current* or *Thermostat Circuit Current.* It is stamped on or inside the control box, gas valve, or relay.

Scale · Pointer

7. If the anticipator rating is (for example) 0.2 amps, set the pointer on the anticipator scale, inside the thermostat, to *0.2.* Then, fine-tune the anticipator as explained in the text on p. 422.

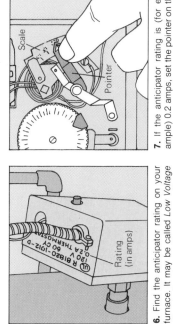

Thermometer adjustment is made inside cover on this model

8. Set thermometer reading to match that of an accurate room thermometer. Use a small screwdriver or Allen wrench to change reading. Keep hands off both thermometers. Replace cover.

Saving fuel at night

According to the American Society of Heating, Refrigeration, and Air Conditioning Engineers, setting the thermostat 5° to 10°F lower at night can save you 5 to 16 percent on your heating bill, depending on the area in which you live.

City	Percent saved by setting thermostat back at night	
	Reduce 5°F	Reduce 10°F
Atlanta	11%	15%
Boston	7	11
Buffalo	6	10
Chicago	7	11
Cincinnati	8	12
Cleveland	8	12
Dallas	11	15
Denver	7	11
Des Moines	7	11
Detroit	7	11
Kansas City	8	12
Los Angeles	12	16
Louisville	9	13
Milwaukee	6	10
Minneapolis	5	9
New York City	8	12
Omaha	7	11
Philadelphia	8	11
Pittsburgh	7	11
Portland	9	13
Salt Lake City	7	11
San Francisco	10	14
St. Louis	8	12
Seattle	8	12
Washington, D.C.	9	13

Tillers

General maintenance

Rotary tillers differ in detail from one manufacturer to another, but most use a one-cylinder engine to drive a series of sharp metal tines, which break up the earth. The rotary action of the tines pulls the machine along. The wheels are not driven by the engine but simply provide a pivot point for lifting the tines.

Follow the engine maintenance and storage procedures in *Lawn mowers* (pp.394–396). It is especially important to keep the tiller engine's cooling fins and air filter clean. Sharpen tiller tines as you would a lawn mower blade (p.399), but

do not balance them. Periodically oil cables and controls with the lubricant recommended in your owner's manual (usually No. 30 motor oil). Also, check the oil level in the gear case and refill it as needed. If the gear case leaks oil, tighten the bolts or replace the gasket. Check V-belts periodically for wear (p.384) and proper adjustment (right). Make a sketch of the tiller's belt arrangement so that you can replace the belts correctly. Use only the tiller manufacturer's recommended replacement belts. See *Small engines*, pp.370–387, for engine problems.

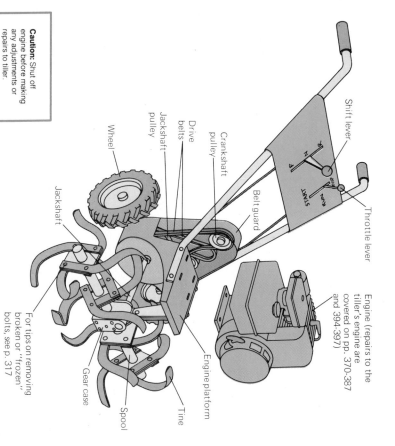

Shift lever
Throttle lever
Belt guard
Engine (repairs to the tiller's engine are covered on pp. 370-387 and 394-397)
Crankshaft pulley
Jackshaft pulley
Wheel
Jackshaft
Drive belts
Gear case
Spool
Tine
Engine platform
For tips on removing broken or "frozen" bolts, see p. 317

How the transmission works

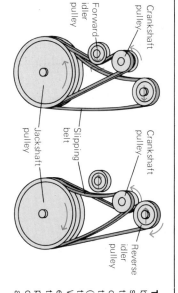

Crankshaft pulley
Forward idler pulley
Crankshaft pulley
Jackshaft pulley
Slipping belt
Reverse idler pulley

Tiller belt drives vary from one brand to another. On this one, seen from the operator's viewpoint, the crankshaft pulley rotates in a counterclockwise direction. When the *Forward* idler pulley is engaged (far left), the outermost belt turns the jackshaft counterclockwise. When the *Reverse* idler pulley is engaged, the inner belt ruts against the underside of the crankshaft pulley and the jackshaft turns clockwise. Another popular arrangement is shown on page 384.

Adjusting drive belts

1/2"
Test made with engine off

1. Belts stretch in use. To check tension, put the transmission in gear and push down on the engaged belt midway between the pulleys. It should give ½ in. or less.

Idler
Jackshaft
Crankshaft

2. Put the transmission in *Neutral*, loosen the idler pulley mounting bolt, and move the pulley so as to reduce belt slack. Shift into gear to check for ½-in. give.

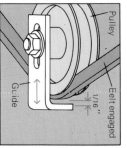

Pulley
Guide
Belt engaged
1/16"

3. Start engine and operate tiller. If belt grabs pulleys when it is disengaged, reduce tension until it slips freely. Position the guide 1/16 in. from engaged belts.

Replacing tines

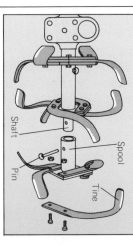

Shaft
Spool
Pin
Tine

Severely bent, worn, or damaged tines should be replaced. Pull retaining pin to remove each tine spool. Open the two bolts that hold the damaged tine to the spool and replace tine. Replace only one tine at a time.

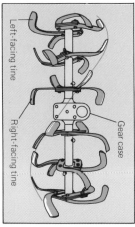

Gear case
Left-facing tine
Right-facing tine

There are two kinds of tines: left-facing and right-facing. To prevent confusion during reassembly, lay out tines and spools in order. The knife edges of the tines on a properly assembled tiller form a spiral.

Water softeners

Care and repair

A water softener removes calcium and magnesium—the minerals that cause soap to form a scummy film—from tap water and replaces them with sodium. People on low salt diets, therefore, should not drink softened water; they may have to buy bottled water, if unsoftened water in their area is unappetizing.

The water softener works by passing hard water through a tank full of plastic beads that are impregnated with sodium. Through a chemical process called ion exchange, the sodium is drawn out of the beads and the calcium and magnesium are deposited in its place. Eventually, all of the sodium is used up, and the unit must be recharged. A 24-hour timer recharges most modern softeners automatically, usually between 1 a.m. and 3 a.m. When the timer cuts in, the control valve diverts tap water around the unit while the built-up calcium and magnesium deposits are flushed down the drain. The tank is then rinsed with a brine, and sodium ions are again absorbed by the plastic beads.

Refill the brine tank with salt when the level drops to less than one-quarter full. Use only salt pellets especially designed for water softeners. Table salt or rock salt

may clog the control valve. When adding new salt, remove any sludge that may have collected on the tubular salt platform screen. Periodically clean the screens in the control and bypass valves, as shown below. If there is a power failure, reset the timer to the proper time of day when power is restored. If your tap water is rusty, clean the softener with a commercial cleaner made for this purpose, following the instructions on the container. If rust persists, you may have to install a special filter ahead of the water softener. If tap water stains tubs and sinks a bluish-green, it is overly acidic; have a neutralizing filter installed. If the water smells like rotten eggs, have your dealer test the water and install the proper type of activated charcoal filter.

If the unit fails to supply soft water, first check for a blown fuse, then check the salt supply and timer. If they are all OK, activate the manual recharge control. If the unit will not recharge or still does not soften water, disassemble the control valve and check for faulty seals and O-rings, or clogged nozzles and screens (below). Do not attempt any repair if the softener is leased or covered by a service contract—call your dealer.

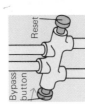
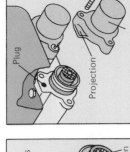
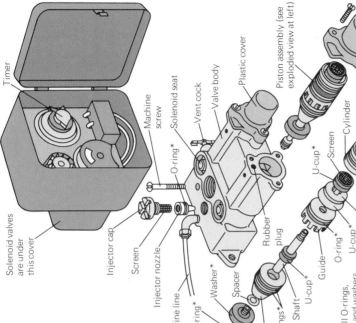

Timer

Solenoid valves are under this cover

Machine screw
Solenoid seat
O-ring*
Vent cock
Valve body
Plastic cover
Piston assembly (see exploded view at left)

Injector cap
Screen
Injector nozzle
Brine line
Washer*
O-ring*
Spacer
Stem
Seat
O-rings*
Shaft
U-cup*
Guide
O-ring*
Rubber plug
Piston
O-ring*
U-cup*
Cylinder
Screen
U-cup*
Plastic cover

*Coat all O-rings, U-cups, and washers with silicone grease before reassembly

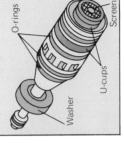

Plug
Projection

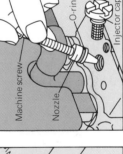

O-rings
Screen
Washer
U-cups

6. Reinstall the plastic covers. Make sure the projection on each one covers the rubber plugs in the valve body. Replace worn O-rings and U-cups. Close vent cock on control valve. Turn lever on bypass valve to *Service* position.

5. Clean piston screen with water and brush. Replace worn O-rings and U-cups. Push piston assembly back into cylinder. Repeat Steps 4 and 5 on second piston assembly. Store screw in valve body.

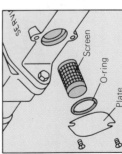

Thread screw into hole in screen, then pull

4. Remove the transparent plastic cover from one of the pistons. Screw the No. 1/4-20 machine screw into threaded hole in the center of the piston. Pull screw with pliers to remove piston assembly.

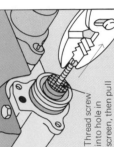

Machine screw
Nozzle
O-ring
Injector cap

3. Remove the No. 1/4-20 machine screw from the valve body, screw it into the injector nozzle, and lift out nozzle. Clean nozzle with a fine wire. Replace worn O-rings. Refit nozzle, screen, and cap.

Control valve service

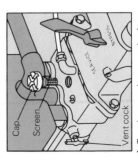

Vent cock
Cap
Screen

Screen
O-ring
Plate

1. Turn lever on bypass valve from *Service* to *Bypass* position. Open vent cock to relieve air pressure in tank. Unscrew injector cap, remove screen, and clean with an old toothbrush and water.

2. Remove side plate and screen from bypass valve. Clean screen with brush and water. Replace O-ring if it is damaged. Always lubricate all O-rings and U-cups with silicone grease before reassembly.

Water heaters

Common problems

Most water heaters are little more than 40- to 50-gallon storage tanks with a gas burner or electric heating elements attached. Homes that are heated by oil often have coils of pipe built into the furnace to heat tap water. Such systems are not practical to service yourself.

Tank-type water heaters have a thermostat that is normally set at 150°F. It can be set as low as 120°F to conserve fuel, or up to 180°F if the water gets cold while passing through pipes in unheated basements or poorly insulated walls. Only 70 percent of the water in a heater tank reaches the desired temperature—about 30 percent near the bottom remains cooler. A 40-gallon tank will therefore contain only 28 gallons of hot water—enough to fill a typical 52- by 22-inch bathtub to about a 5½-inch depth. Once this supply is exhausted, it may take an hour to heat the incoming 28 gallons of water to the thermostat setting. The number of gallons that can be heated from 50° to 150°F in an hour's time is known as the heater's recovery capacity. This figure, along with the total capacity of the tank, is stamped on a plate affixed to every heater. This plate also gives the required voltage for electric heaters, and detailed directions for lighting the pilot on gas heaters.

The common problem of insufficient hot water is often caused by a failure to realize how little water the heater contains, and how long it takes to reheat a new supply. Activities requiring large amounts of hot water should be spaced to allow proper heater recovery time.

To drain the heater for repairs, shut it off, close the cold water inlet valve, then open a hot water tap until the flow ceases. Attach a hose to the draincock and drain the rest into your basement sump or outdoors. Never operate the heater when the tank is empty. Close the drain and refill the tank until water flows from an open tap before you turn the heater on.

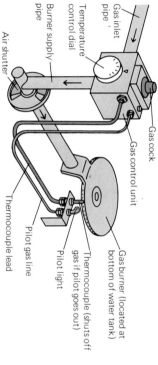

Gas water heater

Gas inlet pipe
Temperature control dial
Burner supply pipe
Air shutter
Gas cock
Gas control unit
Thermocouple (shuts off gas if pilot goes out)
Gas burner (located at bottom of water tank)
Pilot light
Pilot gas line
Thermocouple lead

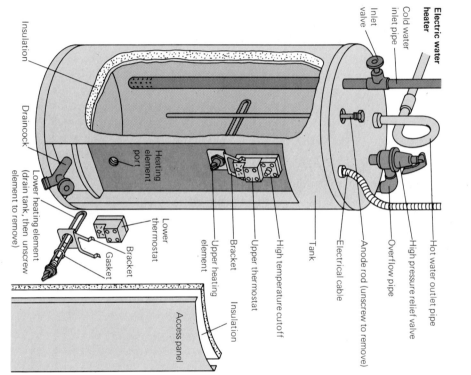

Electric water heater

Cold water inlet pipe
Inlet valve
Insulation
Draincock
Lower heating element (drain tank, then unscrew element to remove)
Heating element port
Lower thermostat
Gasket
Bracket
Upper heating element
Upper thermostat
Bracket
High temperature cutoff
Tank
Electrical cable
Anode rod (unscrew to remove)
Overflow pipe
High pressure relief valve
Hot water outlet pipe
Insulation
Access panel

Troubleshooting guide

Problem	Action for electric water heaters
No hot water	Check that master switch has not been turned off. Check fuses or circuit breakers (p.127); check house wiring or call an electrician if failure persists. Push *Reset* button on high temperature cutoff (upper element). Test thermostats and elements (p.427); replace faulty units
Insufficient hot water	Check thermostat setting; reset if necessary. Check voltage (p.427); call utility if it is too low. Test thermostat (p.427); replace if defective. Clean and check heating elements; replace if necessary. Look for and repair leaking hot water faucets (pp.36-37)
Water too hot	Lower thermostat setting. Test thermostat (p.427); replace if defective. Test high-temperature cutoff (p.427); replace if faulty. Test heating element (p.427); replace if defective
Water leaks from heater	Tighten heating element mounting bolts; if leakage from element persists, replace gasket. Tighten pipe fittings; repair or replace leaking draincock. Place bucket under pressure relief valve; have a plumber replace valve and check heater if discharge is frequent
Heater noisy	Whistling and sizzling may indicate sediment in tank; drain and refill tank (see text at left) until water drains clear. Remove elements and soak in vinegar to loosen scale; scrape off scale and reinstall elements
Hot water discolored at tap	Drain and refill tank (see text) to remove sediment. Remove and clean or replace encrusted elements. Unbolt and remove anode rod; replace it if deteriorated. Have plumber check for and replace corroded supply pipes

Problem	Action for gas water heaters
No hot water	See first two *Actions* under electric water heaters (above). If pilot is out, relight it following instructions on unit. If pilot will not stay lit, clean orifice (p.427); tighten thermocouple nuts (p.427) or replace thermocouple (p.427). If pilot is lit, press *Reset* button; if burner still will not start, adjust pilot flame (p.427) or call repairman
Insufficient hot water	Check temperature control setting; reset if necessary. Look for and repair leaking hot water faucets (pp.36-37). Make sure burner flame is blue; if it is orange, clean out burner shutters or call repairman to clean burner ports. With gas cock on, turn temperature control to *Hot* and open hot water tap; if burner does not light in two to three minutes, have a repairman test and calibrate or replace thermostat
Water too hot	Lower temperature control setting. Have repairman test and recalibrate or replace thermostat. Check for hot air coming out of draft hood (on chimney at top of unit); if it is, have repairman clear blocked flue
Water leaks from heater	Tighten pipe fittings; repair or replace leaking draincock. Place a bucket under pressure relief valve; have plumber replace valve and check heater if discharge is frequent
Heater noisy	Rumbling may indicate sediment in tank; drain and refill tank (see text at left) until water drains clear. Whistling and popping may indicate a faulty burner; call a repairman to clean burner ports
Hot water discolored at tap	Drain and refill tank (see text at left) to remove sediment. Unbolt and remove anode rod; replace it if deteriorated. Have a plumber check for and replace corroded supply pipes

Testing electric heater elements

Turn off the power at the master switch or fuse box before attempting any tests or repairs on an electric water heater. Remove the access panel and carefully cut away the insulation with a sharp knife. Use a volt-ohm meter capable of reading at least 250 volts (p.124) for all tests. For Test 1 (right), you must turn the power back on momentarily. You must drain the heater (p.426) to replace heating elements or gaskets. After completing your work, reconnect all wires and reinstall the insulation and access panel.

Caution: Do not touch the heating elements or test leads while the power is on.

1. Turn off power. Set volt-ohm meter to the 250 VAC scale and attach clips to uppermost terminals of high temperature cutoff. Turn power on. If voltage is not within 10% of value on heater identification plate (120, 208, or 240 volts—see p.126), call utility company. Turn off power and remove meter. Push in *Reset* button.

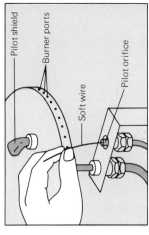

Meter leads — Reset button — Cutoff — Thermostat

2. With meter on RX1 scale, touch clips to screws 1 and 2 on high temperature cutoff, then to screws 3 and 4. If needle does not move toward zero in both tests, replace the cutoff. Remove metal straps, pull cutoff out of spring clips, snap new unit into place, reattach wires and straps.

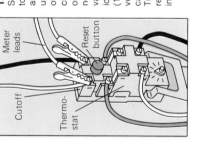

Tests 2-5 made with power off at master switch — Screw 3 — Metal straps — Screw 1

3. Remove wires from heating element. Touch clips to screws 1 and 2 on upper thermostat. If the water in the tank is cold, the meter needle should swing toward zero. If it does not, replace thermostat. Transfer wires, metal straps, and cutoff module to new thermostat and snap it into place.

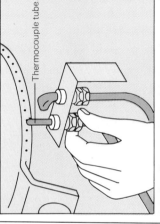

Spring clip — Heating element

4. Clip meter leads to screws 3 and 4 on upper thermostat. If water in tank is cold, meter needle should remain on ∞. If water is hot, needle may swing toward zero. If it does, advance thermostat to its highest setting. Thermostat should click, and meter needle swing back to ∞. If not, replace thermostat.

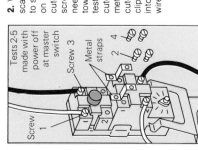

Use a screwdriver to change temperature setting

5. Put thermostat back to normal setting. Touch clips to heating element screws. Any meter reading means element is OK. If needle stays on ∞, replace element. Clip one meter lead to element bracket. Touch second lead to each element screw. If needle moves, replace element. Repeat Tests 3 to 5 on lower unit.

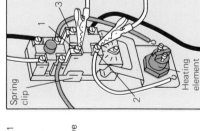

Reconnect wires after testing — Bracket — Touch both heating element screws

Correcting gas heater defects

1. Clean air shutters periodically to assure the proper supply of air to burner and pilot light. If shutters are frequently clogged, vacuum basement floors instead of sweeping them (sweeping raises dust).

Clean shutter with a brush; do not vacuum or pilot light will be blown out. — Air shutter

2. If pilot frequently goes out, unscrew or pull off pilot shield and clean out pilot orifice with a thin copper wire. Do not use a needle or paperclip, as these hard metals may enlarge the orifice.

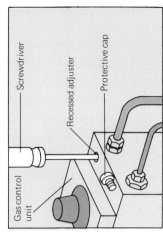

Pilot shield — Burner ports — Soft wire — Pilot orifice

3. If pilot will not stay lit, check for loose thermocouple connections. Do not force thermocouple nuts. Screw them on finger tight, then give them less than a quarter turn with a small wrench.

Thermocouple tube

4. If pilot continues to go out, adjust pilot flame following directions in owner's manual. On this model, you must unscrew a protective cap and turn adjuster until flame is between 1 and 1½ in. long.

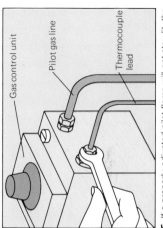

Screwdriver — Recessed adjuster — Protective cap — Gas control unit

5. If a properly adjusted pilot flame will not stay lit, the thermocouple may be faulty. If it is several years old, replace it. Unscrew thermocouple lead from gas control valve. Attach replacement lead.

Gas control unit — Pilot gas line — Thermocouple lead

6. Unscrew old lead from thermocouple tube. Remove old thermocouple tube from pilot bracket. Attach new thermocouple tube to bracket, and end of new lead to tube. Tighten nuts a quarter turn past finger tight.

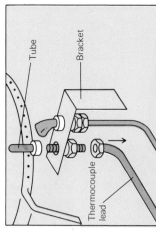

Tube — Bracket — Thermocouple lead

Sports and Camping

The chapter on bicycles covers virtually every job that can safely be performed on a bike at home. The other chapters in this section, like the one on bicycles, provide not only instructions for quick immediate repairs, but also the means for restoring to serviceability various types of long unused outdoor equipment, including rods, reels, skis, rackets, and tents.

contents

General care

When a bicycle is in regular use, lubricate the freewheel, brake calipers, cables, and derailleurs every two weeks. Use a bicycle oil or a petroleum distillate spray, available at hardware stores or bicycle shops. Do not rely on ordinary household lubricating oils for your bicycle; they are too thin for heavy-duty performance.

If the bike has oiling holes on the hubs, pedal axle, bottom bracket, or headset, oil them all at the same time. If there are no holes, these parts are packed in grease and should be disassembled and repacked every 6 to 12 months (pp.432, 435, 442–444). Once a month, or more often in dusty areas, remove and lubricate the chain (p.438).

While you are lubricating the bike, check the wheels, brakes, chain, crank arms, and bearings for looseness, as shown below. Adjusting and cleaning these items when they first need it should result not only in a safer ride but in a greatly increased lifetime for most of these parts.

Many bicycle owners fail to realize the importance of adjusting the handlebars and seat so that the bike is perfectly fitted to the rider (opposite page). Proper adjustment makes a bike less tiring to ride. It also makes the bike easier to control and, therefore, safer.

Periodic checks

1. Check front hub by grasping the frame and wheel. Try to move the wheel from side to side. If you feel a click, the bearings are loose. (See pp. 434–435.)

2. Grasp frame and back wheel to check the rear bearings. Again move wheel from side to side. If you can feel the bearings click, they are loose. (See pp. 434–435.)

3. Press down on the headset and try to roll the wheel forward and backward. If there is play between fork and frame, the headset needs tightening. (See p. 432.)

4. Place cranks horizontally and press down on both at the same time. Rotate them 180° and press down again. If you feel play, check cotter pins (p.442).

5. Keeping pedals horizontal, try to flex them back and forth. If you feel play or clicking, the bottom bracket bearings are worn or loose. (See pp. 442–444.)

Lubrication

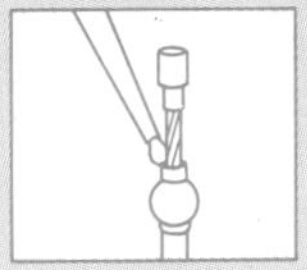

Remove brake and gear cables from their holders (pp. 436, 439), hold them upright, and run oil between the inner cable and the outer casing.

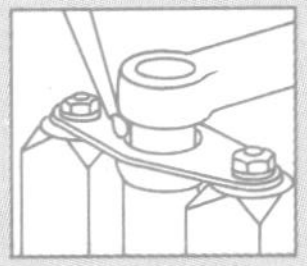

Tilt the bike and oil each pedal where it joins the crank so that oil runs into the pedal shaft. Do not oil all-metal "rat trap" pedals.

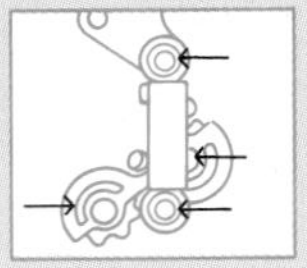

Put a few drops of your bicycle lubricant onto the freewheel mechanism, cable, and all moving parts of the front and the rear derailleurs.

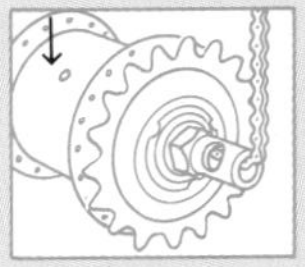

Oil freewheel mechanism and rear sprocket. On 3-speed bikes, oil the toggle chain (see p. 439) and put 15 drops of oil into oiling hole (arrow).

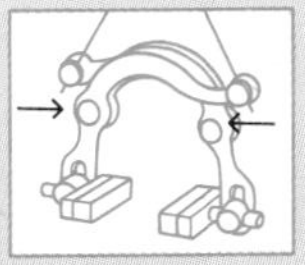

Oil the pivot bolts on each brake caliper (one each on side-pull brakes, two each on center-pull brakes—see pp.436–437). Keep oil off pads, tires.

Ten-speed bicycle

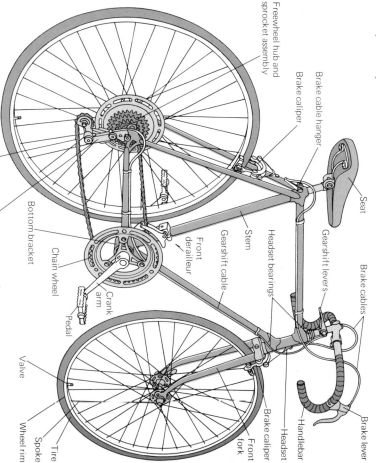

Freewheel hub and sprocket assembly

Brake cable hanger

Brake cable

Brake caliper

Seat

Gearshift levers

Headset bearings

Brake cables

Stem

Headset

Gearshift cable

Handlebar

Front derailleur

Brake caliper

Front fork

Chain

Bottom bracket

Rear derailleur

Chain wheel

Crank arm

Pedal

Valve

Brake lever

Wheel rim

Tire

Spoke

Fitting your bicycle to you

Seat height and angle

1. Adjust seat height. With a wrench or socket and ratchet, loosen seat post nut. Hold rear wheel between your legs and lift out seat, twisting as you pull.

2. After wiping post clean, mark a safety line 2½ in. from its bottom. After adjustment, line must not show above seat tube. If it does, get a longer post.

3. Reinsert post into seat tube. With pedal crank arm parallel to tube, set seat so your heel rests on pedal when your leg is extended. Check safety line.

4. Loosen seat clamp nut under saddle and tilt seat so that either it is parallel to the ground or its front end is slightly higher than its back end.

Handlebar height

Expander bolt · Binder bolt · Stem · Wedge · Plug

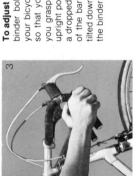

1. After adjusting seat, loosen expander bolt on stem; turn counterclockwise until head is ¼ in. (but no further) above stem.

2. Place wooden block on bolt head and tap on wood until the bolt is driven down flush with stem. This loosens expander inside stem.

3. Holding front wheel between your knees, lift the handlebar free. Wipe stem. Inspect expander; if damaged, buy a replacement.

4. Mark a safety line 2½ in. from stem bottom (see Step 2, above). Set bar height so that expander bolt is level with front of seat.

Handlebar angle

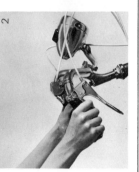

To adjust handlebar angle, (1) loosen binder bolt on handlebar stem; **(2)** If your bicycle has an upright bar, set it so that your wrists are straight when you grasp the grips while sitting in an upright position; **(3)** If your bicycle has a dropped bar, adjust it so that the top of the bar is parallel to the ground or tilted down slightly. Finish by tightening the binder bolt.

Troubleshooting the pump

If your bicycle pump fails to generate sufficient pressure, first, make sure that the connection between the pump body and hose is tight. Next, remove the hose and block one end with a finger. If you can blow air through it from the other end, the hose is leaky and should be replaced. If the pump still does not work, follow the steps shown below. Unless the washer is damaged, clean and reuse it; a replacement may not be available.

1. Pull out the pump handle and unscrew the threaded cap. Then, remove entire plunger assembly from pump body.

2. Unfasten screw holding washer to pump shaft. If washer is not torn or badly cracked, wipe it clean with a damp sponge; it can be reused.

3. Soften a stiff washer by working oil into it with your fingers. Remount washer with convex side to pump shaft, and fasten the screw.

4. Fill washer cup with light grease. Insert plunger assembly into pump body at an angle and twist. Screw on threaded cap firmly.

Bicycles

Servicing the front fork

If a bicycle pulls to one side when you ride it, hands off, the fork is bent. Have a bike shop replace it. Once a year, or whenever the fork binds or clicks as you steer, inspect and grease the bearings. If any bearings are worn, pitted, or discolored, replace them all.

Each set of bearings rides between a cup and a cone. The balls may be loose or held in a frame called a cage. Tightening the upper cone will eliminate play in both sets of bearings. If the top cone is set too tight, the fork will bind and be hard to turn. Tightening the locknut may cause the cone to rotate too, requiring its readjustment (see Step 9).

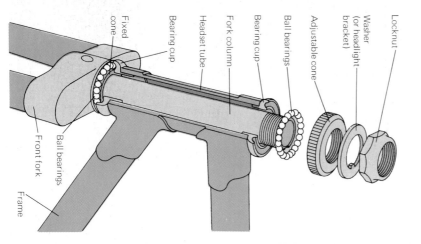

Locknut

Washer (or headlight bracket)

Adjustable cone

Ball bearings

Bearing cup

Fork column

Headset tube

Bearing cup

Fixed cone

Ball bearings

Front fork

Frame

1. Remove handlebar (see p.431) and temporarily hang bar on frame. Unscrew locknut, which may be either a hexagonal nut (left) or a slotted C-nut (right).

2. Lift off locknut and headlamp bracket (if any). You may then disconnect the cables (pp.436,439) to free handlebar completely or let bar remain hanging from frame.

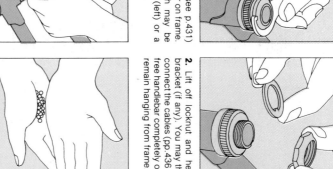

3. Unscrew top bearing cone and remove upper bearings. Replace pitted or flattened bearings with a new set of the same size. Clean old grease from parts with kerosene.

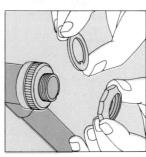

4. Holding frame tightly to fork, bike on its side atop newspapers. Separate fork and frame, catching loose bearings in folds of paper. Clean cup and cone.

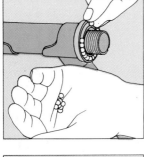
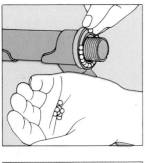

5. If bearings are not worn or damaged, clean each set of them separately in kerosene. Dry them between the palms of your hands or in clean, lint-free toweling.

6. Fill the lower bearing cup with multipurpose grease, sold in bicycle shops. Press the correct number of bearings well into the grease so that they will not fall out.

7. Spread grease on bearing cone and lower the cycle frame over the fork column, being careful not to dislodge any of the bearings. Inspect and clean any balls that drop.

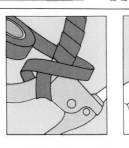

8. Partially fill top cup with bicycle grease and install upper bearings, taking care to install the right size and number of balls and not to drop or damage any of them.

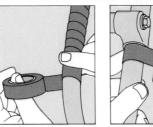
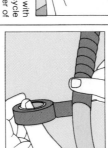

9. Grease top cone and screw it on finger tight. Replace bracket and locknut. Adjust cone to eliminate all play. Tighten locknut; check for binding. Readjust if necessary.

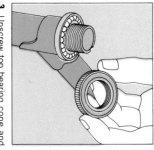

Taping the handlebars

Dropped handlebars do not have rubber grips, but you can give your hands a good surface to grasp by taping the bar. A light-colored tape makes the bike more visible at night. Plastic tape withstands weather best, but cloth tape feels warmer in cold weather and provides a better grip. Before you begin, remove the end plugs and old tape. Clean the bar with nail polish remover or a commercial solvent, being careful not to get any onto the painted frame.

1. Begin from the center of the handlebar. Make first winding square to the bar, then unroll the tape at a slight angle.

2. Press tape down firmly, stretching it as needed to follow handlebar curves. For an even surface, cover half of previous winding with each new turn.

3. To incorporate such attachments as mirrors and levers into the taping, draw tape straight down for half a turn before angling it back and over.

4. Finish each side by extending windings ¼ in. beyond end of bar. Cut and tuck these free edges back inside tubing. Replace end plugs.

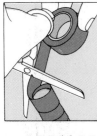

How to change a wheel

The most troublesome step in changing a wheel, or removing a wheel to fix a tire, is keeping tabs on the nuts and washers and the order in which they are arranged. Study the arrangement on your bicycle—sketching it on paper, if necessary—before you begin disassembly. If you must remove hub fasteners, place the parts in a container to prevent loss. On bikes with cable-operated brakes, it may be necessary to loosen the cable anchor bolt (pp.436–437) in order to open the calipers far enough to clear the tire. You must then readjust the brakes.

The formidable-looking 10-speed, or derailleur, rear wheel is usually easy to change. Many manufacturers now install quick release levers (see below). In addition, the guide mechanisms on derailleurs automatically adjust chain tension.

Front wheel

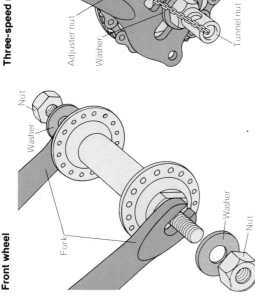

Nut
Washer
Washer
Fork
Washer
Nut

Three-speed rear wheel

Left side nut and washer
Sprocket
Adjuster nut
Washer
Tunnel nut

Single-speed rear wheel

Right side nut and washer
Sprocket
Left side nut and washer
Clip
Brake arm

Turn bike upside down. Disconnect adjuster nut. Loosen left side nut and tunnel nut. Push away fender braces and lift axle from its slots. Free chain from sprocket. To remount, loop chain on sprocket and slide axle into slots. Pull the wheel back until chain has ½-in. play; finger-tighten nut on left. Center wheel, tighten nuts, connect adjuster.

Loosen both right and left axle nuts, removing them only if the bicycle has fender braces. Then, slide wheel downward until axle clears slots in fork. To remount, slide axle into slots and replace the fender braces, if any. Tighten both nuts with your fingers. Center the wheel in the fork, then firmly tighten both nuts with a wrench.

Remove brake-arm clip, nut and bolt. Loosen axle nuts (remove them only if bicycle has fender braces) and slide wheel from axle slots. To remount, loop chain over sprocket and slide wheel into slots. Pull wheel back until chain has ½-in. play, then tighten right nut. Center wheel in frame and firmly tighten both nuts. Replace the brake-arm clip.

To remove, shift to highest gear while turning pedal and wheel. Loosen axle nuts or open quick release mechanism. Swing derailleur up into its *Open* position and push wheel forward until it clears chain.

To remount, lay chain on smallest sprocket. Pull derailleur to *Open* position and slide wheel into place. Center wheel in frame and tighten axle nuts or engage quick release mechanism. Chain adjusts itself.

Derailleur rear wheel

Axle nut and washer
Axle nut
Washer
Multigear sprocket
Rollers

Quick release mechanism

When engaged, the lever must always stand parallel to the frame and point to rear so that it cannot snag spokes or passing objects.

To release, pull lever out and away, never rotate it. To engage, push it in toward wheel.

To set tension, turn adjuster knob, with lever released. A lever with the proper tension requires three fingers to release and firm palm pressure to engage.

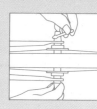

Fixing a flat tire

To locate the cause of a flat, rotate the wheel slowly and inspect the tire. If you find a cut or puncture, mark it on the tire with chalk. Its position relative to the valve will help you find the leak in the inner tube. Remove nails from the tire with pliers and pry out glass with a screwdriver. If there is no obvious puncture in the tire, test the valve (right). If the valve is OK, remove the inner tube to locate the leak.

First, remove the wheel (p.433). Unseat the tire with bicycle tire irons, or with spoon handles. Sharp-edged tools such as screwdrivers may cause more punctures in the inner tube.

After removing the tube, check the rubber around the valve. If it is torn or cracked, replace the tire. If air is leaking from under an old patch, replace the tube. Do not patch over it. Patch other kinds of leaks as shown below. Complete patching kits are sold in bicycle shops. Before remounting the tire, inspect it to make sure that no glass or metal fragments remain inside.

Use a good hand or foot pump and a pocket gauge to inflate tires to the pressure listed on the sidewall. Service station gauges are notoriously inaccurate, and the volume of air the pumps give can quickly burst a bicycle tube.

Checking valves

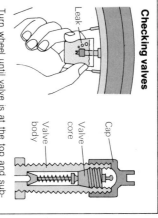

Turn wheel until valve is at the top and submerge valve in a small glass of water. Unscrew leaking valve core with needle-nose pliers, or special slotted valve cap, and replace it.

Leak — Cap — Valve core — Valve body

Unseating the tire, patching the tube

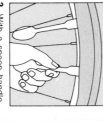

1. If tire is still partially inflated, then deflate it. Unscrew valve-holding nut, if any, and carefully push the valve stem up inside the wheel rim.

2. With a spoon handle, pry a 9-in. section of tire over the rim. Leaving first spoon as a wedge, run a second spoon around entire rim to free tire.

3. With one side of tire clear of rim, carefully work the inner tube out. Check valve stem for damage. If none is found, partially inflate tube.

4. Pinpoint leak by passing the partially inflated tube through the water, stretching it slightly to enlarge any small holes. Look for telltale bubbles.

5. Mark the puncture with chalk. Deflate inner tube and clean the area with emery cloth or sandpaper. Apply a light, even coat of adhesive and let dry.

6. Peel backing from the patch and press patch, sticky side down, over the puncture. Rub edges of patch firmly with spoon. Inflate after 5 minutes.

Reseating the tube and tire

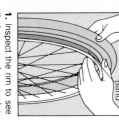

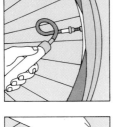

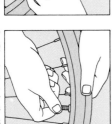

1. Inspect the rim to see that no spoke nipples protrude and that the rim band is smooth and perfectly centered.

Band

2. Pull back the tire's free edge to expose the valve opening. Insert valve stem and draw tire back over that section of tube.

3. Inflate the inner tube until it just begins to take shape. Overinflation will make the next steps more difficult.

4. With your thumbs, tuck tube under tire and onto rim. Then, begin to press the tire's free edge inside the rim lip.

5. When about 9 in. of free edge remain outside the rim, use your fingers to work this final section tightly into place.

6. Check that both tire edges are properly seated. Replace valve-holding nut, if any, and inflate tire to correct pressure.

Servicing wheel bearings

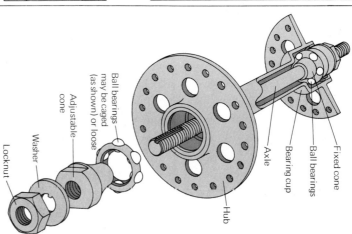

Fixed cone — Ball bearings — Bearing cup — Axle — Hub — Adjustable cone (as shown) or loose — Washer — Locknut — Ball bearings may be caged

Bearing wear is caused by dirt, lack of grease, or overtightening of the cones. It can be detected by removing the wheel and spinning it as you hold the axle. If you feel grating or vibrations, disassemble the bearings and check for worn parts, as shown at right. If even one bearing shows wear, get a new set with the same size and number of balls. Play or binding is eliminated by adjusting the cones. Grease the bearings twice a year.

Most bikes have one adjustable cone (it has notches for the wrench) and one fixed cone (no notches). If a wheel has two adjustable cones, leave one on the axle during cleaning and reassembly. If it is worn, wait until the opposite cone is properly adjusted, then replace and adjust this cone.

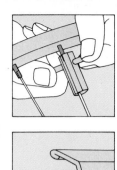
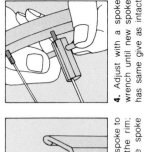

Cross-three pattern

Cross-four pattern

Replacing a spoke

Bicycle spokes look fragile, but they withstand tremendous pressures in keeping the wheel true. To be true, the wheel must be perfectly round, while its plane of rotation is constantly perpendicular to the axle. A single damaged or improperly tensioned spoke can throw the wheel off and lead to a wobbly ride and erratic braking.

A wheel obviously out of true, or one with several damaged spokes, should be brought to a qualified repairman, but you can safely replace one or two spokes yourself, as shown below. It is important to properly lace the replacement into the existing pattern (right). Study the arrangement of the spokes closely before beginning any work. You may have to remove the freewheel sprocket.

4. Adjust with a spoke wrench until new spoke has same give as intact spokes. It must not protrude through nipple or it may puncture tube.

3. Engage tip of spoke to the nipple on the rim; tighten until the spoke appears taut and straight and the nipple is flush with the rim surface.

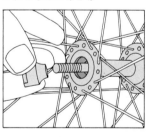

2. When head is properly seated, swing the spoke up and lace it into the network, ending with the tip of the spoke near its hole in the rim.

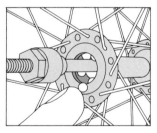

1. With wheel dismounted and tire off, remove broken spoke. Note the side of the hub to which its head connects. Thread the new spoke through hub.

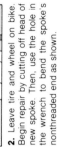

3. Hook bent end into hole in hub. Lace spoke into network, then flex it to insert into nipple. Adjust spoke tension. This repair should be regarded as only temporary.

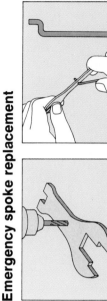

2. Leave tire and wheel on bike. Begin repair by cutting off head of new spoke. Then, use the hole in the wrench to bend the spoke's nonthreaded end as shown.

Emergency spoke replacement

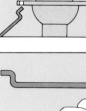

1. Repairs can be made on the road if you carry a wrench with a ⅛-in. hole drilled in the handle and replacement spokes about 1 in. longer than those already on the wheel.

---

5. Clean the cones and axle in kerosene. If the cones show any wear, replace them. The cones and axle are usually sold as a set. Clean the bearings in separate containers. Replace the set if any bearings are worn.

1. Remove wheel and place the axle into a vise, fixed cone downward. (Line jaws of vise with wood to protect the axle threads.) Hold cone with a thin wrench and loosen locknut, then remove cone.

6. Half fill both cups with bicycle grease. Loosely fit the axle and replace bearings on this side, being sure to put back the same number you removed.

2. Open vise. Remove wheel and invert it. Catch bearings and count them. If any are worn, replace the entire set. If they are reusable, store them in a container.

7. Hold the axle tightly in place so that the bearings cannot fall out and invert the wheel. Put axle in vise and replace the remaining bearings and adjustable cone.

3. Lift axle out of hub, invert wheel, and spill out the other set of bearings. If they can be reused, store them in a second container.

8. Tighten the cone until the wheel can be spun without any side-to-side play. If wheel binds, loosen the cone. Hold cone with a thin wrench and tighten the locknut, then recheck adjustment.

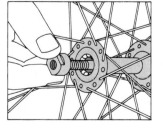

4. Clean the cups at either end of the hub (arrow) with kerosene and inspect. If cups are worn, replace the wheel (which is less expensive than fitting the old spokes and rim to a new hub).

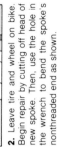

435

Bicycles

Cable brakes

Brakes should be serviced frequently. On cable-brake bicycles, begin by inspecting pads for wear and shoes for proper clearances (see *Servicing brake shoes,* this page.) Check wheel rims for distortion or damage (p.435). Replace cables that are frayed, kinked, or cut. Next, squeeze the brake levers. If they hit the handlebar, adjust them (see below for side-pull brakes; facing page for center-pull). Oil cable housings every two months (p.430).

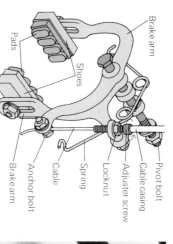

Labels: Brake arm · Pads · Shoes · Brake arm · Anchor bolt · Cable · Spring · Locknut · Adjuster screw · Cable casing · Pivot bolt

Adjusting side-pull brakes

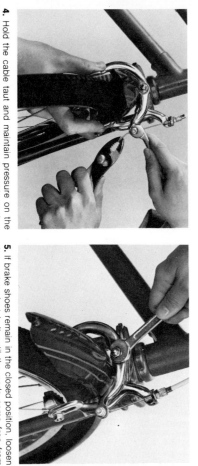

1. If brake lever hits handlebar, loosen locknut on brake assembly at the wheel and turn adjuster screw by hand. When lever clears bar, retighten the locknut.

2. If brake shoes are still more than ⅛ in. from wheel rim after lever has been adjusted, the cable has gone slack. Loosen the cable anchor bolt.

3. Squeeze brake shoes against the wheel with one hand. Using pliers, grasp the free lower end of the cable and pull it downwards to take up the slack.

4. Hold the cable taut and maintain pressure on the brake shoes. Have a helper tighten the cable anchor bolt. Release cable and brakes.

5. If brake shoes remain in the closed position, loosen the center pivot bolt until the pads come free from the rim, but not so much that they wobble.

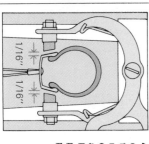

6. Check to see that the wheel is centered between the shoes. If it is not, lightly tap spring on arm farthest from the rim until unit is centered around wheel.

Replacing brake cables

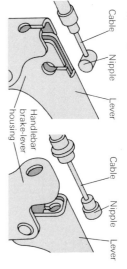

Labels: Cable · Nipple · Lever · Handlebar brake-lever housing · Cable · Nipple · Lever

To replace a faulty brake cable, open the anchor bolt at the wheel and pull cable out of adjuster (see diagrams on this and facing pages). Pull the cable casing out of the brake lever housing on handlebar and push the cable to disengage nipple. Two types are shown disengaged here.

Attach new nipple and casing. Slip end of casing into adjuster at wheel, and fit free end of cable through hole in anchor bolt. Pull cable taut, tighten bolt, adjust brake.

Servicing brake shoes

1. Loosen nut holding shoe to brake arm. If pads are worn, remove shoes and replace with shorter-lived but better-gripping red racing pads. Always install new pads in pairs.

2. Adjust shoe height so that entire pad surface closes on wheel rim without touching tire. Then, tighten nut. If shoes have an open end, make sure it faces the back of the bicycle.

3. Make sure that handbrake lever is in fully open position. Regulate distance of pads to wheel rim by first loosening adjuster screw locknut with a wrench, and then turning screw.

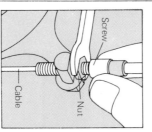

Labels: Screw · Cable · Nut

4. Pads are correctly set when they clear wheel rim by 1/16 in. on each side. Tighten adjuster screw locknut after the pads have been properly set.

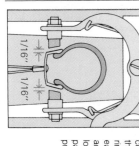

Labels: 1/16″ · 1/16″

Adjusting center-pull brakes

1. To adjust lever, loosen locknut and turn adjuster with your fingers. Then, retighten locknut.

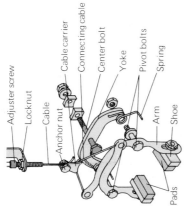

— Adjuster screw
— Locknut
— Cable
— Anchor nut
— Cable carrier
— Connecting cable
— Center bolt
— Yoke
— Pivot bolts
— Spring
— Arm
— Shoe
— Pads

2. To take up slack in the cable, loosen the anchor nut on the cable carrier, above the brake arms.

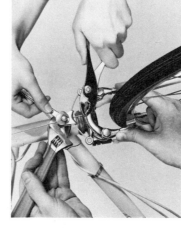

3. Have a helper press brake shoes tightly onto wheel rim while you grasp cable end with pliers.

4. Pull cable downward until it is taut. Keep pressure on cable and shoes and tighten anchor nut.

5. If brake shoes are not equidistant from wheel, loosen brake holding nut (behind fork or bracket).

6. Move brake yoke by hand until brake pads are centered on rim. Retighten nut.

Adjusting coaster brakes

A coaster brake is located inside the rear hub and activated by backpedaling. It is most commonly used on single-speed bicycles. Designed and built for durability, it requires no preventative maintenance other than oiling. Eventually, its bearings and cones will wear with use. The coaster brake may look simple, but it is not. Have any internal work done by a qualified repairman.

You can adjust the brake yourself if the rear wheel begins to wobble or bind. These problems will occur if the retaining clip breaks, allowing the brake lever to rotate, or if you accidentally turn the brake lever when changing wheels on your bicycle.

Adjust the brake so that the wheel spins freely, yet has no side-to-side play (see *Periodic checks*, p.430).

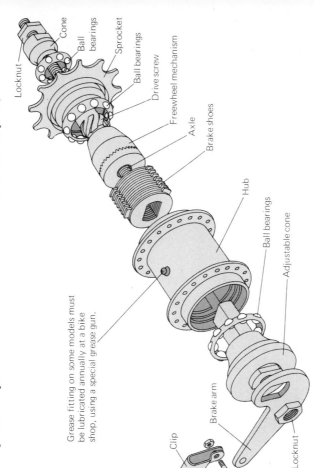

Locknut
Cone
Ball bearings
Sprocket
Ball bearings
Drive screw
Freewheel mechanism
Axle
Brake shoes
Hub
Ball bearings
Adjustable cone
Brake arm
Clip
Locknut

Grease fitting on some models must be lubricated annually at a bike shop, using a special grease gun.

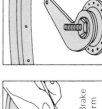

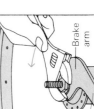

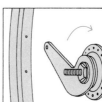

1. Dismount the wheel (p.433). Clamp the wheel in a vise that has been lined with wood or copper to protect the soft threads of the axle.

2. With wrench or channel pliers, loosen locknut next to coaster brake arm. Take care not to strip the threads by applying too much force.

3. To tighten hub, turn brake arm clockwise until wheel no longer wobbles. It should spin smoothly and freely with no noticeable binding or drag.

4. Holding brake arm in position, tighten locknut. Mount wheel on bicycle and secure brake arm with clip (p.433). Test brakes on a level surface.

Bicycles

Servicing a chain

The chain absorbs more punishment than any other bicycle part. Although chains rarely snap, they do become worn and loose. To lessen this wear, wipe the chain with a solvent-soaked cloth whenever dirt builds up on the links. Several times a year remove the chain for cleaning and lubrication.

Periodically check chain tension on one- and three-speed bikes. You can tighten a loose chain at the rear wheel, as shown below. (For derailleurs, see pp.433 and 441). If there is no more room for adjustment at the rear axle, the chain has worn and stretched. Fit a new one. If the chain clatters or grates as you

pedal, inspect it for wear. Sound links should sit firmly between the teeth, not ride up on them.

Worn chain

Sound chain

You can replace the chain of a one- or three-speed bike yourself, but take derailleurs to a bike shop. Replacement chains are usually too long. To find out how many links you must remove, test-mount the chain. Do not use the old one as a gauge; it may have stretched.

Cleaning a chain

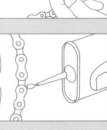

Remove chain and soak it in kerosene for one hour. Clean off residue with a stiff wire brush (left). When chain has dried, install it. Then, drip chain oil into the links as you turn the chain through two complete cycles.

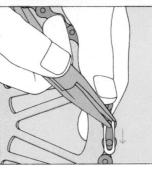

1. Locate chain connector and, with pliers, disengage clip or other fastener holding side plate in place.

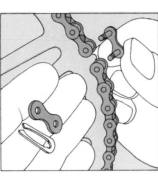

2. Remove side plate. Pull connector free to release the chain ends (also see p.403). Remove chain from bicycle.

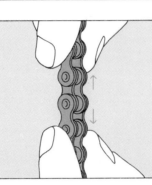

3. Test chain by pulling on any two adjacent links. If there is a lot of play, replace the chain; if not, clean it.

4. Loosen rear wheel nuts and move wheel forward as far as possible in its slots. Holding it there, replace the chain.

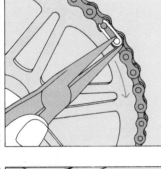

5. Pull chain tightly over both sprockets. If necessary, shorten chain by removing the proper rivet (arrow).

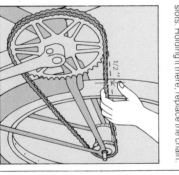

6. Center rivet over hole in a small nut and drive it out with a punch. If rivet is hardened, grind off its head.

7. Replace chain, connector, and side plate. Crimp fastener in place. Its closed end must face direction of travel.

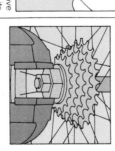

8. Slide wheel back until chain has only ½ in. of play; tighten wheel nuts. Be sure axle is even or wheel will wobble.

Replacing a freewheel

The freewheel must be replaced if a tooth chips off it or if wear causes it to begin slipping. You must also remove the free-wheel when changing a spoke on that side of the wheel. For either job you need a freewheel extractor. When you buy one, take the wheel to the bike shop, for there are many types of extractors. In purchasing a freewheel, make sure it has the same number of teeth as the old one. When replacing it, be careful not to strip the soft aluminum hub threads.

1. Put wheel axle in a vise, freewheel side up. Position extractor; make sure its pegs fit into slots in freewheel. Screw on wheel nut and tighten firmly.

2. Remove wheel from vise and turn over, placing extractor between jaws of vise. Tighten vise.

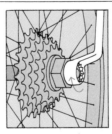

3. Grip wheel rim and turn it counter-clockwise until freewheel loosens. Turn wheel over in vise again, and, with a wrench, remove wheel nut.

4. Grip extractor and unscrew it and freewheel. To install new freewheel, just tighten it by hand and mount the wheel; normal pedalling will tighten it correctly.

Servicing a hub gear

A three-speed bicycle's shift mechanism rarely causes trouble if you lubricate the gear lever housing, rear cable pulley, and the rear hub every month. If the mechanism binds or slips, check the control cable. A kinked, frayed, or severed cable must be replaced. Bike shops sell replacement cables, complete with the outer casing. If the cable is sound, adjust it as shown in Steps 1, 9, 10, 11, and 12. Note the two types of fine adjustment mechanism illustrated in Step 11. Test shift action before riding bike.

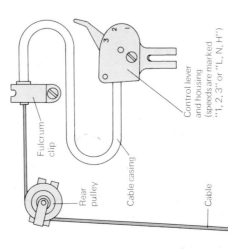

Fulcrum clip

Rear pulley

Cable casing

Cable

Adjuster

Locknut

Control lever and housing (speeds are marked "1, 2, 3" or "L, N, H")

Hub

Sprocket

Tunnel nut

Toggle chain

---

1. Loosen cable locknut near hub and detach cable adjuster from toggle chain. To adjust only, skip to Step 9.

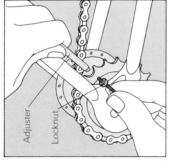

Adjuster

Locknut

---

2. Loosen the fulcrum clip with a screwdriver, then pull the cable forward until adjuster passes through clip.

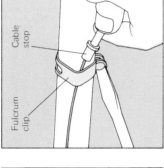

Fulcrum clip

Cable stop

---

3. Flip gear lever to 3, or H, and push inner cable into gear housing to free its nipple. Draw up and back to remove.

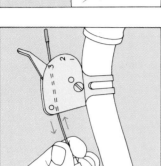

---

4. Lightly lubricate end of new inner cable with bicycle oil. Depress gear lever and push cable through housing.

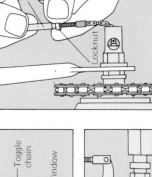

---

5. As shown in this top view, check that nipple is properly seated and that cable runs over slot in lever.

Slot

Nipple

---

6. Slide outer casing end into wide part of slot in gear housing and push it upward to lock it into place.

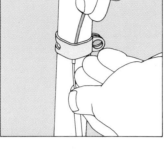

---

7. Pass cable adjuster of the replacement cable under fulcrum clip and pull it until cable stop sits beneath clip.

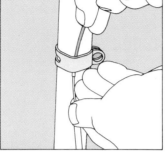

---

8. Lubricate the rear pulley with bicycle oil and make sure that it spins freely. Then, feed the new cable over it.

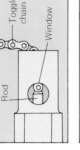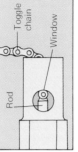

---

9. Grasp toggle chain, hold it perpendicular to axle, and turn clockwise until tight. Then, unwind half a turn.

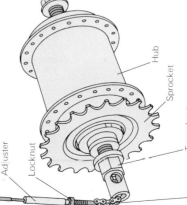

---

10. Attach cable to toggle. Then, slide fulcrum clip forward until cable is barely slack and tighten it. Shift to 2, or N.

---

11. Turn cable adjuster clockwise until rod appears in window (top) or until 2, or N, and line are centered in keyhole.

Rod

Toggle chain

Window

Letter "N"

Keyhole-shaped window

Line

---

12. Flip control lever to 3, or H, position, then screw locknut upward until it rests firmly against cable adjuster.

Adjuster

Locknut

Bicycles

Replacing a derailleur gear cable on 5- and 10-speed bicycles

The derailleur is a mechanism that shifts the chain from gear to gear in order to give multiple forward speeds. A lever on the right side of the frame tube operates the rear derailleur, usually over a cluster of five gears. To obtain 10 speeds, bikemakers combine this rear cluster with a two-gear chain wheel, controlled by a lever on the left side of the frame.

If you encounter binding or slippage as you shift, check the cables and replace any that are kinked, frayed, or broken. To remove the old cable, loosen its anchor bolt at the gear cluster (Step 6) and pull cable forward through the guides. Finally, adjust lever to attain proper cable tension (Step 8).

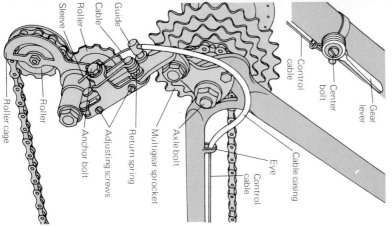

- Control cable
- Center bolt
- Gear lever
- Sleeve
- Roller
- Cable
- Guide
- Roller
- Roller cage
- Anchor bolt
- Adjusting screws
- Return spring
- Multigear sprocket
- Axle bolt
- Eye
- Control cable
- Cable casing

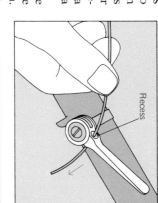

Recess

1. After removing old cable, set the gear lever at its halfway position and thread the entire length of new cable through the hole in the lever. Make sure that the nipple at the end of the cable is seated in its recess.

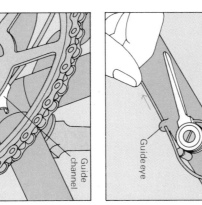

Guide eye

2. Pull the lever back as far as it will go. Feed the cable back through the lever's guide eye and pull it tight.

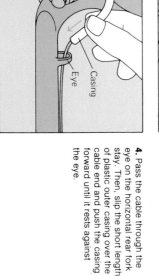

Guide channel

3. Feed the cable through the guide channel just above the bottom bracket of the bike.

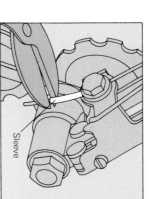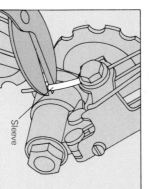

Eye
Casing

4. Pass the cable through the eye on the horizontal rear fork stay. Then, slip the short length of plastic outer casing over the cable end and push the casing forward until it rests against the eye.

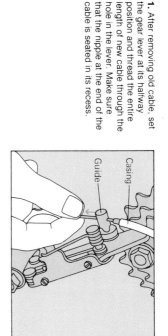

Casing
Guide

5. Slide the cable through the cylindrical guide on the carrier mechanism. Pull the cable downward until the end of the outer casing touches the guide.

Anchor bolt
Lip

6. Move the gear lever all the way forward. Slip the cable between anchor bolt washer and the lip on the anchor bolt flange. Pull the cable taut and tighten the bolt.

7. Push plastic protector sleeve (if supplied) up over the cable end until it rests against the anchor bolt. Snip off any surplus cable.

Sleeve

8. Test-ride the bike. If the gear lever is too loose, the chain will slip into high gear constantly. If it is too tight, the lever will be difficult to move. Adjust the center bolt of the lever for proper tension, if necessary.

Tuning a derailleur system

Derailleur systems slip out of adjustment more frequently than three-speed hub gears. You can avoid many problems by handling the bike with reasonable care. Limit the amount of off-pavement riding, which tends to loosen the delicate cages that transfer the chain from gear to gear. Shift gears while pedaling, not while coasting, and do not backpedal. Never lay the bike on its right side. If the shift lever binds, do not force it; inspect the system and make adjustments.

First, check the cables, as shown on the preceding page. Clean the sprockets and chain with a solvent-soaked cloth. If the chain is worn (see p.438), have a qualified repairman replace it. Finally, check the shift cages. If they are damaged, have them replaced. If they are only misaligned, adjust them yourself.

There are two types of cage adjuster, double screw and single screw. Adjusting either type is a trial and error operation. Have a helper raise the rear wheel clear of the ground and shift gears while you turn the pedal by hand. (A special stand, sold in bike shops, can make this a one-man job.) The adjusting screws must be set so that the chain does not overshoot the sprockets and fall off when it is shifted. But it should not rub against the cage in any gear between shifts.

Adjusting the rear derailleur

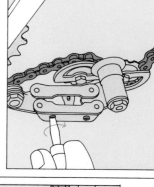

1. Pull right-side shift lever all the way back. Screw in lower adjuster until the chain rides on the center of the large sprocket without overriding. Test for position and overriding after every quarter turn of adjuster.

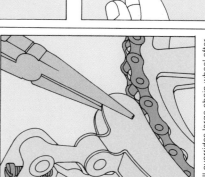

2. Check the clearance between the cage and the spokes. If it is less than 1/8 in., take the bike to a bicycle shop for adjustment.

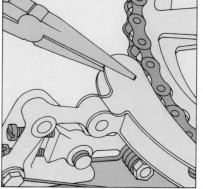

3. Push right-side shift lever all the way forward. Screw in upper adjuster until the chain rides on the center of the smallest sprocket without overriding. Test for position and overriding after every quarter turn of adjuster.

Adjusting the front derailleur

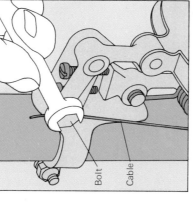

1. Set system in high gear and loosen clamp bolts. Position cage so that it is 1/8 in. above the large chain wheel.

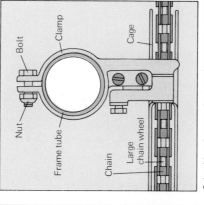

2. Looking down on the cage from above, make sure it is parallel to the large chain wheel, then tighten clamp bolts.

3. Push left gear lever all the way forward. Then, loosen cable anchor bolt. Pull cable taut and tighten bolt.

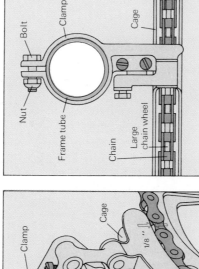

4. Some adjusters have separate screws for high and low gear; set them so that chain does not override sprockets or hit cage.

5. On one-screw models, back off screw just enough so that chain shifts from small to large sprocket without overriding.

6. If chain still overrides large chain wheel after adjustment, carefully bend outer edge of cage slightly inward and test again.

Bicycles

Servicing a three-piece bottom bracket

A three-piece bottom bracket is used on most imported bicycles. American-built bikes usually use a one-piece bracket (see p.444). The bottom bracket assembly consists of the chain wheel, its arms, and the axle that connects them. The axle rides on two sets of ball bearings that are packed in grease. One of the two cups that holds these bearings can be adjusted to take up play in the axle.

The bracket assembly needs periodic maintenance. If your bike's crank arms are fastened to the axle by cotter pins, you can do this work yourself. If the arms have no cotter pins, you must either buy

the special tool required to remove the arms or leave the job to a bike shop.

Disassemble the crank and bearings once a year and repack the assembly with multipurpose bicycle grease. Do it sooner if you hear grating noises coming from the bracket as you pedal. Check the bearings and axle for damage and replace them if they are bad. These parts are not standardized, so bring the old ones along when you buy replacements. If the axle wobbles or binds, adjust the cups (Steps 3, 4, 10, and 11, facing page). If the crank arm is loose, adjust or replace the cotter pin (right).

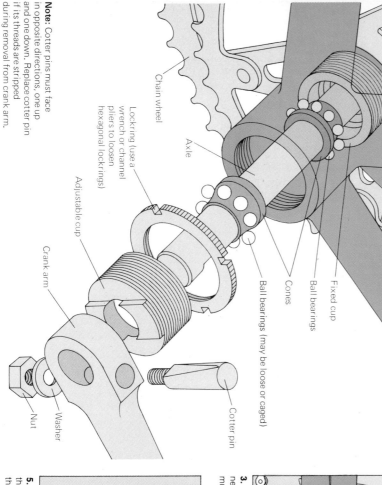

Chain wheel

Locking (use a wrench or channel pliers to loosen hexagonal lockrings)

Axle

Adjustable cup

Crank arm

Nut

Washer

Cotter pin

Ball bearings (may be loose or caged)

Cones

Ball bearings

Fixed cup

Note: Cotter pins must face in opposite directions, one up and one down. Replace cotter pin if its threads are stripped during removal from crank arm.

Fitting a cotter pin

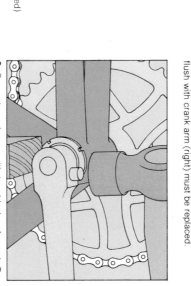

Pin

Crank arm

1. A cotter pin with a protruding head (left) can be adjusted; tap it down and retighten nut. A pin already flush with crank arm (right) must be replaced.

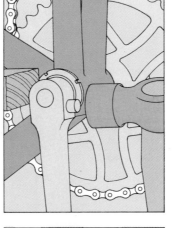

2. To remove old pin, first, remove nut and washer. Hammer the threaded end of the pin flush with the arm, then drive it out with a punch and hammer.

3. Support crank arm with two blocks of wood. Tap new pin into place, threaded end first. Enough thread must be exposed to accept nut and washer.

4. If pin will not pass far enough through crank, use a wooden block to protect its threads and tap pin flush with arm. Drive it out with a punch.

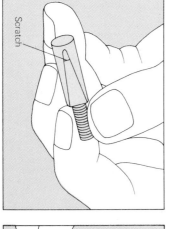

Scratch

5. Examine flat side of pin for scratches caused by the sides of the crank arm hole. You must file down the replacement pin at these marks.

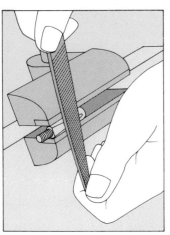

6. Place pin, flat side up, in a vise so that its threads are clear of the jaws. Using a metal file just remove the scratches. Refit pin and washer, then tighten nut.

Adjusting and repacking a bracket

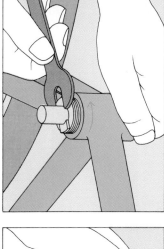

1. Remove chain (p.438), both cotter pins (p.442), and chain wheel. If chain wheel sticks, hold left crank arm firmly and twist wheel from axle.

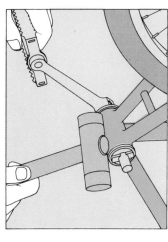

2. Remove left crank arm. If it is wedged on tightly, strike arm as close as possible to its axle with a soft-headed hammer or mallet.

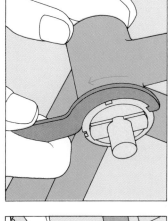

3. Remove lockring on right side. Use a C-wrench if the ring is notched (above) or an adjustable wrench if it is hexagonal. Turn ring counterclockwise.

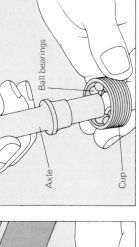

4. Lay bicycle on its right side and unscrew adjustable cup. Hold free hand below fixed cup to catch loose bearings as you draw out axle and adjustable cup.

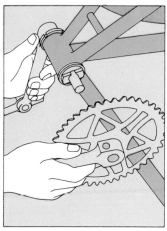

5. Poke remaining fixed cup bearings out through hole. Clean adjustable cup, axle, and all bearings in kerosene. Inspect parts for wear; replace if needed.

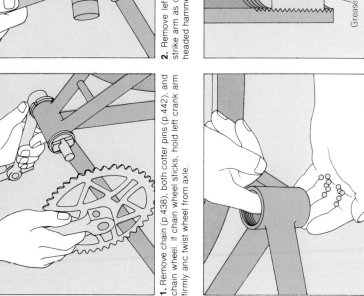

Cup

Grease

6. Clean fixed cup with kerosene and inspect. Have a worn cup replaced by a repair shop. Fill both cups with bicycle grease. Pack caged bearings with grease.

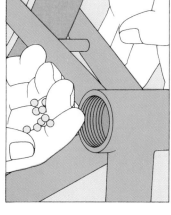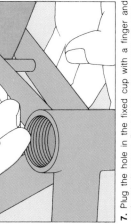

7. Plug the hole in the fixed cup with a finger and replace its bearings. Push loose bearings into the sticky grease to keep them from falling through hole.

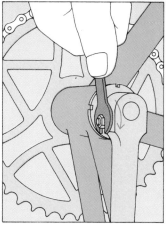

Ball bearings

Axle

Cup

8. Replace ball bearings in adjustable cup, pressing them securely into the grease. Carefully insert shorter end of axle through hole in the cup.

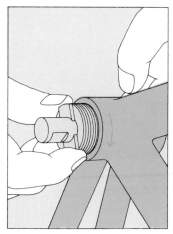

9. Gently lower axle and adjustable cup into housing, taking care not to disturb bearings in fixed cup. Screw adjustable cup clockwise until snug.

10. Tighten adjustable cup with your fingers. It is correctly adjusted when there is no side-to-side axle play, or wobble, but the axle still turns freely.

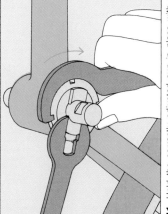

11. Hold the correctly adjusted cup in place with a wrench as you replace lockring. Tighten lockring with C-wrench or adjustable wrench; recheck adjustment.

12. Replace both crank arms and insert cotter pins, fitting them as shown on the preceding page. Replace each washer and tighten nut until it is snug.

443

Bicycles

Servicing a one-piece bottom bracket

Unlike the three-piece bottom brackets found on bicycles built in Europe and Japan (see pp.442–443), the assembly used by most American manufacturers is in one piece. In this design, the crank arm can never loosen and flop about.

Like the three-piece bottom bracket, the one-piece design should be greased annually or whenever you hear grating noises as you pedal. If the crank binds or exhibits play (see *Periodic checks*, p. 430), adjust the cones, following Steps 2, 3, 7, and 8 at right. If the cones are too tight, the crank will be difficult to turn; if they are too loose, it will wobble.

Pedal

Crank arm

Frame

Cone

Locknut

Ball bearings

Chain wheel

Cone

Ball bearings

Cup

1. Remove the chain (p.438), then take off the left pedal by turning its axle clockwise with a wrench.

2. Grasp left crank firmly and loosen locknut by turning it clockwise with a wrench or pliers.

3. Place a punch or the tip of a screwdriver into notch on cone and tap so that cone turns clockwise.

4. Slide locknut and cone off crank arm. Pull out crank arm and chainwheel from right side of bike.

5. Remove bracket bearings—taking care not to lose any—and clean them and the cup with kerosene.

6. Place a bead of multipurpose bicycle grease around the inner edge of the cup and replace bearings.

7. Replace crank arm. Install cup bearings and cone, and turn counterclockwise until there is no play.

8. After adjusting the cone, replace locknut and tighten it counterclockwise until snug.

9. Check bracket again for play or binding, then replace left pedal and tighten counterclockwise.

Camp stoves

Lubricating the pump cup, replacing the generator

A gasoline-fueled camp stove that is operating properly will have a blue flame that is yellow only at the tips. To accomplish this, the pump must be able to build up adequate pressure in the fuel tank and the generator must be clean. To keep the pump in good condition, lubricate it once a month during the camping season or

more often if the stove is in constant use. At times it may be necessary to remove the pump plunger from the fuel tank and apply oil to the leather pump cup, as illustrated in the first photograph below.

The stove's generator vaporizes the liquid fuel into a gas. Eventually the generator becomes clogged with carbon, and

so it is a good idea to keep a spare one on hand. Always burn camp stove fuel; never use automobile gasoline. The latter contains additives that will cause the stove to flicker or burn with a blunt yellow flame, and will quickly clog the generator so that the stove will not light at all. In some cases, the flame may continue burning

after the generator has been turned off. Any of the above symptoms are also signs that the generator requires cleaning, or better, changing. The illustrations at the bottom of this page show the key steps in changing the generator. Because of the danger of igniting the fuel, never work on these pieces until they are cool.

Fuel mixing mechanism

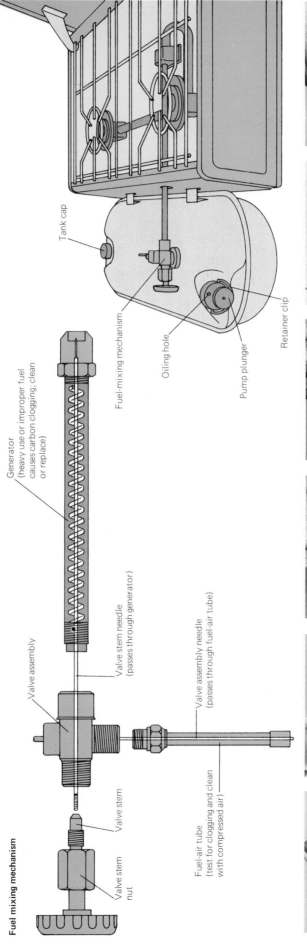

Tank cap

Fuel-mixing mechanism

Oiling hole

Pump plunger

Retainer clip

Generator
(heavy use or improper fuel
causes carbon clogging; clean
or replace)

Valve stem needle
(passes through generator)

Valve assembly

Valve assembly needle
(passes through fuel-air tube)

Valve stem

Fuel-air tube
(test for clogging and clean
with compressed air)

Valve stem
nut

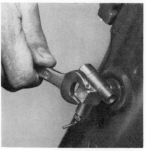

Clamp fuel tank in vise and remove nut holding valve assembly, as shown. Then, unscrew the fuel-air tube by hand and carefully withdraw it. Blow out the tube with compressed air at a garage.

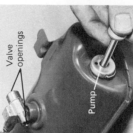

Valve openings

Pump

While the valve assembly is broken down, test for a clogged fuel-air tube. Pump up pressure in capped tank, as shown. If air does not stream from both openings in valve, proceed with the next step.

Valve assembly

Generator

Unscrew generator, using vise-grip pliers or, if there is a nut holding it, a wrench. If necessary, hold valve assembly steady with a second wrench. To install new generator, simply reverse these steps.

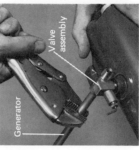

Valve stem

Unscrew old needle from stem and screw in needle that comes with new generator. If you cannot unscrew it, use a wrench and straighten fine wire at its end. If this wire is missing, buy a new stem.

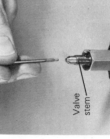

Replacing generator: Take generator and tank out of stove and empty the tank. Then, use a wrench to unscrew nut holding valve stem as shown. Carefully withdraw stem and long needle attached to it.

Leather cup

Oiling pump cup: If pressure fails to build up after lubricating through oiling hole, remove retainer clip with pliers. Take pump plunger out of fuel tank and apply oil to leather cup. Replace a brittle cup.

Canoes

Fiberglass hulls

Fiberglass boat hulls are handmade and consist of several layers of woven glass fiber cloth bonded together with polyester or epoxy resin. The color is often contained in an outer gelcoat, but both the interior and exterior may be painted with enamel. Protect the finish with an annual waxing, using a hard, automotive paste wax. Shallow scratches may be filled by brushing on additional gelcoat—obtained from the canoe manufacturer—and buffing lightly. Fiberglass tends to fade when exposed to sunlight, and the new gelcoat may not be a perfect color match, but the repaired area will also fade and become invisible, given time. Deep scratches may have to be first filled with resin (see below). If large areas of the hull are scratched from repeated beaching or contact with the stream bottom, it is less expensive to paint the entire canoe with a quart of enamel than to coat the bottom with gelcoat. Severe impact damage, whether it includes holes or not, weakens the hull fibers. Cut out the entire affected area and rebuild it with glass cloth and resin, sold in kits. Do not work in temperatures below 60°F.

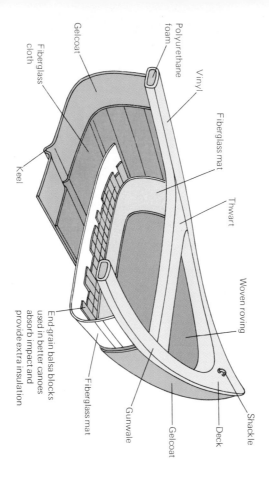

Polyurethane foam
Gelcoat
Fiberglass cloth
Keel
Vinyl
Fiberglass mat
Thwart
Woven roving
Shackle
Deck
Gelcoat
Gunwale
Fiberglass mat
End-grain balsa blocks used in better canoes absorb impact and provide extra insulation

Repairing deep scratches

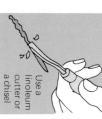

Use a linoleum cutter or a chisel.

Use a small, sharp chisel point to scrape out a V-shaped groove along a deep scratch that goes through the gelcoat. Buy a fiberglass patch kit and mix a small batch of resin and hardener.

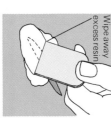

Wipe away excess resin

Press resin into groove with plastic applicator supplied in most kits. Let cure overnight, then rub down with No. 240 wet/dry sandpaper. (see p.91) Finish with soaked No. 400 paper. Apply gelcoat or enamel.

Repairing small holes

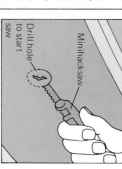

Minihacksaw
Drill hole to start saw

Holes under 2 in. in diameter can be fixed with auto patch kits. One other to fit hole exactly and apply from outside of hull. Add more patches to match hull thickness. Apply patch larger than hole, inside hull.

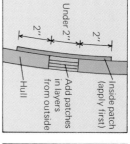

Inside patch (apply first)
Under 2"
2"
2"
Hull
Add patches in layers from outside

When inside patch cures, cut another to fit hole exactly and apply from outside of hull. Add more patches to match hull thickness. Let each cure before adding next.

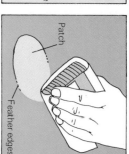

Patch
Feather edges

Use No. 80 sandpaper to feather edges of hardened patch into canoe's surface. Apply auto filler. Finish as you would car repair (p.319). Apply enamel or gelcoat.

Repairing large holes

1. You can repair holes up to about 10 in. yourself. Have dealer repair bigger holes. Cut around damaged area with a hacksaw. Remove as little of sound hull as possible.

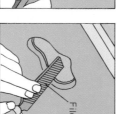

File

2. Use a file to bevel the edges of the cut from both sides and form a V-shaped edge with a 45° apex. This will help to hold the flush-finished patch in place.

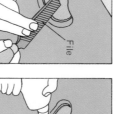

3. To provide grip for the backing mat (Step 8), roughen up the inside of the hull for at least 2 in. around the hole. Use a disc sander with a medium (No. 80) paper.

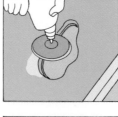

Tape
Plastic
Outside of hull
Cardboard

4. For small holes, cut a cardboard backing plate and cover it with a piece of polyethylene plastic (use a drycleaner's bag). Tape cardboard tightly to outside of hull.

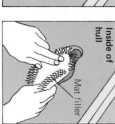

Plate
Outside of hull

5. For holes larger than about 5 in., screw a piece of aluminum or hardboard over the hole. Coat the inside of this backing plate with fiberglass release agent.

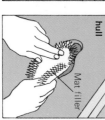

Brush gelcoat over polyethylene or release agent
Inside of hull

6. Working in the shade, mix up just enough gelcoat to cover the backing plate. Spread a thick layer of gelcoat onto the polyethylene, hardboard, or aluminum from inside hull.

7. Mix no more resin than you can apply in 30 minutes. When gelcoat becomes tacky, apply alternating layers of resin and glass mat. (Mat is heavy duty glass cloth.)

Mat filler
Inside of hull

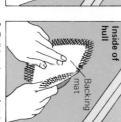

Backing mat
Inside of hull

8. Build up layers of resin and mat until hole is filled. Add a backing mat 2 in. larger than hole. After 24 hours, remove outside plate, fill in screw holes (if any) with resin.

Foam sandwich hulls

Foam sandwich hulls have a core of buoyant, closed-cell foam material surrounded on both sides by several layers of plastic. The material absorbs impact well, and small dents that do not show on the inside of the craft tend to work themselves out in time simply by using the canoe. Dents that show inside the canoe can be removed by applying heat. Special flexible resin, cloth, glue, and paint are available from the canoe manufacturer for repairing large holes and gouges. New seats, thwarts, gunwales, and decks should also be ordered from the manufacturer to assure proper fit.

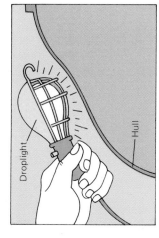

To remove a dent, heat the hull with an electric iron on the *Rayon* setting, a hair dryer, or a 75-watt light bulb with a reflector. Apply heat to the outside of the hull only, in the area of the dent.

Droplight — Hull

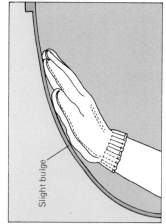

Press on the inside of the dent with a gloved hand. When hull begins to move, remove the heat from the outside and continue to press until the outside surface bulges slightly. Keep pressing until canoe cools.

Slight bulge

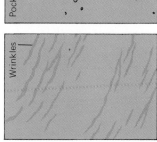

Watch the hull surface carefully; too much heat will burn it. If the finish begins to wrinkle or form tiny pockmarks, remove the heat immediately and let the hull cool until wrinkles or pockmarks disappear.

Wrinkles — Pocks

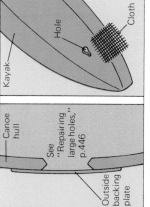

To fix a hole, buy a repair kit from the canoe maker that includes flexible resin and cloth. Use kit as you would fiberglass. Patch a canoe from the inside, a kayak from the outside. Let cure; sand and paint.

Canoe hull — Kayak — Hole — Cloth — Outside backing plate — See "Repairing large holes," p.446

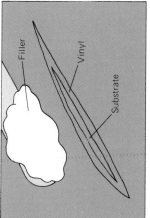

To fix a shallow gouge, buy special flexible glue and paint from the canoe manufacturer. Mix glue and fill gouge with it, using plastic trowel supplied in kit. Paint hull only if gouge has exposed black substrate.

Filler — Vinyl — Substrate

Aluminum hulls

Holes near or below the waterline of an aluminum boat should be covered with a watertight fiberglass patch (see opposite page and *Body and interior*, p.319). A riveted metal patch will leak unless it is backed up by a thick rubber gasket. Some sheet aluminum sold in hardware stores will deteriorate rapidly if exposed to salt water or air. Dents can be hammered out of an aluminum hull in the same way as dents in a car fender, but the metal will get brittle if it is stretched or overheated. To prevent electrolysis corrosion, remove fishhooks and other metal objects from the hull before storing it.

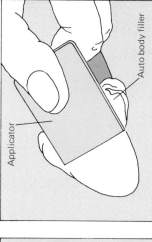

Large dents, such as a buckled keel, can be partially removed by jumping up and down inside beached canoe. Cut pieces of 2 x 4-in. lumber as shown and use a hydraulic auto jack to force the keel straight.

Jack — 2 x 4's

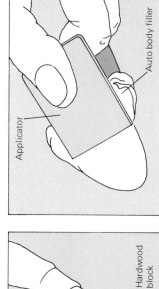

Hold a piece of hardwood over small dents and hammer them out gently from the inside, using a soft-faced mallet. Start at outside of dent and hammer around edges, working slowly toward center.

Hardwood block — Mallet

If you cannot reach the back of the dent, drill one or more small holes into it, about 1 in. apart. Drive a self-tapping screw part way into each hole and pull out dent with a claw hammer. Use filler on screw holes.

Wooden block

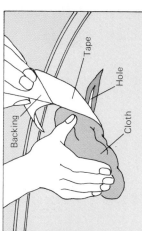

Fill any remaining depressions or wrinkles with auto body filler (see p.319). Apply filler in several coats, sanding the area with progressively finer paper between each coat. Finish with aluminum or marine paint.

Applicator — Auto body filler

Patch small holes above the waterline with aluminum tape. Sand off corrosion around hole. Remove grease with rubbing alcohol. Apply tape to dry surface with a cloth pad, stripping off the backing as you go.

Backing — Tape — Hole — Cloth

Canoes

Wooden hulls

Wooden canoes are made of steamed and formed cedar planks covered with surfaces, enamel to canvas or fiberglass, formed cedar planks covered with canvas. The canvas is waterproofed by coating it with a thin fiberglass shell, or with a special filler and enamel paint. Lightly sand and recoat exposed surfaces when needed; apply varnish to wooden surfaces, enamel to canvas or fiberglass. Patch small holes in the fabric with cellulose adhesive (see p.10). Have a canoe dealer replace rotted canvas or repair major hull damage.

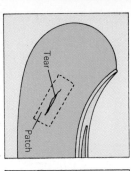

To fix a tear that has not damaged the planking below, cut a piece of canvas about 1 in. bigger than the slit. Insert the patch into the slit and work it into position between the planking and hull canvas. Smooth patch until it lies flat.

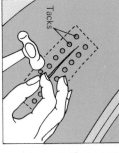

Coat patch with cellulose adhesive, then close the cut and smooth the flaps with your fingers, working excess adhesive out of the slit. Wipe excess adhesive smooth. If the cut is long, secure its edges with brass tacks, crimped inside hull.

If some of the canvas has been torn away, cut off remaining flaps. Cut a patch of heavy canvas large enough to cover the damaged area. Apply with cellulose adhesive. Smooth, then tack edges. Crimp tacks over inside the hull.

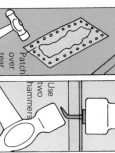

Replacing gunwales

The gunwales, decks, thwarts, and seats on fiberglass and foam sandwich canoes are made of plastic or foam sandwich and are screwed or riveted to the hull. Rivets are preferable, because they cannot work loose as the hull flexes. These parts are made of stamped or extruded aluminum on aluminum hull canoes, and are also riveted in place. Replacements can be ordered through a dealer who handles your brand of canoe. Considerable skill and special woods are needed to replace wooden gunwales, decks, or seats. Leave this work to a dealer.

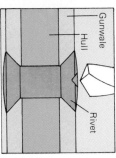

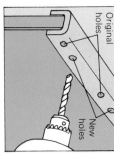

1. Order new parts before removing the old ones; make sure the replacements match the originals exactly in size and shape. Use power drill with a 3/16-in. high-speed steel bit to drill out the old rivets.

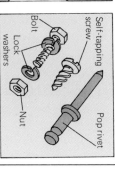

2. Remove old part and fit the new one snugly into place.Drill 3/16-in. holes for the new rivets through both the replacement part and the hull, keeping well away from the original holes in the hull.

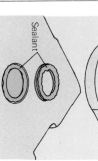

3. Secure the parts with 3/16-in. pop rivets made of aluminum or other noncorrosive material. (see *Riveting*, p.369). If you cannot find rivets of the proper size, use self-tapping screws or nuts and bolts.

Chemical toilets

Care and repair

Portable chemical toilets that flush have three main parts—the bowl, a chemical supply tank, and a waste holding tank. The bowl and chemical tank can be detached from the holding tank when the latter is full and must be emptied. Use only the chemicals recommended by the toilet manufacturer, and handle them with care; most are highly poisonous. Use the manufacturer's antifreeze solution if the unit will be exposed to freezing temperatures. Clean with a mild household detergent that contains no ammonia, abrasives, acid, or petroleum distillates. If the tank sealing valve sticks, free and lubricate it with silicone spray.

Common repairs

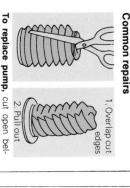

To replace pump, cut open bellows from top to bottom. Fold bellows inward and pull out. Align new bellows and valve assembly, then snap it into place.

To remove a faulty waste tank sealing valve, first remove the four or five self-tapping screws.

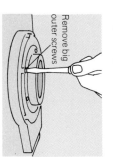

Replace damaged gaskets or valve parts. Place an uninterrupted ring of the manufacturer's sealant or glazing putty between tank and valve during reassembly.

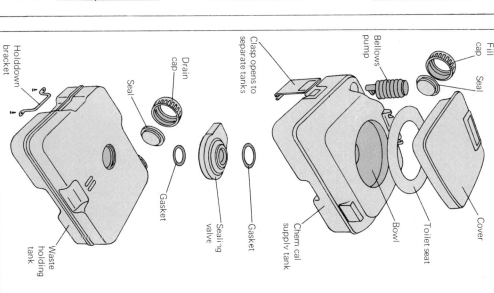

Fishing tackle

Caring for tackle

After a day of fishing, make a spot check of your tackle—your rods, reels, lines, hooks, lures, nets, and leaders—for any damage or loose fittings. Wipe grit and scum off all surfaces with a damp cloth, and then wipe them dry with a clean, soft cloth. Following saltwater fishing, give your equipment a thorough freshwater rinse, and then dry it. When you are fishing every day, give your reel a few shots of oil or grease to keep its gears running smoothly, and spread a little oil on metal surfaces.

If a piece of tackle breaks, do not throw it away. Nine times out of ten, broken tackle can be fixed—if not at home, then by sending it back to the manufacturer or to a professional tackle repair shop. Making a repair is always less expensive than buying new equipment. Experienced fishermen are usually more than willing to share do-it-yourself techniques. Replacement parts and repair materials can almost always be found, although to do so may take some sleuth-ing. If a local tackle shop cannot help you, check the ads in fishing magazines.

Fiberglass, graphite (HMG), and cane rods have many common maintenance needs. Unlike fiberglass and graphite, however, cane rods require revarnishing every year or so. If a rod has metal ferrules, take it apart at least once a week, or the ferrules are likely to "freeze" (see p.453). Keep ferrules clean with a pipe cleaner dipped in nail polish remover (acetone). Do not oil them.

Frayed guide wrappings can be temporarily mended with tape or by applying clear nail polish. But to make the repair permanent they should be completely undone and rewrapped (see illustrations at right). Nicked guides can break the line and should be replaced.

Dirty cork grips should be scrubbed with soap and water. At the same time the reel's seat threads should be cleaned and then lightly oiled. Rods should never be left for long in sun or in dampness, or with tips leaning against a surface.

Wrapping a guide

There are several specialty manufacturers of guides, as well as of the winding threads that are used to rewrap guides. A well stocked tackle shop should have both guides and threads.

Begin the job by cutting a 3-inch piece of thread. Twist it to make a pull loop, and place this within easy reach. Position

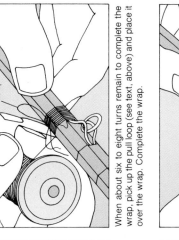

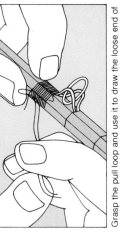

the guide and secure one of its two guide feet with masking tape. Start wrapping the free foot. To anchor the thread, lay the loose end lengthwise along the rod, so that the first few windings will bind the end of the thread. Hold the spool in one hand and rotate the rod to draw thread off the spool.

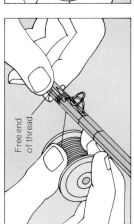

Free end of thread

Wrap the first few windings over the free end of thread. As you rotate the rod, keep even tension on the thread. Do not overlap thread. Align with thumbnail.

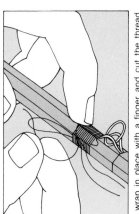

When about six to eight turns remain to complete the wrap, pick up the pull loop (see text, above) and place it over the wrap. Complete the wrap.

Grasp the pull loop and use it to draw the loose end of the wrapping thread under the wrap. Discard the loop. Trim the end of the thread flush with the wrap.

Hold wrap in place with a finger and cut the thread coming from the spool, leaving a loose end of 1 in. Push this end through the pull loop.

Fitting a tip-top

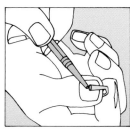

Select a tip-top with socket diameter a bit smaller than rod tip diameter. Carefully sand the rod tip with fine finishing sandpaper until it can just be pushed into socket. Dab rod tip with epoxy cement.

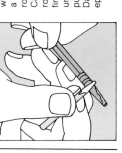

Let a drop of cement slide into socket of tip-top from rod tip, then join parts. Twist tip-top to align with other guides. Use toothpick and nail polish remover to clean up any excess adhesive.

Tip-top (top guide)

Ferrule (female)

Ferrule (joined)

Fore grip

Guide wrappings

Guide

Reel seat

Ferrule (male)

Rear grip

Butt

Fishing tackle

Fly reels

There are four basic types of fishing reels: fly, open-face spinning, closed-face spinning (or spincast), and bait (or plug) casting reels. All new reels come with a booklet telling how to service the reel and identifying its parts. If you are buying a second-hand reel, be sure to ask for its instruction booklet.

Reel manufacturers are noted for keeping a large inventory of replacement parts. You can write directly to the manufacturer for a part if you are not able to obtain it at a tackle shop.

The fly reel is the simplest reel to dis-

assemble and service. Usually, simply by pressing a catch you can release the spool and slip it out of its frame.

Fly reels are vulnerable to grit and sand, which get between the spool and frame. After a fishing trip, separate the halves and wipe the inner surfaces clean with a cloth dipped in gasoline, kerosene, or alcohol. Then, lubricate the reel with lightweight oil. Remember to give reels a freshwater bath after saltwater fishing, then clean and lubricate them. Use pipe cleaners to clean out the axle cylinder. Put a dab of grease on the axle itself.

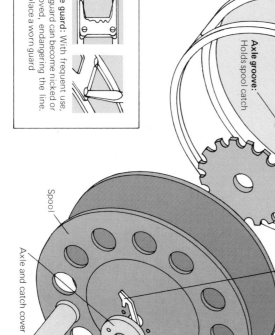

Axle groove: Holds spool catch

Axle

Springs

Thumbscrew brake: Regulates spool and line tension

Spring tension regulating block

Pawls: Engage ratchet gear on underside of spool

Pawl retaining stud

Spring retaining stud

Frame

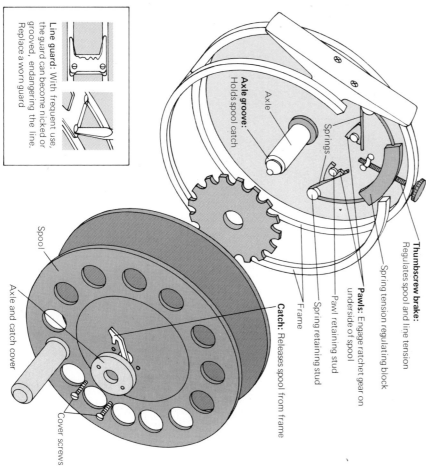

Spool

Axle and catch cover

Cover screws

Catch: Releases spool from frame

Line guard: With frequent use, the guard can become nicked or grooved, endangering the line. Replace a worn guard.

Replacing a broken spring and pawl on a fly reel

The spring and pawl mechanism of a fly reel prevents the spool from turning on its own within the frame. In the type of reel illustrated on this page, a second spring and pawl mechanism is present and makes a clicking sound as line is

reeled in or played out. Also shown is a reel featuring a thumbscrew-type friction brake; when present in a reel, it adjusts the spool tension, which assists in playing a large fish. With only a few such critical parts, not much can go wrong with a fly reel.

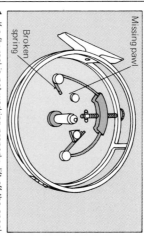

Missing pawl

Broken spring

1. If a fly reel is not working properly, lift off the spool and examine the parts in the frame. This illustration shows a broken spring and missing pawl.

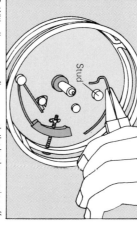

Stud

2. With pliers or your fingers, push the broken spring off its retaining stud. Spring might have snapped because thumbscrew was not released during storage.

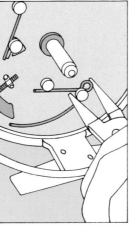

3. With a kerosene-soaked rag, wipe away any grease or grit that has accumulated under the spool. Then, use pliers to squeeze the head of new spring onto the stud.

4. Note how the other spring is held against the tension-regulating block and, with the pliers, position the long end of the new spring in the same way.

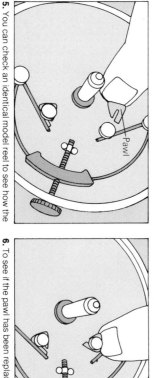

Pawl

5. You can check an identical model reel to see how the new pawl should be placed on the stud. Here, pawl's long straight side is being placed against spring.

6. To see if the pawl has been replaced properly, put the spool back on. If reel action is wrong, push pawl clockwise so that rounded edge is against spring.

Spinning reels (fixed-spool reels)

There are two types of spinning reels, open and closed face. The closed-face model is also known as a spincast reel.

Both types of spinning reels are technically fixed-spool reels. However, the spool of the open-face reel (illustrated below) is not literally stationary. Although the spool does not revolve when line is being wound in, it does move back and forth—in conjunction with the turning of the rotating head and bailing arm.

The open-face spinning reel has a relatively large number of external moving parts. Oil them regularly, and apply grease containing water repellant. Once a year remove the gearcase plate, clean out the old grease with gasoline or kerosene, and repack with new grease.

Replacing a ball spring

When the fisherman cranks the handle of an open-face spinning reel after a cast, the bail snaps over and catches the line in the bollard, permitting retrieval of the line. If the ball spring is broken, the bail will not snap over.

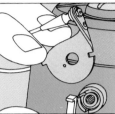

Remove screw securing bracket. Take off bracket to reveal the spring. Work spring out with a steel knitting needle or a similar tool.

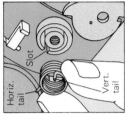

Insert the new spring so that its horizontal tail fits into the slot of the spring cylinder.

Horiz. tail   Slot   Vert. tail

Replace the bracket on top of the spring. The up-pointing vertical tail of the spring must be inserted into the hole provided for it in the bracket.

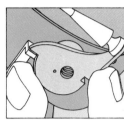

Press bracket firmly down over the new spring, and replace and tighten the bracket screw.

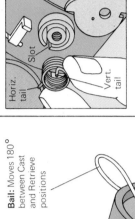

Bail: Moves 180° between Cast and Retrieve positions

Spool: Holds line

Bollard (see inset)

Rotating head: Rotates bail, not spool, during retrieve of line

Body: Houses main gearing

Bollard: Guides line onto spool during retrieve. With heavy use, bollard may become nicked and grooved and break line. Nicked or grooved bollard should be replaced

Spool catch

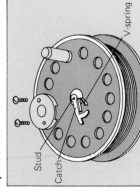

V-spring

Stud   Catch

A loose spool probably means the spring of the spool catch is broken or fatigued. Take off the axle cover and remove the old spring. Make sure the spool catch is on its stud, then place the straight side of the new V-spring against the catch, as shown here.

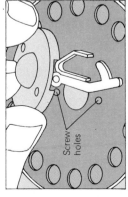

Screw holes

Slide the axle cover back over the stud, spool catch, and spring. Note that the cover is indented on one side to allow the spool catch to protrude. Make sure the cover lines up with the screw holes in the spool.

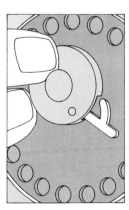

Carefully press the cover down so as not to displace either the spring or the catch. The cover will slip out of position if not held firmly. Replace the two screws and tighten them. Test the action of the spool catch.

Installing new bail on open-face spinning reel

The bail of this reel may break at either of its two ends, which are attached to the rotating head. The manufacturer will probably have a replacement bail, if your local tackle shop does not.

In performing this or any other fairly complex reel repair job, a compartmented reel repair tray or box, such as an egg box or an ice cube tray, is useful. Place the reel parts into the container compartments in the order in which they are removed. This will avoid mix-ups in reassembling the reel. Before starting the job check the condition of the bollard and bollard collar. Replace them if necessary. Note that the pivot screw holding the bail cannot be undone with an ordinary screwdriver but requires pincers.

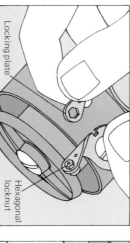

1. The bail is most likely to break on the bracket side, where it is subject to heavy stress. Soldering would be useless. Obtain a new bail to replace the broken one.

Bail
Bracket
Broken here

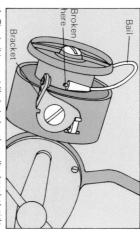

2. On the side of the reel opposite the bracket, loosen the bail's pivot screw with pincers and remove the screw. Detach the broken bail from the reel.

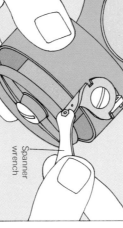

3. On the bracket side of the reel, use screwdriver to undo locking plate screw. This screw is usually very small. Be careful not to lose it.

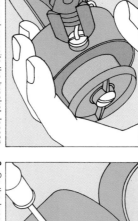

Locking plate screw

4. With the locking plate screw removed, the locking plate itself can be lifted off the hexagonal locknut. Clean the locking plate with a dry rag.

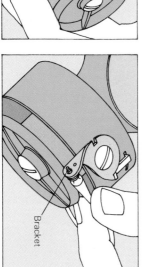

Locking plate
Hexagonal locknut

5. After you have loosened the locknut with a small spanner wrench, remove the nut with your fingers and lay it carefully aside.

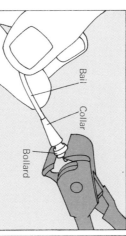

Spanner wrench

6. Discard the old bollard and bollard collar if they are worn. Replace with new ones. Slide bollard and collar together at end of bail; tighten them with pincers.

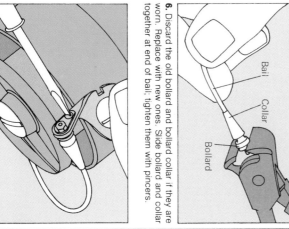

Bail
Collar
Bollard

7. After starting the pivot screw in the new bail with your fingers, finish tightening it with pincers. **Caution: An overtightened pivot screw can break the bail.**

8. Push the end of the bail through its hole in the bracket. Screw hexagonal locknut into place with spanner wrench. Do not overtighten.

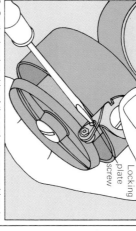

Bracket

9. Fit the locking plate back over the hexagonal locknut. Replace the locking plate screw and tighten it firmly with a screwdriver.

Closed-face spinning reel

To disassemble and clean a closed-face spinning, or spincast, reel, first remove the conical front cover plate, which usually twists off with a half turn. Beneath it is a second cone, usually of plastic, over which the line passes from the spool. Wipe old lubricant off these parts and off the spool shaft. Apply fresh lubricant to these same areas.

The main gears are usually housed under the back cover plate. Twist it open to service them. Use a small brush dipped in kerosene or gasoline to remove old, gummy lubricant from around gears.

Overloading is a problem shared by spincast reels with both open-face spinning reels and bait-casting reels. Overloading is caused by the use of line that is too heavy for the reel, which results in a severe strain on the gears. In choosing line, be sure to follow the reel manufacturer's recommendations.

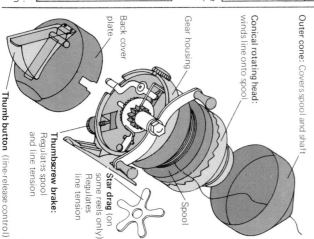

Outer cone: Covers spool and shaft
Conical rotating head: winds line onto spool
Gear housing
Back cover plate
Thumb button (line-release control)
Thumbscrew brake: Regulates spool and line tension
Star drag (on some reels only): Regulates line tension
Spool

Bait-casting reels

The bait-casting reel is built around a rapidly revolving spool, distinguishing it from spinning reels and the much slower fly reel. Moisture from wet line flying off the reel sprays into the small gap between the spool and sideplates. These spots must be regularly oiled to prevent rusting and corrosion.

A level-wind mechanism is found on most bait-casting reels. It takes the line evenly on and off the spool. To work properly, the level-wind guide needs to have its gear and pawl continually replenished with grease. After every fishing day, give the reel a light oiling at oil ports on either end of the spool axle, star drag (if equipped with one), handles and handle shaft, and the groove into which the top of the level wind guide fits.

Most big saltwater reels are only giant versions of the bait-casting reel, usually without level winds, but with powerful star drags. Always loosen the drag on the spool at the end of a fishing day.

Angler's tips

About half the work in caring for fishing tackle is simply fighting moisture-related problems—rust, corrosion, and loss of finish. Most of the rest is fighting dirt and grit. Here are four ways to make the fight a bit easier.

1. Spray reels with one of several available demoisturizing agents.

2. Keep rods and reels in cases until ready to fish.

3. Follow manufacturer's recommendations for cleaning, oiling, and greasing. Old toothbrushes are ideal for cleaning tackle, and pipecleaners will come in handy for any number of odd jobs.

4. Build up a kit of servicing tools.

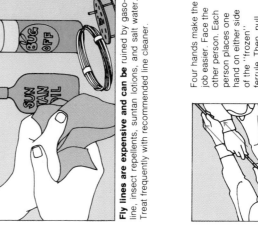

Flies that get matted and bedraggled with heavy use can be restored by holding them in steam from a boiling tea kettle. Let them dry, then apply fly dressing.

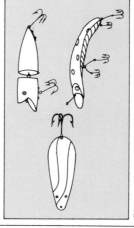

Dull hooks are the cause of many "fish that got away." Even new hooks are rarely as sharp as they might be. Sharpen point and barb with file or whetstone.

Plugs and spools used in salt water should be soaked afterwards in fresh water. On most, damaged hooks can be replaced. Touch up bodies with enamel.

Fly lines are expensive and can be ruined by gasoline, insect repellents, suntan lotions, and salt water. Treat frequently with recommended line cleaner.

Rods with "frozen" ferrules

Parting ferrules: If alone, hold rod behind knees. Grasp rod close to ferrules. Slowly spread—do not jerk—knees apart. Usually, ferrules will part with two or three efforts.

Four hands make the job easier. Face the other person. Each person places one hand on either side of the "frozen" ferrule. Then, pull in unison, steadily. If unsuccessful, give rod half turn and repeat.

Side plate

Spool

Level-wind guide

Worm gear controls level wind

Spool bearing cover

Screw holds pawl that rides worm gear's slots

Pillars

Star drag (on some reels)

Handle nut

Handle

Fishing tackle

Revarnishing

On all kinds of rods, periodic varnishing will help preserve the guide wrappings. Graphite rods never require full top-to-bottom varnishing, fiberglass rods need it only for appearance, but cane rods must be periodically revarnished to stop moisture from reaching the cane. Appearance is the signal: If a rod's finish is thin and worn in several places, it is time for top-to-bottom revarnishing.

Whether doing only a touch-up or a complete job, apply two or three coats of color preservative, letting each dry to touch.

Varnish will discolor winding thread. Before varnishing guide wraps, apply two or three coats of color preservative, letting each dry to touch.

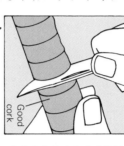

Before touching up a worn spot, rub the rod briskly with a piece of felt. The resulting ultrasmooth surface will be ideal for accepting varnish.

Varnish can be applied with a small paint brush (as shown), with a lint-free cloth, or with your fingers. The thinner the coat, the better it will look.

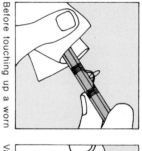

Hold rod horizontally and rotate it gently back and forth between your thumb and forefinger. This will allow the varnish to seep evenly over the rod.

7. Use coarse sandpaper or a file with rounded edge to begin shaping new rings to the contour of the grip.

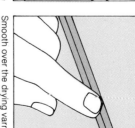

Smooth over the drying varnish with a finger. Some master rodmakers do the full revarnishing of a rod—three coats—using their fingers only.

Repairing a cork grip

Almost all cork grips on rods are built up from standard 1/2-inch-wide rings. Both through tackle shops and mail order firms, the cork rings are available in outside diameters of 1-1/8 and 1-1/2 inches, with inside diameters bored to 1/4, 5/16, 3/8, 7/16, 1/2, and 5/8 inch.

In one method of repair, rings are cut in half and reglued around the rod section, thus eliminating the need to strip the rod of guides and wrappings to slide the rod of guides and wrappings to slide whole rings on. In the method shown at right, however, whole cork rings are used. The use of whole rings eliminates the problem of fitting cork ring halves snugly around the rod and gluing them.

Rod section (or blank)
Cork rings
Glue line
Butt
1/2"

1. Use razor-sharp knife. (Cork is easy to sand and file, but tough to cut.) Make first cut in damaged cork about 1/8 in. from nearest good cork on butt side (right, in drawing). Cutting at glue line might damage sound cork.

Good cork

2. After cutting away most of old, damaged cork, carefully shave away shreds of old cork clinging at glue line to face of undamaged cork ring.

4. Push new ring down rod to check fit. If at all loose, use ring with boring of smaller diameter. If necessary, use rattail file to enlarge bore so that ring barely pushes on.

5. Apply small amount of resin-based waterproof glue to rod and face of old ring. Do same to face of new ring and slide it down rod to fit tightly against old ring.

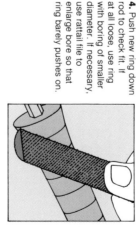

8. Finish the shaping by going over the whole grip with medium, then fine sandpaper.

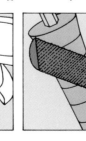

3. To remove bits of cork still sticking to rod and ring face, use a medium-grade file, such as the toothless side of a warding file or fine sandpaper stretched over a wood block. Work for sharp 90° angle between rod and cork ring.

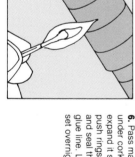

6. Pass match flame under cork. Heat will expand it slightly, push rings together, and seal them along glue line. Let glue set overnight.

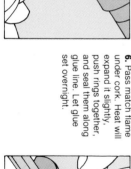

9. If there are cracks and very visible glue lines, fill them with a mixture of clear glue and cork dust. Smooth in with knife.

Flashlights and lanterns

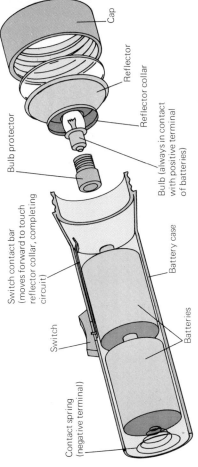

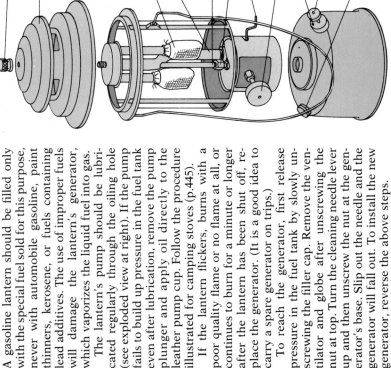

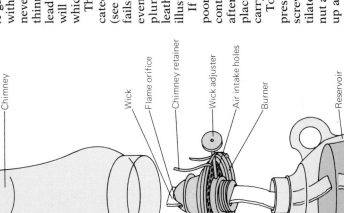

Flashlights

In a typical flashlight, the bulb seats in its socket on a flange (see exploded view at right). The bulb is held in place by a plastic protector that either snaps onto or screws over the base of the bulb. The threaded cap at the head of the flashlight holds the lens, reflector, and bulb in position—with the bulb's base making contact with the positive battery terminal.

At the base of the battery case is the contact spring. This spring makes contact with the negative battery terminal. It carries the negative half of the circuit either through the metal battery case or, in plastic cases, through a metal strip, as

far as the switch. Only when the switch is pushed forward to the *On* position does its contact bar extend far enough to touch the collar of the reflector (or the reflector itself in most older flashlights), completing the electrical circuit so that the bulb lights.

If a dead flashlight does not light with new batteries and a new bulb, look for a bent switch contact. Straighten it so that it makes contact with the reflector collar when the switch is on. Also look for corrosion, especially on the contact spring. Remove corrosion with a strip of sandpaper wrapped around a pencil or dowel.

Oil (kerosene) lamps

Oil lamps should be fueled only with kerosene or commercially bottled lamp oil, never with gasoline. Before lighting a new wick, wait for it to become saturated with kerosene all the way to the flame orifice (see exploded view at right). To light the lamp, remove the chimney and turn the wick up far enough to be able to ignite it with a match in the orifice. Then, put the chimney back on the lamp and adjust the wick height to achieve a bright, smokeless flame. The tip of the wick will usually be considerably below the top of the flame orifice. To extinguish the lamp, simply blow into the top of the chimney. Do not extinguish the flame by turning down the wick.

If one side of the flame burns higher than the other, trim the wick square with scissors. When the lamp burns with a smoky flame even though the wick is correctly adjusted, clean out the air intake holes in the burner.

Never touch the chimney until it has had time to cool. Soot can be cleaned from the chimney with soap and water. If the inside of the reservoir becomes discolored, clean it with a strong detergent and hot water. Slip out the needle and chimneys are available at hardware stores.

Gasoline lanterns

A gasoline lantern should be filled only with the special fuel sold for this purpose, never with automobile gasoline, paint thinners, kerosene, or fuels containing lead additives. The use of improper fuels will damage the lantern's generator, which vaporizes the liquid fuel into gas.

The lantern's pump should be lubricated regularly through the oiling hole (see exploded view at right). If the pump fails to build up pressure in the fuel tank even after lubrication, remove the pump plunger and apply oil directly to the leather pump cup. Follow the procedure illustrated for camping stoves (p.445).

If the lantern flickers, burns with a poor quality flame or no flame at all, or continues to burn for a minute or longer after the lantern has been shut off, replace the generator. (It is a good idea to carry a spare generator on trips.)

To reach the generator, first release pressure in the fuel tank by slowly unscrewing the filler cap. Remove the ventilator and globe after unscrewing the nut at top. Turn the cleaning needle lever up and then unscrew the nut at the generator's base. Slip out the needle and the generator will fall out. To install the new generator, reverse the above steps.

Pools and equipment

Buying considerations

Above-ground swimming pools are more widely owned than in-ground pools for a number of reasons: They are relatively inexpensive; they can be installed by a do-it-yourselfer; they can be taken down and reassembled should the owner move; and they are normally not subject to the problems of frost heaves that can affect in-ground pools in many parts of the country. Furthermore, in many areas taxes and insurance rates are lower for above-ground pools than for in-ground pools. This section deals mostly with above-ground pools.

Before shopping for a pool, check your local building codes. Some communities ban above-ground pools outright, others subject them to discouraging building code restrictions. You may need building, plumbing, or electrical permits; inspections; an occupancy certificate; a new property survey; or protective fencing. A pool may have to be set back a minimum distance from your property line.

The framework of an above-ground pool should be made entirely of aluminum—even the nuts and bolts. Otherwise it may weaken from corrosion. Wood, even redwood, will rot and split in time, especially when exposed to pool chemicals. Steel rusts; painted or coated steel will inevitably be scratched during assembly, and rust will set in. A weakened frame will eventually burst; Bathers may be swept over the jagged edges and injured; thousands of gallons of chemically-treated water will be released onto your property and perhaps onto neighbors' property or into the local water system. Lawsuits may result.

Pool uprights and coping should be aluminum extrusions at least 4 to 6 inches thick for maximum strength. Curved coping is stronger than straight coping; it also overhangs the pool less, so that swimmers are not likely to bump their heads on it. The pool liner should be of at least 20-gauge vinyl.

Types of pool construction

Inexpensive pools have frame uprights and coping made of sheet metal stampings less than 2 in. thick. Strength is marginal, even on the smallest (under 16-ft) pools.

Moderately priced pools have extruded uprights and coping that are at least 6 in. thick. Frame will withstand surging of pool water; coping is wide enough to sit on.

Expensive pools have 6-in. uprights and curved coping 8 in. thick. The coping is clad in vinyl to make it less slippery than painted metal. It should withstand years of use.

This 28-ft. round pool collapsed after four years of use when the steel frame and bolts were weakened by rust. More than 16,000 gallons of water escaped in a few minutes.

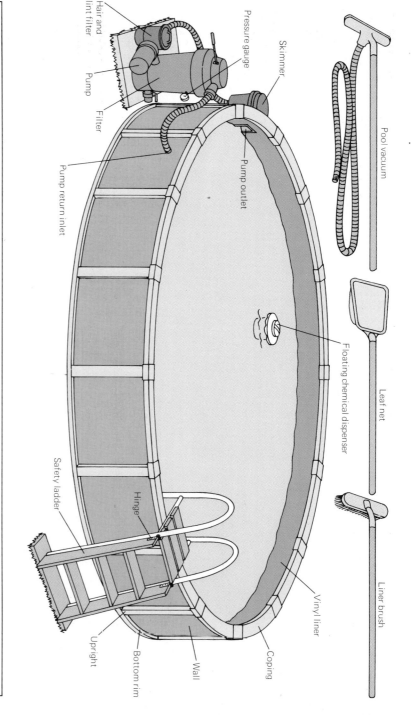

Hair and lint filter

Pump

Filter

Pressure gauge

Skimmer

Pump outlet

Pump return inlet

Pool vacuum

Floating chemical dispenser

Leaf net

Liner brush

Safety ladder

Hinge

Bottom rim

Upright

Wall

Vinyl liner

Coping

Installation pointers

An above-ground pool sold for do-it-yourself installation should come with a set of detailed directions, but many have only sketchy instructions. Follow the directions you have, but keep the points illustrated here in mind. Even if the pool is being installed professionally, make sure the procedures shown here are observed. See that a building permit is obtained, whether it is technically required in your community or not. When a permit is issued, all building and electrical work must be inspected before an occupancy certificate is issued. This may prove to be an inconvenience, but it provides your best guarantee against shoddy construction and dangerous electrical hookups.

1. Pick a site that is clear of overhead wires or branches and fairly level. Use a stake and string to mark out two circles—one the size of the pool, the other 2 ft wider.

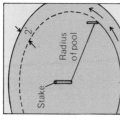

Stake · Radius of pool · 2'

2. Level the area by digging into ground, never by building up with fill. Remove all sod, rocks, sticks, and roots within the area of the larger circle. Tamp earth until it is hard, smooth, and level, then redraw inner circle.

Dig into slope
Check for level with long 2" x 4" and spirit level

3. If you must dig into a slope to level the site, install a retaining wall and curtain drain to prevent rainwater from undermining pool foundation and frame.

Wall · Gravel · Drain pipe

4. Dig a series of shallow holes along the circumference of the inner circle just deep enough to hold a 2-in. patio block. Tamp bottoms of holes firm. Position blocks under and midway between each frame upright.

Patio block · Hole 2" deep

5. Assemble the bottom rim of the pool so that the uprights rest on alternate patio blocks. Drive stakes into the ground to keep the rim from wandering off the circle as you work.

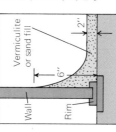

Upright flange · Block · Stake · Rim

6. Recruit several helpers and fit the pool wall into bottom rim. Position wall so that its skimmer and return knockouts are near the proposed pump site, and seam of wall falls along a frame upright.

Joint · Wall · Upright

7. Do not dent or crease wall. Do not try to install wall in a high wind. Touch up all paint chips on wall, then assemble frame uprights. Cover all bolt and screw heads on inside of wall with duct tape to protect liner.

Screw head · Joint · Tape

8. Fill bottom of pool with 2-in. layer of dead sand (sold by pool dealers) or vermiculite (sold at building supply stores). Moisten and tamp fill, then trowel and level it as you would wet concrete when laying a patio floor.

Tamp down 2" layer of sand or vermiculite · Earth

9. Build up fill at pool wall, as shown, so that the weight of the water cannot force liner under bottom rim. If fill level is too low, the liner will stretch and weaken; if fill is too high, the liner will wrinkle.

Vermiculite or sand fill · 2" · 6" · Wall · Rim

10. Remove shoes and install liner. (You will need several helpers.) Center the bottom-sidewall seam exactly in the frame, then spread liner up walls. Adjust liner position to eliminate all wrinkles.

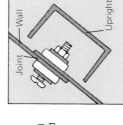

Wall · Liner seam · Distance from seam to wall must be uniform

11. Push home vacuum cleaner hose through skimmer hole and tape in position. Vacuum will hold liner to wall while you eliminate wrinkles. If sun is very hot, spray liner with cool water to keep it from stretching.

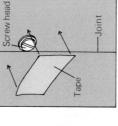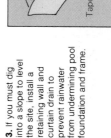

Tape · Home vacuum

12. Put 6 in. of water into pool and measure distance from water's surface to top of wall at several points. If it varies by more than 1 in., drain water and relevel pool structure. When level, install coping, skimmer, filter, and pump.

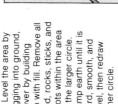

Distance must not vary by more than 1" all around pool · Wall · Water

Electrical grounding

The pool pump, heater, lights, and other electrical equipment must be scrupulously grounded to prevent any possibility of shock. The pump and heater should each be on a separate fused and grounded electrical circuit. Use a ground fault interrupter (GFI) instead of an ordinary outdoor receptacle (see *Electricity in the Home,* p.127). Be sure the pool is at least 10 feet from any electrical outlet. Do not mount electrical cables or outlet boxes on the pool frame. Ground the frame, ladders, slides, and filter housing separately, with grounding rods.

GFI's interrupt the flow of electricity if there is a short circuit that is not massive enough to blow a fuse or trip a circuit breaker. Use GFI's on lines to pump, heater, and lights.

RESET · TEST

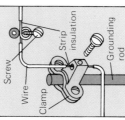

Use three grounding rods, copper or aluminum wire (depending on local codes), and self-tapping sheetmetal screws to ground the pool frame, ladders, slides, and pump housing.

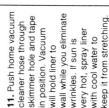

Screw · Wire · Clamp · Strip insulation · Grounding rod

Run grounding wire completely around pool, attaching it to the frame in several places; this will provide a good ground even if the frame corrodes or the wire is broken.

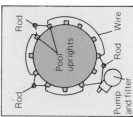

Rod · Pool uprights · Wire · Rod · Pump and filter

Pools and equipment

Pool chemistry

Because it is expensive and impractical to drain and refill a large pool frequently, water purity must be maintained by filtering and chemical treatment. Filtering removes dirt, sand, and other solids that are tracked or blown into the pool. Chemicals (mainly chlorine) kill bacteria, neutralize unfilterable wastes, and impede the growth of algae.

For chemical treatment to be effective, the pool water must have the proper mineral balance, which is measured on a pH scale of 0 to 14. A slightly alkaline pH of 7.4 to 7.6 is best for pool water. Water below 7.0 pH is acidic—it may stain the pool liner, cause eye irritation, and speed the corrosion of pool hardware, pumps, ladders, or piping. Water above 8.0 pH is too alkaline—it will hamper the disinfectant action of the chlorine and cause scale buildup on pump impellers, piping, and heater coils. Chemicals are available to raise or lower pool pH levels. Use them according to their directions.

When the pool is filled for the first time, take a sample of the water to a pool dealer for analysis. He will tell you what treatment is required. This may keep you from overtreating or undertreating the water. Have the water analyzed again at the start of each new swimming season, or when unusual problems occur. Collect the sample in a clean quart jar from about 18 inches (arm's length) below the surface. Bring the dealer a sample of your tap water as well. A conscientious dealer will keep a record of your pool chemistry from season to season and, through comparison, foresee problems that may arise in the future and tell you how to avoid them.

Before the pool is used for the first time, the water should be stabilized by adding a stabilizing compound to the skimmer. Keep the pump in use for 24 hours after stabilizing the water. Do not swim in the pool or backflush the filter during this time.

Chlorine disinfectant is available in powder and solid forms. Stabilized organic chlorine in solid pellets is the most effective type. It is fed into the water continuously at a fixed rate from a dispenser that floats in the pool or hangs inside the skimmer. Powdered chlorine must be added daily by hand.

Chlorine should be added continuously, even if you are away from home, because it is dissipated by heat and sun, diluted by rain, and exhausted in fighting the bacteria that are constantly introduced into the pool. A chlorine level of one part per million (1 ppm) is best. More than 2 ppm will irritate eyes and skin; less than 0.5 ppm will not disinfect.

Reagent kits are sold for testing the pH balance and chlorine level of your pool. Test the water daily for the first two weeks of pool use, then twice a week for the rest of the season.

Perspiration, urine, saliva, suntan lotions, and cosmetics cannot be removed by the filter. They will accumulate and cause the water to become murky. An oxidizing agent, used about every two weeks, will neutralize these organic wastes. Nearly fill a clean plastic bucket with water, then mix in either a commercial oxidizing agent or 5 to 10 times the normal daily dose of powdered chlorine. Pour the mixture into the deep end of the pool. Do this in the evening, operate the pump overnight, and keep out of the pool for 12 hours. This treatment is sometimes called superchlorination.

Algae (tiny one-celled plants) are hard to kill once they begin to multiply. Add an algae inhibitor to the pool every two weeks, preferably in the morning, after the oxidizing treatment. You may swim immediately after this treatment.

Caution: Do not mix concentrated oxidizing agents and algae inhibitors. An explosion may occur. Use them at least 12 hours apart, and run the pump to disperse them thoroughly.

Using the test kit

Several brands of chlorine and pH test kits are sold by pool dealers. Buy one that is easy to read accurately. Fill the test tube to the line with pool water obtained at least 18 inches below the surface and away from the pump inlets. Do not test water immediately after adding chemi-

cals to the pool; let the pump run for at least six hours before testing. Buy fresh test reagents at the start of each swimming season; discard phenol red reagent if it develops an orange cast. Discard pool water samples after testing; do not pour them back into the pool.

1. Rinse test tube in pool, then fill to line. Add specified amount of reagent. Hold bottle vertically and squeeze slowly to obtain drops of the correct size.

2. Cap tube, shake. Do not cover tube with your finger; skin oils will affect readings. Match test colors to shade of sample to determine pH or chlorine level.

How to correct undesirable water conditions *

Problem	Action
Water stings eyes	Test pH level. If low, sow soda ash granules into pool with pump running. Do not use high pH laundry bleach or inorganic chlorine granules in pool; use only stabilized, organic chlorine products
Pool liner stained	
Aluminum pool parts corrode	
Scale formations on heater coils, pipes, pool parts	Test pH level. If high, add 1 pint of muriatic acid or sodium bisulfate to a bucket of water; add to pool with pump running, allow to circulate overnight. Test pH next day. Add more muriatic acid or sodium bisulfate if needed, but no more than 1 pint per day
Pool liner bleached	
Rapid filter clogging	
Heavy chlorine demand	
Cloudy water	
Cloudy water	When caused by abnormal amounts of wind-blown dirt and other nonfilterable wastes, add oxidizing agent or 5–10 times normal daily chlorine dose to bucket of water; pour into deep end of pool; run pump for 12 hours
	For red-brown iron oxide buildup, follow procedure given above but run pump for 48 hours; then, vacuum up particles that have settled on bottom
	When accompanied by a green algae scum, follow procedure above, but sow chemicals directly over algae deposits. Vacuum up dead algae after 12 hours
	When accompanied by black or blue-green algae deposits, brush algae buds vigorously. Stop pump. After 4 hours, sow algecide granules over algae deposits. After 12 hours, start pump, brush and vacuum algae
	If none of the above apply, bring a sample of pool water to a dealer with a testing lab. Follow dealer's instructions. If too much stabilizer has been added, partially drain pool and dilute with tap water

*Do not backflush filter or swim in pool during treatment period. If repeated treatment does not solve the problem, consult a professional pool maintenance service or a pool dealer with a testing laboratory

Periodic cleaning

1. Use leaf net to remove debris not trapped by skimmer. Catch debris before it sinks to the bottom.

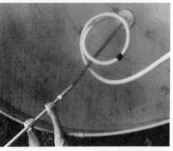

2. Brush down liner or tiles with a stiff bristled brush and tile soap. Brush fits leaf net pole.

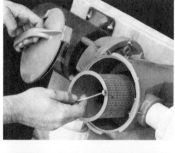

3. Remove catch basket from skimmer; discard leaves and debris. Hose off basket and reinstall it.

4. Turn off pump, remove hair and lint filter basket from pump housing. Clean basket, then reinstall it.

5. Fill pool vacuum hose with water by holding it to return inlet. Assemble vacuum. Clean pool bottom.

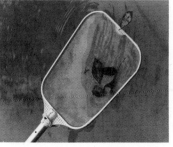

6. If pool wall or frame is steel, check for paint chips and rust. Repair as you would a car (p.319).

Preparing the pool for winter

In parts of the country where it is not warm enough to swim the year around, a pool must be especially prepared for any long period of inactivity. Pool dealers refer to this preparation as winterizing. The water must be chemically treated with a winterizing kit, the filter must be backflushed (p.460) and stored indoors, and the pool must be covered to keep out leaves, dirt, and unauthorized swimmers.

Freezing water is not a problem; the ice expands upward and exerts little extra pressure on the sides of the pool. But if the pool has a leak, the constantly collapsing ice may cut the vinyl liner. Water that has leaked under the pool bottom may cause frost heaves that will stretch the liner, ruin the sand filler, and weaken the pool. Check carefully for leaks before winterizing the pool (see *How to patch a pool liner,* p.461).

Buy a pool cover that can be locked in place. A woven mesh cover will keep out leaves, snow, and most dirt, but allow water to pass through. Excess water will flow out through the skimmer. Solid covers are more expensive but not as strong as mesh covers, and water accumulation can be a problem.

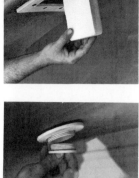

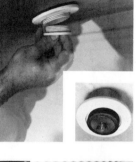

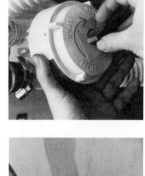

1. Buy a chemical winterizing kit of the proper size for your pool (ask dealer). Add chemicals according to directions. Some will dissolve in float for months.

2. Clean pool thoroughly (see above), then flush or drain filter (see p.460). Turn valve to *Waste* setting until water level drops just below the skimmer.

3. Block the pump return inlet with a screw-in plastic cap or an expandable rubber stopper. Both are sold by pool dealers and manufacturers.

4. Put a chunk of styrofoam into the skimmer to absorb pressure and prevent ice damage in case the skimmer should clog and fill with overflow water.

5. Disconnect electrical lines and hoses; clean and drain the filter thoroughly. Store filter and pump in a warm, dry, well-ventilated room.

6. Inflate vinyl pillow and check it for leaks. Patch leaks as you would a pool liner (p.461). Center pillow in pool and secure with slightly slack ropes.

7. Use net to remove any additional leaves that may have fallen into the water up to this point, then position cover over inflated pillow and pool.

8. Thread cable under cover between closely spaced grommets and over cover between widely spaced grommets; secure with turnbuckle.

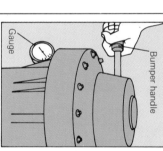

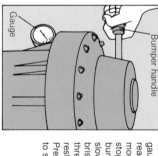

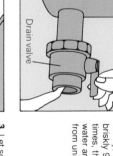

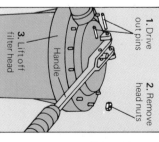

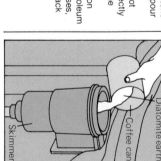

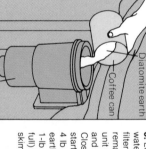

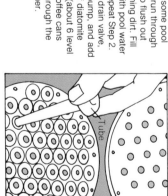

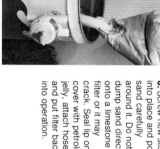

Sand filter service

A sand filter traps dirt and some other impurities by passing the pool water through a foot or more of special fine filter sand, then through a limestone filtering element. When the filter becomes saturated with dirt, water flow will be restricted and back pressure will rise above the normal level—usually 15 called diatomite earth as a filtering medium. The flow of water through the filter deposits this earth evenly over a number of mesh tubes. When the tubes become clogged with dirt, simply turn off the pump and bump the tubes up and down pounds per square inch (psi). This may happen immediately after vacuuming the pool (the vacuum hose is attached directly to the skimmer or pump inlet) or after treating it to eliminate algae. The filter must then be backflushed.

1. Check pressure gauge every day and shortly after you vacuum or add chemicals to pool. When the pressure exceeds the level recommended by the filter manufacturer (in this case 15 psi), shut off pump motor.

2. Adjust the directional valve to the *Backflush* or *Backwash* setting and turn on the pump. This reverses the normal flow of water through the filter. Shut off pump when water leaving waste hose turns clear.

3. Check the sand inside the drum occasionally. If the top levels contain embedded debris that cannot be flushed out, remove the dirty sand. Dry it and sift out debris, or replace it with new sand. Remove all sand before moving filter indoors for winter storage.

4. If sand and dirt are being pumped into the pool at the return inlet, the filter stone is cracked. Remove sand and unscrew the filter stone. Replace it with a new one from a pool dealer.

5. There are two kinds of filter stones. Genuine limestone (left) can be cracked in transit or during installation. New plastic "stones" (right) are less fragile. Both keep sand from being pumped into pool.

6. Screw new stone into place and pour sand carefully around it. Do not dump sand directly onto a limestone filter or it may crack. Seal lip on cover with petroleum jelly, attach hoses, and put filter back into operation.

Diatomite earth filter service

This type of filter uses a fine powder called diatomite earth as a filtering medium. The flow of water through the filter deposits this earth evenly over a number of mesh tubes. When the tubes become clogged with dirt, simply turn off the pump and bump the tubes up and down to dislodge and redistribute both the dirt and the diatomite earth. There is no need to backflush the unit. After several clogging and bumping cycles, the filter will reach a saturation point; it must then be drained, and the diatomite earth replaced with a new supply.

1. When the pressure gauge on the filter reads 7 to 10 psi more than normal, stop pump. Move bump handle down slowly, then up briskly. Repeat three times, then restart pump. Pressure should drop to start-up level.

Gauge

Bumper handle

2. If pressure rises 10 psi within 24 hours of the last bumping operation, stop the pump. Move bump handle down slowly, then up briskly 9 or 10 times, then drain water and earth from unit.

Drain valve

3. Let some pool water run through filter to flush out remaining dirt. Fill unit with pool water and repeat Step 2. Close drain valve, start pump, and add 4 lb of diatomite earth (about 6 level 1-lb coffee cans full) through the skimmer.

Skimmer
Diatomite earth
Coffee can

4. If dirt and diatomite earth are being pumped into the pool at the return inlet, the diaphragm gasket or one or more mesh tubes are leaking. Stop pump. Drain all valves. Remove filter head and bump handle.

1. Drive out pins
2. Remove head nuts
3. Lift off filter head
Handle

5. Separate tube retaining plates and check diaphragm gasket for wear, rips, or holes. Replace the gasket if it is defective. Look down each mesh tube. If the inside is dirty, the tube is leaking.

1. Remove bolts
2. Pry off C-clip
3. Lift plate
4. Check gasket
5. Check tubes for dirt

6. Pull out and replace leaking mesh tubes. If no tubes are leaking and the gasket is sound, the retaining plates were not tight. Coat bump shaft with petroleum jelly, align all tube holes, and reassemble filter. Tighten all bolts securely.

Tube

How to patch a pool liner

A leak in a pool liner must be stopped immediately or it will get much worse. Sand will be washed out from around the leak and the liner pushed into the gulley, which will further stretch and weaken the liner. If the liner then tears, vast amounts of sand will suddenly be washed away, possibly weakening the pool framework to the point of collapse. If such a leak develops, get out of the pool quickly and evacuate the area.

To help prevent leaks, observe these simple rules: Use only plastic plates, cups, and utensils in and around the pool; forbid children to play with sharp toys or BB guns in the vicinity of the pool; and see that swimmers' toenails are trimmed to a reasonable length. Keep a pool patch kit and extra patching material handy. Even when it is too cold to use cement (below 45°F), water pressure will usually hold a temporary patch in place.

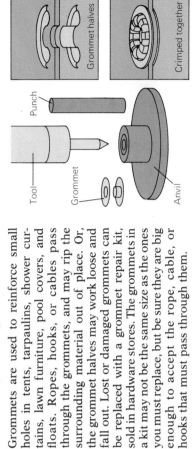

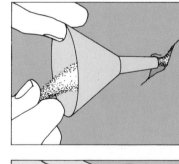

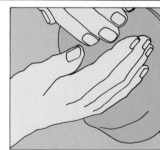

1. Wear goggles to look for leak. Washed-out sand may wrinkle or depress liner. Dirt released at pool bottom will be drawn to a leak.

2. Place a piece of patch material, inner tube, or heavy plastic over the leak immediately. Water pressure will hold it in place.

3. If escaping water has created a deep gulley, drain the pool, raise the liner, and pour dry sand through a funnel to fill the void.

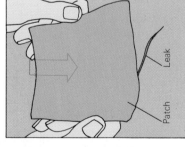

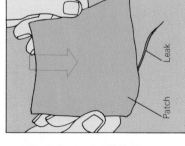

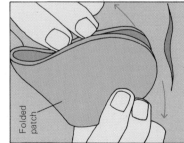

4. Cut a patch from material supplied in kit, and coat with cement. Patch should be circular and twice the size of the tear.

5. Spread cement over entire surface of patch. If tear is under water, fold the patch in half to keep the patch as dry as possible.

6. Working quickly, remove temporary patch. Open adhesive-coated patch immediately and apply. Smooth out any air bubbles.

How to replace a grommet

Grommets are used to reinforce small holes in tents, tarpaulins, shower curtains, lawn furniture, pool covers, and floats. Ropes, hooks, or cables pass through the grommets, and may rip the surrounding material out of place. Or, the grommet halves may work loose and fall out. Lost or damaged grommets can be replaced with a grommet repair kit, sold in hardware stores. The grommets in a kit may not be the same size as the ones you must replace, but be sure they are big enough to accept the rope, cable, or hooks that must pass through them.

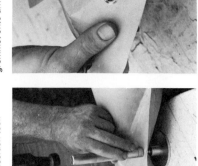

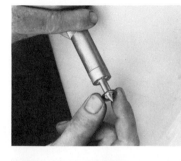

1. Cut a hole into an undamaged portion of material, using punch.

2. Place top (plain) half of grommet over point on insertion tool.

3. Place lower (flanged) half of grommet onto anvil, with flange up.

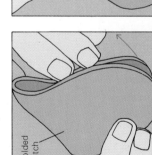

4. Place point of tool through material and into hole in anvil.

5. Hammer sharply on tool to join grommet halves.

6. Hammer until halves are crimped firmly together, with no play.

461

Rackets

Mending techniques

Although a total restringing job is better left to your sports or pro shop, you can easily mend a broken string on a tennis, squash, or badminton racket, using a few simple tools. An old broomstick handle or a thick piece of wooden doweling can be fitted with wood screws and employed as a stretcher. Knitting needles can act as wedges to maintain string tension; the needles must be narrow enough to fit snugly into the frame holes.

New string should match the old in strength and gauge. Replace gut with gut and nylon with nylon. New string should be strung as tightly as possible, but the tension need not be exactly the same as that of the old string.

Before restringing, wrap a thick cloth around the racket shaft to buffer it, then lock the shaft firmly in a vise, as nearly vertical as possible. After you have finished, snip off any loose string ends with a pair of small scissors, or carefully saw them off with a razor blade.

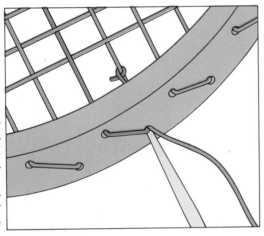

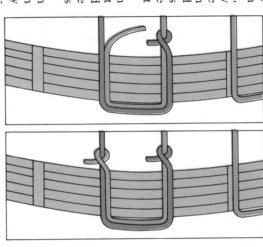

You can improvise a tool to help you stretch string to proper tautness. Simply fasten a pair of screws to a wooden shaft, such as a broomstick. To use tool, wind string around shaft and screws, then turn shaft.

Knitting needles are wedged into frame holes to maintain string tension while tying off the ends of the string. Insert the needle while string is stretched tight, and only then remove the stretching tool.

New string is locked into racket by tying it to the old string. First, end of new string is looped around old string (left). Later, old string is looped around new (right). Pull knots snugly against frame.

Restringing a racket

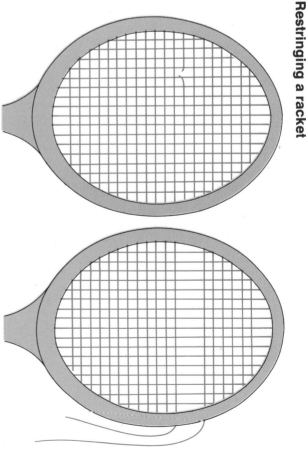

1. At left, a string is shown broken at a typical location in racket. To provide ample lengths to work with (considerable string is needed for the stretching operation), partly unstring the racket, as shown at right.

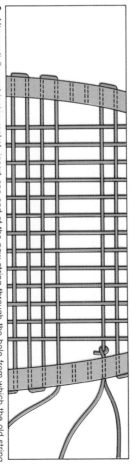

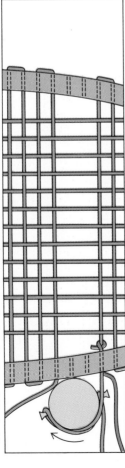

2. After partially unstringing racket, insert one end of the new string through the hole from which the old string emerges at top. Loop it about the old string on the inside of the frame.

3. Pull the loop made in Step 2 snugly into inner frame hole, then wrap the old string onto the stretching tool (see illustration at far left). Since string is slippery, you will get a better grip if you wear gloves.

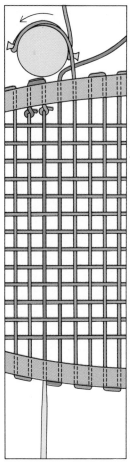

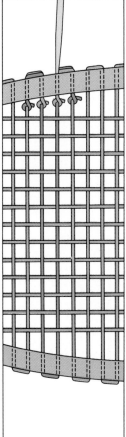

4. Turn the stretching tool to tighten the old string. This will also pull the loop made in Step 2 more snugly into the hole. Keep the string taut and insert a knitting needle into the outer hole to maintain tension.

8. Take the bottom free end of the old string and wrap it about the stretching tool. Tighten this length of old string by turning the stretching tool.

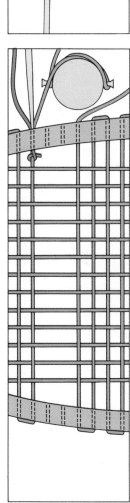

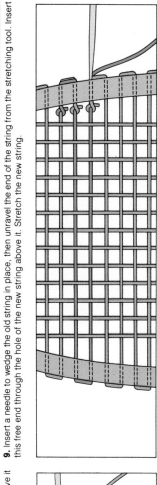

5. Unravel old string from stretching tool. Insert end of new string through hole immediately beneath it and weave it across racket, over and under vertical segments of old string, and out left side.

9. Insert a needle to wedge the old string in place, then unravel the end of the string from the stretching tool. Insert this free end through the hole of the new string above it. Stretch the new string.

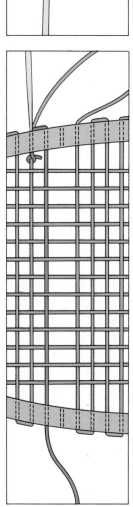

6. Wrap the free end of the new string about the stretching tool and tighten it as done previously on the right side. Insert a knitting needle to maintain tension on the new string.

10. Insert a needle to maintain tension on the new string. Loop the old string about the new and pull the loop tight. Then, remove both the needle at left and the needle maintaining tension on the old string at right.

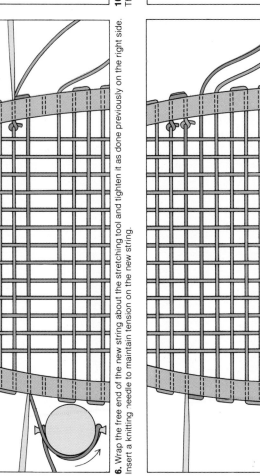

7. On right side, loop loose end of old string over new string. Remove the needle. On left side, pass the loose end of the new string through next hole down. Weave it across the racket and out through hole on right.

11. Feed the free end of the new string through the hole of the old string beneath it. Loop it about the old string and pull the loop snugly into the hole, or push it in with a needle. Remove the remaining needle.

463

Filling downhill (fiberglass) skis

With frequent use skis develop railed edges, dull edges, and worn bottoms. Even new skis may not have the running surface you prefer. Many authorities on skiing believe that perfectly flat bottoms with squared edges are more responsive and easier for the average recreational skier to control. Others argue that a slightly concave running surface tracks better and holds on ice better than a flat surface. Downhill racers may desire slightly rounded, or convex, bottoms.

You can maintain the running surface you prefer by regularly filing your own skis. You will need a flat bastard file and a mill bastard file, each preferably 12 inches long; a woodworker's cabinet scraper, to act as a straightedge and for removing wax; and a carding tool, for cleaning the files. The flat bastard file is coarser; use it first. Wear protective gloves and back one file with the other to keep the cutting file stiff. Fix gouges (see *Filling gouges*, at right) in the skis before filing.

Concave

Convex

Railed edges

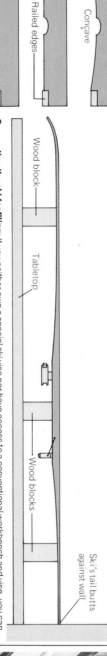

Wood block — Tabletop — Wood blocks

Ski's tail butts against wall

Supporting the ski for filing: If you neither own a special ski vise nor have access to a conventional workbench and vise, you can improvise supports. In this setup, the ski rests on three wood blocks placed on top of a table, with the tail of the ski butted against a wall. Should you employ clamps or vises, buffer the points of contact with the skis.

Hold two files (one as a brace behind the other) flat on ski, angled as shown. Push with long strokes in one direction only, keeping pressure even.

As file fills up with material, clean it on carding tool, running bristles in the direction of the file's ridges. At same time wipe filings from ski.

To make a final check for flatness, use the scraper as a straightedge. Hold it as shown and move it in one direction along the full length of the ski.

To sharpen edges, clamp ski in a vise. Hold the mill bastard file at a 90° angle to the edge, and file with a few light strokes. Do not oversharpen.

Filling gouges

When snow cover is sparse, the plastic base of your skis may suffer scratches and gouges that impair the maneuverability of the skis. A deep gouge that goes into the ski's core should be patched by a ski repair shop, but a gouge in the plastic base is easily filled using a polyethylene candle and a soldering iron or torch.

Clamp ski in vise, buffering the ski's edges with wood or cardboard; if you have no vise, make supports as shown at left. Clean wax and dirt from gouge with a knife or screwdriver. Heat the ski bottom around the gouge with a soft torch flame or by holding a soldering iron close to the area.

When plastic around gouge is soft, hold polyethylene candle close to gouge in the heat of the torch or soldering iron. Fill the gouge with candle drippings while keeping the whole area warm. Slightly overfill the gouge. Let material cool and harden. File the area flush with bottom.

Preparing wooden cross-country skis for storage

While fiberglass cross-country skis with a polyethylene base are repaired like downhill skis, wooden cross-country skis call for different treatment—filling the gouges with epoxy adhesive or plastic wood (see *Filling gouges*, at right).

Wooden skis lose their camber over a period of several years. They will last longer if, before they are stored for the summer, they are coated with pine tar and paraffin to keep out moisture. Store them horizontally, on edge, on a rack.

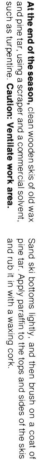

At the end of the season, clean wooden skis of old wax and pine tar, using a scraper and a commercial solvent, such as turpentine. **Caution: Ventilate work area.**

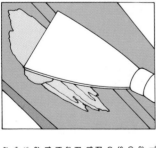

Sand ski bottoms lightly, and then brush on a coat of pine tar. Apply paraffin to the tops and sides of the skis and rub it in with a waxing cork.

To fill a gouge in a wooden (cross-country) ski, mix a small batch of epoxy compound or use plastic wood. Apply the filler with a putty knife. After allowing 12 to 24 hours for the filler to harden, smooth area with fine sandpaper and steel wool. Restore base and running wax.

Tents, backpacks, and sleeping bags

Materials and techniques

Camping equipment is generally sturdy and should last many years with proper care. Barring misadventure or carelessness that results in tears in the fabric, tents, backpacks, and sleeping bags are likely to need repairs only to those parts that take the most stress and wear: zippers, grommets, tent peg loops, lines, and seams.

Frequently the weak point gives out while you are using the equipment on a trip, so it is wise to carry a small kit for field repairs. Include nylon cord, adhesive-backed nylon ripstop tape, split rings (p.467), some device to use as a temporary substitute in case a peg loop or grommet tears out (p.466), a melt-and-patch stick of rubber glue, and duct tape with a dull finish. These materials are available at most camping supply, hardware, and army and navy stores.

You can make permanent repairs at home. For strengthening stress points, and replacing straps and peg loops, use

Repairs to tent pole cords, grommets, peg loops, strap ends, and zippers are illustrated on pp. 466-467

nylon webbing; it is available in widths of 3/4, 1, or 2 inches. Nylon tape is thinner than nylon webbing and not as strong, but it is easier to use as a peg loop or grommet tears out. Nylon tends to ravel when it is cut. To prevent raveling, either heat-seal the webbing or tape by passing a match flame along its cut edges or make the cuts with the hot point of a wood-burning tool.

For sewing repairs, use a thread with a polyester core and an outer wrapping of cotton. It is stronger and stretches less than nylon. If your sewing machine can handle heavy fabrics and the job is manageable on a machine, you may find it more convenient to use the machine than sew by hand. However, most work will require hand-stitching. Use a needle no heavier than necessary to go through the fabric—the needle opens up holes that will let water through. For very thick fabrics, use an upholsterer's needle or a sewing awl.

Sealing the stitching. In all cases, after sewing anything into a pack or tent, apply seam sealant over both sides of the stitching to prevent leaks. Rewaterproof cotton tents only. If you waterproof nylon, condensation is likely to occur inside the tent; moreover, nylon does not retain waterproofing well. Most nylon tents come with a rain fly of coated nylon with which to cover the tent in wet weather.

Patching fabrics. Use a patch similar in type and weight to the fabric being repaired. For a cotton tent, use waterproofed cotton duck or canvas; for a nylon tent or sleeping bag, use adhesive-backed ripstop tape. (Ripstop tape has an extra heavy thread woven in at equal intervals in both directions to prevent tearing.) You can mend small tears in backpacks with ripstop tape, but for a large area make a more durable patch of coated nylon duck or pack cloth. To make a field repair with ripstop tape permanent, simply stitch around the edges of the tape.

Patch a cotton tent on the inside of the tent with a piece of fabric larger by several inches than the hole or tear. Turn the edges of the patch under ¼ inch and hemstitch around the outside of the patch and the edges of the hole or tear. For a tear near a seam, where there is extra strain on the fabric, put a smaller patch directly over the tear and stitch around its edges before placing a larger patch on the inside of the tent.

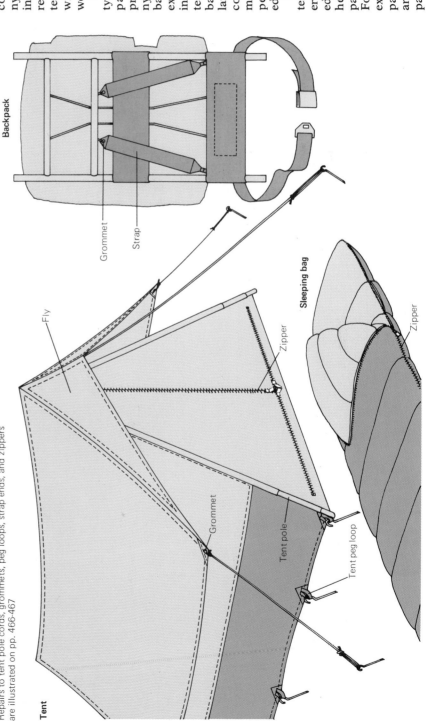

Backpack

Grommet

Strap

Fly

Zipper

Sleeping bag

Zipper

Grommet

Tent pole

Tent peg loop

Tent

Tents, backpacks, and sleeping bags

Repairing peg loops

Frequent usage wears out the peg loops around the bottom of a tent, especially in a cotton tent where contact with the damp ground encourages fabrics to rot. Loops may also pull out of their seams. To make new loops for a large cotton tent, use nylon webbing. For the lighter weight backpacking tent, use nylon tape.

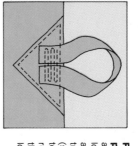
Grommet
Tent pole

Reinforcement patches: When you are replacing a peg loop at the side of a tent, first sew a triangular patch (see above) to reinforce the area; then, stitch the new loop in place.

Setting grommets in loops: Grommets can be set in loops and used to hook over tent poles. One layer of webbing is strong enough to hold a grommet positioned as shown.

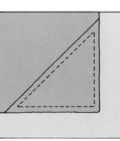

If the tent floor is torn or weakened at a corner, make a triangular patch; stitch the patch in place on the underside of the tent floor.

Reinforcement patches. Reinforce the area in the tent floor where a corner peg loop is to be sewn if the fabric is torn or weakened. Always reinforce the fabric when replacing a side loop; the patch will help to spread the stress.

Make reinforcement patches from fabric of a weight close to that of the fabric of the tent. When reinforcing a tent floor with a waterproof coating, make the reinforcement of coated fabric. Cut a square of fabric, turn under the edges ¼ inch, and fold the patch into a triangle. Iron it flat before sewing it into place. Finally, apply seam sealant over all stitching on both sides of the fabric.

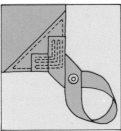
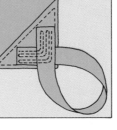

Nylon tape, as opposed to webbing, should be doubled to create a strong enough base in which to set the grommet. Form the loop first, then set the grommet, as shown, before sewing tape to tent.

Cross the ends of the nylon tape or webbing; then, sew the loop to the reinforced underside of the tent floor with several even rows of stitches.

Corner peg loops: Cross the ends of the nylon tape or webbing; then, sew the loop to the tent fabric. Give the disc and fabric a couple of twists and then slide the arms of the U-shaped clamp around the fabric directly underneath the disc. Snap the ends of the U together, one inside the other, so that the two holes are perfectly aligned. Run a length of cord through the holes and tie the ends to form a loop. Use this loop to hold the tent peg until you can make a repair.

If you do not have a gadget like this, you can improvise by using a small, smooth stone and cord.

After setting the grommet in the tape, cross the loop's loose ends; sew the loop's doubled ends to the tent corner as shown. Both the grommet and the stitches pass through a double layer of tape.

Field replacement for a peg loop

If a peg loop breaks so that your tent cannot be properly staked down, you may spend an uncomfortable night if it is windy. Camping supply stores sell field repair kits, containing devices like this two-part snap-on loop.

Break the two lightweight plastic pieces apart. Insert the disc into the tent fabric from inside the tent, and gather the fabric tightly around the disc.

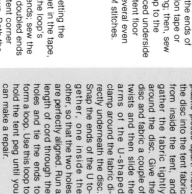

Replacing the shock cord in a lightweight tent pole

Collapsible lightweight tent poles come in three sections, which are often strung together with an elastic shock cord. The cord is always under tension. It runs through the center section of the pole and is attached at each end to one of the other two pole sections. The cord holders are threaded and screwed into the ends of the first and third pole sections. Metal crimp-on stops prevent the cord from slipping through the cord holder. Remove these stops from the old shock cord and use them on the replacement cord. To span a 20-inch pole section, you should use about 14 inches of shock cord.

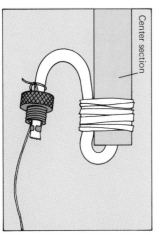
Cord holder
First section
Center section
Cord holder
Stop
String

1. Attach the cord holders to the ends of the shock cord, using the metal stops. Screw one holder into a section of pole. Tie a piece of string tightly to the other end of the cord above the holder and run it through the holder. Feed string through center pole section.

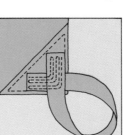
Center section

2. Pull the string to stretch the shock cord until the cord holder and 3 inches of cord emerge from the end of the center section. Double the shock cord back against the center section, and wrap a heavy-duty rubber band around both cord and pole section.

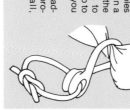
Center section
Third section

3. Remove the string from the end of the shock cord. Screw the cord holder firmly into the third section of pole. The last two sections will spring together to form a single interlocked piece when you release the rubber band holding the shock cord to the center section.

Replacing zippers

Generally, a zipper used in camping equipment is either a flat zipper made of Delrin plastic or a coil-type, or self-mending, zipper. The conventional toothed metal zipper is less than ideal for camping equipment, as it is difficult to zip in cold weather and can even freeze if it gets wet. A coil zipper has one enormous advantage: If it pulls apart it may be rezipped simply by running the slider down and then back up. But it also has certain disadvantages: If flattened, the coils do not resume their shape, and since they are attached to the tape by delicate stitching, they pull out easily; in either case, the zipper must be replaced. Flat zippers of Delrin plastic are relatively trouble free.

If the slider on a zipper breaks, you can replace the slider (see below) and avoid installing a new zipper. Sometimes only the pull tab on the slider will break. If the zipper is a metal one, replace the tab with a split ring, available from camping supply stores, and tie a piece of twine through the ring to make a pull cord.

If camping supply stores do not have zippers in the length you need, you can buy zippers by the yard from a sewing center, and cut strips to the desired length. For backpacks and lightweight tents, a No. 5 zipper is the right size; sleeping bags and cotton tents require a No. 10. Be sure to buy a slider of the correct size for the zipper: single-pull for zipping from one side only, double-pull for zipping from both sides. Make stops as shown below before sewing.

Before replacing a zipper on a down jacket or sleeping bag, slightly open the seam that holds the zipper to see if it the down pops out. If it does, staple or pin the fabric behind the seam. Then, remove and replace the zipper.

Replacing grommets

A number of devices are available for setting grommets, but the tool shown below most closely resembles the one used by professional repairmen. Grommets for outdoor equipment come in sizes 0 to 4, and you need a separate tool for each size grommet. Size 0 is the one usually used in backpacks; tent or fly grommets may be larger—up to 3 or 4. Be sure the new grommet is the same size as the old one if a clevis pin or tent pole must fit through it.

The typical grommet kit includes a supply of flat washer-type grommets. You may prefer to buy spur grommets, which have a row of small teeth that hold the grommet securely in the fabric.

If a grommet tears loose, it is likely that the fabric will need reinforcing before the new grommet is set. Reinforce the fabric with nylon webbing cut to size and heat-sealed at the cut ends.

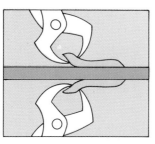

If the old grommet is still in place, use pliers to bend its edges outward on either side of fabric. Grip the bent edges with two pairs of pliers and pull the grommet apart.

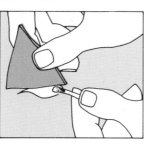

Before inserting a new grommet, reinforce the strap with a piece of 2-in. x 3-in. nylon webbing. Cut the webbing to fit the end of the strap. Heat-seal the cut edges of the webbing with the flame of a match.

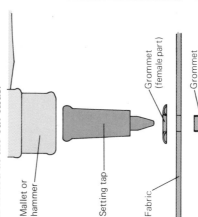

Open up the seams at the end of the strap with a knife or seam-ripping tool. Slide the webbing up inside, fitting the shaped end into place. Resew the seams exactly as they were.

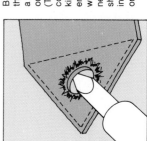

Burn a hole through the webbing with a soldering iron or woodburning tool. (The cutter that comes in grommet kit is not sharp enough to cut heavy webbing.) Set the new grommet as shown at left and, in greater detail, on p.461.

Mallet or hammer

Setting tap

Grommet (female part)

Grommet (male part)

Fabric

Base

Insert male part of grommet through hole in fabric, and place on top of metal base. Fit female, or washerlike, part of grommet on top, rounded side up. Insert point of setting tap into hole, and strike it with a mallet—lightly at first and then with harder blows. Turn tap between blows until grommet parts fit tightly together.

Flat, Delrin plastic zippers: Nip off a few teeth at top, where tape will be sewn in. At top and bottom, form stops: Melt two bits of plastic with a soldering iron or woodburning tool. Fuse them to the teeth to form the stop. For stops on metal zippers, see p.23.

Slider: To replace the slider, remove the stops at the top of the zipper and take off the old slider. After tracking new slider, remake the stops as above. For metal zippers, see p.23.

Tab: On metal zippers, replace a broken tab with a split key ring or a small key ring. Slip the ring through the hole in the slider, then tie cord to it to act as pull

Stops

Stop

Consumer information

Going metric

In December 1975 the President of the United States signed into law a bill that to use a 1-inch bolt and simply give it the name of its converted metric equivalent, 25.4 millimeters. There is no such metric bolt size. Thus, the presently established sizes for hardware, pipe fittings, tools, and so forth will eventually cease to be manufactured; they will be replaced by totally new sizes that will rarely if ever match the old ones.

The home handyman, similarly, will have problems of his own when he discovers that many of his tools, calibrated to the old measures, will be virtually useless for working with metrically calibrated nuts and bolts. No wrench in the English system precisely fits any nut of the metric system, though wrenches made to fit nuts measuring 15/64, 5/16, 15/32, and 5/8 inch come tolerably close to fitting nuts measuring 6, 8, 12, and 16 millimeters respectively. Even with these near-equivalents, however, it is not advisable to attempt to use a wrench calibrated in fractions of an inch on nuts measured in millimeters, for either the wrench or the nut is likely to be damaged in the effort. Slip-in sleeves may now be purchased to convert U.S. wrenches to metric measures. Perhaps the best solution is to purchase two sets of wrenches for use during the changeover period.

Tables to help you convert from one system to the other appear at right. The linear conversion table gives you already worked-out conversions for some linear measurements, including commonly employed fractions of an inch and units such as 1 inch, 1 foot, and 1 yard, 1 millimeter, 1 centimeter, and 1 meter. To use this chart, simply read the appropriate figures from the appropriate columns. Formulas for converting from degrees Celsius (centigrade) to degrees Fahrenheit and vice versa are given below this table. The tables to the far right give factors for converting from one standard unit to another.

put the nation firmly on the road toward adopting the International System of Units, or as it is more commonly known, the metric system of weights and measures. The 1975 legislation does not require nationwide use of the metric system by any particular date. But it established a coordinating committee to oversee progress in changing from pounds, ounces, inches, feet, yards, and miles to grams, kilograms, centimeters, meters and kilometers.

The United States is the only large industrial nation that still uses the old, awkward and basically illogical English system of weights and measures. Indeed, one of the major reasons for adopting the metric system is to facilitate America's international trade, which has suffered because U.S. products bear quantity designations that are confusing or meaningless to most of the rest of the world.

In the years ahead, this is all likely to change. In the long run, the changeover should be an asset to Americans, precisely because the metric system is logical, with every unit of measurement divisible by 10 or multiples of 10. In metric weights, for example, 1 kilogram contains 1,000 grams, or 100 dekagrams, or 10 hectograms. Similarly, in linear measure, 1 kilometer contains 10 hectometers, 100 dekameters, 1,000 meters, 10,000 decimeters, 100,000 centimeters, and 1,000,000 millimeters. Compare this with our measures of 12 inches to 1 foot, 3 feet to 1 yard, and 1,760 yards to 1 mile. In the short run, however, the change-over may cause widespread confusion as Americans slowly adjust to thinking in kilograms, liters, and kilometers. Even more important is the fact that manufacturers will have to retool, at no small expense, to adjust their products to the new system. It will not simply be a matter of calling an old size by a new name. For

instance, manufacturers will not be able

Linear conversion table

	Inches (in.)	Feet (ft)	Yards (yd)	*Millimeters (mm)	*Centimeters (cm)	*Meters (m)
	1/64			0.40	0.04	
	1/32			0.79	0.08	
	1/25			**1**		
	1/16			1.59	0.16	
	1/8			3.18	0.32	
	1/4			6.35	0.64	
	3/8			9.53	0.95	
	2/5			**10**	**1**	
	1/2			12.7	1.27	
	5/8			15.9	1.59	
	3/4			19.1	1.91	
	7/8			22.2	2.22	
	1			**25.4**	**2.54**	
	2			50.8	5.08	
	3			76.2	7.62	
	4			101.6	10.16	
	5			127	12.7	
	6			152	15.2	
	7			178	17.8	
	8			203	20.3	
	9			229	22.9	
	10			254	25.4	
	11			279	27.9	
	12	**1**		**305**	**30.5**	**0.30**
	36	3	**1**	914	91.4	0.91
	39.4	**3-1/4****	**1-1/12****	**1,000**	**100**	**1.00**

* Metric values are rounded off; ** approximate fractions

Note: To find the metric equivalent of quantities not in this table, add the appropriate entries. For example, to convert 2% inches to millimeters, add the figure given in the table for the millimeter equivalent of 2 inches, 50.8, and the millimeter equivalent of ⅝ inch, 15.9, to obtain 66.7 millimeters.

To change degrees Fahrenheit to degrees Celsius, or centigrade, subtract 32°, then multiply by 5/9. For example: 68°F − 32° = 36°; 36° × 5/9 = 20°C

To change degrees Celsius to degrees Fahrenheit, multiply by 9/5, then add 32°. For example: 20°C × 9/5 = 36°; 36° + 32° = 68°F.

Conversion factors

To change:	Into:	Multiply by:
English system to metric system		
Inches	Millimeters	25.4
Inches	Centimeters	2.54
Feet	Meters	0.305
Yards	Meters	0.914
Miles	Kilometers	1.609
Square inches	Square centimeters	6.45
Square feet	Square meters	0.093
Square yards	Square meters	0.836
Cubic inches	Cubic centimeters	16.4
Cubic feet	Cubic meters	0.0283
Cubic yards	Cubic meters	0.765
Pints	Liters	0.473
Quarts	Liters	0.946
Gallons	Liters	3.78
Gallons (Canadian)	Liters	4.55
Ounces	Grams	28.4
Pounds	Grams	454.0
Pounds	Kilograms	0.454
Tons	Metric tons	0.907
Metric system to English system		
To change:	**Into:**	**Multiply by:**
Millimeters	Inches	0.039
Centimeters	Inches	0.394
Meters	Feet	3.28
Meters	Yards	1.09
Kilometers	Miles	0.621
Square centimeters	Square inches	0.155
Square meters	Square feet	10.8
Square meters	Square yards	1.2
Cubic centimeters	Cubic inches	0.061
Cubic meters	Cubic feet	35.3
Cubic meters	Cubic yards	1.31
Liters	Pints	2.11
Liters	Quarts	1.06
Liters	Gallons	0.264
Liters	Gallons (Canadian)	0.22
Grams	Ounces	0.035
Kilograms	Pounds	2.2
Metric tons	Tons	1.1

Warranties, service contracts, and appliance parts

Historically, one of the great confusions of the American marketplace has been the degree to which a manufacturer, distributor, or retailer should stand behind his wares. Both law and custom have varied widely from state to state, while warranties issued by manufacturers have often been so vaguely worded or so complex that it has been difficult for the consumer to tell whether he was buying a fully guaranteed product or one with no worthwhile guarantee at all. In some cases, mailing a warranty card to a manufacturer has actually operated to relieve the seller of any responsibilities, while failing to impose any meaningful obligations on the producer. In 1975, however, Congress passed and the President signed into law, the Magnuson-Moss Warranty Act intended to protect consumers against deceptive warranty practices, inferior products, and poor service.

Implied Warranties. Under the terms of the act, no manufacturer or retailer is forced to provide a written warranty, but this in no way prevents a dissatisfied customer from complaining about a failed product, trying to get a replacement, or taking the offending producer or retailer to court. It is a well-established principle of law that every new product carries a so-called implied warranty—unless a disclaimer on the merchandise, such as "sold as is" or "damaged goods," expressly states otherwise.

What specifically is an implied warranty? Suppose, for example, a consumer purchases a set of molded plastic chairs from a department store and two weeks later the chairs begin to buckle and crack under the weight of their occupants. As the function of a chair is to be sat upon, there is an implied warranty that these pieces of furniture are strong enough to support the weight of adults. Should the chairs fail in this function a complaint to the store is legitimate. If the store fails to make satisfactory repairs, replacement, or refund, the customer may go to his state consumer protection agency, the Better Business Bureau, or to court.

A word of warning, however: An object must be used for the purpose intended. If the chairs in question had been advertised solely for the use of children or specifically marked as "supporting weights up to 100 pounds," then the customer has no legal recourse if they buckle and break under the weight of adults.

Implied warranties also cover several other types of contingencies. Clear title is one of these. If a consumer purchases an item from a store only to discover that the goods will never be delivered because one of the retailer's creditors has exercised a lien, then the customer is entitled to a full refund.

Similarly, if a consumer relies upon a salesperson to choose an item for a specific purpose and the product then proves unsuitable for that purpose, a full refund is in order. But here, too, a word of caution is necessary. Suppose someone wants a machine to shred vegetables and is under the impression that an ordinary blender will do the job. If he walks into an appliance store, points to a blender, and buys it, only to find that it liquefies rather than shreds, he then has no legal right to a refund. If, however, he asks the salesperson for an electric vegetable shredder and is sold a blender with the assurance that its function is to shred, then the implied warranty is in effect.

Express Warranties. Another form of guarantee with which just about all consumers are familiar is the written, or express, warranty. These come packed with thousands of different manufactured goods, ranging from television sets to typewriters, and from hand calculators to refrigerators.

Under the terms of the Magnuson-Moss Act, a manufacturer's express warranty can no longer relieve a retailer of his implied warranty. Many stores, in fact, will issue their own supplementary warranties for the items they sell. It is, however, to the manufacturers' express warranties that the Magnuson-Moss Act primarily addresses itself. The legislation requires the Federal Trade Commission to set standards for express warranties and to enforce their terms. Under the act manufacturers have three choices: to issue no warranty at all; to issue a full warranty for a clearly stated period of time; or to issue a limited warranty.

The lack of a written warranty does not automatically mean that an item is defective or that the producer will not stand behind his product. Often a letter to the customer relations department of the manufacturer will bring quick and effective relief to a dissatisfied customer. In any case, the retailer's implied warranty automatically takes effect when an item is purchased. Even though a fly rod carries no written warranty, if it breaks under the weight of a brook trout the retailer may be held legally responsible to make good on a customer's complaint. Take it back to where you bought it and demand a replacement or a refund.

Important facts about warranties. If a manufacturer offers either a full or a limited warranty, several requirements must be fulfilled:

1. The warranty must be available to the consumer before he purchases the item. It is no longer sufficient to have the document packed away in the carton, leaving the consumer to discover its limitations only after he has paid out his money. The retailer may attach the warranty to a floor model or may post it in a conspicuous place, but the consumer must have the opportunity to examine its terms before making the purchase.

2. The terms of the warranty must be written in clear English, understandable to any literate person. Highly legalistic language must be avoided. If the warranty is a full one (that is, if it requires the manufacturer, distributor, or retailer to repair or replace a defective article at no expense to the consumer), then the period of time that the warranty is in effect must appear in large type at the top of the document. Typically, this will read: "Full 12-month warranty," or "Full 2-year warranty."

Limited warranties must also include the period of time they are to be in force, though this may be stated in the body of the document rather than in the title. These warranties must also outline exactly what is included and what is excluded from their terms. For example, a kitchen appliance that is warrantied for all parts and service costs, except the power cord and plug, must include a disclaimer in the body of the document regarding those parts. Similarly, if only parts, but not labor, are covered, this too must be clearly indicated.

3. Full warranties must apply to any owner of the item in question during the time the document is in force. For example, if a consumer buys a fully warranted electric drill, he may transfer ownership of the tool to another, and the new owner retains all rights under the warranty. A limited warranty need not be transferable, but this must be clearly stated in the body of the document. If you are giving an appliance with such a warranty to someone as a gift, be sure the recipient is registered as the owner.

4. Under the new law, a warranty does not have to be mailed to the warrantor for it to take effect. However, a manufacturer or a retailer is within his rights to demand some proof of purchase—such as a canceled check with a notation describing the article, a receipt of purchase, or the warranty itself—at the time the item is presented for repair.

5. The Magnuson-Moss Act includes a so-called antilemon provision, which requires the warrantor to replace an item or refund its cost after he has tried and

Consumer information

Warranties, service contracts, and appliance parts (continued)

failed to fix it a "reasonable number" of times. What constitutes a "reasonable number" is left to the Federal Trade Commission to decide.

6. Every warranty—full or limited—must include clear directions concerning the method to be used in filing a complaint about the product as well as information about repair facilities. The issuer of a full warranty may no longer require that the purchaser pay mailing costs when he returns the product to an authorized repair shop. These costs must be borne by the warrantor.

7. The holder of a warranty who fails to obtain satisfactory service from the warrantor may seek relief in a number of ways. Informal means will often suffice. These include a complaint to the local appliance retailer, a call or letter to the customer relations department of the manufacturer, or finally a letter to the president of the firm that made the product. Should these initiatives fail to provide a satisfactory response, you can make a formal complaint to your state consumer protection agency or to the Federal Trade Commission itself, either of which can intercede in your behalf or even bring legal action against the warrantor. Finally, you as consumer can go directly to court and if you win your case the warrantor must then pay your legal fees in addition to making good on his warranted obligations.

A consumer with an unsatisfied grievance against a warrantor may find that the mere threat of hauling a manufacturer before the Federal Trade Commission (which has the power to levy fines) is often sufficient to insure a satisfactory response to his complaint.

The Consumer's Responsibilities. Although the Magnuson-Moss Act has greatly increased the range of protection open to consumers, the old saying, "Buyer Beware!" remains an adage to be heeded. The wise consumer, for example, will compare warranties. If one manufacturer offers a "reasonable" limited one-year warranty, while another offers a similar model for $15.95 but with a full one-year warranty, the more expensive product might be considered a better buy. Similarly, it is a good idea to check the literature accompanying a warranty for the nearest authorized repair facility.

Another item to scrutinize is the availability of a free replacement for a product being repaired. In general, most manufacturers will not lend you a drill or an electric typewriter while yours is in the repair shop, but occasionally this service is offered.

Always use a warranted item only for the purpose intended and take care not to abuse the product. If an appliance has been clearly abused or used for some task it was not intended to perform, the warrantor's responsibility is at an end. A toaster that has been dropped on the floor or an air conditioner that has burned out because it was plugged into the wrong electric line will not be repaired under the warranty.

Do not attempt to repair products under warranty. Finally, a customer must follow the guidelines established by the warrantor in securing repairs and service. During the period covered by the warranty, service must be performed only by the warrantor's authorized agents. A consumer should never attempt to repair an appliance himself while the warranty is in effect, as this will almost always automatically cancel the manufacturer's or retailer's obligations.

Automobile Warranties

All of the regulations of the Magnuson-Moss Act apply to automotive warranties, but because of the complexity and high costs of automobiles and their servicing, additional words of caution are in order. All automobile warranties, whether they apply to new or used cars, are limited, both in their nature and in duration. The typical new-car warranty covers the first 12 months or 12,000 miles, whichever comes first. Some manufacturers have offered a 24-month or 24,000-mile warranty on their cars, but not all items covered in the first year are covered in the second. Another manufacturer, in addition to the standard 12-month warranty, has offered a 5-year warranty on one type of engine. A used car bought from a dealer generally carries only a 30- to 90-day warranty, and this is often limited to certain parts only and may not include the cost of labor. A used car bought from a private party generally carries no warranty at all.

Despite the general similarity among manufacturers' warranties on new cars, such differences as exist should be carefully considered before a purchase is made. No auto manufacturer, for example, will give a warranty on the tires that come with his cars, but the tire manufacturer may do so. One manufacturer, however, has offered warranties on spark plugs and mufflers. In short, before purchasing a new car, it is wise to read and carefully compare the warranties offered by rival manufacturers.

Remember that it is necessary to follow the service schedule set forth in the owner's manual if the warranty is to be maintained in effect. Use only the manufacturer's authorized agents (usually the service department of the auto dealer) to perform scheduled servicing and to make warranted repairs. It may not be sufficient merely to bring a car into an authorized facility and announce that the time has come for the 6,000-mile servicing. Instead, leave written instructions, taken from the owner's manual, about the specific work needed, and then see to it that you receive written confirmation that the required servicing has been performed. While such explicit record keeping may appear excessive, it is the only way a car owner can make sure that his warranty will be kept in force.

Service Contracts

Appliance dealers—sometimes in conjunction with manufacturers—routinely offer their customers service contracts. For a fee, which generally rises as the appliance gets older, the contractor will undertake to perform all repairs—either without additional charge or according to a specified schedule of charges. While a service contract *may* offer a consumer a way out of high repair costs, he should remember that he is buying a form of insurance. As with any insurance policy, a service contract is based upon mathematical probabilities. In the past, these have frequently favored the contractor rather than the consumer. If, for example, an all-inclusive one-year service contract on a new dishwasher cost $30.00, the buyer could assume that the contractor had based his price on the knowledge that the average appliance would need less than $30.00 in repairs during its first year in operation.

Once the consumer is aware of this fact, he can then judge the advisability of purchasing a service contract in a rational light. There are often very good reasons to have a contract. Things do go wrong with appliances, and the appliance owner may well decide that it is advisable to pay out a relatively modest sum to assure himself that if the unexpected happens (say a breakdown requiring parts and labor not covered or no longer covered by the warranty), he will not be hit with an enormous bill.

Judging Service Contracts. As with warranties, not all service contracts are the same. There are many variables to consider before buying one, among them the following:

1. Is the contract redundant? If a consumer buys a service contract for an

Manufacturers' addresses

Admiral Group, 1701 East Woodfield Rd., Schaumburg, Ill. 60196
Airtemp Corp., 1301 Lyons Rd., Dayton, Ohio 45459
Amana Refrigeration, Inc., Amana, Iowa 52203
Braun North America, 55 Cambridge Parkway, Cambridge, Mass. 02042
Brother International, 8 Corporate Pl., Piscataway, N.J. 08854
Caloric Corp., Topton, Pa. 19562
Electrolux Div., Consolidated Foods, Stamford, Conn. 06905
The Eureka Co., Bloomington, Ill. 61701
Farberware, 100 Electra Ave., Yonkers, N.Y. 10704
Fedders Corp., Edison, N.J. 08817 (also Norge appliances)
Friedrich Refrigeration, Inc., Div. of Wylan, 4200 North Pan Am Expressway, San Antonio, Tex. 78295
Frigidaire, 300 Taylor St., Dayton, Ohio 45442
General Electric Co., Bridgeport, Conn. 06602 (large appliances)
General Electric Co., Appliance Park, Louisville, Ky. 40225 (small appliances)
The Hoover Co., 101 East Maple St., North Canton, Ohio 44720 (Hoover, Knapp Monarch, and Nesco appliances)
Hotpoint, Appliance Park, Louisville, Ky. 40225
Kelvinator Appliances Co., 4248 Kalamazoo St. SE, Grand Rapids, Mich. 49508
KitchenAid Div. of Hobart Corp., World Headquarters Bldg., Troy, Ohio 45374
Matsushita Electric Corp. of America, 1 Panasonic Way, Secaucus, N.J. 07094 (Panasonic appliances)
Maytag Co., Newton, Iowa 50208
Monarch Kitchen Appliances, Dept. NR-76, Beaver Dam, Wis. 53916
Montgomery Ward, 619 West Chicago Ave., Chicago, Ill. 60607
National Presto Industries, Eau Claire, Wis. 54701
North American Phillips Corp., 100 East 42d St., New York, N.Y. 10017 (Norelco appliances)
Oster Corp., 5055 North Lydell Ave., Milwaukee, Wis. 53217
Philco-Ford Corp., Union Meeting Rd., Blue Bell, Pa. 19422
Proctor-Silex, 700 West Tabor Rd., Philadelphia, Pa. 19120
The Regina Co., Regina Ave., Rahway, N.J. 07065
Ronson Corp., 1 Ronson Rd., Woodbridge, N.J. 07095
Roper Sales Group, 1905 West Court St., Kankakee, Ill 60901
Roto Broil Corp., 29 Riverside Ave., Newark, N.J. 07104
Schick Inc., 33 Riverside Ave., Westport, Conn. 06880
Scovill Manufacturing Co., 99 Mill St., Waterbury, Conn. 06720 (Hamilton Beach, Dominion appliances)
Sears Roebuck & Co., 925 South Homan Ave., Chicago, Ill. 60607
The Singer Co., 30 Rockefeller Plaza, New York, N.Y. 10020
Son-Chief Electrics, Inc., Winsted, Conn. 06098 (Black Angus, Coronet, Magic Maid appliances)
Speed Queen Div. of McGraw Edison, Doty St., Ripon, Wis. 54917
Sperry Remington Shaver, 60 Main St., Bridgeport, Conn. 06602
Sunbeam Appliance Co., 2001 South York Rd., Oak Brook, Ill. 60052
The Tappan Co., Tappan Park, Mansfield, Ohio 44901
Toastmaster Div. of McGraw Edison, 333 River Rd., Elgin, Ill. 60120
Waring Products, New Hartford, Conn. 06057
Waste King Div. of Norris Industries, 5119 District Blvd., Los Angeles, Calif. 90040
West Bend Co., West Bend, Wis. 53095
Western Auto Supply Co., 2107 Grand Ave., Kansas City, Mo. 64108 (Wizard appliances)
Westinghouse Electric Corp., Gateway Center, Pittsburgh, Pa. 15222
Whirlpool Corp., Benton Harbor, Mich. 49022

---

appliance at the time he purchases the appliance, he may find that many, or all, of the items covered by the contract are also covered, for a year or two, by the warranty. In that case he is really paying twice for the same protection.

2. Is the contract all-inclusive? Some contracts may allow an extra charge for labor but not for parts. Others may require the appliance owner to pay for the repairman's travel time. And some contracts cover only a portion of the appliance, such as the motor in a washing machine or the heating elements in an electric range. Do not take the salesman's word for what a contract covers and excludes. Read the contract yourself.

3. Does the contract offer preferential service, or is there an extra charge for speedy, seven-day-a-week repairs? A consumer with a service contract on his hot water heater may think he is entitled to free Sunday and holiday service only to discover that the fine print of the agreement allows a significant charge for such emergency calls.

4. Does the cost of the contract rise significantly with the age of the appliance? In most cases this is true. The cost of a service contract during the first two years after an appliance is bought may be extremely modest, but this is also the time when minimal repairs are needed and warranties are in effect. After that, the price of maintaining the contract may rise astoundingly and by the time the appliance is five or six years old the cost of the contract may be prohibitive. Some contractors may lower rates on older appliances if the contract has been in force since the item was purchased. This is something to ask about.

5. Is the consumer in a position to make minor repairs himself? If a service contract only includes major elements of an appliance it may still be worth while if the owner has the time and knowledge needed to make small repairs and ad-justments. This is particularly true when the cost of a contract is adjusted according to the degree of service anticipated. A home handyman who feels confident that he can deal with most contingencies may find it advantageous to buy a contract that covers only major repair work.

6. Can the contract be transferred? Some contracts apply only to the purchaser and cannot be assigned to others should ownership of the appliance be transferred. Similarly, contracts from local retailers may have no value if the appliance owner moves to a distant area or if the store owner goes bankrupt.

Buying appliance parts

Appliance owners may find that buying replacement parts is not always easy. Even if the appliance retailer or manufacturer authorized service representative has the parts in stock he may try to convince the owner not to attempt his own repair work. This attitude may legitimately stem from the belief that the appliance owner lacks the skill to make his own repairs. And, of course, the owner should not attempt his own repairs on an appliance under warranty. However, the shop may quite naturally prefer to make a profit from repair work, rather than see the customer do the work.

Frequently an appliance dealer may not have the part that the customer requires. The dealer may be able to tell the customer where to locate the part, usually at a nearby parts distributor. Failing that, the customer should look in the yellow pages of his telephone directory under such headings as "Electrical Appliances—Small, Repairing," and "Electrical Appliances—Major, Repairing." A variety of outlets will be listed, some of which sell parts as well as service. Other headings are determined by the appliance itself. Parts for a faulty refrigerator, for example, may be found under "Refrigeration Equipment—Supplies and Parts—Retail," or "Refrigerators and Freezers—Servicing."

Information concerning the availability of parts may be included with the literature that accompanied the appliance at the time it was purchased. The owner's manual may contain a directory of outlets. A last resort, and one that will usually work, is to write the manufacturer's customer relations department (See addresses at right).

Finally, you should know as much as possible about the new part you want. If you are dealing with a parts outlet, it is a good idea to remove the old part from the appliance and take it along with you, together with a notation of the name and model number of the appliance. Manufacturers' diagrams are very useful for anyone attempting repair work. They usually contain an exploded view of the specific appliance and all its working parts, with part numbers and names clearly indicated. Sometimes an appliance will come with such a diagram in its package. If not, you may be able to secure a copy from the manufacturer.

When writing the manufacturer for a part, give the name and model number of the appliance; also give the part name and number (if you have the number from the manufacturer's diagram).

Manufacturers' addresses

If the manufacturer you wish to contact is not listed at right, and you cannot find his address on the appliance itself or in your owner's manual, consult a corporate directory at your local library. The company addresses listed carry no department headings. In most cases, you should address your request for information on acquiring parts to the Customer Relations Department. From there it should be routed to the proper department within the company.

Index

T